MACMILLA
CHILDREN'S
ENCYCLOPEDIA

General Editor: Leonard Sealey M.Ed.

Second Edition

General Editor
Leonard Sealey M.Ed.

Consultants
John Blackie C.B., M.A., Formerly H.M. Chief Inspector for Primary Schools
Lord Briggs, Provost of Worcester College, Oxford
Professor Sir Bernard Lovell O.B.E., F.R.S., Director of the Nuffield Radio Astronomy Laboratories, Jodrell Bank, Cheshire
Rosemary Sutcliff O.B.E., Children's author

Executive Editor
Philip M. Clark B.A.

Designers
Faulkner/Marks Partnership

Cover Designer
Julian Holland

Picture Researchers
Trisha Pike
Anne-Marie Ehrlich B.A.
Caroline Adams B.A.

Contributors
John E. Allen C.Eng., F.R.Ae.S., F.R.S.A.
Dr Martin Angel
Neil Ardley B.Sc.
Sue Becklake
Dr Maurice Burton
Robert Burton M.A.
Michael Chinery M.A.
Kenneth Gatland F.R.A.S.
Michael Gibson M.A.
Hugh Gregor M.A.
Bill Gunston
Peter Hildreth M.A.
Michael Hoyland
Josephine Kamm
Robin Kerrod
Keith Lye B.A., F.R.G.S.
Robert May
Brian Murphy M.A.
Geoffrey Trease M.A.
Ian Tribe B.Sc.
Deysia Tuddenham B.Sc.
P. F. Whiteley B.A., M.Sc.
A. R. Williams M.A.

Artists
Richard Bonson
Terry Collins F.S.I.A.
Gerry Embleton
Garden Studios
Hatton Studios
Richard Hook
Illustrators London
David Jefferis
Eric Jewell
Angus McBride
Ben Manchipp M.S.I.A.
Rodney Shackell
Bill Stallion
John Sibbick

This one volume edition published in 1984 by Macmillan Children's Books, a division of Macmillan Publishers Limited,
4 Little Essex Street,
London WC2R 3LF and Basingstoke
Associated companies in New York, Toronto, Dublin, Melbourne, Johannesburg and Delhi

Reprinted 1985

Printed in Hong Kong

ISBN 0 333 383214

MAN

Our Body and Our Health

Our body is like a very complicated machine. It is made up of thousands of different parts. All these parts work together to keep us alive and to help us move around. Some of the things we do require the strength of our MUSCLES. Other activities need the work of our BRAIN. All the parts of our body need to be kept strong and healthy. For example, we must have the right FOOD for our BONES and TEETH to grow strong and hard. We must sleep to rest our body and take exercise to keep it fit.

Above: This man is using strength, co-ordination and balance to dive into the water.

Below: Cells vary in size and shape. Each cell is designed for a different job.

Cells

All living things are made up of tiny parts called cells. Our body consists of millions and millions of these cells. Each cell takes in food and oxygen from the BLOOD.

Cells are many different shapes and sizes and each of them has a different job to do. BONE cells need to be strong and firm so they are linked together in circles. The nerve cells are very small, but they have long nerve fibres. Messages travel along these fibres. Some fibres carry messages to the BRAIN, telling it what is going on. Others carry messages from the brain, telling each part of the body to do a particular job. MUSCLE cells are long and thin. They are arranged in groups for strength. The cells in our small intestine are tall and thin. They absorb digested FOOD.

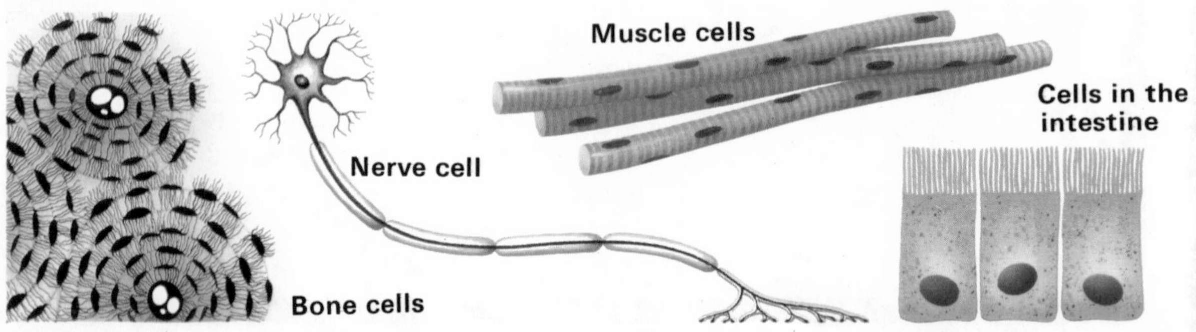

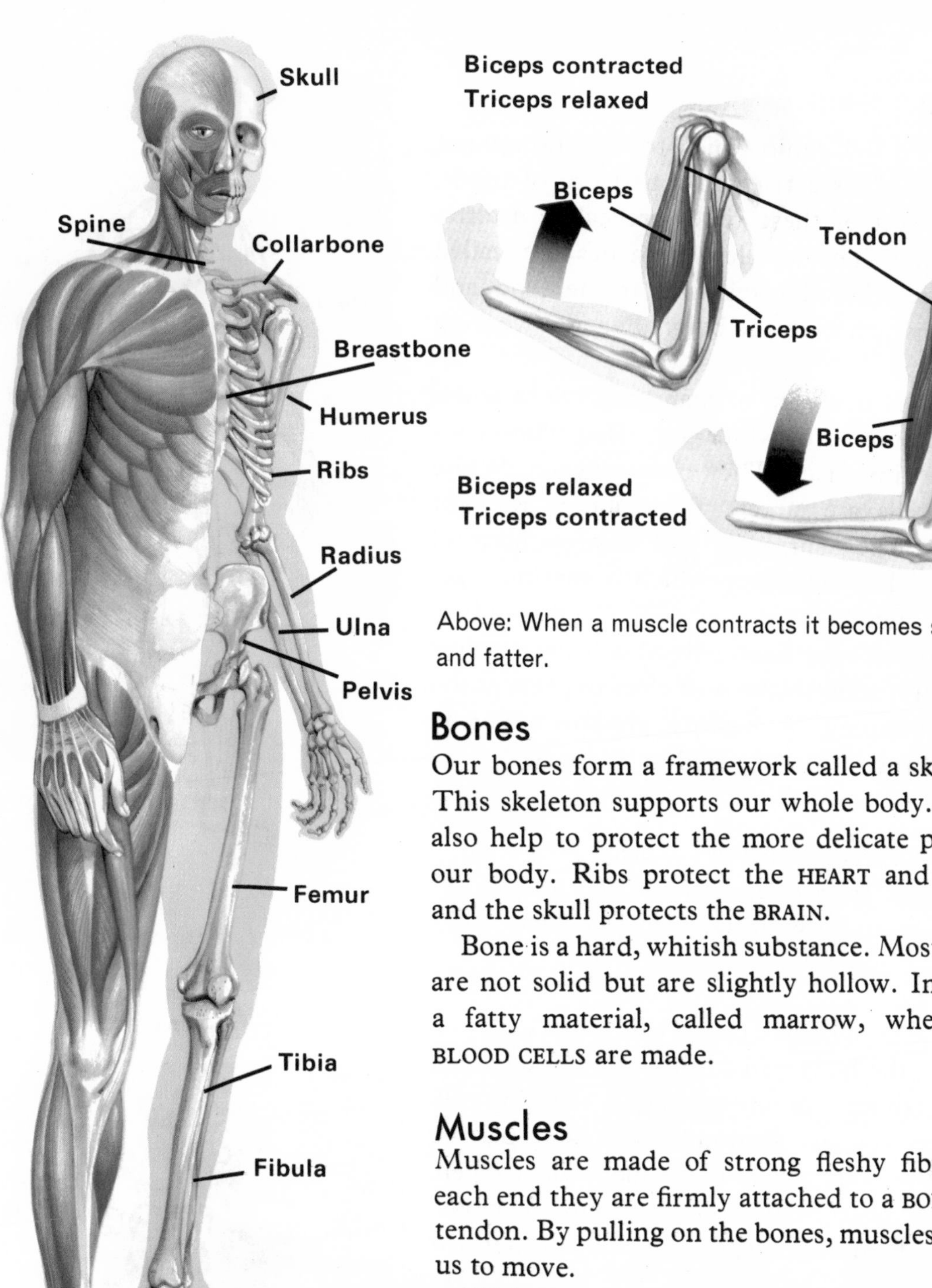

Above: When a muscle contracts it becomes shorter and fatter.

Bones

Our bones form a framework called a skeleton. This skeleton supports our whole body. Bones also help to protect the more delicate parts of our body. Ribs protect the HEART and lungs, and the skull protects the BRAIN.

Bone is a hard, whitish substance. Most bones are not solid but are slightly hollow. Inside is a fatty material, called marrow, where the BLOOD CELLS are made.

Muscles

Muscles are made of strong fleshy fibres. At each end they are firmly attached to a BONE by a tendon. By pulling on the bones, muscles enable us to move.

Without muscles, it would be impossible for us to make any movements at all. The HEART is made up of a special kind of muscle. As this muscle contracts, the heart beats.

Left: Muscle layers cut away to show the bones.

Blood

Blood is a red liquid which travels throughout the body. It is carried in a network of tubes. The largest of these tubes are called arteries and veins. The smallest branches are called capillaries. Blood takes with it the food and oxygen which keep the body alive and working properly.

Blood is made up of many red CELLS and a smaller number of white cells. Red blood cells are like tiny discs. They carry oxygen. White blood cells are larger. Their job is to fight disease. They surround and destroy harmful particles like BACTERIA which sometimes get into the blood.

If you cut your finger, blood will start to flow out. But it soon thickens or clots to prevent too much escaping. A healthy grown-up person has about six litres of blood in his body.

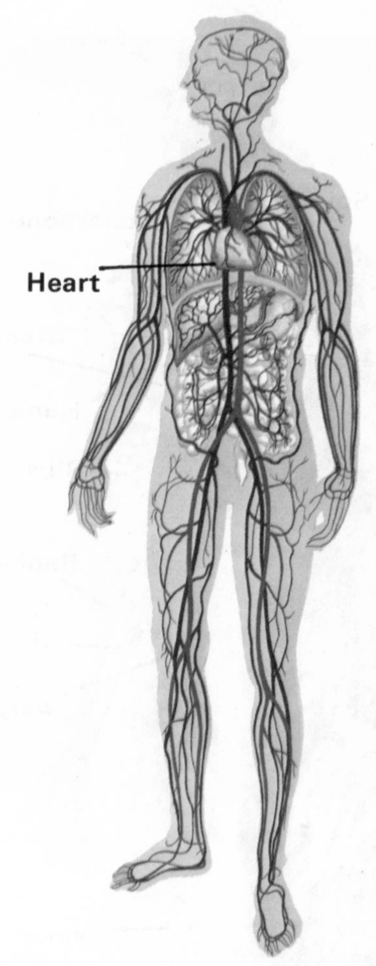

Top right: Part of the network of blood vessels.
Below right: The auricles receive blood coming into the heart. The ventricles pump blood out.

Heart

The heart is a kind of pump which drives BLOOD through the body. An adult's heart beats about 70 to 80 times a minute when he is standing still.

When you are running about and playing hard, the body needs more food and oxygen. Then the heart beats faster, pumping the blood, with its food and oxygen, quickly through the body.

Blood flows along the veins into the right side of the heart. From there it is pumped to the lungs where it takes in oxygen from the air. It comes back from the lungs into the left side of the heart. From there it is pumped into all parts of the body through the arteries.

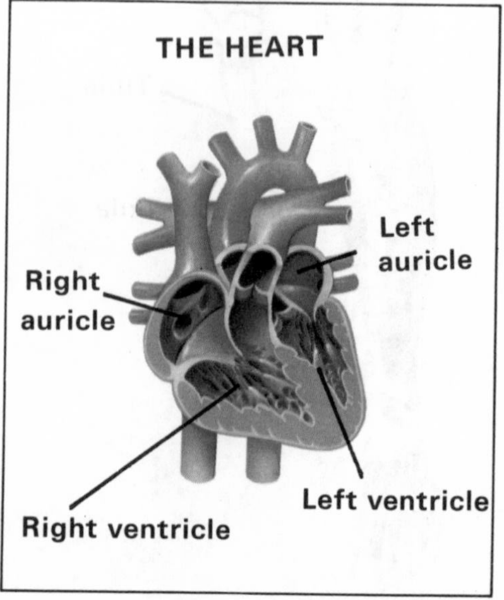

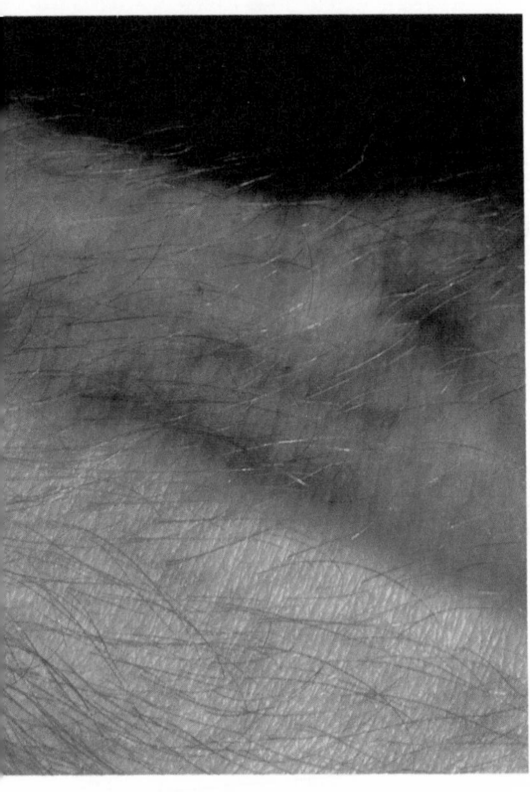

Skin

The whole of our body is covered by skin. In some places, such as the soles of our feet, it is very thick. In other places, like our eyelids, it is much thinner. Skin protects the body against injury and germs and also gives it information about changes in temperature.

The skin is divided into two layers. The outer layer is dead. CELLS flake off from this layer all the time. Underneath this protective layer there are thousands of sensitive cells. All over the skin are tiny openings called pores. Sweat escapes through these pores to cool the body.

Hair

Hair grows on nearly every part of the human body. It is most noticeable, however, on the head. The hair on our head usually grows about 15 centimetres a year.

Each hair grows from a root in its own follicle, or opening, in the SKIN. Every follicle has a GLAND which supplies oils to the hair and to the skin. The follicle also has a MUSCLE attached to it which makes the hair stand on end when we shiver.

Above: The hairs on this man's hand are easy to see.
Below: A section through the skin, greatly magnified.

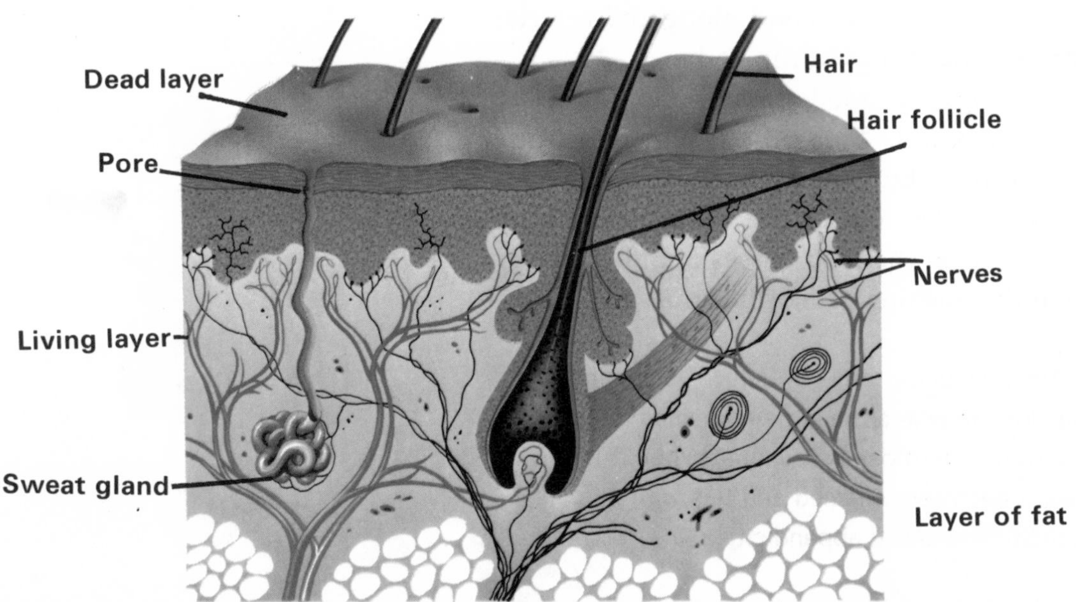

Eating

The FOOD we eat helps to give us energy. It has a long journey to make before all its goodness has been taken into our body.

When we put food into our mouth, it is first chewed into tiny pieces by our TEETH. These pieces of food are then mixed with a juice called saliva. Saliva is made in GLANDS in the mouth. It is produced whenever food is put into the mouth. Saliva contains special chemicals, called enzymes, which begin to digest the food.

The food is then swallowed and goes down the food pipe, or esophagus, into the stomach. Here it is mixed with digestive juices and turned over and over until a thick liquid is formed. The food takes up to six hours to be digested in the stomach, depending on the size of the meal.

A little at a time, this liquid leaves the stomach and passes into the small intestine. The small intestine is a coiled tube about seven metres long. In the small intestine, more enzymes are added to the liquid to complete the digestion process. All the goodness from the food then passes through the walls of the intestine and into the BLOOD. The digested food is carried in the blood along the arteries and veins to the CELLS of the body.

Any undigested food passes into the large intestine or bowel. This tube is wider than the small intestine, but not as long. In the bowel the water is taken out of the waste food. In its more solid form the food passes out of the body through the opening called the anus.

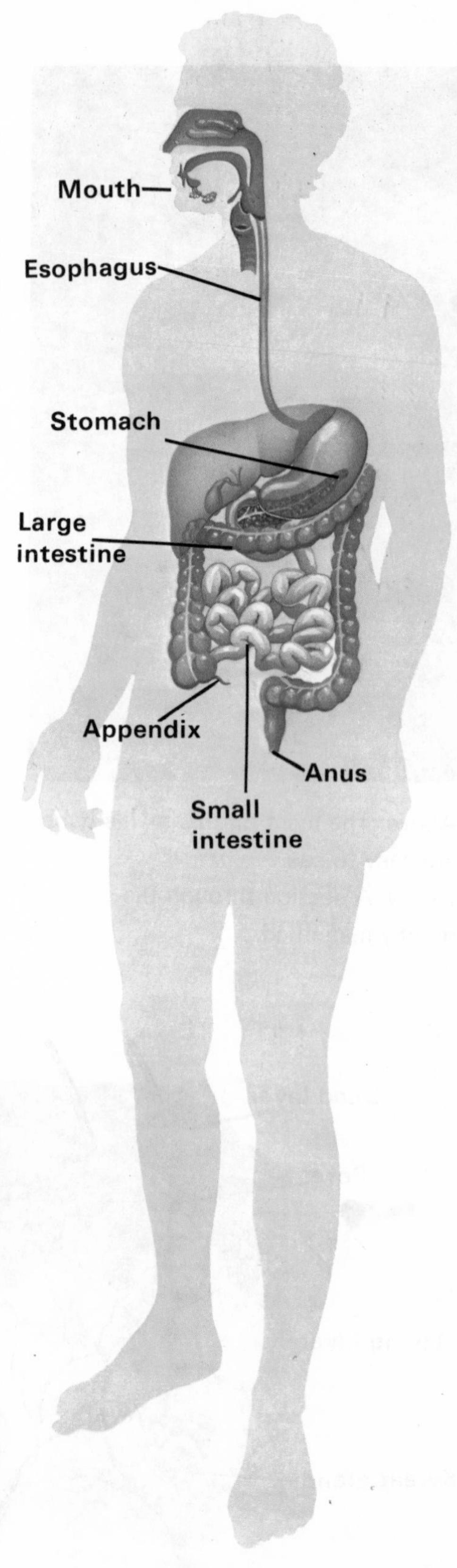

Right: The human digestive system. The appendix, located close to where the large and small intestines meet, serves no purpose in humans. When it is infected, it becomes inflamed and fills with pus. This condition is called appendicitis.

Food

Food is the fuel that operates the human machine. It also provides the materials for building and maintaining our bodies. To be strong and healthy we need a balanced diet. Protein is needed for body-building and growth. Foods like fish, meat, cheese and eggs are rich in protein. Carbohydrates and fats supply our bodies with energy. Bread, rice, potatoes and sugar contain a lot of carbohydrates, and butter and margarine are fats. Our body also needs small amounts of vitamins and minerals. We obtain them from fresh fruit and vegetables.

Left: Many different kinds of food are needed for a balanced diet.

Teeth

Teeth are for chewing FOOD. Most children are born without teeth. At first they do not need food that has to be chewed. At the age of about six months, the first set of twenty teeth begins to grow through the gums. These first, or 'milk', teeth are soon lost. They are replaced by 32 permanent teeth. By the time you are about 14 you should have nearly all your permanent teeth.

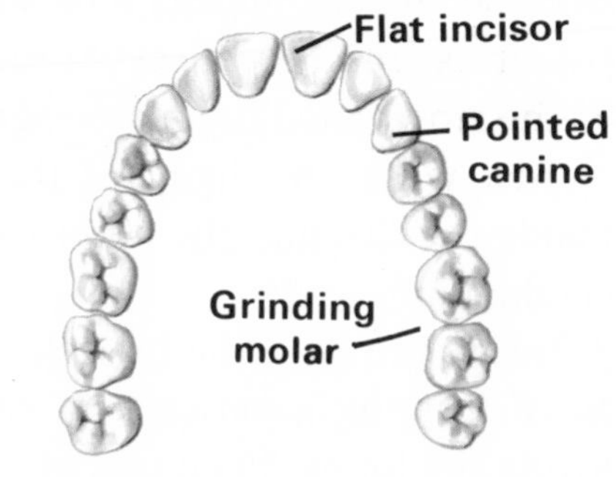

Each tooth is held into the jawbone by a root. You cannot see the roots because they are hidden by your gums. The hard white part that you can see in the mouth is called the crown. The crown is covered by a hard layer of enamel. Under the enamel is a thick layer of strong material called dentine. The centre of the tooth is made up of softer pulp. The pulp contains nerves and BLOOD vessels. It is through these nerves that you feel the pain of toothache.

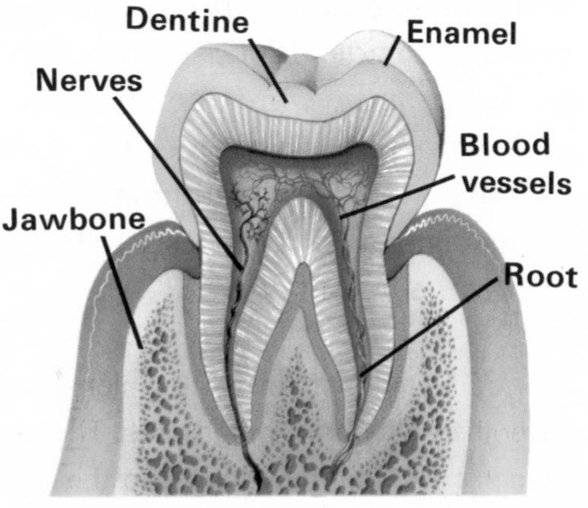

Right: This is what a tooth is like inside. Trapped food particles may dissolve the enamel layer.

Breathing

Breathing is the process of taking in and expelling air. We need air because it contains oxygen. Oxygen enables our body to release the energy contained in our FOOD and keep us moving. When you sit still, you breathe in and out about twenty times every minute. When you run about, you need more energy than when you sit still, and so you need more oxygen. You breathe more quickly when you are running – perhaps as much as fifty times every minute.

Air is drawn in through the nose or the mouth. Next, it passes into the windpipe. The windpipe divides into two passages, called bronchi. One of these goes to each lung. Our lungs are like two large balloons in the chest. When we breathe in, the MUSCLES between our ribs lift the rib cage and the sheet of muscle at the bottom of the ribs, called the diaphragm, pushes downwards. When this happens there is more space inside the ribs and the lungs can swell up as air is taken in.

Inside the lung the bronchi divide again and again forming a network of small air passages inside the lungs. Each one of these air passages ends in a tiny air sac called an alveolus. BLOOD collects oxygen from the alveoli and carries it round the body to all the CELLS. When the cells use the oxygen, they produce another gas called carbon dioxide. Blood carries this gas back to the lungs and we breathe it out.

We do not have to think about breathing because we do it automatically. The BRAIN sends signals to the chest, telling it how often to breathe in and out.

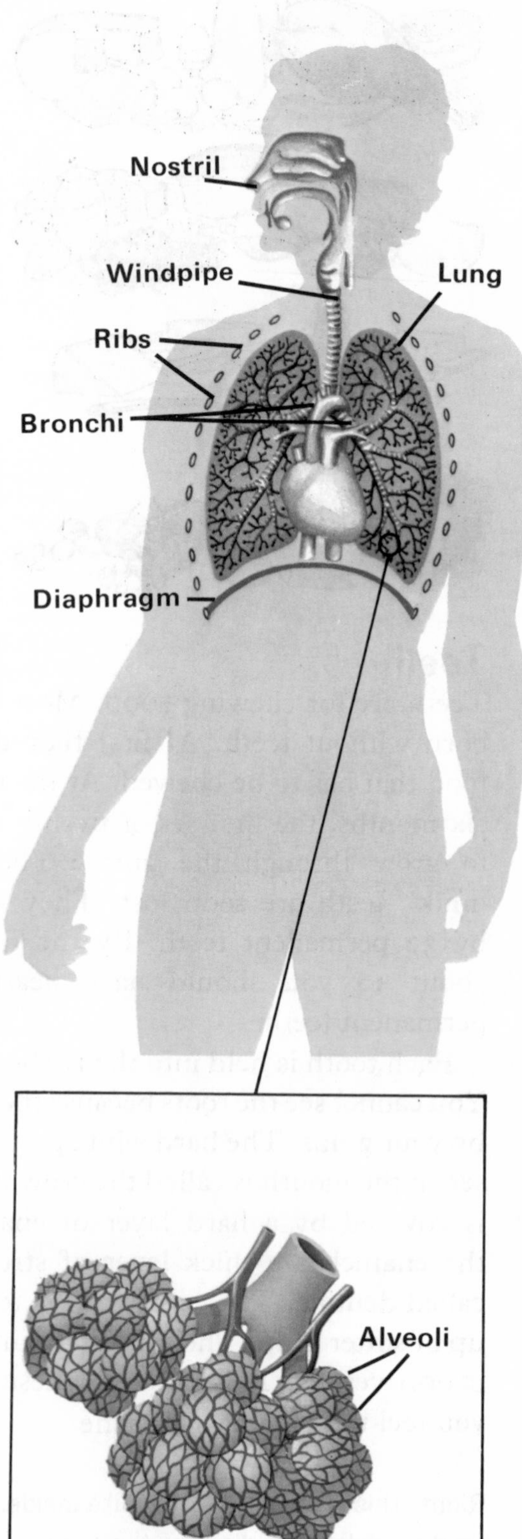

Right: The main organs with which we breathe. Alveoli are tiny branching tubes. Through these, oxygen gets from the lungs into the bloodstream.

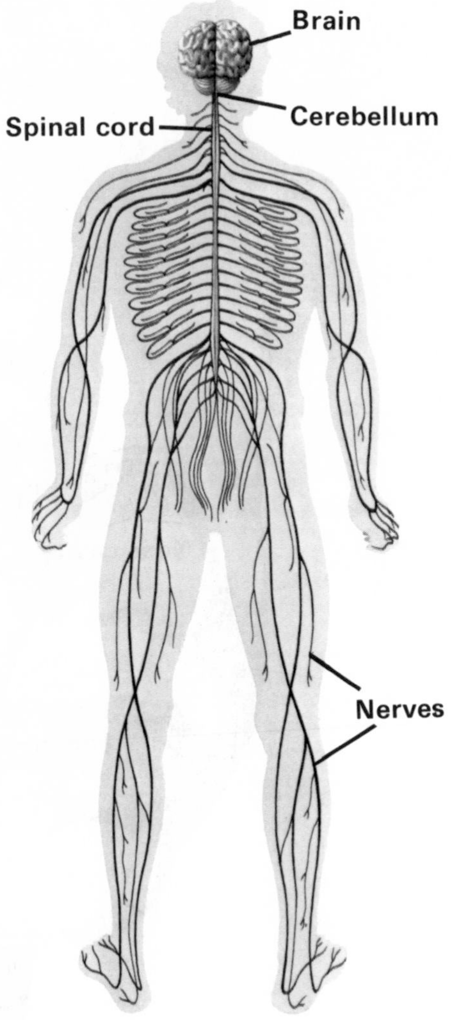

Nervous system

The nervous system gathers information about what is going on inside and outside our body using the SENSES and nerves. The BRAIN and spinal cord receive this information. They then send messages back which can make MUSCLES or GLANDS work. In this way we respond to situations in the world around us. Sometimes we can respond very quickly and without thinking. If we touch something hot, we soon take our hand away. Often we choose what to do. When we cross a busy street we look, listen and think before we decide that is is safe to step forward.

Brain

The brain controls almost all the things that we do. Messages from all over the body pass to and from the brain along the spinal cord. Each part of the brain controls a different activity. Parts of the outer layer receive messages from the SENSES, such as smell, taste and sight. Another area of the brain governs speech.

The brain stores some information as memory. We learn from this memory and can use its information when we have to make decisions.

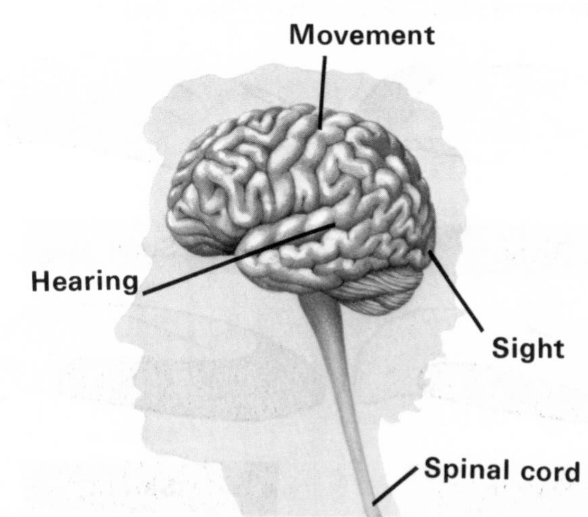

Above: Our nervous system is a network of millions of nerve cells. Most of the nerve cells are in the brain and spinal cord. Others make up the nerve fibres which carry messages all over the body. Some nerves carry messages to the brain and spinal cord, others carry messages away. Nerve fibres only carry messages in one direction.
Right: Different parts of the brain control different actions and functions.

The five senses

The five senses are: sight, taste, hearing, smell and touch. All the sense organs collect information in a different way. But they all send messages along nerves to the BRAIN.

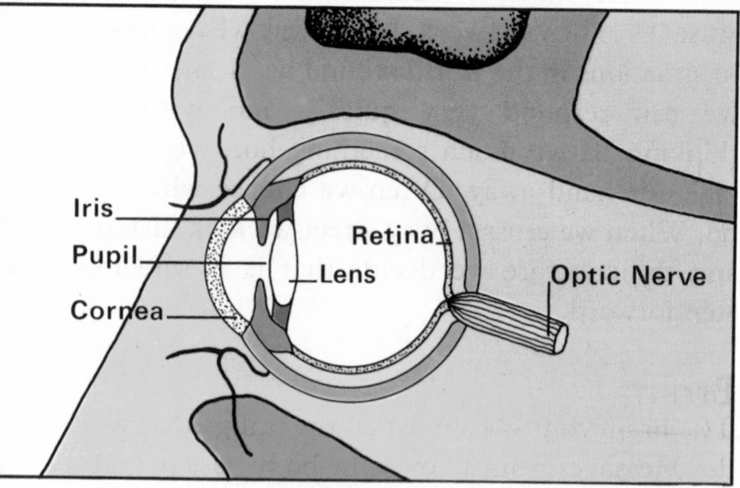

Light enters the eye through an opening at the centre of the iris called the pupil. What we see is focused (made clearer) by the lens, and is recorded on the retina at the back of the eye. Nerves carry messages from the retina to the brain.

Taste buds in the tongue give us a sense of taste. Different taste buds can recognise the four flavours: salt, sour, sweet and bitter.

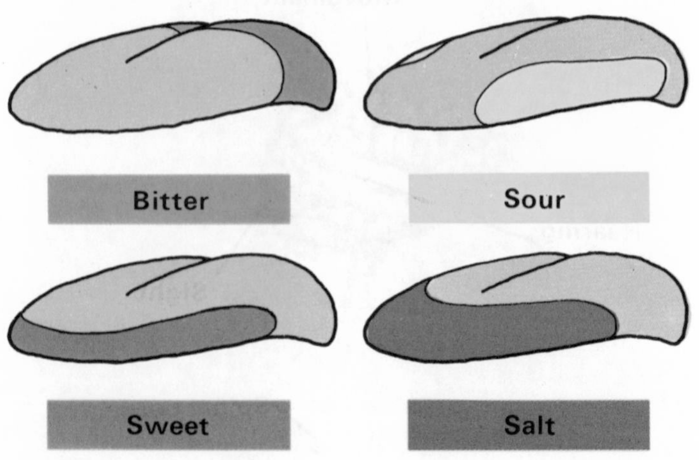

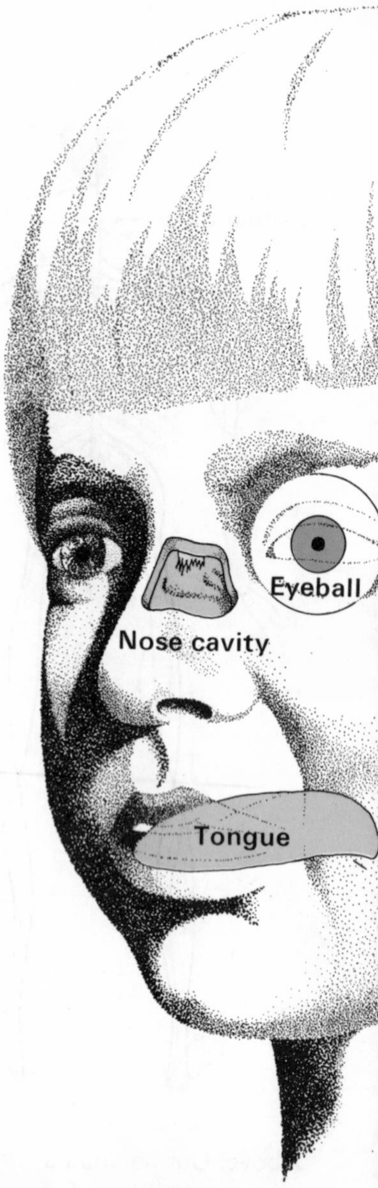

The brain receives information from all our sense organs. The messages are sorted out and co-ordinated before the brain decides what we will do.

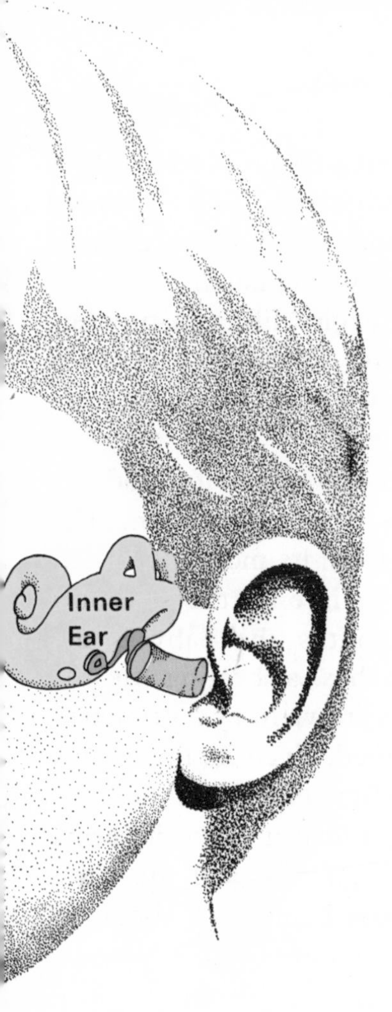

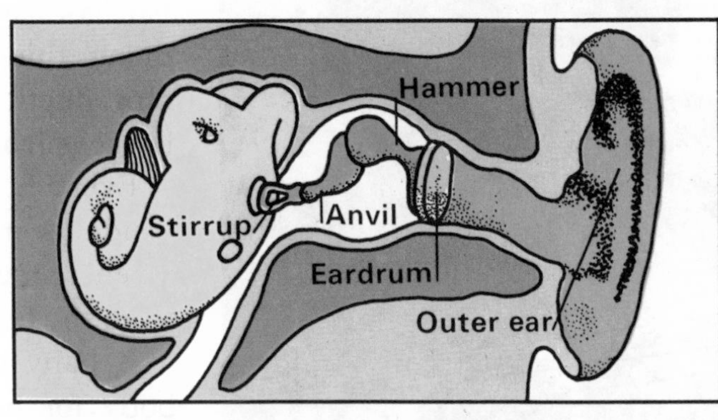

The eardrum vibrates when sounds hit it. This in turn makes three small bones in the middle of the ear vibrate. The vibrations pass to the inner ear where messages are sent to the brain.

Many substances give off a scent or smell. The smell consists of millions of tiny particles which float in the air. We use our noses to detect them. When we smell a flower or a piece of cheese, for example, the particles are drawn up the nose to the smell CELLS in the upper parts of the nose. The smell cells tell the brain what kinds of particles they are.

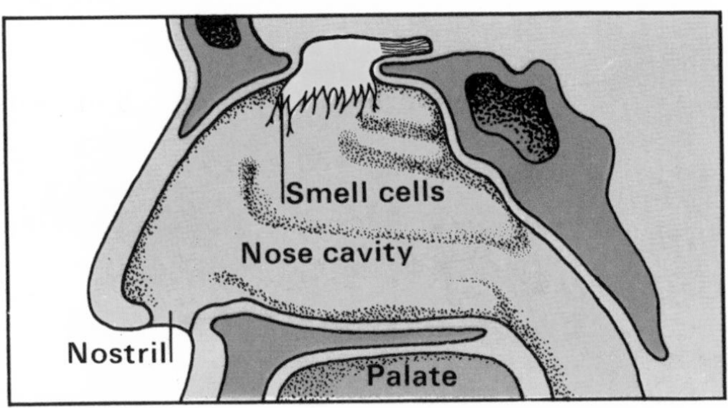

Nerves in our skin give us a sense of touch. We can feel whether objects are rough or smooth, wet or dry and we can respond to sharp pressure. Fingertips and lips are the most sensitive areas.

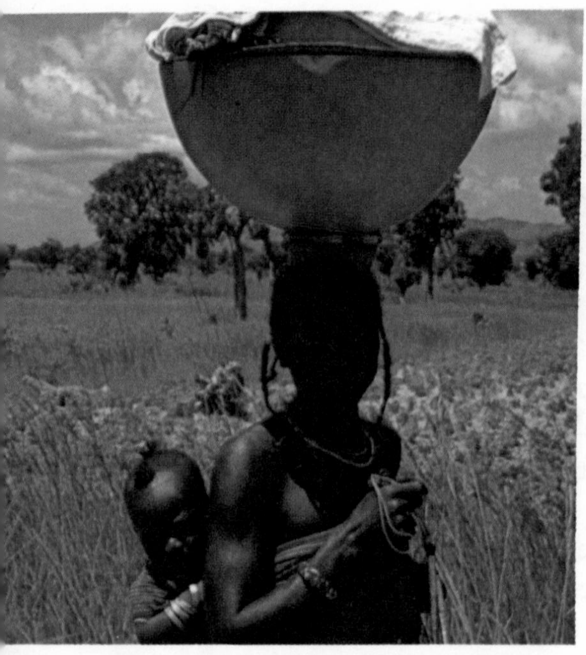

Above: A mother must take care of her baby when it is very young.
Below: The stages of development of a baby inside its mother.

Birth

Life goes on because living things produce other living things like themselves. This is called reproduction. Birds and many other animals lay eggs from which the young hatch.

Every human child begins life as a tiny egg inside its mother's body. This egg is fertilized when it meets a special CELL, called a sperm, from the father's body.

A baby lives and grows inside its mother's body for nine months before it is born. The baby receives its food from its mother's bloodstream. At first the egg is only the size of a pinhead. After two months the baby is 2.5 centimetres long and has a beating HEART. After four months it has grown to 15 centimetres and is almost fully formed. Even its fingernails have started to grow. After six months the baby is 30 centimetres long and can move its arms and legs. The mother can now feel the baby moving inside her. Most babies are about 50 centimetres long when they are born.

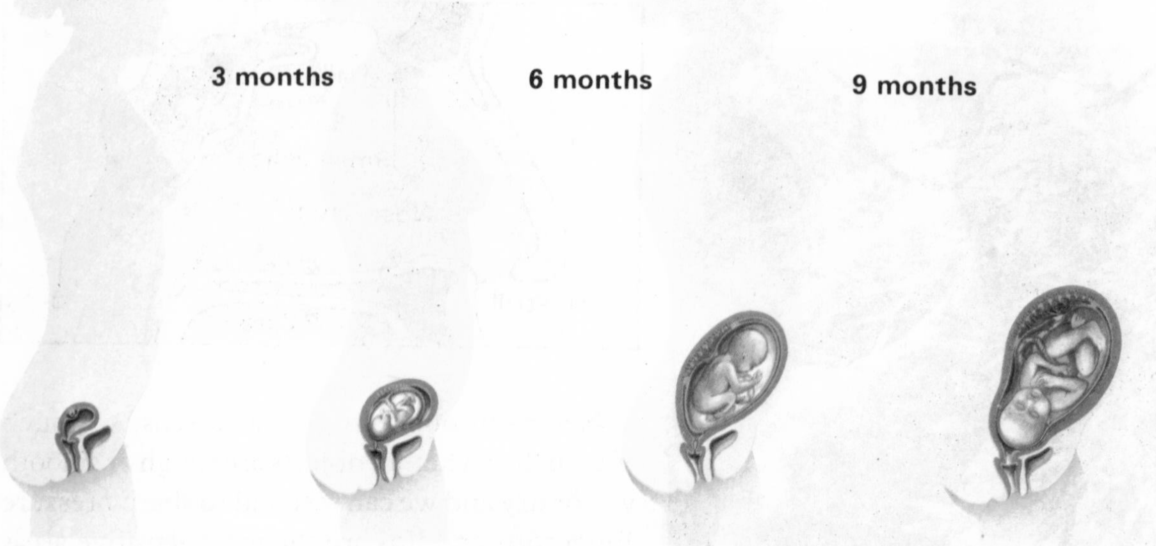

Heredity

Children often look like their parents and their brothers and sisters. This is because every child inherits characteristics from its parents. It may mean that you have brown eyes like your mother and fair hair like your father. We call this heredity.

It is not only appearance that we can inherit. The way we behave or the abilities we have, such as a good singing voice, may also be passed down to us through our parents. Many of these characteristics may be passed on from one generation to the next.

Often there is a gap in heredity. A child may not look like his parents, but he may look like his great-grandfather, or his grandmother.

Above: This child has inherited features very like its mother's.

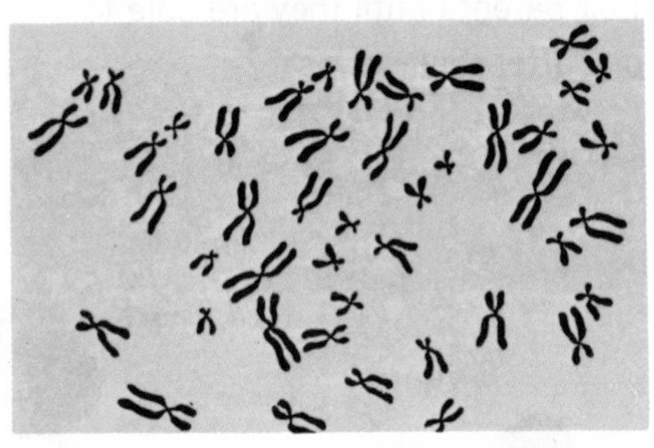

Chromosomes

Every CELL in our body contains thread-like structures called chromosomes. These chromosomes are inherited from our parents. They are made up of a substance called DNA. DNA carries the instructions which tell the cell what to do. The instructions are carried as genes which are arranged along the chromosome in a certain order. Genes determine our characteristics.

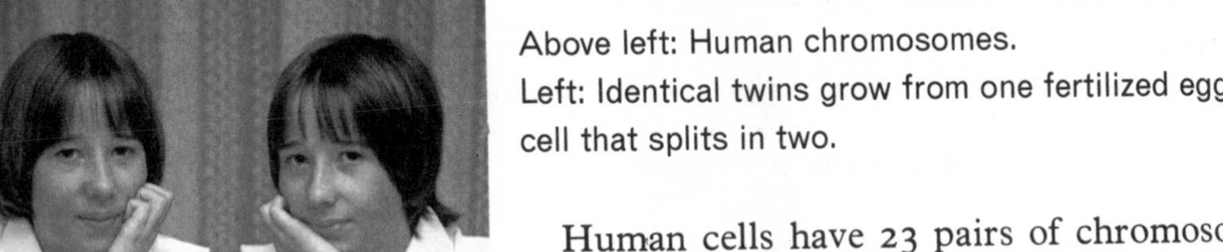

Above left: Human chromosomes.
Left: Identical twins grow from one fertilized egg cell that splits in two.

Human cells have 23 pairs of chromosomes. The twenty-third pair carries the genes which decide whether a baby is a boy or girl. If the chromosomes of this pair are the same, the baby is said to have two 'X' chromosomes and will be a girl. If one chromosome is smaller than the other, the baby has one 'X' and one 'Y' chromosome and will be a boy.

Growing up

A newborn baby can turn its head, grip with its fingers and suck its thumb. But there are many things that it cannot do. Its parents must feed it, keep it warm, and protect it from danger.

Babies grow rapidly for the first few months of their life. Then their rate of growth slows down. As they grow, babies begin to explore and learn about the world around them. By the time they are two years old they can walk and play and begin to think for themselves.

As they get older, children become taller and heavier. Between the ages of eleven and fourteen, boys and girls start to change into men and women. Girls usually start to grow up before boys. They are often taller than the boys for a while. They develop wider hips and their breasts begin to grow. The boys overtake the girls later. They grow taller, their shoulders become broader, their voices deepen and they begin to grow hair on their faces. Most people stop growing altogether when they are about twenty years old.

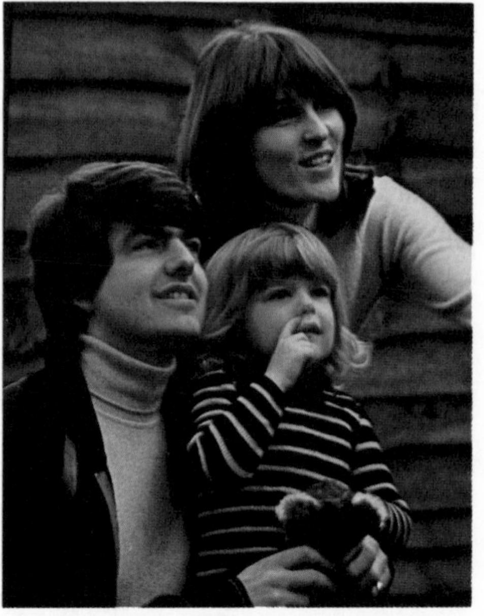

Above: Children are looked after by their parents until they are able to look after themselves.

Below: Up to about 11 years of age, boys and girls look much the same in height and weight. Between 11 and 14 their bodies start to develop adult sexual appearance.

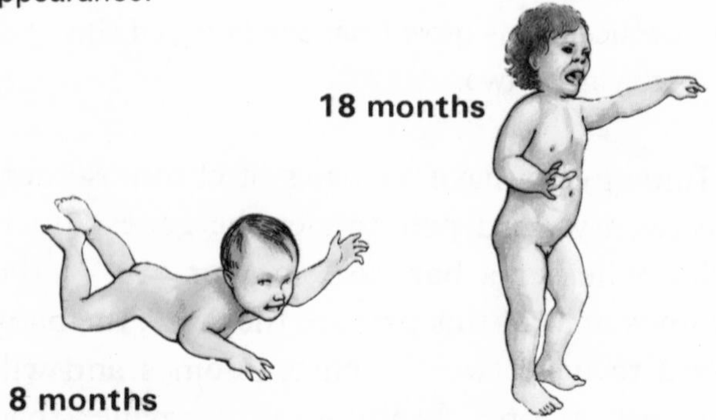

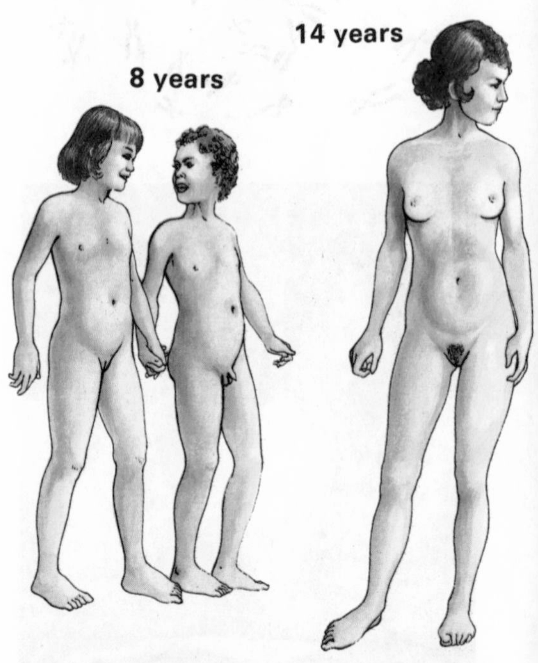

Glands

Parts of the body that release special chemical substances are called glands. For example, saliva is made by glands in our mouth and helps us to digest and swallow FOOD.

Lymph glands help to fight germs in the body. They produce CELLS which destroy BACTERIA. For example, lymph glands in the throat swell up when we have an infection.

Many glands make substances called HORMONES. These are often called chemical messengers. They are released into the BLOOD to reach all parts of the body and keep it working properly. The hypothalamus and pituitary glands produce hormones which control the other glands.

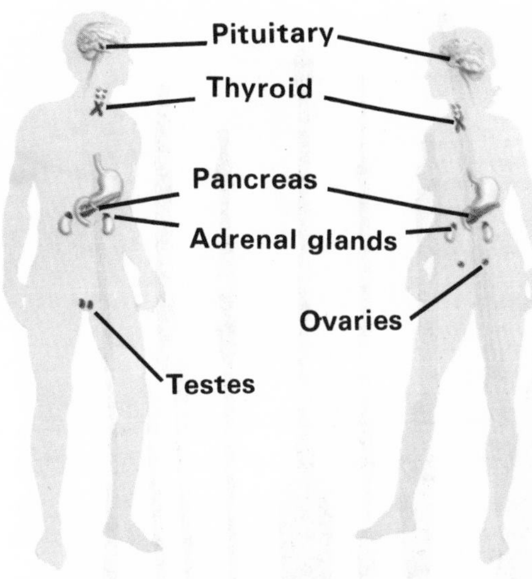

Above: Hormone-producing glands.

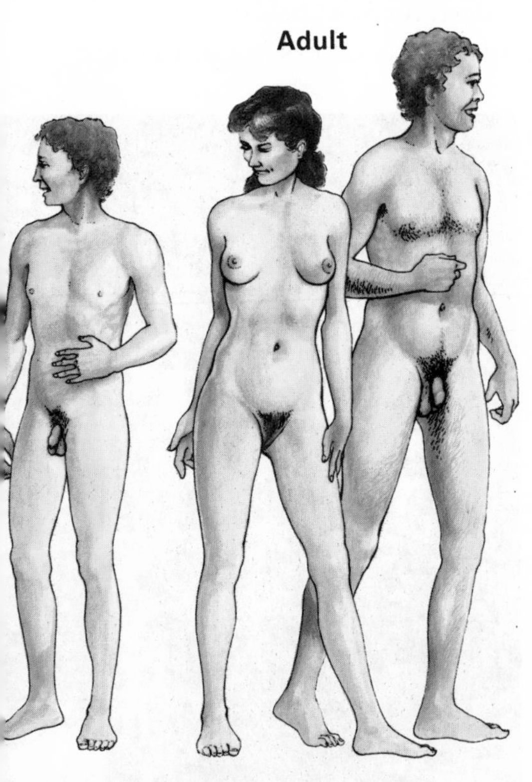

Hormones

Hormones control many of the processes which go on inside our body. They are released into the BLOOD from the GLANDS. Hormones are not released all the time. They are often released in short bursts.

Hormones usually control the activities in our body that happen very gradually. Thyroxine, from the thyroid gland, is produced throughout our life. It controls the speed of many of the body's processes, for example, breathing. Hormones from the pituitary gland control our rate of growth. The female hormones, oestrogen and progesterone, control a woman's feminine appearance. The male hormone, testosterone, controls a man's masculine appearance – beard growth and the development of large MUSCLES.

Some hormones can work quickly. Insulin can rapidly control the amount of sugar in our blood after we have eaten a meal. Adrenalin, from the adrenal glands, controls the speed of our HEART beat and is produced when we are frightened or excited.

Health

From the beginning of history man has suffered from many diseases and has searched for ways to cure them. Signs of surgery have been found in the remains of Stone Age man. Skulls have been found with small holes cut in them. Early man thought that this would release the evil spirits that he thought were the cause of headaches. He also used herbs and berries when he felt ill.

The ANCIENT EGYPTIANS studied medicine, and their priests acted as DOCTORS. But the ANCIENT GREEKS were the first to approach medicine in a logical way. Hippocrates, who lived around 400 B.C., is often referred to as the Father of Medicine. When his pupils became doctors they made a solemn promise to help the sick. This promise is called the Hippocratic Oath. The principles put forward by Hippocrates have guided physicians ever since and form the basis of modern medical practice.

Above: Roman surgical instruments.
Below: An early anatomy lesson.

About 200 years ago doctors began to under-

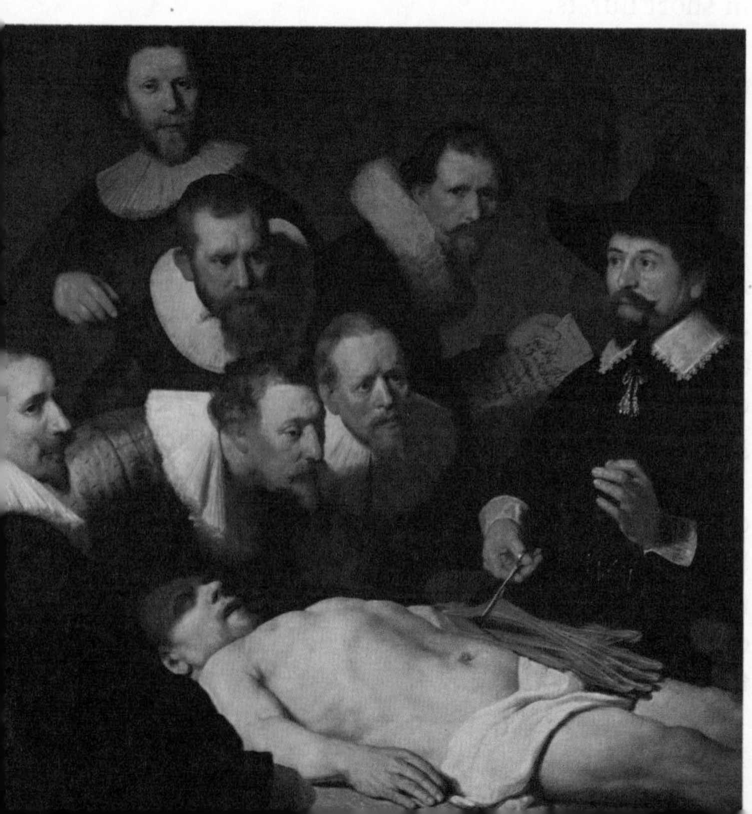

stand more fully how the human body works. They made many important discoveries and this knowledge helped them to understand and cure many diseases.

A part of the body is diseased when it is not working properly or is affected by BACTERIA OR VIRUSES. Today, modern science is successfully preventing and curing many diseases by the use of vaccines or DRUGS. Diseases such as smallpox, diphtheria, and tuberculosis are far less common now. But there are still some diseases for which scientists have not yet found a cure.

The lack of some kinds of food can cause diseases such as scurvy or rickets. Some people get occupational diseases from working with poisonous substances or in difficult conditions. There are also many kinds of mental diseases that affect the way people think and act.

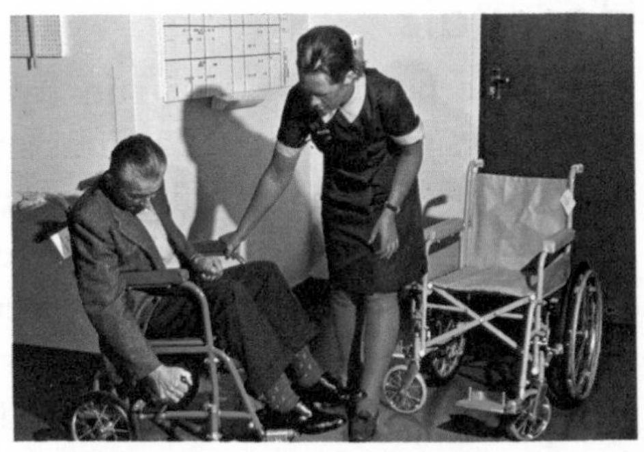

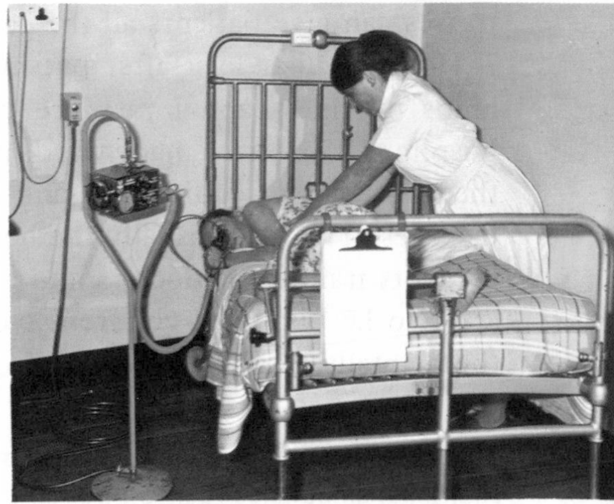

Top right: A patient in a modern hospital being shown how to use a wheelchair.

Right: This patient is breathing with a respirator.

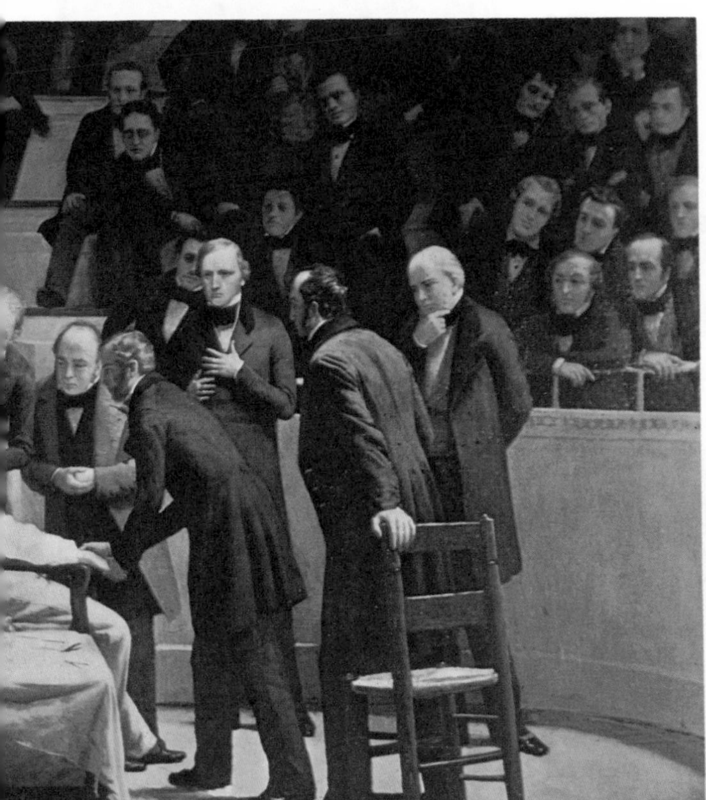

Left: One of the first operations in which anaesthetics were used, in October 1846.

Below: A child being vaccinated against disease in 1883. Vaccines prevent many diseases.

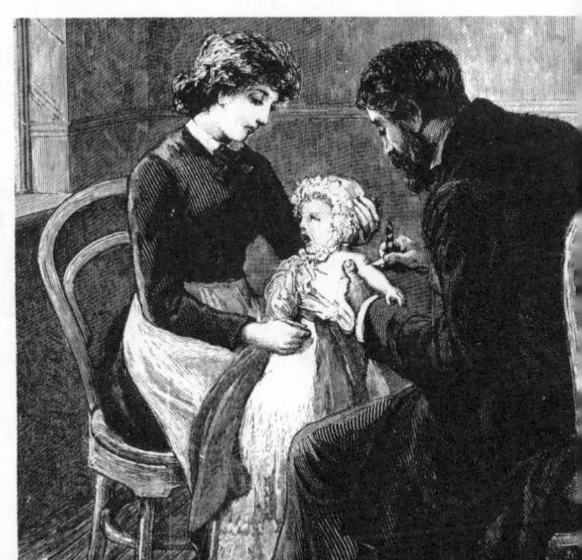

Hospitals

The first hospitals were run by the ANCIENT EGYPTIANS and most civilizations since then have had them. But until quite recently they were very primitive and even dangerous places. Wards were crowded. There were no anaesthetics or antiseptics. The DOCTORS and nurses were ignorant and ill-trained. Modern hospitals are planned so that highly skilled doctors and nurses can give patients all the care they need.

Hospitals that look after patients with most kinds of illness and injury are called general hospitals. They have many wards and operating theatres, X-ray equipment and many other facilities. These are usually the hospitals where students train to be doctors and nurses. There are also hospitals for children, old people and the mentally ill that offer specialized care.

Top right: A hospital at Ashanti in Ghana.
Right: An ambulance rushes through the streets of Chicago.
Below: This man's kidneys have failed. His blood is being purified by a kidney machine.

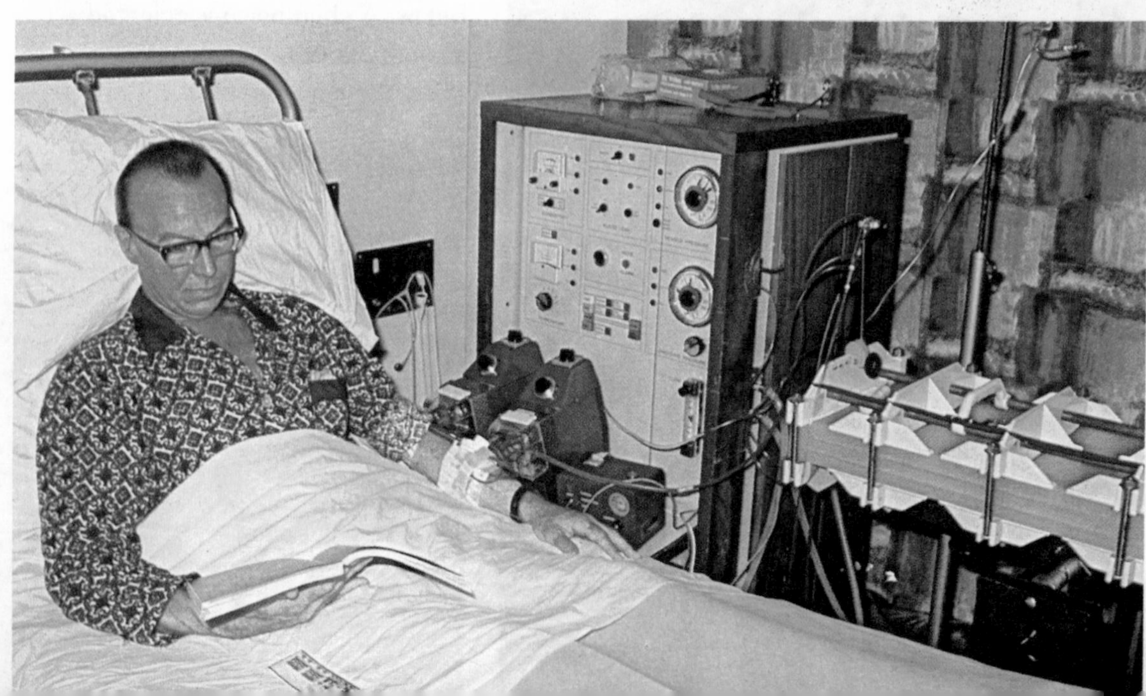

Doctors

Doctors are specially trained to know all about disease, illness and injuries. Some of them become family doctors who work in the community and who know how to deal with all the normal disorders. Others become specialists such as eye or HEART surgeons or psychiatrists. These kinds of doctors usually work in HOSPITALS. Very senior specialists are called consultants.

A doctor's training is long and difficult. It takes many years to qualify as a doctor and much longer to become a specialist. All doctors are taught in special teaching hospitals. Most family doctors work from surgeries, which patients attend. If patients are too sick to go to the surgery, the family doctor will visit them at their homes. Some family doctors prefer to work on their own but more and more of them are joining together to work in groups. This means that they can divide up their work load better and afford better equipment than they could as individuals.

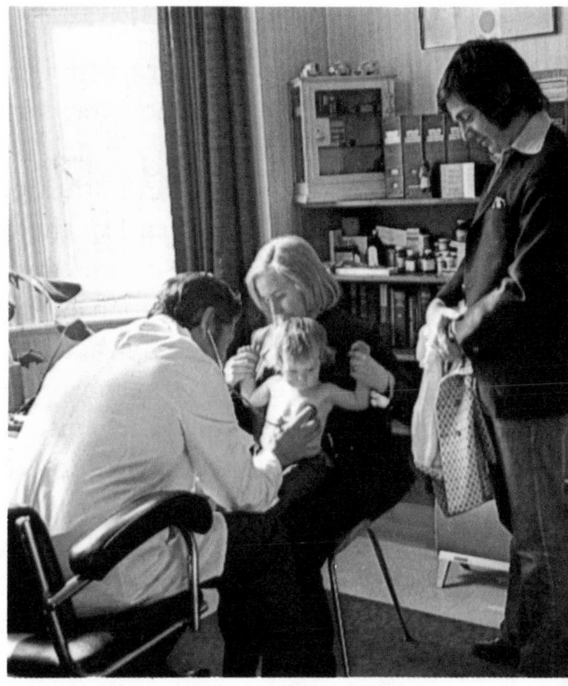

Above: A doctor is checking this child's heartbeat with the aid of a stethoscope.

Below: The dentist checks each of his patient's teeth in turn to decide what treatment is needed.

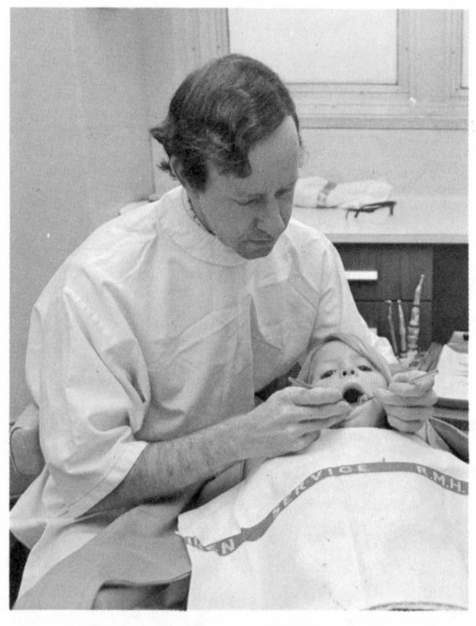

Dentists

Over 100 years ago there were few dentists. When a person had bad TEETH, he went to a blacksmith or a barber to have them pulled out. Today, however, dentistry is a science. A dentist must study for up to six years. He must know how teeth grow, how they are made, and what makes them go bad or decay. He must be able to repair decayed teeth and know how to make dentures (false teeth). A modern branch of dentistry is correcting uneven teeth.

The equipment that dentists use is improving all the time. Modern high-speed drills make work much faster. New materials are being developed for filling holes in decayed teeth.

Virus

A virus is a tiny creature, often called a germ or 'bug'. Viruses are much too small to be seen with the naked eye.

Viruses can grow and multiply and cause DISEASES. Smallpox, measles, the common cold, and many other illnesses are caused by viruses. Some of these diseases, such as smallpox, can be successfully prevented by vaccines. Some can be treated with DRUGS. Others are more difficult to overcome. Even today, in spite of 50 years of research, there is no known cure for the common cold.

Viruses are the cause of many diseases in animals, such as foot-and-mouth disease in CATTLE and distemper in dogs. They also cause a number of plant diseases and can seriously damage crops.

Bacteria

Bacteria are creatures so tiny that they can only be seen under a very strong MICROSCOPE. They live in the SOIL, in the sea and in the air. When anything rots or goes bad, it is probably due to bacteria. Some bacteria invade our bodies and cause diseases, such as typhoid fever, and tuberculosis.

Today vaccines are used to help the body fight bacteria. DRUGS such as penicillin are also used to kill them when they get inside the body.

Some bacteria are useful in industry. For example, some NATURAL FIBRES, such as flax, can be separated by the action of bacteria. The treatment of sewage also relies on bacteria.

Left: A photograph of bacteria, taken through a microscope. Bacteria are very small, but they are larger than viruses. Many diseases are caused by the action of bacteria.

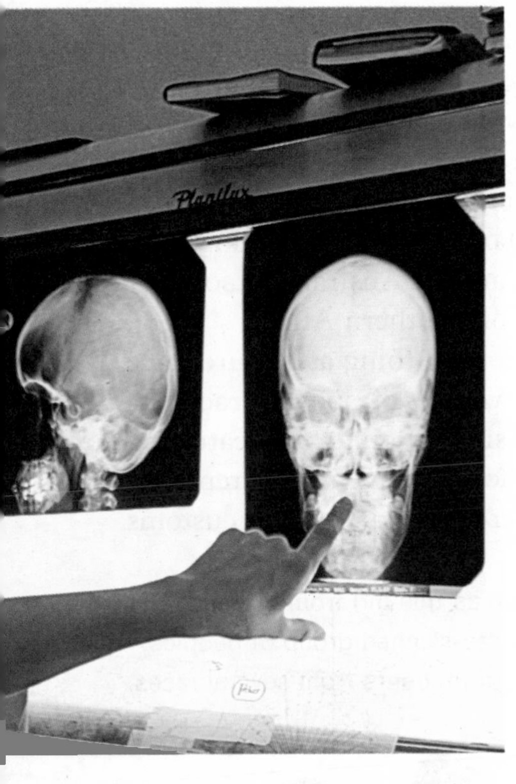

X-rays

If any part of the body is placed between X-rays and a fluorescent screen, a shadow picture of the BONES appears on the screen. If this picture is projected on to a photographic plate, the result is an X-ray photograph (or radiograph). DOCTORS use X-rays to examine bones or other parts of the body we cannot normally see. X-rays can also help to cure certain SKIN diseases, and cancer.

Too great an exposure to X-rays can be dangerous, however. Great care needs to be taken to avoid damage to healthy CELLS.

Left: A doctor examines an X-ray picture of a person's head. By injecting a special chemical into the arteries even organs that are hidden by bone can be made to show on modern X-ray pictures. X-rays were discovered by William Röntgen in 1895.

Microscopes

The optical microscope is an extremely useful tool in many branches of science. It uses a system of LENSES to magnify (enlarge) very small objects (for example BACTERIA) to many times their actual size. Without a microscope, the human eye can see objects down to a quarter of a millimetre in size. A good optical microscope magnifies an object 500 times its actual size.

Objects smaller than the wavelength of visible light (for example VIRUSES) can only be studied with an electron microscope. This uses beams of electrons instead of light. Magnetic lenses work like optical lenses in an optical microscope. Modern electron microscopes can magnify more than 1,000,000 times.

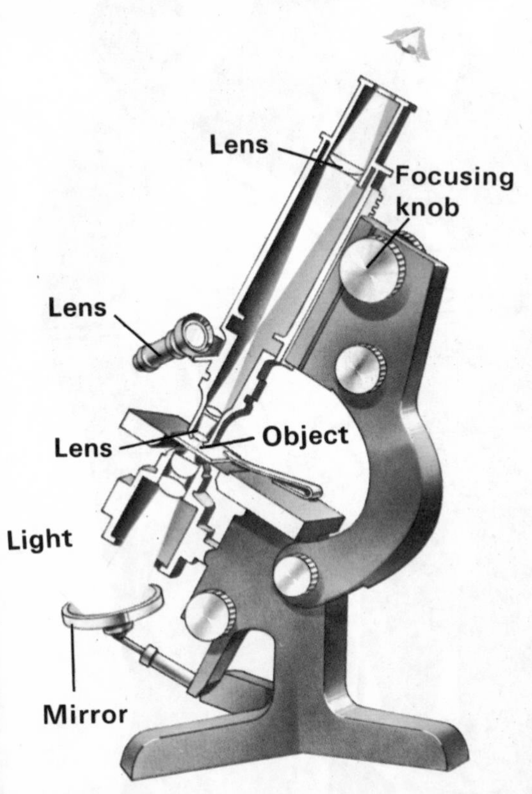

Left: The lenses in some microscopes can magnify objects more than a thousand times. A microscope may have a mirror to catch the light.

Peoples of the World

A group of people having the same skin colour, shape of head, and type of hair is called a race. Scientists divide the peoples of the world into five different races. Most people belong to the three main ones which are: WHITE-SKINNED, BLACK-SKINNED, and YELLOW-SKINNED. Two smaller races are the Australian ABORIGINES and the BUSHMEN of Southern Africa.

There is no such thing as a 'pure' race. Men often marry women of another race and their children may show a mixture of features. People of the same race may live in different countries, and have different languages and customs.

Left: Arabs, such as this girl from Morocco, belong to the white-skinned group of peoples.
Below: A group of students from several races.

Aborigines

'Aborigines' are the first or 'original' dwellers in a country before others came and took over their land.

Today the word is used mainly of the Australian aborigines. They are tall, wiry, dark-skinned people with black curly HAIR. Some still live a hard, primitive life, wandering through the bush. They hunt game with spears or a curved wooden boomerang. Others work on farms and are very good at handling horses and CATTLE. There are far fewer aborigines today than there were when the first white settlers arrived in Australia 200 years ago.

Left: An aborigine dance, in which the dancers imitate the movements of an Australian bird.

Bushmen

The Bushmen were the first people to live in Southern AFRICA. They live in family groups which come together during the rainy season in bands and scatter in the dry season when the game disperses. They are expert hunters and kill the game with poisoned arrows and other primitive weapons. They live on game, bulbs and roots, insects, and other creatures such as FROGS.

Bushmen are very short, with yellow-brown skins, long low skulls, and big cheekbones. They are unlike the various black peoples of Africa, so they are classed in a racial group by themselves.

There are now only about 20,000 Bushmen left in the Kalahari region.

Right: A family of bushmen in the Kalahari desert. One of them is trying to coax a flame out of some ashes.

White-skinned peoples

The peoples we call 'white' are really either pink or pale brown. They vary greatly in type. Their HAIR may be of any shade from blond to black. Their eyes may be brown, blue, grey, or green. They may be tall or short. Their skulls may be long or round. They may be tall, fair-haired Danes or shorter, olive-skinned Italians. They could also be darker-skinned ARABS, Indians, or Pakistanis.

We cannot say what a typical white man looks like. We can only say what he does not look like. If the colour of his skin does not help us, we can look for the features which would mark him clearly as a member of another race. He may have the kind of lips and hair that go with black people or the nose and eyes of the yellow people.

The white-skinned peoples are not only those who live in EUROPE or have left Europe to settle in other lands. They are spread all along North AFRICA and the Middle East, and include many of the people of Central ASIA.

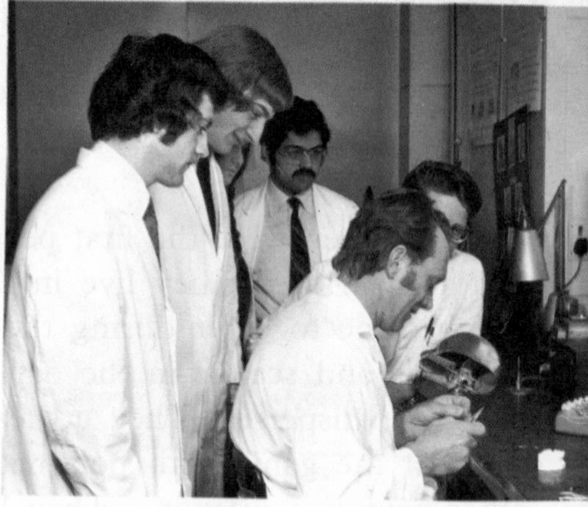

Top: This Arab girl has a very pale skin.
Right: These dental students are all white-skinned, including the Indian at the back of the group.

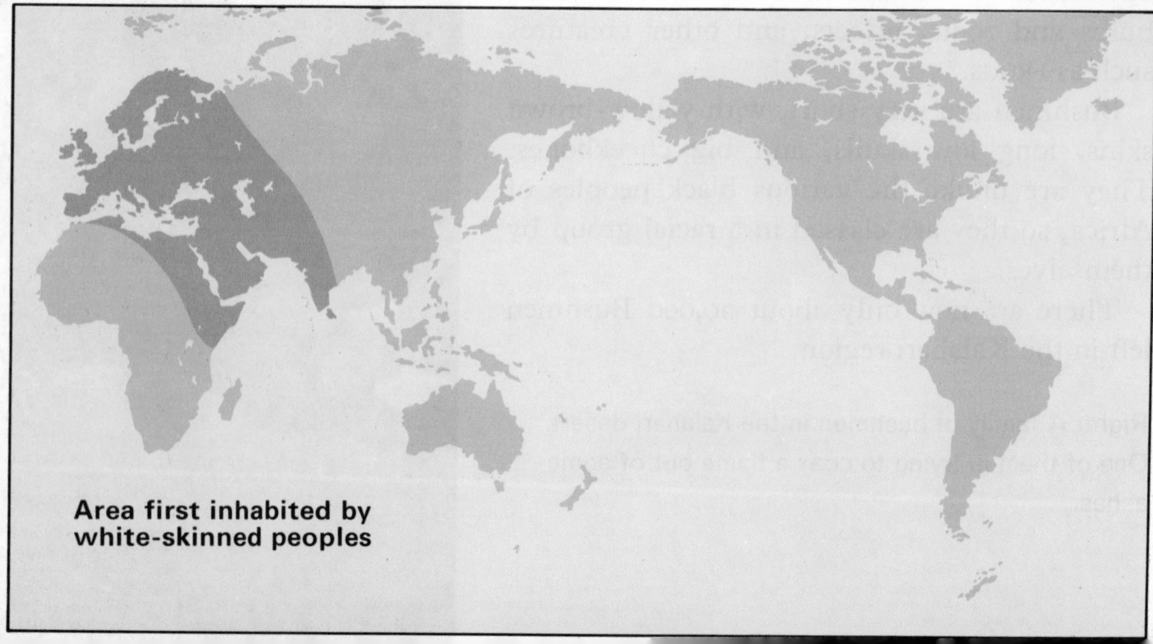

Area first inhabited by white-skinned peoples

Black-skinned peoples

The black race is made up of the black Africans, and of other peoples living in Papua, Melanesia, and nearby lands of South-East ASIA. In the past (early sixteenth to early nineteenth centuries) many blacks were captured and sent to America to work as slaves.

Today, long after the slave-trade has stopped, there are about 15 million black people in the United States. There are also many in BRAZIL and other parts of the American continent. Some have now moved from the West Indies to Britain.

Like the white-skinned peoples, blacks vary in many ways. Their skin may be any shade of brown or black. Some are very tall. Some, like the African pygmies, are very small. Many have short, woolly black hair, broad lips, and a wide nose. Outside AFRICA there has been more inter-breeding with other races and some of these features may not be so marked.

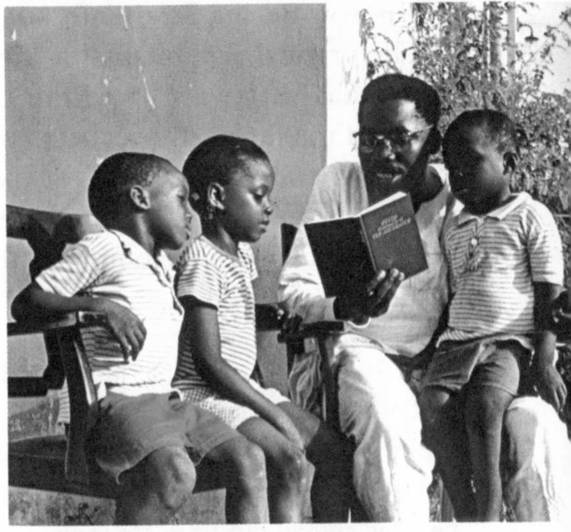

Top right: This girl student comes from Nigeria, in western Africa. She has features typical of the black-skinned race. These include woolly hair, broad lips, and a wide nose.
Right: A black missionary reads to some children.

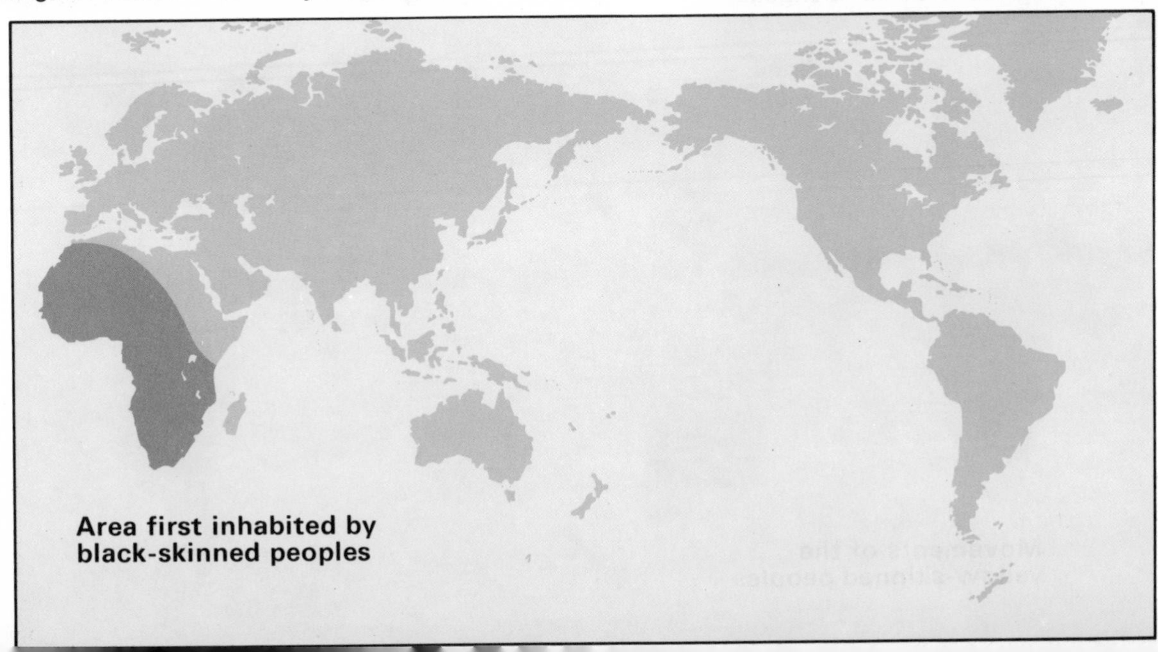

Yellow-skinned peoples

The yellow race is often called the Mongolian or Mongoloid race because its special features are those of the Mongol peoples of Central ASIA. These features are a yellowish skin, high cheekbones, straight black hair, a flattish nose, and a slant-eyed look, caused by a fold of skin at the inner corner of the eye.

The map shows how the other yellow-skinned peoples spread out from Mongolia to occupy other countries: CHINA, Tibet, KOREA, JAPAN, and the nations of South-East Asia. They also crossed the narrow Bering Strait into NORTH AMERICA.

The original inhabitants of Siberia were also Mongolian in type. So are the LAPPS who live today in the far north of FINLAND, SWEDEN, and NORWAY, and so are the ESKIMOS. AMERICAN INDIANS come from this same stock, though their skin is a coppery colour and their noses are 'aquiline' (eagle-like).

Top: An old man and child in Tibet. Both have distinctly Mongoloid features.
Right: A family of Eskimos in Canada.
Below: The map shows how the yellow-skinned peoples spread out from Mongolia.

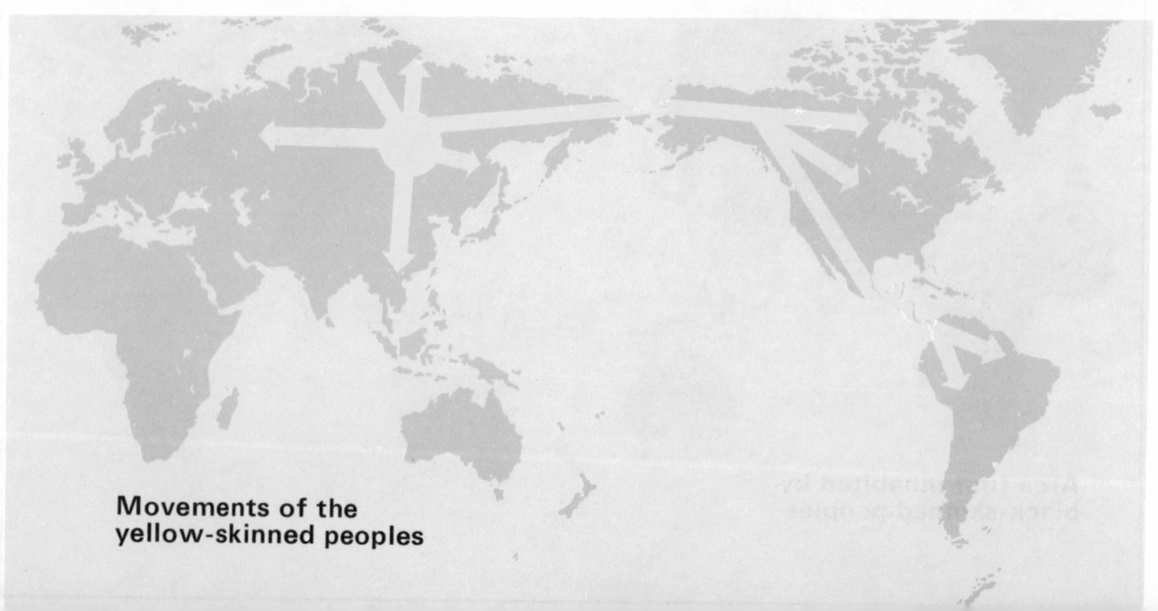

Movements of the yellow-skinned peoples

Top: A present-day Indian in South Dakota, U.S.A. In the background are the carved heads of Mt. Rushmore.
Below: A weaver of the Choctaw tribe.

American Indians

The American (or 'Red') Indians got their name by mistake. When COLUMBUS discovered America he thought he had reached INDIA. He therefore called the natives 'Indians'.

Although the Indians had similar features, they were divided into many tribes. Their languages, customs, and lives were very different. Many hunted the BISON, from which they obtained food and clothing. This animal also provided them with covering for their tepees (tents), and even with fuel.

When the white man came to America, the life of the Indians changed greatly. The white men treated the Indians cruelly, took away their lands and killed most of the bison. In CANADA and the United States, most of the Indians who are left now live in reservations – land set apart for them. In SOUTH AMERICA, most Indians live as very poor peasants, though a few wild tribes still survive in the AMAZON jungle.

Lapps

The Lapps live in the far north of Scandinavia, mostly beyond the Arctic Circle. They are a small, dark-haired people. They speak a language similar to Finnish.

Until very recently most of them followed the great herds of REINDEER that wander about Lapland. The reindeer provided them with everything they needed – meat, milk, clothes, boots, tent-covering, transport and even tools. There are still many Lapp reindeer herdsmen. Most Lapps, however, have settled down to become farmers, fishermen or craftsmen.

Lapp men are expert bone-carvers, and the women are equally good at embroidery. Lapps often wear beautifully decorated clothes.

Left: A Lapp in traditional costume. In the background there is a reindeer.

Eskimos

There are not many more than 50,000 Eskimos living today. They live in arctic lands, such as Greenland, Labrador, Hudson Bay and Alaska. They live by HUNTING and FISHING. The climate makes any kind of FARMING impossible.

During the summer months Eskimos generally live in sealskin tents. In the fierce arctic winters they move to permanent stone or turf houses. Igloos – houses made from blocks of snow – are only used temporarily while the Eskimos are hunting SEALS. Eskimos travel by sleds drawn by dogs called huskies. They also use canoes called kayaks.

Eskimos originally came from ASIA. They belong to the YELLOW-SKINNED group of peoples.

Right: An Eskimo waits with his gun for a seal to appear in a hole in the ice.

Polynesians

The Polynesians are a brown-skinned people who live on many islands in the South PACIFIC. Some scientists believe that their ancestors sailed thousands of miles in frail canoes from ASIA to their island homes. Others believe they first came from SOUTH AMERICA. Among these is Thor Heyerdahl, who built and sailed the raft *Kon-Tiki*.

The Maoris of NEW ZEALAND are of Polynesian stock. They arrived in New Zealand about six hundred years ago from some Polynesian island or islands. Today New Zealand has about 280,000 Maoris.

The Maoris were once a very warlike people. They fought fiercely against the British who colonised New Zealand. But today they are a peaceful people, often working as farmers, craftsmen, and shepherds.

Above: This old Maori woman is standing by the gateway to her village.

Peoples of the Past

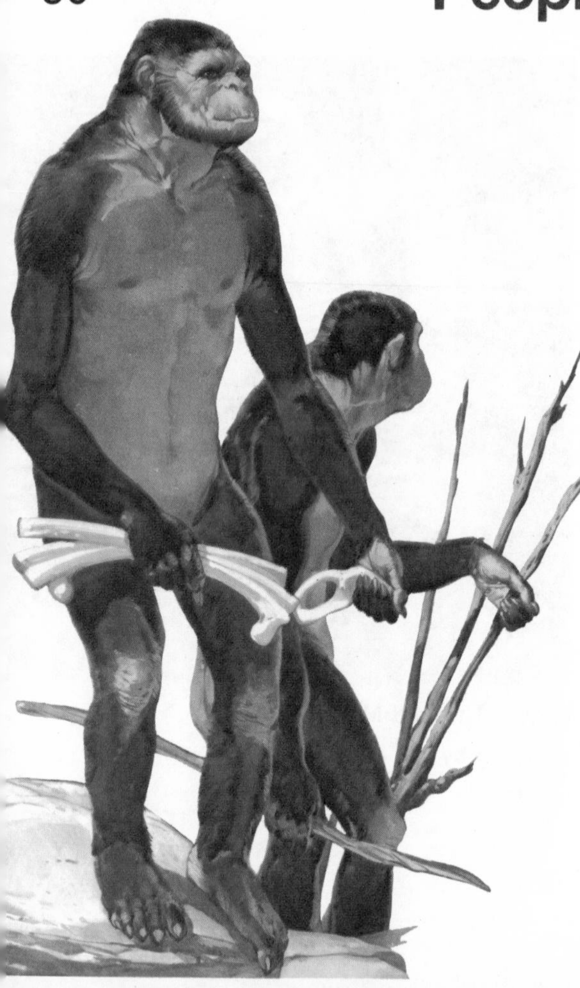

No one knows for certain how long Man has lived on the EARTH. The first man-like animals probably existed about five million years ago and lived mainly in Africa.

Man's first tools were sticks and the stones which he learned to chip into rough axes. He used these axes as weapons, and they helped him when he hunted animals. He also caught fish with spears, and fish-hooks made from thorns. Almost the only things that remain from this period, which is called the Old Stone Age, are some of the stone tools.

In the New Stone Age, people began to live together in larger groups. They learned to tame flocks and herds of domestic animals. They made picks from deer antlers and shovels from the shoulder blades of CATTLE. They also began to make pottery.

Left: Australopithecus was one of Man's earliest ancestors.
Below: These Cro-Magnon cave painters of the Old Stone Age lived 40,000 years ago.

Bronze Age

Five or six thousand years ago men first learned to mix COPPER and tin together to make bronze. This knowledge spread slowly through the world. People could now make better tools and weapons. They had helmets, shields, and armour.

They wove fine clothes and built ships. Their chiefs drove in chariots and lived in palaces.

Iron Age

In some parts of the world, the Iron Age began about four thousand years ago. Men learned to make IRON, and found that it was harder and better than bronze.

The use of the new metal spread slowly. The Iron Age began in Europe in about 900 B.C. It began in CHINA three hundred years later, and in Britain later still. Man made great progress in this period and invented many things.

Right: An Iron Age shield.

Below: An Iron Age lakeside settlement.

The Sumerians

The Sumerians were a nomadic people who settled down in what is now southern IRAQ in about 4000 B.C.

They split up into a number of city states which were soon at war with each other. But in about 2500 B.C. the city of Ur became the most powerful. It stayed so for about 600 years. Then power passed to Babylon.

The Sumerians were the first people to leave written records. These were in the form of clay tablets. Many thousands of these have been found.

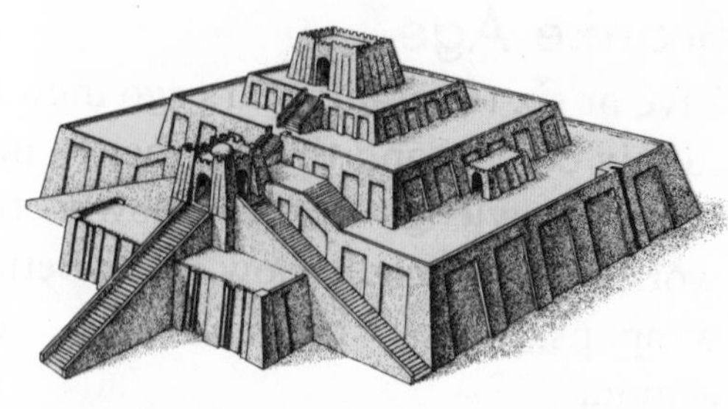

Above: The ziggurat (temple tower) at Ur, about 4000 years ago.
Below: A mosaic panel from a tomb at Ur.

Above: Part of an Egyptian scroll.
Below: The ancient Egyptian Temple of Abu Simbel fronted by four colossal stone figures.

Egyptians

One of the first great civilizations was in the fertile valley of the NILE. The first Pharaoh, or King of Egypt, ruled about 3200 B.C. The kingdom remained powerful for almost 3000 years. Then, the Egyptians were conquered by the Assyrians, then by the PERSIANS, and later by the Greeks led by ALEXANDER THE GREAT.

In that long period the Ancient Egyptians built up a rich empire with strong ARMIES and fleets. Using thousands of slaves, they constructed huge TEMPLES and statues, and put up pyramids to cover the tombs of their kings. The Great Pyramid was built for the Pharaoh, Cheops, in about 2700 B.C. and took nearly five million tons of stone.

The Egyptians studied the STARS and had mapped out the sky by 3000 B.C.

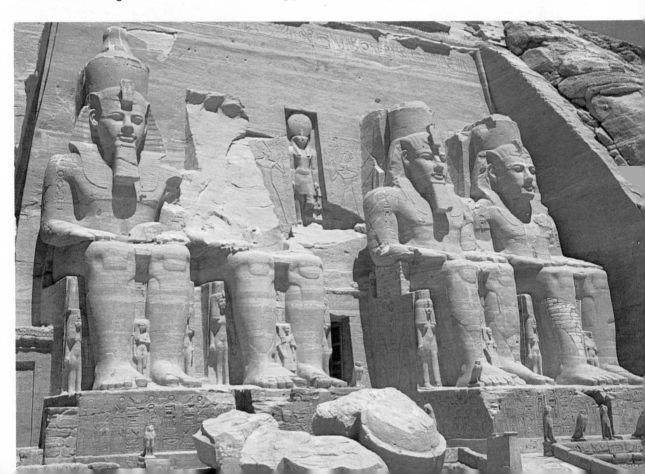

Babylonians

Babylonia was the name of the land between the rivers Tigris and Euphrates. (The area is now part of Iraq.) Civilization began there at about the same date as it did in EGYPT.

Much later, the city of Babylon became the capital. The city had magnificent TEMPLES, PALACES, and bridges over the Euphrates, which flowed through the city. The Hanging Gardens, in terraces, were one of the SEVEN WONDERS OF THE WORLD.

King Hammurabi gave the Babylonians strict but fair laws. Most writing was on clay tablets. Thousands of these have been found, bearing poems, stories, and writings about science. Some of them date back to 1790 B.C.

In 689 B.C., Babylonia became part of the Assyrian Empire. 150 years later it was conquered by the PERSIANS.

Above: A close-up of a figure on the Ishtar Gate, one of eight gateways into Babylon.
Below left: Slaves being driven through the Ishtar Gate.
Below: A Babylonian clay tablet, showing cuneiform writing.

Persians

The Ancient Persians were a nation of warlike people. Cyrus the Great founded their empire by conquering Babylon about 2500 years ago. Later kings, Cambyses and Darius I, enlarged this empire by conquering EGYPT, Asia Minor (modern TURKEY), and other lands.

When the Persians tried to invade EUROPE, they were driven back by the GREEKS, and it was the Greeks under ALEXANDER who conquered the Persians in 331 B.C. Today Persia is called IRAN.

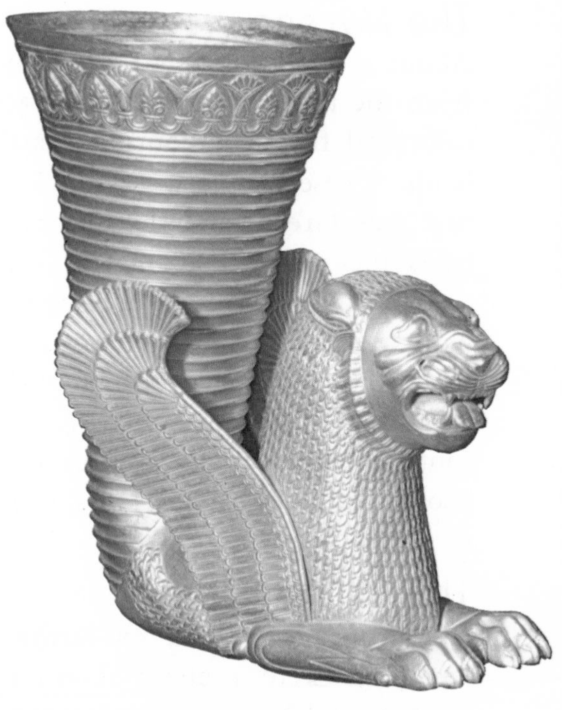

The Hebrews

In about 3000 B.C. the Hebrews were a tribe of nomads wandering with their flocks. In about 1400 B.C. they settled in what is now JORDAN and established the kingdom of ISRAEL. What distinguished them from all the other people around them was their belief in one God, Jehovah. After many battles with their neighbours they were finally overrun and captured by the Assyrians. As their history ended, the history of their descendants, the Jews, began.

Above: A 5th-century B.C. Persian gold cup.
Below: Solomon, king of the Hebrews from 970-931 B.C. , watches his temple being built.

The Myceneans

About 1900 B.C., a new people invaded GREECE from the north. Over the next 300 years they colonized the neighbouring coastlines and islands. These people were the Myceneans, the first true Greeks and the heroes immortalized by Homer in the *Iliad* and the *Odyssey*.

The Myceneans soon became rich by trading with their neighbours. Many beautiful things that they made have been found all over the MEDITERRANEAN. But around 1200 B.C. their sea routes were blocked by barbaric sea-faring peoples and the Mycenean culture crumbled.

Above: A gold mask found in a grave at Mycenae.

The Minoans

The Minoans were a sea-faring people who settled in Crete in about 2000 B.C. They were the first real European civilization. They built a great PALACE at Knossos which was the home of the king and queen and their court. It also served as a religious and administrative centre. The Minoans also traded throughout the Mediterranean in POTTERY, metal artefacts, oils and wine. Their civilization was destroyed by a mighty volcanic explosion in about 1470 B.C. However, by this time their influence had spread to the nearby mainland of GREECE.

Above: The palace of Knossos.
Below: A wall painting found inside the palace of Knossos showing the sport of bull-leaping.

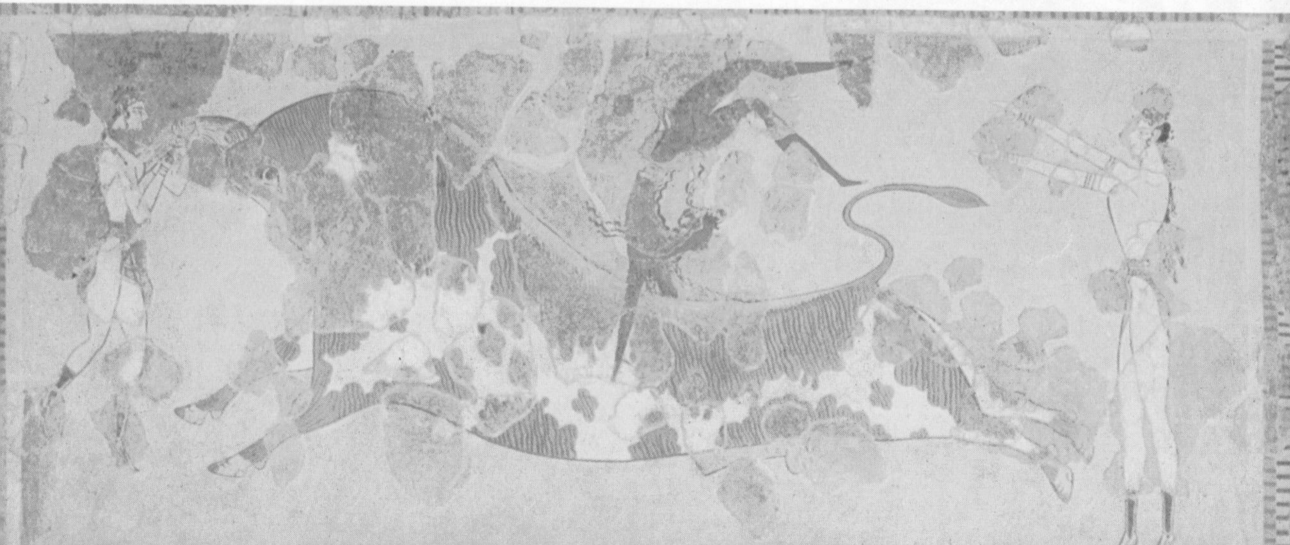

Greeks

Greek history began in about 2000 B.C., in Crete, an island in the Aegean Sea. Then came the splendid age (1400–1000 B.C.) of the city of Mycenae on the mainland. A new tribe, the Dorians, entered the country. Many small separate 'city states' grew up in the next few centuries.

The Greeks founded trading ports throughout the MEDITERRANEAN. In time, two states, ATHENS and Sparta, became rivals for the leadership of Greece. They fought a long war which left them both weak. Then, in 338 B.C., the whole country was conquered by a northern Greek king, Philip of Macedon, father of ALEXANDER THE GREAT.

The Greeks were brilliant and original thinkers. We can still read many books they wrote, recite their poems, and act their plays.

Right: A statuette of the goddess Aphrodite.
Below: Alexander the Great leading his army.

Romans

ROME was founded in about 753 B.C. by one of the Latin tribes of central ITALY. Until 510 B.C. the Romans had kings. Then they formed a REPUBLIC. Two consuls were elected to govern for one year, instead of the kings. They were helped by a senate of elder citizens.

The Romans had many enemies, but they were a tough people. They invented a fighting unit – the legion – so well trained that few could stand against it. The Romans conquered all Italy. They went on to take over EUROPE west of the Rhine and Danube, along with North AFRICA and Western ASIA to make a great empire.

In time, the consuls could no longer control this huge empire. A strong man was needed to

Above: The Romans built fine roads all over their vast empire.

Below: The Romans enjoyed watching battles between gladiators.

rule for life. JULIUS CAESAR (murdered 44 B.C.) was the first of these men, but his great-nephew, Augustus, became the first emperor.

The empire lasted about 500 years. It was overthrown by barbarian invaders between A.D. 300 and 400. Until then, despite disasters and civil wars, it mostly gave its subjects peace and good government. Famous emperors included Claudius, who brought Britain under Roman rule, the soldiers Trajan and Hadrian, and Constantine the Great.

The Romans copied many of their ideas from the GREEKS. They were, however, a more practical people than the Greeks. They were better at building straight roads, bridges and arched AQUEDUCTS to carry clean water to their cities.

Byzantine Empire

Byzantium (now called ISTANBUL) was an ancient Greek city. When the ROMAN Empire became so big that it had to be divided, Byzantium became the capital of the Eastern Empire. It was known as Constantinople. When the Western Empire fell, the Eastern half continued for a thousand years, until the Turks conquered it in A.D. 1453.

The Byzantine emperors kept a magnificent court, where visitors were dazzled by the rich robes and complicated ceremonies. Church robes are still copied from Byzantine styles. Greek, not Latin, was spoken.

Byzantium has left us beautiful churches and MOSAICS (pictures made with small pieces of stone).

Right: A mosaic (a picture made up of hundreds of tiny coloured stones) of the Byzantine Empress Theodora. She is surrounded by ladies of the court.

Arabs

It is believed that people were living in what is now Saudi Arabia around 1000 B.C. But Arabs remained a little-known desert people until they found a great leader in MOHAMMED (about A.D. 570–632). He gave them a new religion (ISLAM) and just before his death he launched them on a holy war, or 'jihad', against unbelievers.

The Arabs, who were also called Saracens, were fine horsemen and soldiers. In the next hundred years, their armies conquered much of western ASIA, North AFRICA, SPAIN and PORTUGAL. But they were driven back in FRANCE. They created a rich civilization, especially in Baghdad, Sicily, and Spain, with beautiful PALACES (such as the Alhambra, near Granada, in Spain), gardens and fountains. For many years they led the world in science and medical skill.

Right: The Arabs were great astronomers. In this picture you can see an astronomer using an astrolabe (an instrument for calculating the position of the sun and stars) like the one shown in the picture below.

Indians of Asia

Many millions of people, with different languages, customs and religions, live in the area which in 1947 was divided into INDIA and PAKISTAN. This region has had many rulers and has often been invaded. Nevertheless, Indian civilizations are among the most ancient in the world.

Around 2500 B.C. an advanced civilization grew up in the Indus Valley. Prosperous cities such as Mohenjo Daro came into being, but in about 1700 B.C. these cities were suddenly abandoned. Early in the third century B.C., most of northern and central India was united in a single empire known as the Mauryan Empire. It reached its height during the reign of Ashoka. The Gupta Empire, A.D. 320–500, was a golden age of HINDU culture. Later, Moslem conquerors established the Mogul Empire, A.D. 1505–1707, which produced fine art and architecture.

Above: An Indian holy man in front of the Hindu temple of Minakshi in Madurai.

Right: Ashoka, an Indian ruler of the third century B.C., sets out on a pilgrimage.
Below: The desert Arab's way of life has changed very little since the time of Mohammed.

Anglo-Saxons

The Angles, Saxons, and Jutes were tribes of ancient GERMANY. They used to raid Britain during the Roman occupation. Then, from A.D. 449, they began to make Britain their home, slowly driving the Celtic Britons westwards into Wales and Cornwall. This slow conquest was completed in A.D. 825. In this year England was united for a time when King Egbert became master of all the country except for the far north.

The Anglo-Saxons were farmers and country-dwellers. Most modern English villages have grown from their early settlements. At first the Anglo-Saxons worshipped pagan gods. Then St Augustine arrived from ROME in A.D. 597 and soon all Anglo-Saxons had become Christians.

Above: The Great Buckle, from the Sutton Hoo burial ship.
Below: Anglo-Saxons ploughing.

Vikings

The Vikings were known also as Northmen, Norsemen, or Danes. Most of them were farmers. They were a fierce, warlike people.

The Vikings were overcrowded in their bleak northern lands, and so they sailed in their long-ships to Iceland, Greenland, and even NORTH AMERICA. From A.D. 787 they began invading Britain, Ireland, and FRANCE, and seized large

A carving from the prow (or front) of a Viking ship.

areas. They raided as far south as SPAIN and ITALY.

The Vikings were not mere pirates. They were also traders. They founded Dublin, Nottingham and many other towns. Their adventures are told in long stories called sagas.

Normans

The French king allowed some Northmen (or VIKINGS) to settle in northern FRANCE in A.D. 911. They were known as Normans. They became Christians, learned civilized ways, and in time spoke Norman French, but they kept the warlike and adventurous spirit of the Vikings.

In 1066 their duke, WILLIAM THE CONQUEROR, claimed the crown of England and won it at the Battle of Hastings. At the same time, other Normans seized southern ITALY and Sicily. Both there and in England they established strong governments. Some of their fine stone CATHEDRALS and CASTLES can still be seen.

Above: The reconstructed Viking ship of Oseberg.
Below: The Battle of Hastings as shown on the Norman Bayeux Tapestry.

Chinese

The Chinese civilization is one of the oldest in the world. Pottery with picture-writing has been found in CHINA dating from about 4500 B.C.

Early China was made up of many small states. Then it was united under one ruler. Each ruler was thought to be sent by the gods. He was known as the Son of Heaven. In 551 B.C., the great philosopher CONFUCIUS was born. At that time, there were many writers, artists, and philosophers, and they were treated with great honour.

The Chinese invented many things – gunpowder, paper, PRINTING, and the ship's compass. They excelled in the making of PORCELAIN (which we call 'china' because they invented it), in water-colour painting, and in carving.

Right: A fifteenth-century Chinese porcelain factory.
Below right: A figure representing the Chinese earth spirit.
Below: The Great Wall of China today.

Japanese

The ancient Japanese peoples came to their islands from the mainland of ASIA several centuries before CHRIST. All their emperors have been descended from their first ruler, Jimmu.

The Japanese learned much of their civilization from the CHINESE – arts, buildings, government, even costume. They altered it, however, to suit their own needs. They made beautiful metalwork, sculpture, and pictures.

In the ninth century, a class of warriors called *samurai* appeared in Japan. They followed a code of conduct called *bushido*, or 'knightly path'. Their power lasted until 1876, when they were forbidden to carry SWORDS.

Below left: A Japanese mask.
Below: A samurai on horseback.

Mayas

The Mayas were an ancient AMERICAN INDIAN people living in Yucatan, on the south-eastern borders of MEXICO. Their great period was A.D. 300–900, but their civilization revived later. It lasted until the Spaniards came in about A.D. 1500.

They were talented architects and artists. Many of their stepped pyramids and the TEMPLES where they made sacrifices to their gods are still standing. Their priests studied the stars and mathematics. They worked out an accurate calendar and reckoned time from 3113 B.C.

Aztecs

The Aztecs were a wandering AMERICAN INDIAN people who moved southwards from what is now the U.S.A. They settled in MEXICO about A.D. 1200, where they built their capital Tenochtitlan in A.D. 1325.

They made fine clothes, carvings, and coloured pottery. They also built pyramids, and sacrificed prisoners to the God of War. Their last emperor, Montezuma, was defeated by the Spaniards in A.D. 1520.

A stepped Mayan temple. The three figures on the right are priests. As children, their heads were tightly bound up. This made their heads very long.

Incas

The Incas were an AMERICAN INDIAN tribe. They ruled an empire of subject peoples extending over Peru, Ecuador, and the north of Chile. They came from the south about A.D. 1100 and made their capital at Cuzco, high in the Andes. Their important buildings were covered with sheets of gold. The ruler of the empire was called the 'Unique Inca', and was treated like a god.

The Incas built bridges, paved roads, and made AQUEDUCTS. They could move ten-ton blocks of stone. They had no system of writing, however, and had not thought of the wheel. The Spanish general, Pizarro, conquered them in A.D. 1533.

Religions and Sects

From the earliest times, men have held religious beliefs. Religions arise from the idea that forces more powerful than man control him and the universe. Primitive man worshipped objects, such as rivers and mountains, or the sun or moon. Later peoples, such as the EGYPTIANS and the GREEKS and ROMANS, believed in many gods.

Many religions today teach that there is only one God. Jews and Christians share this belief. The followers of most of the main religions also believe in some kind of life after death. In addition, all religions tell their followers how they should behave on earth. A sect is a group of members of one religion, who have certain beliefs of their own. Most of the main religions are divided up into a number of sects.

Above: The Buddhist Temple of Dawn in Bangkok, Thailand.

Below: Jerusalem is a holy city for three major religions: Judaism, Islam and Christianity. Jews offer prayers at the Western, or 'Wailing', Wall.

Islam

Islam means 'to submit'. It is the religion of the Moslems who live in the ARAB countries, PAKISTAN, and other parts of ASIA. They have one God, Allah, and their sacred book is the Koran.

Like Jews and Christians, Moslems believe in the Old Testament prophets, or teachers, such as Moses. They say also that JESUS was a great prophet but not the Son of God. They think that the greatest prophet of all was MOHAMMED, the founder of Islam, an Arab who died in A.D. 632.

Left: The Kaaba is an important Moslem shrine in Mecca. Inside, it is empty. The band around the black covering contains writings in gold. All Moslems try to visit Mecca once in a lifetime.

Judaism

Judaism is the religion of the Jews. Jewish teaching is based on the books of the Old Testament, and a collection of writings called the Talmud. The Jews believe that when Moses was leading them out of Egypt, God gave them the Ten Commandments.

Judaism is more than a religion. It is a complete philosophy and way of life. Since it was founded, around 3500 years ago, Judaism has evolved a complete social and civil law of its own. Like Christians, Jews believe in one God. Strict Jews keep Saturday as their Sabbath, or day of rest. They must not marry non-Jews. They may not eat pork. Their ministers are called rabbis, and their services are held in synagogues.

Today, Jewish people live all over the world as well as in ISRAEL.

Left: A Rabbi reads from the Scriptures in a synagogue in Tunisia.

Above: The Buddha preaching to his followers.
Below: A statue of the Buddha, at Kamakura in Japan.

Buddhism

Siddhartha Gautama, the founder of Buddhism, was a HINDU prince, born about 550 B.C. He is called the Buddha, or 'the enlightened one'. He had been brought up in great luxury. But his life changed when he was twenty-nine, for he happened to see a sick man, an old man, and a dead man, one after the other. For the next six years he lived as a beggar, and thought deeply about the best way to live in the world. He spent most of the rest of his life teaching people to follow the law of *Karma*, which meant giving up earthly desires to reach the perfect peace of *Nirvana*. In order to do this a man must follow the Noble Eightfold Way, which lays down rules for correct behaviour.

Buddhists believe that creatures are born many times. They also consider it wrong to kill. Buddhist teachings were not written down until about 100 B.C. Today about one-fifth of the human race follow Buddhism. Most Buddhists live in CHINA, JAPAN, and other parts of ASIA.

Shinto

Shinto is the main religion of the people of JAPAN. It is a mixture of nature-worship and ancestor-worship. Shinto was established before the arrival of BUDDHISM in Japan in A.D. 552. After that time the two religions became mixed together. The main divinity is Amaterasu, the sun. The rising sun is the national symbol of Japan and appears on the Japanese flag.

The Emperor of Japan is traditionally thought to be descended from the sun-goddess. Until recently he was worshipped by his people as a kind of god.

In modern Japan, the Shinto religion exists alongside Buddhism and CHRISTIANITY and the Japanese people are allowed to worship as they please.

Right: A worshipper at a Shinto shrine in Japan.

Hindus

Hinduism is INDIA's main religion. Its oldest scriptures, the Veda hymns, are thousands of years old. Hindus worship God in many different forms. The three most important forms are Brahma the Creator, Vishnu the Preserver, and Shiva the Destroyer.

Hindus believe that they are born again many times. They are born in a higher or lower state depending on the life they have led. They believe that they can live a series of better and better lives until they attain the state of *moksha*. At this point they are freed from the need to be born again. Not all Hindus have exactly the same customs and beliefs.

Left: A carnival horse at a Hindu festival in Madras, India. Festivals like this one are part of India's colourful tradition.

Above: Jesus was crucified by his enemies in about A.D. 30. This painting shows the body of the dead Christ.

Christianity

Christianity is the faith of those who believe that JESUS, a young Jewish teacher, was in fact the Son of God sent on earth to show men how to live. Thousands flocked to hear Jesus preach, but He also had powerful enemies who put Him to death in about A.D. 30. However, His disciples, or followers, said that He had risen from the dead. They went on spreading the Gospel or 'good news' that God was the loving Father of all and that there was a better life after death.

Several wrote down all they remembered about Jesus. These writings are called the Gospels of Matthew, Mark, Luke, and John. They form the beginning of the New Testament. With the Old Testament, it forms the Bible.

Jesus was also called 'Christ', a Greek word meaning 'the anointed one'. His followers came to be called Christians. Soon they spread all over the Roman Empire. In A.D. 380, Emperor Constantine made Christianity the official religion.

Above: Martin Luther being formally excommunicated (expelled) from the Catholic Church by Charles V, the Holy Roman Emperor.

Protestants

After the Middle Ages, some Christians thought that the ROMAN CATHOLIC faith was no longer true to Christ's teaching. A German monk, MARTIN LUTHER, led their protest in 1517. His followers (the PROTESTANTS) broke away and formed their own churches. They refused to obey the Pope and also changed the services.

The breakaway of the Protestants from the Roman Catholic Church led to great turmoil throughout Europe.

Protestant churches include the Church of England, the Church of Scotland, and the Lutheran Churches of NORWAY, DENMARK, SWEDEN, and GERMANY itself. A later development was the Protestant Episcopal Church of the United States.

Above: An open-air Christian religious service being held in the Republic of Zaire.

Roman Catholics

Early Christians belonged to one 'catholic' (world-wide) church, but in time they divided into the Roman Catholic and the EASTERN CHURCH. The head of the Roman Catholics is the Pope, the bishop of ROME, but there are other bishops and priests in most parts of the world. These bishops and priests may not marry.

Catholics (laymen) must keep the Church's rules, confessing their sins and going to the service called Mass each Sunday. They believe that Christ's Mother, the Virgin Mary, and the Saints can help them when they pray to God.

Below: A painting by Raphael of Pope Leo X who held office from 1513 to 1521.

Eastern Church

The Eastern (or Orthodox) Church began after the capital of the Roman Empire had been moved to Constantinople, now ISTANBUL. Later, it refused to accept the Pope as the head of the Christian Church. In 1054 it separated from the Western (ROMAN CATHOLIC) Church.

The Eastern Church spread to a number of countries, mainly GREECE and Russia. The Russian Church has survived attempts to suppress it by the Communist Party, which does not approve of religion.

The archbishops of the Eastern Church are known as patriarchs or metropolitans. Saints are considered to be very important. They are often represented by small images called icons.

A typical Greek Orthodox Church in Thessalonica.

Quakers

'Quakers' was the name given to the Society of Friends because they sometimes trembled with excitement at their meetings in the early days. The Society was founded by George Fox in 1652. The Quakers were widely persecuted during the early years of their existence but the movement spread quickly through Britain, and by 1656 had its first members in NORTH AMERICA. One Quaker, William Penn, founded the state of Pennsylvania.

Quakers practise simplicity in dress, speech, household furniture, marriage and funerals. They believe in a strict and sincere way of life, based on the goodness of every man. They worship God in quiet meetings.

Quakers have been active in opposing slavery and capital punishment. They will not fight as soldiers but will risk their lives to help the wounded.

Presbyterians

These Christians, who follow the teachings of the reformer, John CALVIN (1509–1564), believe that the Church should be directed by 'Elders' (Senior Church Members), not bishops. 'Presbyter' is the Greek word for 'Elder' and so they are called Presbyterians in some parts of the world.

In other countries, the followers of Calvin are known as Calvinists; for example, the Dutch Reformed Churches of South Africa. There are three such Churches: Nederduitse Gereformeerde Kerk, the Gereformeerde Kerk, and the Nederduitsch Hervormde Kerk van Afrika. The French and Swiss Reformed Churches are also Calvinists.

Left: The Swiss reformer John Calvin.

Mormons

The official name of the Mormon Church is the Church of Jesus Christ of the Latter-Day Saints. Joseph Smith claimed he had seen a vision of God and had been given a new gospel, the Book of Mormon. He founded the Church in 1830.

The Mormons settled first in Missouri, and then in Illinois. In both places there were conflicts with their neighbours, and Joseph Smith was killed.

In 1847, Brigham Young, their second leader, led them to what is now Utah, where they founded Salt Lake City. At first, the men often had several wives, but later Mormons gave up this practice, as it was against U.S. law. Today they are a wealthy church and send missionaries to other countries.

The choir of the Mormon Tabernacle, in Salt Lake City, Utah. The choir is famous all over the world.

Folklore and Belief

The stories and ideas of a group of peoples, which are handed down from parents to children, are called folklore. Early religions were closely connected with folklore. The ANCIENT GREEKS told stories, not only about gods, but about the heroes who were nearly as powerful as the gods.

Before people understood the scientific reasons for things happening, they explained them by magical or superstitious ideas. People thought that natural events like tides and seasons were caused by the gods. It was therefore important not to make the gods angry. Even today we have a number of SUPERSTITIONS.

Many old customs survive long after their original purpose has disappeared. Holly and mistletoe were used in religious ceremonies long before Christianity.

The Greeks and Romans worshipped a number of gods and goddesses. They believed that the gods lived on the top of Mount Olympus. The king of the gods was called Zeus (1). The Romans called him Jupiter. The queen was called Hera (Juno to the Romans). Other gods included Apollo (3), the sun-god; Artemis (2) (Diana), goddess of the moon and hunting; Aphrodite (Venus), goddess of love; Ares (Mars), god of war, Poseidon (5) (Neptune), god of the sea; Dionysus (4) (Bacchus) was god of wine and drama; Hermes (6) (Mercury) was the messenger of the gods.

Myths

Myths are the stories that have grown up among various peoples to explain things they could not fully understand. The GREEKS, for example, said the SUN was really a young god, Apollo, driving a golden chariot across the sky. Myths were passed down by word of mouth before there were any books. Each people has its own group of myths, but some groups of myths have been influenced by others.

Different peoples have had different stories to explain similar things. Some held that the world was supported by the giant Atlas. Others believed that it rested on four elephants riding on the back of a swimming turtle.

Left: A painting of a mythical subject-the Birth of the Milky Way, by Tintoretto.

Norse gods

Before they became Christians, the ANGLO-SAXONS and other German tribes believed in many gods. The king of the gods was Odin, or Woden, the All-Father, the Lord of Hosts. He lived in Asgard (heaven) and had a hall, Valhalla, where dead heroes led a life of fighting and feasting.

Odin's wife was named Frigg, but a much more important goddess was Freya, who drove a chariot drawn by cats. Odin's sons were the mighty thunder god Thor, and the gentle Balder, who was killed by the evil god, Loki. Wednesday is named after Woden, Thursday after Thor, and Friday after Freya.

Below left: Three of the most important Norse gods. Odin is on the left, and Thor is in the centre. Balder stands on the right. Thor was believed to cause thunder with blows from his hammer.

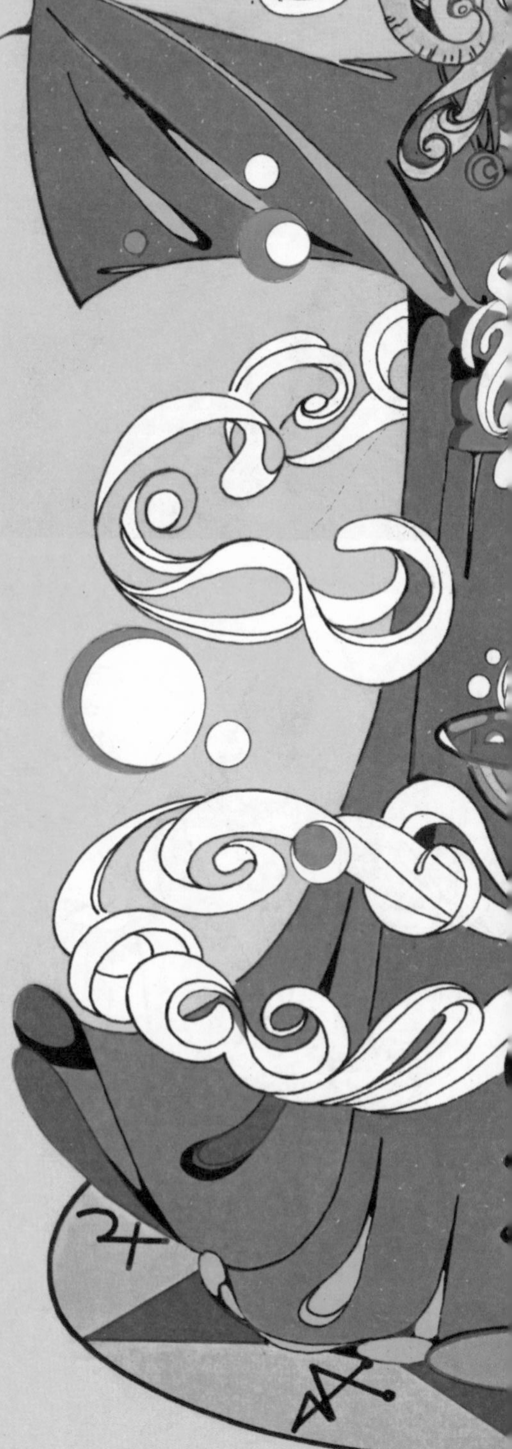

Superstitions

Not walking under ladders, not spilling salt, 'unlucky 13' – these are just a few of many superstitions.

Superstitions are old ideas that are left over from the days of magical beliefs. In those days people knew nothing of science and often did not understand the real reasons why certain things happened. Most people do not seriously believe in superstitions, but they remain as habits.

Witches

Until about three hundred years ago, most people believed in witches. Some still do. Witches were people who claimed that they could help or harm other people with MAGIC charms or spells.

We normally think of witches as women, but there were men witches as well. Men witches used to be called wizards, or witch-doctors in AFRICA (where they are still occasionally found).

Top left: Some of the things that are connected with superstitions. In some parts of the world black cats are thought to be unlucky. In other countries they are considered lucky.

They sometimes appeared to have magical powers by frightening simple people so that they became ill. In the past almost everyone believed in witches, who were sometimes cruelly put to death.

A coven was a secret group of thirteen witches, meeting at night.

Magic

Before men studied science, they thought that it was possible to influence the laws of nature. They believed that some people could make things happen just by thinking about them. They thought that it was possible to influence the weather, or to ensure a good harvest, by magical means.

Magic carpets, rings, wands, lamps, cloaks, and swords appear in many old stories.

A conjurer is someone who performs tricks, but he knows that what he does only *looks* like magic. We still say a thing is done 'by magic' if we cannot understand it.

Centre: A warlock, or wizard. He is wearing a magic cloak, and ram's head cap. He is standing in a circle containing magical symbols.
Top right: Some tools of the conjurer's trade.

Government

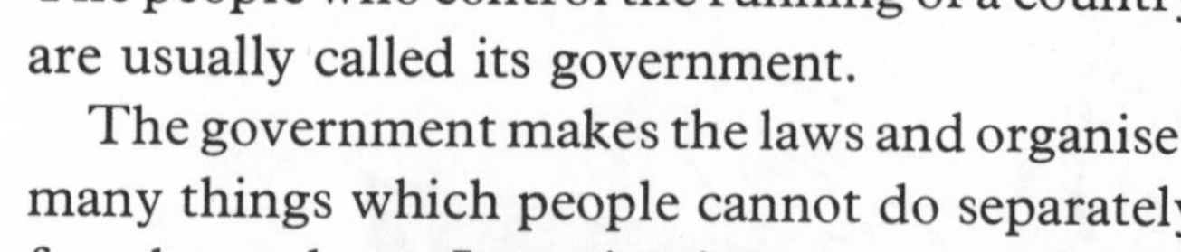

The people who control the running of a country are usually called its government.

The government makes the laws and organises many things which people cannot do separately for themselves. It maintains an ARMY and a POLICE force, and builds ROADS. In some countries the government also builds many of the houses, owns the RAILWAYS, runs the postal services, and provides schools and hospitals.

The government needs money to pay for these things and for many other purposes, such as old age pensions and sickness benefit. It collects the money it needs from the people in TAXES.

The pictures on this page show some of the ways in which the Government spends the taxpayers' money: aid to agriculture, scientific research and exploration, including space expeditions.

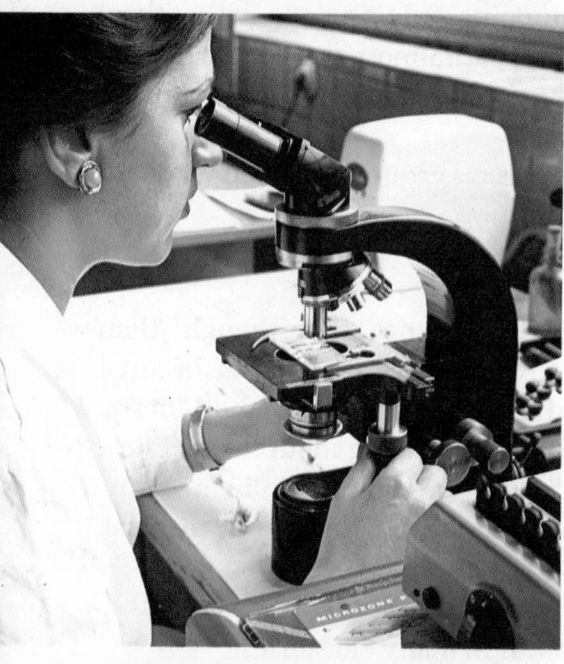

Monarchy

Monarchy means a system of government by one ruler for his lifetime. A monarch is usually a king or queen, emperor or empress. He or she comes to power as the child or the nearest relative of the monarch before.

An absolute monarchy is one in which the sovereign has complete power to make and carry out the laws of the country. A limited monarchy is one in which the sovereign rules a country with a constitution and established laws.

Modern monarchs, like the Queen of England and the King of NORWAY are the heads of limited monarchies. They leave the running of the government to their MINISTERS, who have been elected to their job. But the monarch still acts as the head of the nation.

Above: The Queen of England and the Duke of Edinburgh with the Queen of Denmark and her husband, Prince Henrik.

Below: This painting shows the U.S. Congress voting for independence from Britain in 1776. From being a colony, the United States became a republic, with a President as its ruler.

Republic

The term 'Republic' comes from the Latin *res publica*, which means 'commonwealth'. Throughout history, republics have usually come about because people did not like being ruled over by a monarch.

Nowadays a republic is a government where there is no sovereign. The leader is usually called a PRESIDENT.

The ANCIENT ROMANS had a republic from 510 to 31 B.C. Later on, EUROPE was mainly ruled by emperors and kings, until republics were founded again by the Swiss, the Italians, and the Dutch. England was a republic for a time under OLIVER CROMWELL. The U.S.A. became the first of the great modern republics.

Fascism

Fascism is a form of government which believes that the state is supreme. Fascist states are often DICTATORSHIPS. People who oppose the state are often put into jail, sent into exile or murdered.

Often the leader of a fascist state makes the people believe that their country is better than all other countries. This can sometimes lead to war. In 1939, the fascist states of GERMANY and ITALY invaded and overran their neighbours. This led to WORLD WAR II. However, they were finally beaten by the western allies, who had come to the support of the invaded countries.

Fascist dictatorships still exist in many countries of the world.

Right: The fascist ruler Franco came to power after the Spanish Civil War (1936-9). This is a political poster from that war.

Dictatorship

A dictator is a man who takes over the government of a country, often by force, after a REVOLUTION. Often he breaks the law of that country and makes new laws to suit himself, without letting people vote. He may also abolish TRADE UNIONS and other groups of people who try to oppose him. Sometimes people who disagree with the way a country is being run are put into prison or killed.

Modern dictators have included Adolf HITLER (GERMANY), Benito Mussolini (ITALY), Joseph Stalin (RUSSIA), Francisco Franco (SPAIN), and Idi Amin (UGANDA). All of these countries became more free when the dictators died or were overthrown.

Left: Charlie Chaplin played a character very like Hitler in the film *The Great Dictator.*

Democracy

Democracy is a Greek word and means 'government by the people'. One of the phrases still used today to define democracy is 'government of the people, by the people, and for the people'. In a true democracy, everyone has a say in the way the country is run. Democracy is the opposite of totalitarianism, or one-party DICTATORSHIP.

Democracy was a form of government developed in ANCIENT GREECE when each state was so small that every man could go to a meeting and vote. Now that states have millions of citizens, people have to choose a few men to speak and vote for them. Different countries choose these men in different ways, and systems of democracy are very varied.

Modern examples of democracies include GREAT BRITAIN, the U.S.A., FRANCE, GERMANY and ITALY.

Above: Counting the votes after a local council election in Britain.

Communism

Communism is the theory that all people are equal and that all property should be owned by the state. In return the state should give everyone everything he or she needs. This theory was put forward in the nineteenth century by KARL MARX and is often called Marxism. CHINA, the Soviet Union and several other countries are trying to work towards this situation.

Communists do not believe in God. They believe that the state is the main authority. Some communists believe in REVOLUTION to further their aims. Many people object to communism because they do not want total control by the state.

Left: Soldiers of the Communist Chinese army assembled in the capital, Peking.

Political parties

People with the same ideas on how to run the government often join a political party. They hold meetings, give out leaflets, and try in every way to get their leaders elected.

In a free country, any group of people can form a party. In the U.S.A., there are two big parties, the Democrats and the Republicans. In Britain the main parties are the Conservatives (Tories) and the Labour Party, or Socialists.

Some countries have even more parties. Social Democrat parties are much the same as the Labour Party in Britain. In some countries where the COMMUNIST Party is in power, no other parties are allowed. Anyone trying to form one may be put in PRISON.

Above: Outdoor elections on the island of New Guinea.

Right: The election of the Democratic candidate for the 1972 U.S. presidential election, which was won by Richard Nixon.

Revolutions

Revolutions happen when people are not satisfied with the way their country is run. After a revolution a country has new rulers (the word *revolution* means 'to turn around'). Russia had two revolutions in 1917.

Robespierre (3) was a leader in the French Revolution. He executed many opponents by guillotine (4). The Russian Revolution of 1905 (1) failed, but the Bolsheviks (7) under Lenin (2) were successful in 1917. In 1956 the Russians crushed a revolution (6) in Hungary. 'Che' Guevara (5) was a revolutionary in South America.

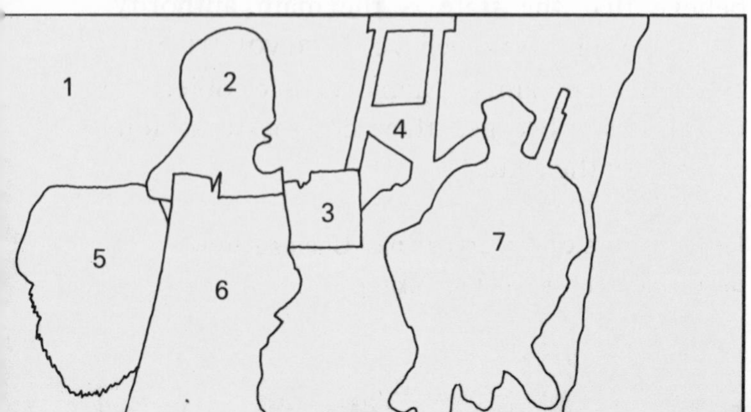

Elections

Elections are held so that citizens can choose people to run their government. Countries have different systems. Usually, there is a secret ballot. Nobody knows how anyone else votes.

The U.S.A. has an election for PRESIDENT every four years. In Britain, PARLIAMENT must hold a General Election at least every five years. The election may come sooner if it seems necessary to choose a new parliament. In some countries elections are not free, because the government allows votes for only one person or candidate.

Women were not allowed to vote at all until the twentieth century. Even today there are countries which do not allow certain groups of people to vote.

Parliament

A parliament is the place where laws are made, TAXES are fixed, and all matters of government are discussed.

The British Parliament meets at Westminster, in LONDON, and is often called 'the mother of parliaments' because it is so old and has been copied in so many other countries. Often these other countries use a different name, such as Congress or National Assembly, but the basic idea is the same. When the people of a country are free to elect the government they want, the system is called 'parliamentary DEMOCRACY'.

The British Parliament consists of three parts: the Queen, the House of Lords and the House of Commons. Laws have to be passed in both Houses and signed by the Queen. The House of Commons has about 630 M.P.s (Members of parliament), each chosen by voters in one area.

Below: The Queen, the Duke of Edinburgh, Prince Charles and Princess Anne at the opening of the British Parliament in 1979.

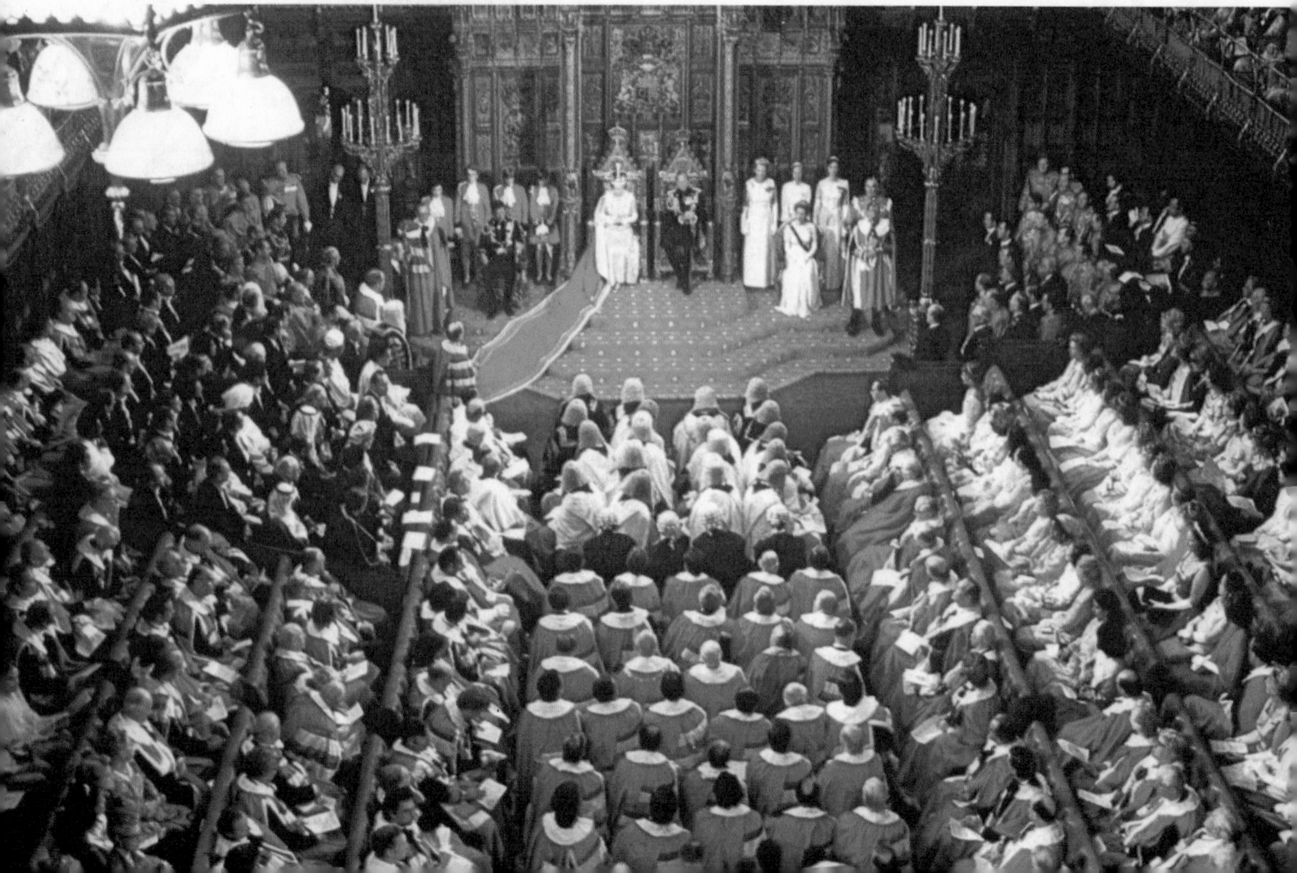

Above: The Parliament buildings in Canberra, Australia.
Right: William Pitt the Younger, Britain's youngest ever Prime Minister.

Prime Minister

A Prime Minister is the head of the governing party. Sometimes, as in FRANCE, the Prime Minister has less power than the PRESIDENT. In Britain the Prime Minister has more power than anyone else.

In Britain when a political party is elected into office the Queen asks its leader to 'form a government'. The leader, who becomes Prime Minister, chooses other MINISTERS for the various departments and offices in the government. The British Prime Minister is given a house and office at 10 Downing Street in London near the House of Commons as well as a quieter country home at Chequers in Buckinghamshire. When the Prime Minister cannot get PARLIAMENT to vote as he or she wishes then he or she must either resign or hold an ELECTION.

Above: Margaret Thatcher, the first woman to become Prime Minister of Britain.

Congress

Congress is the body which makes laws for the United States. Like the British PARLIAMENT, it meets in two parts, the Senate and the House of Representatives. They use the north and south wings of the great Capitol building in WASHINGTON, D.C.

Congress is bound by the rules, or Constitution, of the United States and needs a two-to-one vote to alter those rules. The PRESIDENT can put a ban or veto on what Congress decides, unless there is a two-thirds majority against him.

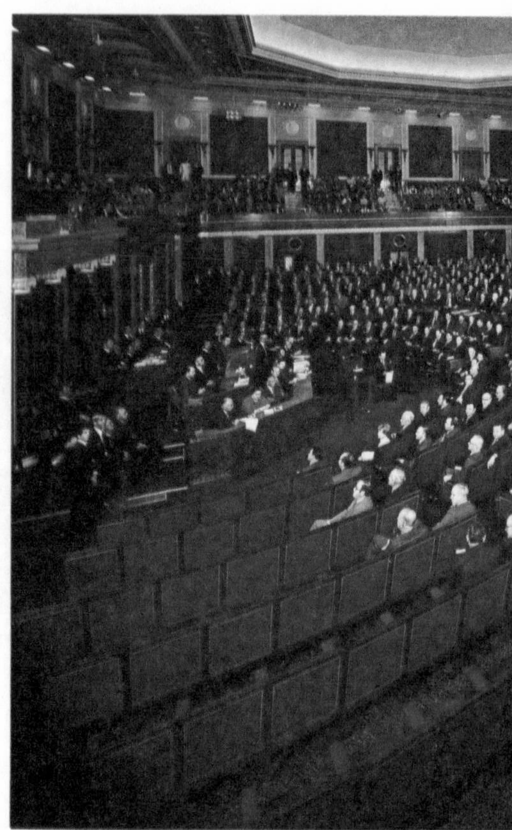

Senate

The first senate was in ancient ROME. Now it is the name given in many countries to the 'upper house' of the body making their laws. The United States Senate is part of CONGRESS. It has 100 members. Two senators are elected from each of the 50 states and serve for six years each. But one third of the senators retire every two years. In this way, the people can vote to change their senate by degrees, but not all at once.

President

In a REPUBLIC, the president is head of the state and is treated almost like a king. He is often elected for life but sometimes for a fixed term –

PRESIDENTS OF THE UNITED STATES
(1) George Washington. (2) Thomas Jefferson.
(3) Andrew Jackson. (4) Abraham Lincoln.
(5) John F. Kennedy.

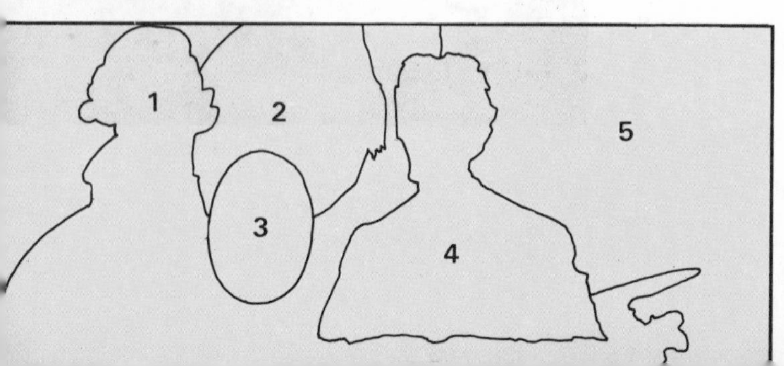

The United States House of Representatives.

four years in the United States unless the people vote for him again. He cannot now serve more than two terms.

Like modern kings, some presidents have little real power – for example, in ITALY and INDIA the government is actually run by the PRIME MINISTER. In many other republics, for example the ones in SOUTH AMERICA, the president is the most important man in the country.

House of Representatives

The House of Representatives is much bigger than the SENATE. It is also part of the United States CONGRESS. It has 435 members. Each state sends its two senators, whether it has a large population or a small one. However, the number of its Representatives depends on the number of voters. Unlike senators, they have to stand again for ELECTION every two years.

Civil Service

Civil servants are men and women who work in the different departments or agencies, of a government. These departments include defence, health, education, and housing. Civil servants carry out the policies of the government, even if they do not agree with them. Today many countries have a large civil service, which employs thousands of people. Senior civil servants may be highly paid, expert officials.

In the United States, civil servants used to be changed when a new PRESIDENT was elected. This practice was called the 'spoils system'. In 1883 an act was passed which introduced the 'merit system'. The new system meant that people could only get into certain grades in the civil service by passing an examination.

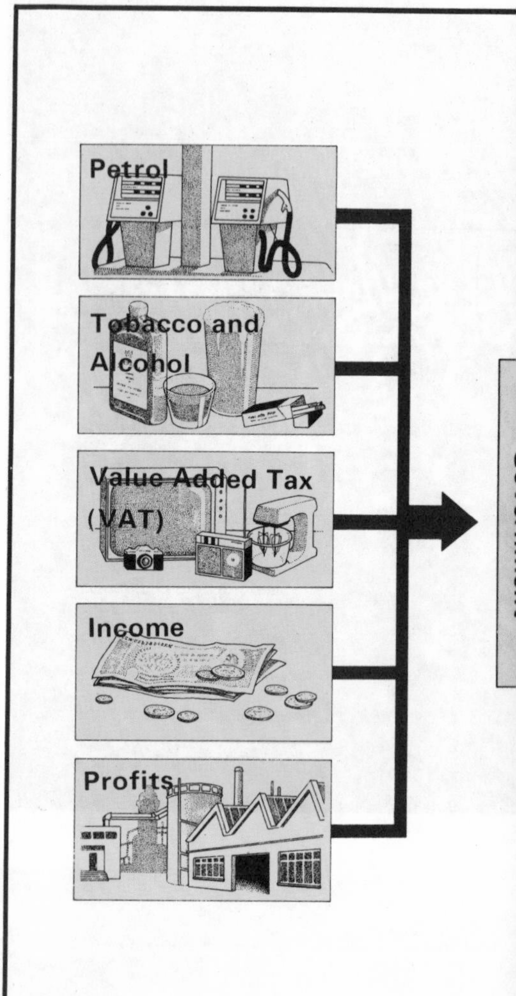

Ministers

In Britain, and some other countries, the head of a government department is called a minister. He is a member of the government. The most important ministers have places on a special committee called the cabinet. It is presided over by the PRIME MINISTER. When it meets, ministers offer advice on what policies the Prime Minister should follow.

Examples of ministerial positions are: the Minister of Defence who is responsible for the ARMY, AIR FORCE and NAVY of a country, the Home Secretary, who looks after the administration of the POLICE, PRISONS and immigration, and the Foreign Secretary, who is responsible for foreign affairs.

Right: The splendid British Embassy in Moscow viewed from the Kremlin, the main building of the Russian Government.

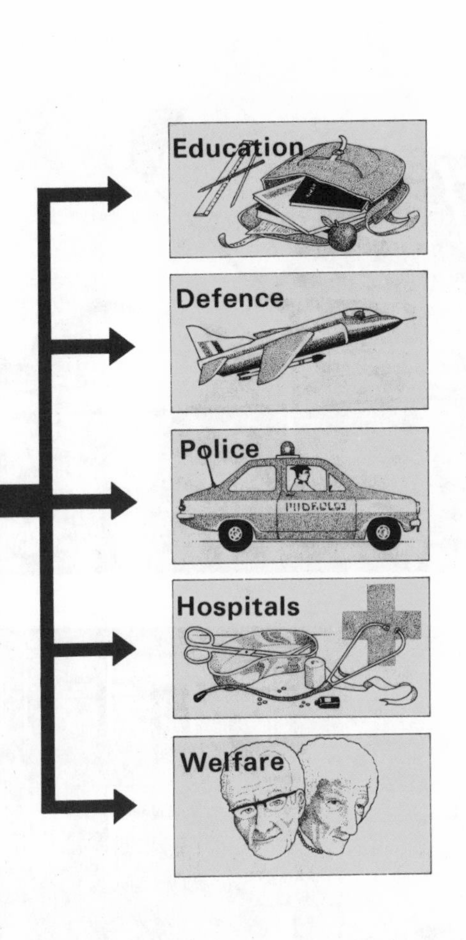

Taxes

Taxes are the money that people in some countries have to give their government to pay for ARMIES, HEALTH SERVICES, schools, pensions, and many other things. People pay taxes both directly, out of their pay, and indirectly, every time they buy certain things.

The largest direct tax is Income Tax, which is based on how much money a person earns in a year. In Britain, most people pay income tax through the Pay-As-You-Earn System (PAYE). Tax is deducted from their wage packets before they receive them. People pay indirect taxes on such goods as beer, tobacco, and cars.

Companies have to pay tax on their profits. In some countries, the money people leave when they die is also heavily taxed.

Taxes change from time to time, and each country has its own system. In Britain there is a system of local taxes called rates. In the United States there are separate state and city taxes.

Left: Most of the money spent by the Government has to come from taxes. This diagram shows where some of the money comes from and shows where most of it is spent.

Ambassador

An ambassador represents his country in a foreign land. He explains to the rulers of that country what his own government is doing or thinking about certain matters. He also looks after his country's affairs and interests in the country to which he is sent.

He tries to settle arguments between the two countries and to help them understand each other better. He has a big official house called an embassy, and often has a large staff of officials who are called diplomats.

Local government

Government in most countries is conducted at a national and a local level. The national government looks after the interests of the population as a whole. Local government, on the other hand, is concerned with the more immediate needs of the people. Among the many services provided by local government are the POLICE force and the fire services, public HEALTH and SOCIAL SERVICES, housing and education, town and country planning, ROADS and engineering works, public LIBRARIES and MUSEUMS, and parks and swimming pools. Money for local government comes from the national or state government and from local taxes. In Britain the main local tax is the rates, which are paid by property owners.

Refuse disposal (top right) and the fire services (below) are both paid for and run by local governments. They are financed through local taxes called rates.

Above: An elderly man is being visited by a local government worker and a nurse. The sick are regularly visited at their homes.

Social services

A century ago in many countries it could be a terrible fate to be poor and old or young and out of work. If you did not have a family or friends to help you, you had to go to a workhouse. This was a grim place where people were given little to eat or drink, cheap rough clothes and made to do horrible and degrading work. Life was made as unpleasant as possible.

Today most governments provide social services to aid such people. Some of these services are paid for and run by the national government. People out of work or sick can receive social security benefits to make sure that they have enough to eat and somewhere to live. Fuel for the elderly, clothing and bedding may also be supplied by the state benefit system.

But most social services are run at LOCAL GOVERNMENT levels. For the elderly there are home helps to do their housework, health visitors and, if necessary, old people's homes. Child care is another social service. It involves looking after children who, for some reason, are unable to live with their parents.

The probation officer supervises people who have been put on probation by the COURTS after breaking the LAW. The probationer must report regularly to a probation officer, who tries to keep him or her out of further trouble. HOSPITALS also provide social services. Special departments try to help patients with personal problems.

Much of the money to pay for these services comes from national government and is raised by way of TAXES. The rest of the money needed comes from the rates.

Left: Local governments usually pay for educational facilities, such as schools.

Law

Laws are the rules people need to agree upon if they are to live in peace together. From the earliest times, and in the most savage tribes, laws have been made to say what men may do and what they may not. People cannot obey the law, however, unless they know what it is. One of the first marks of a civilized people is to have its laws clearly written down and known by everyone.

One important set of laws was the Ten Commandments, given by Moses to the Israelites. The ANCIENT ROMANS had a fine legal system, on which much modern law is based. Today, not all countries have the same laws.

Below: The United States Supreme Court is situated in Washington.

Courts of law

Courts are where cases are tried. A case may be about a criminal offence, such as stealing. Or it may be a civil offence, like a dispute between two business firms.

A court has a high seat for the JUDGE, or magistrate, tables and seats for LAWYERS and newspaper men, and seats for the public. If there is a prisoner, he stands inside a little enclosure called the dock. People who are connected with the case may be called to give evidence. They have to swear to tell the truth, and can be punished for not doing so.

Left: The famous Old Bailey court of law in London. The statue of justice sits on top of the tower.

Crime

Crime usually means breaking the law in a serious way. Murder (killing someone), assault (injuring someone), and stealing are crimes. A person who has committed a number of crimes is called a criminal. Parking a car in the wrong place is not a crime. It is an offence, however, and the motorist can be punished for it.

When a crime has been committed, the POLICE are mainly responsible for catching the criminal. They must catch the right person. It would be wrong to punish an innocent man who has done nothing. So the police must take the man they catch to COURT, and a magistrate – or a JUDGE and JURY – must decide whether he is innocent or guilty.

If he is guilty, a criminal can be sent to PRISON for a serious crime. If the crime is not serious, he can be fined (made to pay a sum of money). A criminal can also be put on probation. He will not be punished unless he commits another crime. A probation officer is put in charge of him.

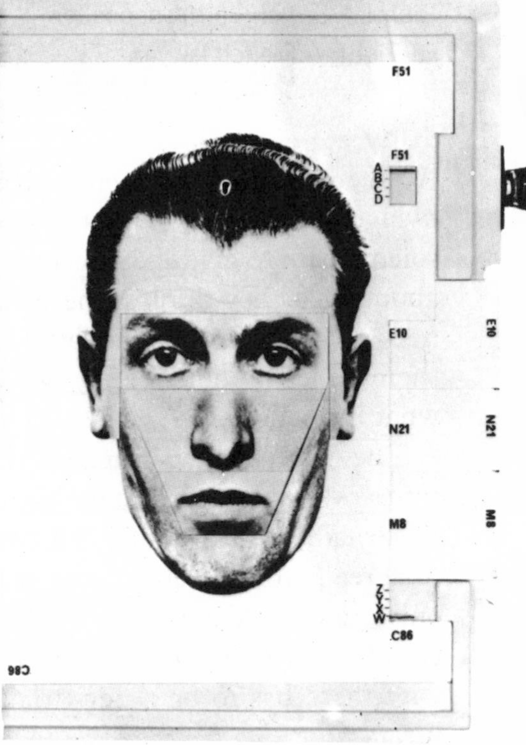

Above: A method of constructing the face of a criminal from parts of many different photographs.

Judge

A judge is a LAWYER who has worked for most of his life in the courts and knows the law thoroughly. He needs a very keen brain and must be fair to both sides.

In some countries, such as Britain and the United States there is a JURY to help him, and he does not have to decide whether the prisoner is guilty or not. The jury settle guilt or innocence, but the judge helps them by explaining the law. He also sees that the trial is properly run, and sums up the main points before the jury decide. The judge fixes any punishment or sentence.

In civil cases (disputes that are not crimes) judges often decide the matter themselves without a jury.

Right: A British Lord Chancellor.
Far right: A French lawyer.

Jury

A jury is a group of men and women, usually twelve, who listen to a law case. They take a solemn oath to give an honest verdict or decision about what they think is the truth. They do not need to be experts in the law. The JUDGE helps them on legal points. They only have to decide what happened.

The first juries in England were in NORMAN times. Many countries have copied this system. In Britain, until recently, all twelve jurors had to agree before a verdict was reached, but now only ten have to agree. In the United States, all twelve have to reach the same decision. Otherwise there has to be a new trial, with different jurors.

In AUSTRALIA, in civil cases, there are sometimes only four people in a jury. In Scotland there may be as many as 15.

Lawyer

People who wish to become lawyers have to study the law for several years. Lawyers earn their living by advising people and speaking for them in the COURTS. The law is too complicated for most people to understand without help. In Britain there are two kinds of lawyer: a solicitor works mainly in his office and may speak only in the Magistrate's Court; a barrister's job is to speak in all kinds of courts. At present only a barrister may become a JUDGE.

In the United States the words are attorney and counsellor, but the same lawyer may do the work of both barrister and solicitor.

International courts

In 1899 a group of statesmen met in HOLLAND to discuss ways of stopping wars and solving disagreements between nations. One of the ways they found of doing this was to set up the International Court of Justice.

Countries who quarrel can go to the International Court where fifteen JUDGES from different countries decide who is in the right. Decisions are based on a majority of judges present. Before they go to court the countries in dispute have to agree to accept the decision. Disputes are very often about where exactly frontiers between countries are drawn.

Another International Court is the European Court of Justice which sits in LUXEMBOURG. This was set up by the countries of the European Community. It makes sure that all the countries of the COMMON MARKET obey the rules and it can fine countries who disobey very heavily. Every member country appoints a judge.

Left: The Peace Palace in the Hague, seat of the International Court of Justice.

Police

The first duty of a police force is to see that people obey the law. But the police are not only concerned with catching criminals. They have to do such jobs as direct traffic, control crowds, find lost children, rescue people in danger, and give first aid in accidents. In many countries people often go to a policeman for help when they are in trouble.

Most policemen and policewomen wear uniforms, but those doing detective work wear 'plain' clothes, so that criminals will not know what they are. If a policeman sees a person actually committing a CRIME, he can arrest him on the spot. To make an arrest at other times he must get a court order called a warrant.

The police cannot try to punish people themselves – they must take them to the COURTS. In some countries, there are secret police who arrest people who protest against the government.

Right: Policemen using Alsatian dogs in a search in Epping Forest, near London.

Below: A mounted British policewoman outside the gates of Buckingham Palace.

Prisons

When a person has been tried, and is found guilty of a CRIME he may be sent to prison for a certain time. He may, however, be let out early if he behaves well. Sometimes people are put in prison while they are waiting for their trial.

Prisons used to be very harsh places where people were cruelly treated. In some countries they still are. But most civilized countries are trying to make prison a better place, where criminals can learn how to fit into an ordinary working life and live honestly when they come out. Today, there are many 'open' prisons, where certain prisoners are not kept locked up in cells, but have a certain amount of freedom.

Police uniforms from different countries. (1) Traffic policeman of Thailand. (2) French policeman. (3) Dutch policeman. (4) Motorway patrolman from the United States of America. Britain is one of the few countries with unarmed policemen.

Warfare

Warfare is fighting between two or more countries, or between two parts of the same country. In the past, men have always fought wars, but the kind of war has changed from one age to another. New weapons have been important. The side that could produce a new weapon has often won. Even simple inventions like the stirrup have made great differences. Without stirrups it was very difficult to fight on horseback.

Sea warfare has its own history of change. So has the war in the air. War has become more complicated and more terrible as nations have become bigger and science has produced new weapons. Today most people want to avoid war.

Above: A carving of an ancient battle from a Roman frieze.

Below: A cutaway view of a medieval castle.

Fighting during the English Civil War.

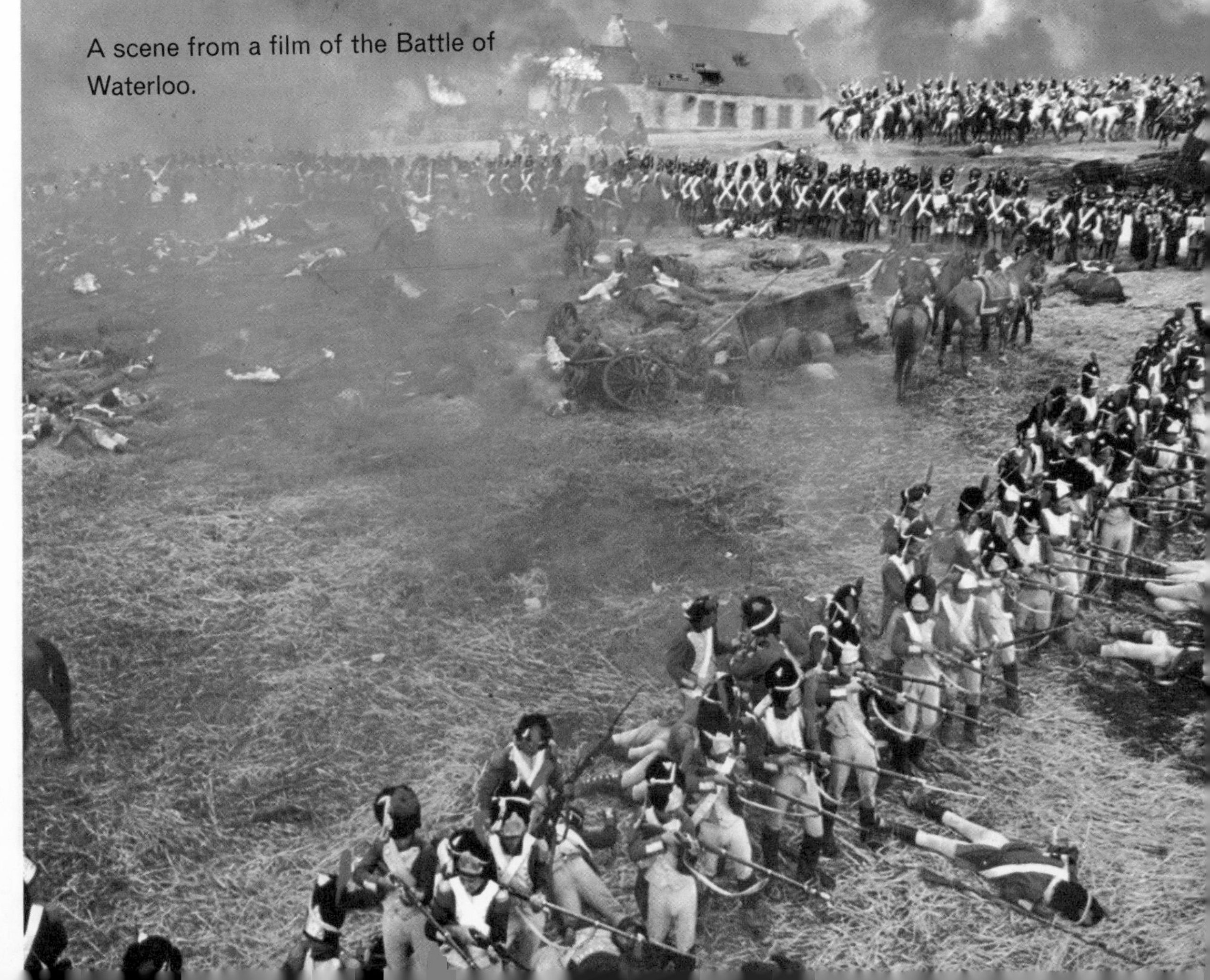

A scene from a film of the Battle of Waterloo.

World War I

The Great War (as it used to be called) lasted from August 1914 to 11 November 1918. On one side were the two empires of GERMANY and Austria-Hungary, later joined by Bulgaria and TURKEY. They were called the Central Powers.

Against them were the Allies – that is, the Russian Empire to the east, the French to the west, the British, and the Belgians. Later the Italians, the Japanese, the United States, and many smaller nations joined the Allies. Because so many countries were involved, it later came to be called a world war.

After four years, the nations that had started the war were weary and exhausted. More than ten million soldiers had been killed. By coming fresh into the struggle, the United States tipped the scale, and the Central Powers collapsed in defeat.

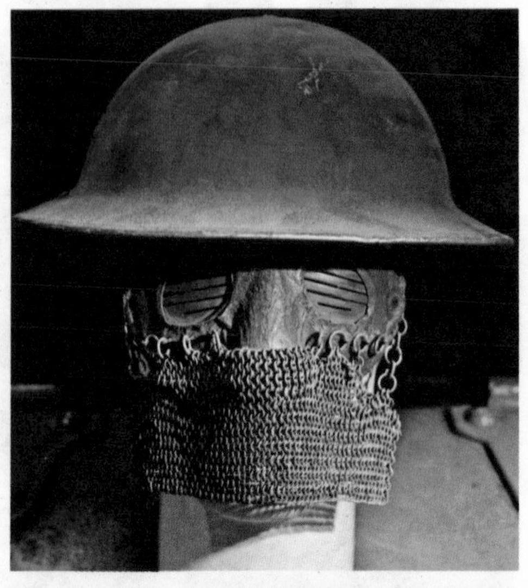

Above: A British helmet and face mask worn in World War I.
Below: The trench warfare of World War I meant that neither side gained much ground for four long years, but millions lost their lives.

Above: An American soldier watches as reinforcements come ashore during the D-Day landings on the beaches of Normandy in 1944.
Below: Whole cities were destroyed by bombs during World War II.

World War II

The Second World War began when the German DICTATOR, ADOLF HITLER, sent his soldiers to attack two small neighbouring countries (AUSTRIA and CZECHOSLOVAKIA) and nobody stopped him. But when he attacked POLAND on 1 September 1939, the Poles fought back. The British and French then stepped in to help.

Hitler conquered Poland and then launched a surprise attack in the west, overrunning DENMARK and NORWAY, the NETHERLANDS, BELGIUM and FRANCE. He then tried to break the spirit of the British but lost the Battle of Britain against the R.A.F. in 1941. Meanwhile, Hitler's allies had come into the war, the Italians, under the dictator, MUSSOLINI, and then JAPAN.

By 1944 the tide was turning. The American, British, and other forces landed on the Normandy beaches (D-Day) and drove the Germans out of France. In 1945 they swept across Germany to meet their Russian allies. Germany surrendered. A few months later the first atomic bombs were dropped on the Japanese cities of Hiroshima and Nagasaki. Japan surrendered and the war ended.

Armies

The first battles were fought between small groups of men. Usually these men did not stay together for long. Military leaders found that they could keep a band of fighting men together, however, if they trained them well. The ANCIENT ROMANS worked out an efficient army, with regiments called legions (4,000 to 6,000 men) and officers called centurions (in charge of 100 men).

An army includes infantry (foot soldiers), gunners (in charge of the artillery), and cavalry (soldiers on horseback or, nowadays, in tanks).

Until 200 years ago, armies were small (rarely more than a few thousand men). NAPOLEON started using all the men available to him, and armies became much bigger (100,000 men or more). In WORLD WAR I, some armies contained over a million men. Today wars are fought using machines, and the armies of some countries have become smaller again.

Above: A French hussar of 1807.
Right: A modern tank of the Rhine army in Germany.

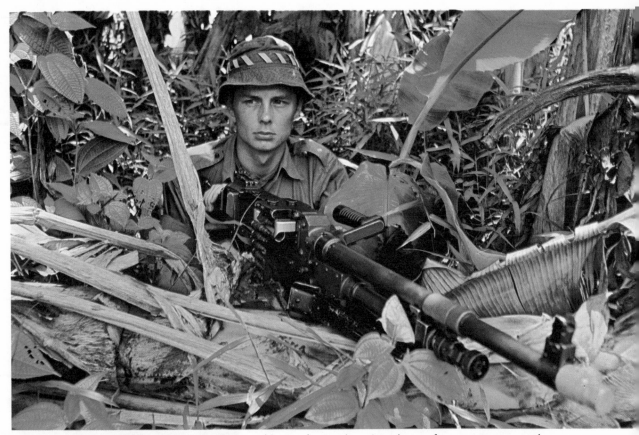

Above: In modern jungle warfare, weapons and uniforms are camouflaged so that they cannot be easily seen by the enemy.

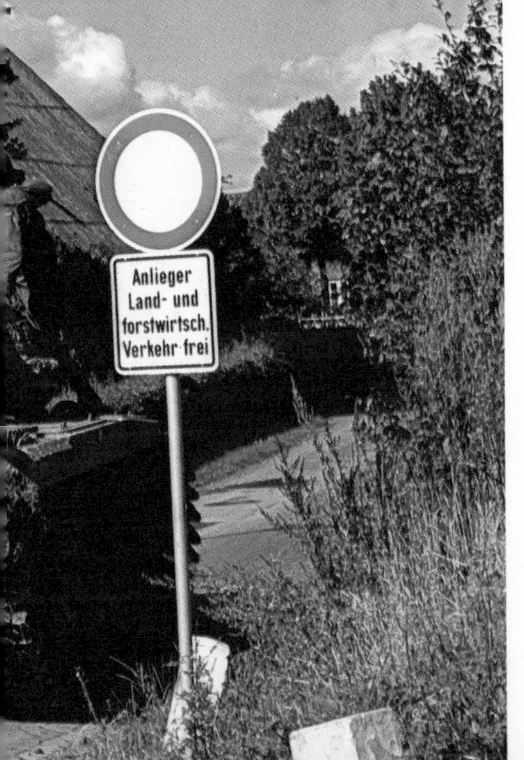

National service

National service, or conscription, means that every fit young man must join the ARMY or serve his country in some way if he is 'called up' or 'drafted'. If the doctors find a man unfit, he is let off or 'exempted'.

Conscription was begun by NAPOLEON. He wanted to create big enough ARMIES to fight in his many campaigns. He also needed to replace the thousands of soldiers who were killed and wounded in his battles.

Many countries still have conscription. Britain had it only in the two World Wars and for some time afterwards.

Navies

A navy is made up of all the marine military forces of a country. This includes men, vessels, stores and yards. Large navies are made up of several fleets. Each fleet is stationed in a different part of the world (such as the PACIFIC fleet). Fleets may have smaller divisions such as squadrons. Ships that are engaged in trade with other countries are said to form part of the merchant navy.

In ancient times sea battles between the navies of opposing countries were fought like land battles on board ships. The object was for the crew of one ship to board the enemy ship and kill its crew. Later on, ships carried heavy

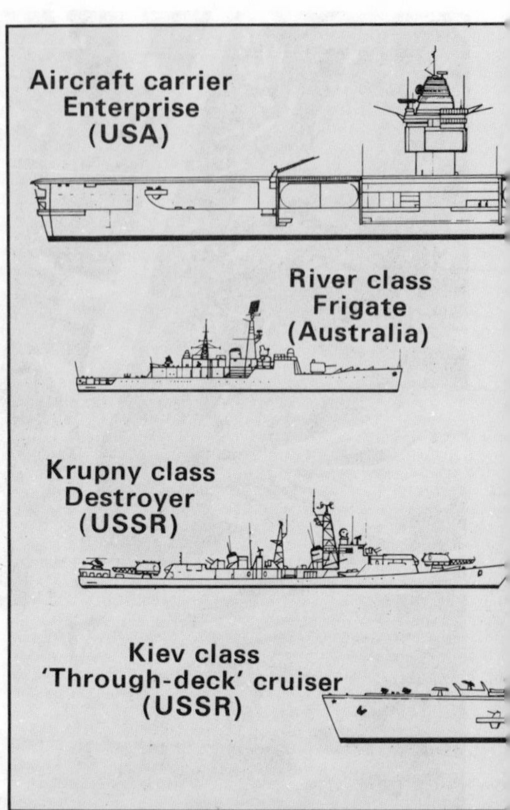

Below: Naval dress has changed a great deal over the years. The sailor on the left is wearing the naval uniform of 1799. The man in the centre is dressed in 1880s' uniform, while the sailor on the right is in modern dress.

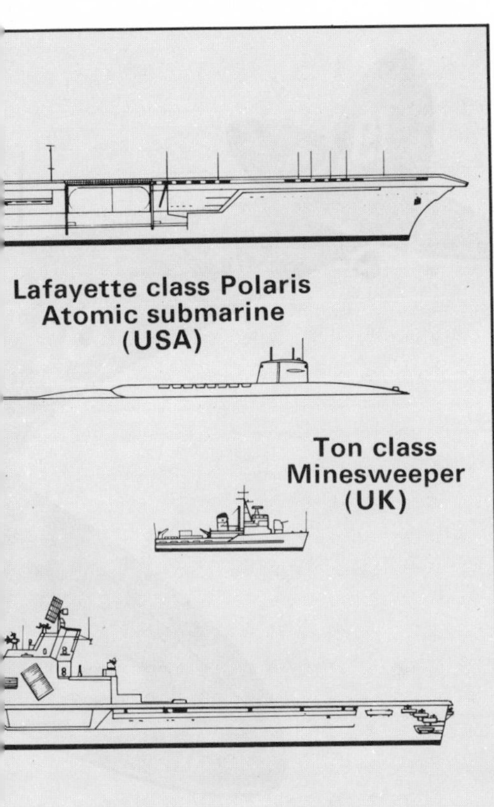

guns. The guns enabled them to sink an enemy ship from a distance.

Britain has had a navy since King Alfred's time, over 1000 years ago. For a century after NELSON, the British Navy was the biggest in the world and even its UNIFORM was imitated by others. In the last century, it claimed to keep the seas peaceful all over the globe. Now the biggest navies are those of the United States and the Soviet Union.

A modern fleet is made up of ships of various sizes and types – battleships, aircraft carriers, cruisers, destroyers, frigates, and submarines. Today, the new nuclear-powered submarines are one of the most important parts of a navy. They are able to remain under water for months.

Left: A modern navy is made up of many different types of ships and submarines.
Below: A frigate of the British Navy, HMS *Ardent.*

Air forces

There were no air forces before WORLD WAR I. When the war broke out in 1914, the first aircraft had only just been invented. Military leaders of the time did not immediately see that aircraft had a useful role to play in warfare. At first they were only used for reconnaissance (scouting) missions over enemy territory. Later, the pilots and observers started firing at the enemy with handguns. This led to machine guns being fitted to aircraft.

Air forces became more and more important as the war went on. The British Royal Air Force, originally called the Royal Flying Corps, was formed in 1911. By 1918 it had 27,000 aircraft. Different types of aircraft were built to carry out a wide variety of tasks. Among them were light combat aircraft, heavy bombers and seaplanes, which worked closely with the navy.

Below: Two Hawk trainers of the RAF.

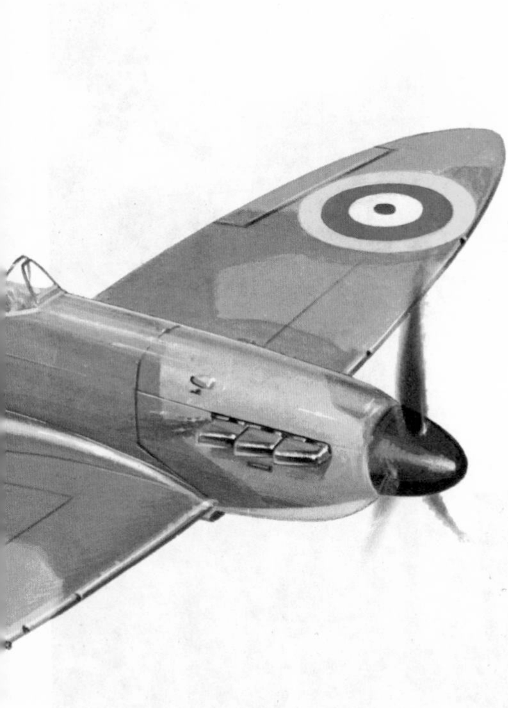

In WORLD WAR II aircraft played an important role from the start. Navigation had greatly improved, particularly through the development of radar. A huge number of bombing raids took place against enemy FACTORIES, towns and armed forces. Fighters were used to protect shipping and to sink SUBMARINES. Other aircraft were sent in deep behind enemy lines so that troops could parachute down.

Until very late in the war, all aircraft were powered by engines with propellers. But by the end of the war jet-powered aircraft were also in use. Since then, they have almost completely taken over. Today, however, these fast jet aircraft are being replaced by long-range ROCKETS with powerful nuclear explosives in their warheads. These may soon make fighters and bombers out of date.

Above: The Spitfire was a fast fighter plane of World War II.

Below left: The Harrier can take off without a runway.
Below: A Wessex helicopter on manoeuvres.

International Organizations

From the beginnings of history, nations have formed pacts and alliances. In the past, only a small number of countries entered into an alliance, usually to defeat a more powerful enemy or to gain territory. Today the world is far too complicated for this kind of treaty.

International organizations are much bigger and with much longer-term aims. They are concerned with nations helping each other, particularly the rich nations helping the poorer nations. Organizations like this are the U.N., the COMMONWEALTH and UNESCO. There are also military organizations, such as NATO and the WARSAW PACT. The countries that belong promise to support each other in case of war.

Right: The huge UN office building in New York.
Below: The Headquarters of the European Economic Community (the Common Market) in Brussels.

COMMONWEALTH COUNTRIES

Antigua and Barbuda
Australia
Bahamas
Bangladesh
Barbados
Belize
Botswana
Brunei
Canada
Cyprus
Dominica
Fiji
The Gambia
Ghana
Grenada
Guyana
India
Jamaica
Kenya
Kiribati
Lesotho
Malawi
Malaysia
Malta
Maldives
Mauritius
Nauru
New Zealand
Nigeria
Papua New Guinea
St Kitts-Nevis
St Lucia
St Vincent and the Grenadines
Seychelles
Sierra Leone
Singapore
Solomon Islands
Sri Lanka
Swaziland
Tanzania
Tonga
Trinidad and Tobago
Tuvalu
Uganda
United Kingdom
Vanuatu
Western Samoa
Zambia
Zimbabwe

Commonwealth

The Commonwealth is the name now given to the old British Empire. All but the very smallest Commonwealth countries (like the little islands of the PACIFIC OCEAN) now have their own governments and are not governed by Britain. But many, such as CANADA and AUSTRALIA, still regard the Queen as their queen. Even those which have become REPUBLICS, like INDIA, remain members of the Commonwealth and accept her as its head. The prime ministers of the Commonwealth countries meet from time to time.

A few countries, such as South Africa and Pakistan, that were once part of the Empire, have chosen to leave the Commonwealth.

Commonwealth once meant government without a MONARCHY. After the execution of King Charles I of England, the rule of OLIVER CROMWELL was known as the Commonwealth.

Below: Commonwealth Leaders with Her Majesty Queen Elizabeth II during a meeting in London.

United Nations

The United Nations came into existence in 1945. It began as an association of 50 countries, but many more joined later. Its first aim is to stop future wars by giving governments a chance to meet and settle their disputes peacefully.

It also tries to get countries to work together and help each other. The richer nations give or lend money to the poorer ones. When there is a flood, famine, or an EARTHQUAKE, the other countries send food, tents, DOCTORS, and medicines. When certain illnesses break out, governments help each other so that the infection does not spread.

Meetings are held at the headquarters in NEW YORK, where the Secretary General works with his staff. Each nation votes in the General Assembly, but only 15 are chosen for the Security Council, which has more power.

Above: The United Nations symbol. Below: A meeting of the Security Council. Fifteen countries are represented on the Council. The U.S.A., Great Britain, France, Russia, and China are always on it. Other countries are on it in turn.

Above: The headquarters of the E.E.C.'s European Commission in Luxembourg.

Common Market

The Common Market is the simple name for the European Economic Community (E.E.C.). It began in 1957 when the Treaty of Rome was signed by six nations, FRANCE, GERMANY, ITALY, BELGIUM, THE NETHERLANDS, and Luxembourg. They agreed to work together in trading and many other matters as if they were all one country. Britain at first formed a separate group with some other countries, the European Free Trade Association (EFTA), but later with two other countries she joined the Common Market in January, 1973.

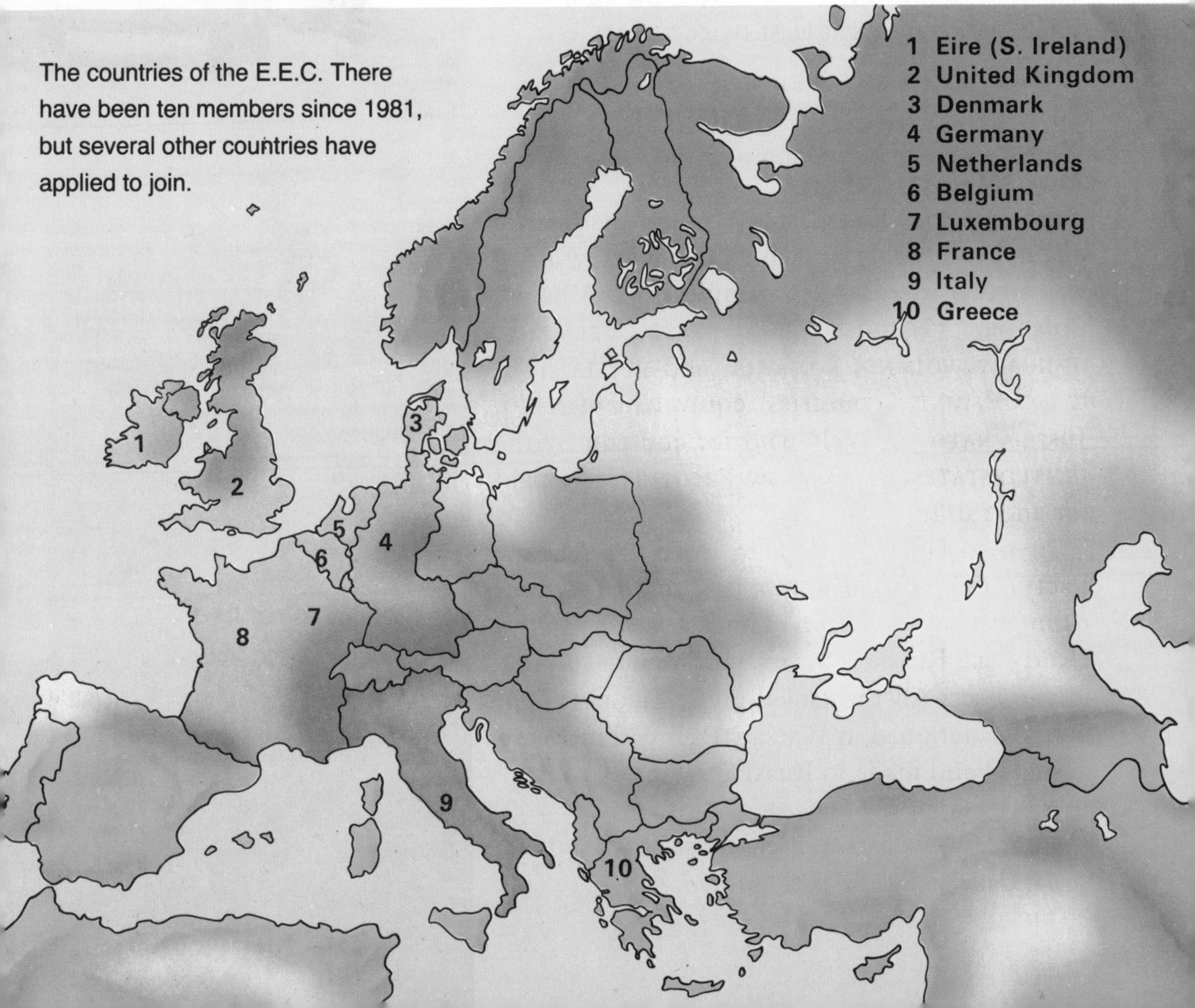

The countries of the E.E.C. There have been ten members since 1981, but several other countries have applied to join.

1 Eire (S. Ireland)
2 United Kingdom
3 Denmark
4 Germany
5 Netherlands
6 Belgium
7 Luxembourg
8 France
9 Italy
10 Greece

Nato

NATO stands for the North Atlantic Treaty Organization. It was set up in 1949 to defend the western nations against any military threat from the COMMUNIST nations. These are RUSSIA and the other WARSAW PACT countries – POLAND, CZECHOSLOVAKIA, HUNGARY, ROMANIA, Albania, Bulgaria, and EAST GERMANY. The original member countries of NATO were BELGIUM, CANADA, DENMARK, FRANCE, ICELAND, ITALY, LUXEMBOURG, the NETHERLANDS, NORWAY, PORTUGAL, GREAT BRITAIN, and the UNITED STATES. GREECE, TURKEY, WEST GERMANY and SPAIN joined later. NATO is run by the North Atlantic Council which has a member from each of the countries. The Council meets at least twice a year.

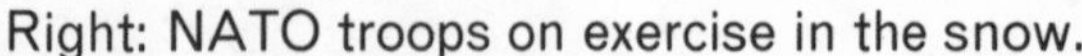

Right: NATO troops on exercise in the snow.

The Warsaw Pact

The Eastern European Mutual Assistance Treaty, commonly known as the Warsaw Pact, was signed in 1955. Its members are Albania, Bulgaria, CZECHOSLOVAKIA, EAST GERMANY, HUNGARY, POLAND, ROMANIA, and RUSSIA. It is the COMMUNIST countries' equivalent of NATO. Just as NATO is largely paid for and run by the UNITED STATES, the Warsaw Pact is largely paid for and run by Russia.

In 1956 Hungary tried to leave the Warsaw Pact but the Russians stopped them by overrunning the country. This invasion shows clearly that Russia is the most dominant country in the Pact. All the tanks, guns, AIRCRAFT and ROCKETS stationed in Warsaw Pact countries are designed and made in Russian factories.

Right: A May Day parade of the armed forces of the Soviet Union in Red Square, Moscow.

Seato

SEATO stands for the South-East Asian Treaty Organization. This organization was formed in 1955. Its original member countries were AUSTRALIA, FRANCE, GREAT BRITAIN, NEW ZEALAND, PAKISTAN, the Philippines, THAILAND and the UNITED STATES. France and Pakistan later withdrew from SEATO in protest at the United States' involvement in the war in VIETNAM.

Like NATO, SEATO came into being to defend western-style DEMOCRACIES in South-East Asia from the threat of war by COMMUNIST countries in the area. Its members see communist RUSSIA as the biggest threat.

SEATO differs from NATO, however, in that the member nations do not have to work closely together.

Red Cross

The Red Cross was started by a Swiss banker, Jean Henri Dunant, who was horrified by the sufferings of the troops wounded at the Battle of Solferino in 1859. He organized the villagers of the surrounding communities into volunteer groups to help the soldiers.

Until that time, ARMIES had few DOCTORS and nurses, and soldiers often died where they fell. Dunant got a number of countries to make a Convention (agreement) at Geneva, promising not to shoot at Red Cross men who were not fighting but helping the wounded.

To show who they were, these men were to use the Red Cross flag. It was the exact opposite of the Swiss flag, which is a white cross on a red background. When Moslem countries took up the idea they did not want to use a red cross because they thought it was a Christian sign. They were allowed to use the Red Crescent.

MAN
FACTS AND FIGURES

OUR BODY AND OUR HEALTH. There are 206 bones in the human body. The longest bone in the body is the femur. Gold has long been used in dentistry: The Ancient Egyptians fixed loose teeth with gold wire.

PEOPLES OF THE WORLD. Today, there are more than 4,500 million people in the world. It has been estimated that there will be more than 6,000 million by the year 2000. The most heavily populated country is China, with over 1,000 million inhabitants.

PEOPLES OF THE PAST. It is thought that man originated in eastern Africa. The population of Ancient Egypt was about 5 million – the same as modern Cairo. The Great Wall of China, man's largest construction, is nearly 2700 kilometres long.

RELIGIONS AND SECTS. Every year 100,000 Moslems make a pilgrimage to Mecca, Mohammed's birthplace. More people follow Christianity than any other religion. In Judaism, a boy becomes a man at the age of 13 in a special ceremony called Bar Mitzvah.

FOLKLORE AND BELIEF. The sphinx of Greek mythology ate people who could not answer its difficult riddle. An old legend describes how Faust sold his soul to the Devil in return for a longer life. In England, the last execution for witchcraft was in 1716.

GOVERNMENT. One of the oldest parliaments is the *Althing,* the parliament of Iceland, founded in A.D. 930. The first British Prime Minister was Sir Robert Walpole, who headed the government from 1721 to 1742.

LAW. The first country to abolish the death penalty was Liechtenstein in 1798; the first American states to do so were Michigan in 1846 and Wisconsin in 1853. During the nine days of the General Strike of 1926, $1\frac{1}{2}$ million British people stopped work.

WARFARE. Gunpowder was first used in the West in the thirteenth century. It was known even earlier in China. In World War II, about 55 million people were killed. The world's greatest bomb was a 57-megaton hydrogen bomb tested by the U.S.S.R. in 1961.

INTERNATIONAL ORGANIZATIONS. The E.E.C. is the world's largest trader. Comecon, Eastern Europe's economic community, was founded in 1949. The world's largest political unit is the British Commonwealth of Nations. The United Nations had 157 member countries in 1982.

ANIMALS

Insects

The body of an insect is divided into three sections. The head is small and has ANTENNAE and EYES. The thorax is the middle part and carries the wings and legs. Behind the thorax is the abdomen, the largest part of the body.

All insects have six legs. SPIDERS and ticks have eight legs and so are not insects. Most insects can fly, and most have two pairs of wings.

Insects do not have BONES; their bodies are stiffened by a hard skin. Because the skin is hard, an insect cannot grow bigger gradually as we do. It has to moult, or shed its skin, and replace it by a new and larger skin.

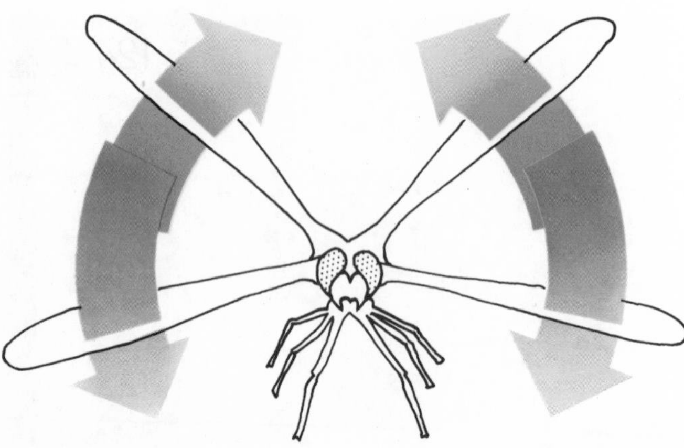

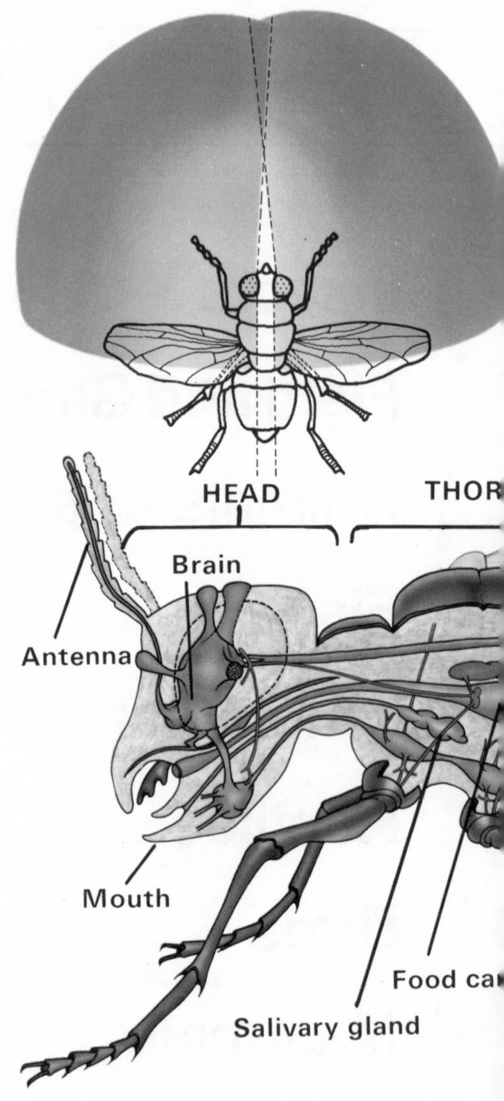

Above: The dragonfly moves its wings separately. Most insects move their wings together.
Right: The main internal organs of an insect.

Most insects lay eggs, although a few give birth to live young. Some young insects, called nymphs, look like their parents. Others have soft bodies and look like worms. They are called larvae, and change into adults inside a pupa. BUTTERFLIES and MOTHS grow in this way.

There are over a million different kinds of insects in the world. They are found almost everywhere, from the icy polar regions to the tropical forests.

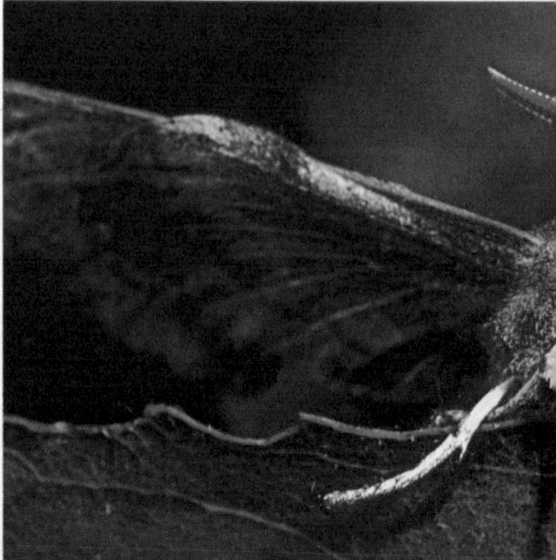

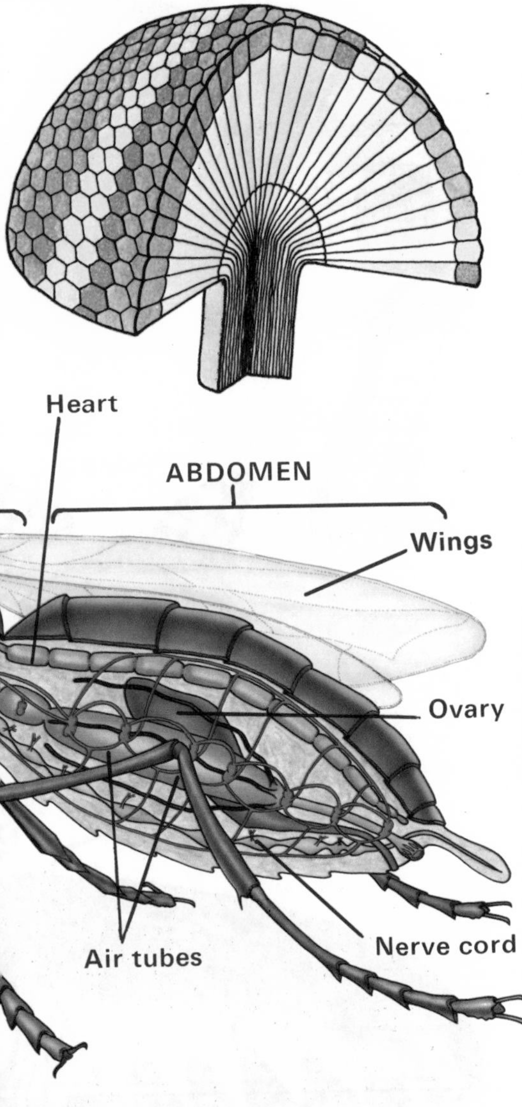

Eyes

The eye of an insect is not like ours. It is made up of lots of cone-shaped units packed close together. Their surfaces are called facets and they fit together like tiles on a floor. Each facet has a LENS and a retina.

Insects with good vision have eyes with many facets. DRAGONFLIES have over 10,000 in each eye.

Far left: A fly's eyes give it all-round vision.
Left: The cone-shaped units of an insect's eye. Each is joined to the brain by a nerve.
Below: The facets of a fly's eye.

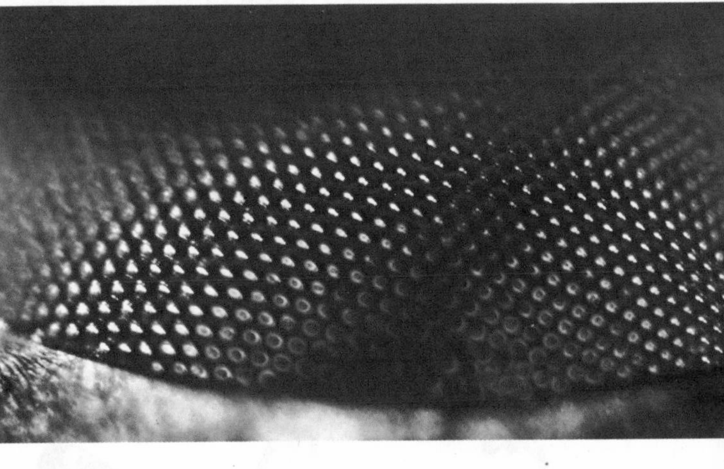

Antennae

An insect has two antennae sticking out from the top of its head. They look like long hairs or delicate fans, although DRAGONFLIES and some other insects have tiny bristle-like antennae.

Antennae are often called 'feelers' because they are sometimes used by the insect for feeling its way forward. They can also be used for smelling and tasting food. When flying, insects use their antennae to feel currents of air.

Left: The head of a poplar hawkmoth, showing the delicate antennae which pick up scent.

Butterflies and moths

There are a number of differences between butterflies and moths. Butterflies are brightly coloured and fly by day. Most moths are active at night. Butterflies have knobs on the ends of their ANTENNAE, but most moths do not.

The wings of butterflies and moths are covered with small scales. The scales are very delicate and will come off if the wings are touched.

There are four stages in the life of a butterfly or moth: egg, caterpillar, pupa, and adult. The caterpillar is the larva or young insect. It has a soft, worm-like body. There are three pairs of true legs behind the head and several pairs of prolegs, or false legs, at the rear end.

Swallowtail butterfly

Monarch butterfly

Fritilla butterf

Most caterpillars eat LEAVES. Some can do great damage to crops. The caterpillar of the clothes moth eats wool, fur, and feathers. Some adult moths and butterflies sip nectar from FLOWERS. Others do not feed and die soon after laying their eggs.

After it has been eating for some time, the caterpillar forms a pupa. The pupa of a butterfly is called a chrysalis. It is a hard case in which the adult develops. When the adult has developed, it crawls out of the pupa. Most moth caterpillars spin a silk cocoon around themselves before turning into a pupa. Cocoons of the silk moth are used for making silk fabrics.

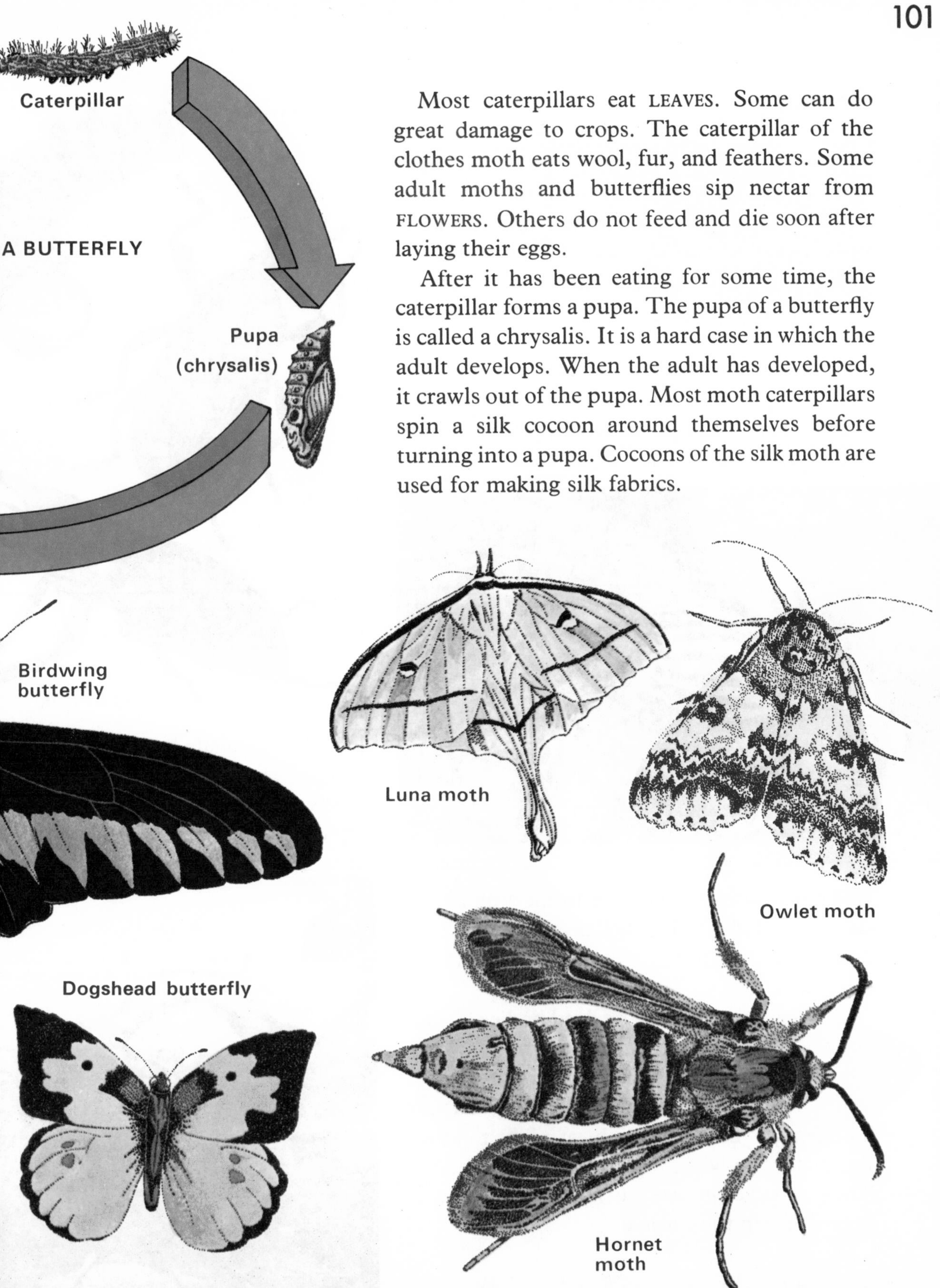

Beetles

Beetles have hard, shiny front wings. These cover almost all of the body and protect the delicate hind wings. They are often beautifully coloured.

There are a quarter of a million different kinds of beetles. Some are so small that they cannot be seen easily. Others, the Goliath and Hercules beetles, for example, are almost the size of a man's hand.

The larvae of beetles are called grubs. The grubs of powder-post beetles and death-watch beetles make tunnels in wood. These tunnels ruin furniture. The larvae of click beetles are called wireworms. They live in the SOIL and eat the ROOTS of plants. If a click beetle is turned over on its back, it leaps into the air with a loud clicking sound.

Burying beetles bury the dead bodies of small animals and lay their eggs in them. The grubs hatch out of the eggs and eat the bodies.

Fireflies and glow-worms make their own light. The females flash their light at night to attract the males. Ladybirds are small, round beetles. They eat other insects, such as APHIDS, and are very useful in the garden.

Left: The Colorado beetle damages potato crops.
Below: Two male stag beetles fighting with their 'antlers' (jaws).

Houseflies

Unlike most other insects, flies have only one pair of wings instead of two. Each hind wing is represented by a little club-shaped part called a balancer. It helps to balance the insect when it is flying.

Houseflies very often come into our houses in the summer, but they do not always live indoors. Large numbers of them live in farm yards and rubbish dumps. They pick up all kinds of disease-causing germs and they should not be allowed to land on food when they come into the house.

Houseflies lay their eggs on manure and other decaying matter. The eggs hatch into legless larvae called maggots. Each female housefly lays about 900 eggs. In warm weather it takes only three weeks for the maggots to grow up into flies.

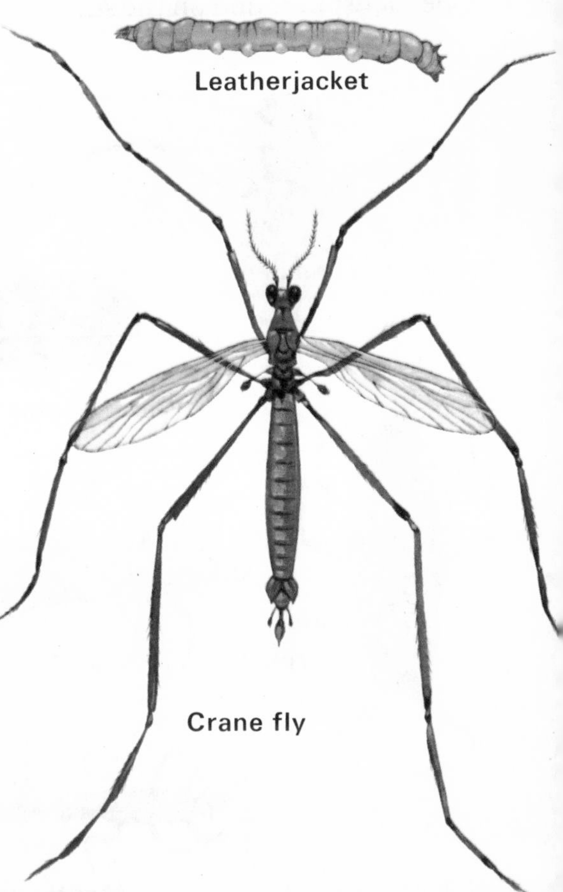

Right: The housefly and the crane fly, with larvae.

Crane flies

The crane fly is also called daddy long legs. It is a two-winged fly with long spindly legs which easily break off if you try to catch it. The club-shaped balancers are easily seen in the crane fly. The insects are attracted to lights and they often come in through the windows at night and buzz around the house. They are quite harmless. Out of doors the crane flies can be seen flying over the meadows, or resting among the long grass. They are most common during the late summer.

The larvae of crane flies are called leatherjackets. They are brown or grey and they usually live in the SOIL, where they eat the ROOTS of plants. They sometimes turn lawns brown by eating the roots of the grass. Some crane fly larvae live in decaying wood, and some live in the mud or shallow water of ponds.

Pond insects

There are several insects that are easy to find in ponds or in slow-running streams. Young DRAGONFLIES, mayflies, and caddis flies live at the bottom of ponds, although the adults live in the air above.

The larvae of caddis flies are called caddis worms. They live in tubes or cases. The silk cases have small pebbles and pieces of plants stuck to them. The caddis worms carry their cases with them, as a SNAIL carries its shell.

Several bugs and BEETLES spend all their lives in the water. They carry little bubbles of air under their wings so that they can breathe. They include the water boatmen that 'row' themselves along with two long legs. Backswimmers are similar insects that swim upside down. Other insects skate on the water surface. Whirligig beetles spin round on the surface like small black boats.

Above: The water stick insect, a slender bug which creeps slowly among the water weeds and eats other small animals.

Below: Some common pond insects.

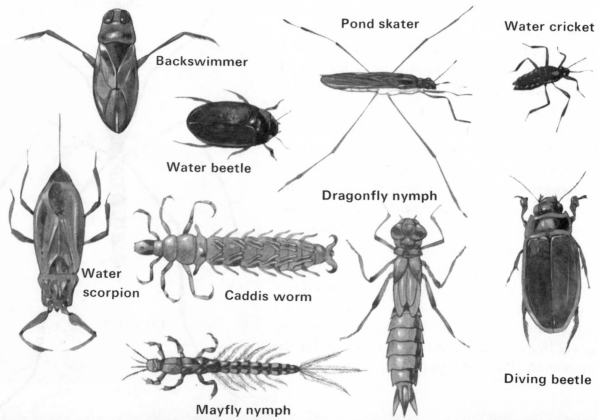

Backswimmer

Pond skater

Water cricket

Water beetle

Dragonfly nymph

Water scorpion

Caddis worm

Diving beetle

Mayfly nymph

Dragonflies

Dragonflies hunt other insects. They have huge eyes and when they see a smaller insect they pounce on it quickly. Dragonflies are very fast fliers and they can also hover and fly backwards. Unlike most other insects, the front and rear pairs of wings do not beat in time with each other.

Damselflies are close relatives of dragonflies, but they are smaller and more delicate. Unlike dragonflies, they fold their wings back when resting.

Dragonflies usually live near ponds and RIVERS. The females lay their eggs in the water or in the STEMS of water plants. The young live in the water. They are called nymphs. They hunt small water animals, such as TADPOLES and worms. When they are fully grown they crawl out of the water and climb up the reeds. Their skins then split and the adult dragonflies come out.

The largest insects that have ever lived were dragonflies with wings about 67 centimetres across. They lived in the age of the DINOSAURS.

Above: This dragonfly has just emerged from its nymph skin. It will remain on a pondside reed for a few hours until its wings dry and harden, ready for flight.

Below: This young green locust will change its skin and emerge as a fully winged adult. When locusts swarm, they can strip the vegetation from vast areas of land.

Locusts

Locust eggs are laid in sand. The young locusts that emerge at the surface are unable to fly. They travel along the ground until they become adults with fully developed wings.

For most of the time locusts live alone, like their relatives the grasshoppers and crickets. Every now and then, however, they gather together to form a vast swarm. The swarm starts to fly and is carried by the WIND.

The Bible tells us stories of locust plagues. The swarms land on crops and eat all the LEAVES. Locusts are one of the worst pests of agriculture, especially in AFRICA. Nations today help one another to find and destroy the locust swarms before they do any damage.

Above and below: Honey bees collect pollen and nectar from flowers.
Right: The three kinds of bees which are found in a hive.

Bees

Honeybees live in large nests called hives. In each hive there is a queen bee (who lays all the eggs). There are also several hundred males, called drones, and thousands of workers. The worker bees look after the hive. They build the comb and care for the young bees. They also leave the hive to gather nectar and pollen from flowers. The nectar is turned into honey.

New nests are started when a queen leaves the old nest with some of the workers and finds another place to settle. This is called swarming.

There are many other kinds of bees. They all collect pollen and do the work of plant POLLINATION. Bumblebees make small nests under the ground. The queen is the only member of the colony to survive the winter.

Solitary bees do not nest in hives. They live alone and lay their eggs in burrows in soil, logs or walls. There are no workers and the young bees have to look after themselves.

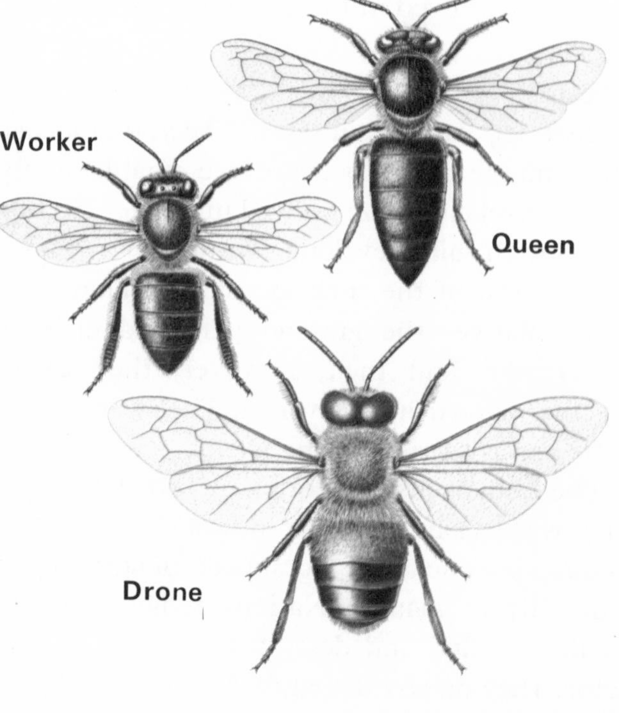

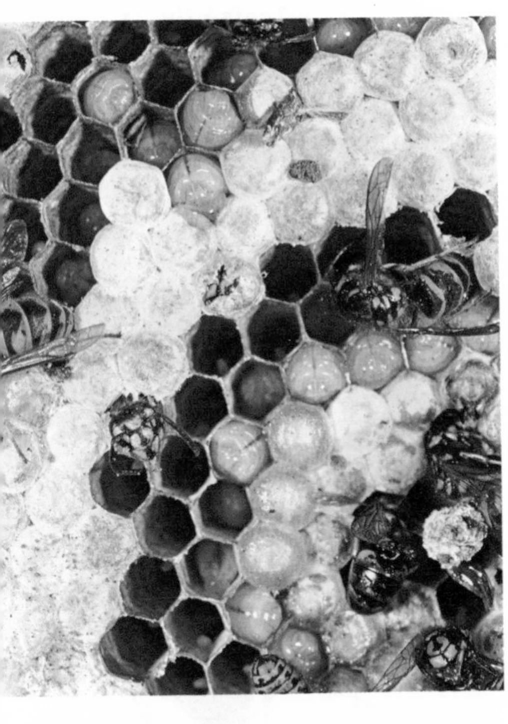

Wasps

The best-known wasps have yellow-and-black striped bodies. They have stings which they use to defend themselves. The yellow stripes warn animals to leave them alone.

Wasps live in large nests like honeybees, but they do not make honey. They drink nectar and the juices of rotten fruit. They also catch small insects to feed the grubs or larvae.

Other wasps live alone. They catch insects or SPIDERS for their larvae to eat. The victims are paralysed by the sting and carried to the wasp's little nest.

Left: Part of a wasp nest, showing the little six-sided cells in which the grubs live. The nest is made of chewed wood, called wasp paper.

Ants

Ants are related to BEES and WASPS. They, too, usually live in large nests. Army and driver ants do not have a nest but wander through the countryside. They live only in warmer countries.

Ants fly only when the queens and males leave the nest to mate and start new nests. When the queens land, they tear off their wings, disappear into crevices, and start to lay eggs. These eggs produce worker ants, which then start to build the nest.

The workers have a language of smells. If one worker finds food, it lays a trail of scent for others to follow. The ants also 'tell' each other about the food they have found by rubbing their ANTENNAE together. The army and driver ants eat nothing but animal matter, but most ants eat animal *and* plant material. A few only eat SEEDS.

Right: Ants are very fond of sweet things and they often stroke aphids (see page 110) to get honeydew.

Insects that carry disease

Some insects spread serious diseases. In tropical countries mosquitoes carry malaria and yellow fever. They suck the BLOOD from people with the disease and pass on the germs when they suck the blood of healthy people.

In AFRICA the tsetse fly carries sleeping sickness and a serious disease of CATTLE called nagana. Man can prevent these diseases from spreading by killing the insects with poisons or destroying the places where they live.

Fleas suck blood from people and animals by piercing the skin with a tube-shaped mouth. When they do this, they can pass on the germs of diseases. The body of a flea is very narrow. Its shape allows it to run easily through the hair or feathers. When disturbed it jumps into the air.

A louse is very flat in shape. Some lice live in the hair of mammals and suck their blood. Others live on birds and eat their feathers.

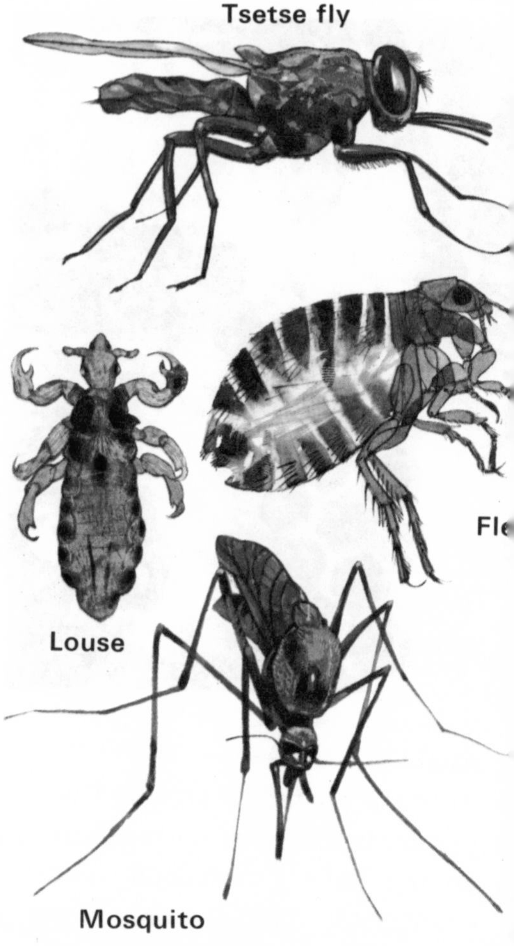

Right: Some important disease-carrying insects.
Below: The map shows the regions of the world in which malaria is still a problem.

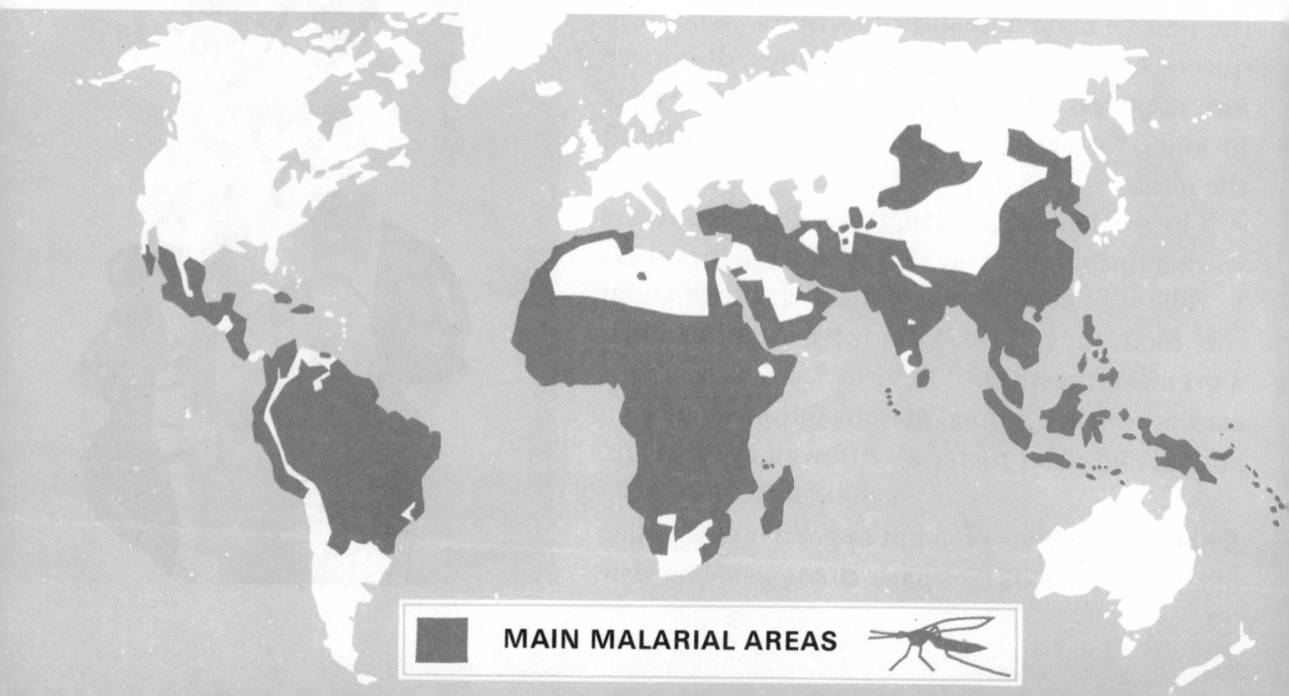

MAIN MALARIAL AREAS

Insects that sing

A familiar sound during summer is the chirping, squeaking songs of grasshoppers and crickets. The males sing to attract the females. They rub two wings together or scrape a back leg against a wing to produce their song.

Each kind of grasshopper and cricket has its own special song. The American katydids are so named because their song sounds like 'Katy-did-she-did'. Grasshoppers sing only when the sun shines, but crickets often sing at night.

Cicadas are another kind of insect which sing. They have a sound-making mechanism in the abdomen and are the noisiest insects in the world. They are common in many countries which have warm climates.

Right: A grasshopper on a blade of grass.
Below: A female bush cricket.

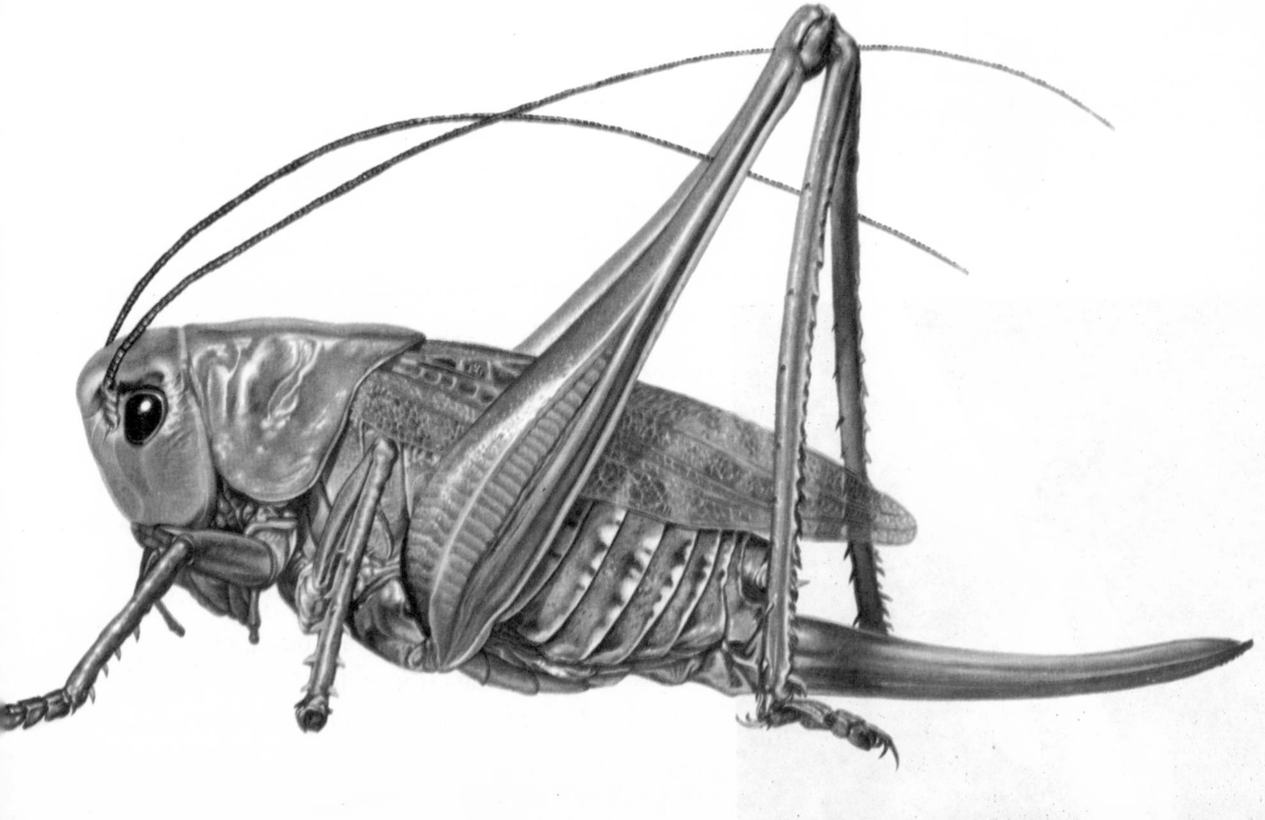

Insect frauds

Many animals eat insects. They know, however, that some insects are dangerous, or unpleasant to taste, so they leave them alone. For example, few animals will try to eat a WASP, because of its painful sting.

Some insects are able to protect themselves because they look like the unpleasant insects. In the summer you may see flies with black and yellow stripes feeding on flowers in the garden. They are harmless. Yet animals do not eat them because they look like wasps.

There are many other examples of such frauds in the insect world. Sometimes the dangerous and the harmless insects are so alike that even experts cannot tell them apart.

Left: Enemies leave the hoverfly (top) alone because it resembles the wasp (left).

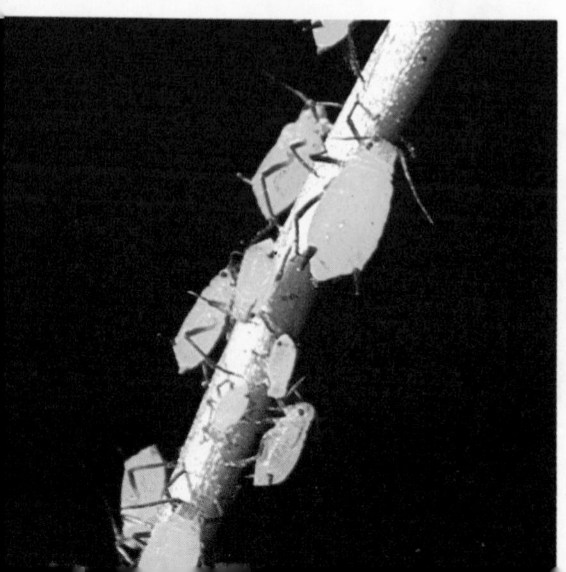

Aphids

Aphids are small insects that suck the juices, or sap, of plants. Some of them cause serious damage to the plants. Greenfly and black fly are aphids that harm ROSES and beans. As well as simply taking the sap, the aphids spread plant diseases. Some aphids have wings and some do not. The wingless ones do not move very far and, because they breed so quickly, they soon get very crowded on the plants.

Aphids suck sap up tubes in their bodies like hollow needles. Some of the sap oozes out of the body of the aphids as sugary honeydew. ANTS like to eat honeydew, and they herd aphids as man herds cows.

Left: Aphids are usually green, black, or brown. Winged ones (top) often fly about, but the wingless ones stay on the stems and leaves.

Insects that eat wood

Very few animals can eat wood, because it contains substances that they cannot digest. But termites (insects that look like ANTS) are very good at eating wood. Their bodies contain tiny animals that digest the wood for them.

Termites are a great nuisance in many parts of the world, especially in hot countries, because they destroy wooden buildings. They dislike the open air, so they eat away the inside of planks and posts until only a thin shell is left.

Termites live in huge nests which are made in the ground, in trees or in fallen logs. In each nest, there is a queen, who lays thousands of eggs, and a king. As in beehives and ants' nests, food is gathered by workers. The nests are guarded by soldiers armed with huge jaws.

Right: The towering nest of a termite colony.
Below: There are four different types of termites in a termite colony. (1) A Queen. (2) Soldiers. (3) Workers. (4) A King.

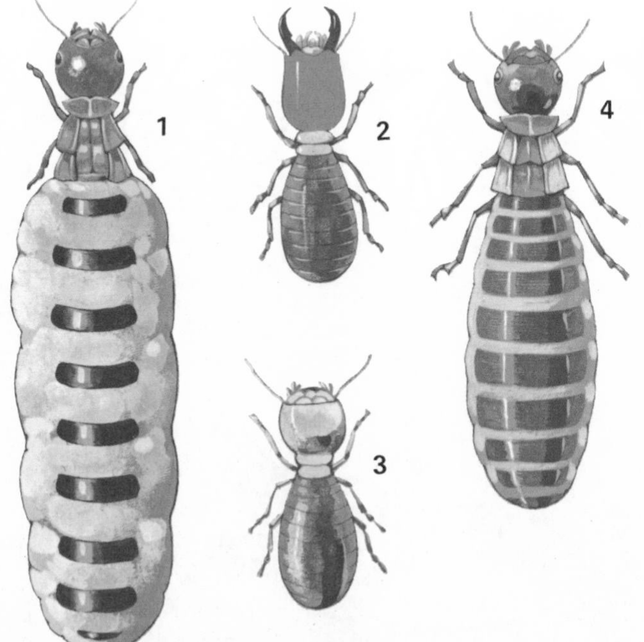

Field and Garden Animals

If you look closely under bushes or stones in a field or garden, you will find many kinds of small animals. They differ from man and other large animals because they have no backbones. Scientists call them invertebrates. Some, such as the EARTHWORM, have soft bodies. Others, such as the insects, have a hard skin. This is an outside skeleton that protects them.

Some of these animals are a nuisance to the gardener, but most of them are harmless or even useful. The earthworms are very useful animals.

A thousand square metres of SOIL may contain about a million earthworms. Their burrows help to drain the soil, and also to let air into it. As an earthworm burrows, it eats the soil. Bits of undigested soil are sometimes left on the surface. These are the wormcasts which can be seen on lawns. Earthworms also pull LEAVES into their burrows, where they eat them.

Gardens are full of small animals. Spider webs hang from the plants, and worms tunnel in the soil.

Earthworms

A close look at an earthworm shows that it is made up of about 150 rings or segments. All the segments look alike, except for a broad band near the middle of the body. This band is called the saddle, or clitellum. It makes a cocoon for the eggs, which are laid in the SOIL.

Earthworms have no proper EYES, but the skin is sensitive to light.

Above: A spider with its prey.

Spiders

Spiders feed on small animals. They kill them with their poisonous fangs. Large spiders can give painful bites to humans. The American black widow can even kill people.

The best-known spiders build silken webs to catch their prey. Some webs are closely woven sheets. Others are wheel-shaped and are suspended in the twigs of bushes. The spider lies in wait on or near the web until an insect becomes trapped. Some spiders do not spin webs but chase their prey.

Snails and slugs

Snails and slugs belong to the group of soft-bodied animals called molluscs. The SEA SNAILS are their close relatives.

Snails have a long, moist body. They carry a shell on their back. When a snail is disturbed, it can pull its body back into the shell. It also retreats into the shell and seals the entrance in dry weather. This prevents its soft body from drying up. The eyes of a snail are on the tips of two tentacles on the head.

Snails move by creeping on a flat 'foot' underneath the body. Slime comes out of the front of the body to make a slippery track. It hardens in the air to make a glistening trail. Snails eat LEAVES by scraping them with a rough tongue.

Slugs are snails without a shell or with a small shell hidden in the body.

Above: A thrush's 'anvil', where the bird breaks snail shells open and extracts the bodies.

Below: (1) African giant snail. (2) Large red slug. (3) Garden snail. (4) Roman or edible snail. (5) Large black slug. (Not on the same scale.)

1

2

3

4

5

Woodlice

If you pull the BARK off an old log or turn over a large stone, you may find some woodlice underneath. They like to tuck themselves firmly into damp corners, and very often several woodlice squeeze together. They come out at night to feed on scraps of dead plants.

The body of a woodlouse is covered with a row of hard plates. Some woodlice can roll themselves into a ball for protection.

Right: Two kinds of woodlice huddle together on a damp piece of wood.

Above: A common millipede.
Below: A centipede, showing the single pair of legs on each segment.

Centipedes and millipedes

Centipedes and millipedes look alike. They have long bodies made up of small sections, like beads on a string. They also have many legs. Centipedes have one pair of legs under each section. Millipedes have two pairs of legs for each section.

Both centipedes and millipedes live in moist places – under dead LEAVES or in damp SOIL. Centipedes eat other small animals. Large centipedes can give a painful, poisonous bite. Millipedes eat plants and are harmless to man, although they sometimes damage crops. Some millipedes can roll up into a ball.

Animals of the Seashore

Not all seashores are the same. Some face steep cliffs and are very narrow and rocky. Others can be wide, flat, sandy beaches. Many animals live in sandy beaches, but we seldom see them because they burrow under the sand when the tide is out. Many kinds of animals can be found on rocky beaches where there are small pools. Most seashore animals are invertebrates (without backbones).

The animals of the seashore live in an area that the TIDES cover every day. They lead a special sort of life, because they are not quite land animals and not quite sea creatures. All seashore animals have to be able to live out of water when the tide is out, but few can live out of water for long.

Left and below: Rocky shores at low tide are home for a wide variety of animals, including crabs, barnacles and sea slugs.

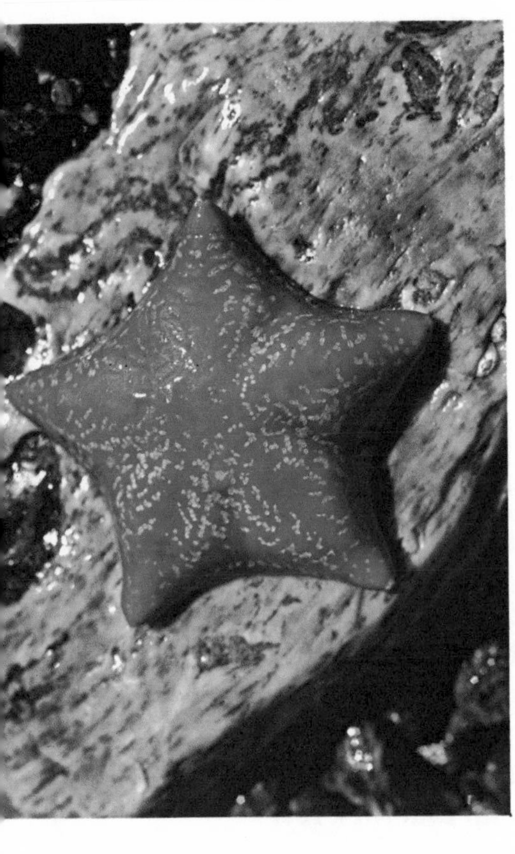

Starfish

Starfish are mostly all arms and no body. They usually have five arms, but some kinds have as many as 50.

Starfish eat BIVALVES, LIMPETS, fish, and other small animals. Underneath the starfish's arms there are rows of small suckers, called tube-feet. These help the starfish walk and also catch hold of its food. The starfish eats by pushing its stomach out of its mouth and folding it around its food.

If a starfish's arm is cut off, together with a part of the central disc, that arm will grow into a new starfish. The rest of the original starfish will also survive, and it will produce a new arm after a while.

Left: A cushion star, one of the starfish with short arms. Most starfish have longer arms and smaller bodies. The mouth is on the underside.

Sea urchins

Sea urchins are usually round animals with a thin chalky shell just under the skin. They are covered with rows of movable spines. Between the spines are suckers or tube-feet like those of the STARFISH. Most kinds crawl over the sea bed by means of their tube-feet, but some use their spines. The spines of the burrowing types are flattened and used for digging. Most urchins scrape up seaweed with the teeth on their undersides, but some pick up food with their tube-feet or with the tiny pincers among the spines. We usually find just their empty shells on the beach. They show the scars of the spines and the holes through which the tube-feet passed.

Right: The edible sea urchin extends its slender tube feet beyond its sharp spines.

Sponges

Sponges are animals, not plants. Their skeletons are made up of hard spines or tough fibres. These spines make a frame to hold the soft tissues. The larger sponges come from the coasts around warm countries. Bath sponges are collected by divers and dried. A bathroom sponge is only the fibrous skeleton of the animal. Most 'sponges' today are man-made.

Right: The purse sponge growing among red seaweeds. It is cup-shaped when in the water.

Coral

Corals are like small SEA ANEMONES. They have soft, round bodies and tentacles armed with stinging cells. Their bodies are protected by hard, chalky skeletons. When a coral dies, its skeleton remains. In time, millions of coral skeletons pile up to form a reef.

Left: A coral reef surrounds a tiny island.
Below: Gently swaying coral tentacles.

Sea anemones

In clear rock pools, sea anemones can often be seen, with their rings of tentacles waving above their bodies. If a sea anemone is prodded, it quickly folds away its tentacles. It also folds them away if the pool is emptied. This prevents the sea anemone from drying up.

Sea anemones eat small animals, which they catch with their tentacles. The tentacles are armed with stinging cells. These shoot out poisonous threads, like miniature harpoons, which hold the prey. When the prey is dead, the tentacles pass it in to the sea anemone's mouth.

Above: A beadlet anemone has caught a small fish with the stinging cells on its tentacles.

Worms

The lugworm is a worm that lives in the sand. It looks like a large red EARTHWORM, but it has a row of feathery GILLS down each side of its body. Lugworms are used as bait by fishermen.

Ragworms sometimes swim by wriggling their bodies from side to side like SNAKES. They eat small animals and SEAWEED.

The sea mouse does not look like a worm. It has a flat, pointed body and rows of golden brown bristles. It burrows in the mud and sand.

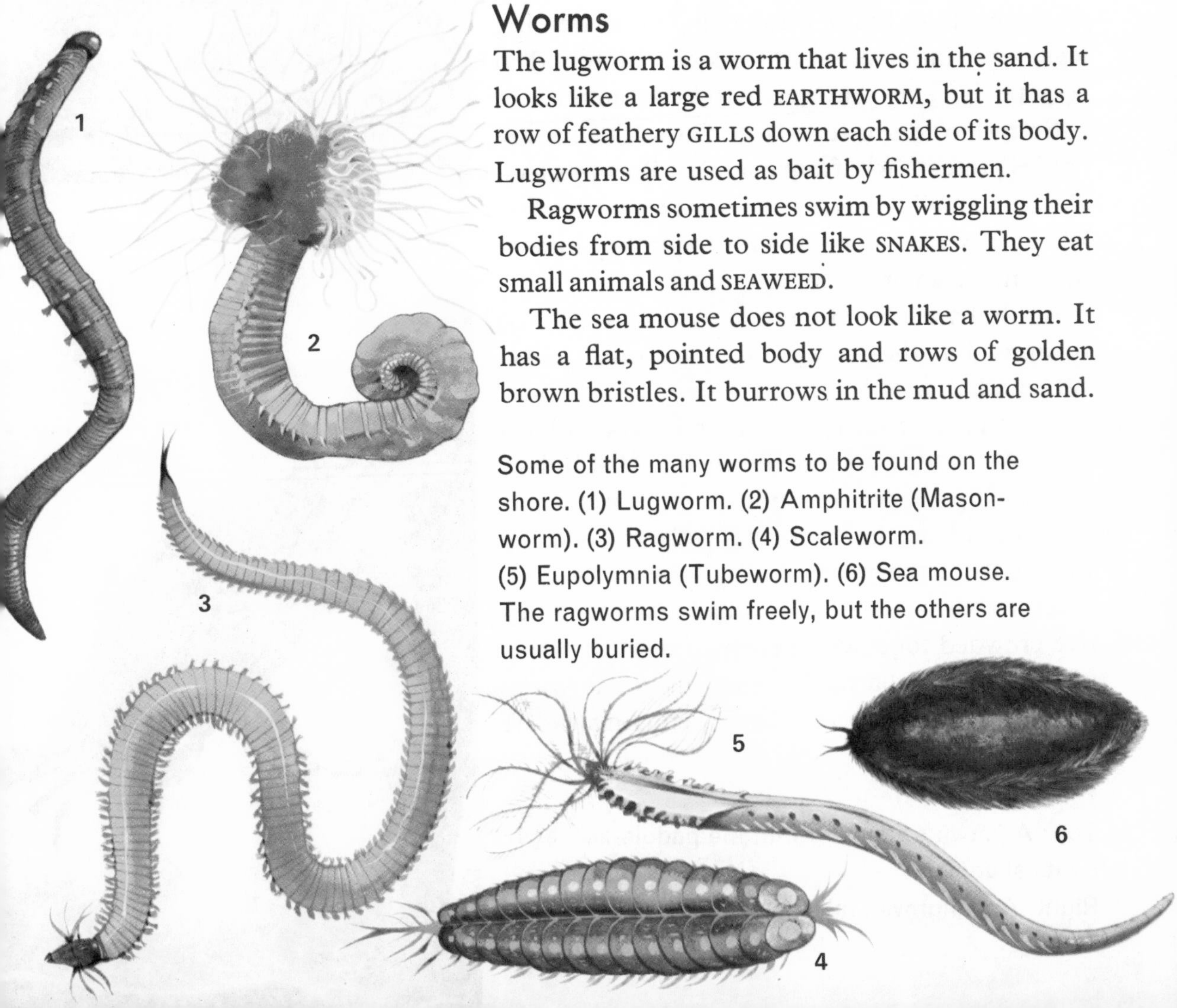

Some of the many worms to be found on the shore. (1) Lugworm. (2) Amphitrite (Mason-worm). (3) Ragworm. (4) Scaleworm. (5) Eupolymnia (Tubeworm). (6) Sea mouse. The ragworms swim freely, but the others are usually buried.

Crabs, lobsters, and barnacles

Crabs, lobsters, and shrimps all have hard shells and five pairs of legs. Four pairs are used for walking and swimming. The front pair has large claws that are used for fighting and catching food.

Crabs can be found in rock pools and in the sand. They eat small animals and dead fish, which they tear up with their claws.

Some crabs can live out of water. Robber crabs can climb trees. The largest crabs are the long-legged spider crabs.

Lobsters and shrimps are different in shape from crabs. Behind the shell there is a long abdomen that has several pairs of swimming legs, or swimmerets. Lobsters can be found in rock pools. They can weigh 16 kilogrammes.

Spiny lobsters have no large claws. Their spiny bodies protect them from enemies. Shrimps look like very small lobsters with transparent bodies. When they are not looking for food, they hide in the sand or among SEAWEED.

Adult barnacles do not look like CRABS or shrimps, but the young stages are much alike. When a barnacle is young, it swims in the sea. Then it glues itself to a rock and grows a hard shell. At low tide it shuts the shell so that it does not dry up. When the tide is in, the shell is opened. Then the barnacle collects food by waving its feathery legs through the water.

Acorn barnacles look like small LIMPETS. They live crowded together on rocks and on the hulls of ships. Goose barnacles hang upside down on long stalks, and are also found clinging to the hulls of ships.

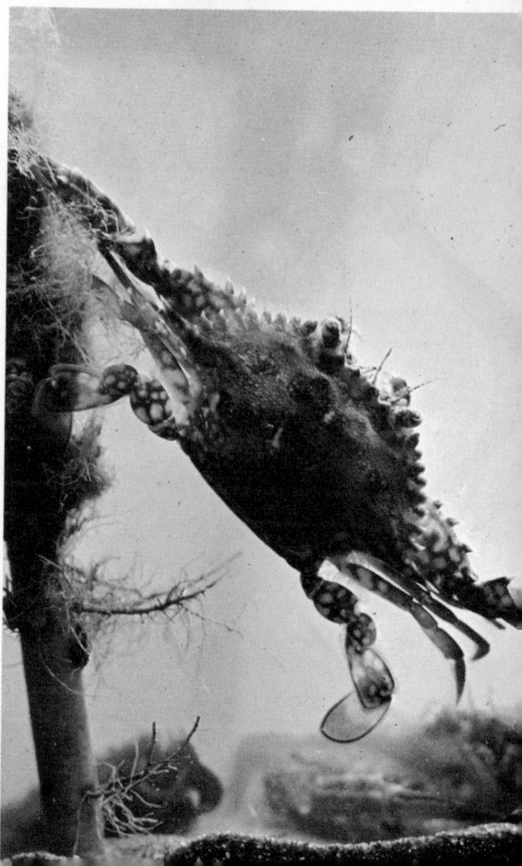

Top: A prawn swimming with the paddle-like legs on its abdomen.

Right: A mangrove crab swimming.

Above: (1) Lobster. (2) Edible crab. (3) Fiddler crab waving its large claw. 
Right: Acorn barnacles clustered on a rock. When the tide covers them the shells open and the animals 'comb' food from the water.

Limpets

When the tide goes out, a limpet holds tightly to the rock with its sucker-like foot. The cone-shaped shell is pulled close to the rock to make a watertight joint. It is very difficult to knock the limpet off.

When the tide is in, the limpet crawls about feeding on seaweed. It scrapes weeds off the rock with the same kind of rough tongue that SNAILS have. Limpets always return to the same place on the rock when the tide goes out.

Right: Common limpets, with their shells pulled tightly down around them.

Bivalves

Bivalve means 'two-shelled'. It is the name given to animals with two shells covering their bodies. The shells are connected by a hinge so that they can open and shut like a suitcase.

Mussels are fastened to rocks by fine threads. Oysters usually have one half of the shell cemented to a stone on the sea bed. A pearl is formed inside an oyster to cover up a sand grain that is irritating its soft tissues.

Clams have flat shells. Some are anchored to the sea bed by threads. Others swim by clapping their shells together. Cockles and razorshells burrow in sandy beaches. The shipworm is not a true worm. It is a bivalve that bores holes with its sharp shells in the timbers of ships.

Right: Mussel shells, with barnacles attached.

Octopus, squid, and cuttlefish

The eight arms (tentacles) of an octopus have rows of suckers that it uses to catch crabs. Octopuses live in shallow, warm seas. They walk on their tentacles or swim by squirting jets of water.

Octopuses escape from their enemies by changing colour to match their surroundings and by squirting out clouds of an inky liquid.

Squids live in the open sea. They have ten arms. Cuttlefish live on or near the sea bed. Squids and cuttlefish swim in a similar way to the octopus – by jet propulsion, and also by flapping the fins on their sides. Giant squids can be 20 metres long.

Left: The octopus rests on the sea bed and spreads its eight arms while waiting for food.

Sea snails

Sea snails are closely related to land SNAILS. The most common kind of sea snail is the periwinkle. Each kind of periwinkle lives in a particular part of the shore. Some live in very shallow water and can survive out of water for a long time. Periwinkles eat seaweed.

Whelks are sea snails with heavy, rough shells. They eat BIVALVES and CRABS. The cones live in tropical seas. They have beautiful cone-shaped shells, but the animals inside them are poisonous. They can kill a man. Cowries are sea snails whose shells were once used as money.

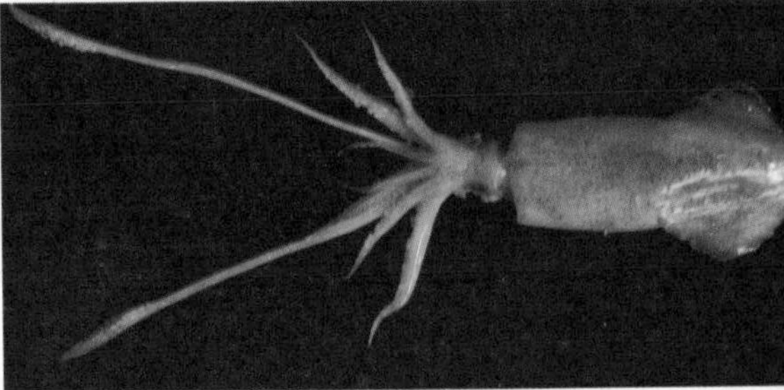

Left: A variety of sea shells.
Above right: A squid puts out its two long sucker-covered tentacles. These are its main food-catching weapons.
Right: A flat-topped periwinkle crawls over the seaweed at low tide.

Fish

LIFT BALANCE DRIVE

Above: A shark moves forward by waving its tail from side to side. The other fins control lift (up and down movement) and balance. The coloured arrows show which fins control different movements.

There are 25,000 kinds of fish. They live in water, but some, such as LUNGFISH, can live on land for short periods. Nearly all fish are covered with scales.

A typical fish has a streamlined body covered with a layer of silvery scales. There are a number of slender FINS on its body. The typical fish breathes by means of GILLS and swims by wriggling its tail from side to side. Many fish have an air-filled pouch in their bodies. It is called the swim-bladder and, by altering the amount of air in it, the fish can float easily at any depth it chooses.

Fish are cold-blooded animals. Most of them lay eggs, but some give birth to live young. A few even make nests for their eggs and young.

There are three main groups of fish. The FISH WITHOUT JAWS are sometimes not classed as fish. The SHARKS and their relatives have skeletons of soft cartilage instead of BONE. All other fish are called 'bony fish'.

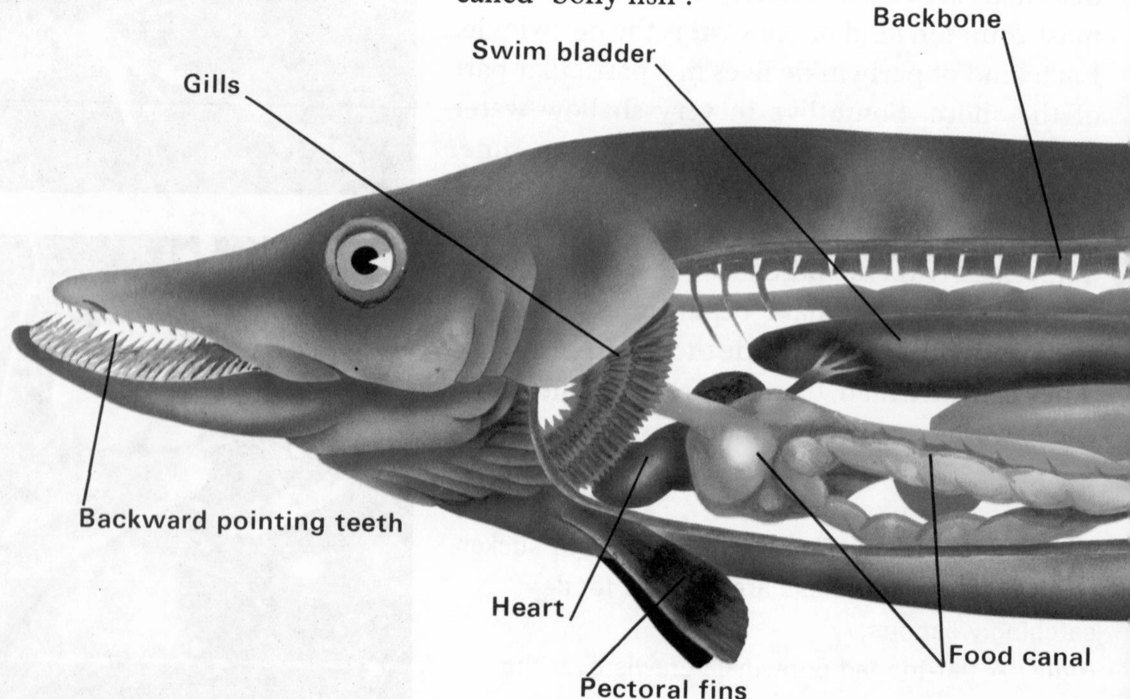

Gills and fins

A fish breathes by taking mouthfuls of water and squirting it out through the gills. The gills are feathery organs enclosed in pouches on each side of the head. They have a supply of blood. Oxygen from the water passes into the gills and carbon dioxide passes out. Oxygen is needed to provide the fish with energy.

Some fish have lungs as well as gills. A lung-fish, for example, can breathe air and live out of water for a time.

A fish swims by waving its tail from one side to the other. These movements push water back-wards and drive the fish forwards. The tail fin increases the area that is pushing against the water. Other fins are used for steering and balancing. Pectoral fins are mostly used as paddles when the fish is swimming slowly.

Some fish use body fins and not their tails for swimming. The skates and rays swim by flapping their large pectoral fins.

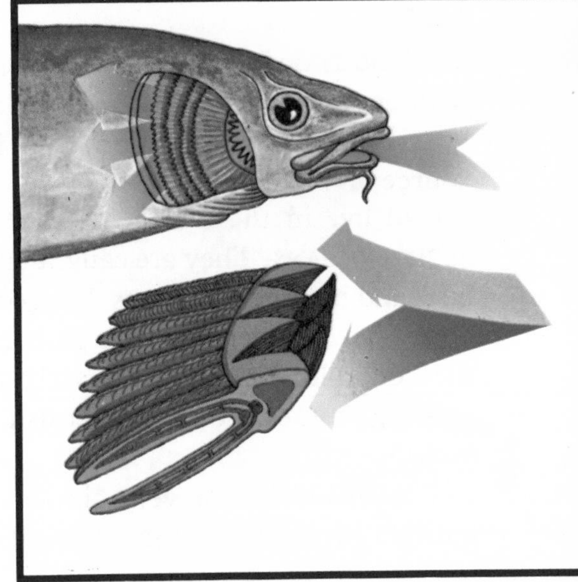

Above: A fish breathes by taking water in through its mouth and forcing it out over the gills. Part of the gills is shown enlarged. They contain a lot of blood. Oxygen goes into the blood from the water.

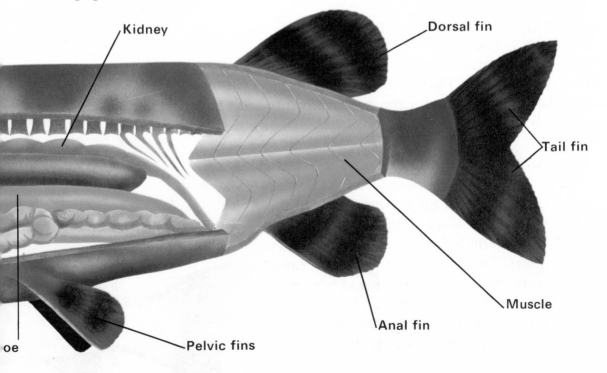

Cod

The cod is one of the world's most useful fish. Millions of kilogrammes of codfish are sold every year for food. In addition, cod liver oil is a source of Vitamin D.

Cod live in the North ATLANTIC and North PACIFIC OCEANS. They are caught on long fishing lines and in large trawl nets dragged over the sea bed. They can weigh up to 27 kilogrammes, but the cod sold for food are rarely heavier than 10 kilogrammes. Cod eat other fish, worms, and crabs.

The haddock is a very similar fish, distinguished by a dark spot just behind the head.

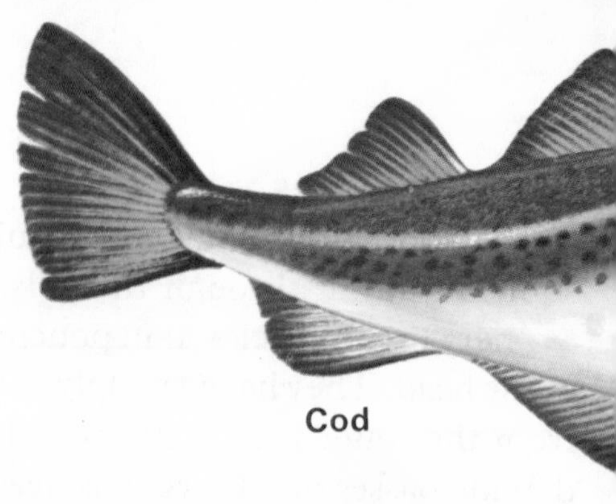
Cod

Herring

The herring is so useful as food that wars have been fought over the right to fish for it. Many seaside towns started as fishing villages where herring were caught. Today, far fewer herring are caught as they have been fished so heavily in the past.

Herring live in huge groups called shoals. They swim close together and feed on tiny animals that are strained out of the water passing through their GILLS. Herring prefer cooler water, and the shoals appear near the coast when they are ready to lay their eggs.

Common eel

Moray eel

Herring

Mackerel

The mackerel is an important food fish. Several different kinds live in the northern parts of the ATLANTIC and the PACIFIC. They are about a foot long, with greenish backs marked with wavy black stripes. The belly is silvery blue. There is a row of very small fins on the top and bottom of the body just in front of the tail fin. The fish spend the summer in shoals near the surface, but they move down to the sea bed for the winter.

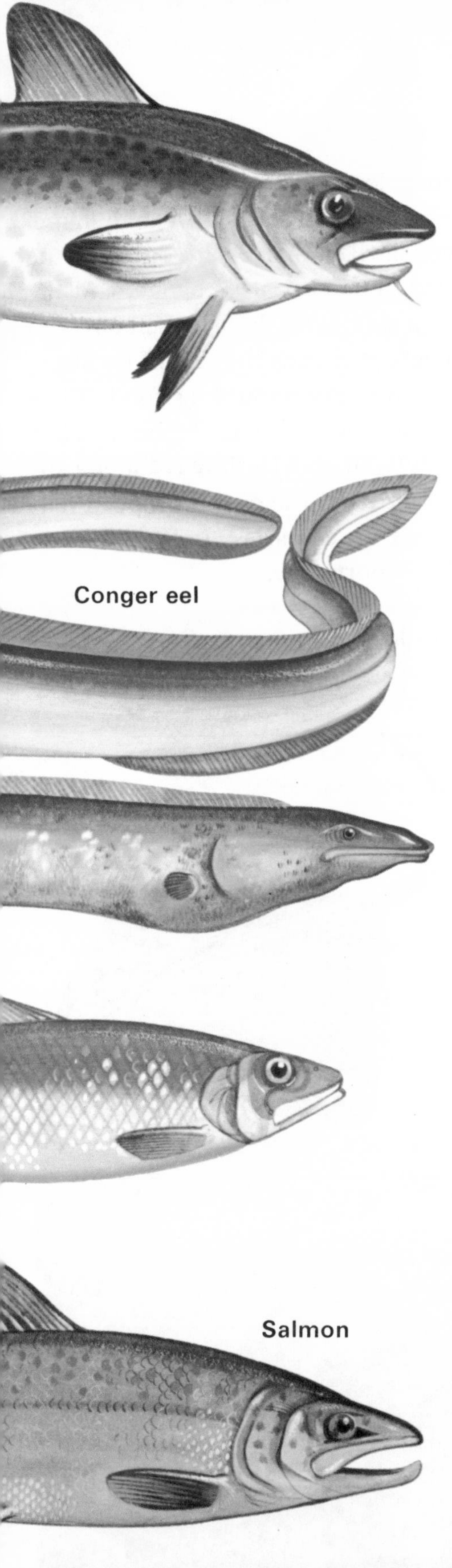

Eels

Eels have long, slender bodies, which are extremely slippery. They spend the day under stones in the water and come out at night to eat small animals.

When freshwater eels grow up, they migrate down the RIVERS and lay their eggs in the sea. European and North American eels lay their eggs in the SARGASSO SEA. The baby eels swim back to the coasts and make their way into the rivers. The young European eels take about three years to make this journey, but the American eels reach the coasts in about one year. The adult eels do not come back to the rivers and they die soon after spawning.

Moray eels and conger eels spend their whole life in the sea. Their sharp teeth can give a very nasty bite. Some moray eels are poisonous. They eat fish and crabs.

Salmon

The salmon and its relative, the trout, are the angler's favourite fish. They can be distinguished from other fish by the fleshy FIN on the back, just in front of the tail. The largest salmon ever caught weighed 58 kilogrammes.

Salmon spend most of their lives at sea, but they swim up RIVERS and streams to lay their eggs. While swimming upstream they often make tremendous leaps to get over weirs and waterfalls. They are very tired and thin when they reach the spawning grounds. The eggs are laid on the stream bed and the young salmon swim down to the sea when they are one or more years old. They spend a few years in the sea and then swim back to the coasts. They usually enter the very rivers in which they started their lives. PACIFIC salmon lay only one batch of eggs and then die. ATLANTIC salmon may spawn every year for several years.

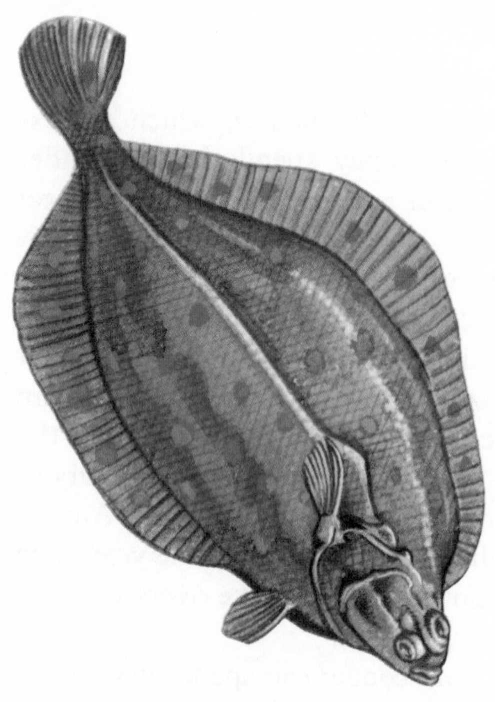

Flatfish

A young flatfish looks like a normal fish, but when it is a few days old it starts to change shape. One eye moves until both eyes are on the same side of the head. The FINS also change, and the fish turns on its side. The flatfish then sinks to the seabed, where it spends the rest of its life.

Some flatfish are very popular as food. They include sole, plaice, halibut, and flounder. They are caught in nets, or trawls, dragged along the seabed. The flounder is the only European flatfish that migrates up estuaries. It even lives in fresh water for a short time.

Left: The plaice, like most other flatfish, lies on its left side.

Sharks

The sharks are fish whose skeletons are made of soft cartilage instead of BONE. Their skin is covered with sharp scales. Most sharks have very sharp teeth. They eat other fish. Some will attack humans. The two largest sharks, the basking shark and the whale shark, are harmless. The smallest sharks are the dogfish.

Right: A skate, related to the shark family.
Below: A grey shark.

Deep-sea fish

Many kinds of fish live hundreds and even thousands of metres beneath the surface of the sea. They are not usually very large but they often have very strange shapes. At these depths it is very cold and there is no light. Some of the fish have luminous spots on their bodies. These help them to find their food and they also help them to recognise each other. The gulper eel has an enormous mouth, and can eat other fish as large as itself. Over its mouth the angler-fish has a kind of 'fishing rod'. This rod has a luminous tip that brings other fish close enough for the angler-fish to snap them up.

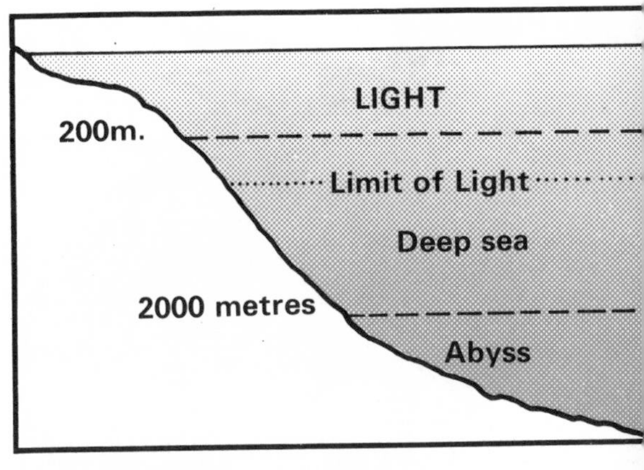

Above: Most deep-sea fish live more than 300 metres down.

Below: Some creatures from the deep sea.

Above: Flying fish can glide several hundred metres.

Flying fish

Flying fish live up to their name. They leap out of the water and glide through the air on their large wing-like FINS. They launch themselves into the air by swimming rapidly up to the surface and breaking right through it. Gliding helps them to escape from other fish which might eat them. Most flying fish live in warm seas.

Squid, which are related to the OCTOPUS, can also 'fly'. They do this by pumping out water which forces them up and forward.

Left: Sometimes flying fish gain extra speed in the air by putting the tail fin into the water and wriggling it to drive themselves forward.

Electric fish

The electric ray lives in warm seas. When touched, it gives a painful electric shock. The electricity is generated in 'batteries' made of special muscles. Normal muscles contract (get shorter) when they receive electrical signals from the brain and they cause movement. The 'battery' muscles, however, pass on the electrical charges and send them out into the water. The electric ray gives out charges of up to 200 volts. The electric catfish of AFRICA and the electric EEL of SOUTH AMERICA also give severe shocks. The eel can give out 550 volts. The shocks are used to stun the fish's prey and to drive away enemies.

The electric eel cannot see well. It sends out weak electric currents which help it to find its way about.

Right: The electric ray's electric charges come from its 'wings'. It wraps itself around its prey to kill it.

Sticklebacks

Salmon, freshwater bass, and other fish make nests for their eggs. These nests are no more than small pits in the sand. The stickleback, however, makes a nest by gluing together pieces of weed. The nest is made by the male, whose belly turns red during the nesting season. He drives away other males and then performs energetic 'dances' to attract the females. Next, he leads the females to his nest where they lay their eggs. The eggs and newly hatched sticklebacks are then guarded by the male, who stays by the nest and fans it with his FINS. This fanning sends currents of fresh water over the eggs and young fish and ensures that they get plenty of oxygen.

Left: The red belly of the male stickleback (top) helps it to attract the females.

Seahorses

The strangely-shaped seahorse is found in warm, shallow seas. It swims with its body held upright. It is propelled by the FIN on its back. When resting, it wraps its long tail around a piece of SEAWEED. Some kinds of seahorse have long trailing 'ribbons' of skin on their bodies. These resemble the SEAWEEDS and the animals are thus very well camouflaged when resting.

The female lays her eggs in a pouch on the male's belly. After the babies hatch, they are squeezed out of the pouch. The seahorses are closely related to the pipefish. These are very slender snake-like fish. They have a long snout like that of the seahorse and a very long tail. Like the seahorse, the pipefish usually have bony rings on their bodies.

Right: The seahorse's strange body is strengthened by lots of bony rings.

Sturgeons

The sturgeon looks like a shark with a long, curved snout and an up-turned tail. Its skeleton is made largely of cartilage, but it really belongs with the bony fishes. It is covered with large bony plates. It is the fish which produces caviar. Caviar is a delicacy made from the eggs of the sturgeon.

Most sturgeons live in the sea and go up RIVERS to breed. A few kinds spend all their life in fresh water. Sturgeons can grow to a great size. The Russian beluga can weigh 1450 kilogrammes and can yield about 200 kilogrammes of caviar.

Today, in the U.S.S.R., sturgeons are bred in special tanks. They are then released into the sea.

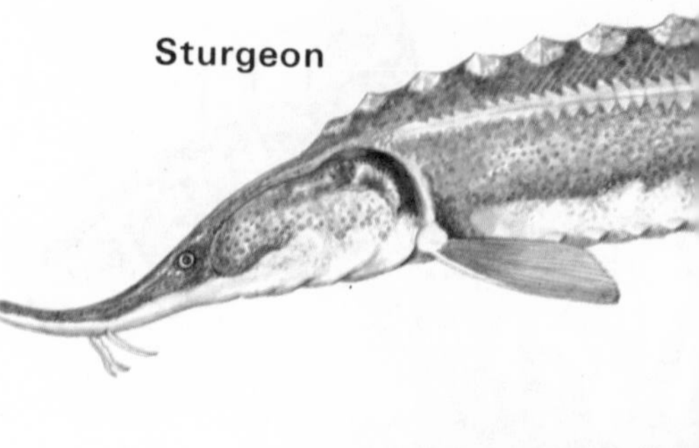

Top right: The sturgeon's mouth is right underneath its snout.

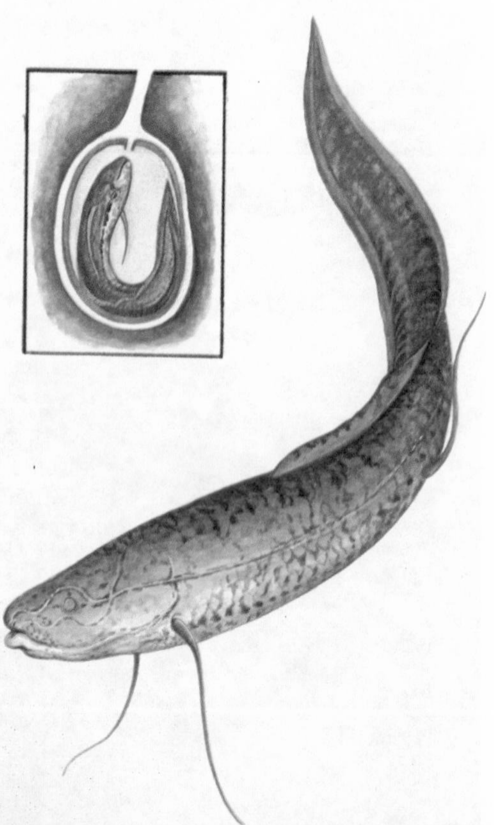

Lungfish

Millions of years ago lungfish lived all over the world. They are now found only in SOUTH AMERICA, AFRICA, and AUSTRALIA. A lungfish has GILLS as well as lungs, but the lungs are very important for breathing. If a lungfish is held under water, it will drown.

Because lungfish can come to the surface to breathe air, they can live in foul water where other fish cannot survive. In summer, when the lakes and RIVERS dry up, the African and South American lungfish live in burrows in the mud. The Australian lungfish cannot live for very long when it is out of the water. It is much heavier than the other lungfish.

Left: The eel-like African lungfish has very slender fins . In dry weather it burrows into the mud and leaves a little air hole.

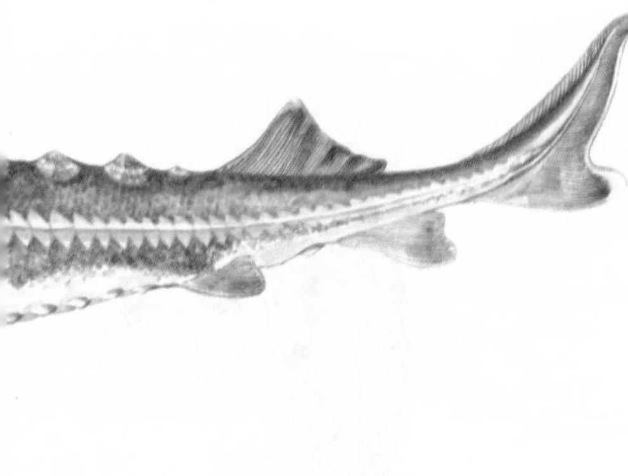

Coelacanths

Scientists used to believe that the coelacanth (pronounced *see*-la-kanth) had become extinct 70 million years ago. But in 1938 a live coelacanth was caught by a South African trawler. Since then, other coelacanths have been caught. They are peculiar fish in many ways. Their FINS are very strong, with bones in them that look like those in the legs of a land animal. The fins probably help the fish to creep around on the sea bed. At one time these fins made scientists think that the coelacanths were the ancestors of land animals. It is now known that this is not true, but the fish that first started to come on to the land must have been something like the coelacanths.

Coelacanth

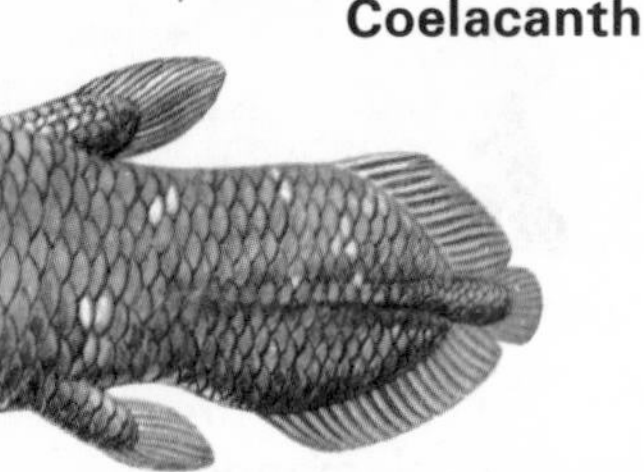

Left: The coelacanth is a heavily armoured fish. The large scales overlap, so that almost every part of the fish has three layers.

Fish without jaws

Some scientists think that the lamprey and the hagfish are not really fish at all. They look like eels, but they have no jaws and no pectoral and pelvic FINS. The mouth is a small round opening surrounded by a powerful sucker and lots of sharp, horny teeth. The lampreys attach themselves to other fish by means of the sucker and they use the teeth to rasp away the flesh. They then suck the blood of their victims. Some of the smaller lampreys feed on water snails and other small animals.

The hagfish lives in the sea. There are several different kinds of lampreys. Some live in the sea and others in fresh water.

Right: The lamprey has a long, thin body like an eel's. It has a row of seven gill openings on each side of its body.

Amphibians

Amphibians are cold-blooded animals that can live either in the water or on land. Even when they live on land, they must never be far from water. Their eggs need moisture. Their larvae, called TADPOLES, swim in pools and streams until they change into adult amphibians. The adults can live on land. They usually have to stay in damp places, however, so that they do not dry up. Some TOADS can survive in DESERTS by storing water in their bodies.

The mud puppy and the siren of NORTH AMERICA spend their whole life in water. They look like newts, but they never lose their GILLS.

Other amphibians can manage to live with almost no water. The greenhouse FROG of the south-eastern United States lays its eggs on moist ground. Its young have no tadpole stage and the eggs hatch into tiny frogs.

Above: The orange-eyed tree frog has suckers on its toes.
Below left: The fire salamander.
Below: A female great crested newt under water.

Salamanders

Some amphibians look like LIZARDS. These are the salamanders. They can be distinguished from lizards by their soft, damp skins. Like other amphibians, salamanders live in wet places. They come out at night to eat insects and worms.

Some salamanders make burrows in the SOIL. The olm lives in caves in southern EUROPE. The giant salamander of JAPAN is the largest living amphibian. It grows to 150 centimetres and is often caught by fishermen.

Newts are a kind of salamander. They hibernate (sleep) during the winter. In the spring they return to ponds to lay their eggs. During this time the males become brightly coloured.

If newts are kept in an aquarium they can sometimes be watched as they shed their skin. All amphibians do this, but newts can shed their skin in one piece. It floats in the water as if it were a transparent animal.

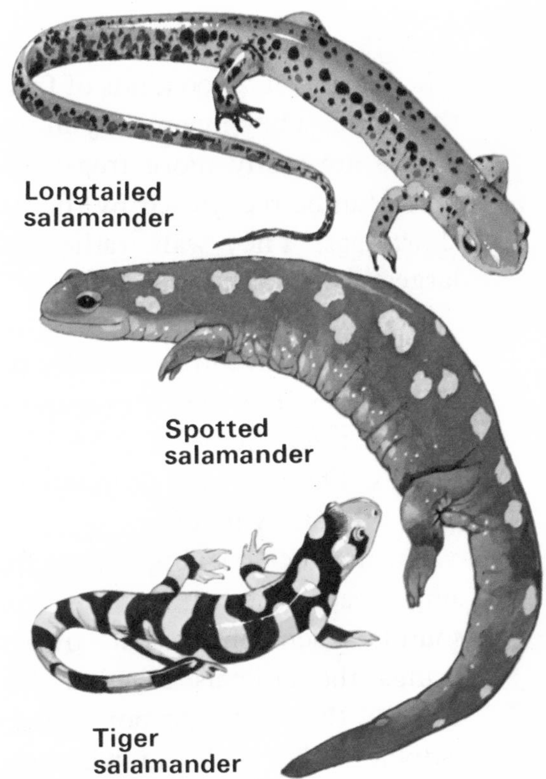

Axolotls

Axolotls are most unusual animals. They are SALAMANDERS that do not grow up. Their whole life is spent as TADPOLES living in water. They can, however, lay eggs.

Above: Three types of salamander with their bright coloured markings.
Below: The axolotl retains its red gills all its life.

Frogs and toads

There are over 2,500 kinds of frogs and toads in the world. They live mainly in warm countries. There are many more frogs than toads. The toads can be recognised by their fat bodies and short legs. They walk rather than hop. The largest frog is the Goliath frog of West AFRICA.

Frogs and toads usually live in damp places, but some can live in DESERTS by storing water in their bodies. The tree frogs spend almost all their lives in trees. Some of them lay their eggs on LEAVES. The TADPOLES drop into pools under the trees when they hatch.

During the breeding season frogs and toads sing to each other with croaks, grunts, and other sounds. Each kind has its own 'song', which brings the animals together for egg laying. Usually the adults do not guard the eggs and tadpoles. The male midwife toad of EUROPE, however, wraps strings of eggs around his legs.

Toads have poisonous glands in their skin that stop enemies from eating them. The brightly coloured arrow-poison frogs are used by South American Indians to poison their arrows.

Tadpoles

An amphibian hatches out of its egg as a tadpole. The tadpole of the common FROG takes about ten weeks to turn into a froglet.

At first a tadpole has no mouth and no GILLS. The gills grow gradually until they look like feathers on each side of the head. Later they become covered by flaps of skin. Finally they disappear. By this time the tadpole has lungs.

When the legs grow, the back pair seem to grow first, but the front pair are hidden by the gill flaps. When the legs are fully grown, the tadpole looks like a frog with a tail. Then the tail disappears, and the frog hops on to the land.

Reptiles

Reptiles are cold-blooded animals whose bodies are covered with scales. An important difference between reptiles and ourselves is that our HEART has four compartments, but a reptile's heart has only three. Most reptiles lay eggs. The eggs of some reptiles, however, hatch inside the mother's body, and the young are born alive.

For millions of years the reptiles were the most important animals in the world. During this time there lived the many kinds of DINOSAURS and other large reptiles. These included the plesiosaurs and the fish-like ichthyosaurs, the flying PTERODACTYLS, and many others.

Nearly all of the reptiles died out, or became extinct, over 100 million years ago. No-one exactly knows why. The only kinds of reptiles left are TORTOISES and TURTLES, CROCODILES and ALLIGATORS, LIZARDS and SNAKES, and the tuatara.

The tuatara, or sphenodon, looks like a large lizard with a row of spines down the back. It lives on islands off the coast of NEW ZEALAND.

Above: The Australian thorny devil, a desert lizard.
Below left: A skink lizard.
Below: A land iguana.

Tortoises and turtles

Tortoises and turtles are reptiles whose bodies are protected by a shell. There are about 230 kinds living in the warmer parts of the world. The name tortoise is usually given to the kinds that live on land. Those living in water are called turtles. The shell is made up of horny plates. The upper part, or carapace, is attached to the ribs and backbone.

The tortoises can draw their head and legs into the shell for protection. They are slow moving and are very long-lived. The giant tortoise grows to 150 centimetres long and can live for 150 years. The small tortoises are often kept as pets. In temperate climates they hibernate (sleep through the winter) from October to March. The tortoises are mostly vegetarians.

The freshwater turtles eat other animals. The marine turtles live in the sea, but they come ashore to lay their eggs in the sand.

Top right: A giant tortoise from the Galapagos.
Right: A green turtle swimming.
Below: Terrapins, fresh-water turtles.

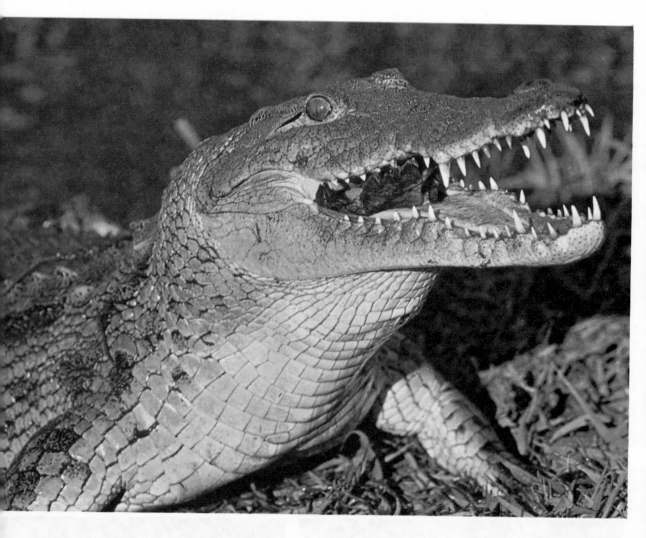

Above: A crocodile showing its huge, powerful jaws.
Below: An American alligator.

Crocodiles and alligators

Crocodiles spend much of their time basking in the sun. They can run very fast but they rarely go far from the bank of the RIVER. When disturbed, they slip into the water. Crocodiles are found in most tropical parts of the world. They reach six or seven metres in length.

The alligator looks like the crocodile. One kind lives in the south-eastern United States. Another kind lives in CHINA.

Crocodiles and alligators lay their eggs in nests. The mother stays near the nest until the eggs hatch.

Lizards

Lizards are reptiles with slender bodies and long tails. They are fast runners and are difficult to catch. The slow-worm and the grass snake are lizards that have lost their legs and look like snakes. Some lizards can shed their tails when attacked. They run away, leaving their tail with the enemy.

The largest lizard is the Komodo dragon, which grows to three metres. The flying dragon of ASIA can glide from tree to tree. The geckos are lizards that often come into houses in warm countries to search for insects. They can hang upside-down from ceilings.

The gila (*heel*-a) monster and the beaded lizard of the south-western United States and MEXICO are the only lizards with poisonous bites.

Two large Australian lizards. The eastern water dragon (left) and (below) the bearded dragon displaying its beard and its strong teeth.

Snakes

Snakes are legless reptiles. Unlike legless lizards, such as the slow-worm, they have no movable eyelids and eardrums. Snakes cannot hear sounds, but they can feel vibrations in the ground. Some snakes, like the boas and pythons, still have a tiny pair of hind legs.

Snakes move by pushing the body forwards in waves or by pushing with the scales on the belly. They do not move as fast as many people think. The fastest snake is the black mamba, which can travel at 11 kilometres an hour.

Snakes are most common in hot countries, but the adder can live north of the ARCTIC circle. They usually live on the ground, basking in the sunshine, or hiding in crevices when the weather is cold. The African boomslang lives in trees. Several kinds of snakes make burrows.

Below left: A snake bites into a rubber-covered jar to provide venom for making snake-bite serum. Below right: A diamond python with its eggs.

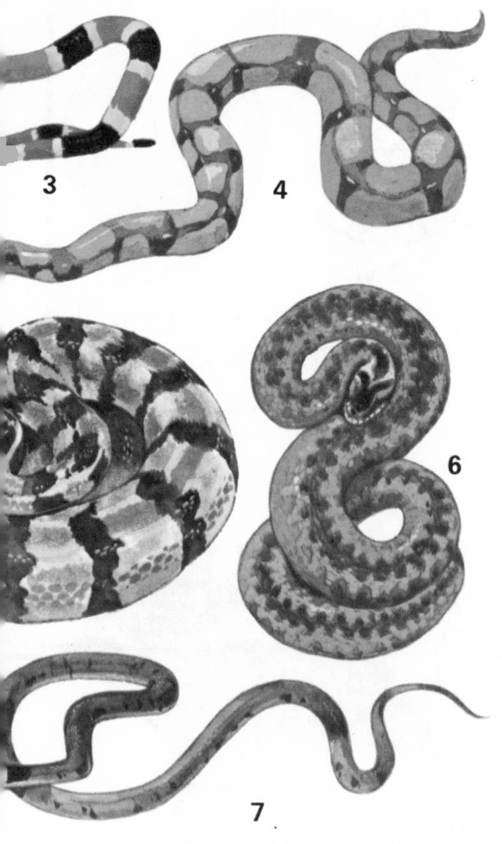

In south-east ASIA there are sea snakes. The largest snake of all is the South American anaconda, which grows to 11·4 metres.

Snakes eat live animals, or the eggs of birds and other reptiles. The prey is eaten whole after being killed by poison or by constriction. Constriction means that the snake winds its body around the prey to stop its breathing.

Snakes can swallow large animals because their jaws are very loosely attached to the skull and they can open their mouths very wide. A large meal may satisfy a snake for many weeks.

Poisonous snakes inject poison, or venom, into their victims through hollow teeth called fangs. In some countries people are killed every year by snakes. The most dangerous snakes are the krait of Asia, the Australian tiger snake, and the sea snakes.

Left: (1) Wagler's pit viper. (2) Cobra. (3) Coral snake. (4) Boa constrictor. (5) Rattlesnake. (6) European viper or adder. (7) Grass snake.

Chameleons

The chameleons (ka-*meel*-yans) are a strange kind of LIZARD. Their eyes can point in different directions. For example, one eye can look forwards while the other looks backwards. The skin of the chameleon changes colour to match its background or to show that it has been disturbed.

Chameleons live in the forests of AFRICA and in parts of EUROPE and ASIA. A chameleon moves very slowly along branches. It catches insects by shooting out its long tongue. Its tongue, when fully extended, is as long as its body.

Right: The chameleon can look backwards with one eye and forwards with the other.

Birds

Birds are flying animals whose bodies are covered with FEATHERS. They are warm-blooded.

Millions of years ago the birds developed from reptiles that lived in trees. A bird's legs are covered with scales like those of a LIZARD. At first birds could only glide from tree to tree. Later birds were able to fly by flapping their wings. Eventually many kinds of birds appeared.

Kiwis, ostriches, and PENGUINS cannot fly. Swifts and albatrosses, however, can keep flying for days on end. Puffins and guillemots use their wings for swimming as well as for flying.

Most birds have their eyes on the sides of the head, so they can see almost all around them. OWLS have forward-looking eyes and can judge distances very well.

Below: A drawing to show the main internal organs of a pigeon.

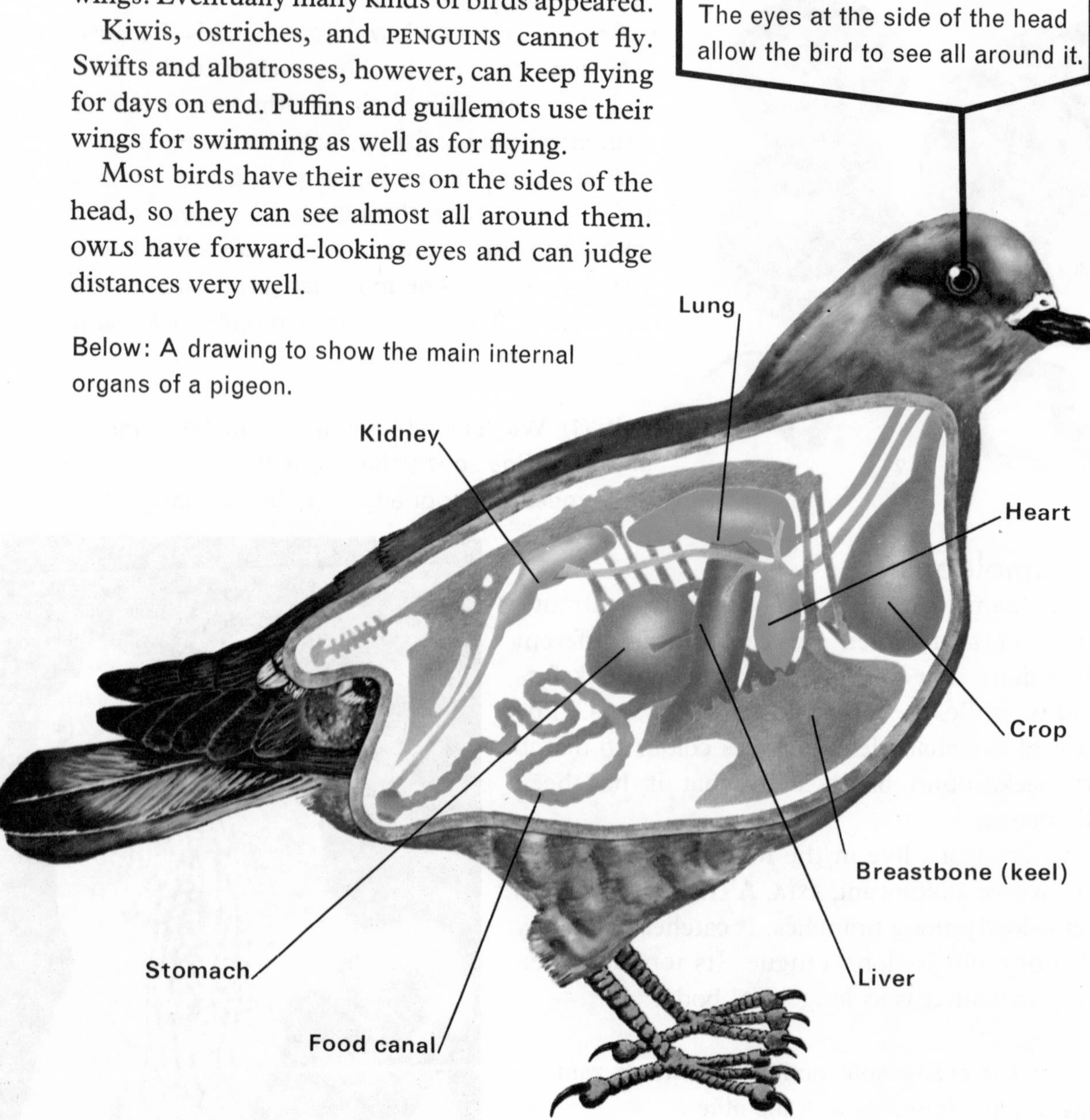

Beaks

A bird has no hands with which to hold things. Instead, it uses its beak, or bill. Its beak is an extension of the jaws. It is covered by horny plates and contains the bird's nostrils. Today's birds have no teeth, although some extinct birds did, such as ARCHAEOPTERYX.

The shape of a bird's beak shows us what it eats. Finches and sparrows have stout, cone-shaped bills for opening seeds. OWLS and hawks have sharp curved beaks for tearing flesh. Beaks are also used for NEST building and for preening (looking after the FEATHERS). The pelican uses its large beak as a fishing net, and beaks are also used as weapons.

Left: The beaks of (1) Toucan. (2) Eagle. (3) Woodpecker. (4) Finch. (5) Nuthatch. (6) Heron. Each beak is shaped for a special job.

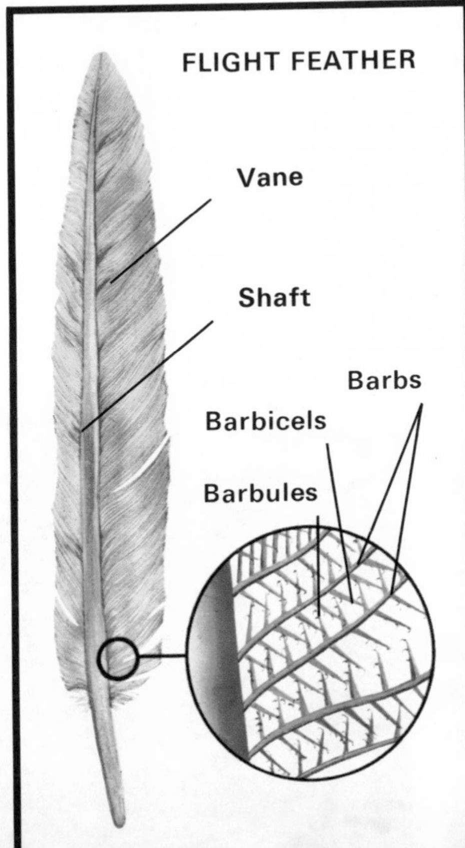

Feathers

Feathers are made of the same substance as human HAIR. They keep the bird warm. Wing feathers are important for flying.

There are two kinds of feather. One kind, called down, is soft and fluffy. Baby birds are covered with down. As they grow up, the adult feathers grow over the down. Adult feathers are made up of a shaft, or quill, and a flat vane. The vane can bend and is made up of rows of barbs and barbules, which are neatly hooked together by barbicels.

When a bird preens, it uses its beak to make sure that the barbs and barbules are in their proper places.

Left: A feather from the wing of a bird. The smaller picture shows how the feather is made up.

Top: Flight. The stages in the movement of a duck's wings.
Above: The wing of a bird, showing how the feathers overlap to give a smooth outline.
Below: (Left) Herring gull in flight. (Centre) Sacred ibis taking off beside a lake. (Right) A gannet coming in to land.

How a bird flies

A bird flies by flapping its wings. On the down-stroke the wings are forced down and back to push the bird upwards and forwards. On the up-stroke the wings are bent and the FEATHERS are separated to let air through. This prevents the bird from being pushed down again. The tail is used for steering and slowing down.

A bird needs strong MUSCLES to fly. Its wings are worked by the very large breast muscles. To make flying easier, a bird has light, hollow BONES and a strong HEART. The lungs are connected to bags of air called air sacs. These increase the amount of oxygen that the bird can breathe in.

Different birds have different types of wings. The type depends on the bird's method of flying. The albatross glides on long, thin wings. The humming-bird hovers on short, broad wings.

Nests

Nests are used to hold eggs until they hatch. Some baby birds stay in the nest until they can fly. There are many different kinds of nest. Some birds only make a slight hollow in the ground. Nests in trees are more elaborate. Twigs and grass are woven together in the shape of a cup. Mud, feathers, or moss may be used as linings. Nests in burrows in the ground, like the kingfisher's, or in holes in trees, like the woodpecker's, are especially safe from enemies.

The emperor penguin of the Antarctic does not have a nest at all.

Eggs

Birds' eggs differ in size and colour, but in other ways they are similar. Inside a hard, oval shell is the white, the fluid that protects the yolk. The yolk is food for the growing chick. The chick starts as a tiny disc on the top of the yolk. The shell lets in air so that the chick can breathe.

The egg must be kept warm all the time to grow properly. When the chick is ready, it makes a hole in the shell with its BEAK and crawls out.

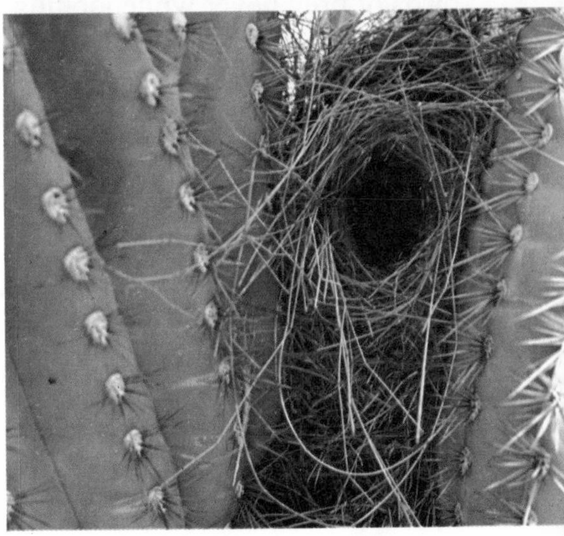

Right above: Cattle egrets at their nest.
Right: A well protected nest in a cactus plant.
Below: An opened egg, showing the yolk and the white, and a variety of eggs.

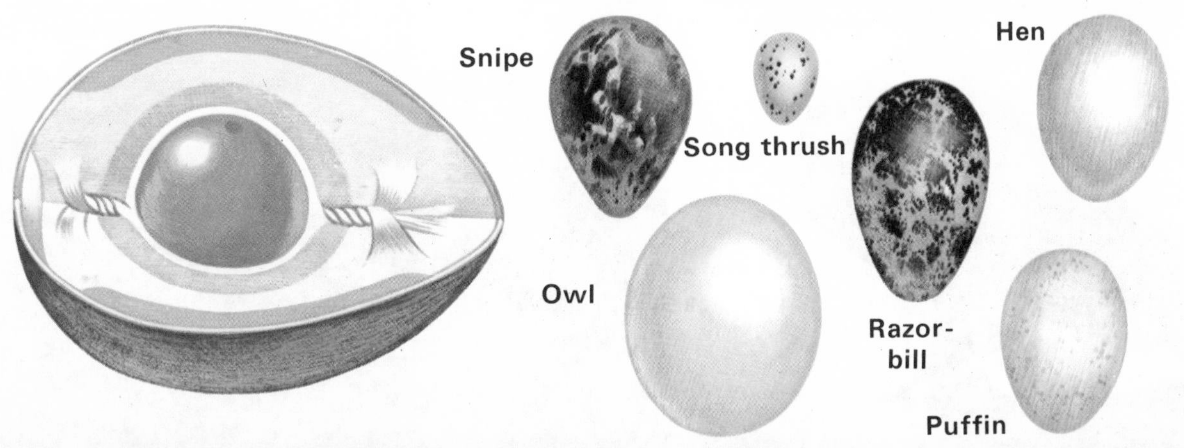

Birds of prey

Birds that hunt and eat animals are called birds of prey. The OWLS are birds of prey, but usually only hawks, falcons, and vultures are so called. All birds of prey have sharp hooked BEAKS and long claws or talons, which they use for catching and killing their prey.

The hawks include the eagles, harriers, the kites, and the fish-eating osprey. The largest eagles are the harpy eagle of SOUTH AMERICA and the monkey-eating eagle of the Philippines.

The falcons are fast-flying hunters. They dive or 'stoop' at their prey. The peregrine falcon can spot its prey three-quarters of a kilometre away, and stoop at nearly 300 kilometres an hour. Some birds of prey hover while looking for food.

The vultures are birds of prey that eat dead animals. They have no FEATHERS on their head. The secretary bird is a long-legged bird of prey that looks like a stork. It runs after its prey.

Above right: The peregrine falcon.
Below: The bald eagle.
Below right: A flock of vultures.

Owls

Owls are BIRDS OF PREY that usually hunt in the dark. They have excellent eyesight and hearing. They can easily find mice and other small animals at night. Their FEATHERS are so soft that the owls make no noise when flying. They can hear the slightest rustling on the ground, and the animals cannot hear them coming. During the daytime the owls sit in trees or old buildings. They are hard to see, but they sometimes give themselves away by spitting out pellets containing the fur and feathers of their prey.

Most owls nest in trees. The barn owl nests in old buildings, however, and the snowy owl nests on the ground. The burrowing owl of the Americas lives in holes in the ground.

Left above: A tawny owl brings home a frog.
Left: The Australian boobook owl.

Game birds

Game is the word used for animals that are killed for sport. Many kinds of birds can be called game birds, but the name is usually used for the pheasants, grouse, quails, and partridges. These birds live on the ground. They eat seeds, leaves, and insects. When disturbed, they fly up very fast, but they do not usually fly very far.

Female game birds are called hens. They are dull-coloured and are difficult to see when they are sitting on their eggs. The cocks, or male birds, are brightly coloured as a rule. Many of them put on displays to attract their mates in the spring. Strict laws control the shooting of game birds. They cannot be killed in the spring, when they are rearing their young.

Right: A cock capercaillie (top) and a red-legged partridge.

Hummingbirds

Hummingbirds have bright, shining FEATHERS. They feed on nectar and small insects, which they collect while hovering in front of flowers. While collecting nectar, hummingbirds pick up pollen on their feathers and carry it to the next flower they visit. In this way, they pollinate the flowers.

Although they are very small, hummingbirds are strong fliers. The ruby-throated hummingbird migrates hundreds of kilometres across the sea. Hummingbirds' wings make a humming sound and can beat at up to 80 times a second.

Most hummingbirds live in the forests of tropical America, but the rufous hummingbird nests in Alaska and migrates to the tropics for the winter.

The smallest bird in the world is the bee hummingbird of Cuba. It has a wingspan of 4 centimetres and weighs just 2 grammes.

Right: Hummingbirds normally take nectar from flowers, but can learn to feed from a bottle.

Cuckoos

The European cuckoo gets its name from its call, which it utters in spring. The hen cuckoos lay their eggs in the nests of other, smaller birds. When the baby cuckoo hatches, it pushes the other eggs out of the nest. It is fed by its new parents. When the young cuckoo grows up, it flies to AFRICA. It can find its way there without being shown by its parents.

There are many kinds of cuckoos in the world. Some of them look after their own eggs and chicks.

Left: A reed warbler feeds a young cuckoo which will soon be bigger than the warbler itself.

Seabirds

The best-known seabirds are the gulls. They spend their time near the shore and sometimes come inland. The terns look like the gulls but are smaller. They nest in large groups on sandy ground and dive for fish.

Many seabirds come near the land only when they are breeding. During the summer, some cliffs are filled with guillemots and razorbills, which crowd together on ledges.

The cormorant and the shag have long, slender necks and narrow beaks. They swim after fish. When they return to the rocks, they stand with their wings open to dry them.

The gannet dives for fish from a great height. In tropical seas frigate birds steal fish from boobies (relatives of the gannet) as they bring them home to their young. The frigate birds chase the boobies to make them drop their catch.

The albatrosses are superb gliders.

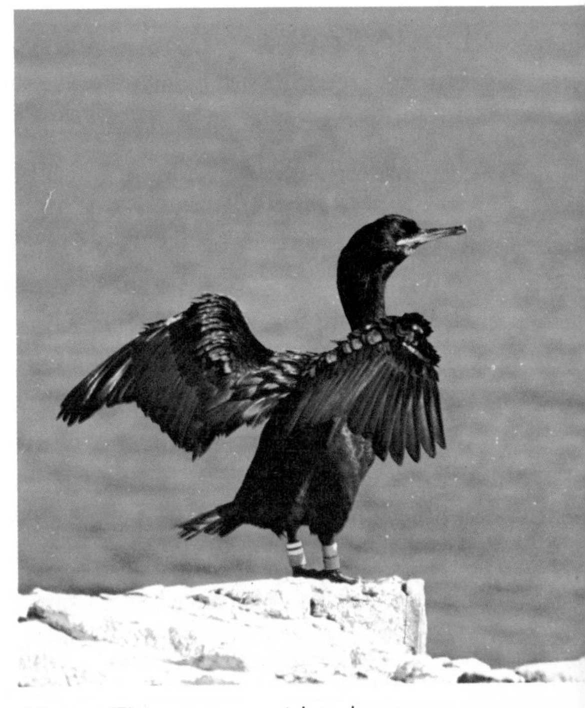

Above: This cormorant has been diving for fish. Now it stretches its wings to dry them.

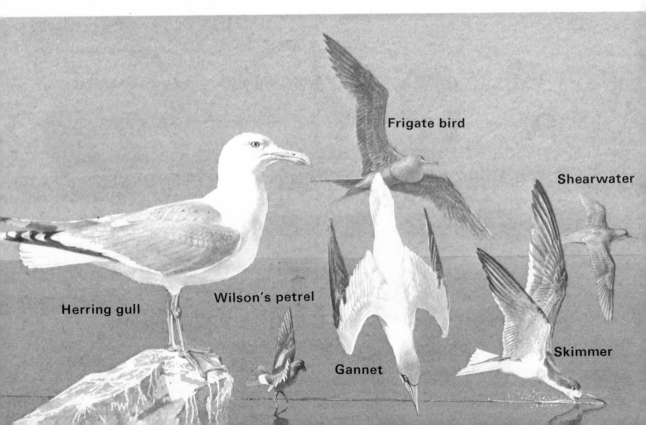

Frigate bird
Shearwater
Herring gull
Wilson's petrel
Gannet
Skimmer

Ducks, geese, and swans

Ducks, geese, and swans are called 'wildfowl'. The long-necked swans are the largest. Geese are smaller, and the ducks are smallest of all.

The graceful mute swan, which can be recognised by the knob on its BEAK, has been domesticated for hundreds of years. The male is called the cob, the female is the pen, and the babies are cygnets. The black swan lives in AUSTRALIA.

Many of the geese nest in the ARCTIC and fly to warmer countries for the winter. The farmyard goose is a descendant of the greylag goose. The male goose is called a gander. The babies are goslings. The Hawaiian goose, or néné, nearly became extinct. It was saved from extinction, however, by being kept in captivity.

The familiar kinds of ducks live on ponds and feed in shallow water by dabbling on the bottom, with their tails in the air. The mallard is the ancestor of domestic ducks. The eider duck lines its nest with fine down FEATHERS. These are collected to make eiderdowns.

Above: Bar-headed and emperor geese together in a wild-life reserve. Most geese normally live in flocks.

Mallard duck

Eider duck

Black swan

Canada goose

Songbirds

The small birds that nest in woods and gardens and come to bird-tables are called songbirds. The males sing to keep other males out of their territory and to attract females.

Not all songbirds have such beautiful songs as the blackbird, nightingale, or robin. The sparrows do not sing well; neither do the crows. The birds of paradise have harsh voices, but they show off colourful FEATHERS instead of singing.

The songbirds are the largest group of birds. They are found all over the world. The woods and fields may be full of them. But we may not notice them if they are not singing. The trees are full of warblers and tits feeding on insects and finches feeding on seeds. Flower-peckers, sunbirds, and honey-eaters of tropical countries are songbirds that eat nectar.

Right: Four common songbirds. Their songs are heard mainly during the nesting season.
Below: The Australian red-browed finch.

Blackbird

Chaffinch

Nightingale

Thrush

Parrots

The parrots live in forests in tropical parts of the world. They have sharp, hooked BEAKS. They have been kept as pets for hundreds of years. The macaws, amazons, and lorikeets have brilliant plumage of many colours. Budgerigars are small Australian parrots which live in large flocks. They eat seeds and they sometimes damage fields of WHEAT.

Their ability to 'talk' makes parrots popular as pets. The African grey parrot, the green amazon, and the budgerigar are the best talkers. Although the birds can say many words, and even sentences, they do not understand what they say. They can imitate mechanical sounds such as saws as well as human voices.

Right: The eastern rosella parrot, one of Australia's many brightly coloured parrots.

Flightless birds

Some birds have lost the ability to fly. PENGUINS, for instance, have become swimmers. Some large birds have become fast runners. The African ostrich is the largest living bird. It has a long neck and long legs, but its wings are very small. Ostriches have been recorded as running as fast as 60 kilometres an hour. They live on the plains of AFRICA and often mix with herds of ZEBRA and antelopes. Ostriches feed mainly on plants.

The rheas of SOUTH AMERICA and the cassowaries and emus of AUSTRALIA resemble the ostrich. The kiwi of NEW ZEALAND is the size of a chicken. It has a very long BEAK. It is active at night and uses its keen sense of smell to hunt for worms.

Left: The male ostrich may reach a height of two and a half metres. The cassowary lives in forests.

Penguins

Many people think that all penguins live in the ANTARCTIC. There are, however, penguins living in AUSTRALIA, SOUTH AFRICA, and SOUTH AMERICA. Penguins cannot fly, but they use their wings as stiff flippers for swimming. They eat shrimps, fish and squid. Their legs are short, and they can only waddle slowly on land. When a penguin wants to hurry, it lies on its belly and pushes itself along with its flippers and feet.

Penguins spend much of their time in the water and they are protected from the cold by a dense coat of FEATHERS and a layer of blubber.

Penguins build NESTS of pebbles or grass. Jackass and Magellan penguins live in burrows. The Emperor penguin holds its egg on its feet.

Right: King penguins, second largest of the 17 different kinds of penguins.

Migration

Many kinds of birds fly from one part of the world to another. After they have raised a family and winter is setting in, they fly to a warmer place where there will be more food. In the spring they fly back to their nesting place. This is called migration. The European swallows fly to AFRICA for the winter because the cold weather kills off the flying insects that they eat. The North American swallows fly to SOUTH AMERICA. The arctic tern flies more than 30,000 kilometres in a year, spending part of the time in the ARCTIC and part in the ANTARCTIC.

When birds are migrating they use the sun or stars to steer by, just as a ship's navigator does. Some mammals, fish, and insects also migrate.

Above left: Gentoo penguins on the shore.
Left: An Adélie penguin incubates its eggs.

Mammals

Mammals are animals with fur or HAIR. They are warm-blooded. This means that their temperature stays the same at all times. We are mammals and our temperature stays at about 37° centigrade. Our clothes help keep our body warm. Other animals rely on their fur or a thick layer of fat under the SKIN.

Nearly all mammals give birth to live babies. The mother feeds them on milk, which is made in special GLANDS on her body. Only two kinds of mammals lay eggs. They are the duck-billed platypus and the spiny anteater or echidna of AUSTRALIA and New Guinea.

Below: Duck-billed platypus.
Below right: A koala eating eucalyptus leaves.

Pouched mammals

Kangaroos and their relatives keep their babies in a pouch. They are called marsupials, or pouched mammals. When a baby kangaroo is born it is very small, but it can crawl through its mother's fur and into her pouch. The mother's milk GLANDS open into the pouch, and the baby stays there, in complete safety, until it is larger.

Pouched animals are found mainly in AUSTRALIA and New Guinea, but a few, such as the opossum, live in the Americas. Wallabies are small kangaroos. The koala is a marsupial that looks like a small BEAR and lives in gum trees.

The Tasmanian wolf is a very rare marsupial that looks like a true wolf and also has the same meat-eating habits. The animal was once common in Australia, but men hunted it. It is now confined to Tasmania and it may be extinct.

Above: A kangaroo with a baby in her pouch.
Right: An opossum with her babies.

Moles

Mounds of fresh earth in a field or garden may show that a mole is at work. A mole spends its life in underground tunnels. It digs these tunnels with its powerful hands and pushes the earth up to the surface to make the mounds.

A mole's fur is velvety and can be brushed either way. The mole can move forwards or backwards in its narrow tunnel. A mole's eyes are very small, and it is almost blind.

Moles are very active. They spend their time running along their tunnels looking for insects and EARTHWORMS to eat. When worms are plentiful the moles bite their heads off and store them in special chambers of the nest.

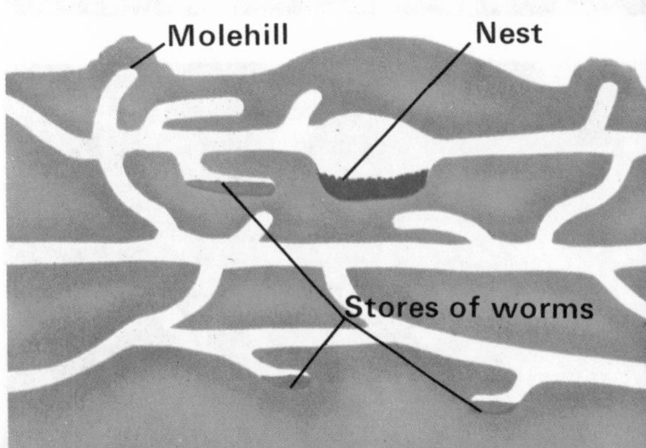

Right: A mole's tunnel system.

Rats and mice

Many mammals belong to the group called rodents, or gnawing animals. They have front teeth shaped like chisels that they use to gnaw through tough food such as nuts, BARK, and ROOTS. SQUIRRELS, porcupines, chipmunks, and guinea pigs are rodents, but the most common kinds are the rats and mice.

Rats and mice are pests. They eat our food and spread disease. The Black Death was a disease spread by the black rat, which came into EUROPE from central ASIA in the Middle Ages.

Rats have climbed into ships, and have been carried all over the world. The house mouse is another rodent that once lived only in central Asia and is now found everywhere.

There are many other kinds of rats and mice in different parts of the world. They usually live in burrows or among plants and come out only at night. They are seldom seen by man. Yet if crops are grown nearby the rats and mice will probably eat them.

Top: A jumping mouse, showing its long back legs.
Above: A muskrat at the entrance to its riverside nest.

Squirrels

There are many kinds of squirrels, and most of them live in trees. The red squirrel is common in EUROPE and parts of ASIA. The grey squirrel came originally from NORTH AMERICA. It was introduced into Britain about a hundred years ago.

Both the red and grey squirrel are agile creatures with large, bushy tails, which help them keep their balance. Squirrels eat nuts and BARK. They also like fruit and young birds.

There are also members of the squirrel family that live on the ground, including the prairie-dogs and chipmunks of North America.

Left: A grey squirrel (top) and a family of red squirrels at their nest.

Beavers

The beaver lives in RIVERS and streams in NORTH AMERICA and parts of EUROPE. Beaver families live in pools they have made by damming streams with branches and mud. In the middle of the pool they build a lodge, or house. It has underwater entrances leading to a nest above the water level. Here the beavers are safe from enemies and winter frost. Beavers get the branches for the dams and lodges by cutting down trees with their teeth. They eat the BARK from the twigs.

Beavers swim very well, using their broad tails as rudders. The tail is also used to warn other beavers if danger approaches: it produces a tremendous crack when slapped on to the water.

Right: A beaver at work on its lodge. It quickly gnaws through logs which are too long.

Rabbits and hares

Rabbits and hares are not rodents, although they look like some of them. Rabbits came originally from southern EUROPE, but they have been taken to many other parts of the world. They are often kept as pets. Wild rabbits live in GRASSLAND and open woodland. They eat plants and often damage crops. Rabbits live in burrows and their babies are blind and naked. Similar animals living in the Americas are called cottontails, but they do not burrow.

Hares are usually larger than rabbits, with longer legs and ears. They run very fast and they do not burrow. They live in the grass in shallow nests called forms. Baby hares are born with their eyes open and with all their fur. Hares in cold countries often turn white in winter.

Right: (1) Arctic hare. (2) Brown hare. (3) Common European rabbit. (4) American jack rabbit.

Cat family

Cats have been kept as pets for thousands of years. They can see well at night because the pupils of their eyes open wide to let in as much light as possible. The different kinds of pet cats are all descended from a wild African cat.

There are about 40 kinds of wild cat. Most are about the size of our pet cats. They live mainly in the warmer parts of the world. Five kinds of cats are called the 'big cats': the lion, tiger, leopard, snow leopard, and jaguar. The big cats roar and lie with their front legs stretched out in front of them. Small cats usually lie with their legs curled up.

Lions live on the plains of AFRICA and ASIA. They once lived in EUROPE. Families of lions are

1 ▲ 3 ▼

(1) Caracal or desert lynx. (2) Canadian lynx. (3) Tiger. (4) Jaguar. (5) Cougar (puma). (6) Cheetah. (7) Lion. All are meat-eating animals.

2 ▼

6 ▼

called prides. Most other cats live by themselves. The tiger lives in Asia, in high mountains and in jungles. The snow leopard also lives in the mountains of Asia, but the leopard is found in the forests of Asia and Africa. The jaguar lives in the forests of SOUTH AMERICA. Sometimes the big cats become 'man-eaters', usually when they are old or sick.

The cheetah is the fastest animal on land. It can run at 120 kilometres an hour over short distances. At one time cheetahs were trained to catch ANTELOPES.

The American puma, also called the cougar or mountain lion, is as big as a leopard. It is very strong but rarely dangerous.

4 ▼

5 ▶

7 ▼

Bears

Bears can walk on their hind legs but usually they run on all fours. They have short legs and long, sharp claws. Small bears – the black bear, for example – can climb trees well. The largest are the brown bear and grizzly bear, which can weigh over 500 kilogrammes. They eat berries, leaves, fish, insects, and other small animals. Bears can be very dangerous if they are disturbed.

The polar bear lives in the far north. Its hairy feet give it a good grip on the ice and snow. It eats fish and SEALS. The polar bear is one of the most dangerous of all animals.

The giant panda is a close relative of the bear. It lives in CHINA and eats BAMBOO shoots, LEAVES, and small animals.

Mongooses

The mongooses of AFRICA and ASIA are famous SNAKE killers. They can leap at a snake and sink their teeth into its neck before it can strike. They also like to eat EGGS, insects, reptiles, MICE, and other small animals.

Right: Brown bear (top), Polar bear (centre) and Sun bear.

Below: A pair of banded mongooses.

Weasel family

The slender, agile weasels and their relatives, the stoats, martens, and mink, are expert hunters. They have short legs and can slip through the grass like snakes.

The weasel is only 30 centimetres long but can kill animals as large as a RABBIT. The martens are like large weasels and live in trees. Mink live in marshes and near river banks.

Otters are good swimmers. They have webbed feet and waterproof fur. They usually live near RIVERS and LAKES. The sea otter of the PACIFIC spends all its time at sea. It eats shellfish which it breaks open with a stone.

Badgers look like small BEARS. They live in burrows and come out at night. The wolverine is famous for its big appetite and ferocity. It can kill DEER. The skunk is another large member of the weasel family. It is famous for the terrible smell that it makes to get rid of enemies.

Some of the weasel family are trapped for their pelts (coats). The stoat turns white in winter and it is the source of ermine fur.

Raccoons

The raccoon can be identified by the black mask over its eyes and by its long tail with black rings. It lives in woods near streams in America. It is famous for washing its food, but it does this only when kept in captivity.

The relatives of the raccoon are other small flesh-eating animals like the coati and kinkajou which also live in America.

Above right: (1) Otter. (2) Weasel. (3) Marten. (4) Badger. All are flesh-eating members of the weasel family. Martens have valuable fur.
Right: A raccoon. Sometimes they come into towns to look for food.

Dog family

The wolf is probably the ancestor of the domestic dog. It lives in NORTH AMERICA, EUROPE and ASIA. Small family groups, or packs, of wolves live together. Sometimes packs join with other groups to form a larger pack. Usually each pack has its own territory, which it guards against others. Wolves can kill large animals such as caribou and moose, but they sometimes eat small rodents.

The coyote of North America and the jackals of AFRICA and Asia are small relatives of the wolf.

The foxes are common in many parts of the world. The red fox lives in Europe, Asia, and America. Sometimes it even lives in towns. Although foxes usually hunt at night, they are sometimes seen during the day. The small, arctic fox lives in the far north. The fennec is a small DESERT fox with enormous ears.

The Cape hunting dog lives in the savannas of Africa. It hunts in packs, chasing and killing ZEBRAS and ANTELOPES. The dhole, or wild dog of INDIA, also hunts in packs.

Right: Four members of the dog family. (1) Coyote or prairie wolf. (2) Bat-eared fox. (3) Grey or timber wolf. (4) Dingo.
Below right: The spotted hyena.

Hyenas

Laughing hyena is the name often given to the spotted hyena of AFRICA, which makes a noise like a man's laugh. There are two other kinds of hyena: the brown hyena of southern Africa and the striped hyena of north Africa and INDIA.

At one time hyenas were considered cowardly animals that only ate the remains of other animals' meals. In fact, hyena packs kill ZEBRA and ANTELOPES. They have powerful jaws that can crush the largest BONES.

Whales

Whales live in the sea and swim by means of their powerful tails, which have two paddles called flukes. Although whales have no fur, they are warm-blooded mammals. They are kept warm by a layer of fat, or blubber, under the skin. A whale's nostril, or blowhole, is on top of its head. When it breathes out, or 'blows', a puff of vapour can be seen.

There are two main kinds of whales: the whalebone whales and the toothed whales. The whalebone whales are the largest animals that have ever lived. Blue whales can grow more than 33 metres long.

The dolphins and porpoises are small whales.

Right: A number of kinds of whales (not on the same scale).

Dolphin

Narwhal

Sperm whale

Greenland right whale

Blue whale

Seals

Seals are mammals that live in the sea but come ashore to breed. The popular seal of the circus is the sea lion. It can run on land by tucking its hind flippers under its body.

Seals are most common in the cold waters of the ARCTIC and ANTARCTIC. They often have their babies, called pups, on ice floes. Seals eat fish and other sea animals. The leopard seal sometimes eats PENGUINS and baby seals.

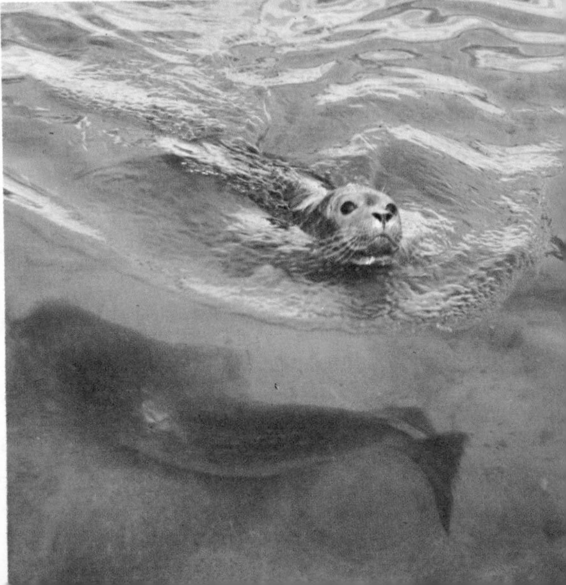

Right: Seals swimming.

Giraffes

Giraffes live in the open GRASSLANDS of AFRICA. Their light brown skin is covered with dark brown patches. This colouring gives good CAMOUFLAGE. They are famous for their long necks and can be nearly six metres high. Their height enables them to eat leaves from the tops of trees. In order to eat grass or to drink, they must spread their front legs.

Giraffes usually live in small herds. When they are frightened, they run away. They appear to be moving in slow motion, but actually they can gallop at great speed. The giraffe has a relative with a shorter neck called the okapi. Okapis are much less common than giraffes. They are solitary creatures that live in forests.

Right: A giraffe leaves a water hole.
Below right: A young deer or fawn picks its way across a stream. Even here the dappled coat helps to break up its outline and camouflage it.

Deer

Deer are rather shy, hoofed mammals which usually live in woodlands. They eat GRASS and LEAVES. They normally live in small herds and, in autumn, the males or stags challenge each other to fights. The winners take charge of the females. Baby deer (fawns) can run when they are only a few hours old. They have dappled coats and are difficult to see when lying still.

Nearly all male deer carry branched antlers, which are quite different from horns. They are made of bone and are grown and lost each year. Freshly grown antlers are covered with skin. Each set of antlers is larger than the previous set until the deer is fully grown. Female reindeer carry antlers as well as the males. The largest deer is the North American moose.

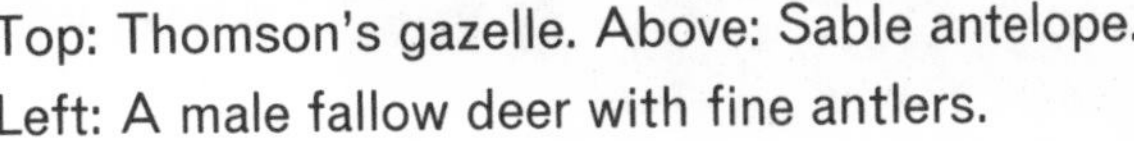

Top: Thomson's gazelle. Above: Sable antelope.
Left: A male fallow deer with fine antlers.

Antelopes

Antelopes look like DEER but they have horns like those of GOATS or CATTLE, rather than antlers. Most of them live in AFRICA but the saiga lives in central ASIA. The blackbuck lives in INDIA. Large herds of wildebeestes (also called gnus) and gazelles live on the African plains. Oryx live in DESERT regions of Africa and Arabia. These antelopes escape from lions and cheetahs by running. Duikers, kudu, and bushbuck live in thick woods and forests, where they are difficult to find. The largest antelope in the world is the eland, which has been domesticated.

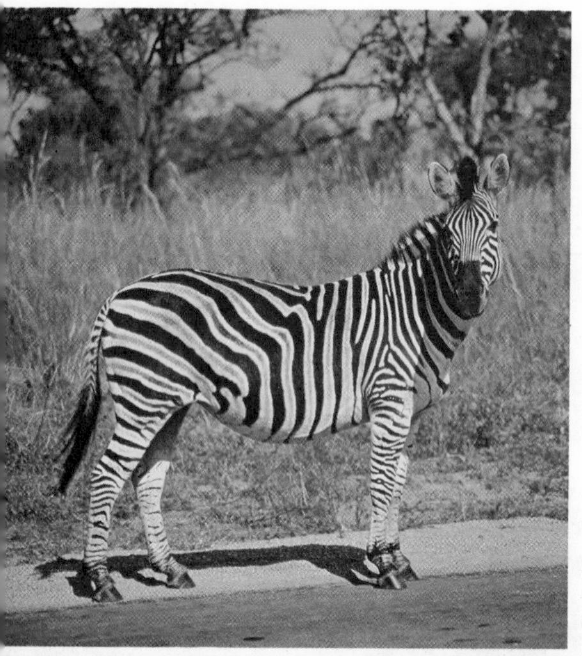

Zebras

Most zebras live on the plains of AFRICA. They are a kind of wild HORSE. They have vivid stripes of black or brown and white, and a tufted mane. The stripes help to break up the outline of the zebra, and make it more difficult to see at a distance. The largest kind of zebra is Grévy's zebra. The mountain zebra is now rare. The quagga, another kind of zebra, became extinct about 100 years ago.

Rhinoceros

The rhinoceroses live in AFRICA and ASIA. They are large, powerful animals with horns on the nose. The Indian rhinoceros has one horn; its thick skin is in folds. The black and the white rhinoceroses of Africa have two horns.

The rhinoceros eats leaves and grass. Rhinoceroses can be very dangerous. In spite of their size, they can charge at 40 kilometres an hour. They cannot see very well, and depend on their senses of smell and hearing.

Above left: The zebra.
Left: The wide-mouthed white rhinoceros.
Below: The black rhinoceros has a pointed snout.

Bison

Bison are related to domestic CATTLE. They have powerful shoulders, a massive head, and short horns. The males have a thick mane.

Thousands of bison once roamed the plains of NORTH AMERICA in vast herds. But many were killed by the white settlers for meat or simply for sport. A few small herds now live in reserves.

The European bison is even rarer. It is sometimes called the wisent. It used to live in the forests of EUROPE, but few of these animals are alive today.

Above: A herd of American bison. Bison are grazing animals and they thrive on the long grasses. They used to live in herds of many thousands.

Buffalo

BISON are often called buffalo, but the true buffalo is quite different. Buffalo are grass-eating animals that live in AFRICA and ASIA. The African and Asian kinds look alike, but they are not closely related. They are both heavy animals with large, sweeping horns.

African buffalo are fierce and very dangerous. The Asian buffalo are sometimes called water buffalo, from their habit of wallowing in mud or water. They have been successfully domesticated. They are used for many tasks, such as pulling carts.

Below left: A water buffalo pulling a plough in a rice paddy field in the Philippines.

Below: African buffalo, also known as Cape buffalo, are among the most dangerous of animals because they charge fearlessly at anything that disturbs them. They live in herds in open woodland.

Elephants

The elephant is the largest living land animal. Its natural home is AFRICA and ASIA. The African elephant may weigh up to 6000 kilogrammes. It has larger ears and longer tusks than the Indian elephant. The ears help to keep the elephant cool. The tusks are very long teeth.

The trunk is a very long nose with nostrils at the tip. It has many uses. It is used for lifting food to the mouth, moving heavy objects, and even for stroking other elephants. Water can be sucked up the trunk for drinking or squirted out as a shower bath.

The African elephant lives on plains and in forests, but the Indian elephant lives in jungles. Both kinds live in small herds, although old bulls (males) may live alone. Their food is fruit and leaves and they can push down whole trees to get at the high branches.

Indian elephants have been domesticated for thousands of years. They are used to lift tree trunks, draw wagons, or to take part in parades.

Above left: The African elephant has large ears.
Left: An Indian elephant at work pulling logs.
Below left: The hippopotamus is a large relative of the pig.

Hippopotamuses

The hippopotamus can weigh as much as 4000 kilogrammes. Among land animals only the ELEPHANT is larger. Hippopotamuses live in the African tropics. They spend most of their time in RIVERS and SWAMPS with their eyes and nostrils above the water. They eat plants on the banks of the rivers, but they can also do great damage to crops. Hippopotamuses have huge mouths, and large tusk-like teeth.

The pygmy hippopotamus is much smaller and is quite rare.

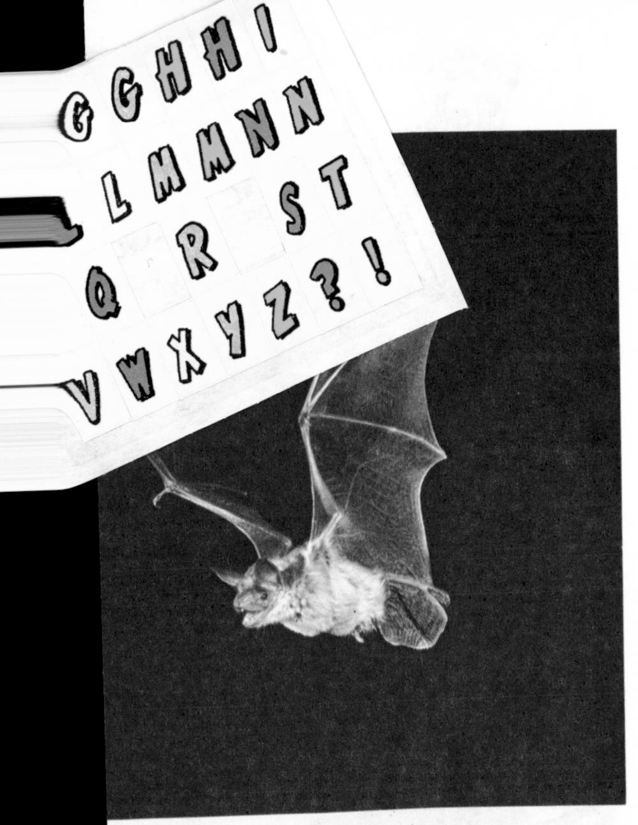

Mammals that fly

The only mammals that can really fly are the bats. (Flying squirrels and flying lemurs only glide from tree to tree.) The wings of bats are made of a thin web of skin. It is stretched between the body and the fingers. Another web is stretched between the hind legs and the tail.

Nearly all bats fly in the evening and sleep during the day. They find their way about in the dark and find their food by means of sonar. They let out a continuous, high-pitched squeaking and listen for the echoes of the squeaks coming back from nearby objects.

Small bats eat insects. Those that live in temperate countries hibernate (sleep through the winter), since in winter there are few insects about. In the tropics there are large bats called fruit bats. They eat fruit and sip nectar. The largest is the flying fox.

Vampire bats drink the blood of sleeping mammals. Fish-eating bats of SOUTH AMERICA catch fish that come to the surface of the water.

Above: A bat in flight, showing the very long fingers of the wing.
Below: Two gliding mammals – a phalanger (left) and a red and white flying squirrel.

Apes and monkeys

The apes are man's closest relations. Apes can be distinguished from monkeys because they have long arms and no tail. The Barbary ape of Gibraltar is really a monkey with a very small tail. Apes can stand upright but usually walk about on all fours.

The chimpanzee of African forests is the most intelligent of the apes. It lives in small groups. It spends most of its time on the ground. Chimpanzees can use tools. They use sticks to scrape ANTS out of the nests, stones to crack nuts, and leaves to wipe their fingers.

The gorilla is the largest of the apes. Old males can weigh as much as 200 kilogrammes, but they are not fierce animals. Gorillas live in African forests and eat fruit.

Right: A variety of monkeys and apes – all are members of the large group called primates.

The orang-utan and the gibbons live in south-eastern ASIA. Their home is in the trees. Gibbon families call loudly to each other.

There are many different kinds of monkeys. In tropical America there are the spider monkeys and woolly monkeys, which can hang from branches by their tails, and the tiny marmosets and tamarins.

The rhesus monkey of INDIA is sacred to the HINDUS. It is also used for medical research. The hanuman, or entellus, monkey is also sacred. It is one of the langurs, a group of monkeys that eat leaves.

The baboons are the largest monkeys. Unlike the others, they live mainly on the ground. Baboons live in families called troops. The males are very strong and have long teeth. They defend the rest of the troop against enemies.

Orang-utan

Baboon

Chimpanzee

Lar gibbon

Gorilla

Mammals in armour

The armadillos of America are protected by an armour of bony plates covered with tough skin. The armour is flexible. Some kinds of armadillos can curl up into a ball.

The pangolins live in AFRICA and ASIA. Their bodies are covered with a layer of scales that overlap like the tiles on a roof. The African pangolin can roll up into a ball.

Right: The furry armadillo has bony plates under its hair. The strong claws are used for digging. Armadillos eat ants and other insects.

Domestic Animals

Perhaps man could not have become civilised without the help of domestic animals. When animals were tamed instead of being hunted, men could settle in one place. Domestic animals gave men food and clothing without the effort of having to hunt. As the animals became tamer, they could be used for riding or carrying loads. As life became easier, animals could be kept as pets – just for fun.

Animals were first domesticated at least 10,000 years ago. No one knows what the ancestors of many domestic animals looked like, or when they were first domesticated. Over the years, animals have been bred for special purposes and their appearance has changed. Only a few domestic animals still also live as wild animals. The ELEPHANT, the RABBIT, the turkey, and the llama of the ANDES are examples.

There are also many kinds of animals that we do not usually think of as being domestic animals. The silk moth is domesticated to produce silk, and the honeybee to produce honey.

Above: Indian zebu cattle take a rest from pulling their cart.

Below left: The elephant is also used in some countries to pull heavy loads.

Below: A domesticated cat.

Dogs

The dog became the friend of man at least 10,000 years ago, during the Stone Age. Many people think that the dog is descended from the wolf. Others believe it may have come from another kind of wild dog that is now extinct. There are now many breeds. The largest dogs are the St. Bernards and the smallest are the chihuahuas.

The first breeds of dogs were probably sheep dogs, which were used to defend their owners' flocks against wild animals. The Alsatian is such a guard dog. Other dogs were bred to help in hunting. Hounds follow animals by scent, and retrievers bring back animals that have been shot. Terriers chase foxes and badgers out of their holes in the ground. Dogs are used to guard property and to carry loads. The huskies are famous for pulling sledges.

Many of these 'working dogs' are now kept as pets. There are also dogs that are specially bred as pets.

Above right: This dog has been trained as a guide dog for blind people.
Right: An Alsatian guard dog.
Above: A sledge-pulling husky dog.

Cattle

Cattle are descended from the aurochs (*ore*-ox) which lived in the forests of EUROPE and ASIA. It became extinct in 1627. There are two main kinds of cattle. Dairy breeds have been developed to produce milk. Some cattle give up to 13,000 litres of milk each year. Beef cattle are kept for their meat. Other cattle breeds give both milk and beef.

The zebu of AFRICA and Asia is another kind of cattle. It has a hump on its shoulders. It is used to draw ploughs and carts, and is also kept for its meat.

Above: Hereford cattle are a famous beef breed. You can recognize them by their white faces.

Horses

In the past, man has depended on the horse for transport, and for moving heavy goods. Horses used for pulling loads are large and strong. They have large hoofs to support their weight. Horses that are used for riding are smaller and lighter. The smallest are called ponies. The Arabian horses are graceful and very fast. Modern race-horses are descended from this breed.

In some parts of the world horses are still kept for their meat and milk. The donkey is descended from the wild ass, a relative of the horse. The mule is a cross between a female horse and a male donkey.

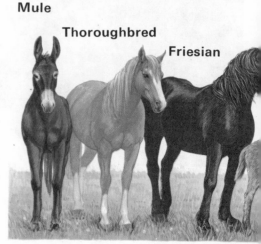

Mule
Thoroughbred
Friesian
Donk

Sheep

The first domestic sheep lived in ASIA during the BRONZE AGE. The 450 modern breeds have been produced to live on different kinds of grazing and in different climates. The blackface sheep lives on heather-covered hills. The finest wool comes from the merino. Not all sheep, however, are kept for wool. Their meat is an important product. The East Friesian is milked. The lambs of the karakul sheep give astrakhan fur.

Above: A big-horn sheep in the Canadian Rockies. Its woolly coat keeps it warm in the snow.

Goats

Goats look like SHEEP, but their horns never grow out to the sides of the head, as sheep's horns do. The male goat, or billy, has a beard.

Goats are kept in many parts of the world for milk and meat, as well as for their hides. They will eat almost anything. They can live on poor grass where SHEEP and CATTLE would not survive. They will climb trees to get at the LEAVES, and will even eat the BARK. They have sometimes made DESERTS by destroying all the plants.

The first domestic goats lived in eastern EUROPE and the Near East. They were descended from wild mountain-living goats.

Pigs

Man has used the pig for many things. For example, pigs are kept for their meat. The skin of pigs is used for leather, and pig bristles are put in brushes. In the past, pigs have even been used for pulling carts.

Domestic pigs are descended from the European and Chinese wild pigs. Both kinds still live in the wild. Pigs eat all sorts of things, including acorns, ROOTS, and small animals. They are basically woodland animals and, in the past, the swineherds used to take their pigs out into the forest each day to feed.

Many breeds of pigs exist today, each with its own shape and appearance. Some are used mainly for fresh meat, others for bacon.

Left: Pigs easily get sun-burn and they often wallow in mud to protect their skin from the sun.

Reindeer

The reindeer of Scandinavia and the caribou of NORTH AMERICA are the same animal, but the reindeer has been domesticated. Reindeer are no larger than a donkey. Both sexes have antlers.

The animals spend the summer time out on the treeless TUNDRA of the far north. They feed on LICHENS and other small plants. In the winter they move south into the forests.

The LAPPS and other peoples of the ARCTIC first tamed reindeer about 1500 years ago. These people depend on their reindeer for many things. They eat reindeer meat and drink the milk. The skin makes soft leather for clothes, and the bones make needles. The reindeer are also used to pull sledges.

Left: Reindeer manage to feed on very sparse grasses and lichens.

Camels

There are two kinds of camel: the one-humped Arabian camel, and the two-humped Bactrian camel whose home is in the rocky DESERTS of Central ASIA. Both have been domesticated. The Arabian camel has been taken to such places as AUSTRALIA and the south-western desert in the United States.

Camels are very useful in hot, dry countries. They have broad feet which allow them to walk easily over loose sand without sinking into it. They can stand great heat and can go for many days without drinking. They are used for carrying loads and for pulling ploughs. The dromedary is a special breed of Arabian camel which is used for riding.

Left: Arab tribesmen use dromedaries for journeys in the desert.

Poultry

Chickens, or domestic fowls, are descended from the jungle fowls that live in the dense forests around the HIMALAYAS. They used to be kept for religious sacrifices and for telling the future. Chickens have always been kept for their eggs. They were not specially bred for eating until about 150 years ago. The 37 breeds of chicken are divided into egg-layers and table birds (for eating). There are also ornamental chickens, such as the long-tailed Yokohama.

The turkey is a much larger bird which comes from MEXICO and the United States. It was domesticated a long time ago by the AZTECS and it was taken to EUROPE in the sixteenth century. Millions of birds are reared each year for meat.

Right: Three kinds of poultry. (1) Rhode Island Red chicken. (2) Guinea fowl. Turkey.

Animal Defence

Only the largest and strongest animals can live without fear of being killed by meat-eating animals. Nearly every animal has some way of defending itself against its enemies.

Some animals are swift and can outrun their enemies. Other, slower animals cannot escape by running away. They defend themselves by hiding in a safe place.

If an animal cannot escape its enemies, it has to try to protect itself. Many animals do this by biting, by kicking, or by using their horns or antlers. Others have special defences, such as STINGS or spines, which teach their enemies to leave them alone.

Animals use many methods of defending themselves. Deer often run, but if cornered they will kick with their hooves and attack with their antlers. Impala and other antelopes escape with bounding leaps. The opossum pretends to be dead, while the black and white skunk squirts a smelly liquid at its enemies. Wasps and scorpions sting, and snakes inject poison with their teeth.

Animal smell

When a skunk is attacked, it squirts a jet of fluid from special glands at the base of the tail. The fluid is foul-smelling. If the enemy is hit by the fluid, he will start to choke and may be blinded for a short time. Skunks have white stripes on their bodies that warn animals not to attack them.

The grass snake also protects itself by giving off an unpleasant smell if disturbed.

Skunk

Stings

A sting is a sharp, hollow tube that an animal uses to inject poison into other animals. It is like the needle that a doctor uses for injections.

SEA ANEMONES and cone shells sting the animals that they eat, but they also sting their enemies. A BEE uses its sting for defence. Any animal that tries to break into the hive is attacked by a swarm of bees.

Scorpions have a sting at the tip of the tail. Some kinds can kill a man.

Scorpion

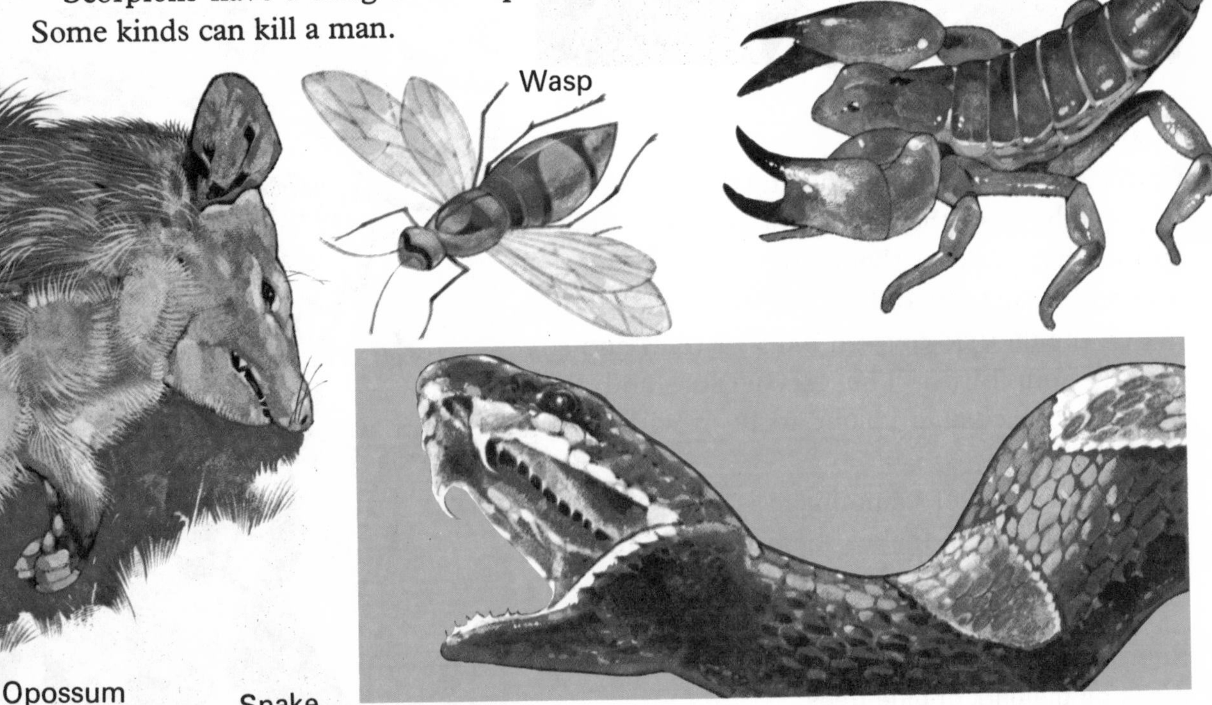
Wasp

Opossum

Snake

Spiny coats

The hedgehog's back is covered with a dense coat of prickles. When alarmed, it raises the prickles. Then it rolls into a ball. It tucks its head and legs under its belly so that its enemy can find nothing but prickles.

The porcupines have coats of spines, which are much longer than the hedgehog's prickles. The spines of the African porcupine come out easily and stick deep into the flesh of any animal that touches them.

Right: A hedgehog asleep for the winter.
Below: A twig-like stick insect.

Camouflage

Camouflage is a way of disguising the appearance of something so that it cannot be seen. Many animals have colours that match their surroundings and make them difficult to see. Some moths match the LICHEN-covered BARK of trees and so escape from birds. The CHAMELEON and the OCTOPUS can change colour to fit in with their surroundings.

Another kind of camouflage is used by animals whose shape makes them difficult to see. The stick insect looks like a twig.

Right: The pine hawkmoth is not easy to see when it sits on the bark of pine trees.

Colours

Many insects are boldly marked with red and black, or yellow and black patterns. Many of these creatures have an unpleasant taste, and they may be poisonous. The bright colours warn their enemies of this. Animals learn to leave yellow-striped WASPS and BEES alone because of their STINGS. The burnet MOTH of Britain and Europe has bright, metallic colours. Its body contains the poison cyanide, and birds learn not to eat brightly coloured moths. American monarch BUTTERFLIES are also brightly coloured. Their bodies contain a heart poison.

Not all brightly coloured insects are unpleasant. There are many INSECT FRAUDS. They have bold patterns, but they are harmless.

Left: The bright colour of ladybirds warns birds of their unpleasant taste.

Bluff

One way that a helpless animal can defend itself is to pretend that it is large and fierce. The frilled LIZARD of AUSTRALIA gets its name from a frill of skin around its neck. The lizard is one metre long, but it is harmless. When attacked, it spreads its frill. The frill looks like an open umbrella. It makes the lizard look enormous and the frightened enemy runs away.

The peacock butterfly sits on a twig with its wings closed. When frightened, it opens its wings and shows its large, coloured spots. These look like eyes, and the way they suddenly appear startles enemies. Several other kinds of butterflies and moths have 'eyes' on their wings.

Above left: The emperor moth's 'eyes' suggest a larger and stronger animal than it really is.
Left: The frilled lizard pretends to be fierce.

Early Animals

The first living things appeared on the Earth over 1500 million years ago. At first, there were only simple creatures living in the sea. We do not know what these first creatures looked like. WORMS, shellfish, and other sea creatures very much like those alive today existed 750 million years ago. The first fishes appeared 500 million years ago.

The amphibians came out on land 100 million years later. Then the reptiles appeared. When the DINOSAURS died out about 100 million years ago, the mammals and birds had already appeared. Man is a newcomer. He has lived on earth for perhaps two million years.

Most of the kinds of animals that lived millions of years ago are now extinct. We do not always know why these animals disappeared. It may be because of great changes in the climate.

Above: Fossilized shells of belemnites – early relatives of the squid.
Below: A fossilized fish.

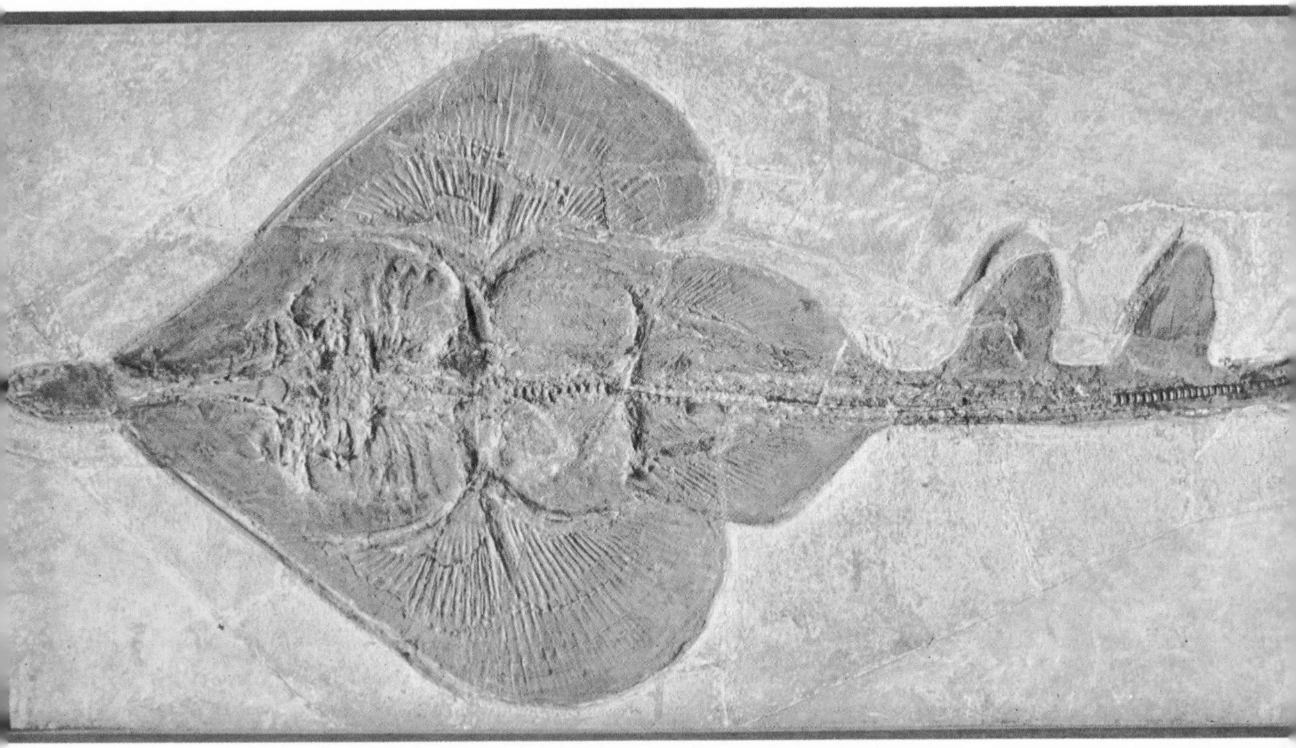

Animal fossils

We know about animals that became extinct millions of years ago because scientists have found their fossils. A fossil is an animal's skeleton preserved in rock. This happens when its body becomes covered in mud. The mud gradually buries the skeleton and turns into rock around it. Millions of years later it is discovered when coal is being mined or when the sea washes part of a cliff away.

By studying fossils, scientists discover what extinct animals looked like and how they lived. They can tell the age of a fossil by measuring how deep it is buried, and by studying the layers of rocks around it.

Very few animals become fossilized, because usually their bodies are eaten by other animals or else their bones decompose. Sometimes only parts of a skeleton become fossilized. Some animals are well preserved; every detail of the bones is seen, sometimes with the outline of the body.

Trilobites

Long before fish appeared, there were animals in the sea that looked like large WOODLICE. Some of them were about a metre long. These were the trilobites.

The front part of a trilobite's body was covered with a hard shield. The back part was made up of rings or segments. Some trilobites could roll up like woodlice. They had a row of legs down each side of the body. The legs were used for walking on the bottom of the sea or for swimming. The legs are rarely preserved in fossils, but the head shields are very common in the older rocks. Trilobites became extinct about 250 million years ago.

Ten thousand kinds of trilobites are known. Most of them were under four centimetres long.

Right: Trilobites used to crawl on the seabed.

Ammonites

Ammonites lived in the sea hundreds of millions of years ago. They are distantly related to the OCTOPUS and squid, but their bodies were protected by shells. Over the course of millions of years the shells changed shape. The first ammonites had straight shells. Then ammonites with curved shells appeared. These were followed by ones with tightly coiled shells. Others were straight with a coiled tip. The largest ammonites had shells one metre across. If these could be unrolled, they would be ten metres long. An ammonite could withdraw its body into its shell, and close the entrance with a kind of door. As only the shell became fossilized, we do not know what the body of an ammonite was like. It probably had tentacles like an OCTOPUS.

Right: A fossilized ammonite shell.

Pterodactyls

The pterodactyls, or pterosaurs, were flying reptiles. The wings were a thin fold of skin. The wings stretched from a very long finger to the sides of the body and hind legs. The first pterodactyls had long tails, but these gradually disappeared. The largest pterodactyl was Pteranodon, which had a wingspan of eight metres. The smallest was the size of a sparrow.

Pterodactyls had large wings and very light bones. They were not able, however, to fly well by flapping their wings. They probably glided over the sea like the albatrosses, coming ashore to lay their eggs. Some of them ate fish.

Above: Pteranodon, the largest pterodactyl.

Below: Scientists can tell from the bones that Archaeopteryx was not a good flier but glided from tree to tree.

Archaeopteryx

Birds are descended from the reptiles. One of the most important fossils ever found is Archaeopteryx. This was an animal that was half bird, half reptile. Its skull was like that of a reptile and its BEAK had rows of teeth, which no modern bird has. Archaeopteryx had a long bony tail and its front limbs, although in the form of wings, still carried claws.

But Archaeopteryx was clearly a bird, because it was covered with FEATHERS. The outlines of its feathers were well preserved when it became a fossil. Archaeopteryx was alive about 150 million years ago.

Dinosaurs

We usually think of all the large extinct reptiles as being dinosaurs, a word that means 'terrible LIZARDS'. In fact, there were many different groups of giant reptiles that existed alongside the dinosaurs. These include the PTERODACTYLS, plesiosaurs, and ichthyosaurs.

Not all dinosaurs were giants. Some were no bigger than a chicken. The most famous dinosaurs, however, are the large ones. These were the huge four-footed dinosaurs with long necks and tails. Diplodocus was 27 metres long and weighed 25,000 kilogrammes. It probably lived in swamps. Brontosaurus was another monster.

Triceratops and Stegosaurus were four-footed dinosaurs whose bodies were protected by armour. Triceratops had three horns on its head and a bony frill protecting the neck. The back of Stegosaurus carried bony plates and spikes.

Some kinds of dinosaurs had very small front legs and looked rather like today's kangaroos.

Footprints found in rocks show that they walked with their front legs and tails held off the ground. The duck-billed dinosaurs, or hadrosaurs, lived in swamps. One fossil shows that the front feet were webbed. This showed scientists that it could swim. Hadrosaurs ate tough plants, and their beaklike jaws had 2000 small teeth.

Iguanodon was a 10-metre long dinosaur that ate leaves and twigs. The largest of the two-legged dinosaurs was Tyrannosaurus rex. It had a head 1·3 metres long and teeth up to 15 centimetres long. It ate other dinosaurs.

When the dinosaurs lived on land and the pterodactyls lived in the air, there were many reptiles living in the sea. The plesiosaurs had long necks and paddle-shaped legs. They ate fish and squid.

The ichthyosaurs looked like fish or dolphins. They had a fin on the back, and the tail ended in a fishlike fin. They could not come on land to lay eggs. Instead, they gave birth to live young.

Extinct animals

We have already seen that some kinds of animals flourished and then became extinct, the DINOSAURS and the MAMMOTH, for example. This is something that is still happening. There are animals that became extinct only a few hundred years ago or are becoming very rare now. Many animals are dying out because men hunt them or destroy their homes.

The moas were flightless birds that looked like giant ostriches. They lived in NEW ZEALAND and were hunted by the Maoris. The last moas died not long after Europeans arrived in New Zealand. The dodo was another flightless bird. It lived on Mauritius and became extinct about 300 years ago.

The passenger pigeon of NORTH AMERICA lived in huge flocks that sometimes darkened the sky. It was hunted so much that the last one died in a zoo in 1914. The quagga of southern AFRICA was hunted by settlers. It had disappeared by 1878.

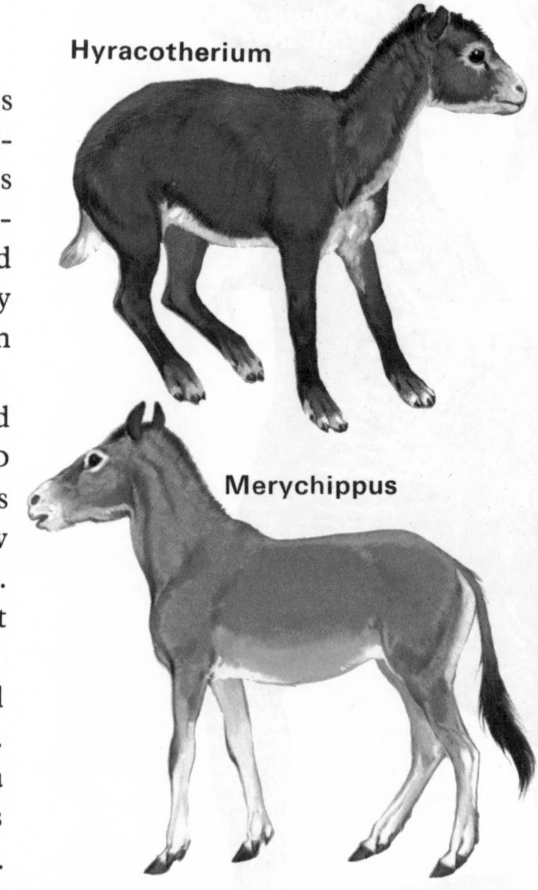

Above: The evolution of the horse.

Below: Some of the animals that man has hunted to extinction.

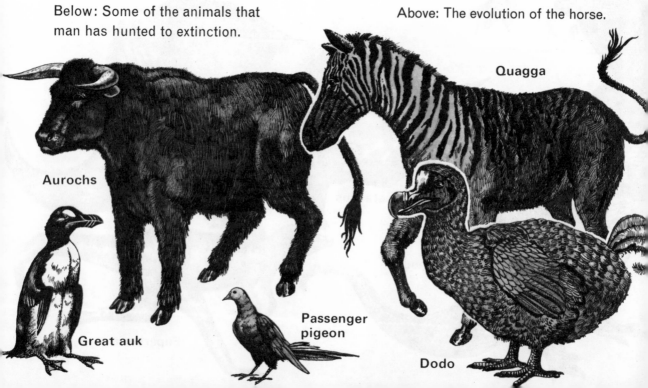

Quagga

Aurochs

Great auk

Passenger pigeon

Dodo

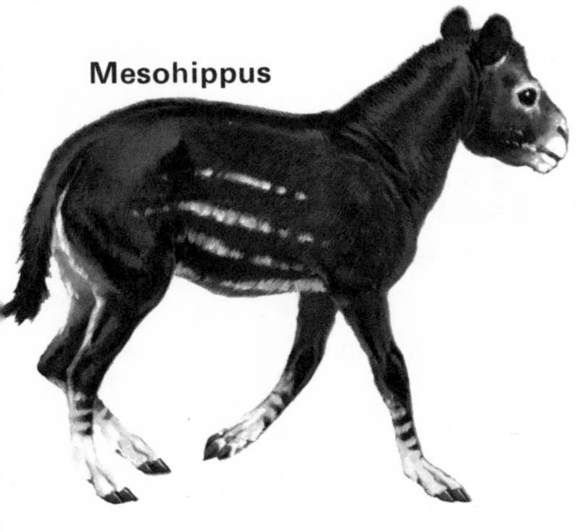

Mesohippus

Primitive horses

The first ancestor of the HORSE lived 50 million years ago. It was called Hyracotherium, and it was the size of a small DOG. Instead of hooves, it had four toes on the front feet and three on the back feet. Thirty million years later it was replaced by Mesohippus. This was a larger animal and had three toes on each foot.

Later still, horses appeared in which the outer toes on each foot were smaller and the weight was placed on the centre toe. Finally, the modern horse appeared with just one toe (the hoof) on each foot.

Equus (modern horse)

Mammoths

The woolly mammoths were large ELEPHANTS with huge tusks and thick coats of fur. They lived at the same time as primitive man who hunted them for food. Bodies of woolly mammoths have been found in the frozen soil of Siberia.

Other kinds of mammoths did not live in cold places, and did not have thick coats.

Below: Woolly mammoths.

ANIMALS
FACTS AND FIGURES

INSECTS. The heaviest living insect is the African Goliath beetle. The size of a man's fist, it weighs about 100 grammes. A silkmoth cocoon may contain one kilometre of unbroken silk thread. An American cicada bug spends 17 years under the ground before becoming adult.

FIELD AND GARDEN ANIMALS. Earthworms gradually bury objects by bringing soil up from underneath them and leaving it at the surface. Some slugs eat earthworms and actually follow them into their tunnels. Rolled-up woodlice and millipedes were once used as medicine.

ANIMALS OF THE SEASHORE. A Californian mussel pumps over two litres of water through its body every hour. Some sandy shores have more than 300 cockles under every square metre of sand. Several thousand acorn barnacles may grow on a square metre of rock surface.

FISH. The largest fish in the world is the whale shark. This fish reaches lengths of more than 15 metres. Sturgeons have been known to live over 70 years. The skins of dogfish and other small sharks are so rough that fishermen used to scrub the decks with them.

AMPHIBIANS. One group of amphibians, known as caecilians, have no legs. They look like large earthworms and they burrow in the soil. The paradoxical frog has a tadpole nearly 300 millimetres long, but the adult frog is only 90 millimetres long.

REPTILES. Turtles and tortoises have no teeth, but their jaws have very sharp edges. When most of the crocodiles were killed in one part of Africa, there was a plague of hippos. The crocodiles had been controlling the hippo population by killing some of the babies.

BIRDS. The heaviest flying bird is the mute swan, which weighs about 16 kilogrammes. The Arctic tern migrates regularly between the Arctic and Antarctic regions. It covers about 35,000 kilometres each year. A cockatoo has been known to live more than 100 years.

MAMMALS. The world's smallest mammal is the Etruscan shrew, whose head and body are less than 50 millimetres long. The tallest mammal is the giraffe, which reaches a height of about 6 metres. Sperm whales and bottle-nosed whales can submerge for up to two hours.

DOMESTIC ANIMALS. The ornamental chicken called the Yokohama fowl has tail feathers up to 7 metres long. Some of the long-woolled breeds of sheep give fleeces weighing 6 kilogrammes or more when they are shorn. Some breeds of chicken lay more than 300 eggs in a year.

ANIMAL DEFENCE. Skunks can squirt their foul liquid for a distance of four metres. When a minnow is attacked it gives out a scent which sends the rest of the shoal diving for cover. Spider crabs camouflage themselves with pieces of sponge and seaweed.

EARLY ANIMALS. The earliest animals all lived in the sea. Land animals probably came into existence about 400 million years ago. The largest land animals that ever lived were dinosaurs, such as Diplodocus and Brontosaurus. Their brains were the size of hens' eggs.

PLANTS

Parts of a Flowering Plant

Most plants produce flowers. The best-known flowering plants are garden flowers, vegetables, fruits, and grass. Many trees and shrubs have flowers. But such plants as MOSSES, FERNS, SEAWEEDS, and fungi do not produce flowers.

Flowering plants have many parts in common: STEMS, ROOTS, LEAVES, buds, and SEEDS. Each part has a different purpose. For example, leaves make food for the plant. Stems support the leaves and carry the food to all parts of the plant. The roots take up water and minerals from the soil. They also help to anchor the plant in the ground. The flower itself makes seeds.

The parts of the plant all work together. If any part is damaged, the life of the whole plant is affected. If buds are destroyed by birds, insects, or FROST, the plant may not produce flowers until the following year. The plant could even die.

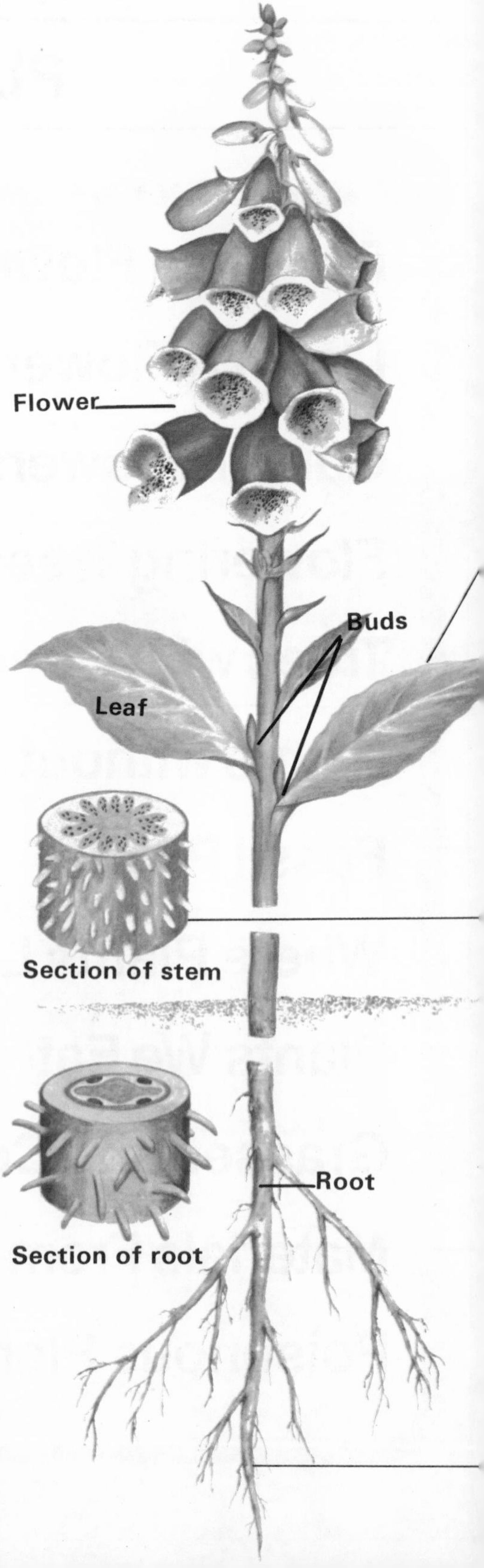

Right: The main parts of a flowering plant. Shapes and sizes vary a lot, but nearly all flowering plants have roots, stems, and leaves.
Below: The beautiful Chinese Hibiscus flower.

Flower
Buds
Leaf
Section of stem
Root
Section of root

SECTION THROUGH 'SKIN' OF LEAF (GREATLY ENLARGED)

Guard cells

Wax coating

Hair

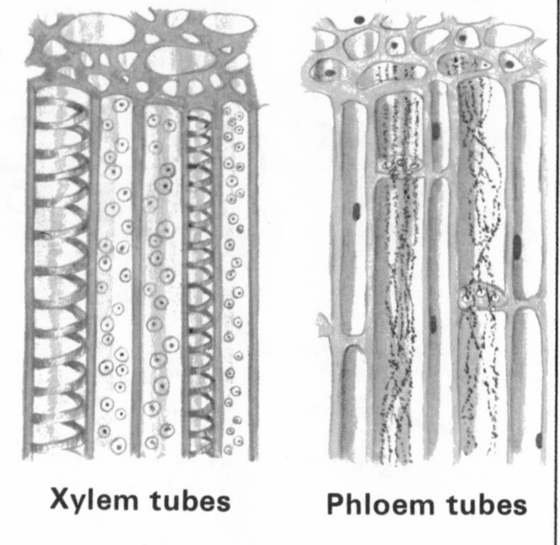

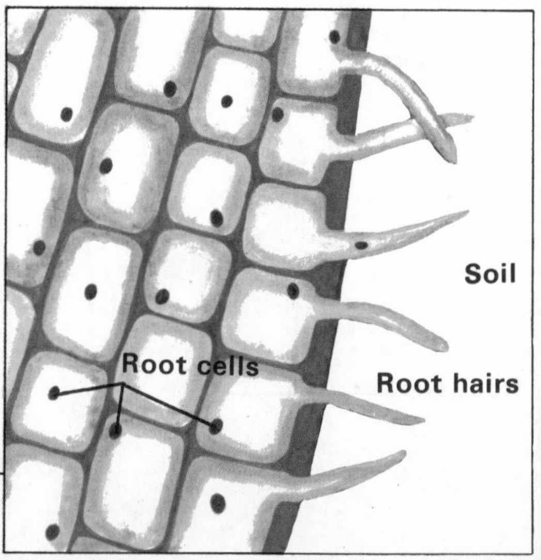

Plant cells

All living things are made of small units called cells. A large plant contains many millions of cells. A small plant has a much smaller number of cells. It may even consist of only one cell. Many simple plants are single cells and are too small to be seen without a MICROSCOPE.

Cells differ in their shape, size and contents. Some cells are round, some are brick-shaped, and others are long and thin. A flowering plant contains at least 25 different types of cell.

Most plant cells build around themselves a wall made of a material called cellulose. The cellulose helps to join the cells together and to give them some protection and strength. Animal cells do not have these cellulose walls.

Left: Four kinds of plant cells. Guard cells are special 'skin' cells which control the size of the breathing pores. Phloem tubes carry food. Xylem tubes carry water and provide support. Root hairs absorb water from the soil.

Below: Tiny water plants seen under a microscope. They are made of cells, but they have no roots, stems, leaves, or flowers.

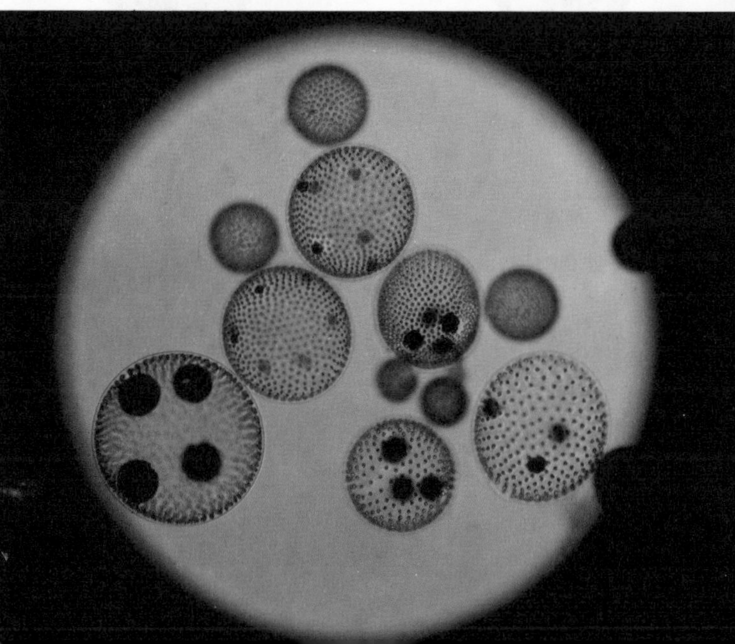

Roots

Roots normally grow down into the ground away from the light. They are white or brown in colour. They differ greatly in size and length. Some plants, such as most garden WEEDS, have many hair-like roots growing near the surface of the SOIL. These are called fibrous roots.

The roots we see when a weed is pulled out of the ground are only a small part of the whole root system. Most of the roots remain in the soil. Some plants, such as the carrot, have one big root, called a tap root, going deep into the soil.

All roots do two things. One of these is to anchor the plant in the soil. A strong wind can make the top of a tree sway many metres, putting a great strain on the roots. The second job of the roots is to take up water and minerals from the soil. The plant needs water and minerals in order to grow.

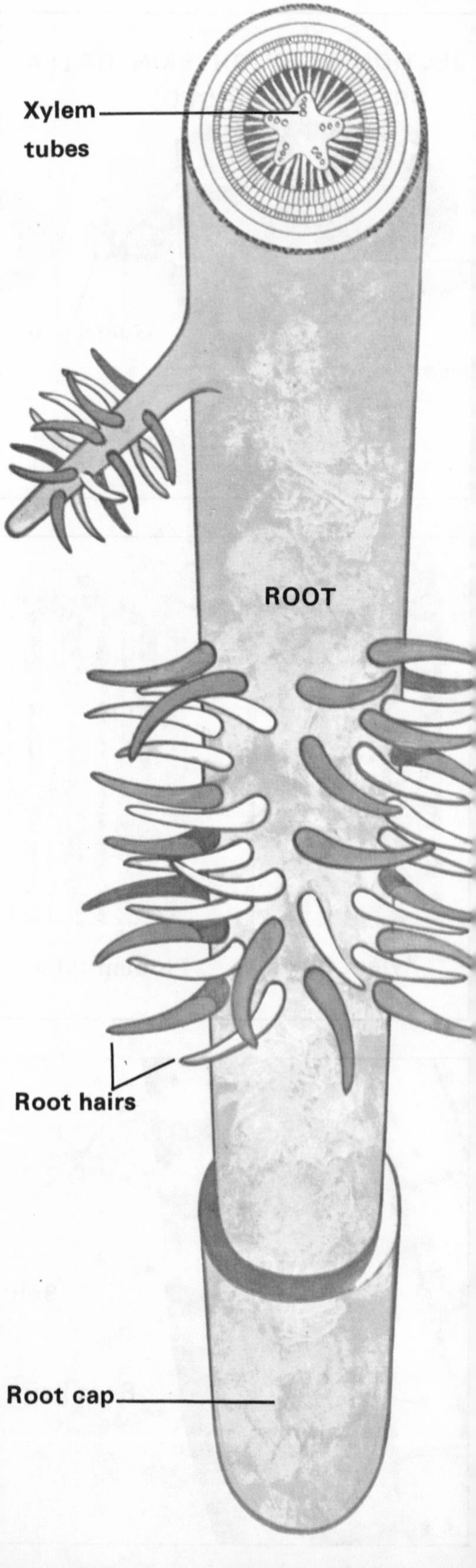

Right: A root showing the inside and outside. The tough woody part is in the centre. The root cap protects the root tip pushing through the soil
Below: The two main kinds of roots.

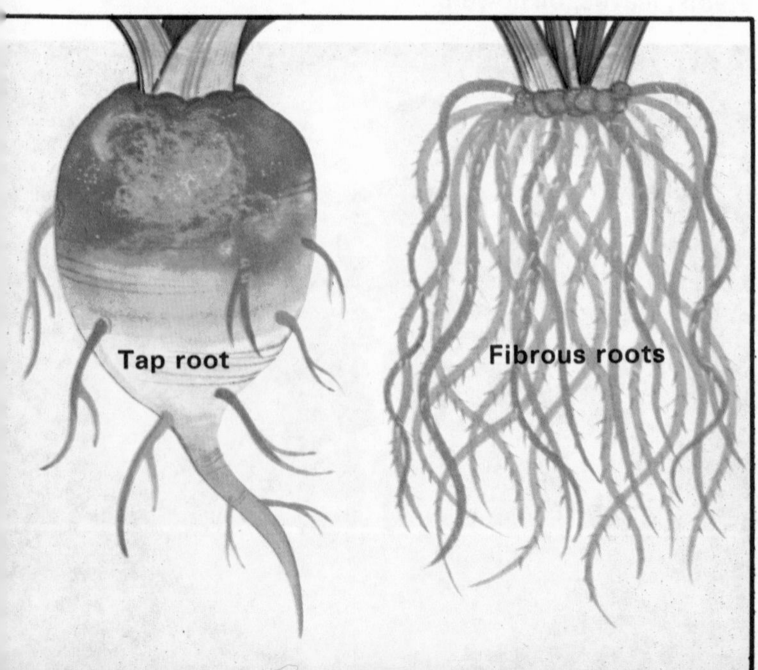

Xylem tubes

ROOT

Root hairs

Root cap

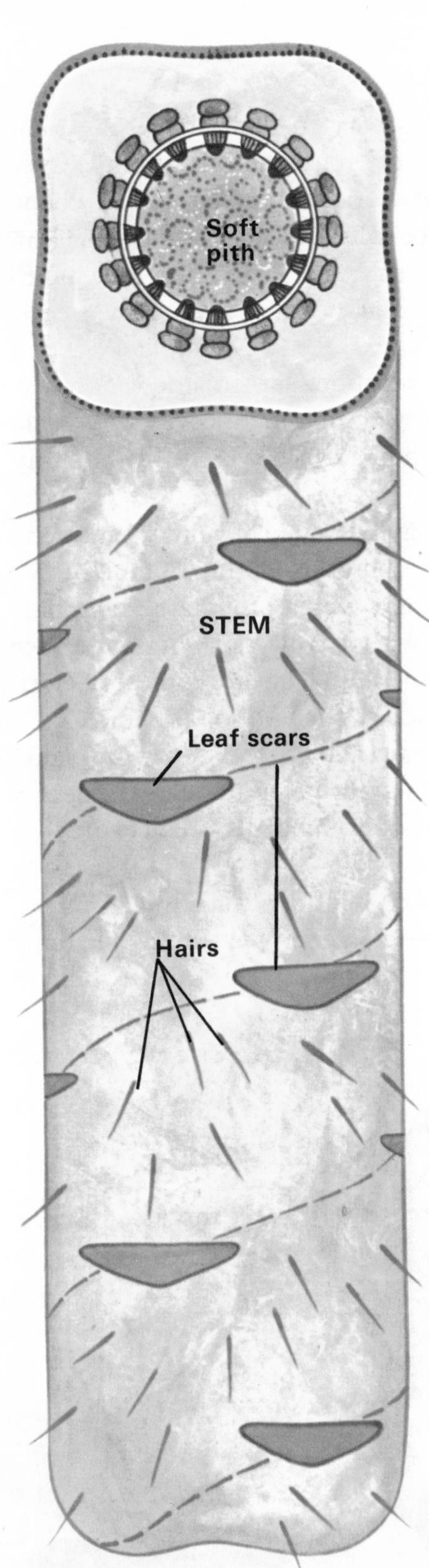

Stems

A stem links the ROOTS to the rest of the plant. It usually grows upwards towards the sunlight, though some stems grow under the ground. Most stems are green or brown in colour. The stem holds the LEAVES and FLOWERS so that sunlight can reach them and help them to grow. A stem also has to be strong. It has the weight of the plant to support and it must resist the force of the wind.

The stem contains many different kinds of CELLS. An older stem is made up mostly of tube-shaped cells. These cells carry water and food up and down the plant. Some cell walls are very tough, making the stem very strong. A tree trunk contains many of these woody tubes. New ones are formed every year, and each year's tubes form an annual ring.

Left: A young plant stem. The woody parts form a ring. As the stem gets older the bundles of woody tubes join up and lots more are produced so that they make up most of the stem.
Below: The underground stem of Solomon's Seal. Leaves and flowers come up from the buds.

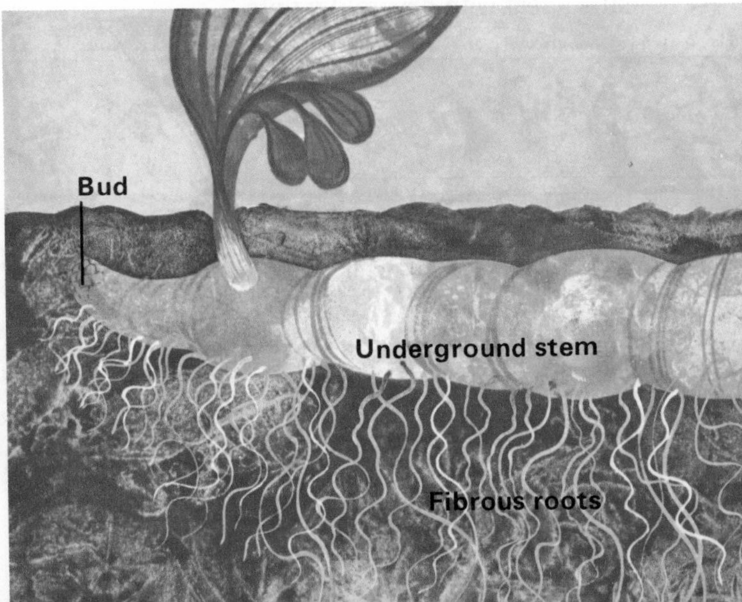

Top: The simple leaf of the privet.
Above: The Chile rhubarb has huge spiny leaves.
Below: The rose has a compound leaf – a leaf with several leaflets.

Leaves

Although leaves vary in their shape, size, and colour, they are often thin and flat. Some leaves, such as the privet, are very simple in shape. Other leaves are split into smaller parts, or leaflets. Some are arranged like a fan (the HORSE CHESTNUT) or in pairs (PEA OR ASH). Other leaves are divided so finely that they look like lace.

The edge of a leaf may be smooth, toothed, or spiny. Another way in which leaves vary is the appearance of their surface, which may be shiny, hairy, or plain.

Leaves also have a system of veins. Some veins run parallel to each other. Others branch in all directions. Parallel veins are most commonly found in plants with narrow, upright leaves, such as GRASSES. Branching veins are typical of horizontal leaves such as the RHODODENDRON.

All leaves are attached to the STEM, sometimes by a stalk. This stalk helps to keep the leaves apart. The part of the rhubarb plant which we eat is a leaf stalk.

The main function of the leaf is to make food. To do this job it needs energy from the sun. Tiny holes in the leaf surface, called *stomata*, help in this process.

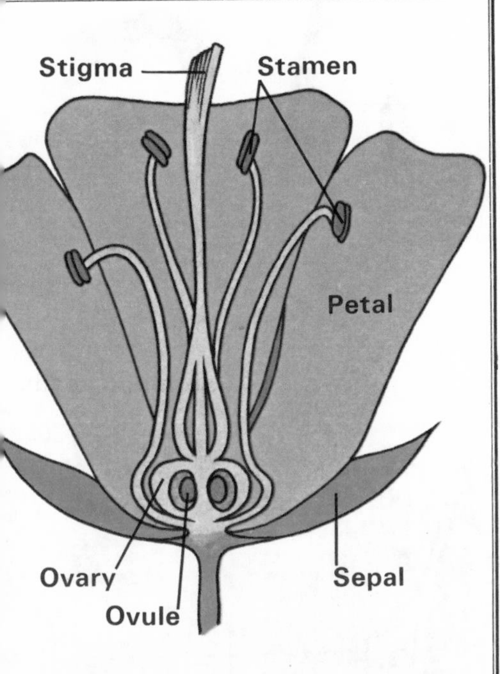

HE MAIN PARTS OF A FLOWER

Below: The ginger plant has an unusual flower head.
Below right: Thistles, like daisies, have hundreds of tiny flowers packed tightly together in a single head.

Flowers

The job of a flower is to produce SEEDS for the next generation of plants. Like all other parts of the plant, flowers differ very much in their size, shape, and colour.

Many flowers are brightly coloured to attract insects, which help in POLLINATION. But the flowers of many trees are small and green or colourless. Those of the POPLAR, OAK and BEECH, for example, are small and dull compared with the flowers of the ROSE, orchid or marigold.

Some plants, such as the TULIP, have only one flower each year. Others may produce hundreds. Each daisy flower head, for example, contains a large number of tiny flowers packed tightly together.

The outer parts of the flower, known as the sepals and petals, protect the inner parts. The inner parts are concerned with producing the seeds. The male parts are called stamens and produce pollen. The female part, the pistil, includes the ovules which will become the seeds. Not all flowers contain both male and female parts. Some holly trees, for example, are male and others are female. Only the female trees produce the red berries containing seeds.

Fruits and seeds

The pistil, the female part of the flower, produces the fruit and seeds. Seeds are formed inside fruits. They contain the young plant and its food supply. For example, a peapod is the fruit which contains the seeds (PEAS). Seeds have very little water and are protected by a tough skin. Sometimes a fruit contains only one seed, as in the case of the cherry. WHEAT grains and dandelion parachutes are other fruits with one seed.

Fruits are either fleshy or dry when ripe. Berries and other fleshy fruits are often brightly coloured and they are attractive to birds and other animals. These creatures peck at the fruits and scatter the seeds inside them. Small seeds, such as those of the blackberry, may be swallowed. They pass right through the animal but they can still grow afterwards.

Some fleshy fruits spread their seeds by shooting them away from the fruit. The squirting cucumber bursts open when it is ripe, throwing its seeds for some distance. Other squirting cucumber plants may then begin to grow nearby.

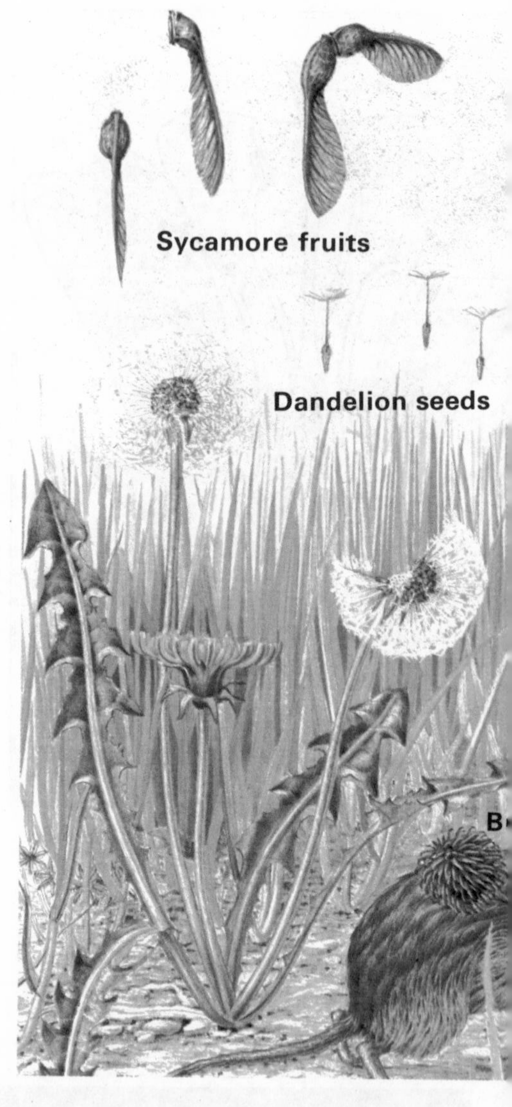

Right: Fruits and seeds are spread in different ways.
Below: All these fruits contain one or more seeds. They are nearly all scattered by animals.

Dry fruits are much lighter and can be blown away by the wind. The fruits of thistles can be carried by wind for great distances. If the fruit itself is not blown away, the wind can shake the seeds out.

The poppy capsule contains a large number of black seeds. At the top of the capsule are small slits. When wind shakes the capsule, the seeds are thrown out through the slits.

The fruits of gorse are pods, which become black as they dry. On a hot day, the pods twist and burst loudly, scattering the seeds. Fruits with hooks, such as goosegrass and burrs are spread by catching on to the fur of animals.

Life of a Flowering Plant

Like animals, plants have to grow. They grow from a seed until they can produce FLOWERS and SEEDS of their own. During their life they must make a vast amount of food so that they can build ROOTS, STEMS, and LEAVES.

The soil, rain, wind, sun, and air all play their part in the life of a plant. They provide all the materials and energy which a plant needs. The energy usually comes from sunlight, which the leaves trap and use for making food.

Plants compete with each other for space, light, and food. In woods, for example, the trees take up much of the light and water, leaving very little for smaller plants. So the small plants flower early in the spring, before the tree leaves come out.

When fruits and seeds are released from the plant, they must be spread some distance away. Otherwise, too many plants would be trying to grow on the same patch of ground.

Right: Three kinds of places where plants can live: 1. The soil. 2. In or on other plants. 3. In water. Below: These pictures show what happens to a plant (right) when it is not watered.

1

3▽

2

Plant growth

An animal usually reaches a time when it stops growing. Plants, however, can go on growing until they die. A tree that lives for 1000 years or more becomes bigger every year. Plants that live for many years are called perennials. Some may be 30 years old before they start to flower. Biennials, which live for two years, spend the first year of their life making and storing food. In their second year they grow quickly to produce flowers and seeds. Annuals are plants that live for only one year. They grow very quickly, flower and then die.

Conditions must be right for growth. The speed with which a plant grows depends upon a number of things. Temperature, the amount of sunlight, the type of SOIL and the amount of water or RAIN are all important. Different plants need different conditions. A tropical plant, for example, needs a lot of heat in order to grow.

Below left: Many garden plants are annuals and live for only one year.
Below centre: The wallflower is a biennial.
Below right: The hollyhock normally lives for several years. It is a perennial.

Soil

Soil is formed from different substances. ROCKS are broken down by ice, FROST, WIND, and RAIN into small grains or particles. These particles vary greatly in size. Some are very small and others are large enough to see. When humus, a substance which is made of dead plants and animals, is added to these particles, a soil is formed.

A clay soil is made of very small particles which stick together, holding a lot of water but very little air. This type of soil contains a lot of the minerals needed by plants, but it is not a good soil. The ROOTS cannot breathe properly in it. Clay soil is also very heavy and hard to dig.

A sandy soil has many more air spaces because the sand grains are large. It is a poor soil. It holds very little water and lets the minerals needed by plants wash down too deep into the ground.

Peat is made entirely from plant remains which do not decay. A peaty soil is usually acid and has very few minerals. Peat is sometimes used for fuel where coal is scarce.

The best type of soil is a loam, a mixture of clay, sand, and humus. It contains plenty of air, water, and minerals for plant growth. Loam is dark in colour and it warms up quickly in spring.

Above: Loam has balanced amounts of sand, clay, and humus. Below: (Left) water drains through sand. (Centre) water becomes trapped in clay. (Right) peat soils contain a lot of humus.

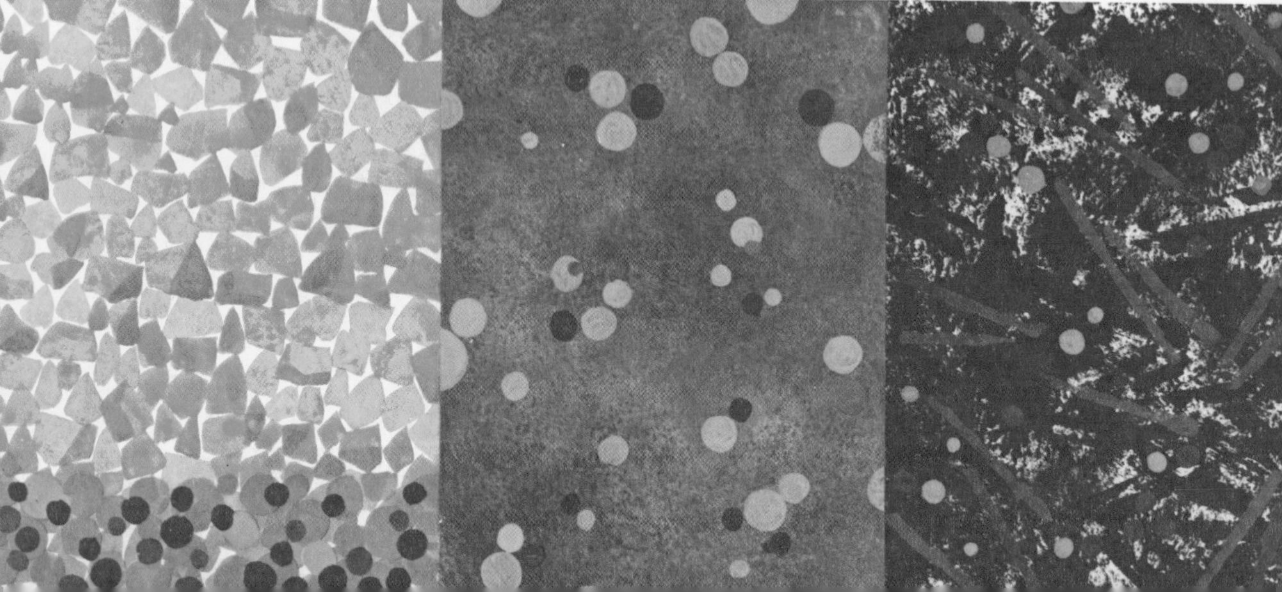

Food

Food is necessary to provide energy. It is also needed to build and repair the body of the plant or animal. The main difference between plants and animals is that plants are able to make their own food; animals cannot.

This food is made by using sunlight, water, minerals, and carbon dioxide (a gas found in the air). The energy from sunlight is absorbed by a green substance in the leaves called chlorophyll. It helps to combine water and carbon dioxide to form sugar. All animals get their food from plants, either directly or indirectly. Since the plant makes its food by using the energy of sunlight, it is quite clear that all living things depend on the sun.

Above: The lower tomato plant has been starved of minerals.
Below: The diagrams show how water and gases move through a plant by day (left), and by night.

Energy from sunlight
Water and minerals
Oxygen
Carbon dioxide

Parasites

Parasites are plants, or animals, which 'steal' food from other living things. Unlike other plants, parasites are not able to make their own food. The plant or animal that the parasite feeds on is called the 'host'. Parasites are attached to their host by special sucking ROOTS.

Plants that can make some of their own food are called semi-parasites. The mistletoe is the best-known example of this kind of plant. It is found growing on various trees, particularly APPLE trees. It buries its roots in the branches, and sucks out food. The yellow rattle is a green plant, but it grows on to the roots of grass. It obtains extra food from these roots.

Top: The toothwort, like the broomrape, gets food by sending suckers into the roots of other plants.
Right: Mistletoe growing on an apple tree. It buries its roots in the branches.
Below: The Australian strangler fig is not a true parasite, but it kills other trees by smothering them and cutting off the light.

The dodder is an example of a complete parasite. It grows on gorse and heather bushes, and sucks out food from their STEMS. Broomrapes are also parasites. They take food from the roots of many plants, including ivy, thistles and clovers.

Many fungi are parasites. They cause a number of plant diseases. WHEAT rusts, garden mildew, and grape and peach diseases are all caused by fungi. Fungi also cause a number of skin diseases in Man.

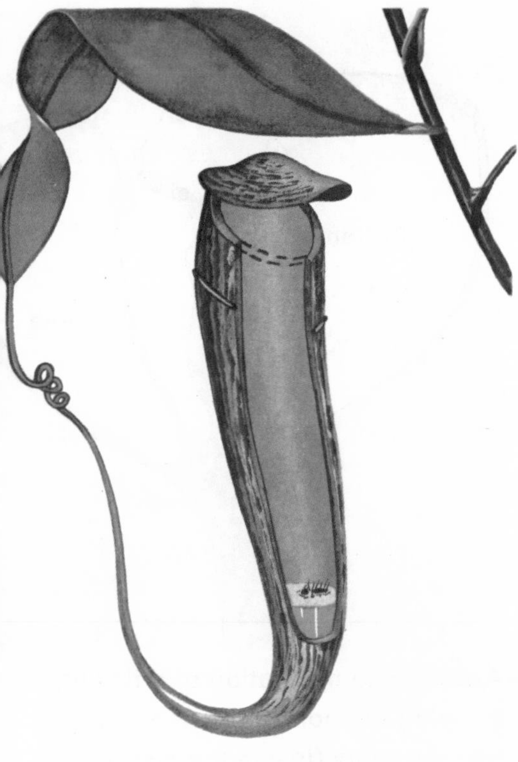

Above: Inside the pitcher of a pitcher plant.

Below: The Venus' flytrap comes from North America.

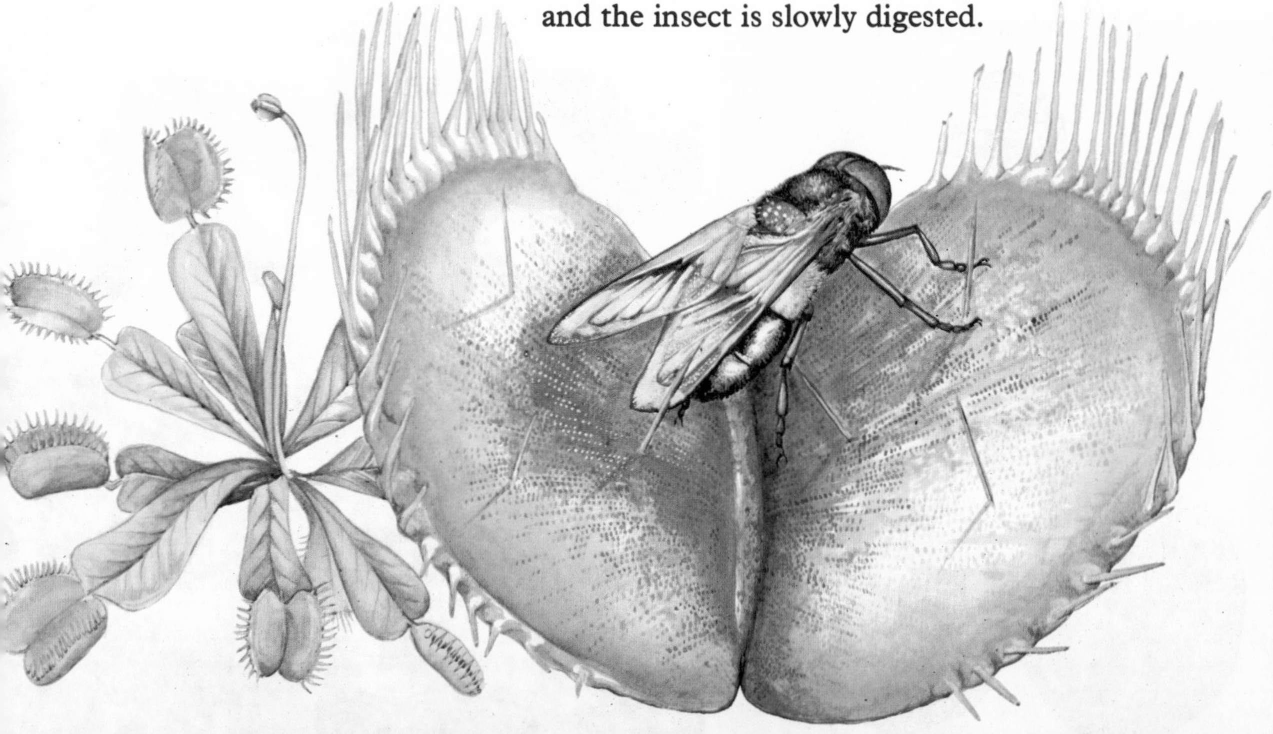

Plants that eat insects

Many animals eat plants, but not many plants use animals as food. Some plants which live in poor conditions are not able, however, to make enough food for themselves. They obtain extra food by catching insects.

Pitcher plants catch insects in their special LEAVES. Once an insect is trapped inside the pitcher, it dies and is broken down, or digested. Thus the plant gets the food it needs.

Sundews have leaves covered with many small hairs. These hairs are very sticky. Any insect which lands on a leaf gets stuck, like a fly in a SPIDER'S web. The hairs then slowly close round the insect, holding it tightly and then digesting it. These plants have been used as flypaper.

In the butterwort, the whole leaf is sticky. The edges of the leaf are rolled inwards to prevent the insect from escaping.

The Venus' flytrap, often grown as a pot plant, has leaves with two flaps, each having long teeth. When an insect lands on a leaf, the flaps close, trapping it. Juices pour out from the leaf cells and the insect is slowly digested.

Pollination

In order to make seeds, pollen from the male part of the flower (stamen) must be moved to the female part (pistil). This process is called pollination. Pollen cannot move on its own, so it must be carried by wind or insects or some other means.

Grasses and many trees are pollinated by the wind. They produce a lot of very light pollen which is easily shaken out and carried away by the wind. The stigma, or tip of the pistil, traps any pollen which blows on it. Many trees flower and produce pollen in early spring. Grasses flower rather later.

Many flowers are pollinated by insects, such as BEES, MOTHS and BUTTERFLIES. The insects are attracted to the flower by the bright colour and by the sugary nectar it produces. The bee uses nectar to make honey. As the insect lands on the flower and pushes its tongue down to the nectar, it transfers pollen to the stigma. It can also carry pollen away to other flowers.

In tropical countries, bats and HUMMING BIRDS help to pollinate flowers.

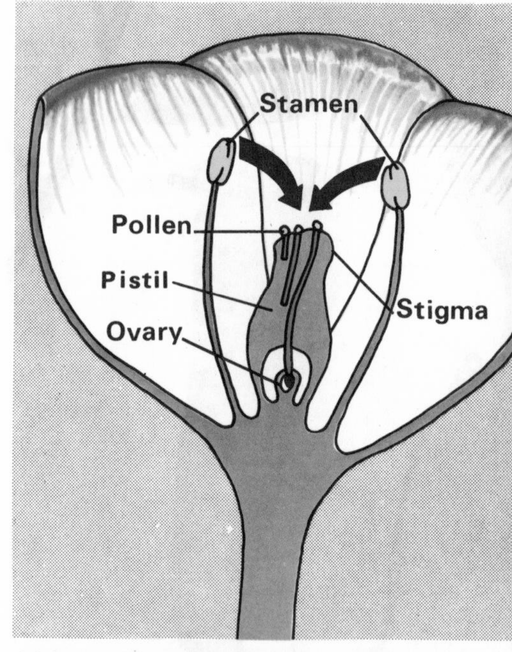

Above: The pollination of a flower, showing the pollen growing down into the ovary (inside the pistil).
Below left: The pollen of the Caucasian pine, magnified 800 times.
Below: Crocus flowers exposing their large stigmas for pollination.

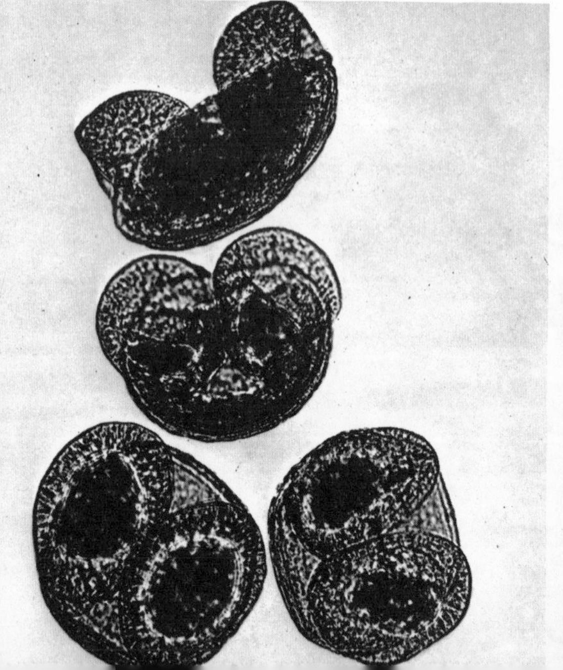

Development of fruits

When a plant has been pollinated, the pollen starts to grow. It grows down the pistil towards the egg-cells and fertilizes them to make SEEDS. The pistil becomes the whole fruit.

As soon as pollination and fertilization are over, most parts of the flower begin to die. The petals fall from the flower and the stamens wither. Both the petals and the stamens have done their job and are no longer needed.

The pistil starts to swell and to become harder. Inside, the seeds are growing and food is stored in them. The fruits and seeds ripen and are shed from the plant.

Poppy capsules, acorns and hazel nuts are among the many kinds of dry fruits. They lose water as they ripen. Many dry fruits split open and scatter their seed. The fruits themselves do not fall until much later.

The juicy part of the APPLE (the part we eat) is not formed from the pistil. It is formed from the flower stalk which swells up around the pistil. It takes several months to grow and it changes colour as it ripens. The tough core which contains the seeds is the actual pistil.

This kind of fruit, which does not grow just from the pistil, is called a *false fruit*. The strawberry is another well known false fruit. Like the apple, it is formed from the flower stalk, but here the flower stalk does not enclose the pistil. The pistil consists of several distinct parts, each of which forms a pip on the surface of the strawberry. Each pip contains a seed.

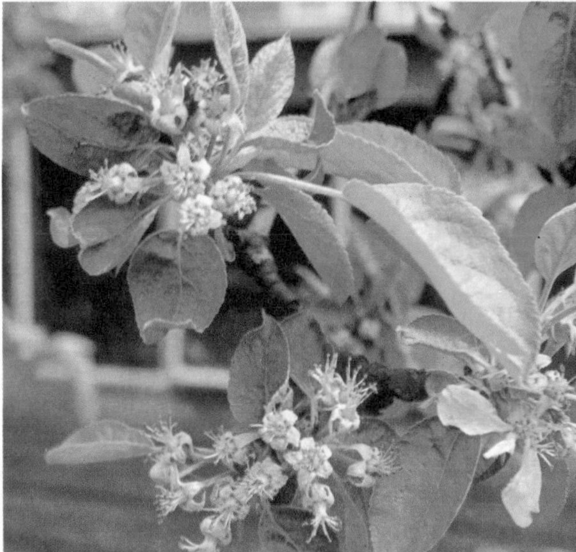

Top: Apple flowers open and ready for pollination by bees and other insects.
Centre: After pollination the petals fall and the fruit begins to swell.
Below right: Ripe apples.

Seeds and seedlings

The life of a new plant begins with the seed. It contains food to keep it alive and to help it grow when conditions are right.

A seed may have to wait a very long time before conditions are right for it to start to grow, or germinate. Even when conditions are right, some seeds do not start to grow at once. Their most important need is water. A dry seed placed in water or damp soil soon starts to swell. It gets much larger than it was. The seed also needs the right temperature and the presence of oxygen from the air.

The first stage of germination cannot be seen from the outside. The young plant, or embryo, grows rapidly by using up its food supply. Soon, it is large enough to burst through the seed coat. The first part to appear is the ROOT, which is soon covered in hairs. The root takes in more water and minerals for the plant. Next, the shoot appears. It rapidly grows towards the light, where it becomes green and starts to make food. The plant is now a seedling. Gradually it will grow into a mature plant.

Right: Stages in the germination of a pine seed.
Below: A beech seedling starting to make its food.

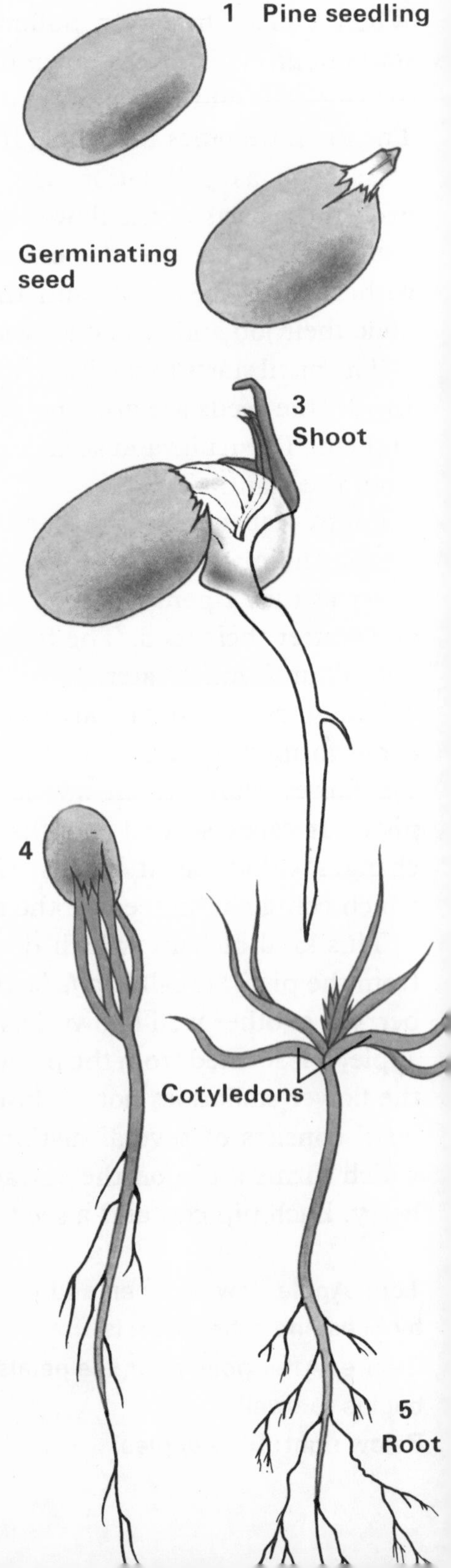

1 Pine seedling

2 Germinating seed

3 Shoot

4

Cotyledons

5 Root

Plant support

The bigger a plant becomes, the more weight the STEM has to support. Usually, the stem becomes woody and thick in large plants, such as trees and shrubs. Special roots sometimes grow out from the stem. They grow down into the soil, and act like the ropes that support a tent.

Many plants support their weight without forming a thick stem. The ivy supports itself on trees and walls by small roots which anchor the climbing stem. Various creepers use the same method.

Many climbers, such as the blackberry and the climbing ROSE, scramble over other plants. The thorns on the stems help to support them. The whip-like tendrils of PEAS are part of the LEAF, and help the plant to climb. They are sensitive to touch and curl round any support. With the honeysuckle and runner bean, however, the whole stem twists round the support.

Water also plays an important part in support. It fills up the cells and makes them firmer. When pot plants are left unwatered they droop, or wilt. But they quickly recover if given more water.

Above: The swamp cypress has a thick base to its trunk.
Below: Stilt roots growing out from the stem like guy ropes.
Below right: Ivy on a tree trunk.

Garden Flowers

Above: The wild ancestors of these garden lupins were much smaller.
Below: These large and showy flowers all came from wild plants.

There are several thousand kinds of garden flowers. Although many garden flowers are very like their wild relatives, most have been improved by gardeners so that they are bigger and more colourful. The wild lupin, for example, has much smaller flowers than the plants which are grown in gardens. The garden lupin was produced by using only seeds from the largest wild lupins. Horticulturalists (experts in growing plants) repeated this process many times to give the garden lupin. Varieties with new colours have been produced by taking seeds from freaks.

Another way in which new varieties are obtained is to cross one type with another. Sometimes horticulturalists use two or more different kinds of plants to make a new variety. For example, the Shasta daisy comes from daisies from England, America, and JAPAN.

Some plants were once grown because of the colour of their flowers, but today are grown for other reasons. The runner bean, for example, was first a garden flower but today is grown as a vegetable.

Roses

The rose is famous for its colour and smell, even though many types of garden rose do not have a very strong perfume. The petals of the rose are large and brightly coloured, forming a cup when the flower is open. Inside, there are many yellow stamens which produce pollen. Insects such as bees are attracted to the flowers by the colour and scent and pollinate them. The fruits of the rose, called hips, are red or orange when ripe and very fleshy. They must be cut off if the plant is to produce plenty of flowers.

There are many types of wild roses which have been used to make the garden varieties. There are several hundred garden roses, and the number increases every year. Garden roses usually have many more petals than wild roses.

Garden roses can be put into several groups, but there are two main types. One is the bush rose, which is cut back each year and produces many large flowers. The other is the climber or rambler, which has a weak stem and has to be supported.

Above: Spek's yellow rose.
Below: Bush roses.
Below right: Climbing roses supported on a trellis.

Dahlias

The dahlia is a member of the daisy family. Each flower head is really a collection of many flowers with large, brightly-coloured petals. The range of colours is very great and some kinds even have several colours in one flower.

The shape of the flower head varies a good deal. Some dahlias look like daisies, while others have rounded or spiky heads.

Dahlias were called after Anders Dahl, a Swedish scientist. They come from hot countries and they are the national flower of MEXICO. The wild dahlias are about two metres high and they have single purple flowers. All dahlias have fleshy STEMS and swollen ROOTS. Food is stored in the roots. The plants are easily killed by frost. Gardeners growing dahlias in cooler regions must dig up the roots every autumn and store them indoors until the spring.

Right: Orange and yellow cactus dahlias. Each coloured spike is actually a separate flower.

Chrysanthemums

The chrysanthemum, like the dahlia, is a member of the daisy family. It is very popular as a garden flower. It normally flowers in autumn, but when grown indoors can be made to flower at any time of the year.

There are many varieties of chrysanthemum, and some still look like daisies. The first garden chrysanthemums were yellow, and were grown in JAPAN.

New plants are grown from cuttings taken in spring when the old plants start to grow again.

The chrysanthemum takes its name from a Greek word meaning 'golden flower'.

Left: One of many beautiful chrysanthemum varieties.

Sweet peas

The sweet pea flower has five petals. The largest petal stands at the back of the flower. It is known as the standard. The two petals at the side are called the wings. The other two form the keel. They are joined together, and are shaped like the keel of a ship. They hide the stamens and pistil.

The flower has a sweet smell and is attractive to BEES. When a bee lands on the flower, the keel is weighed down and the other parts are exposed. POLLINATION can then take place.

The sweet pea is a climbing plant. When it is grown in a garden it often has to be supported on sticks. Some of the upper leaflets of its LEAVES look like little fingers. They are called tendrils, and enable the plant to climb.

The first sweet peas came from Sicily. Today the sweet pea has a very large range of colours.

Right: Sweet peas are very colourful and they have a pleasant smell. The climbing tendrils are clearly seen at the top of the picture.

Carnations

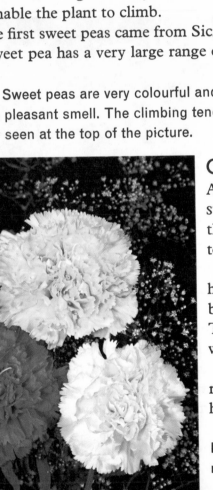

All carnations have waxy, blue-grey LEAVES and STEMS. The leaves are narrow and pointed and the stems are swollen where the leaves are joined to them.

Carnation plants are large, up to 1·5 metres high if grown indoors. The flowers are large and brightly coloured. Some of them are striped. There are many petals covering the entire flower, which has a sweet smell.

The garden pinks are flowers that are closely related to carnations. Pinks are smaller, but they have a stronger scent.

Left: The sweetly scented carnation comes in many colours.

Tulips

One of the most popular garden plants of late spring is the tulip. It has large, brightly-coloured flowers, with broad, waxy petals. Some types of tulip have pointed or feathery petals.

The flower grows on a long stalk from the centre of a bulb, which is planted in autumn. When cut open, the bulb looks like an onion, consisting of fleshy scales packed tightly together. The bulb contains stored food. Tulip growing is an important industry in the NETHERLANDS.

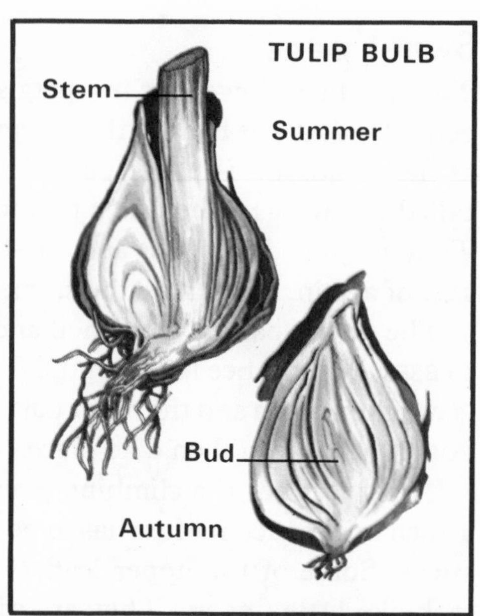

Right: Tulip bulbs opened to show the scales.
Below: Tulips have large waxy petals.
Below right: Tulip flowers showing the stamens.

Pansies

The garden pansy is a small plant with large flowers. The flowers, which may be almost any colour, look as though they have a face painted on them.

The pansy is a perennial and is easily grown from seed. It makes a good plant for edging flower borders or on rock gardens.

The wild relatives of the pansy, such as hearts-ease, have much smaller flowers but are very attractive.

Left: Pansies often have petals of two colours.

Weeds

A weed is a plant that grows where we do not want it. Weeds choke off other plants and ruin gardens and lawns. They grow very quickly, covering any patch of bare ground.

The groundsel, chickweed, and shepherd's purse are common weeds. They make large numbers of seeds in a few weeks, having several crops each year. These plants often flower throughout the winter. They are very easy to kill by digging or pulling up.

Weeds such as the dandelion and dock take much longer to produce flowers, but each plant may release several hundred seeds each year. These plants are often difficult to remove because of their deep tap roots. They may grow again if cut back or dug up.

Another type of weed spreads itself by using creeping stems. Buttercups, couch and nettles are common weeds which have stems spreading in all directions near the surface of the soil. They are very difficult to destroy because almost any part which survives is able to make another plant. An easier way of killing these weeds is to spray them with special chemicals.

Above: The dandelion, a difficult weed to remove.

Below: Some garden weeds. Apart from the cornflower, all are common.

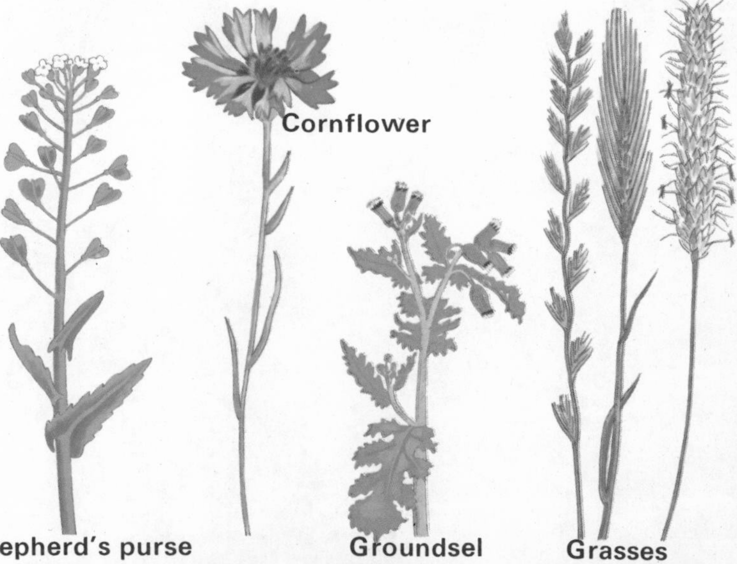

Flowering Trees and Shrubs

Many of the trees and shrubs found in cool countries lose their LEAVES in autumn. The leaves change colour, then drop off and rot. Trees that lose their leaves in this way are called deciduous. The buds of deciduous trees are able to withstand FROST, RAIN, and SNOW. In the spring, their flowers appear.

Trees that do not lose their leaves in autumn are called evergreens. Evergreens lose their leaves throughout the year, but are continually growing new ones. The tree or shrub is never bare of leaves, as deciduous plants sometimes are.

Many trees are pollinated by the wind. Their flowers are usually not very colourful and are often small. Trees which have large, coloured flowers are pollinated by insects.

Right: Many shrubs bear bright berries.
Below: Japanese maple trees of various kinds.

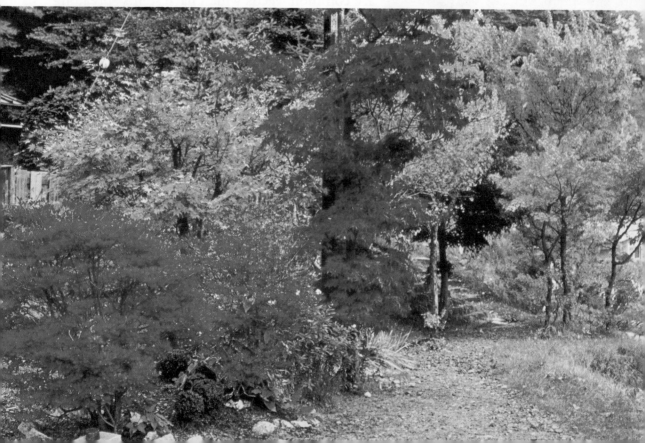

Bark and wood

The outer covering of the woody parts of a plant is called the bark. The bark helps to protect the plant from damage caused by frost, animals, or disease.

Some barks are much thicker than others. The bark of some trees, such as the OAK, may have deep cracks. Other barks, such as the silver BIRCH, can be peeled off in thin strips.

The inner layer of bark contains special CELLS. These transport food up and down the plant. Underneath the bark is the wood. New wood is added each year.

The wood is formed in rings. Usually one new ring is produced each year.

There are many kinds of wood. Balsa wood, for example, is very light and easily cut, while teak is very hard. Each tree can be recognised by its wood.

Wood helps the plant in two ways. One is to transport water and minerals up the plant from the SOIL. The other is to give the plant greater strength. Wood is also one of man's most important raw materials.

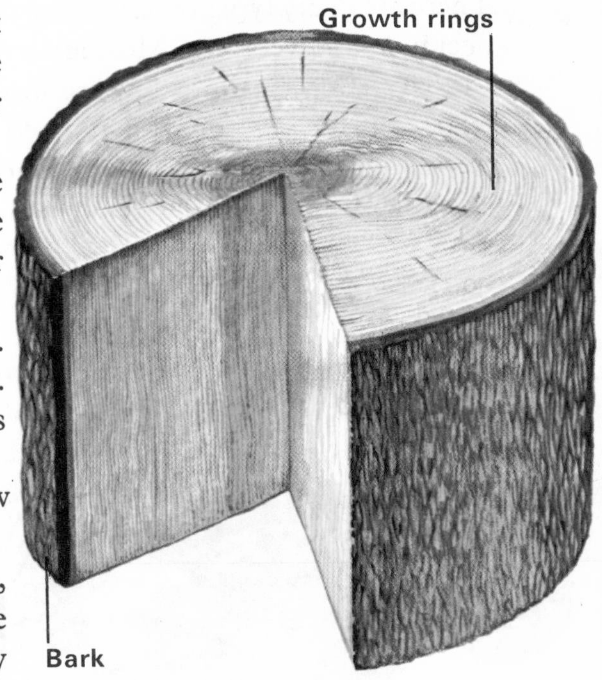

Above: Part of a tree trunk. The growth rings can be clearly seen. Below: The bark of the Scots pine (left), Tibetan cherry (centre), and paper-bark maple.

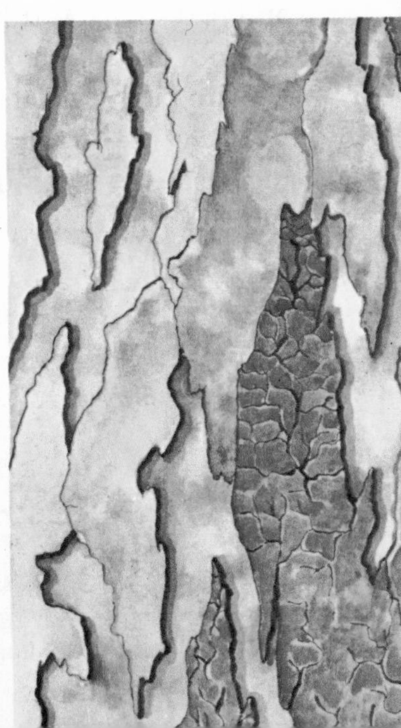

Oak

There are many types of oak. They can be either deciduous or evergreen. Most are large trees, up to 40 metres high. But a few are shrubs.

The oak grows slowly, compared with other trees, and can live for a very long time. The wood is very hard and has a number of uses. The European cork tree is also an oak. The cork used for bottle stoppers comes from its outer bark.

Oak

You can recognise the oak by its grooved bark, by the shape of its leaves, and by its acorns.

Fruit (acorn) Leaves Winter outline

Ash

The ash is a fairly tall deciduous tree (15–40 metres high). It grows in EUROPE, North AFRICA and parts of ASIA. It has a smooth grey BARK, and black buds in winter. It has large LEAVES, divided up into many leaflets.

The wood is tough and used for making tennis rackets, as well as the handles of tools. Other types of ash are found in NORTH AMERICA.

Ash

The ash has greyish bark and twigs. In the winter it has black buds.

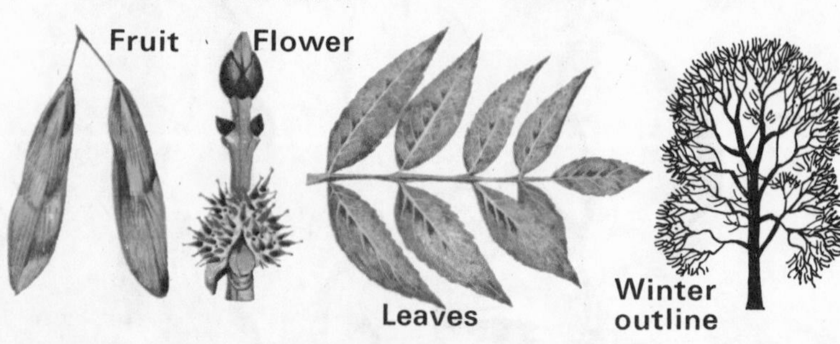
Fruit Flower Leaves Winter outline

Beech

The common beech is a large tree which reaches a height of 30 to 50 metres. It is found growing in chalk, limestone, and sandy SOILS. It is often planted by man. The common beech and its relatives in EUROPE and America are deciduous. Those of AUSTRALIA and NEW ZEALAND are sometimes evergreen. Beechwood is often used for furniture.

The beech is a large, graceful tree. Like the ash, it has smooth grey bark.

Beech

Birch

There are 40 types of birch. They are found in NORTH AMERICA, EUROPE, and the U.S.S.R. In Europe, one of the most common types is the silver birch, which is found in sandy, acid SOILS. It is a tall, graceful tree growing to a height of 30 metres. It has a silver-coloured bark.

The wood of birch trees is used mainly for making plywood and some light furniture.

The silver birch is one of the commonest of the birches. Birch flowers grow as catkins.

Birch

Lilac

The lilac can be either a planted shrub or small tree. It grows up to seven metres high. The garden varieties have large, brightly coloured FLOWER heads which appear in early summer. The lilac is related to the ASH.

Lilacs first grew in Eastern EUROPE and ASIA, before they were taken to other countries. They give their name to a colour, which is a kind of pinkish purple.

The lilac has large, heart-shaped leaves.

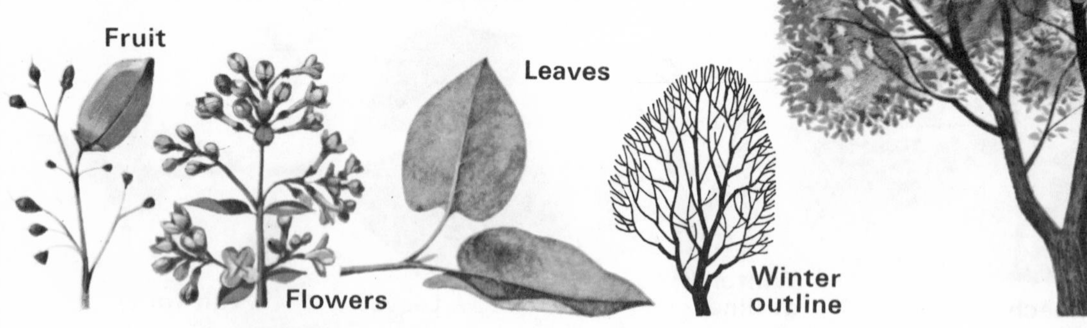

Mountain ash (Rowan)

Mountain ash

The mountain ash is found mainly in EUROPE. It grows in many types of soil. It is slender and grows to a height of 15–20 metres. It is called the mountain ash because it can survive exposure high up on MOUNTAINS, and because its LEAVES look like those of the ASH. The amelanchiers of NORTH AMERICA are related to it, but they are smaller and have simpler leaves. The mountain ash is also called the rowan.

The mountain ash has compound leaves.

Maple

There are many types of maple trees. The most familiar are the sugar maple of NORTH AMERICA, the sycamore, and the Japanese maple. All of these trees are deciduous and have deeply-lobed LEAVES.

Maple syrup comes from the sap of the sugar maple. The sap is taken from the tree in late winter or early spring.

Many kinds of maple are grown in gardens for their brightly coloured autumn leaves.

Maple

Horse chestnut

The horse chestnut is a large tree, growing up to 40 metres in height. It is deciduous and found in ASIA, EUROPE, and NORTH AMERICA. It is called the horse chestnut because in the past the seeds (or conkers) were used as a medicine for horses.

The horse chestnut is not related to the sweet chestnut.

The horse chestnut, or buckeye, is a large tree. The spikes or flowers are often called 'candles' and the seeds are called conkers.

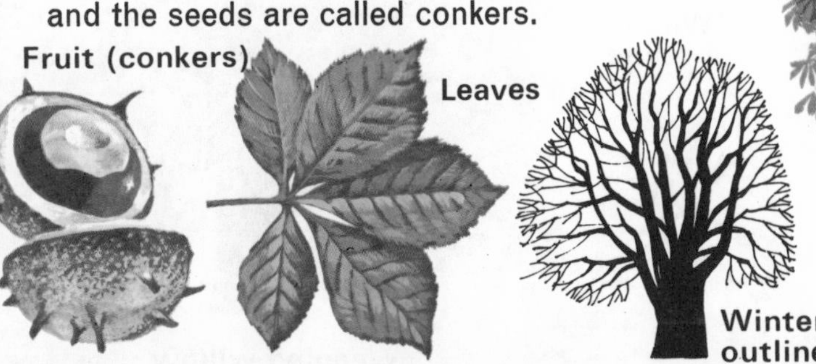

Horse chestnut

Plane

Plane

Various types of plane trees are found in EUROPE, ASIA and NORTH AMERICA. Plane trees are often planted in cities because they are not much affected by polluted air. One of the best-known types is the London plane. Its bark peels off in large flakes each year.

The wood of plane trees is very hard and tough, and has a number of uses.

Plane trees are often called buttonwoods because the fruits hang in round clusters.

Willow

There are over 300 types of willow. Some of these are found in most countries. Willows can be either trees or shrubs. Their wood is usually soft and pliable, and is ideal for making wicker furniture, baskets, and some kinds of fences. One of the most beautiful willow trees is called the weeping willow. Like other kinds of willow, it is usually found near water.

Weeping willows have graceful hanging branches.

Weeping willow

Elm

The elm is a tall tree growing up to 30 or 40 metres in height. It is common in many countries. There are about 30 different types, all of which can live for several hundred years. Because the wood of the elm does not split easily, it is often used to make furniture.

Dutch elm disease is a serious problem in several European countries.

The flowers of the elm open very early in the year, long before the leaves.

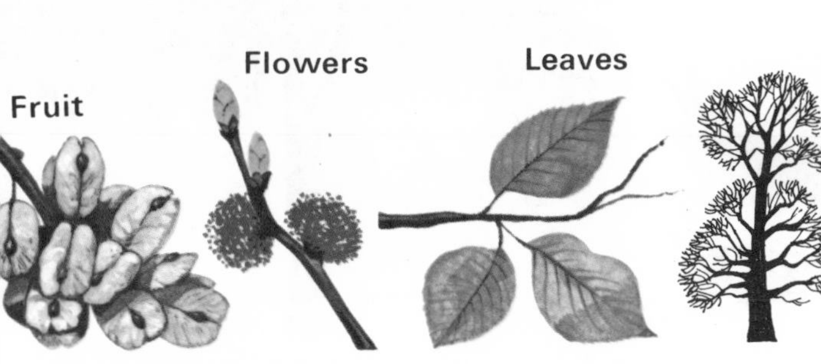

Magnolia

The magnolia is famous for its large FLOWERS, which appear in spring. There are many types of magnolia, which can be either trees or large shrubs. Magnolias are either deciduous or evergreen. The bull bay, one of the American magnolias, can reach heights of 25 metres. Most of the magnolias grow in eastern ASIA, but they are cultivated in gardens all over the world.

Magnolia

An evergreen magnolia, with its leathery leaves.

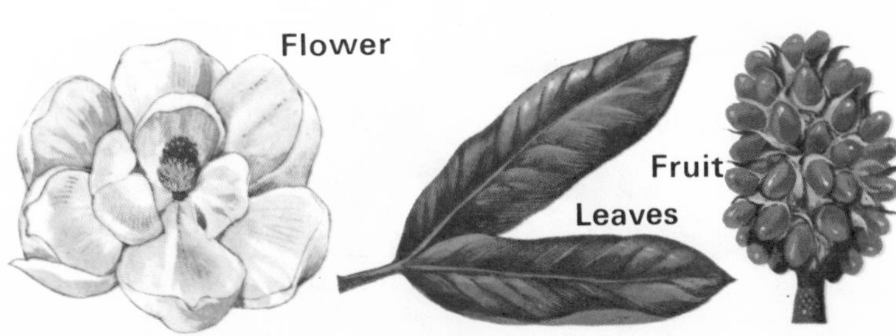

Holly

The holly is a very common evergreen growing to a height of 15 metres or more. There are over 300 types, including many garden varieties. Some of these have mottled green and yellow leaves. The trees are either male or female, but only the female trees produce the red berries. These berries are very poisonous to humans.

Holly has prickly evergreen leaves. The female trees have bright red berries. Holly is used in some countries as a Christmas decoration.

Fruit (berries) Leaves

Holly

Eucalyptus

There are many types of eucalyptus. They are found wild only in AUSTRALIA, and the islands to the north of Australia. They are now grown in many countries, especially in parks.

Many of the eucalyptus have rather blue, waxy LEAVES. The blue gum tree has leaves of this type. Some are tall trees found growing in forests and high up on MOUNTAINS. Others are small shrubs which can live in DESERTS.

Eucalyptus leaves are the food of the koala bear.

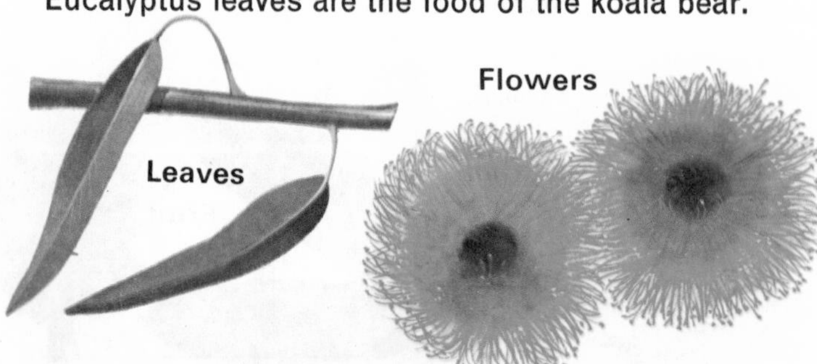

Leaves Flowers

Eucalyptus

Rhododendron

Most of the 600 types of wild rhododendron are found in ASIA, particularly in the HIMALAYAS. Most rhododendrons are evergreen, with large shiny LEAVES. They also have huge bell-shaped FLOWERS.

Azaleas, commonly planted in gardens and parks, are types of rhododendron. Azaleas are deciduous, rather than evergreen. They drop their leaves in the autumn.

Rhododendrons are large shrubs with many stems.

Rhododendron

Flower

Leaves and bud

Broom

Broom

Broom is a small shrub belonging to the PEA family. It has many slender green branches, without spines, but the LEAVES are small and sparsely scattered over the plant. Most of the food is made in the green STEMS. The plant is covered with pretty yellow FLOWERS in early summer. The flowers are then followed by black pods which explode when ripe and throw their SEEDS out.

Broom usually grows on sandy soils.

Trees with Cones

PINES, FIRS, CYPRESSES and SPRUCES are some of the many types of trees which have FLOWERS in the form of cones. They are called conifers. Like flowers, these cones also produce SEEDS. But they have no petals or sepals, and no stamens or pistils.

The cones are either male or female. The male cones produce masses of pollen. They are smaller and softer than the female cones, which produce the seeds. The seeds are protected by hard, woody scales.

The cones are pollinated by the wind. The pollen often has small air-filled wings to help it float. Many female cones take two or more years to grow their seeds, which are released when the scales dry and open up.

Most trees with cones are evergreen and have long, thin LEAVES called needles. Their timber is known as softwood and vast amounts are used in buildings.

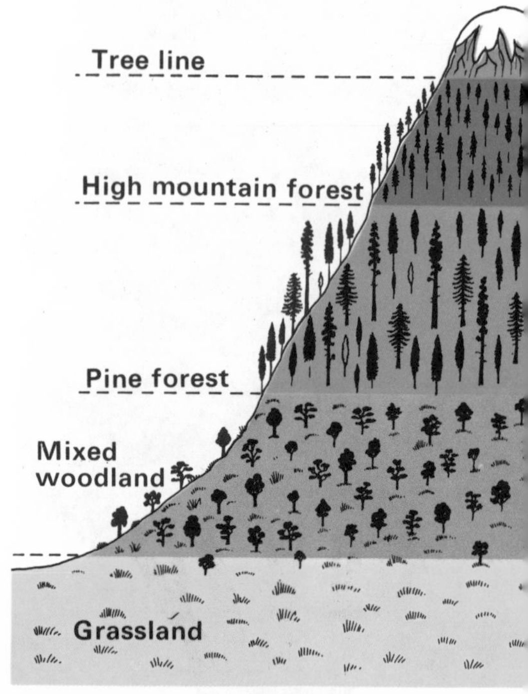

Above: Conifers can live higher up on mountains than other trees.
Below: A pine forest in autumn.

Pine

There are at least 80 different kinds of pine. They are found mainly in northern countries. Some pines are also found in the MOUNTAINS of tropical countries.

All pines have evergreen, needle-like LEAVES in small tufts. These tufts are found on small shoots growing off the main branches.

One of the most important European pines is the Scots pine. Each tuft of leaves consists of two blue-green needles. The Scots pine is a tall tree, growing to 30, 40 or even 50 metres high. The upper BARK, which is a bright red-brown or orange colour, tends to fall off in patches. The lower bark is thick and dark brown.

The eastern white pine of NORTH AMERICA has its tufts of leaves in groups of five. It grows to a maximum height of 60 metres. It is a very useful tree for timber.

The lodgepole pine is found in western North America, but is planted elsewhere. Its leaves grow in pairs, like those of the Scots pine, but they are a darker green in colour.

Fir

The firs are tall, cone-shaped trees. Their LEAVES do not have stalks and are flat with a blunt tip. When they fall off, they leave a circular scar behind. Fir trees can be recognised by these scars. Fir cones are very long and grow upright.

The Douglas fir, one of North America's most important timber trees, is not a true fir. It is much bigger than the true fir trees, and its cones hang downwards from the branches.

The balsam fir produces a sticky gum, or resin.

Balsam fir

Spruce

The spruce is an evergreen tree that bears cones and is a member of the PINE family. There are about 40 different kinds of spruce growing in the Northern Hemisphere.

The spruce tree is shaped like a pyramid. Each LEAF stands on a woody peg. When the leaf falls, the peg remains on the tree. The spruce cones, which hang down from the branches, take one year to ripen.

Timber from spruces is used for building.

Norway spruce

Larch

The larch is one of the few deciduous conifers. (The other is the swamp CYPRESS of the southern states of NORTH AMERICA.) Larches grow to a height of 60 metres and cover vast areas of land in the far north. They also cover many MOUNTAIN regions. They are often planted for timber. The wood is used for poles and fences and for building. One of the North American larches is called the tamarack.

Larches have leaves in tufts, and small cones.

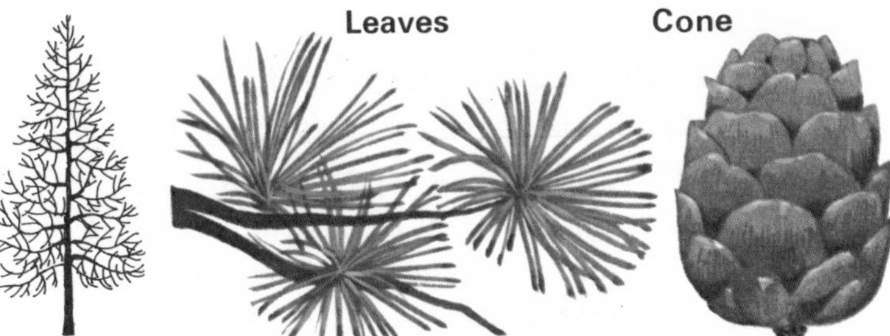

Cedar

The cedars are massive, spreading trees. They are found wild in the MEDITERRANEAN region and in the HIMALAYA Mountains. Because they are very impressive trees, they are sometimes planted in large gardens and parks.

Three types of cedar are well known. These are the cedar of Lebanon, the deodar, and the Atlas cedar. The Western red cedar is not, in fact, a true cedar.

The cedar has large, barrel-shaped cones.

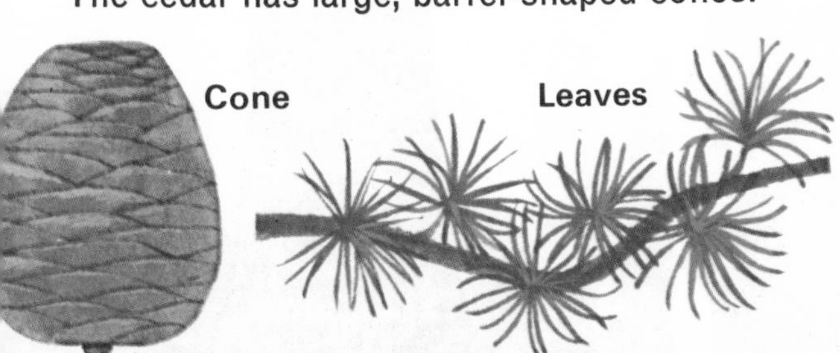

Giant trees

The giant trees of NORTH AMERICA are the largest known living things. They may live for several thousand years. Some of them are very famous and have been named after people. Even the stumps of these trees have been given names. One is called the Mark Twain Stump.

There are three kinds of giant tree. One is the redwood, which grows wild only near the coast of California. The tallest redwood trees are over 115 metres high. Their bases are over 7 metres across. Their LEAVES are like flattened needles and they have small, round cones. The BARK, which is thick and soft, is a red-brown colour. It protects the tree from heat and fire. These trees are not often damaged by forest fires. If they are burnt, they will quickly sprout new leaves.

Another type of giant tree is called the big tree or Wellingtonia. It is also known by its Indian name of Sequoia. Like the redwood, it is found wild only in California. But it grows farther away from the sea. It can grow to a height of at

Right: A young Californian redwood.
Below: A baobab tree in southern Africa. The Land Rover gives an idea of its size.

least 100 metres. The trunk becomes thinner towards the top, but can be as much as 10 metres across at the bottom. The leaves are small and narrow and grow close to the branch. The cones are twice as big as those of the redwood and are egg-shaped. This tree is sometimes planted in parks and gardens in other states and countries.

The third giant tree, the Douglas fir, can grow to a height of 95 metres. It grows over large areas of western North America, but it is often planted in other countries for its useful timber. The bark is thick and often has deep grooves in it. AMERICAN INDIANS are supposed to have used the bark to heal wounds. In North America, young Douglas firs are the most popular Christmas trees. The leaves are short, with dark green needles growing all round the twigs.

Far left: The Wellingtonia.
Left: The Douglas fir, a valuable timber tree.

Dwarf trees

Some trees are naturally small. Centuries ago, however, the JAPANESE discovered a way to make large trees small. They called these dwarf trees by the name of *bonsai*.

The secret of the bonsai method is to grow the plants in small pots, cutting the LEAVES, shoots, and ROOTS often. Bonsai trees as old as 150 years can be as small as 60 or 70 centimetres in height. The leaves and everything else are on the same scale as the miniature trunks and branches. These trees can also be trained to grow in any shape by using wire. Several trees can be grown together to look like tiny forests.

Right: This bonsai needle juniper tree is 70 years old.

Cypress

All cypress trees have very small, flat LEAVES which lie over each other. These leaves often completely cover the smaller shoots. There are a number of different types of cypress. They are found in many countries and can reach a height of between 50 and 60 metres. Some of them are important for the tough wood which they produce. The Western red CEDAR is grown mainly for its wood. The Lawson's cypress is grown in parks and as a hedge. The Italian cypress is shaped like a pillar.

Cypress

Juniper

Many junipers are stout, spreading, evergreen shrubs or small trees about 10 metres high. Some are creeping plants, which are often grown in gardens. Junipers are found wild in America, and from EUROPE and AFRICA to the HIMALAYAS, and CHINA.

The berries, which can be red or blue, are in fact very fleshy cones. These cones take two or three years to ripen. Oil from the cones is used in medicines, and also to flavour certain drinks, such as gin.

Leaves

Berries

Monkey-puzzle

The monkey-puzzle comes from Chile, where the SEEDS are sometimes used as food. The monkey-puzzle is also called the Chile pine. It is a large tree, growing up to 50 metres high. The lower branches die and drop off as the tree grows.

The LEAVES can live for as long as 15 years. They are triangular in shape and spiny. The cones are quite large. The monkey-puzzle gets its name because the thick, spiny leaves make it very difficult to climb. It would indeed puzzle a monkey to try to climb it.

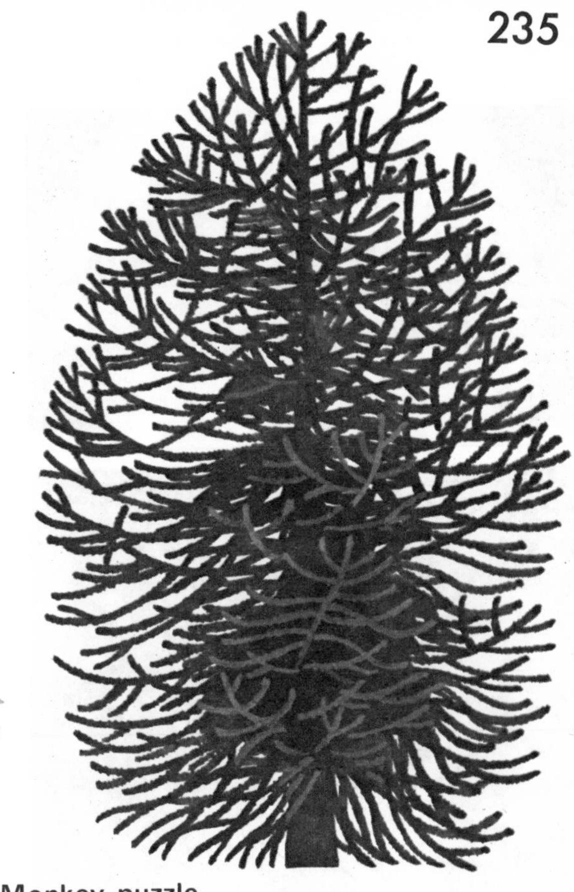

Monkey puzzle

Yew

Yew

The yews grow to a height of 20 metres or more. They live for a very long time. New shoots often grow up alongside the trunk from the base of the tree, making it appear twisted and gnarled. The wood is very hard and useful.

The LEAVES of the yews are flat. They grow in two rows on either side of the branch. The seeds are not carried in cones. Each seed is separate and it is surrounded by a juicy red cup which attracts the birds.

Plants without Seeds

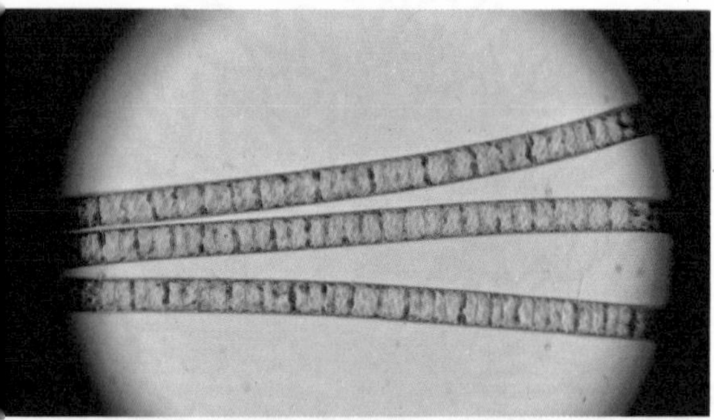

There are about 350,000 different kinds of plants. About 250,000 kinds produce SEEDS in cones or FLOWERS. The remaining 100,000 plants do not produce seeds. They form spores, which are smaller and much simpler than seeds.

Spores are found everywhere: in the air, in soil, in water, and on the surface of everything we touch. Different spores vary greatly in shape, size and colour. Like seeds, they grow into new plants.

MOSSES, FERNS, SEAWEEDS, and MUSHROOMS are some of the types of plant which do not produce seeds. These plants are generally smaller than the seed-producing plants, and most of them will grow only in damp places. Seaweeds, for example, will not live for very long out of the sea. Some of these plants are so small that they can only be seen with a MICROSCOPE.

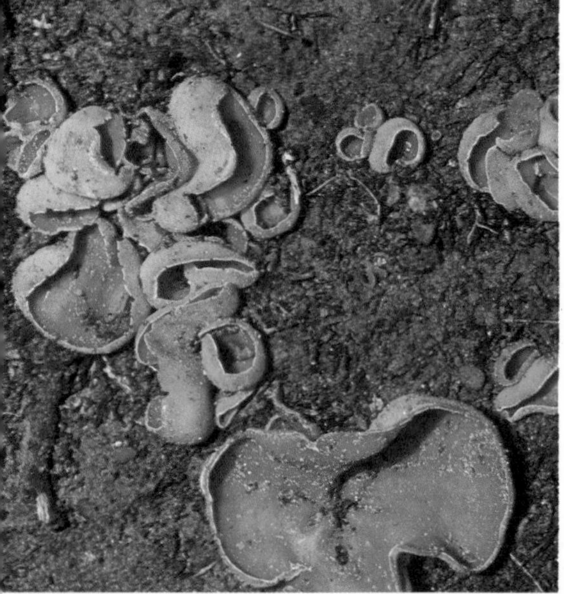

Top: Thread-like freshwater plants (algae) seen through a microscope.
Left: Orange-peel fungus.
Below left: Lichens growing on a stone.
Below: Two kinds of peat moss.

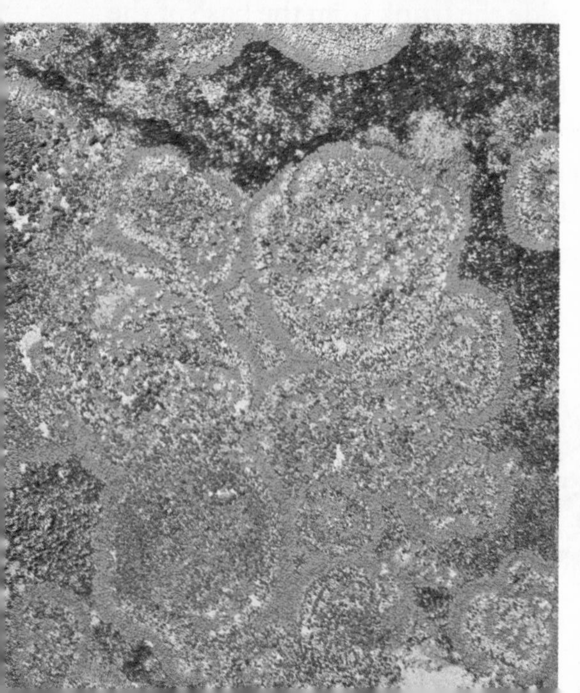

Plants too small to see

Algae is the name given to an enormous group of plants. Some of these are large (for example, kelps, which are a kind of SEAWEED). But most algae are very small. A lot of them have only one cell. We can only see them through a MICROSCOPE. Most algae are found near water.

Diatoms are a kind of algae. They are single-celled plants that are found near the surface of LAKES and seas. They have a cell wall made of glassy material. It is often composed of two halves which fit together like a box and its lid. Diatoms normally increase their numbers by splitting into two. The variety of their shape and colour is enormous. They provide food for fishes and many other animals.

Other single-celled plants common in water are able to move about by using their small, whip-like tails. They are green and able to make their own food, but have many animal-like features. Ponds and pools sometimes turn green because so many of these plants are present.

BACTERIA are often described as plants. In some ways, however, they behave more like animals.

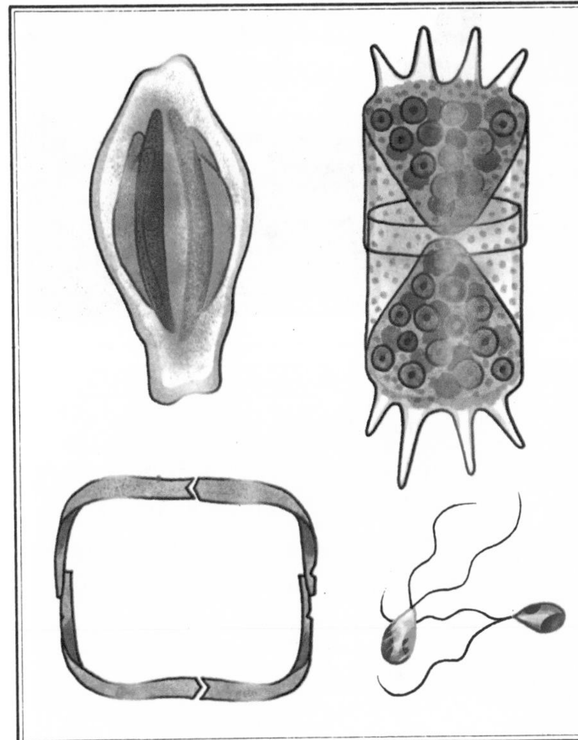

Above: Some of the many kinds of diatoms, with their elaborate box-like cell walls.
Below: Some of the single-celled flagellates or whip-plants.

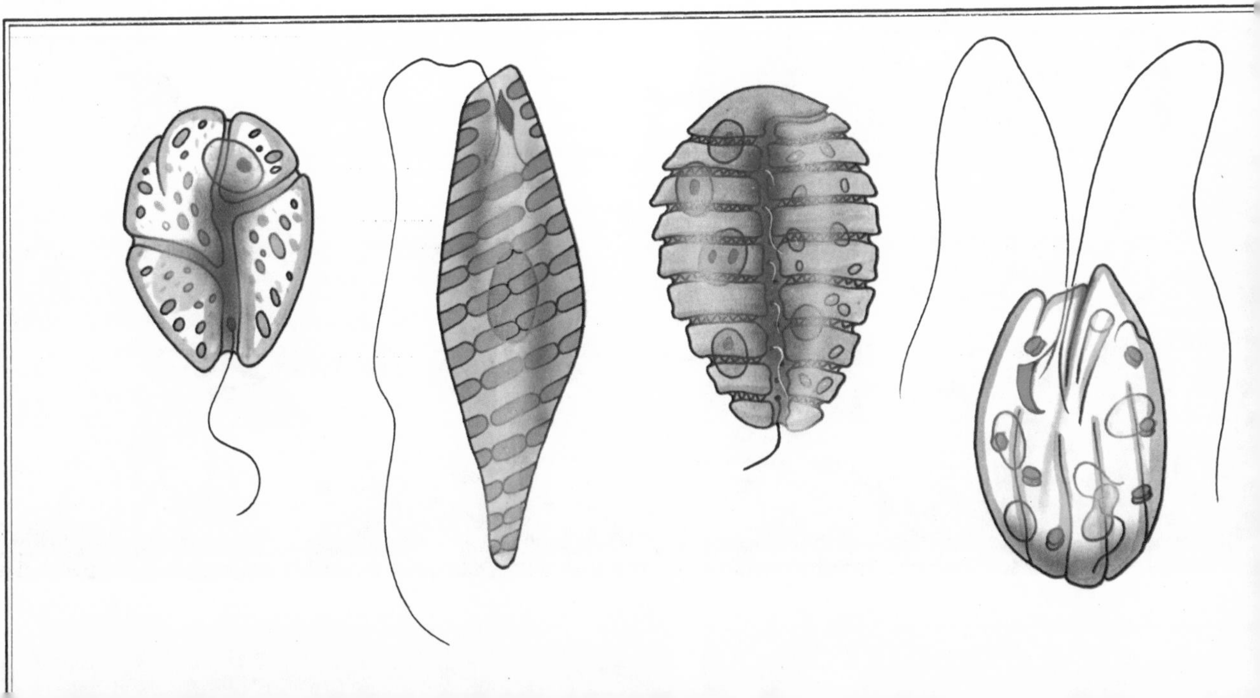

Seaweed

There are three main kinds of seaweeds; the greens, the browns and the reds.

The most common kind of green seaweed is the sea lettuce. It is flat and thin, and resembles a lettuce leaf. It is common on mud flats.

Brown seaweeds are very common on rocky shores. As the tide goes out, bladderwracks or rockweeds are exposed. Their small air bladders enable them to float, so they are not damaged by the waves. Low down the shore and in deeper water grow the kelps. They are very long and some American kinds grow over 30 metres long. Extracts of kelps are used in making ice cream.

Red seaweeds are also quite common on rocky shores. Irish moss is one common kind and is used in making jellies. Many red seaweeds are eaten in countries like JAPAN. An important red seaweed is the CORAL seaweed which is coated in lime and helps to build coral reefs.

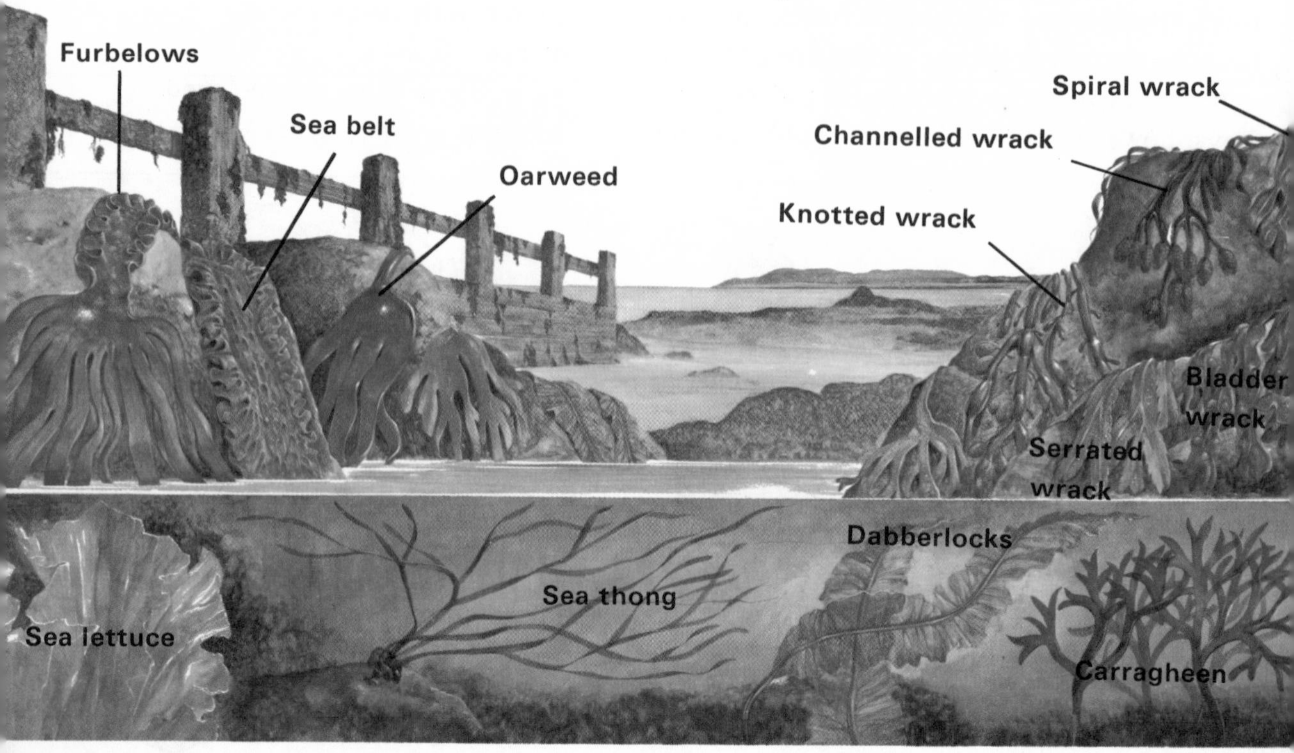

Above: Brown seaweeds cover the rocks and are often exposed when the tide goes out.
Below: Some types of seaweeds growing at their different levels on the seashore. A few seaweeds float freely in the water, but most are attached to rocks by suckers called holdfasts.

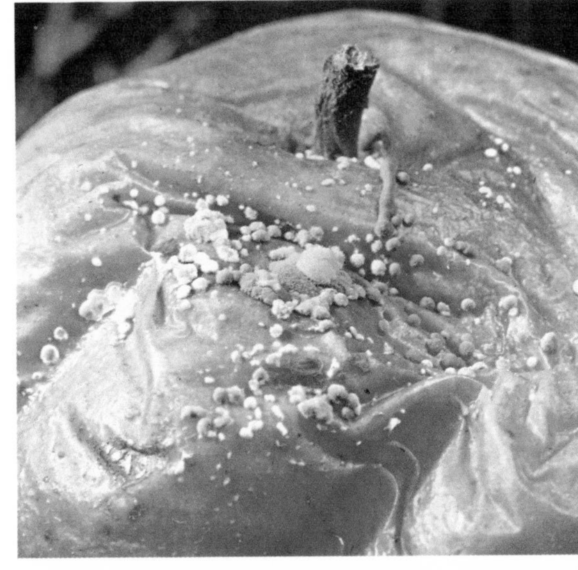

Mould

Moulds are often found growing on old bread, fruit, or leather. They make food unfit to eat and they ruin goods. Moulds are usually white or grey in colour, but they can also be blue, green, or yellow.

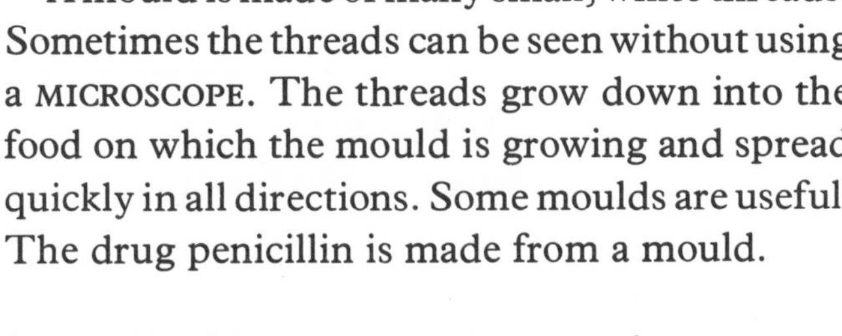

A mould is made of many small, white threads. Sometimes the threads can be seen without using a MICROSCOPE. The threads grow down into the food on which the mould is growing and spread quickly in all directions. Some moulds are useful. The drug penicillin is made from a mould.

Right: Mould growing on a rotten apple.

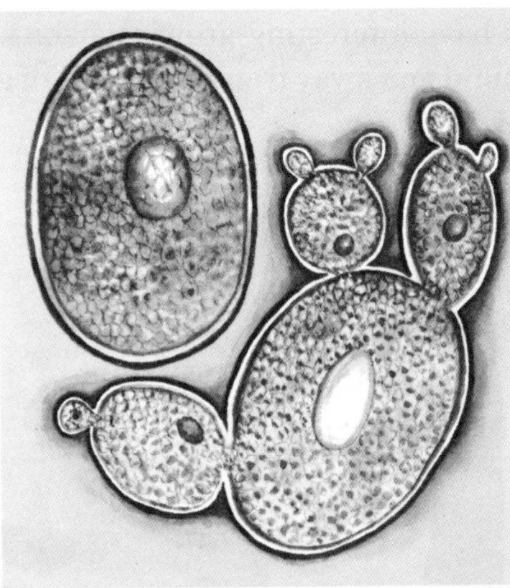

Yeast

Yeast is a single-celled plant. It grows very quickly and produces great numbers of CELLS. Each cell is too small to see without a MICROSCOPE.

Bakers and brewers use yeast to make bread rise or to make wines and beers.

Yeast can be bought as dried pellets, or fresh in greyish lumps. It is found growing on the skin of many fruits such as plums and grapes.

Left: Yeast multiplies by budding off new cells.
Below: Frothy yeast in a vat during beer-making.

Chanterelle

Mushrooms and toadstools

Most mushrooms and toadstools have a cap and a stalk. They grow from an underground mass of white threads which feeds on manure, dead leaves, or other buried food. They cannot make their own food.

The cap produces spores which grow into new plants. Both the cap and the stalk may be brightly coloured. They may have many different shapes and patterns. If you look under the cap you may see the gills, spreading out like the spokes of a wheel. The spores grow on these gills. Some toadstools look more like a sponge underneath. They have hundreds of tiny holes through which the spores fall.

Mushrooms have interesting growing habits. They grow around and away from the centre of a

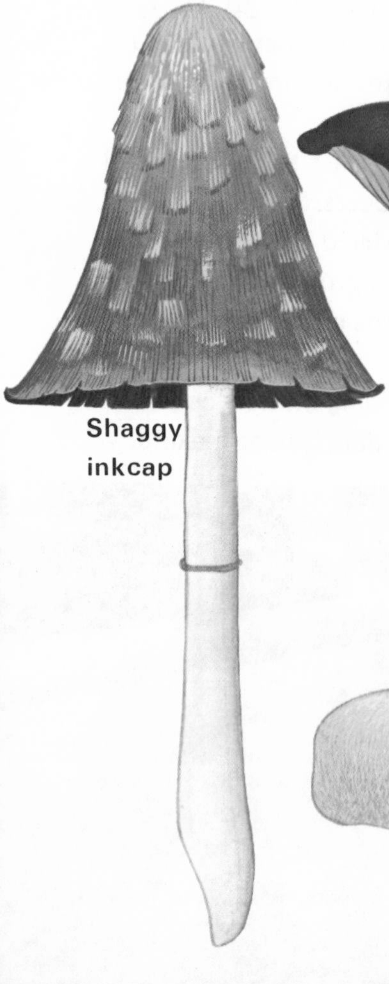

Shaggy inkcap

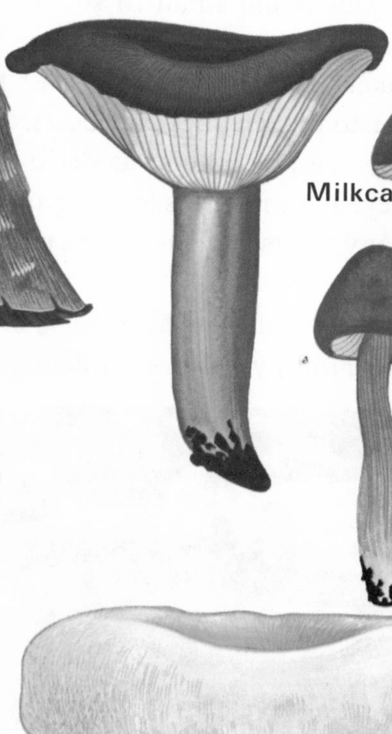

Milkcaps

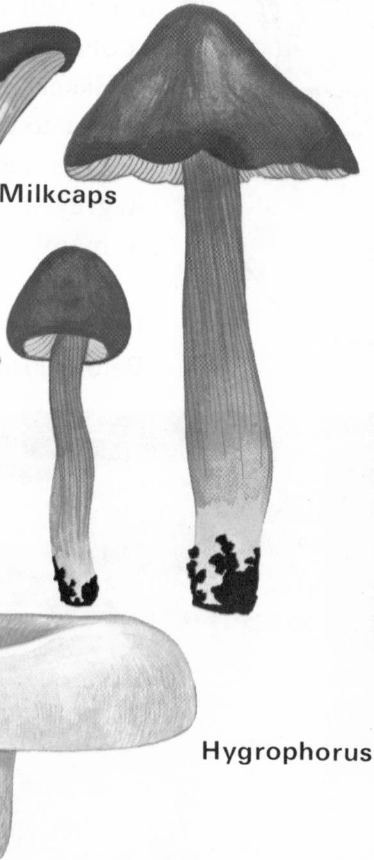

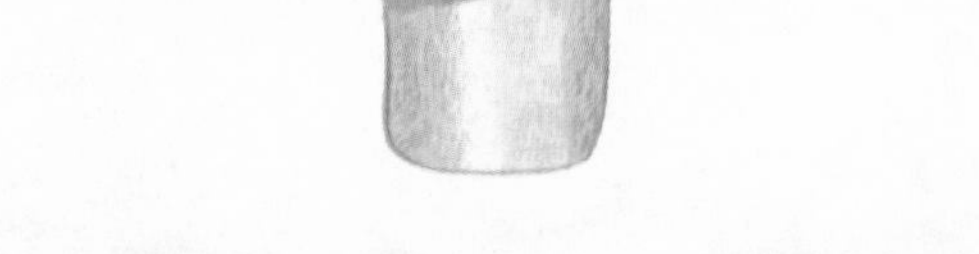

Edible mushroom

Hygrophorus

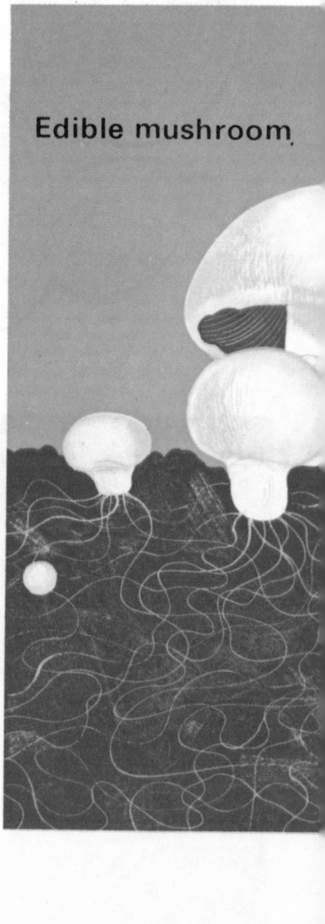

supply of food. The so-called fairy rings we sometimes see on lawns are really toadstools growing farther and farther away from the centre of the ring. Some fairy rings become 30 metres or more across. Some toadstools do not grow on the ground at all. They grow on old tree trunks and form shelf-like caps without stalks. These toadstools are called bracket fungi.

Both mushrooms and toadstools can grow very quickly and often appear overnight. Mushrooms are toadstools that are good to eat. Most toadstools taste unpleasant, and some are very poisonous. The DEATH CAP is the most poisonous of them all. The bright red fly agaric is also very poisonous. Several kinds of toadstool are shown on these pages.

Fly agaric

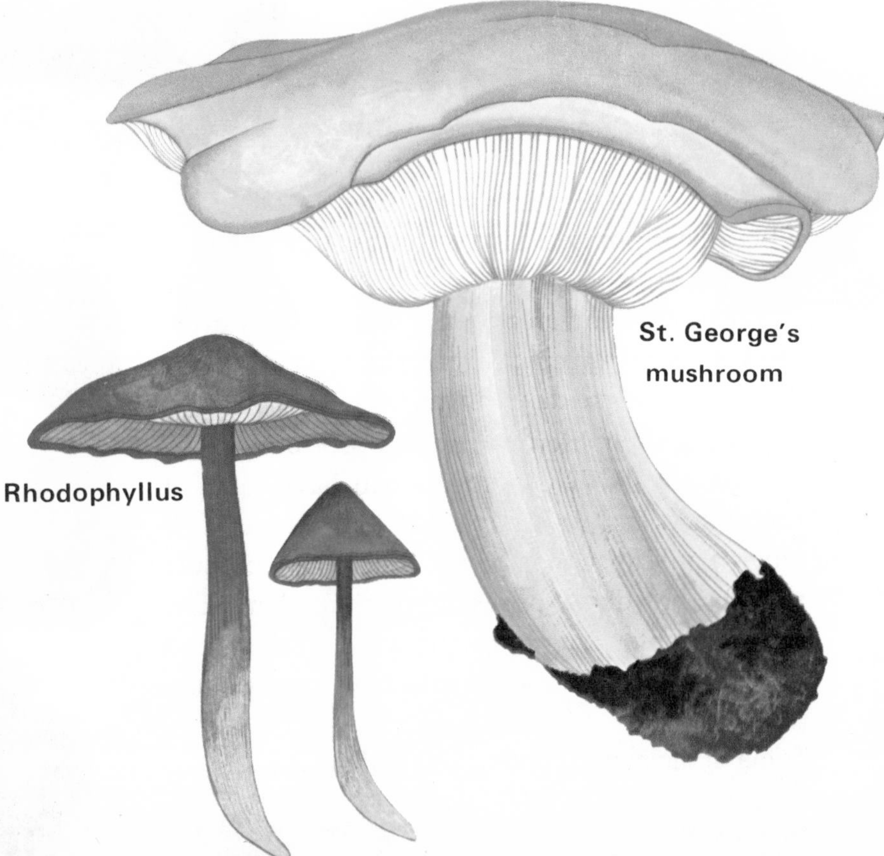

St. George's mushroom

Rhodophyllus

Lichens

There are about 15,000 different kinds of lichen. They are all small plants, but they differ greatly in colour and shape.

Lichens are hardy plants that grow quite slowly. Some grow as little as one or two millimetres each year. They are among the first plants to grow on bare surfaces such as roof tiles, walls, and tree trunks. Lichens can live on very little food and water. Some lichens can survive without water for over a year. But they grow best in damp climates.

Some lichens are used as food and others are used to make dyes.

Some lichens look like dry mould. Others have slender branches or leaf-like lobes.

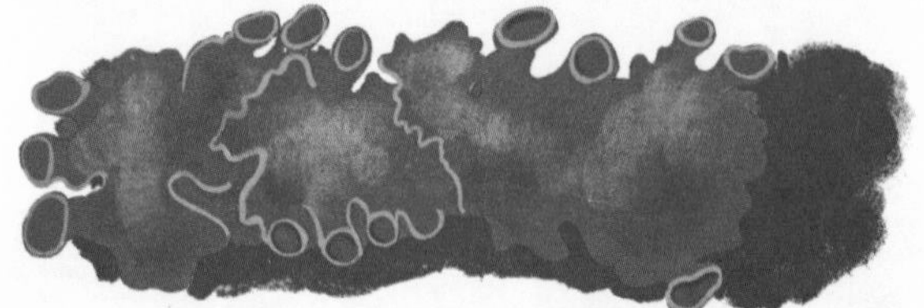

Mosses

Mosses are small plants with thread-like ROOTS. They have pointed LEAVES on an upright or a creeping STEM.

They are found all over the world. They grow in every kind of place from the tropics to the Arctic. They like damp areas best.

During their lifetime mosses produce a capsule on a stalk. This capsule can have teeth at the tip and is covered by a cap. The cap is shed when the capsule is ripe. Then the capsule releases powdery spores in dry weather. The spores are blown away by the wind. If they land in moist places they grow into new moss plants.

Some of the many different kinds of mosses.

Ferns

Most ferns are tropical, but they are found all over the world. Some grow as trees to a height of 20 metres. In EUROPE and NORTH AMERICA, they are much smaller and have LEAVES which grow up from an underground STEM.

The leaves are tightly curled up at first and uncurl as they grow. Each leaf is made up of a number of leaflets. These produce the spores which form new fern plants.

Ferns are commonly found in shady or damp places. Some, such as the water fern, float on the surface of LAKES and RIVERS.

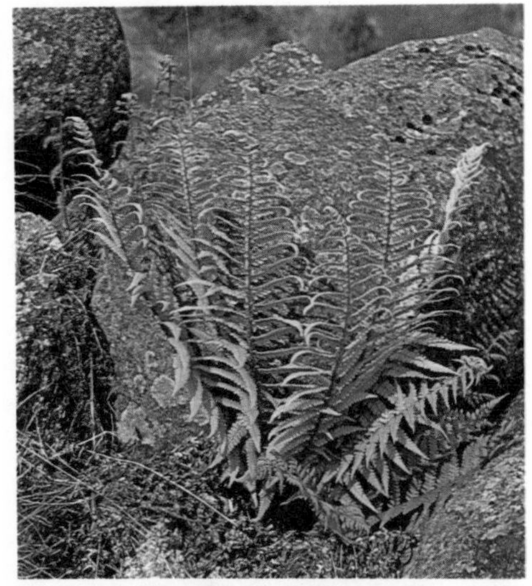

Above: Mountain Buckler fern.
Left: The curled young leaves of the male fern.
Below: The leaf or frond of a fern.

Horsetails

Horsetails have jointed, bushy STEMS which give them their popular name. The stems are very rough and were once used for cleaning pots and pans. Their LEAVES are very small and pointed.

The shoots are produced from a creeping, underground stem. At the tip of the stem is a small cone which releases minute spores. The spores are blown away by the wind and grow into new plants.

Horsetails are found all over the world except in AUSTRALIA and NEW ZEALAND.

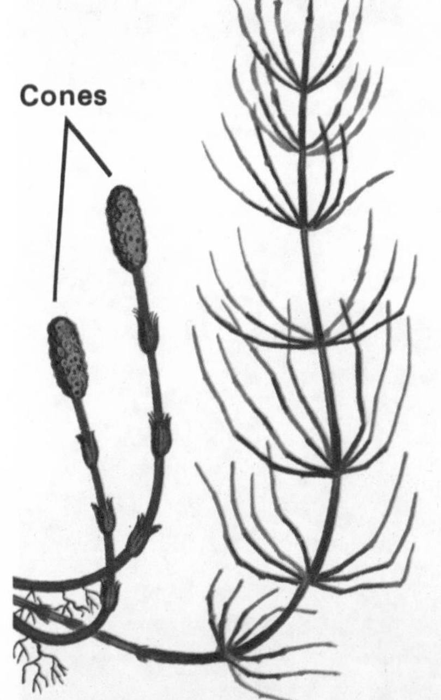

Horsetail shoots showing the little cones.

Fossil Plants

Above: A fossil leaf.
Below: Whole trees may become fossils. This trunk is in the Petrified Forest in Arizona.

During the history of the earth, many thousands of different plants have completely disappeared. The only record we have of them is as fossils, preserved by accident in COAL, ROCKS, peat or ice.

Our record of early plants is not complete. A great many types of plants have not been preserved. Dead plants usually decay easily like the leaves which fall in autumn. Only very rarely are plants preserved, and then only a small part of the whole plant may survive.

Plant fossils help us to discover the history of plant life. Experts can work out what the first plants looked like and how they changed. Fossils can also give us some idea of how long ago PINES and flowering plants first appeared. The history of plant life goes back over many hundreds of millions of years to a time when the earth was quite different. The fossils tell us something about what the earth was like then.

Fossil plants are also important in other ways. They have formed all the world's coal.

Early land plants

Plant life began in the seas. Only after many millions of years did plants start growing on the land. The early land plants had to survive the problems of living in dry air. It took a very long time for plants to spread all over the earth.

Many of the early land plants did not have LEAVES, but had bare, forked STEMS. The tips of the stems produced spores to make new plants.

Other early land plants had many small leaves and looked like some of the plants which still exist today.

The FERNS were among the most successful early land plants. Some of them grew to the size of very large trees. Some of these giant ferns still grow in NEW ZEALAND.

Many of the first plants which grew on land were quite different from the plants found today. Some, like the tree ferns, can still be found in tropical and sub-tropical countries.

Coal plants

About 250 million years ago, great forests covered the earth. Most of the plants that grew in these forests were not trees with cones or FLOWERS. They were kinds of giant HORSETAIL that grew as tall as the trees of today. Much of the land they grew on was swamp.

These plants died and fell into the swampy ground. As time passed, they became squashed under more dead trees. Over millions of years they turned into COAL. Many fossil plants can be found in coal. These fossils tell us what plants were like during earlier times.

The fossil horsetails had enormous, jointed STEMS up to 30 metres high. At each joint, branches grew out of the stem. Other large coal-age plants produced spores in cones. They did not, however, have jointed stems. The stems were covered in scars where LEAVES and branches had fallen off. In some cases only the very tip of the tall trunk had leaves and cones.

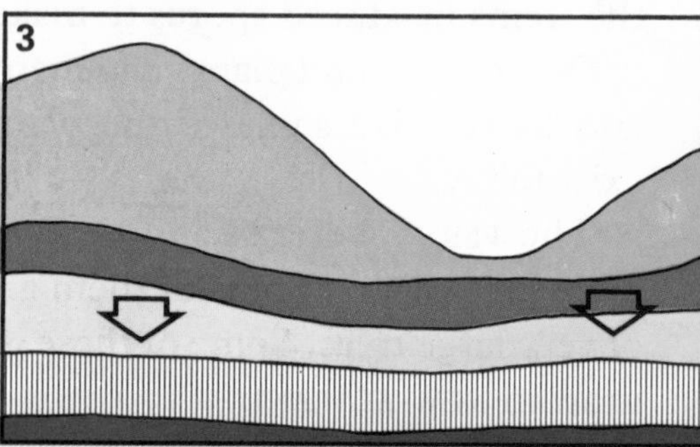

Above: Stages in the formation of coal.

Below: The Coal Age swamps were covered mainly by large horsetails.

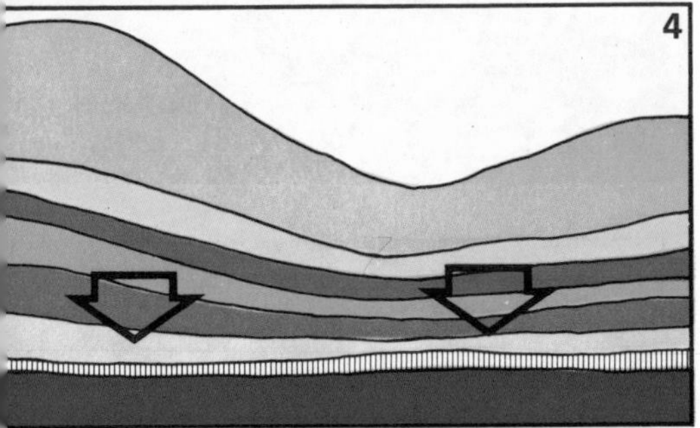

Below: A variety of early seed plants. Some, such as the thick-stemmed cycads, can still be found alive today.

Early seed plants

After millions of years the swamps of the COAL age disappeared. The climate became drier and warmer. This was the age of the DINOSAURS. The giant HORSETAILS died out, and plants that produced SEEDS took their place. These plants are cycads or false sago palms, and are relatives of the PINES and FIRS. A few of them are still found today in tropical countries. During the age of the dinosaur they were very common and many different kinds have been found as fossils.

Cycads all had thick STEMS. Their LEAVES were like those of palms or BANANAS. Some false sago palms were small, and none of them grew as tall as the trees of the coal age. They produced seeds in large cones, usually at the top of the plant.

Another kind of plant that became common towards the end of the coal age was the seed fern. Seed ferns were large plants with fern-like leaves but with seeds instead of spores. The flowering plants probably arose from seed ferns.

Where Plants Live

Over three-fifths of the earth's surface is covered by water. Yet large plants do not live in most of this water. It is too deep and not light enough. Most of the plants that do grow in the sea are very tiny and float near the surface.

The land is therefore a better place for flowering plants. But there are problems for plants living on land. One is water. Plants need water to grow, which they get mostly in the form of RAIN. Some plants, however, need a great deal of water. Others need very little.

Heat is another problem. Not all plants need

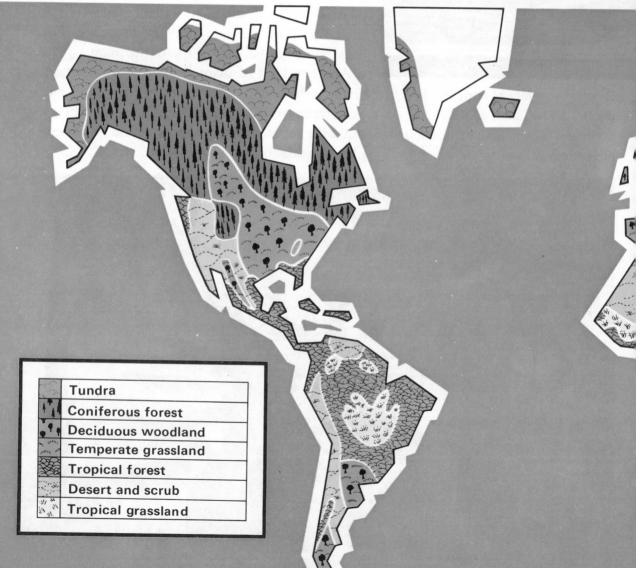

Tundra
Coniferous forest
Deciduous woodland
Temperate grassland
Tropical forest
Desert and scrub
Tropical grassland

the same amounts of heat in order to grow properly. The SOIL, which provides minerals as well as water, also affects plant life and growth.

The amounts of rainfall and heat vary from place to place. So does the makeup of the soil. For these reasons, different parts of the earth have their own kinds of plant life. The forests of tropical countries, for example, have very different plants from the forests of colder countries.

Far left: The lush vegetation of the tropics.
Left: The sparse tundra vegetation.

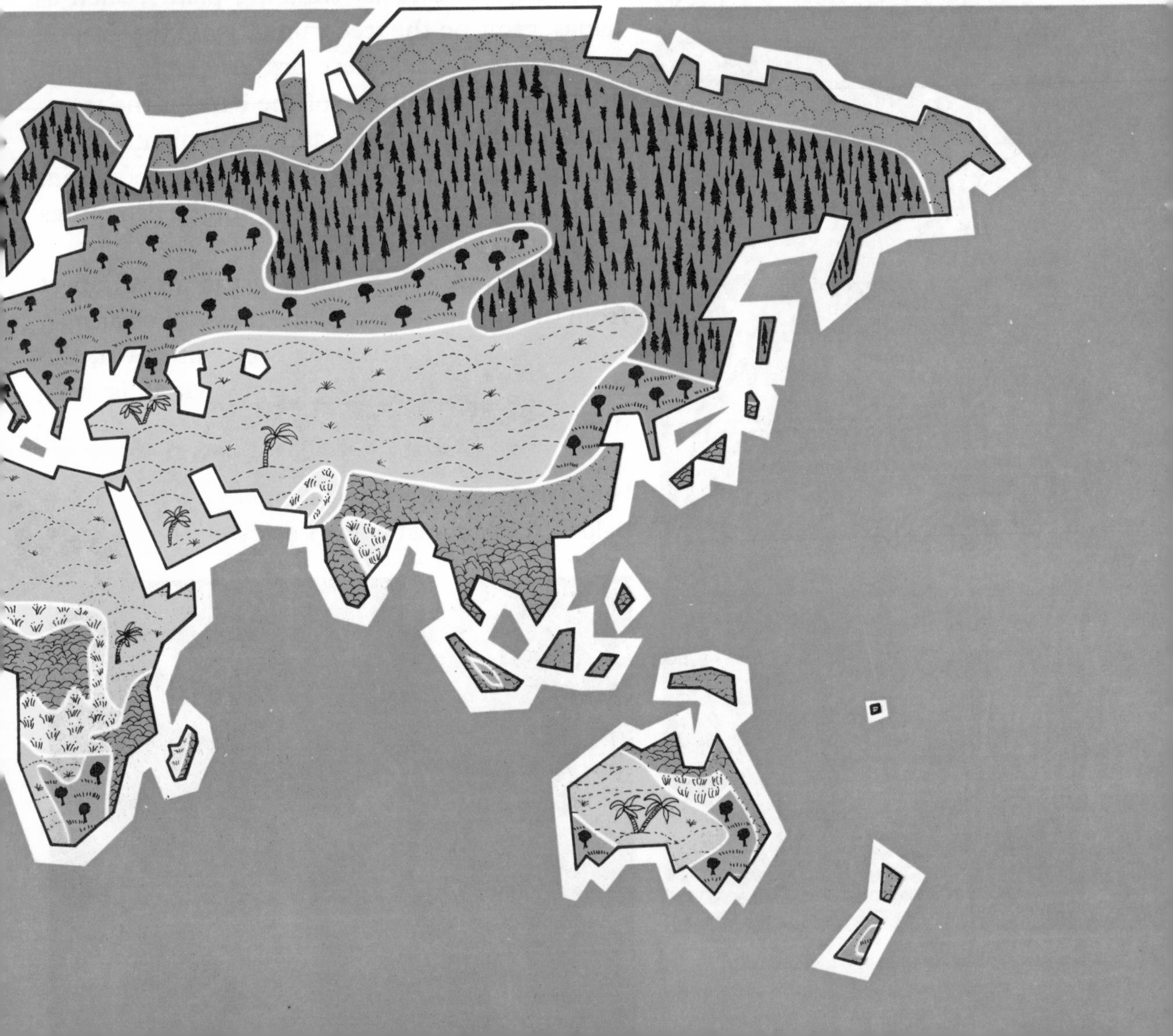

Tropical forests

Tropical forests are very hot and there is heavy RAIN most days. As the weather is like this month after month, the plants in these places grow very quickly.

Most trees in tropical forests are much taller than those in other types of forest. The LEAVES of the trees are usually broad. They are often split into many small parts called leaflets. It is easier for the light to get through between the leaflets to the lower leaves. This type of leaf is not so easily damaged by the heavy rain.

In tropical forests, climbing plants, such as lianas, grow on the tree trunks, from the ground to the tree tops. There are also many plants growing on the surface of the bark of the trees. These include orchids, and some plants of the pineapple family. These plants take no food from the trees. They get minerals from the droppings of birds and other animals.

Little grows on the floor of the forest, apart from the twisting roots of the trees. In clearings, where trees have fallen or been cut down, the undergrowth is often so thick that it is very difficult to walk through.

Left: The layers of a tropical forest.
Below: A rain forest in the tropics.

Deciduous woodland

Deciduous woods are common in places that have warm summers, and winters that are not too cold. They also need regular rainfall throughout the year. A few of the trees in them may be evergreens, such as HOLLY, but most of the trees have no leaves for at least one third of the year.

Some of these woods consist of only one main kind of tree. Others have a mixture of trees, with far more open spaces. The type of tree depends mainly on the SOIL.

There are usually plenty of small plants under the trees. The kinds of plants vary with the soil

Left: A plantation of oaks in winter.
Above: Beech trees in autumn.

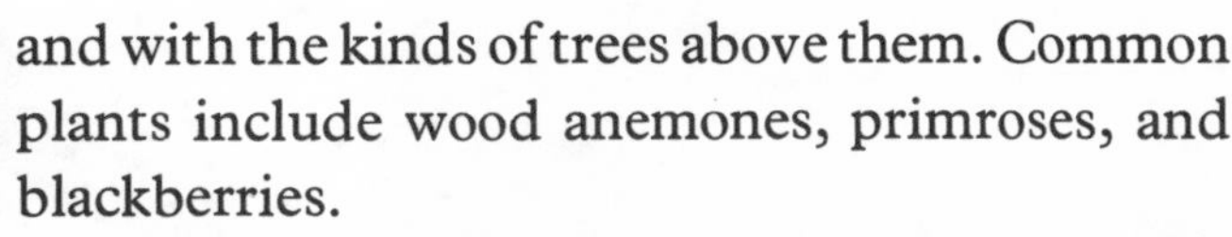

and with the kinds of trees above them. Common plants include wood anemones, primroses, and blackberries.

In BEECH woods very little light reaches the ground during the summer. Not many plants can live there. Those that do live there usually come up early in the year. They include bulbs such as snowdrops and bluebells. They flower and make their food before the beech leaves come out and cast their shade.

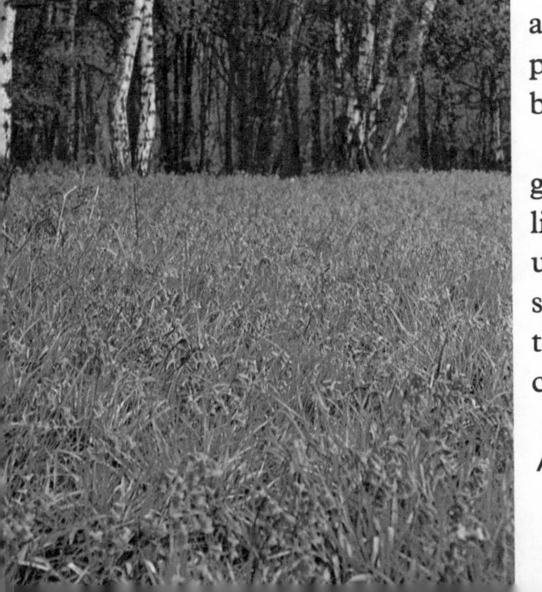

A carpet of bluebells in deciduous woodland.

Coniferous woodland

Coniferous woods are made up of PINES, and other trees with cones. Many of these trees are not affected by the cold, so they flourish in the north and on high mountains. They survive in dry conditions or poor soil.

Coniferous trees are usually tall. The lowest branches are very often dead or missing altogether. The trees therefore have straight trunks with all the leafy branches at the top. Natural woodlands are often quite open, and plenty of light can reach the ground. Small plants, especially FERNS, can grow on the ground beneath the trees. Heather is also very common.

Many coniferous trees, however, are specially grown for their wood in plantations. They are planted so close together that very little light gets in. Hardly any small plants can grow at all in these plantations.

The tough, needle-shaped LEAVES do not decay very quickly. They lie on the soil, which turns acid so that other plants may not be able to grow, even if there is enough light.

Right: A forest of Japanese larch.
Below: Coniferous forests on the Yukon, Canada.

Top: A North American prairie.
Above: Sisal plants (agaves) growing on the South American grasslands.
Below: The South African veldt.

Grasslands

Most of the world's grasslands are in the centre of continents, where the rainfall is too low to allow trees to grow. Grasslands have different names in different parts of the world. The savannas of AFRICA and many of the plains of SOUTH AMERICA are tropical grasslands. The prairies of NORTH AMERICA and the steppes of the U.S.S.R. are temperate grasslands.

The height of the grass in the different areas varies greatly. Much of the grass of the African savannas is very tall, often as high as four metres. It is called elephant grass. The grass of the prairies, however, is sometimes only a few centimetres high.

Many other plants grow among the grasses. Acacia trees and palms may grow on the slightly damper areas of grassland.

The grasslands of western EUROPE have been made by man and his domestic animals. Man cut down the original forests, and his SHEEP and CATTLE prevented new trees from growing by nibbling them off. The land then slowly turned into grassland.

Desert plants

The only water in the DESERT comes from a small amount of RAIN, DEW, and a little water deep underground. In some years there may be no rain at all.

The plants that can grow in the desert have all found ways of overcoming the lack of water. Some have very long ROOTS which can reach down many metres to the underground water. Other plants store water in their fat stems. These plants do not have LEAVES, which would allow some water to escape. Instead, they have spikes to protect themselves from animals looking for water. These plants are mainly cacti. Travellers in the desert can get water from them.

Some plants with leaves lose them when the weather is very dry. They then turn brown and look dead. As soon as there is enough water for them however, they start to grow again and produce new leaves.

Other desert plants do all their growing while there is water. Then, in the dry season, they die. Their seeds can live, however, until water is again available.

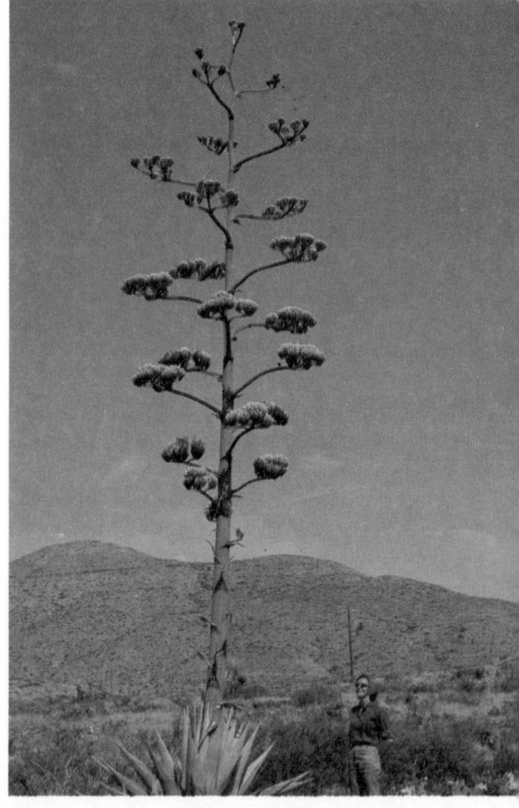

Above: The century plant, a long-lived plant of the American deserts.
Below left: Organ pipe cactus.
Below: The Joshua tree.

Mountain plants

Only small plants can grow high up on MOUNTAIN sides. The SOIL on high mountains is usually thin and poor. The plants are often covered by SNOW in winter. They also have to survive strong WINDS. Many of the plants form dense mats or 'cushions' very close to the ground. In this way they escape the worst of the wind and they also gain a certain amount of heat from the ground. Many of them are hairy and this also helps to keep them warm.

Most mountain plants have long ROOTS, which grow deep into cracks in the rock. Sometimes, they grow on banks of loose stones, called scree. Among the better-known mountain plants are the edelweiss, which has white and yellow flowers, the mountain pansy, and saxifrage.

Above: Alpine rhododendron.
Below: Silver thistle.

Tundra

Tundra is the name given to the cold, barren lands that surround the ARCTIC OCEAN. They are found in the far north of NORTH AMERICA, EUROPE, and ASIA, beyond the coniferous forests. The temperature rarely rises above ten degrees centigrade. The plants which grow there have to put up with poor SOIL, which is frozen for much of the year. They also have to survive strong WINDS. None of the plants is very large. Tundra plants grow very slowly because they have only a short time each year to make food.

LICHENS, such as reindeer moss, are the commonest plants. Some dwarf plants such as creeping birches and willows can also live in these areas. In the short summer, the tundra is transformed into a colourful 'carpet', as many plants hurriedly flower and set their SEEDS. Hundreds of little pools are formed by the melting snow.

Canadian tundra ablaze with colour in the summer.

Heath

Heaths are found mainly in EUROPE. Some have sandy SOIL which drains very easily and is dry for much of the year. Others grow on damp, peaty soils.

The most common plant found on heaths is the heather. Like many heath plants, it is small and grows by creeping over the soil. Bracken and gorse are other plants commonly found on heaths.

PINES and BIRCHES can thrive on the heathland, but few other trees can survive on the acid SOIL.

Grey LICHENS, looking like miniature bushes, often spring from the ground or from the heather stems. The insect-catching sundew plant grows on many of the damper heaths.

Heathland in summer. Heather covers much of the ground, but there are also a number of silver birch trees.

Bog

Bogs are wet, swampy areas of land. They are formed where there is high rainfall and very poor drainage. Some bogs are like quicksand and can trap a person walking across them. Most bogs are not dangerous, however.

Bogs are made up largely of peat. Peaty SOIL comes from dead plants that have not been completely broken down, as in normal soil. All bogs are acid and only certain plants can grow on them. The most common bog plant is the peat MOSS, or sphagnum, which is used by gardeners both to improve the soil and to pack plants.

The remains of forests are often preserved in bogs.

A bog, composed of peat moss (sphagnum) and dotted with pools. The white spots are the fluffy seeding heads of the cotton grass.

Freshwater plants

There are many different kinds of freshwater plants. Some live completely under the water. Others are rooted in the SOIL below the water and send their LEAVES and FLOWERS up above the surface of the water. Still others float entirely in the water, with only their flowers above the surface.

Small freshwater plants that grow in streams and rivers are often in danger of being washed away by flowing water. The larger plants are anchored to sand, soil, or stones. Even though plants in LAKES and ponds are not threatened by flowing water, many of them are anchored to the soil. Water lilies, for example, have STEMS and ROOTS growing in the mud. They send up leaves to float on the surface.

Some freshwater plants float completely on the surface, where they get plenty of light, air, and water. Sometimes these plants cover the entire surface of the water. They make it difficult for other plants to live. The water hyacinth, for example, can smother the surface of lakes.

Above: The water lily holds its beautiful flowers up clear of the water.
Below: Water plants may float freely or root in the mud.

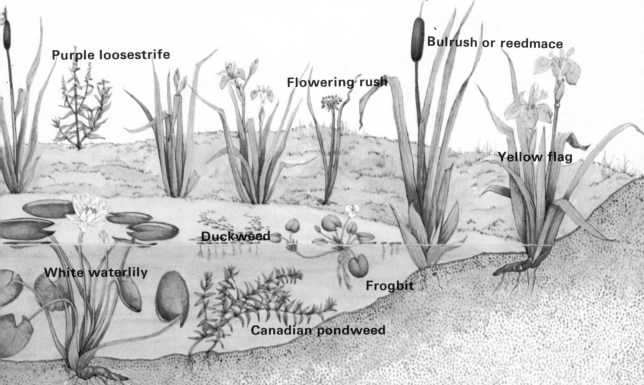

Plants We Eat

Most of the plants eaten by man have flowers. The only plants without flowers which we use as food are MUSHROOMS, some SEAWEEDS, and the SEEDS of a few PINE trees.

Most food plants come from just a few families. The most important is the family which includes GRASSES and CEREALS.

The palm family is also important. It provides us with DATES, coconuts, and many other foods. The PEA and BEAN family also gives us a great many food plants. The ROSE family includes APPLES, plums and pears. The CABBAGE family also contains a number of important food plants. POTATOES, tomatoes, and peppers all come from one family, and CITRUS FRUITS from another.

Different parts of different flowering plants are used as food. For example, apples and tomatoes are fruits, peas are seeds, while cabbage and spinach are leaves. Rhubarb and celery are leaf stalks, CARROTS and beetroot are roots, and potatoes and YAMS are stems.

Above: Some popular fruits and vegetables.

Below: Man has carried several food plants from their native homes and grown them elsewhere. Not all the 'journeys' are shown.

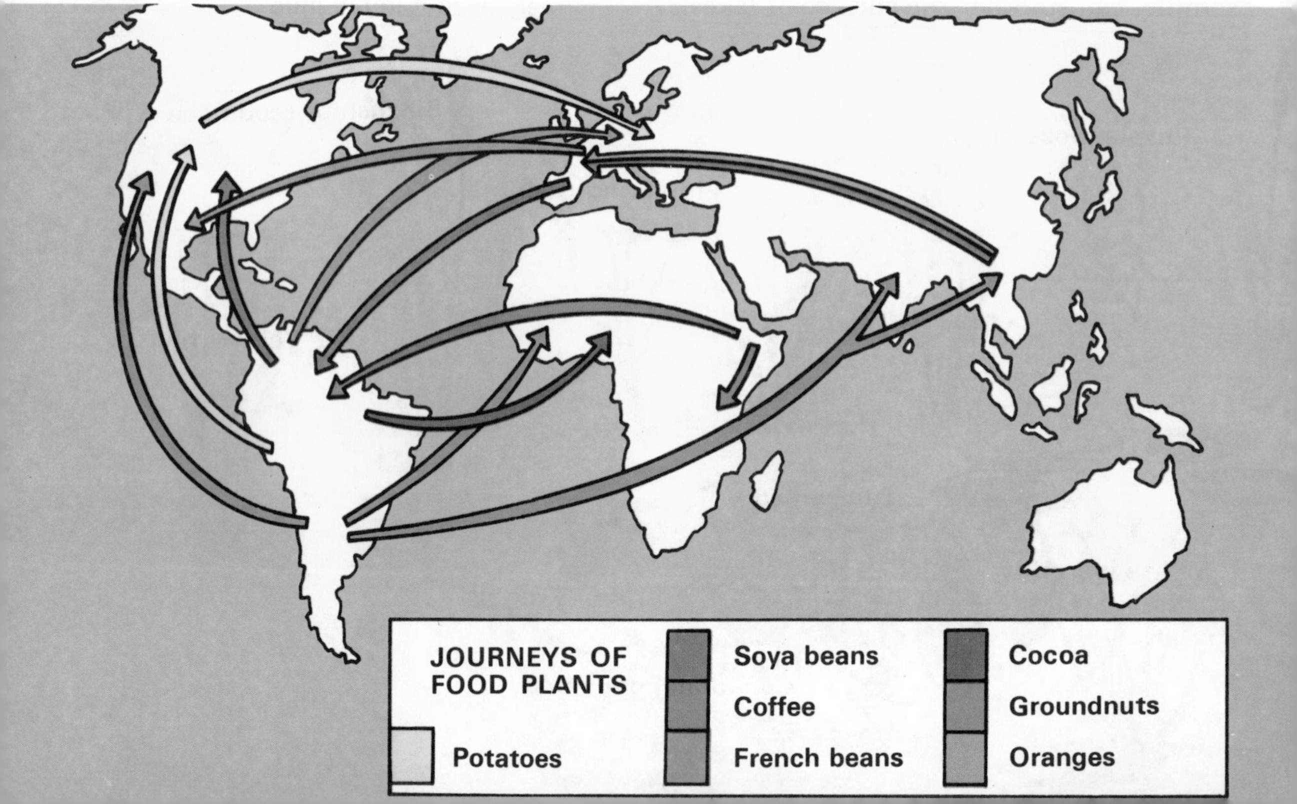

JOURNEYS OF FOOD PLANTS

Potatoes

Soya beans

Coffee

French beans

Cocoa

Groundnuts

Oranges

Carrots and other roots

ROOTS, like underground STEMS, are used by plants to store their food. A large number of plants are grown by man for the food contained in their roots.

The carrot has a red or orange tap root. This contains much sugar and many vitamins. The shape of the root varies a great deal.

Parsnips have large yellowish roots with a strong smell and taste. They have been grown for food since Roman times.

The turnip and swede are very similar, having round tap roots which are white or purple in colour. One difference between them is that the swede has a long neck bearing several leaf scars.

Top right: Autumn King carrots.
Above: The rounded roots of the swede.
Right: Sugar beet roots. The roots are shredded up and boiled to extract the sugar.

Radishes were first grown in EGYPT over 2,000 years ago. Most radishes have small round red roots with a strong taste. They are eaten raw in salads.

The beetroot, like the SUGAR BEET, contains a large amount of sugar. The root is usually round and purple.

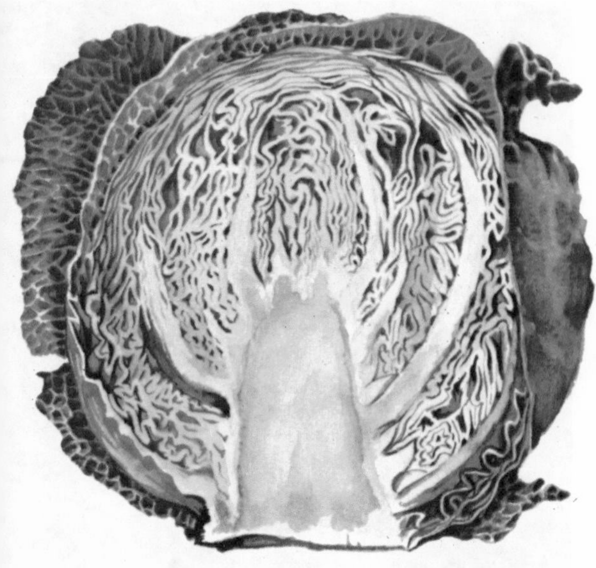

Cabbages

The cabbage was first eaten by the ANCIENT GREEKS and the ROMANS. All the cabbages we eat today have probably come from the wild cabbage which is found by the sea in many parts of EUROPE.

The part we eat is a very large bud made of many LEAVES tightly packed together. The inner leaves are usually pale green or have no colour because the light can not reach them.

Some other types of cabbage are kale, brussel sprouts, and savoy. The cauliflower is also a form of cabbage in which food is stored in young flowers.

Above: A cabbage cut in half to show the tightly packed leaves.
Right: Kale, a leafy type of cabbage widely used for feeding cattle and sheep.
Below: Wild potatoes are much smaller than cultivated ones.

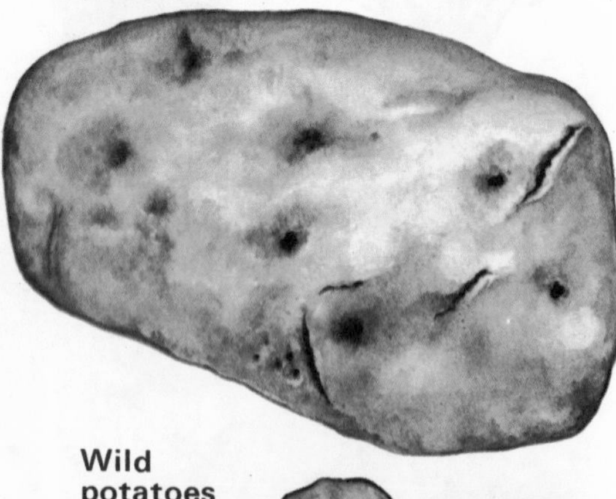

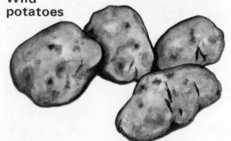

Potatoes

Potatoes come from SOUTH AMERICA, where they have been used as food for 2,000 years.

Part of the STEM of the potato plant grows underground and branches out like a ROOT. The ends of these branches are swollen into tubers. It is these tubers which we eat as potatoes. They contain a lot of starch.

On the surface of the potato there are small buds, called eyes. These eyes grow into new shoots if the potato is not dug up and eaten. Each shoot then produces more tubers.

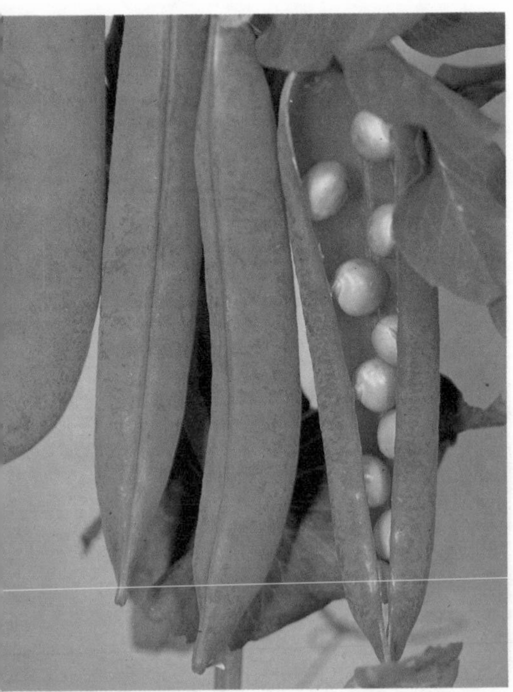

Peas and beans

The FRUITS of pea plants and bean plants are called pods. Inside the pods are the SEEDS, which are the part we usually eat. With many beans, such as kidney beans, we eat the pod as well.

Pea plants have white flowers. Their leaves end in curled-up tendrils, and these coil round supports such as sticks and help to hold the plant up. There are many different kinds of peas, some big and some small.

Some bean plants grow very tall and need sticks to climb on. Others grow close to the ground. All the different kinds of beans have long, thin pods. Runner beans and kidney beans come from SOUTH AMERICA and have red or white flowers. One of the most important is the haricot bean.

Broad beans grow in fat, bright green pods. Their flowers are white with black spots. Butter beans and mung beans, used in Chinese cooking, belong to the runner bean family. Some kinds of beans are used to feed CATTLE.

Above: The peas we eat are the seeds of the plant.
Below: French beans (left) and runner beans. We eat the seeds *and* the pods of both these beans.

Sugar cane

Sugar cane is a large kind of grass cultivated in many countries for its sugar. It grows best in tropical countries such as INDIA and the West Indies, but is also planted in the U.S.A., SPAIN, and AUSTRALIA.

The sugar is found in the STEMS, which are squashed to remove the juice. Brown sugar and molasses, or treacle, are made from this juice. The brown sugar can be treated again to give pure white sugar and golden syrup.

Above right: Cutting sugar cane by hand in the West Indies.
Above: Carrying the canes out by train.
Below: Harvesting sugar beet.

Sugar beet

Sugar beet is a kind of beetroot, but its ROOT is white rather than dark red. This root is swollen, like a CARROT, and can be as much as 30 centimetres long.

Each beet yields a large amount of sugar. After growing from six to nine months underground, the beet is dug up. The root is then cut into pieces. The pieces are boiled in water to remove the sugar.

Sugar beet is cultivated in many countries of EUROPE, and in the U.S.A. and CANADA. It is grown in places where the weather is too cold to grow SUGAR CANE.

Yams and sweet potatoes

Yams and sweet potatoes take the place of the ordinary POTATO in many tropical countries. They are full of starch and other food. Yams are swollen underground stems, but sweet potatoes are swollen roots rather like DAHLIA roots.

Yams are much larger than potatoes and have a brown, cracked skin. They are mainly grown in West AFRICA, South-east ASIA, the West Indies and PACIFIC Islands. They must be boiled before eating to destroy a poison which they contain.

Sweet potatoes originally came from SOUTH AMERICA, but they are now also grown in the U.S.A. and CHINA. They are about the same size as potatoes, but have a purple or white skin. Sweet potatoes are usually cooked by boiling, and have a slightly sweet taste, as their name suggests.

Top: Sweet potatoes came originally from South America.
Left: Yams in Tamale market, Ghana.
Below: A date palm showing the dates hanging in large bunches near the top of the tree.

Date palm

Most dates come from hot and dry parts of North AFRICA, the Middle East, and INDIA. They are the FRUITS of the date palm, which grows to a height of 25 metres and lives for about 80 years. The trees are either male or female. The dates grow on the female trees, which give between 40 and 60 kilos of fruit each year.

The dates grow at the top of the tree in large bunches which hang down below the LEAVES. Each date has a very hard, long SEED in the middle. It can be planted and grown as a pot plant. The dates contain a lot of sugar which provides plenty of energy.

Apples

More apples are eaten today than almost any other kind of fruit. The first apples eaten by man were crab apples. These are grown today in gardens for their colour and for making jam. They are also found wild in hedges.

There are many other types of apple. Cooking apples are usually large and need sweetening with lots of sugar. Eating apples range from the very sweet red ones, such as 'The Delicious' and 'Beauty of Bath', to the harder, sharper-tasting ones such as 'Granny Smith' and 'The Northern Spy'.

Apples are easy to store, and so they can be obtained all the year round. Something like 20 million tons of apples are sold each year, most of them coming from Europe.

Left: Loading a bin with apples in an orchard.
Below: A banana plantation in Queensland, Australia. Notice the huge leaves of the banana plants.

Bananas

The banana is grown in tropical countries. Bananas are an important food crop. Those we buy in shops are in small bunches, called hands. These are only small parts of the enormous bunches which grow on the banana tree. A bunch may have as many as 200 bananas.

The bananas we eat are cut from the tree before they are ripe and while the skins are still green. They slowly ripen and turn yellow on their journey to other countries.

The banana tree is not really a tree at all. Its 'trunk' consists of LEAF stalks, and not wood. The leaves and fibres from the plant are used for making roofing material, and for mats, bags, and baskets.

Citrus fruit

Oranges, lemons, grapefruit, limes, and tangerines are some of the many different citrus fruits. They are all really berries with thick skins. They come from shrubs or small trees in tropical or warm countries.

Sweet oranges are grown in many countries, including the U.S.A., ISRAEL, and SOUTH AFRICA. These oranges are eaten fresh or used to make orange juice. The Seville, or bitter, orange comes from SPAIN and is used to make marmalade.

Kinds of citrus fruit. Oranges (top), Grapefruit (above left), Lemon (above).
Below left: Lime saplings in a nursery in Ghana.

The lemon has a very sharp taste and the juice is used in cooking. It is grown mainly in ITALY, Spain, and California. The fruit of the lime tree looks like a very small, green lemon. It also tastes something like a lemon.

The grapefruit looks like a large yellow orange, but it is not as sweet. Large numbers of grapefruit are grown in North and Central America and South Africa.

Tangerines resemble small oranges and are also very sweet. The tree can live in slightly colder countries than the orange tree. It is grown in the United States and Southern EUROPE.

Tea

Tea is made from the LEAVES of a small tree grown in ASIA. The trees are cut back to make bushes so that the leaves can be picked easily. Only the leaves from the tips of the shoots are removed. Tea leaves are usually picked by hand, but now machines also do this work.

As soon as the leaves have been picked, they are taken to a factory where they are specially treated. During the treatment they are broken into small pieces and turn black. They are then packed in wooden tea-chests lined with metal foil, and sent off to other countries.

Tea is a very popular drink in at least half the countries of the world. CHINA grows the most tea, but the Chinese people use nearly all of it themselves. INDIA and Sri Lanka also produce large crops of tea. The best quality tea comes from the mountain regions of India. It is now also grown in parts of East AFRICA.

Above: The leaves of the tea plant. Below: Picking tea leaves by hand in Sri Lanka. Only young leaves are picked.

Coffee

About one-third of the people in the world drink coffee. It comes from the fruits of a small tree grown in parts of SOUTH AMERICA and AFRICA, especially in BRAZIL and KENYA.

The fruits are small red berries which usually contain two seeds, which we call coffee beans. A machine removes the beans from the berries. Then they are dried in the sun.

The beans have to be roasted and ground to a powder before they can be made into a drink.

Right: A woman with a child on her back, picking coffee beans in Kenya.

Above: Workers spreading cocoa beans out on a drying floor.

Below: A cacao tree with its pods.

Cocoa

The cocoa powder used for making drinks and chocolate comes from the SEEDS of a small tree grown mainly in West AFRICA. The tree, called the cacao tree, needs a lot of RAIN and a rich SOIL.

The seeds, called beans, grow inside a large pod about 15 centimetres long. Flowers and pods hang down from the main trunk of the tree.

Cocoa beans are cooked and then dried by the heat of the sun before the cocoa is removed.

Grasses and Cereals

There are about 10,000 different kinds of grass. The grass family is one of the largest and most important groups of flowering plants. It includes the ordinary grasses as well as the cereals and the BAMBOOS. The grasses of fields and slopes are important because they help to stop the SOIL from being washed away by the rain. They are also important as food for farm animals.

The cereals are the grasses which provide us

Above: The large grasses called reeds are still used to make thatched roofs in many places.
Right: Various kinds of grasses. Their flowers are small and have little colour.

with much of our food. Bread, cakes, RICE, spaghetti, and macaroni are made from cereals. Some are used to make beer and other alcoholic drinks. SUGAR CANE is another grass which provides us with food. Bamboos are mainly giant, tropical grasses. Some grow very quickly. They are important building materials in some countries.

Grasses have other uses such as making perfumes, paper, hats, mats, and ropes. Some grasses are also used to make thatched roofs.

Hay

Many grasses are an important food for farm animals and HORSES. Hay is dried grass, cut in the summer and dried by the heat of the sun. In some countries the hay is dried on special wooden frames.

During the winter, when the grass grows very little, the animals are fed on hay. The hay contains most of the food found in fresh grass. Special grasses are often sown in the hay fields to make sure that good quality hay is grown.

Grass is often stored in silos without being dried out. Then it is called silage. It has a strong smell, but it is just as good for animals as fresh grass. It is often used in place of hay.

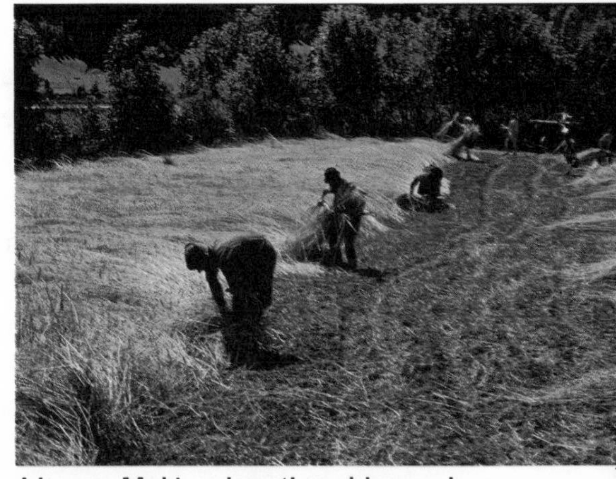

Above: Making hay the old way, by hand. It is now usually done by machine.

Below: Some common hay grasses.

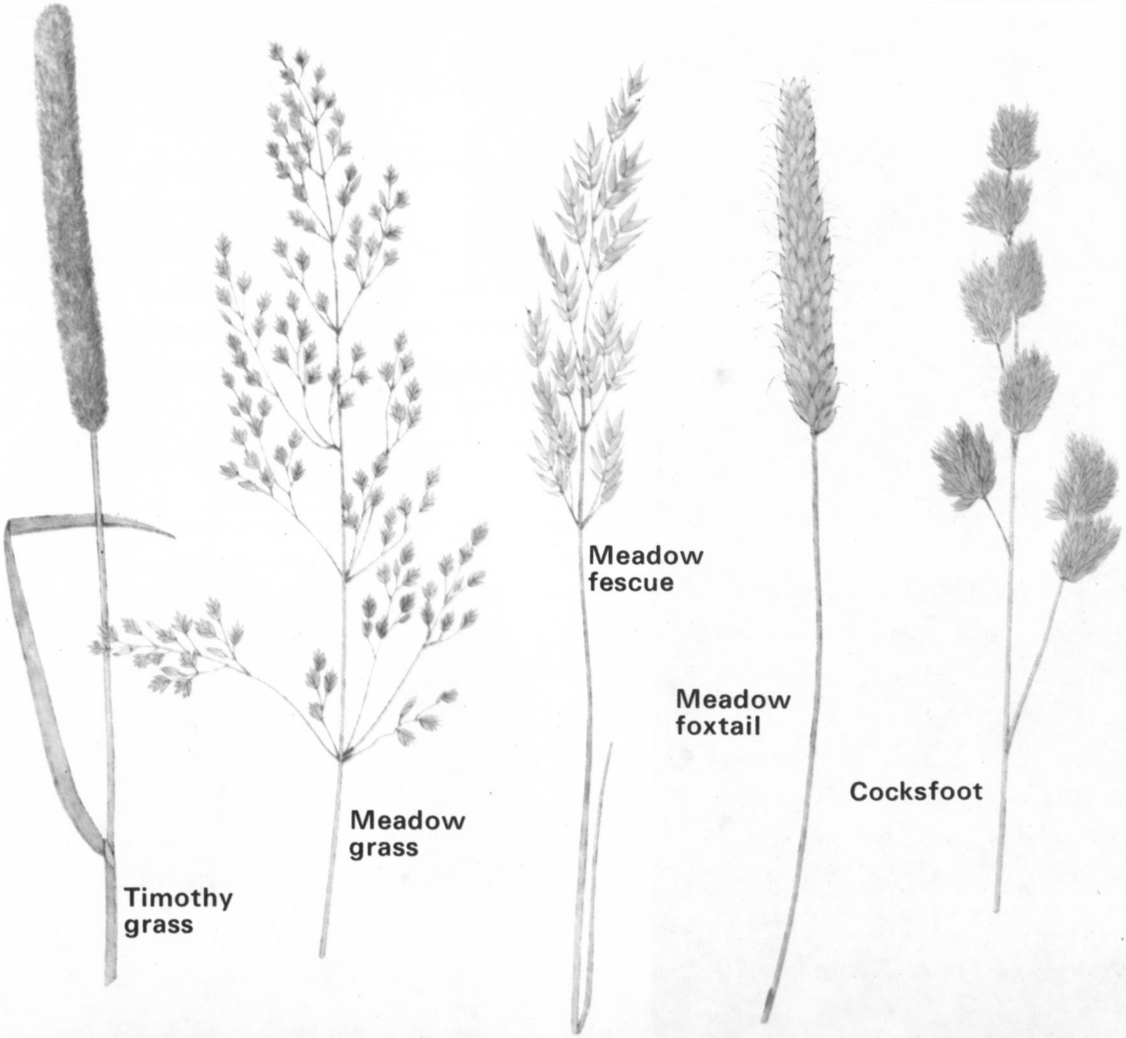

Timothy grass

Meadow grass

Meadow fescue

Meadow foxtail

Cocksfoot

Bamboo

The bamboos are the largest grasses known. Some grow to a height of 30 metres with stems of up to 20 centimetres thick.

Bamboos are used in tropical countries to build houses and boats. Furniture and paper can also be made from bamboos.

A lot of bamboo shoots are eaten in East ASIA. The shoots are thick and pointed, growing from an underground stem. They are picked when young and eaten after they have been boiled. The shoots can also be pickled for storing.

Millet

Below: Bamboos grow in dense clumps. The stems are hollow and have many uses.

Millet

There are many different kinds of millet grown around the world. Millets do not grow well in harsh northern climates, but they prosper in very dry SOILS.

Millets have smaller grains than other cereals. They are used as food for humans in parts of ASIA and EUROPE, where they are ground into flour. In CANADA and the U.S.A., millets are mainly used as animal food. Ground millet seeds are fed to livestock, POULTRY, and other birds.

Below: Red sorghum is mainly a tropical crop, used for making beer and for feeding animals.

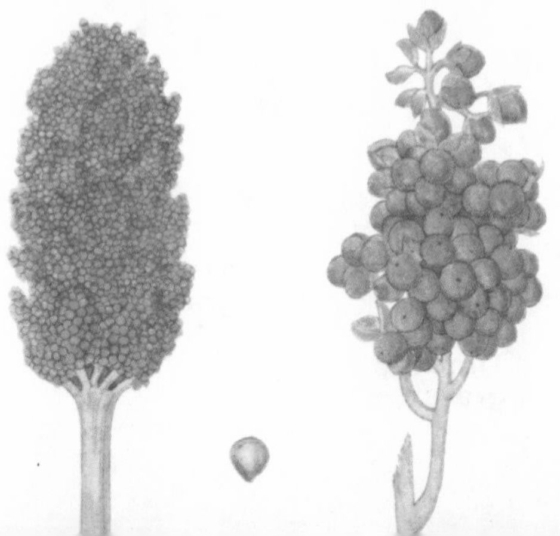

Rice

Rice is the main food of about half of the world's population. It is eaten mainly in ASIA, particularly in INDIA and CHINA. The rice plant comes from Asia, but it is now grown in parts of EUROPE, particularly in ITALY. It is also grown in the U.S.A.

Rice plants are grown in flooded fields. These are called paddy fields. The rice is sometimes planted from seeds, but is often planted as seedlings. The plants grow to between one and two metres in height. When the rice plants are ripe, the fields are drained. The plants are then gathered, usually by hand. It takes about four months to produce a crop of rice.

After the rice plants have been picked, they are beaten to release the hard white grains which we eat. They contain a great deal of starch. Rice can be made into flour. It is also sometimes used as a food for animals.

Right: Rice originally grew in lowland swamps. In hilly regions it is grown on flooded terraces cut out from the hillsides.

Maize

Cooking oil, corn-flakes, cornflour, and corn-on-the-cob are some of the uses for maize or sweet corn. As with other cereal crops, it is the fruit or grain which is eaten.

The plant grows to a height of two or three metres. It has large, bright green leaves. Male flowers are found at the top of the plant. Female flowers grow lower down and produce the 'cobs', which have many fruits.

Maize came originally from America, but it is now grown all over the world.

Ripe cobs of corn or maize. The individual fruits or grains can be clearly seen.

Wheat

Wheat is the most important cereal crop grown in temperate countries. The fruits of the plant, known as grains, are ground up to make flour.

Wheat was one of the first cereals to be cultivated. It came originally from western ASIA and several wild forms still live there. Many cultivated varieties now exist.

One type of wheat – bread wheat – is used for making bread and cakes. It is grown on a vast scale in many countries.

Another type of wheat – durum or macaroni wheat – is important in the making of pasta for spaghetti and macaroni. Its flour is much stickier than that of the bread wheat. It is also grown in many countries, but mainly in drier regions.

The ear of wheat is made up of plump grains, normally without any whiskers or awns.

Rye

Rye is one of the most important cereal crops grown in colder countries. It is planted in the northern parts of EUROPE where other cereals will not survive because of the cold. It is also widely grown in the U.S.S.R. It grows well on poor sandy SOIL. It does not become diseased as easily as WHEAT.

The grain is used for making black bread and rye bread. It is also used in the brewing of alcoholic drinks, such as whisky and beer. Rye is also grown in the Americas, where it is mainly used as food for animals, particularly HORSES. It also provides grazing for SHEEP and CATTLE.

The stems of the plant are used as straw for making hats and paper.

The ear of rye is rather similar to that of wheat, but the grains always possess awns.

Barley

Barley is an important cereal grain grown in many parts of the world. Only WHEAT, RICE, and MAIZE are more important.

Unlike those of other cereals, barley grains are fat and ridged. The ears of barley have long bristles called awns or beards.

Barley has been grown for thousands of years. Once it was commonly used for making bread. (WHEAT is now used instead.) Today barley has many uses. Huge quantities of it are fed to PIGS and other domestic animals. It is also used to make beer. First the grains are soaked in water, to make them start growing. Then they are dried to form what brewers call malt. YEAST is added to the malt to make beer.

Barley can be recognised by the long awns or whiskers. The ripe ears usually hang down.

Oats

Oats are mainly used as an animal food. They are not greatly used by man, except in the form of oatmeal and porridge. Porridge is very popular in Scotland, where good quality oats are grown. The U.S.A. and CANADA are the world's largest producers of oats.

The flower shoots are large and spreading, unlike other cereals such as WHEAT, RYE, and BARLEY. Oat grains are also longer and thinner than those of other cereals.

Wild oats look very similar to the cultivated crops but their grains are smaller. They grow as WEEDS in other cereal crops and are a serious problem. Cultivated oats were probably derived from them about 2,000 years ago.

Oats differ from most other cereals in not having their grains in ears or spikes.

Materials From Plants

At one time, man depended on plants for almost all his materials. Wood, PAPER, medicines, RUBBER, CORK, COTTON, oils, perfumes, and dyes are all made from plants.

Today there are many man-made alternatives to some of these materials. Many medicines and perfumes, for example, are now artificial. ROSES, lavender, and mint, however, are still important as natural perfumes. The use of wood in buildings has been partly replaced by the use of steel and concrete.

Over 2,000 different dyes can be made from plants. In the past these plant dyes were very important. Today, man-made dyes are common, and plant dyes are less often used. Madder (red), indigo (purple), and saffron (yellow), are among the most popular plant dyes.

The tannins, however, are still important. Many trees, such as the OAK, sweet chestnut, and wattle contain large amounts of tannin in their bark. Tannins are used to tan or cure animal skins. They were once used to make inks.

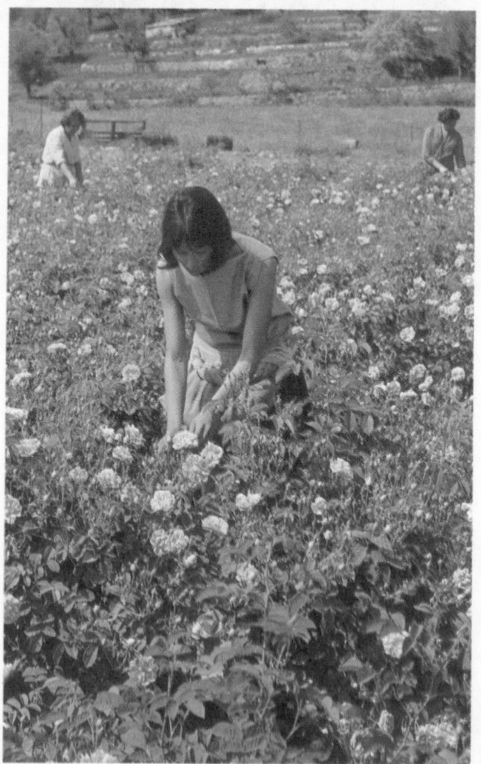

Plants provide many useful chemicals. Mint (top) is a source of menthol. Roses (right) and lavender (below) provide perfumes. Bark (below right) provides tannin when stripped from the trees.

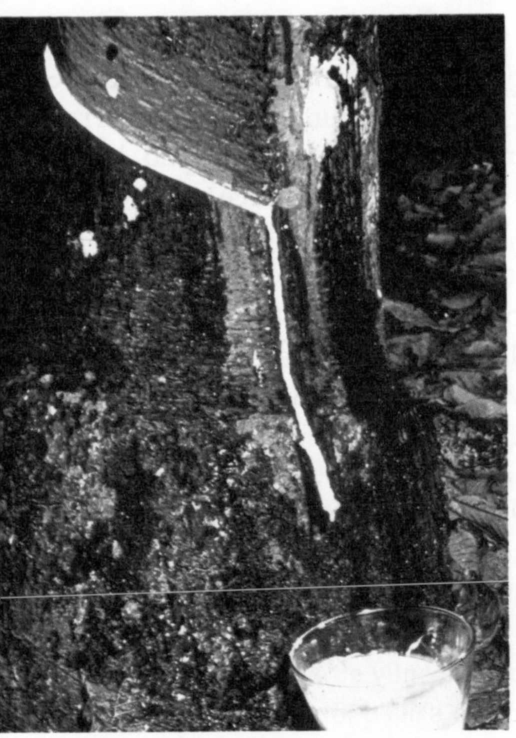

Rubber

There are two kinds of rubber used in the world today. One is natural rubber, which comes from the sap (juice) of a tree. The other is synthetic, or man-made, rubber, which can be made from OIL and other materials.

Rubber trees originally grew in the wild. Once natural rubber trees were found mostly in BRAZIL, but now most natural rubber comes from plantations in south-eastern ASIA.

Natural rubber – a sticky, milky liquid called latex – comes from the BARK of the tree. To obtain the latex, a man called a tapper cuts a slit into the bark of the tree. He fixes a small cup under the slit, and the latex drips into it.

When they are full, the cups of latex are taken away and treated in many ways. The latex hardens into a material called crude rubber. Ultimately, crude rubber is used to make tyres, boats, shoes, raincoats, and many other things.

The rubber plants that people grow indoors in pots are young india rubber trees. The rubber that comes from these plants is of little value.

Above and below: Rubber tapping: a slanting cut is made in the bark and the latex runs into a bowl. Below right: The familiar household rubber plant.

Cork

Cork is a spongy, light material which comes from the BARK of a tree found in many MEDITERRANEAN countries. SPAIN, PORTUGAL, and Algeria are the countries which produce most of the world's cork.

The cork tree is a type of OAK, but it is evergreen. The bark is stripped off the tree when it is 10 years old. More bark can be removed after another 10 years. Cork is made by boiling the bark to clean it.

Cork has a large number of uses, including floor and wall tiles. It is also used to make bottle stoppers. It contains a great deal of air, and therefore floats easily.

Left: A cork oak recently stripped of its outer bark. Cork stripping is a skilled job.

Cotton

Cotton has been used now for thousands of years. Although man-made fabrics have now partly replaced it, it is still one of our most important natural materials.

The cotton plant produces FRUITS which are large and fluffy. These are called bolls. The cotton SEEDS are hidden in the bolls. The bolls are picked by hand or machine and then treated in several ways to obtain pure cotton. The boll weevil is a small insect that attacks cotton plants. In the past it has done a lot of damage, and is still a danger.

Cotton plants need a warm, sandy SOIL and a lot of water. They grow best in the southern states of the U.S.A. and along the rivers of INDIA and EGYPT.

Examining the cotton bolls to see if they are ready for harvesting.

Jute

The coarse cloth used for making sacks is called hessian. It comes from fibres in the stem of the jute plant. This plant is grown mostly in INDIA. It is a tall annual, growing to a height of two to three metres, or even more.

The stems are 'retted' (left to rot) in water tanks for a few days and then beaten to remove the jute fibres. Afterwards, the fibres are washed, and then dried. They are specially treated so that the fibres can be woven. These fibres are often two metres or more in length. They are stiff and yellow but not very strong. Although used mainly for making sacks, the hessian is also used as backing for mats and 'lino'.

Left: Jute stems being harvested before the jute fibres are removed from them.

Sisal

Sisal comes from the LEAVES of plants called agaves. They are spiky, cactus-like plants. They came originally from the DESERTS of MEXICO, where they are still grown. Today sisal is also grown in other parts of the world, including AFRICA, and South-east ASIA.

The leaves are long and pointed and contain many long fibres. The fibres are removed from the leaves by hand or by machine. They are extremely tough. Hard-wearing mats and carpets are made from sisal. So are some kinds of rope.

Sisal leaves are cut a few at a time. Taking too many would weaken the plant: leaving too many would allow the plant to flower. It would then die, for agaves normally flower only once.

Cutting leaves from a sisal plant. Not all the leaves are removed at any one time.

Spices

Spices are plants used for flavouring food. Different parts of the various plants are used.

Vanilla is used in cooking and for flavouring ice cream. It comes from the seed pods of a tropical orchid, which are black when dry.

The cinnamon tree is grown mainly in Sri Lanka. The spice used in sweets and curries is the BARK of the young twigs.

Nutmeg can be bought as a nut or as a powder. It comes from a tropical tree which has fleshy

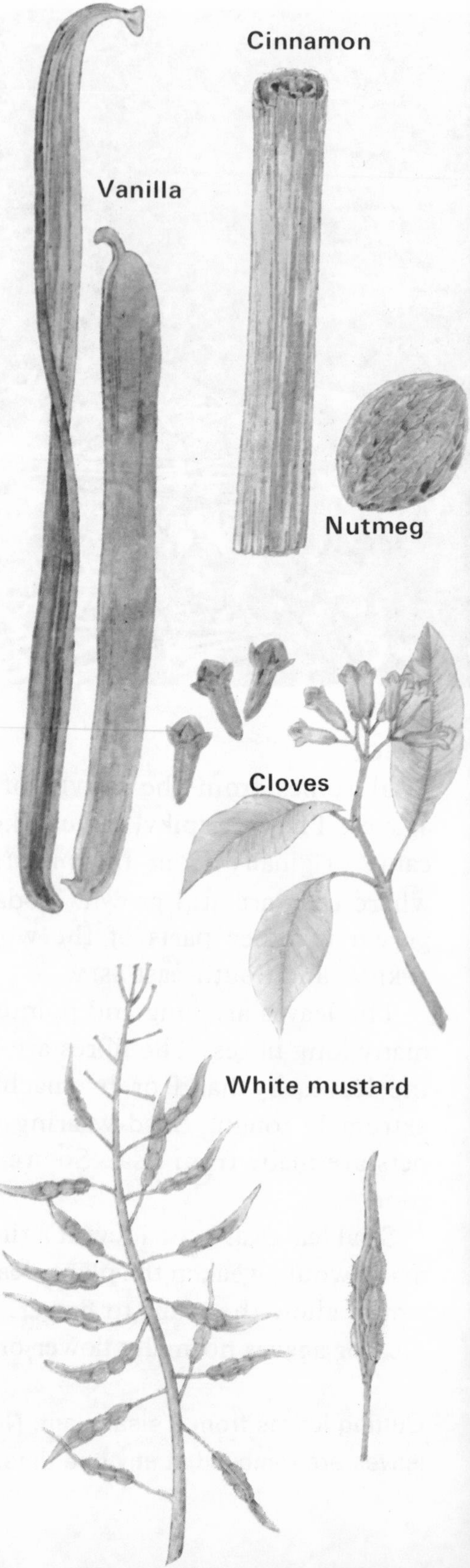

Spices come from many parts of the plant, but especially from the fruits and seeds.

FRUITS. Inside the fruit is a SEED, which produces the spice.

Cloves are the dried flower buds of a tropical tree. The tree is grown in East AFRICA, mainly in Zanzibar and Madagascar.

Mustard is made from the ground-up seeds of the two mustard plants – the black and the white. The plants are members of the CABBAGE family and fields of their bright yellow flowers are often seen in the summer.

There are many different types of pepper, such as sweet peppers, chillies and peppercorns. Peppercorns are ground to give the familiar pepper powder.

Cinnamon

Vanilla

Nutmeg

Cloves

White mustard

Oil-producing plants

One of the most important oil-producing plants is the coconut palm. It is a tropical plant found mainly on beaches. The oil comes from the white flesh of the coconut fruit. It is used in the making of soap and margarine.

The oil palm is another tropical palm. Its nuts produce an oil also used in making soap and margarine.

The fruits of the olive tree are crushed to give the oil used in medicine and cooking. The tree is found in warm countries, mainly in EUROPE.

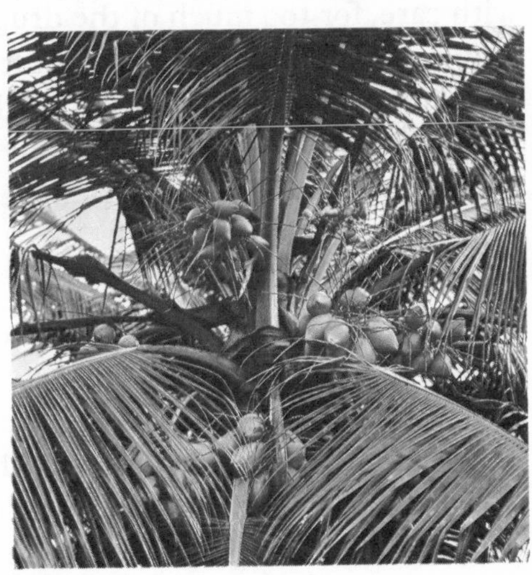

Top: The disc of the sunflower will develop into a mass of oil-rich fruits.
Above left: Separating cotton fibres from the seeds which are full of useful oil.
Above right: Clusters of coconuts on the palm.
Left: Spreading peanuts or groundnuts out to dry.

Peanut oil is another important plant oil. It is used in cooking, making margarine, the canning of fish, and as a salad dressing. Large crops of peanuts are grown in NIGERIA, INDIA, and CHINA.

Sunflower fruits (seeds) contain an oil which is useful in cooking. It is also used for varnishes and soaps.

Medicinal plants

Man has used plants for treating and curing diseases for many thousands of years. Nearly 2,000 years ago the Roman doctor Dioscorides described about 500 different plants which were then in use for this purpose. Some of these plants are no longer used, but many new ones have been discovered since Roman times. A large number of the medicines we take today come from plants. Any plant used for making medicine is known as a medicinal plant. These plants must be used with care, for too much of the drug they contain may be dangerous. Many of the medicinal plants are, in fact, very poisonous. The deadly NIGHTSHADE is an extremely poisonous plant, but it provides *atropine*, which is a very important muscle-relaxing drug.

Only part of a medicinal plant may contain the drug or drugs used as a medicine. The opium poppy, for example, produces opium only in the unripe capsule (fruit). Other parts of the plant contain little or no opium. The white juice of the capsule contains a number of pain-killing drugs, such as morphine and codeine.

Two important drugs come from the BARK of trees. Quinine, used for treating malaria, comes from the cinchona tree of PERU. The people of Peru used the drug for many years before it was taken to EUROPE and NORTH AMERICA. Another drug is curare, originally used by the South American Indians as a poison to put on their arrows. Today, the drug is used to relax muscles during surgical operations.

Various drugs come from plant LEAVES. The leaves of the foxglove, for example, contain a powerful drug (digitalin) given to people with weak hearts. Cocaine, which dentists can use to deaden the NERVES in gums, comes from the leaves of a South American shrub.

Poppy

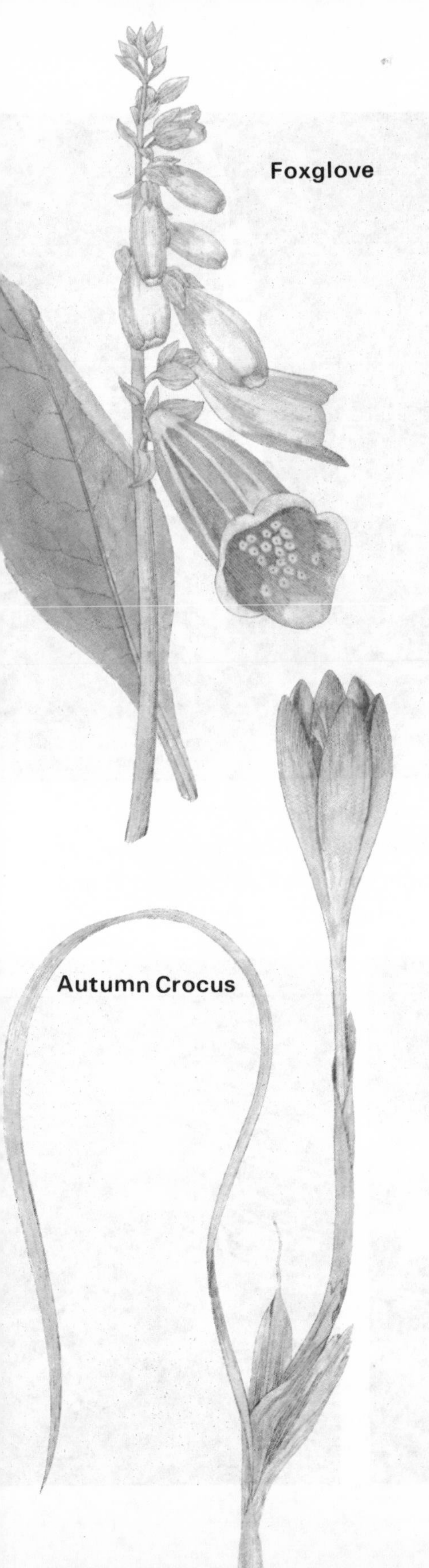

The underground parts of some plants are useful as medicines. The autumn crocus, a plant which grows in southern EUROPE and north AFRICA, contains a drug used in curing rheumatism. The garlic and onion, normally used as food, are sometimes used to treat high BLOOD pressure. They can help people with other diseases of the blood and HEART. Relatives of the YAMS are used to make cortisone. This is another drug used for treating rheumatism and arthritis.

Drugs can affect the working of the brain and mind as well as other parts of the body. Reserpine, a drug used to calm the mind and reduce anxiety, is obtained from the roots of an Indian shrub called Rauvolfia. The HINDUS have known the value of this plant for nearly 3,000 years, but reserpine itself was not discovered until a few years ago.

Many plants grown for decoration also have medicinal properties. The leaves of the laurel can help stomach upsets and rheumatism. The cones of the CYPRESS are used for blood diseases.

Some of the most important drugs, the antibiotics, are made from MOULDS. The best-known antibiotic is penicillin, used for curing diseases caused by BACTERIA. The green penicillin mould is grown in huge tanks of specially prepared 'soup'. Warm air is blown through the tanks and the mould grows very rapidly. The tanks are then emptied and the penicillin is separated from the 'soup'. It is purified and packed in measured doses ready for the doctor or nurse to give it to the patient. Penicillin kills a very wide range of disease-causing bacteria.

The poppy, the foxglove, and the autumn crocus, or meadow saffron – three attractive plants which also provide useful medicines.

Poisonous Plants

Although many plants are good to eat, many others are very poisonous. They contain poisons which interfere with our BREATHING, or with our BLOOD or our NERVES. These plants can make us very ill and some can even kill us if we eat them. Luckily, these very poisonous plants are usually rare, but we should still be careful how we handle wild plants. Even some garden flowers are poisonous if we get them into our mouths.

Red berries are very attractive and tempting to eat. Often, however, they are the most poisonous part of the plant, as are the berries of the CUCKOO PINT. Even food plants may have poisonous parts. Nothing could be safer to eat than a tomato, and yet the stem of the tomato plant is very poisonous. If a POTATO is left exposed to light, it turns green. This is a sign that a poison is present and that the potato should not be eaten.

Just because a plant is poisonous to us it does not mean that it is poisonous to other animals. Birds frequently eat berries that would make us very ill.

Above: Monkshood.
Below: Three other poisonous plants: spindle (left), henbane, and yew (right).

Death cap

The death cap is the most poisonous of all toadstools. It grows mainly in DECIDUOUS WOODLANDS and nearby GRASSLAND in the autumn.

Although it is about the same size as a MUSHROOM, it looks different. It has a ragged collar on the stalk like the mushroom, but it also has a cup at the base. The colour of the cap varies from white to greenish-yellow. The stalk is white. The gills are also white. The common mushroom has pink or brown gills.

After the death cap has been eaten, six to 15 hours can pass before signs of poisoning are noticed. By this time it is too late to do anything about it and certain death will follow. Nearly all the deaths from toadstools result from eating the death cap in mistake for a mushroom. But it need not be mistaken if you look out for the cup at the base and the white gills.

Ergot

Ergot is a fungus which grows on RYE plants. It feeds on the rye fruits. It appears as thick, dark purple spikes.

When the rye is harvested, the ergot gets mixed in with the grain. It then goes into the flour and so into the BREAD. When someone eats the bread, there can be many unpleasant effects. In some cases, the person may even die.

The ergot has some good points, however. Drugs can be extracted from it for use in controlling migraine and internal bleeding.

If the ergot is not harvested with the rye the black or purple spikes fall to the ground. In the spring they send out fleshy pink branches which scatter spores to infect new rye flowers.

Ergot poisoning used to be so common in EUROPE that it sometimes wiped out whole villages. Today, it is quite rare.

Thorn apple

The thorn apple, or jimsonweed, belongs to the POTATO family. It grows as a WEED in many parts of the world, but we do not know for certain where it came from in the first place.

It can reach a height of one metre and has large, jagged LEAVES. Its FLOWERS are either white or purple and are shaped like trumpets. They appear from July to October. The fruit is a spiky case containing the SEEDS.

The entire plant is poisonous, but the leaves and seeds are particularly dangerous. Even the nectar is supposed to be poisonous.

The plant's American name of jimsonweed is derived from the town of Jamestown in Virginia. It was near here that a company of soldiers died through eating the cooked leaves.

Above right: The thorn apple is recognised by its white trumpet-shaped flowers and spiky fruits. Below right: The deadly nightshade, with its bell-shaped flowers and very poisonous fruit.

Nightshades

There are several common nightshades. All parts of them are poisonous, especially the FRUITS.

The most poisonous kind is the deadly nightshade, often called the belladonna. It has large, bell-shaped FLOWERS which are a light purple-blue. The berries are large and purple-black.

Woody nightshade and black nightshade are both very common plants, closely related to the POTATO. Their star-shaped flowers are all built on the same plan. Woody nightshade is a climbing plant with yellow and purple flowers. Its ripe fruits are bright red.

The black nightshade is a small WEED common in gardens. The flowers are white and yellow. The small berries look like black currants.

Hemlock

The hemlock is a member of the CARROT family. It grows on the banks of streams, on wasteland and in hedgerows.

It is a tall plant having a thick, shiny STEM, which is covered in purplish spots. The FLOWERS are white and grow in the form of open umbrellas. If the plant is crushed, it gives out a musty smell.

Hemlock contains several poisons. If a person eats any part of it, his BREATHING will stop, and he will die. Hemlock is famous as the poison given to the ANCIENT GREEK thinker, SOCRATES.

The purple spots on the stems distinguish the hemlock from most of its relatives, but this does not mean that plants without such spots are harmless.

Above left: The hemlock is usually called the poison hemlock in order to distinguish it from the cone-bearing trees of the same name.
Below left: The privet is a relative of the lilac.

Privet

The privet is a small deciduous shrub growing wild over a large area of Europe, especially in chalky regions. It is very commonly grown as a garden hedge, but it is gradually being replaced for this purpose by the hardier Californian privet from Japan. Yellow-leaved varieties are very commonly grown today.

The LEAVES of the privet are small, quite dark, and shiny. Because people usually keep hedges cut, it does not often have the chance to flower. The flowering time, however, is July and August. The FLOWERS grow in white clusters. They have a very strong smell. The berries, which are black, are particularly poisonous.

One way to stop privet poisoning is to make sure that hedges are cut often.

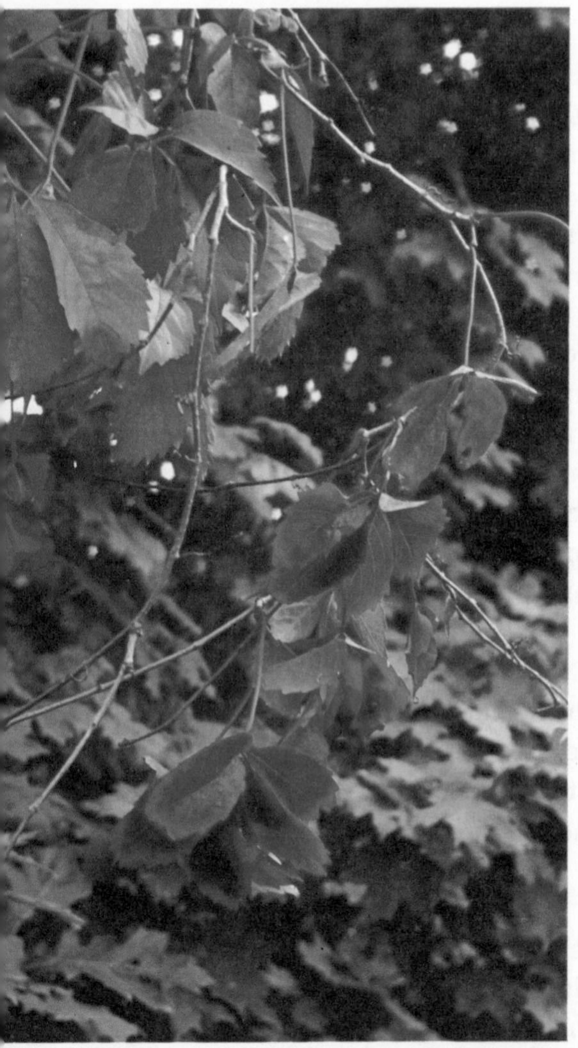

Poison ivy

Poison ivy comes from NORTH AMERICA. It is a deciduous shrub which grows about three metres high. The LEAVES grow in groups of three leaflets. They can be five to 12 centimetres long, but the middle one is the largest. In the autumn they turn to a beautiful red and orange.

The juice of this plant is poisonous. On most people it brings out extremely painful blisters. Persons who have to handle it should wear gloves.

It is sometimes called poison OAK. Poison sumac, a similar plant with more leaves, grows in swampy land and can cause a severe rash.

The attractive leaves of the poison ivy. Touching the leaves may cause painful blisters.

White bryony

The white bryony is a climbing plant which is often seen in hedgerows. Every year it withers, and then sends out new shoots the following spring. The shoots cling to neighbouring plants with long tendrils.

The ROOTS of this plant are thick and long. In June and July the FLOWERS appear. They are small and greenish-yellow. The berries are shiny red.

The whole of this plant is poisonous, but especially the berries. A child can die after eating just a few of the berries.

Below: The white bryony, showing the pale flower and the long coiled tendril. This stretches like a spring and does not snap in the wind.

Laburnum

The laburnum is a tall, graceful tree which is often planted in gardens and parks for decoration.

The trunk of the tree is smooth and greyish-brown. In the spring, long clusters of yellow FLOWERS appear. They hang down from the branches. The FRUIT is a pod, which helps to show that the plant is one of the PEA family. All parts of the laburnum are poisonous.

Left: The laburnum is one of the most attractive garden trees, but it is also one of the most dangerous. Its seeds are very poisonous.
Below: The flower spike of the cuckoo pint.

Cuckoo pint

The cuckoo pint is quite a common plant in many European countries. It grows in shady places such as hedges, woods, and ditches.

The LEAVES are large and arrow-shaped. They are shiny and are often marked with black spots. The flower spike has a leaf-like hood and a purple 'finger', but the real flowers are very small and hidden at the bottom of the spike.

The red berries develop later at the base of the spike. They are clustered thickly round the stalk. These are very poisonous.

PLANTS
FACTS AND FIGURES

PARTS OF A FLOWERING PLANT. The world's largest flower belongs to an Indonesian plant called Rafflesia. About a metre across, it weighs more than 10 kilograms. The world's largest fruit, the double coconut, from the Seychelles Islands, weighs up to 20 kilograms.

LIFE OF A FLOWERING PLANT. The talipot palm grows for nearly 40 years before it has any flowers. Then it produces more than 50 million flowers all at once and dies soon afterwards. A little plant growing in the Sahara Desert lives for only two weeks.

GARDEN FLOWERS. Men have cultivated flowers for thousands of years. The famous Hanging Gardens of Babylon were among the first big gardens devoted to flowers. The oldest botanical garden still in existence is the one in the Vatican, in Rome. It is over 700 years old.

FLOWERING TREES AND SHRUBS. The tallest flowering trees are Australian eucalyptus trees. Some are about 100 metres high. The mesquite tree of the American deserts has roots up to 33 metres long. African baobab trees may have trunks 10 metres in diameter.

TREES WITH CONES. The largest things which have ever lived are the giant redwood trees of California. Some of them are more than 115 metres high. The oldest living things are the bristle-cone pines. Some of them are more than 5,000 years old and they are still growing.

PLANTS WITHOUT SEEDS. Coal was formed mainly from seedless plants living about 250 million years ago. Some of these plants were over 30 metres high. They scattered dust-like spores to reproduce themselves. The largest seedless plants today are tree ferns 20 metres high.

FOSSIL PLANTS. The earliest land plants of which we have any knowledge lived about 450 million years ago. Plants with real flowers did not appear until about 125 million years ago. Arizona's Petrified Forest contains ancient tree trunks which have turned to stone.

WHERE PLANTS LIVE. Lichens are the hardiest of plants. They can grow on bare rocks and walls. Many lichens grow in Antarctica, where only two kinds of flowering plants grow. Tropical forests may contain more than 300 different kinds of trees in one square mile.

PLANTS WE EAT. Man has always eaten plants, but he did not start cultivating them until about 10,000 years ago. China, the Middle East, and Central America were the main centres of early agriculture. Well over 250 million tons of potatoes are grown every year.

GRASSES AND CEREALS. Wheat is the most widely grown cereal, with a world production of about 460 million tons every year. Corn or maize comes next, with about 450 million tons every year. Nearly 800 million tons of sugar cane are harvested in a year.

MATERIALS FROM PLANTS. More than three million tons of rubber are taken from rubber trees each year. Cotton is the most important natural fibre. About 15 million tons are produced every year. Penicillin was discovered in 1928 by Sir Alexander Fleming.

POISONOUS PLANTS. The tobacco plant contains a poison called nicotine, which is used to kill insect pests. Buttercups are all poisonous. Cattle sometimes die if they eat too many buttercups. Stinging nettles inject a mild poison when we brush against their hairs.

THE EARTH AND BEYOND

The Universe

Above: A sixteenth-century star globe.
Below: The Trifid Nebula.

The universe includes everything we know. It extends in all directions as far as TELESCOPES have been able to penetrate.

No one knows how big the universe is. Astronomers can detect bodies so far away that the LIGHT reaching us from them has been travelling for 10,000 million years. As light moves nearly 300,000 kilometres every second, this distance is very great indeed. There might be bodies farther away, but we cannot detect them.

Astronomers believe that the groups of STARS called GALAXIES are all moving away from each other. The universe is therefore getting bigger.

No one knows how the universe began and when it will end. Some astronomers say that the universe has existed for ever and will never end. They believe that new galaxies form to fill the space left as the galaxies in the universe move farther apart.

Other astronomers think that the universe formed at some time in the distant past. They say that a single body of matter exploded to form galaxies. The galaxies spread out through space.

Above: The light of the stars in the Pleiades shows up the nebulae (the light blue patches).

1 2

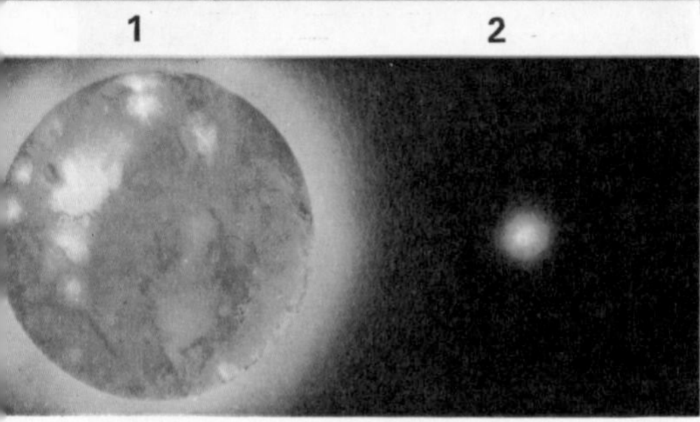

3 4

Stars

All the bodies in the night sky are often called 'stars'. In fact, in our solar system only the SUN is a star. The MOON and PLANETS are not stars.

Stars like the SUN are made up of hot gases, and they give out their own LIGHT. They form in clusters from gas and dust clouds within the GALAXY. As pockets of gas shrink under the force of GRAVITY, their centres become hot and highly compressed. Hydrogen gas is turned into helium gas by an atomic process, and the stars are born.

Stars vary greatly in age, size, temperature, and colour. Dull red stars are the coolest; bluish stars are the hottest. Some stars get hotter and hotter until they explode. They are called supernovae.

Not all stars exist on their own. Some are bound together in pairs, threes, and greater numbers by mutual forces of gravity.

Our galaxy is thought to contain at least 100,000 million stars. They are separated by immense distances. Astronomers measure these distances by the distance LIGHT travels in one year. This unit for measuring star distances is called a light year.

When we look into space we are really looking back in time. Most of the starlight we see started on its journey before we were born. Light from Sirius, the brightest star, takes 8·7 years to travel to us on earth. Light from Castor in the CONSTELLATION Gemini takes 44 years.

Left: Four stages in the life of a normal star. (1) The star forms as a cloud of gas shrinks under the force of gravity. (2) It becomes smaller and hotter and begins to shine, like our sun now. (3) When its gases are burnt up, it becomes a 'red giant'. (4) The star may explode or end its life as a 'white dwarf'.

Nebulae

Nebulae look like misty patches of light in the sky, rather than sharp points of light like the STARS. Most of them are huge clouds of dust and gas within our own GALAXY.

We can see light nebulae as shining patches in the sky. Some shine by reflecting the light from nearby stars. The gas in other light nebulae is made to glow by the energy from bright stars in the cloud.

Many nebulae do not shine at all, but block the light from the stars beyond them instead. These dark nebulae are seen as dark areas, and they hide large parts of the MILKY WAY from us.

Some nebulae seem to be thrown off into space by dying stars. The Crab Nebula is known to be the remains of a giant star which exploded. The supernova explosion was seen by Chinese astronomers over 900 years ago. Other nebulae like the Great Nebula in Orion, are thought to be the place where new stars are born.

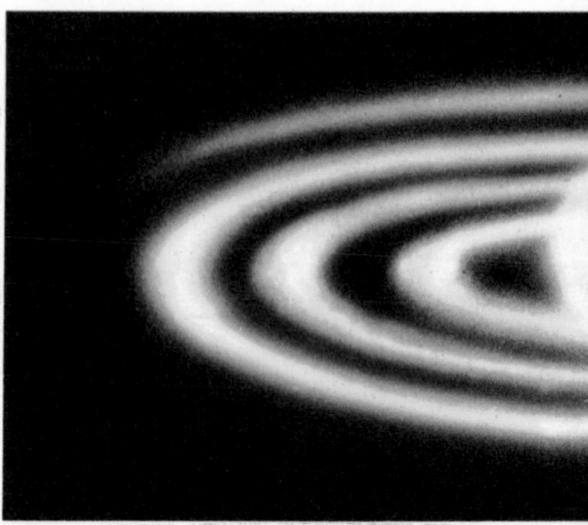

Above: The red arrow shows the position of the sun among the 100,000 million stars in our galaxy.

Below left: The Horsehead Nebula blocks out the light from the stars behind it.

Below: The Great Nebula in Orion is thought to be the birthplace of new stars.

stars. It is the brightest Nebula in the sky.

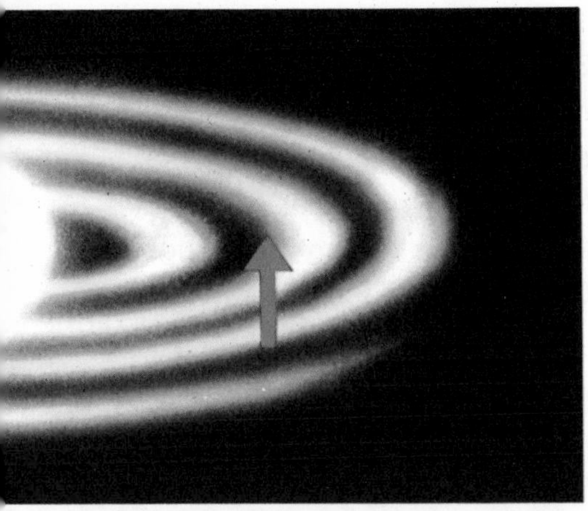

Galaxies

A galaxy is a huge collection of STARS, gas, and dust. Our own star, the SUN, is one of about 100,000 million stars that make up one galaxy. Our galaxy is turning slowly in space like a gigantic wheel.

For a long time astronomers thought that our galaxy was the whole universe. We now know that a very large number of other galaxies exist beyond our own. They are like huge islands of stars separated from one another by vast stretches of space. Not all galaxies are spirals like ours. Some of the brightest are oval-shaped.

Milky Way

On a clear night you can easily see the Milky Way. It is the faint band of light that stretches across the sky. This light comes from the millions of STARS in our own GALAXY, that lie between us and the centre of the galaxy.

Apart from a bulge at the centre, where th
stars are much closer together, the galaxy
flat spiral shape. Our solar system lies in
the spiral arms, towards the edge of the

It is not very easy to study our own g
because we have a side view of most of it. Th
is why the Milky Way does not look spiral-shaped. Also, nebulae in the spiral arms hide parts of the galaxy from us, especially towards the centre. However, radio waves are not stopped by dust and gas clouds, so they reach us from all parts of the galaxy.

Above left: The nearest large galaxy to us is the spiral-shaped galaxy in the constellation of Andromeda. This is what our galaxy would look like from far away.
Left: The Milky Way is the view we have of our own galaxy from the earth. The white streak is a comet.

Constellations

For thousands of years man has divided the night sky into groups of STARS called constellations. Today astronomers list 88 constellations. One of the most famous in the Northern Hemisphere is Ursa Major, or the Great Bear.

Below: The constellations in the Northern Hemisphere. The easiest constellations to spot are Ursa Major (the Great Bear) with its seven stars forming the plough; and Cassiopeia, shaped like a W.

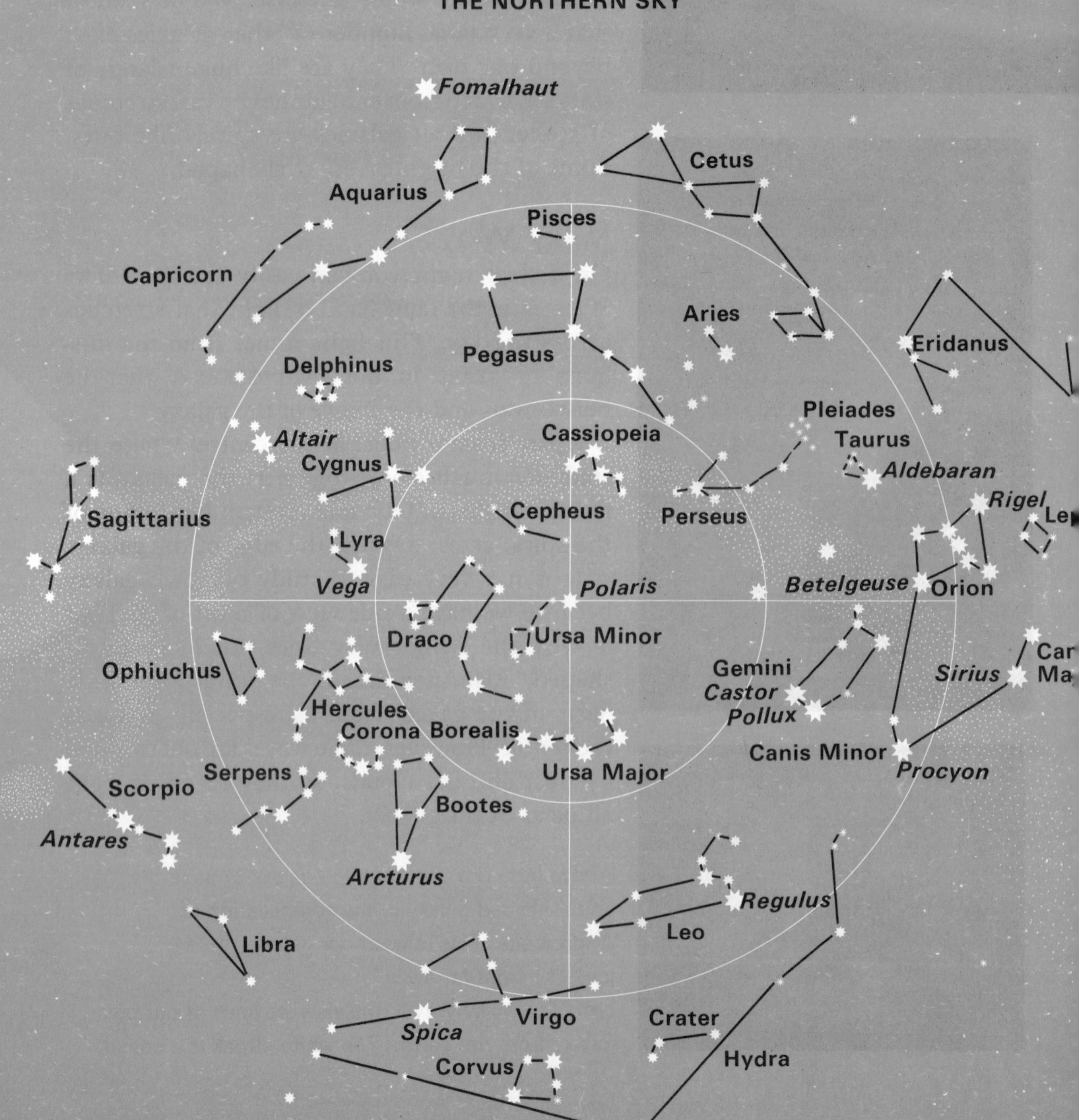

Below: A map of the constellations in the sky of the Southern Hemisphere. The best-known constellation is Crux, or the Southern Cross. Orion can be seen in the northern sky in winter.

One of the easiest constellations to find in the Southern Hemisphere is Crux, or the Southern Cross. Another well-known constellation is Orion, which can also be seen in the northern sky in winter. Its brightest star is the huge red Betelgeuse, more than 250 times bigger than our SUN.

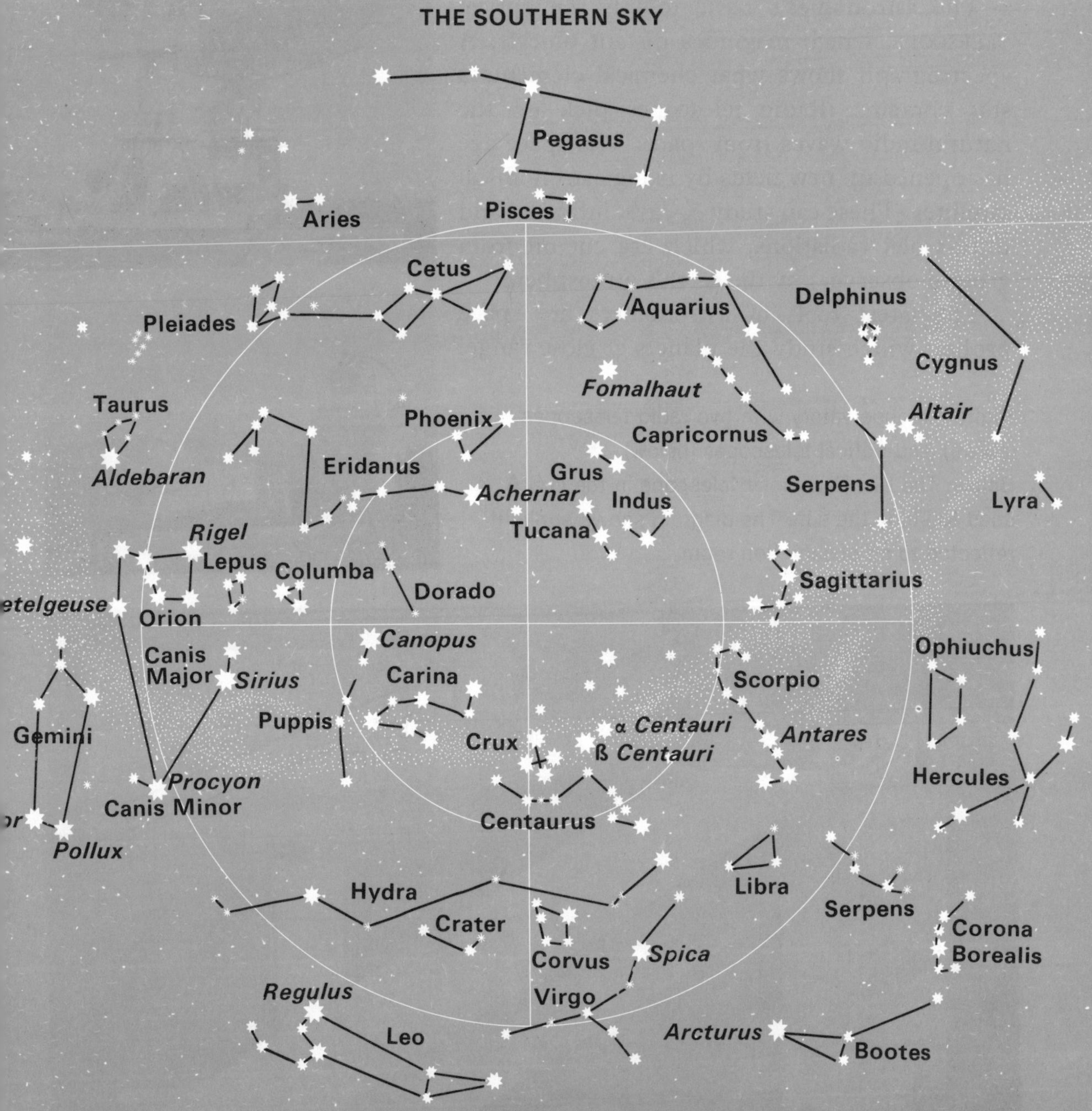

Astronomy

Astronomy is the scientific study of the universe and all it contains – for example, PLANETS moons, COMETS, STARS, NEBULAE and GALAXIES. Astronomers study the movements of the heavenly bodies, the distances between them, and the radiations they give out.

The astronomer's basic tool is the optical TELESCOPE, which magnifies distant objects. A spectrograph shows what chemical elements a star contains. Radio telescopes pick up the natural radio waves from space. The space age has opened up new fields by using astronomical satellites. These can study X-rays, infra-red and ultra-violet radiations, which are cut off from ground observers by the earth's atmosphere.

The latest tools of astronomers are space probes, which study the planets at close range.

Right: An observatory with two radio telescopes (above), and optical telescopes (below).
Below: The Kitt Peak solar telescope in the U.S.A. is used to study the sun. The diagram shows sunlight reflected to an observation room.

Above: A refracting telescope inside the protective dome of an observatory. Below: Jodrell Bank, a radio telescope in England. Radio telescopes receive radio waves from space.

Telescopes

The telescope is an instrument that makes distant objects like the STARS and PLANETS appear closer and therefore more detailed. It forms an image of the distant object and magnifies (increases the size of) this image.

Two main types of telescope are used in ASTRONOMY, the refractor and the reflector. The earliest type is the refractor. This consists of tubes in which are mounted a LENS at the front and a magnifying lens in the eyepiece.

A reflecting telescope uses a concave mirror to collect and focus the light. The light is then reflected by smaller mirrors on to a photographic plate, or through an eyepiece to the observer.

Early astronomers looked through their telescopes and drew what they saw. Now astronomers photograph the stars. To see very faint stars and far-away galaxies, the photographic plates are sometimes exposed for hours. The earth's spinning motion makes the stars appear to move, so the whole telescope must be moved to follow the stars being photographed. Spectrographs are often used with a telescope to split the star light into its basic colours. This spectrum can tell the astronomer what chemical elements are in a star.

Apart from light, the only kinds of radiation from stars that can reach ground level are some radio waves. These are picked up by radio telescopes, which work in much the same way as reflecting telescopes. A metal dish collects the radio waves, reflecting them on to a receiver.

Radio telescopes can also be used for radar. Radio signals are sent out towards a planet, for example. The reflected signals from the planet are then collected by the radio telescope. Radar can measure the exact distance of another planet, its size and its spin rate.

convex lens

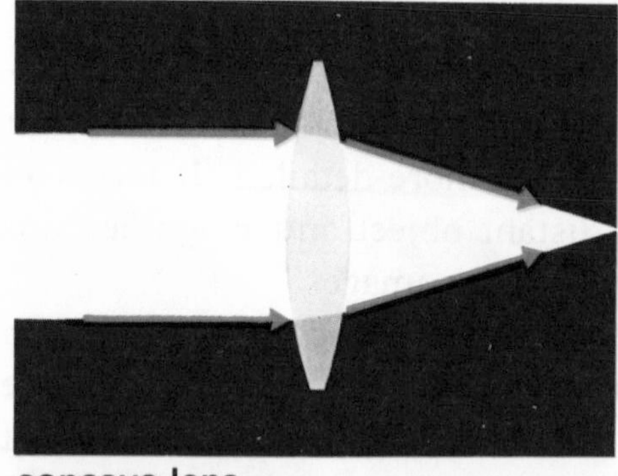

concave lens

Lenses

A lens is usually made of GLASS. It has a special shape that permits a beam of light passing through it to diverge or converge (become wider or narrower).

When light rays enter the lens, they are refracted (changed in direction). Because of the curved surface of the glass, the refraction is greatest towards the rim. It is least at the centre, where the rays pass through without bending.

In a refracting TELESCOPE a system of lenses allows us to enlarge distant objects.

Left: There are two basic kinds of lenses. They are convex lenses and concave lenses. A convex lens (top) has a bulge in the middle. It makes light rays converge to a point, called the focus. A concave lens (bottom) is thin in the middle. It spreads out light rays.

Mirrors

Mirrors, which reflect light, have a special place in ASTRONOMY. They are used with LENS systems in reflecting TELESCOPES to obtain clear images of distant objects.

Mirrors are used for big telescopes because big lenses do not give very good images. Most giant telescopes, for example the one at Mount Palomar Observatory in California, are reflecting telescopes. They have a large mirror which is formed into a concave shape (curves inwards in the shape of a saucer). The mirror is then polished and silvered to reflect the maximum amount of light on to a point in front of it.

Right: The Hale telescope at the Mount Palomar Observatory uses a concave mirror that is 5 metres in diameter to collect and focus the light from the stars.

Light

The SUN and the STARS are the natural sources of light. There are also forms of light we cannot see – for example, infra-red and ultra-violet light. We cannot see them because our eyes are not sensitive to them.

Light belongs to a large group of radiations known as electro-magnetic waves. They include RADIO waves, X-rays, and gamma rays. We call the group the electro-magnetic spectrum.

Visible light can be thought of as energy flowing continually in a wave motion. But it can also be regarded as a stream of tiny particles, or corpuscles. Light travels at a speed of 299,792 kilometres per second. It takes about 8½ minutes to reach us from the sun and 4¼ years to reach us from Proxima Centauri, the nearest star beyond the sun. The distance that light travels in one year is known as a light year.

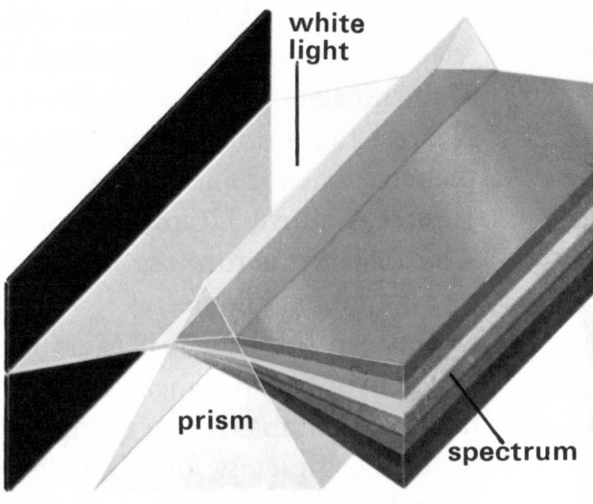

Above: White light is a mixture of colours. A prism can split up a band of white light into its 7 basic colours. These are called the spectrum. Each colour varys in wavelength.

Spectrum

When LIGHT is passed through a glass prism, it splits into its basic colours – red, orange, yellow green, blue, indigo, and violet. This range of colours is called the spectrum.

Each of the colours consists of waves of different lengths. The shorter waves are bent more than the longer ones, so the colours are spread out. Sunlight shining on raindrops produces the same effect – in the form of a RAINBOW.

When starlight from a TELESCOPE is passed through a spectrograph, a photograph of the star's spectrum is produced. This band of colours from red to violet is crossed by many dark lines. This is because the gases at the surface of the star absorb particular colours. Each chemical element has its own individual pattern of dark lines. The spectrum can therefore reveal what the star is made of.

The Solar System

The SUN, and all the bodies which circle it in space, make up the solar system. We live on one of the nine PLANETS that revolve around the SUN. Nearest the sun is Mercury, the smallest of the planets. Then come Venus, the EARTH, Mars, Jupiter, Saturn, Uranus, Neptune, and Pluto. The distance across the solar system is about 13,000 million kilometres.

Between the orbits of Mars and Jupiter is a belt of many small planets called asteroids. These may be the remains of a tenth planet that failed to form completely into a single body. Millions of meteoroids – from nearly 800 kilometres in diameter to small rock and dust particles – are also circling around the sun in this belt. COMETS, too, are part of the sun's family.

To get a rough idea of the sizes of the planets, we can think of Mercury as a small seed, Venus and the earth as peas, Mars, an orange pip, Jupiter an orange, Saturn a smaller orange, Uranus and Neptune large cherries, and Pluto as another small seed. On this scale the sun would be a ball 600 millimetres across, and the earth would be 65 metres from the sun.

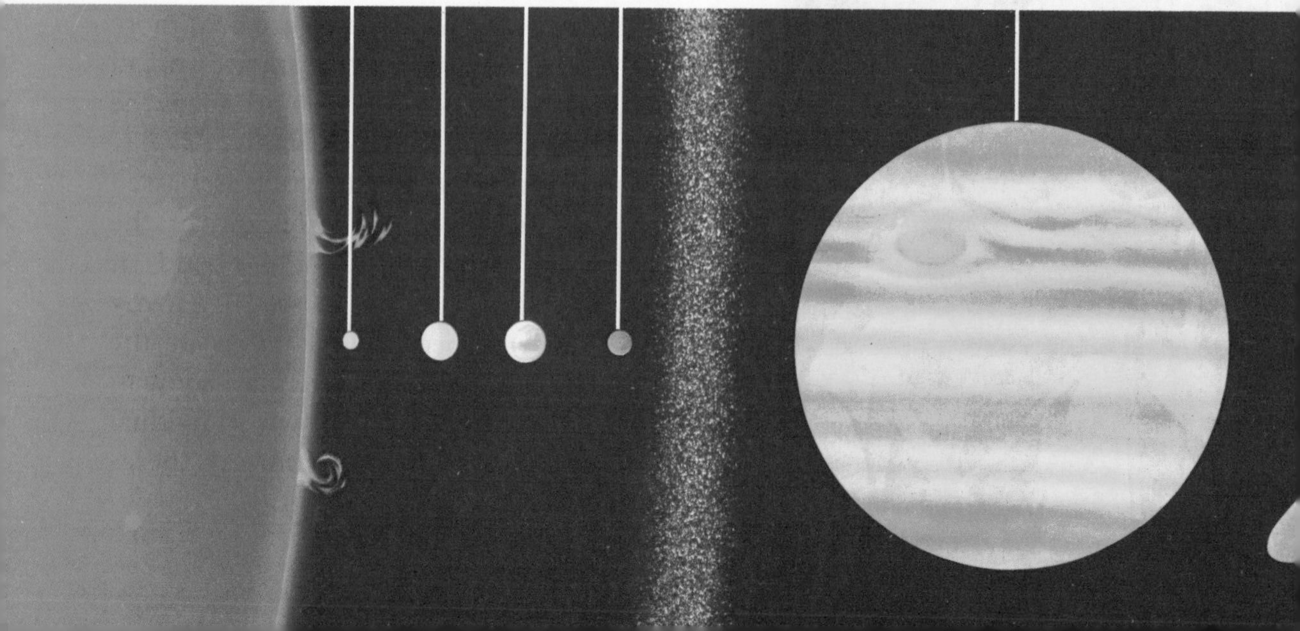

Sun Mercury Venus Earth Mars Asteroids Jupiter

Gravity

All bodies in the universe have an invisible force of attraction – gravity – which tends to draw them together. How strong the attraction is depends on how much matter the bodies contain – their mass – and how far apart they are from each other.

When we throw a ball up into the air, the EARTH'S gravity pulls it back down. The same force prevents us from being flung from the face of our spinning world.

It is the SUN's gravity that keeps the circling PLANETS from flying off into space. In the same way the MOON is trapped by the gravity of the earth, and remains in orbit around it. Man-made satellites also stay in orbit around the earth because of its gravity.

Sir Isaac NEWTON was the first man to understand and explain the idea of gravity.

Left: The sun's gravity keeps its family of planets circling around it.
Below: The solar system. The size of each planet is to scale, but the distances are not.

Sun

The sun is one of 100,000 million STARS in our GALAXY. It is the star around which the PLANETS of our solar system revolve. Many other stars are bigger and brighter. It is only because the sun is so near that it appears so huge and bright. Light from the sun takes about 8½ minutes to reach the earth.

The sun is an immense ball of glowing gas, taking up over one million times as much space as the earth. The gas is mainly hydrogen. Deep inside, hydrogen atoms are constantly combining to make atoms of helium. In the process energy is released in the form of heat and light. We call this process a thermo-nuclear reaction.

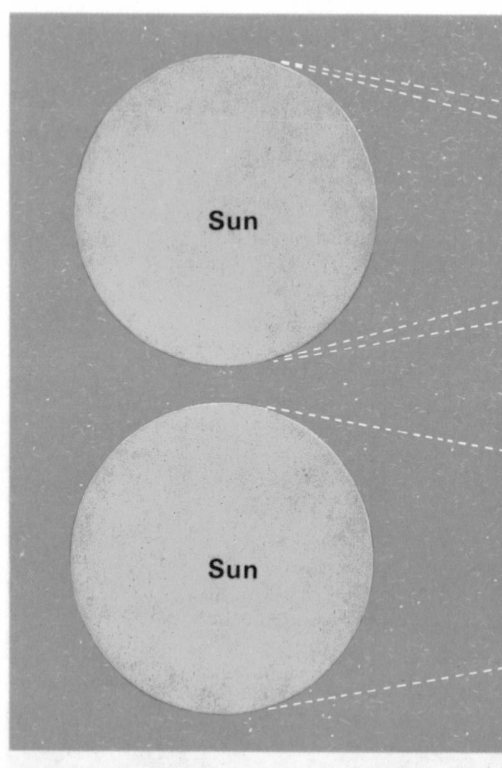

Below: The sun's surface is sometimes disturbed by sunspots. Ribbons of glowing gas burst into space.

WARNING

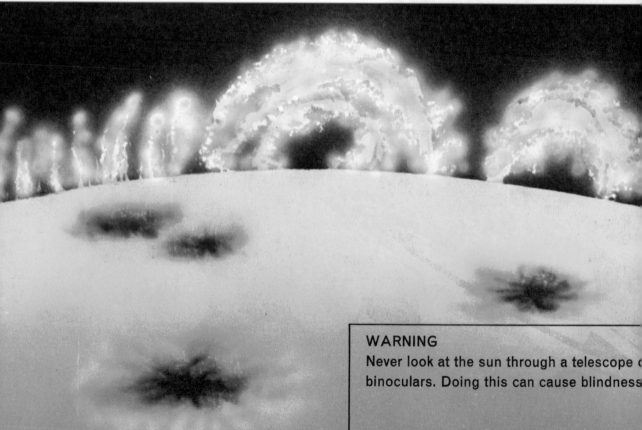

Never look at the sun through a telescope or binoculars. Doing this can cause blindness.

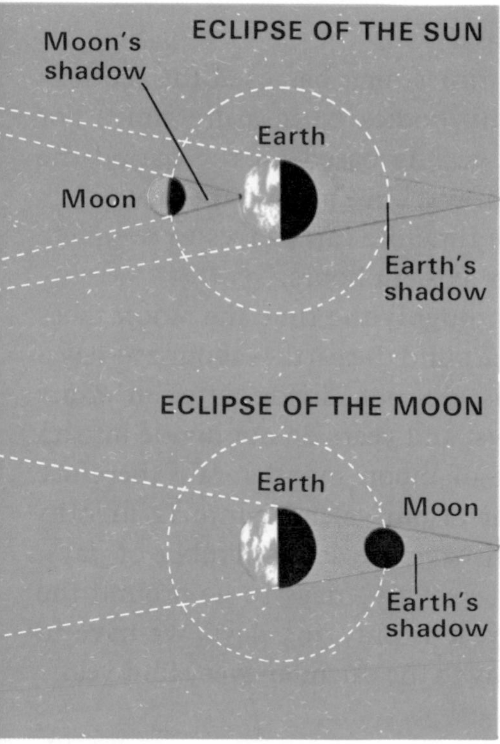

Eclipses

When the MOON passes between the SUN and the earth, the sun's rays are cut off and the sky grows dark. We call this a solar eclipse. An eclipse may be total (when little light gets through), or partial. In a total eclipse, the sun's flaring outer atmosphere (corona) can be seen.

We have an eclipse of the moon when the earth passes between the sun and the moon, and the moon is in the earth's shadow. The sun's rays are cut off from the moon and it appears to grow dim.

Astronomers can predict when eclipses will happen because they have measured the precise movements of the earth and the moon in relation to the sun.

Below: A partial eclipse of the sun occurs when the moon covers part of the sun.

Northern Lights

Sometimes when flares (sunspots) erupt from the SUN, many small electrified particles are thrown into space. Some of these bombard the earth and are trapped in its magnetic field. They cause gas atoms in the earth's upper atmosphere to glow, creating spectacular displays of *aurora borealis*, the Northern Lights.

The glowing lights that play across the northern skies are best observed when storm conditions on the sun coincide with cold, clear winter nights. They often appear as swaying curtains of white, yellow, green, or pink light.

The corresponding displays in the Southern Hemisphere are called aurora australis, or the Southern Lights.

Right: The Northern Lights are usually seen only in the far north.

Above: A calendar used by the Aztec people of Mexico. They measured time very accurately.

The calendar

From ancient times man has used the motions of the heavenly bodies to measure time. For example, our year is based on the period the earth takes to travel once around the SUN.

A day is the time the earth takes to complete one turn on its axis, 24 hours.

A month is roughly the time the MOON takes to travel once around the earth – about $27\frac{1}{2}$ days. Moon months do not divide into an exact number of days, and years do not divide into an exact number of moon months. We therefore divide the year of our calendar into 12 months that do not all have the same number of days.

The earth takes $365\frac{1}{4}$ days to go around the sun. Since a year is only 365 days, we have to add another day to the calendar every four years.

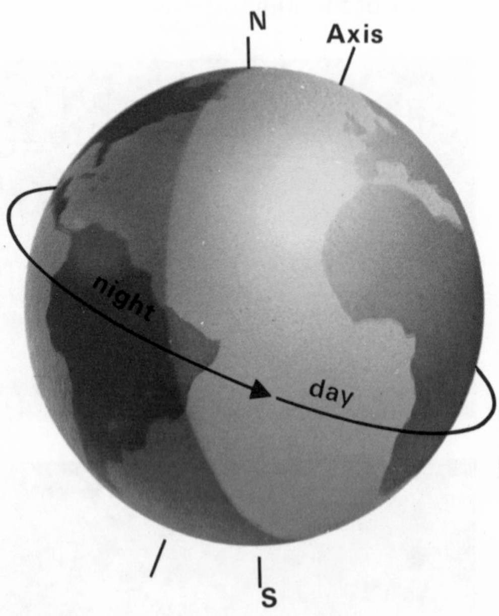

Above: Where the earth is illuminated by the sun, it is day. When it is night, we are in the earth's shadow. As the earth turns, night follows day.

That day is always 29 February. A year of 366 days is called a leap year.

The earth moves through space like a huge spinning top leaning over at $23\frac{1}{2}$ degrees. When the North Pole tilts towards the sun, it is summer in the Northern Hemisphere and winter in the Southern Hemisphere.

Six months later, when the earth is on the other side of the sun, the North Pole tilts away from the sun. Then it is winter in the north and summer in the south.

summer

winter

Above: The Devil's Punchbowl, Surrey, England, in summer (top), and winter (above).
Below right: The world is divided into time zones, each one usually an hour apart.

International Date Line

In 1884 scientists divided the world into 24 time zones. These were based on an imaginary line running through Greenwich Observatory. (Greenwich is in south-east LONDON, on the River Thames.) The time in the zone containing Greenwich is called Greenwich Mean Time.

Going westwards around the world from Greenwich, we subtract an hour for each 15 degrees of longitude. Going eastwards from Greenwich we add an hour for each 15 degrees of longitude.

At 180° longitude we arrive at the International Date Line. This imaginary line runs north–south through the PACIFIC OCEAN. When crossing the International Date Line, the date is put forward one day going west (a day is lost). The date is put back one day going east (a day is gained). In other words, if we are travelling east and it is Monday when we reach the date line, it is Sunday again when we have passed through.

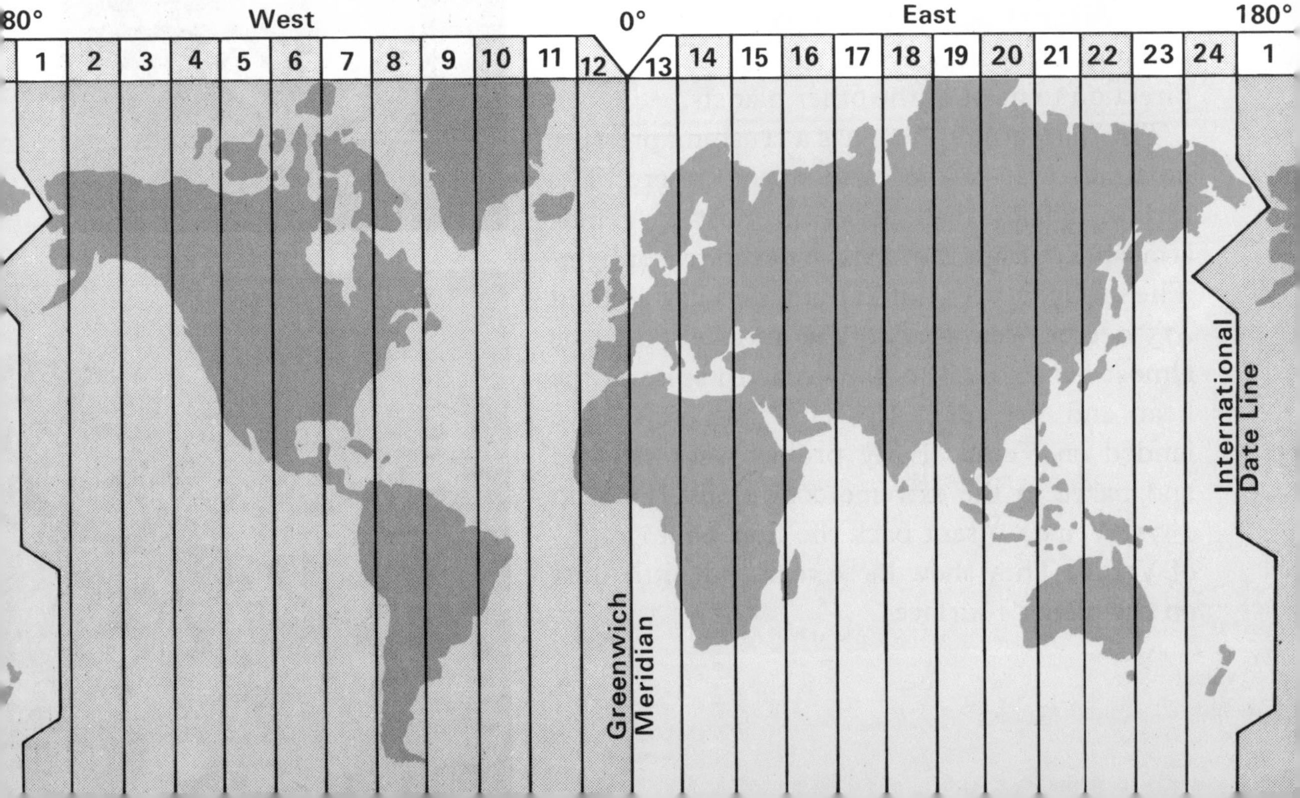

80° West 0° East 180°

1 2 3 4 5 6 7 8 9 10 11 12 13 14 15 16 17 18 19 20 21 22 23 24 1

Greenwich Meridian

International Date Line

The inner planets

Mercury is the smallest of the four inner, rocky planets. It is not much bigger than the MOON. It is the closest planet to the SUN. The temperature on the side facing the sun is so high that lead would melt there. It has no atmosphere to hold the heat so the side away from the sun freezes at 170 degrees centigrade below zero.

Mercury spins slowly on its axis (an imaginary line through its centre), taking 59 days to turn once. It is the fastest planet in the solar system. It takes just 88 days to circle the sun at a speed of more than 170,000 kilometres an hour.

Mercury cannot easily be seen from the earth because it is so close to the sun. The Mariner 10 spacecraft which flew past it revealed a rocky surface covered with craters that looked surprisingly like the moon.

Venus is the nearest planet to us. It is the brightest object in the night sky, apart from the moon. Its surface is always hidden by thick CLOUDS which race round the planet in only four days. Venus itself moves very slowly, making one turn every 243 days. It turns in the opposite direction to most of the other planets.

The thick atmosphere has a crushing pressure 90 times that of the earth's atmosphere. The carbon dioxide that makes up most of Venus' atmosphere traps the heat produced by sunlight. The surface is even hotter than Mercury's, about 475 degrees centigrade. The surface would be almost hot enough to glow red. In spite of the heat and pressure, Russian spacecraft have landed on Venus. Early probes were crushed and baked in the extreme conditions. Then in 1975, Venara 9 sent back the first photographs of Venus. They show loose rocks but little dust on the planet's surface.

Above: Mercury as seen from the Mariner 10 spacecraft.
Below: Earth from space.

Above: A picture of Venus taken by Mariner 10.

Below: The planet Mars.

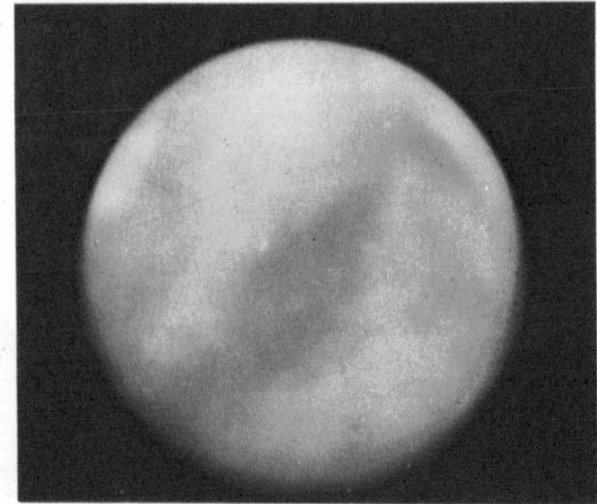

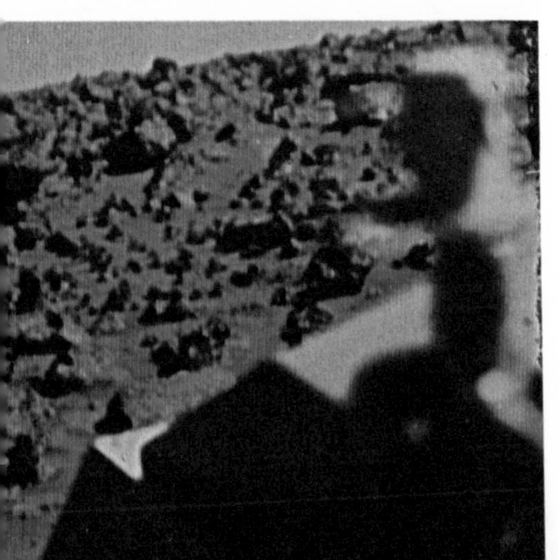

Mars is a cold, dry planet only about half the size of the earth. Clouds sometimes float in its thin atmosphere of carbon dioxide. The highest temperatures on Mars are the same as the lowest temperatures on earth. The whole surface of Mars has been photographed by orbiting space probes. There are many craters like the moon, but there are also deep valleys and volcanic mountains more like the earth. There appear to be dry river beds, but there is no liquid water on Mars now. The two Viking spacecraft that landed on Mars showed us a rock-strewn desert. Winds raise the red dust to make the sky look pink. Sometimes dust storms rage over the whole planet. The spacecraft scooped up soil and tested it for signs of life, but they did not find any.

Earth is like a huge spaceship that carries us through space at an average speed of about 107,000 kilometres an hour. This is about 30 kilometres a second. It takes 365$\frac{1}{4}$ days to travel once around the SUN. All the time our planet is spinning like a top. Its speed at the equator is about 1670 kilometres an hour.

The earth is the only planet in the solar system with oceans and seas. Beneath a constantly changing pattern of clouds, seven-tenths of its surface is covered by the oceans. The North and South Poles are permanently covered with SNOW and ice.

The air we breathe – our atmosphere – is held in place by GRAVITY. Its gases are mainly nitrogen (78 per cent) and oxygen (21 per cent). The atmosphere protects us from METEORS and dangerous radiation from outer space.

Left: The Martian landscape where one of the Viking spacecraft landed. The red colour of the rocks and soil shows up clearly.

The outer planets

Jupiter, the giant of the sun's family, contains more material than all the other planets put together. Its diameter is more than 10 times the earth's diameter, and it is quite different from the inner, rocky planets. It is liquid with a deep atmosphere, but it may have a small solid centre. It is made up of the gases hydrogen and helium, like the sun, but it is not big enough to be a star. It spins faster than any other planet, turning once every 10 hours. This makes its clouds spread out into coloured bands around its equator. The lighter-coloured 'zones' are higher and cooler than the darker-coloured 'belts'.

Jupiter's famous 'Red Spot' may be an enormous storm. It is so big that it could easily swallow up the earth. Jupiter has about 14 moons. Three of these are larger than our moon.

Saturn is very like Jupiter except for its spectacular rings. It is another giant ball of liquid hydrogen. The speed at which it spins makes it bulge at the equator and produces cloud bands like Jupiter.

Saturn is surrounded by four thin, flat rings spreading out around its equator. Their outer diameter is more than twice the planet's diameter, but they are not more than a few kilometres thick. Stars are sometimes seen shining dimly through them, so they cannot be solid. They are probably millions of small lumps of ice.

Saturn has about 17 moons. These include Titan, the largest moon in the solar system, and the only one with a real atmosphere.

Uranus is the nearest of the three planets that were not known to the ancient astronomers. It

Top right: Saturn, the ringed planet.
Above right: The giant planet Jupiter.
Right: As yet no space probe has visited Neptune.

was discovered by accident in 1781, by the British astronomer, Sir William Herschel. He realized that this 'star', which moved against the background of stars, must be a planet. It is too far away for us to discover much about it, even with the largest telescopes, but it is probably a liquid planet with a solid core. It is the only planet whose spin axis does not point in a north-south direction. Its axis is tilted so that it appears to be lying on its side. In 1977 astronomers discovered a faint ring system round Uranus. The rings cannot be seen with a telescope. However, when a star passed behind Uranus, the star disappeared several times on each side of the planet.

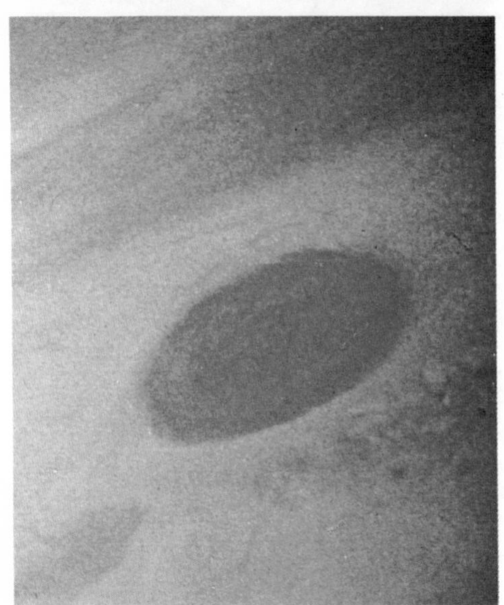

Neptune seems to be a twin planet to Uranus. They are almost the same size, and are made up of the same gases. However, Neptune is about twice as far from the sun as Uranus, and appears bluish rather than greenish. Neptune was discovered in 1846. Astronomers noticed that Uranus was not following its expected path round the sun. They thought that another planet must be pulling it off course. They calculated where this outer planet should be, and found Neptune.

Pluto is the lonely wanderer at the edge of the solar system, though some astronomers think that there may be other planets beyond it. Pluto is smaller even than Mercury and is believed to be a frozen ball of ice and rock like a giant dirty snowball. It takes 248 years to travel round the sun and sometimes comes nearer the sun than Neptune. Pluto may once have been a moon of Neptune.

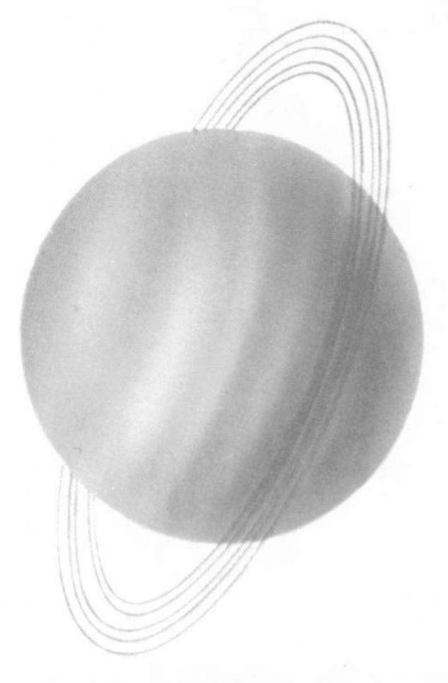

Above left: A close-up of Jupiter's Red Spot.
Left: Astronomers discovered a ring system around Uranus in 1977.

THE MOON

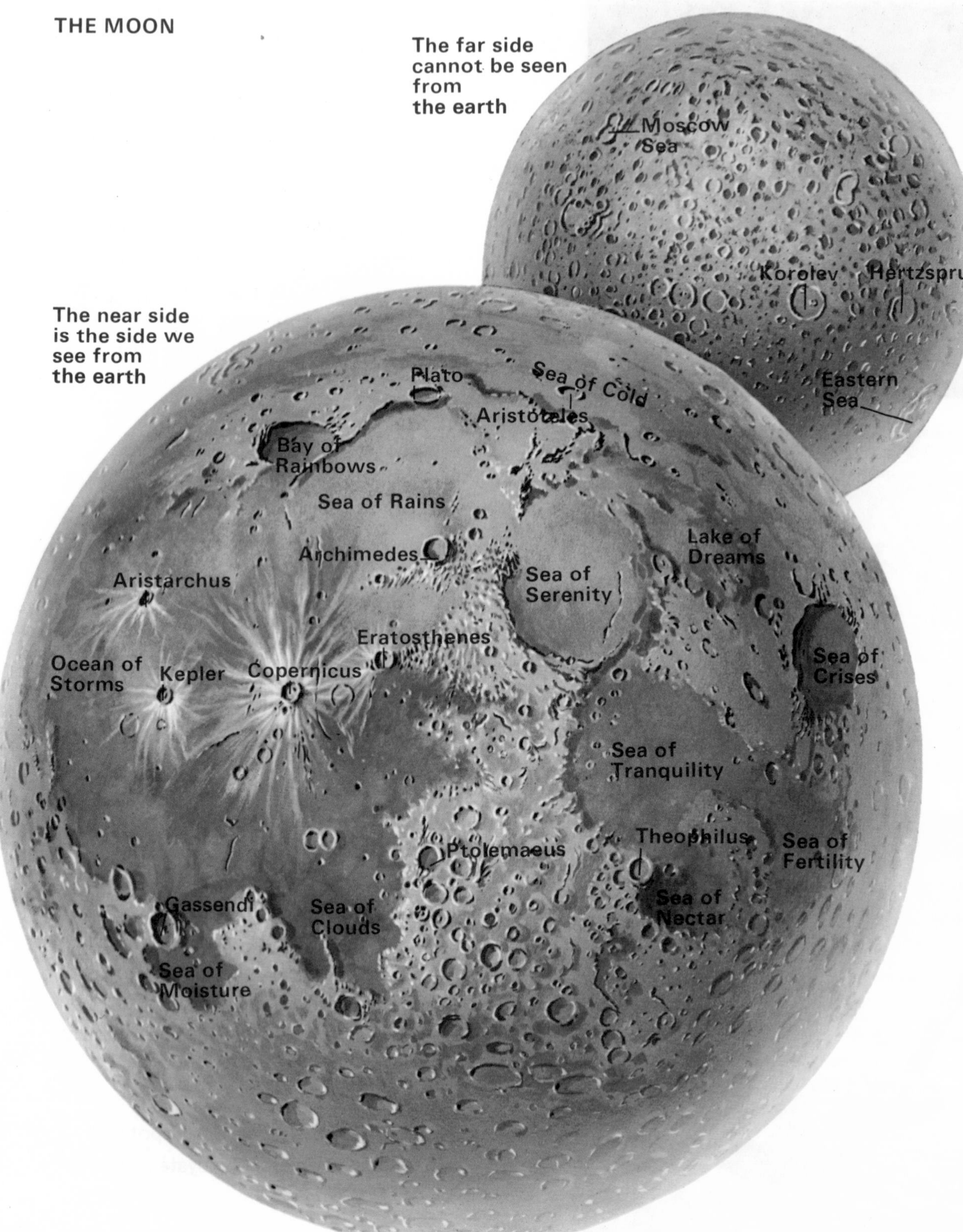
The far side
cannot be seen
from
the earth
Moscow
Sea
Korolev
Hertzsprung
Eastern
Sea
The near side
is the side we
see from
the earth
Plato
Sea of Cold
Aristoteles
Bay of
Rainbows
Sea of Rains
Archimedes
Lake of
Dreams
Aristarchus
Sea of
Serenity
Eratosthenes
Ocean of
Storms
Kepler
Copernicus
Sea of
Crises
Sea of
Tranquility
Theophilus
Sea of
Fertility
Ptolemaeus
Gassendi
Sea of
Clouds
Sea of
Nectar
Sea of
Moisture

Moon

The moon circles around the earth every 27 days 8 hours. In the same period of time it completes one turn on its axis. Therefore the same side is always facing towards the earth. The average distance between the moon and the earth is about 384,000 kilometres.

The moon is about one-quarter the diameter of the earth. Its GRAVITY is only one-sixth that of the earth.

Its airless surface is hot in sunlight and cold in shadow. It has thousands of craters. They range in size from small pits to over 100 kilometres across. There are mountains and large dry plains called 'seas'. The U.S.S.R. was the first country to crash land a space probe on the moon in 1959. The first working instruments were landed in 1966, by the U.S.S.R. in January and by the U.S.A. in May. American ASTRONAUTS Neil Armstrong and Edwin Aldrin were the first men to land there – on the Sea of Tranquillity – on 20 July 1969.

Moon samples brought to the earth so far, as expected, contained no evidence of life. Igneous ROCKS – those which had become solid after melting – were similar to volcanic rocks on the earth.

The moon also has chunks of rock and soil cemented together by temperature and pressure. In places the soil is so fine that the astronauts' boots made firm impressions. Some of this dark grey soil contains small beads of glass, which are formed by the shock and heat of rocky bodies crashing on to the moon at high speed.

Top: The Lunar Module of the Apollo spacecraft in orbit around the moon. The earth can be seen above the moon's horizon.
Centre: A footprint in the moon's soil.
Bottom: Edwin Aldrin stands beside a leg of the lunar module on the Sea of Tranquillity.

Comets

One day you may be lucky enough to see a comet as it moves around the sun. The most famous is Halley's comet, which takes 76 years to travel around the sun. This comet last appeared in 1910 and is due to return in 1986.

Comets are made up of frozen gases and dust. They travel in very long, thin orbits, bringing them from the edges of the solar system to swing round very close to the sun. We can only see them when they are near the sun. Then they reflect sun-light and glow as they react to solar radiation. When they approach the sun, an enormous glowing tail forms stretching out from the comet's head.

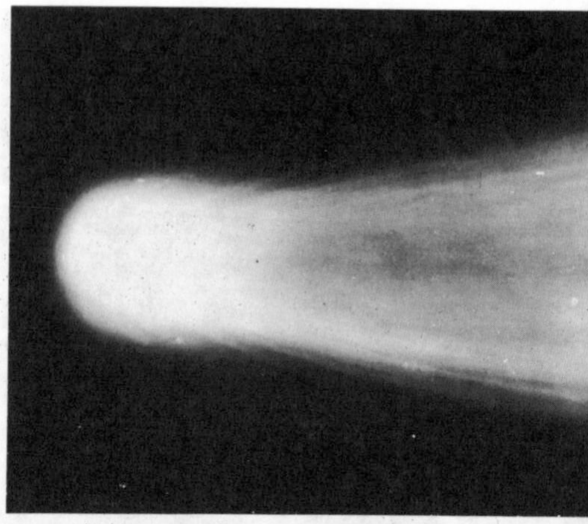

Above: The head of Halley's Comet. Below: The path of Halley's Comet through the solar system. The tail always points away from the sun.

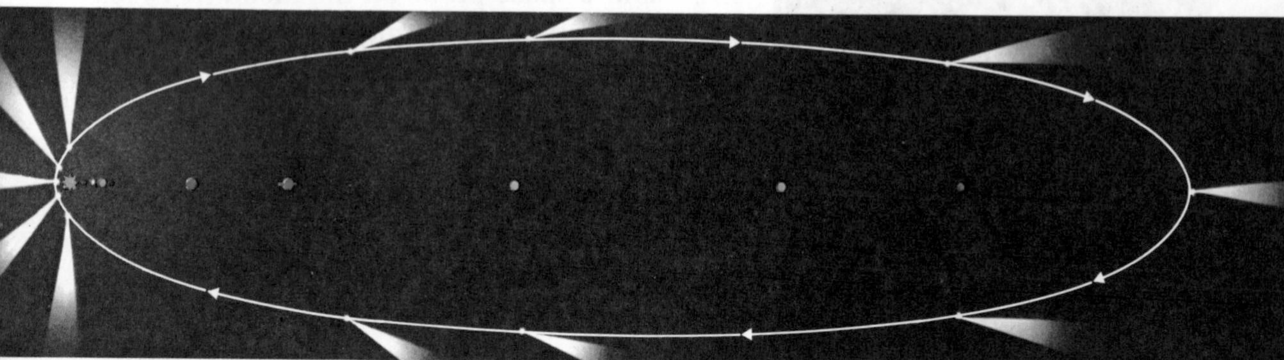

The tail of a comet is millions of kilometres long, but it does not contain very much material. It is almost transparent. In fact most of the material in a comet is in the nucleus, which may be only one kilometre in diameter.

Some comets take thousands or even millions of years to make one orbit of the sun. Others leave the solar system never to return. Comet Encke returns to the sun most frequently, every 3.3 years.

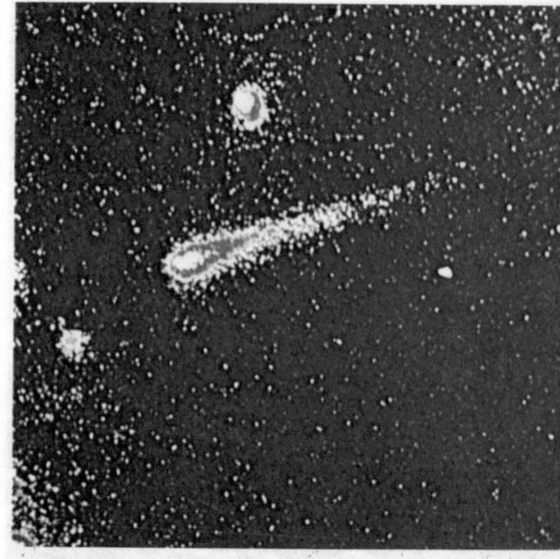

Right: Comet Kohoutek. It was the first comet to be studied from space, by the Skylab astronauts.

Meteors

In its journey around the SUN, our planet collides with millions of fragments of rock and dust. Most of these particles are smaller than a grain of sand. But they move at tremendous speeds – an average of about 17 kilometres per second.

When one of these particles strikes the EARTH's atmosphere, friction with the air makes it white hot. It then burns up in a spear of light. We call this a meteor or a 'shooting star'.

Meteors large enough to get through the atmosphere and to reach the ground are called meteorites. They are made of stone or iron, or both.

Meteorites range in size from small pebbles to huge boulders weighing many tons. A large meteorite fell near Flagstaff, Arizona, in prehistoric times. It weighed about a million tons, and left a crater about 1290 metres across and 175 metres deep.

Top right: This crater was formed by a giant meteorite which hit the ground.
Right: A meteor crossed the sky as this photograph was being taken.

Asteroids

The sun's family of planets includes thousands of minor planets called asteroids. Most of these circle the sun in a belt between Mars and Jupiter. They are jagged chunks of rock, and the largest is only about 1,000 kilometres across, much smaller than our moon. Most of them are very much smaller than this. A few do not stay in the asteroid belt but follow paths that bring them close to the sun and sometimes to the earth.

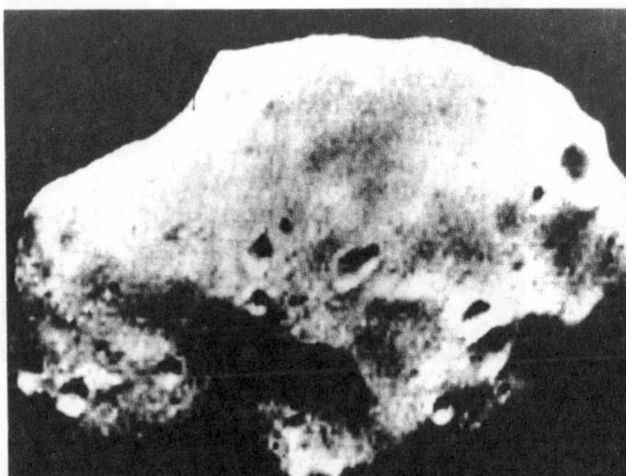

Right: Phobos, the tiny moon of Mars. It could once have been an asteroid.

Our Earth

The earth was formed about $4\frac{1}{2}$ thousand million years ago. Some meteorites are this age, and scientists think the earth is as old as the meteorites. But they do not know *how* the earth was formed. It was most likely created at the same time as the other PLANETS in the solar system. But no one knows for sure how the solar system was formed.

Like other STARS, the SUN formed as clouds of dust and gas gathered together in space. Perhaps the earth and planets formed at the same time, from small pockets of dust near the sun. Another possibility is that the sun gathered a disc-shaped cloud of dust as it moved through space. This dust then condensed to form the planets. As the dust condensed, it heated up. Over millions and millions of years, balls of molten rock gradually formed, producing the new planets.

Other theories suggest that the earth was once part of a star. This star came near the sun and the sun's GRAVITY pulled out hot material from the star. This material broke up into several new planets.

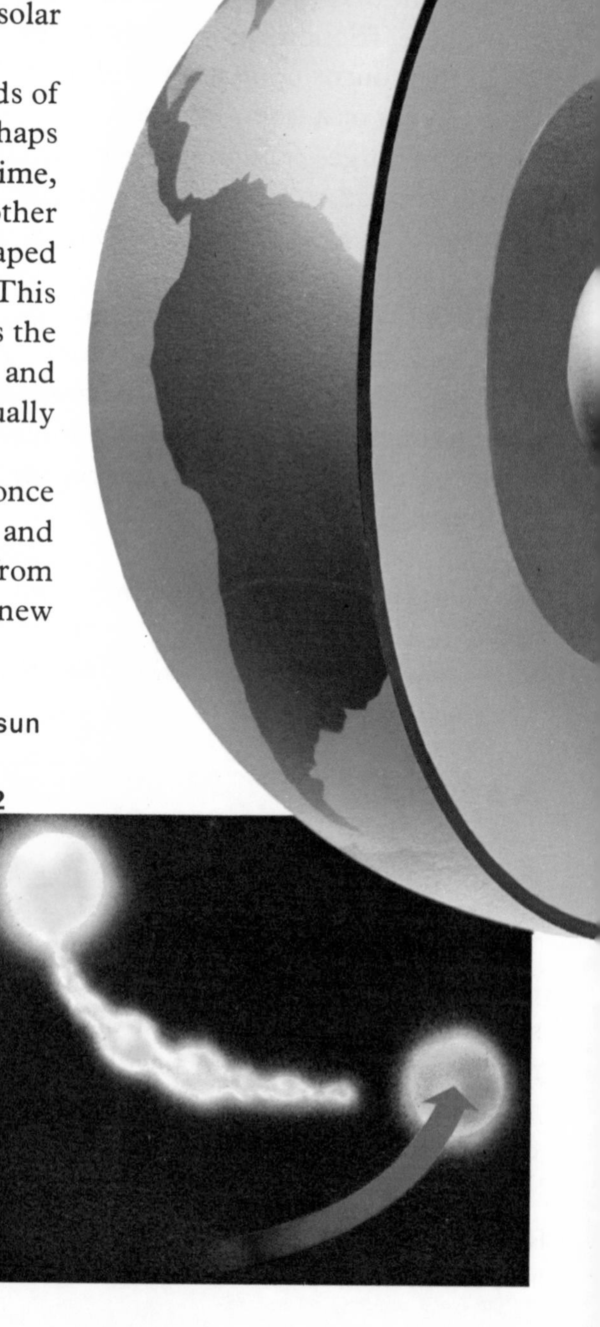

Below: The planets may have formed with the sun (1), or by being pulled out of a star (2).

1

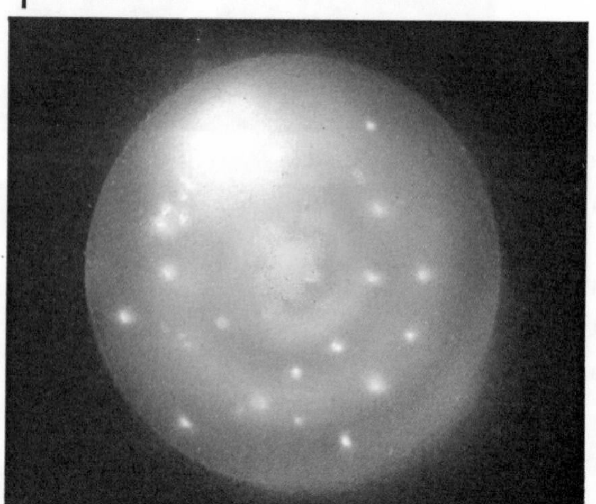

2

The layers of the earth.

Yet another suggestion is that the sun was once one of a pair of stars. The other star blew up, leaving pieces of the star moving round the sun. These pieces became the planets.

Perhaps we shall soon find out which of these theories is correct, or whether the earth formed in yet another way. We may find the answer by exploring the planets, and not here on earth.

Whatever its origin, the earth was probably born as a ball of rock. Gradually, it gained heat and its interior melted. A solid shell of rock was formed around the centre, and over it an outer skin. The skin is called the crust, and the solid shell is the mantle. The centre of the earth is called the core. It is in two parts: a liquid outer core and a solid inner core. We live on a few metres of soil on top of the crust.

Crust	About 100 kilometres thick
Mantle	2790 kilometres
Outer core	2260 kilometres thick
Inner core	1220 kilometres *radius*
Radius of the earth	6370 kilometres

Below: The planets may have formed from a dust cloud around the sun (3), or an exploding star (4).

Continental drift

If you look at a map of the world you will notice that the ATLANTIC coasts of SOUTH AMERICA and AFRICA are a similar shape. If they could be moved together, they would fit closely. For years some geologists have believed that all the continents of the world once fitted closely together. A new idea to support this is that 200 million years ago, one huge super-continent existed, surrounded by ocean. Then it began to break up into separate pieces, and the pieces slowly drifted apart. These pieces of land are called plates, and the continents lie on different plates. As the plates move, the continents also drift slowly apart. Today the Americas are continuing to move farther away from EUROPE and Africa. But the movement is very slow. The plates move at speeds of only 10 to 100 millimetres a year.

The plates are located beneath the land and the oceans. They make up the bottom part of the earth's crust. Some plates are large and others are small. Almost all the PACIFIC OCEAN lies above one large plate, called the Pacific plate.

150 million years ago

100 million years ago

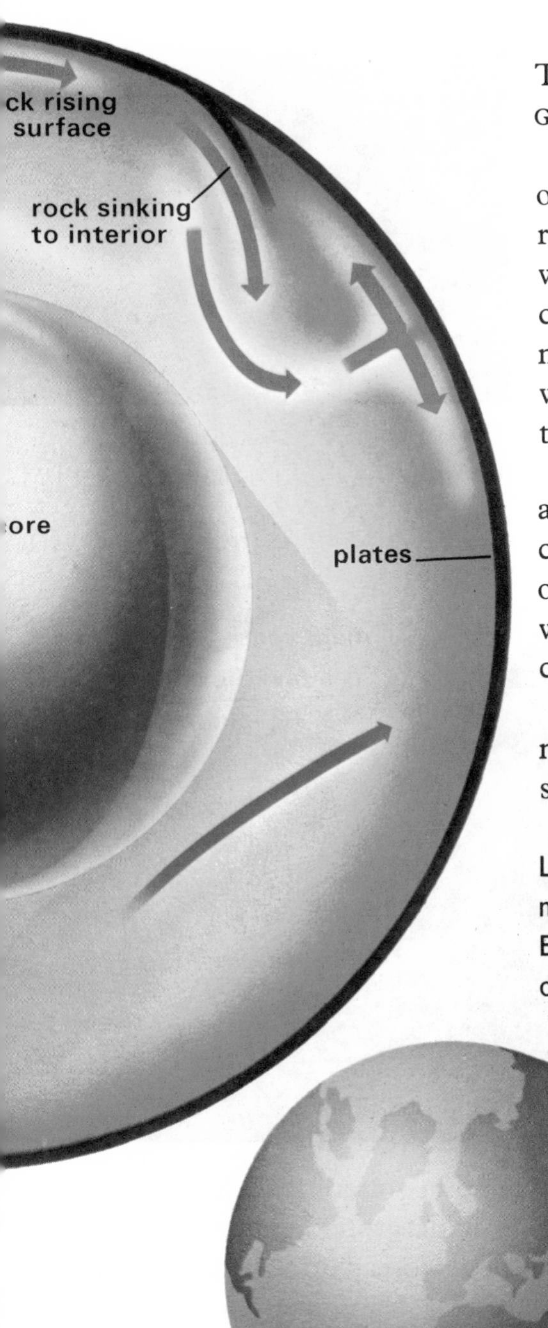

The small Aegean plate is covered by only GREECE, the Aegean Sea, and the coast of TURKEY.

Some people think that heat from the inside of the earth makes the plates move. Hot, molten rock beneath the ground moves gradually towards the surface. When it meets the earth's crust, it spreads out and flows sideways. As the molten rock moves sideways, it carries the plates with it. When it cools, the rock sinks back into the earth's interior.

The hot rock reaches the crust in several places and spreads out over the globe. Some plates are carried into each other, others scrape past each other, and some move away from each other. But where two plates collide, the land will start to change shape.

Although they are moving slowly, the plates meet with great force. Nothing can stop the result: volcanic eruptions, and EARTHQUAKES.

Left: Movements of hot rock in the earth's interior make the surface plates move.
Below: 200 million years ago, the continents fitted closely. Then they began to drift apart.

50 million years ago

today

Volcanoes

A volcano erupts when a passage or vent opens up through the crust of the earth. The vent reaches down to a chamber of molten rock beneath the ground. The molten rock is forced up the vent and flows out on top as lava.

On the surface, the lava cools and becomes solid rock. A cone-shaped volcano sometimes builds up with a crater at the top. Eventually the vent becomes blocked and the eruption stops. But, if pressure builds up underground, the vent may re-open and the volcano explode again.

Above: Crater Lake in Oregon in the United States. It fills the crater of an extinct volcano.

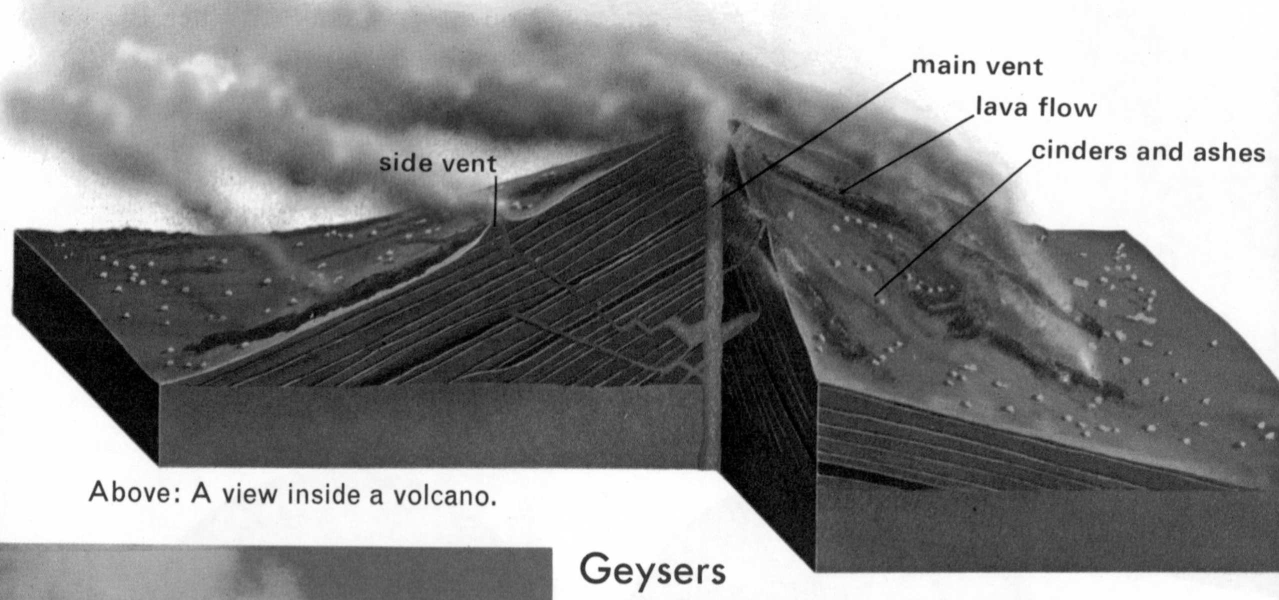

Above: A view inside a volcano.

Geysers

Geysers are found in volcanic regions. The heat causes water in underground chambers to boil. The boiling water is forced up a crack in the rock to the surface. There it spurts out in a column of hot spray.

A geyser is a special kind of hot water spring. Hot springs occur where water is warmed underground.

Left: A geyser sends a plume of hot steam and spray shooting into the air.

Above: An explosion of lava from a volcano in Iceland.

Earthquakes

Earthquakes occur when one mass of rock suddenly moves in relation to another. The movement does not have to be very great to cause severe destruction in cities.

Earthquakes usually occur in the same regions as VOLCANOES. This is explained by CONTINENTAL DRIFT. Great strain results where two plates are colliding or moving past each other. Pressure builds up between masses of rock and then they suddenly give way and move, causing earthquakes. The split produced where rocks break under such pressure is called a fault. If molten rock lies underneath faults, vents may open up and volcanoes erupt.

When an earthquake occurs beneath the sea, it shakes the sea floor. This movement produces a powerful wave at the surface of the sea. The wave is not very high but it moves very fast. As the wave approaches the shore, it piles up into a huge wave in the shallows. Then it smashes into the shore with great violence. These waves are often wrongly called tidal waves. Their correct name is tsunami.

Right: Damage from an earthquake in Nicaragua.

Shaping the land

High MOUNTAINS, deep VALLEYS, and all the other features of the land may look very permanent. But they are slowly changing all the time.

Two actions keep changing the shape of the land. One action is that of underground forces. These forces bend the layers of ROCKS, forcing them up and down into mountains and valleys. Geologists think that the movement of rock plates beneath the earth's surface – CONTINENTAL DRIFT – causes the earth's crust to buckle and fold.

The other action is the slow wearing down of the mountains and other features. This action is called erosion. The heat of the SUN, RAIN, and frost, and the motion of RIVERS, GLACIERS, seas, and WINDS help to break down the rock into small particles and to carry the particles away. The action of water can also dissolve some rocks. The rock particles are eventually deposited elsewhere. As soon as the underground forces have raised a chain of mountains, the forces of erosion begin to wear it down.

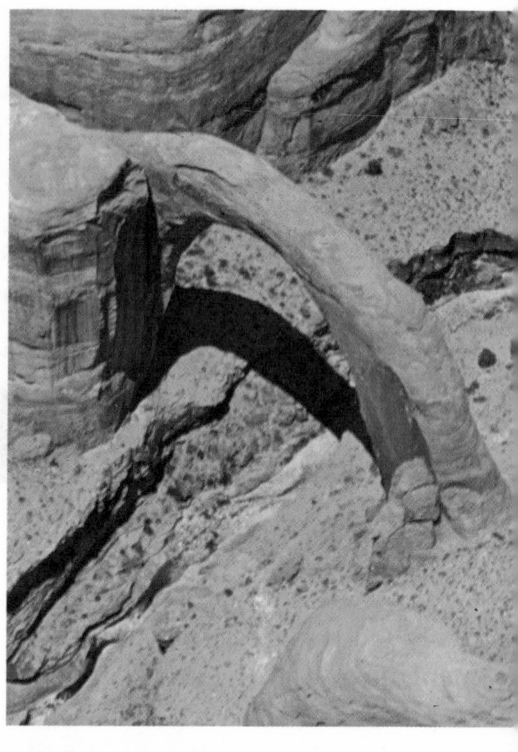

Above: Rainbow Bridge, Utah, a sandstone arch formed by erosion. Below: Columns left when erosion made Monument Valley, U.S.A.

Mountains

Mountains are formed in different ways. One way is when the earth's crust bends. Then great folds that are many thousands of metres high and many kilometres apart are produced. The movement of the earth's crust may also jam together or even overturn the folds on top of one another. This kind of action forms mountains and VALLEYS of all kinds and sizes.

Folding produces great stresses on the layers of rock. Often the layers break, producing splits called faults. Cliffs and scarps in mountainous areas may sometimes be faults. The layers of rock are often exposed to view at faults. The bends in the layers caused by the folding can easily be seen in cliffs.

Mountains are also formed by erosion. If a hard block of rock is surrounded by softer rock, erosion may wear away the soft rock but not the hard rock. The block is left standing and forms a mountain.

VOLCANOES are another kind of mountain. They are built up in layers of solid lava.

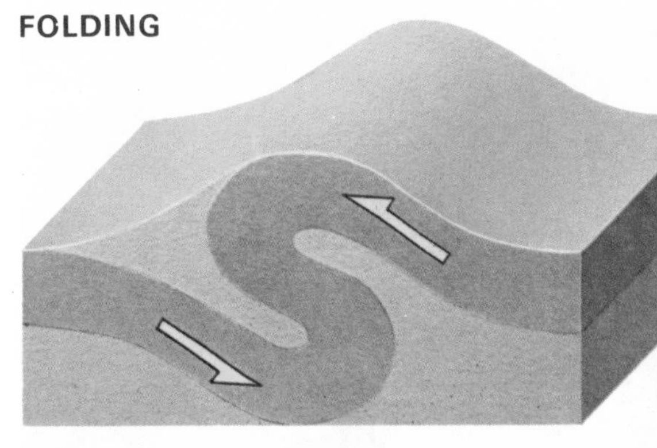

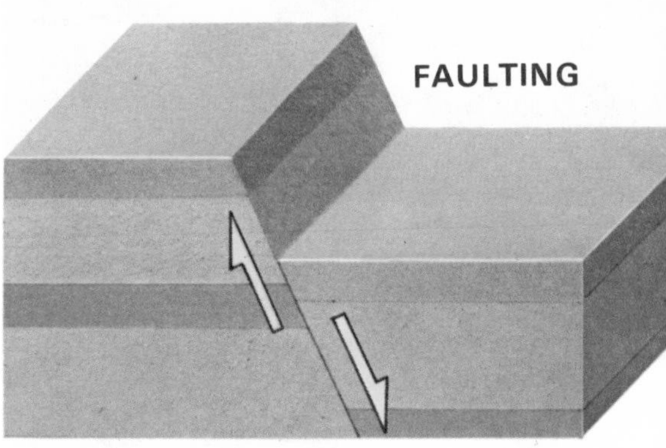

Below: Mount McKinley is the highest mountain in North America.

The Rockies

The Rocky Mountains, or Rockies, are a long chain of mountains that stretches along the western side of NORTH AMERICA. They extend from Alaska to MEXICO. They are situated some distance from the sea and act as a divide. This means that the rivers on the two sides of the Rockies flow in opposite directions. On the east all the rivers flow towards the ATLANTIC OCEAN. On the west they all flow towards the PACIFIC OCEAN. There is little volcanic activity in the Rockies, and EARTHQUAKES do not often happen there.

Left: One of the highest peaks of the Rocky Mountains is Grand Teton in Wyoming.

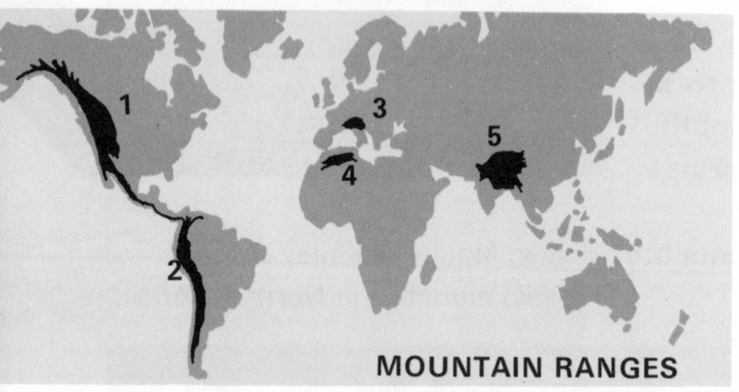

Left: A map of the world showing five great mountain ranges: the Rocky Mountains (1), the Andes (2), the Alps (3), the Atlas (4), and the Himalayas (5).
Below: This pass in the Andes is as high as the top of the highest mountain in the Alps. It is situated in Bolivia.

The Andes

The Andes are the long chain of mountains that runs along the western coast of SOUTH AMERICA from the isthmus of Panama, south to Cape Horn. The Andes are very different from the ROCKIES. They are near the sea, and have many VOLCANOES and EARTHQUAKES. Some scientists believe that the Nazca plate beneath the south-east PACIFIC is being pushed beneath the South American plate. The edge of the descending plate is melted, and this liquid rock is rising through volcanoes. The Rockies are some distance from plate edges, so there is less activity.

The Alps

The Alps are the greatest mountain range in EUROPE. They extend from southern FRANCE, through SWITZERLAND and northern ITALY into AUSTRIA. The mountains rise steeply in the south, but more gently in the north. They are formed by Italy moving very slowly northwards. If the earth's crust were not buckled up to form the Alps, Europe would be 100 kilometres wider than it is today.

Left: Muerren is a small town lying high up among the Swiss Alps. It is situated near the Jungfrau, one of the highest mountains in the Alps.
Below: The Atlas Mountains above Marrakesh, Morocco.

The Atlas

Across the other side of the MEDITERRANEAN SEA, AFRICA is moving north, like ITALY. This action is raising the level of the Atlas Mountains on the north coast of Africa. It is also gradually reducing the distance between the north and south shores of the MEDITERRANEAN SEA.

Below: Annapurna, one of the highest peaks in the Himalayas, overlooks Pokhara, Nepal.

The Himalayas

The Himalayas make up the world's greatest mountain range. This range contains the world's highest peaks, of which the tallest is Everest. The Himalayas started to form about 50 million years ago, when the Indian plate came into contact with ASIA.

INDIA is still moving slowly north. So are Arabia and AFRICA. This action is raising a new range of mountains from the Himalayas at one end to the ALPS at the other.

Valleys, canyons, and gorges

Valleys, canyons, gorges, ravines, and gullies are all kinds of long depressions in the land. As a RIVER or stream flows over the ground, it wears away the rock. Gradually it carves out a depression. A small channel formed in this way is called a gully. A larger, deeper channel is a ravine.

At first the river cuts deeply into the land as it descends towards the sea, forming a narrow valley. But as the river cuts away the land, its course becomes less steep and it flows more slowly. The cutting action widens the valley bottom and erosion makes its sloping sides gentler. Rock particles (silt) carried in the water are deposited to give the valley a flat bottom.

If the rocks are being slowly pushed upwards as the river cuts them, a gradually deepening gorge is formed. It will have steep, vertical sides. A canyon is a large gorge. Canyons are very deep and narrow at the bottom, but they open out at the top.

This valley has the U-shape of a valley formed by a glacier.

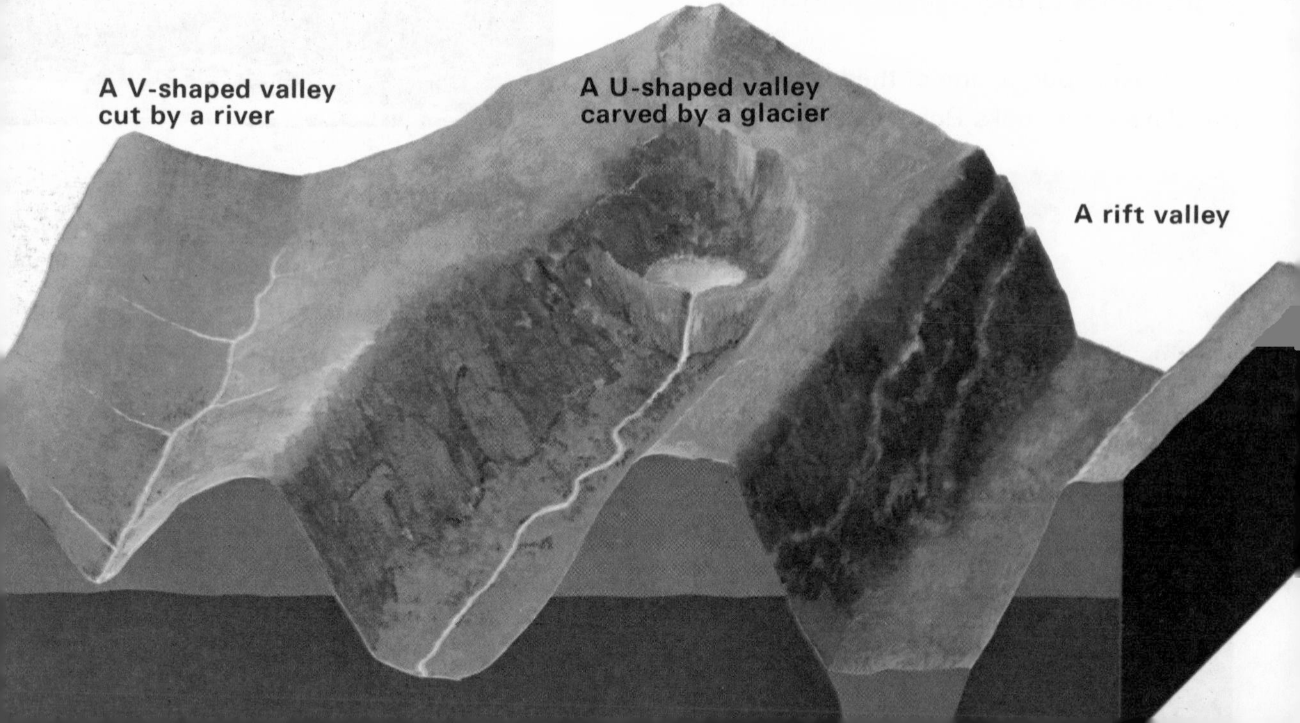

A V-shaped valley cut by a river

A U-shaped valley carved by a glacier

A rift valley

The most spectacular canyon in the world is the Grand Canyon in the United States. It was formed in Arizona by the Colorado River cutting into a gradually rising plateau. The river has cut more than 1500 metres down through different layers of rock. These layers can be seen along the sides of the Grand Canyon. Some layers are made of harder rock than others.

Valleys are also formed where GLACIERS gouge out channels in the land. A river usually forms a V-shaped valley. A glacier makes a U-shaped valley.

Above: The Grand Canyon was formed as the Colorado River cut deep into a high plateau.
Left: The Grand Canyon from the air.

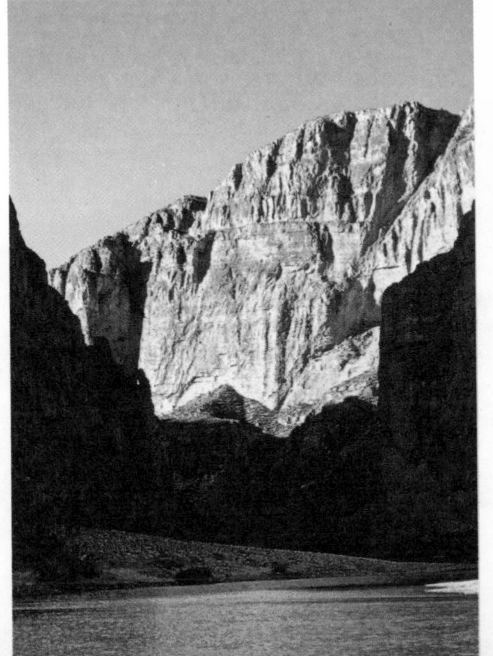

Rift valleys are different from ordinary valleys. They have steep sides, but they are wide at the bottom. A rift valley is like a huge trench or trough in the land. Rift valleys are not formed by erosion. The sides of smaller rift valleys are faults in the rock. The land slips down between the faults.

Large rift valleys are slightly different. The Great Rift Valley in eastern AFRICA has formed where two plates are moving apart. It is at the southern end of a system of rifts, which includes the Dead Sea and the Red Sea.

Left: A canyon formed by the Rio Grande in Texas.

Rivers

A river begins on high ground. The place where a river starts to flow is its source. Rivers can begin where several tiny streams or rivulets come together. The source may also be a spring. Some rivers begin by flowing out of LAKES, and others are formed where GLACIERS melt.

The river flows downhill from its source until it reaches another river or the sea. Rivers that flow into other rivers are called tributaries. The main river gets bigger as more water flows into it from tributaries. By the time it gets to the sea, it may be very wide. The part of the river that enters the sea is called the mouth of the river. The wide region at the mouth is called an estuary.

The river cuts a VALLEY in the land as it flows. It carries away SOIL down towards the sea. Fine particles of soil carried by rivers are called silt. When the river approaches the sea, the land becomes almost flat. The water travels too slowly to carry all the silt. A flat plain builds up over the floor of the valley as silt is left behind.

Above: Seen from space, the Nile delta appears as a green triangle of vegetation amid the desert.

River rises on high ground
River grows as tributaries join, and cuts valley
Waterfall where river flows over cliff

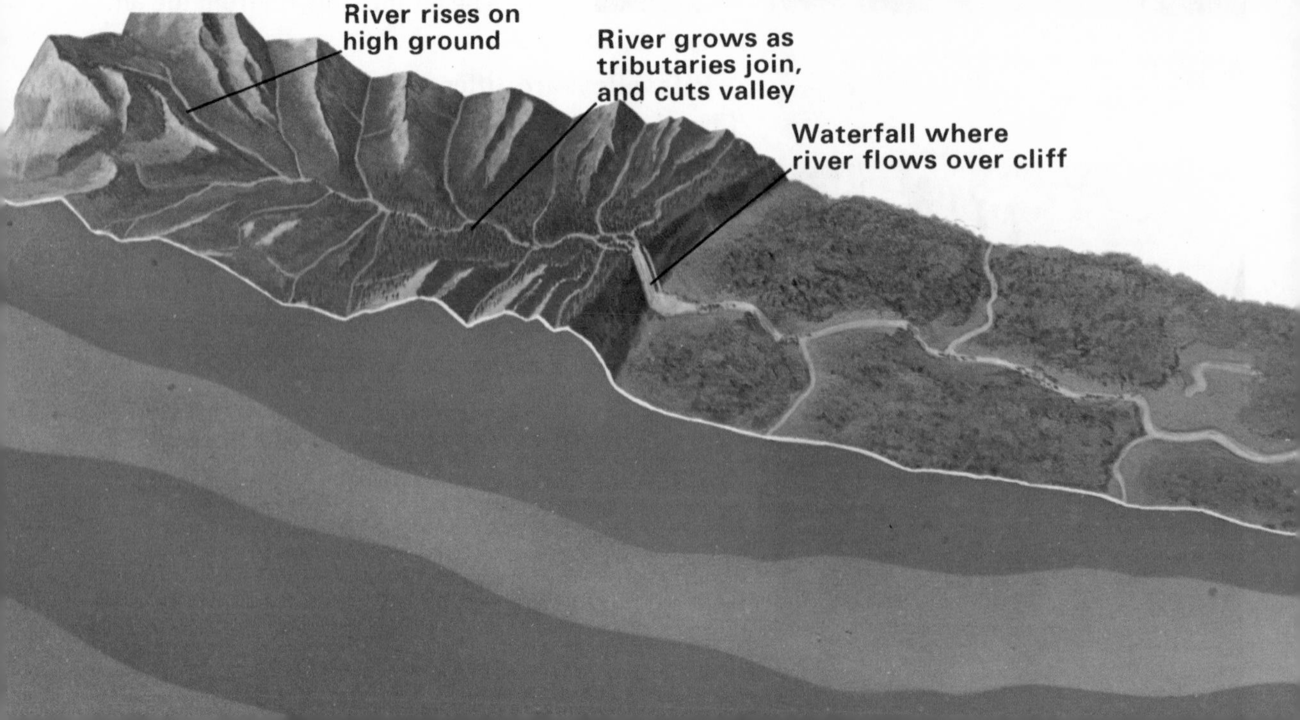

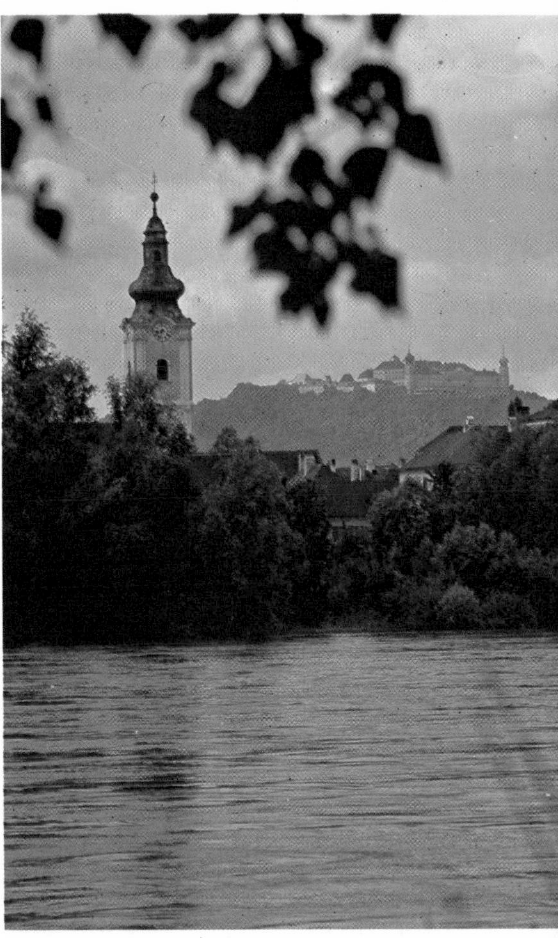

The river often starts to curve over the plain, forming meanders in its course. Large rivers carry so much silt that the deposits at the mouth break the river up into small channels. The network of channels spreads out in the shape of a triangle before the river finally enters the sea. This region is called a delta, after the triangular Greek letter called delta.

Every continent has several great rivers. They rise in the middle of the continent and flow across the land to the ocean. Some rise in mountains on one side of the continent and flow right across it to the other side. These rivers are important as a source of water for man and as a means of transportation. Civilization began alongside rivers. Man still needs water to survive.

Left: The Nile begins life in the centre of Africa. Other rivers flowing from lakes join the Nile in its long course to the sea.
Right: The Danube is the second longest river in Europe. It flows across Europe to the Black Sea. The longest river in Europe is the Volga.

A RIVER FROM SOURCE TO MOUTH

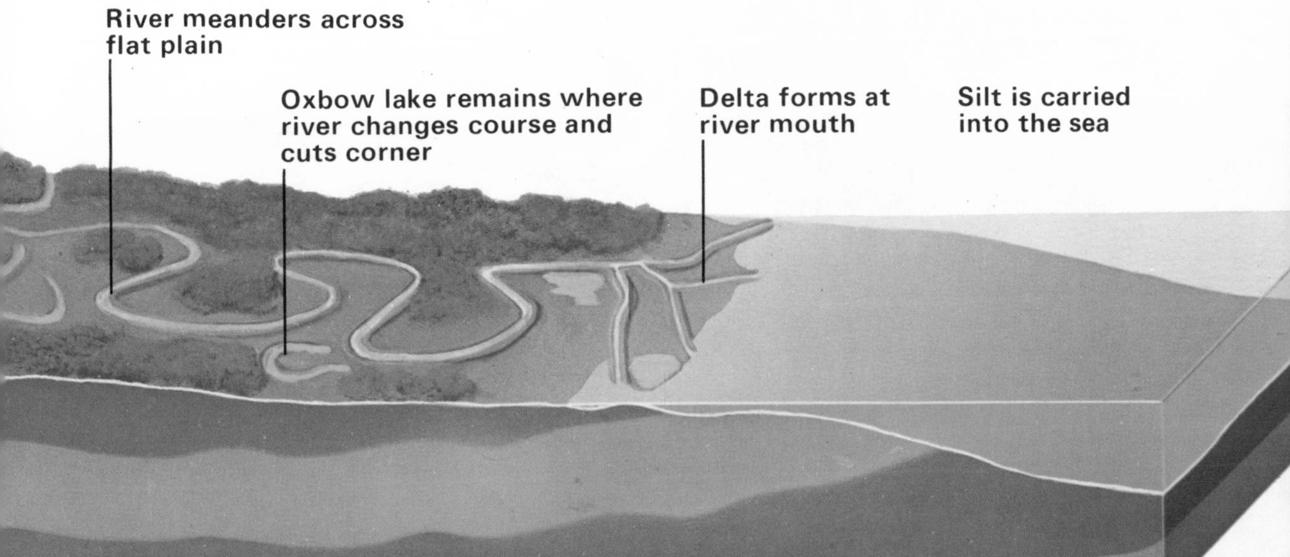
River meanders across flat plain
Oxbow lake remains where river changes course and cuts corner
Delta forms at river mouth
Silt is carried into the sea

Waterfalls

If a RIVER comes to a cliff, it spills over in an often spectacular curtain of water. We call this a waterfall.

Cliffs, which may be formed by a fault in the rock, are not the only way waterfalls are born. Waterfalls may also appear where the river flows over ground containing a hard bed of rock. The river wears away the softer rock on both sides of the hard bed. Once the hard rock is exposed, it forms a ledge over which the water plunges.

If there is a layer of soft rock in a cliff, this will be worn away too. A space is formed behind the waterfall. A ledge hangs over the space. From time to time, pieces of the ledge fall away. In this way, the waterfall gradually moves back up the river. The Horseshoe Falls at Niagara Falls are receding at a rate of a metre a year for this reason.

The highest waterfall in the world is Angel Falls in Venezuela. It is 980 metres high.

Sometimes a RAINBOW can be seen in a waterfall. This happens when sunlight falls on the droplets in the spray around the waterfall.

Above: The Marmore waterfall in Italy. A rainbow can be seen in the bottom of the picture, where sunlight strikes the spray.

ACTION OF WATERFALLS

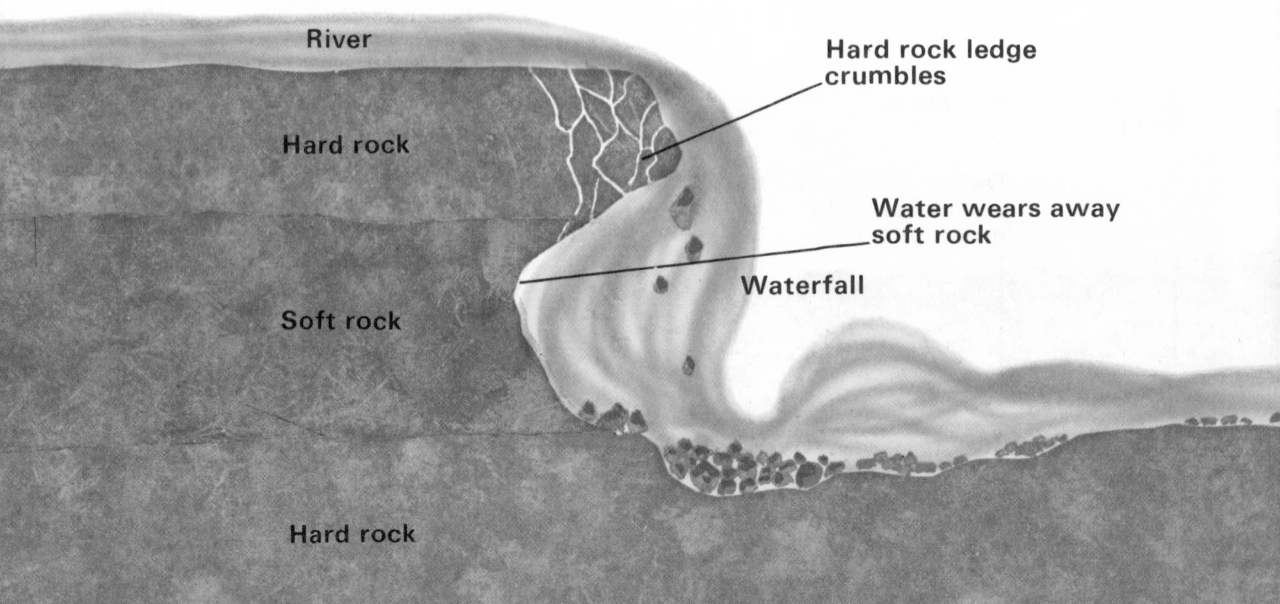

Caves

When a RIVER flows over a bed of limestone, the limestone will be worn away like other rocks. But the water also dissolves a little of the mineral calcite, of which limestone is mostly made. The dissolving action happens because the water contains some carbon dioxide gas from the air. It enables the water gradually to hollow out passages and chambers underground.

The caves that form are often beautiful. The roof and walls may be covered with columns of white calcite. The hanging columns are called stalactites. They form because the water drips from the roof or down the walls, and the dissolved calcite crystallizes again to form layers of solid calcite. It takes many thousands of years to form a stalactite. Where the drops of water hit the cave floor, columns start to build up. These rising columns are called stalagmites.

Right: A cave in South Africa. Water dripping through the ceiling of the cave carries minerals that form the hanging stalactites.

FORMATION OF LIMESTONE CAVES

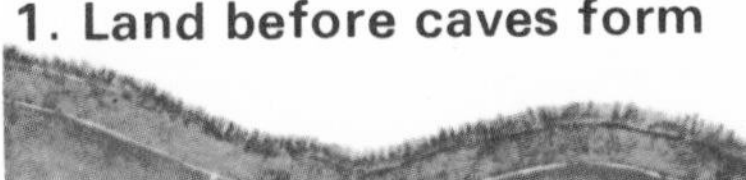

1. Land before caves form

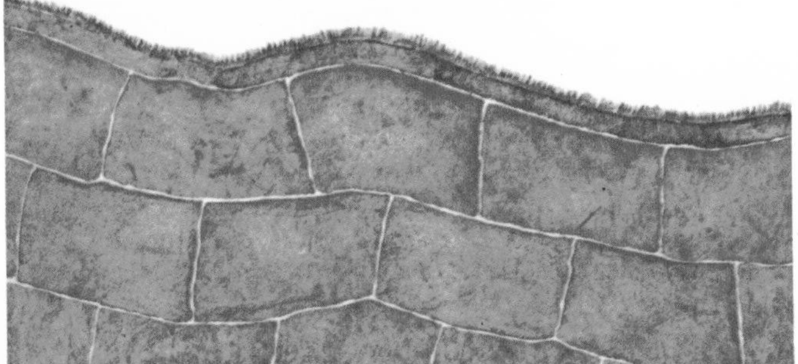

2. Water action widens cracks in rock

3. Passages open underground

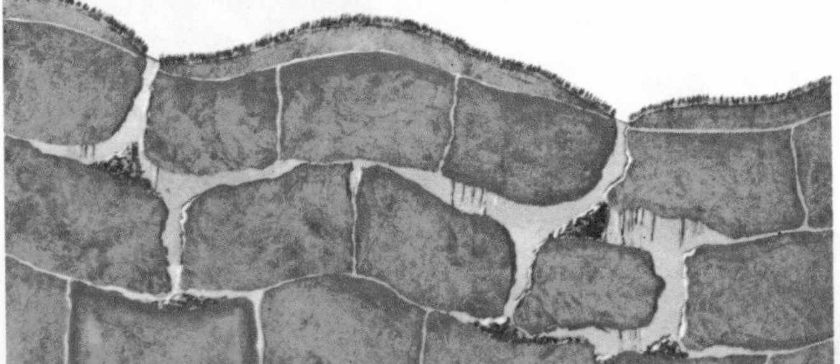

4. Passages widen into caves

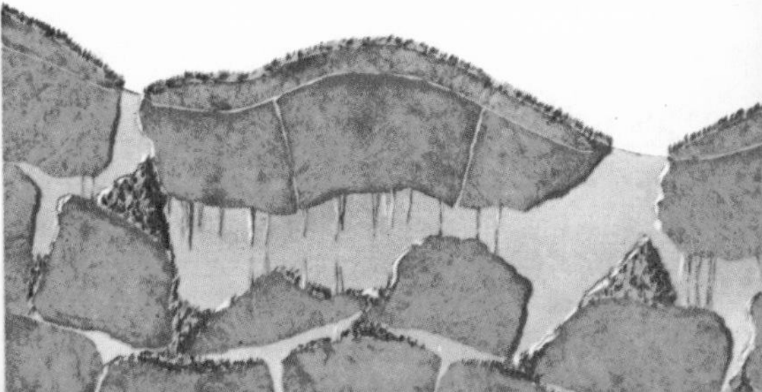

Glaciers

Glaciers are RIVERS of SNOW and ice. They are formed near the tops of high MOUNTAINS or on the ground in lands near the ARCTIC and ANTARCTIC oceans. The masses of ice are produced by snowfalls.

Glaciers move slowly, from as little as a centimetre a day to about 30 metres a day. They dig out rocks from the land and carry them to the sides and end of the glacier. A glacier ends when it gets down to where the air is warm enough to melt the ice.

Ice sheets

The falls of snow on land in the ARCTIC and ANTARCTIC cause huge sheets of ice to form on the ground. Because all the ice does not melt in summer, the ice gradually gets thicker and thicker as the years go by. Great ice sheets cover Antarctica and almost all of Greenland. They are as much as 3000 metres deep in places. Smaller sheets of ice are called ice caps. Ice caps cover islands in the ARCTIC OCEAN.

Above: The Gorner glacier in Switzerland. The lines of rocks that form at the sides and ends of glaciers are called moraines.
Below: The edge of an ice sheet.

Ice ages

Over thousands of years the world's climate changes, causing ice sheets to spread and melt. An ice age occurs when the ice sheet is large. The last ice age was at its height 18,000 years ago. Then ice covered the land as far south as the Great Lakes in NORTH AMERICA. It reached to the southern part of the British Isles, and covered Scandinavia, northern GERMANY, northern POLAND, and northern Russia.

Icebergs

Icebergs are huge lumps of ice that float in the sea. They are formed where GLACIERS or ICE SHEETS meet the sea. Large blocks of ice break off and float away. The ice is lighter than water, and so it floats. But only a ninth of the iceberg can be seen above the surface. The other eight-ninths of the berg is below the water.

Most icebergs form at the edges of the ice sheets on Greenland and ANTARCTICA. The ocean currents eventually carry the icebergs into warmer waters. There they slowly melt away.

Above: 18,000 years ago, the last ice age was at its height. The northern ice sheet reached to where London is today. Then it began to retreat. It reached its present size about 6000 years ago.
Below: A medium-sized iceberg in the Antarctic Ocean. Icebergs there may be over 60 kilometres long.

Lakes and inland seas

If a RIVER meets a hollow on its journey to the sea, it will fill the hollow with water. A lake will then be formed. If the lake is very large, it is sometimes called an inland sea. The largest is the Caspian Sea in ASIA, and the next biggest is Lake Superior in NORTH AMERICA. Often there is a river flowing out of the other end of the lake. If water is continually flowing through a lake, the water of the lake stays fresh, and its level does not change.

Some lakes do not have an outlet. All the surrounding rivers flow into the lake, but none flows out. These lakes often form in hot regions. The heat of the SUN makes most of the water evaporate, so that its level stays low. The water cannot rise high enough to find an outlet. If the lake has no outlet, its water becomes very salty. In some places, the sun's heat makes lakes dry out during the summer.

The hollows in which many lakes form have usually been dug out by GLACIERS. The Dead Sea, however, has filled a large rift VALLEY.

Below left: Lake Seefeld, Austria.
Below right: The shore of the Dead Sea.

Swamps and marshes

LAKES do not last for ever. Gradually they fill up with silt. Plants start to grow where the water is shallow. Areas called SWAMPS develop where the SOIL is always wet and overgrown with vegetation. Swamps also form on low-lying, soft ground where water does not easily drain away. They often form near RIVER mouths. Mangrove swamps are found along tropical coasts. Mangrove trees grow in thick tangles in the wet ground.

A marsh is slightly different from a swamp. Marshes are covered with a thin layer of water from time to time. Marshes often form on sea coasts, where high tides flood land near the shore with water every day. A BOG is a swamp in which large quantities of MOSS grow. Bogs may look firm enough to stand on, but are often not solid enough to support a man's weight. Over thousands and thousands of years, the moss forms peat and eventually COAL.

Swamps and marshes can sometimes be drained to produce rich land for farming.

Left: A lake in New Zealand formed by a glacier.
Below: The Everglades swamps in Florida, U.S.A.

Deserts

Deserts are very dry regions where few plants will grow because there is little rainfall. Some grass and scrub may survive as well as plants such as cacti, which need little water. But few men and animals can live in the desert.

Some deserts have a surface of sand, which the WIND blows into dunes. Other deserts are stony or rocky. A desert often is very hot during the day but cold at night. The continual changes of temperature break the rock and stones into fragments. Because the wind blows the smaller fragments away, SOIL cannot form.

Deserts usually have some RAIN during the year. Sometimes there are thundery showers. The water runs quickly away or evaporates in the heat and is lost. But some water remains underground and comes to the surface at an oasis.

Deserts are found in broad bands around the world both north and south of the equator. They occur in regions where the air pressure is usually high.

1

3

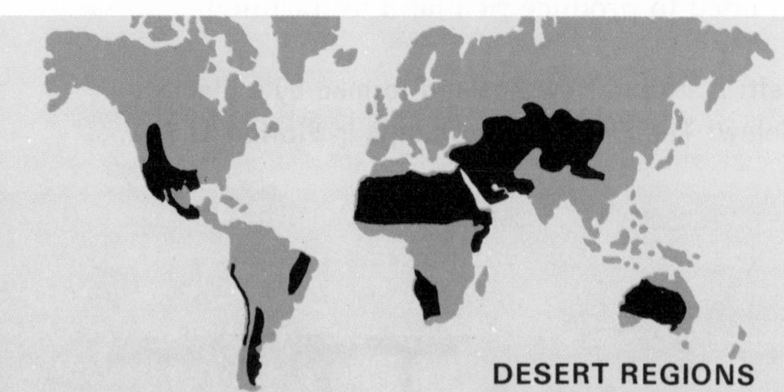

Above: The world's main areas of desert (black), form two bands either side of the equator.
Right: Four desert scenes. (1) Sand dunes, formed by the wind. (2) Cactus growing in Arizona.
(3) Bleached bones lying in the Australian desert.
(4) A stony part of the Sahara.

2

4

Fiords

Fiords are long, narrow bodies of water that cut into a COAST. They occur where the coast is mountainous. They often wind back and forth and may be many kilometres long.

Fiords formed in an ICE AGE when GLACIERS dug out deep VALLEYS as they descended towards the sea. The glaciers have now disappeared, and the sea has invaded the valleys. Fiords are found along the coasts of NORWAY, CANADA, Alaska, Chile, and NEW ZEALAND.

Above: The Naerovfjorden is one of many beautiful fiords along the coast of Norway.

Coasts

Coasts form the border between the land and the sea. There are several different kinds of coasts. Some are smooth beaches of sand or pebbles where the water is shallow. This kind of coast is partly caused by the action of WAVES, which break up rocks. Much sand on beaches, however, is brought to the sea by RIVERS.

Beaches do not form where the water is deep along the shore. The shape of a coast depends on the kind of ROCKS there. If there is a mixture of hard and soft rocks, the soft rocks will wear away much more quickly. Then coves, islets, and rock pinnacles will be formed. If there is only one kind of rock, a smooth cliff may result. If the rock is soft, the waves will cut into the rock at the foot of the cliff. Pieces of the cliff will start to fall away, and over many years the coastline changes.

In some places, silt from rivers and raising of the land may extend the coast. Then the sea recedes. In south-eastern England, several ancient ports are now about three kilometres inland.

Right: Pictured Rocks, a section of coast in the United States. The sea has eaten into the cliff, causing rocks to fall into the sea. Caves sometimes form by the action of the waves.

Islands

Islands near the COAST are partly submerged hills and MOUNTAINS of the mainland. The water surrounding them is not very deep. But some islands are found in the middle of oceans, where the water is extremely deep. Such islands, often called seamounts, are the tops of VOLCANOES that build up from the ocean floor.

Chains of islands form in mid-ocean where the underground plates are moving apart. Rock comes up from below to produce the islands.

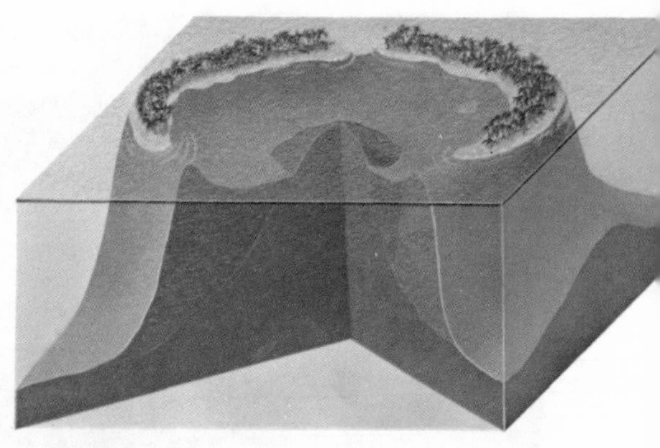

Above: Coral reefs form rings around an island, or lines near a coast. They grow from the seabed to the surface. Sand and soil may then cover the reefs, and trees may begin to grow, forming coral islands. Sometimes, the island within a ring of reefs sinks beneath the sea together with the reefs. But the reefs start to grow again up to the surface. An atoll is a ring-shaped coral island.

Below: A coral island in Malaysia.

Atolls

CORAL reefs grow under the water along coasts and around islands. They are formed by tiny animals. The animals live in large colonies, and the limestone reefs are formed from millions of their skeletons. A coral island forms where sand and soil cover the reef. Coral will only grow in certain conditions of depth, light, and warmth.

An atoll is a ring-shaped reef, with a quiet lagoon of water in the middle. Atolls grow when islands with reefs around them submerge.

Rocks and Minerals

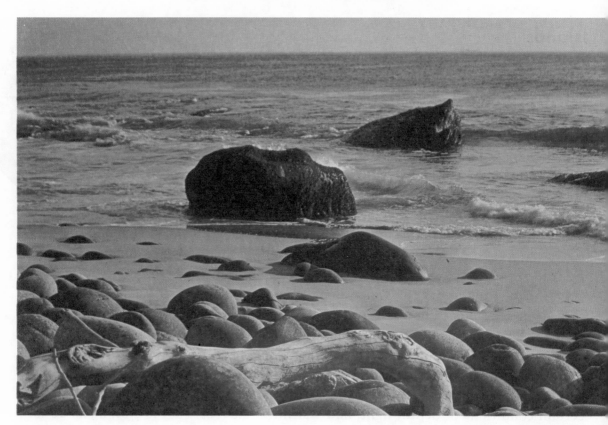

The whole earth, apart from the air and water and living things, is made of ROCKS. The MOON and the PLANETS are made of rocks too. ASTRONAUTS have brought rocks from the moon back to earth. The moon rocks are similar to rocks found on the earth.

The earth is made of many different kinds of rocks and minerals. Minerals are the chemical compounds found in rocks. For example, limestone is a very common rock. It is made up mostly of the mineral called calcite. Granite is another well-known rock. It contains three minerals: feldspar, quartz, and (usually) mica. Ores are rocks with minerals that are useful to man.

Some rocks, such as granite, are very hard. They do not wear away very easily with the action of water and the weather. Softer rocks, like sandstone, crumble more easily.

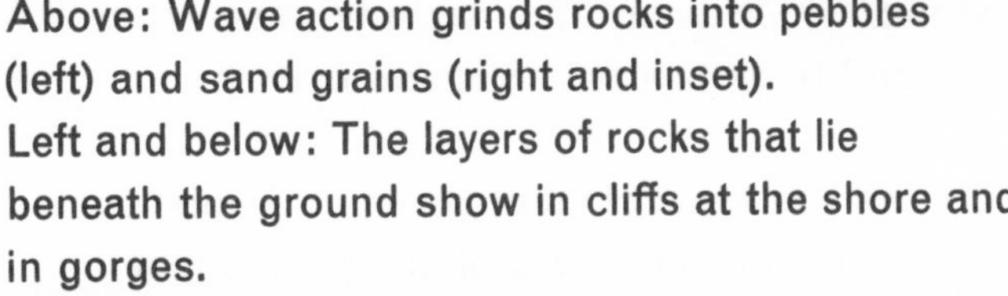

Above: Wave action grinds rocks into pebbles (left) and sand grains (right and inset).
Left and below: The layers of rocks that lie beneath the ground show in cliffs at the shore and in gorges.

Rocks

There are three main groups of rocks in the world. Geologists – scientists who study rocks – are able to tell one group from another by the way the rocks are formed. The first group of rocks is called igneous rocks. These rocks form when hot, liquid rock cools and becomes solid. The word *igneous* comes from a Latin word meaning 'fire'. Igneous rocks include granite and basalt. Basalt sometimes forms large six-sided columns. The steps of the Giant's Causeway in Northern Ireland are the tops of basalt columns.

The second group is called sedimentary rocks. The rocks are made from layers of small rock particles. These layers are called beds or strata. Over a long time the particles become pressed together, forming a sedimentary rock. The particles may have been made by the action of the weather or water on rocks. Sand grains formed in this way are pressed together to become sandstone. Shale is another sedimentary rock. It is formed from layers of silt and clay.

Below: The white cliffs of Dover on England's southern coast are made of chalk. This is a sedimentary rock that was formed beneath the sea.

Limestone and chalk are also sedimentary rocks, but the particles forming these rocks came mostly from animals, not other rocks. In prehistoric times millions of sea creatures died and sank to the bottom. Layers of their tiny skeletons and shells built up. As time passed, the layers stuck together to form rock. In places the sea floor has risen above the water to become dry land.

The third group is called metamorphic rocks. Rocks of any kind are changed by underground heat and pressure into different rocks. Marble is formed from limestone and slate from shale, for example. The name metamorphic comes from Greek words meaning change of form.

Above: Igneous rocks originate as hot, liquid rock beneath the ground. This rock reaches the surface as fiery lava (left). Sometimes when the rock cools, it cracks up to form large columns such as those in the Devil's Postpile, California, U.S.A. (right).
Left: A quarry of marble, a metamorphic rock.

Precious minerals

When ROCKS form, the minerals in them nearly always consist of crystals. The crystals are symmetrical pieces of the mineral with natural flat faces and regular edges. Crystals of quartz can be found in many kinds of rocks. They are usually colourless and transparent and have faces with six edges.

Many transparent crystals are used as gems. Jewellers usually cut them and polish the faces. Diamonds are the best-known gemstones. They are formed deep underground by great heat and pressure on black carbon. Rubies are red crystals and sapphires are blue crystals of the mineral corundum, which normally has no colour. The colours of these gems are produced by small amounts of other substances. Emerald is a green variety of the mineral beryl. An interesting semi-precious mineral is Blue John, which is a purple variety of fluorspar. It is found only in Derbyshire, England, and in JAPAN.

All these minerals are precious because they are beautiful and rare. Amethyst is an attractive red-purple variety of quartz. Amethysts are fairly common.

Not all precious minerals are clear and gleam with light. Jade is a precious stone that is opaque (cannot be seen through). It is valued for its beautiful green colour. Opals have an unusual internal structure. They are milky white or deep blue-black, but glisten with colours. Opals are made of silica.

Precious minerals are always found as small crystals or veins (thin layers) in common rocks. Some rocks contain nuggets (pieces) or veins of precious metals. Gold is the best known precious metal. It is mostly used as a form of money and stored in banks. Silver is another precious metal.

1

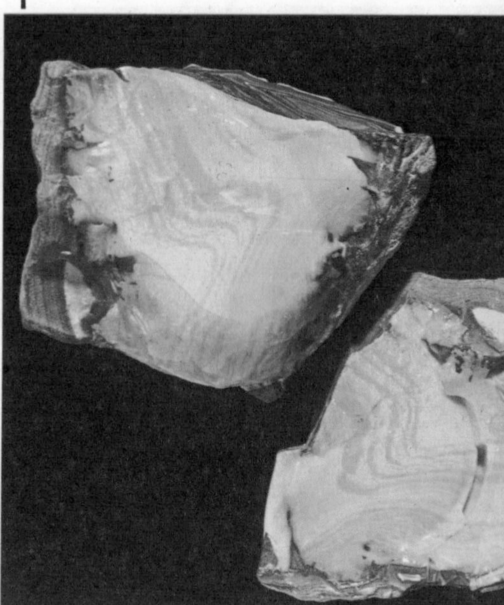

4

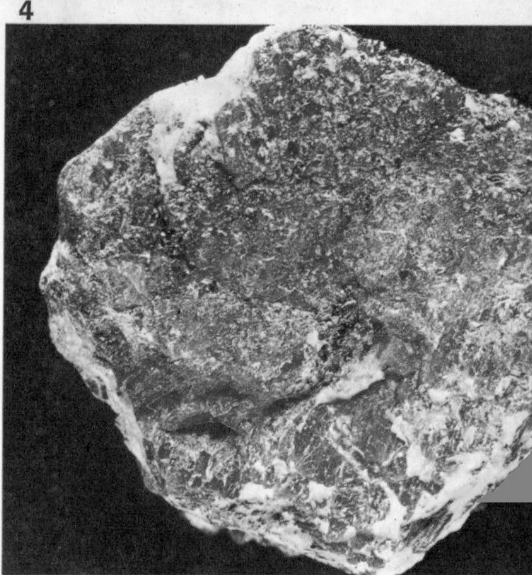

Eight minerals as they are found.
(1) Opal in ironstone.
(2) A blue crystal of sapphire in basalt.
(3) Amethyst crystals.
(4) Natural ruby.
(5) A collection of diamonds.
(6) Crystals of silver in calcite.
(7) A vein of gold.
(8) Prisms of emerald in calcite.

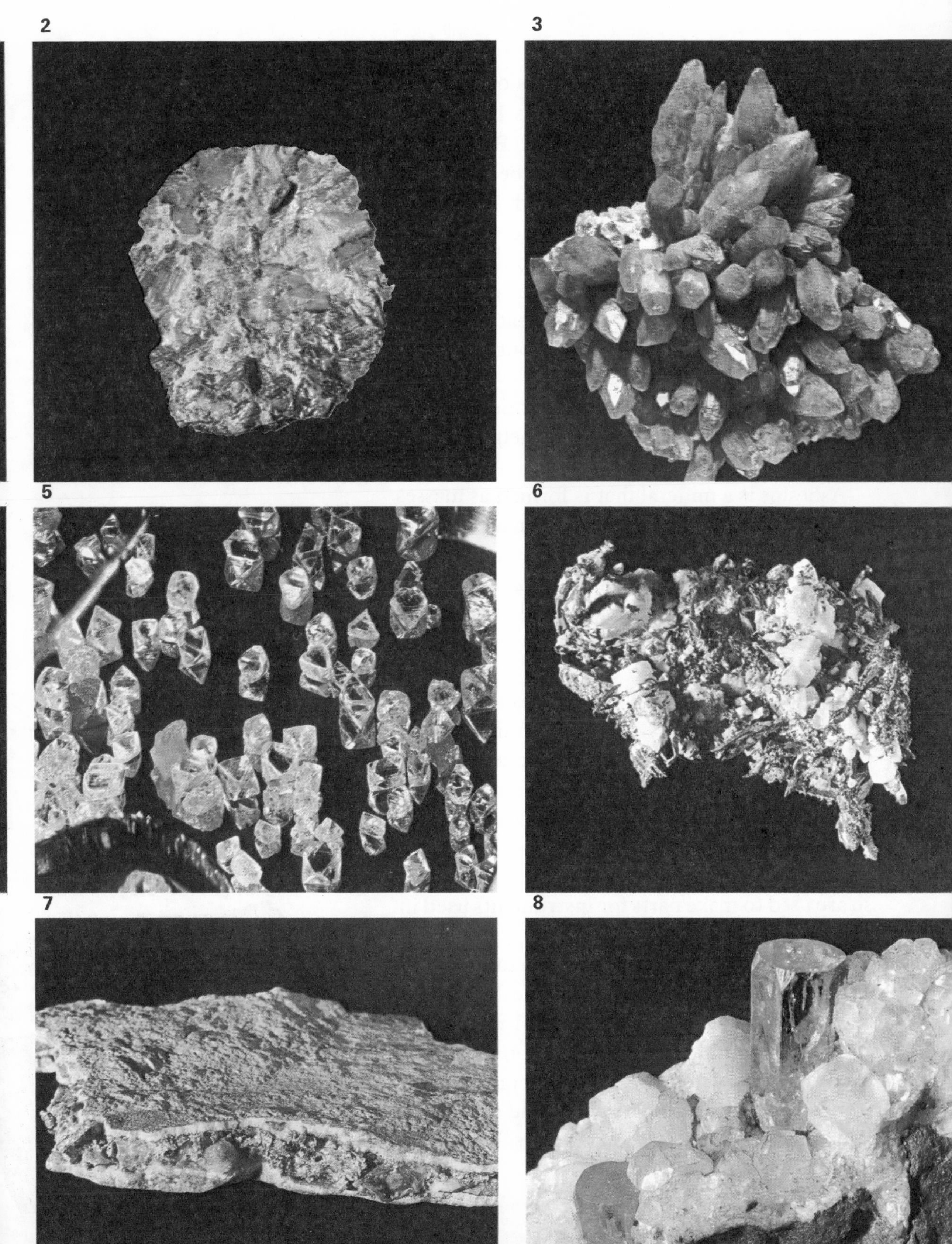
2
3
5
6
7
8

Useful minerals

Men dig mines to take many kinds of minerals from the earth. PRECIOUS MINERALS have value because of their beauty and rarity. But several plentiful minerals are also valuable because they are useful to us. Limestone and basalt are quarried for use as building stone and road-making materials. CLAY is used to make BRICKS, and limestone and gypsum to make cement and plaster. We burn COAL to make heat and electricity. OIL is used largely as fuel, but has many other uses.

Phosphate rocks and nitrate minerals are mined to make FERTILIZERS that help crops to grow.

Asbestos is a mineral that is formed as masses of fibres. The fibres can be woven in a cloth that resists fire and heat, because it is made of a mineral that does not burn. Quartz has uses in electrical devices. Sulphur is one of the raw materials found in the earth. It is used in the CHEMICAL INDUSTRY.

Even precious minerals have uses apart from decoration. Diamonds and corundum are very hard minerals. They are used to make special kinds of drills and abrasives for sanding and polishing. Some precious metals are used in electrical machines because they conduct electricity very well. Also, they do not rust or corrode and so are used to make parts for instruments used in DENTISTRY and SURGERY.

Some of the most important minerals contain useful metals. The minerals have to be treated to get the metals. The most useful metals are ALUMINIUM and IRON. To get aluminium, electricity is passed through the mineral bauxite. Iron is made by heating hematite and other iron minerals in blast furnaces. Iron is important because steel is made from it.

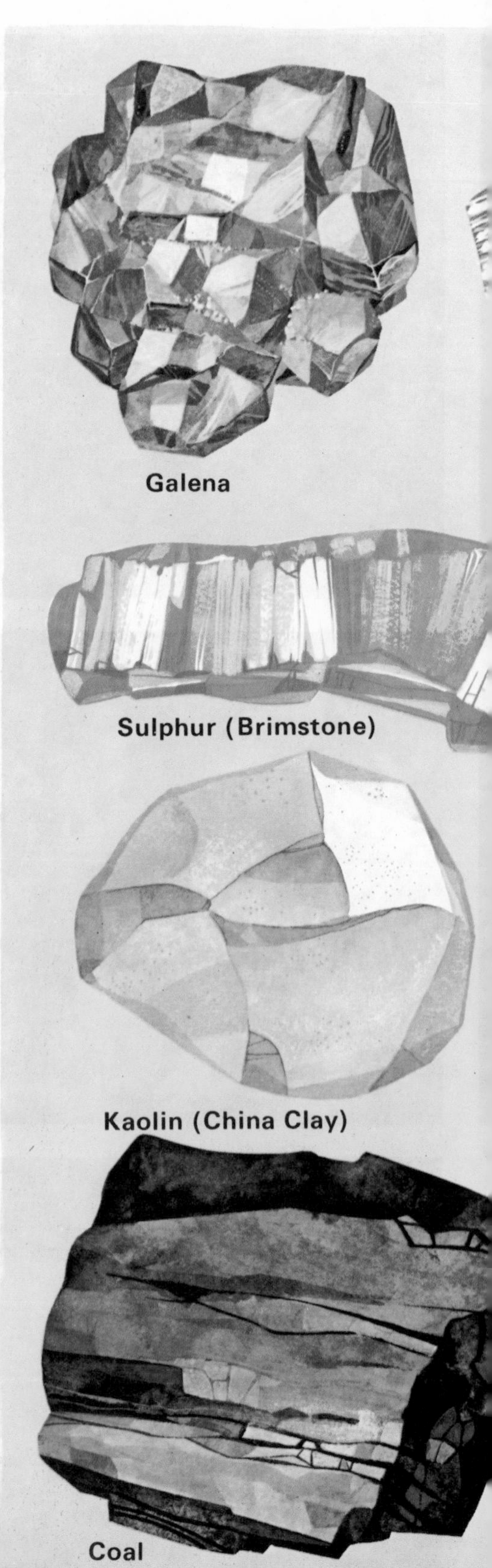

Galena

Sulphur (Brimstone)

Kaolin (China Clay)

Coal

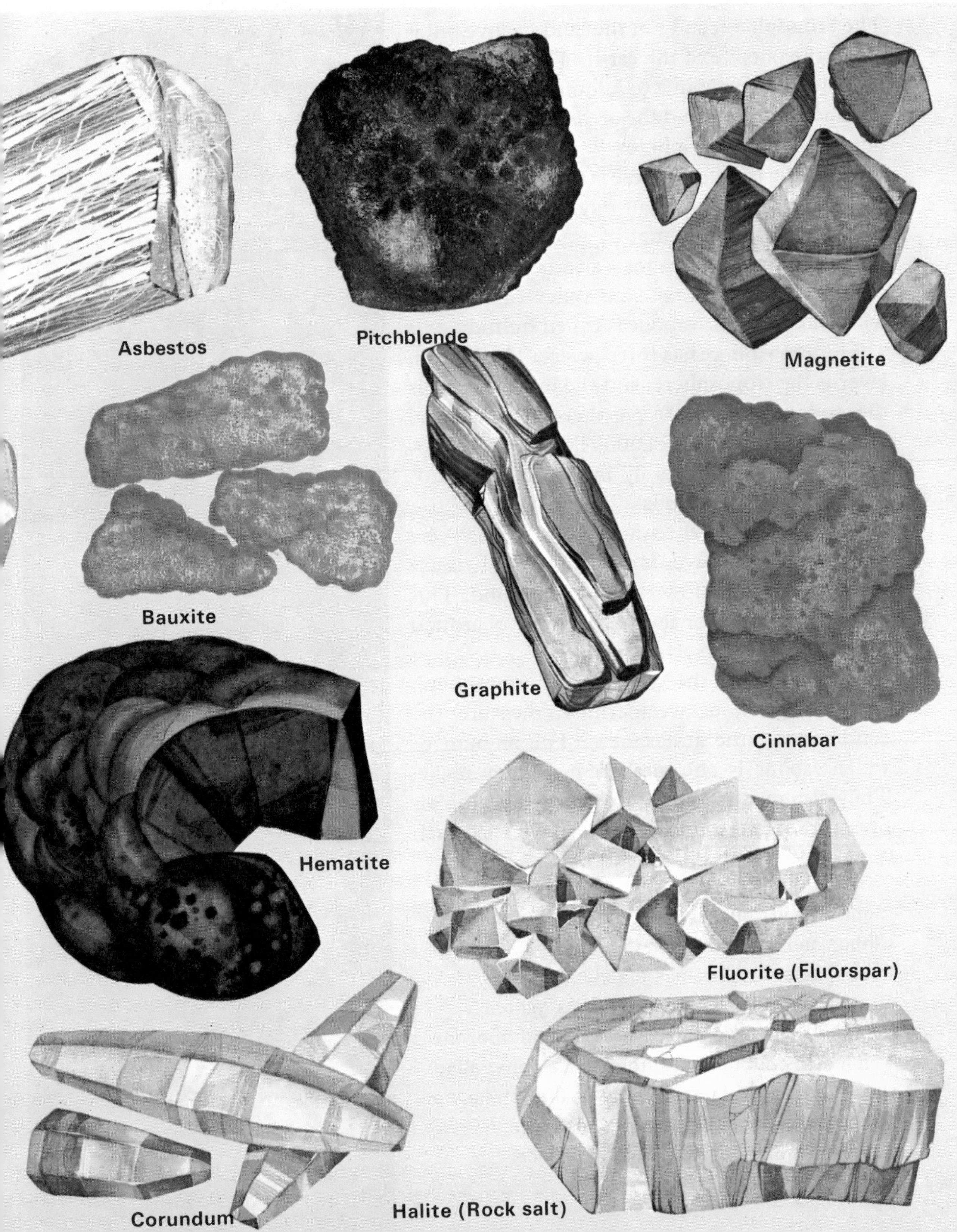
Asbestos
Pitchblende
Magnetite
Bauxite
Graphite
Cinnabar
Hematite
Fluorite (Fluorspar)
Corundum
Halite (Rock salt)

The Atmosphere

The atmosphere, and not the land we live on, is really the outside of the earth. The atmosphere is a layer of air about 150 kilometres thick, that lies above the land and the oceans. We live at the bottom of the atmosphere.

The air in the atmosphere is a mixture of gases. It consists of 21 per cent oxygen, 78 per cent nitrogen, a small amount of argon, and a little carbon dioxide. There may also be some water vapour. Dry air contains no water vapour. Air with a lot of water vapour is called humid.

The atmosphere has three layers. The bottom layer is the troposphere, and the middle layer is the stratosphere. The troposphere is from 8 to 16 kilometres thick. The CLOUDS float in the troposphere. Many airliners fly in the lower stratosphere, above the clouds.

The layer above the stratosphere is called the ionosphere. This layer is useful to man because it reflects back RADIO waves to the ground. This makes it possible for the waves to travel around the earth's curved surface.

Meteorology is the study of the atmosphere. Meteorologists, or weathermen, measure the conditions in the atmosphere. The amount of water vapour is one measurement they make. They also measure the temperature and the air pressure of the atmosphere, as well as such things as WIND speed and rainfall.

Right: The various layers of the atmosphere. Clouds and mountains are in the lowest layer, the troposphere. Then comes the cloud-free stratosphere. This is where airliners generally cruise. At the top of this layer is a band of ozone, which stops harmful rays from space penetrating to the ground. Meteors burn up as they strike the upper atmosphere. The auroras also form there. Satellites orbit above this layer, in space.

Thermometers

We use thermometers to record the temperature. The level of coloured liquid or silver mercury in a tube shows how hot or cold it is. A special thermometer that weathermen often use is the maximum-minimum thermometer. It is like two thermometers in one. One half shows the highest temperature reached during the day. The other half indicates the coldest temperature in the night.

It usually gets colder the higher we go in the atmosphere. This is why there is SNOW at the tops of very high mountains.

1

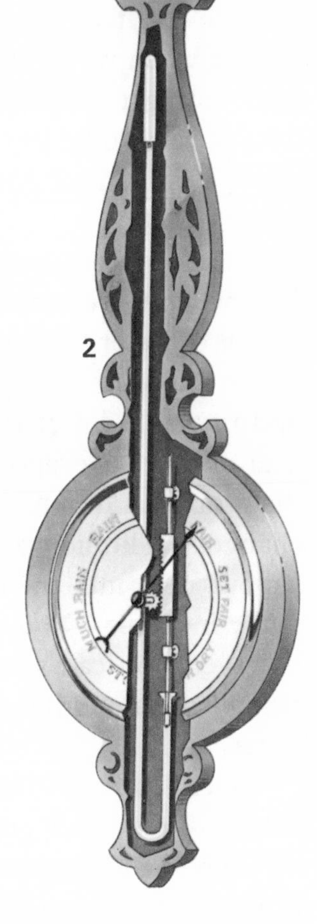

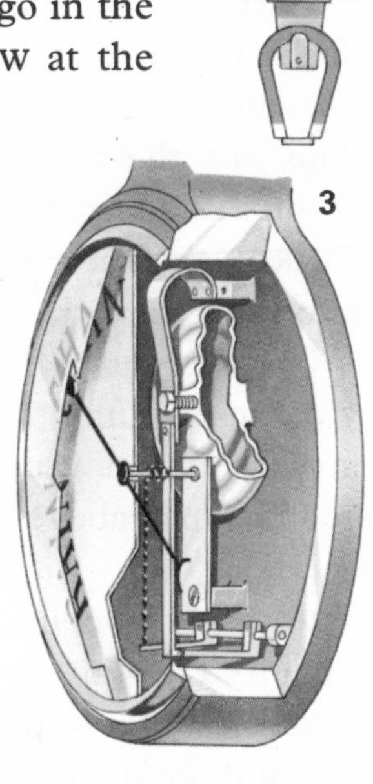

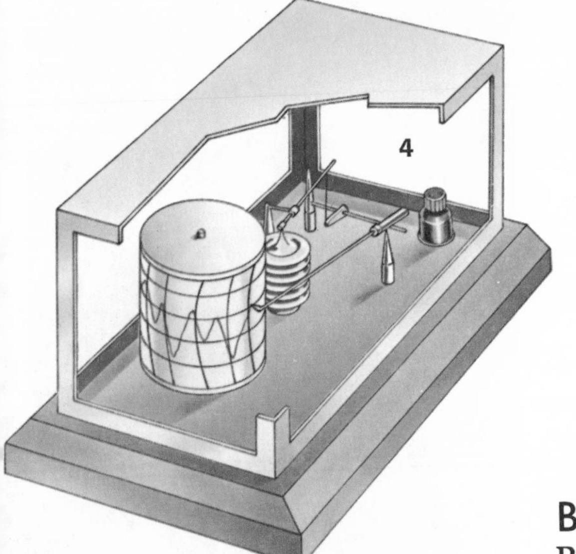

Above: Four instruments for measuring conditions in the atmosphere. (1) A maximum-minimum thermometer. The magnet is used to reset it. (2) A mercury barometer. Changes in air pressure make the level of mercury in the long tube rise or fall. This turns the pointer. (3) An aneroid barometer. (4) A barograph. The pen records changes in pressure automatically.

Barometers

Barometers measure the pressure of the air. There are two main kinds of barometer. The mercury barometer contains a tube of mercury, rather like a large THERMOMETER. The level of mercury indicates the pressure. The aneroid barometer has a thin box connected to a pointer. When the pressure changes, the box changes shape and moves the pointer. The pointer shows the pressure on a dial. Air pressure gets less as we go higher. The air at the top of Mount Everest for example, is so thin that mountaineers have to carry their own oxygen to breathe.

Water cycle

Weather changes when the temperature and the amount of water in the atmosphere change. We can see and feel water coming from the atmosphere when we have RAIN. But the water must somehow get back to the atmosphere. (Otherwise the air would lose all its water, and it would never rain again.) Meteorologists call this the water cycle.

There are many stages in the water cycle. Rain falls when water vapour in CLOUDS condenses. Drops of water form and fall to the ground. The water soaks into the ground and feeds streams and rivers. A lot of rain falls into the sea. The heat of the SUN evaporates some of the water in the ground and in RIVERS, LAKES, and the sea. It changes the liquid water into water vapour. The vapour rises into the air. Water vapour is normally invisible. On a very damp or humid day, however, you can sometimes see water vapour rising from a puddle or pond in a mist above the water.

Water vapour also gets into the air from living things. Trees and other plants take in water through their roots and give off water vapour from their LEAVES. People and land animals drink water and breathe out water vapour. In all these ways the water returns to the air. There it gathers to form clouds and condenses to form rain. The rain falls to earth, and the cycle starts again. It continues even if SNOW or HAIL fall instead because both eventually melt to form water.

The amount of water vapour in the air depends on the temperature. The air is more moist in the tropics, where it is hot, than in the cold polar regions. If all the water in the air suddenly fell as rain, there would be an average rainfall of three centimetres.

Below: Water falls on the land as rain and snow. It flows to the sea by rivers, and also through rocks. Water gets back into the air by evaporating from sea and land.

1

Clouds

A cloud is a large collection of droplets of water or miniature crystals of ice. Clouds form where water vapour in the air condenses or freezes. Therefore clouds form high in the air, where it is colder than at ground level.

There are several different kinds of clouds. Large, heavy thunderclouds with tops shaped like cauliflowers are called cumulonimbus clouds. The high wisps of cloud known as 'mares' tails' are called cirrus clouds, and a 'mackerel sky' is cirrocumulus.

Five kinds of clouds. (1) Cumulus. (2) Stratocumulus. (3) Altocumulus. (4) Altostratus. (5) Cirrus.

2

3

4

5

Fog and mist

Fog and mist form when water vapour condenses in the air at ground level. This happens when the ground is cold, which is why there is often fog or mist on cold mornings. The fog or mist is a thick mass of water droplets, like a cloud on the ground. The droplets evaporate when the air warms later in the day, and the fog or mist disappears. A mist is less dense than a fog. If you can see less than one kilometre ahead, you are in a fog. If the visibility is less than two kilometres, it is a mist.

Left: Layers of mist on an autumn morning. Fog would completely cover the hills.

Dew and frost

Early in the morning, the grass and trees are often covered with drops of water. This happens even if there has been no rain. The drops are called the dew. The ground gets so cold at dawn that water vapour in the air condenses into drops of water on the ground. The temperature at which dew forms is called the dew point. If the ground temperature falls below freezing, the water vapour freezes and the ground is frosty. If the air gets colder than freezing, the trees become coated with frost.

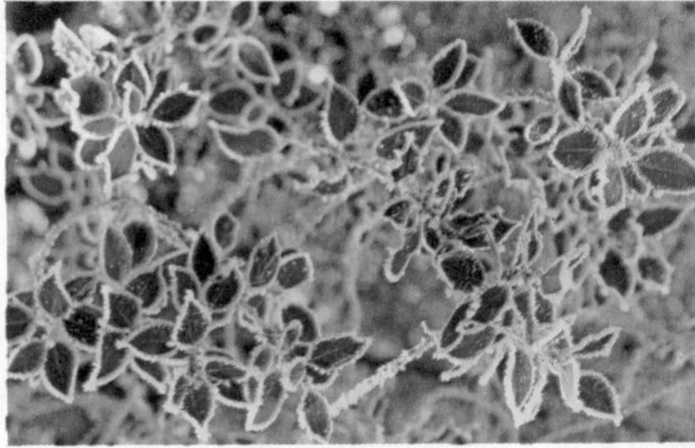

Above: Leaves near the ground become coated with frost on cold mornings, as the dew freezes.

Above: A snow-plough forces its way along a blocked road, flinging the snow to one side.

Snow

Snowflakes fall from CLOUDS when the cold changes the water vapour in the clouds into tiny ice crystals. When the crystals stick together, they become heavy and fall as snowflakes. If the weather is dry, the flakes will be smaller because dry crystals do not stick together well. The wind may drive the snow into deep snowdrifts. About ten centimetres of snow will fall where only one centimetre of rain would fall.

Rainbows

You can see a rainbow only if the SUN is shining on the RAIN from behind you. The drops of water in the rain reflect the sun's light back towards you. But as they do so, each drop splits the LIGHT up into the colours of the SPECTRUM. A large circle of coloured bands of light is formed. You only see the upper part of the circle, as a bow. The lower part of the circle is out of sight below the horizon. In fact, two bows form, one outside the other. The inner, or primary, bow has red on the outside. The outer, or secondary bow, is usually much fainter. It has red on the inside.

Above: A rainbow forms as sunlight is reflected inside raindrops. In a secondary bow, light is reflected twice in each drop.

Rain and hail

Rain falls when droplets of water suspended in the CLOUDS flow together and form large drops. When the drops get heavy enough, they can no longer stay up in the air and fall to the ground as rain. In thunderstorms and cloudbursts the raindrops are large and fall in a torrent from the sky. Drizzle is a kind of spray of small drops.

Weathermen measure rainfall. They record in a special gauge the depth of water produced by falling rain during a certain time, usually a day.

Hail consists of frozen raindrops. They form when the air cools very rapidly, which sometimes happens high up in unusual weather conditions. The hailstones increase in size as water vapour freezes and forms extra layers of ice. When the hailstones reach a certain size, they are too heavy for the air currents. Then they fall to the ground as hail. The hailstones usually are only about five millimetres across, but the largest have measured up to 190 millimetres across.

Thunder and lightning

Thunderstorms occur when there is much water vapour in the air and the air starts to move in rapid upward currents. Thunderstorms most often occur in summer and in the tropics when the ground is hot and heats the air. Huge CLOUDS form, and large charges of static electricity are produced in them by the violent conditions in the atmosphere. When the electric charges become very great, huge sparks fly between the clouds and the ground. These sparks are lightning flashes. They heat the air so much that the air instantly expands and causes a clap of thunder.

Right: A huge flash of lightning strikes a city during a violent thunderstorm.

Winds

A wind is a current of air moving over the land or the sea. The direction of a wind is the direction *from which it has come*, and not the direction in which it is going. For example, a south wind is blowing from the south towards the north. A wind vane points in the direction of a wind. The strength of a wind can vary from a light breeze to a HURRICANE. The Beaufort scale is the system that weathermen use to describe the strength and speed of a wind.

Winds are produced because the pressure of the air is different in different places. Air flows from a region of high pressure to a region of low pressure, causing a wind. The heat of the SUN on the earth produces pressure differences and winds.

In the tropics, the heat makes the air expand. As it expands, it gets lighter and rises. Cooler air from surrounding regions moves in to take the place of the rising air. This change causes winds to blow towards the tropics. These winds are called the trade winds.

Above: Winds blowing mostly in the same direction have made this hawthorn tree grow to one side.

THE BEAUFORT WIND SCALE

Number	*Wind*	*Speed (km/h)*
0	Calm	0–2
1	Light air	3–5
2	Slight breeze	6–10
3	Gentle breeze	11–20
4	Moderate breeze	21–30
5	Fresh breeze	31–40
6	Strong breeze	41–50
7	High wind	51–60
8	Gale	61–75
9	Strong gale	76–90
10	Whole gale	91–105
11	Storm	106–120
12	Hurricane	over 120

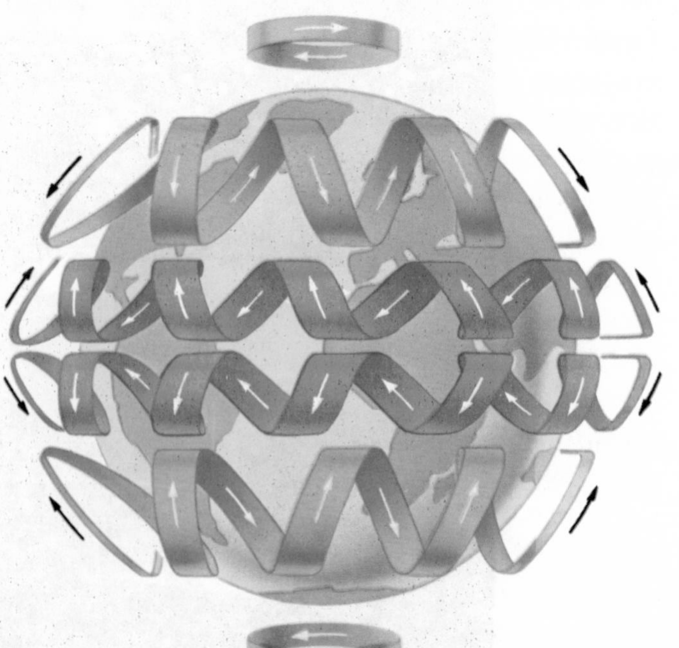

Left: The main winds of the world are the westerlies (green) and the trade winds (red). The rotation of the earth makes them move with a corkscrew motion.

Hurricanes

A hurricane or a tropical cyclone is the most destructive kind of storm. It starts in mid-ocean in the tropics. Hot air heavy with moisture starts to rise in the heat. The rotation of the earth starts the rising air spinning. This action lowers the air pressure at the centre of the spinning column of air. More air flows towards the low-pressure region but is caught up in the spin. The spinning gets more and more violent, and a howling storm starts to move across the ocean. When it hits the land, it may cause immense destruction. As it crosses the land, the hurricane loses its force.

Similar, but smaller, storms can form on land. These are called whirlwinds or tornadoes. They consist of tall, thin spinning columns of air. Waterspouts happen when air columns spin over the sea. Water is sucked up in them.

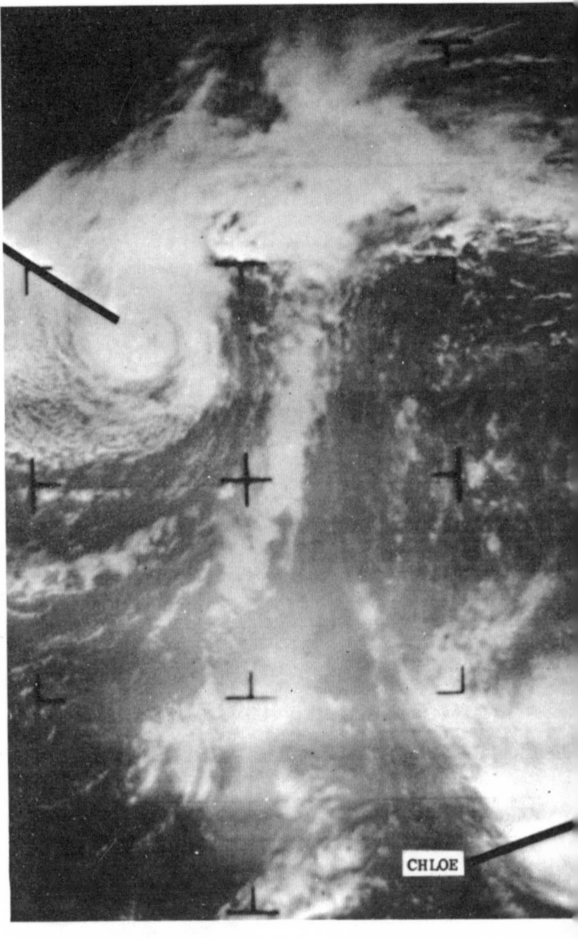

Right: A photograph of two hurricanes taken by a weather satellite in space. Hurricanes are given Christian names, such as Chloe.

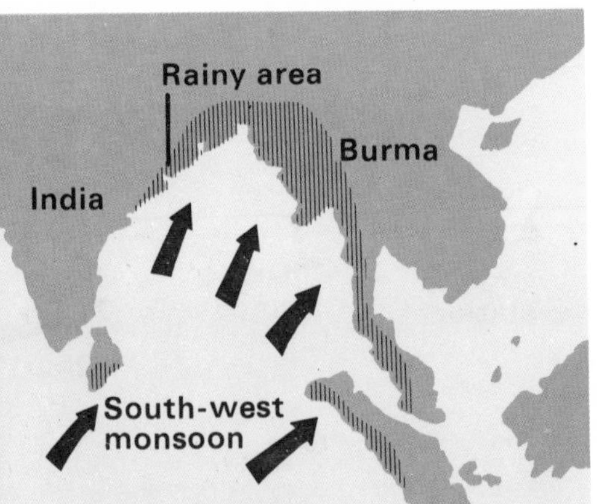

Above: Wet monsoon winds blow over the Indian Ocean in summer. They pick up much water vapour and drop it as rain on the land.

Monsoons

A monsoon is a WIND that changes direction from season to season. The monsoon winds of south-eastern ASIA are well known. In the summer, the heat of the land lowers the air pressure. Winds come from the south-west over the ocean. There they pick up moisture which then drops as RAIN on the land. Then in the autumn, the land cools, and the wet winds stop. In their place come dry monsoon winds from the north-east. These last until the following spring, after which the wet monsoon comes again.

Other monsoon winds blow over the south-eastern United States, eastern AFRICA, and northern AUSTRALIA.

Weather forecasting

Forecasting the weather can be done in two ways. The weathermen can find out what happened the last time there were similar conditions. Then they can predict that the same thing will happen again. This method works well for regular events, such as MONSOONS. In unpredictable climates, however, the weathermen have to observe and measure day after day. Then they must work out scientifically what will happen. They must know what series of events to expect after atmospheric changes. Weathermen have learned a great deal in recent years. Although their work is very complicated, they can use computers to help them make forecasts quickly. Weathermen are also known as meteorologists.

Weather conditions must be measured over a wide region. The measurements are sent to a central weather station where they can be ex-

Above: Sunlight hour metres on the roof of the Weather Centre in London.

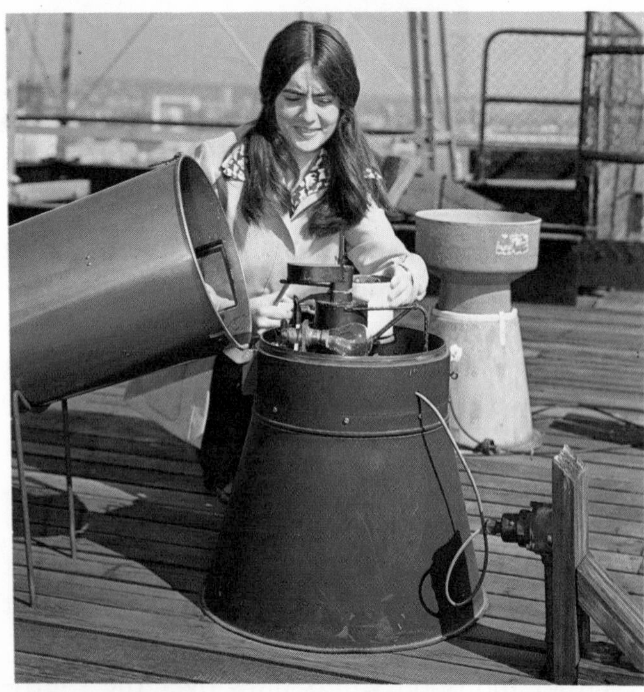

Above: Taking a rain gauge reading in London.

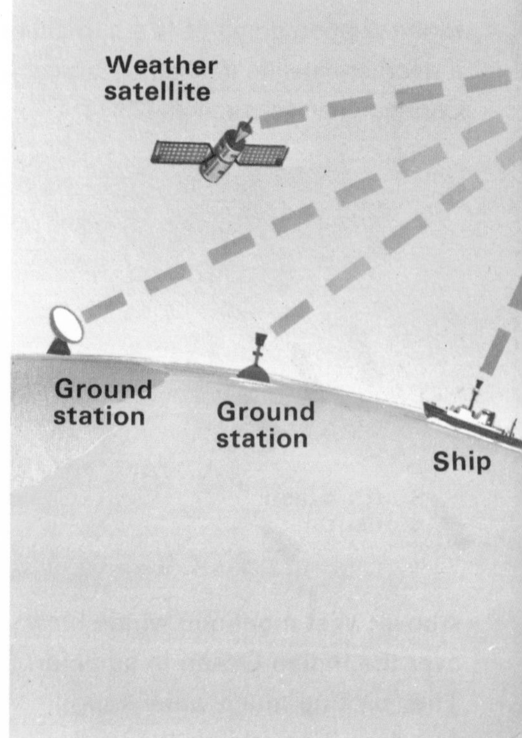

amined and used. Most towns have a set of weather instruments, such as THERMOMETERS, BAROMETERS, and anemometers. The instruments are read regularly and the results are sent to a central weather station.

Other measurements come from radiosondes, which are high-flying BALLOONS that carry automatic instruments. Satellites circling the EARTH send down pictures of the CLOUDS from space, and RADAR stations can locate distant storms. With these and other aids, forecasts can be made.

Below: Meteosat is a weather satellite. It relays information back to a ground station on earth.

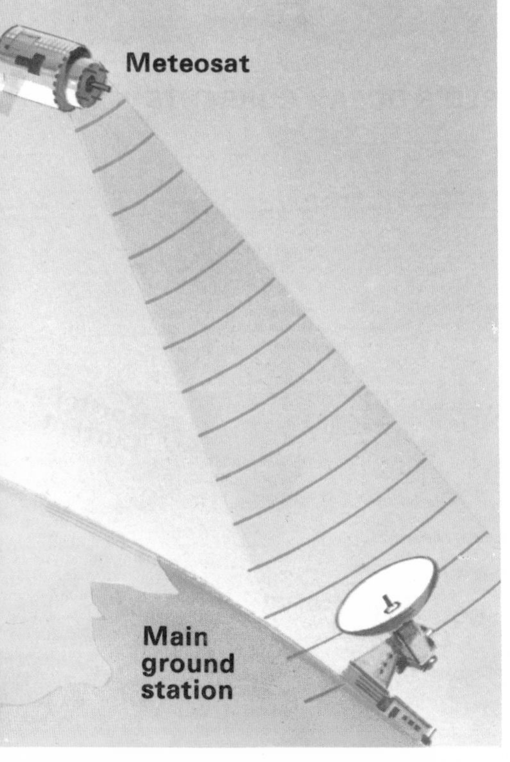

Above: Automatic weather recording instruments may be carried on buoys.

Oceans and Seas

Although its name is earth, our world is mostly covered with water. The oceans and seas make up seven-tenths of the surface of the globe. Near the land the water is not very deep. A sea floor forms what is called a continental shelf about 200 metres deep near most parts of the continents. At its edge, the sea floor slopes more steeply to the ocean floor. The ocean floor is fairly level and is about 3000 to 6000 metres deep. Here and there, deep trenches cut through the ocean floor. These are called deeps. Ranges of underwater MOUNTAINS are called mid-oceanic ridges.

Great currents of water flow through the oceans. They are mainly blown by the winds. Differences in temperature between one part of the ocean and another also cause currents to flow. The rotation of the earth makes big currents take curving paths. It turns them to the right in the Northern Hemisphere and to the left in the Southern Hemisphere.

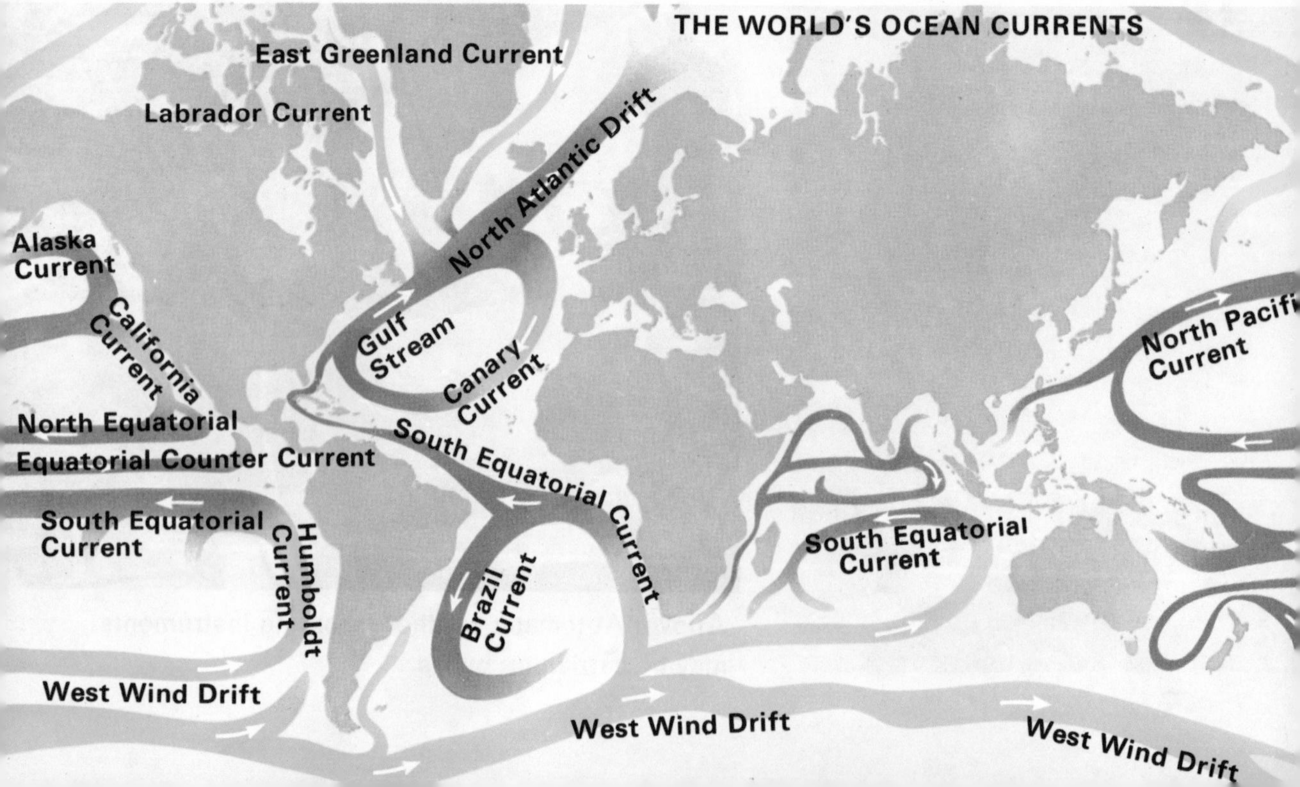

THE WORLD'S OCEAN CURRENTS

East Greenland Current
Labrador Current
North Atlantic Drift
Alaska Current
California Current
Gulf Stream
Canary Current
North Pacific Current
North Equatorial
Equatorial Counter Current
South Equatorial Current
South Equatorial Current
Humboldt Current
Brazil Current
South Equatorial Current
West Wind Drift
West Wind Drift
West Wind Drift

Waves

Waves are caused by the wind blowing on the surface of the water. The water in the waves, however, does not move along with them. A boat is not pushed along by the waves; it just bobs up and down.

Sea waves are just like waves made in a rope by fastening one end and shaking the other end. When the wave gets to very shallow water near the shore, the motion of the bottom of the wave gets slower. But the top, or crest, of the wave continues on and soon topples over. The wave breaks and splashes onto the shore. The destructive waves called tsunamis are caused by EARTHQUAKES shaking the ocean floor. Tsunami, a Japanese word, is a better name than tidal wave, because these waves are not caused by the tides.

Left: The waves battering the shore have a very destructive effect. Here, a sea wall of wooden stakes has been built to protect the shore.

Tides

The tides are changes in the level of the sea, which usually rises and falls twice a day. Tides happen because the SUN and MOON pull on the oceans. Their force of GRAVITY makes the water rise a little. Two rises in level occur, one on each side of the earth. As the earth rotates once in 24 hours, the water in an ocean rises once every 12 hours. This is high tide. Six hours later the water falls in level between each of the rises, and low tide occurs. Spring tides happen when the rise and fall is large. The sun and moon are then in line with the earth, and they pull together. The neap tides happen when the sun and moon are at right angles and do not pull together. Neap tides do not rise or fall very much. Spring and neap tides occur once every month.

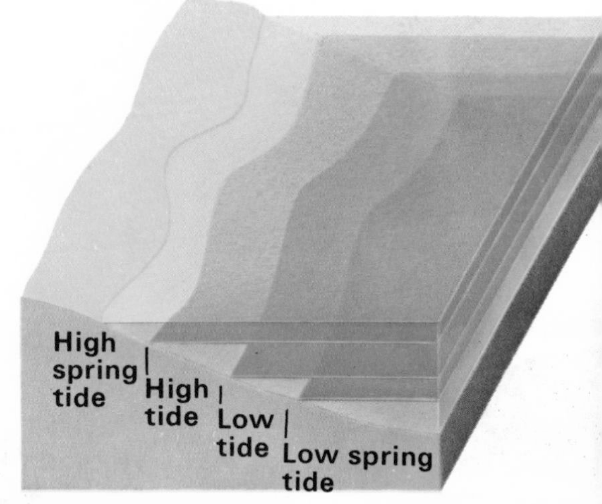

Above: Several different zones are produced by the rise and fall of the tides on the shore.

Pacific Ocean

The Pacific Ocean is the largest of the world's five oceans. It is so large that it covers almost a third of the globe. It is larger than all the land put together. From the Philippines to SOUTH AMERICA, it stretches halfway round the world.

The Pacific Ocean is almost sealed off by land to the north. But to the south it joins other oceans. The Pacific Ocean has many ISLANDS. They are mostly volcanic in origin. Some are CORAL islands. There are four main groups of islands. Hawaii lies to the north and Polynesia to the south. Micronesia is east of the Philippines, and the islands of Melanesia lie to the south-west, near AUSTRALIA and New Guinea.

The deepest point on the earth is probably the Challenger Deep, part of Marianas Trench in the western Pacific Ocean. Trenches occur at the edges of plates where rock is being forced to sink back into the earth's interior.

Area: 165 million sq. km.
Average depth: 4250 metres
Greatest depth: 11,033 metres in Marianas Trench

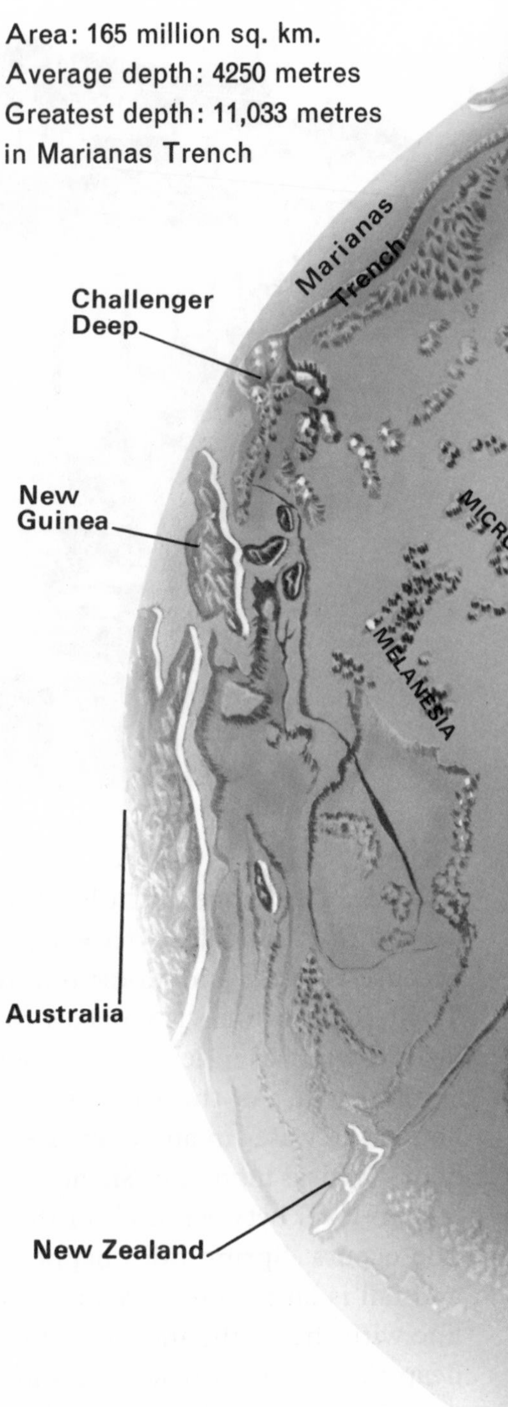

Below: Lion Island in Broken Bay, North of Sydney, Australia.

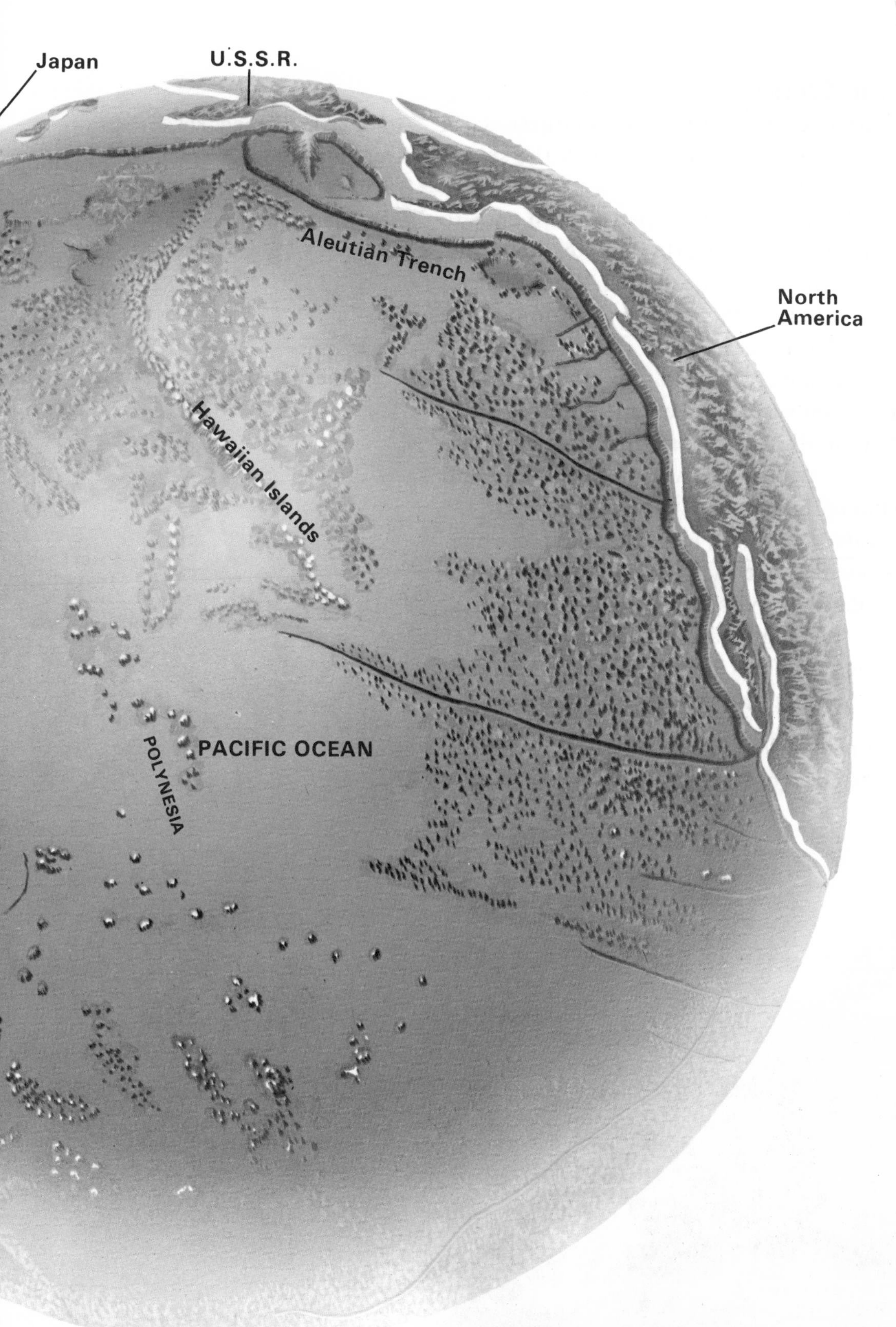
Japan
U.S.S.R.
Aleutian Trench
North America
Hawaiian Islands
PACIFIC OCEAN
POLYNESIA

Atlantic Ocean

The Atlantic Ocean is the second largest ocean in the world, but it is only about half the size of the PACIFIC OCEAN.

The Atlantic Ocean lies open at both ends to the other oceans of the world. Unlike the Pacific, it has few ISLANDS. The British Isles are not really Atlantic islands, because they do not rise from the Atlantic ocean floor. They rise from the continental shelf attached to EUROPE. Most Atlantic islands are part of an undersea ridge that runs midway between the Americas and Europe and AFRICA. ICELAND is at one end and the island of Tristan da Cunha at the other.

This ridge is thought to be the point at which the continents on either side of the ocean are drifting apart. It marks the edges of the plates, which are moving away from each other. Hot rock comes up from below to fill in the gap, forming the ridge and causing volcanic activity.

Below: A natural arch formed by Atlantic waves striking the coast of Portugal.

Area: 82 million sq. km.
Average depth: 4250 metres
Greatest depth: 8738 metres near Puerto Rico

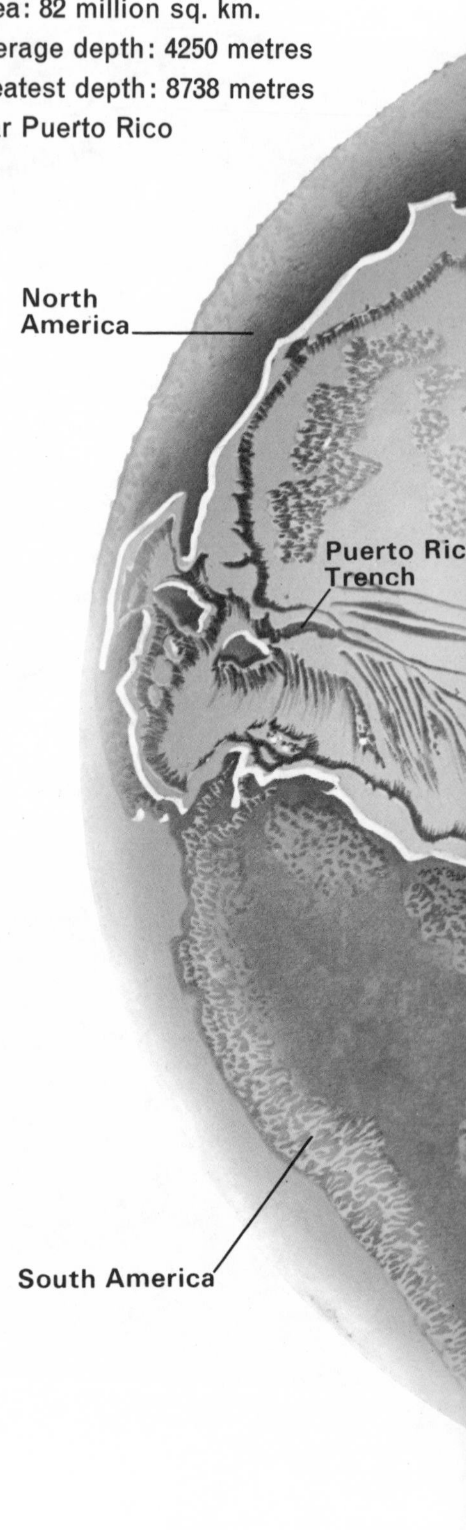

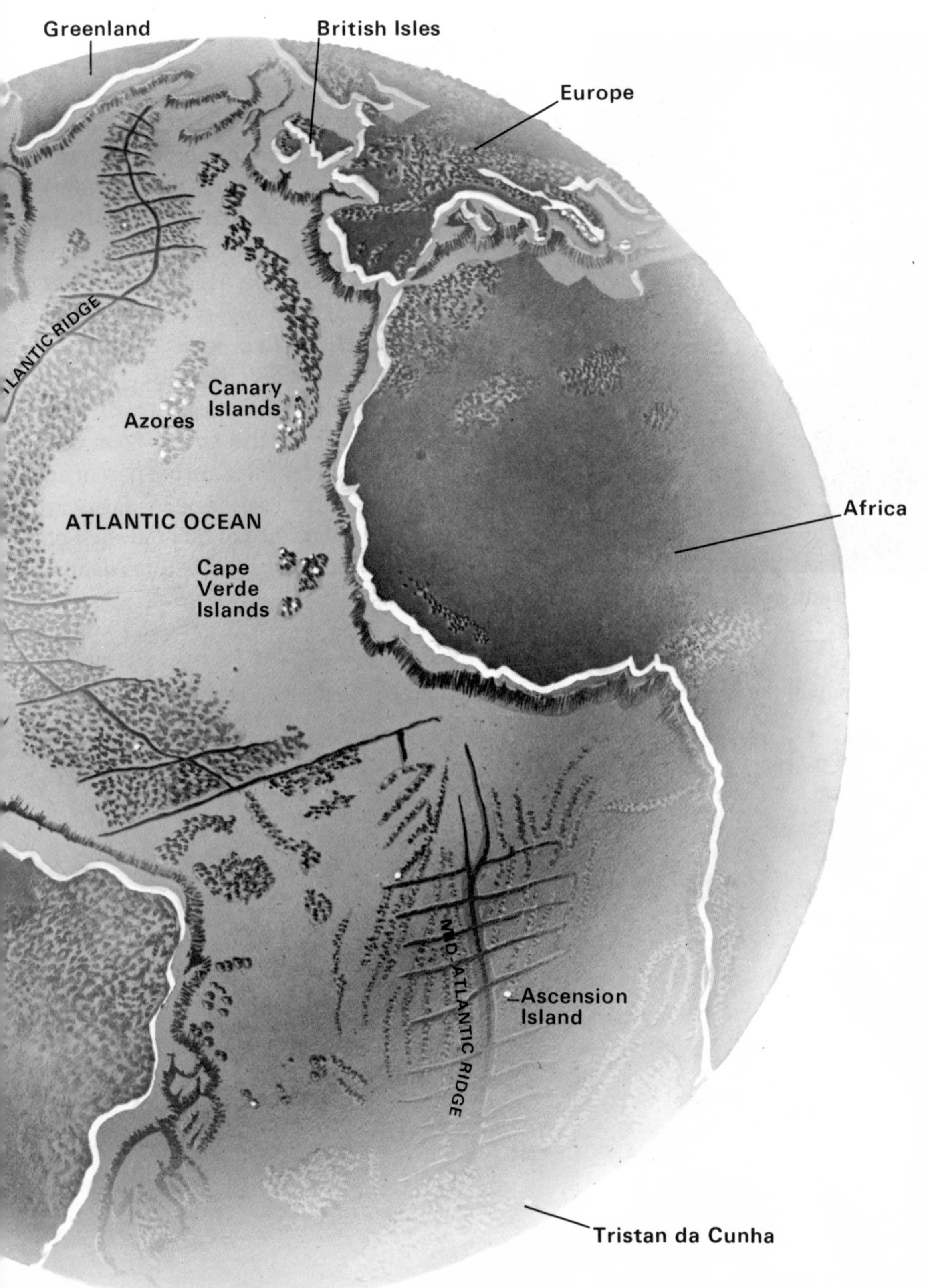
Greenland
British Isles
Europe
ATLANTIC RIDGE
Canary
Islands
Azores
ATLANTIC OCEAN
Africa
Cape
Verde
Islands
MID-ATLANTIC RIDGE
Ascension
Island
Tristan da Cunha

Above: The sun sets over the shore of the Indian Ocean in South-east Asia.
Below: A map of the Indian Ocean.

Indian Ocean

The Indian Ocean is the third largest ocean. It is bordered by AFRICA, ASIA, and AUSTRALIA on three sides, but it is open to the south. Like the ATLANTIC OCEAN, the Indian Ocean has an undersea ridge running along its centre. It extends north from near ANTARCTICA to the Red Sea. Several islands rise from this ridge, which has two side branches. One runs north-west and ends at the Seychelles. The other extends to INDIA and carries the Maldive Islands.

The Cocos Islands in the eastern Indian Ocean rise straight from the ocean floor like most of the Pacific Islands. They are not part of an undersea ridge. The large islands of Madagascar and SRI LANKA are part of the continental shelf of AFRICA and India. They are not oceanic islands.

Area: 73 million sq. km.
Average depth: 4000 metres
Greatest depth: 8047 metres in Diamantina Deep.

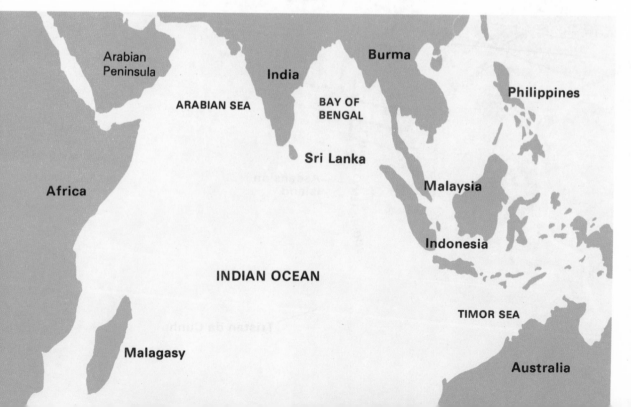

Arabian Peninsula
India
Burma
Philippines
ARABIAN SEA
BAY OF BENGAL
Sri Lanka
Africa
Malaysia
Indonesia
INDIAN OCEAN
TIMOR SEA
Malagasy
Australia

Arctic Ocean

The Arctic Ocean at the North Pole is bounded by the north coasts of CANADA and Alaska, Greenland, Scandinavia, and the U.S.S.R. The narrow Bering Strait connects it with the PACIFIC OCEAN. It merges with the ATLANTIC OCEAN on both sides of Greenland along the Arctic Circle. Most of the Arctic Ocean is covered with a layer of floating ice. In the winter this layer is firm and solid. In the summer, however, the ice breaks up into large pieces called floes.

Area: 14 million sq. km.
Average depth: 1500 metres
Greatest depth: 5449 metres

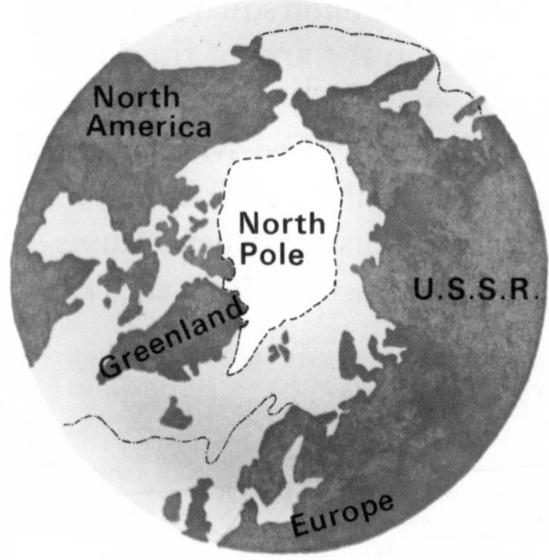

Left: Their thick coats help polar bears to survive in the cold Arctic regions.

Antarctic Ocean

The Antarctic Ocean or Southern Ocean has no proper boundaries like the other oceans. It is the ocean that surrounds the continent of ANTARCTICA at the South Pole. It extends from Antarctica to the southern tips of the surrounding continents. Many geographers consider that the Antarctic Ocean is not a separate ocean. They think of it as being the southern parts of the PACIFIC, ATLANTIC, and INDIAN OCEANS.

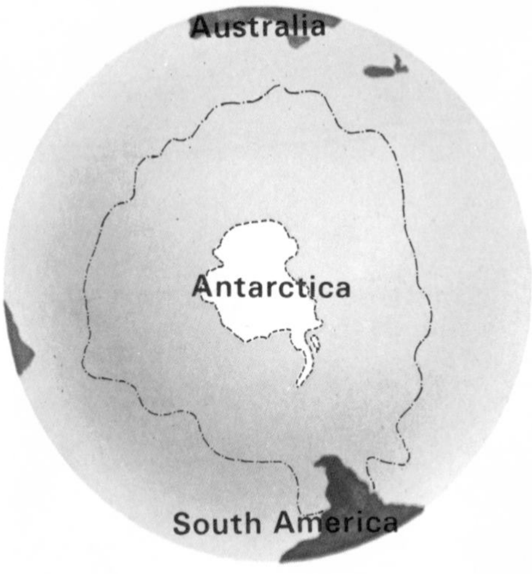

Left: An elephant seal bellows on an Antarctic island.

Mediterranean Sea

The Mediterranean Sea lies between EUROPE and AFRICA. Narrow straits connect it to the ATLANTIC OCEAN in the west and the Black Sea in the east. The Mediterranean has an area of nearly two and a half million square kilometres. The deepest point is in the arm of the Mediterranean called the Ionian Sea, where the depth increases to 4350 metres. The Mediterranean is gradually getting smaller as Africa moves slowly towards Europe. This movement causes EARTHQUAKES in the north-east Mediterranean.

Above: The Rock of Gibraltar guards the west end of the Mediterranean. It lies at the southern tip of Spain.

North Sea

The North Sea lies between Britain and NORWAY, DENMARK, GERMANY, and the NETHERLANDS. It is an arm of the ATLANTIC OCEAN. The North Sea has an area of 570,000 square kilometres. It is a very shallow sea because its bed is part of the continental shelf surrounding the British Isles. The average depth is only 30 metres in the southern part of the North Sea. The deepest point is off the coast of Norway, where the depth is about 800 metres. The Dogger Bank is a shallow fishing ground in the centre of the North Sea.

Caribbean Sea

The Caribbean Sea is a tropical sea that lies between the West Indies and Central and SOUTH AMERICA. It is a western arm of the ATLANTIC OCEAN. To the north, it connects with the Gulf of MEXICO through the Yucatan Channel. The Caribbean Sea has an area of about two million square kilometres, and its greatest depth is 6950 metres near the Cayman Islands.

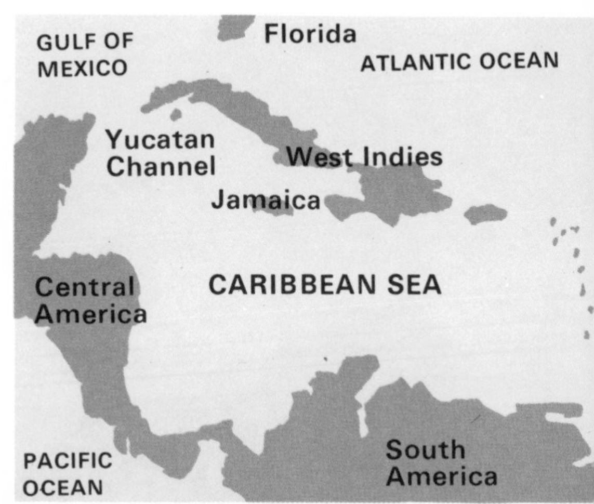

Below: The Blue Lagoon in Jamaica, a typical Caribbean scene.

Sargasso Sea

Unlike other seas, the Sargasso Sea is not bounded by coasts. It is an oval-shaped region of the ATLANTIC OCEAN lying between Bermuda and the Azores. A great system of ocean currents runs around the edge of the northern half of the Atlantic Ocean. The Gulf Stream and North Atlantic Drift are Atlantic currents. The Sargasso Sea lies in the middle of the ocean, where there are no great currents. Seaweed gathers in the motionless water and floats in great clumps at the surface of the sea.

The Continents

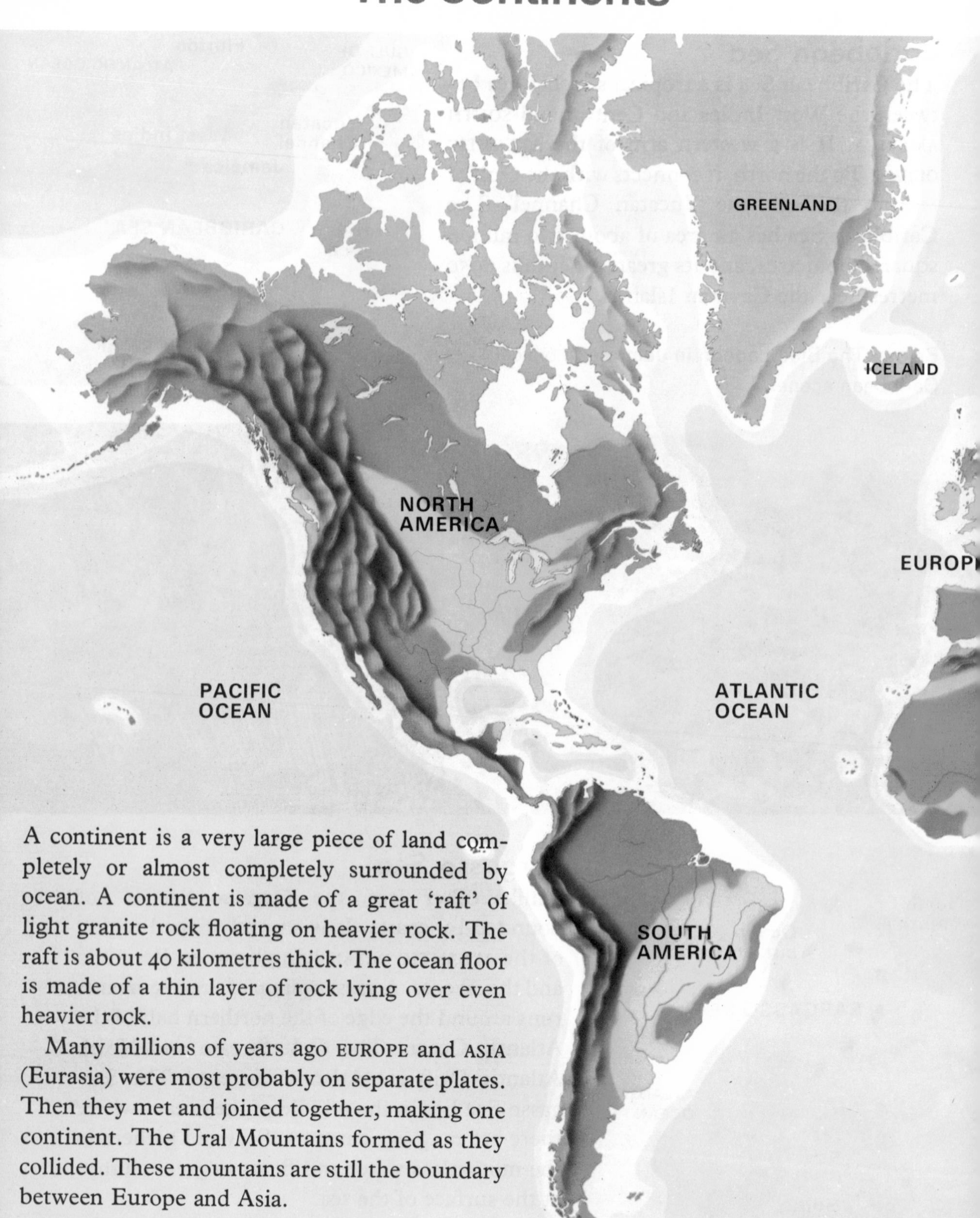

A continent is a very large piece of land completely or almost completely surrounded by ocean. A continent is made of a great 'raft' of light granite rock floating on heavier rock. The raft is about 40 kilometres thick. The ocean floor is made of a thin layer of rock lying over even heavier rock.

Many millions of years ago EUROPE and ASIA (Eurasia) were most probably on separate plates. Then they met and joined together, making one continent. The Ural Mountains formed as they collided. These mountains are still the boundary between Europe and Asia.

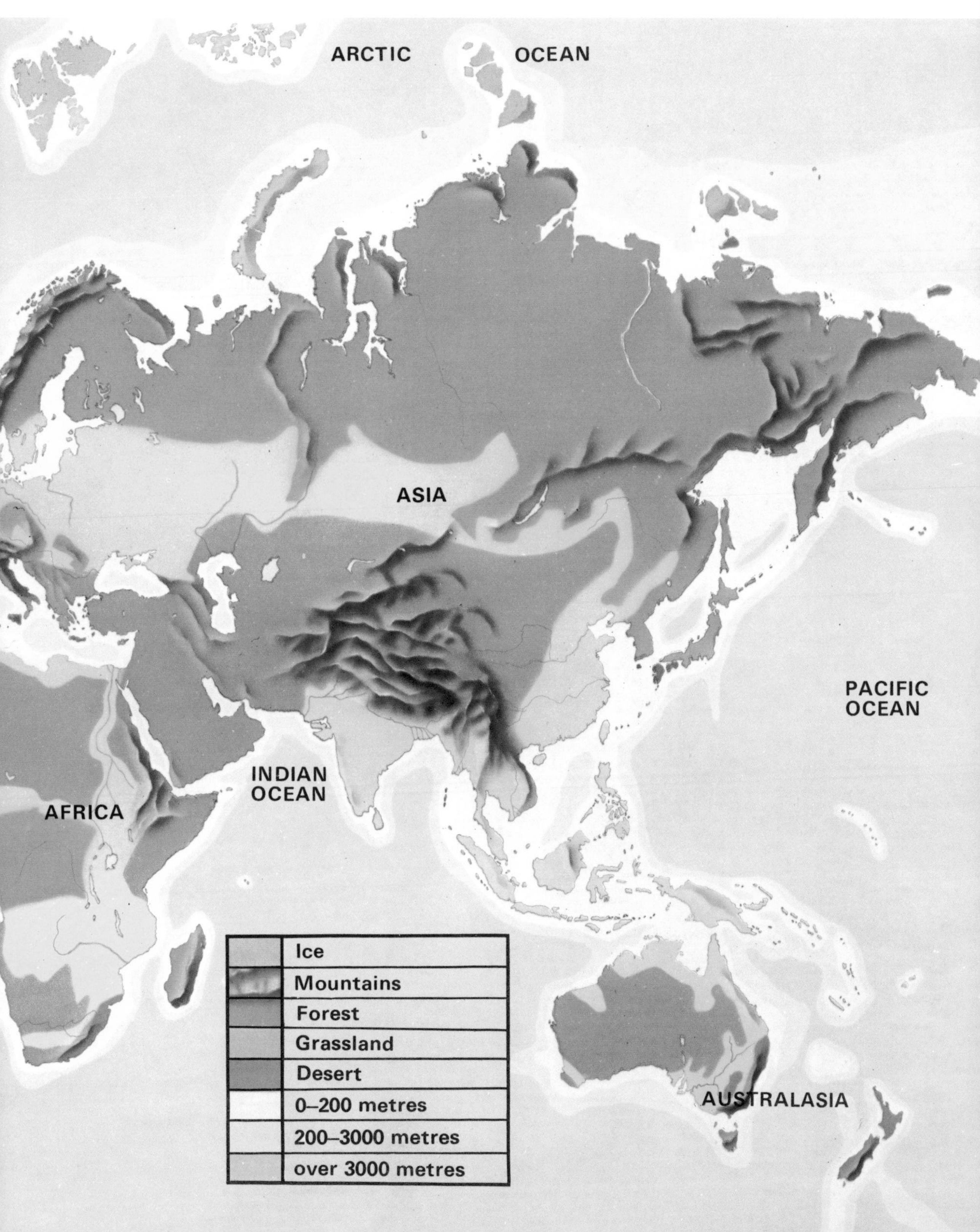
ARCTIC
OCEAN
ASIA
PACIFIC
OCEAN
INDIAN
OCEAN
AFRICA
AUSTRALASIA
Ice
Mountains
Forest
Grassland
Desert
0–200 metres
200–3000 metres
over 3000 metres

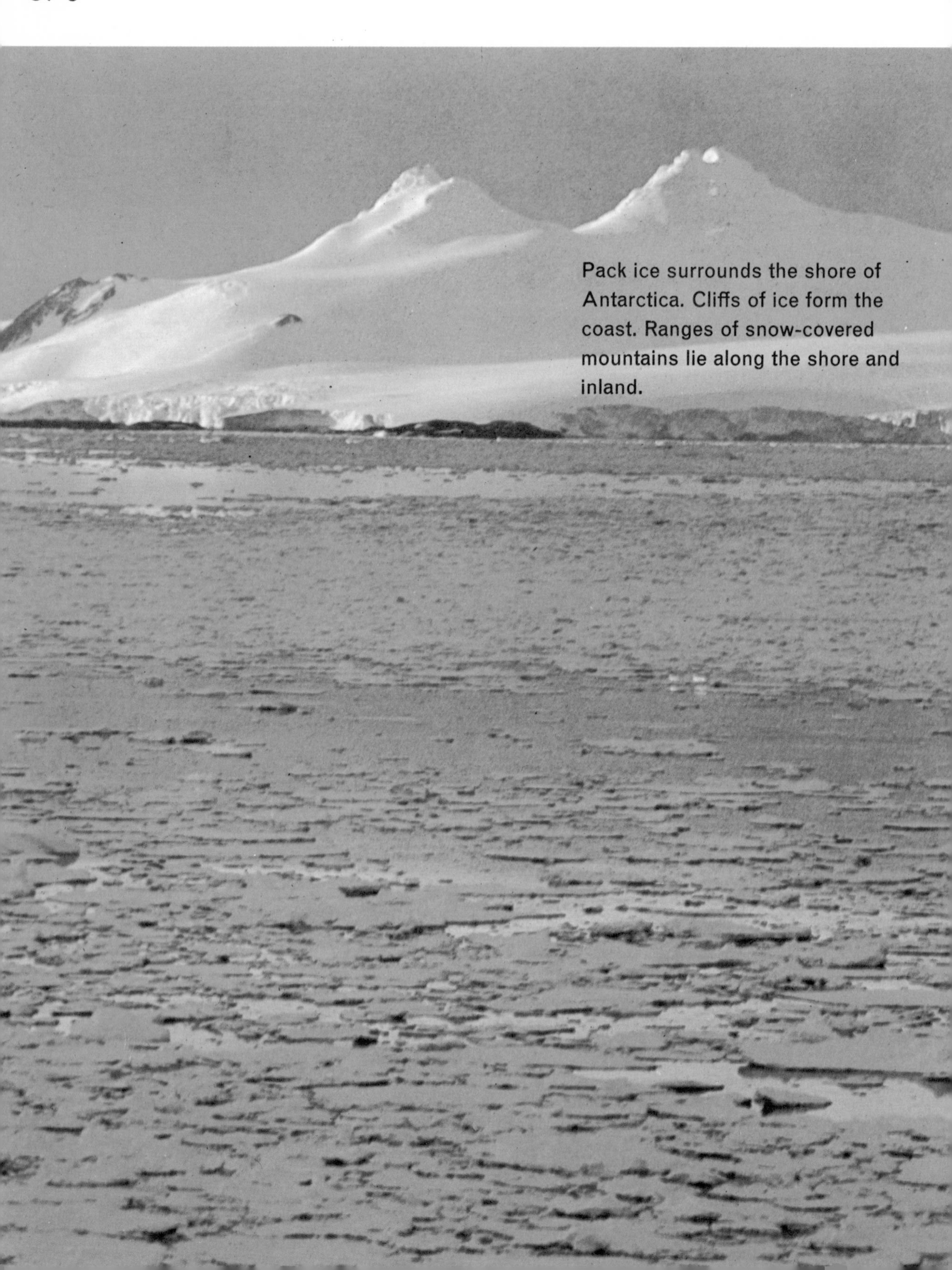

Pack ice surrounds the shore of Antarctica. Cliffs of ice form the coast. Ranges of snow-covered mountains lie along the shore and inland.

Antarctica

Antarctica is the continent surrounding the South Pole. It has an area of 15 million square kilometres. It is so cold that a thick ice sheet always lies over the land. In some places the ice goes down to below sea level. This means that if the ice melted, some land would be under the sea.

Right: A research station in Antarctica.

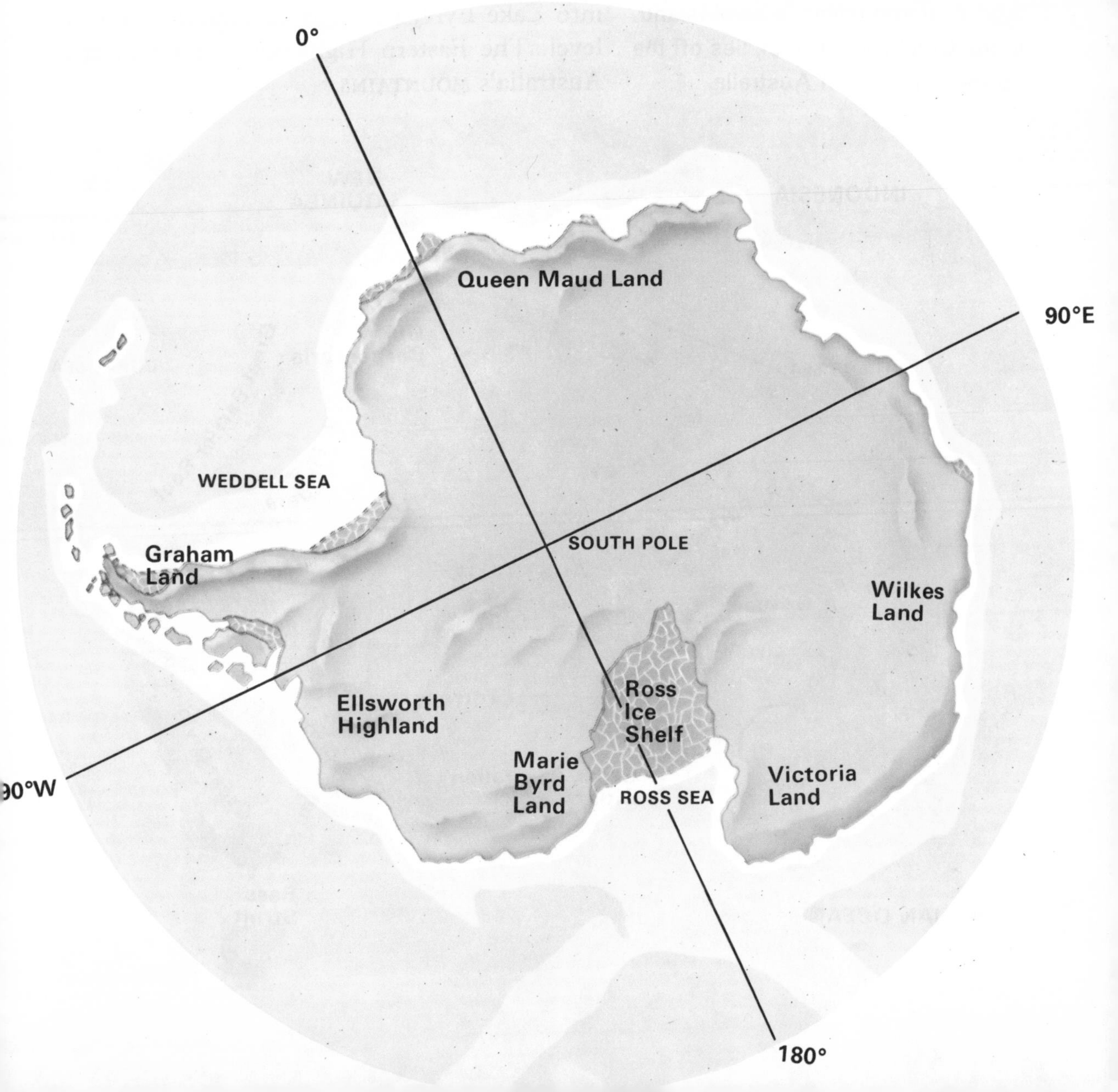

0°
Queen Maud Land
90°E
WEDDELL SEA
Graham Land
SOUTH POLE
Wilkes Land
Ross Ice Shelf
Ellsworth Highland
Marie Byrd Land
ROSS SEA
Victoria Land
90°W
180°

Above: Heron Island, a coral island in the Great Barrier Reef, lies off the north-east coast of Australia.

Australasia

Australasia is the region made up of AUSTRALIA, the islands of NEW ZEALAND and New Guinea, and other small nearby islands. Australia has an area of 7,700,000 square kilometres. It has three main regions. The Western Plateau covers the western half of Australia. It is an area of DESERTS about 400 metres high. The Central Lowlands consist of low, arid plains. Some RIVERS drain into Lake Eyre, which is 12 metres below sea level. The Eastern Highlands contain most of Australia's MOUNTAINS.

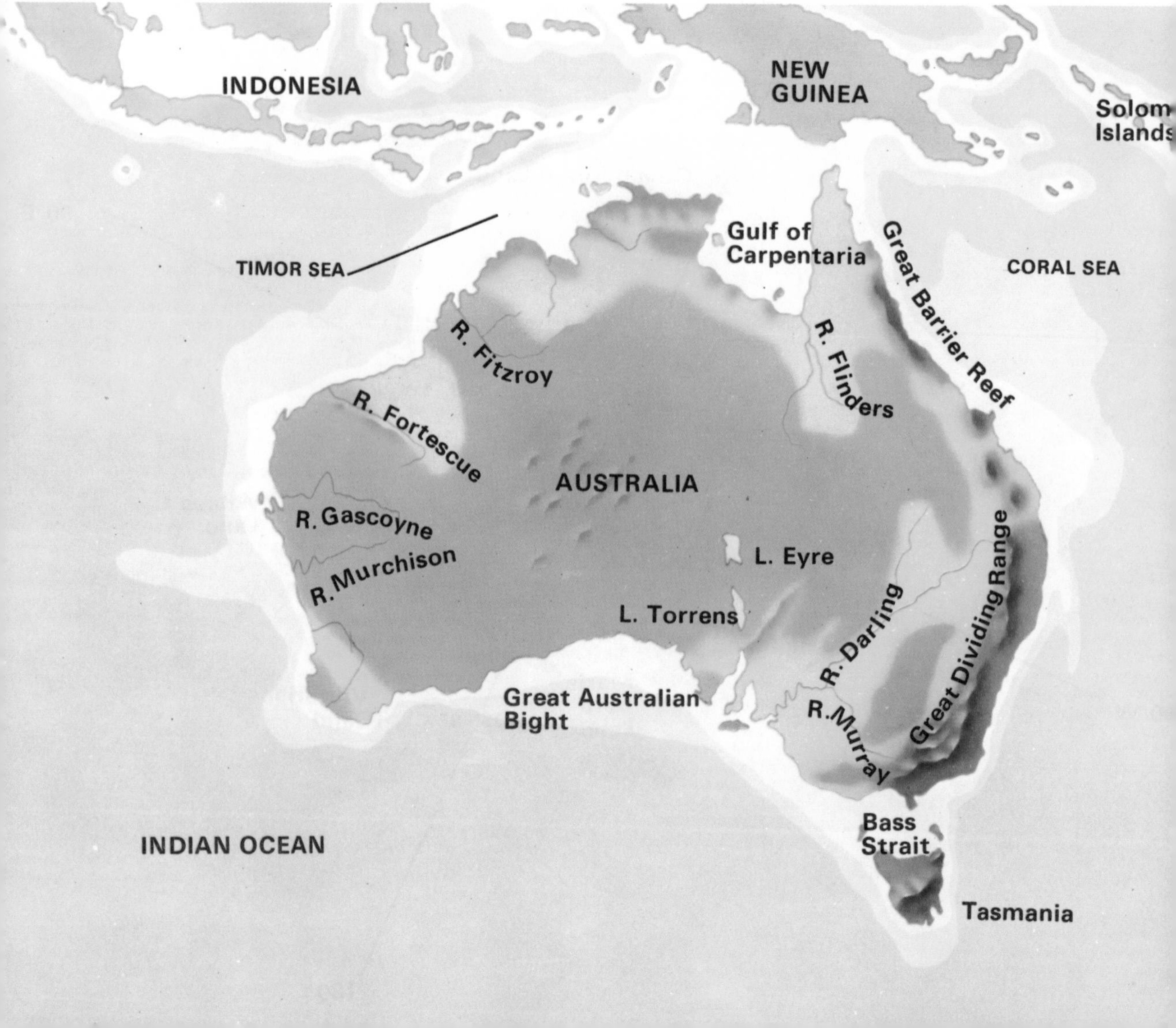

Above: Ayer's Rock lies in the arid Australian desert. It is the biggest rock in the world.
Below: The Shotover River in New Zealand.

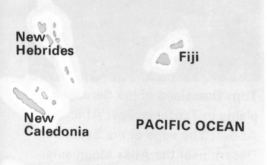

New Zealand is made up of two islands. A chain of high mountains extends along the western coast of South Island. The coast has magnificent FIORDS in the south-west. To the east of the mountains is a great grassy plain. The North Island has lower mountains than the South Island. But there are many VOLCANOES and GEYSERS in the centre of North Island. The climate of New Zealand is generally warm and rainy.

Africa

Africa has an area of 30 million square kilometres. North Africa mostly consists of the Sahara Desert. To the north-west are the ATLAS Mountains. The coast beyond has a MEDITERRANEAN climate, wet in winter and dry in summer. In the east the Nile Valley provides a fertile region.

South of the Atlas, most of Africa is made up of a vast plateau about 1000 metres high. A narrow, low plain surrounds this plateau at the coast. Great RIVERS occupy huge shallow hollows in the plateau.

A series of rift VALLEYS extends through eastern Africa. The Great Rift Valley is one. The formation of rift valleys has produced high mountains from ETHIOPIA to southern Africa. But there is no great backbone of MOUNTAINS in Africa, unlike other continents. The large island of Madagascar is separated from the African mainland by the Mozambique Channel.

Around the equator in west and central Africa, it is hot and wet. Thick forest covers much of the land. To the north and south, and on the higher land to the east, it is less wet. GRASSLAND and woodland are found. In south-west Africa, it is dry and there are DESERTS. Along the coast of SOUTH AFRICA, the climate is Mediterranean.

Top: Grassland of the Serengeti plains in Tanzania, East Africa.
Above: The edge of the Sahara Desert, near the Atlas Mountains.
Below: Table Mountain rising above Cape Town in South Africa.

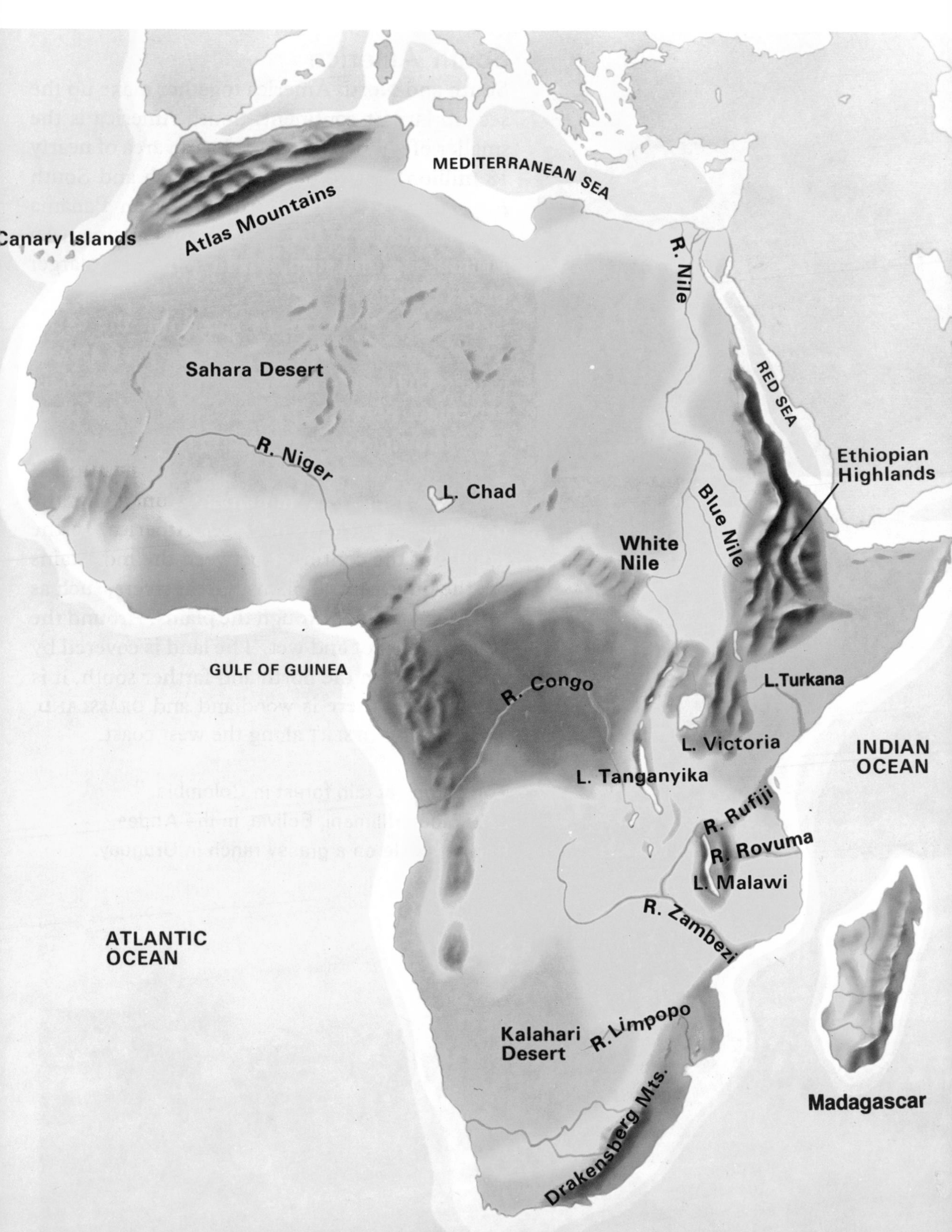
MEDITERRANEAN SEA
Canary Islands
Atlas Mountains
R. Nile
Sahara Desert
RED SEA
R. Niger
Ethiopian Highlands
L. Chad
Blue Nile
White Nile
GULF OF GUINEA
R. Congo
L.Turkana
L. Victoria
INDIAN OCEAN
L. Tanganyika
R. Rufiji
R. Rovuma
L. Malawi
R. Zambezi
ATLANTIC OCEAN
Kalahari Desert
R. Limpopo
Drakensberg Mts.
Madagascar

South America

South and North America together make up the second largest continent. South America is the smaller of the two halves. It has an area of nearly 18 million square kilometres. North and South America meet at the border between Panama and Colombia, in the Isthmus of Panama. (An isthmus is a thin strip of land joining two larger pieces of land.)

The ANDES Mountains run down the entire western coast of South America. They are the longest chain of mountains in the world, and are very high. Between the Andes and the sea there is a narrow plain. In the south, the sea comes up to the mountains and there are many ISLANDS.

Lower ranges of mountains run along the north and east coasts of South America. In the middle of the continent between the mountains are the huge central plains. Great rivers, such as the Amazon, run through the plains. Around the equator it is hot and wet. The land is covered by thick forest. In the north and farther south, it is less wet and there is woodland and GRASSLAND. There is also DESERT along the west coast.

Top: Tropical rain forest in Colombia.
Left: Mount Illimani, Bolivia, in the Andes.
Below: Cattle on a grassy ranch in Uruguay.

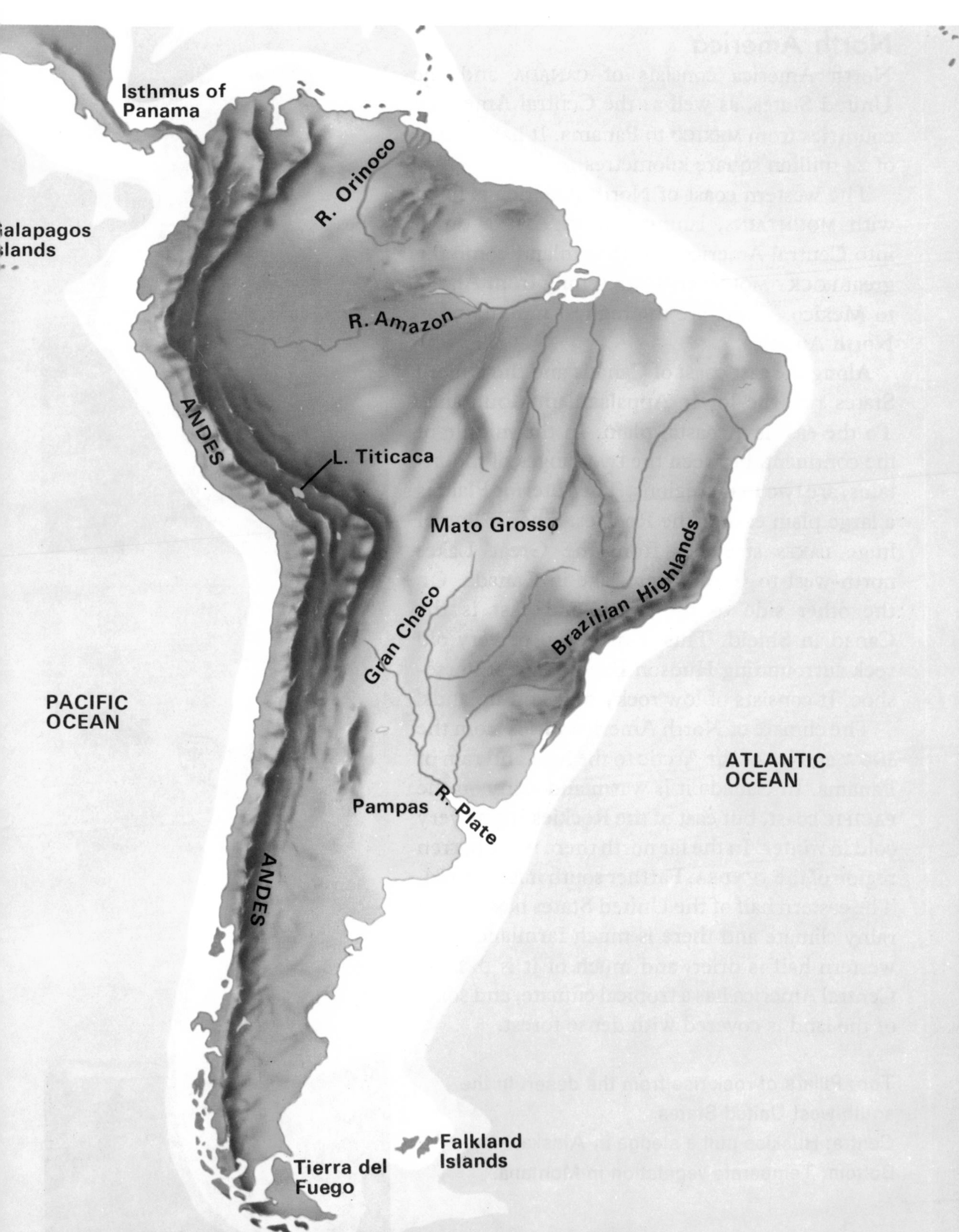
Isthmus of Panama
R. Orinoco
R. Amazon
ANDES
L. Titicaca
Mato Grosso
Brazilian Highlands
Gran Chaco
PACIFIC OCEAN
ATLANTIC OCEAN
Pampas
R. Plate
ANDES
Falkland Islands
Tierra del Fuego

North America

North America consists of CANADA and the United States, as well as the Central American countries from MEXICO to Panama. It has an area of 24 million square kilometres.

The western coast of North America is lined with MOUNTAINS, running from Alaska down into Central America. Further inland come the great ROCKY MOUNTAINS, stretching from Alaska to Mexico. These are the highest mountains in North America.

Along the east coast of Canada and the United States run the lower Appalachian Mountains. To the east is a coastal plain. In the middle of the continent, between the two ranges of mountains, are two main regions. The Interior Plain is a large plain east of the Rockies. Then a line of huge LAKES stretches from the Great Lakes north-west to Great Bear Lake in Canada. On the other side to the north and east is the Canadian Shield. This is made up of very old rock surrounding Hudson Bay in a great horseshoe. It consists of low rocky hills and uplands.

The climate of North America varies from the SNOW and ice of the Arctic to the heat and rain of Panama. In Canada it is warm and rainy on the PACIFIC coast, but east of the Rockies it gets very cold in winter. In the far north there is the barren region of the TUNDRA. Farther south it is forested. The eastern half of the United States has a warm rainy climate and there is much farmland. The western half is drier, and much of it is DESERT. Central America has a tropical climate, and some of the land is covered with dense forest.

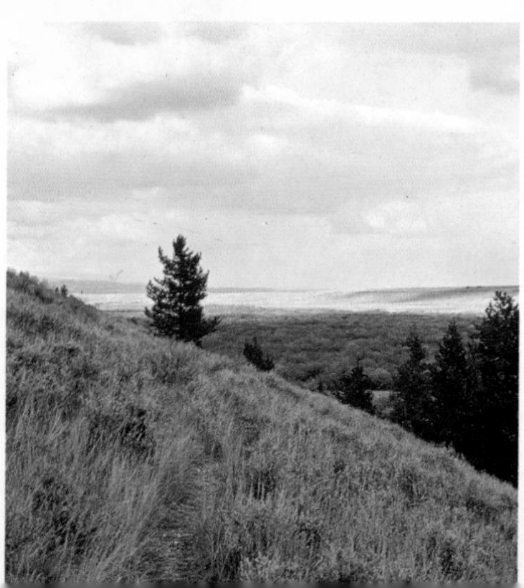

Top: Pillars of rock rise from the desert in the south-west United States.
Centre: Huskies pull a sledge in Alaska.
Bottom: Temperate vegetation in Montana.

GREENLAND
ARCTIC OCEAN
BAFFIN BAY
Baffin Island
BEAUFORT SEA
Davis Strait
ASKA
NORTHWEST TERRITORIES
Great Bear Lake
R. Mackenzie
Great Slave Lake
HUDSON BAY
LABRADOR
ROCKY MOUNTAINS
CANADA
L. Winnipeg
Great Lakes
St Lawrence
R.Missouri
R. Ohio
Appalachian Mts
UNITED STATES
R. Mississippi
Red River
Sierra Nevada
ATLANTIC OCEAN
Rio Grande
PACIFIC OCEAN
MEXICO
GULF OF MEXICO
Sierra Madre
Gulf of California
CUBA
WEST INDIES
YUCATAN
CARIBBEAN SEA

Contrasting European scenery.
Above: Loch Creran, a bleak inlet on the coast of Scotland.
Below: A green valley lying among the Alps in Switzerland.

Europe

Europe is really a huge peninsula joined to the western end of ASIA. A peninsula is a stretch of land that sticks out into the sea. Europe lies west of the Ural Mountains in the U.S.S.R. It has an area of over 10 million square kilometres.

Europe has a north-west boundary of MOUNTAINS and uplands. These run from Ireland through Wales, northern England, and Scotland to NORWAY, SWEDEN, and northern FINLAND. South and east of these mountains is a huge central plain that stretches from west to east across Europe. It begins in southern England, crosses northern FRANCE, BELGIUM, the NETHERLANDS, DENMARK, northern Germany, and POLAND, and then continues across the U.S.S.R. to the Urals. The plain is very low and rarely gets any higher than 200 metres above sea level. Farther south comes a range of mountains, stretching from PORTUGAL through SPAIN and France to southern Germany.

There are a number of great mountain ranges in Europe, starting with the Sierra Nevada in southern Spain. Then come the Pyrenees, the ALPS, the Carpathians, and the Caucasus, which are Europe's highest mountains. Branches lead off this chain of mountain ranges. The Apennines form a backbone for ITALY. Other mountains rise through the Balkans and TURKEY to join the Caucasus at the Caspian Sea. Beyond the mountains lies the MEDITERRANEAN SEA, Europe's southern boundary.

Europe has a mild, rainy climate and much of the land is farmed, except in mountainous regions. It does not get very cold because of warm winds from the ATLANTIC OCEAN, where a warm current starts in the Gulf of MEXICO. This flows north-east, first as the Gulf Stream, and then as the North Atlantic Drift, before reaching Europe.

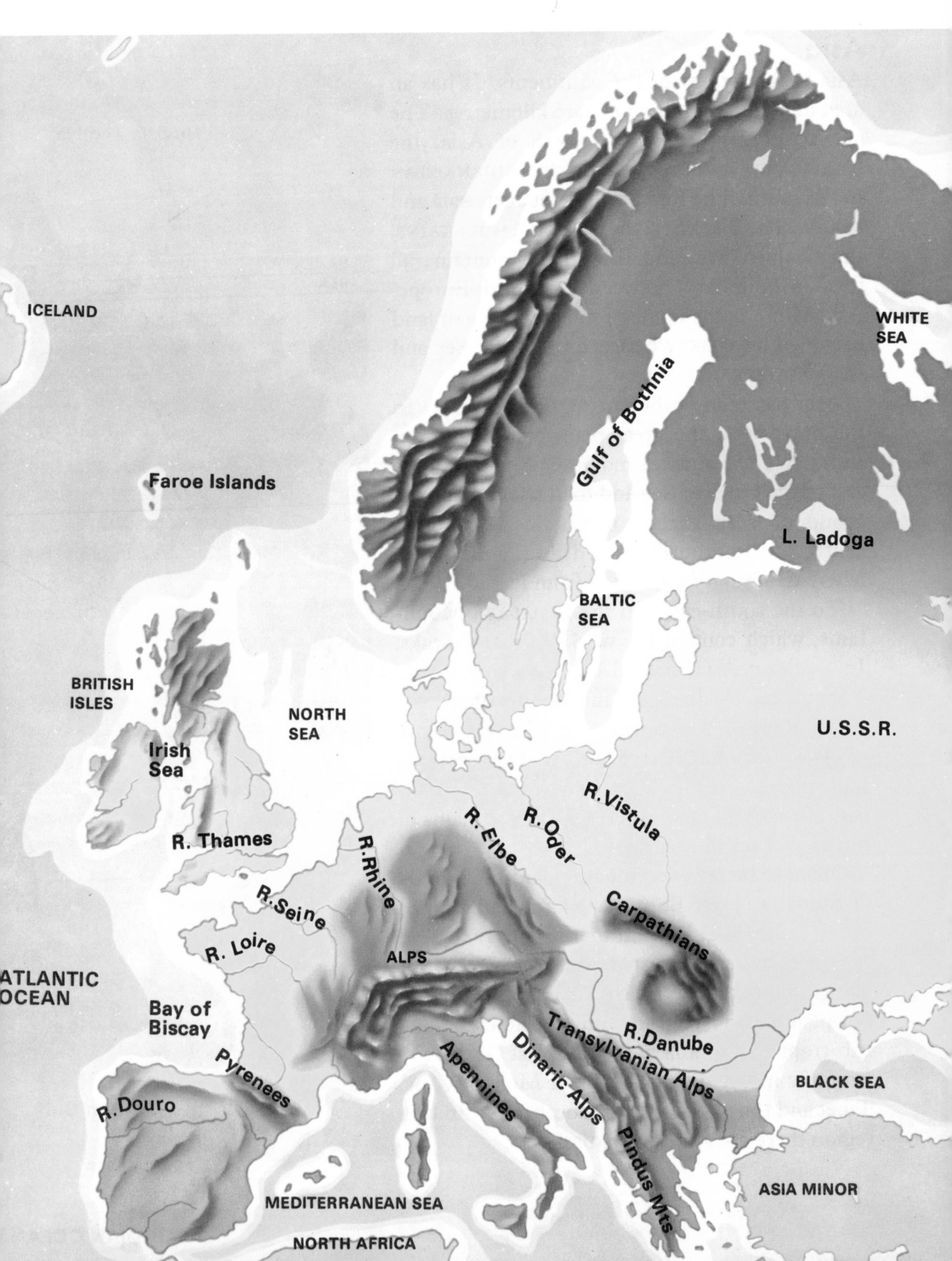
ICELAND
WHITE SEA
Gulf of Bothnia
Faroe Islands
L. Ladoga
BALTIC SEA
BRITISH ISLES
NORTH SEA
U.S.S.R.
Irish Sea
R. Vistula
R. Oder
R. Elbe
R. Thames
R. Rhine
R. Seine
Carpathians
R. Loire
ALPS
ATLANTIC OCEAN
Bay of Biscay
R. Danube
Transylvanian Alps
Dinaric Alps
Apennines
Pyrenees
BLACK SEA
R. Douro
Pindus Mts
ASIA MINOR
MEDITERRANEAN SEA
NORTH AFRICA

Asia

Asia is the largest of the continents. It has an area of about 44 million square kilometres. The ARCTIC OCEAN lies to the north of Asia, the PACIFIC OCEAN to the east, and the INDIAN OCEAN to the south. The Red Sea lies between Asia and AFRICA. The Black Sea, the Caucasus MOUNTAINS, the Caspian Sea, and the Ural Mountains all form a boundary between Asia and Europe. Asia Minor is the name of the peninsula of land occupied by TURKEY between the Black Sea and the MEDITERRANEAN SEA.

Asia has many different natural features. In the north-west the great plain continues from Europe. The Caucasus mountains extend to the east of the Caspian Sea and then rise into a large group of very rugged mountains. The high centre of the group is called the Pamir Knot. Many mountain ranges lead from it.

To the south-east run the HIMALAYA Mountains, which contain the world's highest peaks. In southern Asia, several high plateaus extend from the mountain ranges into Arabia, IRAN, and INDIA. Ranges of mountains run from the centre of Asia to its north-east corner. They contain high plateaus in Tibet and MONGOLIA. To the east of these mountains are the coastal plains of CHINA and south-east Asia.

Offshore lie JAPAN to the east, and the islands of Sumatra, Java, Borneo, and the Philippines to the south-east. Beyond them is AUSTRALIA.

The climate is moist in the eastern coastal plains, where there is much farming. The northern plain is very cold in winter. The climate is sub-tropical in India and south-east Asia. It is very dry in the high plateaus of Mongolia and Tibet and the plateaus to the south-west. In this region there are also several DESERTS.

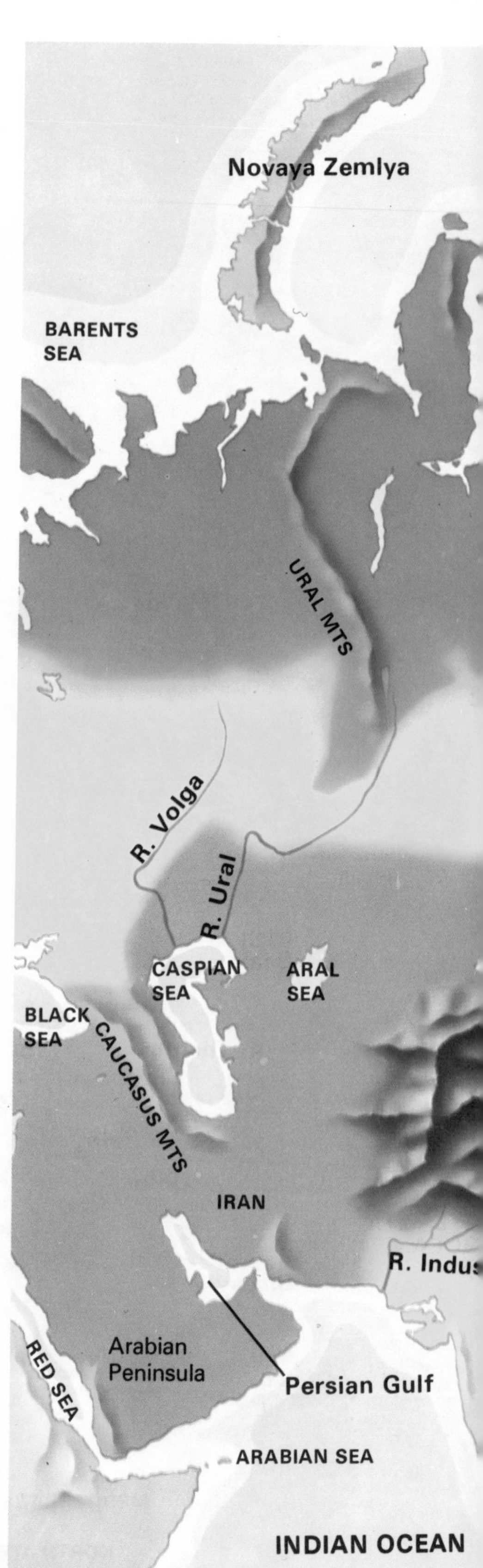

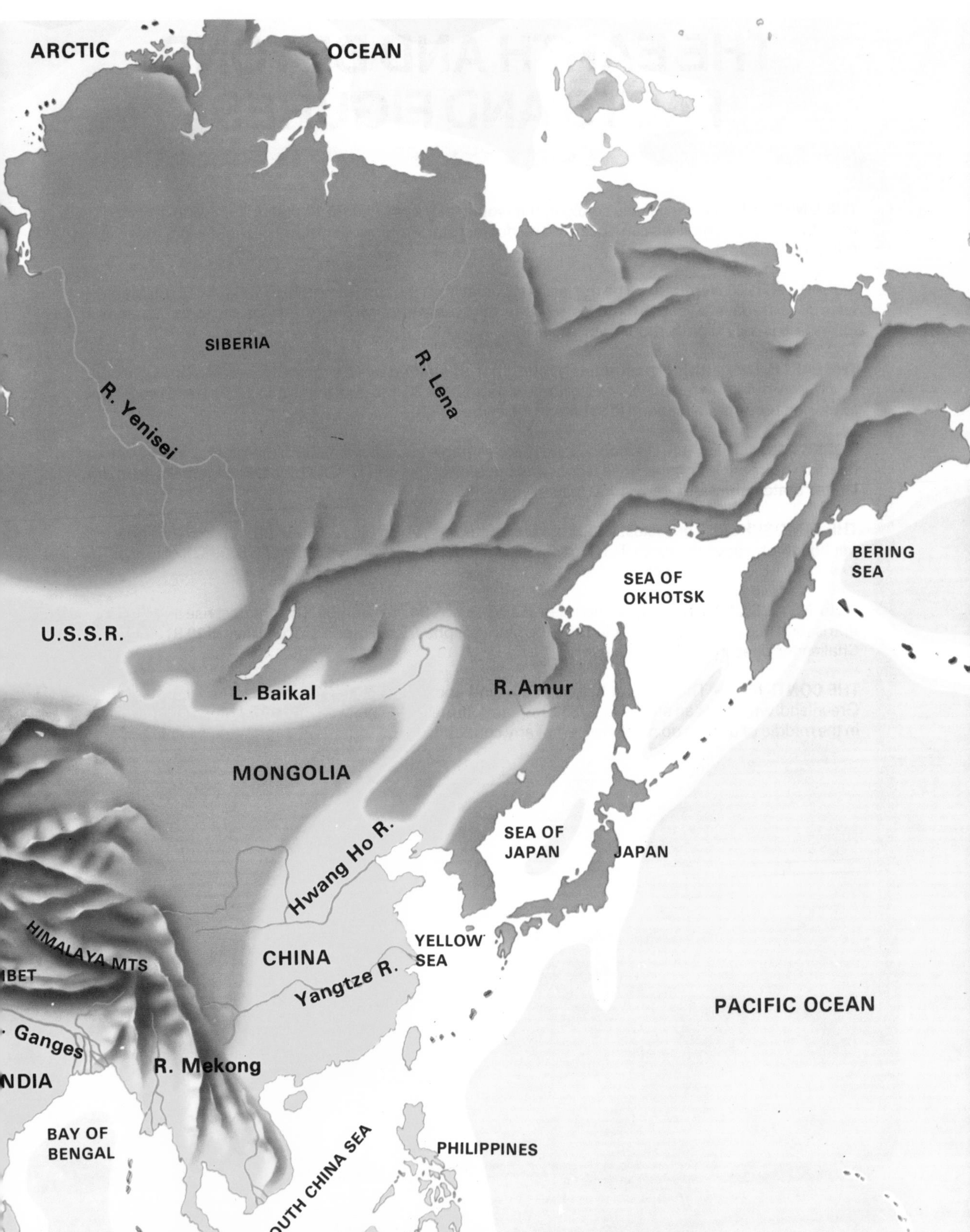
ARCTIC
OCEAN
SIBERIA
R. Lena
R. Yenisei
U.S.S.R.
L. Baikal
R. Amur
SEA OF
OKHOTSK
BERING
SEA
MONGOLIA
Hwang Ho R.
SEA OF
JAPAN
JAPAN
HIMALAYA MTS
IBET
CHINA
YELLOW
SEA
Yangtze R.
PACIFIC OCEAN
Ganges
R. Mekong
NDIA
BAY OF
BENGAL
SOUTH CHINA SEA
PHILIPPINES

THE EARTH AND BEYOND FACTS AND FIGURES

THE UNIVERSE. The universe is so big that it would take a ray of light 10,000 million years to reach us from the farthest region we can observe. The nearest star, Proxima Centauri, is $4\frac{1}{4}$ light years (40 million million kilometres) away.

SOLAR SYSTEM. Neptune will be the farthest planet from the sun from 1979 to 1999. A year on Mercury lasts 88 earth-days; a year on Pluto lasts 248 earth-*years*. Although Saturn is huge, the force of gravity at its surface is only slightly more than on earth.

THE EARTH. The earth is not completely round, but is flattened by 42 kilometres between the poles. The most powerful known volcanic explosion was about 1470 B.C. on the island of Thera, Greece. The explosion produced a tsunami (tidal wave) 54 metres high.

ROCKS AND MINERALS. Diamond is the most valuable as well as the hardest mineral. Pumice stone floats on water; it is light because it contains bubbles of gas and air. The oldest known rocks are in the United States; they are nearly 4000 million years old.

THE ATMOSPHERE. The fastest winds are the jet steams, which blow at speeds of up to 500 kilometres per hour high above the earth. The highest recorded temperature on the ground is 59°C in Algeria. The lowest is –88°C in Antarctica.

OCEANS AND SEAS. The largest recorded sea wave was 34 metres high. The greatest rise and fall of the tide is 16·3 metres in Nova Scotia. In 1960, the bathyscaphe *Trieste* made a record dive of 10,917 metres in Challenger Deep in the Pacific Ocean.

THE CONTINENTS. The average height of the land above the sea is 750 metres. The largest island is Greenland, which has an area of 2,180,000 square kilometres. Greenland and most other islands that lie in the middle of oceans do not form part of any continent.

FAMOUS PEOPLE

Painters and Sculptors

The first artists were probably the hunting folk of the Stone Age, who painted animals on the walls of their caves. Then came the ANCIENT EGYPTIANS, ANCIENT GREEKS, and other peoples, who made temples, statues, and paintings in honour of their gods.

Artists of the BYZANTINE EMPIRE made MOSAICS, and painted FRESCOES, which are a kind of mural, or wall picture. Some of the greatest frescoes were painted by Italian artists of the Middle Ages, such as Giotto.

In the fifteenth century, artists started to move away from religious subjects. Later, Dutch and German painters became some of the world's greatest artists. The Spaniard Velasquez was a very fine seventeenth-century artist. In the next century great English and French painters appeared. England produced magnificent portrait painters such as Gainsborough and Reynolds.

In the nineteenth century, the IMPRESSIONISTS tried to paint things as they themselves saw them. Today, when it is possible to make life-like photographs of people and scenes, many artists paint 'abstract' pictures that do not look like anything we can see around us.

Botticelli

Alessandro di Mariano dei Filipepi was born in Florence in ITALY, in about 1444, and died in 1510. He seems to have gained the name Botticelli in a strange way. His brother, who had charge of him, was a merchant whose trade sign was a *botticello*, or little barrel, so Alessandro became known as Sandro Botticelli.

Botticelli studied painting under the artist Fra Filippo Lippi. Working on his own, he became famous for such paintings as *Primavera* (Spring) and *The Birth of Venus*. These colourful paintings are full of light, and the figures almost seem alive. Later, Botticelli painted many religious pictures such as *The Nativity*, which hangs in Britain's National Gallery.

Leonardo da Vinci

Anybody asked to name the most famous picture in the world might well reply, '*The Mona Lisa*'. This is the PORTRAIT of a mysteriously smiling woman by Leonardo da Vinci (1452–1519). Leonardo, son of a LAWYER from Vinci, near Florence in ITALY, was a friend of the artist BOTTICELLI. Another well-known painting by Leonardo is *The Last Supper*, a FRESCO in a church in Milan.

Leonardo was not only one of the greatest painters, but also a sculptor, architect, philosopher, scientist and engineer. He was always trying to find out, and then draw, how things really were, and how they worked. He also studied anatomy in order to draw and paint the human body accurately.

Far left: *The Adoration of the Magi* by Botticelli shows the three wise men with the Holy Family. Left: Leonardo da Vinci's *Madonna of the Rocks* has an atmosphere of mystery.

Dürer

Albrecht Dürer, born in Nuremberg in 1471, was one of the greatest of German artists. After learning the trade of book illustration, he travelled around EUROPE, and visited VENICE where he met the artist Bellini. From 1512, Dürer was employed in Germany by the Holy Roman Emperor, first Maximilian I, and then Charles V. In 1520 he visited Flanders (modern BELGIUM and NETHERLANDS) but returned to Germany until his death in 1528.

Dürer's greatest works are his WOODCUTS and copper ENGRAVINGS. They combine vivid imagery and symbolism with great accuracy and detail. Most of the engravings portray a world filled with grim warriors and strange monsters. His drawings, such as *The Hare*, have the same detail.

Left: Dürer's *The Knight, Death, and the Devil.*

Titian

Tiziano Vecelli (about 1477–1576), who is called Titian by English-speaking people, was an Italian painter. He studied art and worked for some time in VENICE, especially on FRESCOES (murals), such as *The Assumption* in the Frari Church. He also worked for the Pope and Emperor Charles V. One of his best-known PORTRAITS is that of Charles V. For his successor, Philip II of SPAIN, Titian painted many portraits and pictures on mythological subjects.

Titian's works are remarkable for their technical skill and magnificent use of rich colours. A certain red colour is now called titian after him. Titian died of the plague in Venice. Unlike the other victims, he was buried inside the city with great honour.

Left: *Bacchus and Ariadne* by Titian.

Michelangelo

Michelangelo Buonarroti-Simoni lived from 1475 to 1564. He was a painter, architect and poet. He was also probably the greatest of Italian sculptors. As a boy he showed such talent that he was chosen to work in the household of Lorenzo de Medici who provided money and encouragement for many great artists.

Among Michelangelo's finest sculptures is the huge figure of David. This figure is very beautiful and also very lifelike. Michelangelo preferred sculpture to painting, but he spent over four years painting the ceiling of the Sistine Chapel in the Vatican in ROME for the Pope. This huge painting shows the creation of the world and other scenes from the Bible.

Left: An ancient Greek priestess from Michelangelo's Sistine Chapel paintings.

Raphael

Raphael Santi (1483–1520), son of a painter, was born in Urbino in ITALY and studied with the artist Perugino. In 1504 he went to Florence where he learned much from LEONARDO DA VINCI.

In 1508 Raphael went to ROME where he met MICHELANGELO, who had much influence over his work. Raphael painted a series of FRESCOES (murals) for the Vatican. He also made cartoons (sketches) for a series of tapestries. One of Raphael's greatest paintings is the *School of Athens* which is a fresco in the Vatican representing Philosophy.

Raphael also planned many buildings, and was one of the architects of ST PETER'S basilica in Rome.

Left: A portrait of a lady – *La Donna Velata* – by Raphael.

Brueghel

Pieter Brueghel (about 1520–1569) was born at Brueghel (near Bruges in modern BELGIUM). He was the son of a peasant. Brueghel first worked as an engraver, cutting designs in wood or metal. Later, he travelled in FRANCE and ITALY before settling in Antwerp and then Brussels. Brueghel's most famous pictures show scenes of peasant life. They are full of fascinating, active figures. Among them are *Peasant Dance* and *Peasant Wedding*. Two of Brueghel's sons also became painters: they are known as 'Hell Brueghel' and 'Velvet Brueghel'.

Above: Brueghel's *Peasant Wedding*. Below: Rembrandt painted this self-portrait when he was 34.

El Greco

Domenikos Theotokopoulos (about 1541–1614) was born in Crete, an ISLAND near GREECE. He became known as *El Greco*, meaning The Greek. El Greco studied in VENICE under TITIAN and began to paint in his master's style. Then he settled in Toledo in SPAIN and his style changed completely. He painted strange, stormy pictures in brilliant colours, with figures which looked much shorter or much longer than in real life.

Many of his finest paintings are still in Spain: the best-known is *The Burial of Count Orgaz*. *View of Toledo,* now in the Metropolitan Museum, NEW YORK, is his only LANDSCAPE.

Rembrandt

Rembrandt van Rijn (1606–1669) was the son of a miller. He was probably the greatest of the Dutch painters. He studied and worked chiefly in AMSTERDAM and Leyden.

Rembrandt was especially famous for his PORTRAITS. His finest gifts were his clever use of dark and light tones, and his power to reveal the characters of the people he painted. His most famous painting is *The Night Watch*.

In all, Rembrandt produced over 600 OIL PAINTINGS (including about 60 self-portraits), 2,000 drawings, and 300 ETCHINGS. Rembrandt made a fortune as a young man but he died poor. People grew tired of his pictures and his genius was forgotten.

Goya

Goya (1746–1828), whose full name was Francisco José Goya y Lucientes, was one of SPAIN'S greatest artists. He was also a hot-tempered man. It is said that he once threw a plaster cast at a sitter who had annoyed him. The sitter was England's hero, the Duke of WELLINGTON.

Goya was painter at the Spanish court. His PORTRAITS are strong and vivid but not flattering. They show clearly any bad qualities in his sitters. His ETCHINGS and drawings are also sometimes cruel. The series of etchings, *Disasters of War*, for which he made drawings when NAPOLEON'S armies entered Spain in 1808, are grim and terrifying. But, like most of Goya's pictures, they are impossible to forget.

El Greco and Goya have also left portraits of themselves. El Greco's self-portrait (below) is very formal, but Goya's (below right) is honest and unflattering.

Turner

Joseph Mallord William Turner (1775–1851) was the son of a LONDON barber. Even as a child, it was clear that he would become an artist.

Turner's early work was greatly influenced by other artists, such as the Frenchman, Claude. Later, when in his fifties, Turner began to try to paint the effects of light and air. He was particularly fond of painting sea scenes. To find out what it was like, he once had himself tied to the mast of a ship during a storm at sea. *The Fighting Téméraire*, (an old SAILING SHIP), is one of his best-known paintings. Some of his later paintings are almost entirely abstract (they contain no recognisable objects).

Above right: A self-portrait by Cézanne. Cézanne was shy by nature, and painted few portraits except of himself and his wife.
Far right: This self-portrait by Van Gogh is sometimes called *Vincent in Flames*.

Cézanne

The French painter Paul Cézanne (1839–1906) was born in Aix-en-Provence and studied in PARIS. There he met a group of artists called IMPRESSIONISTS, including Monet, Manet and Degas. The Impressionists tried to paint the reflection of light on objects. They gave an impression of an object, not its exact form.

Cézanne soon returned to Aix to paint LANDSCAPES, PORTRAITS, and STILL-LIFES. He was more interested in the actual shape of an object than the Impressionists were. In planning a picture, he formed the objects into a richly-coloured pattern. Cézanne and his followers were called Post- (after) Impressionists. People disliked his work but he took no notice. His genius was not understood until after his death.

Van Gogh

The Post-Impressionist painter Vincent Van Gogh (1853–1890) was the most important Dutch painter after REMBRANDT. His life was one of sadness and poverty. In a fit of despair he once cut off part of one ear. Nobody believed in his genius except his brother Theo, who supported him out of his own small earnings.

Vincent (as he signed his pictures) did some of his best work in FRANCE. He painted whatever he saw around him: LANDSCAPES, STILL-LIFES, and PORTRAITS, making marvellous use of colour. Like CÉZANNE, he was interested in pattern, but his own feelings kept coming in, to give his pictures extra life. Eventually, thinking himself a failure, friendless, and a burden on Theo, Van Gogh killed himself.

Matisse

Henri Matisse (1869–1954) was one of the greatest French painters of this century. At first, he intended to be a LAWYER. At the age of 20, while recovering from an illness, he decided to become a painter.

Matisse greatly admired the work of the IMPRESSIONISTS. He was also influenced by the Post-Impressionists, including CÉZANNE. He became a member of a group of painters who were known as *Les Fauves* (wild beasts) because their style at that time was thought to be crude.

Matisse travelled around the world for several years, and then, in 1917, settled in the south of FRANCE. He designed a chapel for the Dominican nuns at Vence which was completed in 1951. He also painted the large murals which cover its walls.

Left: A painting by Matisse. He is noted for his use of strong, bold colours.

Picasso

Pablo Ruiz Picasso (1881–1973) has been called the greatest painter of modern times. He was a sculptor, etcher and designer as well as a painter. He was the son of a Spanish art teacher, and he settled in PARIS in 1903.

Picasso painted in many different styles. At first, he used strong colours, then he painted chiefly in blue, then in rose. Later, he evolved one style of Cubism, with pictures made up of a series of cones and cubes. But he also painted in a style closer to real life. For each picture he chose the style which seemed to suit the subject best. After about 1925, his work became more and more abstract. He was more concerned with painting ideas and feelings than simply painting scenes and objects.

Left: *The Three Dancers*, by Picasso.
Below: Picasso, aged 87, points to one of the pictures that surround him. He continued painting until the very end of his life.

Above: A bust by Rodin of Balzac, the great French novelist and short-story writer.

Rodin

François Auguste Rodin was born in 1840. He studied sculpture in PARIS, where he worked as a sculptor before moving to Brussels. Later, he returned to Paris, where he made his mark. Copies of his statues were bought by collectors all over the world. He lived in the house which is now a MUSEUM of his work. Here, most of his famous sculptures can still be seen. They include *The Thinker*, and the massive *Gate of Hell*. The latter work was inspired by DANTE's poem *The Inferno*. *The Kiss* is another of Rodin's more famous sculptures.

Rodin made a number of portrait sculptures of the great men of his time, including the writers Honoré Balzac and Victor HUGO. He also produced a great number of ETCHINGS and drawings.

Rodin died in 1917.

Henry Moore

Many people consider that Henry Moore is the greatest sculptor of our day. He was born in 1898, the son of a Yorkshire COAL miner. He studied art, and when he came to LONDON, he spent hours in the Natural History MUSEUM and the British Museum. He examined the shapes made by nature in stone and wood, and the carvings made by peoples in ancient times. His own style developed from these early studies.

Moore works in wood, bronze, and stone. His sculptures can be viewed in the round, that is, from a number of different points. At each point there is something different to see. His work can be seen in museums all over the world. Some of his sculptures are sited in the open air in London and other places.

Left: This bronze sculpture by Henry Moore can be seen beside the River Thames, in London.

Composers

Until a few hundred years ago, music was hardly ever written down. For this reason, we do not know the names of the earliest composers (writers of music). Early music was based on single tunes, or melodies. Later, several tunes were combined into one song, or piece of music. Among early composers of many-tuned music were Palestrina in ITALY, and the Englishman William Byrd.

A further musical development was opera. This has a story set to words and music. Monteverdi was the first great operatic composer. Among others are Purcell, MOZART, WAGNER, Verdi, Puccini, and Richard Strauss.

Music was also written for instruments played alone, or together in an ORCHESTRA. Eighteenth century music is often called CLASSICAL MUSIC, though some call all 'serious' music classical. The greatest classical composers include BACH, HANDEL, HAYDN, Mozart and BEETHOVEN. Some also wrote church music, opera and songs.

Above: Johann Sebastian Bach. Below: The seventeenth-century English composer, Henry Purcell.

During the nineteenth century, many composers wrote romantic music. This kind of music appeals to the listener's feelings and imagination. Among the best-known composers born in the nineteenth century are SCHUBERT, Berlioz, Mendelssohn, CHOPIN, Schumann, Liszt, BRAHMS, TCHAIKOVSKY, DVORÁK, Elgar, Mahler, DEBUSSY, and Sibelius.

Twentieth-century music frequently sounds different from earlier music. A composer whose work is often performed now is the Hungarian Béla Bartök. Two popular Russian composers of our century are Prokofiev and Shostakovich.

The Austrian Arnold Schoenberg invented a new method of composition. He introduced 12-note music instead of the old scale of eight notes. Today, a number of composers write ELECTRONIC MUSIC as well as ordinary music.

Bach

Johann Sebastian Bach (1685–1750), one of the greatest musicians of all time, belonged to a musical German family. He began his career as a church organist, and was soon composing ORGAN preludes (opening pieces) and fugues (pieces arranged for several contrasting parts). Then he was made court musician to the ruling prince of Cöthen, and had his own ORCHESTRA to direct.

At Cöthen he composed some of his finest chamber music (music written for a small number of players). Later, as organist at Leipzig, he composed church music, including his St Matthew and St John Passions, and the *Mass in B minor*.

Three of Bach's sons became well-known musicians. They were Wilhelm Friedmann, Carl Philipp Emanuel, and Johann Christian.

Handel

The world's most popular oratorio (a composition for voices and orchestra, usually on a religious subject) is Handel's *Messiah*. George Frederick Handel was born in Germany in 1685. He was already known as a composer of operas when he settled in England in 1711. He had little success with his operas but made his name with his oratorios, among them *Israel in Egypt*, *Samson*, and *Judas Maccabeus*.

When the Elector of Hanover became King George I of England, Handel was out of favour for leaving Germany. He was forgiven, however, when he wrote his famous *Water Music* for one of the royal water parties on the River Thames in LONDON. Handel died in 1759 and was buried in Westminster Abbey.

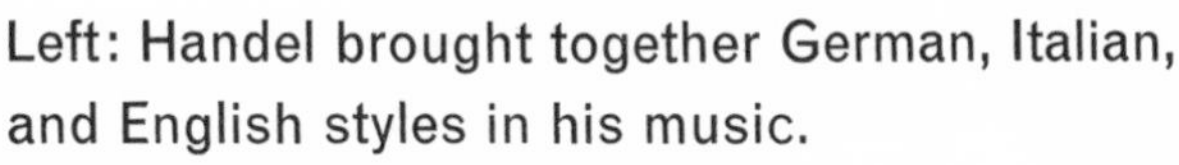

Left: Handel brought together German, Italian, and English styles in his music.

Above: Joseph Haydn.

Haydn

After hearing *God Save the King* played in LONDON, the Austrian musician Joseph Haydn (1732–1809) wrote a national anthem for his own country. Haydn, the son of poor parents, had been a choir boy in VIENNA Cathedral. Later, he played in street bands, taught singing, and began to write music.

In 1761 Haydn was made musical director to the rich Esterhazy family, and composed vast amounts of music of many kinds. He wrote more than a hundred symphonies (full-length works for a complete ORCHESTRA). Later composers followed Haydn's outline plans for his symphonies and other works. Haydn also wrote a number of operas.

As an old man, Haydn wrote his oratorio *The Creation* and another equally splendid work for voices, *The Seasons*.

Mozart

HAYDN described his young friend Wolfgang Amadeus Mozart (1756–1791) as the most extraordinary and original musical genius ever known. Born at Salzburg, AUSTRIA, where he is honoured today with music festivals, Mozart started playing the harpsichord (which is similar to the PIANO). He began composing at the age of five, and toured the courts of EUROPE with his father.

Mozart wrote marvellous operas, among them *The Marriage of Figaro*. He also wrote many symphonies, sonatas (pieces for single instruments), chamber music, and concertos (for one or more instruments and ORCHESTRA). Yet he remained so poor that a friend calling one winter's day found Mozart, who could not afford a fire, waltzing with his wife to keep warm. His last work, a Requiem (funeral) Mass, was written as he lay dying.

Above: Wolfgang Amadeus Mozart.

Beethoven

Ludwig van Beethoven was born in Bonn, Germany, in 1770. He made his name early as a musician. Like MOZART, he performed at concerts as a child.

In his twenties, Beethoven settled in VIENNA. There he studied under HAYDN, and wrote symphonies, sonatas, chamber music, and songs. However, he began to go deaf, and had to give up playing the PIANO at concerts.

Many people consider Beethoven's nine symphonies as the finest ever written. He also wrote one opera – *Fidelio*. In later life Beethoven became totally deaf. But he continued to compose and conduct music even though he could not hear a note. He died in 1827.

Left: This portrait of Beethoven gives some idea of his strong and fiery personality.

Schubert

One of the world's best-known songs is the vivid *Erl King* by the Austrian composer Franz Schubert (1797–1828). It describes a father, his little son in his arms, galloping on horseback in a vain attempt to save the child from death.

Schubert was the son of a schoolteacher and began to compose at the age of 13. For a time he taught in his father's school, but he hated teaching and later managed to earn just enough to live from his music.

Schubert wrote a number of symphonies among other musical works. He is best known, however, for his many songs, written for voice and PIANO.

During his lifetime, Schubert was very poor, and was never well-known. He died aged 31.

Right: Franz Schubert.

Chopin

The composer and pianist Frédéric François Chopin was born near Warsaw, POLAND, in 1810. Chopin was half Polish and loved Poland, although he did not live there after the age of 21. In 1831 he settled in PARIS where he remained until his death in 1849 after many years of illness.

Chopin wrote almost entirely for the PIANO and was an excellent pianist himself. Many of his compositions are based upon dance forms and rhythms, such as mazurkas, waltzes, and polonaises. The gaiety and lightness of his work were in contrast to his own sad nature. Chopin's work was quite different from that of the other musicians of his time.

Right: A portrait of Frédéric Chopin, by the great French painter Delacroix.

Brahms

The German composer Johannes Brahms (1833–1897) had his first music lessons from his father. At the age of 15, Brahms began to play the PIANO in public, but went on with his studies, learning to compose as well as to play. Brahms became a close friend of Robert Schumann who was full of enthusiasm for his work and encouraged him.

At first, Brahms' music was considered too modern. Later, Schumann's wife, Clara, a well-known pianist, helped to make it known by performing it at concerts. As well as grand, powerful music for the piano, symphonies, concertos, and chamber music, Brahms wrote about 300 songs. He destroyed much of the music he had written because he was not satisfied with it.

Left: An early photograph of the composer Brahms in his study.

Above: Richard Wagner liked to dress in extravagant and romantic costumes.

Wagner

There cannot have been many composers whose operas were so much admired by a king that he was willing to spend vast sums of money in order to see them performed. But this is what happened to the German composer Richard Wagner (1813–1883) when he met Ludwig II of Bavaria.

Wagner is important as the creator of a new kind of opera which he called music-drama. He wrote both the words and the music for his operas, which are based on ancient German stories. Among his operas are the four works that make up the *Ring of the Nibelungs, Tristan and Isolde, The Mastersingers of Nuremberg,* and *Parsifal,* his last work. *The Ring* was first performed at a specially-built opera house in Bayreuth, Germany.

Today, a festival of Wagner's operas is held in Bayreuth every year.

Tchaikovsky

Some of the best-known music in the world was written by the Russian composer Peter Ilich Tchaikovsky (1840–1893). Almost everybody has heard his ballet music for *Swan Lake, The Sleeping Beauty,* and *The Nutcracker*. His *1812 Overture* has the sound of bells pealing and cannon firing. It recalls NAPOLEON's retreat from MOSCOW in 1812.

Tchaikovsky first studied music at home. He also studied law and worked in a government office. Then he made music his career and composed, among other things, operas, symphonies, piano concertos, and chamber music. Tchaikovsky was greatly helped by a rich widow who gave him money on condition that they never met. He wrote his Fourth Symphony for her.

Right: Tchaikovsky, painted in 1893.

Dvořák

Antonin Dvořák (1841–1904) was born in a village near Prague in CZECHOSLOVAKIA, where his father was both an innkeeper and a butcher. At the age of 16, Antonin went to Prague to study. Five years later, he joined the ORCHESTRA of the Prague National Theatre.

Dvořák made a number of visits to England. Between 1892 and 1895 he lived in NEW YORK. His stay in the United States resulted in his ninth symphony *From the New World* – probably his best-known work. Dvořák was interested in the folk music of both EUROPE and NORTH AMERICA. This had a strong influence on his music. Dvořák also wrote a number of other symphonies and nine operas.

Right: Dvořák, who started life as a poor village boy.

Debussy

Claude Debussy (1862–1918) was a remarkable French composer who had a great influence on MODERN MUSIC. He shared the views of the French artists called IMPRESSIONISTS. This meant that he did not write music that told a story in a bold theatrical way. Instead, he suggested feelings and happenings in his music.

Debussy's best-loved composition is called *Clair de lune* (Moonlight) which he wrote for the PIANO. His finest music includes *La Mer* (The Sea). In this piece, he suggests the sea and the waves as an Impressionist painter might.

His opera *Pelléas and Mélisande* was very different from any operas written before it. In it the singers do not sing splendid tunes. Instead their words come closer to everyday speech.

Right: The French composer, Claude Debussy.

Stravinsky

In the late nineteenth century, some composers began to break away from the old forms to use different tones and rhythms. The Russian composer Igor Stravinsky (1882–1971) used both the old and the new. Stravinsky's music was always changing. Sometimes it sounds a little like TCHAIKOVSKY, sometimes more like BACH. But Stravinsky never copied the work of others. He let his own music develop from it.

Stravinsky wrote some of his best-known music for ballets: *The Firebird, Petrushka,* and *The Rite of Spring*. His music is always lively and exciting.

Stravinsky left Russia in 1914 and settled in FRANCE. He went to live in the United States in 1939, and later became an American citizen.

Right: Igor Stravinsky in later life.

Britten

The famous English composer, Benjamin Britten, helped many young people to understand music better. He is well-known to children through *A Young Person's Guide to the Orchestra* and *Let's Make an Opera*.

Britten was born in 1913 and began to write music while he was still very young. He wrote a number of religious works, particularly songs and carols. He is well-known for his operas, which include *Peter Grimes* and *Billy Budd*. Britten was also an excellent pianist.

In 1948 Britten started the Aldeburgh Festival. This important musical occasion takes place every year. He became a Life Peer – Lord Britten – in 1976 and died the same year.

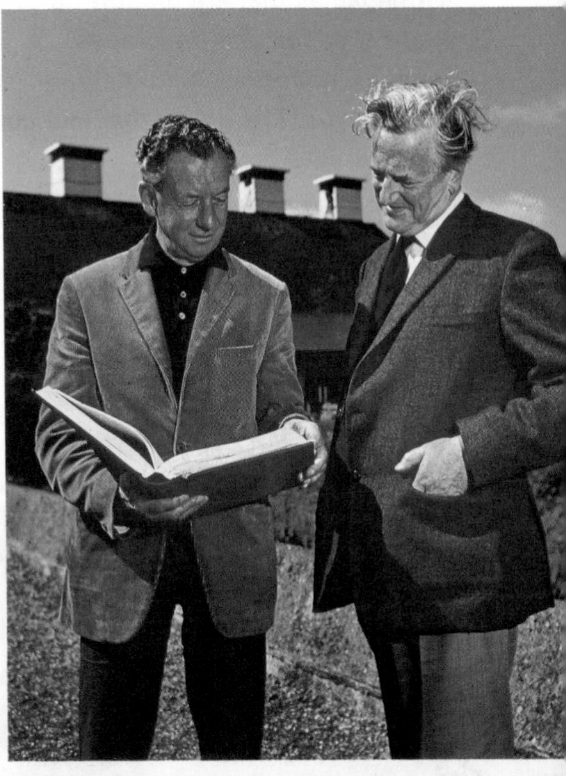

Right: Benjamin Britten (left) with Peter Pears, the English tenor.

Writers

Long before people learned how to write, they told one another stories and poems. The first writers had the job of collecting these stories and writing them down.

Many of the earliest writings, such as the epics of HOMER, are in the form of long poems. Much poetry written later is in the form of lyrics, which are much shorter.

Today, most stories are written in the form of novels. These are descriptions of life that seem true, but are in fact made up. Many great novelists, such as Jane AUSTEN, were women.

Another important kind of writing is drama – the writing of plays. Many people consider that SHAKESPEARE is the greatest ever writer of plays. Other great writers of plays are GOETHE, and such ANCIENT GREEK dramatists as Aeschylus and Sophocles.

Three fables that are thought to be by Aesop.
Right: The fox and the grapes.
Below: The tortoise and the hare.
Below right: The goose that laid golden eggs.

Above: A sculptured bust of Homer.

Homer

Very little is known about the Greek writer Homer who may have lived in the ninth century B.C. There are many legends about him. He is said to have been blind and to have wandered from city to city reciting tales.

Homer is generally believed to have written two epic poems (story poems) which rank among the world's masterpieces of writing. *The Iliad* tells of the war between the ANCIENT GREEKS and the Trojans. *The Odyssey* describes the adventures of the Greek hero Odysseus on his way home from the war.

Ovid

Publius Ovidius Naso (43 B.C.–A.D. 17) was one of the greatest of the ANCIENT ROMAN poets. He was the son of wealthy parents who wanted him to become a LAWYER. Instead, young Ovid travelled to GREECE and other countries.

Ovid's best-known poems are the *Metamorphoses* and *The Art of Love*. Ovid had a great gift for fantasy. *Metamorphoses* deals with all kinds of changes, such as stories of gods changing into human or animal shape. The emperor took offence at *The Art of Love*, and Ovid was exiled (sent away) from ROME.

Aesop

Aesop was a Greek writer who probably lived in the sixth century B.C. Little is known about his life. He may have been a slave who was later freed.

Aesop wrote fables (short stories which teach a particular lesson). Most of them are about animals that speak and act like people; for example, the TORTOISE and the hare who run a race. There are many collections of his fables. However, no-one knows which ones he actually wrote and which are just said to be by him.

Dante

Dante Alighieri (1265–1321) is the greatest poet of ITALY. He is best known for his long poem *The Divine Comedy*. The subject of this work is Dante's imaginary journeying through hell and heaven. Dante also wrote a number of books and shorter poems. He wrote mainly in Italian; before him, most writers had written in Latin.

Dante was born in the city of Florence. Much of his early poetry tells of his love for a lady called Beatrice, who died young. In about 1285, Dante married Gemma Donati. Later, he became involved in a struggle between two rival political parties in Florence. He was unjustly accused of crimes, and the last twenty years of his life were spent in exile.

Right: Behind Dante is a scene from his *Divine Comedy*. On the right is his native city, Florence.

Chaucer

The most vivid description of life in fourteenth-century England was given by the poet Geoffrey Chaucer (about 1340–1400). His *Canterbury Tales* are stories told by an imaginary band of pilgrims on their way to the shrine of the murdered St Thomas à Becket at Canterbury. The stories are not only entertaining but also reveal the characters of the pilgrims who tell them.

Chaucer was in the ARMY which invaded FRANCE under King Edward III in 1359. He was captured, but set free on payment of a ransom which the King himself helped to pay. Later, he was in the service of the King's son, John of Gaunt. When Chaucer died he was the first man to be buried in Poet's Corner in Westminster Abbey, LONDON.

Right: Chaucer, author of the *Canterbury Tales.*

Cervantes

The Spanish writer Miguel de Cervantes Saavedra (1547–1616) is famous as the author of *Don Quixote*. This is a book which makes fun of books of chivalry. It is both funny *and* sad. It tells of Don Quixote, a knight who travels in search of adventure with his faithful companion Sancho Panza. The pair meet with all kinds of comic adventures.

Cervantes was a soldier before he became a writer. He served in the great sea battle of Lepanto, in which he lost the use of his left hand. He was in prison several times during his life, and it was as a prisoner that he began work on *Don Quixote*.

Above: The hero of Cervantes' *Don Quixote* attacks a windmill, thinking it to be a knight.

Shakespeare

William Shakespeare (1564–1616) is England's greatest poet and dramatist (writer of plays). His plays are performed in nearly every country in the world and are generally thought to be the finest ever written. He also wrote more fine roles for actors than anyone else.

Shakespeare was born at Stratford-on-Avon and almost certainly went to the local grammar SCHOOL. He married Anne Hathaway and had three children. We think he went to London in 1587 to earn his living in the theatre, returning to Stratford in 1597.

As well as many poems (among them *Venus and Adonis*), Shakespeare wrote 35 plays, mostly in blank verse (verse which does not rhyme). He wrote comedies such as *Twelfth Night, As You Like It*, and *A Midsummer Night's Dream*; histories such as *Richard III* and *Henry V*; and tragedies such as *Hamlet*, *Macbeth*, and *King Lear*. He found plots for many plays in old stories.

Julius Caesar, The Taming of the Shrew

Right: An engraving of William Shakespeare.

Romeo + Juliet, The Tempest.

Above: Milton as a young man.

Milton

Paradise Lost by John Milton (1608–1674) is considered the greatest epic poem in the English language. An epic is a long poem that tells a story.

Milton started writing poetry at about the age of ten. He went to St Paul's School, LONDON, and Cambridge UNIVERSITY. There he wrote his well-known poem for music, *Ode on the Morning of Christ's Nativity*. When the English civil war broke out in 1642, Milton was on the side of PARLIAMENT against King Charles I.

Among Milton's best known poems are *Lycidas*, *Paradise Regained*, and *Comus*. The sonnet (14-line poem) *On His Blindness* was written after Milton himself had become blind. He had to dictate his later poetry so that someone else could write it down.

Above: Molière, like Shakespeare, was both actor and playwright.

Molière

Sir Walter SCOTT once called the French playwright (writer of plays) Molière (1622–1673) 'the prince of comic writers'.

Molière's real name was Jean Baptiste Poquelin. He studied law, but was only interested in the theatre. For 12 or 13 years Molière both acted for, and managed, a company of strolling players. During this period he began to write the brilliant comedies which made him famous and enabled him to establish his company permanently in PARIS. Some of his plays were written to entertain the court of LOUIS XIV.

Among his plays are *Le Bourgeois Gentilhomme* (The Middle-class Gentleman); *Le Médecin Malgré Lui* (A Doctor Despite Himself); and *Le Malade Imaginaire* (The Imaginary Invalid).

Molière was acting the part of the Invalid when he was suddenly taken ill. He died a few hours afterwards.

Defoe

Many people have heard of *Robinson Crusoe*, the adventures of a sailor, shipwrecked on a desert island. The author, Daniel Defoe (1660–1731), was the son of a London butcher called James Foe. Daniel changed his name to Defoe because it sounded grander.

Robinson Crusoe was based upon the experiences of a man called Alexander Selkirk who had recently been rescued after spending five years on an uninhabited island.

Defoe wrote several other novels, including *Moll Flanders*. He also wrote many short books and newspaper articles about the problems of the day. Like CERVANTES, Defoe was in prison several times, mostly for debt. Much of his best work was written in the last 15 years of his life.

Above left: Defoe had to stand in the pillory for attacking the government in his writings.
Below left: Gulliver in Lilliput, towing away ships from the enemy fleet.

Swift

Captain Gulliver of *Gulliver's Travels* has many adventures in strange countries. One country is Lilliput, whose people are only a few centimetres high. Another country is Brobdingnag, the land of giants.

The book was not written for children, but in a shortened form it has always been popular with them. The author Jonathan Swift (1667–1745) wrote it as a satire, showing the silliness of, or making fun of, people and things.

Swift was born in IRELAND. He became a priest in 1694. His satires include *The Battle of the Books* on literature and *The Tale of a Tub* on religion and learning. He also wrote *Journal to Stella*, a book of letters to a girl he loved.

Goethe

Germany's greatest writer, Johann Wolfgang von Goethe (1749–1832) wrote poetry, plays and novels. He was also a scientist who made discoveries in anatomy (the study of the human body) and botany (the study of plant life). His romantic story, *The Sorrows of Young Werther*, appeared in 1774, and made him famous.

At the age of 26, Goethe became a counsellor to the young Duke of Weimar, in south Germany. Goethe became a minister of state at the court. Ten years later he spent some time in ITALY. On his return to Weimar, he gave more time to writing.

Goethe's best-known work is the dramatic poem *Faust*. This tells the story of a man who often does wrong, but never loses his faith in the right and good. Goethe worked on this poem at intervals over 50 years.

Above: A painting of Goethe against a background of ruins.

Scott

Sir Walter Scott (1771–1832) was the first great writer of historical novels (stories that are set in the past). He became a LAWYER in Edinburgh, the capital of Scotland, and began writing long story poems such as *The Lay of the Last Minstrel*. His poetry was very successful, and he was famous as a poet before he started to write novels.

Scott's first novel was called *Waverley*. It was the first of a series that are called the Waverley Novels. These were tremendously successful. In all, Scott wrote 28 novels. In 1826 a company with which Scott was connected fell into debt. Scott determined to earn enough money from his writing to pay off the debts. He died, however, before he could complete this task.

Right: Sir Walter Scott was one of the most popular writers of his day.

Jane Austen

In eighteenth-century England, many people liked 'horror tales'. The English novelist Jane Austen (1775–1817) made fun of this fashion in *Northanger Abbey*, one of her six novels.

Her other novels are *Emma, Mansfield Park, Persuasion, Pride and Prejudice,* and *Sense and Sensibility*.

Jane, a clergyman's daughter, lived a quiet life. She never married but stayed at home when she was not visiting relatives or friends. Her novels give a picture of the English middle classes of the day. They are written with humour, imagination, and an understanding of people. The Hampshire house in which most of them were written is now a Jane Austen MUSEUM.

Byron

George Gordon Byron (1788–1824) became the sixth Lord Byron as a schoolboy of ten. He published his first poems when he was still at Cambridge UNIVERSITY. On leaving the university he travelled widely in EUROPE. On his return to England, he quickly became famous as a result of the success of his verse stories.

Following the failure of his marriage, however, Byron left England. He never returned. He died of fever at the age of 36 in GREECE, while helping the Greeks in their fight against the Turks.

Two of Byron's best-known long poems are *Childe Harold's Pilgrimage* and *Don Juan*. *Don Juan* is a poem in which the reader seems to hear the poet himself talking and making fun of things.

Left: Lord Byron in Greek costume. He was famous for his good looks and extravagant dress as well as for his poetry.

Grimm Brothers

Jacob (1785–1863) and Wilhelm (1786–1859) Grimm were two German brothers who made a collection of German fairy tales. Many of these tales had never been written down before. Both the brothers were professors at German UNIVERSITIES. They wrote books about the German language and worked on a dictionary which they never finished.

Some of the Grimm brothers' stories are now very well known. They include *Snow White* and *Hansel and Gretel*. *Snow White* has been made into a cartoon film by Walt DISNEY.

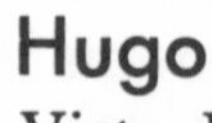

Left: In *Hansel and Gretel* by the Grimm brothers, two children find a house made of gingerbread in a wood. They start to eat the house and are made captive by the witch who lives there, but in the end they manage to escape.

Hugo

Victor Hugo (1802–1885) was the son of a general in the ARMY of NAPOLEON. He was a great French poet, novelist, and dramatist (writer of plays).

Hugo wrote his first play when he was only 14 years old. His first book of poems was published when he was 20. He continued to write poetry throughout the rest of his life. His best-known novel is probably *Les Misérables* and his best-known play *Hernani*.

In 1848 Hugo was banished from FRANCE because he opposed the Emperor Napoleon III. He returned in 1870 after Napoleon's fall from power. He had become an important person in France. When he died, huge crowds gathered to watch his funeral procession.

Left: Victor Hugo, painted in 1836, with François-Victor, one of his sons.

Andersen

One of the world's greatest writers of fairy tales was the Danish writer, Hans Christian Andersen (1805–1875). Hans' father, a poor shoemaker, died when Hans was 11 years old. In order to earn some money, the boy built a toy theatre and made clothes for the puppets. He also read aloud plays, especially plays by SHAKESPEARE, which had been translated into Danish.

Andersen wanted to be an OPERA SINGER, but his voice was not good enough. Instead, he began to write. His best book is known everywhere as Hans Andersen's Fairy Tales. Among the best-known of these tales are *The Ugly Duckling*, *The Emperor's New Clothes*, and *The Brave Tin Soldier*.

Left: Hans Andersen (centre) wrote many fairy stories. *The Ugly Duckling* (above) tells of a duckling that none of the other animals liked because he was so ugly. In the end, he becomes a beautiful swan. *Thumbelina* (below) is a little girl so tiny that her cradle was a walnut shell.

Poe

The inventor of the modern detective story was an American, Edgar Allan Poe (1809–1849). His famous book *The Murders in the Rue Morgue* first appeared in 1841.

Poe's father was American; his mother was English. Both died while he was still a child, and he was cared for by an American family called Allan. In 1836 he married a young cousin. She died in 1847, and he wrote a poem, *Annabel Lee,* in her memory. Poe was a brilliant writer of weird, fantastic stories and poems. They include *The Fall of the House of Usher* and *The Raven,* perhaps his best-known poem. A number of Poe's stories have been made into FILMS.

The Brontës

The Brontë sisters were brought up on the bleak Yorkshire moors in the north of England. They became one of the most famous family of writers that has ever lived.

Their father was the rector of Haworth, and three of his daughters, Charlotte (1816–1855) Emily (1818–1848) and Anne (1820–1849) wrote books and poems. The Yorkshire moors often came into their writing. Tragically, they all died when they were quite young.

Charlotte's most famous book is *Jane Eyre* and Emily's is *Wuthering Heights*. Both are strong, romantic stories which are widely read today. Anne's books are less well known. The home where they lived is visited by thousands of people every year.

Right: Charlotte Brontë, author of *Jane Eyre.*

Dickens

In the nineteenth century, people who got into debt often had to go to prison. This happened to the father of the English novelist Charles Dickens (1812–1870). Young Charles went to work in a FACTORY that made blacking for shoes. He described this unhappy time in his novel *David Copperfield.*

In 1831 Dickens became a reporter of debates in Britain's PARLIAMENT. He also wrote stories for MAGAZINES. His first success, published as a serial, was *The Pickwick Papers*. Dickens' novels frequently describe social conditions. *Oliver Twist*, for example, showed how badly the poor were treated. Other novels by Dickens are *A Christmas Carol* and *A Tale of Two Cities.*

Right: An imaginative drawing of Dickens surrounded by characters from his books.

Verne

Jules Verne (1828–1905) was a French writer of scientific stories. Today, such stories are called science fiction. Verne wrote more than 60 stories, of which the first was *Five Weeks in a Balloon*. Among his most famous works are *Twenty Thousand Leagues under the Sea,* and *Around the World in Eighty Days*.

Like other great writers of science fiction, such as H. G. Wells and Arthur C. Clarke, Verne wrote about things that later came true. He foresaw such things as SUBMARINES, and voyages to the MOON. Some of his characters are well known, partly through the FILMS that have been made of his books. They include the mysterious Captain Nemo, and the Englishman Phileas Fogg.

Right: A photograph of Jules Verne.

Twain

Samuel Langhorne Clemens was the real name of the famous American writer Mark Twain (1835–1910). Mark Twain was born in Florida, Missouri, the son of a LAWYER. Halley's Comet appeared in the sky at his birth. He always believed he would die when it reappeared; he did.

As a young man, Twain worked as a river pilot on the Mississippi. 'Mark twain' was a call used by pilots, meaning that a depth of two fathoms had been measured.

After the U.S. civil war, Twain became a journalist. His first success was as a humorous writer with *The Innocents Abroad,* the adventures of a party on a trip to EUROPE. His best-known books are *The Adventures of Tom Sawyer* and *The Adventures of Huckleberry Finn*.

Right: Mark Twain in later life.

Above: A drawing by Tenniel of a scene from *Alice in Wonderland*.

Carroll

Probably the most famous of all children's books is *Alice's Adventures in Wonderland* by Lewis Carroll (1832–1898).

Carroll's real name was Charles Lutwidge Dodgson. He was a lecturer in mathematics at Oxford UNIVERSITY. He was fond of children, and wrote *Alice* and *Through the Looking Glass* for Alice Liddell, the young daughter of Oxford friends.

Both books deal with a make-believe world, but Carroll writes of it as though it were real. The books contain some of the best nonsense poems ever written, such as *Father William* and *Jabberwocky*. Carroll also wrote a long nonsense poem called *The Hunting of the Snark*.

Above: Robert Louis Stevenson.
Below: Kipling in his study.

Stevenson

One of the most frightening stories ever written is *The Strange Case of Dr Jekyll and Mr Hyde*. It tells of respectable Dr Jekyll who, every now and then, turns into Mr Hyde, a criminal.

The author, Robert Louis Stevenson, was born in Scotland in 1850. Owing to poor health he travelled abroad a great deal, and in 1888 he settled in Samoa in the PACIFIC OCEAN where he died in 1894. The people of Samoa were very fond of him and treated him like a chief.

Stevenson wrote poems, novels and essays (short pieces). He also wrote adventure stories. The two most famous are *Treasure Island* (originally called *The Sea Cook*) and *Kidnapped*.

Kipling

The English writer Rudyard Kipling (1865-1936) wrote a number of stories and poems about INDIA, where he was born. *The Jungle Books*, and *Just So Stories*, a collection of animal tales, were written for children. So was *Puck of Pook's Hill*.

This and its sequel, *Rewards and Fairies*, are stories about English history. *Stalky & Co.* is a collection of school stories for boys. It is partly about Kipling's own school days in Devonshire.

Kipling also wrote books and poems for adults. In 1907 he was awarded the NOBEL Prize for Literature.

Hemingway

The American author Ernest Hemingway (1899–1961) started work at the age of 16 as a NEWSPAPER reporter. He used his experience in *A Farewell to Arms*, one of the best war novels ever written. In 1936 he went to SPAIN to write about the Spanish civil war. This gave him the idea for his famous novel *For Whom the Bell Tolls*. Other works include the novel *The Sun Also Rises* and the essay *Death in the Afternoon*, which is about bullfighting.

In 1954 Hemingway was awarded the NOBEL Prize for Literature for the art of story-telling as shown in his novel *The Old Man and the Sea*.

Above: Hemingway working at his home in Cuba, in the West Indies. Below: Orwell in the churchyard of the English village of Wallington.

Orwell

The real name of novelist and essayist George Orwell was Eric Blair (1903–1950). As a young man, Orwell served as a policeman in BURMA. When he returned to EUROPE he had several jobs but was sometimes out of work. He described this period in *Down and Out in Paris and London*. In 1936 he was wounded while fighting in the Spanish civil war. *Homage to Catalonia* is about this period.

Orwell's novel *Animal Farm* can be read as a fairy tale. But it also shows the weaknesses of COMMUNISM. In *Nineteen Eighty Four*, Orwell shows what can happen under a DICTATORSHIP. Orwell also wrote essays. Some of these appear in the collection *Inside the Whale*.

Entertainers

We all like to be entertained. After working hard all day, people want to relax and let someone else work at keeping them happy. In earlier days, a family would entertain itself. Occasionally they would go to see professional entertainers at their local MUSIC HALL or THEATRE. Today, however, most people look to others to entertain them. Entertainment has become a big business.

With the invention of the CINEMA, some entertainers gained a world-wide following. The first stars were comedians and ACTORS of the silent screen, such as Charlie CHAPLIN and LAUREL AND HARDY. When talking FILMS began, a new set of film actors appeared. Humphrey Bogart was one of the stars of the screen in its most successful days. Barbra Streisand is an example of a film actress of the 1970s. She is also a singer. The men who make films are also important – for example, Walt DISNEY who pioneered cartoon films.

Today, RADIO and TELEVISION bring comedians, actors, musicians, singers, and dancers right into our homes. The record player, also, has made stars of many musicians and singers. Frank SINATRA, Elvis PRESLEY and the BEATLES achieved fame and set trends in popular music with the help of recordings of their songs.

Classical musicians usually have a smaller, but more constant audience. Yehudi Menuhin is a classical musician. He is a violinist whose playing is known all over the world. Opera is an entertainment that combines great music, singing and acting. OPERA SINGERS, such as the soprano Joan Sutherland, work mainly in the great opera houses of the world, such as La Scala in Milan. They have a very specialised audience. BALLET DANCERS are also entertainers. Two of the best-known today are Margot Fonteyn and Rudolf Nureyev.

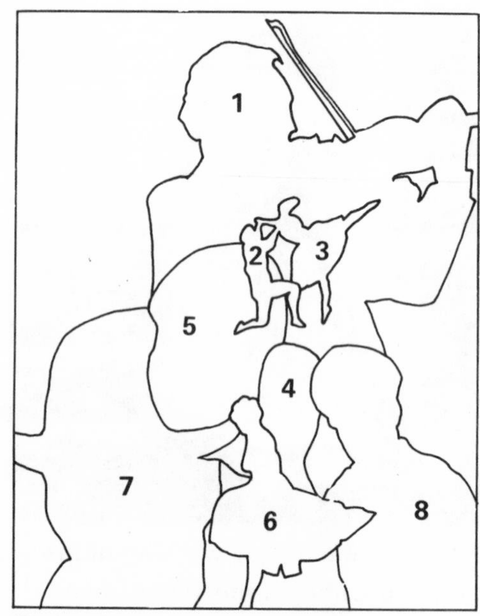

Right: Entertainers work in many different fields. Classical musicians, such as Yehudi Menuhin (1), entertain with brilliant performances of well-known music. Famous ballet dancers and opera singers have loyal audiences flocking to see them. Among the most admired are the dancers Rudolf Nureyev (2) and Margot Fonteyn (3), and the late singer Maria Callas (4). All-round entertainers, such as Barbra Streisand (5), can sing popular songs, dance and act. They make films and records as well as television and stage appearances. Some film actors are known for a particular style of acting. Marilyn Monroe (6) often played light, glamorous parts, and Humphrey Bogart (7) the tough detective. Marlon Brando (8) is known for his many different rôles.

Chaplin

Charles Spencer ('Charlie') Chaplin was born in LONDON in 1889. He had a hard childhood, and as a young man became a comedian (a person who makes you laugh). As part of a company of MUSIC HALL ACTORS, he went to the United States in 1910. He made his first FILM three years later. Soon afterwards, he appeared in the costume that made him famous – bowler hat, cane, and baggy trousers.

Chaplin's early films included *The Kid* and *The Gold Rush*. His first 'talkie' was *The Great Dictator* which made fun of HITLER. Among his later films were *Limelight* and *A King in New York*. Chaplin wrote, directed, and acted in his films. He died in Switzerland in 1977.

Above right: Chaplin as he appeared in early films.

Laurel and Hardy

Stan Laurel (1890–1965) and Oliver Hardy (1892–1957) are famous for the series of comedy FILMS they made together. Laurel's real name was Arthur Stanley Jefferson. He was born in England and later went to the United States. Hardy was an American. It is not difficult to tell them apart in their films. Hardy is the fat one, and Laurel is thin and sad-looking.

Fred Astaire and Ginger Rogers

Fred Astaire and Ginger Rogers form one of the most famous dancing partnerships in history. Fred Astaire was born in 1899 and Ginger Rogers in 1911. Although most of their FILMS together were made in the 1930's, they are quite often shown on television today. Many fans consider *Top Hat* to be their finest film. Others include *The Gay Divorce* and *Flying Down to Rio*.

Disney

Walt Disney (1901–1966) was born in Chicago, U.S.A. After studying art, he spent some years in advertising. Then he went to Hollywood and started Disney Studios with his brother Roy.

Disney soon began to make cartoon FILMS. Cartoons are made up of thousands of drawings, with a different drawing to show each movement. His first 'talkie' cartoon was *Steamboat Willie*, in which Mickey Mouse appeared. Disney's first full cartoon film was *Snow White and the Seven Dwarfs*, based on a story by the GRIMM BROTHERS. He made many other cartoon films, including *Pinocchio*, *Alice in Wonderland*, and *The 101 Dalmatians*.

Disney also made a number of non-cartoon films, such as *Twenty Thousand Leagues Under the Sea*. *Mary Poppins* was an experiment in mixing cartoons with real ACTORS. Disney's nature films include *The Living Desert* and *The Vanishing Prairie*.

In 1955 Disney built Disneyland in California, U.S.A. which is part amusement park and part MUSEUM. There is now a Disneyland in Florida, too.

Above left: Fred Astaire and Ginger Rogers dancing on roller skates in *Shall We Dance*.
Left: A scene from the Disney film *Pinocchio*.

Coco

Coco was the CIRCUS name of Nicolai Poliakoff (1900–1974). He was born in Russia, but he later became the most famous CLOWN in Britain.

Coco's big red nose and his wild hair, his baggy clothes and his comic genius made him adored by children and grown-ups alike.

Coco takes his place here as a great entertainer from the circus. Only a few clowns in history have become really famous.

Houdini

Harry Houdini (1874–1936) was an American magician who amazed his audiences by seeming to do the impossible! He became famous for his incredible escapes from chains and handcuffs, and from behind locked doors.

One of his best tricks was to be flung chained up in a sack into a river. After it seemed certain that he would drown, he would come smiling to the surface. For another trick, he would be locked in a vault and yet would manage to get out. He was nicknamed the 'Handcuff King' and the 'Man who walked through walls'.

Above: Coco the clown.
Below: Marcel Marceau.

Marceau

Marcel Marceau was born in 1923. He is a great French actor and is most famous for his mime performances. This means that he acts with his eyes, his face and his body, but he does not speak. He can tell quite complicated stories just with gestures. He is able to make his audiences 'see' things that are not there.

He can portray with great humour a man walking into the sea, a group of people at a party, or even a man trying to paste a poster on a hoarding. His work is also serious, and in one of his best-known mimes he shows with great realism how a person changes as he gets older.

Above: Louis Armstrong.
Below: Frank Sinatra.

Louis Armstrong

Louis Armstrong was born in 1900 in New Orleans in the United States. New Orleans is the birthplace of jazz music and Armstrong grew up surrounded by the new music. He left New Orleans in 1922 to join 'King' Oliver's band in Chicago. He soon became world famous for his superb trumpet playing.

Armstrong was one of the first musicians to create a solo style in jazz. He also became famous for his rough-voiced singing and for his cheerful personality on stage. Armstrong died in 1971.

Sinatra

Frank Sinatra was born in the United States in 1917. He rose rapidly to fame as a singer with Harry James' band and with Tommy Dorsey's band in the early 1940s. Sinatra was the first singer to gain a great following among young people, such as many singers have today. But Sinatra has remained a popular singer ever since because his romantic songs appeal to a wide range of people. Sinatra is a FILM ACTOR as well as a singer. His many films include *From Here To Eternity*, *On The Town*, and *High Society*.

Elvis Presley

Elvis Presley was born in the United States in 1935. His singing, backed by the sound of electric guitars and a hard beat, revolutionised popular music in 1956. Rock and roll music, headed by Presley, overthrew the earlier romantic music.

With his great appeal to young people, Presley became a teenage idol like SINATRA before him. His records, including *Heartbreak Hotel*, *Blue Suede Shoes*, and *Hound Dog*, sold in millions. Elvis also made a number of musical FILMS. He died at the early age of forty-two in 1977.

Scientists and Inventors

Science in its modern form began only a few hundred years ago. One of the first great scientists was GALILEO. He used his observations to prove new theories. Before him, most people had accepted the ideas of ANCIENT GREEK scientists such as Aristotle, without checking to see if they were right. Galileo laid the foundations for the work of NEWTON, who is considered one of the greatest scientists of all time.

However, science in the twentieth century has changed greatly since Newton's day. Discoveries are now often made by scientists working together, who may compete with others to make a discovery first. An example of this was the discovery of how a chemical called DNA in body CELLS is made up. The discovery was made in 1953 by James Watson and Francis Crick, and makes an exciting detective story.

Modern science can be very expensive. Earlier in this century, men such as Ernest Rutherford found that atoms are made of smaller particles, by using simple apparatus. Other scientists, such as Niels Bohr, then developed theories about how these particles fitted into the atom. But to discover new sub-atomic particles today takes giant accelerators costing millions of pounds, with dozens of scientists and engineers involved.

Atomic scientists have given us power – including the power to kill. In 1942 Enrico Fermi built the first nuclear reactor, in which uranium atoms were split to release energy. This soon led to the first atomic bomb.

Medical scientists are always working to save lives. Surgery has become much safer since Joseph Lister realized the need to kill germs when operating. Equally important advances in saving lives have been the introduction of vaccination and antibiotics.

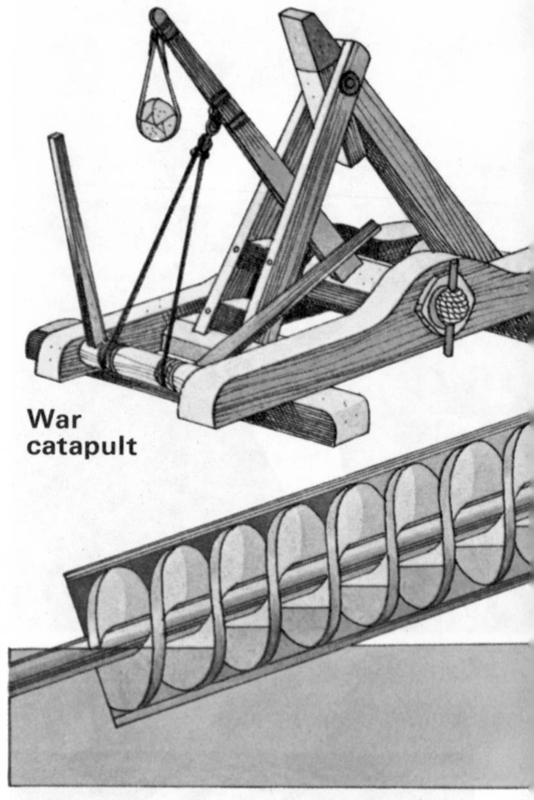

War catapult

Below: Leonardo da Vinci sketched, but never constructed, this flying machine. The notes are in his so-called 'mirror writing'.

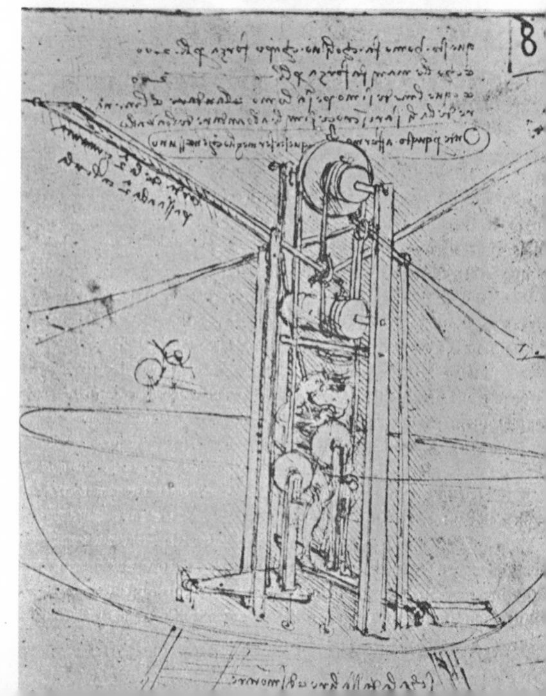

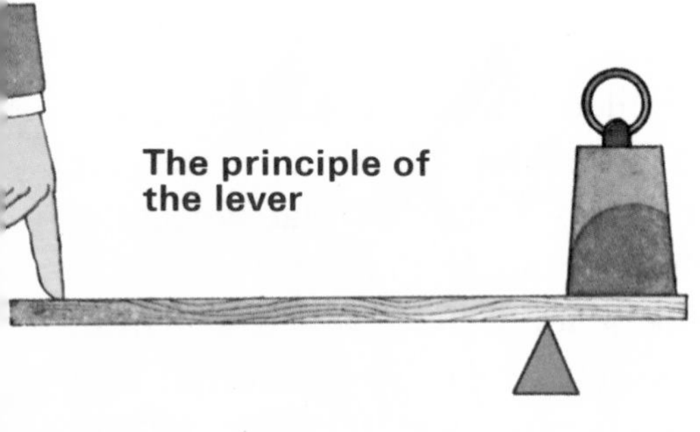

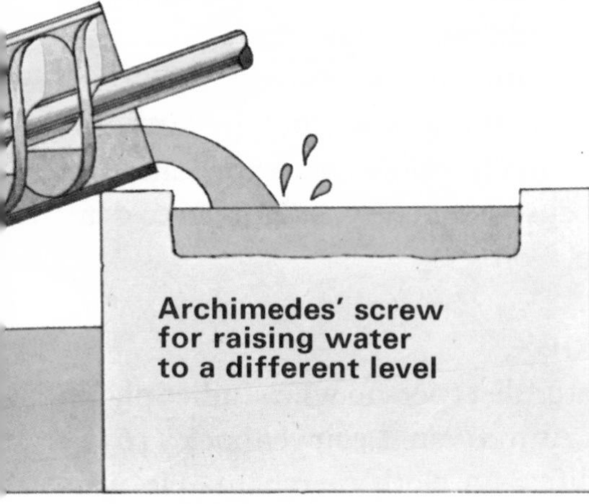

Above: Some of Archimedes' inventions and discoveries. Below: A portrait of Nicolaus Copernicus, the astronomer.

Archimedes

There is a well-known story about the ANCIENT GREEK engineer and mathematician Archimedes (287?–212 B.C.). The king of Syracuse had ordered a goldsmith to make him a crown, and had given him a certain weight of gold for the task. When the crown was finished, the weight was correct, but the king suspected that SILVER had been added, and some of the gold stolen. Archimedes was thinking about the problem when he stepped into a bath full of water. He noticed that some of the water overflowed. Suddenly the answer came to him. Forgetting to dress, he rushed off home shouting 'Eureka' ('I have found it'). After he had done some experiments he was able to tell the king how much of his gold had been stolen.

Archimedes also worked out the laws of levers and pulleys. With these machines, small forces can move heavy loads. He also did important work in mathematics.

When the ROMANS besieged Syracuse, Archimedes invented machines which helped to hold them back. He was killed when they at last entered the city.

Copernicus

The founder of modern ASTRONOMY was a Pole named Nicolaus Copernicus (1473–1543). Copernicus proved that the SUN is the centre of the solar system and that the EARTH and the PLANETS revolve around the sun. Before this, it was thought that the earth was still, with all the planets revolving around it.

Copernicus refused to make his discoveries public for many years because he feared that they would not be believed. When he did publish them, there were many arguments. These led the way to fresh discoveries.

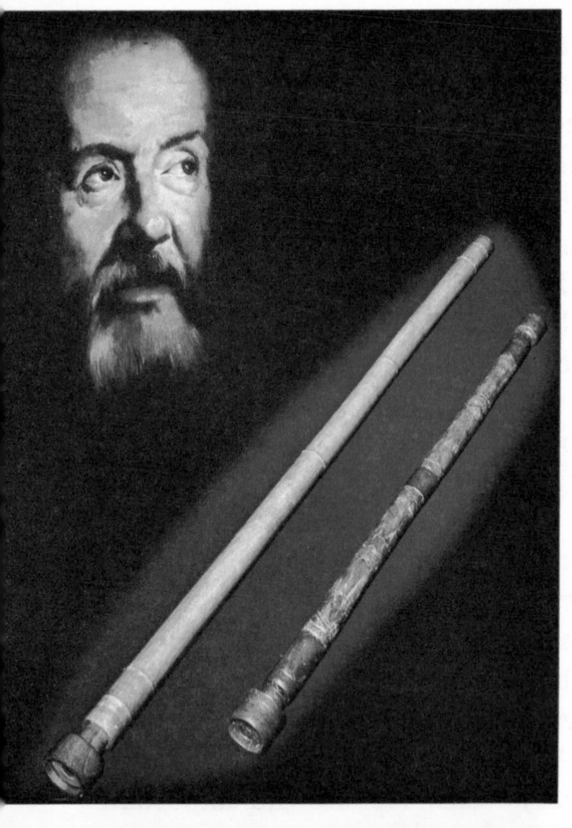

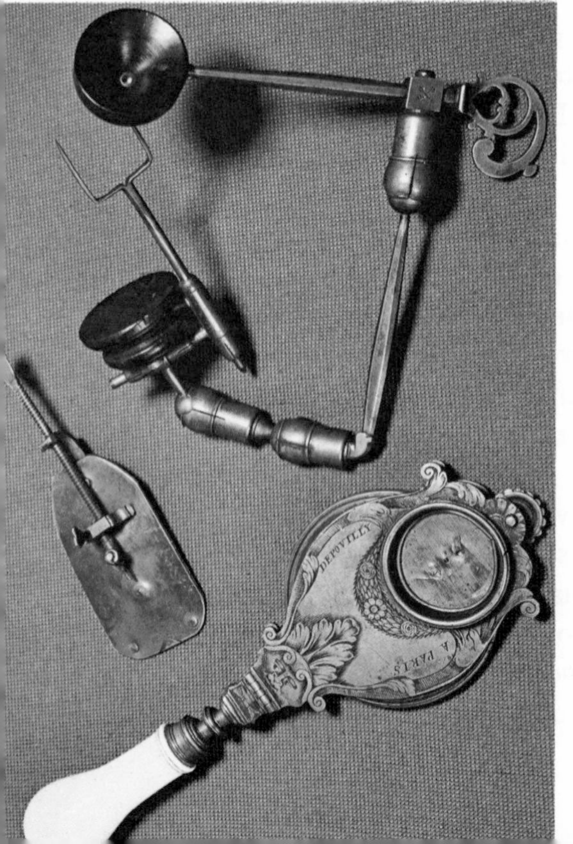

Galileo

The Italian, Galileo Galilei (1564–1642), was a scientist who gained knowledge by observing and experimenting. He showed that objects of different weights all fall at the same speed, in opposition to the belief of the time. He also built a TELESCOPE through which he discovered that the MOON has MOUNTAINS and VALLEYS, the SUN has spots, and, among other things, that the MILKY WAY is made up of many STARS.

Galileo also studied the movement of the EARTH around the sun as described by COPERNICUS. When he made public his explanation of this, he was accused of heresy and forced to deny it by the Pope.

Leeuwenhoek

The Dutch naturalist (person who studies plants and animals) Anton van Leeuwenhoek (1632–1723) began life as a cloth merchant. He was, however, more interested in making magnifying (enlarging) LENSES for MICROSCOPES.

Van Leeuwenhoek used a simple kind of microscope with only one lens. With the help of his lenses, he made important discoveries about the BLOOD, and the make-up of man's SKIN, TEETH, MUSCLES, and HAIR.

Newton

It is said that the falling of an apple to the ground helped the great mathematician and scientist Sir Isaac Newton (1642–1727) to work out the laws of GRAVITY. His knowledge of the laws of gravity enabled him to calculate how the MOON revolves around the EARTH, and the earth and PLANETS round the SUN.

Top left: Galileo with two of his telescopes.
Left: Some of Leeuwenhoek's microscopes.

Above: Sir Isaac Newton.
Below: A cartoon of Darwin.

Newton laid down the laws by which all matter (objects which occupy space) moves. He made discoveries about the nature of light, and constructed the first reflecting TELESCOPE.

Newton, a farmer's son, studied at Cambridge UNIVERSITY. In 1669 he was appointed the University's professor of mathematics. Later, he became President of England's most famous scientific society, the Royal Society.

Faraday

Michael Faraday (1791–1867), the son of a blacksmith, became one of the greatest scientists in history. In 1833, he was made Professor of Chemistry at the Royal Institution in London.

His most important work was concerned with the study of ELECTRICITY and magnetism. His discoveries made possible the large-scale generation of electricity.

Faraday was a brilliant lecturer and he started lectures for children at the Royal Institution. These lectures, called the Faraday lectures, continue to this day.

Darwin

Most people today believe that the kinds of plants and animals around us did not always exist. They have developed over millions of years from other, quite different kinds of living things. Even man and the APES probably had the same ancestor millions of years ago.

Charles Darwin (1809–1882), the son of a doctor, was the scientist who established this idea of evolution. As a young man, he spent five years on a scientific expedition round the world in a ship, H.M.S. *Beagle*. He returned to England to study, to experiment, and to write books about his ideas on evolution. The most famous are *The Origin of Species* and *The Descent of Man*.

Jenner

Thousands of people died from smallpox each year in the eighteenth century. In 1778 an English doctor, Edward Jenner (1749–1823), began to experiment with methods of preventing it. Jenner knew that country people who had caught a milder disease called cowpox believed they could not catch smallpox. Jenner began experimenting, and discovered a method of giving people cowpox. These people were then immune to (would not catch) smallpox.

At first, many people in England opposed Jenner's method of injection (vaccination) but he soon became famous. Injections of this sort are now used to prevent many other diseases. They have saved lives all over the world.

Left: Edward Jenner, who discovered vaccination.

Pasteur

In 1885 a boy who had been bitten by a mad dog infected by rabies was given a newly-discovered inoculation (injection) and did not develop the disease. Without the inoculation, he would almost certainly have died.

The inventor of this life-saving inoculation was Louis Pasteur (1822–1895), a French chemist who had studied BACTERIA. Pasteur made other important discoveries which have helped to prevent germ-carried diseases in man and animals.

Pasteur also carried out work on the action of bacteria in beer. This led to the purifying process called *pasteurisation* (after its inventor). Today, not only beer, but most milk is treated in this way.

Right: Louis Pasteur discovered that germs could be killed by heat or by various chemicals.

Koch

Robert Koch (1843–1910) was a German doctor who was interested in the study of BACTERIA. He invented a method of keeping bacteria alive in the laboratory, so that he could study their behaviour. Koch also experimented with dyes, which he used to colour bacteria. In this way, he could recognise different kinds under a MICROSCOPE.

In 1891 Koch was made director of the Berlin Institute for Infectious Diseases. Five years later, he went to SOUTH AFRICA to study a CATTLE disease – rinderpest – which he helped to cure. He also did work on human diseases, such as cholera and sleeping sickness, in AFRICA and INDIA. In 1905 Koch won a NOBEL prize.

Left: Robert Koch with two of his assistants.
Below: Fleming studying bacteria.

Fleming

Penicillin, grown from a green mould, is a powerful means of destroying harmful germs in the human body, and so of saving lives. It was discovered and named in 1928 by a professor of bacteriology, Alexander Fleming (1881–1955). A scrap of mould came into contact with some BACTERIA which Fleming was examining. He noticed that the bacteria near this mould died off.

During WORLD WAR II scientific workers solved the problem of how to use, and produce, penicillin and thus saved the lives of countless soldiers. Penicillin was the first of the many antibiotics used today. Antibiotics kill germs without harming the cells of our bodies.

Fleming was knighted in 1944 and in 1945 he shared the NOBEL Prize for Medicine with two others who worked on penicillin.

Nobel

Once a year, at a special ceremony, a few distinguished people are awarded Nobel Prizes. The founder of these Prizes was Alfred Bernhard Nobel (1833–1896), a Swedish scientist.

Nobel discovered the explosive called dynamite. This was much safer to use than earlier explosives. He made a large fortune from this and other discoveries and inventions. However, it saddened him that his explosives were so widely used for warfare.

Nobel left most of his money to establish five prizes. They are awarded for services to physics, chemistry, physiology (the study of the working of the body) or medicine, literature, and peace. It is considered a very great honour to win one of these prizes.

Left: Alfred Nobel, the inventor of dynamite.

Mendel

Gregor Johann Mendel (1822–1884) discovered the laws of HEREDITY. In humans, these laws mean, for example, that children often look like their parents. Mendel did most of his experiments with PEA plants. He discovered what he called 'factors', such as tallness or shortness, red colouring or white colouring. By pollinating different kinds of pea plants, he worked out why the new plants were tall or short, red or white.

Mendel was born in Heinzendorf in Silesia, which used to be part of AUSTRIA, but is now in CZECHOSLOVAKIA. He became a monk in the monastery of Brno. Later, he was made abbot of the monastery. He published the results of his work in 1866, but it was only much later that scientists agreed with his ideas.

Right: Gregor Mendel as Abbot of Brno.

Röntgen

Wilhelm Konrad von Röntgen (1845–1923) was a great German scientist. In 1895, he noticed that when he passed ELECTRICITY through a vacuum tube, a piece of paper nearby, coated with a chemical called barium platinocyanide, glowed. He became intrigued and experimented further. He discovered that rays like LIGHT rays, but much more penetrating, were producing this strange effect. He had in fact discovered the X-RAY. In 1898 he took the first X-ray picture of his wife's hand.

Röntgen was awarded a NOBEL Prize in 1901 for his discovery. X-rays have had an enormous effect on medicine. DOCTORS use them to find out what is wrong with a patient so that he can be given the correct treatment.

Left: Röntgen, the discoverer of X-rays.

Pierre and Marie Curie

The most famous husband and wife team in scientific history is probably the Curies. Pierre (1859–1906) was French. Marie (1867–1934), a Pole, was trained partly at the Sorbonne, the UNIVERSITY of PARIS. There she met and married Pierre, a professor of physics. Together, they began the work which resulted in the discovery of radium, an entirely new element (basic substance). Radium, a radio-active METAL, is widely used in the treatment of certain diseases.

The Curies shared the NOBEL Prize for Physics in 1903 with Antoine Becquerel, who had discovered radio-activity in the metal uranium. After Pierre's death, Marie became the first woman professor of physics at the Sorbonne. In 1911 she won a Nobel Prize for Chemistry.

Right: A cartoon of Pierre and Marie Curie.

Bell

The TELEPHONE sends voices over a distance by means of electric currents. It links person to person, country to country, and is now part of everyday life.

The inventor of the first really successful telephone was Alexander Graham Bell (1847–1922). He was born in Edinburgh, Scotland. As a young man, he lived first in CANADA, and later in the United States. He became professor of Vocal Physiology at Boston UNIVERSITY.

In 1876, after several years of experiments, Bell produced his first telephone. He also invented the photophone, which sends out sounds by means of a beam of light. He took a great interest in the education of deaf-mutes (people who cannot hear and so have not learned to speak).

Above: Bell as an old man.

Edison

The American inventor Thomas Alva Edison (1847–1931) was born in Milan, Ohio. At the age of 12 he was working as a newsboy on the Grand Trunk railway line running to Detroit. Edison printed and distributed the first NEWSPAPER to be issued from a train. He also learnt all he could about telegraphy (sending messages by TELEGRAPH) from a kindly stationmaster.

In 1876 Edison set up a laboratory and works at Menlo Park, New Jersey. His very many inventions included a system of telegraphy by which more than one signal could be sent on a single line at the same time.

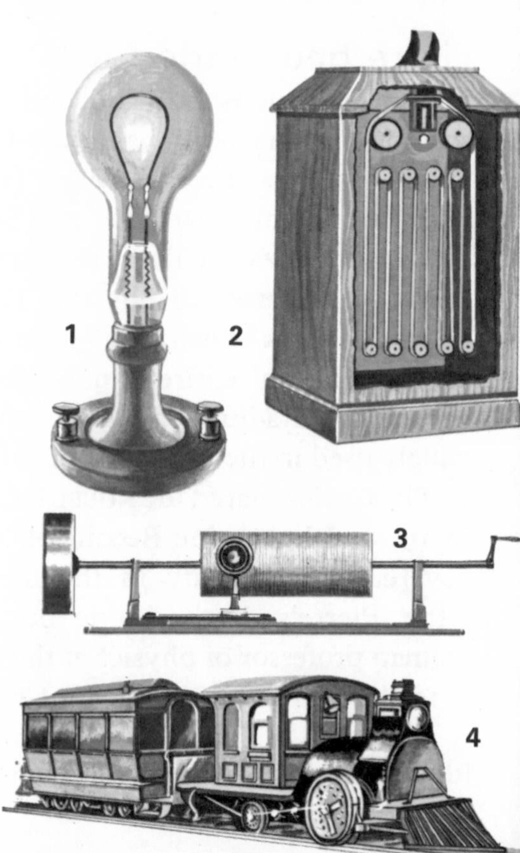

Right: Some of Edison's inventions. (1) Carbon filament lamp. (2) 'Kinetoscope' – a moving-picture viewing box. (3) The first phonograph (early gramophone). (4) A train fitted with Edison's electric storage battery.

Above: Marconi (left) with early wireless equipment.
Below: A bust of Einstein by the sculptor Jacob Epstein.

Marconi

Guglielmo Marconi (1874–1937) developed wireless telegraphy. In this system, messages in MORSE code can be sent and received without the use of connecting wires. Marconi's father was Italian, his mother Irish. He was educated in ITALY but, after making a series of experiments, came to England. There he showed his discoveries to Sir William Preece, engineer-in-chief of the Post Office TELEGRAPH system.

In 1899 Marconi produced an instrument which sent wireless messages across the English Channel to FRANCE. In 1901 the first signals were sent across the ATLANTIC OCEAN between Cornwall in England, and Newfoundland. This was the beginning of the transatlantic telegraph service.

Marconi won the NOBEL Prize for Physics in 1909. In 1915 he became a member of the Italian PARLIAMENT. He was made a *Marchese* (marquis) in 1929.

Einstein

Among many famous Jews driven out of GERMANY by the Nazi DICTATOR, Adolf HITLER, was Albert Einstein (1879–1955).

As a child, Einstein was shy and slow in learning to speak. Later, he decided to become a teacher. He taught for a time, then turned to mathematics and physics. In 1914 he was appointed to an important post in Germany, but in 1933 he was forced to leave. He went first to England, then settled in the United States.

Einstein is world famous for his work on the mathematical theory of relativity. This gave scientists new ideas about the nature of time and space.

Einstein was awarded the 1921 NOBEL Prize for Physics.

Engineers and Architects

The world around us is largely the work of builders and engineers. They influence the way we live. Just over 20 years after Karl BENZ patented the first modern motor car, Henry Ford began mass-producing the famous Model T. The internal combustion engine brought to the man in the street the transport revolution that began with the development of the STEAM ENGINE and the introduction of railways. Steam also became the principal means of propulsion at sea. BRUNEL was a major influence, building an extensive rail system in western England, as well as building passenger ships to cross the seas.

Today, for passenger travel, ships are less important than aeroplanes. After the WRIGHT brothers' pioneering efforts, the flights of daring fliers captured the public imagination. But it was the development of AIRCRAFT as a result of WORLD WAR II, and the extra speed provided by jet engines, that made flying possible for large numbers of people.

Our cities are changing rapidly too, to meet the requirements of modern living. Wide highways, flyovers, and shopping precincts are being built to meet the needs of people and cars in many cities.

The development of engineering methods, and of materials such as steel, concrete, and GLASS, have allowed architects to develop bold new designs in building.

Modern buildings do not need the pillars and arches of classical architecture. The new techniques have brought about the plain, towering SKYSCRAPER, and the geodesic dome invented by R. Buckminster Fuller, which can roof over a very large area without any support. Architects rarely use unnecessary decoration but now make their buildings functional. Modern architecture can still, however, be pleasing to look at.

Above: A building designed by Palladio in Vicenza.
Left: Inigo Jones, who was much influenced by Palladio's work.

Palladio

Andrea Palladio (1518–1580) was a great Italian architect. He began his career as a stone mason. Then he went to ROME to study for two years. There he saw many buildings that had been constructed by the ancient ROMANS, and was very impressed by them. When he returned home to Vicenza, he began to design houses, theatres and government buildings in a similar style to those he had seen in Rome.

Palladio's ideas did not inspire other Italian architects in his own day, but after his death his influence was great. The English architect, Inigo Jones (1573–1652) was inspired by him, and so were many later British and American architects. Many of their buildings are described as being in the 'Palladian' style, although many are simpler and less ornamented than his were.

Wren

In the Great Fire of LONDON of 1666, many buildings were destroyed, among them St Paul's CATHEDRAL. Christopher Wren (1632-1723), the most famous English architect of the day, was invited to rebuild St Paul's.

Wren was a scientist, mathematician, and professor of ASTRONOMY. He became an architect in about 1662 when he designed the Chapel of Pembroke College, Cambridge. The rebuilding of St Paul's lasted from 1675-1710. Wren also designed 52 churches to replace the ones burnt in the Great Fire. He also made plans to rebuild London, but he was never allowed to carry them out. Among his other works are the more modern part of Hampton Court, and hospitals at Chelsea and Greenwich. Wren was buried in St Paul's.

Left: A portrait of Sir Christopher Wren by Sir Godfrey Kneller.

Above: The Scottish engineer James Watt.
Below: George Stephenson.

Watt

The STEAM ENGINE first appeared in about 1700. One of the first steam-driven pumps was made by Thomas Newcomen in 1705. But Newcomen's pump wasted steam, and used a lot of COAL. The Scottish engineer James Watt (1736-1819) began to think about these problems when he was repairing Glasgow UNIVERSITY's model of Newcomen's pump. Watt built a steam engine that was stronger, more reliable, and used less coal. It was first used to pump water out of mines, but was later made to drive many different kinds of machinery.

In 1775 Watt went into partnership with Matthew Boulton who owned a large FACTORY. Watt's engine was one of the main causes of the INDUSTRIAL REVOLUTION.

Fulton

The American engineer Robert Fulton (1765-1815) invented the first successful steamboat. He studied art, but soon turned to engineering. In 1800 he built a SUBMARINE, the *Nautilus* (illustrated on page 526). His steamboat *Clermont* was launched in 1807.

Stephenson

The English engineer George Stephenson (1781-1848) never went to SCHOOL, but he went to evening classes and learned arithmetic and about machinery. He worked as an engineer in COAL mines.

Stephenson designed and built a LOCOMOTIVE (moving STEAM ENGINE) to draw coal trucks. Then he was made the engineer of a railway to be built between Stockton and Darlington in Durham. In 1825 he drove his engine, *Locomotion,* on the line, pulling wagons and coaches. It was the first ever public passenger train.

Above: The French architect and engineer Ferdinand de Lesseps.

With an improved engine, the *Rocket*, Stephenson proved that steam engines were reliable and faster than horses for pulling trains. In 1830 he completed a railway line between Manchester and Liverpool.

De Lesseps

Until the middle of the nineteenth century, ships sailing from EUROPE to INDIA had to sail round AFRICA. Ferdinand de Lesseps (1805–1894), a French engineer, drew up a scheme to cut through the narrow Isthmus (neck of land) of Suez which joins Africa to western ASIA. Work on the SUEZ CANAL, which is about 160 kilometres long, was finished in 1869.

De Lesseps failed to cut through the Isthmus of Panama, which joins North and SOUTH AMERICA. Work on the PANAMA CANAL, which he started, was finished by United States engineers.

Brunel

The British engineer, Isambard Kingdom Brunel (1806–1859) built BRIDGES, DOCKS, CANALS, and railways. He built the more difficult parts of England's Great Western Railway and drew up the plans for Clifton Suspension Bridge, in Bristol, England. He also built the *Great Western*, the first STEAMSHIP to make regular trips between England and the U.S.A. His *Great Britain* was the first large ship to be built of metal.

Brunel's next steamship, the *Great Eastern*, was a commercial failure. It was six times larger than any other ship of the time; too big for the size of her engines, and too big to pass through the SUEZ CANAL. This ship was a great disappointment to Brunel.

Left: I. K. Brunel, photographed in front of the cable chains of the *Great Eastern*.

Wright Brothers

In 1903 the American inventors, Wilbur Wright (1867–1912), and his brother Orville (1871–1948), became the first men to fly in a power-driven aeroplane.

The brothers knew about German gliding experiments. They thought of some improvements, and built their own gliders. Then, they fitted a PETROL ENGINE to a glider, and on December 17th, 1903, near Kitty Hawk in North Carolina, they made four flights. The longest, by Wilbur, lasted 59 seconds. They called their AIRCRAFT *Flyer*, later renamed *Kitty Hawk*.

In 1905 Wilbur managed to stay in the air for 38 minutes. In 1908, in a new machine, he set up a record of 140 minutes. The brothers were asked to supply planes for the U.S. government. This led to the formation of the Wright Brothers Company to build aeroplanes.

Above: The Wright Brothers, with *Kitty Hawk* in the background.

Benz and Daimler

Karl Benz (1844–1929) and Gottlieb Daimler (1834–1900) have both been called 'fathers' of the modern MOTOR CAR. Both German engineers, Benz lived in Mannheim and Daimler in Cannstatt. They were both working towards the same goal at the same time, but neither knew about the other's work until after the first car had been produced.

Benz completed the first successful petrol-driven car in 1885. Daimler produced the world's first 4-wheeled car in 1886. He founded the Daimler Automobile Company in 1890. In 1895 the first real motor race was held in France. It covered 1,178 kilometres. The race was won by a car with a Daimler engine.

Left: Karl Benz. It is generally believed that he and Gottlieb Daimler never met.

Wilbur Wright

Gropius

Walter Gropius (1883–1969), the architect, was a pupil of one of the founders of modern architecture, Peter Behrens. In 1919 Gropius became head of the Bauhaus, a German college of practical art and architecture. His students learned about building as well as design.

Gropius designed mainly FACTORIES but was also responsible for Harvard Graduate Centre. He also designed Impington Village College in England with Maxwell Fry, a British architect. Gropius used mainly concrete and GLASS in his buildings and often gave them huge glass 'curtain' walls.

In 1937 Gropius settled in the United States.

Le Corbusier

Charles Edouard Jeanneret (1887–1965), or Le Corbusier as he was called, came from SWITZERLAND. Like GROPIUS, he was a pupil of Peter Behrens in BERLIN.

Le Corbusier designed buildings and planned cities in many parts of the world. He was one of the group of architects who designed the UNITED NATIONS building in NEW YORK. He believed that a house is 'a machine for living in', so it should be practical, labour-saving, and comfortable.

Frank Lloyd Wright

Most of the buildings designed by the American architect Frank Lloyd Wright (1869–1959) are dwelling houses. Many were built on an open-plan system, with the main rooms running from the back to the front of the house. Wright was the leader of modern American architects.

Above left: The Bauhaus.
Far left: Le Corbusier.
Left: Frank Lloyd Wright.

Explorers

From earliest times, man has had an urge to explore his surroundings. The first explorers were primitive men who were looking for better land on which to grow their crops and to feed their cattle.

With the development of trade, merchants searched for new places to buy and sell goods. The PHOENICIANS, who were also skilled navigators, sailed all over the MEDITERRANEAN SEA, exploring and trading with many countries.

Another reason why men explored new lands was curiosity. This helps to explain why so many explorers were able to endure such great dangers and hardships.

Today, most of our world has been explored and mapped. In recent years, man has begun his next great adventure – the exploration of the solar system and the universe itself.

Left: A thirteenth-century world map centred on Jerusalem.

Leif Ericsson

The VIKINGS sailed to many parts of the world in their longships. Eric the Red, a Norwegian chief, discovered Greenland in about A.D. 982.

Eric's son Leif Ericsson, or son of Eric, is believed to have continued the exploration of Greenland. He probably took part in expeditions sent by his father to NORTH AMERICA in about A.D. 1000. It seems fairly certain that he reached the part of the North American coast between Labrador and Cape Cod, Massachusetts. He called this land Vinland (Wine Land) because of the wild grapes that he found growing there.

Left: Vinland is shown on the far left of this map. The map, probably a forgery, was once believed to date from the fifteenth century.

Below: This old manuscript shows Marco Polo arriving in Venice.

Marco Polo

In 1271 a young man left VENICE (then an independent state) with his father and uncle and started on a long trading journey. The young man was Marco Polo (1254–1324).

The party travelled through Persia (modern IRAN), AFGHANISTAN, and northern Tibet, often over country unknown to Europeans. Then they reached PEKING in CHINA and the court of the emperor Kublai Khan to whom they gave a message from the Pope.

Marco Polo stayed as an honoured guest in China. He travelled about, and visited countries as far away as BURMA. The Polos returned home by sailing around the southern tip of INDIA, and then journeying through Persia. They had been away for 24 years.

Three years later, Marco Polo was captured in a sea battle between Venice and Genoa. He told his story to a fellow prisoner who wrote it down in a book called *The Travels of Marco Polo*.

John and Sebastian Cabot

John Cabot (1450–1498), who explored the coast of NORTH AMERICA, may have reached the mainland of America before COLUMBUS. Cabot, who was born in Genoa, settled in Bristol, England, as a merchant. In 1497 he sailed westwards with his son Sebastian in the hope of finding a new trade route to ASIA. Instead he discovered what was probably Newfoundland or Labrador.

John Cabot made another voyage the following year. This time he sailed further down the North American coast. He died before his ship returned.

In 1509 Sebastian Cabot (about 1483–1557) sailed from the port of Bristol looking for the north-west passage to Cathay (CHINA). He reached the entrance to Hudson Bay. Later, in the service of SPAIN, he explored the South American rivers Plate and Parana. Sebastian returned to England in 1548.

Diaz

In the fifteenth century, ships from EUROPE began to visit the west coast of AFRICA. Their object was to find a sea route round Africa to INDIA and to search for gold. The Portuguese were the first Europeans in west Africa. A navigator, Diogo Cão (his dates are unknown), explored more than 2200 kilometres of the coast. In 1484 he discovered the mouth of the River Congo (now Zaire).

After Cão came Bartholomew Diaz (about 1455–1500). Starting from the Congo, Diaz explored the coastline to the south, and discovered the Cape of Good Hope. He rounded the Cape and sailed on to reach the Great Fish River.

By 1488 Diaz had discovered over 2000 kilometres of coastline.

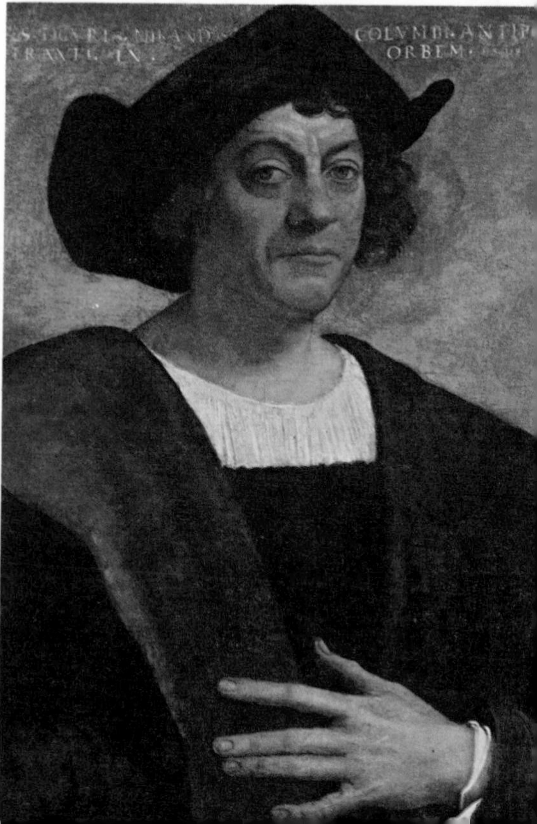

Columbus

The explorer who is considered the discoverer of the Americas, Christopher Columbus (1451–1506) was an Italian. He settled in PORTUGAL and changed his name from Cristoforo Colombo. Columbus believed that the world was round, and worked out that he could reach ASIA by sailing westward.

In 1492, in the service of SPAIN, he sailed across the ATLANTIC OCEAN, and arrived at the ISLANDS of the Bahamas off the American coast. He also discovered the West Indies. On his third voyage, in 1498, Columbus reached the mainland of SOUTH AMERICA. But some of his men were jealous of his power and he returned to Spain a prisoner. He was freed, and made a last journey in 1502. He never realised that the lands he had visited were not part of Asia.

Left: The main voyages of the early explorers.

Vasco da Gama

The search for a sea route from EUROPE to INDIA was begun by DIAZ and Diogo Cão. The task was completed by the adventurous Portuguese navigator, Vasco da Gama (about 1460–1525).

Vasco da Gama started from Lisbon and he sailed to the Cape Verde Islands. He then sailed southwards, rounded the Cape of Good Hope, then followed the east coast as far north as Malindi in what is now KENYA. He crossed the INDIAN OCEAN and in 1498 reached the south-west coast of India, where he established a settlement. In 1499 he returned to PORTUGAL and was greatly honoured. He made two more trips to India in 1502 and 1524.

Far left: A painting of Christopher Columbus.
Left: Vasco da Gama, from an old manuscript.

Magellan

The Portuguese explorer Ferdinand Magellan (about 1480–1521) set sail in 1519 in command of an expedition to find a western route to the East Indies.

Magellan sailed across the ATLANTIC, down to the tip of SOUTH AMERICA, and through the straits afterwards named Magellan in his honour. When he came to the other side he named the ocean the PACIFIC OCEAN because it seemed so peaceful. He then sailed on to the Philippine ISLANDS where he was killed in a fight with the natives. The crew of one of his ships completed the voyage.

Above: Magellan. His ship's route around the world is shown below.

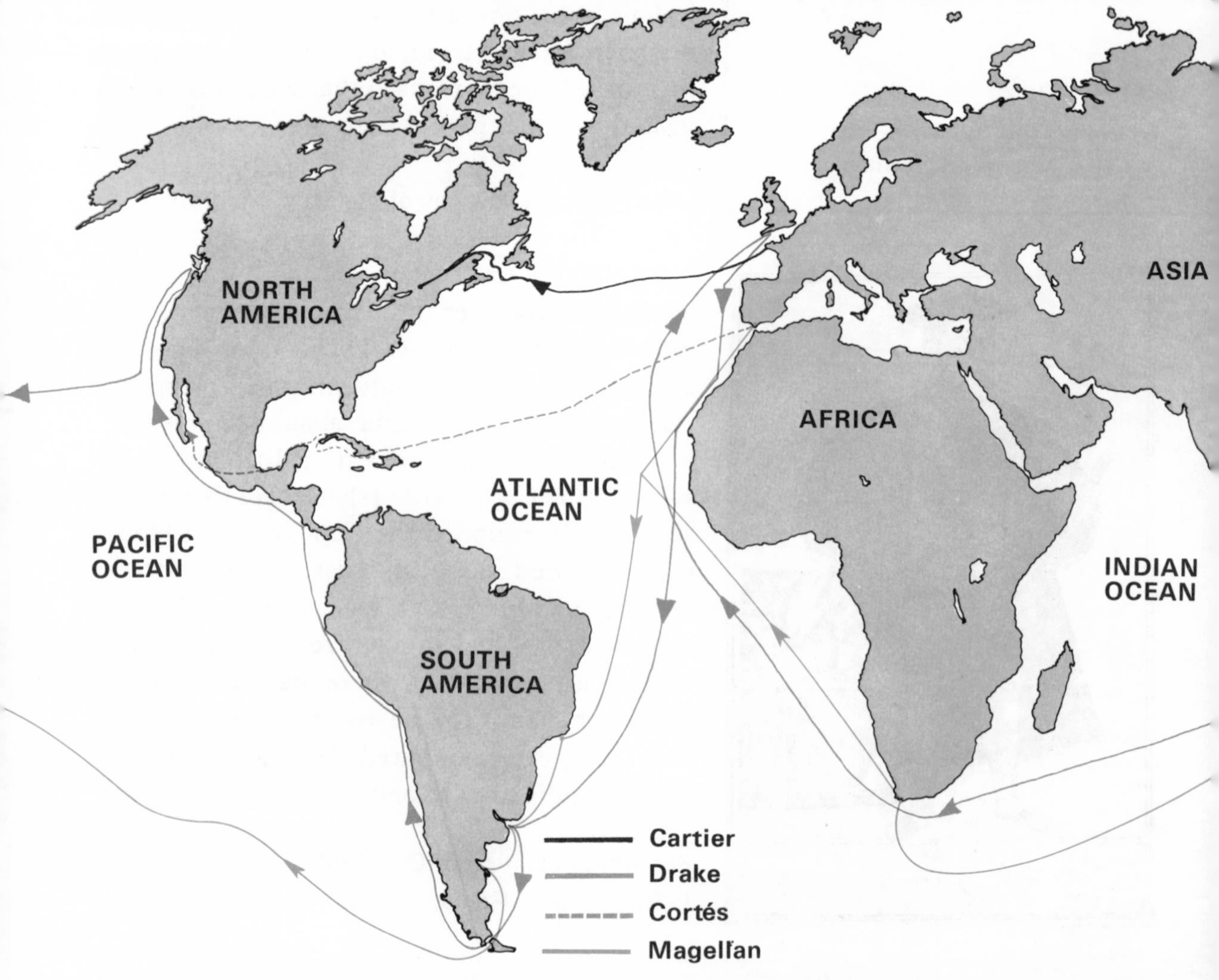

NORTH AMERICA
SOUTH AMERICA
AFRICA
ASIA
ATLANTIC OCEAN
PACIFIC OCEAN
INDIAN OCEAN
Cartier
Drake
Cortés
Magellan

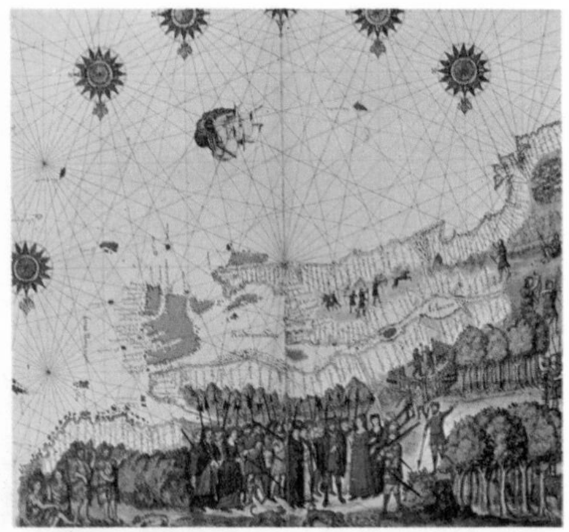

Above: Part of an old map of Cartier's travels.

Cartier

In 1534 the French navigator Jacques Cartier (1491–1557) tried, without success, to find a north-west passage to CHINA around NORTH AMERICA.

In 1536 Cartier returned and discovered and explored the Gulf of St Lawrence and the St Lawrence River. He learned from an Indian tribe that he was in a land which they called CANADA. Cartier followed the St Lawrence inland as far as what is now the city of MONTREAL, capital of the province of Quebec.

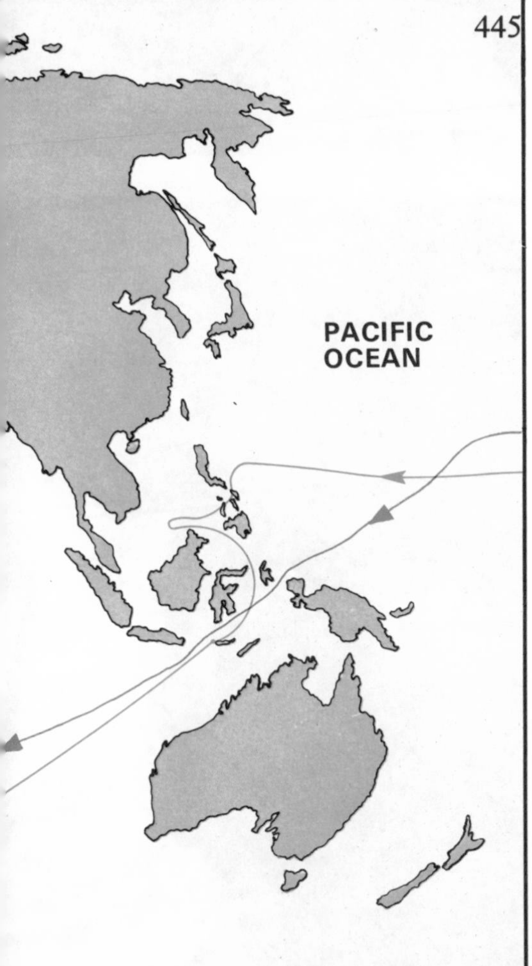

Cortés

MEXICO (or New Spain, as it was called) had only just been discovered when, in 1518, the Spanish adventurer Hernando Cortés (1485–1547) was chosen to lead an expedition there.

In 1519 he was received with honour by the AZTEC people of MEXICO in their capital, Tenochtitlan. Cortés did not, however, trust the Aztecs so he captured their emperor, Montezuma, and kept him hostage. Later, Montezuma was killed and the Aztecs drove the Spaniards from their city with great loss of life. With Indian allies, the Spanish re-took the city, then all Mexico.

Drake

In 1577 Francis Drake (about 1543–1596) began a voyage around SOUTH AMERICA and up the PACIFIC coast of NORTH AMERICA. He returned to England by way of the Philippines and the Cape of Good Hope in SOUTH AFRICA. He was the first Englishman to sail round the world.

In 1588 Sir Francis Drake was one of the commanders of the English fleet when the King of SPAIN sent his powerful fleet, the Armada, to invade England. The English fleet prevented the Spanish ships from landing.

Hudson

After the discovery of America, traders began to look for westward routes from EUROPE to ASIA. Some people thought that it would be possible to sail around the top of NORTH AMERICA. They believed that there was a sea route, which they called the north-west passage.

A gallant attempt to find the north-west passage was made in 1610. An English navigator, Henry Hudson (about 1550–1611), visited North America and the Canadian ARCTIC. He and his crew suffered dreadful hardships during the Arctic winter. The crew mutinied, and set Hudson, with a few loyal men, adrift in an open boat. They were never found.

Hudson Bay, Strait, and River are all named in his honour.

Above right: Henry Hudson was set adrift in an open boat by mutineers and left to die.
Below right: A portrait of Cook by Nathaniel Dance.

Cook

The English navigator James Cook (1728–1779) made three voyages of discovery. He proved that NEW ZEALAND consists of two ISLANDS and that AUSTRALIA is not part of another continent. He explored the eastern coast of Australia, and named it New South Wales.

In 1773 Captain Cook made the first crossing of the ANTARCTIC Circle, and made important discoveries in the South PACIFIC. Among them were the Society Islands, named in honour of the Royal Society; and New Caledonia. He also discovered a group which he named the Sandwich Islands after Lord Sandwich, then First Lord of the Admiralty. They were later renamed the Hawaiian Islands. Cook was killed in Hawaii by hostile native people.

Hudson Bay

Canada

U.S.A.

.... Franklin

———— Hudson

.... Cook

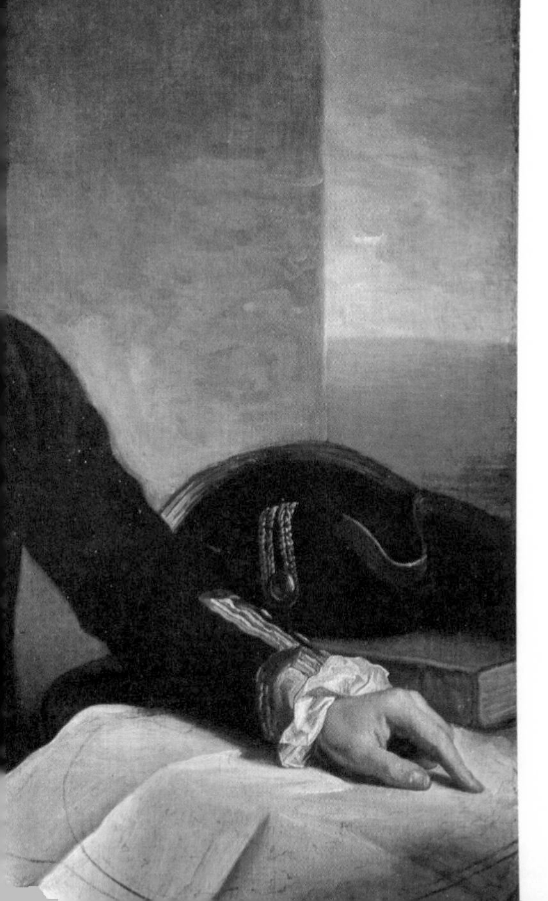

Franklin

In 1845 an English explorer, Sir John Franklin (1786–1847), was sent to the ARCTIC to find the north-west passage to the PACIFIC OCEAN. He was in command of two ships, *Erebus* and *Terror*. The ships were last seen near the entrance to Lancaster Sound, north-west CANADA. Then they vanished.

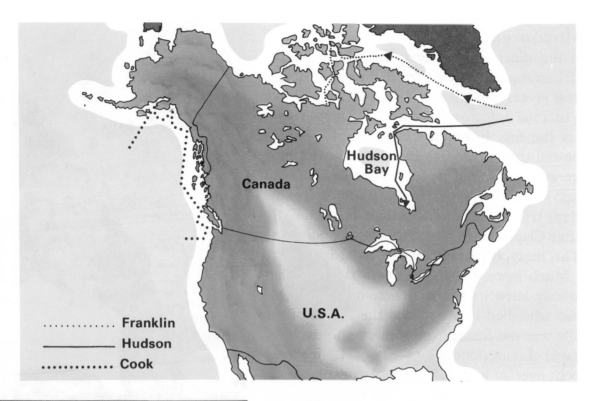

The story was gradually put together by expeditions sent to discover the truth. The ships had been trapped by ice. After 18 months in the ice, Franklin died. The crews left the ships and tried to march to safety. No-one survived. Although the expedition ended in disaster, Franklin had shown that the north-west passage existed. His ships had in fact nearly reached a point already reached from the west by previous expeditions.

In 1875 a monument was raised in honour of Sir John in Westminster Abbey, London.

African explorers

In the nineteenth century, the aims of most African explorers were to trace the course of two great RIVERS, the Niger and the Nile.

In 1796 a doctor, Mungo Park (1771–1806), was the first European to see the Niger. He showed that it rose in a mountain district near the west coast, and traced its course for about 1500 kilometres. Then Hugh Clapperton (1788–1827) tried to follow the Niger to its mouth. After Clapperton's death, Richard Lander, one of his party, reached the sea by canoe in 1830.

Much more was known about the Nile, but nobody knew its source (where it began). One man who died trying to find the source of the Nile was the Scottish missionary and explorer David Livingstone (1813–1873). Livingstone spent over 20 years in AFRICA. His explorations were intended to open up the interior of the continent to other missionaries and thus end the slave trade. On his travels he traced the course of the Zambezi, and discovered the Victoria Falls and Lake Nyasa (Malawi).

In 1871 people feared that Livingstone was dead and H. M. Stanley (1841–1904) was sent to look for him. He found him ill, but alive, on the shores of Lake Tanganyika. Stanley later crossed Africa from east to west, and traced the course of the River Congo (now Zaire).

Earlier, John Hanning Speke (1827–1864) and Sir Richard Burton (1821–1890) had also set out to find the source of the Nile. They discovered Lake Tanganyika, one of the world's largest freshwater lakes. Speke went on to find the Nile's source, in Lake Victoria. His story was not, however, generally believed.

Among those who helped prove that it was true were Stanley and Sir Samuel White Baker who explored Lake Albert.

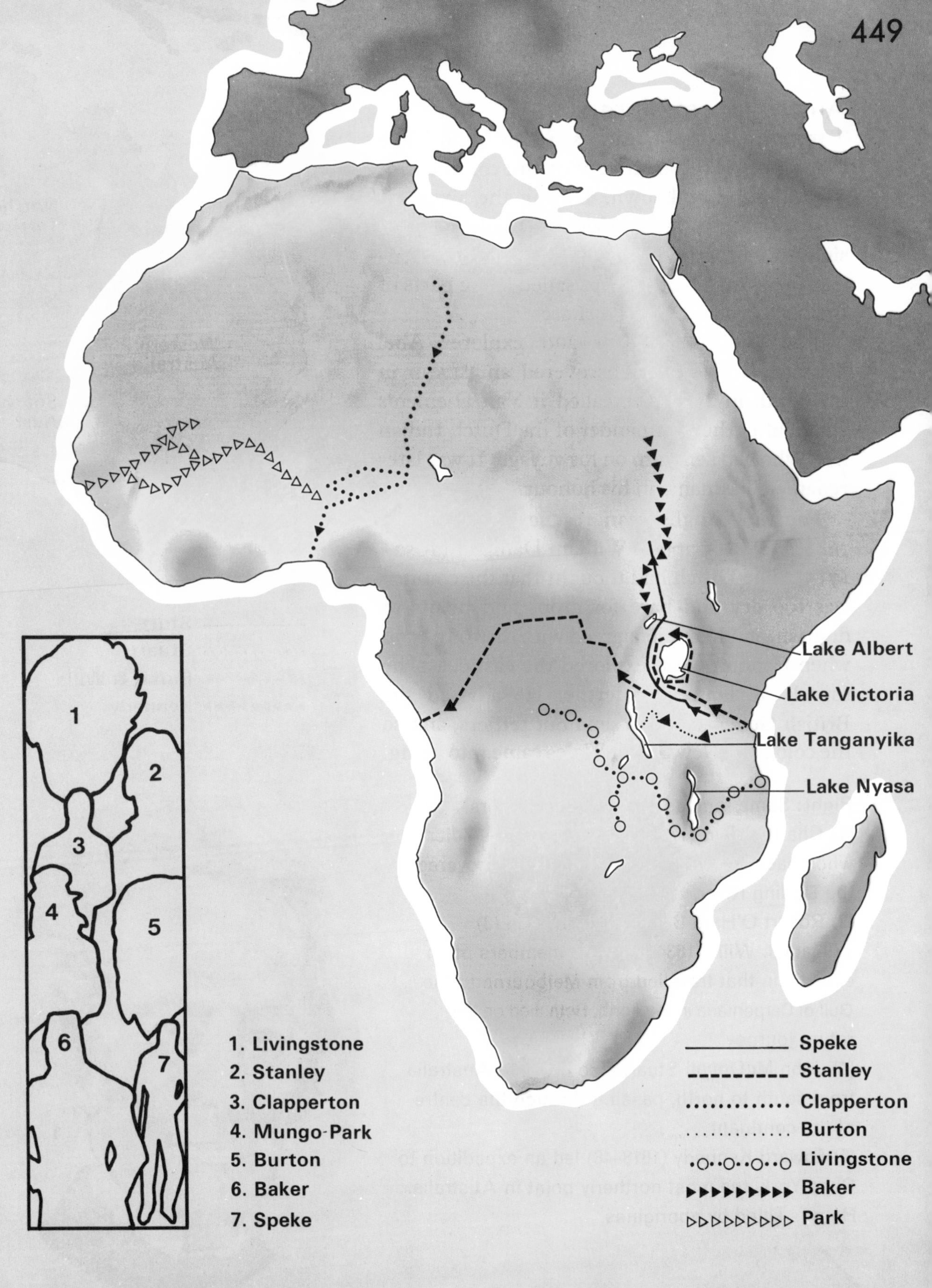
Lake Albert
Lake Victoria
Lake Tanganyika
Lake Nyasa
1
2
3
4
5
6
7
1. Livingstone
2. Stanley
3. Clapperton
4. Mungo-Park
5. Burton
6. Baker
7. Speke
Speke
Stanley
Clapperton
Burton
Livingstone
Baker
Park

Australian explorers

The word AUSTRALIA means 'South Land.' The exact date of the discovery of the continent of Australia is not known. During the sixteenth century, Portuguese navigators sailed within sight of its coasts. In the first half of the seventeenth century Dutch ships sailed along parts of the northern and western shores.

The Dutch navigator and explorer Abel Tasman (1603–1659) discovered an ISLAND in the south in 1642. He called it Van Diemen's Land, after the commander of the Dutch Indian fleet who had sent him on his voyage. It was later renamed Tasmania in his honour.

The first Englishman reached Australia in 1688. He was Captain William Dampier (1652–1715). The Dutch had thought that the country was too dry and bare for crops and plants to flourish, and Dampier agreed with them. In 1770 when Captain COOK explored the east coast, he found the land very fertile. He advised the British Government to send out settlers, and so the colony of New South Wales came into being.

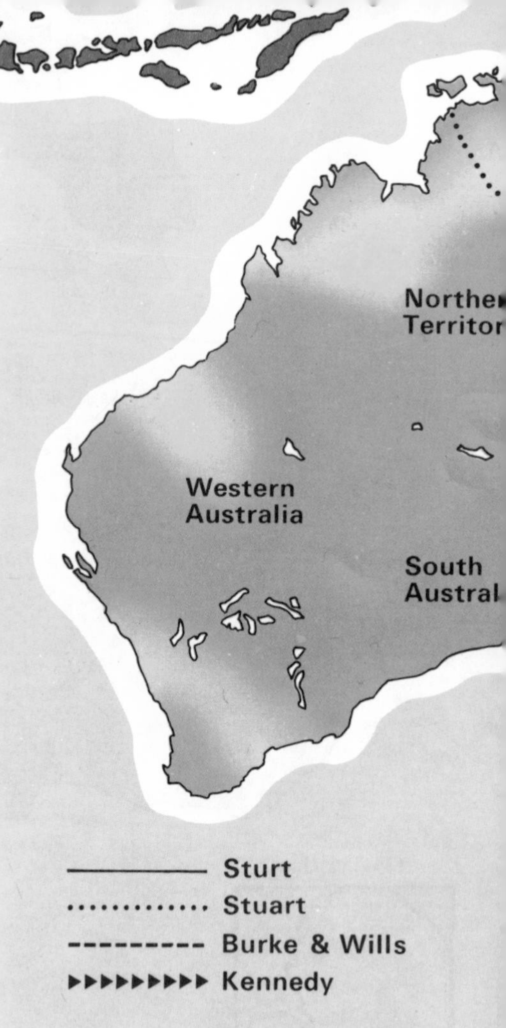

Right: Some famous Australian explorers.
(1) Charles Sturt (1795–1869) was an ex-soldier who headed several expeditions. He discovered the Darling River.
(2) Robert O'Hara Burke (1820–61) and (3) William J. Wills (1834–61) were members of an expedition that travelled from Melbourne to the Gulf of Carpentaria in the north. Both died on the return journey.
(4) John McDouall Stuart also crossed Australia from south to north, passing through the centre of the continent.
(5) Edward Kennedy (1818–48) led an expedition to Cape York, the most northerly point in Australia. He was killed by aborigines.

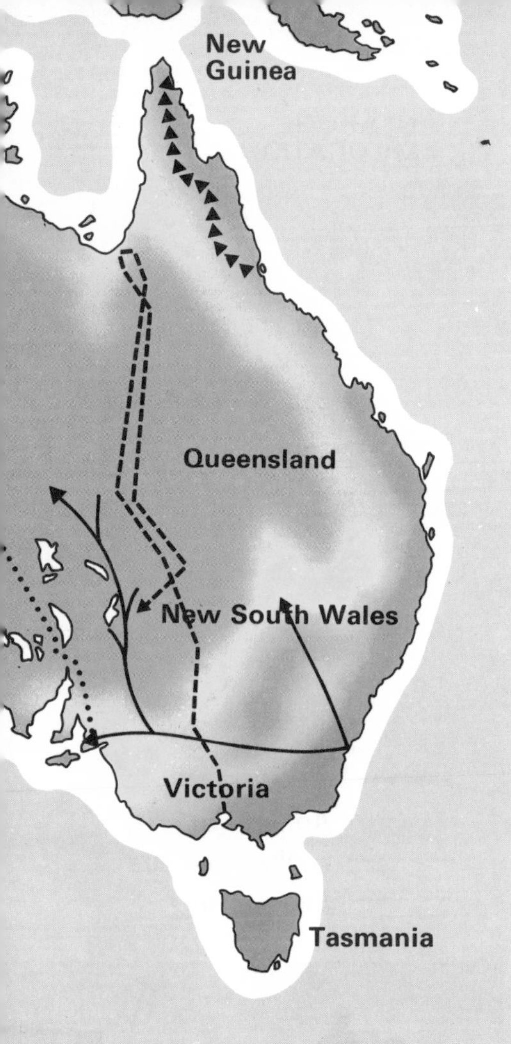

Important discoveries along the coasts of Australia were made by Matthew Flinders (1774–1814). Flinders and a surgeon, George Bass, left England in the ship *Reliance*. In 1797 they sailed in open boats along the coast of Victoria, Britain's second Australian colony. They proved that Tasmania is an island. Bass Strait, between Tasmania and the mainland, was named after the surgeon, who died in 1812. Flinders, meanwhile, continued his survey of the coasts and sailed round the whole continent.

Once the coastal districts were known, explorers pushed into the interior. Among them were Sir Thomas Mitchell (1792–1855) and Charles Sturt (1795–1869). Mitchell was Surveyor-General of New South Wales. He made four expeditions into the interior, and added greatly to knowledge of the country. Sturt went to live in Australia in 1826. He followed the course of the Murrumbidgee and Murray Rivers, and found where the inland rivers of New South Wales flow. The information he collected helped the growth of South Australia.

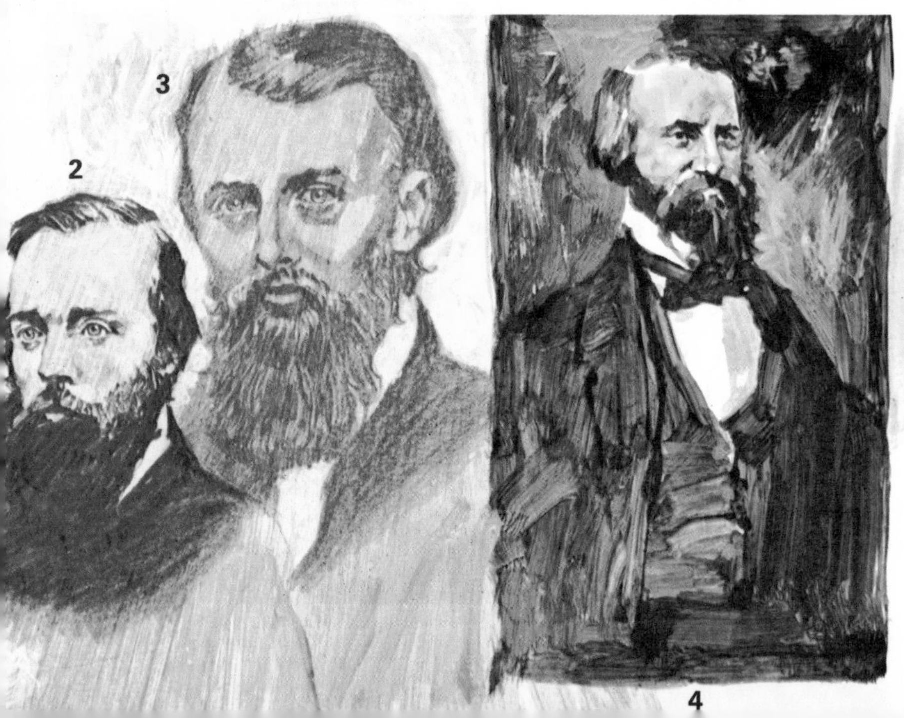

Polar explorers

The North and South Poles are the ends of the axis (line) around which the EARTH turns daily.

Attempts to find the north-east passage from the PACIFIC to the ARCTIC continued until 1879, when a Swede, N. A. E. Nordenskjöld (1832–1901) navigated the channel.

Many attempts were made to find the north-west passage. The expeditions sent to discover the fate of Sir John FRANKLIN and his men returned with new information. In 1906 the Norwegian, Captain Roald Amundsen (1872–1928) successfully navigated the passage.

Meanwhile, explorers from several countries were trying to reach the North Pole. Another Norwegian, Fridtjof Nansen (1861–1930) made a brave but unsuccessful attempt in 1893. He let his ship drift with the ice-pack as far north as possible, and then tried to push his way across the ice by sledge.

The North Pole was finally reached by an American, Robert Peary (1856–1920). Peary had already crossed North Greenland by sledge, a journey of almost 2000 kilometres. In 1908, with ESKIMO companions, he set out on a sledge journey to the Pole. He got there in April 1909.

Exploration of the ANTARCTIC continent, where the South Pole is situated, really began in 1773, when Captain COOK crossed the Antarctic Circle. In the nineteenth century, explorers from several countries sighted various parts of the coastline. In 1841 the British explorer James Clark Ross (1800–1862) reached the Ross Sea (which was named after him) and explored that part of the continent known as Victoria Land.

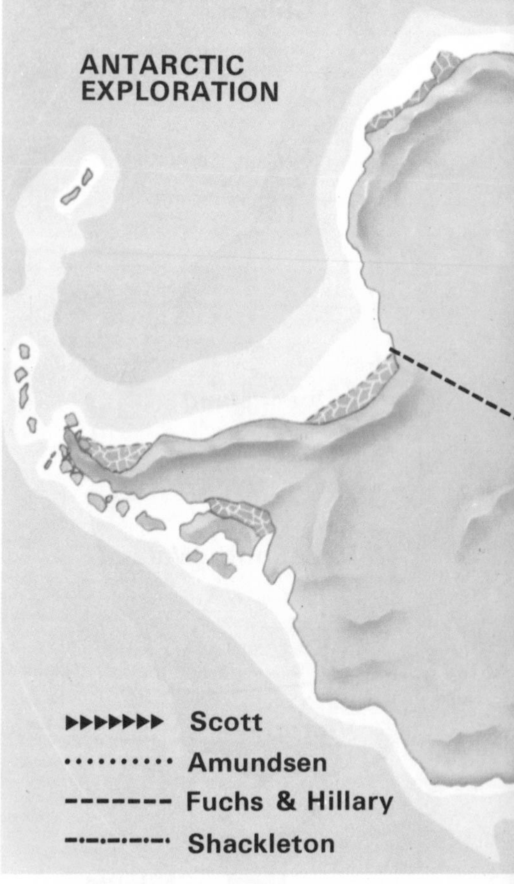

Right: A Sno-Cat vehicle has a narrow escape. In 1957 Vivian Fuchs and Edmund Hillary made the first crossing of Antarctica.

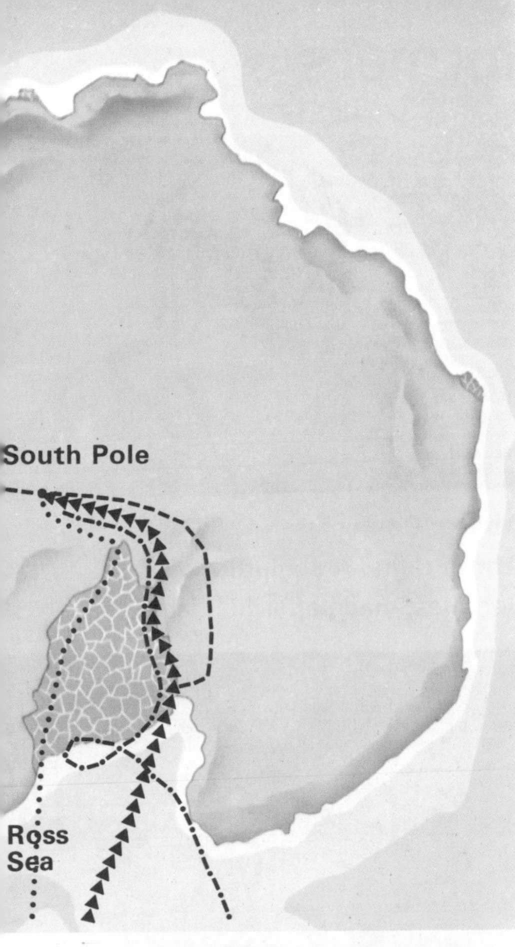

Exploration continued into the twentieth century. Between 1901 and 1904, the British explorer Captain Robert Falcon Scott (1868–1912) commanded an expedition which got to within 800 kilometres of the South Pole. Between 1907 and 1909, a second expedition, commanded by the British explorer Sir Ernest Shackleton (1874–1922) got to within two hundred kilometres of the Pole.

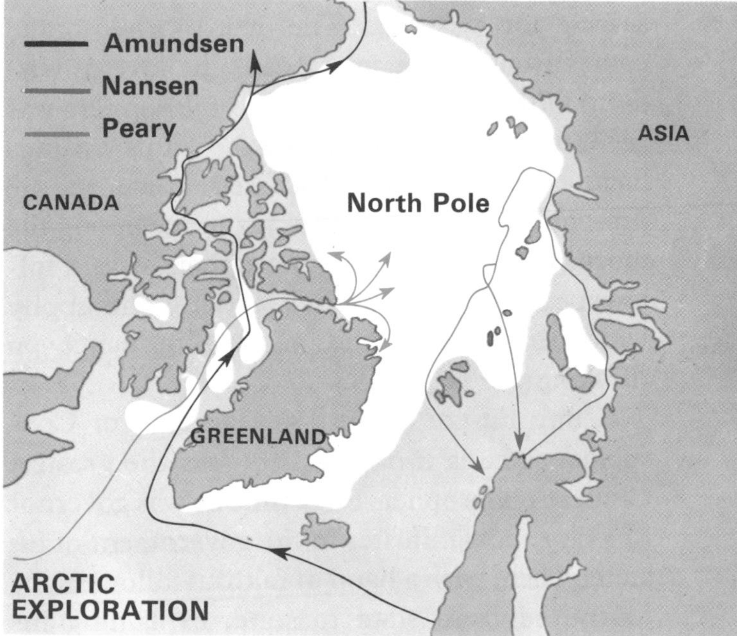

In 1910 Scott sailed for the Antarctic once more. With four companions, he reached the South Pole in January 1912. He arrived to find that Amundsen and his companions had beaten him by one month. Scott and his companions, Captain Oates, Dr Wilson, Lieutenant Bowers, and Seaman Evans, died on the return journey. They were within 20 kilometres of safety. Later that year, a search-party found their tent and three of the bodies. They also found the records and scientific instruments which Scott had left in perfect order.

Thinkers and Reformers

Some of the world's great thinkers are religious leaders who teach how people should think and act. Among these can be counted Buddha, whose teachings are followed by many, and John Wesley who started the METHODIST movement in England. At two very different periods in history, the ideas of these two men greatly influenced the thinking and lives of millions of people, and still do.

Others are philosophers who, in their studies, search for wisdom. The word 'philosophy' comes from Greek, and means the love of wisdom. One of the world's great philosophers was the Greek, Plato (428–347 B.C.). Plato's writings have been read and discussed down to the present day. Aristotle (384–322 B.C.), among the most famous of Greek philosophers, was a follower of Plato. He founded a school of philosophy which has always had a great influence on thinking people.

K'ung Fu-tzu (about 551–479 B.C.) or Confucius, as he is usually called, was the greatest Chinese philosopher. For a time he was governor of a city and a minister in the government of his state. Then, with a band of faithful followers, he journeyed from state to state, explaining his beliefs. Rulers, he taught, should be more interested in the welfare of their people. All people should learn to love and respect one another, and be kind, generous and forgiving.

All reformers are thinkers, but reformers do more than think and study. They try to do away with things which they believe to be bad or wrong. They try to replace these things with others which are good and right. Reformers are often condemned in their lifetime as trouble-makers. But most have followers who are ready to continue their work and, where necessary, to add to it new reforms.

Above: Confucius.
Above right: A sculpture of Socrates, made after his death.

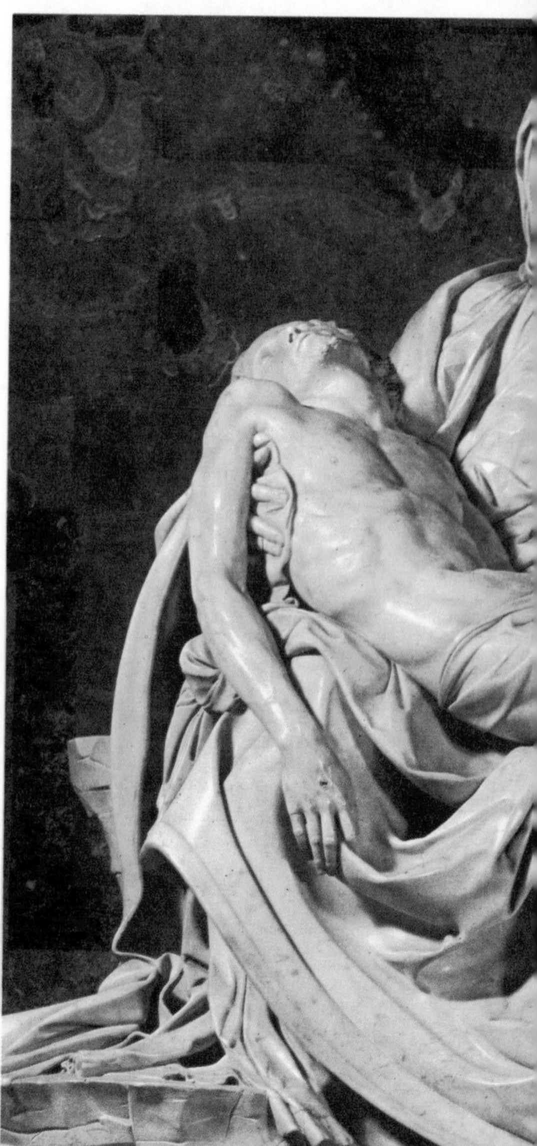

Below: Michelangelo's *Pietà*, now in the Vatican, Rome, shows Mary with the dead Jesus.

Socrates

The Greek philosopher Socrates (about 470–399 B.C.) lived in the city-state of ATHENS. He had many followers, among them Plato. Socrates taught people to question old ideas, and to believe only those things which they really understood. He also taught them to trust their own reason to decide what was right.

In 406 B.C. Socrates was made a member of the Council of Athens. Later, he was accused of encouraging young people to criticize the ideas and beliefs of the day. He was tried, and condemned to die by drinking poison. When the fatal drink was brought to him he swallowed it calmly.

Jesus

Mary, the mother of Jesus, and her husband, Joseph, lived in Nazareth in the land that is today called ISRAEL. Jesus was born in Bethlehem in about 4 B.C. Joseph and Mary were Jews, and Jesus was brought up as a follower of JUDAISM.

At about the age of 30, Jesus left Nazareth. He collected together a band of disciples (followers) and went about the country teaching. He also used a gift of healing to cure the sick.

Jesus had great sympathy for the poor, the oppressed, and the humble. He taught them a simple form of religious faith. He also criticized the Jewish religious leaders of the time. The ROMANS, overlords of the country, feared that Jesus would lead a rising against them. He was arrested, tried by Roman law, and, about A.D. 33, suffered the cruel death of crucifixion.

Christians throughout the world believe that Jesus rose from the dead and was seen by the disciples. They believe that he is the Son of God. Today, CHRISTIANITY has more followers than any other religion.

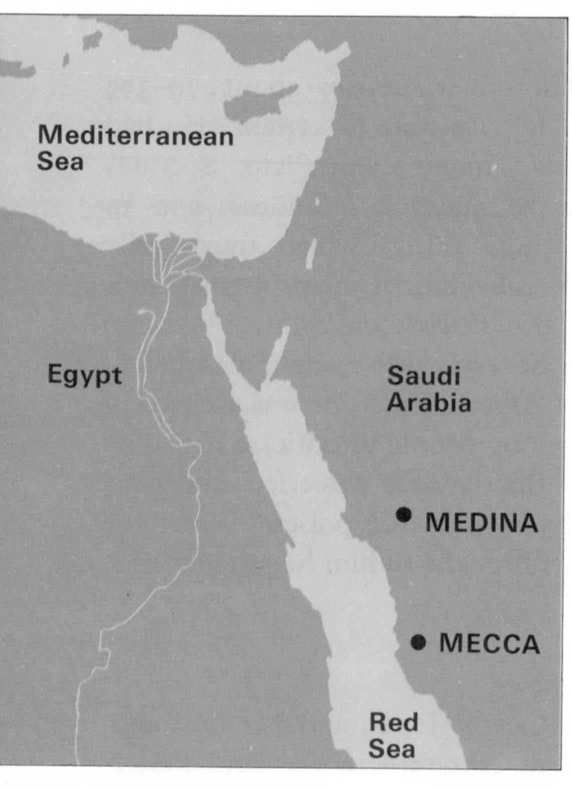

Mohammed

Mohammed (about A.D. 570–632) founded the religion of ISLAM. He was born in the Arabian city of Mecca. As a camel-driver on trading journeys, Mohammed met Christians and Jews, and became interested in their beliefs. He thought that the ARABS also needed a religion with high ideals. Islam is founded on belief in one God (Allah) and in Mohammed as the prophet of Allah. The Koran is the sacred book of Islam. It consists of the revelations made to Mohammed by God.

Islam made little headway at first. In 622 Mohammed fled from Mecca to Medina. He gathered round him a band of loyal, fierce believers, ready to spread Islam by force. He and his followers beat off a number of attacks by their enemies. In 630 Mohammed returned to Mecca in triumph.

Luther

A German priest, Martin Luther (1483–1546) started the religious revolt known as the Reformation. He was a professor at the UNIVERSITY of Wittenberg. Luther condemned the practice of selling indulgences (pardons) to people who had committed sins. The Pope sent him a stern message about this. Luther burnt it openly. Luther was excommunicated (expelled) from the ROMAN CATHOLIC Church for questioning some of its teachings. He then began to preach the Reformed Religion, a different form of CHRISTIANITY. Luther's ideas gave much more freedom of thought to the individual.

Luther's followers were called Lutherans, or PROTESTANTS (because they protested against a decision to outlaw their faith).

Right: Martin Luther.

Calvin

Jean Chauvin (1509–1564) was a Frenchman who called himself Calvinus, or Calvin, the Latin form of his name. He left the ROMAN CATHOLIC Church and settled in Geneva, SWITZERLAND, where he set out to reform religious teaching and to improve the thoughts and behaviour of the people. He developed a strict set of rules. His chief religious teaching is about *predestination*. This states that God destines (intends) some people to enjoy salvation (everlasting happiness in an after-life), but dooms others to everlasting punishment.

Calvin's form of religion is called Calvinism. It spread to many European countries. In Scotland, its followers are called PRESBYTERIANS.

Left: This picture of Calvin shows his stern, humourless character.

Erasmus

The Dutch priest Desiderius Erasmus (about 1466–1536) was one of the leading European scholars of his time. He was very fond of England, but never learnt English. He became a friend of Sir Thomas More, who was later beheaded for refusing to recognise King Henry VIII as head of the Church in England.

Erasmus travelled about EUROPE, teaching, writing, and studying. He carried on a long public argument with LUTHER about religion. Erasmus was a Humanist. He believed that ordinary people should be allowed to think for themselves and to learn more. He thought that reforms were needed in religious teaching. One of his important works was a new translation, into Latin, of the GREEK New Testament.

Right: A portrait of Erasmus by Hans Holbein.

Florence Nightingale

In 1854, England, FRANCE, and TURKEY were at war with Russia in the Crimean Peninsula in the Black Sea.

An Englishwoman, Florence Nightingale (1820–1910), was horrified to learn how badly the hospitals for the wounded were run. She went out to the Crimea with a small band of nurses, and reformed the work of the hospitals. Patients, who had been neglected, were made clean and comfortable, and many lives were saved. The British soldiers called her 'The Lady with the Lamp' because she always visited the wards last thing at night carrying a lamp.

On her return home, Florence Nightingale was given £45,000 as a reward for her work. She spent it on a school at a LONDON hospital for training nurses. This was the beginning of modern nursing.

Above: Florence Nightingale in the Turkish hospital at Scutari, where many soldiers wounded in the Crimean war were sent.

Marx

COMMUNISM is based on the teachings and writings of Karl Marx (1818–1883), a German philosopher. Together with his friend Friedrich Engels, in 1848 Marx wrote a booklet called the *Communist Manifesto* which set out a programme for socialist REVOLUTION.

Marx supported the German revolution in the same year. When it failed, he and Engels went to live in England, where Marx spent the rest of his life. There, among other works, he wrote his famous book *Das Kapital* which develops his theories about capitalism.

Marx's followers are called Marxists, and his ideas have had an enormous effect on the whole world.

Left: Karl Marx was born in Germany but spent most of his adult life in England.

Gandhi

Among the many Indians who wanted independence from British rule for INDIA was Mohandas Gandhi (1869–1948). Gandhi, a HINDU LAWYER, was known as Mahatma – wise and holy leader. As a young man, Gandhi fought for equal rights for Indians in SOUTH AFRICA. He used non-violent methods, such as publicly breaking unjust laws to draw attention to them. When he returned to India in 1915, he used the same methods to force the British to grant independence.

Gandhi also worked for friendship between Hindus and Moslems, but was assassinated by an extremist on his way to a prayer meeting.

elow: Sigmund Freud with his pet ow dog at his home in Austria. His eatment is still used today.

Freud

Sigmund Freud (1856–1939) was an Austrian doctor who thought of a way of treating people suffering from mental illness. He called it psychoanalysis.

Patients being treated would be encouraged to talk about themselves and particularly about their dreams. Freud believed that people's secret hopes and fears are hidden in their dreams. If a patient could face up to these hidden feelings he might come to understand himself better.

Martin Luther King

Martin Luther King (1929–1968) was a black American clergyman who wanted equal civil rights for black people and an end to segregation in the south of the United States. He organised a boycott of buses to protest against segregation on them, and a march to WASHINGTON to persuade the government to back his movement.

In 1964 King was awarded the NOBEL Peace Prize. Like all reformers, King had enemies. He was shot and killed by one of them.

Rulers and Leaders

Some modern rulers and leaders. Above: Queen Elizabeth II (United Kingdom) came to the throne in 1952. Below (left to right): President Nyerere (Tanzania), ex-Queen Juliana (Netherlands), and Prime Minister Lee Kuan Yew (Singapore).

In the past, MONARCHS (kings and queens) gave orders which their subjects had to obey. A king generally came to the throne because his father had been king. He expected to remain king for the rest of his life. Some kings used their power badly, however, and their subjects rebelled. In England, in 1215, the barons forced King John to sign the Magna Carta, which took certain rights away from the king.

The power of kings slowly lessened. First groups of advisers and then PARLIAMENTS were set up to guide them. In modern times, most monarchs have no power to take any action or decision on their own. Most decisions are taken by their governments.

The PRESIDENT of the United States and the PRIME MINISTER of England are leaders, but they do not rule. They are not appointed for life but can be turned out of office within a few years if the people they represent dislike what they are doing. This is called DEMOCRACY. In a DICTATORSHIP, leaders like STALIN and HITLER may be as powerful as the kings of the past and can only be turned out of office with great difficulty.

Some people, such as NAPOLEON, become leaders because others will follow them eagerly. Such leaders have helped to change the course of history.

Above: Part of a mosaic, showing Alexander the Great fighting against the Persians.
Below: A bust of Julius Caesar.

Alexander the Great

In 331 B.C. the GREEK King of Macedon, Alexander the Great (356–323 B.C.) captured Persia (modern IRAN) and its provinces. Alexander was a general who wanted to build a great Greek empire. He captured many cities along the coast of the MEDITERRANEAN Sea. He then went on to conquer EGYPT and to found the city of Alexandria, named after him. He even conquered the western part of INDIA.

Alexander wanted to convert people to Greek ideas. He therefore encouraged Greeks to settle in the conquered cities.

Hannibal

The most important enemies of the ANCIENT ROMANS were the people of Carthage, in North AFRICA. The greatest of Carthage's generals was Hannibal (247–183 B.C.). Hannibal took his ARMY over the ALPS to get into ITALY. He won many battles but never attacked ROME itself.

After many years in Italy, Hannibal returned to defend Carthage against the Romans. He was defeated at the battle of Zama. Hannibal later killed himself to avoid capture.

Julius Caesar

Julius Caesar (about 100–44 B.C.) was one of the world's greatest generals. He was also a good historian and speaker. After an adventurous military career, he became DICTATOR of the city of ROME. Rome was then the centre of an empire which Caesar did much to extend.

Among Caesar's conquests were Gaul (FRANCE) and EGYPT. He also came to Britain. The ROMANS invited him to become emperor but he refused. His enemies feared that he might accept and become even more powerful and so they killed him.

Cleopatra

Cleopatra (about 69–30 B.C.) was the beautiful daughter of the ANCIENT EGYPTIAN king, Ptolemy XI. She had enemies who drove her out of EGYPT. She then appealed to JULIUS CAESAR for help. He made her queen of Egypt again.

After Caesar's murder, civil war broke out in the Roman Empire. One side wanted control over Egypt, but Mark Antony, a Roman general, supported Cleopatra against them. Mark Antony and Cleopatra were defeated in battle. Both of them killed themselves.

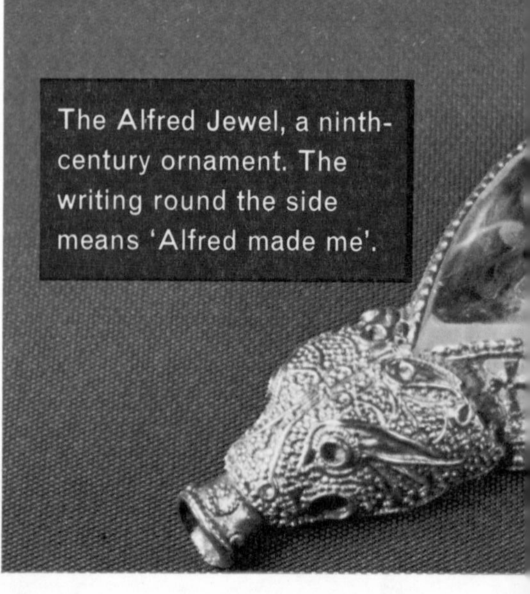

The Alfred Jewel, a ninth-century ornament. The writing round the side means 'Alfred made me'.

Above: A picture from an old manuscript, showing Pope Leo III crowning Charlemagne Emperor.

Attila the Hun

Attila (about A.D. 400–453), king of the warlike Huns, ruled an empire which stretched from the Baltic Sea to western Russia. He gained many victories over the forces of the Roman Empire.

In 451 Attila marched through Germany, crossed the River Rhine, and went on to invade Gaul (FRANCE). There he met his only defeat. He re-formed his army and invaded ITALY. He died suddenly, possibly by poison, on his wedding day. After his death, his empire collapsed. Attila is said to have been very cruel and proud.

Charlemagne

Charlemagne, or Charles the Great (about 742–814), was King of the Franks. His kingdom was what is now FRANCE but by the time he died it included Germany and much of ITALY.

Charlemagne championed the cause of CHRISTIANITY against German and Italian tribes. In 800 Pope Leo III crowned him Emperor of the Holy Roman Empire. Charlemagne's empire was well-governed and his court a centre of art and learning. When he died the empire fell apart but some of it continued to be called the Holy Roman Empire for about a thousand years.

Alfred the Great

Alfred (849–899) succeeded his father as king of Wessex in southern England in 871. At the time, a large part of England was overrun by the Danes (VIKINGS).

Alfred spent the first years of his reign fighting the Danes. In order to defeat the Vikings at sea, he built up an English navy. When he had secured peace, he started to improve the towns, and to build fortifications and SCHOOLS. He invited scholars and teachers from EUROPE to his court. He also translated Latin books into English.

William the Conqueror

William I, called The Conqueror (1027–1087), was a son of the Duke of Normandy. He claimed that Edward the Confessor, King of England, had promised him the English crown. After Edward's death, however, Harold, Duke of Wessex, was chosen as king. William invaded England and defeated Harold at the Battle of Hastings in 1066. Harold was killed and William was crowned King of England.

William set up a French nobility and soon established control over the whole country.

Above: A drawing of William the Conqueror, made about 400 years after his death.

Genghis Khan

The Mongol emperor Genghis Khan (1162–1227) was a powerful and ruthless leader. Genghis Khan means 'very mighty ruler'. His armies won many victories over the tribes of MONGOLIA and northern CHINA, and went on to invade Russia. Captured towns were destroyed and the people killed. When Genghis Khan died, his empire stretched from the Yellow Sea, off the east coast of China, to the River Dnieper in Russia.

Genghis Khan's grandson, Kublai Khan, completed the conquest of China.

Joan of Arc

In 1429 a girl of seventeen led an army towards the French city of Orléans, which was surrounded by English troops. She was Jeanne d'Arc (1412–1431), called Joan of Arc in English.

From childhood, Joan believed she heard the voices of saints. They commanded her to free FRANCE from the English invaders. They also ordered her to escort the French king to the city of Rheims to be crowned.

Joan drove the English from Orléans, and went on to win battle after battle. She saw the king crowned at Rheims. But the war was not over. In the end Joan was captured and put to death by burning, but her example encouraged the French to drive out the English. Joan was declared a saint in 1920, about 500 years later.

Above: A romantic picture of Joan of Arc. Joan was a peasant girl from a remote village in Lorraine. Right: A portrait of Oliver Cromwell.

Elizabeth I

Elizabeth I (1533–1603), daughter of Henry VIII and Anne Boleyn, was 25 when she came to the throne of England. Her long reign was a time of danger. England, a PROTESTANT country, was threatened by ROMAN CATHOLIC Spain. There were Catholic plots to kill Elizabeth and put the Catholic Mary Queen of Scots on the throne. In 1587 Mary was executed.

Elizabeth never married. When she died, the throne went to her cousin, James, who was King of Scotland. In this way, Scotland and England were joined together.

Elizabeth's reign was a time of much exploration and trade, and of the strengthening of England's power. It was also a time of great writing, such as that of William SHAKESPEARE, great music, and great buildings.

Right: Queen Elizabeth I, painted in 1588, the year of the Spanish Armada.

Cromwell

Oliver Cromwell (1599–1658), a member of PARLIAMENT, became a general when civil war broke out between the forces of Parliament and King Charles I. He raised and trained first a regiment, and then an army which defeated the royal troops. Cromwell became ruler of England when the King was arrested and executed in 1649. England was declared a COMMONWEALTH in 1653, with Cromwell as Lord Protector.

Cromwell was a very religious man who became a stern but wise ruler. He strengthened England's power overseas and kept the peace at home. This period was a time of restrictions on public entertainment, style of clothes and religious views.

Cromwell's son, Richard, succeeded him but only ruled for a year. Then England became a MONARCHY again under King Charles II.

Louis XIV

One of the greatest rulers of FRANCE, Louis XIV (1638–1715) is sometimes called the Sun King. Before Louis became king, the French nobles had caused a lot of trouble. Louis, therefore, decided to keep them under his eye, away from their estates. He built a magnificent palace at Versailles, just outside PARIS. All the important nobles were members of the court, and were expected to be there. Louis did a lot to encourage the arts. Some of France's greatest thinkers, writers, and painters lived and worked during his reign, often at his court.

During Louis' reign, however, France was often at war, and lost many of her lands overseas, particularly in America. The wars made France poor and increased discontent among her people.

Right: Louis XIV on horseback.

William of Orange

William, Prince of Orange (1650–1702) was a ruler of the NETHERLANDS who married Mary, the daughter of James II of England, and succeeded him as King.

William was invited to become King by the English nobility who did not like James's method of government or his ROMAN CATHOLIC religion. William and Mary were crowned joint sovereigns in 1689. James had fled. He tried to fight his way back but was defeated at the Battle of the Boyne in IRELAND. The victory on the Boyne earned William the hatred of Irish ROMAN CATHOLICS and his connection with the 'massacre of Glencoe' earned him the dislike of many Scots. He was respected but not popular in England.

Left: William of Orange, a Dutchman, became King William III of England.

Frederick the Great

The greatest of the many states that joined together to form Germany was Prussia. Prussia's most important king was Frederick II (1712–1786), known in history as Frederick the Great. As a boy, Frederick was interested in music and literature. His father, King William I of Prussia, forced him to have an ARMY training. He hated this so much that he made an unsuccessful attempt to escape to England.

Frederick became king in 1740. He proved to be a brilliant army commander. During his reign, the size and power of Prussia greatly increased. As ruler, Frederick made a number of wise reforms. Although he kept his love of music and writing, he never put his own interests before his duty to the state.

Right: Frederick the Great reviewing troops.

Maria Theresa

The Empress Maria Theresa (1717–1780) was a great ruler of AUSTRIA. When her father, Charles VI, died, he left behind a huge empire. Despite promises made to him, several European powers refused to recognise the new Empress as ruler of Austria and Hungary. As a result, the War of Austrian Succession (1741–48) broke out.

Prussia and FRANCE were Maria Theresa's chief enemies. Britain supported her and her Hungarian subjects rallied to the Austrian cause. She lost some territory in the war but the powers were forced to accept her as Empress.

Farming and trade prospered under her rule and she became a very popular monarch. She even lowered taxes. Like ELIZABETH I of England, she had a powerful personality.

Right: The Empress Maria Theresa.

Catherine II

The Empress Catherine II of Russia (1729–1796) is often called 'the Great'. She was the daughter of a German prince and married the future emperor, Peter III, when she was only 16 years old. Peter was murdered in 1762 and Catherine came to the throne. She was clever, strong, and full of energy, and she ruled Russia for 34 years.

Catherine made many plans for reform, but few took place. For example, some SCHOOLS were opened, but her plan to start primary education on a big scale failed through lack of money.

Catherine worked hard to make Russia more powerful. She waged successful wars against TURKEY, and made Russia much larger than it had been before.

Left: Catherine the Great on horseback, wearing a soldier's uniform.

Above: George Washington.
Below: Thomas Jefferson.

Washington

The first PRESIDENT of the United States of America, George Washington (1732–1799), was the great-grandson of an Englishman who had settled in America. As a young man, Washington served in the British ARMY which was fighting the French.

In 1775 the War of Independence broke out. It was fought between British troops and British settlers (Americans) in Britain's 13 North American colonies. Washington was Commander-in-Chief of the American army. The war ended in 1783 with an American victory. Britain then acknowledged the independence of the United States.

With Washington's help, the United States formed themselves into a REPUBLIC. Washington was elected President in 1789. He was trusted and loved by the people, and was re-elected President in 1793. Many people consider Washington the greatest figure in American history.

Jefferson

Thomas Jefferson (1743–1826) was the third PRESIDENT of the United States, and one of the greatest. In 1776 he helped draw up the famous Declaration of Independence, which stated that Britain's American colonies were 'of right Free and Independent States'.

It was due to Jefferson, and also to WASHINGTON, that the United States capital – now the city of WASHINGTON – was founded on the banks of the Potomac River. Jefferson was twice elected President. His most important act is known as the Louisiana Purchase. By this purchase from France he gained for the United States vast lands west of the Mississippi River. NAPOLEON was prepared to sell the land to the United States, rather than let Britain take it over.

Above: Abraham Lincoln.
Below: The log cabin in Hodgenville, Kentucky, U.S.A., where Lincoln was born.

Lincoln

One of America's greatest heroes was born of poor parents in a log cabin in Kentucky. This was Abraham Lincoln (1809–1865). Lincoln had no schooling, but his mother taught him to read and write. He worked in a number of jobs, and studied law, eventually becoming a LAWYER.

In 1861 Lincoln was elected the sixteenth PRESIDENT of the United States. At that time the Sourthern States still kept black slaves. Lincoln spoke out strongly against slavery. The Southern States did not want to lose their slaves, and so they left the Union. As a result, civil war broke out between the Northern and the Southern States. Lincoln was anxious that the North and the South should not be divided. The North won the war. The two sides were reunited as a nation, and slavery was abolished (made unlawful).

Just after the war ended in 1865, Lincoln was shot and killed in a THEATRE in WASHINGTON. It was a tragedy for both North and South.

Nelson

The great English naval commander, Horatio, Lord Nelson (1758–1805), first went to sea at the age of 12. In 1793 when England was beginning a long war with FRANCE, he was given the command of a battleship. He lost his right eye in one battle, his right arm in another.

In 1798 Nelson faced NAPOLEON's fleet at the Battle of the Nile. He completely defeated the French. Without ships Napoleon could not get supplies to his ARMY in EGYPT. His plans for an empire in the east came to nothing.

In 1801 Nelson took a fleet into Copenhagen harbour. There, he put the Danish fleet out of action. Napoleon was not able to make use of the Danish ships.

In 1805 Nelson commanded the British fleet against the French at the Battle of Trafalgar. Before the action started he hoisted from the flagship *Victory* his famous signal: 'England expects that every man will do his duty'. The French lost the battle but Nelson was killed.

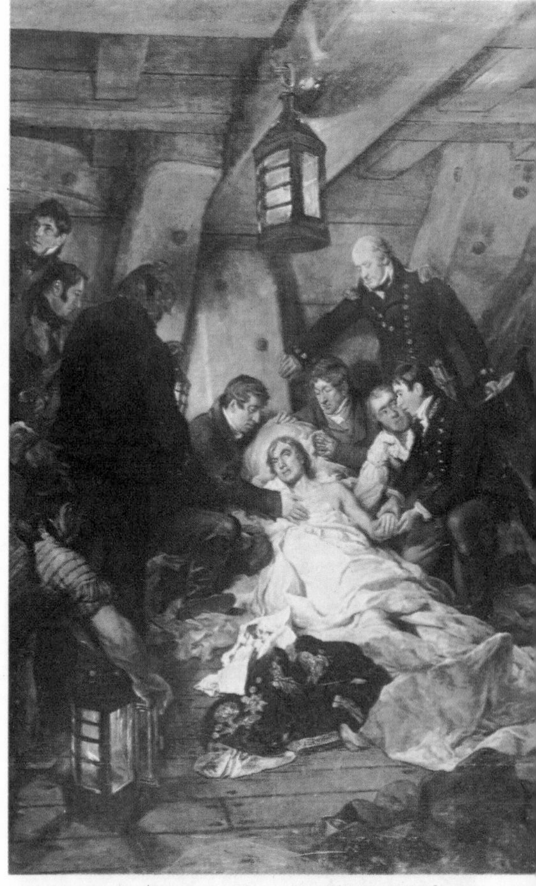

Above: The death of Nelson.

Wellington

Arthur Wellesley, first Duke of Wellington (1769–1852), was both a soldier and a statesman. In 1808, after fighting successfully in INDIA, Wellington led the British ARMY in the six-year Peninsular War. His aim was to drive NAPOLEON'S forces out of SPAIN and PORTUGAL. He won several victories which helped to hasten Napoleon's downfall.

After his final great victory over Napoleon at the Battle of Waterloo in 1815 in BELGIUM, Wellington went back into politics. In 1828 he became PRIME MINISTER of England. He was not always popular, but his influence was enormous.

Right: Wellington acknowledges a salute.

Above: Napoleon as First Consul. He and Wellington were born in the same year.

Napoleon

Napoleon Bonaparte (1769–1821) was born in Corsica and educated in French army SCHOOLS. He served in the French army and in 1795 was made Commander-in-Chief. In 1797 he defeated the Austrian forces in ITALY. Next year he led an expedition into SYRIA and EGYPT.

Napoleon returned to PARIS a national hero. He became head of the government as First Consul. In 1804 he crowned himself Emperor.

A series of great victories followed against the allied forces of England, Russia, AUSTRIA, and Prussia. Napoleon was now the most powerful man in EUROPE. In 1812 he set out to conquer Russia but was forced to retreat. He surrendered to the Allies and was imprisoned on the ISLAND of Elba.

Napoleon escaped, but in 1815 was finally defeated at the Battle of Waterloo by the English under the Duke of WELLINGTON, and the Prussians under Field-Marshal Blücher.

Napoleon died in exile on the island of St Helena.

Toussaint L'Ouverture

The black general Toussaint L'Ouverture (1743–1803) was brought up as a slave on the island of Hispaniola in the West Indies, part of which was a colony of FRANCE. Toussaint learned to read and write. Later, he led the slaves in a revolt against the French, and in 1793 the slaves were freed.

In 1801 Toussaint set up a government and named himself PRESIDENT. Then NAPOLEON sent a large force against him. Napoleon wanted to re-establish slavery. Toussaint's ARMY took to the MOUNTAINS. The French were too strong for them, and Toussaint had to ask for peace in 1802. He was sent to France and put in prison, where he died.

Right: Toussaint L'Ouverture.
Below: Simón Bolívar.

Bolívar

Simón Bolívar (1783–1830) is known as the hero of South American independence. He was born in Venezuela, then ruled by SPAIN. He studied in MADRID, the Spanish capital. He also visited PARIS just after the French REVOLUTION.

Bolívar decided that Venezuela should be free. He led a revolt against the Spaniards, and finally won independence in 1821. He then united Venezuela with New Granada in the REPUBLIC of Colombia, and became the first PRESIDENT. He added Ecuador to the new Republic, and also helped the Peruvians, who were fighting for their own independence. The Republic of Bolivia, formerly part of Peru, was named in Bolívar's honour. Bolívar would have liked to have united all Spanish-speaking SOUTH AMERICA.

Venezuela separated from Colombia in 1829, and Bolívar gave up the Presidency.

Above: Sir John Tenniel's famous cartoon of the Emperor William II dismissing Bismarck (the Pilot).
Below: Queen Victoria in old age.

Bismarck

The German statesman, Prince Otto von Bismarck (1815–1898), is sometimes called the 'Iron Chancellor'.

Bismarck was born at a time when Germany was still divided into a number of small kingdoms and states. He was determined to unite the country under the leadership of the Kingdom of Prussia. He worked for this unity for many years, and gained it in 1871 after fighting short wars against AUSTRIA and FRANCE. The king of Prussia then became Emperor of the German Empire, as William I. Bismarck was made Imperial Chancellor and a prince. He strengthened Germany at home and increased her importance in EUROPE.

In 1888 William I died, and was succeeded by his grandson, William II. He quarrelled with Bismarck, who was forced to resign.

Queen Victoria

Queen Elizabeth II's great-great-grandmother was Queen Victoria (1819–1901). She was only 18 years old when she came to the throne. She married her cousin, Prince Albert of Saxe-Coburg-Gotha (now part of Germany) (1819–1861), and had nine children.

The Queen had some influence on people and events but, as with other kings and queens in modern times, her governments had the real power. Lord Melbourne was PRIME MINISTER when Victoria became queen. He guided her wisely through the first difficult years of her reign, when England had many problems. Later, his place as counsellor was taken by a later Prime Minister – Benjamin Disraeli.

Victoria was Queen of Great Britain and IRELAND, and Empress of INDIA. She reigned longer than any British king or queen before her.

Roosevelt

Franklin Delano Roosevelt (1882–1945) could walk only with difficulty after a bad attack of poliomyelitis (paralysis). Yet he was the only man ever to be elected PRESIDENT of the United States four times.

In response to the world-wide financial depression of the 1930s, Roosevelt brought in his famous 'New Deal'. This was a series of far-reaching reforms which helped to revive the economy and relieve unemployment.

In WORLD WAR II, Roosevelt was a good friend to the Allies even before the United States had declared war. During the war, Roosevelt had several important meetings with Winston CHURCHILL and STALIN. Roosevelt died only a few months before final victory in the war.

Right: F. D. Roosevelt (front of picture).

Eisenhower

Dwight David Eisenhower (1890–1969) was educated for the ARMY at West Point Military Academy. At the outbreak of WORLD WAR II he held the rank of lieutenant-colonel. Yet in 1943 he was the Supreme Commander of all the Allied forces in EUROPE.

After the war – in 1948 – Eisenhower left the army and became President of Columbia University, NEW YORK. In 1952 he was elected PRESIDENT of the United States. He was re-elected in 1956, with Richard Nixon as vice-president.

As President, Eisenhower made three 'good-will' tours of countries overseas. These formed part of his work for peace and friendship among nations. As a leader, his greatest gift was that he was able to persuade people of all nations to work together in a friendly way.

Below: Eisenhower (right) with U.S. soldiers during World War II.

Top: Lenin.
Above: Josif Stalin.

Lenin

Lenin's real name was Vladimir Ilyich Ulyanov (1870–1924). He studied law and the writings of Karl MARX. He organised TRADE UNIONS for the workers but unions were forbidden in Russia. Lenin was imprisoned and then exiled (in 1897) to Siberia, in the far east of Russia.

In 1900 Lenin was released, and went to Western EUROPE. He became a leader of a revolutionary party, which soon split into the Bolsheviks (majority) and the Mensheviks (minority). Lenin was a Bolshevik. He lived in SWITZERLAND during WORLD WAR I, returning to Russia in 1917. The Bolsheviks overthrew the government in the November REVOLUTION, and Lenin became the country's leader. As head of government, he carried out many changes and reforms in a very short time.

Stalin

LENIN called Josif Dzhugashvili Stalin (1879–1953) 'the man of steel'. This was because he was hard and cool in times of danger. Stalin was a revolutionary. He was imprisoned, then exiled to Siberia. He escaped, and later joined Lenin and the Bolsheviks.

Stalin was a leader of the 1917 REVOLUTION. This led to the birth of the new Russia, the U.S.S.R. After Lenin's death, Stalin became head of the government. He aimed to build up Russia's industry and transform agriculture by a series of five-year plans. He also carried out 'purges'. Thousands of people who opposed his rule were purged (imprisoned or executed).

In WORLD WAR II, Stalin defended the U.S.S.R. against the invasion of Nazi Germany in 1941. After the war, he ruled harshly until his death. He was a ruthless man, but, by the time he died, Russia had become a major world power.

Mussolini

Benito Mussolini (1883–1945) was the son of an Italian blacksmith. He came to power as leader of the Fascist Party in October 1922. Later he became DICTATOR of Italy and the ally of HITLER in WORLD WAR II.

The Fascists were patriotic and very anti-COMMUNIST, and they bullied their way to power. As their leader, Mussolini was ruthless both at home and abroad. In 1937 he invaded and conquered Abyssinia (now ETHIOPIA) while the world stood by and looked on.

Mussolini saw himself as the founder of a new Roman Empire. In 1940, when Hitler seemed set to conquer most of Europe, Mussolini was quick to join him. But few Italians wanted to fight and many turned against him. He fell from power but was reinstated by Hitler when the Germans invaded Italy. At the end of the war Mussolini was caught and executed by his Italian opponents.

Above: Hitler (right) with Mussolini.
Below: Churchill at his desk.

Churchill

In May 1940 WORLD WAR II was going badly for Britain and her allies. The PRIME MINISTER, Neville Chamberlain, resigned. His place was taken by Winston Churchill (1874–1965).

Churchill was a soldier, historian, writer, and painter as well as a politician. He had seen action in SOUTH AFRICA and INDIA. In 1900 he became a Member of PARLIAMENT, and later held important government posts.

Churchill was a great wartime leader. His defiant speeches inspired Parliament, the armed forces, and people at home with hope and courage. He made several journeys overseas to meet STALIN and President ROOSEVELT. In 1945, however, his party lost the general ELECTION. In 1951 he became Prime Minister again and finally resigned in 1955.

Hitler

The DICTATOR of Germany, Adolf Hitler (1889–1945), was born in AUSTRIA. He went to live in Germany in 1912. He fought in WORLD WAR I.

After Germany's defeat in the war, Hitler became the head of a new party, the National Socialists (or Nazis). In 1933 the Nazis came to power and Hitler became Führer (Leader).

The Nazis hated COMMUNISTS and Socialists. They also hated Jews, Slavs, gypsies, and others who were not, they said, of 'pure' German blood. As a result, millions of innocent people were killed, or died in concentration camps.

Hitler took possession of Austria and CZECHOSLOVAKIA. In 1939 he invaded POLAND. As a result of this invasion, Britain and FRANCE declared war on Germany. In 1941 he rashly invaded the U.S.S.R. Germany was defeated in 1945. It is thought that Hitler killed himself as Russian troops advanced on BERLIN.

Below: General de Gaulle, great French soldier and statesman.

De Gaulle

In 1940, during WORLD WAR II, FRANCE surrendered to Nazi Germany. A high-ranking army officer, Charles de Gaulle (1890–1970) refused to surrender. Instead, he flew to England. In LONDON, he raised and led the Free French fighting forces, who continued the war.

After the war, General de Gaulle returned to France a national hero. He was made head of a new government and chief of the armed forces. In 1946 he resigned.

In 1958 de Gaulle returned to power as PRESIDENT of the French Republic. Until his resignation in 1969 de Gaulle did a lot to stimulate economic growth and national pride in France. He negotiated with ALGERIA for independence in 1962, and in 1963 vetoed (stopped) the British application to join the COMMON MARKET.

Mao Tse-tung

The Chinese leader, Mao Tse-tung, was born in 1893, the son of a farmer. He studied the writings of Karl MARX at UNIVERSITY. He helped to form the Chinese COMMUNIST Party, and later gained control of it. Mao won the support of CHINA's peasants and organised a peasant ARMY.

After JAPAN's defeat by the Allies in WORLD WAR II, Mao's army defeated China's ruler, General Chiang Kai-Shek. The Communists then came to power. In 1949 Mao was elected Chairman (Chief of State) of the new Communist People's Republic of China.

Under Mao China became a leading country in international politics. Mao Tse-tung died in 1976.

Right: Mao Tse-tung claps to thank his audience for their applause at a political rally.

Jan Christian Smuts

Jan Christian Smuts was born in the Cape, SOUTH AFRICA, in 1870. 'Jannie' was a brilliant scholar and studied law at Stellenbosch and Cambridge Universities. He married Isie Krige and they had seven children. During the Boer War he fought against Britain but after the Peace of Vereeniging was signed, he worked hard to establish friendship with Britain.

At the end of WORLD WAR I, he became one of the founders of the League of Nations. After the Second World War he helped to draft the UNITED NATIONS Charter in 1945. In 1946 he was the leader of the South African delegation to the United Nations Assembly in New York. He died in 1950.

Left: Jan Christian Smuts in the uniform of a British Field Marshal.

Kennedy

The youngest man, and the first ROMAN CATHOLIC, to be elected PRESIDENT of the United States was John Fitzgerald Kennedy (1917–1963).

Kennedy served in the NAVY in WORLD WAR II. In 1943 the motor torpedo boat which he commanded was rammed and sunk by a Japanese destroyer. Kennedy and the other survivors swam almost five kilometres to safety.

After the war, Kennedy went into politics. He was elected PRESIDENT in 1960. He helped to show the American people how to meet the problems of a scientific age. He fought against racial discrimination – the idea that black Americans should not have the same rights as whites.

Kennedy's murder by Lee Harvey Oswald shocked the whole world.

Right: President Kennedy with his wife.

Castro

The PRIME MINISTER of Cuba, Fidel Castro, was born in 1927. Cuba is a large ISLAND in the CARIBBEAN SEA. Castro studied at UNIVERSITY, and was active in student protest. Then, for two years, he worked as a LAWYER.

Under the rule of President Fulencio Batista, Cuba was a police state. In 1953 Castro headed an ARMY which sought to overthrow Batista. In 1959, at the third attempt, the army won. Batista was forced to flee. Castro became the most powerful man in the new government.

Castro has worked hard to improve Cuba's agriculture, education, and industry. He is a COMMUNIST. Under him, Cuba is friendly with the U.S.S.R. and other Communist countries.

Right: Fidel Castro, the Cuban Prime Minister, addresses workers at a tractor factory.

FAMOUS PEOPLE FACTS AND FIGURES

PAINTERS AND SCULPTORS. The most valuable painting in the world is the *Mona Lisa* by Leonardo da Vinci. Rembrandt painted about 60 self-portraits from 1629 to his death 40 years later. In his old age Renoir, crippled by arthritis, painted with brushes tied to his hands.

COMPOSERS. Mozart composed his first music at the age of six and wrote his first opera when he was 12 years old. Mahler's 8th symphony, the *Symphony of a Thousand,* requires about 750 performers. Haydn wrote 104 symphonies, 84 string quartets, and about 50 concertos.

WRITERS. The earliest-known writing, made about 6000 years ago, used pictures instead of words. The longest poem, written in ancient India, contains three million words. The world's best-selling book is the Bible; it has been translated into 1400 different languages.

ENTERTAINERS. Bing Crosby sold more gramophone records than any other single entertainer, and the Beatles have sold more than any other group. Walt Disney won 35 Oscars (Film Academy Awards) for his motion pictures – far more than any other person.

SCIENTISTS AND INVENTORS. Einstein was only 26 years old when he published his theory of relativity. The first words ever recorded, by Edison in 1877, were 'Mary had a little lamb'. American scientists have won more Nobel prizes than those of any other country.

ENGINEERS AND ARCHITECTS. The first school of architecture was established in France in 1671. In 1829 Stephenson's engine, the *Rocket,* set a rail speed record of 47 kilometres per hour. The unit of power, the watt, is named after James Watt, who developed the steam engine.

EXPLORERS. The most distant exploration – as far as 400,187 kilometres from earth – was made by the astronauts of *Apollo 13* in 1970. The first people to travel around the world were the surviving crew of the expedition led by Ferdinand Magellan from 1519 to 1521.

THINKERS AND REFORMERS. Socrates left no written works and is known only through the works of his followers. Mohammed's birthplace, Mecca, is a holy city that only Moslems may enter. Martin Luther King was the youngest person ever to receive the Nobel Peace Prize.

RULERS AND LEADERS. The largest empire ever known was the Mongol Empire founded by Genghis Khan. Louis XIV reigned for 72 years, longer than any other European monarch. Four U.S. Presidents have been assassinated while in office: Lincoln, Garfield, McKinley, and Kennedy.

TRAVEL AND COMMUNICATION

Space Travel

Less than a hundred years ago only a few people thought that man would ever travel in space. Yet now men have left the planet EARTH and have even travelled to, and walked on, the MOON.

Just how do we get things into space? When you throw a ball into the air, it rises up and then falls back because of the earth's pull, or GRAVITY. The harder you throw, the higher the ball rises. If you could throw it at 40,000 kilometres an hour, the ball would overcome gravity altogether and escape into space. At the lower speed of 28,000 kilometres an hour, you could make the ball circle the earth in orbit.

Using a ROCKET for propulsion, these very high speeds are possible. In October 1957 the U.S.S.R. launched an artificial moon (satellite) into orbit up to 900 kilometres above the earth. At such heights there is scarcely any air to push against a satellite to slow it down. The satellite therefore keeps circling at a steady speed without the need for an engine. Since 1957 thousands of different types of SPACECRAFT have been launched into orbit and deep into space.

Above right: Apollo astronauts in pressurized spacesuits rehearsing a moon walk.
Below: The first space traveller, a dog named Laika, before its flight in *Sputnik II* (1957).

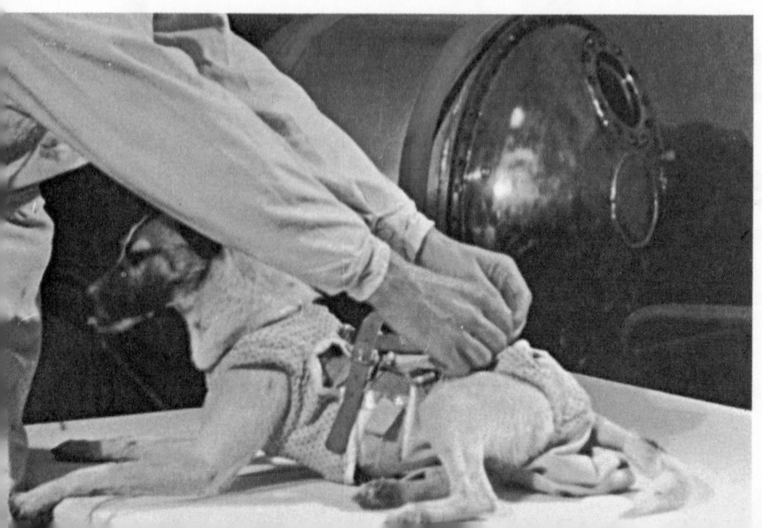

Astronauts

The Russians began the Space Age when they launched *Sputnik I* SPACECRAFT in 1957. They also pioneered the manned exploration of space. In April 1961 they sent a spacecraft manned by Yuri Gagarin into orbit around the EARTH. Gagarin was the first astronaut (*cosmonaut* in Russian). Many other Russian and U.S. astronauts have since travelled into space in one-, two-, and three-man spacecraft, and lived on board space laboratories. In July 1969 two U.S. astronauts made the first MOON landing.

Astronauts have to undergo a long period of training for their flights through space. They spend many hours in dummy spacecraft (simulators). These behave on the ground as the real spacecraft do in space. The men are whirled round in huge machines to get them used to the forces they will experience in space flight. But it is difficult to get them used to weightlessness.

As there is no air in space, astronauts carry a mixture of oxygen and other gases to breathe.

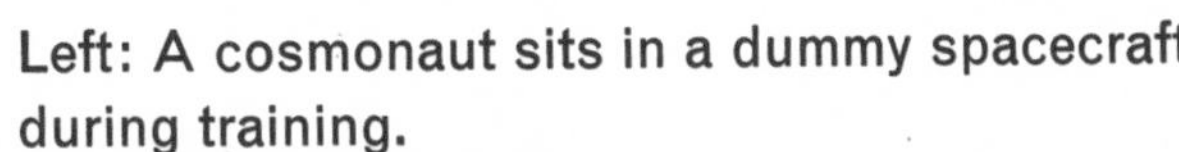

Left: A cosmonaut sits in a dummy spacecraft during training.

Below: U.S. astronauts land at sea and are then taken by helicopter to a recovery ship.

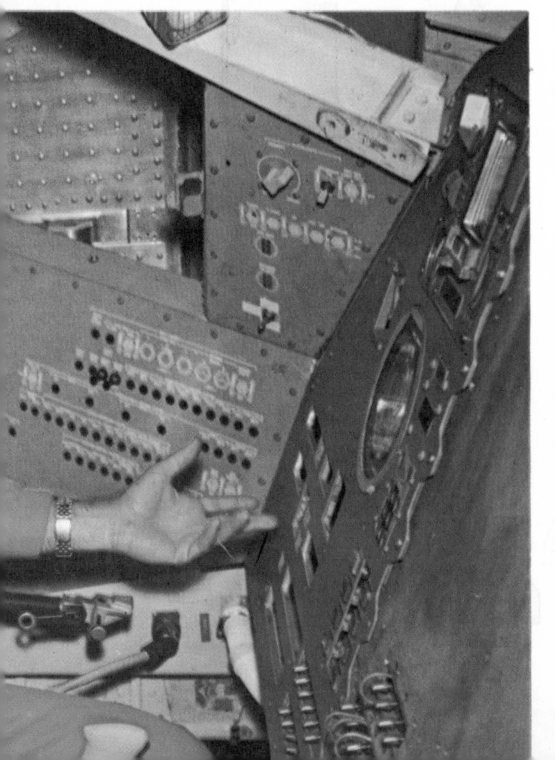

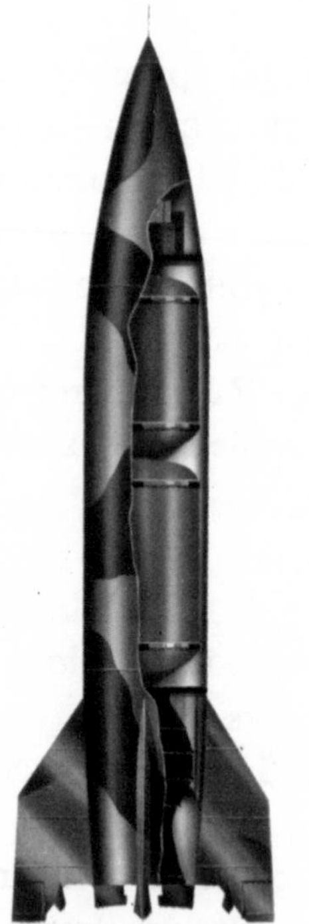

Rockets

Every SPACECRAFT is carried into space by a powerful rocket. The rocket is the only kind of engine that can work in space, where there is no air. It can do so because it carries its own oxygen to burn its fuel. Other engines, such as AIRCRAFT jet engines, rely on oxygen in the air to burn their fuel.

Above: The V2 rocket, first built in Germany during World War II.

Below: Bigger and bigger rockets have been built over the years.

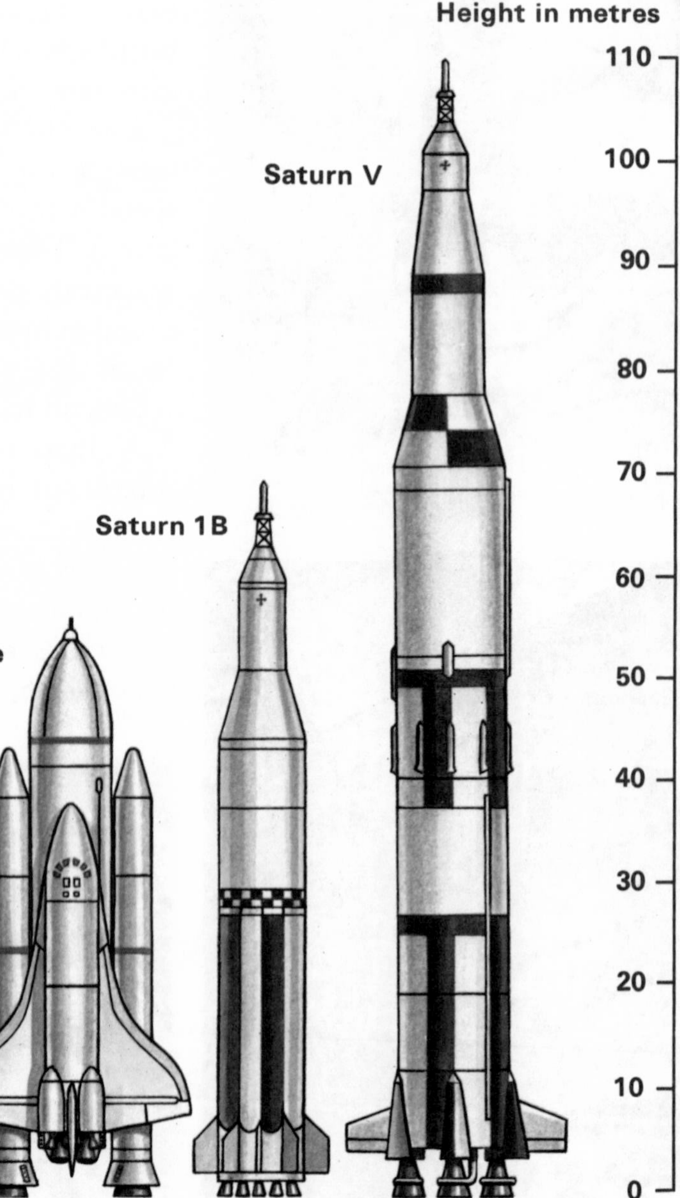

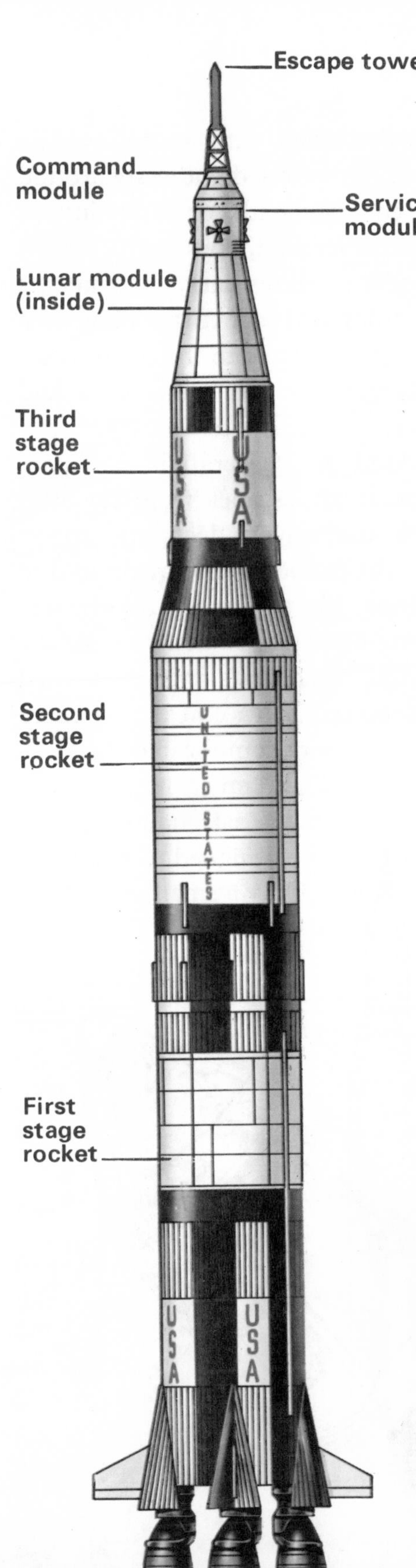

The rocket does, however, work much like a jet engine. It burns fuel in a chamber to make a stream, or jet, of hot gases. The action of the jet shooting backwards out of the rocket causes a reaction that pushes the rocket forwards.

Most space rockets use liquid fuels, such as kerosene (paraffin), and hydrogen gas that has been cooled into a liquid. Rockets need huge quantities of fuel for space flights.

Even so, no single-stage rocket is powerful enough to escape from the EARTH's pull or GRAVITY. It is necessary to string two or more rockets together so that the bottom ones give the top one a lift into space before dropping off.

A huge Saturn V rocket, weighing nearly 3000 tonnes, is needed to send a three-man rocket to the moon and back. The three rocket stages that make up Saturn V contain 41 rockets in all. The largest rockets are for propulsion and use about two tonnes of liquid every second. Smaller, solid rockets with a thrust of only 30 kilograms, are used to change direction. The direction and speed of a spacecraft are controlled by computers on board and by radar from earth.

Left: Saturn V Apollo moon rocket.
Below: Saturn V's engines.

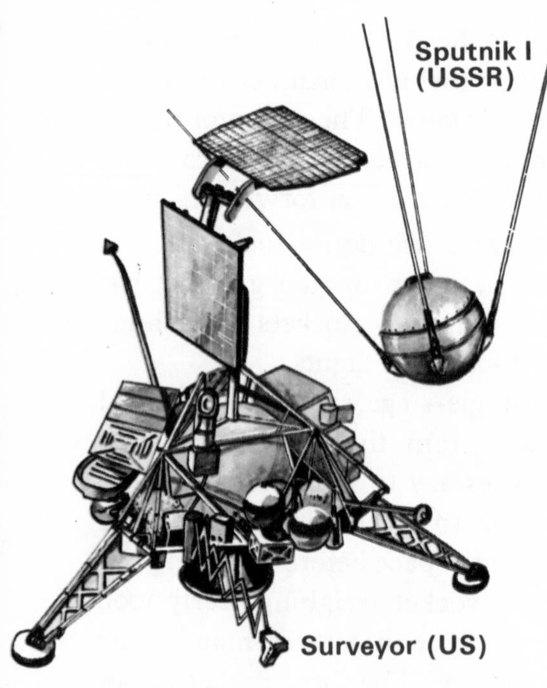

Spacecraft

The first craft launched into space was an artificial satellite. This circled endlessly around the EARTH in a constant path, or orbit, just as the MOON, a natural satellite, does.

Today, scientific satellites carry instruments to measure such things as magnetism. They then radio the measurements back to the earth. COMMUNICATIONS SATELLITES relay messages and TV programmes from country to country.

The second kind of spacecraft is the space probe. This spacecraft escapes from its orbit round the earth and travels deep into space. Scientists have sent probes to the moon and to the PLANETS Venus, Mars, Jupiter, Saturn and Mercury, carrying many instruments.

A third kind of spacecraft is the manned spacecraft that carries ASTRONAUTS. Manned spacecraft are much more complicated than unmanned spacecraft. They must have a life-support system to keep the astronauts alive in space. They must also be designed to bring the astronauts safely home. Only a small part of the spacecraft returns to the earth.

Above: Sputnik I, first man-made satellite of the earth, and a Surveyor moon probe.
Below: A Mariner Venus probe.
Below right: Part of the Apollo spacecraft.

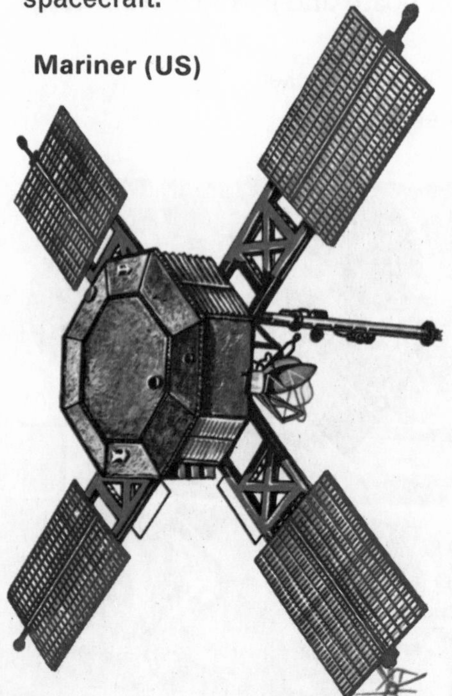

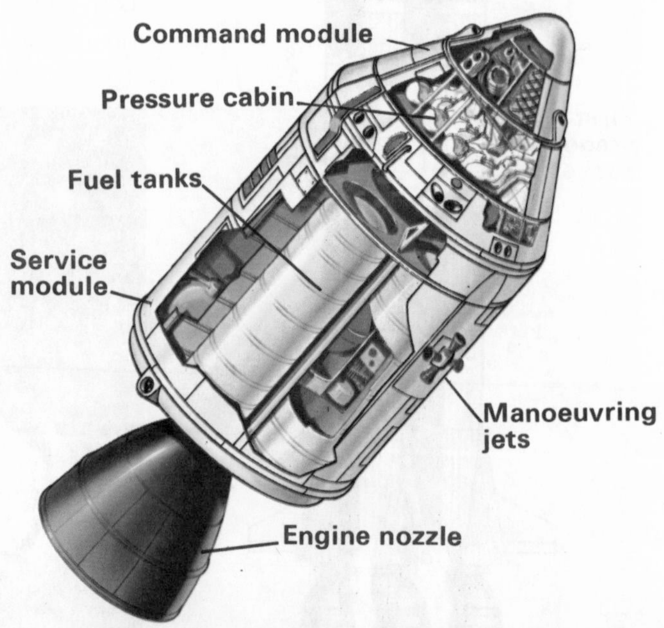

Skylab was an American space station launched in May 1973. It was sent into orbit, unmanned, by a Saturn V rocket. The three-man crew were sent up later in the Apollo Command and Service Modules launched by the smaller Saturn I rocket. The first crew manned the station for 28 days, the second stayed for 59 days and the third for 84 days. Skylab re-entered the earth's atmosphere in July 1979. It had been hoped that it would stay up long enough for the Space Shuttle to fly up to it.

The Space Shuttle is the first of a new family of space vehicles that can fly both in the atmosphere and also in space. It has large rocket motors at the rear; it carries a very large fuel tank and two massive solid rocket boosters. It weighs nearly 2000 tonnes and all the rockets fire together to launch it vertically. The main part of the Shuttle can stay 30 days in orbit and then must return through the atmosphere to land on a runway like an ordinary aircraft.

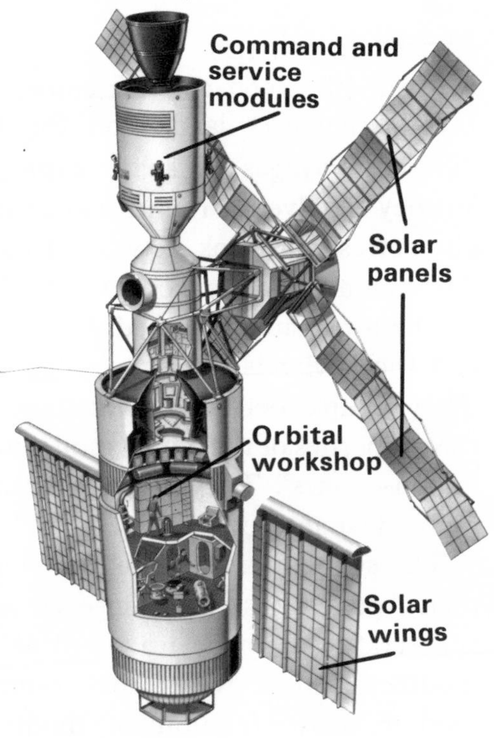

Above: The Skylab space station.
Below: Testing the Space Shuttle.

Moon landings

Between July 1969 and December 1972 twelve U.S. ASTRONAUTS landed on the MOON in six different voyages of space exploration. Each journey involved a round trip of over 800,000 kilometres, and took between 10 and 13 days. The first man on the moon was Neil Armstrong.

The astronauts explored the lunar highlands and the lowlands – the so-called *maria* (seas). They set up experiments, which included testing the properties of the moon's soil, and registering 'moon-quakes'. They also collected samples of moon dust and rocks.

The astronauts used the same kind of three-man Apollo SPACECRAFT on each journey. The spacecraft was made up of three sections, or modules. These were: the command (crew) module, service (equipment) module, and lunar module. The last was the craft which actually landed on the moon. Two astronauts descended in the lunar module, leaving the main craft circling above. After their moon walks they used the upper part of the lunar module to return to the main craft for the journey back to the EARTH.

Above: The Lunar Rover (moon buggy) used during the Apollo 17 landing, 1972.
Right: The Apollo Lunar Module.
Below: The Russian 'moonwalker' Lunokhod on the moon's surface.

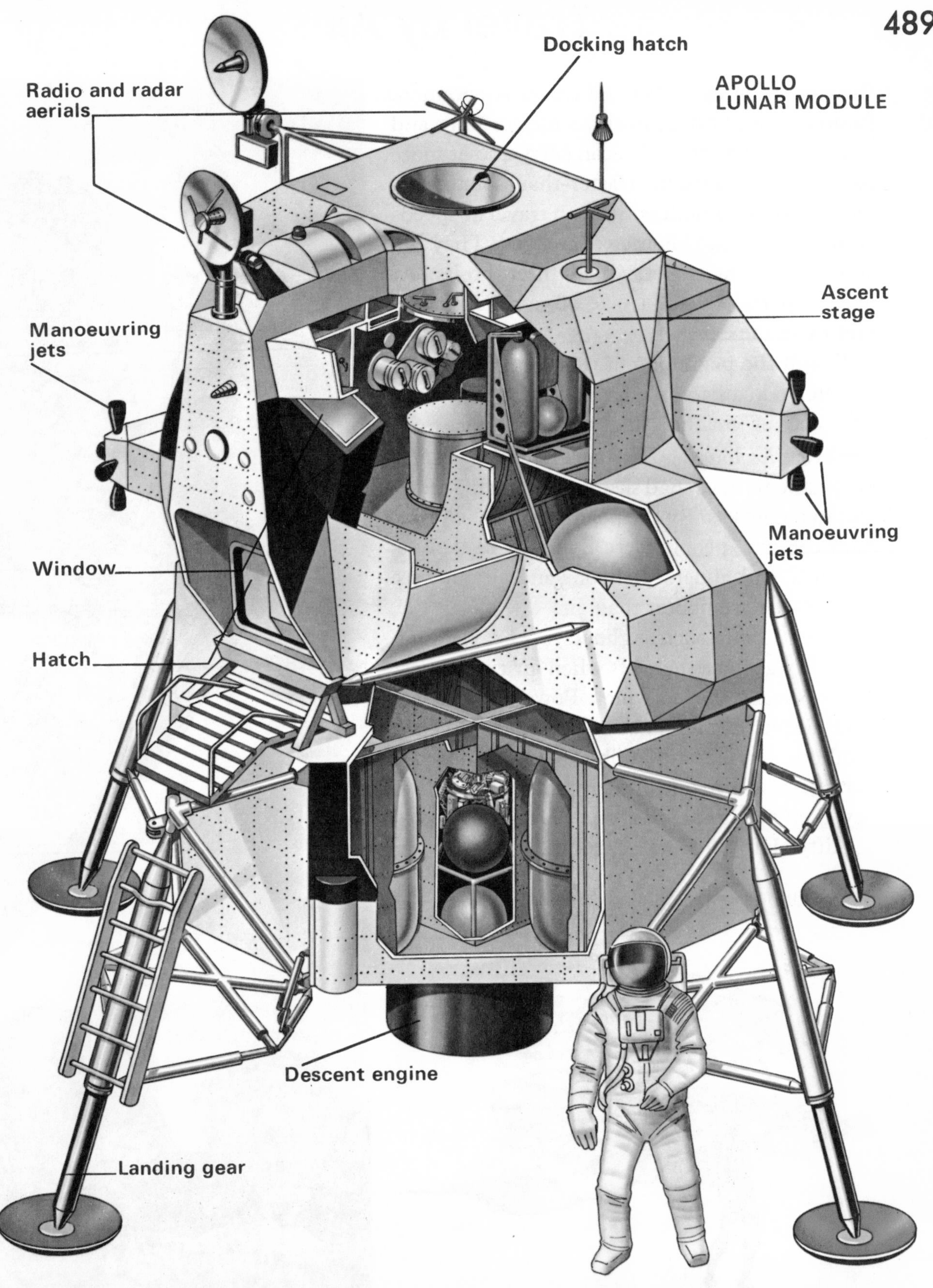
APOLLO
LUNAR MODULE
Docking hatch
Radio and radar aerials
Ascent stage
Manoeuvring jets
Manoeuvring jets
Window
Hatch
Descent engine
Landing gear

Travel by Air

We live in an age when air travel is common. Jumbo jet AIRLINERS, over 70 metres long and weighing 350 metric tons, can carry 400 or more passengers. Supersonic (faster-than-sound) airliners have been built which can travel at speeds of more than 2000 kilometres an hour. They can cross the ATLANTIC OCEAN in three hours. At busy airports, AIRCRAFT take off and land every minute of the day.

Yet, at the beginning of this century, no-one had flown in an aeroplane at all. Many men had dreamed of manned flight before this time, however. As long ago as the fifteenth century, LEONARDO DA VINCI had sketched flying machines and HELICOPTERS. By the beginning of the twentieth century, people were flying in BALLOONS, AIRSHIPS, and gliders. Balloons and airships are aircraft that are lighter than air.

Other aircraft, such as gliders, are heavier than air. They achieve their lift when air rushes past their specially shaped wings. Powered, heavier-than-air (aeroplane) flight began when two U.S. brothers, Orville and Wilbur WRIGHT, fitted a PETROL ENGINE to one of their gliders. They first flew their machine, *Flyer*, on 17 December 1903, at Kitty Hawk in North Carolina.

Below: Otto Lilienthal gliding (1890s).

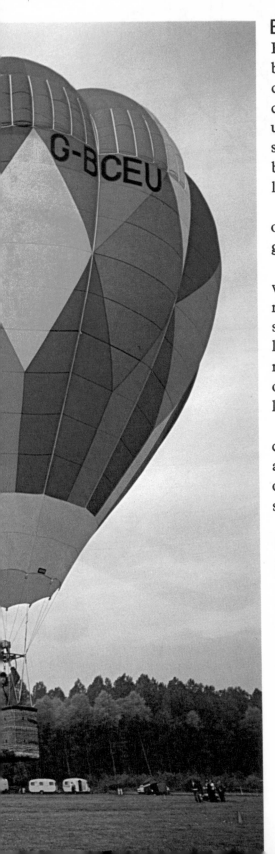

Balloons and airships

French brothers Joseph and Etienne Montgolfier built the first balloon craft in 1783. It flew because it contained hot air, which is lighter than cold air. Montgolfier balloons had a fire slung under the balloon to keep the air hot. At about the same time, another Frenchman, J. A. C. Charles, built a balloon that contained hydrogen, the lightest of all gases.

Ballooning became a new and exciting means of travel and a popular sport. Today, people still go ballooning for pleasure.

The main problem with balloons is that they will go only where the WIND blows them. They need an engine and propeller before they can be steered. In 1900 Ferdinand von Zeppelin fitted lightweight PETROL ENGINES to a 195-metre-long rigid balloon. This craft, called a Zeppelin, was one of the first really successful steerable balloons, or airships.

Other Zeppelins and similar craft eventually carried passengers across the ATLANTIC (in 1919) and around the world (in 1929). But after a series of fires and crashes in the 1920s and 1930s airships went out of use.

Left: Hot air ballooning (1970s).
Below: The British airship R.100 (1930).

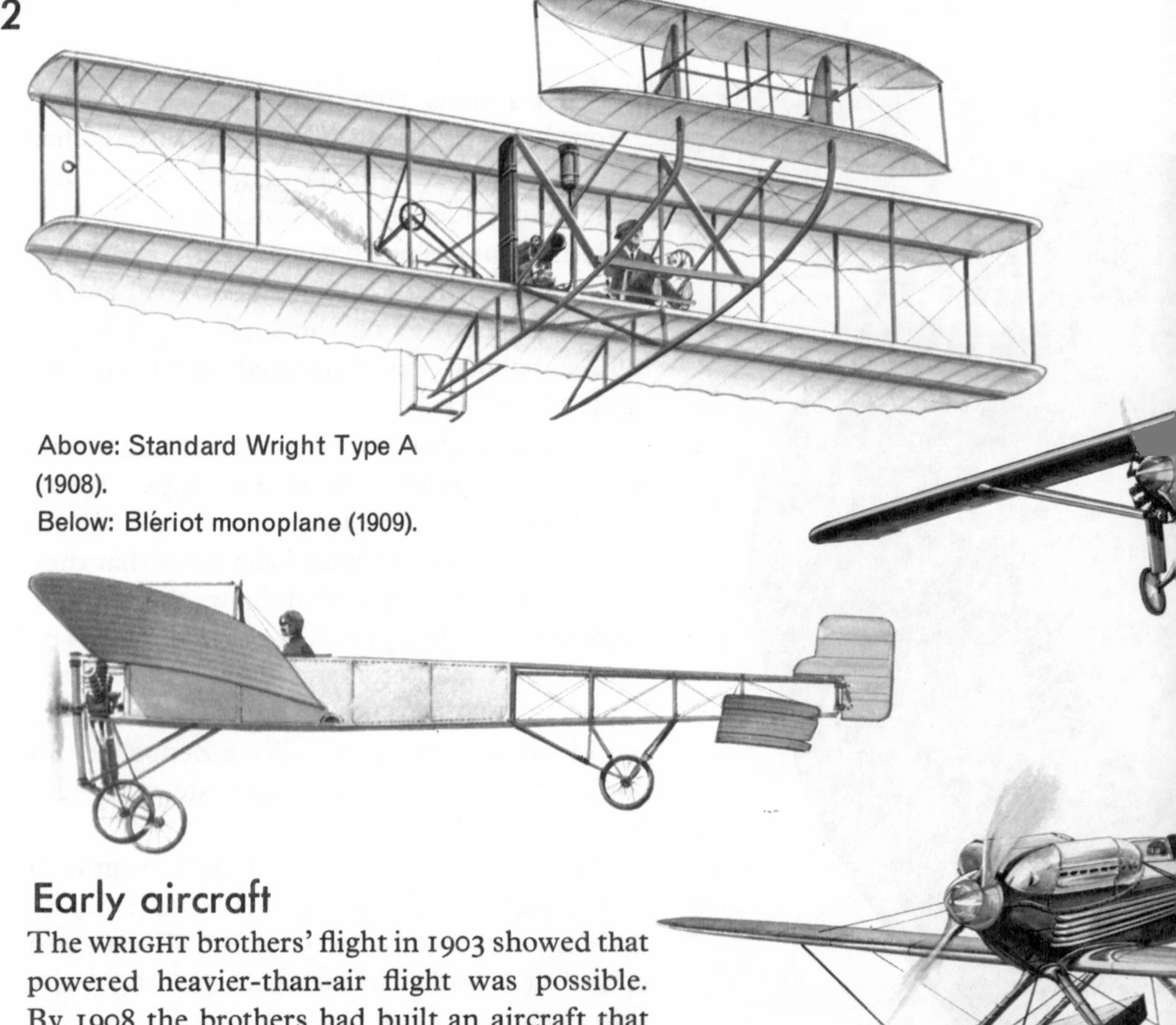

Above: Standard Wright Type A (1908).
Below: Blériot monoplane (1909).

Early aircraft

The WRIGHT brothers' flight in 1903 showed that powered heavier-than-air flight was possible. By 1908 the brothers had built an aircraft that could remain in the air for more than two hours. In the same year they gave flying demonstrations in EUROPE that caused a sensation.

The 'flying machine' developed rapidly from then on. In 1909 Louis Blériot flew across the English Channel. Ten years later John Alcock and Arthur Whitten Brown flew non-stop across the ATLANTIC OCEAN. In the years between, aircraft developed out of all recognition, especially during WORLD WAR I. Small fighter planes flew faster, farther and higher than anything before. Bombers were many times heavier than the fighters and could be converted into passenger-carrying airliners.

Above: Supermarine seaplane (1931).

Below: Lindbergh's *Spirit of St Louis.*

The aeroplanes of today are very different from the flimsy wood-and-cloth machines of the early 1900s. Yet they work on the same principles. Four forces act on a plane travelling through the air – weight, lift, thrust, and drag.

The weight acts downwards. It must be balanced by an upward lift. A plane gets its lift from its wings. They are more rounded on the upper surface than underneath. They develop lift when they are moved through the air because the air pressure on top is reduced.

Thrust is the force needed to move the plane through the air. In early planes a propeller turned by a PETROL ENGINE provided the thrust.

Drag is the force a plane experiences as it pushes through the air. Aircraft are designed to be as streamlined as possible to reduce drag. The first really 'streamlined' airliner was the Douglas D.C.2 of 1933. The design made the D.C.2 the fastest and most comfortable airliner of its day.

Above: Douglas D.C.2 of 1933.

Jet aircraft

Most modern aircraft are propelled by a stream of hot gases from a jet engine, or GAS TURBINE.

The pilot controls his aircraft in flight in much the same way as the pioneers did, by moving control surfaces on the wings and tail. He can make the wings dip left or right by moving the ailerons on the rear surfaces of the wings. He can increase lift at take-off and landing by lowering the wing flaps. He can make the nose go up or down by moving the elevators on the tailplane. The rudder, which is on the tail fin, is used to turn the nose left or right. In flight, the automatic pilot normally operates the controls.

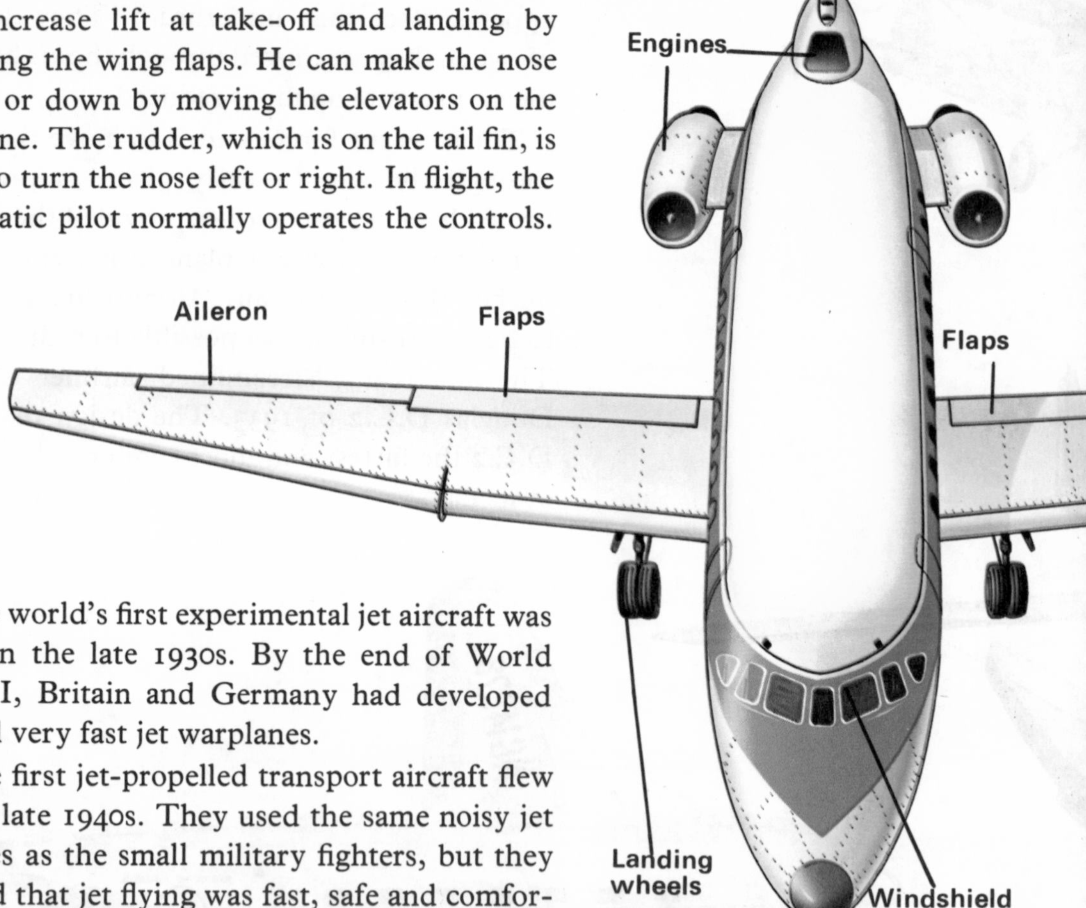

The world's first experimental jet aircraft was built in the late 1930s. By the end of World War II, Britain and Germany had developed several very fast jet warplanes.

The first jet-propelled transport aircraft flew in the late 1940s. They used the same noisy jet engines as the small military fighters, but they proved that jet flying was fast, safe and comfortable. Every year more and more passengers wanted to fly in the new jets, so much bigger versions were planned. They required very large and different engines that had to be much quieter than the older ones. They were called fanjets.

The first of these large fanjet airliners was the Boeing 747. More 'wide-bodied' jets followed, such as the D.C. 10 and the Airbus.

Above: The control surfaces on a plane include the ailerons and flaps on the wings, and the elevators on the tail. Not seen here is the rudder at the rear of the tail.

Above: Experimental Whittle jet aircraft E28/39.
Below: Caravelle jet airliner (1959).
Bottom: Lockheed TriStar wide-body fanjet.

The growth of the world's fleet of jet airliners was slowed down by the oil crisis of 1973 and the rise in the price of aviation fuel. But the number of passengers is still increasing and another family of jet airliners is being built. These include the Boeing 757 and 767 in the U.S.A. and the Airbus A 310 in Europe. These aircraft have engines that make much less noise and burn less fuel.

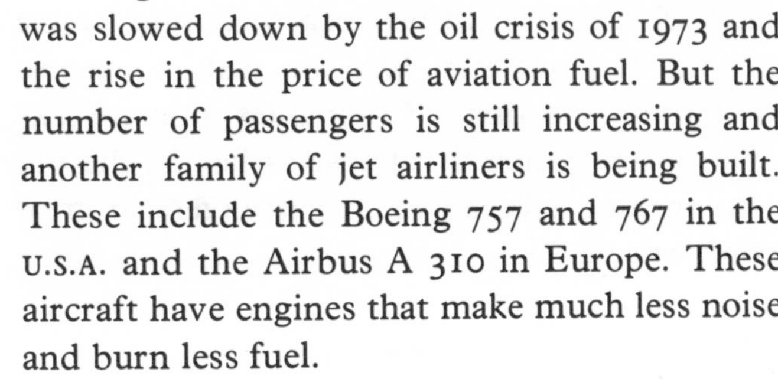

Passenger aircraft

Over 250 million passengers fly every year. Many fly as far as 9000 kilometres at a time but most people travel much shorter distances.

Small jet airliners holding 150 to 250 passengers are a very common form of transport. They carry millions of holidaymakers every year to places such as the Mediterranean and the Canary Islands. Some propeller-driven aircraft still fly today, ferrying 40 to 100 passengers at a time from the small airports to the main ones. Remote regions may be served by small air taxis which can hold between three and twelve people. Businessmen hire air taxis to get to important meetings. Companies operate executive jets which fly almost as fast as the big Boeings and take up to 20 passengers in great comfort.

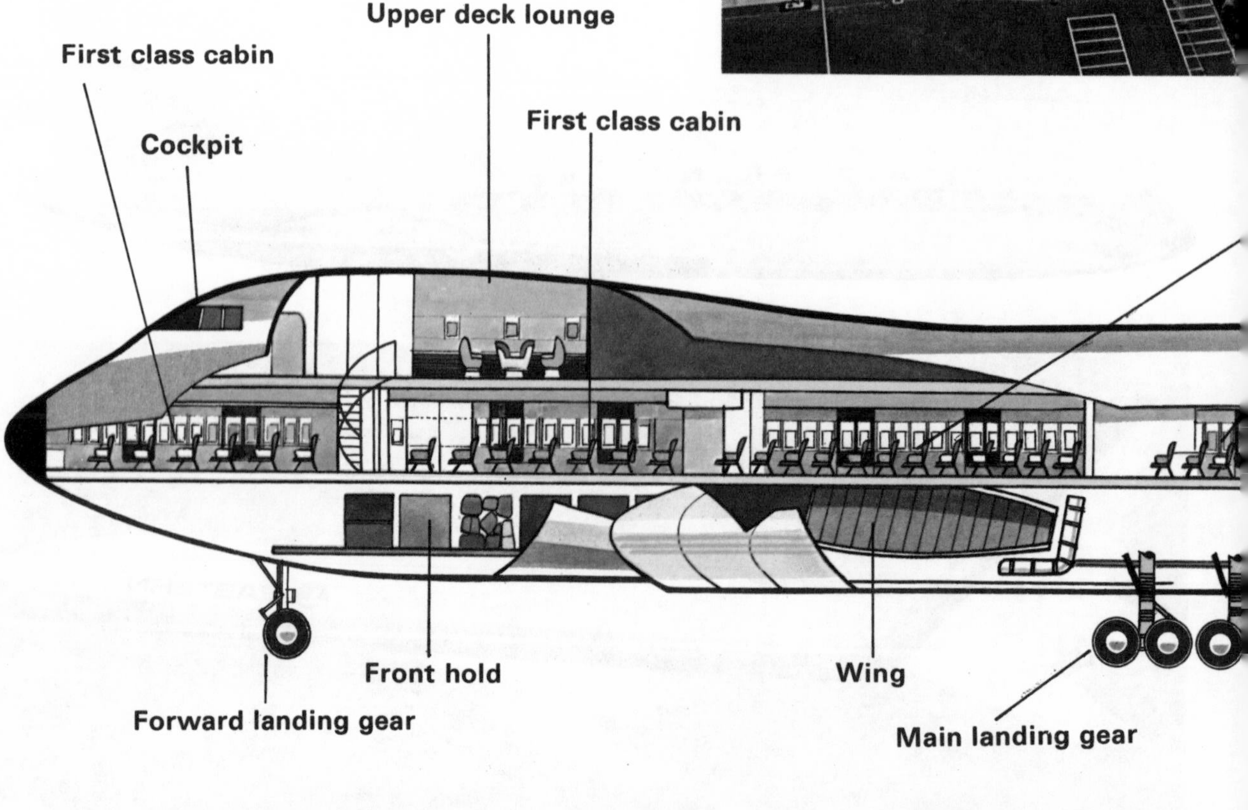

Upper deck lounge
First class cabin
Cockpit
First class cabin
Front hold
Wing
Forward landing gear
Main landing gear

Airports

The first airports were grass fields and were called aerodromes. As aircraft became bigger and heavier, concrete runways were built. Today, giant international airports may contain as many as 30,000 full-time workers at any one time, and as many passengers. They are really like cities with their own shops, hospitals and restaurants.

Finding a site for a new airport is a difficult job, as there is rarely enough space near to a big city. An airport may be as far as 80 kilometres from the city. Getting all the passengers to the airport can be a problem.

Left: Charles de Gaulle airport in Paris, France.
Below: The Boeing 747, the world's largest airliner.

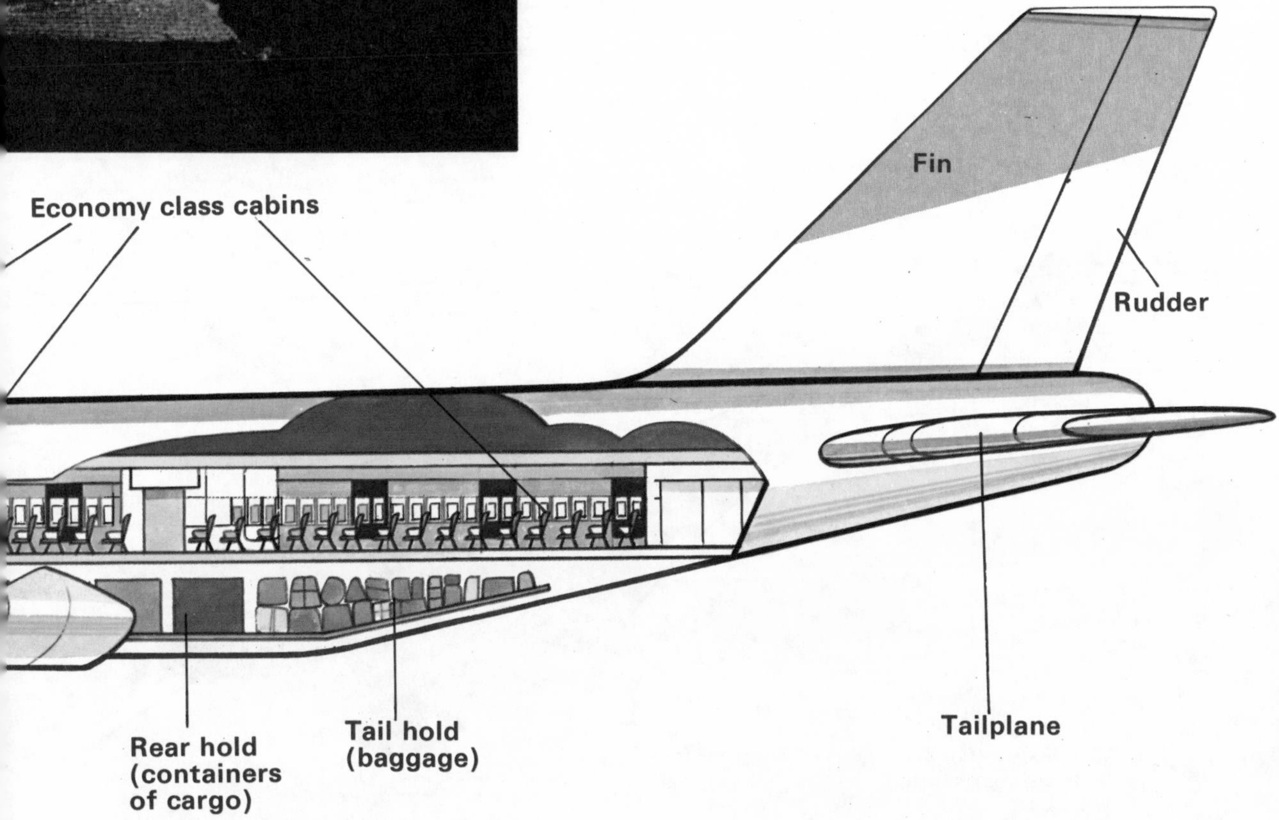

Fin
Economy class cabins
Rudder
Rear hold (containers of cargo)
Tail hold (baggage)
Tailplane

Supersonic flight

Supersonic speeds are those that are greater than the speed of sound (sonic speed). Several modern fighter aircraft and one airliner can fly at supersonic speed. The Anglo-French *Concorde* flies at 2333 kilometres an hour. (At the height *Concorde* flies, sound travels through the air at 1060 kilometres an hour.)

AIRCRAFT that fly so fast are shaped quite differently from the other airliners. The air cannot move out of the way of the aircraft quickly enough and it becomes compressed and hot. This increases the drag, so supersonic aircraft have to be carefully streamlined with a needle-like nose and thin, swept-back wings. Air-conditioning systems have to be fitted to remove the excess heat from the cabins.

Above: The Tornado supersonic warplane.
Below: The Anglo-French *Concorde*.

Right: The F-16 supersonic fighter.
Below right: A model in a water flow tunnel.

Wind tunnels

An AIRCRAFT designer first tries out a design for a new aircraft at ground level. He tests a scale model in a WIND tunnel. In the tunnel, air is blown past the model. This creates the same conditions as if the model were actually moving through still air.

The designer observes the airflow over the model and takes measurements of lift and drag. His observations and measurements will show him how he can improve his design. He must then carefully scale up his design to build a test plane, or prototype.

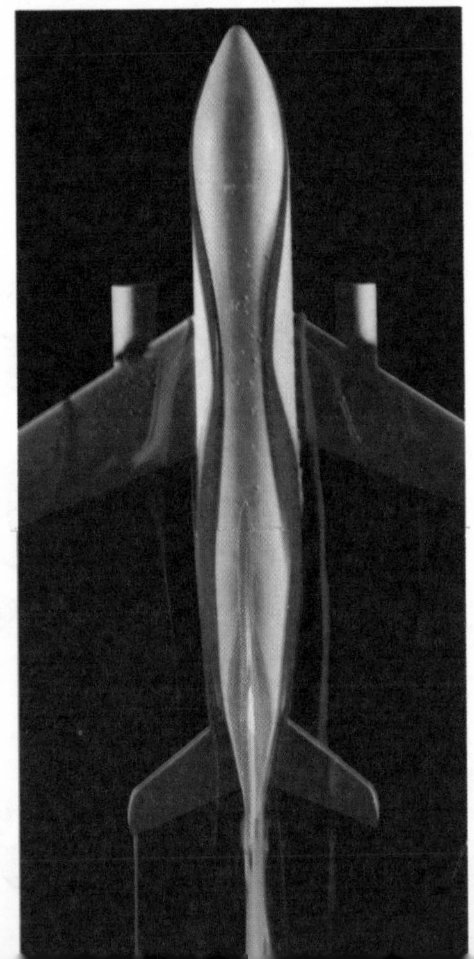

Automatic pilots

It would be very tiring for an airline pilot to keep his hands on the controls for a whole flight lasting up to ten hours. The automatic pilot does this for him. The pilot controls the take-off and the start of the climb and then programmes the aircraft to fly at the desired height and speed.

Helicopters

Helicopters can fly forwards, backwards, up, down, and sideways. They can also hover and do not need a runway. They can land and take off from a flat roof or a clearing in the jungle.

Helicopters are widely used by the armed forces. They are useful for sea and MOUNTAIN rescue operations. In some cities they are used for regular passenger flights.

The helicopter has a many-bladed rotor on top. This is driven by the engine. The rotor blades are the same shape as wings and they provide lift for the helicopter when they turn. A small rotor on the tail points the helicopter the right way. The pilot manoeuvres his craft by altering the angle of the rotor blades. The spinning rotor also propels the helicopter. The helicopter cannot fly as fast as winged aircraft.

Above: This Swiss helicopter is fitted with skis for landing on snow-covered mountainsides.

Below: Igor Sikorsky designed the first practical helicopter in 1939. Modern helicopters have a similar design.

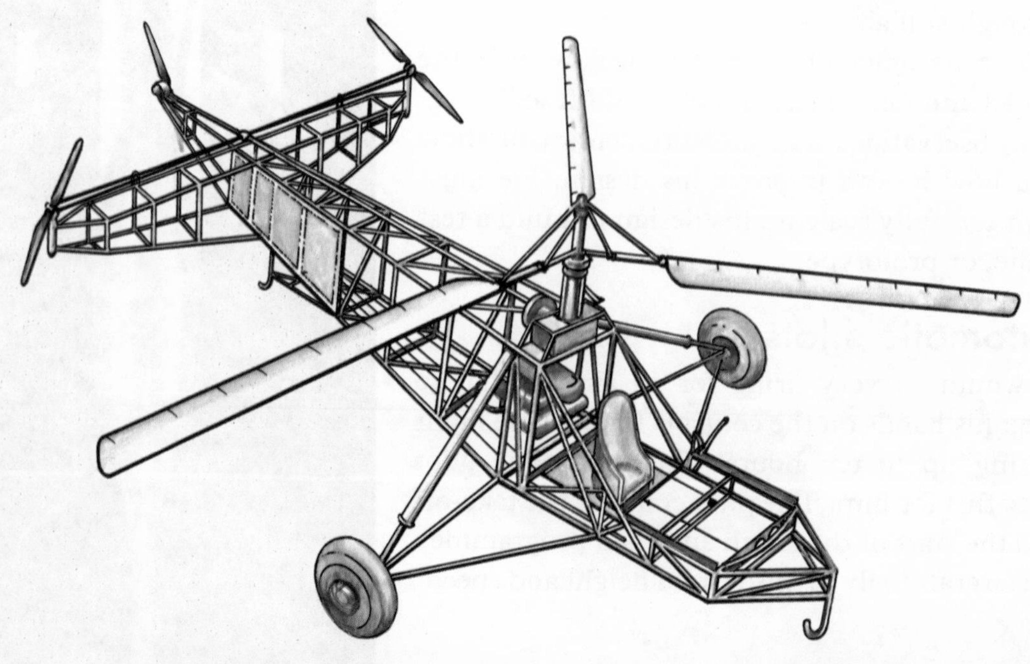

Vertical take-off aircraft

The British Aerospace *Harrier* is a jet warplane which can take off and land vertically. It does not work like a helicopter or an ordinary jet aircraft. Instead of pumping jets of air out backwards, it pumps the air out through nozzles in the sides.

When the nozzles face downwards, the aircraft can rise or come down vertically. When the *Harrier* is right off the ground the nozzles are slowly turned backwards and it moves forward. It gradually gains speed until, with the nozzles pointing straight back, the *Harrier* becomes a jet fighter capable of flying at near supersonic speeds.

The *Harrier* operates from fields and clearings in woods.

Below: The *Harrier* jump jet.

Ships and Boats

There are today a great number of different kinds of ships and boats. Some of these ships carry passengers. Many more carry cargo (goods). Cargo ships are often called FREIGHTERS. They are used mainly for carrying large amounts of heavy goods. Such loads would be much too expensive to send by AIRCRAFT. Bulk liquids, such as OIL, are usually transported by TANKERS.

It is probable that primitive man was able to travel by water long before he had learned to tame animals or use the wheel. At first he clung to floating logs. Later, he found out how to use a paddle, to make the log go where he wanted.

Over thousands of years, the floating log developed into rafts and CANOES. Then came the age of SAILING SHIPS, which ended little more than a hundred years ago. The STEAMSHIPS that replaced them were faster and more reliable.

Among the most recent developments have been the introduction of HYDROFOILS and HOVERCRAFT, which skim over the surface of the water.

Arab dhow

Chinese junk

Canoes

Early man made the first practical boat when he hollowed out a log so that he could sit inside it. This kind of vessel, generally called the dugout canoe, is still used today in parts of AFRICA and in some of the islands of the PACIFIC OCEAN.

The canoes used by many of the Pacific islanders are outriggers. These are made by lashing the canoe to another log, which acts as a float and makes the canoe more stable. Some craft are like two canoes fixed side-by-side and are called catamarans.

The AMERICAN INDIANS improved upon the dugout with the birchbark canoe. They stretched the BARK of BIRCH trees over a wooden frame. In the ARCTIC, the ESKIMOS developed a fast canoe called the kayak. Kayaks are made of animal skins stretched over a wooden frame, with a hole in the top for the canoeist.

Another type of canoe is the coracle, which was used by the ancient Britons. This is a round, fragile vessel made with animal skins stretched over a light frame.

Above left: A modern passenger liner designed for long-distance pleasure cruising.
Below: Boats from many parts of the world which have been in use for hundreds of years.

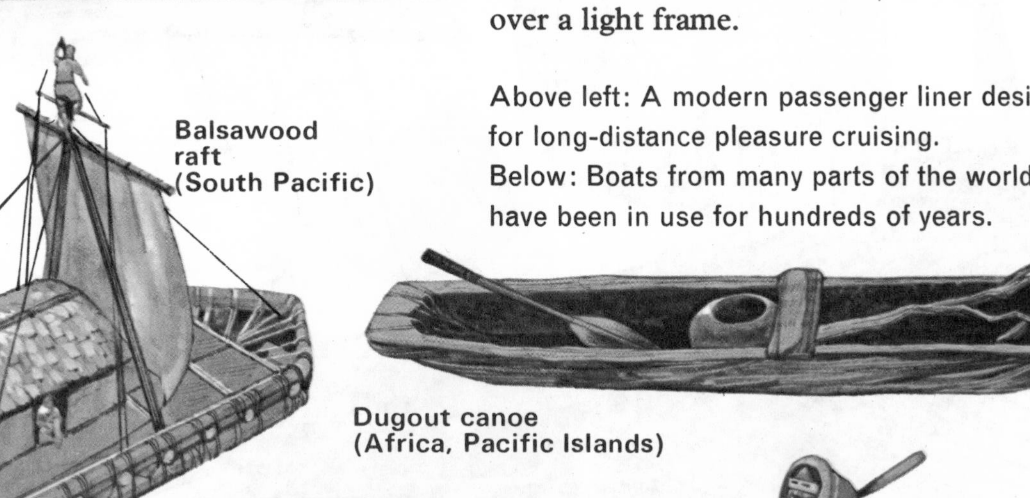

Egyptian galley (1500 B.C.)

Sailing ships

The WIND is a source of energy. Early man discovered how to use the wind to move his CANOE. He put a hide or a piece of cloth on a pole, and stood it upright. He had invented the sail.

The first big sea-going vessels were built by the Cretans. They were galleys – open vessels worked by slaves pulling the oars. The ANCIENT EGYPTIANS, the PHOENICIANS, the GREEKS, and the ROMANS developed the galley as a fast fighting vessel. Their galleys had a sail, but still relied mainly on oars. The later galleys had two or more banks of oars to give extra power. A trireme, for example, had three rows of oars.

FROM GALLEY TO CLIPPER

Roman cargo ship (A.D. 200)

Greek trireme (300 B.C.)

In about A.D. 1000 a new type of sail came into use. It was the lateen, or fore-and-aft sail, which enabled ships to sail into the wind as well as with it. Sailing ships developed slowly until the fifteenth century. It was then that the number of masts and sails was increased, giving greater efficiency and speed.

The design of sailing ships continued to improve for several hundred years. The fastest merchant sailing ships ever built were the clippers. These ships were graceful and very fast, being able to reach a speed of 20 knots (37 kilometres an hour). They were built especially for the Far Eastern TEA and wool trades.

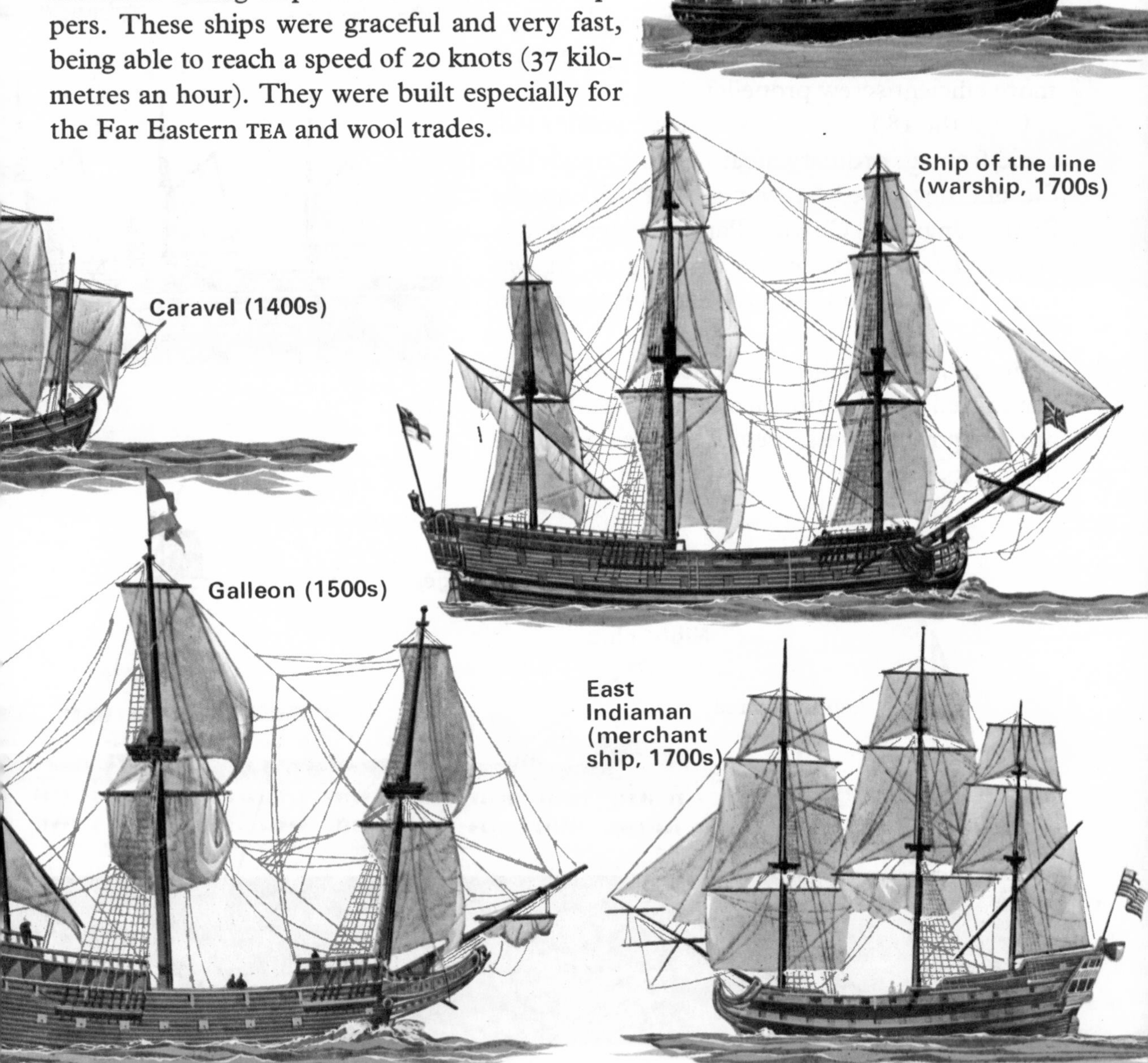

Steamships

In the early nineteenth century, when the first clippers were being built, men were already trying to find a way of using the newly invented STEAM ENGINE to drive ships. In 1807 the American engineer Robert FULTON built the first successful steamboat, the *Clermont*. In 1819 the U.S. ship *Savannah* became the first steamship to cross the ATLANTIC.

Like all the early steamships, the *Savannah* was propelled by paddle wheels. By the 1840s the paddle wheel was being replaced by the much more efficient screw propeller.

Until the 1890s, the power in steamships still came from an ordinary steam engine much like the one developed by James WATT. Then the British engineer Charles Parsons developed a STEAM TURBINE that would drive ships. It was more powerful and worked better than earlier engines.

From the 1900s the largest ocean LINERS have been fitted with steam-turbine engines. Even a nuclear-powered vessel requires a steam turbine to turn its propellers.

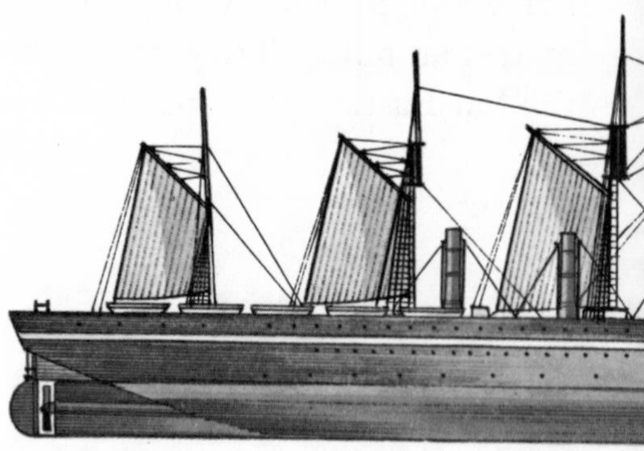

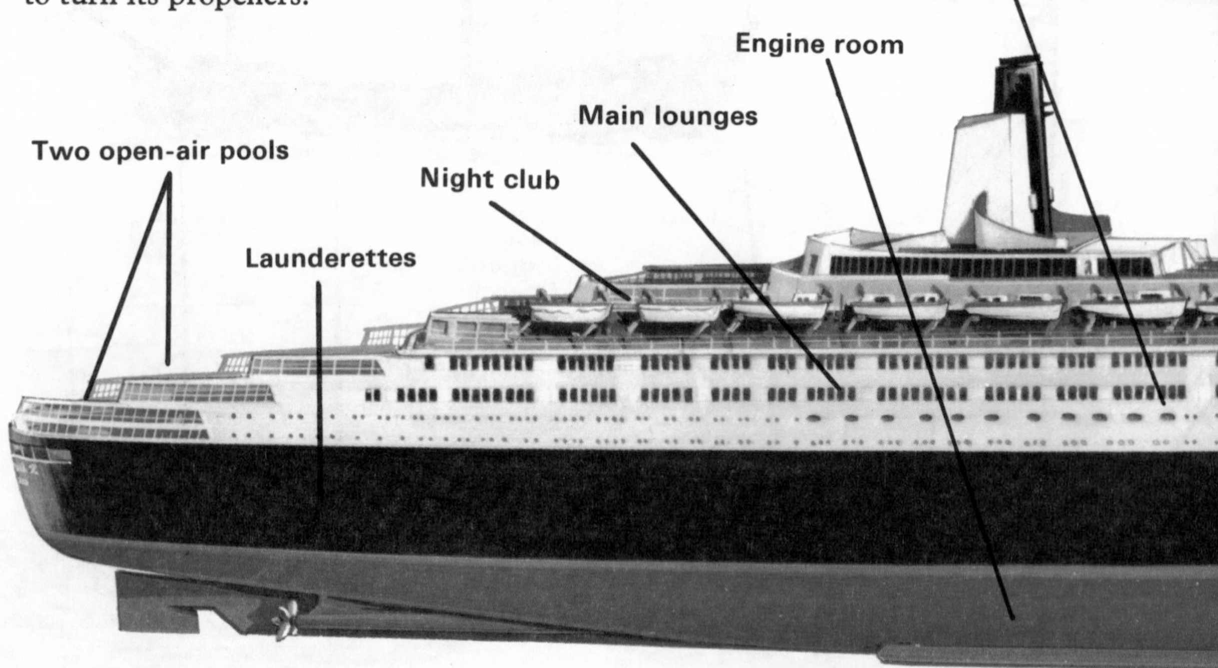

Liners

The ocean liner is the most luxurious of all the ships at sea. The finest, such as the *France* and the *Queen Elizabeth 2*, are like huge floating hotels. They have comfortable cabins for passengers, and fine restaurants and lounges. They also have swimming pools, sun decks, and many other facilities for entertainment and sport. Most liners have CINEMAS, ballrooms, hairdressing salons, and SHOPS.

Liners differ from other big ships in having a large superstructure (the part of a ship above deck level). Most liners are fitted with underwater side fins called stabilizers. In rough weather the stabilizers reduce the rolling of the ship.

Above left: Robert Fulton's paddle steamer *Clermont*.
Left: Brunel's *Great Eastern* was a very large steamship launched in 1859.
Below: The *Queen Elizabeth 2* provides a regular service across the Atlantic during summer. In the winter it is used for cruises.

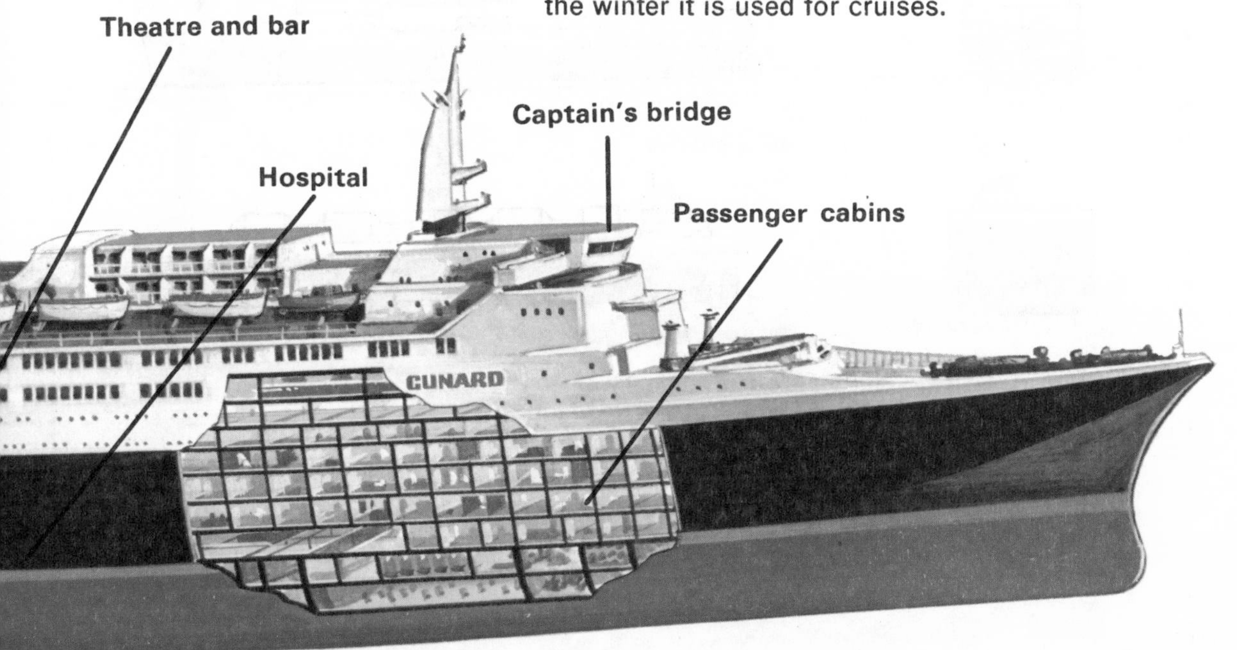

Above: A modern freighter. Note the tall lifting masts, or derricks, on deck. They are used to lift cargo into and out of the ship's holds. Below: The shapes of three common kinds of freighters.

Freighters

There are more freighters, or cargo ships, in use today than any other kind of sea-going vessel. These ships can carry almost any cargo around the world. They may carry general cargo or be designed and equipped for special use. Meat and FRUIT carriers, for example, contain large refrigerators to keep their cargo fresh during a long sea voyage. Container ships are designed to carry goods in standard-sized containers. This makes the goods easier to load and unload. Many freighters have cabins for a few passengers.

Freighters that sail to a more or less regular timetable are known as cargo liners. Tramps are freighters that sail when and where there is cargo to be moved. Coasters are small, general-purpose freighters that remain mostly in coastal waters.

Today, many freighters have DIESEL ENGINES, and not STEAM ENGINES OR TURBINES.

Coastal freighter

Bulk carrier

Container carrier

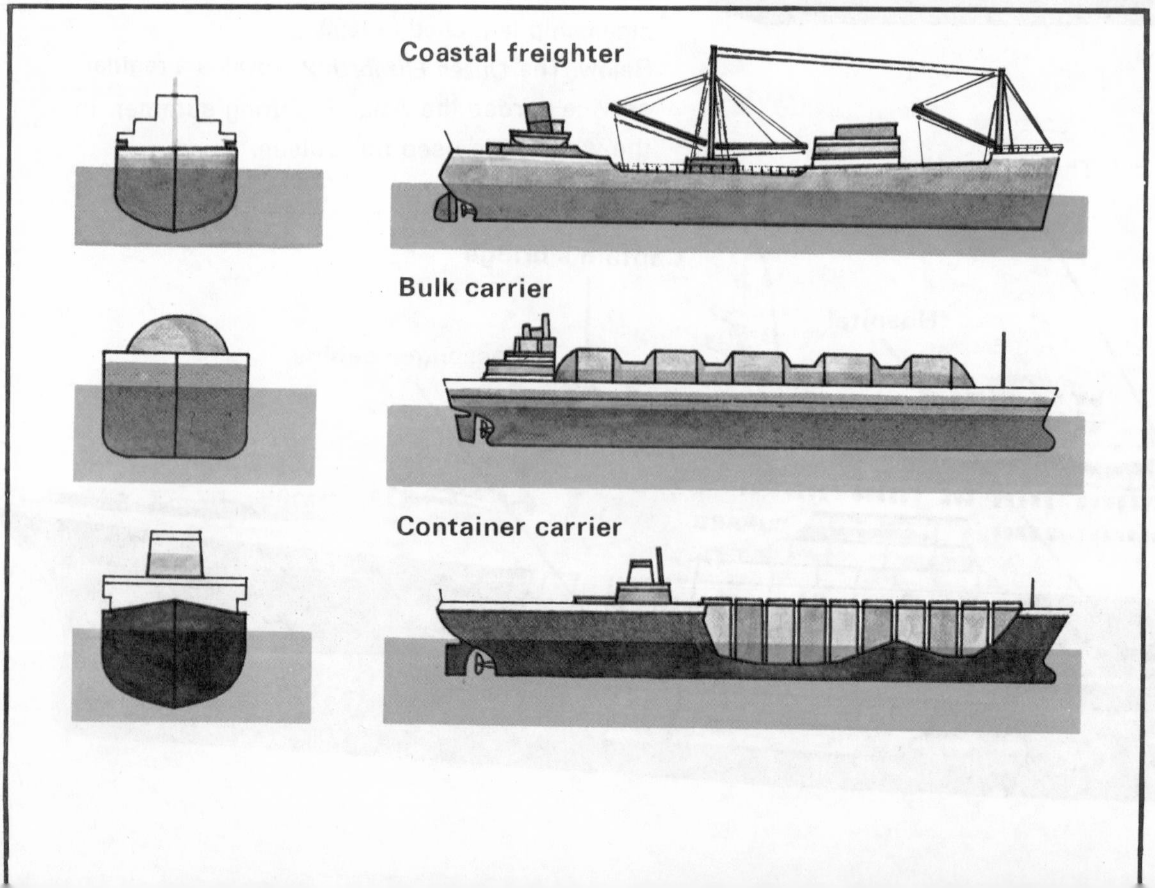

Tankers

Tankers carry liquid cargoes, particularly crude OIL, or petroleum, in bulk. The biggest ships afloat now are oil tankers. The giant Japanese tanker *Globtik Tokyo*, for example, is 379 metres long, and 62 metres wide. Most tankers are too big to be able to use existing ports. They usually discharge their cargo by pipeline away from the shore at the end of long jetties.

Below: A tanker loaded with crude oil. It rides low in the water because it is fully laden. It has a superstructure aft (at the stern). This contains the navigation bridge and the crew's living quarters. The oil is carried in separate tanks within the vessel.

Above: A car ferry unloading.
Below: Tugs towing a huge oil tanker close to shore.

Ferries

Ferries are boats that are used for short journeys on water, such as wide RIVERS, estuaries, and sea channels. For example, a large number of ferries cross the English Channel. The cross-channel passenger ferries connect with trains on either side. They are like small LINERS, and are fitted with stabilizers and powerful engines (often DIESELS). They can keep up their speed even in bad weather.

Different ferries are designed to carry different vehicles – railway coaches (which are always loaded at the stern), private cars, and commercial vans and trucks. These ferries usually have a large lower deck to hold the vehicles and an upper deck for passengers. In some countries HOVERCRAFT are also used as passenger and car ferries.

Tugs and icebreakers

Tugs are designed for towing and pushing ships and barges. One of their main jobs is getting large LINERS and FREIGHTERS in and out of port. These ships are often too big to move safely in ports and harbours under their own power. There are ocean-going tugs designed for salvage work, that is, towing damaged ships to safety.

The icebreaker is another kind of ship that helps other vessels. Icebreakers are strong, thick-hulled ships, designed to break up sea ice. They are used to keep northern shipping lanes open during the winter.

Hydrofoils

As a boat moves, the water tends to slow it down. This is called drag. The more of the hull that is in the water, the greater is the drag. One kind of boat, the hydrofoil, overcomes drag by lifting itself out of the water as it moves along. Attached to the hydrofoil's hull are underwater wings, called foils. Movement of the foils through the water produces an upward lift. As the boat goes faster, the hull is lifted out of the water. Some hydrofoils can travel at speeds of over 100 kilometres an hour.

Hovercraft

Like the HYDROFOIL, the hovercraft is able to skim over the water. Unlike the hydrofoil, some hovercraft can also travel across the land. They are amphibians. The hovercraft gets its lift by riding on a 'cushion' of air at slightly above atmospheric pressure. The air supply needed to maintain the cushion is provided by one or more fans. Nearly all amphibious hovercraft are fitted with a flexible 'skirt'. This helps to stop air leaking from the cushion, and allows the craft to ride over obstructions.

A hovercraft is propelled by air propellers, water propellers, or air jets from the fan, often driven by a GAS TURBINE engine. The craft is steered by swivelling the propellers, or by rudders that move in the propellers' airstream.

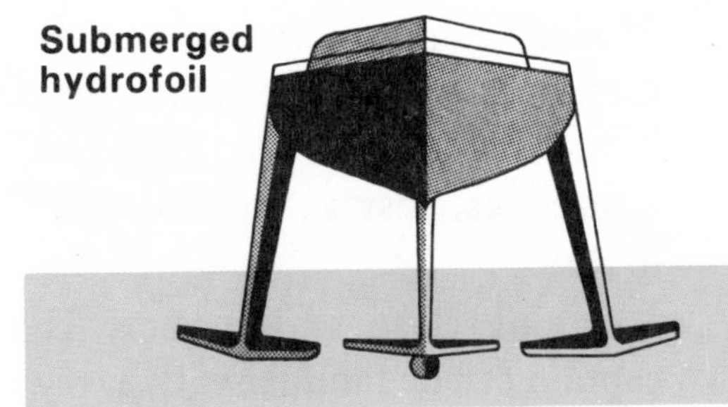

Two types of hydrofoils, with the hulls out of the water.

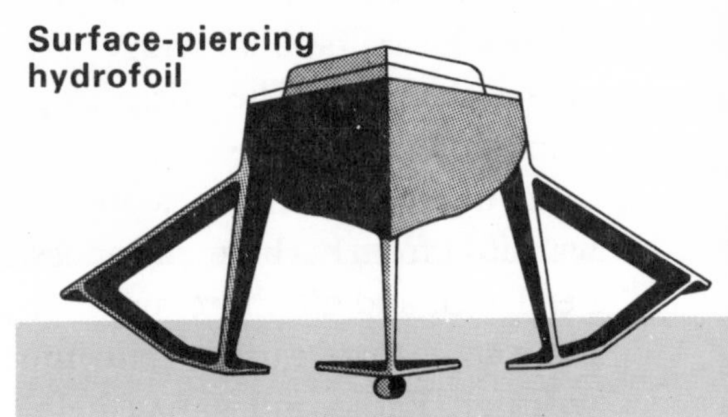

Below: One of the SR-N4 hovercraft used as a car ferry across the English Channel. It can carry 30 cars and 250 passengers across in only 35 minutes.

Safety At Sea

Modern ships are fine pieces of engineering, but they still have to fight against the elements. They have to avoid rocks and wrecks, shallows and sandbanks, just as the old SAILING SHIPS had to do.

Sailing close to the shore is not easy. No captain can be familiar with every piece of coastline or navigation channel. So floating markers, or buoys, are used to indicate safe channels and such dangers as sandbanks. Many ports have pilots who are familiar with every twist and turn of the channels. They help to guide the larger ships into the port.

At night, LIGHTHOUSES and LIGHTSHIPS flash warnings from harbour entrances, as well as from headlands and off-shore rocks. Weatherships remain at sea to give up-to-date information on the weather. Radio and RADAR help to make navigation more accurate and reduce the danger of ships wandering off course. They are very valuable at night and when there is FOG or mist.

However, despite all these aids, hundreds of ships are lost at sea each year. Some sink in heavy seas or collide with other ships. Others are wrecked when they are driven on to rocks by HURRICANE-force WINDS. Fire is another great danger. Fortunately, most ships these days can call for immediate assistance on the radio with a 'Mayday' distress call (from the French *m'aidez* – help me), or an SOS transmission in MORSE code. They may also fire off a signal rocket. When this happens, neighbouring ships go to the rescue. LIFEBOATS and coastguards may also give assistance.

Right: Four kinds of buoys. Red cone-shaped buoys mark the right-hand side of a channel going into harbour. Black-and-white buoys mark the middle of a channel.

Red cone-shaped buoy

Mid-channel buoy

Gong buoy

Lighted buoy

Lighthouses and lightships

Seafaring countries usually have a large number of lighthouses around their shores. Around the British Isles, for example, there are some 350 major lighthouses, as well as over 40 lightships. Lightships are boats which act as lighthouses. They are anchored in places where it is not possible to build a proper lighthouse.

A lighthouse consists of a tall tower. On the top is a lantern that flashes a powerful light out to sea. The light may be provided by an electric lamp, or by a lamp burning acetylene gas or OIL. In many lighthouses the lamp is switched on and off automatically. These lighthouses do not have to be manned all the time. Every lighthouse sends out a different kind of flashing signal.

Left: The Eddystone lighthouse in the English Channel, which is 51 metres high.
Below: A lifeboat standing at the top of a boat-ramp ready to put to sea.

Lifeboats

Lifeboats are stationed at various points around the COAST of a country. They go to the help of vessels that are in difficulties. They are strong and almost unsinkable. Their powerful DIESEL ENGINES enable them to make headway in the roughest seas. Lifeboats are not large craft. They are often no more than ten metres long.

The world's first lifeboat service was started in Britain in 1824. Later it became the Royal National Lifeboat Institution. This body is not paid for by the government, and the crews of its 140 boats are volunteers. In many other countries the lifeboat service is paid for by the government.

Small inshore rescue boats are increasingly used in shallow waters near the coast.

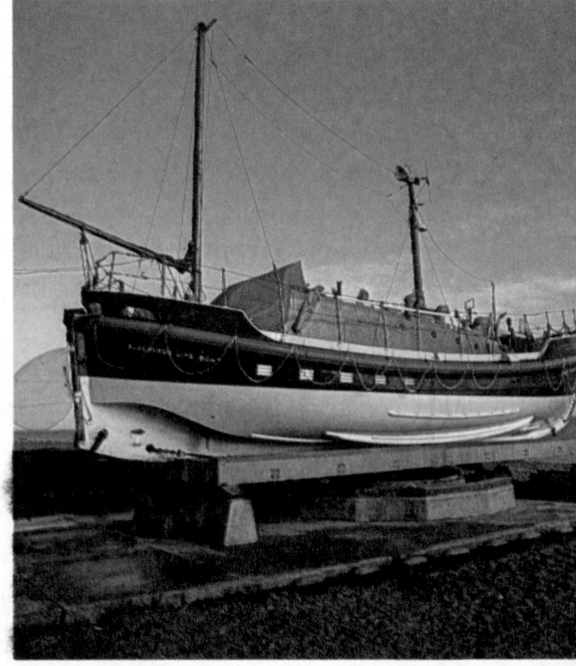

Navigation

Navigating means finding your way from place to place, preferably by the shortest and most direct route. We all have to do some simple navigating at times. For example, we sometimes find our way around the countryside by observing landmarks.

Navigating at sea can be almost as simple, provided that the ship is within sight of landmarks. The ship's navigator notes their position on a CHART. Navigating out of sight of land is more difficult. Unless the navigator knows the position of the ship, he cannot tell the captain which direction, or course, to steer.

The navigator may fix his position by 'celestial' navigation – observing the SUN and STARS. For his observations he requires a SEXTANT, and an accurate chronometer to measure the time. He also requires an accurate COMPASS. The other method is electronic navigation, which includes the use of RADAR and RADIO DIRECTION FINDING.

Constant fixes of position are needed during an ocean voyage. This is because the WIND and ocean currents are continually pushing the ship off course.

A navigator uses latitude and longitude to describe his position on the EARTH'S surface. The latitude of a ship's position is a measure of the ship's distance from the equator. The longitude is a measure of its distance east or west of Greenwich, in LONDON.

On maps and CHARTS there are lines of latitude running parallel to the equator, and lines of longitude running north-south. The lines are circles drawn over the surface of the globe for reference.

A circle can be divided into 360 degrees. Each degree is divided into 60 minutes. Latitude and longitude are measured in degrees and minutes.

Above: Taking a reading with a sextant.

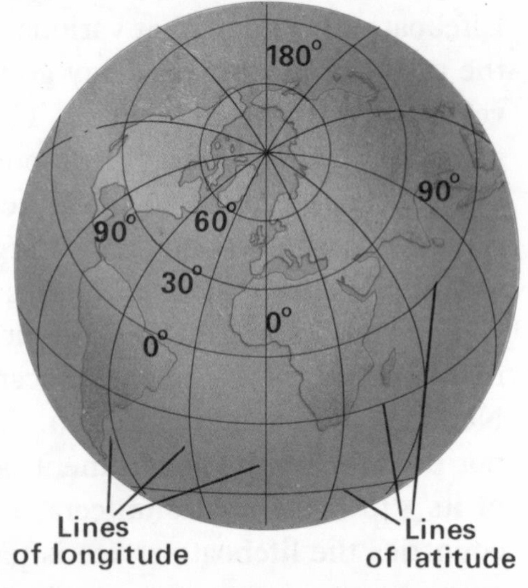

Above: World map marked with some lines of latitude and longitude.

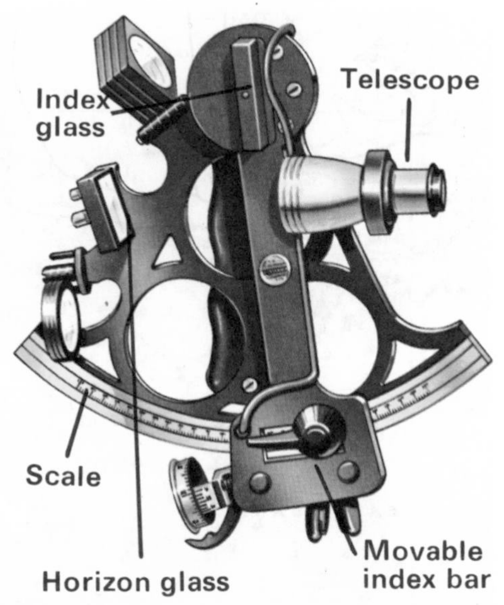

Above: The main features of the sextant. The sextant has been a useful instrument for navigation since its invention in 1731.

Sextants

The sextant is an instrument that helps the navigator work out his position. He measures the angle above the horizon of the SUN or a STAR. The navigator looks at the horizon through the telescope and the fixed, half-silvered mirror (horizon glass). Then he moves the index bar, which holds another mirror (index glass), towards the sun. He stops when he sees the reflected image of the sun appear to touch the horizon. Then he reads the angle from the scale.

At the same time he notes the direction of the sun by using a COMPASS. He also records the exact time on a chronometer.

From the sextant and chronometer readings the navigator can work out his ship's position accurately. He does so with the help of the *Nautical Almanac*. This is a book of tables that lists the positions of the stars and PLANETS over the earth at any time throughout the year.

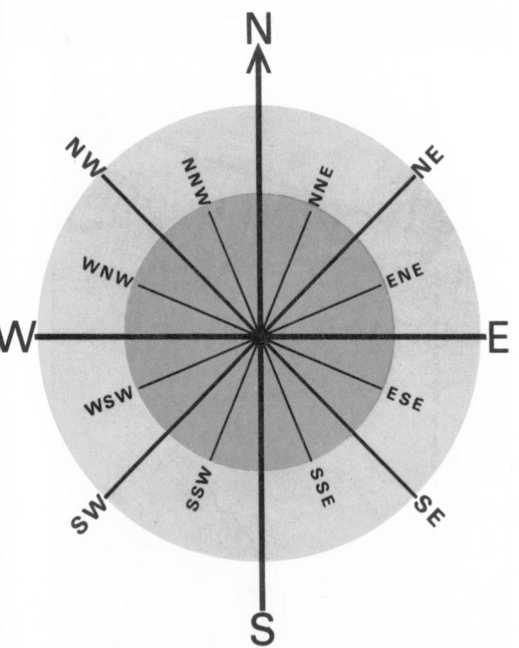

Above: The main compass points. (N = North, E = East, S = South, W = West.)

Compasses

The compass is a basic instrument for navigation. The simplest type is the magnetic compass. This consists of a magnetized needle on a pivot. Because of the EARTH's magnetism, the needle always points north-south. (It does not point to north but to magnetic north, usually a few degrees off.) The modern mariner's compass is a refined form of the compass. It is mounted on a stand called a binnacle. Various devices keep it steady while the ship rocks beneath it.

Most modern ships and AIRCRAFT are also equipped with a much more accurate compass called a gyrocompass. A rapidly spinning gyroscope is the heart of a gyrocompass. Once the gyroscope is set spinning, it remains pointing in the same direction. It is undisturbed by the movement of the ship or aircraft.

Charts

The navigator uses a mariner's chart, which gives accurate information about coastlines and the depth of water. It gives details of harbours and the navigable channels leading to them. It shows every rock, reef, shoal, and sandbank that might endanger shipping. It also shows where dangerous CURRENTS are found.

Mariner's charts are also called hydrographic charts. Hydrography is the study of surface waters. All seafaring countries have a hydrographic department. The British Admiralty set up its Hydrographic Department in 1795. It used specially equipped survey ships. It set a new standard of accuracy in chart-making.

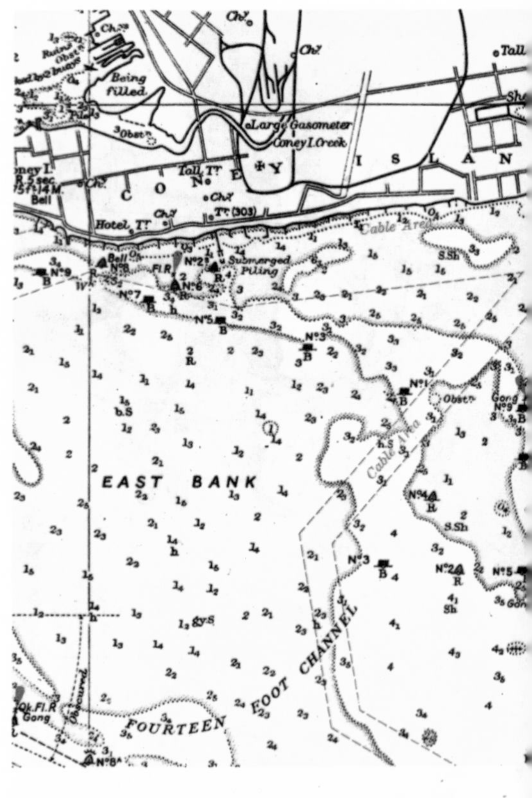

Right: Part of a mariner's chart, showing water depths, buoys, and many other features. Depths are shown in fathoms.

Radio direction finding

The use of radio waves completely changed communications and navigation at sea and in the air. MARCONI developed the 'wireless telegraph', and used it for communication at sea as early as 1897. In 1906 a system of radio direction finding came into operation. In this system, radio beacons on shore or on LIGHTHOUSES send out radio signals. By means of a radio direction finder, a ship's navigator can pinpoint his own position by taking bearings on two such beacons.

More accurate electronic navigation systems include Loran and Decca. In these systems, several shore transmitters send out powerful radio signals. Equipment on the ship picks up these signals, and calculates the ship's position.

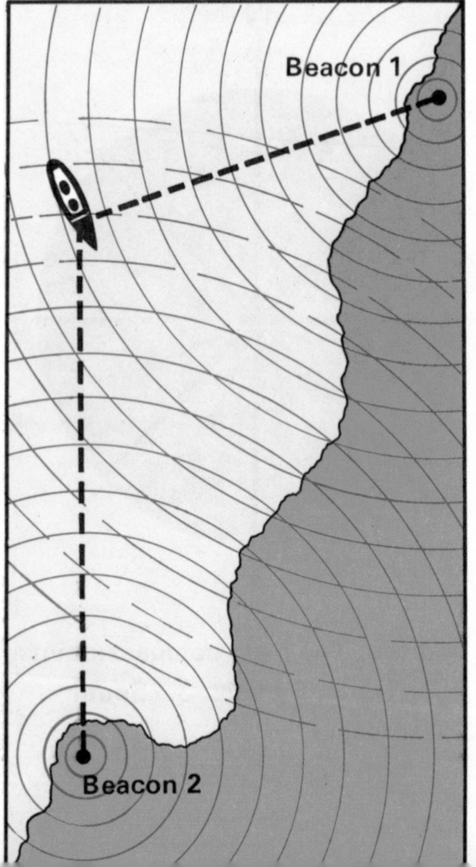

Right: The signals from radio beacons on shore are picked up by passing ships.

Radar

Radar is one of the most useful aids for short-range navigation. The word RADAR stands for 'RAdio Detecting And Ranging'. It is a means of 'seeing' objects by bouncing pulses of radio waves off them. Unlike light waves, radio waves can penetrate CLOUD and FOG. Thus navigators no longer have to sail blind in bad weather or at night. Practically all large ships are now equipped with radar. It is also installed at many ports and airports. Airliners and other large planes carry radar for detecting thunderstorms, as well as other planes nearby.

One of the most common radar systems is used in ships. It consists of a transmitter, an aerial, and a receiver. The transmitter sends out radio pulses through the aerial. This turns round and scans the surrounding area. The pulses are reflected back when they strike another ship or anything else in their path. The reflected pulses are received by the aerial as a kind of echo. By electronic means the echo can be made visible on a screen. This is rather like a television screen. From the position of the echo, the direction and range (distance) of the object can be calculated.

Above: Observing a radar screen.
Below: Sound waves are bounced off the seabed to find out the depth of the water beneath a ship.

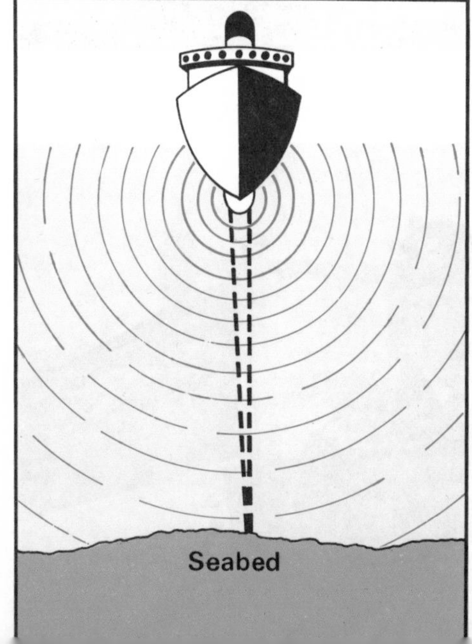

Echo sounders

The echo sounder is an accurate device used for sounding (measuring the depth of the water beneath a ship). It works rather like RADAR, but uses sound waves instead of radio waves. It sends pulses of sound waves downwards and receives echoes from the seabed. The difference in time between sending the signal and receiving its echo is a measure of the depth of water. Automatic equipment continuously records the depth of water. Similar equipment is sometimes fitted to fishing trawlers so that it can be used to detect shoals of fish.

Ports and Harbours

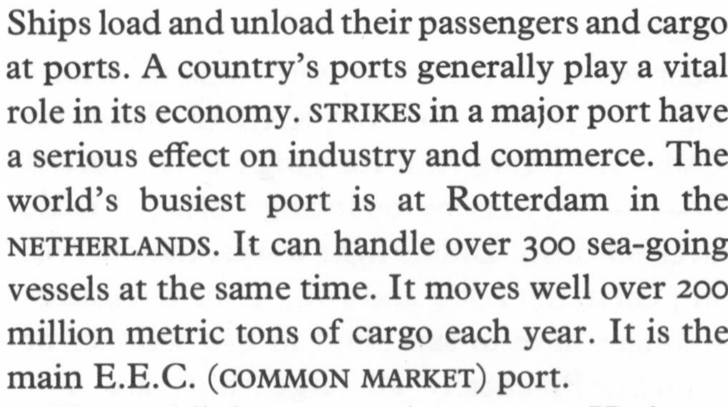

Ships load and unload their passengers and cargo at ports. A country's ports generally play a vital role in its economy. STRIKES in a major port have a serious effect on industry and commerce. The world's busiest port is at Rotterdam in the NETHERLANDS. It can handle over 300 sea-going vessels at the same time. It moves well over 200 million metric tons of cargo each year. It is the main E.E.C. (COMMON MARKET) port.

The world's largest port is NEW YORK Harbour. It covers an area of 240 square kilometres and has a waterfront of 1000 kilometres or more.

Top left: The harbour at Camden, Maine, U.S.A.

Left: A view across the busy dockland area of Sydney, Australia.

Bottom left: A British Customs and Excise Department official going to a newly docked ship.

Ports may be situated on the sea COAST, as at SAN FRANCISCO and SYDNEY. Or they may lie inland up-river, as at LONDON or Bordeaux. A modern port needs all the necessary facilities for handling passengers and cargo. It must have wharves, jetties, or DOCKS for the vessels to berth at. It needs warehouses to store cargo. It should have accommodation for passengers. And there must be handling equipment such as cranes, fork-lift trucks, and so on. In particular, the port must have good ROAD and rail communications with the rest of the country it serves.

The port should be in a sheltered position. Many ports lie on natural harbours – stretches of water sheltered by cliffs or hills. The port of Rio de Janeiro is a magnificent natural harbour. Other ports lie on artificial harbours. These are made by building a protective wall, called a breakwater, out from the shoreline. Dover, in England, is an example of an artificial harbour.

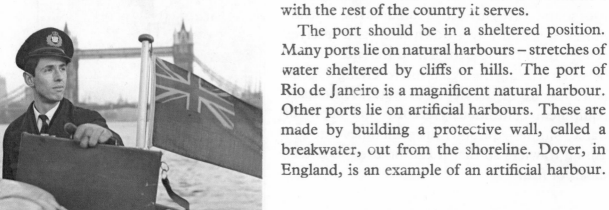

Docks

One thing that affects the operation of a port is the TIDE – the regular rise and fall of the sea twice a day. In some parts of the world, for example, along the MEDITERRANEAN coast, there is little change in level. Ships can load and unload their cargo with little trouble.

However, in other parts of the world, the tides may cause a difference of as much as 12 metres between high and low water. In such places the loading and unloading of cargo from ships would be very difficult.

Top right: Dockside and floating cranes are being used to unload this fruit ship.
Right: A container ship being loaded.
Bottom right: Freighters being unloaded at the world's busiest port – Rotterdam.

At ports where there is much rise and fall in the TIDES, docks have been built. Docks are enclosed basins that can be shut off from the sea. Ships sail into the docks at high water, and watertight lock gates are closed behind them. A fall in water level outside the dock when the tide goes out therefore has no effect on the water level inside. The ships can unload more easily, and then sail out at the next convenient high tide.

Lining the dockside are a variety of fixed and mobile cranes and derricks. These are used for transferring cargo between ship and shore. Bulk cargoes of ore and COAL are unloaded by cranes fitted with scoops (or grabs). Bulk grain is shifted by elevators that suck it through a long pipe. Special equipment is installed at some docks for handling goods in containers. The containers may hold several packages. This reduces the amount of handling needed. They are carried to and from the docks by train or truck.

Dredging

Most ports are troubled by silting. Silt is a build-up of mud and sand. RIVER and sea currents as well as the TIDES drop the sand and mud in navigation channels, harbours, and DOCKS. If the silt were allowed to remain, the port area would fill up and become too shallow for navigation. Dredging is therefore carried out regularly to remove the silt.

Several types of dredging vessels are in use. One is the bucket dredger, which uses an endless chain of buckets to scoop up the silt. The buckets move round an arm that points down towards the seabed. The dredged silt is discharged into a hopper barge alongside.

The suction dredger is also widely used. It sucks up the silt through a pipe.

Dry docks

Most ports have dry docks. These are also called graving docks. Dry docks differ from ordinary DOCKS because the water inside them can be pumped out. Ships go into dry dock when they need work carried out below the waterline.

The ship enters the flooded dock, and the lock gates are closed behind it. Water is then pumped out until the ship's keel rests on blocks on the bottom of the dock. Spars (poles) are wedged between the sides of the ship and the dock. The rest of the water is pumped out. Work below the waterline can then proceed. After repairs have been completed, the dock is again flooded, and the ship can sail out.

Another form of dry dock widely used for ship repair is the floating dock. This is a large steel structure which has walls at the sides and is usually open at both ends. The walls and bottom of the dock contain compartments that can be flooded or pumped dry.

Bucket dredger

Suction dredger

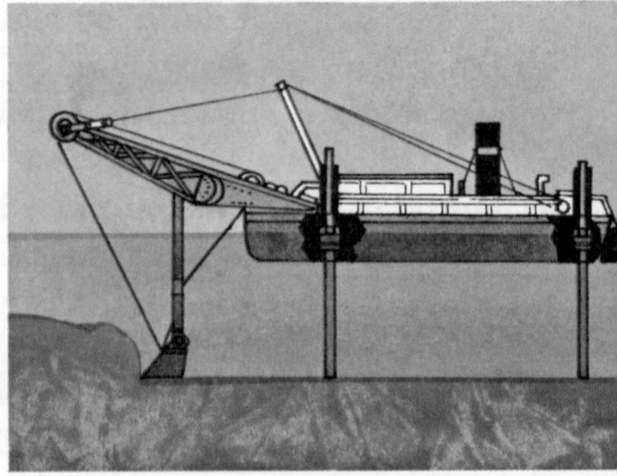

Dipper dredger

Above: Three common kinds of harbour dredgers.

Right: Maintenance work being carried out below the waterline on a ship in a floating dock.

NETUNO

Undersea Exploration

Many rich deposits of OIL and NATURAL GAS have been found in the seabed. Other minerals are undoubtedly there as well. There are many other reasons why men wish to descend into the sea – for example, to repair ships and harbour equipment, to examine WRECKS, and to recover sunken treasure.

However, man cannot live for long without air. So he must take air with him when he ventures under the sea. By holding his breath he can remain underwater for only a minute or two. He cannot do much exploring or go very deep in that time. Even if he could hold his breath longer, and go deeper, the pressure of deep water would be great enough to crush him.

With suitable equipment, however, men can survive in the underwater world. The heavily-clad DEEP-SEA DIVER can descend to depths of 100 metres of more. The more lightly-equipped FROGMAN can venture down to more than 30 metres. Men may also descend in specially built chambers, such as the diving bell and, for great depths, the bathysphere and BATHYSCAPHE.

Above: An old diving bell in which men descended to the seabed.

Below: A modern research submarine with mechanical grab.

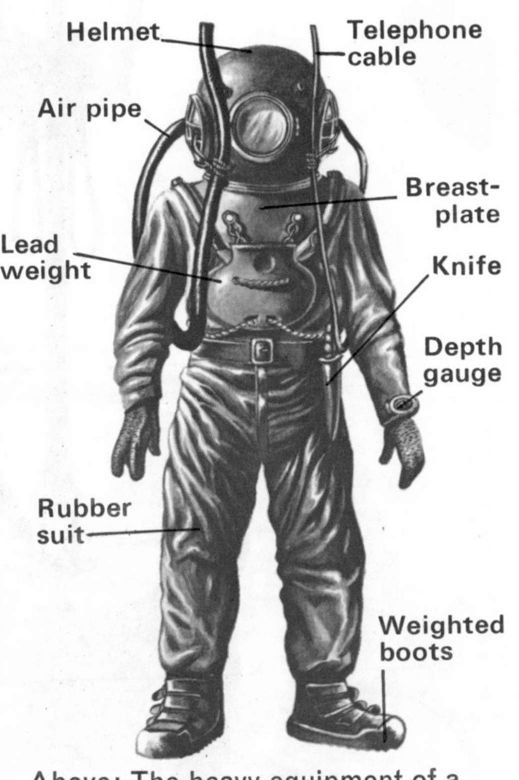

Above: The heavy equipment of a deep-sea diver.

Below: A diver emerging after a practice dive.

Deep-sea divers

Divers who dive deep, or remain under water for any length of time, wear a diving suit and helmet supplied with air from the surface. A round COPPER helmet with thick GLASS windows bolts on to a breastplate attached to the heavy RUBBER suit. The diver has lead weights at his waist, and his boots have lead soles. A lifeline from his breastplate connects the diver with the boat he is working from. A TELEPHONE cable enables him to communicate with the surface. Air is pumped into the diver's suit through an air pipe.

As the diver descends into the water the pressure around him increases. At 10 metres it is twice as great as at the surface. At 100 metres it is 11 times as great. To help the diver resist this pressure, the pressure of air in his suit is increased accordingly. When the diver goes back up, the pressure is gradually reduced. This must be done slowly, otherwise gases in the diver's BLOOD form bubbles. He then gets an attack of very severe cramp known as 'the bends'. If the diver's ascent is very swift, he may even be killed.

To reduce the danger, a diver has to rest several times on his way up. A diver who has been working for some time at 50 metres might have to rest five or six times on his way up. His ascent might take an hour or more. Sometimes a decompression chamber is used to bring a diver to the surface quickly. The chamber, which is at the same pressure as the diving suit, is lowered to him. He climbs inside and is hauled to the surface. Then the pressure in the chamber is gradually reduced to normal.

For dives down to 45 metres or so, the diver breathes compressed air. For deeper dives he breathes a mixture of oxygen and helium. Breathing ordinary air at great depths makes the diver dizzy.

Frogmen

A frogman is a specially trained diver who takes his own air supply under the water with him. He wears what is called 'Self-Contained Underwater Breathing Apparatus' (or SCUBA). Since he is free of surface help, the frogman can move about much more easily. But he cannot go as deep or remain down as long as a DEEP-SEA DIVER.

The frogman usually wears a tight-fitting rubber suit and large flippers on his feet to help him swim faster. This makes him look rather like the FROG from which he gets his name.

The most widely used form of SCUBA is the aqualung. This was invented by the famous French underwater explorer Jacques-Yves Cousteau in 1942. The aqualung feeds compressed air or oxygen through a sensitive valve to the diver's mouth when he breathes in. Another valve lets the air he breathes out escape into the water. The gas is contained in cylinders strapped to the diver's back.

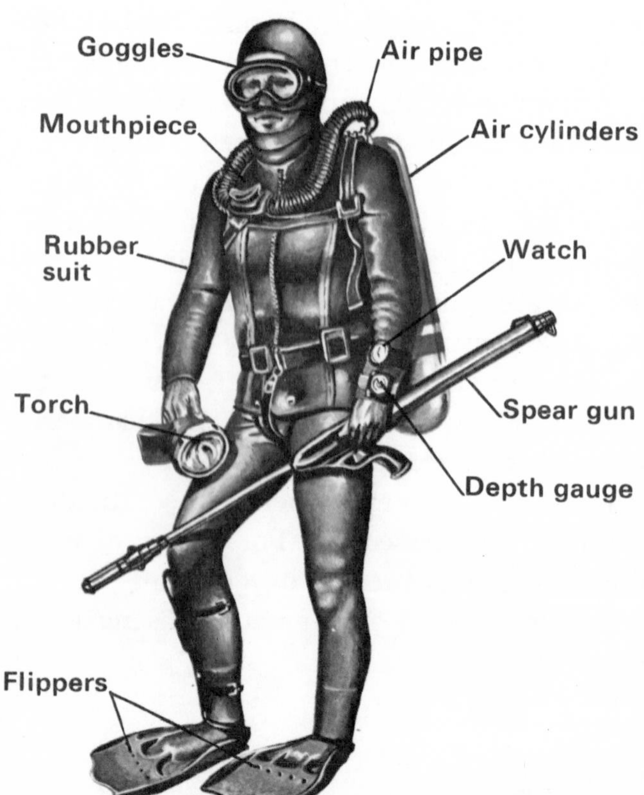

Bathyscaphes

Even DEEP-SEA DIVERS cannot go down very far below the surface of the sea. Scientists have, however, gone down much further in special observation chambers. These chambers have thick metal walls to withstand pressures hundreds of times greater than at sea level.

The U.S. scientist William Beebe began deep-water exploration in the 1930s, using what he called a bathysphere. It was a big steel ball, lowered down by cable to depths of up to 1000 metres. In 1960, a Swiss physicist named Auguste Piccard invented a diving craft called the bathyscaphe which could descend more than ten kilometres into the ocean. It had a large tank of petrol which helped it to get back to the surface, as petrol is lighter than water.

Submersibles

In recent years, new miniature submarines, called submersibles, have been built. They are used particularly in the offshore oil industry. Submersibles are powered by propellers, which are driven by electric motors. They are used to carry out a wide variety of tasks under water.

Left: Frogmen with 'snorkel' breathing tubes on a submarine research vessel.
Below: Piccard's bathyscaphe *Trieste*.

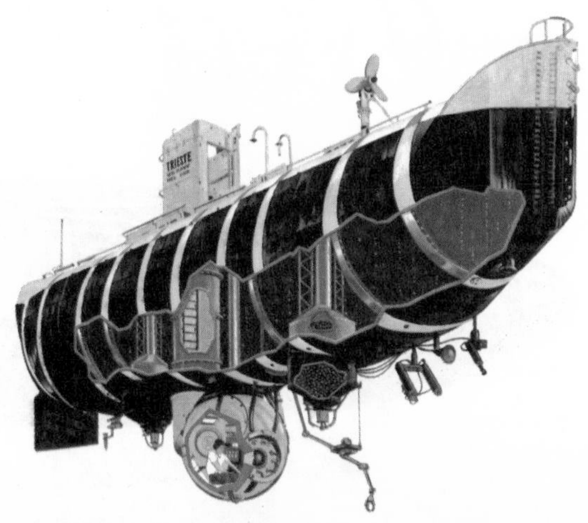

Submarines

Submarines are vessels designed to travel underwater. *Submarine* means 'under the sea'. Most submarines are warships operated by the world's NAVIES. They can attack surface ships with torpedoes while underwater, unseen by their target. The largest submarines can also fire guided missiles from beneath the sea that can reach targets thousands of kilometres away.

Submarines may also have a future as cargo vessels, especially as TANKERS. One advantage of submarine craft is that, once they are submerged, they are 'below the weather' and are not affected by WIND and WAVES. Several experimental submarine craft have been built for exploring the seabed. Jacques-Yves Cousteau, for example, built a two-man 'diving saucer' for underwater research. It was propelled by water jets.

Early submarines were long but not streamlined. The modern naval submarine is cigar-shaped, long and slim. This shape gives greater speed underwater. On the submarine's hull is the conning tower, or 'sail', which contains the navigation bridge and one or more periscopes. Like an ordinary ship, a submarine is driven by

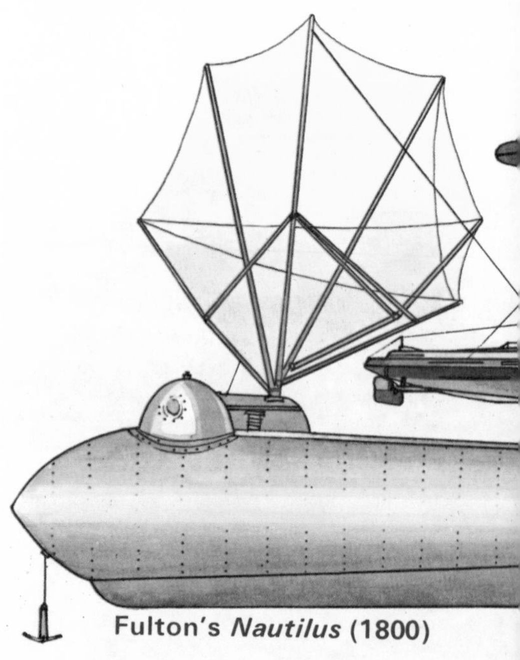

Fulton's *Nautilus* (1800)

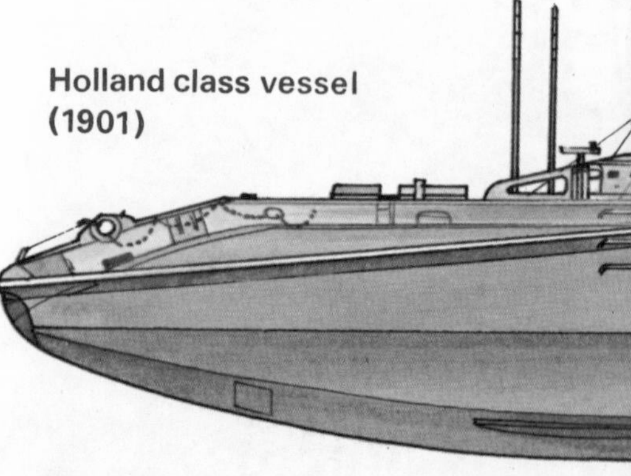

Holland class vessel (1901)

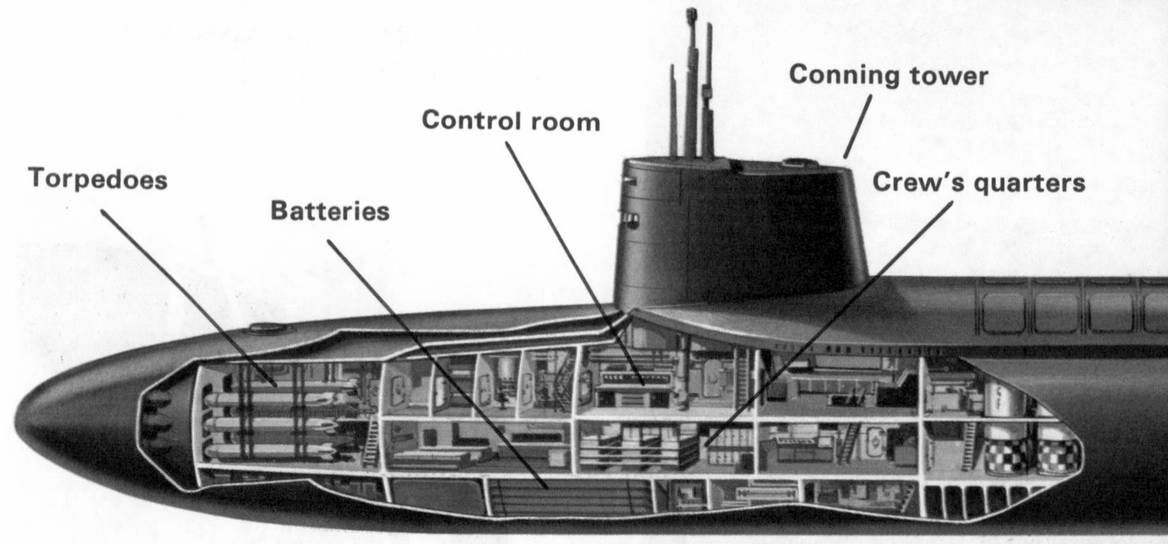

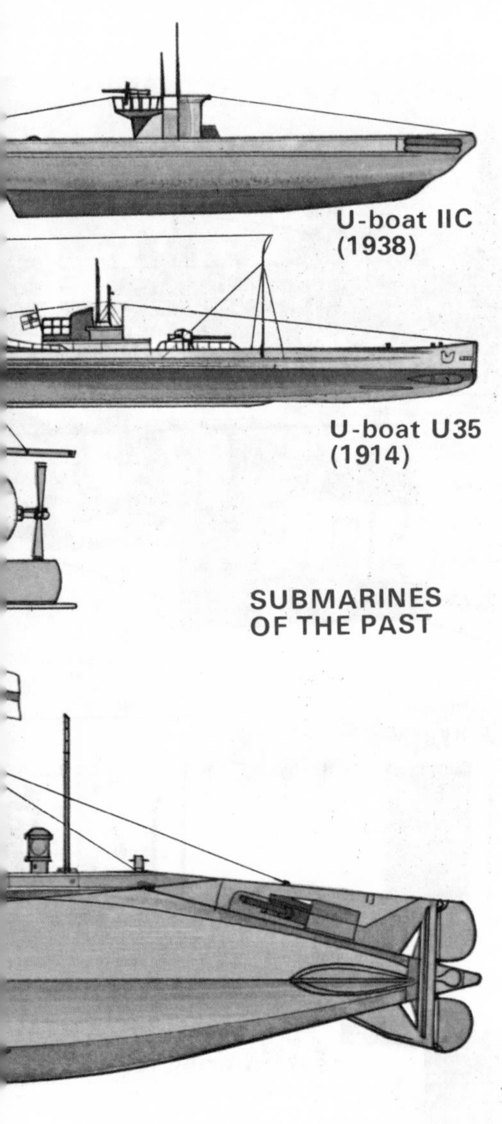

a propeller and steered to left and right by a rudder. It also has hydroplanes, or diving planes, at bow and stern to guide it up or down through the water. A submarine dives by allowing water to flow into its ballast tanks. These are tanks surrounding the main hull of the vessel. It surfaces by blowing the water out.

There are two types of submarine. The smaller submarines use a DIESEL ENGINE to turn the propellers while on the surface. But they use electric motors powered by batteries when submerged. Diesel engines cannot be used underwater because they need air. These submarines use their diesel engine to recharge their batteries. They must therefore surface regularly.

Nuclear submarines can, however, remain submerged for months at a time. They are powered by a nuclear reactor, which needs no air to operate. And their 'fuel' will last for a year or more. The nuclear reactor produces heat to turn water into steam. The steam is then used to drive turbines, which turn the propellers.

Left: Various submarines of the past. They are not all drawn to the same scale.
Below: A modern nuclear-powered submarine. More than 120 metres long, this vessel carries 16 missiles which it can fire while submerged. A crew of 140 is needed to operate the vessel.

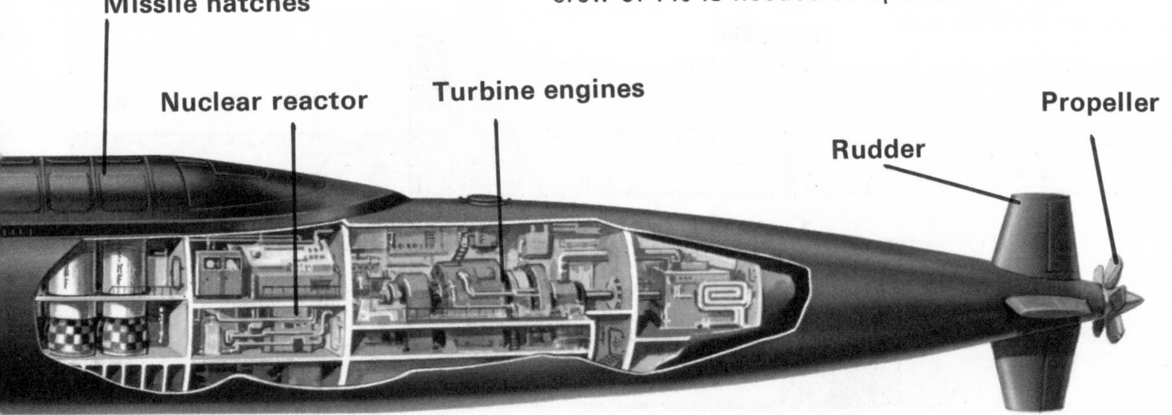

Inland Waterways

In most countries there are navigable RIVERS and LAKES. These provide a natural route for travel and transport by boat, barge, and even by ship. The use of these waterways, however, is limited. So, over the years, artificial waterways, or CANALS, have been built to reach places not served by rivers.

Canals have also been built to link rivers or lakes into a longer inland waterway. Existing rivers that are not suitable for navigation have been straightened, widened, and deepened to allow traffic to pass.

A change in water level – caused by rapids, a WATERFALL, or a DAM – can be overcome by building locks to raise or lower boats between the different levels.

In general, inland waterways are not as important as they once were. A great deal of their trade has been taken by rail, road, and air.

Below: How a lock works.

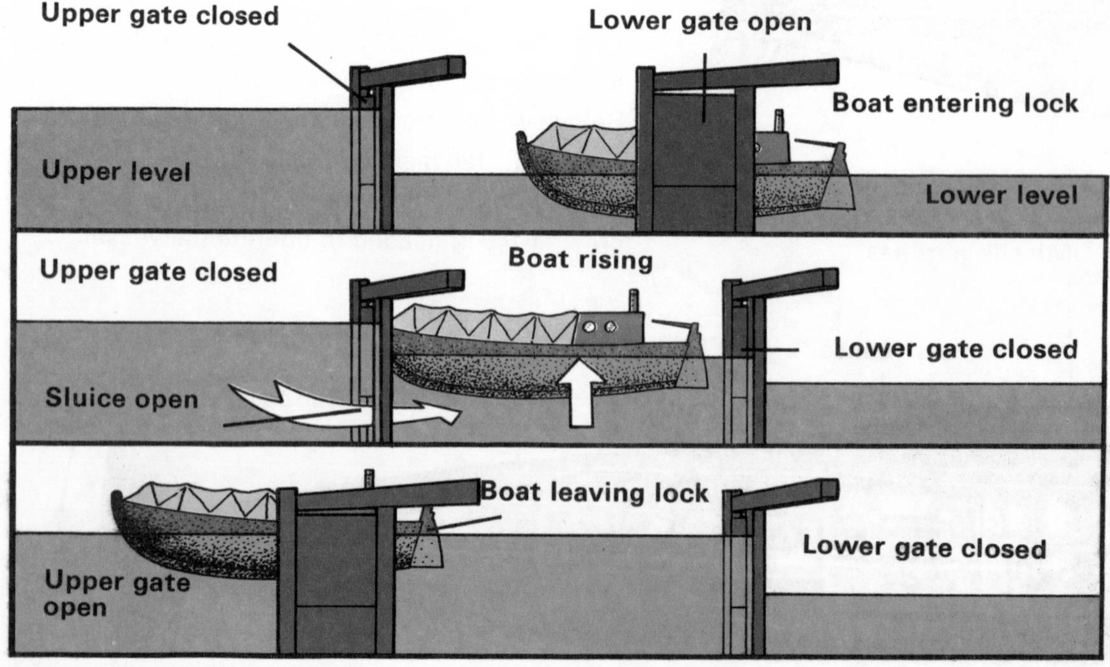

Above: Basle harbour on the Rhine, Europe's main waterway. It is one of the world's busiest.

Below: Horses are the traditional way of pulling along canal boats.

Canals

The great era of canal building began in the 1700s as the INDUSTRIAL REVOLUTION got under way. The new industries demanded larger and better transport systems. The ROADS were almost useless for moving freight, and the railways had not yet been built. James Brindley built Britain's first industrial canal, the Bridgewater, in the 1750s. By 1840, Britain had 6000 kilometres of canals. Today, only 500 kilometres are important for trade.

The first U.S. canal was built in Massachusetts in 1792. Today the U.S.A. still has a number of canal systems. The most important is the Great Lakes–St Lawrence River system. The ST LAWRENCE SEAWAY opened up great areas of NORTH AMERICA to ocean-going ships.

EUROPE, FRANCE, GERMANY, BELGIUM and the NETHERLANDS have extensive and interlinked canal and RIVER systems. The U.S.S.R. has the longest canal system in the world, the 3000-kilometre Volga–Baltic Canal.

Sea canals, which offer short cuts across narrow strips of land, are of international importance. Foremost is the PANAMA CANAL in Central America.

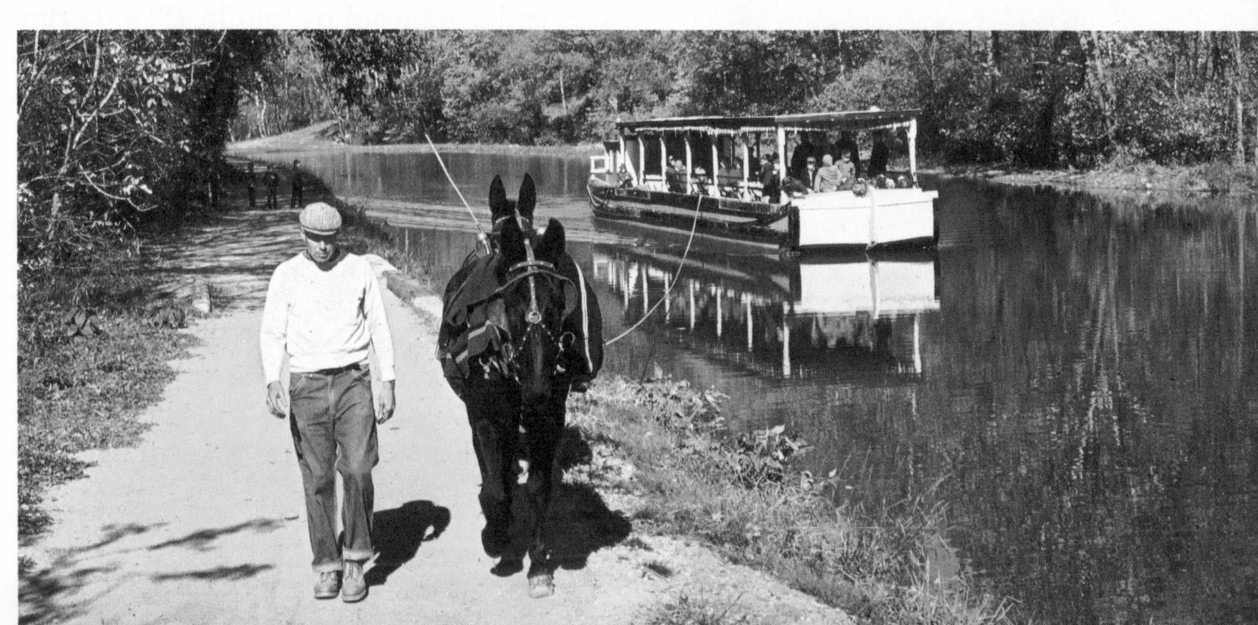

Panama Canal

An average of about 40 ships sail through the Panama Canal every day. This CANAL runs across the Isthmus of Panama in Central America. It links the ATLANTIC and PACIFIC oceans. Using the canal saves ships a long and difficult voyage around the tip of SOUTH AMERICA. Construction of the 80-kilometre canal was a great engineering feat. It involved building a DAM to form a LAKE 50 kilometres long, and blasting a trench through the Continental Divide.

Three sets of locks raise and lower ships between lake and sea levels. One set – the Miraflores locks – are the world's biggest. Ships are towed through the locks by LOCOMOTIVES.

The French, under Ferdinand DE LESSEPS, attempted construction of the canal in the 1880s but failed. American engineers took over the project in 1904 and completed it 10 years later.

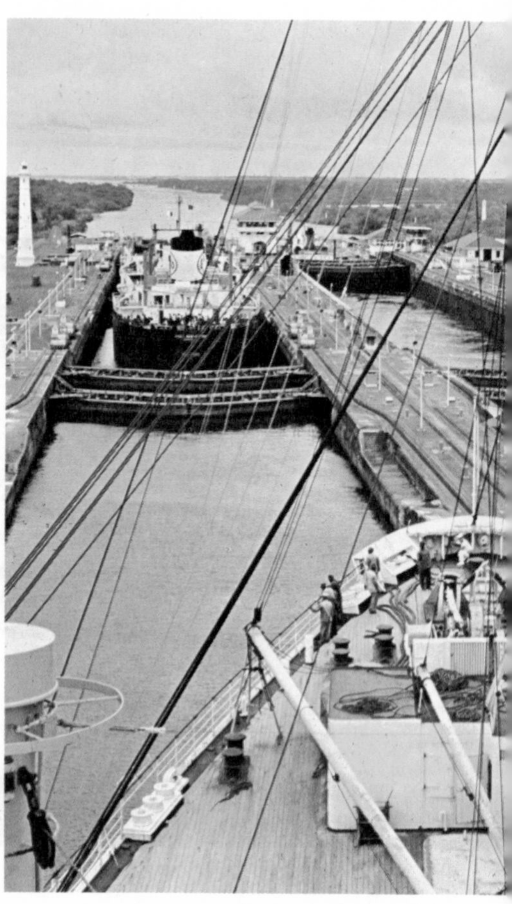

Right: One of the locks on the Panama Canal.
Below: Ships passing through the Suez Canal.

Suez Canal

The Suez Canal links the MEDITERRANEAN and Red seas. It was planned by Ferdinand DE LESSEPS and completed by him in 1869. It runs 160 kilometres across sandy DESERT from Suez on the Red Sea to Port Said on the Mediterranean.

There are no locks on the Suez Canal as there is very little difference in level between the two seas. The Suez Canal can save ships sailing between EUROPE and the Far East an extra journey. The canal was closed by the Arab-Israeli war of 1967, but was re-opened in 1975. Sometimes it is cheaper to send giant bulk carriers round AFRICA than it would be to use the smaller vessels necessary to get through the Canal.

St Lawrence Seaway

One of the greatest CANALS of recent times is the St Lawrence Seaway. It is on the St Lawrence River between CANADA and the United States. It runs about 300 kilometres south-west from MONTREAL to Lake Ontario.

The seaway is part of the vast St Lawrence River system that extends from the North ATLANTIC into the Great Lakes (Lakes Superior, Michigan, Huron, Erie, and Ontario). The Great Lakes form the world's largest inland waterway. Building the seaway opened up the Great Lakes to ocean-going ships, which can now sail 3750 kilometres inland.

Construction of the seaway meant widening existing channels and cutting new ones. It also involved building DAMS to raise water levels, and constructing huge locks to lift ships from one level to another.

Two locks on the St Lawrence Seaway: above, a vertical-lift bridge over St Lambert Lock; below, Welland Flight Lock.

Travel by Road

Ancient civilizations were using the wheel at least 5000 years ago. The wheel probably developed from the technique of rolling heavy objects along on logs. The first true wheels were solid wooden discs. But, in about 2000 B.C., the Assyrians and EGYPTIANS began using wheels with spokes on their chariots. They built two-wheeled chariots for fighting and racing. As spoked wheels were lighter, greater speed was possible.

Later, the ROMANS developed a four-wheel wagon with a bar which allowed the front wheel axle to turn for steering. They also built good ROADS.

After the Roman Empire crumbled, the fine Roman roads were allowed to decay. By the Middle Ages, roads had become so bad that wagons could scarcely use them. The safest way of transporting goods was by packhorse. There were few passenger carriages. Most people walked or travelled on horseback. Transport became a little faster after 1760. During this period the enclosed stagecoach was used for long-distance travel.

Road conditions improved considerably in the 1800s with the need for faster transport following the INDUSTRIAL REVOLUTION. Some people tried to build steam-powered carriages, but with little success.

The main revolution in road transport did not come until 1885. Then, two German engineers, Karl Benz and Gottlieb Daimler independently built 'horseless carriages' powered by PETROL ENGINES. These vehicles were the ancestors of the modern MOTOR CAR. A little while later, Rudolf DIESEL, another German engineer, developed an efficient engine that burned OIL instead of petrol. The diesel engine now powers LORRIES and BUSES, LOCOMOTIVES and ships.

Bullock cart

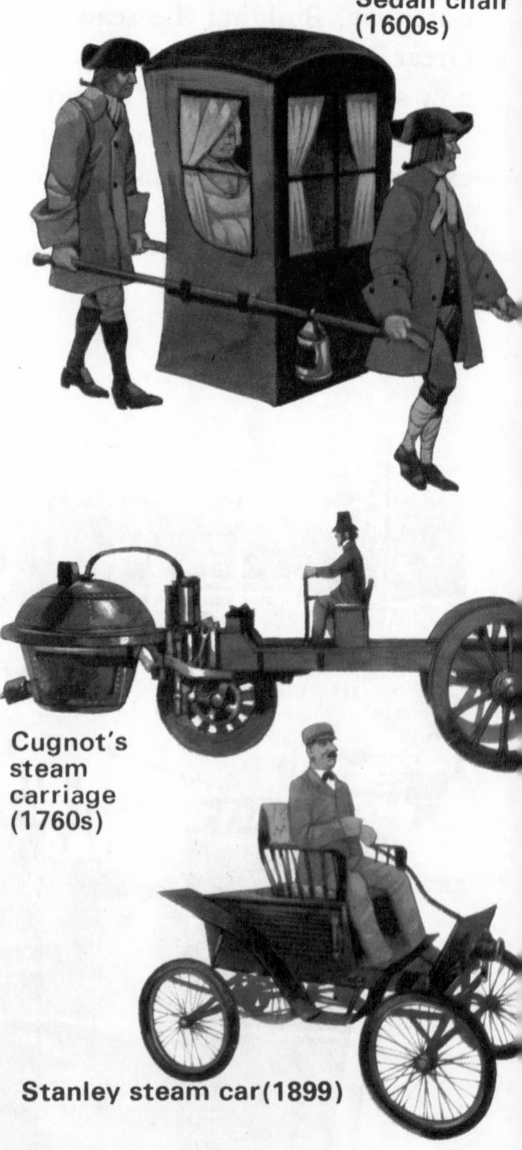

Sedan chair (1600s)

Cugnot's steam carriage (1760s)

Stanley steam car(1899)

Egyptian chariot
(1500s BC)
Packhorses
(Middle Ages)
Stagecoach
(1830)
Bugatti
(1910)
Benz Velo
(1893)
Rolls-Royce
Silver Ghost
(1909)
Model 'T'
Ford (1915)
Volkswagen
(1938)

Early cars

The first cars were called 'horseless carriages'. They had wooden spoked wheels and solid rubber tyres. Their bodies, springs and seats were also the same as on fashionable carriages and they were built by the same craftsmen.

There was a surprising variety of different designs among early cars and all sorts of new devices were tried out. Not every car even had a steering wheel. Instead, some were fitted with a tiller, like on a boat. Large oil lamps in huge brass frames were in use for many years before electric generators and the light bulb were able to operate in the car.

By 1900 many car manufacturers still famous today had set up their own factories. Renault in France, Ford in America and Lanchester in England were developing many new ideas.

Right: A de Dion Bouton motorcar of 1902.

Below: An early Rolls-Royce. The passengers were protected from the weather.

Left: Henry Ford.

Lanchester made a car driven by steam and Ford set up the first mass-production line to make his Model 'T' or 'Tin Lizzie'. 14 million Model 'T's were eventually produced. In the U.S.A. Thomas Edison tried unsuccessfully to make an electrically propelled car helped by a large team of scientists.

In 1907 the famous Rolls Royce Silver Ghost appeared. It was powerful, comfortable and rode smoothly on pneumatic tyres. It set a new pattern for car design and at last gave the car an identity of its own, quite different from the horse carriage. Later, windscreen wipers were fitted and the closed-in saloon appeared. Starting handles gave way to the electric starter.

Below: Ford Model 'T's rolling off the production line in 1919.

Petrol engines

Most cars have an engine which uses petrol as fuel. It is called an internal combustion engine because burning (combustion) of the fuel mixture takes place inside closed cylinders. Most car engines have four, six, or eight cylinders arranged in line or in a V-formation.

Inside the cylinders are gas-tight pistons. The gases produced by burning the petrol expand and force the pistons along the cylinders. A connecting rod sends the piston movement to the crankshaft. This changes the up-and-down (reciprocating) movement of the piston into a turning (rotary) motion. Only rotary motion can be used to turn the car wheels.

The petrol engine works according to a repeated sequence, or cycle, of operations. It is called a four-stroke cycle because in each cylinder the cycle repeats itself after every four piston strokes (movements up or down).

On the first stroke of its cycle, the piston moves down. A mixture of petrol and air is pulled into the cylinder through an open valve. Next, the valve is closed and the piston moves up. The fuel mixture is thus compressed. When the piston nears the top of its stroke, an electric spark from a sparking plug ignites the mixture. The hot gases produced force the piston down on its power stroke. As the final upstroke begins, another valve opens and the spent gases are forced out. Then the cycle begins again.

A few cars and MOTOR CYCLES have piston engines that work on a two-stroke cycle of operations. Two-stroke engines are generally simpler but less efficient than four-stroke engines.

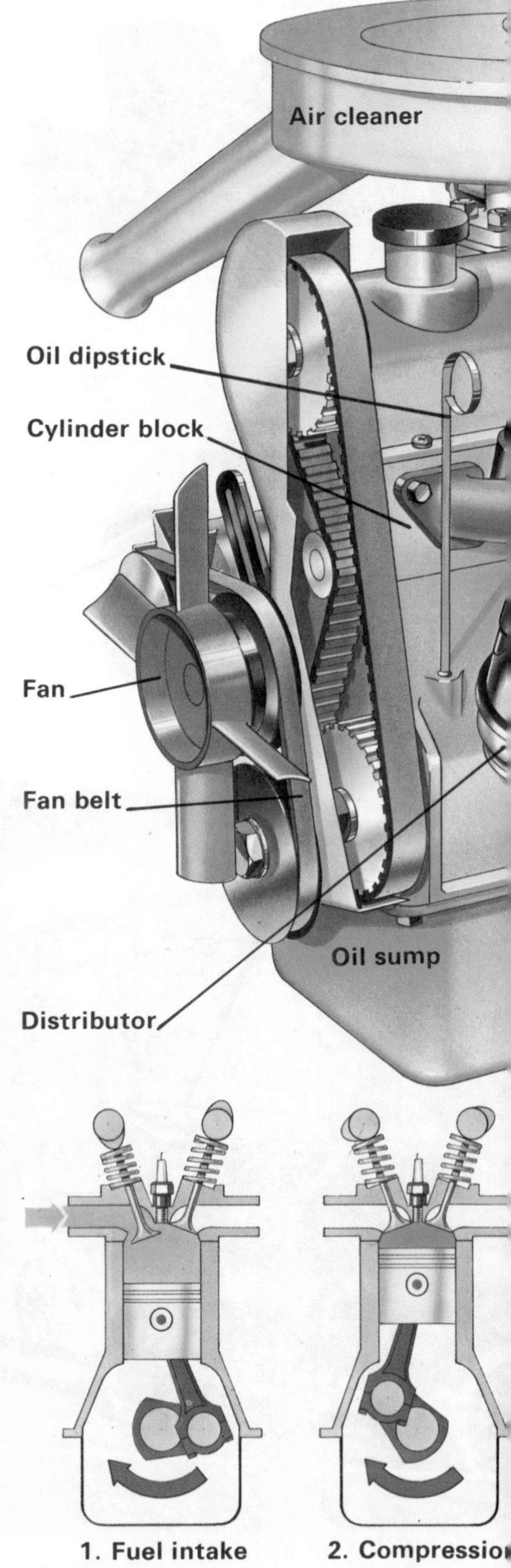

Above right: Some of the main parts of an ordinary four-cylinder petrol engine.
Right: The stages of the four-stroke cycle.

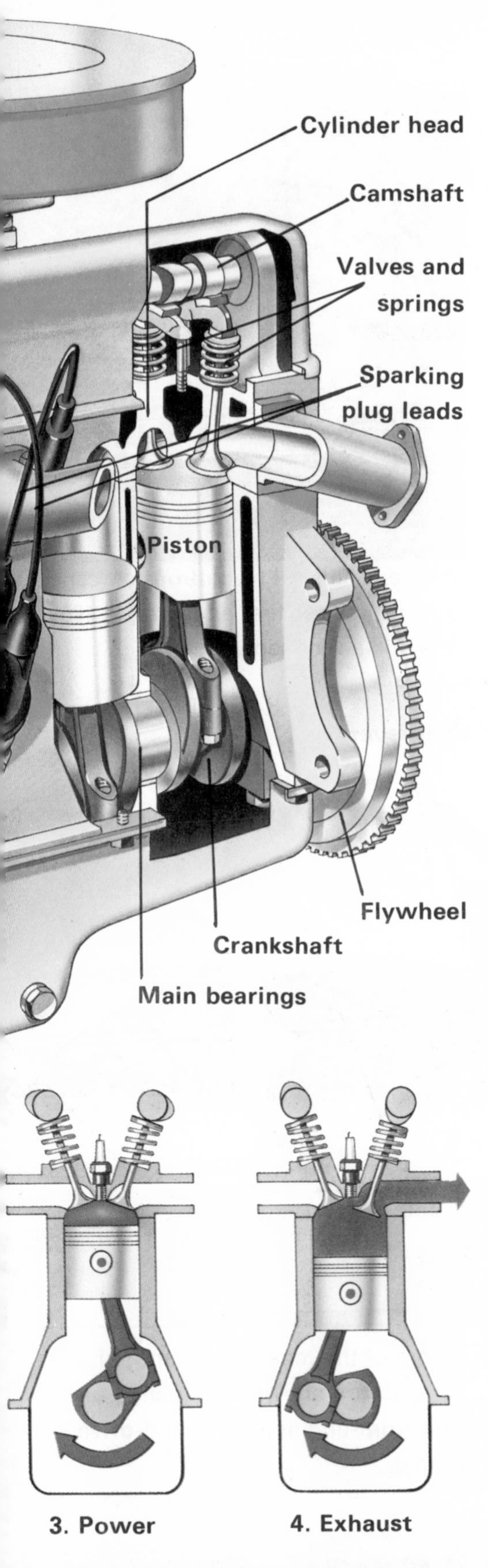

3. Power

4. Exhaust

Petrol is usually mixed with air in a carburettor before it enters the engine. The ignition system sends a spark to ignite the mixture. Pulses of electricity go to the sparking plugs in each cylinder at just the right times. Heat given out by the burning fuel is removed by the engine's cooling system. The engine is kept well oiled by its lubrication system.

The Wankel engine is a special kind of petrol engine. It has cylinders shaped like a figure of eight. The cylinders each contain a nearly triangular rotor. The hot gases produced by burning the fuel mixture turn the rotor around inside the cylinder. The Wankel engine is therefore called a rotary engine. It is much simpler than an ordinary petrol engine and runs more smoothly.

Most car engines have a serious drawback, however. They cause POLLUTION. Large cities are especially affected. Car makers are looking for ways to make engines run more cleanly.

Diesel engines

The diesel engine is another kind of internal combustion engine. It uses a light OIL (diesel oil) and not petrol as fuel. Diesel engines are stronger than petrol engines and cost less to run. They are used to power LORRIES and BUSES, as well as some cars and many ships and LOCOMOTIVES. They can be huge. Some diesel engines in ships are as big as houses.

The diesel works on a two- or four-stroke cycle of operations, as does the petrol engine. But there is an important difference. The diesel does not use a spark to ignite its fuel. Instead, air is drawn into the cylinders and greatly compressed (squeezed). As a result, the air gets very hot. Then the fuel oil is injected into the hot air as a spray and burns at once. The diesel engine therefore needs no sparking plugs.

Modern cars

The car of today is one of man's most important forms of transport. In less than a hundred years it has developed from the simple 'horseless carriage' into the modern fast, streamlined machine. In the United States alone, there are about 90 million registered cars.

A car is a complicated piece of machinery made up of hundreds of different parts. These can be grouped into systems that perform certain essential operations. The engine, for example, has fuel, ignition, lubrication, and cooling systems.

The transmission system transmits power from the engine to the driving wheels of the car. It consists of the gearbox, clutch, propeller shaft, and rear axle. Using the gears in the gear-

Above: The Mini revolutionized car design when it first appeared in 1959. It is still a very popular car.

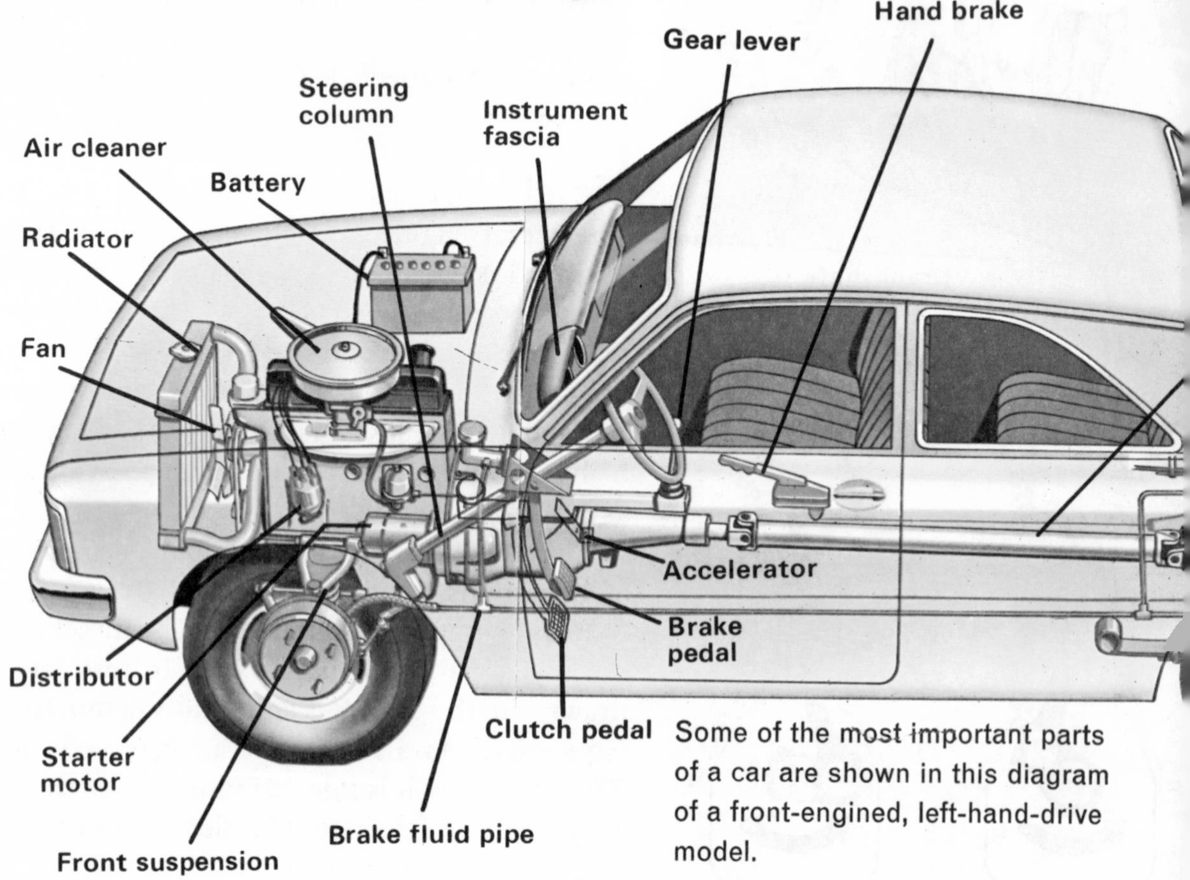

Hand brake
Gear lever
Steering column
Instrument fascia
Air cleaner
Battery
Radiator
Fan
Accelerator
Brake pedal
Distributor
Clutch pedal
Starter motor
Brake fluid pipe
Front suspension

Some of the most important parts of a car are shown in this diagram of a front-engined, left-hand-drive model.

Above: The Alfasud Sprint is equipped with a very powerful engine.
Above right: The Lotus Esprit is a good example of modern, streamlined car design.

Above: The Mercedes is one of the most luxurious cars of today.

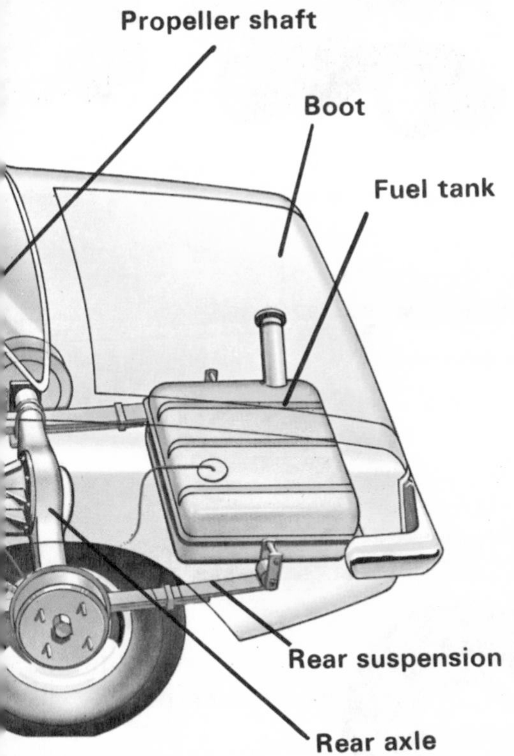

box, the driver can vary the speed of the engine in relation to the speed of the car. The clutch disconnects the gearbox from the engine when the driver wishes to change gear. Cars with automatic transmission have no clutch as the gears change automatically.

The steering system turns the front wheels to guide the car. The braking system stops the car. The main brake acts on all four wheels, and works by liquid pressure. It is operated by a foot pedal. The hand brake acts only on the rear wheels. It works by cable. The suspension system is designed to absorb shocks from the road. The electric system operates the lights, ignition, horn and radio.

Lorries

Lorries, or trucks, are vital for transporting a wide variety of freight (goods).

Many different kinds of lorries are used, each designed to do a certain job. When a manufacturer builds a lorry, he puts a standard engine into a standard frame, or chassis. Then he adds one of a variety of bodies. He might add on a flat body for transporting timber, or a closed 'box' body for furniture. A 'tank' body is used for bulk liquids such as milk, and a 'tipper' body for sand and gravel.

Many goods are transported by articulated lorries. These consist of two parts – a powered tractor (or truck tractor) and a half-trailer. The tractor can move about independently and serve more than one half-trailer.

Most lorries have DIESEL ENGINES, except in the U.S.A. where they usually have PETROL ENGINES.

Right: Three contrasting kinds of lorry bodies.

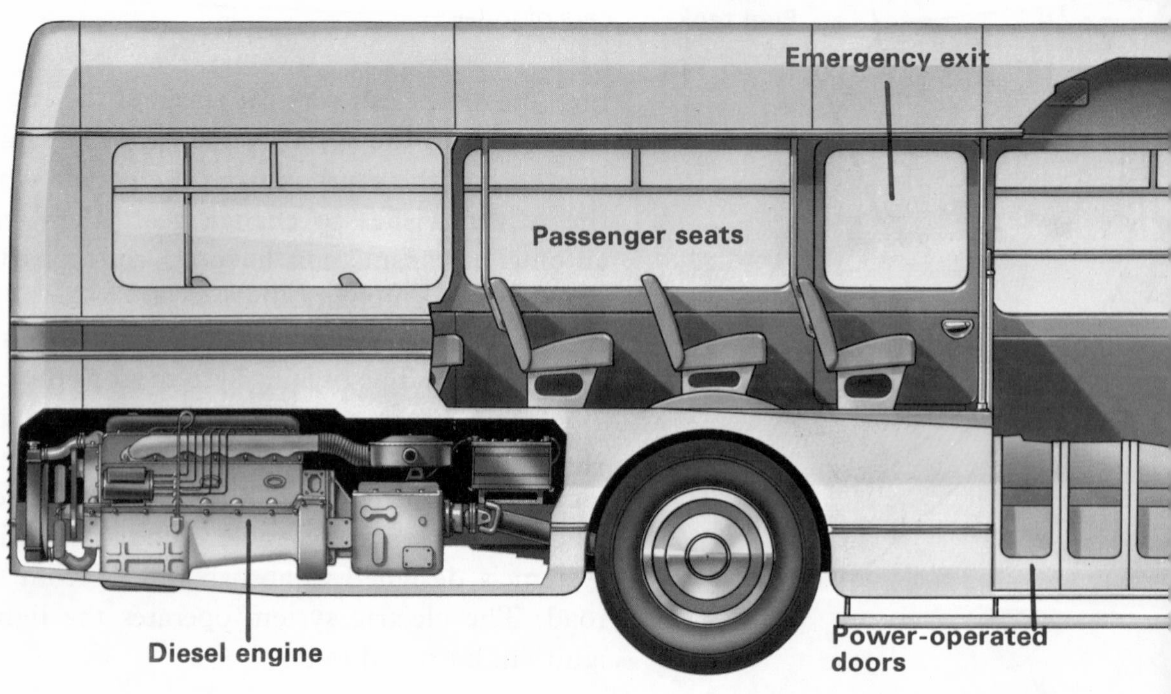

Buses and coaches

Buses are large motor vehicles used for public passenger transport. The word *bus* is short for *omnibus*, meaning 'for all'. Most buses have DIESEL ENGINES and are similar mechanically to LORRIES.

Buses can carry many people. Single-deck buses usually have seats for 40 or more passengers. Double-deck buses, which are common in Great Britain, can seat nearly twice that number. Buses halt regularly at stops to set down or pick up passengers.

City buses intended mainly for short journeys usually have few comforts. For long-distance travel, coaches with well-upholstered seats, air conditioning, and toilets, are generally used.

Truck mixer

Above left: A heavy articulated lorry leaving a car ferry.

Below: A modern bus showing the diesel engine at the rear.

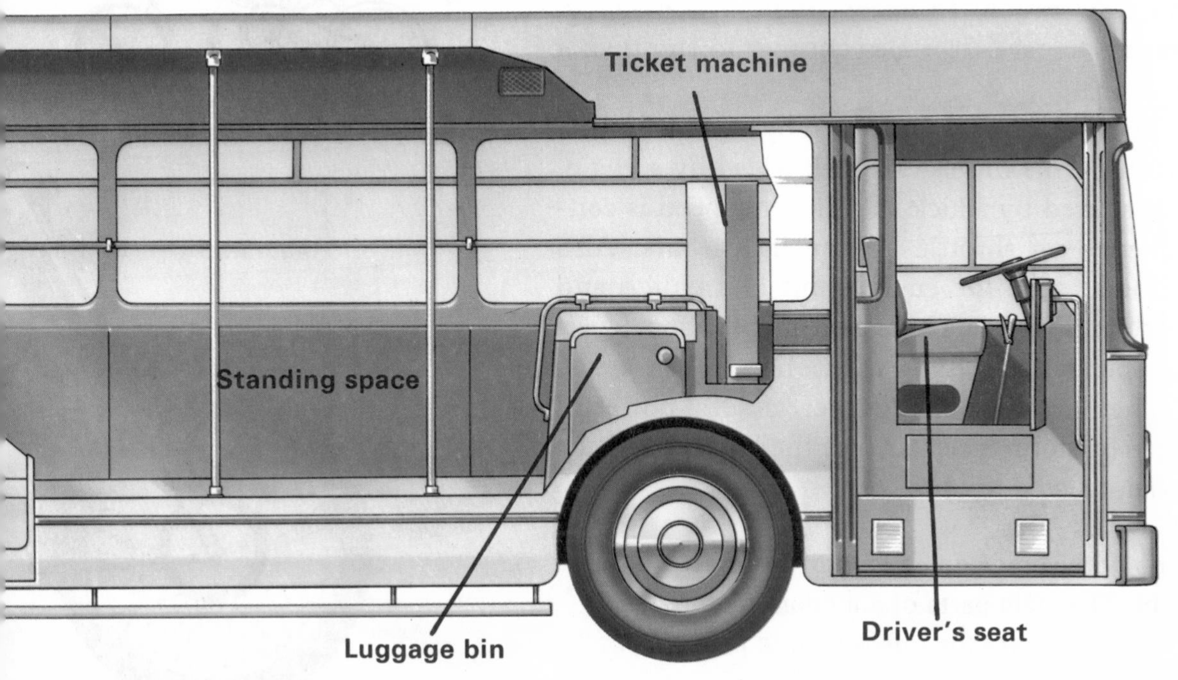

Bicycles

The two-wheeled bicycle is the simplest, cheapest and most silent form of transport there is. Almost anyone from the age of about five can learn to ride one. In flat regions, such as BELGIUM and the NETHERLANDS, bicycles are very widely used. The 75 million bicycles in the world are used for getting to work as well as for pleasure and BICYCLE RACING.

The modern bicycle has two wheels of equal size. In many bicycles made today the wheels are much smaller than in older designs. The bicycle is steered by handlebars attached to the front wheel. It is propelled by means of pedals that drive the back wheel through sprockets (toothed wheels) and a chain. The brakes are worked by levers on the handlebars.

Motorcycles

The motorized BICYCLE, or motorcycle, is a very popular means of transport. Though it is not as comfortable as a MOTOR CAR, it has great speed and acceleration. In heavy traffic it is easier to use and to park. It is also cheaper to run than a car.

The motorcycle is powered by a small PETROL ENGINE. This drives the back wheel by a chain. It is started by a kick starter, and speed is controlled by a throttle on the handlebars. Also included with the engine unit is a clutch and gearbox. The rider changes gear with a foot lever. He operates the clutch with a hand lever.

There are also other, lighter, and less powerful kinds of motorcycle, such as the scooter and the pedal-assisted 'moped'.

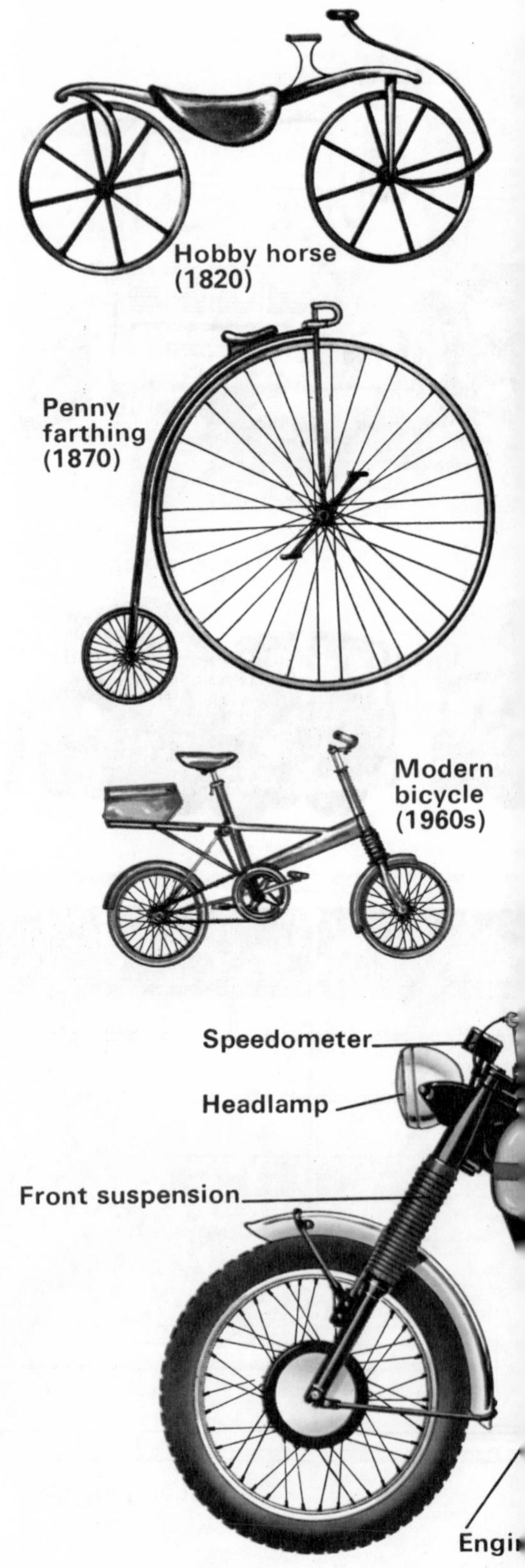

Top right: Three generations of bicycles.
Right: The main parts of a modern motorcycle. The seat will take the rider and one passenger.

Road safety

Since there are hundreds of millions of vehicles on the ROADS, it is not surprising that there are many accidents. In the United States alone, each year some 55,000 people are killed and two million injured in road accidents.

Government organizations, such as the U.S. National Highway Traffic Safety Administration, or private bodies, such as Britain's Royal Society for the Prevention of Accidents, set regulations and publish information aimed at reducing the number of road accidents. Local authorities keep road surfaces in good repair, improve existing roads, and build new ones.

To prevent accidents, everyone must obey the highway code – the rules of the road. They must be familiar with the meanings of the road signs. These warn of danger ahead and give other useful information. People must obey traffic lights, and signals given by the POLICE.

A car or BICYCLE owner should make sure his vehicle is always in good condition, especially the tyres and brakes. He should not drive if he is tired or if he has drunk too much alcohol. He should not drive too fast in bad weather. Car drivers should always wear a safety belt. Motorcycle riders should wear a helmet.

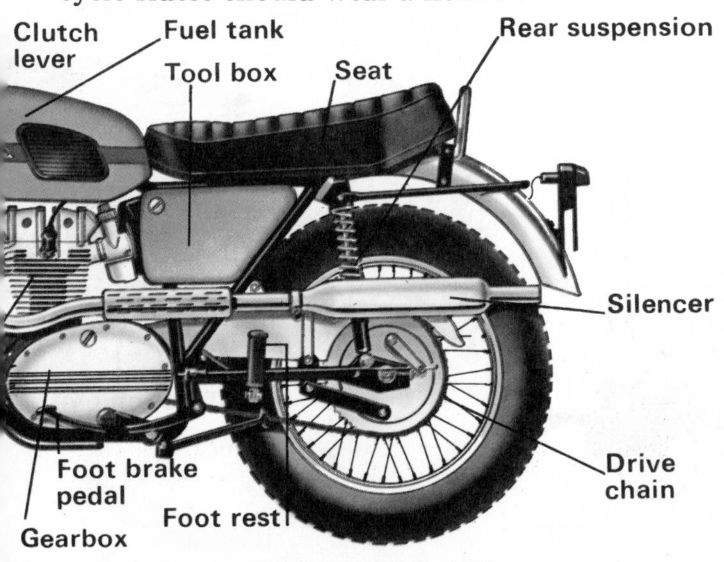

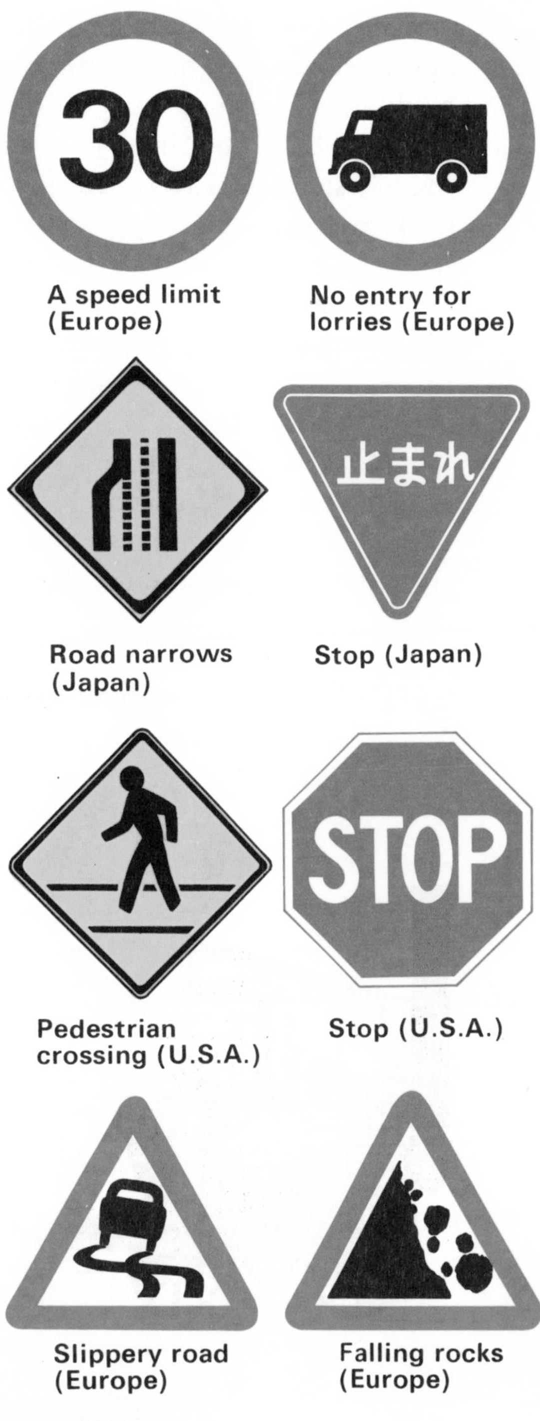

A selection of road signs, which inform drivers of restrictions or warn them of hazards.

Travel by Rail

It is only about 150 years since the true beginning of the railways. The British engineer George STEPHENSON opened one of the world's first public railway lines in 1830 – the line between Manchester and Liverpool. Stephenson's first really successful railway engine was his famous *Rocket*. This was a STEAM ENGINE on wheels. It was the ancestor of all later steam locomotives.

Stephenson was not, however, the inventor of the railway. The Cornish engineer Richard Trevithick developed a crude steam locomotive in 1804. The use of rails for transport dates back at least to the sixteenth century, when 'tramways' were used in COAL mines. The tramway was a track of iron or wood rails, along which the coal trucks were pushed.

The coming of the railways revolutionized communications throughout the world. In particular, it opened up the continent of NORTH AMERICA in the nineteenth century.

Above: A long train of the Canadian Pacific line winds its way through the Rockies.
Left: Two early locomotives.

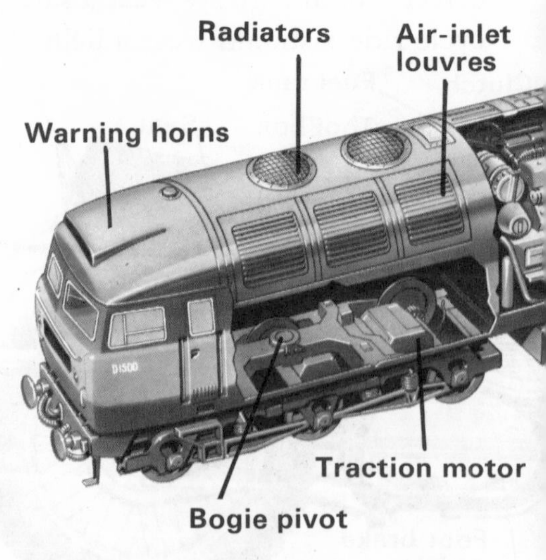

In some countries, especially the U.S.A., the railways are less important than they once were. Competition from the car, LORRY, BUS, and AIRCRAFT has led to this decline. Passenger traffic has decreased, and many lines have been forced to close. The railways still carry a great deal of freight however. They are an economical way of transporting heavy goods over a long distance.

In an attempt to attract more customers, the railways are continually improving their services and efficiency. Faster, cleaner, diesel and electric locomotives have taken over from the steam engines. Speeds of 180 kilometres per hour are becoming commonplace. Long welded lengths of rail are replacing the short ones, and this results in a smoother ride. Many trains now have lounges, restaurants, and sleeping cars.

UNDERGROUND RAILWAYS are being improved and extended in many cities to relieve the traffic congestion on the streets. Experiments are being carried out with new forms of railways, such as HOVERTRAINS.

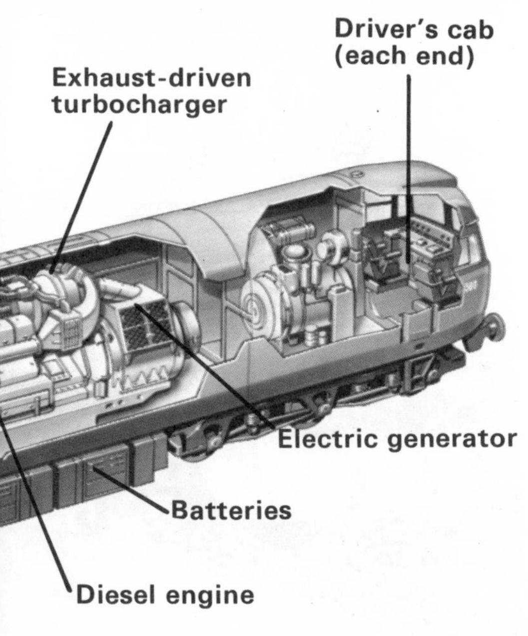

Below left: A modern diesel-electric locomotive used by British Rail.

Below: Japan's fast New Tokaido railway.

Locomotives

There are two main kinds of locomotives on the railways today – diesel and electric. Diesels can run on any railway track. Electric locomotives can run only on a special, electrified track.

Diesel locomotives are powered by one or more DIESEL ENGINES. These burn OIL as a fuel. The power is carried from the engine to the driving wheels of the locomotive by way of the transmission system. Systems may be electric, hydraulic, or mechanical.

In diesel-electric locomotives, the diesel engine turns an electric generator to make electricity. The electricity is then fed to electric motors that turn the driving wheels. In diesel-hydraulic locomotives, moving oil transmits the power from the engine to a shaft driving the locomotive's wheels. In a diesel-mechanical locomotive, power is transmitted from the engine through a gearbox, as in a BUS.

Electric motors drive the wheels of electric locomotives. The electricity is supplied to the locomotive from the outside. Often the power comes from an overhead cable. The locomotive picks up the electricity by means of a sprung arm (or pantograph) on the roof. In other electric locomotives the electricity is picked up from a third rail alongside or between the tracks.

A few locomotives have GAS-TURBINE engines. This engine is much the same kind as is used in jet planes. Oil or gas is burned in the engine in a blast of air. This process produces hot gases that spin a turbine wheel. The wheel drives a generator that produces electricity. The electricity is fed to electric motors on the driving wheels.

Above: The British High Speed Train.

Right: A Russian gas-turbine locomotive, which is suited to long-distance operation.

Above: A French overhead-wire electric train travelling at speed.

Below: The control tower at a marshalling (sorting) yard.

Signals

For safety, a train driver must always know whether the track ahead of him is clear. Various kinds of signals give him that information. The signals are inside and outside his cab. In the past, track signals were of the SEMAPHORE type. Different positions of the arms meant Stop and Go. The signals were worked by men in tall boxes. Each man was responsible for a certain section of track.

Modern signals are more like traffic lights. Coloured lights tell the driver if it is safe to proceed. Signals are now often set electrically from a central control point which may be up to 80 kilometres away.

Automatic devices have been introduced for extra safety. Almost always, the train itself automatically sets the signals behind it at Stop. Many LOCOMOTIVES have an automatic warning system that tells the driver how each signal is set as he approaches. The system puts on the brakes automatically if the driver passes a Stop signal.

Underground railways

Underground railways can be found in many big cities. LONDON has its Underground (or 'Tube'). NEW YORK has its Subway. PARIS and MOSCOW have their Metros. Underground systems provide a fast means of transport in these cities.

London has had underground railways since 1863. The early lines were worked by steam LOCOMOTIVES and ran just below the surface. They were built by the 'cut-and-cover' method. A big trench was cut in the ground and covered over afterwards. The first deep line was not built until 1890. All systems are now electric.

An underground train can start and stop quickly. This helps it to go swiftly between stations. The carriages are often rounded so that they fit snugly into the TUNNELS. They have sliding doors that open and close automatically. They have both sitting and standing room, so that each train can take as many passengers as possible. The electric motors driving the wheels are located beneath the passenger carriages. Electric power comes from a third rail alongside the track or from an overhead wire.

Top right: A station on the Metro in Paris, France.

Right: An ornate hallway in Kievskaya Metro station in Moscow, U.S.S.R.

Below: An underground station in Tokyo, Japan.

Monorails

Ordinary trains run along a track of twin rails. But there are now special trains that run along a single rail. They are called monorails. The idea is not new. Germany has a monorail (the *Wuppertal Schwebebahn*) which has been in operation since 1901. The monorail has, however, been most used in JAPAN.

There are two types of monorail systems. In one, the passenger cars hang from an overhead rail. In the other, the car sits astride the rail. In both types, electric motors turn the driving wheels.

Hovertrains

The HOVERCRAFT is a vehicle that glides over a surface on a 'cushion' of air. Experimental trains have been built using this principle. The hovertrain, as it is called, glides above a MONORAIL track. There is no friction (rubbing) to slow the train down. It can therefore travel very fast. A French *Aérotrain*, for example, has reached a speed of 375 kilometres an hour. Some hovertrains have a propeller. Others are powered by a special kind of electric motor.

Below: One of France's Aérotrains. This one is designed for use over short distances. It is powered by electric motor.

Language and Code

The main way in which we communicate with one another is by speaking. Two people who speak the same language use words which they both know represent certain objects or ideas. They link these words together in a certain way and thus communicate.

If, however, two people do not understand each other's words, then they cannot communicate by language. They may even have to return to the oldest means of communication and use gestures and signs.

Early man communicated by such sign language. He also made use of a few basic sounds. As his BRAIN and his faculties improved, he became able to make different sounds to describe different things. He had, in fact, begun to use words. He was well on the way to developing a spoken language. He also found that he could communicate by drawing objects. In so doing he took the first step towards a written language.

A total of about 5000 languages and dialects are spoken in the world today. Nearly 900 of these come from INDIA.

The language spoken by more people than any other is Mandarin Chinese, which is spoken by about 600 million people. English is spoken in the largest number of countries. It is spoken by more than a tenth of the population in about 30 different countries.

Above: Japanese pupils learning English in a language laboratory.

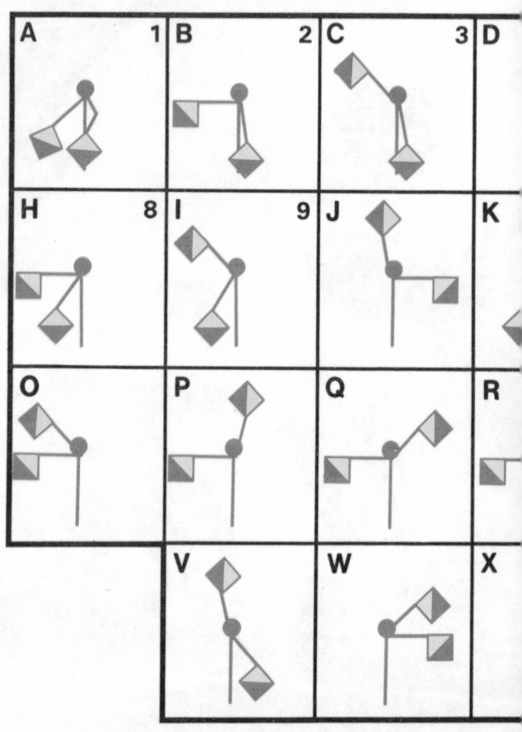

Writing

Early man first began to write in the form of pictures and symbols. In the simplest form of picture-writing, the pictures represented exactly what they showed. A circle stood for the SUN, a lion for a lion, and so on.

As time passed, people began to use pictures in a different way. The pictures stood not only for the objects themselves, but also for ideas

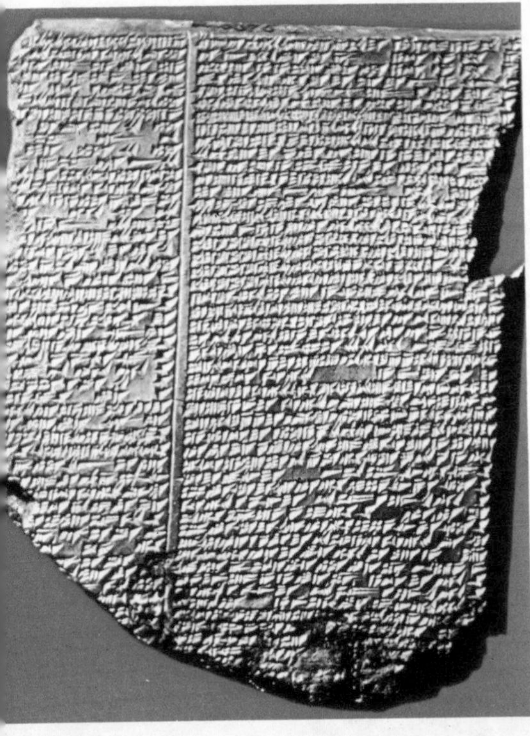

Above: Cuneiform writing.
Below: The semaphore code.

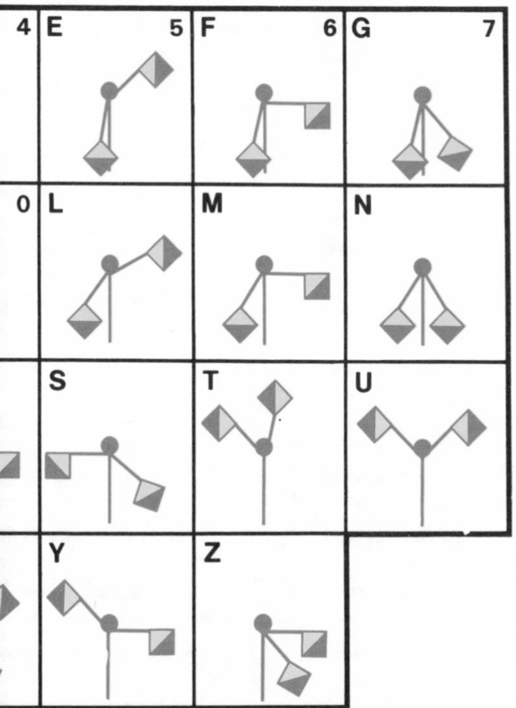

associated with the objects. The circle symbol for the sun could also have the meaning Heat or Day. The lion could also mean Strength or Courage.

Eventually people began to use picture symbols to stand for the words in an idea. In this 'word-writing' the idea 'The man hunts deer in a wood with his two dogs' might be represented by picture symbols of a man's head, two strokes, a dog, a bow and arrow, a deer, and a tree.

Later, symbols came to represent not only a certain word but also the sound of that word. The next stage was for each letter to stand for a sound.

The Sumerians used this form of writing 5000 years ago. They wrote in cuneiform (wedge-shaped) strokes. The EGYPTIANS developed their own form of word picture and phonetic writing, which we call hieroglyphic.

Eventually, a language was broken down into a number of basic sounds. Each sound was given a symbol. This marked the beginnings of an alphabet. Today, western countries use an alphabet based on an early Roman system. But in CHINA no alphabet has ever been developed. Chinese consists of symbols called characters.

Semaphore

One way of communicating over a distance is by semaphore. Semaphore is a system of signalling by two FLAGS held in the hand. Sailors sometimes use semaphore to signal from ship to ship at short range. The signaller holds the flags in various positions to represent letters or numerals.

An 'optical telegraph' using a semaphore system was used for long-distance communication in EUROPE in the early nineteenth century. It was replaced by MORSE's electric TELEGRAPH.

Morse

Morse code is a very useful system of signals which was devised by the inventor of the electric TELEGRAPH, Samuel F.B. Morse. He developed a code of dots and dashes so that he could send messages along the telegraph wires. The dots and dashes are pulses of electricity.

Letters of the alphabet, numerals, and punctuation are represented by different combinations of dots and dashes. Certain other combinations are employed to indicate such things as End of Message or Error.

Morse code is still widely used for long-distance communication by telegraph cable (wire) or RADIO (wireless). Radio operators on ships often use it, and so do amateur radio enthusiasts (hams).

There are other ways in which messages can be sent by Morse code. At sea, ships within sight of each other but out of earshot can communicate by flashing lamp (blinker). This is a searchlight with a shutter which is opened and closed to give short and long flashes. These flashes stand for the dots and dashes of the code.

Above: A signaller tapping out a message in Morse.
Below: The Morse code.

A	•—	J	•———	S	•••	2	••———
B	—•••	K	—•—	T	—	3	•••——
C	—•—•	L	•—••	U	••—	4	••••—
D	—••	M	——	V	•••—	5	•••••
E	•	N	—•	W	•——	6	—••••
F	••—•	O	———	X	—••—	7	——•••
G	——•	P	•——•	Y	—•——	8	———••
H	••••	Q	——•—	Z	——••	9	————•
I	••	R	•—•	1	•————	0	—————

The heliograph was once in widespread use on land for flashing messages in Morse. It used the reflected rays of the SUN to send messages. The sender made the flashes by tilting the mirror reflecting the sunlight.

Braille

Braille is a special code made up of raised dots on PAPER. It enables blind people to read by touch. In this code, different arrangements of up to six dots represent letters of the alphabet, short words such as 'the' and 'and', numerals, and punctuation. The blind person reads braille by lightly running his fingertips over the dots. With practice he can read quite fast. He can write braille by means of a keyboard machine called the braillewriter.

The code is named after a Frenchman, Louis Braille, who introduced it in 1829. Braille was himself blind from the age of three. He was a fine musician and later devised a braille system for writing music.

Deaf-and-dumb language

The problems of communication among some handicapped people are very great. People who cannot speak or hear cannot use language in the ordinary way. Such people may have to rely on gesture or sign language in order to communicate. Or they may use finger spelling, or deaf-and-dumb language. The letters of the alphabet are indicated by different positions of the fingers on one or both hands. Another way deaf people can 'hear' is by watching a person's lips while he is speaking. This is called lip reading. It is difficult to learn and not always accurate.

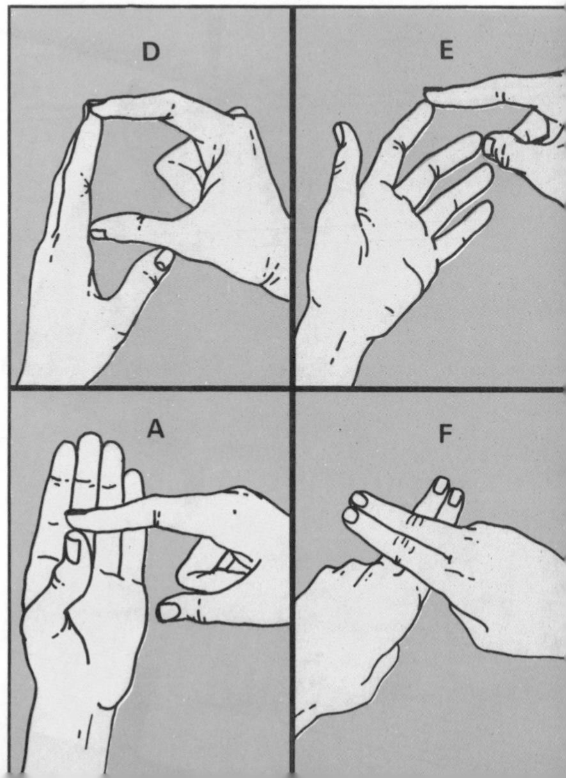

Top right: A blind girl reading a Braille book.
Right: 'DEAF' spelt in deaf-and-dumb language.

Number

At first, western countries used the Roman number system. The ROMANS, like the GREEKS before them, used letters of their alphabet as number symbols, or numerals. The value of a number was obtained by adding together the values of the individual numerals. Thus, as X was the symbol for ten, XXX meant thirty.

The Roman numeral system was very clumsy. It made calculating very difficult. In about A.D. 700 the ARABS introduced a much better system to EUROPE. They had learned it from the HINDUS. The new system was based on powers of ten. It became known as the decimal system (*decem* is Latin for ten). It had symbols for each number from 1 to 9 and also a zero symbol. The system worked on the principle of place value. Thus 1296 meant 1 thousand, 2 hundreds, 9 tens, and 6 ones. We use this Arabic system today.

Mathematicians use other number systems, based on units other than 10. The binary system, for example, is based on multiples of 2.

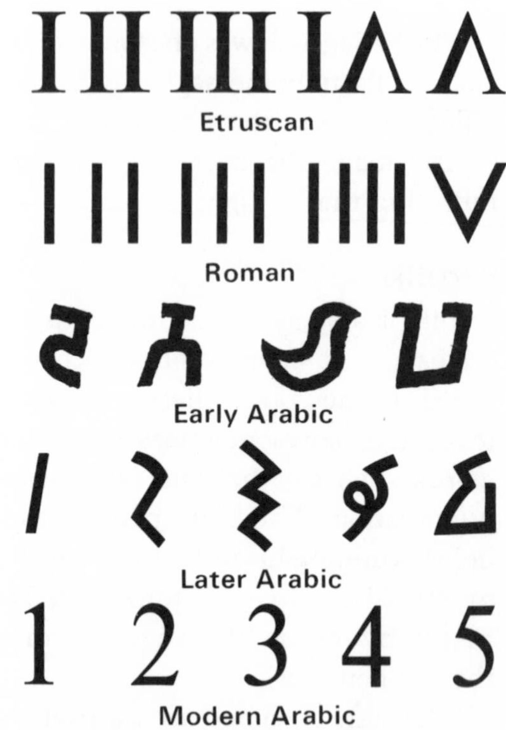

Above: Some numeral systems.
Bottom left: Calculating devices.
Below: A comparative scale of feet and metres.

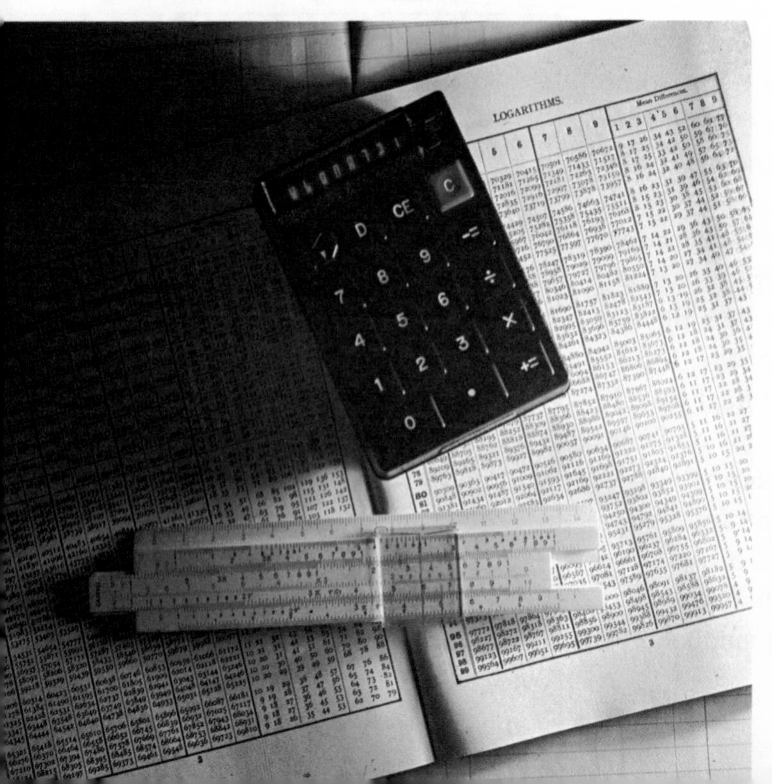

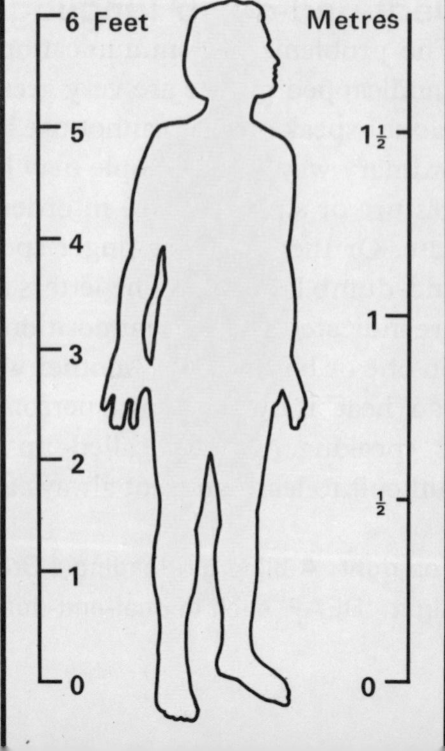

Weights and measures

The most widely used system of weights and measures is the metric system. It is a logical decimal measuring system first worked out by the French in the 1790s. Each unit in the metric system is ten times bigger than the one before it. The term metric system is used because all other units are based upon the metre.

The basic unit, the metre, is precisely defined. Originally it was intended to be one ten-millionth of the distance between the North Pole and the equator. Now it is defined as 1,650,763.73 wavelengths of the light given out by a form of the gas krypton.

Before most countries adopted the metric system, there were many different ways of weighing and measuring things. In the English length measurement, for example, there were 12 inches in a foot, 3 feet in a yard, 22 yards in a chain, and so on. The yard, which became the standard unit, was first defined as the distance from King Henry I's nose to his fingertips.

1 ounce	= 28·35 grammes
1 pound	= 453·6 grammes
	= 0·45 kilogramme
1 U.S. ton	= 907 kilogrammes
	= 0·91 metric ton
1 English ton	= 1016 kilogrammes
	= 1·02 metric tons
1 inch	= 25·4 millimetres
1 foot	= 304·8 millimetres
1 yard	= 0·91 metre
1 mile	= 1·61 kilometres
1 U.S. pint	= 0·47 litre
1 English pint	= 0·57 litre
1 U.S. gallon	= 3·79 litres
1 English gallon	= 4·55 litres

Comparison of measures. In the jugs (left to right): 1 English pint, 1 litre, and 1 U.S. pint. In front, a kilogramme of butter (left) compared with a pound.

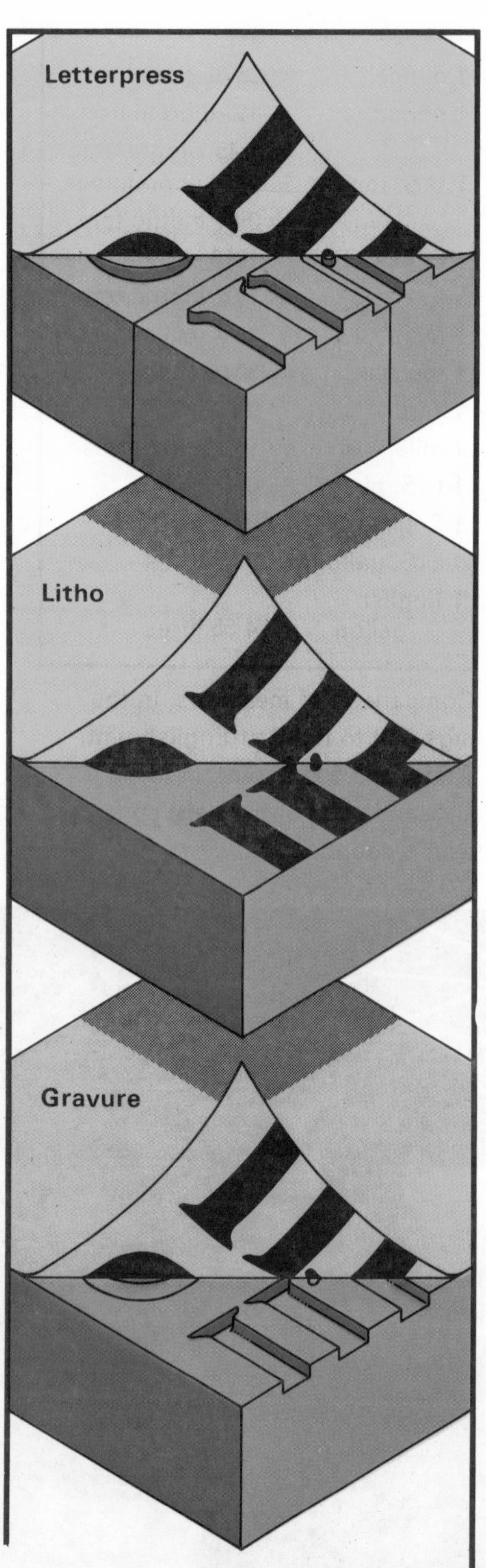

Printing

More than 500 years ago, a German, Johann Gutenberg pioneered modern printing methods with his invention of movable type. Type is the term for the pieces of metal from which printing is carried out. Gutenberg cast his type in tiny moulds. He assembled the type letters into words, the words into lines, and the lines into pages. Then he locked the pages into frames, inked the type surface, and pressed a sheet of PAPER against it. An image of the words was transferred to the paper.

The method of printing Gutenberg used is called the letterpress process. It is still widely used, in an improved form, especially for printing NEWSPAPERS. A more recent and increasingly popular method is litho (short for lithography). The printing is done from a flat surface. The type image is transferred to the surface photographically. A third printing method is gravure, in which printing is done from a pitted surface.

Methods of typesetting are now completely mechanized. Monotype and Linotype machines have long been widely used. In Monotype setting, each letter is cast separately in a mould. In Linotype a whole line of type is cast at once. A more recent method is photosetting. The type image is made on photographic film.

Before pictures can be printed they must be 'screened', or reduced to a pattern of dots of various sizes. (You can see the dots clearly in newspaper pictures.) Most colour printing is done using four colours. All the colours must be broken down into combinations of black, yellow, magenta (red), and cyan (blue). Separate printing plates are made for each colour.

Left: The principles of the main printing processes showing the different kinds of printing plates.

2

4

Above: The four pictures show how full colour in printing is built up stage by stage. 1. Blue. 2. Yellow added. 3. Red added. 4. Black added.
Right: The golf-ball head used in the modern electric typewriter shown below it.

Typewriters

The typewriter is a writing machine with which an expert can type 140 or more words a minute. This is considerably faster than anyone can write.

The basic principle of typewriter operation has changed little. The typist strikes a key on the keyboard. This forces a piece of type against an inked ribbon in contact with the PAPER. But today's machines have many refinements which make for faster, more accurate typing. Electric machines are particularly fast and easy to use.

The typewriter was invented in 1868.

Reference books

In order to study any subject properly, you will need to be able to use reference books. You are reading a work of reference at this moment.

Reference books can give general information, or they can deal with one subject. Encyclopedias try to cover the whole field of knowledge. An encyclopedia for adults may have thousands of pages, and may be in many volumes.

Atlases and dictionaries are other important kinds of reference books. Atlases are basically collections of maps, though they may contain much other information. Dictionaries explain the meaning of words, and you can also use them to check how a word is spelt.

Right: The reading room at the British Museum.

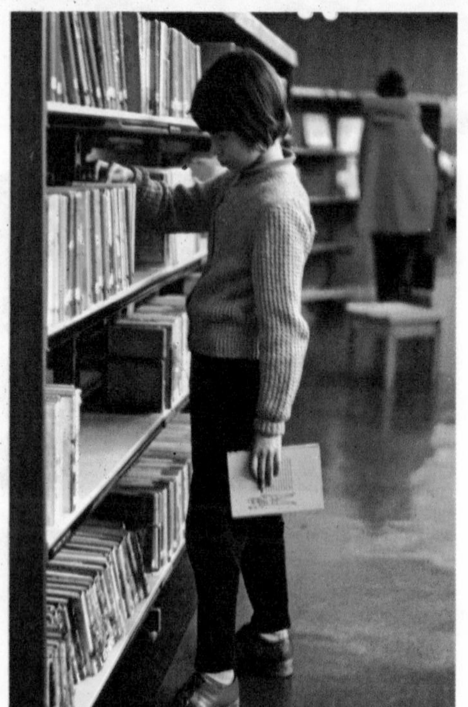

Above: Inside a children's library. Most public libraries have a children's section.

Libraries

No-one can hope to own all the books he may want to read or use. Fortunately, there are libraries in most towns that will lend us the books. Some are school libraries, others are public libraries.

A good library contains thousands of books on all kinds of subjects. They are arranged on the shelves in a certain order so that any particular book is easy to find. Fiction books (novels), for example, are usually arranged alphabetically, according to the names of the authors. Non-fiction books are arranged subject by subject. Each subject is given a number according to a standard method of classification. The most common system is the Dewey decimal system.

Most libraries have a reference section as well as the ordinary lending section. The books in the reference library are REFERENCE BOOKS and are for use in the library only. This section often has a variety of NEWSPAPERS and MAGAZINES.

Above: Some well-known international magazines.

Newspapers

Newspapers provide us with up-to-the-minute news of the world about us. National newspapers, such as the *Daily Telegraph*, provide information about events world-wide; local newspapers concentrate on items of local interest, such as town planning.

Newspapers work to very strict deadlines. Morning papers must go to press in the early hours of the morning so that they can be printed for distribution by breakfast-time.

Above: Setting newspaper copy.

Magazines

Magazines are usually less concerned with day-to-day news than NEWSPAPERS. They appear less often than newspapers (usually by the week, month, or perhaps four times a year). Some have millions of readers. Others have no more than a few hundred. It is possible to find magazines on almost any subject – business, sports, hobbies, science, and books. Some magazines report and discuss the news. Others publish stories and poems. Magazines are printed to last longer than newspapers.

Flags

Sailors of all countries can communicate with one another by means of the international flag code. Each letter of the alphabet is represented by a flag of a different colour and pattern. Each numeral from 0 to 9 is represented by a coloured pennant (a flag that narrows at one end). Messages can be sent from ship to ship by spelling out the words letter by letter in a string of flags.

In addition, each alphabet flag has a separate meaning. So have combinations of other alphabet flags. Here are some examples of the code. The flag for the letter A, when hoisted by itself, means 'I am undergoing speed trials'. O by itself means 'Man overboard!' P, the so-called 'Blue Peter', means 'I am about to proceed to sea'. The combination NC means 'I am in distress and require immediate assistance'. The combination PYU means 'Have a good voyage'.

Many phrases that are likely to be used at sea are represented by one or a group of code letters. Ships carry a code book that explains the code in several languages. When a ship is using the international code it flies the 'code flag and answering pennant'. Three other flags, called substitutes, complete the international code. A substitute is used for a repeated letter in a signal.

Several other flags may be flown by a ship. Merchant ships fly a house flag of the company that owns them. They also fly the national flag, or the merchant flag of the country where they are registered. Britain's merchant flag, for example, is the Red Ensign, often called the 'Red Duster'. Naval ships also fly an identifying flag at the stern to indicate their country of origin. This can be the same as the national flag.

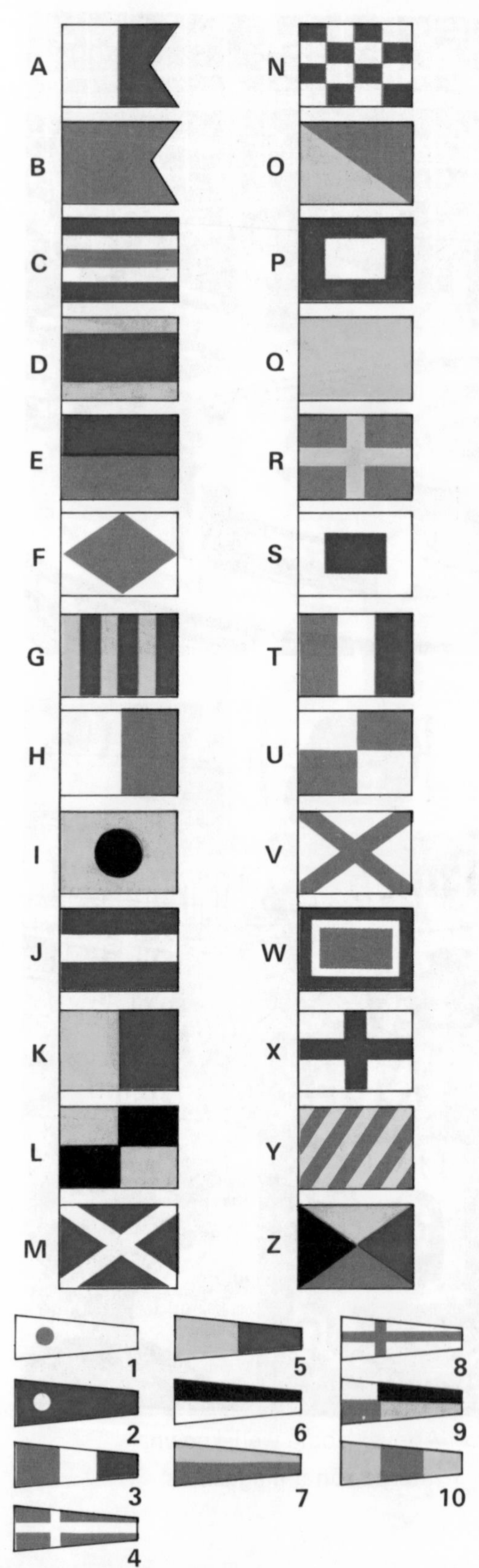

Right: Alphabet and number flags of the flag code.

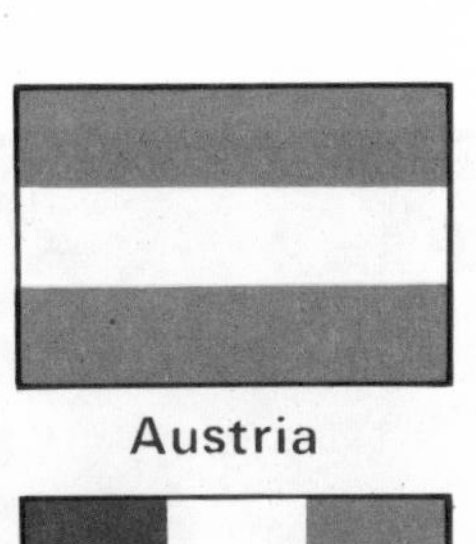
Austria

Belgium

Denmark

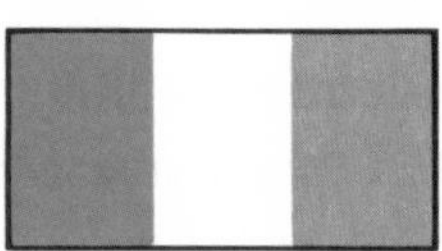
Ireland

Finland

France

West Germany

Greece

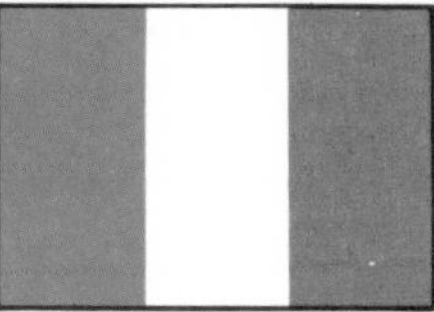
Italy

Netherlands

Norway

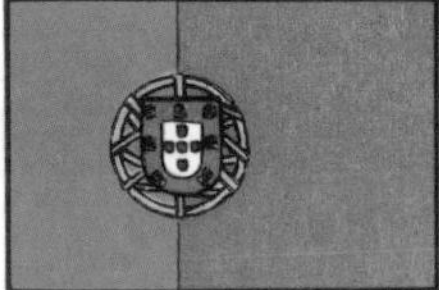
Portugal

Spain

Sweden

Switzerland

United Kingdom

Brazil

Canada

Jamaica

Mexico

United States

South Africa

Egypt

Ghana

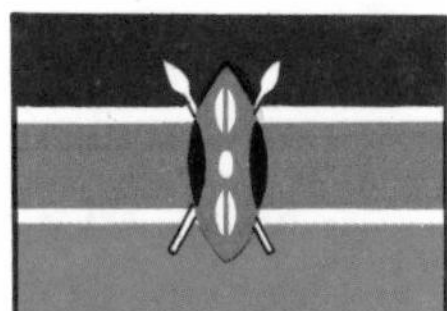
Kenya

Nigeria

India

Lebanon

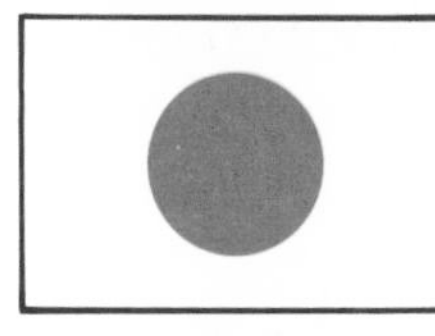
Japan

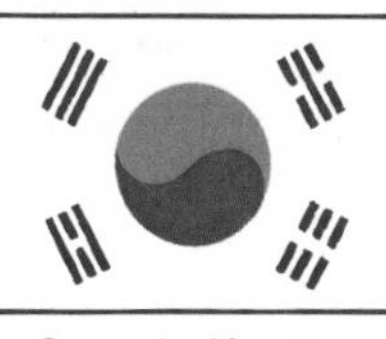
South Korea

Nationalist China

Sri Lanka

Indonesia

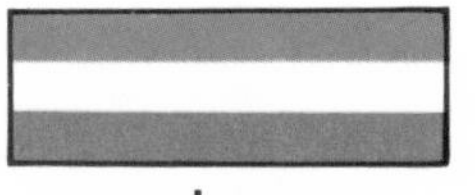
Iran

Malaysia

Nepal

Thailand

U.S.S.R.

Australia

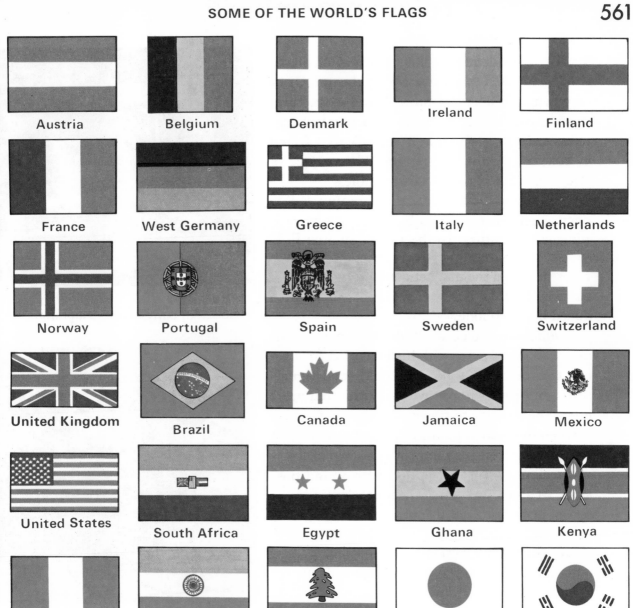

New Zealand

Today, someone in NEW YORK may switch on the RADIO and listen to a concert from Boston. Or he may switch on his TELEVISION set and see pictures transmitted live from PARIS via a COMMUNICATIONS SATELLITE. He may even talk to a friend in TOKYO over the TELEPHONE. The science of electronics has made all this possible.

Telecommunications, or communications over a long distance, really began in the early nineteenth century. In the 1830s, Samuel F. B. MORSE was sending coded messages through wires. He used the magnetic effect of an electric current. In 1876 Alexander Graham BELL produced his telephone.

Guglielmo MARCONI made the next communications advance with his invention of wireless telegraphy in 1896. He could send signals through the air without wires. Within ten years it became possible to transmit voice by wireless. By then the motion picture was well established, though silent. In 1927 improved SOUND RECORDING techniques made pictures with sound possible. At about the same time, experiments were taking place with television.

Above: Bell's original telephone.
Below: An early Morse telegraph.

Below: Marconi (far left) in Newfoundland, watching preparations for the first transatlantic wireless transmission, 1901.

Microphones

Before sound can be recorded or transmitted by wire or RADIO, it must be changed into electrical signals. This is done by the microphone. Microphones contain a thin metal disc or strip (the 'diaphragm') that vibrates when sound hits it. These vibrations are then made to set up tiny electric currents in various ways.

In one common microphone the diaphragm is connected to a coil placed between the ends of a magnet. A current is set up in the coil when the diaphragm moves it. In another kind of microphone the vibrating diaphragm presses on a certain kind of crystal and sets up a current.

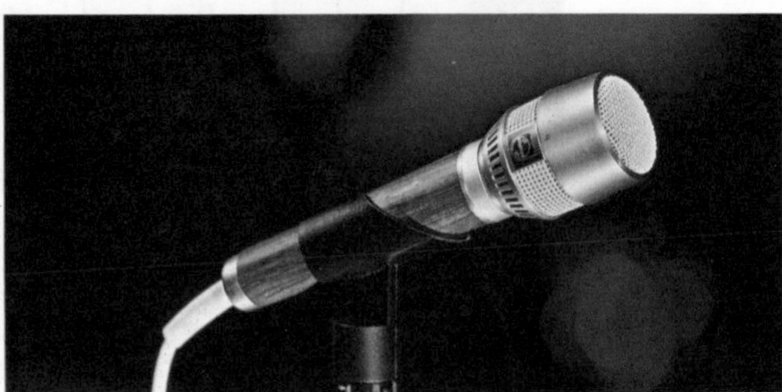

Above: One type of microphone widely used for broadcasting and recording.

Loudspeakers

A MICROPHONE is needed to change sound signals into electrical impulses. In order to change the impulses back into sounds, you need a loudspeaker.

The loudspeaker is, in fact, a microphone in reverse. It contains a device that vibrates when electrical signals are passed through it. Many loudspeakers change electrical signals into vibrations by means of a coil and magnet. These vibrations are then transmitted to a large, cone-shaped diaphragm. The diaphragm vibrates in the air and makes sound waves.

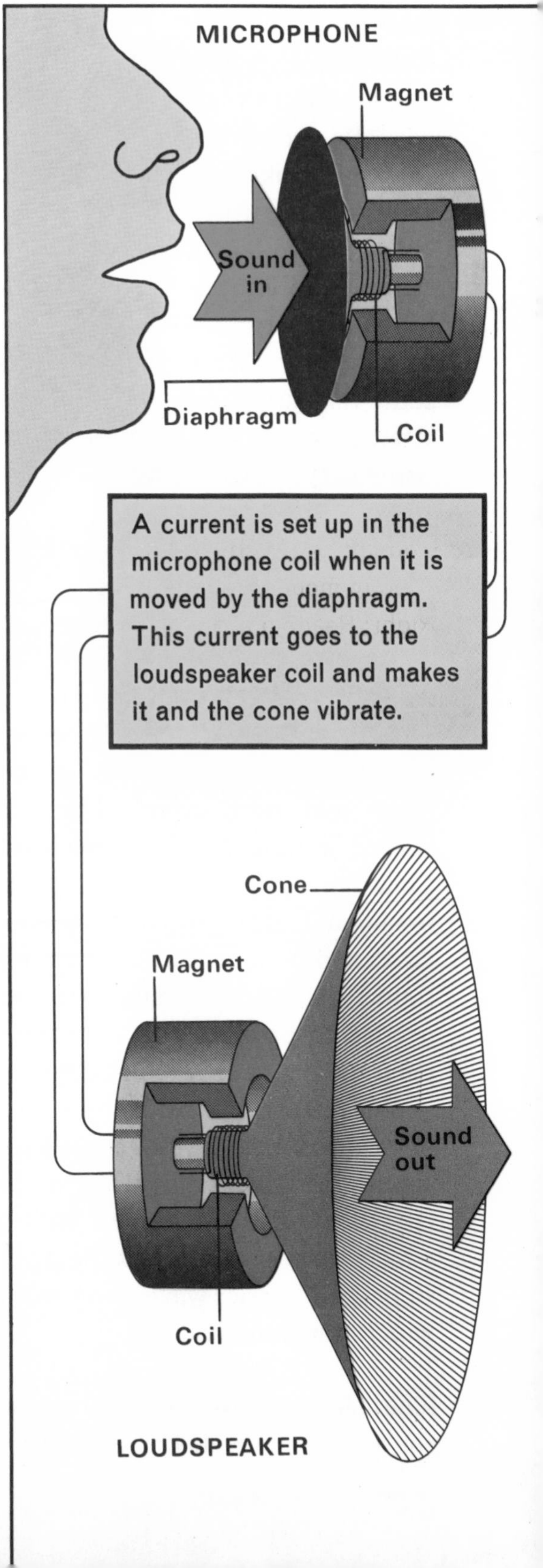

MICROPHONE

Magnet

Sound in

Diaphragm

Coil

A current is set up in the microphone coil when it is moved by the diaphragm. This current goes to the loudspeaker coil and makes it and the cone vibrate.

Cone

Magnet

Sound out

Coil

LOUDSPEAKER

Radio

Most countries have radio broadcasting stations that send out a variety of programmes to inform, educate, and entertain their listeners. There are something like 700 million ordinary radio receivers in the world at present.

Radio also has more specialized uses. Short-range radio is used by ARMIES and the POLICE. Ships use RADIO DIRECTION FINDING equipment in navigation. Most ships, some trains, and even some cars, are equipped with radio TELEPHONES. Passengers can dial into the telephone network while they are travelling.

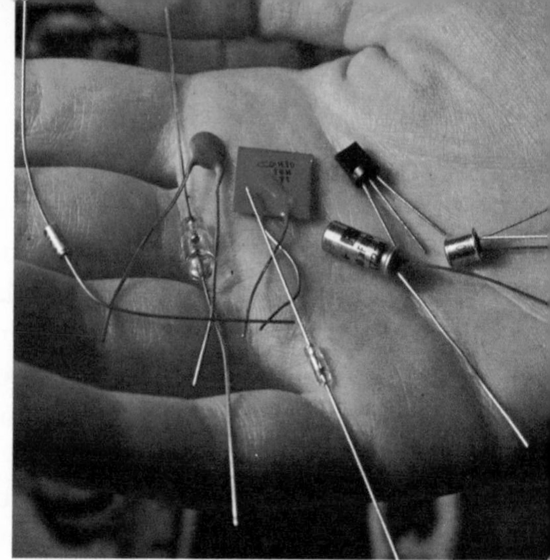

Top left: A handful of transistors of the kind used in modern radio receivers.
Right: Reading a play in a radio studio.

Most radio programmes are recorded in the studio of a radio station. However, other items are broadcast 'live', such as concerts, news items, and sports events. They may also be recorded on tape. At a live broadcast of a play, for example, the performers are in a sound-proof studio and speak into a MICROPHONE. The producer and engineers direct operations and control sound quality. A sound effects man may be needed to produce the right noises to accompany the dialogue, such as doors slamming.

The result of the studio performance is a series of electrical signals from the microphone. These signals cannot be broadcast as they are. First they have to be combined with a radio wave, which can be sent through the air. The combined signal and 'carrier wave' then goes to a tall aerial, which transmits it.

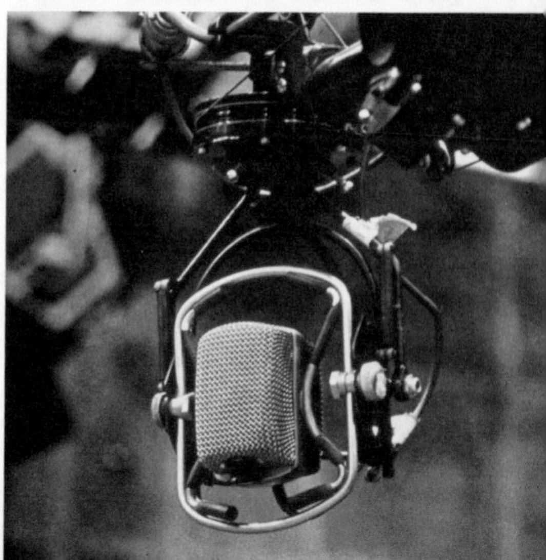

Right: A studio overhead microphone.
Far right: An outside broadcast van and crew.

A radio receiver picks up the combined signal and carrier wave with its aerial. It sorts out the signals from the carrier wave and feeds them to a LOUDSPEAKER. In this way the original sounds that entered the studio microphone are reproduced.

Left: A simple crystal radio which can be made cheaply and easily.

Early radio receivers used gas-filled tubes (valves) to strengthen and sort out the incoming waves. But today most receivers contain tiny transistors instead. They are cheaper and more reliable than valves. They also need less power.

Below: A transmitting aerial for broadcasting. Aerials are built extremely tall so that they can transmit over a great distance.

Sound recording

Not all RADIO programmes are broadcast 'live'. Most have been recorded previously on magnetic tape and then played back on a tape recorder for the broadcast. A great many gramophone records are also played in music programmes. Records and tapes are the main forms of sound recording in use today. Thomas A. EDISON pioneered sound recording in 1877 when he invented the phonograph. This was the forerunner of the gramophone, but it played wax cylinders rather than plastic records.

Before sounds can be recorded, they must be changed into electrical signals. This is done by a MICROPHONE. In gramophone recording, the electrical signals from the recording microphone are made to vibrate a needle. This cuts a wavy groove on a revolving disc. This disc is played back by putting a pick-up needle in the groove as the disc is spinning. The groove makes the needle vibrate. Then a device in the pick-up head changes these vibrations into electrical signals. These signals are fed to a LOUDSPEAKER, which reproduces the original recorded sounds.

In tape recording, the electrical signals from the recording microphone are changed into magnetic signals by a sensitive magnetic device called the recording head. The magnetic signals make an invisible pattern on a moving magnetic tape. To play back the recording, the tape is run past a playback head. This acts in the opposite way to the recording head. It produces electrical signals from the recorded magnetic ones, which are fed to the loudspeaker.

In the modern 'music centre', a cassette tape recorder, record player and radio are built into a single unit.

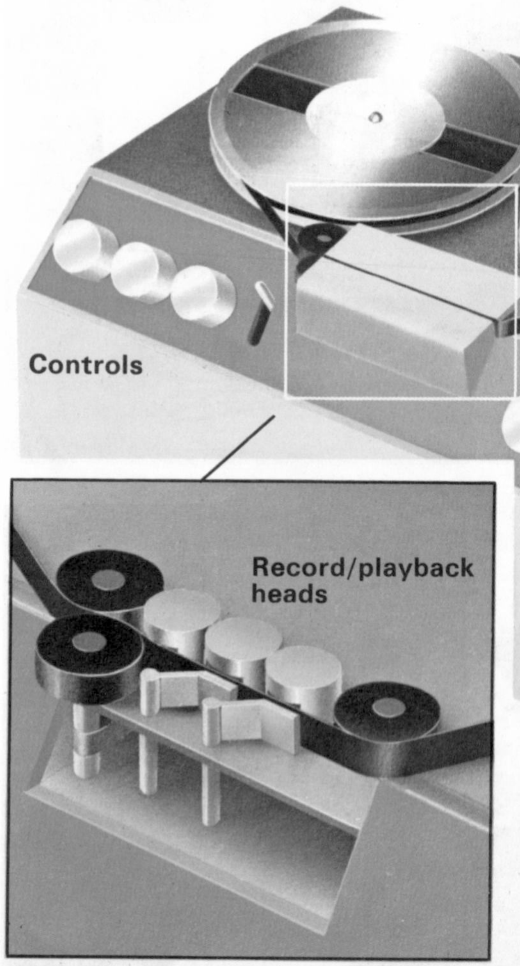

Right: An early Edison cylinder phonograph.

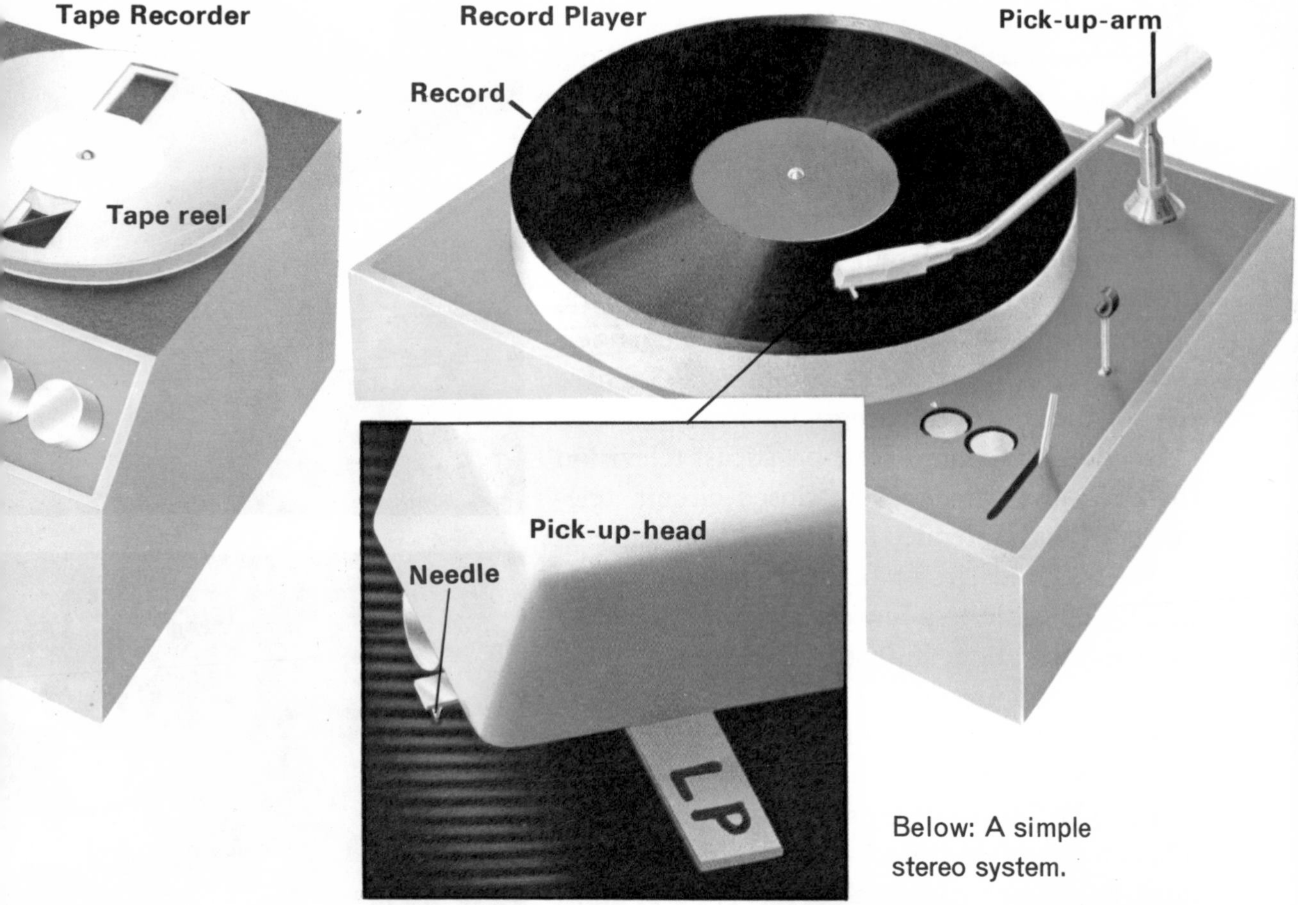

Tape Recorder

Tape reel

Record Player

Record

Pick-up-arm

Pick-up-head

Needle

LP

Top left: A tape recorder. Inset are shown the drive mechanism and record/playback heads.
Top right: A record player. Inset are shown the pick-up head and needle, or stylus.

Below: A simple stereo system.

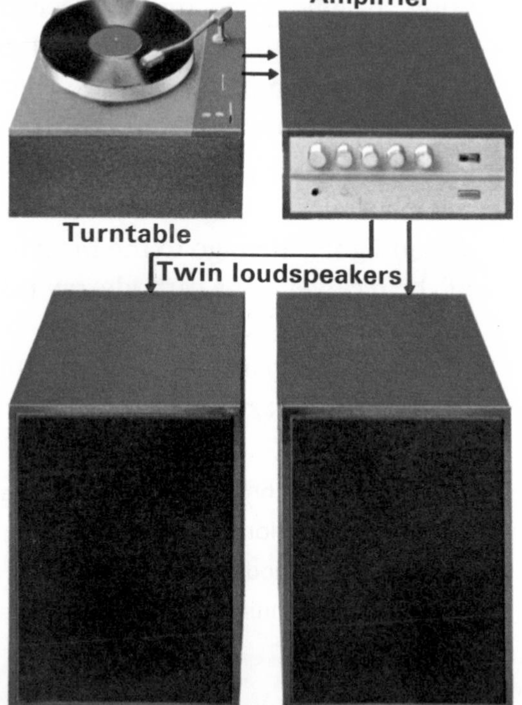

Stereo

Sound recorded with a single MICROPHONE and played back over a single LOUDSPEAKER never sounds quite like the original. It is possible to get a much more realistic effect by using two microphones and two loudspeakers placed to right and left. The result is stereophonic sound, or 'stereo'. We ourselves hear stereophonically because we have two ears. There are stereo record players and stereo tape recorders.

Television

Television broadcasting on a large scale did not begin until the late 1940s. At first, transmissions were only in black and white. Now they are mainly in colour.

Today, viewers have the choice of a variety of programmes on different channels. There are programmes on sport, drama, FILMS, opera, quizzes, and news reports. Some of the channels carry advertising, known as 'commercials'. These pay for the cost of the programmes.

In addition to large-scale broadcast television there is also small-scale 'closed-circuit television'. This is intended for a limited audience. It is called closed-circuit because transmission is usually by cable to a few receivers. It is widely used in education, industry, the POLICE force, and other organizations.

Television is a means of sending moving pictures by RADIO waves. A special camera views the scene to be televised and records an image of it. This image is made up of hundreds of horizontal lines. Each line is composed of tiny spots of light, some bright, some dull. The camera changes these spots into electrical impulses (vision signals). It transmits the picture spot by spot and line by line, moving from left to right.

This process is called scanning. It is done by a beam of electrons from an electron gun. The vision signals then go to the most important part of the receiver – the cathode-ray tube. This tube re-creates the picture.

Colour television is more complicated. First the camera breaks down the colours in a picture

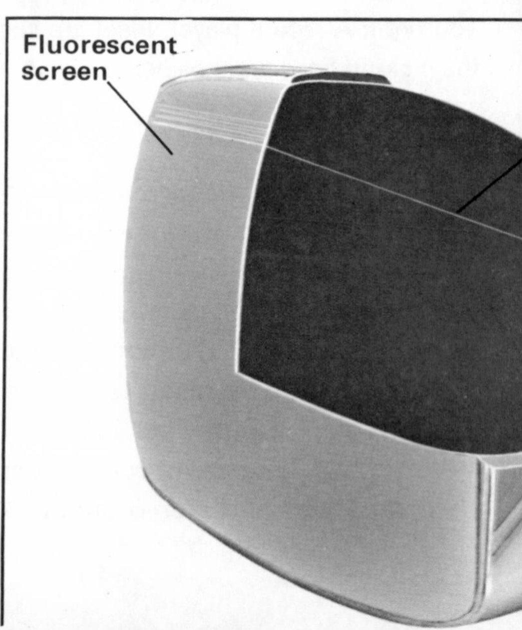

Top: An outside broadcast television camera.
Centre: A television studio controller.
Right: A TV cathode-ray tube, showing a thin beam of electrons scanning across the screen.

Top: Making an adventure serial in the television studio.
Above: Making sets for television productions.

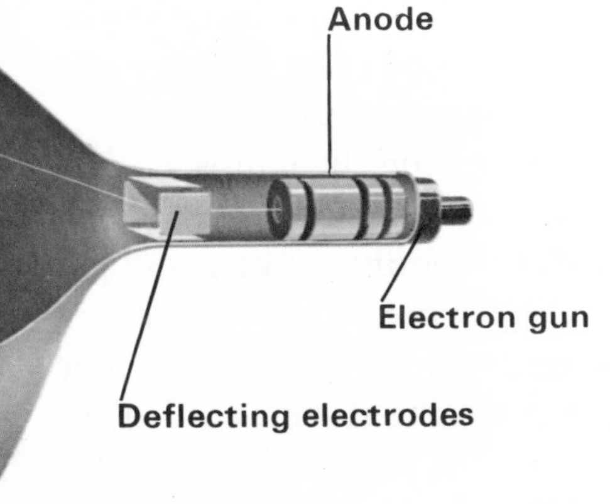

into different combinations of the basic colours red, blue, and green. Then it transmits separate signals representing each colour.

Some television receivers, called teletext, are equipped to receive more than just broadcast programmes. They can receive selected information on their screens about all kinds of subjects from news items to exchange rates. Teletext was pioneered in Britain with such systems as Ceefax (BBC) and Oracle (Independent Television).

Films

Films (motion pictures) are one of the most popular forms of entertainment. They have progressed from flickering, black-and-white silent films to the colourful, wide-screen sound films of today.

The ciné, or movie camera, cannot take a picture that actually moves. The result of trying to do so would be one big blur. The camera takes a series of still pictures, or frames, one after the other. Each frame shows any movement a little further advanced than the frame before it. To show the film, a projector throws the sequence of still pictures rapidly on to a screen. Our EYES continue to see one frame for a fraction of a second after it has disappeared. Our eyes cannot pick up the break between one frame and the next. We therefore have an illusion of movement.

Left: A piece of film, showing the sound track running down the right-hand side.
Right: Shooting a film in a studio.

The ciné camera takes its pictures on film that is sensitive to light. The film is moved past the camera LENS by a motor. A claw mechanism holds the film still briefly while each frame is exposed. While the film is moving between frames, a shutter cuts off the light from the lens and thus prevents blurring. The projector shines a light through the developed film and throws a magnified image on to the screen.

The sound accompanying the film is also recorded on the filmstrip at the side of the frames. It can be recorded as a continuous band of light and dark shades. Or it can be tiny lines of different lengths. Or it can be a very thin strip of magnetic tape. Whatever is used, the result is called the sound track.

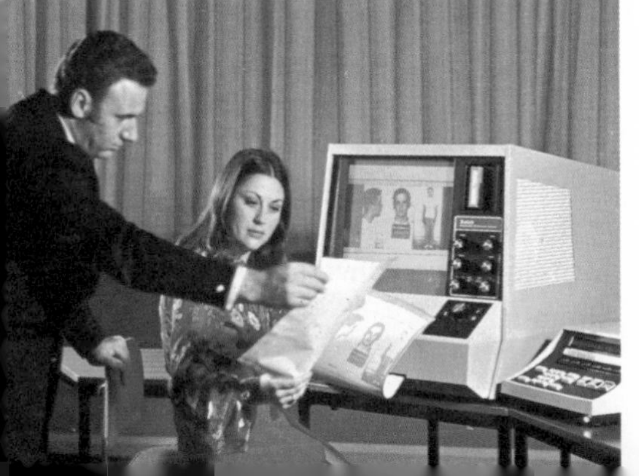

Left: A piece of microfilm (actual size).
Bottom left: A unit for reading microfilm.

Microfilm

Because space in buildings has become expensive, storing the vast amounts of printed paper that is now produced has become quite a problem, especially for reference LIBRARIES.

One solution to the problem is to put the information on film. Several pages of a NEWSPAPER, or many pages of a book, are photographed side-by-side, using a narrow strip of film. A thick book or a pile of newspapers is thus stored on a small roll of film. This is called microfilm. When someone wants to look at the book again, the microfilm is put into a projector, which throws a magnified image on to a viewing screen.

Telephones

One piece of communications equipment we are all familiar with is the telephone. Using the telephone, we can speak to friends in another street, in another town, or thousands of kilometres overseas. Local connections between telephones are made by wires. But long-distance connections may involve the use of microwaves (very short RADIO waves) and even a COMMUNICATIONS SATELLITE. The first workable telephone was made in 1876 by Alexander Graham BELL.

The telephone handset is a combined transmitter and receiver. The transmitter is a kind of MICROPHONE. It is in the mouthpiece. When you speak into it, the sound vibrates a thin diaphragm. This presses against some grains of carbon and causes an electric current passing through the grains to vary. The sound of your voice is changed into electrical signals that can then be transmitted over the telephone wires.

The receiver in the earpiece contains a diaphragm which is vibrated by the electrical signals from other telephones. The vibrating diaphragm sets up sound waves identical to those that entered the far-off transmitter.

Connections are made between one telephone and another through a central exchange. Each telephone subscriber is given an identifying number. When someone wishes to make a call, he picks up his telephone and dials the number of the person he wishes to talk with. Dialling sends a series of electrical pulses through the telephone wire to the exchange. There, the pulses operate a number of switches which select the route to the telephone he is calling, and connect him to it. Telephone operators deal with calls to and from places which are not on an automatic system. They also deal with enquiries and problem calls.

Above: London's Post Office Tower is a transmitting and receiving aerial for telephone conversations and TV signals.

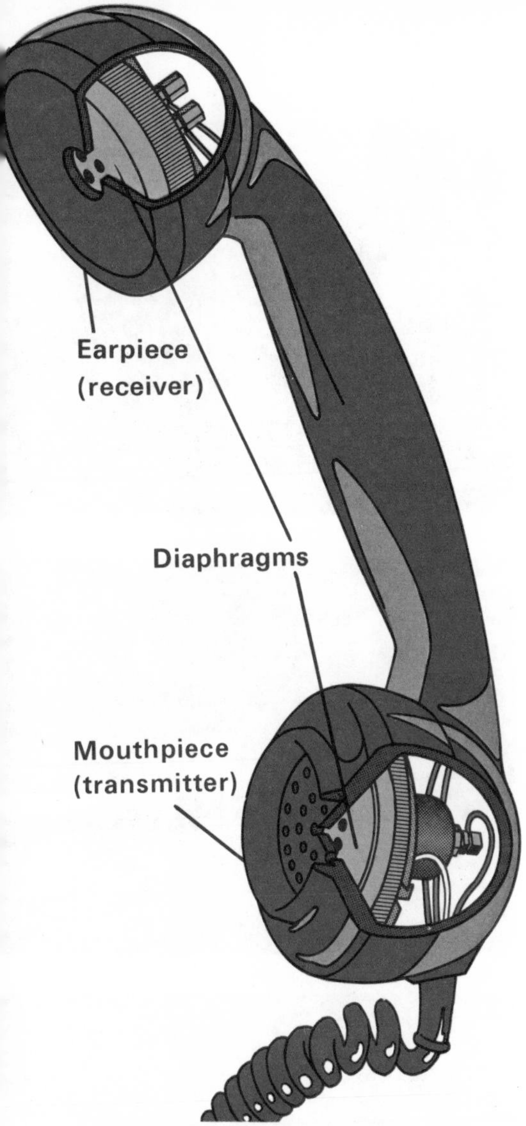

The postal service

In many countries, including AUSTRALIA, BRITAIN and FRANCE, but not the UNITED STATES, the telephone network is one of the services provided by the Post Office. The main function of the Post Office, however, is to deliver mail. To pay for this service it charges for stamps, which must be stuck on every letter before it will be delivered. Many businesses use a franking machine to make a stamp-like mark on the letters, instead of using stamps.

Vast quantities of mail are distributed throughout the country every day, mostly by road and rail. Letters and parcels going abroad are often sent by air. The United States has the largest postal system, which handles some 100,000 million letters and parcels each year.

In recent years, most main post offices have installed automatic machines to cope with the increasing volume of mail. The machines sort the mail into different sizes, cancel the stamps, and put it into piles for different regions.

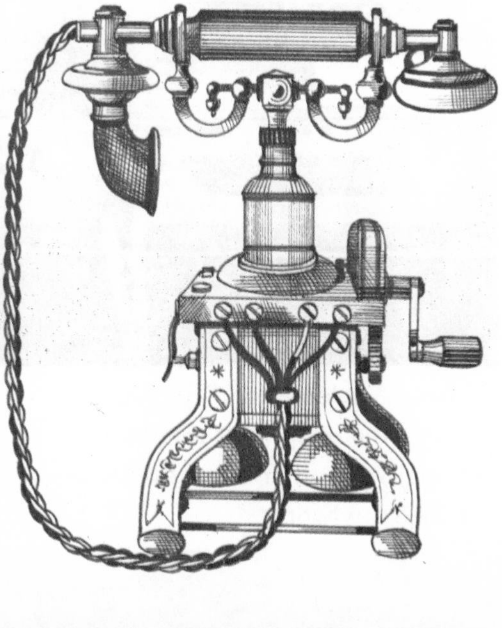

Left: Two British telephones:
above, a modern handset; below, a 1910 model.
Below: Part of the sorting and despatch areas of a modern post office.

Telegraph

Samuel F. B. MORSE began the modern revolution in communications with his invention of the telegraph in the 1830s. The telegraph is a means of sending electric impulses representing letters and numbers through a wire. Morse also devised a suitable code for sending messages (the Morse code). Telegraphy is now less important because of improved TELEPHONE services.

In a simple telegraph the sender taps out his message with a key. When he presses the key down, a pulse of electricity flows through the wires to a receiver, or sounder. The sounder makes a clicking noise when current passes through it. The person receiving can translate the clicks into the message.

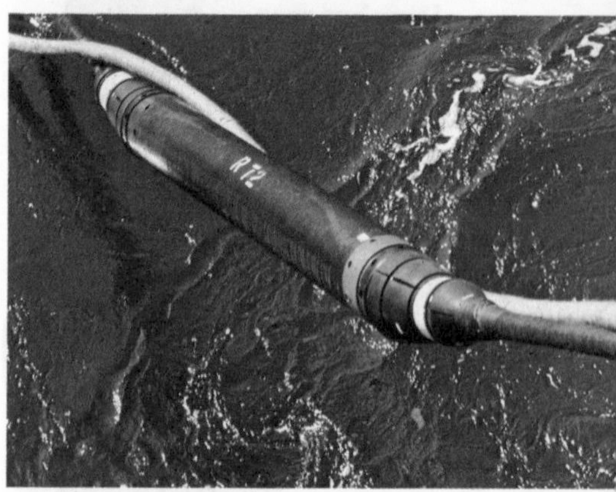

Top right: Looking for a fault in the Atlantic telegraph cable in 1865.
Right: A repeater, used to boost the strength of signals sent through the cable.

Teleprinters

Today, most TELEGRAPH messages are sent automatically by a machine called a teleprinter. This is a keyboard machine that looks like a TYPEWRITER. It transmits each letter as a combination of five electrical pulses. A receiving teleprinter automatically changes the pulses back into letters, and types them out. Regular teleprinter users subscribe to the 'Telex' network and reach each other by dialling.

Telegrams are another way of sending telegraph messages. A telegram is a teleprinter message which is put on a special form and delivered by a telegraph office or post office. Overseas telegrams are called cables, because they are often routed via undersea cables. A network of underseas cables links the continents.

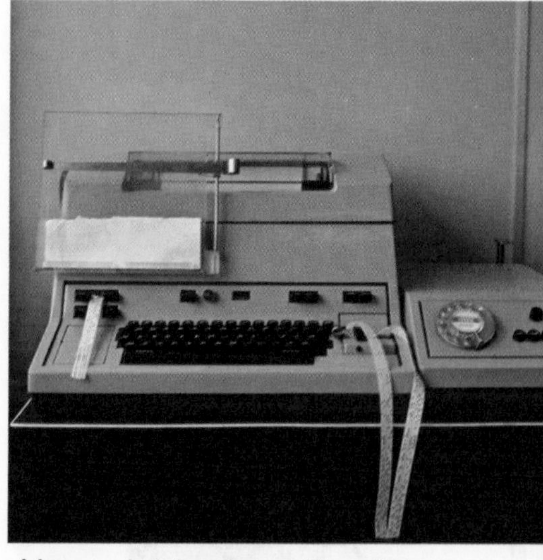

Above: A teleprinter. The dial enables the teleprinter operator to connect with other subscribers on the Telex network.

Communications satellites

Satellites are SPACECRAFT that circle the EARTH in a carefully chosen orbit. Communications satellites are equipped to receive signals from one ground station and then relay them to another. They can relay many TELEVISION programmes and TELEPHONE calls all at once.

The great advantage of a satellite over an ordinary transmitting aerial (antenna) is that it can reach a very much wider area. An aerial is only a few hundred metres tall. But a satellite can be positioned thousands of kilometres up. A satellite above the ATLANTIC can carry signals from EUROPE to the Americas.

The largest satellites are placed in an orbit at about 35,900 kilometres above the earth. At this height they orbit in the same time that the earth takes to rotate. In other words they appear to be stationary in the sky.

Signals are beamed to and received from the satellites by means of huge, bowl-shaped aerials.

Above: A sending/receiving aerial.
Below: Three communications satellites can serve the whole world.

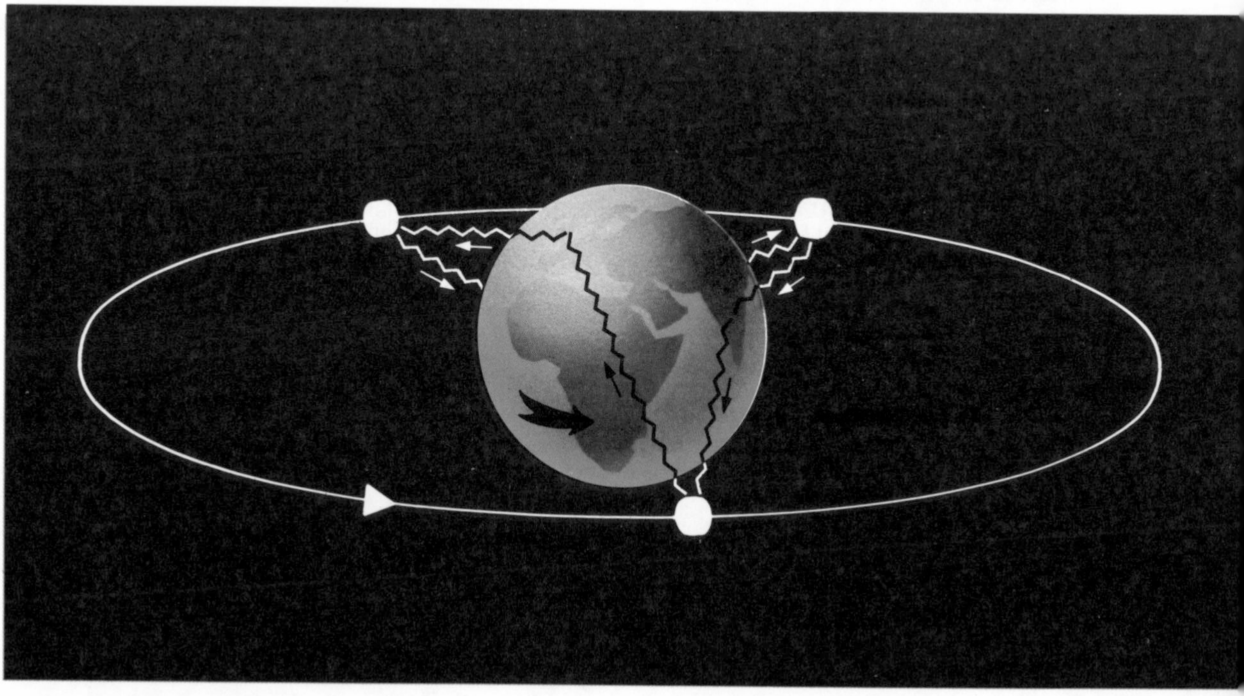

TRAVEL AND COMMUNICATION FACTS AND FIGURES

SPACE TRAVEL. The only woman to venture into space so far is Valentina Tereshkova-Bykovsky, who orbited the earth 48 times between 16th and 19th June, 1963. The oldest rock recovered from the moon by the *Apollo* astronauts is 4600 million years old.

TRAVEL BY AIR. Nearly 500 years ago, Leonardo da Vinci sketched a primitive flying machine, helicopter, and parachute. The first person to be killed in an aeroplane crash was Thomas E. Selfridge, in 1908. He was a passenger in an aeroplane piloted by Orville Wright.

SHIPS AND BOATS. A 200,000-tonne oil tanker, travelling at its top speed of about 32 kilometres an hour takes over a kilometre to make an emergency stop. The fastest crossing of the Atlantic – just under three days eleven hours – was made by the *United States* in July 1952.

SAFETY AT SEA. Merchant ships carry on their hull a series of marks which show how low they can safely ride in the water under certain conditions. They are called Plimsoll lines after the British shipping reformer who caused them to be introduced in Britain in 1876.

PORTS AND HARBOURS. At most ports incoming ships are inspected, and customs duties (taxes) are levied on goods being imported. At free ports, however, ships may enter and leave without customs inspection, and no duties or taxes are payable on goods.

UNDERSEA EXPLORATION. The first successful submarine attack occurred during the American Civil War. The Confederate submarine *Hanley* rammed a Union ship in Charleston harbour. The most gold ever recovered from a sunken ship was £5,000,000 from the *Laurentic.*

INLAND WATERWAYS. The longest canal tunnel in the world is on the Rove canal, which links the River Rhone and the port of Marseilles, in southern France. The tunnel is 7·25 kilometres long, 22 metres wide, and 15 metres high.

TRAVEL BY ROAD. The air-filled, or pneumatic tyre fitted to bicycles, cars, and other road vehicles was invented by Scottish veterinary surgeon John Boyd Dunlop in 1888. The longest regular bus route runs from Miami, Florida, to San Francisco, California – over 5000 kilometres.

TRAVEL BY RAIL. Not all railways have the same track width, or gauge. The U.S.A., Britain, and France use the standard gauge of 1·43 metres. In some countries, both broader and narrower gauges are in use, the most common being 1·67 metres, 1 metre, and 760 and 610 millimetres.

LANGUAGE AND CODE. In the 1880s, Ludovic Zamenhof, a Pole, devised Esperanto, an artificial language for use by people of every country. It uses all the letters of the Roman alphabet except Q, W, X, and Y, together with five extra accented consonants.

TELECOMMUNICATIONS. The German physicist Heinrich Hertz was the first to produce and detect radio waves, in 1887. John Ambrose Fleming invented the radio valve in 1904. John Bardeen, Walter Brattain, and William Shockley together invented the transistor in 1948.

WORK AND INDUSTRY

Farming and Fishing

In prehistoric times, man had to hunt to survive. He killed animals for food and he made clothing from their skins. Only later did he learn to domesticate (tame) animals such as CATTLE and SHEEP. When he did, hunting was no longer a necessity. Man became a farmer and started to lead a more settled life.

Man was also a fisherman from the earliest times. He fished with spears, with lines, and with nets. He soon realized that the sea – and inland waters as well – could keep him supplied with food. In time FISHING, like farming, grew into one of man's greatest industries.

Above right: Cattle drawing a plough in India.

Nearly half the world's population works on the land, growing crops and raising animals. By doing so, they produce food for the rest of the people in the world. The number of farmers varies from country to country. In some countries, almost everyone farms the land. In developed countries, however, there are fewer farmers. In these countries, they use machines and advanced methods of farming to produce more food with fewer people.

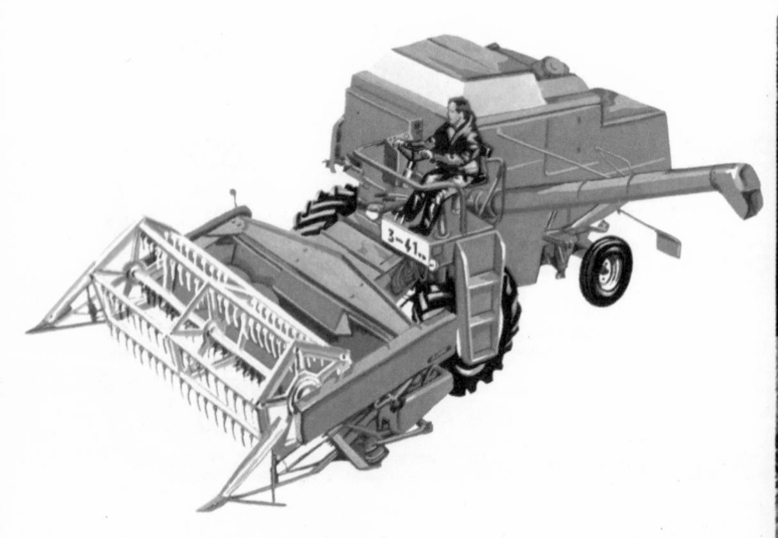

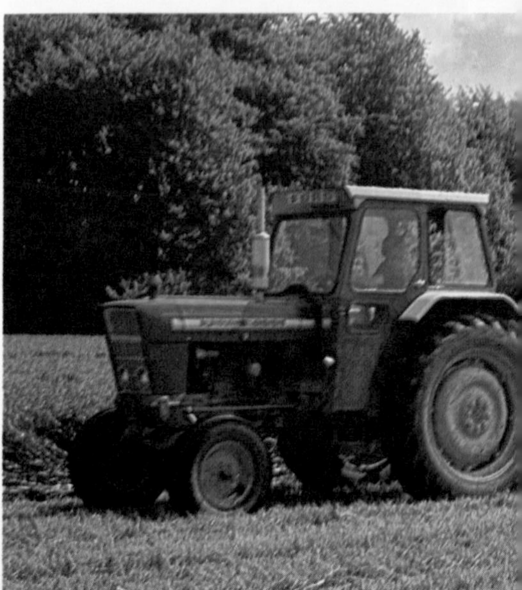

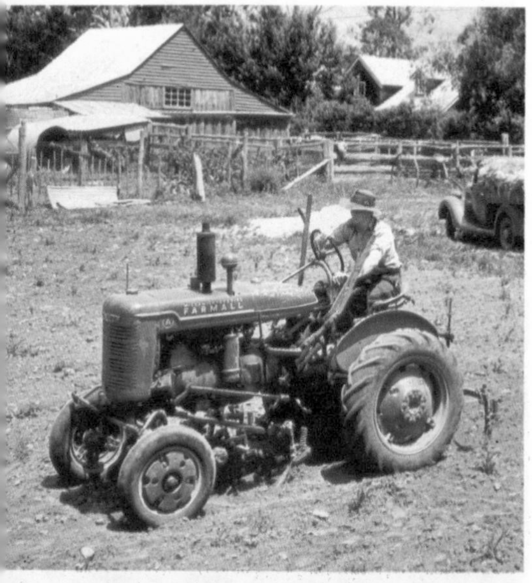

In parts of AFRICA, ASIA, and the Americas, farmers still use old methods of farming. Many use a method called shifting cultivation. They clear a piece of land, grow crops and then graze cattle there until the land can no longer produce crops. They then move on to a fresh piece of land.

Some farmers specialize. They may either grow crops or raise LIVESTOCK. Others do both. Farmers grow different crops and raise different animals for a number of reasons, such as type of climate and the condition of the SOIL.

Above left: Hoeing (clearing the ground of weeds) with a tractor.

Centre left: Harvesting a crop of peas in Australia.

Farm machinery

The tractor is the most important machine on the modern farm. It pulls the many kinds of farm implements that cultivate the SOIL, and that plant and harvest crops.

One of the most useful implements is the plough, which breaks up and turns the soil. The tractor is also used to pull cultivators, harrows, and rollers. When farmers sow SEEDS, they use a seed drill attached to a tractor.

Many kinds of machines have been developed for harvesting different crops. Some dig POTATOES or SUGAR BEET; some cut grass for HAY or silage; others reap WHEAT and other CEREALS. Especially valuable is the combine harvester, which is used to gather wheat, OATS, and other cereals. The combine not only cuts the crop but threshes the grain from it as well.

Far left: A combine harvester.

Left: A forage harvester cuts grass and blasts it through a funnel into a trailer.

Cereals

Cereals are plants of the grass family. Farmers throughout the world grow them as crops. Two important cereals are WHEAT and RICE. For centuries wheat has been ground into flour to make bread. Rice is the basic food of millions of Asians. MAIZE, BARLEY, RYE, and OATS are other cereals.

Maize is used mainly as a LIVESTOCK feed, but it can be eaten as a vegetable or ground into flour. Barley is used for making beer and whisky. Coarse black bread is made from rye. Oats are important as a livestock feed. They are also used for making oatmeal.

Most cereals are sown in cultivated SOIL and harvested by machines such as combines. Rice is an exception. It is usually planted in muddy land, which is flooded as the plants grow. The land is usually drained as the crop ripens.

Forage crops

Forage crops are crops grown for animals to eat. Grass and MAIZE are two of the main forage crops. But farmers also grow others. Lucerne, also called alfalfa, is one of the most important. Lucerne belongs to the same family of plants as clover, another valuable animal feed. Lucerne is nourishing to LIVESTOCK and also acts as a natural FERTILIZER in the SOIL. It can be made into HAY and silage in the same way that grass can. Lucerne yields several crops each year. The soya bean, a member of the PEA family, is rich in protein and is another important forage crop, especially in the U.S.A.

In some parts of the world, livestock graze on WHEAT and corn stubble in the winter. In other areas, kale, a member of the CABBAGE family, is grown as a winter forage crop.

Above: Rice being dried on racks in Japan.
Left: A U.S. wheatfield being harvested.
Right: Potato harvesting, showing the potatoes being dug (bottom) and sorted into sizes (right).

Root crops

Farmers grow many kinds of root crops. They sell them as food for people or store them as feed for animals. POTATOES are a valuable root crop. They make up a major part of the diet of people in many parts of the world. SUGAR BEET is grown as a source of sugar in cool climates. CARROTS and turnips are other root crops used for eating and as animal feed.

The planting, cultivating, and harvesting of root crops is done largely by machine. Root crops are not difficult to weed. This is one reason why they are often included in CROP ROTATION systems. They help to clean and improve the SOIL after CEREALS have been grown.

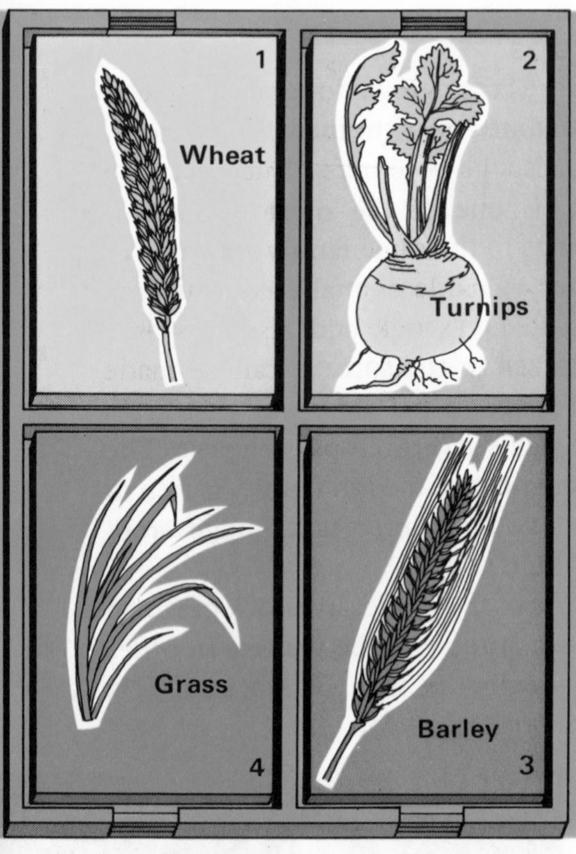

Above: The crops of a common kind of four-crop rotation.

Below: A helicopter spraying crops against blight (a fungus disease).

Crop rotation

Farmers do not usually plant the same crop on the same piece of land year after year. They move their crops from field to field in rotation.

Farmers in different countries rotate different crops. In the United States, for example, farmers might plant MAIZE in one field, OATS in a second, soya beans in a third, and leave a fourth field for grass. The following year the first field would be planted with oats, the second with soya beans, the third would be left for grass, and the fourth would be planted with maize. In some countries of EUROPE, the farmers might rotate WHEAT, turnips, BARLEY, and grass. They continue rotating the crops until they are back where they started. Then they begin the process again.

There are good reasons for rotating crops. For one thing, plant diseases tend to flourish when the same crop is planted again and again in the same field. For another, some crops take so much goodness from the SOIL that it soon becomes barren. Rotation helps the soil recover.

Chemical sprays

Many kinds of insects and diseases attack crops. Insects such as BEETLES, caterpillars, and LOCUSTS can ruin whole fields. Fungus diseases such as WHEAT rust can also do great damage. Farmers can control pests and diseases by spraying or dusting crops with certain chemicals. They can spray them with insecticides (insect killers) and fungicides (fungus killers). These sprays must be used with care, however, so as not to upset the balance of nature or cause POLLUTION.

Farmers can also use chemical sprays to control WEED growth, especially in producing CEREAL crops. These are called herbicides (weed killers). These substances kill the weeds without damaging the cereals.

Above: Seaweed being gathered on the seashore. Once it has rotted, seaweed makes a good fertilizer.
Below: Liquid manure being spread over growing crops. The spreader is attached to a tractor.

Fertilizers

Farmers know that even good CROP ROTATION will not entirely prevent the SOIL from losing its nourishing substances. To prevent the loss of such substances as nitrogen, potassium, and phosphorus, farmers spread fertilizers on the ground. They try to put back into the soil what the crops have taken out.

Farmers may use natural fertilizers such as farmyard manure, which is made up of animal waste and rotted straw. In some countries, guano is used as a fertilizer. It is the droppings of bats or seabirds. Bonemeal (made from the BONES of animals) and sewage sludge are other natural fertilizers. Such fertilizers, however, are often scarce. Farmers therefore use many chemical fertilizers made in FACTORIES. Superphosphate, ammonium sulphate, and potassium sulphate are some of these artificial fertilizers. Lime is also used as a fertilizer. It improves the condition of the soil by overcoming acidity, and this allows better PLANT GROWTH.

Livestock farming

Farmers raise many kinds of animals for their meat, their milk, their wool, their skins (hides), or their eggs. The main livestock are CATTLE, SHEEP, PIGS, and POULTRY. GOATS are also kept in some parts of the world. Some farmers also keep livestock such as HORSES to do work.

Raising cattle is the most important kind of livestock farming. Many breeds are kept – dairy cows for their milk and beef cattle for their meat. Sheep are raised in many countries for their meat (lamb or mutton) and for their wool. No country has as many sheep as AUSTRALIA, which has about 180 million. Sheep are hardy animals, needing little care, except at lambing and shearing time. The finest fleece comes from the Merino breed of sheep. The fleece from a Merino can weigh up to 12 kilogrammes.

Above: A shepherd in northern India tending his flock.
Below: An Australian farmer treating his sheep against disease.

CHINA, the U.S.S.R., and the U.S.A. are the world's largest producers of pigs. Pigs are raised for their meat. It is called pork when fresh and bacon or ham when cured (preserved by salting or smoking). Modern breeds of pigs such as the Landrace have been bred to give leaner meat. They also grow faster. They can gain half a kilogramme in weight in a day. Pigs also breed rapidly. Sows can produce a litter of twelve piglets at a time.

Most goats are kept for their milk. Excellent cheese can be made from goat's milk. French and Norwegian farmers produce much goat cheese. Swiss goats, such as the Toggenberg and Nubian breeds are excellent milk producers.

Some goats are bred mainly for their wool. The most important wool breeds are the Angora and the Cashmere.

Many farmers use a method called intensive farming in raising animals. The growth of such animals as cattle and pigs is carefully controlled. Farmers give these animals a special diet to fatten them quickly. Feeding is often done by machine.

Intensive farming is also used in chicken farming. The chickens are kept indoors. Egg-laying hens are cooped in separate cages in what is called a battery.

Chickens are the most valuable kind of poultry. They are raised for their meat and their eggs. Turkeys, DUCKS, and geese are also kept by farmers, but they are not usually raised by intensive methods.

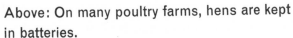

Above: On many poultry farms, hens are kept in batteries.
Left: A box of young chicks. They are raised on a large scale in incubators.
Below: A sow with a litter of piglets.

Cattle farming

Dairy cattle are raised mainly for their milk, one of our most important foods. Milk contains all the things our bodies need for growth, including VITAMINS. Cream, butter, and cheese also come from milk. Some people, however, do not get their milk from cows. They get it from GOATS, SHEEP, and other animals.

Dairy farmers raise different breeds of cows for their milk. The Friesian breed gives the most milk – about 7000 kilogrammes a year. Jersey and Guernsey breeds produce the richest, creamiest milk.

On modern farms, the cows are milked twice a day by suction machines. The milk is then sent by LORRY or pipeline to the dairy. There it is filtered and pasteurized (quickly heated and cooled) to kill any germs it may contain. It then goes into bottling machines. Between cow and bottle the milk is untouched by human hand.

Top: A highland steer on a farm in Scotland.
Right: Hereford beef cattle grazing in a valley in Montana, U.S.A.
Below: On modern dairy farms, the cows are milked by suction machines.

Beef cattle are raised mainly for their meat. They have much squarer, stockier bodies than dairy cattle. The most important beef breeds include the Aberdeen Angus, the Hereford, and the Shorthorn. The French Charolais cattle are also excellent beef animals.

In hot humid climates, farmers raise the Brahman, or zebu. It can be recognized by the hump on its shoulders.

Most beef herds consist of males whose reproductive organs have been removed. They are known as bullocks, or steers. Steers fatten much faster than ordinary bulls.

Beef cattle are raised in large numbers in many countries, especially in GRASSLANDS such as the vast open prairies of NORTH AMERICA and the pampas of SOUTH AMERICA. The big farms that raise them are often called ranches. Some of the biggest ranches cover an area of 10,000 or more square kilometres. Big sheep farms are also often called ranches, but in AUSTRALIA they are called stations.

Below: Branding a calf in South Dakota, U.S.A. Cattle on ranches are identified by their brands.

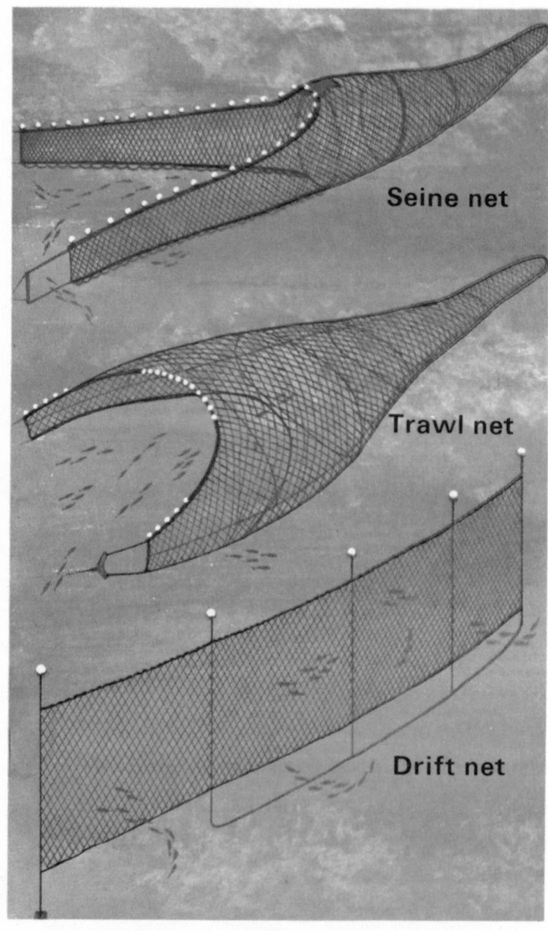

Above: The three most common kinds of nets used by fishermen.
Below: A good catch being landed in Nova Scotia.
Below right: Hauling in a trawl net full of fish.

Fishing industry

Commercial fishermen usually catch fish in nets. Three kinds of nets – the trawl, or drag, the drift, and the seine – are widely used.

In trawling, a fishing boat drags a bag-shaped net along the sea bottom. Fish such as COD, flounder, and haddock are caught in this way. Trawlers are sturdy vessels that may go into Arctic waters to find their catch. Some are equipped as fish factories. The fish are cleaned and deep frozen as soon as they are caught. Factory ships can stay at sea for many weeks.

A drift net is often several kilometres long. It hangs, from floats, near the surface of the water. Fish feeding near the surface, such as HERRING and MACKEREL, get their GILLS caught in the mesh (the holes in the net). In this kind of fishing, the net is put out at dusk. At dawn the fishing boat hauls in the catch.

Seining is the most important of the different kinds of net fishing. A seine is a long net that is drawn in a circle slowly through the sea. Fish are forced into a pocket and caught.

Line fishing is also done commercially. It is usually done near the shore. Fishermen trail lines of baited or unbaited hooks over the side, or leave baited lines on the seabed. Trolling is a kind of line fishing in which boats trail lines from poles hanging over their sides.

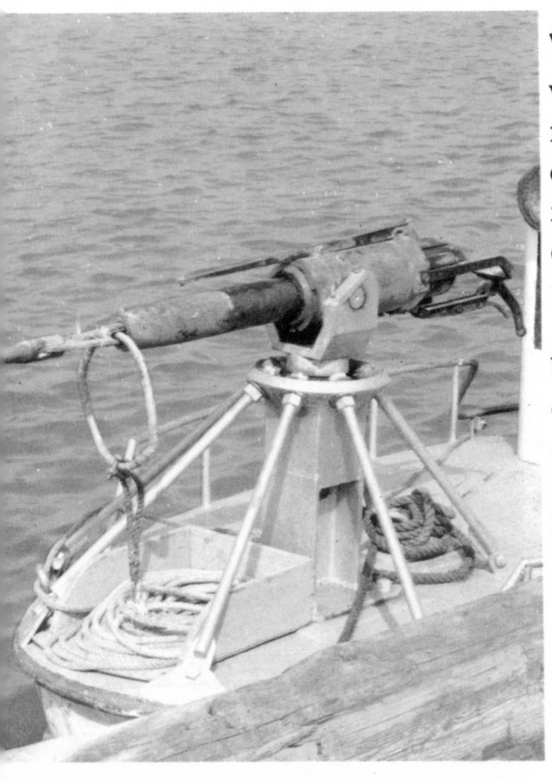

Above: The harpoon gun in the bows of an Icelandic whaler.
Below: A dead whale being cut up at a whaling station in Iceland for its valuable meat and blubber.

Whaling

WHALES have been hunted for hundreds of years for their meat and their oil. People in several countries eat whale meat, but most of it is made into cat and dog food. Whale oil is obtained by cooking the thick layers of blubber fat beneath the whale's skin. It is used to make margarine.

Whales are hunted by harpoon from catcher boats, which operate from a factory ship. A gun on the boat shoots a harpoon into the whale and a charge inside it explodes and kills the animal. Because some whales sink after dying, whalers have to pump air into their bodies to keep them afloat. The catcher boat then returns to the factory ship with the whale. The catch is hauled into the ship for cutting up.

Large numbers of whales, especially finbacks and sperm whales, used to be killed every year. So many have been killed that the whale is in danger of becoming extinct. Some countries no longer allow the sale of whale meat; others do not allow whales to be hunted. Many people feel that if whales are to survive they should not be hunted at all.

Forestry and Timber

Wood is one of our precious natural resources. It is used to build HOUSES and make FURNITURE. It is also made into PAPER, fabrics and explosives. We burn it for fuel. But the supply of TIMBER, as cut wood is called, is limited. Trees must be planted so that we will have enough wood for the future.

Looking after and replanting trees is called forestry. The people who do this work are called foresters. They grow seedlings in a NURSERY to plant out in the forest. They protect the trees from fire, disease, and a variety of pests. If uncontrolled, BEETLES and caterpillars would bore into the wood or damage the buds or foliage.

Right: A forest worker cutting off the side branches of a felled tree with a chain saw.

DEER, SQUIRRELS, RABBITS, and MICE can also do great damage, especially to the buds and tender shoots of young seedlings.

The forester also decides when it is time to fell, or cut down, the trees. Felling is the first of the LOGGING operations, which get the timber from the forest to the SAWMILLS and PULPMILLS.

Fires destroy and damage millions of trees every year. Some fires are started by accident. Others are caused by lightning or by the great heat of the SUN in summer. Once they start, forest fires are hard to control. Fanned by strong winds, they can spread faster than a man can run.

During a hot spell, therefore, foresters must keep a constant fire-watch. Often they watch from tall towers overlooking the forest. At the first sign of smoke, they RADIO or TELEPHONE for the firefighters. The firefighters then move in by truck, HELICOPTER, or even parachute. It is their job to check the spread of the fire before it gets out of hand.

Timber trees

There are two main kinds of timber trees – softwoods and hardwoods. The softwoods are such trees as PINE, FIR, and SPRUCE. They have thin, needle-like LEAVES, and bear their SEEDS in cones. They are therefore called conifers (cone-bearers). Most softwood trees are evergreen, which means that they do not lose their leaves each autumn. One of them – the LARCH – is an exception. It is a needle-leaf conifer that does lose all its leaves every year.

The hardwoods are trees with broad leaves. OAK, BEECH, BIRCH, sycamore, MAPLE, mahogany, and teak are all hardwoods. They are mainly deciduous trees, which means that they lose all their leaves in the autumn. New leaves grow again in the spring.

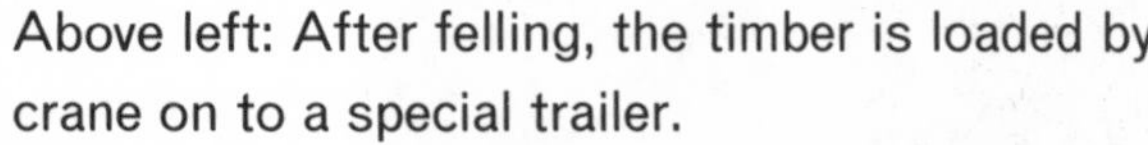

Above left: After felling, the timber is loaded by crane on to a special trailer.
Left: Timber can be towed across lakes inside great floating collars, or booms.

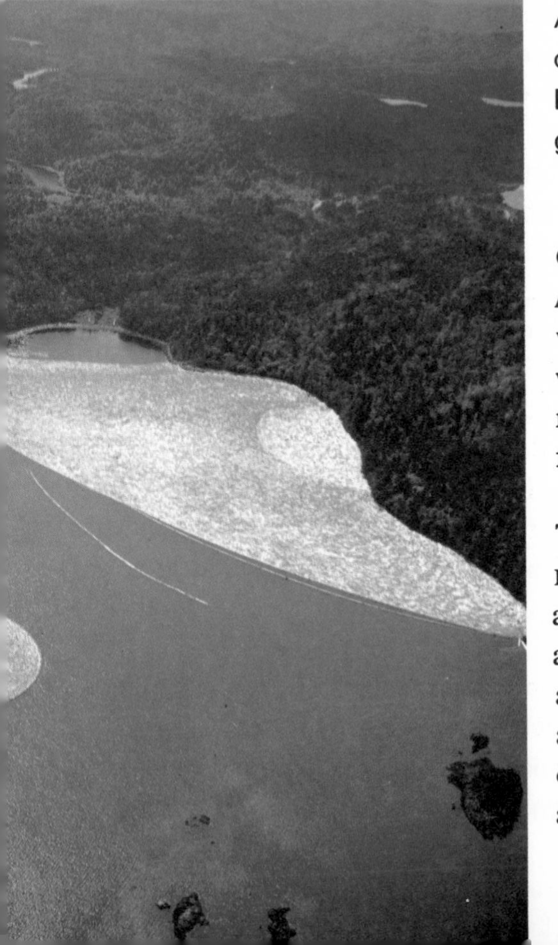

Softwoods thrive in the cold, northern regions. Great belts of softwood forests lie across NORTH AMERICA, Scandinavia, and the U.S.S.R. The hardwoods need a temperate climate, with moister, warmer weather. Tropical hardwoods, such as mahogany, teak, and ebony, grow in the rain forests near the equator.

Softwoods are the most valuable timber trees. They are used for PAPERMAKING. Houses and FURNITURE are made from them. The hardwoods are used mainly to make furniture, for panelling and flooring, and as fuel. Many of the most attractive woods, such as mahogany and walnut, are used as veneer (thin sheet). Veneer is placed over cheap woods to make them look more attractive.

Nurseries

Foresters usually replant a forest with seedlings they have raised in a nursery. They get the SEEDS from healthy trees. Sometimes they collect the seeds from the ground, but they must get conifer seed cones from the branches. They often do this with a net which they throw over the branches.

The seeds they gather are sown in specially prepared seedbeds. When some seedlings are about two years old, they are transplanted into a nursery bed for another year or two. Then they are strong enough to be planted out in the forest. Conifers, however, are not always transplanted before they are planted out in forests.

Logging

The term logging covers all the steps from the time the trees are cut down in the forest until they are taken to the SAWMILLS.

The people who do the work are often called lumberjacks, especially in NORTH AMERICA. In the past, lumberjacks led hard lives, living in rough bunkhouses. Today, they usually have their own homes near the forests and drive to work in cars.

In most countries, logging has become very mechanized. The lumberjack uses a chain saw to fell the trees and cut them into logs. He uses tractors, bulldozers, winches, and cranes to haul and load the logs. He often transports the logs by truck and train. Sometimes they are skidded (dragged) from the forest. In some places timber is still transported by water.

Above left: Logs being sluiced from the Humber Canal into Deer Lake in Canada.

Left: Mechanical handling equipment is now used widely in logging operations.

Sawmills

At the sawmill, logs are stored in a pond until they are needed. Then, one by one, they are fed into the mill by a conveyor called the bull chain. In the mill they are moved back and forth on to a band saw – a narrow, endless saw blade driven at high speed. In this way, the logs are sawn into different shapes.

The timber is then trimmed and cut into standard lengths. Before the timber can be used, it must be dried, or seasoned. Seasoning can be done slowly in the air or quickly in drying kilns.

Some logs are sliced into thin sheets, or veneer, for making into plywood. Plywood is made by gluing sheets of veneer together in a special way.

Right: Sawn lengths of timber being sorted at a timber-yard in Montana, U.S.A.
Below: Wood pulp after being dried and pressed.
Bottom: Logs on their way to be pulped.

Pulpmills

Not every log goes to the SAWMILLS. Many go to the pulpmills to be made into wood pulp. Wood pulp is the raw material for making PAPER and rayon, among other things.

At the pulpmill, the logs are sawn into short lengths, and their BARK is removed. Then they can be made into pulp in one of two ways. They can be ground with a grindstone while being sprayed with water. This ground woodpulp is often used for making newsprint (the paper on which NEWSPAPERS are printed).

Pulp can also be made chemically. The logs are cut up into chips and the chips are 'cooked' in chemicals. This pulp, too, can be made into newsprint. Many papermills make their own pulp, but sometimes it is dried at a pulpmill and sent in sheets to the papermills.

Papermaking

Most paper is made from the wood pulps of softwoods such as PINE and SPRUCE. But some paper is also made from other plant materials such as straw, esparto grass, and rag (COTTON) waste. Some of the best paper is made using rag pulp. Rag paper is strong and lasts longer than pulp paper. It is used for such things as LAWYERS' documents that need to be kept for a long time. Many papers are made from a blend of pulps.

Papermaking begins when the wet pulp is beaten in a machine with revolving knives or bars. This process further breaks down the wood fibres. Then comes mixing. At this point, certain materials, such as rosin, are added to the pulp. Rosin makes the paper more waterproof. The paper may be bleached white, or dyed to give it colour. China clay may be added to give the paper a smoother surface.

Now the pulp is ready to go into a long paper-making machine. At the wet end the pulp flows on to a moving wire-mesh belt. Most of the water drains away, leaving a damp web (or band) of paper. This paper is then squeezed through heavy rollers into a thin sheet.

MAKING PAPER

Paper is often made from dry pulp sheets. First, the sheets are turned into wet pulp again. The pulp then goes to a beater, which shreds the wood fibres. Next, various materials are added to the pulp, which goes to the papermaking machine. The water drains away, leaving a damp layer that is dried and pressed into a thin sheet.

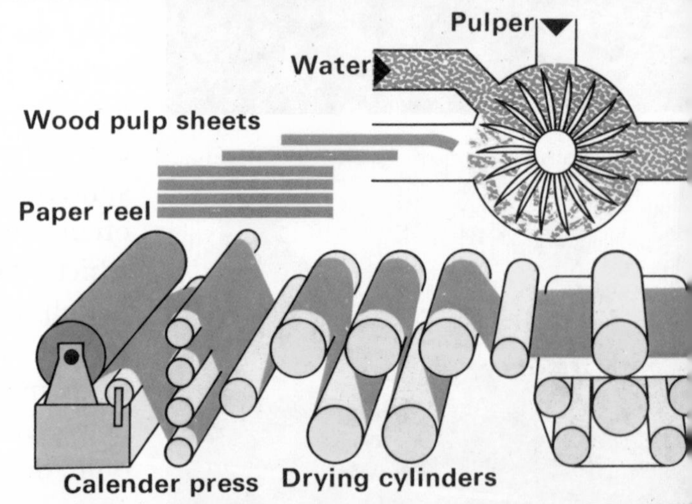

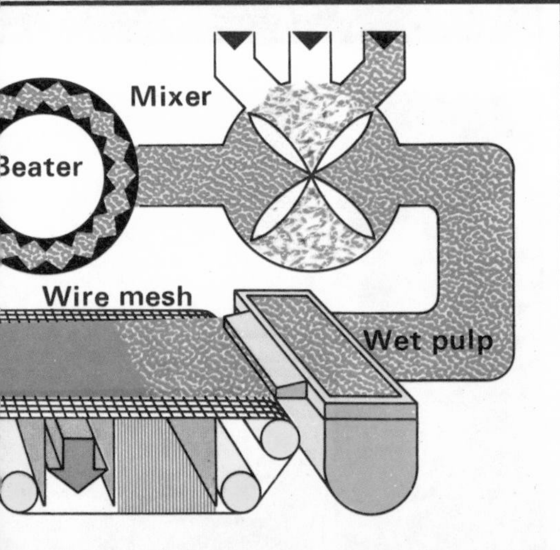

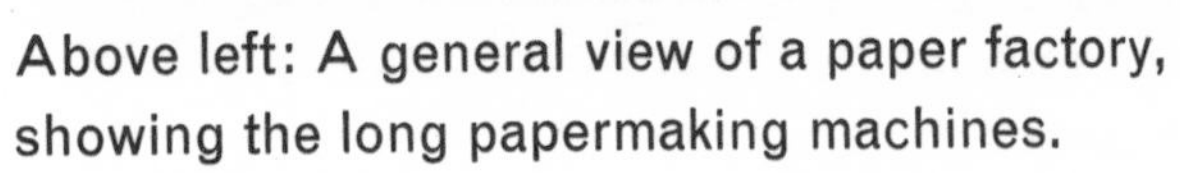

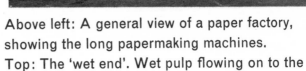

Above left: A general view of a paper factory, showing the long papermaking machines.
Top: The 'wet end'. Wet pulp flowing on to the wire-mesh belt.
Above: The 'dry end'. A reel of paper just off the machine.

The damp sheet next passes over a series of drying cylinders, heated by steam. The dry paper emerging then goes into a calender press. There, heavy rollers give it a smooth surface.

Papermaking is a quick process. The paper sheet leaves the dry end of the machine at a speed of 50 kilometres an hour or more.

Mining

Mining means taking minerals from the ground. Minerals are basic raw materials for other industries, which turn them into useful products.

Sometimes minerals can be used in the state in which they are found. Sulphur is a mineral that is mined either on the surface near VOLCANOES or deep underground. The CHEMICAL INDUSTRY uses sulphur directly and makes it into sulphuric acid. This is perhaps the most useful of all industrial chemicals. The mineral bauxite is very valuable because it can be made into ALUMINIUM. Any mineral that can be processed to give a metal is called an ore.

Most minerals are compounds of two or more chemical elements combined in certain proportions. For example, the mineral magnetite is a compound having three atoms of IRON to every four of oxygen. The iron can be separated out and changed into useful metal. Minerals also have a definite structure, which often gives them a crystal form. Some of these crystals, especially diamonds, sapphires, and rubies, are prized as gems. COAL and OIL are also classed as minerals because they are taken from the ground.

Below: Preparing for the arrival of a supply boat on a North Sea oil drilling rig.

Surface mining

Some mineral deposits are found on or near the surface of the ground. IRON ore and bauxite are two minerals found in surface deposits. To get them, miners use the opencast method.

The miners begin by removing any earth that lies above the ore. They use mechanical excavators, such as draglines. Then the uncovered ore is broken up, usually by explosives. Power shovels then load the ore into trucks or railway wagons, which take it to crushing plants.

Heavy minerals, such as GOLD and tin ore, are often found in stream beds. Such deposits of minerals are called placers. In the days of the great gold rushes in California, Alaska, and AUSTRALIA, miners used to work gold placers by panning. They would swirl gravel and water from a stream in a shallow pan. The heavier gold particles remained in the pan while the lighter materials would be swept away.

Today, many placer deposits are worked by a machine called a dredger. It sends buckets into the stream bed to bring up the gold-bearing gravel. Another method uses jets of water to dislodge loose gold-bearing soil from hillsides.

Above: An opencast mine in Virginia, U.S.A.

Left: A nineteenth-century coal mine. Coal is a very important source of energy.

Below: Bucket dredgers are often used for mining gold.

Underground mining

Many of the minerals we need lie deep under the surface of the ground. They are in veins that run through rock layers. COAL mines are often 800 metres or more deep. To reach gold deposits in SOUTH AFRICA, for example, shafts more than three kilometres deep have been sunk.

A mineral vein usually runs at an angle through the rock layers. To reach the mineral, engineers sink vertical shafts near or through the vein. Then they make horizontal tunnels at various levels from the shaft to the vein.

Miners travel up and down the shafts in 'cages' (LIFTS). They also travel along the tunnels in trucks pulled by electric or DIESEL LOCOMOTIVES. These tunnels in a big mine can extend great distances. One South African gold mine has a total tunnel length of more than 4000 kilometres.

The main tunnels in a mine are well lit and are supplied with fresh air. But it is different at the ore face, where the minerals are mined. There, the air is thick with dust, and only the light from the miners' lamps pierces the gloom.

Miners often use explosives to break up the ore. First they drill holes in the ore face. Then they insert the explosive charges and explode them. Rock drills are also used to break up the ore. Conveyor belts or mine cars carry the broken ore to hoists that haul it to the surface. There the ore may be graded (sorted) before being loaded into railway wagons or barges.

Underground mining can be dangerous. Rock falls may occur and trap the miners in the tunnels. Dangerous gases such as firedamp (methane) may build up and explode. Miners often carry safety lamps which warn them when firedamp and other dangerous gases are present. Many modern mines have an automatic system that can detect the presence of too much gas.

Above: Part of an underground coal mine, showing the winding gear (on the surface) and cages (lifts) serving the different levels. The shaft on the right is for fresh air.

Above: This quarry is being worked for the stone chips used in road construction.
Left: A miner examining a vein of copper in an underground copper mine in Australia.

Quarrying

Within the earth there are many kinds of ROCKS. Unlike minerals, they are not often important for the chemicals they contain. Instead, they are mostly used for different kinds of BUILDING and construction. Removing rock from the ground is called quarrying.

Some of the most important kinds of rocks quarried are granite, marble, slate, limestone, and sandstone. These rocks are all used for building. They are either cut out of the rock or blasted loose with explosives. Stone used for building is usually cut out, because it might be damaged by explosives. One method of cutting out the stone is by drilling holes and driving wedges into them. The stone used in road-making is usually blasted free.

Deposits of CLAY, sand, and gravel are also found in the ground. These deposits can be scooped up with power shovels and dredgers to produce huge open pits.

Fuel and Energy

We live in a world that needs a great deal of power every day. We need power for lighting and heating, for CARS and LOCOMOTIVES, and for machines of many kinds. We get this power mainly by burning fuel – COAL, petrol, OIL, kerosene (paraffin) and NATURAL GAS. The trouble is that we are using these fuels so rapidly that they are becoming scarce. By the year 2000 we will have to be using new sources of fuel.

Much fuel is used to drive different kinds of engines. Burning fuel releases heat, which may be used to drive STEAM ENGINES. It also produces hot gases, which can be made to force pistons up and down (as in PETROL ENGINES). The gases can also be made to move turbines (as in GAS TURBINES).

Our main sources of fuel must run out one day. When this happens, one solution may be atomic, or nuclear, power. This power comes from the metals uranium and plutonium, whose atoms can be made to split. When this fission, or splitting, takes place, very intense heat is produced. This heat can be used to turn water into steam to drive turbines to make electricity. Hundreds of nuclear power stations are already in use in many countries.

Above: This old water mill in Canada has an overshot wheel.
Below left: Steam traction engines were once used for powering machinery on farms.
Below: An experimental atomic reactor at Dounreay in Scotland.

Water power

Many centuries ago, man, when he learned to use WIND POWER, also began to use another natural force – flowing water. He built waterwheels. They turned millstones, which enabled him to grind grain. The waterwheels also drove different kinds of machines.

The modern kind of waterwheel is called a water turbine. Coupled to a generator, it produces what is called hydro-electric power. CANADA and the U.S.S.R. are two of the main producers of hydro-electricity.

Water can flow from one place to another only if there is a difference in level between the two places. The difference in level is called a head. A hydro-electric power station can sometimes make use of a natural head. Often, however, a head must be created by building a DAM across a river VALLEY.

Wind power

Man first used the power of the wind when he hoisted sails on boats and travelled over the seas. Later on, he used sails on land. He built windmills, which caught the wind in their sails. The sails drove a system of wooden shafts and gears to pump water from the ground or grind corn. Many of the later windmills had a revolving turret and a tail vane, which was like a rudder on a boat. Many of the older kinds of windmills can still be seen, particularly in the NETHERLANDS. Few, however, are actually used now.

The modern windmill is made of steel and is often found on farms. At the top of a tower is a wheel with many blades, or a propeller, and a tail vane. Today, windmills are used for pumping water and for generating electricity.

Right: A fine old windmill in the Netherlands.

Coal

Hundreds of millions of years ago, shallow seas and SWAMPS covered much of the EARTH. In the swamps grew giant FERNS and HORSETAILS. When the ferns and horsetails died, they sank into the swamps and began to rot. In time they became covered with mud and vegetation. As the years passed, heat and pressure changed them into the black substance we call coal. Because it was once living, coal is known as a fossil fuel. OIL is another fossil fuel.

Man has used coal for centuries. Until about 1950 it was his most important fuel. Coal heated homes and offices and provided fuel for most power stations, ships, and LOCOMOTIVES. Today, however, oil has replaced coal for many jobs.

Above right: The pithead at Bold Colliery in the north of England.
Right: Electric locomotives are used to haul trains in underground coal mines.

Even so, the world still uses some 2700 million metric tons of coal every year. PLASTICS, perfumes, and insecticides are some of the things that can be made from coal.

Coal mining is one of the world's biggest industries. Some coal lies near the surface of the ground, but much of it lies deep underground. In SURFACE MINING, often called opencast mining, big power shovels scoop up the coal and load it into trucks or railway wagons.

Sometimes coal seams are less than about a hundred metres deep. Then huge dragline excavators, or wheel excavators, are used to strip the SOIL away. Strip mining often ruins the land.

Right: At the coal face. The roof is supported by powerful hydraulic props.

Underground coal mining is more difficult than surface mining. It is like other forms of UNDERGROUND MINING, but there are differences. Most coal seams are horizontal rather than vertical (upright). They are much larger than ore deposits. Unlike ore, coal is soft enough to be cut out. Because of these reasons, coal-cutting machines such as shearers, ploughs, and trepanners are often used in coal mines. In some mines, coal is cut from a wall as long as 70 metres. This operation is called the long-wall method.

Underground coal mining can be dangerous. Great care has to be taken to prevent explosions and cave-ins.

Below: A miner repairing a coal shearer.

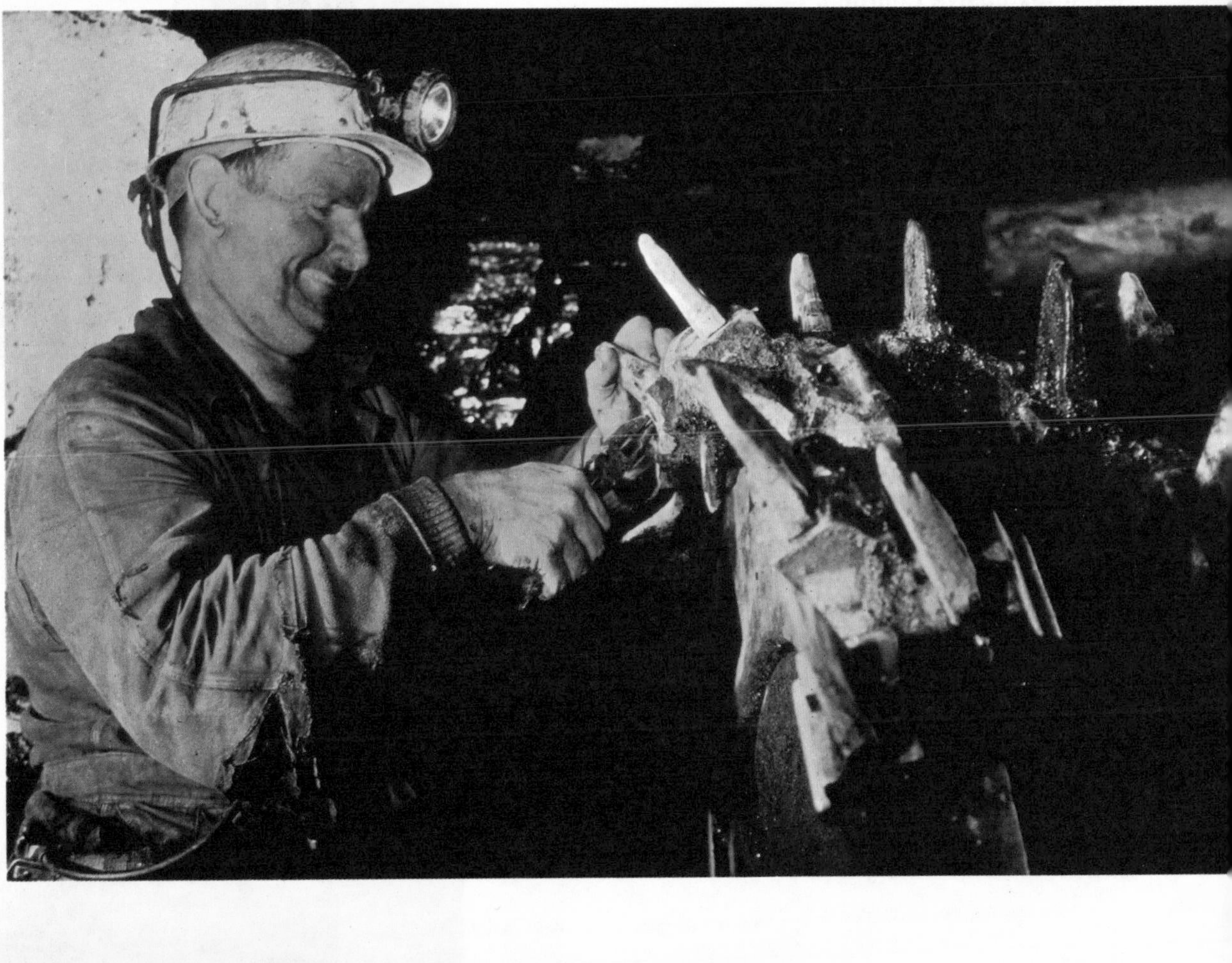

most widely-used fuel in the world. ...e get petrol for our cars, DIESEL oil for our LORRIES, ships, and BUSES, kerosene for our jet planes, and heating oil for our homes, offices, SCHOOLS, and FACTORIES. Oil is also an important raw material for the CHEMICAL INDUSTRY. It can be treated with other chemicals and changed into PLASTICS, insecticides, explosives, detergents, dyes, and even DRUGS.

Some of the leading oil-producing regions of the world include the Middle East, NORTH AMERICA, and SOUTH AMERICA. Large deposits have also been found under the NORTH SEA.

Above: Prospecting for oil in the Libyan desert, using explosive charges.
Right: Changing pipes on a drilling rig.

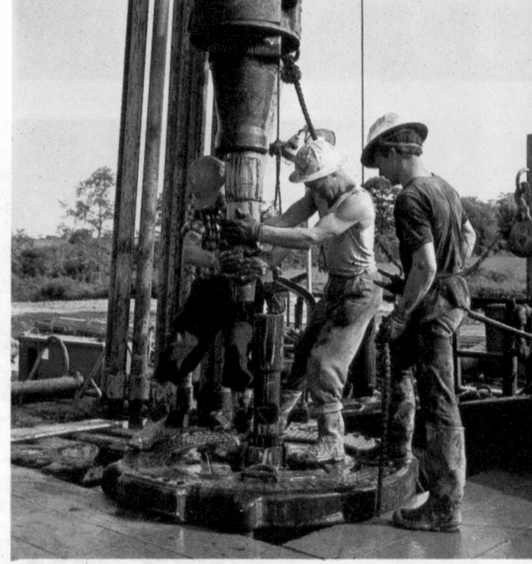

Crude oil, or petroleum, is a thick greenish-black liquid that comes from beneath the surface of the EARTH. It is a mixture of substances called hydro-carbons, which are made up of hydrogen and carbon. Scientists believe that oil was formed from tiny plants and animals that lived in the seas hundreds of millions of years ago. Like COAL, the oil was formed under the pressure of mud and ROCKS.

Oil deposits can be found in different ways. Oilmen make surveys from planes, take rock samples, and even set off explosions. If they think they have found a likely spot, they begin drilling. Drilling is done by rotating a drill bit at the end of a long string of pipes. A tall drilling rig is erected at the site to handle the long drill pipes. Drilling offshore is done from huge platforms, which are floated into position.

Right: An oil refinery in Denmark.

To reach the oil deposits on land, crews may have to drill down three or four kilometres. If oil is struck, the crew cap the borehole with a complicated structure of pipes and valves. This is called a 'Christmas tree'. The pipes connect with pipelines that take the crude oil to refineries for processing, or to storage tanks. Oil TANKERS take the oil from there to refineries.

At oil refineries, oil is split into various parts called fractions by a process called distillation. The most important fractions include petrol, kerosene, and diesel oil. Most refinery processes are almost entirely automatic.

Above: Oil prospectors recording the shock waves caused by explosions in the ground.
Left: The tall derrick of an oil drilling rig.
Below: A distillation tower separates the crude oil into different parts, or fractions.

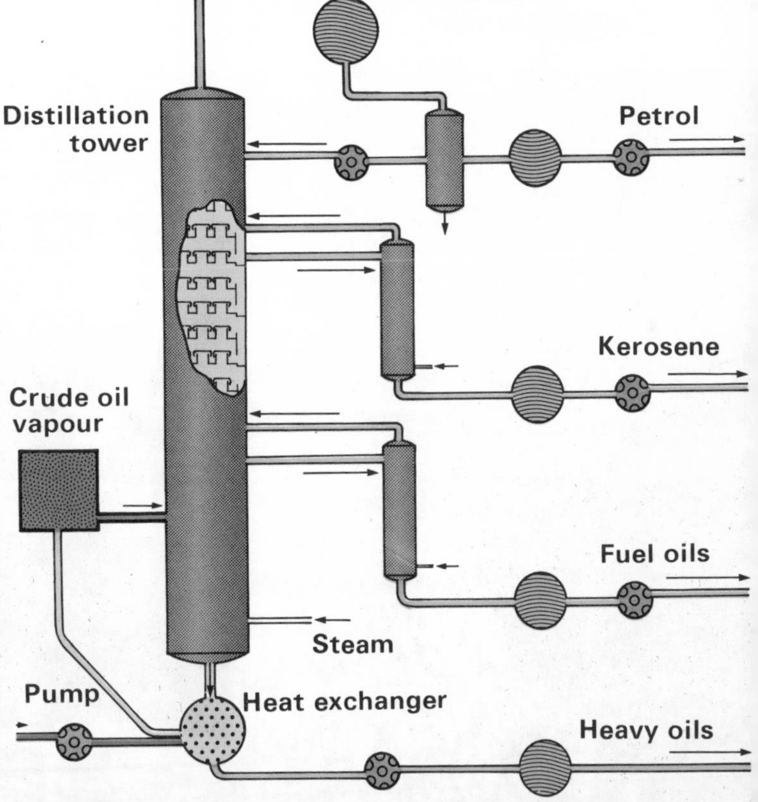

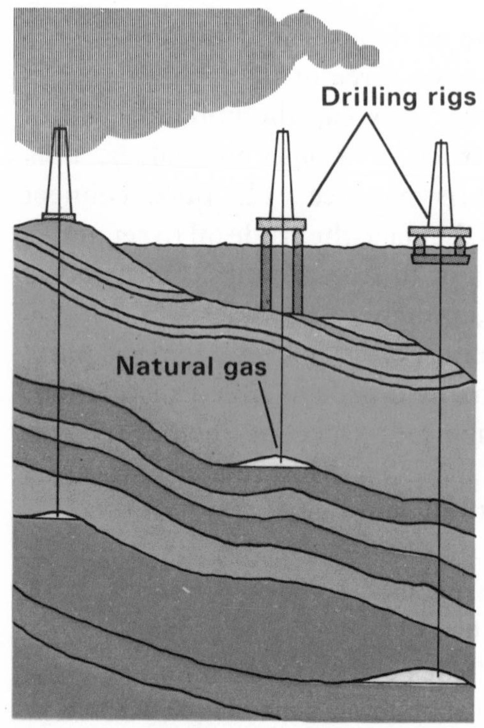

Above: Natural gas is trapped in rock layers deep underground.
Below: A natural gas production platform at sea.

Natural gas

When OIL was formed in underground ROCKS millions of years ago, natural gas was formed too. Like oil, it is a mixture of hydro-carbons. It is mainly made up of methane, a gas that is also formed when plants decay in marshes. Now and then, marsh gas catches fire, producing a strange blue, flickering flame. This flame is called 'will o' the wisp' or 'Jack o' lantern'.

Sometimes natural gas is found in the earth by itself. Often, however, it comes to the surface when boreholes are drilled for oil.

Natural gas is a valuable fuel. It is used to heat buildings and to operate COOKERS and REFRIGERATORS. It is widely used to heat furnaces in industry, to cut metals, and to run machines.

The U.S.A. has huge deposits of natural gas. This gas is sent across the country by a network of pipelines. Natural gas can also be transported as a liquid by sea in refrigerated TANKERS.

The U.S.S.R. and CANADA are also large producers of natural gas.

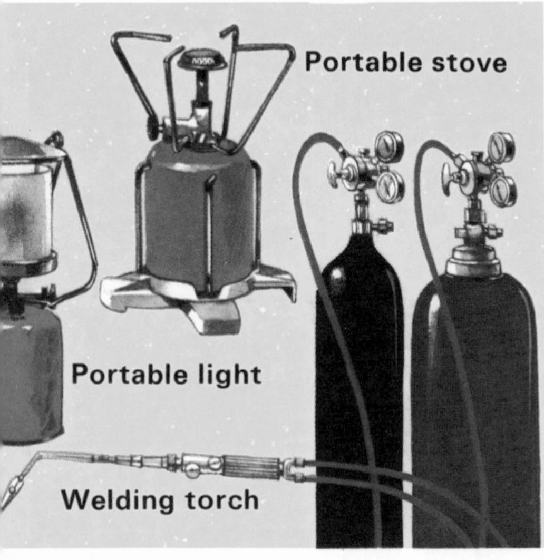

Above: Some of the uses of bottled gas.
Below: A natural gas storage tank (foreground) at a refinery.

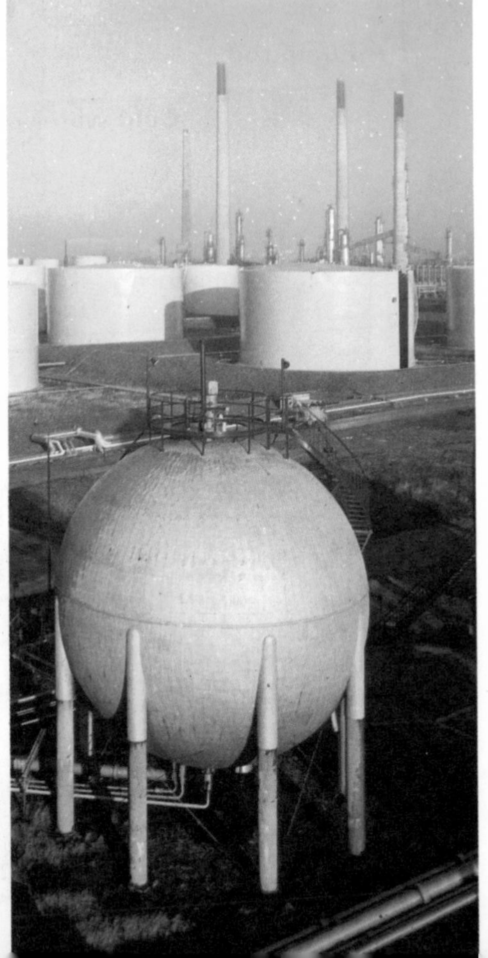

Bottled gas

Two of the gases in NATURAL GAS – butane and propane – can be turned into liquid. They become a liquid under pressure. In this form they are put into bottles. Bottled gas is easy to store and easy to ship. It is a useful fuel, especially in isolated homes where there is no other gas or electricity. It is also used in boats.

Bottled gas also has many uses in industry. For example, it produces a very hot flame for WELDING and cutting metal.

Manufactured gas

Not every country has large deposits of NATURAL GAS. To meet their fuel needs, these countries have to manufacture gas, either from COAL or from OIL. They make different kinds of manufactured gas.

To make coal gas, coal is heated fiercely away from the air. When this is done, a mixture of gases and vapours is given off. Cooling and washing with water remove the unwanted substances. This process leaves a mixture of gases (such as hydrogen and carbon monoxide) that will burn. However, many of the substances removed from the coal gas (for example ammonia) are valuable as chemical raw materials.

Many kinds of gas can be made from oil. All the processes for making oil into gas involve heating the oil so that it breaks down into gas. The oil most used to produce gas is called naphtha.

Water gas is made by blowing steam through red-hot coke. Water gas is often mixed with oil gas or natural gas before use.

Acetylene gas is another manufactured gas. It produces a very hot flame when burned with oxygen, and is used in WELDING and cutting metals.

Steam engines

Until about 200 years ago there were only a few sources of power – the MUSCLES of men and animals, the wind, and water. Then the Scottish engineer James WATT developed a steam engine powerful enough to drive many kinds of machinery. Earlier steam engines did not work well. They were good for little except working pumps.

Watt's engine led to the rapid growth of industry that came to be called the INDUSTRIAL REVOLUTION. His engines also led to the development of the LOCOMOTIVE and the STEAMSHIP.

The steam engine is a reciprocating engine with a piston and cylinder, as is the PETROL ENGINE. Steam from a boiler is let into each side of the piston in turn, forcing it back and forth in the cylinder. The piston's movement is changed into a rotary (turning) movement by means of a connecting rod and crank.

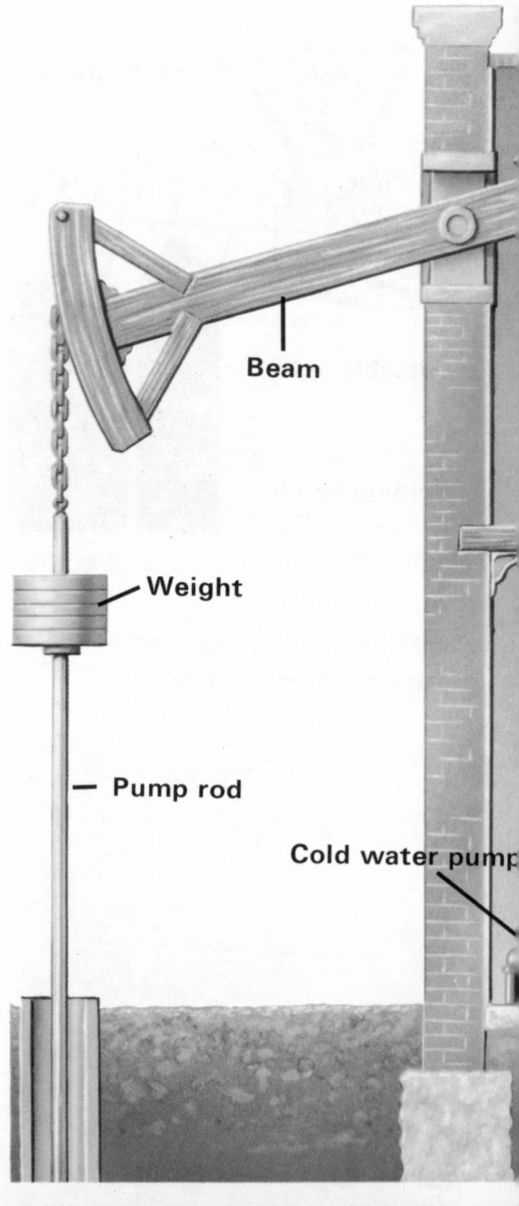

Right: A steam engine of the early 1700s.

Steam turbines

Today, few piston STEAM ENGINES remain. But steam is used to drive another kind of engine, the steam turbine.

The steam turbine consists of a long rotating shaft (rotor) with many-bladed wheels on it. A casing surrounds the wheels and shaft. Steam is blown in at one end and expands through the spaces between the blades, causing the turbine wheels to spin. To produce electricity, the spinning rotor is coupled to a generator. To drive a ship, it is geared to the ship's propeller.

Many power stations use steam turbines of well over a million horsepower.

Right: Steam-turbine electricity generators at a power station.

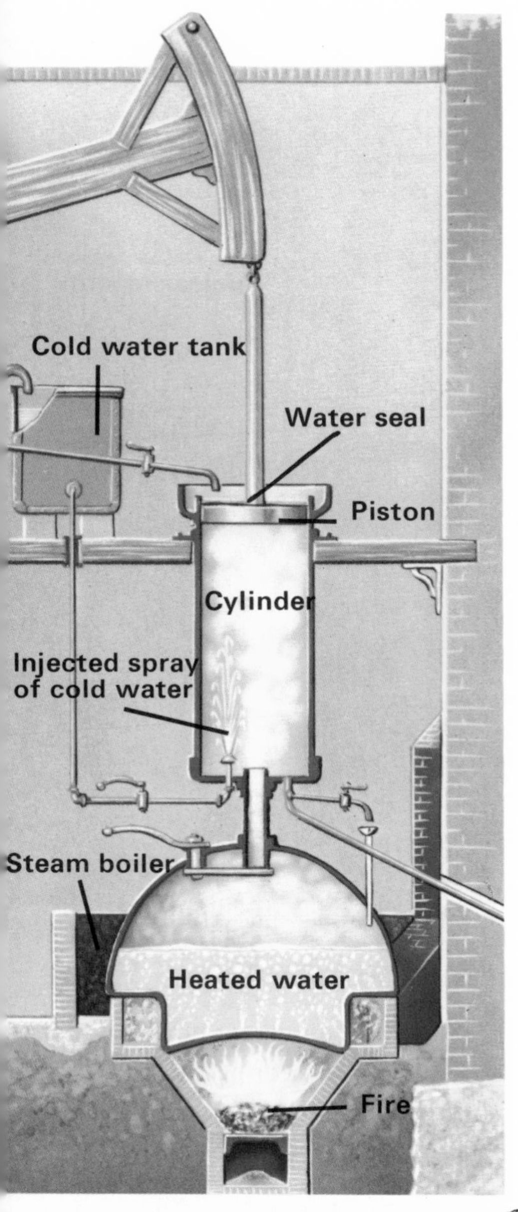

Gas turbines

In a gas turbine, hot expanding gases turn turbine wheels and so make a shaft rotate (go round). The gas turbine drives generators in power stations, as well as working pumps in OIL fields. It has been developed as jet and turboprop engines to propel AIRCRAFT. It is also becoming increasingly important in transportation by ROAD and rail.

A gas turbine has three main parts – a compressor, a combustion chamber, and a turbine. The compressor sucks in and compresses air. It then delivers it to the combustion chamber. Fuel such as kerosene is sprayed into the chamber, and burns in the air. The hot gases produced spin the turbine. The simplest jet engine has just one turbine, which drives the compressor. The hot gases then escape as a jet from the engine and propel it forwards.

Below: A cutaway picture of one kind of aircraft jet engine. The compressor sucks in air which is then compressed. In the combustion chambers, fuel mixes with the air and burns. The hot gases formed in this way spin the turbine before escaping as a jet.

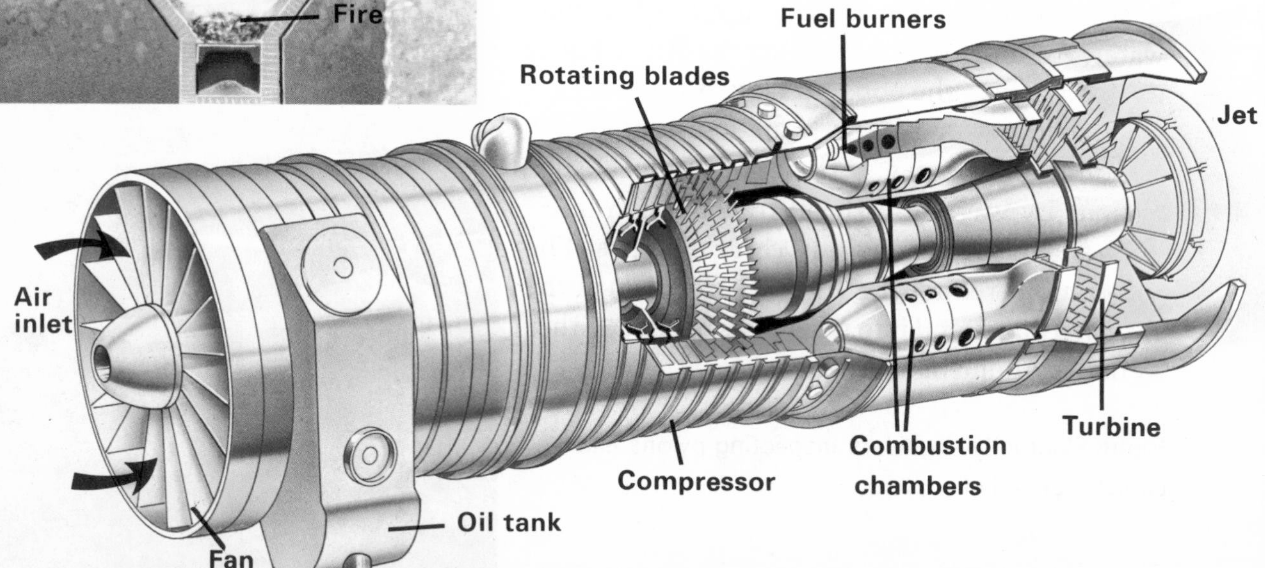

Electric power

Electricity is our most convenient form of power. It is cheap to produce, easy to send from place to place, and clean to use.

Electricity is produced, or generated, in a power station. An engine drives the electricity generator. Electricity is produced by moving coils of conductive wire through a magnetic field. Two main kinds of engines are used in power stations to drive the generators – STEAM TURBINES and water turbines.

Many power stations use turbine-generators (turbo-generators) driven by steam. Various fuels are used to fire the boilers that raise the steam for the turbines. OIL and COAL are widely used; so is NATURAL GAS. Nuclear power stations use uranium in nuclear reactors. The reactors generate heat by splitting uranium atoms. The heat is then used to turn water into steam to drive steam turbines in the normal way.

Power stations that generate electricity by water power are called hydro-electric power stations. The largest power stations are hydro-electric. They use the force of flowing water to spin turbine wheels connected to the generators. Most hydro-electric power stations are built at DAMS, where there is a great supply of flowing water. An unusual one, built on the River Rance in FRANCE, uses the ebb and flow of the tides.

Electric power is sent from a distant power station to our homes. First it goes to local sub-stations by way of overhead transmission lines. High steel towers, or pylons, carry the lines. The sub-stations reduce the voltage (pressure) of the electricity and send it to where it is needed, either by underground or overhead cables.

Above: In a nuclear power station a nuclear reactor produces heat to turn water into steam for driving steam turbines.

Right: Electricity engineers inspecting pylons and cables from a helicopter.

Below: Hydro-electric power stations use the energy of flowing water. Water stored behind a dam is released through a sluice and down a pipe onto a turbine. The turbine spins and turns a shaft connected to a generator, which produces electricity. Right: A dam on the Snake River, Washington State, U.S.A. Such dams are ideal sites for hydro-electric power stations.

Reservoir
Dam
Sluice
Water flow

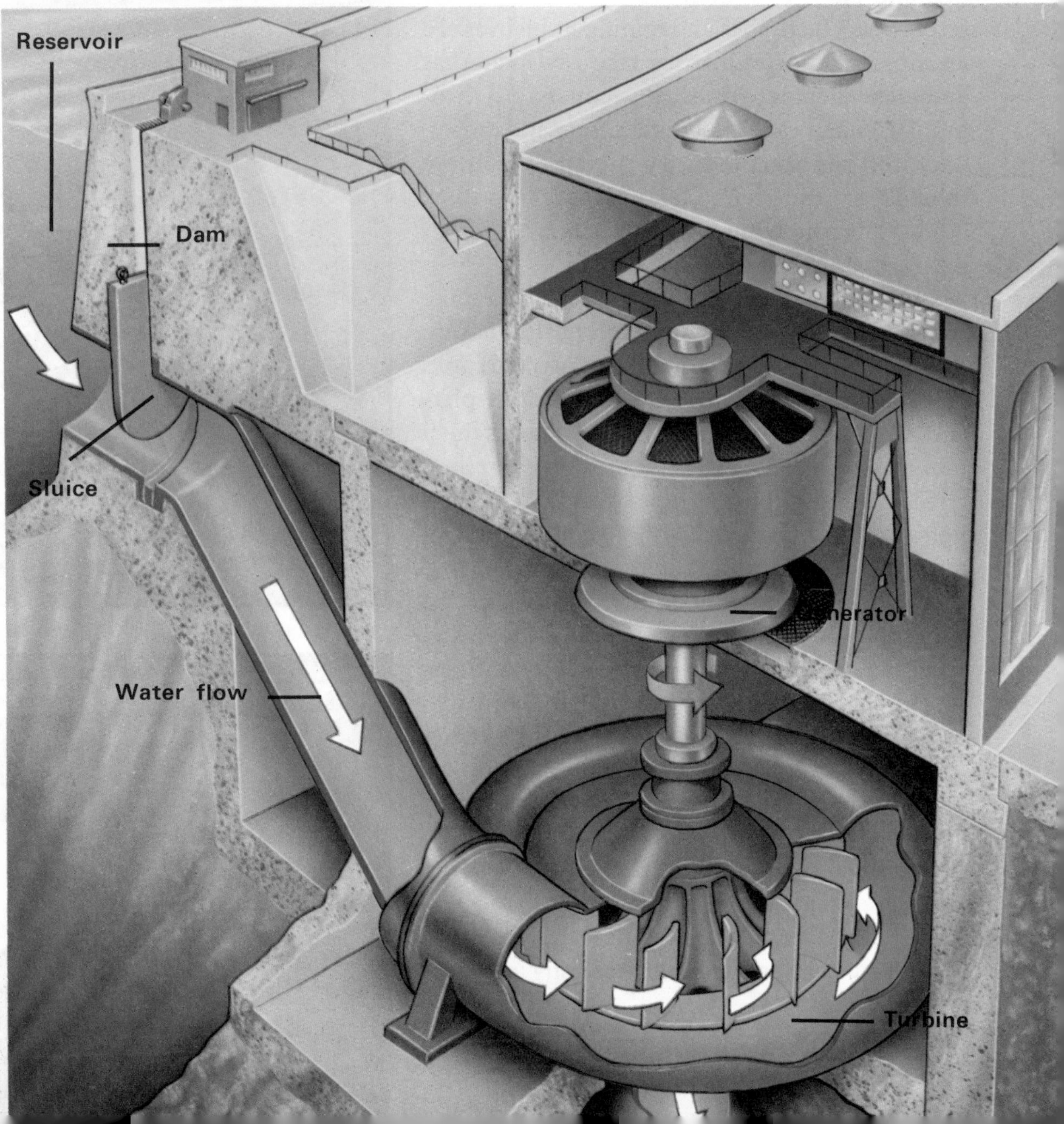

Industry

In today's society, work is highly organized. We have to produce enough goods to meet the needs of a large population. We call any organized and productive activity an industry. There is, for example, the TIMBER industry, the IRON AND STEEL industry, the CHEMICAL INDUSTRY, the construction industry, and the MOTOR-CAR industry.

Some industries make direct use of natural resources. The timber and mining industries are examples. Other industries take raw materials and make them into finished products. All these industries are called manufacturing industries. The iron and steel industry processes iron ore mined from the ground, and turns it into steel. Then it manufactures many kinds of other products from the steel.

SHIPBUILDING and clockmaking are two quite different kinds of manufacturing industries. Shipbuilding is called a heavy industry. It uses large amounts of materials such as steel plate and, with the aid of heavy machines, makes them into massive products.

Clockmaking, on the other hand, is called a light industry. It uses only a small amount of materials to make quite small products.

The main feature of industry today is the widespread use of machines. Using machines, men can produce goods in greater quantities, more quickly, and more cheaply, than they could using their hands. The introduction of machines on a large scale about two hundred years ago brought about the INDUSTRIAL REVOLUTION.

Above: The steelworks at Port Talbot, Wales, one of the biggest steel plants in Britain.
Right: Building the four-engined Boeing 747, often called the 'Jumbo Jet'. Most Jumbos carry up to 500 passengers.

Industrial Revolution

Until a few hundred years ago there was little real industry. Most people lived in the countryside and farmed the land. They could live on the food they produced themselves. They grew their own WHEAT, baked their own bread, and made their own CLOTHES and FURNITURE. The few machines that there were, such as the spinning wheel, were simple and were worked by hand.

Then, in the eighteenth century, a great change took place. In 1709, Abraham Darby made the first successful attempt at using coke for smelting IRON. Thus, more iron became available. Spinners and weavers invented machines that greatly increased output. One of these inventors, Richard Arkwright, put several of his machines in a large building and employed a number of people to work them. Thus he introduced the FACTORY system of working.

James WATT developed a practical STEAM ENGINE that provided a source of power to drive the new machines in the factories. People began to leave the land and work in cities and towns. A revolution in the way people lived and worked had begun. This was the Industrial Revolution.

Below: A nineteenth-century textile factory.

Factories

A factory is a place where men and machines are employed to make a product of some kind. The product could be matches, aspirins, ball bearings, TELEVISION sets, sulphuric acid, or cars. Some products, a television set, for example, are complete and ready for sale when they leave the factory. Others, such as ball bearings, are only used as part of another product.

In a factory the work to be done is usually divided up into a number of operations. This is called division of labour. In a BICYCLE factory, for example, separate departments might make the wheels, the frame, the brakes, and the gears.

Some parts might come from other suppliers. Then another department might put the different parts together to make a finished bicycle.

Very accurate machines are used in production to ensure that individual parts are virtually identical. The product can therefore be assembled from any of the parts produced. This is important. It is the basis of mass production (production on a large scale).

Assembly lines

One of the main ways of making a product from many different parts is by means of a moving assembly line. U.S. car pioneers Henry Ford and R. E. Olds developed the assembly-line system for mass-producing their cars in the early 1900s. The system is still seen best in car making.

On the car assembly line, the basic frame of the vehicle moves slowly through the FACTORY on a long conveyor. There are workers at various points along the line. They are supplied with certain parts that they attach to each frame as it passes. By the time the frame has reached the end of the production line, it has been transformed into a finished car, ready for the road.

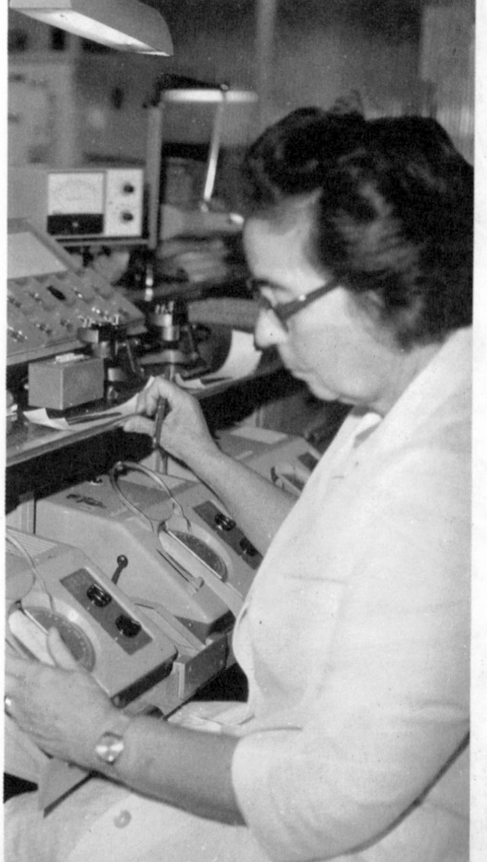

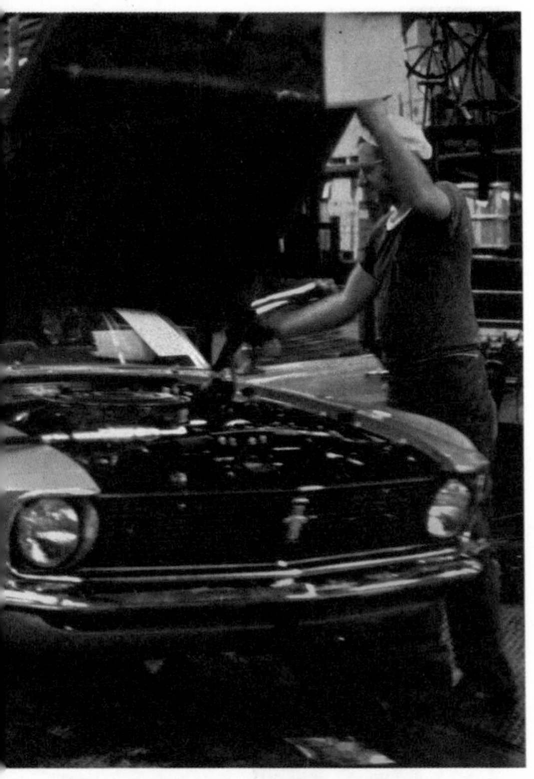

Above: Most cars are mass-produced on an assembly line like this one.
Left: A worker testing watches.
Below: The control room of a factory that is run by computer.
Below right: An automatic machine for filling milk cartons.

Automation

Many machines used in industry carry out complicated operations without an operator, except to switch them on or off. They are often guided by instructions fed into them on punched paper tape, or on magnetic tape, similar to that used in tape recorders. Machines can be linked together to carry out a whole succession of operations automatically, one after the other. The introduction of such automatic machinery into industry is one example of automation. Automation can relieve people of much dull work.

An OIL refinery provides one of the best examples of automation. It is an enormous FACTORY that changes crude OIL into useful products such as petrol and kerosene. Yet there is scarcely a worker to be seen. Almost everything works automatically. A few people in a central control room watch instruments that tell them what is happening in various parts of the refinery.

The real controller is an electronic brain, or computer. It is a machine that can be given a set of instructions about what is to be done everywhere at any one time in the refinery. It is linked to all the refinery controls, such as valves and heaters. It alters them as necessary to keep the operations working properly.

Management

A team of managers is needed in most organizations. It is their job to see that the organization runs smoothly. They have many duties. They must carry out the policies of the directors. They must also see that work is done in the cheapest and most efficient way. To do their job well, they must make the best use of employees, machines, materials, and money.

In an industrial company there might be many different managers. Most companies have managers in production, sales, ADVERTISING, and public relations. There are also accountants (money managers). Personnel managers work closely with the employees. They explain management policies, consider employee problems, and negotiate with UNIONS over such things as pay, working conditions, and welfare benefits.

Above: A meeting of managers in Germany.
Below right: A union official addressing an open-air meeting of union members.

Unions

A great many workers in industry belong to a union. Unions protect the interests of the workers and prevent them being exploited by their employers. The trade union movement began in the late 1700s but did not become well organized until much later. Today many unions have become very large and very powerful. Their demands and actions can have a great effect on the economy of a country.

During the INDUSTRIAL REVOLUTION many workers were badly treated. Today, workers in many countries are no longer exploited by their employers. Their unions have improved their pay and working conditions by negotiating with MANAGEMENT.

Since unions speak for a large number of workers, they can bargain more effectively than a single worker can. Negotiations between unions and management are the most important part of what is called industrial relations. These negotiations are usually an example of compromise. For instance, the union may ask for more pay and shorter working hours for its workers. Management may then make a counter offer – more pay but no change in working hours. The union and management may have to meet many times before reaching an agreement. Even then, the union members usually have the right to accept or reject the agreement by vote. Sometimes, if no agreement can be reached, a third party may be asked to decide the issue. This procedure is called arbitration. In many countries the third party is the government.

If a union will not accept less than they asked for, they may take industrial action and call a STRIKE (tell their workers to stop working). In this way they try to force the employers to give in to their demands.

Left: Union members stage a protest march.

Strikes

A strike takes place when employees refuse to carry on working because they are dissatisfied with their pay or working conditions.

There are two kinds of strike – official and unofficial. Official strikes happen when the elected leaders of a Trade Union tell their members to stop work. Unofficial strikes take place when workers strike without the backing of their union officials.

Although strikes are common in EUROPE and America, they are still forbidden in many countries of the world.

Pollution

Pollution means the poisoning of the land, the seas, and the air. It is one of the greatest problems facing mankind today. Industry is to blame for some of the pollution that exists. Some FACTORY chimneys release dangerous fumes, smoke, and dust into the air. Factory wastes containing dangerous chemicals (lead and mercury compounds, for example) are sometimes poured into our RIVERS. The amounts released at any one time may be small, but they can build up over a period of time and cause real harm to human beings and wildlife.

Water pollution is serious because we all rely on a supply of pure water to live. River pollution can become so bad that fish and plants cannot live. In some countries, LOCAL GOVERNMENT authorities add to the pollution problem by allowing untreated sewage to flow into the rivers and seas. OIL is increasing pollution at sea. A TANKER may discharge oil by accident during a collision, or on purpose when its tanks are being cleaned out. Oil fouls beaches and smothers and kills SEABIRDS.

In most developed countries, exhaust fumes from cars are a major cause of air pollution. Cars give out irritating and poisonous gases and lead compounds. In cities these gases can build up to dangerous levels at times. In the Los Angeles Basin, for example, polluting gases often get trapped with the sea fog, causing very thick and clinging smogs. These smogs are particularly dangerous to health.

Right: In March 1978 the oil tanker, *Amoco Cadiz*, ran aground off the coast of Brittany, France. Fifty thousand metric tons of its cargo of crude oil spilled out into the sea, killing seabirds and fish. Beaches along the French coast were also polluted.

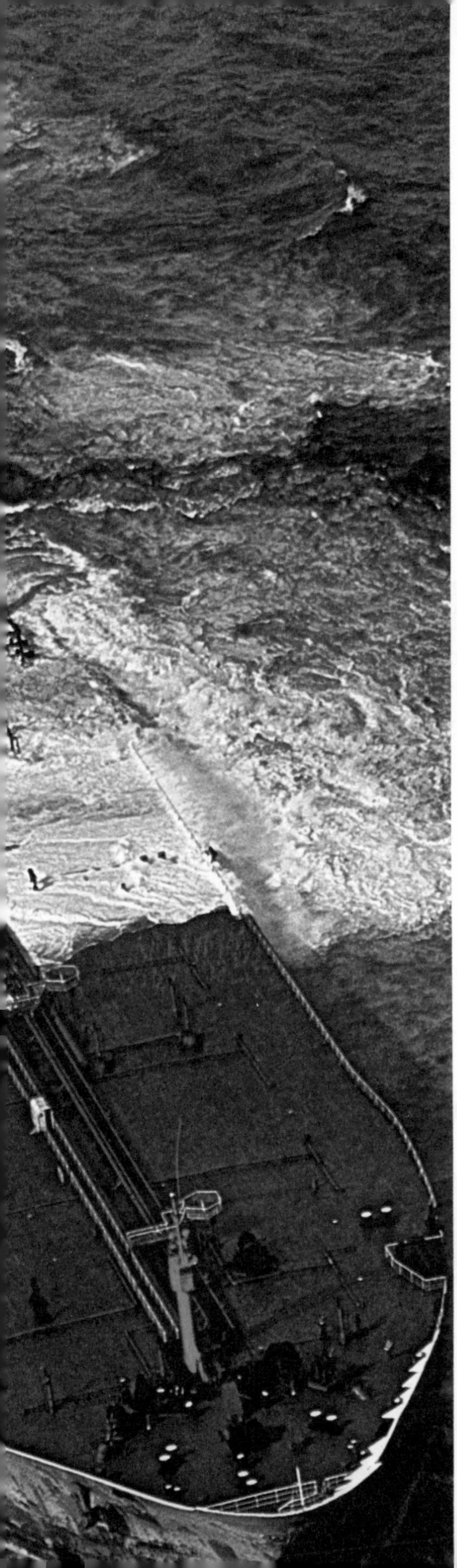

We use insecticides to kill insects that attack crops. In doing so, we may upset the balance of nature by killing the food supply for birds. In some cases, the substances in insecticides may also harm animals that feed on the crops. Not long ago, when certain insecticides containing chlorine were sprayed on SEEDS, millions of birds that fed on the seeds died. These insecticides were then banned. DDT, once the most widely used insecticide, is now banned in many countries.

Over the last few years, people throughout the developed countries of the world have become aware of the long-term dangers of pollution. At last, international action is being taken. Most governments have already passed some anti-pollution laws. The U.S.A., for example, has imposed severe limits on the pollutants permitted from car exhausts.

Factories are ordered to remove the poisons from their wastes before discharging them into the air or the rivers. Already, in some countries, the air is noticeably cleaner, and the rivers are beginning to support fish and plant life again.

Below: Car dumps like this spoil the countryside, and are another form of pollution.

Metals

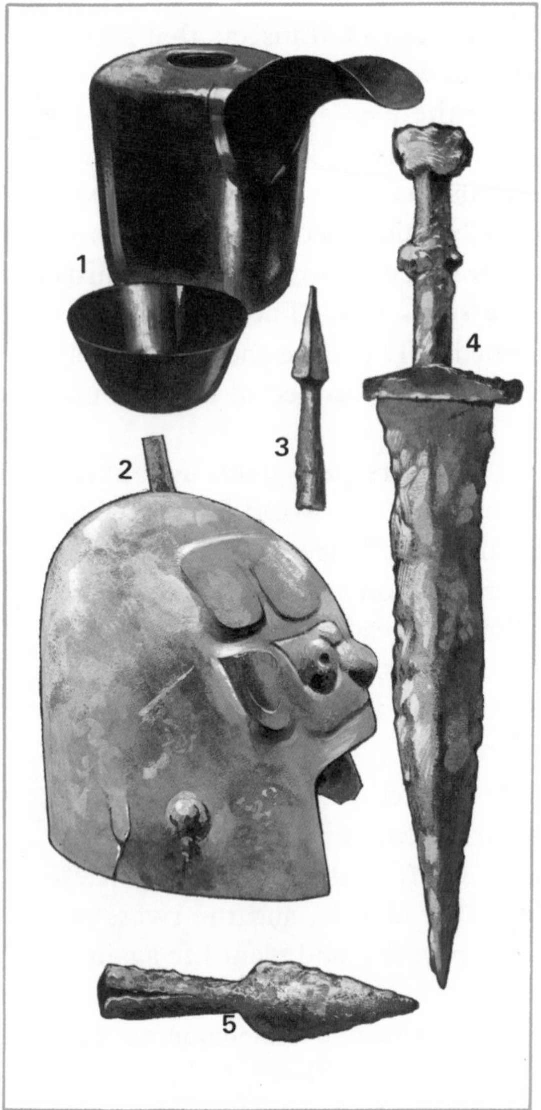

1. Ancient Egyptian copper vessels.
2. Bronze Chinese helmet.
3. Iron Roman catapult dart.
4. Iron Roman dagger.
5. Iron Roman spear head.
6. Gold Ancient British shoulder clasp.

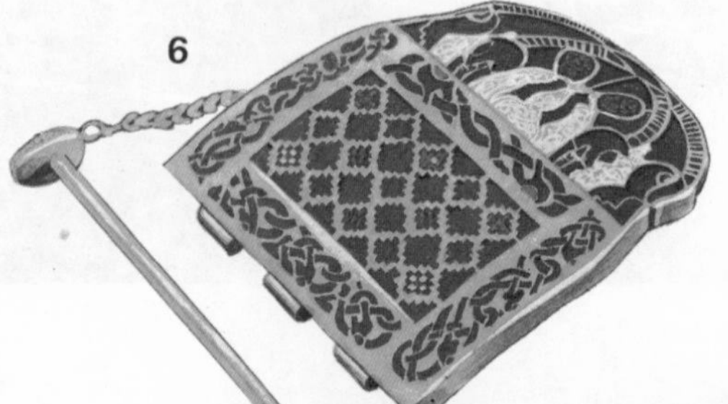

It was prehistoric man's discovery and use of metals that led to civilisation. Without metals we would still be in a stone age, hunting with wooden spears and cutting with stone axes.

By far the most important metal used in industry today is IRON. Pure iron itself is not particularly useful. But when other metals and a little carbon are added to it, it becomes much more valuable in the form of steel. Steel is an example of what is called an ALLOY, or mixture of metals and other chemical elements.

Nearly 70 metals are found in the EARTH's crust. But only about half of them are very useful. Most of these metals are found in the form of minerals. They are combined chemically with other elements, especially oxygen. The handful of metals that can be found in native (metal) form include COPPER, SILVER, gold, and platinum.

When the metal can be easily extracted from a mineral, we call that mineral an ore. The metal can often be extracted by smelting, or heating the ore in a furnace with a substance such as coke. Then the crude metal formed is usually refined, or purified. Impurities are often removed by re-melting the metal in a furnace.

Below: An Indian tinsmith at work.

Above: The biggest ever gold nugget was found in 1872. It weighed 286 kilogrammes.

Alloys

Few METALS are used in their pure state. They are too weak, too brittle, or they corrode (rust) quickly. They may also have some other properties that make them unsuitable for industrial use. Scientists can often improve the properties of a metal by adding another metal, or even a non-metal, to it to form an alloy.

Steel is an alloy of IRON. By adding less than one part of carbon to two hundred parts of iron, a great increase in strength and hardness can be brought about. Iron has other properties that can be improved. Iron by itself usually rusts and stains badly. But with the addition of a little chromium and nickel, it can be made into stainless steel.

COPPER forms several important alloys with other metals. When mixed with tin, it forms bronze. Bronze is much harder and stronger than either copper or tin. Copper is mixed with zinc to form brass. Again, the alloy is much harder and stronger than the parent metals. With nickel, copper forms the cupro-nickel alloys. Cupro-nickel, not SILVER, is the metal now used to make 'silver' coins.

Even our precious metals silver and gold are usually mixed with a little copper to make them harder. Silver and gold alloys with mercury (the only liquid metal) are used by dentists to fill TEETH. Alloys with mercury are called amalgams.

There are hundreds more useful alloys. ALUMINIUM alloys are very important. Invar is an interesting iron-nickel alloy that expands scarcely at all when heated. Type metal used by printers contains lead, tin and antimony. Pewter contains lead and tin.

Left: A bronze statue. Bronze is often used for statues as it is easy to cast and does not rust.

Iron and steel

Steel is the cheapest and most widely used metal in the world. Huge quantities are used in manufacturing, engineering, and construction of many kinds. The world produces about 750 million metric tons of steel every year. In comparison, only about 16 million metric tons of ALUMINIUM are produced each year.

Steel is an ALLOY, or mixture, of iron with a little carbon and usually other METALS as well. There are many kinds of steels. Each contains different amounts of carbon and alloying metals. The most common kind of steel is mild, or low-carbon, steel. It is used for making most car bodies. Important alloy steels include stainless steels and tool steels. Some steels, which are called high-speed tool steels, remain hard and sharp even when they get red-hot.

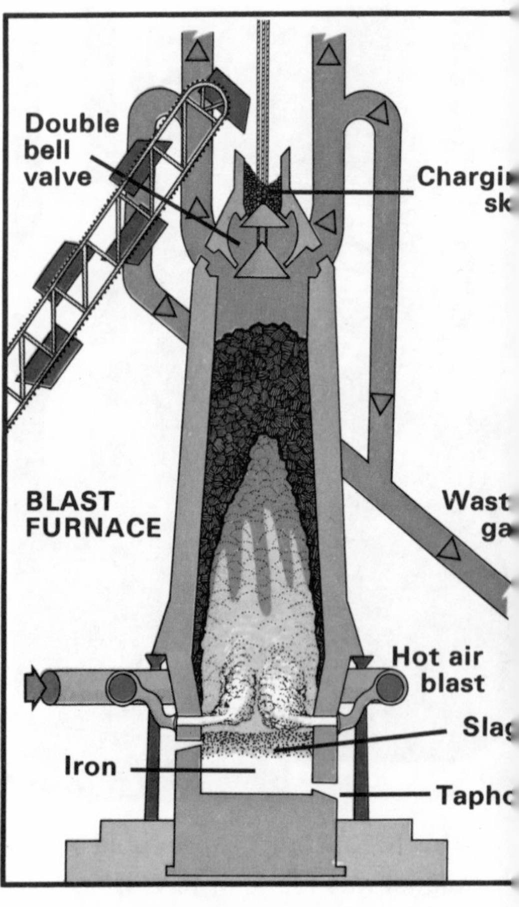

Right: Diagram of a blast furnace.
Below: An opencast iron-ore mine in Australia. The ore-bearing rock gives the landscape a rust-red colour.

There is plenty of iron in the EARTH's crust. It occurs usually in the form of iron oxide (in combination with oxygen). Iron oxide ore is mined in much the same way as other ores. We get iron from the ore by smelting it with coke in a blast furnace.

The blast furnace is so named because hot air is blasted through it to make the coke inside burn fiercely. In the great heat, the coke (carbon) combines with the oxygen from the iron and changes into carbon dioxide gas. The iron melts and falls to the bottom of the furnace. Limestone is also added to the furnace. It melts to form a slag, which combines with the impurities that would otherwise stay in the iron. The slag floats on top of the iron and can be removed separately.

The molten iron is poured from the furnace into a series of hollow moulds called pigs. At this stage it still has too much carbon in it to be useful and it is known as pig iron. The extra carbon is taken out in another furnace by a process called refining.

Most steel is refined in an open-hearth furnace. In this furnace the pig iron lies in a shallow hearth and is heated fiercely by the furnace flames. Iron ore and scrap steel are usually added to the furnace as well. In the furnace most of the carbon is burned out, leaving purified steel.

Much pig iron is also refined in what is called a converter. Air or oxygen is blasted through or onto the molten iron, again causing most of the carbon to burn out. While the steel is still hot, other metals may be added to bring it to the desired composition. A little manganese is almost always added to make the steel less brittle. Electric furnaces, from which the air has been removed, are used for refining steels that need to be very pure. Scrap steel, not pig iron, is used in electric furnaces.

Two common kinds of furnaces used to refine pig iron into steel. Above: An electric arc furnace. Below: A converter.

Aluminium

Aluminium has been known for about a hundred years. After IRON and STEEL, it is used more than any other metal. It is silvery grey in colour and very light in weight. When pure, it is quite soft and not particularly strong. But other metals can be added to it to make much stronger ALLOYS.

Aluminium is produced, not by smelting, but by passing electricity through molten alumina. Alumina comes from ore called bauxite.

Industries around the world use vast quantities of strong, lightweight aluminium alloys. The aircraft industry, for example, makes aircraft bodies, or airframes, out of them. For the home, aluminium and its alloys are used to make window frames, kitchen foil, and cooking utensils. Saucepans are made out of it because the metal conducts heat well and resists staining. Aluminium also conducts electricity well. For this reason it is widely used for electric cables.

Aluminium has replaced iron and steel in the production of some things. TYPEWRITERS, car engines, home appliances, and packaging are increasingly being made out of this metal.

Copper

Copper has been known to man since prehistoric times. It is one of the few METALS that can be found native, or in the form of metal, in the ground. The ANCIENT EGYPTIANS were skilled at working native copper at least 7000 years ago. Later they discovered how to extract copper from its ores by smelting.

Copper has an attractive reddish-brown colour. It is easy to bend and to beat into shape. It can also be drawn out into fine wire easily. A lump of copper the size of a golf ball (40 millimetres in diameter) can make 25 kilometres of wire without breaking.

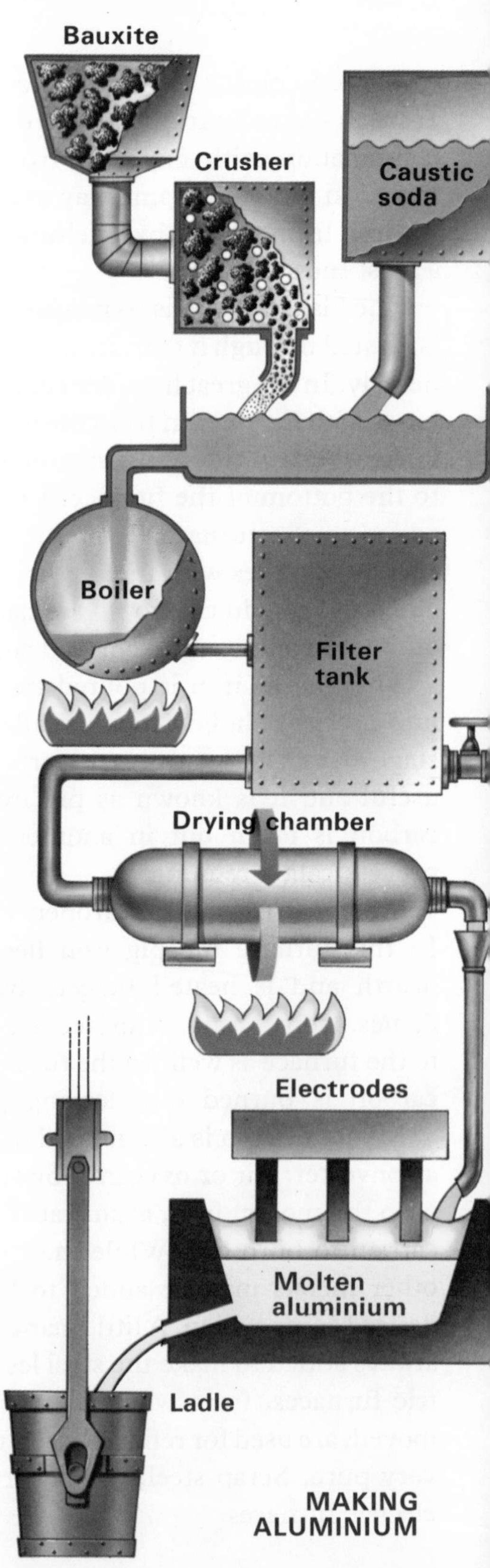

MAKING ALUMINIUM

Copper conducts electricity better than any other metal except SILVER. The electrical industry, in fact, is the biggest user of copper. Great quantities of copper are also used to make such ALLOYS as brass, bronze and cupro-nickel. Another useful property of copper and its alloys is that they do not rust, as IRON and steel do.

The U.S.A., the U.S.S.R., and CHILE are the world's leading copper producers. Native copper is found very rarely in the earth and then only in tiny amounts. For industry, copper is obtained by processing copper ores. Two of the most important ores are copper pyrites and chalcocite. These ores may be mined on the surface or deep underground. They are smelted to produce impure copper. This is then refined using electricity. Copper refined by electricity is one of the purest metals produced commercially.

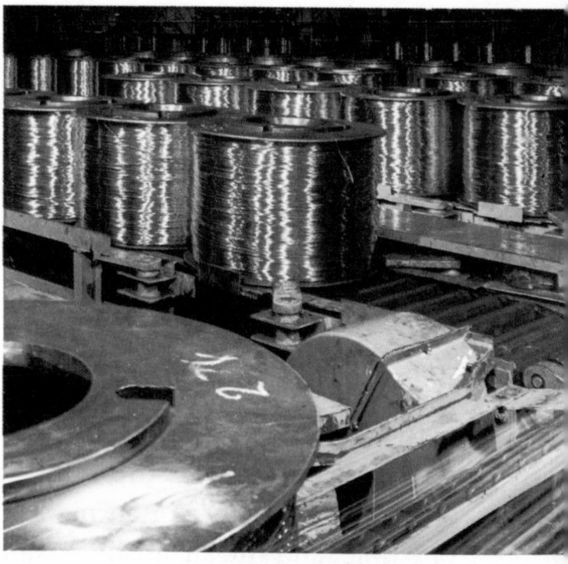

Above: Copper being drawn into thin wire. Most copper wire is used by the electrical industry. It is a good conductor of electricity.

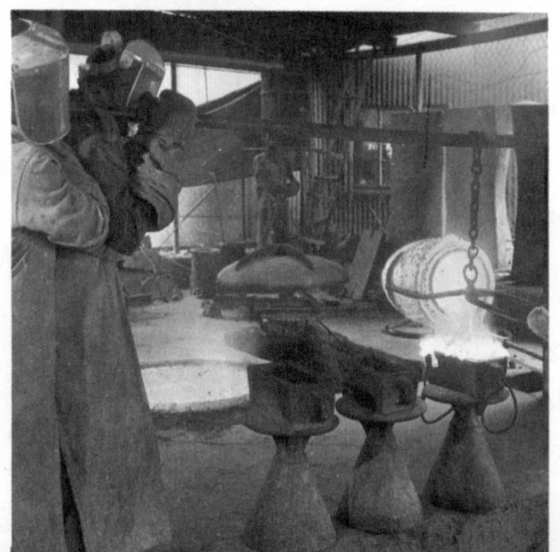

Silver and gold

COPPER belongs to the same chemical family as the precious METALS silver and gold. They are regarded as precious because they are scarce. They have an attractive colour, and keep their appearance for a long time. Like copper, they are easy to shape and draw into fine wire.

Copper, silver, and gold are often called coinage metals. They have been used for making coins for hundreds of years. Today, however, most coins are made of copper ALLOYS. Silver and gold are too expensive.

Silver and gold can be found as metals in the ground. They were therefore well known to the early civilisations, who made them into fine works of art. Today, silver and gold are taken from ores that provide other metals as well.

Above left: Silver being refined in Australia.
Left: Gold being poured into moulds.

Casting

We can shape METALS in a number of ways. One way is by casting. Car engine cylinder blocks, for example, are usually made by casting. This process involves pouring molten metal into moulds. When the metal cools and becomes solid, it takes on the shape of the mould. Casting is done in a foundry.

Many moulds are made of a special firm sand. They are made in two halves that are fitted together, one on top of the other. Two holes are left, passing through the sand into the empty space inside. The molten metal is poured into one hole, and the air inside escapes through the other.

Another casting method uses permanent moulds, or dies, made of metal. They can be used again and again. The molten metal can be poured or injected into the mould under pressure. When the metal is solid, the mould opens to release the casting. This method is called die-casting. It is used especially for shaping small objects, such as toy cars, from ALLOYS.

Many metals, including steel and ALUMINIUM, are cast from the furnace into large blocks called ingots. While the ingots are still red-hot, they are reduced into smaller slabs by rolling. The slabs are then shaped by other methods.

Above: Steel being worked in a forging press to prepare it for further shaping later.
Below: Making a casting from a sand mould.

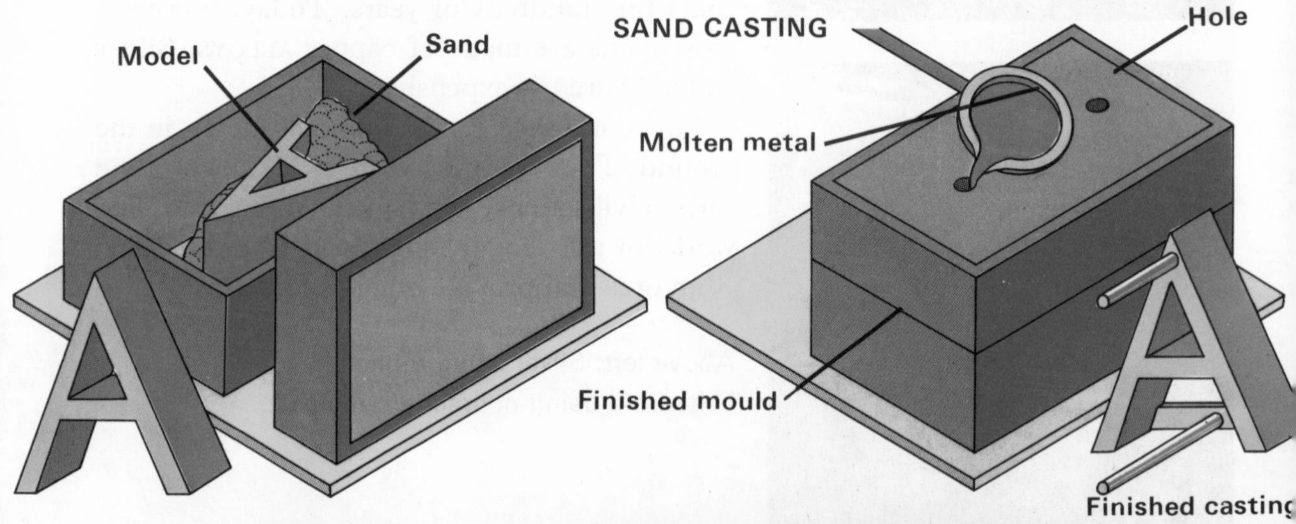

Forging

Forging is one of the most important ways of shaping metal. In forging, hot metal is hammered into shape by a heavy drop hammer. Drop forging is a mechanical way of doing what the village blacksmith once did by hand with a hammer and an anvil.

The drop hammer has a heavy ram, or weight, that is raised by compressed air or steam pressure and then allowed to fall on the metal. Beneath the metal is the bottom half of a mould, or die. Above it is the top half of the die. When the ram drops on the top half, the metal is forced into shape as the two halves of the die come together.

Drop forging is very noisy and violent. It does, however, produce nearly finished parts with no waste. It is not very good for shaping large pieces of metal. They are forged in huge presses worked by liquid pressure. Some of these presses can apply pressures of 10,000 metric tons or more. Presses are also used to shape sheet metal.

Below: A steel ring being finished after forging.

Machining

Many metal products have to be machined after they have been shaped by FORGING and CASTING. Machining is the final shaping process. It is carried out by power-driven machine tools. The casting of a car engine cylinder block, for example, must be drilled with many holes of different sizes to form the cylinders and valve guides. The holes must be precise in size and position. They must also have a smooth, polished surface.

Drilling is one of the most important machining operations. It is done on a drill press, which presses a rotating twist drill against the workpiece (the part to be machined). Like most other machining operations, drilling produces a lot of heat. The friction, or rubbing of the tool against the workpiece, causes the heat. To reduce friction and wear and to cool the parts, a liquid called a cutting oil is poured on them. Boring is an operation carried out to increase the size of a drilled hole.

Turning is another machining operation. It is used to shape round pieces of metal, such as shafts. The workpiece is mounted and turned on a machine called a lathe. Cutting tools can be moved onto the workpiece as it revolves.

Above: A machine tool operator turning metal on a lathe.

Below left: Drilling a metal plate using a drill press.

Below: An automatic milling machine at work on the panels for a modern airliner.

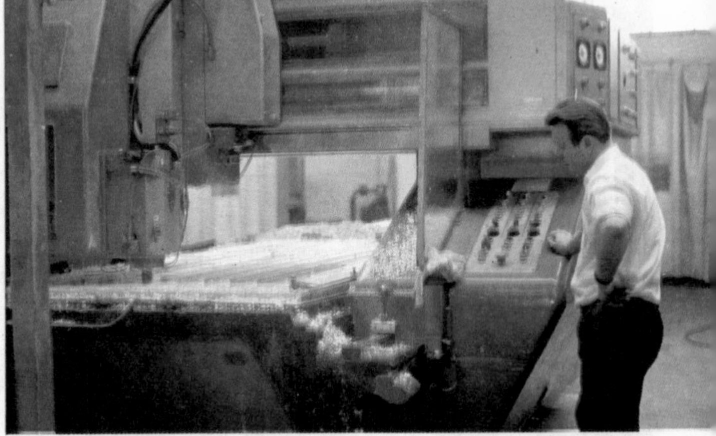

In milling, machining is done by a revolving cutting wheel with sharp teeth. Planing, which produces a flat surface, is done by a knife-like cutting tool. Often the final machining operations are grinding and polishing. Products made out of wood and PLASTICS are also sometimes machined as a final shaping process.

Some machine tools are worked by men. Others work automatically. They follow instructions fed to them on magnetic tape.

Welding

It is not always possible or necessary to make metal objects by shaping and MACHINING. Often it is better to construct them by joining several pieces together. This may be done by welding.

In fusion welding, the welder first heats the edges of the metal pieces with a high temperature flame from an oxy-acetylene torch until the surfaces melt. Then he usually adds more molten metal from a welding rod to fill the gap between the two pieces. The filler metal and the melted edges fuse together. When the metal cools and solidifies, a strong joint forms.

Instead of a gas flame, the welder may use the heat produced by an electric arc to melt the metal. This is known as arc welding.

Another form of electric welding is called resistance welding. When an electric current is passed through two overlapping metal parts, they heat up. A little pressure is applied to join the parts together. Spot welding and seam welding are two forms of resistance welding.

In friction welding, the parts are rubbed together under pressure until they soften and fuse.

The most recent method of welding is by laser beam. Laser welding is often done where delicate parts must be joined very accurately.

Above: Welding an iron frame, using arc welding equipment. The welder is wearing a mask to protect his face and eyes from sparks and the glaring light.

Construction

Above: An excavator clearing away unwanted soil.

The face of the EARTH is changing every day. Men and machines are at work reshaping our cities, towns and countryside. To improve communications they construct ROADS and MOTORWAYS. They build BRIDGES over RIVERS and VALLEYS and across estuaries. They dig railway TUNNELS through MOUNTAINS and hills. To house an expanding population they build tall SKYSCRAPERS. They build DAMS to provide water for irrigation, to produce power, improve navigation, or control flooding.

The people who are in charge of this kind of work are the civil engineers. They receive their training in colleges and UNIVERSITIES and on the job. They must direct the workers and select the best materials. Modern construction engineers have many powerful machines at their disposal. Bulldozers, scrapers, excavators, cranes and pumps – these are some of the machines that help do the work.

Left: Concrete is often brought to a site ready mixed in drums on the backs of lorries.
Below: Re-surfacing a road with asphalt. The asphalt is spread hot and rolled flat.

Above: A section of motorway in South Korea.
Below: The so-called 'Spaghetti Junction', near Birmingham in England. Planning and building motorway junctions is difficult and expensive.

Roads

Newer and better roads have become increasingly important as the number of cars and LORRIES continues to grow each year. Modern roads usually have a base of crushed stone on firmly packed earth. The surface may be asphalt or tarmac (a mixture of crushed stone and bitumen, a kind of tar).

There are also concrete roads in many places. They are usually laid by what is called a concrete train. This consists of a number of spreaders and vibrators that move slowly along rails at the edge of the road.

The ROMANS were the first real road engineers. They built their roads of layers of broken stones of various sizes and covered them with flat stone slabs. They gave their roads a camber (curved surface) for drainage. They also gave them kerbstones, and often a kind of pavement.

Motorways

ROADS built especially for fast traffic are known as motorways in Britain, autobahns in GERMANY, and expressways, freeways, or turnpikes in the United States. These roads are designed to let cars travel at high speeds with maximum safety.

Motorways usually have three or more lanes going in each direction. Often a barrier or a strip of land separates the cars going in one direction from the traffic coming towards them. Other roads cross over or under the motorway. There are no intersections. Traffic enters or leaves the motorway at carefully designed junctions.

Motorways are built as straight as possible. They have gentle slopes so that vehicles need not slow down very much. Because straight roads can make drivers sleepy, motorways are designed with occasional turns and curves to help drivers stay alert.

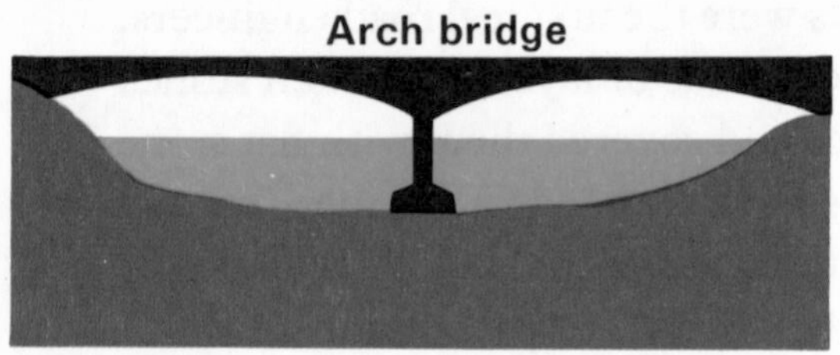

Above: Three common kinds of bridges. The suspension bridge can span the greatest width.
Below: A lifting bridge over a canal in the Netherlands. The bridge deck lifts up to allow canal craft to pass beneath it.

Bridges

Bridge building is one of the most exciting jobs of the civil engineer. One of the longest span bridges is the Humber Bridge across the River Humber in north-east England. It spans a distance of 1410 metres. Like all the biggest bridges, it is a suspension bridge. The bridge deck (roadway) hangs from huge cables. These cables are suspended from towers 155 metres high.

Arch bridges are in widespread use. Their strength lies in their arch shape. The ANCIENT ROMANS perfected the stone arch design more than 2000 years ago. The modern bridge builder, however, uses steel, or concrete reinforced (strengthened) with steel, to construct his arches. Sydney Harbour Bridge in AUSTRALIA is one of the best known steel arch bridges. It was built in 1932 and has a span of 503 metres.

The most common kind of bridge is the beam bridge. The simplest beam bridge is a beam or girder resting on supports at each end. A single beam cannot span more than a few metres because it tends to sag in the middle under its own weight. A truss, or steel framework, is often built on it to make it stronger. In order to span any distance, a series of beams and supports has to be used.

There are many other kinds of bridges, such as the cantilever and box-girder bridges. There are also bascule bridges (such as Tower Bridge in LONDON), vertical-lift bridges, and even submersible bridges, which can be lowered into the water.

In wartime and in peacetime emergencies, ARMIES build temporary bridges to cross RIVERS. They use metal Bailey bridges, which bolt together, or pontoon bridges, in which a deck is laid on a string of pontoons, or floats.

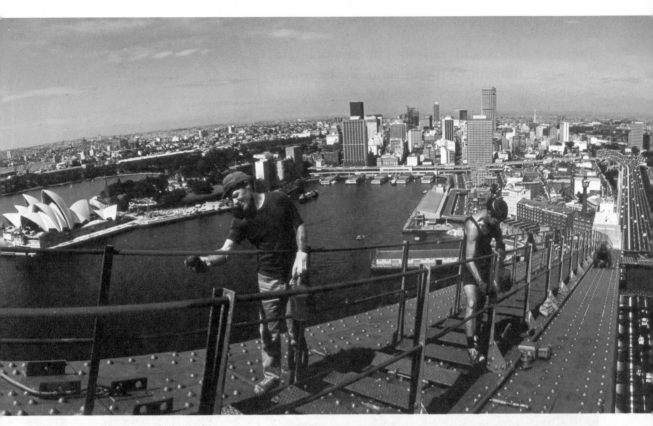

Above: Painting the Sydney Harbour Bridge.
Below: Tower Bridge in London. The two halves of the bridge deck can lift to allow river traffic through.
Right: A stone arch bridge at Antietam, U.S.A.

Tunnels

Building ROADS and railways in mountainous country is difficult. Without tunnels, the routes would have to be either very long or very steep. Many long road and rail tunnels have been dug through the ALPS between FRANCE and ITALY, and between SWITZERLAND and Italy. The 12-kilometre Fréjus rail tunnel, completed in 1871, was the first great Alpine tunnel.

Some of the longest tunnels are built beneath RIVERS or estuaries. In recent years the Japanese have built a number of long underwater tunnels to link their main ISLANDS.

Top: The Thames tunnel at Rotherhithe, London, in 1843.
Above: An open section of the St Bernard Tunnel through the Alps between Switzerland and Italy.
Left: The Hochtor Tunnel in Austria.

Tunnelling through rock is done with the help of explosives. A network of holes for the explosives is drilled into the rock. After the explosion, machines or conveyor belts load the broken rock into freight cars for removal. When workers go through soft or porous ground, a tunnelling shield is used to prevent the tunnel collapsing.

Dams

Dams are built to control the flow of a RIVER or a stream. The water that builds up behind the dam can then be used for many different purposes. Water is needed in the home for drinking, COOKING, and washing. Industry needs it for cooling and processing. In dry climates, farmers use it for irrigation.

Stored water can also be used to produce power, by allowing it to flow from the dam through turbines. The building of dams creates artificial LAKES, or reservoirs.

There are several different kinds of dams. Some are long, low, embankment dams built of earth and rock. Others are high concrete dams. These dams can be gravity dams, which hold back the water by their weight. Or they can be arch dams, which owe their strength to their shape. Arch dams are curved towards the water.

One of the biggest dams in the world is Fort Peck Dam on the Missouri River in the U.S.A. It is nearly six and a half kilometres long and contains 96,000,000 cubic metres of earth and rock.

The Tarbela Dam on the River Indus in PAKISTAN has a volume of 143,000,000 cubic metres.

Above: The Kariba Dam on the border between Zambia and Zimbabwe. It supplies hydro-electric power for both countries.
Below: Hsinan Chiang dam, near Hangchow, in China.

Shipbuilding

The first stage of shipbuilding is design. Someone who designs ships is called a naval architect. It is his job to produce a design that satisfies the needs of the shipowner. Many safety factors need to be taken into account.

The architect streamlines his design at and below the waterline to reduce the drag. The drag is the resistance of the water on the moving hull. Before he is satisfied, he tests scale models of his design in a water tank.

When the design has been accepted, the architect draws up detailed plans. These plans guide the workers who will actually make and assemble the various parts of the ship. The construction of the ship takes place on the slipway, which reaches down to the water. The keel, the backbone of the ship, is laid first. The hull is then built up from the keel and the decks and bulkheads are fitted. The bulkheads divide the ship into a number of compartments.

As the decks are built up, the engineers start moving in the engines and all the other heavy machinery. The hull is painted, and soon the ship is ready for launching. A wooden 'cradle' is built round the ship, and the slipway is greased. There is a ceremony to name the ship, and it slides down into the water.

After launching comes the process called fitting out. The superstructure is completed, and all the rest of the equipment is put in. The cabins are also furnished. The engineers test the engines and get them ready for the sea trials.

Top left: A welder at work in a shipyard. Compare the size of the propeller with that of the welder.
Top right: Part of the superstructure of a tanker being lifted into place on the hull.
Right: A ship being launched stern-first.

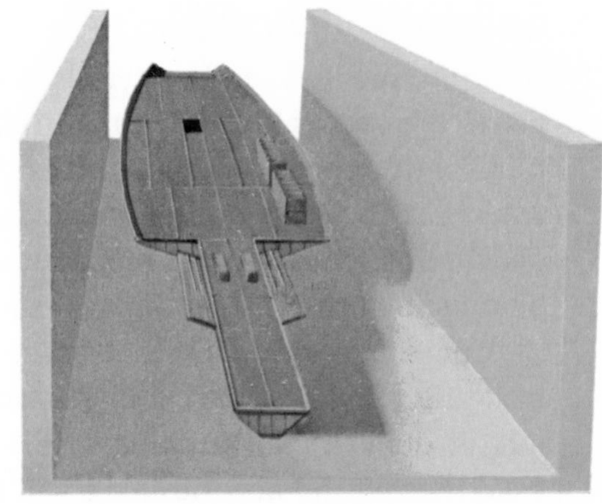

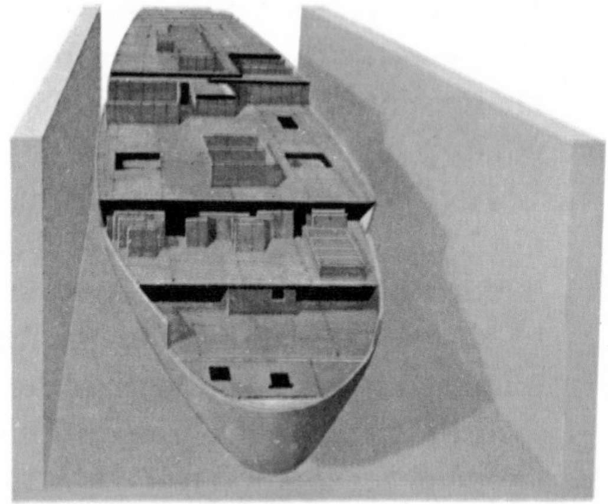

Above: Three stages in the construction of a ship. The structure is built up by welding together panels of sheet steel.

Building industry

Building methods and materials throughout the world are more alike now than in the past. New blocks of offices or flats often look similar wherever they are built. Building a new home or office can take a long time. Much work has to be done before construction can start.

A person or company that wishes to put up a building must first have a plan made of it. This job is done by an architect. His plans show exactly what the new building will look like. An architect is part engineer and part artist. He must make calculations to be sure that his building will stay up when it is built. He has to know how strong the materials are that he wants to use. He must work out the weight that will press on the walls and floors when the building is in use. Only then can he be certain that no part of his building will be overloaded and that the whole structure will be safe.

The architect also tries to make the building look as attractive as possible and designs it so that it fits in with surrounding buildings. He must make sure that the building will be pleasant and comfortable to live and work in. He must also make sure that it will not cost too much to build.

The architect's plans must be approved by the local planners before work can start. The builders begin by digging down into the ground to make foundations for the building. The foundations go down beneath the building and secure it firmly in the ground. The builders also lay pipes for DRAINAGE and WATER SUPPLY, and other services such as electricity and GAS.

If a tall building is being built, the next job is to build a frame or a core of steel or concrete on the foundations. A crane is used to lift the heavy girders or beams into their positions.

Workmen, who must have a good head for heights, then fix them together. Floors and walls are lifted up and fixed on. They are often concrete slabs which are made in a FACTORY and brought to the site. Sometimes a tall building uses the core to house the LIFT shaft. Then each storey (floor) is built around the core.

Next the ROOF and STAIRCASES are constructed so that workmen can work inside the shell of the building. They install wires and pipes for the various services. They fit WINDOWS, doors, wall panels, CEILINGS, floor coverings, and all kinds of other fittings. Then decorators complete the building and it is ready for its first occupiers.

Building a house is a similar but smaller job. In a tall block of flats or offices the frame takes the weight of the building. The walls do not support the building and so need not be thick and strong. In a house there is much less weight to support, and the walls can be made to hold up the floors and the roof. Beams placed across the house from one wall to another support the floors. Walls are usually built of special hollow building blocks cemented together with a facing of brick, stone, or wood on the outside. Inside, a smooth layer of plaster is often spread over the wall blocks. Pipes in the plaster and beneath the floors carry water, gas, electric cables, and sometimes hot air for HEATING.

Left: Different stages in building construction.
1. The architect draws the plans.
2. A surveyor examines the site.
3. Bulldozers clear and excavate the site.
4. Bricklayers build house walls.
5. Laying a reinforced concrete floor.
6. Making reinforced concrete walls.
7. Assembling a frame of girders.
8. Manufactured windows and wall facings.

Chemical Industry

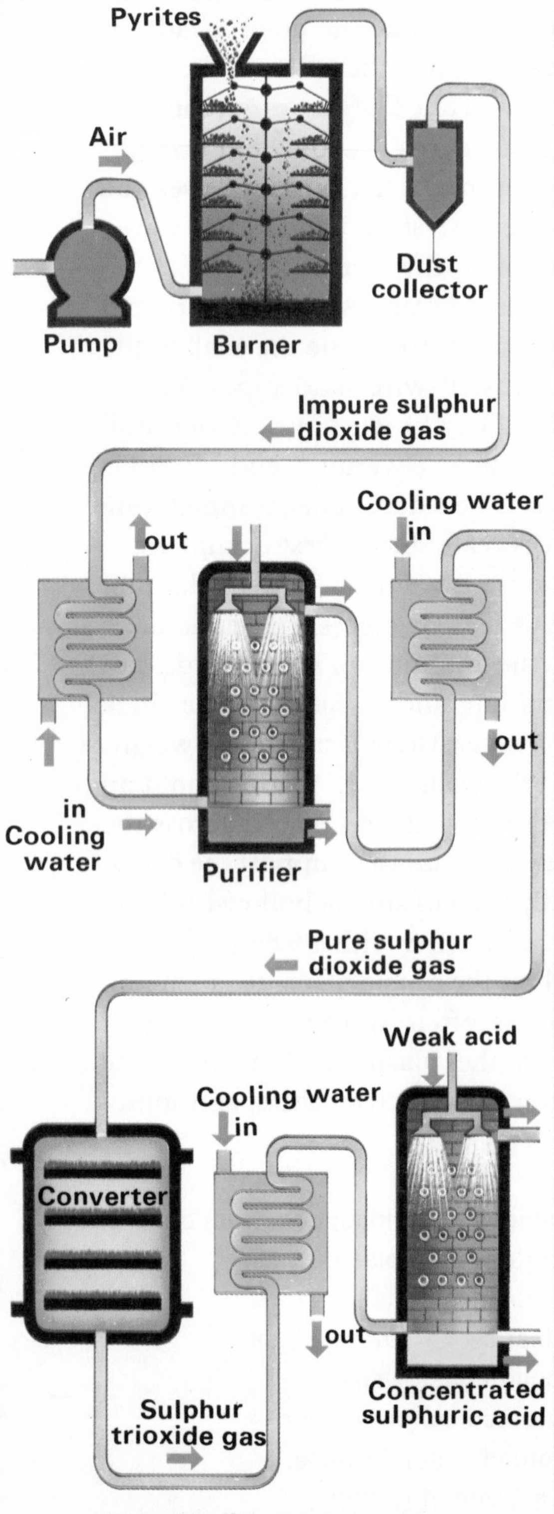

Pyrites
Air
Pump
Burner
Dust collector
Impure sulphur dioxide gas
Cooling water in
out
in Cooling water
out
Purifier
Pure sulphur dioxide gas
Weak acid
Cooling water in
Converter
out
Sulphur trioxide gas
Concentrated sulphuric acid

MANUFACTURE OF SULPHURIC ACID

The term chemical industry covers a large number of industrial activities. The industry makes a great variety of chemicals. It also produces finished products such as PLASTICS, paint, DRUGS, detergents, explosives, synthetic fibres, dyes and insecticides.

The most useful basic chemical that the industry makes is sulphuric acid. It is used in many chemical processes, from making FERTILIZERS to 'pickling' (cleansing) steel. Caustic soda (for making soap, among other things) is also produced in large quantities. So is ammonia (for fertilizers). These and other chemicals are often called heavy chemicals because they are made in very great quantities. Most drugs, however, are produced in relatively small amounts. They are an example of fine chemicals.

The chemical industry uses many kinds of raw materials – ROCKS, minerals, and COAL, mined from the ground. It also uses TIMBER cut from the forest, and many other plant materials.

PRODUCTS MADE FROM COAL OR OIL

Coal
Glues
Detergents
Plastics
Perfumes
Preservatives
Fuels
Soaps
Coated wallpapers

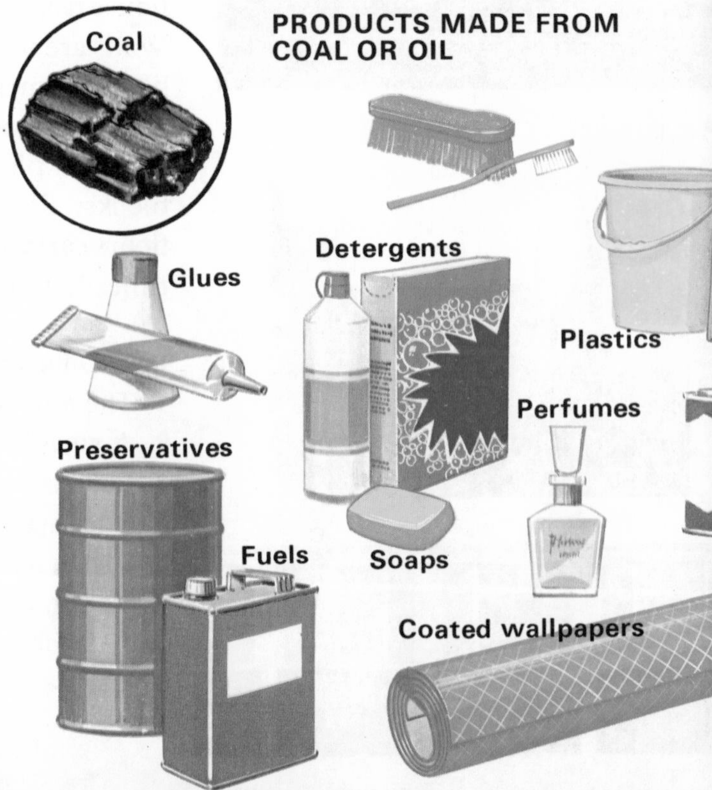

Most important of all, the chemical industry uses petroleum, or crude oil. Petroleum is vital both as a raw material and as a fuel. Unfortunately, supplies of petroleum will not last for ever.

The industry uses different chemical processes to turn these raw materials into useful products. By a process called cracking, it breaks down complicated substances into simple ones. Another process (polymerization) builds up simple substances into complicated ones. The industry also uses physical processes such as mixing, filtering, and drying. These processes help to make raw materials usable both chemically and commercially.

Research is vital to the chemical industry. Scientists are always trying to develop new or better processes and products. If a process looks promising, chemical engineers test it. They design equipment and build a small-scale pilot plant. If the process works there, they may go ahead and build a full-size plant.

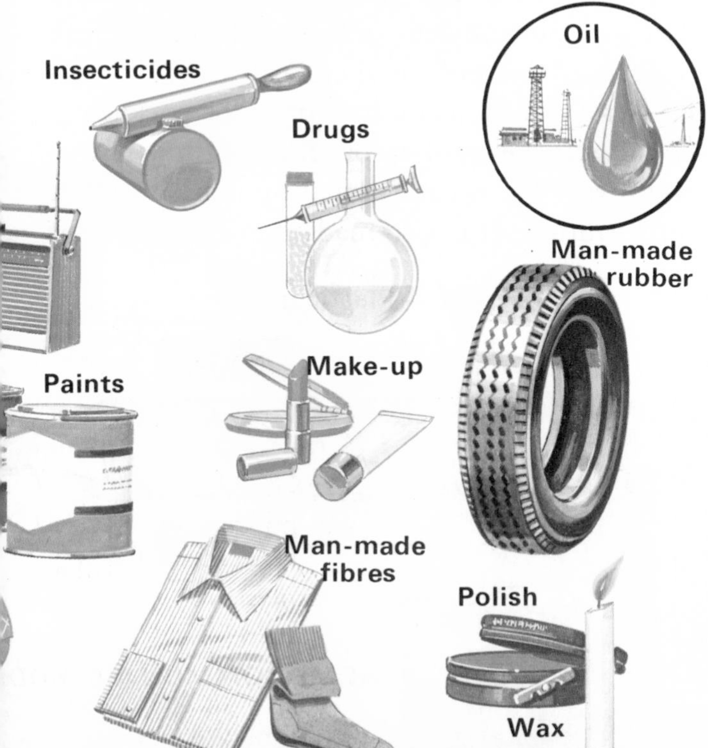

Above: A chemical plant at Salt Lake City, Utah, U.S.A.
Below: Pure sulphur, obtained by processing a crude oil in which it occurs as an impurity.

Polystyrene is a kind of plastic. Above: Light expanded polystyrene for packaging. The white balls are granules of solid polystyrene. Below: Polystyrene furniture.

Plastics

In the early part of this century there were hardly any plastics. Today, the CHEMICAL INDUSTRY has produced hundreds of plastic products for almost every use. In the kitchen alone, plastics are used for floor and CEILING tiles, for heat-proof working surfaces, and for refrigerator linings. Bowls, detergent and bleach bottles, and even tables and chairs are also made of plastic. Elsewhere in the home you may find plastic TELEPHONES, light sockets, pens, raincoats, and boots. Textiles of many kinds can be woven from MAN-MADE FIBRES made from plastic materials.

There are many different kinds of plastics. Each kind has properties that make it useful for certain things. Plastics do, however, have some things in common. When heated, they can all be easily moulded into shape. All plastics are made up of long chains of molecules. They are produced by a chemical process known as polymerization in which small molecules combine.

Two plastics are particularly well known. They are polyethylene (usually called polythene in Britain) and polyvinyl chloride (PVC). Polyethylene can be made into bags for packaging. It can also be used to produce bottles, bowls, and toys. PVC is used to make imitation leather for furniture. It is also made into records, floor

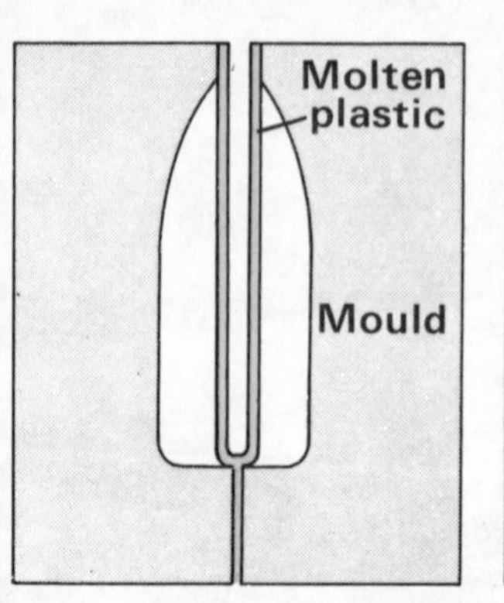

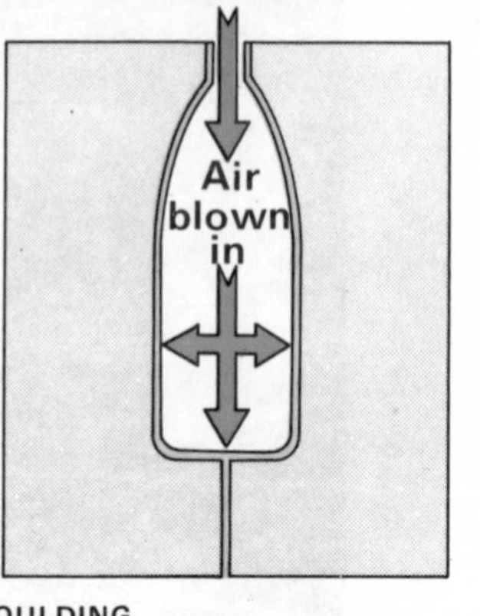

BLOW MOULDING

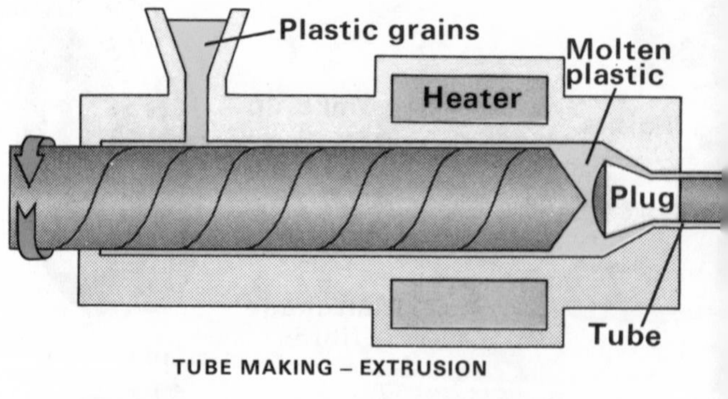

TUBE MAKING – EXTRUSION

SOME COMMON METHODS

tiles, drainpipes and gutters, roofing, hoses, raincoats, and boots. Two other common plastics are nylon and polystyrene.

All these plastics can be softened by heating and, if necessary, reshaped. For this reason they are called thermoplastics, or heat-softening plastics. Some plastics, however, do not soften once they have been set by heat. They are called thermosetting, or heat-setting, plastics. They include Bakelite, a trade name for a plastic used to make heat-proof handles for pans and irons, as well as for heat-proof mats and working surfaces. Bakelite is important in the history of plastics. It was one of the first plastics that was truly synthetic (made entirely from chemicals).

Plastics can be shaped in many ways. One way is by moulding. Bottles are blow-moulded. In this process, air is blown into a blob of molten plastic inside a mould. Another way is injection moulding. Toys, bowls, and many other objects can be injection moulded. Molten plastic is injected into a mould under pressure.

Certain plastics are compression moulded in heated presses. Heat-proof surfaces are produced by laminating. In this process, a kind of sandwich is made of layers of paper or cloth soaked in a plastic solution. These layers are then heated and pressed together.

Above: Plastic strips being moulded for use in refrigerators. Below: Artificial ski slopes are surfaced with plastics.

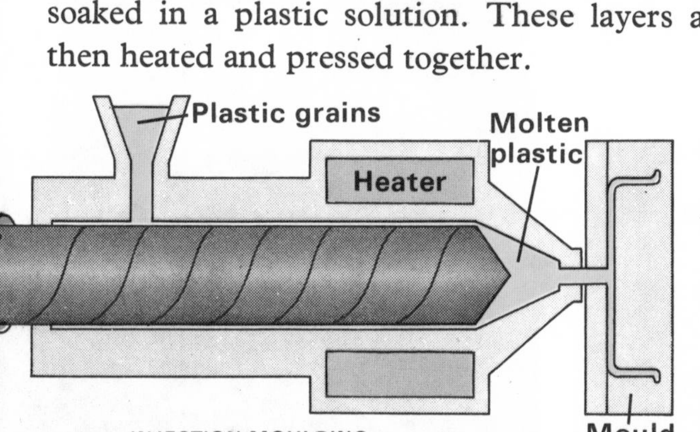

INJECTION MOULDING

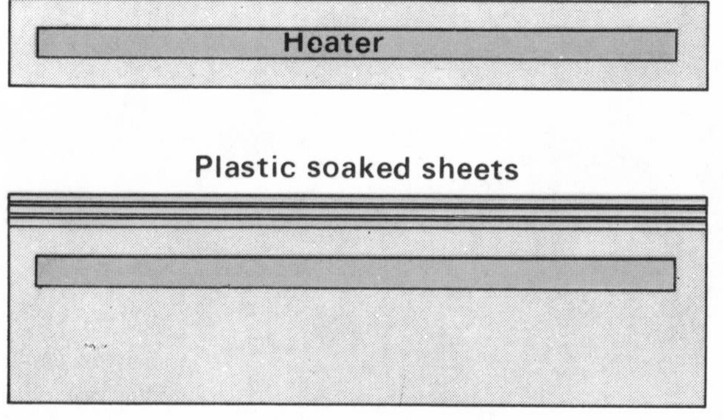

LAMINATING

F SHAPING PLASTICS

Drugs

Today, doctors can do much more for their patients than they could in the past. They have a wider variety of drugs to treat DISEASES and illnesses of almost every kind. Some of these drugs come from what are called MEDICINAL PLANTS. One is quinine (for treating malaria), which comes from the bark of a South American tree. Another is opium (a pain-killer), obtained from certain kinds of poppy.

Other drugs come from animals. An important one is insulin, which is obtained from an organ (the pancreas) in CATTLE and PIGS. Insulin can also be made synthetically in the chemical laboratory. It is used to treat diabetes, a condition in which the BLOOD has too much sugar.

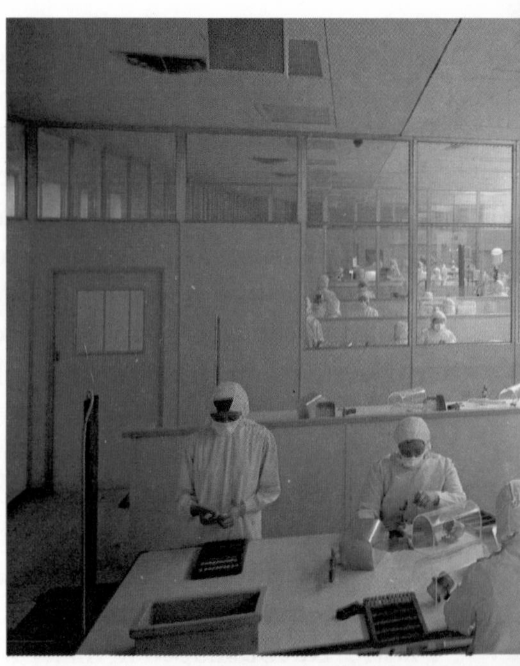

Above right: Absolute cleanliness is essential in any work involving drugs.
Right: Workers checking the machinery at a penicillin factory.
Below: Apparatus used to coat pills with sugar.

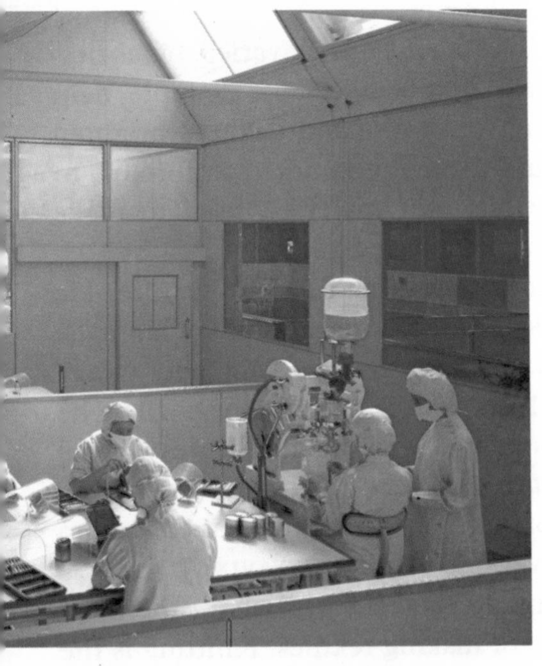

Special drugs, called antibiotics, are obtained from various MOULDS. Many kinds of diseases and infections can be treated with them. Alexander FLEMING discovered penicillin, the first antibiotic, in 1928. Penicillin is still used on a very wide scale.

The majority of drugs today, however, are synthetic. Some of them are identical to natural substances found in plants and animals. But many are entirely new. Especially useful are the sulpha drugs, which are used to treat pneumonia and other dangerous illnesses.

The most widely used drug of all is aspirin. It was discovered in COAL tar in 1838. Today it is used as a pain-killer and is made synthetically on a very large scale.

Soap and detergents

Cleanliness helps to reduce the risk of DISEASE. If our bodies, clothes, and houses are clean, there is less chance of germs spreading. That is why we use soaps and detergents. They are cleansing agents that lift dirt from greasy surfaces. Water by itself will not combine with dirt effectively. But soap, or a detergent, and water will do the job.

Soaps are made by boiling animal fats or plant oils with, for example, caustic soda. This process also produces glycerine. It is a valuable by-product that is used to make the explosive called nitro-glycerine.

Detergents are synthetic cleansing products. They are often made from chemicals obtained from petroleum, or crude OIL. Detergents are used in the home to wash dishes, laundry, and walls. They also have many uses in industry.

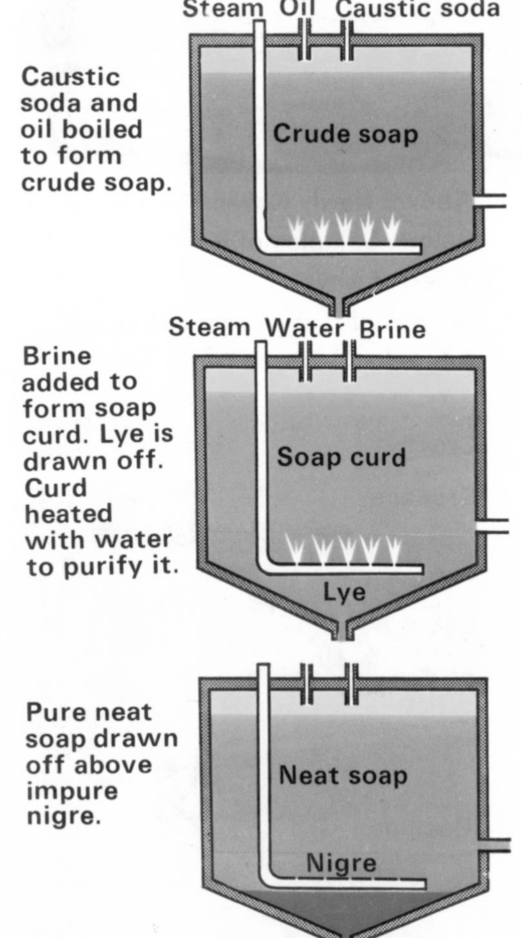
Steam
Oil
Caustic soda
Caustic soda and oil boiled to form crude soap.
Crude soap
Steam
Water
Brine
Brine added to form soap curd. Lye is drawn off. Curd heated with water to purify it.
Soap curd
Lye
Pure neat soap drawn off above impure nigre.
Neat soap
Nigre

Right: Three main stages in the production of soap from fat or oil and caustic soda.

Textiles

Above: Newly woven blankets
Below: Samples of textiles made in different ways.
Below right: A Navajo Indian girl with a hand-woven rug.

In our daily lives we use a great variety of fabrics. Suits, knitwear, and blankets, for example, help keep us warm. CURTAINS and CARPETS brighten our homes and make them more comfortable to live in. The different materials used to make these articles are called textiles.

In very early times, man had no textiles. He clothed himself in the skins and furs of animals. Then he discovered how to spin and weave SHEEP'S wool into a soft, warm fabric. First he would draw out and twist the short fibres of wool into a long yarn (SPINNING). Then he would join many sets of yarns together by passing them under and over one another (WEAVING).

Weaving many sets of yarns is still the most common way of making textiles. Knitting is the next most popular method. Two or more needles are used to loop a single yarn into a loose fabric. Lace is a decorative fabric made by twisting yarns together.

At first man made all his yarn and cloth by hand at home. It was not until the 1760s that machines began to take over. James Hargreaves's 'Spinning Jenny' was the first of them. Textile making became a great industry – the first major industry of the INDUSTRIAL REVOLUTION.

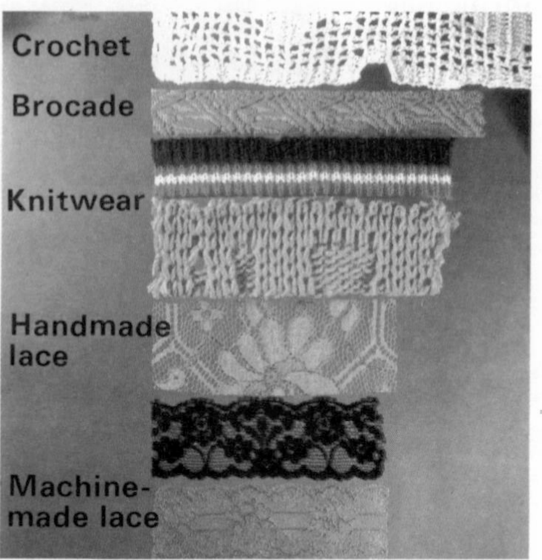

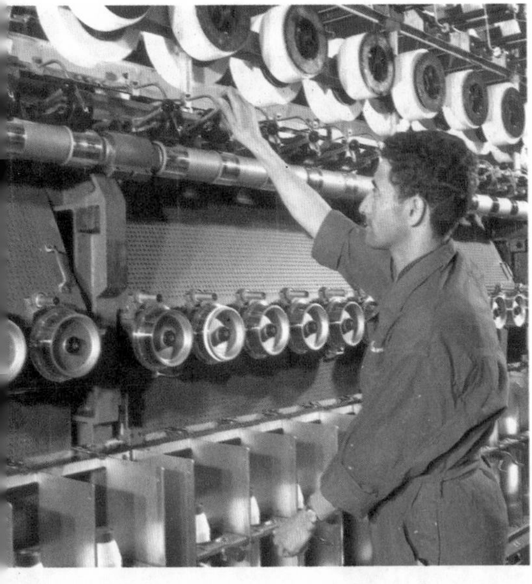

Spinning

Most textile fibres are no longer than the fibres of wool on a SHEEP. They have to be spun (drawn out and twisted) into yarn before they can be made into cloth. In the spinning mill, the fibres are first cleaned. Then a carding machine and a combing machine straighten them out and gather them into a loose rope (sliver). Several slivers are combined and drawn out into a finer rope (roving). The roving goes to the spinning machine. There it is drawn out still more and twisted into firm yarn.

Left: Man-made fibre being drawn into yarn.

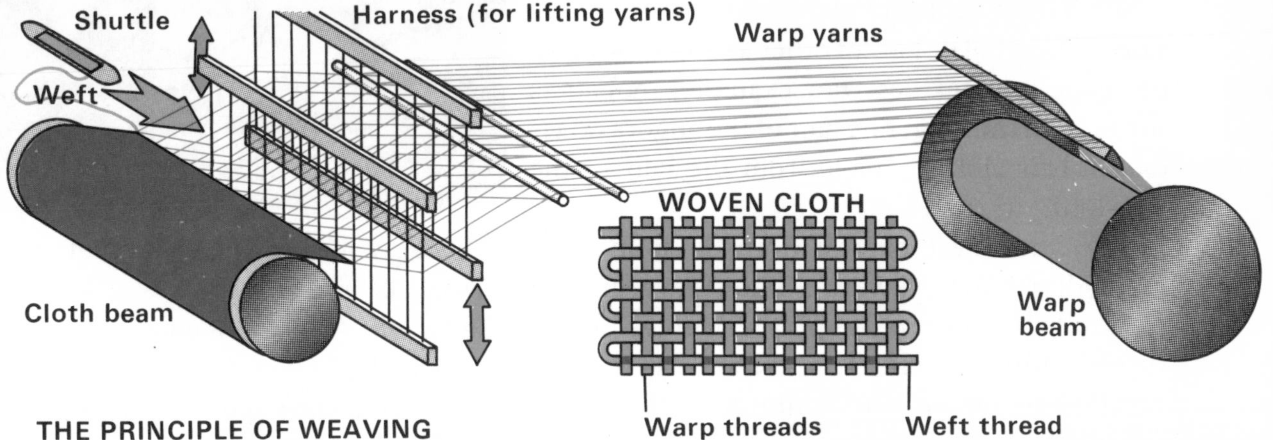

THE PRINCIPLE OF WEAVING

Weaving

Weaving yarn into cloth is done on a loom. One set of yarns (the warp) is stretched over a frame, and runs the whole length of the cloth. Then another yarn is threaded back and forth under and over the warp to form a set of crosswise threads (the weft, or woof). In practice, certain of the warp threads are raised and lowered alternately, and a shuttle containing the weft is shot rapidly through the gap to make a line of weave.

Right: An African woman weaving on a hand loom.

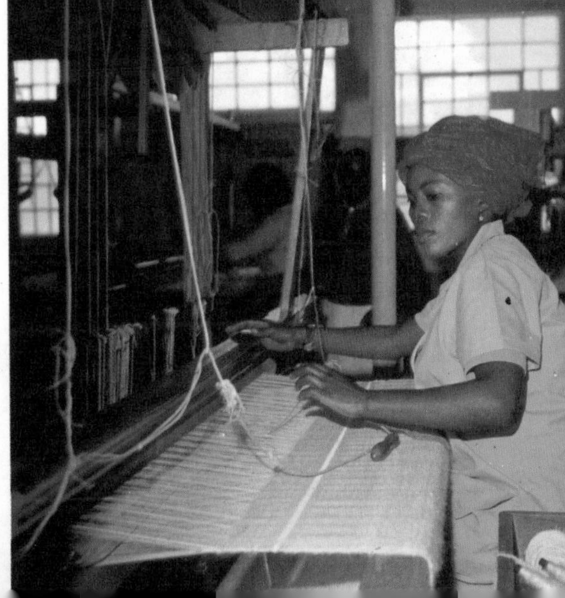

Natural fibres

Nature provides us with a great many textile fibres that we can spin into yarn. Some, like wool, come from animals. Others, such as COTTON, come from plants. One, asbestos, is a mineral. It is used to make fire-proof materials, such as firemen's suits and safety curtains.

Cotton is the most widely used of all fibres. It comes from the ripe seed boll (pod) of the cotton plant. Like all plant fibres, cotton is a pure form of cellulose, the woody substance present in most plants. Some plants, including flax and JUTE, contain long fibres in their stalks. Flax fibres make up into fine linen cloth.

Wool from the SHEEP is the best known animal fibre. The wool or hair of other animals may also be made into textiles. For example, mohair is made from the long, fine hair of the angora GOAT. CAMEL hair cloth is made from the hair of the two-humped camel.

Silk, the finest natural fibre, is spun by a caterpillar – the silkworm. The silkworm lives on mulberry leaves. It spins a cocoon of fine thread around itself. The cocoon can be unravelled to obtain one continuous thread.

Above: A sheep being sheared at Swan Hill, in Australia.

Below left: A silkworm on a mulberry leaf.

Below: A cocoon spun by a silkworm.

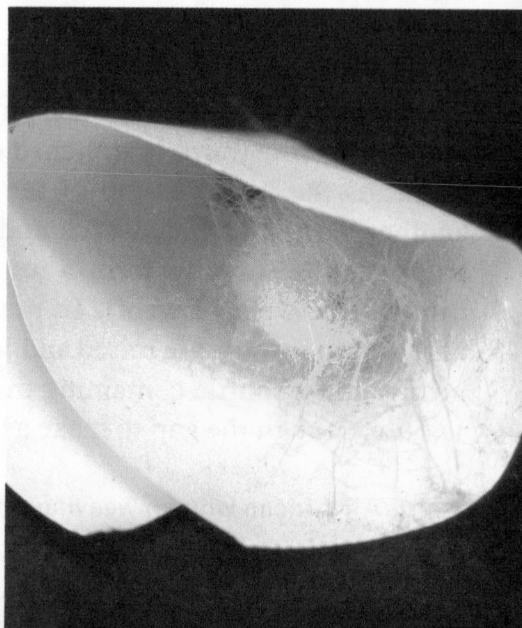

Man-made fibres

A large number of textile fibres are not found in nature. They are made by man. Rayon is one of the most widely used of these man-made fibres. To make rayon, scientists first dissolve the cellulose in COTTON or sometimes wool in certain chemicals. Then they pump the solution through the tiny holes of a spinneret – a metal plate or cap. The fine streams of solution enter an acid bath and change back to pure cellulose. Fabrics made from rayon once used to be called artificial silk. Rayon has other uses besides being a textile fibre. Vast quantities of it are used in car tyres, for example.

Other kinds of man-made fibres are made from cellulose. They are called acetate and triacetate. They consist, not of pure cellulose but of compounds of cellulose. They are made by a process called dry spinning. The cellulose compounds are dissolved in a liquid and then forced through a spinneret into a stream of warm air. The liquid dries, leaving fine fibre threads.

Some fibres are made entirely from chemicals. We call them synthetic fibres. They are really kinds of PLASTICS that we can make into long filaments. Most of them are made from chemicals obtained from petroleum, or OIL. Nylon is the best known synthetic fibre. It was also the first synthetic fibre. To make nylon fibres, nylon chips are melted and then pumped through a spinneret. As they emerge, the fibres solidify in a stream of cold air. Other common synthetic fibres include the polyesters and the acrylics. Polyester fibres are made by melt spinning, acrylic fibres by wet or dry spinning.

Synthetic fibres are much stronger than rayon and the natural fibres. They do not absorb water. They are therefore easy to wash, and drip dry quickly. They need little or no ironing.

The production of rayon fibres. At one stage the cellulose is a yellow syrupy mass (above). Later (below) pure cellulose fibres emerge from the acid bath.

Bleaching

Most fibres are naturally yellowish in colour. But most people want fabrics to be either pure white or coloured. Fabrics are made white by bleaching. In bleaching, chemicals containing chlorine are added to the fabrics. Even when we want to colour the fabrics by dyeing or printing, we bleach them first. Bleaching removes dirt and wax from the fibres and lets them accept dye more easily. Synthetic fibres are more difficult to bleach than natural fibres. They are often treated with a so-called blue whitener to make them appear brighter.

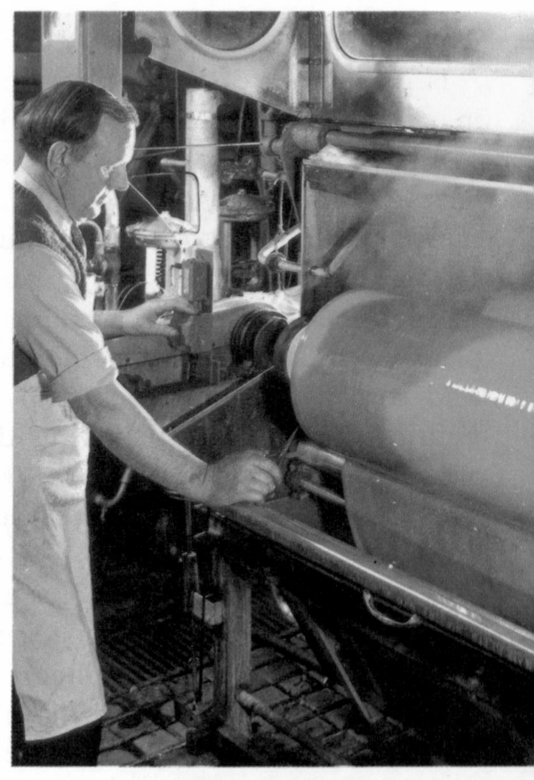

Dyeing and printing

We can colour textiles by dyeing or printing. Dyeing usually means passing the fabric backwards and forwards through a solution of hot dye.

Above right: Dyeing fabric in a dyeing machine, using hot liquid dye.
Right: Colour pattern printing using silk screens.

There are a few natural dyes, such as indigo (blue) and madder (red), which come from plants. But most dyes are synthetic. They are made from chemicals obtained from COAL or petroleum (OIL). Sir William Henry Perkin, an English chemist, made the first synthetic dye (mauve) in 1856. Synthetic dyes can now be made in almost every colour of the rainbow. They scarcely fade at all in the light.

Dyeing colours the whole fabric. Printing is a way of giving the fabric a coloured pattern. The printing may be done from rollers or with silk screens, which are a kind of stencil. In both methods, coloured dye pastes are applied to parts of the fabric to build up the desired pattern.

Textile finishing

Fabrics may be given one or more finishing treatments to make them more suitable for use. One common treatment is called pre-shrinking. Most cloth tends to shrink (get smaller) when it is washed. The threads close up. In pre-shrinking, the threads are shrunk mechanically at the FACTORY.

COTTON and linen are often given a shiny surface by calendering. This is a process in which the fabric is squeezed between heavy rollers. Another finishing operation gives blankets their soft, fluffy surface. They are brushed with the heads of teasels or with fine wires, which makes the fibres in the blankets stand up.

Raincoats and similar garments are given a coating of silicone resin to make them waterproof. Some dress fabrics are also treated with resin, to hold pleats, and to resist creasing.

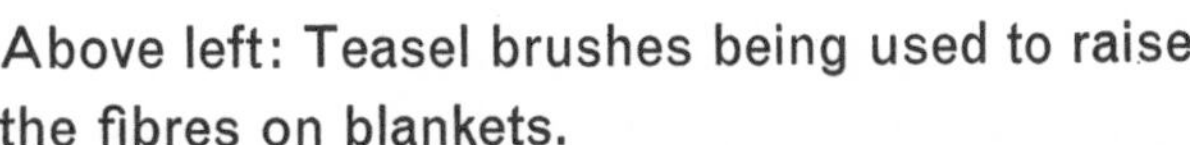

Above left: Teasel brushes being used to raise the fibres on blankets.

Below: A woman from Java applying hot wax to a traditional Batik design before dyeing it.

Pottery and Glass

POTTERY and GLASS are two cheap and common products. They are very useful, especially for tableware and kitchenware. Both are made from common materials – pottery from CLAY and glass from sand. They are quite similar. The finest pottery, called porcelain, is glass-like and translucent (lets through light).

Both pottery and glass are produced in furnaces. In making pottery, the heat from the furnace bonds (joins) the clay particles together without fully melting them. In making glass, the furnace melts the sand and other ingredients completely. The molten glass usually remains clear as it sets. A piece of glass appears to be one big solid crystal, but it is not. It is, in fact, what is called a super-cooled liquid.

Pottery-making was one of man's earliest crafts. His first efforts were little more than sun-dried mud pies. But he soon became skilled and, over the centuries, produced fine works of art. No one has ever surpassed the skill of the early Chinese potters, who first discovered the art of making porcelain. For this reason fine pottery came to be known as china.

Above: A Chinese porcelain vase.
Below: An Indian craftsman decorating pottery statuettes.
Below right: A stained glass window.

Clay

Clay, the basic material from which POTTERY is made, is found almost everywhere. Not all clay is suitable for making pottery. Clay for pottery must contain certain substances that make it easy to mould into shape. It must also have substances that act as binding agents when the moulded clay is baked in a furnace.

Few natural clays can be made into pottery by themselves. Several must be blended together. The best natural clay is pure white China clay, or kaolin. It is used for making porcelain, the finest pottery. China clay is difficult to work by itself. So other clays are blended with it to make it easier to work.

Left: A water jet being used at a china clay pit in Cornwall, in England, to remove soft clay from the rock.

Bricks

Bricks are one of the most common BUILDING materials. They are moulded from CLAY and baked in a furnace in the same way as POTTERY. The clay used for bricks is coloured and relatively coarse. In early times, people made bricks from mud and straw and baked them in the sun. These sun-dried bricks are called adobe. Adobe HOUSES are still built in warm, dry climates.

The clay for brick-making is crushed and kneaded into a doughy mass. Then it is squeezed into a ribbon, which is chopped into separate blocks. The blocks are fired in large ovens, or kilns. In many modern brick kilns, the clay blocks travel through a long tunnel. They are in turn dried, fired into bricks and then cooled.

Right: Clay blocks coming out of a pressing machine ready to be fired into bricks.

Pottery

Potters use different types of CLAY and other materials to make the different kinds of pottery. The three main kinds are porcelain, stoneware, and earthenware. Porcelain is the finest pottery. Delicate and almost glass-like, it is used for the best tableware. Bone china is very similar to porcelain. It is so named because bone ash is used in its manufacture.

Right: Pottery on a stall in a market in North Africa. The style and decoration are traditional.

Stoneware is a strong, hard kind of pottery. It is non-porous (does not absorb liquid), and it is fired at very high temperatures. It is usually buff or brown in colour, and rather rough. Oven-ware, storage jars, and sewer pipes are some of the things made of stoneware.

Earthenware is dull and rough. It is porous. It has to be glazed (given a glossy coating) before it will hold liquids. Cheap china is earthenware that has been given a white glaze.

The potter usually makes his wares by 'throwing' on a potter's wheel. With his hands, the potter shapes his cups, bowls and jugs from wet clay as it is turning on a revolving wheel. In FACTORIES, most pottery is moulded instead of thrown. When it is thrown, the job is done with the aid of simple machines. In each case, the shaped piece of clay must be allowed to dry before it is baked, or fired, in a kiln (oven). Otherwise it will crack, or even shatter.

Most earthenware pottery is glazed to make it waterproof. It is usually decorated. It may be ornamented with figures, and a design may be painted or transferred on to it. Painting can be done before or after glazing.

Below: A potter throwing a pot, using a potter's wheel.

Above: Loading raw clay pottery into the kiln for firing, at the Wedgwood pottery in England.

Ceramics

POTTERY, BRICKS, and GLASS are examples of ceramics – materials that have been subjected to great heat during manufacture. There are many ceramic products. Cement is one. It is made by roasting a mixture of CLAY and limestone, and then grinding the residue to a fine powder.

Different kinds of clays are used to make ceramics. Many modern ceramics are produced by firing metal oxides, such as alumina. Artificial rubies and sapphires can be made by melting alumina in a very hot flame. Engineers use special ceramics to make high-speed tools and abrasives (for grinding and polishing). Many electrical goods include ceramics because they have excellent insulating properties.

Right: A girl decorating a plate by hand.

Glass

Glass is a very useful material. It is translucent (lets through light) and is not affected by the weather. Thus it is ideal for WINDOWS. It can also be shaped easily.

Glass does not affect the taste of food and drink. It is therefore used to make bottles, ovenware, and tableware. Beautiful glassware can have a gem-like sparkle. Designs are often cut, engraved, and etched (with acid) into it.

Right: Milk bottles cooling after they have been blown in a high-speed machine.

The ordinary glass used in windows and much tableware is made from sand, limestone, and soda. These materials are heated in a furnace to a temperature of 1500° Centigrade. They blend together to form molten glass. The result is called soda-lime glass.

Soda-lime glass shatters easily when it is hit or when hot water is poured on it. It can be strengthened by adding borax to the glass-making mixture. Then it is heat-resistant and can be made into ovenware. Other kinds of glass are made by varying the ingredients.

Above: A selection of modern glassware in a range of colours.
Left: Eighteenth-century wine glasses. The delicate decoration was done by engraving.

Glass is shaped while it is hot. Often it is pressed into shape, or cast in moulds. But it can also be blown into shape. Glass-blowing by hand is a skilled art. Most commercial glassware, however, is blown or moulded by machine.

Ordinary flat glass for windows is made by drawing a long sheet of glass upwards from the cool end of the furnace. This glass has a bright finish. It tends to be distorted, however, because of the way it was drawn from the furnace. A better flat glass is made by grinding and polishing both sides of a glass sheet. It is called plate glass. It is not distorted like ordinary glass, but it has a less bright finish. For years now plate glass has been used for shop fronts and picture windows. An even better flat glass is made by floating a layer of molten glass on a bath of molten tin. Float glass has the advantage over plate glass of having a brighter finish.

Fibre-glass

GLASS can be made into delicate fibres finer than a human HAIR. We call this fibre-glass. The fibres can be gathered into yarn and woven into fabrics for tablecloths and CURTAINS. Being made of glass, they are fireproof. They do not stain, and they do not become yellow in sunlight.

Combined with some PLASTICS, fibre-glass makes a strong material. It is used to make such things as fishing rods, suitcases, car bodies, and boat hulls.

Fibre-glass is also made into a fluffy kind of matting. In this form it is an insulator. It is used in many houses to prevent heat loss through the ROOF and walls.

Left: Laying fibre-glass matting. It will help to prevent heat being lost through the roof of the house.

The Electronics Industry

Over the past 20 years the fastest growing industry has been the electronics industry. Transistor radios, pocket calculators and digital watches are just a few of the things we use every day that rely on electronic devices. In industry, electronics has led to the introduction of automatic and robot machines. In space, it has enabled us to send probes to explore the far reaches of the solar system, and to send astronauts to the MOON and back.

What does 'electronic' mean and how does it differ from 'electric'? When we speak of something electrical we are referring to the flow of electricity through wires. Electricity is a flow of the tiny particles of matter we call electrons. In electronics, electrons also flow, but not only through wires. They also flow through a gas or a vacuum, as in VALVES, and through SEMICONDUCTORS, as in transistors.

In valves and semiconductors electrons can be generated and controlled in a variety of ways to produce interesting electrical effects.

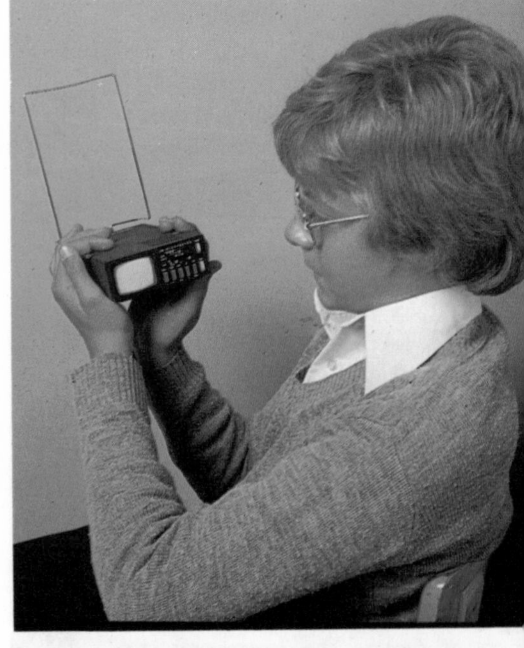

Above: Advances in electronics mean that miniature TV sets can be made. Below: Before the invention of the transistor, radio and TV receivers were very large. They are now much more compact.

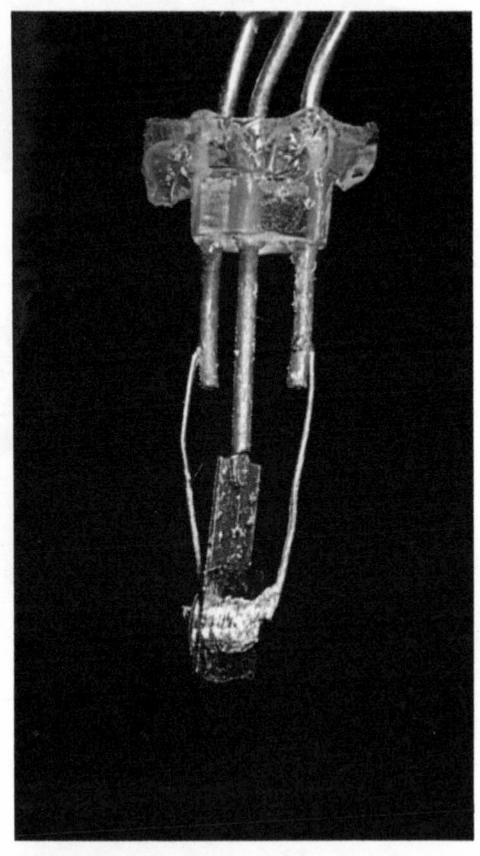

Transistors (above) can be packed together in a tiny space to produce a transistor radio (below).

Valves

In 1904 John Ambrose Fleming invented a device that led to the development of radio. It was the electronic valve. It was so called because it allowed electrical signals to pass through it in only one direction. The valve was a glass bulb which had had all the air drawn out, with two plates, or electrodes, sealed inside. One electrode, the cathode, gave out electrons, which flowed to the other electrode, the anode.

Fleming's valve could rectify, or change, electric current from alternating current (like the mains) into direct current (like a battery). It could also detect radio waves. It was improved in 1906 by Lee de Forest, who added a third electrode, or grid, between the other two. De Forest's triode, as it was called, could amplify, or strengthen weak radio signals. It could also be made to transmit a powerful radio signal. Later, valves with more electrodes were introduced which made possible sensitive domestic radio receivers.

Semiconductors

In 1948 three American scientists – John Bardeen, Walter Brattain and William Shockley – invented the transistor, which was to revolutionize electronics. The transistor gradually replaced VALVES in all electronic equipment. It is made of a special crystal called a semiconductor. It is so called because the crystal conducts electricity only very slightly.

The most common material for making semiconductors is silicon. Silicon crystal can be made electrically different in different places by treating it with chemicals. A single piece of silicon can then be made to behave in exactly the same way as a valve. Then it becomes known as a transistor.

Silicon chips

In the old-fashioned kind of radio set the valves or transistors and other electrical devices are joined together by soldered wires. More recent sets use printed circuits. These are thin films of copper bonded to an insulated baseboard. The use of printed circuits and transistors has meant that electronic equipment is now very compact.

But even smaller devices are needed for some miniaturized equipment, particularly in spacecraft. Such devices are called integrated circuits (ICs). In ICs a single slice, or chip, of silicon forms a complete electronic circuit. Different parts of the chip are microscopically treated so that they act as transistors and other components. A silicon chip only a few millimetres square could hold all the complicated circuitry for a colour television set.

Some silicon chips can be made to behave like a miniature COMPUTER. They are called microprocessors. They are found in such things as digital watches and pocket calculators.

Computers

The word 'computer' really means the same as 'calculator'. But we generally use it to mean an electronic device that can make calculations at unbelievable speed. It is also called a data processor because it can take in, memorize and carry out calculations on all kinds of information, or data. The common computer deals with data in the form of digits, and is called a digital computer. It uses the binary system of arithmetic in which numbers are represented by the digits 1 and 0.

A computer is made up of several units. There is a memory unit, which stores data until it is required. It also stores the program, or set

Above: Computers are being used more and more in the worlds of science, industry and business.

Above: Pocket-size electronic calculators are useful in working out mathematical problems.

of instructions, which tells the computer what to do with the data. An arithmetic unit carries out the calculations. An input unit feeds information into the computer, while an output unit delivers the results. Punched cards and tape, magnetic tape and visual display units are among the common input/output devices.

The coming of the silicon chip has led to a great reduction in the size of computers. Some are now little bigger than a TYPEWRITER.

Above: Part of a computer silicon chip, greatly magnified.

Above: Computer-stored information can be displayed visually on a screen.

Services

There are three main groups of industries. The first, or primary industries use or extract natural materials. They include FARMING and MINING. The secondary industries use the raw materials provided by the primary industries to produce or manufacture goods. The third group, called the service industries, distributes and sells the manufactured goods to the customers – the general public or industrial companies.

Goods sold to the general public are called consumer goods. They are usually sold through wholesalers and retailers. Wholesalers buy goods in bulk from the manufacturers. Then they sell the goods to a number of retailers. Retailers in turn sell the goods to the public in SHOPS and STORES. Producers, wholesalers and retailers all want to sell as much as possible. They hire salesmen and women to persuade people to buy. They also carry out ADVERTISING campaigns.

Advertising, together with packaging, distributing and selling form part of what is called marketing. Large companies often devote much time and money to marketing. They do market research to find out what their customers want.

Another vital service industry is transport. Without it a nation's economy would suffer. In most countries one or more of the transport services are nationally (publicly) owned. In others, they are run by private companies. Many services are provided by local and national governments. They include public HEALTH and social services, housing and education, and the POLICE force. BANKING and INSURANCE are two other essential services.

The scope of the service industries is vast. On a more personal level they include garage repair works, hairdressers and beauty salons. BROADCASTING companies provide information and entertainment.

ADVERTISING

Advertising means any way of trying to persuade people to buy goods or services. Advertisements are carried by RADIO and TELEVISION networks, as well as by nearly all NEWSPAPERS and MAGAZINES. In addition, advertisements in the form of posters appear almost everywhere on walls and hoardings. There are many other ways of advertising, including short cinema films.

Most commercial advertising is handled by agencies. The client, usually a company, goes to the agency with a product that it wishes to advertise. The company has probably already decided which kind of advertising (for example, in a national newspaper) is most suitable for its product. The job of the agency is to suggest ideas, and to produce a finished advertisement from the idea that the client likes best.

Advertising is usually very expensive. However, the advertiser hopes that people will buy more of his products as a result of the advertisements. Many radio and television companies run on the money they make from advertising. Most newspapers and magazines would be a lot more expensive if they did not have advertisements.

SELLING YOUR PRODUCT
The client who requires an advertising campaign for his product comes to an advertising agency

THIS IS MY PRODUCT, CAN YOU HELP ME SELL IT?
SUDZO
YES, COME AND TALK TO OUR MARKET RESEARCH DEPARTMENT AND THE MEDIA BUYER!

Market research into the product is started.
copy, or words are then written...

.... and some "visuals" or rough pictures are then drawn up...
SUDZO!
SUDZO
Gum
.. by the art department

The "visuals" and words have to be approved by the agency and by the client.
SUDZO
FINE! THAT WILL BE EASY ENOUGH.
I LIKE THE IDEA, BUT COULD YOU CHANGE THE COLOUR?

The campaign is now properly underway
CAN YOU SHOW MORE OF THE PACKET PLEASE?
photographs are taken...

... and the copy is set ...
... at the printer's

I THINK WE SHOULD HAVE LESS WRITING AND MAKE THE PHOTOGRAPHS BIGGER, MIKE.
I THINK YOU'RE RIGHT!
With the photographs and type, rough proofs are printed and shown to the client for his general criticism.

Corrections are completed and the finished artwork is delivered to the newspapers and magazines in which it will appear.
PRONTO
DELIVERY SERVICE

ACTION!
If T.V. advertising is required, a film director is briefed in the same way and a short 1½-2 minute film is made.

The advert then appears on television
SUDZO! FOR A MUCH WHITER WASH!!
SUDZO!
and in national magazines and papers.

Markets

In the past, people in the country would gather once or twice a week at a fixed place to sell their products and buy others that they needed. These gatherings were the first markets. Country towns still have weekly markets but they are less important than they used to be.

In cities, street markets also grew up. Some of these are once-weekly, like Petticoat Lane in LONDON, and some daily, like the Bazaar in ISTANBUL. Some sell a great variety of goods, and others specialize – in antiques, for example. There are also wholesale markets, held daily in permanent buildings, such as Billingsgate, the fish market in London.

Left: A market in Tunisia, in Africa, where farmers buy and sell camels, cattle, and goats.

Shops and stores

Unlike most MARKETS, shops and stores are open six or seven days a week. They are located in permanent places. They usually specialize in selling one product, for example, shoes, hardware, or food. In country areas, general stores keep a wide selection of products to serve people who seldom go to the city. These stores may sell clothing, food, and hardware. Often they serve as the post office for the area. Travelling shops and stores also visit rural areas.

In many cities, modern shopping centres have been built in recent years. They have many shops and stores all together. The centres are often fully enclosed, and free of traffic. There is usually plenty of parking space nearby.

Centre left: A tempting selection of pastries in a shop in Cherbourg, France.
Left: A covered shopping centre in New York.

Department stores

Department stores sell a wide variety of goods. They are divided into many sections, each of which sells a different kind of product. They are really many SHOPS in one. A typical department store has several floors that can be reached by LIFTS or ESCALATORS. Its departments will sell clothing and shoes, FURNITURE and bedding, CURTAINS and CARPETS, hardware and electrical goods. There will also be departments for glassware and china, books and toys, cameras and watches, records and musical instruments, sports and gardening equipment. A department store often has one or more restaurants, a pet shop, and a travel bureau.

The world's biggest store is Macy's in NEW YORK. It covers a floor area of 190,000 square metres. It offers about 400,000 different items for sale. Other famous department stores are Harrods in LONDON and GUM in MOSCOW. (GUM stands for state universal store in Russian.) It is opposite the KREMLIN in Red Square.

Above: A shopper looks at a display of glassware in a big department store.

Below: The check-out points at a large self-service supermarket.

Supermarkets

In many modern SHOPS and stores the customers serve themselves. They find the goods they want without the help of sales assistants.

Big self-service stores of this kind are usually called supermarkets. They sell mainly food and common household items – for example, detergents and polishes. Most of the goods are stacked on long shelves and their prices are clearly marked. Fruits and vegetables are in one section; meat is in another. Customers load their purchases into special baskets or trolleys and pay for them at one of the cash desks.

Supermarkets often price their goods lower than small shops do. Their profit comes from large sales rather than high prices.

Money

In early times, people used to trade what they had for what they wanted. A farmer might trade a kilo of butter for a COTTON shirt. He might pay his workers with a dozen eggs or a leg of pork. This form of transaction is called bartering.

In time, people began using objects to represent the value of the things they had. Some of these objects, such as CATTLE, were still difficult to move about. In about 600 B.C. people started using coins. Paper money was not introduced until about 1400 years later.

The coins and notes in circulation are called currency. For many years, coins contained their value in metal. Today, however, the face value of a coin is not the actual value of the metal. The coin is merely a token.

Left: (1) Gold coin of Alexander the Great. (2) Silver Augustus Caesar coin. (3) Silver Viking penny. (4) Bezant of Constantine VII. (5) German florin of 14-15th century. (6) George III halfpenny.

Banking

People put their MONEY into a bank for many reasons. Most people feel that it is far safer there than it would be in their homes. They also use the services that banks provide. For example, they may wish to open a current account. You simply deposit money in the bank, which credits it to your account. The bank also gives you a cheque book. To withdraw your money you write a cheque for the amount you want. The bank then gives you the cash amount and debits (takes the money from) your account.

Cheques can also be used to pay for goods and SERVICES. The cheque tells the bank to pay money from your account to the account of a person or company you name on the cheque.

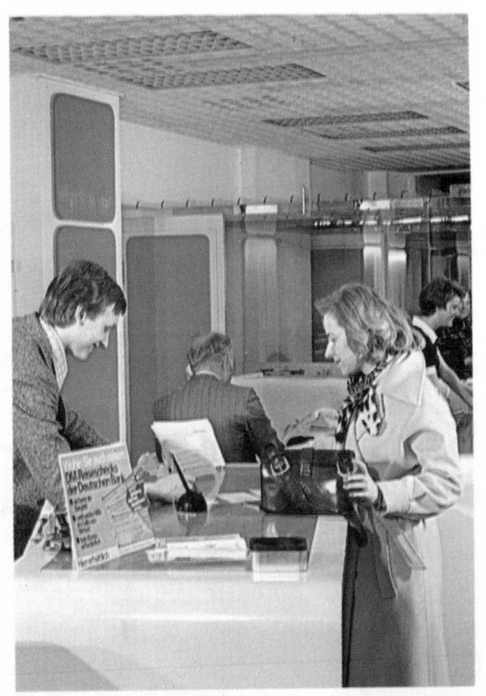

Above: Seeking advice about opening a bank deposit account.
Below: The Underwriting Room of the international insurance market at Lloyd's of London.

You can also put your money into a deposit account. It will earn a certain amount of interest for you. The bank pays you for the use of your money.

You can also borrow from a bank. But then you will pay interest to the bank. In some countries the bank lends you money by allowing an overdraft on your current account. It lets you withdraw more money than you have in your account as long as it knows that you will soon be able to pay it back. The bank may ask for some kind of security to back an overdraft.

You may also borrow money by getting a bank loan. Here you usually borrow a fixed amount at a fixed rate of interest. You agree to pay it back over a fixed period of time.

Large and small businesses could not run properly if there were no bank loans. SHOPS and stores, for example, sometimes borrow money to pay for their stock before selling it.

Insurance

As we grow older, we spend MONEY on such things as cars and HOUSES. We stand to lose a lot of money if our car is in an accident, if our house burns down, or if its contents are stolen. To protect ourselves from such losses, we can take out accident, fire, and theft insurance.

Each year we pay a sum of money, called a premium, to our insurance company. In return, the company promises to pay us for any losses we insure against.

Many people take out life insurance against their own death. Life insurance helps their families if they do die. There are also endowment policies. People take them out to cover their lives over a period of years. At the end of the policy (or sooner if they die), they or their families receive an agreed amount of money.

Schools

In most developed countries the government provides free education for children. It uses money from TAXES to pay teachers and for the cost of school buildings and books. The government is investing MONEY to educate its young people. It realises that educated citizens are useful to the country in their later life.

In many countries there are laws which say at what age children must go to school. There are also laws which say how old they have to be before they can leave. Children usually have to go to school at the age of five or six. In Britain they now have to stay at school until they are 16. In some other countries the school-leaving age is lower.

Education really begins in the home as soon as a baby is born. At the age of three, many children go to nursery school. Two or three years later, they enter a primary school. At the age of about 11 they go to a secondary school. In some countries this is called a high school.

There are many different kinds of secondary school. In Britain, many children now go to comprehensive schools.

Above: An example of a modern school building, in Hampshire, England.
Right: A nineteenth-century classroom scene.

Comprehensive schools take children of many different levels of ability. These schools are replacing the older grammar and modern schools. Children remain at their secondary school until they are between 16 and 18. Then they may have a chance of going on to a UNIVERSITY or college.

The pattern of education varies from country to country. In some countries, the central government has control over all education. In

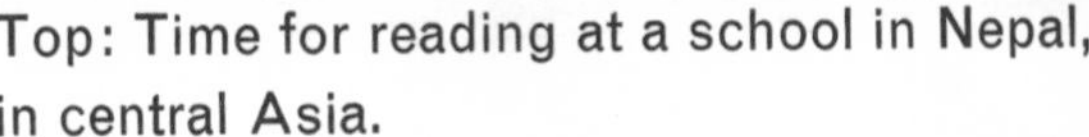

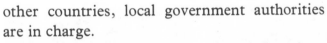

Top: Time for reading at a school in Nepal, in central Asia.
Above: Instruction in a relaxed atmosphere at an English junior school.

other countries, local government authorities are in charge.

Most countries also have private education. This means that parents can pay to have their children sent to certain schools. People who agree with this system say that it gives parents a larger choice of schools. Other people think that private schools give the children that go to them an unfair advantage over other children.

Universities and colleges

Universities and colleges are places where some young people go to continue their education after leaving SCHOOL. Most university students study one main subject, although they may also study a number of others. Teaching is usually by lectures, or by discussions between a lecturer and a group of students.

Most students stay at their university for three or four years. At the end of this time, they take an examination. If they pass, they receive their Bachelor's degree, usually a B.A. (Bachelor of Arts), or B.Sc. (Bachelor of Science). Some students study for several more years in order to get higher degrees, such as M.A. (Master of Arts), or Ph.D. (Doctor of Philosophy).

Most university courses do not train students to do a particular job. Colleges, on the other hand, usually teach skills which enable the students to follow a career, for example, CLOTHES design, or business studies.

Three famous universities.
Above: Bonn, West Germany.
Below: Harvard, U.S.A.
Below right: Cambridge, England.

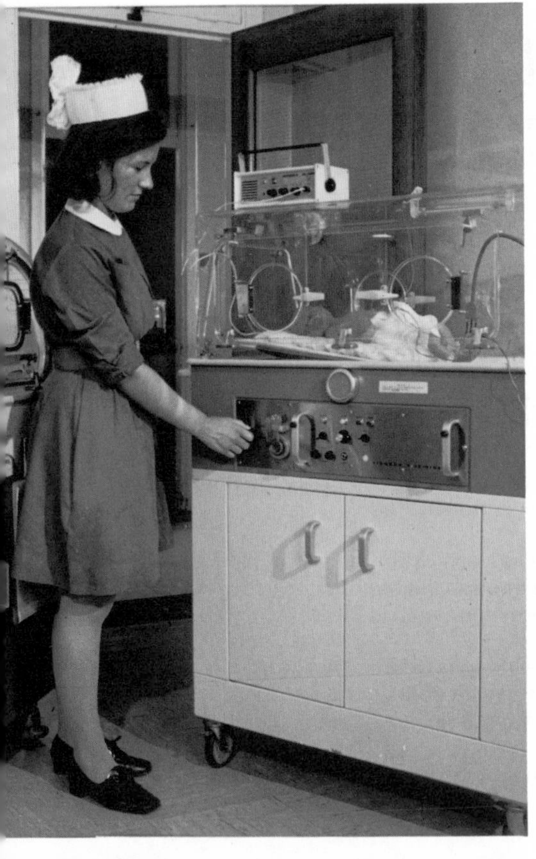

Health service

The health of the population is a major concern of governments. They know that people's health is important to the well-being of the country. There are two areas, or sectors, of health: public and private.

In the public sector, governments must provide enough clean, germ-free water. They must build good sewage systems. They must hire workers to remove rubbish and to clean streets. There must be people to inspect food and control pests.

In the private sector, governments have to be sure that there are enough doctors and dentists. There have to be enough hospitals with trained staff. And hospitals must have the facilities and equipment so that the job can be done well.

Left: A nurse checks the controls of an incubator. Inside is a premature baby. Modern equipment is vital to a good health service.

Public health is financed in different ways. In some countries local government taxes pay for it. The governments may also pay for the private health service. In this system the people pay weekly contributions toward their health service. In other countries, such as the U.S.A., federal and state taxes pay for much public health.

There is, however, no general national health service in the United States. Some employers and unions offer free or cheap medical INSURANCE, but many people have to pay for whatever treatment they receive. To cover themselves, they often take out their own medical insurance. Even in countries with a national health service some people pay for private treatment or take out some form of medical insurance.

WORK AND INDUSTRY FACTS AND FIGURES

FARMING AND FISHING. The foundations of modern farming practice were laid down in the 1700s: Jethro Tull invented the seed drill and Charles 'Turnip' Townshend pioneered crop rotation. In the Far East, fishermen train cormorants to dive and catch fish.

FORESTRY AND TIMBER. It takes the wood of between 15 and 20 pine trees to make one tonne of good quality white paper. A Californian big tree in the Sequoia National Park, U.S.A., contains enough timber to make 40 five-roomed bungalows. It is over 80 metres high.

MINING. The largest diamond ever found was the Cullinan. Found in Pretoria, South Africa, in 1905, it weighed more than half a kilogramme. The *Star of Africa No. 1* in the royal sceptre of the British Crown Jewels was cut from the Cullinan. It is the world's largest cut diamond.

FUEL AND ENERGY. Edwin Drake launched the world oil industry when he bored his first well at Titusville, Pennsylvania, U.S.A., in 1859. Natural gas seeping through the ground in parts of the Middle East has been burning for centuries. These 'Eternal Fires' were mentioned in the Bible.

INDUSTRY. In the early part of the Industrial Revolution, factory wages were so low that whole families – husband, wife, and children – had to work up to 16 hours a day to earn enough money to live. The world's largest trade union is the Metal Workers' Union of West Germany.

METALS. An alloy of bismuth, lead, tin, and cadmium known as Wood's Metal melts when it is put into boiling water. Its melting point is only about 70°C. Gold can be beaten into sheet so thin that you can almost see through it. Mercury is the only naturally liquid metal.

CONSTRUCTION. 'Macadam' road surfaces, made of stone chips and tar, are so called after their inventor John McAdam (1756-1836). Lake Washington Bridge in Seattle, Washington, is the longest floating bridge in the world. It has a floating section two and a quarter kilometres long.

CHEMICAL INDUSTRY. The chemical industry began to develop in the mid-1800s. Important discoveries of the early years included those of coal-tar dyes by William Perkin in 1856; dynamite by Alfred Nobel in 1862; and celluloid plastic by John Hyatt in 1869.

TEXTILES. Fragments of linen cloth found in the remains of Swiss lake dwellings suggest that man was making textiles as early as 4000 B.C. Nylon, Terylene, and Courtelle are three man-made fibres that are produced from oil. Rayon and Tricel are made from wood pulp.

POTTERY AND GLASS. In 1709 Johann Bottger became the first person outside China to discover the secret of making true porcelain. He set up a factory in Dresden, Germany. A natural black glass called obsidian is formed when molten rock from a volcano chills rapidly.

ELECTRONICS INDUSTRY. The first electronic computer, called ENIAC, was an enormous machine that used 18,000 radio valves. Today's most powerful computers can perform over 36 million operations in one second.

SERVICES. Aristide Boucicault founded the first department store, in Paris, in 1852. The term A1, meaning excellent, comes from the classification first used by the London insurance company Lloyds to describe a well-built ship.

COUNTRIES AND HOMES

Europe

EUROPE, which includes a quarter of the U.S.S.R., covers only about one-fourteenth of the land in the world. However, about one-sixth of the world's people live there.

The countries of Europe have fought many wars among themselves. But, after WORLD WAR II, which started in Europe, they joined together to form two main groups. Most of the countries of eastern Europe have COMMUNIST governments, and are closely linked with the U.S.S.R. The countries of western Europe trade with each other, and ten form the European Economic Community (E.E.C.), or COMMON MARKET.

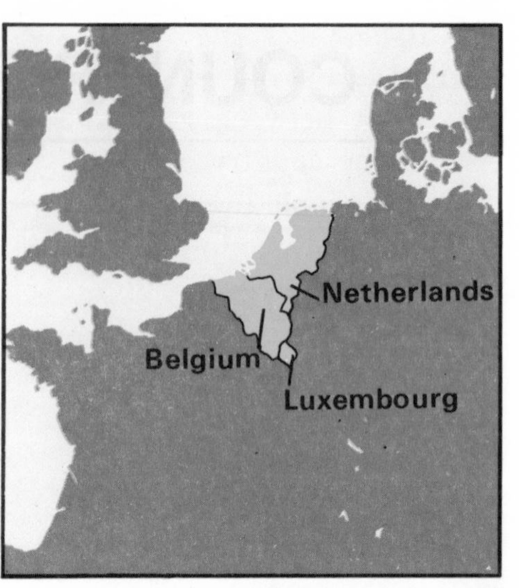

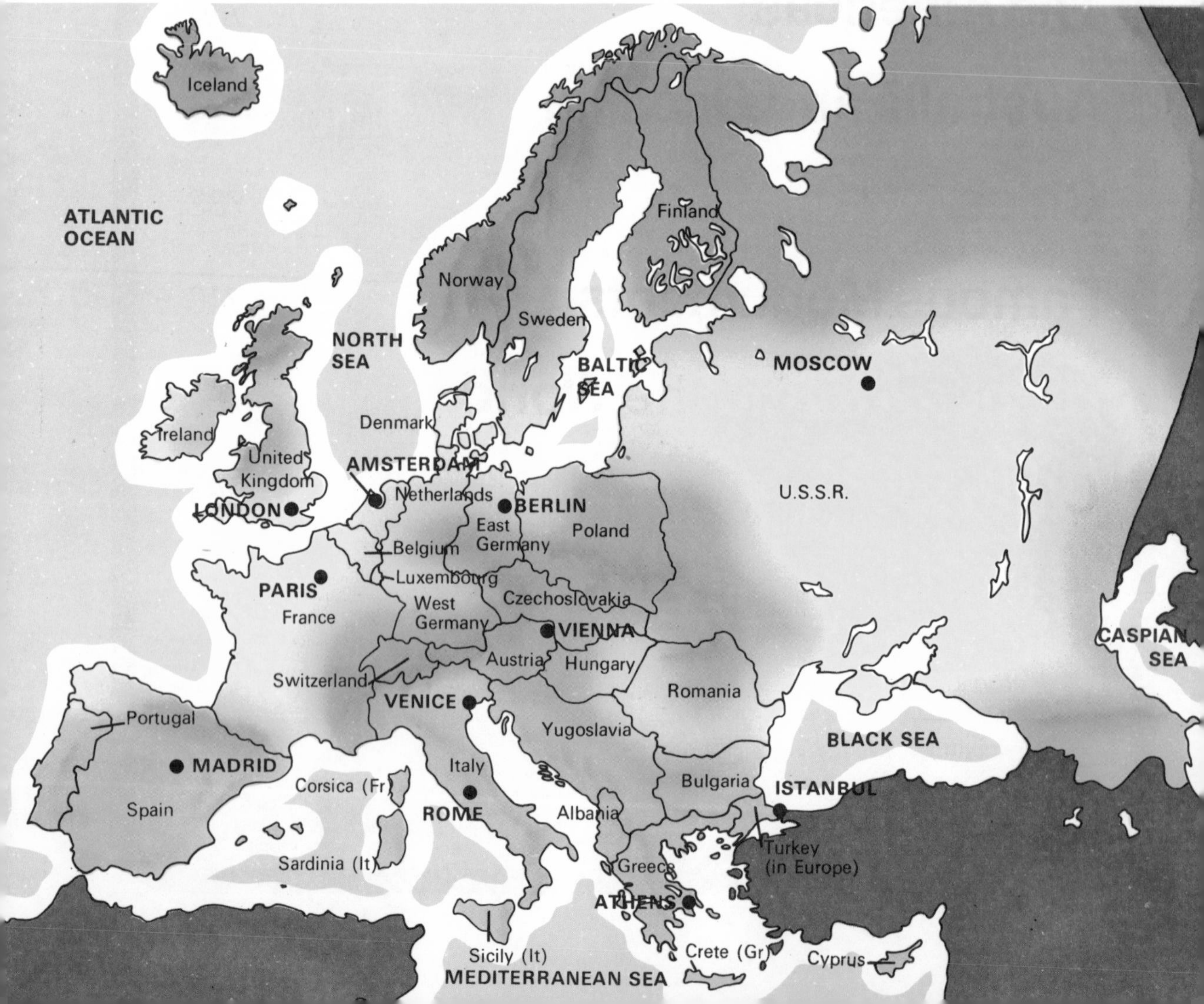

Belgium

Belgium is a small MONARCHY that borders the NORTH SEA between FRANCE and the NETHERLANDS. The country is mostly flat. Two main groups of people live there: the Walloons, who speak French, live in the south, and the Flemings, who speak Flemish, live in the north.

Belgium is an industrial country and has many COAL mines. The headquarters of the COMMON MARKET is in Brussels, the capital.

Above: An old Guild house, now a café, at Ghent in Belgium.
Below: The market at Maastricht in the Netherlands.
Bottom: A castle in Luxembourg.

Netherlands

The Netherlands is also known as Holland. It borders the NORTH SEA between BELGIUM and WEST GERMANY. Much of the country is below sea level, but the Dutch have built huge dykes (walls) to keep out the sea. They have also drained large areas that were covered by water to make new farming land. The country is very flat with a network of CANALS and RIVERS.

Trade is very important in the Netherlands, and the Rotterdam Europoort is the largest port in the world. Dutch is the main language, but most people also learn other European languages.

Luxembourg

Luxembourg is a tiny country sandwiched between FRANCE, BELGIUM, and WEST GERMANY. Belgium, the NETHERLANDS, and Luxembourg together form a trade group known as Benelux. The manufacture of IRON and steel is the most important industry of Luxembourg. The country is governed by a PARLIAMENT and the Grand Duke of Luxembourg is the head of state.

	Belgium	Netherlands	Luxembourg
Population	9,823,000	13,814,000	356,000
Area (sq. km.)	30,513	41,160	2,586
Capital	Brussels	Amsterdam	Luxembourg

Sweden

Sweden is one of the countries of Scandinavia. The others are NORWAY and DENMARK. They are in the northern part of EUROPE. It is cold there in winter, and the days are short. The Scandinavian languages – Swedish, Norwegian, and Danish – are very similar.

Sweden is a MONARCHY that lies along the western shore of the Baltic Sea. Sweden borders FINLAND to the north and Norway to the west. The west is mountainous, but there is lowland in the south and there are many LAKES. Forests cover most of the country, and there are large deposits of minerals.

RIVERS running from the MOUNTAINS provide hydro-electric power for industry. It is these natural resources that have made Sweden one of the richest countries in the world. Sweden did not fight in either of the two World Wars.

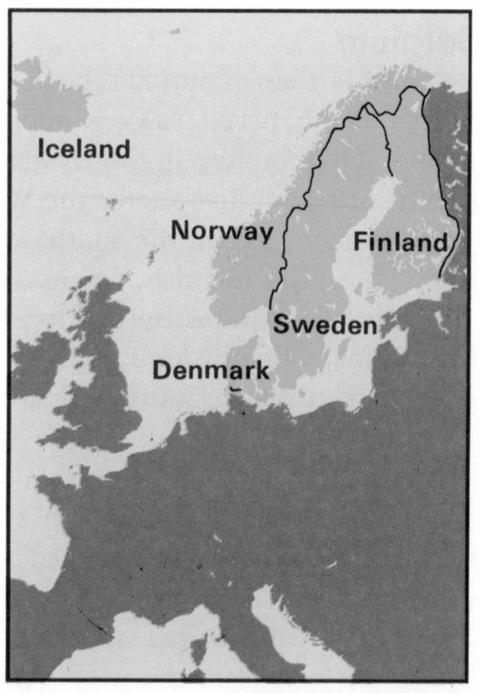

Norway

Norway lies between SWEDEN and the ATLANTIC OCEAN. It is a mountainous country, and along the coast are many inlets called FIORDS. The mountain RIVERS supply Norway with hydro-electric power for its industries. Fishing is also important, and Norway's fleet of merchant ships is one of the largest in the world. Very little of the land is suitable for farming.

During most of the nineteenth century, Norway was ruled by Sweden. It became fully independent in 1905. Norway was occupied by German troops during WORLD WAR II. Today the country is a MONARCHY.

Above: The little town of Geiranger, Norway, stands on a fiord that reaches far inland.

	Sweden	Norway	Denmark	Finland	Iceland
Population	8,236,000	4,035,000	5,080,000	4,742,000	221,000
Area (sq. km.)	411,479	323,886	43,074	337,052	102,819
Capital	Stockholm	Oslo	Copenhagen	Helsinki	Reykjavik

Denmark

Denmark occupies the Jutland peninsula (a long neck of land) which lies north of WEST GERMANY. Several islands in the Baltic Sea are also part of Denmark. The land is flat and there are many farms. Manufacturing and agriculture are the chief industries in Denmark. The Danes produce much meat, cheese, and butter.

The huge island of Greenland belongs to Denmark. Greenland is so cold, however, that few people live there. Denmark is a MONARCHY.

Finland

Finland borders NORWAY and SWEDEN to the north, and the U.S.S.R. to the east. Its coast lies on the Gulf of Bothnia and the Gulf of Finland. It is a lowland country, covered with dense forests. Nearly a tenth of the country consists of LAKES. Finland's industries are based on TIMBER, and paper is an important product.

A PRESIDENT is chosen as head of the state. The people speak Finnish, a language that is similar to Hungarian. Many Finns also speak Swedish.

Top: The Royal Palace at the centre of Copenhagen, Denmark.
Above: Helsinki Cathedral, Finland.
Below: Boats at Reykjavik, Iceland.

Iceland

Iceland is an ISLAND in the northern ATLANTIC OCEAN. It is very cold and there is much SNOW and ice, but hot springs in the ground give people warm water to heat their houses. VOLCANOES sometimes erupt in Iceland, causing great damage. A new volcano, called Surtsey, rose from the sea off Iceland in 1963. There are no railways and few ROADS, and therefore travel by air is common.

The people of Iceland live mainly by fishing. Iceland is governed by a PARLIAMENT. (The first parliament in history was in Iceland.) The language, Icelandic, is similar to the Scandinavian languages.

United Kingdom

The full name of the United Kingdom is the United Kingdom of Great Britain and Northern Ireland. The United Kingdom is often called the U.K. or Britain. Together with the Republic of Ireland (Eire), the U.K. occupies the British Isles in north-western EUROPE. The U.K. is made up of four main regions: England, Wales, Scotland, and Northern Ireland.

The different regions of Britain govern themselves in different ways, but the most important decisions are made by PARLIAMENT in LONDON. The Isle of Man in the Irish Sea, and the Channel Islands in the English Channel, also have their own laws. Queen Elizabeth II is the head of state of the United Kingdom, and she approves the decisions made by Parliament.

Top: Typical old streets in Norwich, the main town in East Anglia in eastern England.
Centre: Holyrood Palace, Edinburgh, Scotland.
Bottom: Hills in Snowdonia, Wales.

The U.K. has many different kinds of scenery. Scotland has great ranges of low MOUNTAINS with deep VALLEYS and lochs (FIORDS) along the western COAST. Offshore are the Hebrides and the Orkney and Shetland islands. Much of Scotland is remote, wild countryside.

In northern England, the Pennine mountains run north from the Midlands to Scotland. In the north-west is the Lake District, a region of beautiful hills, valleys, and LAKES, shaped by GLACIERS during the ICE AGE. South and east of the Pennines, the country is mostly low-lying.

Wales contains much high ground that rises to the mountains of Snowdonia in the north.

Northern Ireland also has high hills, surrounding a large lake called Lough Neagh.

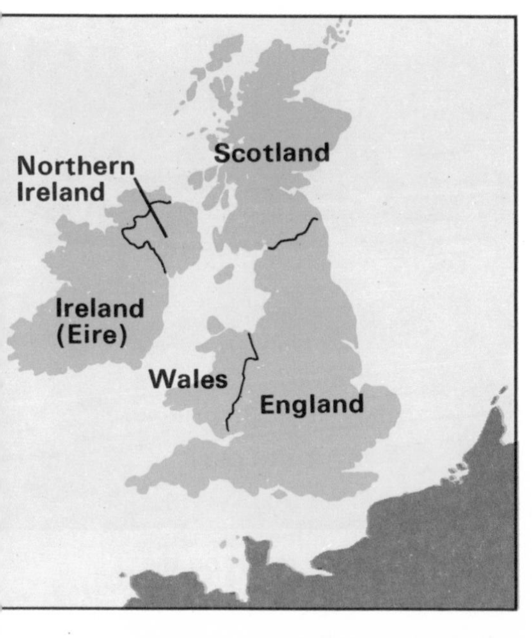

The United Kingdom has large deposits of COAL and IRON ore, and oil comes from wells in the North Sea. The country is mainly an industrial nation. It produces only half of the food it needs. The rest has to be bought from other countries, particularly COMMONWEALTH and COMMON MARKET nations. The main industrial regions are in northern England, the Midlands, the London area, south Wales, and the Scottish lowlands near Glasgow. There is much fertile farmland.

English is spoken everywhere in Great Britain. Gaelic is also spoken by some people in Scotland and Northern Ireland, and Welsh is spoken in Wales.

	England	Scotland	Wales	Northern Ireland	Republic of Ireland
Population	46,221,000	5,116,000	2,790,000	1,490,000	2,443,000
Area (sq. km.)	130,357	78,749	20,761	14,146	68,893
Capital	LONDON	Edinburgh	Cardiff	Belfast	Dublin

Ireland

The Republic of Ireland, and Northern Ireland, which is part of the UNITED KINGDOM, occupy the island of Ireland. The Republic of Ireland is, however, often simply called Ireland or Eire. The head of state is the PRESIDENT. Irish, a form of Gaelic, is the first official language, but most people speak English, the other official language. Eire has a large central plain surrounded by low MOUNTAINS. There are several large LAKES in this mainly agricultural country.

Eire was once part of the United Kingdom. In 1922 it became an independent nation, but Northern Ireland stayed within the U.K. Most people in Eire are ROMAN CATHOLIC whereas Northern Ireland is mainly PROTESTANT.

Left: Mountpleasant Square, Dublin, Eire.

Spain

Together with PORTUGAL, Spain occupies the Iberian peninsula between the ATLANTIC OCEAN and the MEDITERRANEAN SEA. The Balearic Islands in the Mediterranean and the Canary Islands in the Atlantic also belong to Spain. The Spanish COAST and islands are lined with towns that are popular holiday resorts.

Long ago, Spain was occupied by the Moors, a people of Berber and ARAB descent. They built many lovely palaces, but they were driven from Spain between 1200 and 1500 by Christian armies. In the 1500s, Spain became the most powerful country in EUROPE, but later it declined.

Spain is made up of a huge central plateau, largely surrounded by MOUNTAINS. Farming is the main activity, but manufacturing is also important. The official language is Spanish.

Spain has been a MONARCHY for most of its history, with the exception of the period between 1931 and 1975. From 1939, following a three-year civil war, General Francisco Franco ruled as Chief of State. When Franco died in 1975, the monarchy was restored and Juan Carlos I became king. The country is now ruled by an elected PARLIAMENT called the Cortés.

Above: A seaside resort on the north-west coast of Spain.
Below: A church near Valencia, on the same coast.

Andorra

Andorra is a tiny country in the Pyrenees, a mountain range between FRANCE and SPAIN. Most people work on farms or in the tourist industry. Andorra is a principality, but it is ruled by an elected General Council. The official language is Catalan.

	Spain	Andorra	Portugal	Malta
Population	33,824,000	31,000	8,611,000	314,000
Area (sq. km.)	504,879	465	91,631	316
Capital	MADRID	Andorra la Vella	Lisbon	Valletta

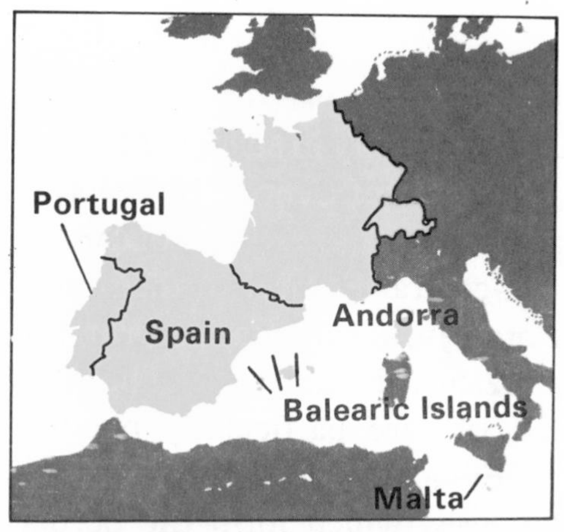

Portugal

Portugal lies along the western coast of the Iberian peninsula. It has a long border with SPAIN. Most of the people are farmers or fishermen and cork, sardines, wines and wood pulp are important products. Many tourists visit Portugal to enjoy its pleasant, sunny climate. Manufacturing industries are now developing around the capital, Lisbon, and other towns.

The country consists mostly of tablelands, surrounded by coastal plains. The volcanic Azores Islands, about 1200 kilometres west in the ATLANTIC OCEAN, also belong to Portugal.

Portugal became important in the 1400s when Portuguese explorers started to build up a great overseas empire in Africa, South America and Asia. Nearly all of Portugal's overseas possessions are now independent. The last large territories to become independent were ANGOLA and MOZAMBIQUE, in Africa. They both gained independence in 1975. Once a MONARCHY, Portugal became a REPUBLIC in 1910. A PRESIDENT is head of state and the country is ruled by an elected National Assembly. The official language is Portuguese.

Above: A view of Lisbon.

Below: A street in Valletta, Malta.

Malta

Malta is a small island country in the MEDITERRANEAN SEA, south of Sicily. It contains three populated islands: Malta, which is the largest, Gozo and Comino. Tourism, farming and fishing are leading industries.

Malta was a British colony and naval base until 1964, when it gained independence. It became a REPUBLIC in 1974, but it remained a member of the COMMONWEALTH. A PRESIDENT is now head of state and an elected House of Representatives governs the country. English and Maltese are the official languages.

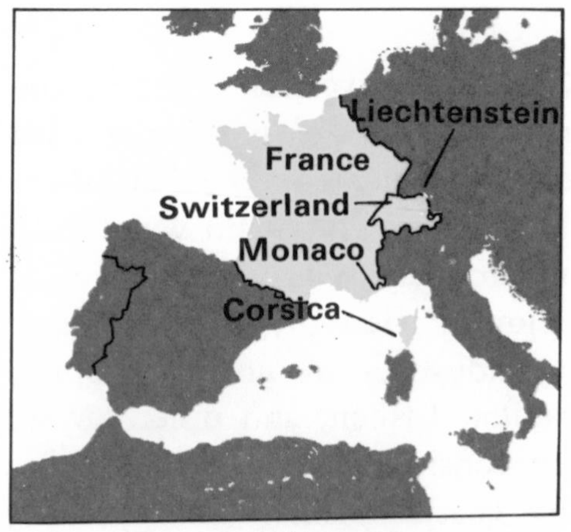

Above: An inn at the port of Honfleur in northern France.
Below: A castle at Saumur, a town in the Loire valley. This region of France is well known for its many beautiful castles built along the Loire river.

France

Apart from the European part of the U.S.S.R., France is the largest country in EUROPE. Much of it is low-lying. The Massif Central, however, is a region of high plateaus and extinct VOLCANOES that lies in south-central France. In the south-east the ALPS and Jura Mountains form the border with SWITZERLAND and ITALY. The Alps and the south coast are particularly popular with visitors to France. Other scenic uplands include the Pyrenees, which form the border with SPAIN, and the Vosges mountains in the north-east.

Because it is a large and fertile country, France can grow most of the food it needs. It also has large reserves of minerals and natural power. Farming and industry are both important.

France is a REPUBLIC governed by a PARLIAMENT. French is the main language, but other languages are spoken in border areas.

France once had many colonies in AFRICA. These are now independent nations, but most of them still have close ties with France. ALGERIA fought a long war for independence. France still has some colonies, mostly small islands. The island of Corsica is also part of France.

Monaco

Monaco is a tiny principality, with a prince as head of state. It lies on the MEDITERRANEAN SEA, in south-eastern FRANCE. It is a famous luxury holiday centre, known for its gambling casino at Monte Carlo and its international car rally.

	France	Monaco
Population	52,656,000	25,000
Area (sq. km.)	543,998	1.89
Capital	PARIS	Monaco

Above: A square in the city of Geneva, Switzerland.
Below: Vaduz, the capital of Liechtenstein.

Switzerland

Switzerland is a small country in south-central EUROPE. It has no coastline. The ALPS and the Jura Mountains cover nearly three-quarters of the country. Between the Alps and the Jura is a plateau region called the Mittelland. Most of Switzerland's people live in this region.

The country has few natural resources. Swiss craftsmen have concentrated on making expensive, high-quality products, such as machines, clocks, and scientific instruments. Today nearly half of the people work in manufacturing and construction industries. Far fewer work on farms, but Switzerland is well known for its dairy products, including cheese and butter.

Switzerland is a REPUBLIC. There is no single head of state, but there is a Federal Council with seven members. These are elected from seven of the 22 cantons (regions) in turn by the parliament, which consists of two elected chambers. The Federal Council changes every four years. German is the language of three-quarters of the people in Switzerland, but French and Italian are also official languages. Switzerland has been a neutral country since 1815.

Liechtenstein

Liechtenstein is a small MONARCHY, ruled by a prince, between AUSTRIA and SWITZERLAND. The country is closely linked with Switzerland, and the people use Swiss money. Switzerland also looks after Liechtenstein's defence, foreign affairs, and other matters. Liechtenstein became independent in 1342. German is spoken.

	Switzerland	Liechtenstein
Population	6,346,000	24,000
Area (sq. km.)	41,288	160
Capital	Berne	Vaduz

Italy

The mainland of Italy sticks out like a boot into the MEDITERRANEAN SEA. The island of Sicily lies at the toe of the boot. Sicily belongs to Italy, as does the island of Sardinia and the smaller Lipari islands. These include the famous volcanoes, Stromboli and Volcano. Other volcanoes in Italy are Etna and Vesuvius.

The Apennine Mountains run the whole length of Italy. They join the ALPS at the border with FRANCE. The Lombardy plain in the north, which contains the River Po valley, is the only large low-lying region. Farming is important on this plain, which also contains most of Italy's industries. Southern Italy is devoted mainly to farming, but the land is dry and the people there are poorer than those in the north. Tourism is important. The ruins of the ancient Roman Empire, Vatican City in ROME, and such beautiful cities as VENICE, are popular with visitors.

Italy is a REPUBLIC, and the PRESIDENT is head of state. Italian is spoken throughout the country. German is also spoken near the border with AUSTRIA.

Above right: The Ponte Vecchio, the old bridge across the River Arno in Florence, Italy.
Right: The dome of St Peter's in the Vatican City. Michelangelo was one of the architects of the church, the largest of all Christian churches.

Vatican City

Vatican City is the world's smallest independent country. It stands on a hill in north-west ROME, ITALY's capital city. It is the centre of the ROMAN CATHOLIC Church, and the home of the Pope. People do not need to show their passports when they enter Vatican City. There they can visit St Peter's Basilica and the Vatican Palace, which house many famous works of art.

Greece

Greece is a mountainous country that juts out into the MEDITERRANEAN SEA, south of YUGOSLAVIA and BULGARIA. Most Greeks are farmers, growing olives, grapes and figs, but manufacturing is the most valuable activity. Tourism is very important. People travel to Greece to see the scenery, the many off-shore islands, and the ancient ruins.

A group of soldiers took over the government of Greece by force in 1967. The king left the country and PARLIAMENT was dissolved. In 1975 Greece became a REPUBLIC, with a PRESIDENT as head of state.

Above: The ruins of an ancient temple at Delphi, Greece.
Below: Dubrovnik, Yugoslavia.

Albania

Albania lies on the Adriatic Sea and is bordered by YUGOSLAVIA and GREECE. Most people in this mountainous country are farmers, growing cereals, grapes, mulberry leaves, and olives. Albania became a COMMUNIST REPUBLIC in 1946. It became an ally of CHINA in 1961, but all links with China were ended in 1978.

Yugoslavia

Yugoslavia borders the Adriatic Sea, north of ALBANIA. The Dinaric Alps line the coast, and the Danube plain lies in the north-east. About half of the people are farmers, but industry is becoming more important. There are several languages, but most people speak Serbo-Croat.

Yugoslavia has had a COMMUNIST government, with a PRESIDENT, since WORLD WAR II. It is not, however, closely linked to the U.S.S.R.

	Italy	Vatican City	Greece	Albania	Yugoslavia
Population	56,323,000	1,000	9,200,000	2,432,000	21,560,000
Area (sq. km.)	301,245	0.44	131,986	28,748	255,804
Capital	ROME		ATHENS	Tirana	Belgrade

West Germany

When WORLD WAR II ended, Germany was occupied by the ARMIES of the United States, Britain, FRANCE, and the U.S.S.R. They governed the country in four zones – American, British, French, and Russian. The first three zones became the Federal Republic of Germany, usually called West Germany. The Russian zone became the German Democratic Republic (EAST GERMANY). The former capital of Germany, BERLIN, was divided into two parts in the same way, although it is in the middle of East Germany. German is spoken throughout both countries.

West Germany borders nine other countries, including East Germany. It has a short coastline on the NORTH SEA and Baltic Sea. The second largest city, Hamburg, is an important North Sea port. Much of West Germany is a large plain. The land rises in the south towards the ALPS. In the west, the River Rhine flows through West Germany on its way from SWITZERLAND to the NETHERLANDS. The Rhine valley, the Black Forest, and Bavaria in the south, are famous for their beauty. The River Rhine is navigable for most of its length and is much used for transport.

West Germany has large resources of COAL and minerals, and is one of the leading industrial countries in the world.

Top: The village of Oberammergau, in Bavaria, West Germany.
Above: The fairy-tale palace of Neuschwanstein, Bavaria, looks like a medieval castle, but it was in fact built by King Ludwig II only a century ago.

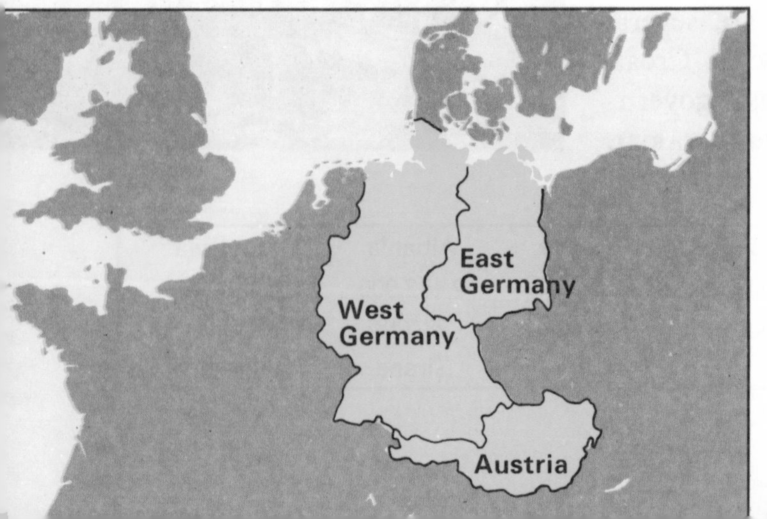

East Germany

Almost all of East Germany lies on a low, flat plain. Before WORLD WAR II, this region was the main farming area of Germany. Now industry has been built up, but East Germany can still grow almost all its own food. East Germany has a COMMUNIST government. The head of state is the chairman of the council of state.

Because the governments of WEST GERMANY and East Germany are so different, the two have not reunited. The border between them is strongly guarded. Non-communist countries only began to treat East Germany officially as a separate country in 1972.

Left: A strongly guarded wall marks the East German—West German border in Berlin.

	West Germany	East Germany	Austria
Population	61,442,000	16,767,000	7,456,000
Area (sq. km.)	248,624	108,179	83,853
Capital	Bonn	East BERLIN	VIENNA

Austria

Austria, a small country in central EUROPE, is bordered by ITALY, YUGOSLAVIA, HUNGARY, CZECHOSLOVAKIA, WEST GERMANY, SWITZERLAND, and LIECHTENSTEIN. Until 1918, it was part of the Austro-Hungarian Empire. The present boundaries were fixed after WORLD WAR II.

Today, winter sports make Austria a popular country with tourists. The ALPS, which extend from Switzerland into Austria, have many SKIING resorts. Both farming and industry are also important. Austria is a REPUBLIC, and German is the official language.

Left: The Tirol, a mountainous region in western Austria, is famous for its beauty.

Below: Prague, the capital of Czechoslovakia, is an old city with elegant buildings.

Poland

Poland, CZECHOSLOVAKIA, HUNGARY, ROMANIA, and BULGARIA are all COMMUNIST countries in eastern EUROPE. They became communist after the end of WORLD WAR II. These countries have close links with the U.S.S.R. They are each ruled either by a PRESIDENT or by the chairman of a council of state.

Poland is the largest country of eastern Europe. It borders the Baltic Sea in the north. The U.S.S.R. lies to the east, and Czechoslovakia to the south. The Oder and Neisse rivers form the western border with EAST GERMANY. Most of Poland is a low, flat plain, but the land rises to the Carpathian Mountains in the south. About one-third of the people are farmers. Poland has much COAL. Industry, especially SHIPBUILDING, is important. The people speak Polish, a language similar to Russian. Most Poles belong to the ROMAN CATHOLIC Church.

Czechoslovakia

Czechoslovakia (pronounced check-o-slo-vak-ya) has two groups of peoples. These are the Czechs who live in the west, and the Slovaks who live in the east. Czechoslovakia is a country of low MOUNTAINS, rolling hills and old towns. Industry is important in Czechoslovakia, which has rich deposits of minerals.

In 1968 the COMMUNIST government tried to make reforms (changes in the political system). The U.S.S.R. did not approve of the reforms. The Russian army invaded Czechoslovakia, put down the reforms, and changed the Czech leaders.

	Poland	Czechoslovakia
Population	34,528,000	14,857,000
Area (sq. km.)	312,677	127,877
Capital	Warsaw	Prague

Hungary

Most of Hungary is on a low plain. The River Danube flows from north to south across the country. In the west is Lake Balaton, which is popular with tourists. In Hungary, more people work in industry than in farming.

Most Hungarians are descendants of the Magyars, a people who came from ASIA long ago and settled in Hungary.

Left: A corner of old Warsaw, Poland.

Romania

The Carpathian Mountains and Transylvanian Alps take up a large part of central Romania. The River Danube flows along the border with YUGOSLAVIA and BULGARIA until it reaches the Black Sea on the Romanian coast. Fertile VALLEYS and plains lie beneath the MOUNTAINS, and farming is very important. But there are large reserves of OIL and COAL, and industry is developing. Romania is often called Rumania.

Right: A view of Bucharest, Romania.
Below right: A church in Sofia, Bulgaria.

Bulgaria

Bulgaria is south of ROMANIA and also borders the Black Sea. Ranges of MOUNTAINS run east-west across Bulgaria. Much of the land, however, is farmed. Agriculture is very important, although industry is developing rapidly. The people speak Bulgarian, a slavonic language written in the Cyrillic alphabet, like Russian.

Romania	Bulgaria	Hungary
21,250,000	8,730,000	10,672,000
237,500	110,911	93,032
Bucharest	Sofia	Budapest

Asia

ASIA is the largest continent in the world. More than half the world's people live there. The world's biggest countries and the countries with the largest populations are in Asia. Some contain hundreds of millions of people.

	U.S.S.R.
Population	257,900,000
Area (sq. km.)	22,400,000
Capital	MOSCOW

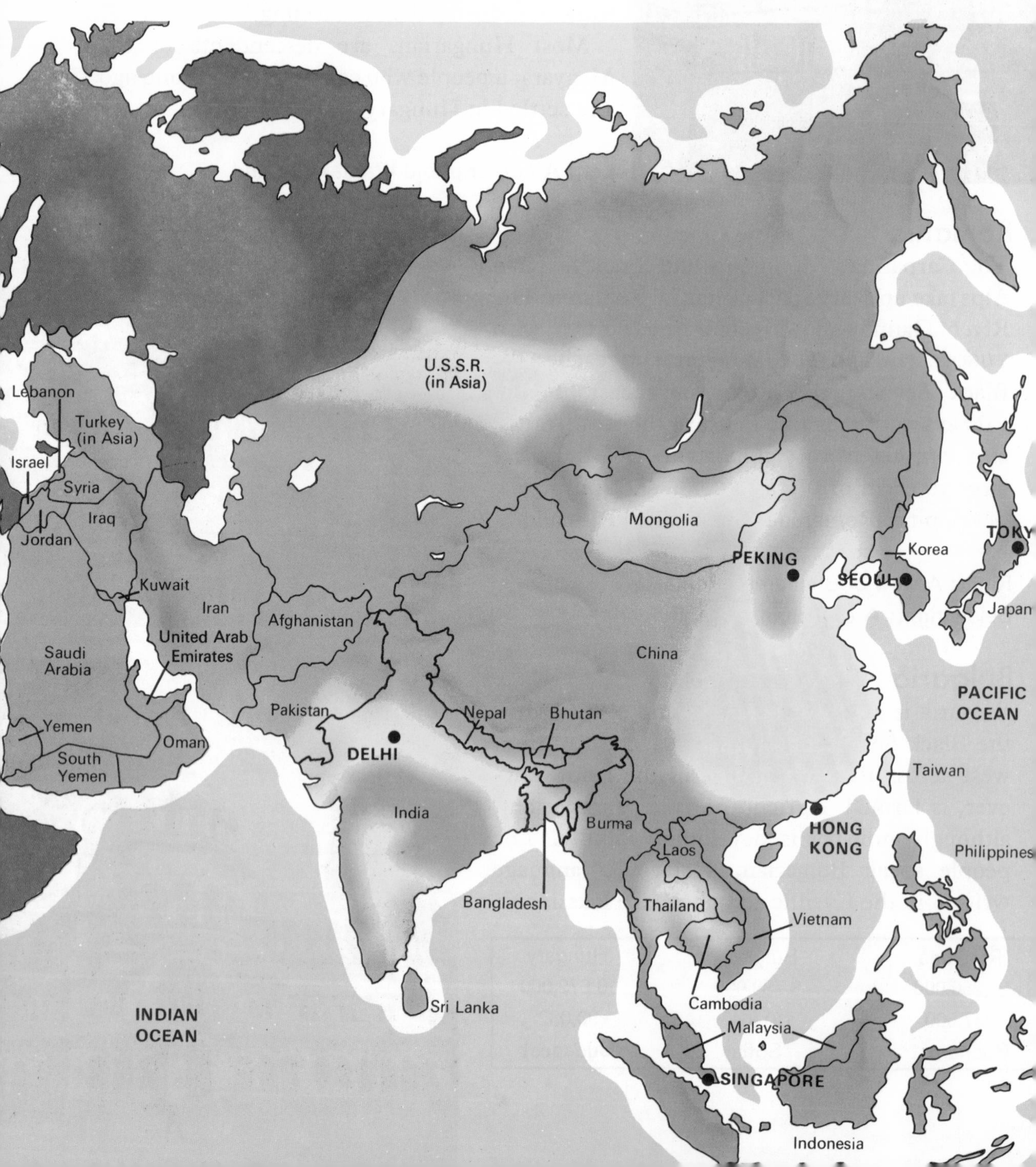

Top: A bridge in Leningrad, U.S.S.R.
Centre: A gorge in Georgia, U.S.S.R.
Bottom: The world's deepest lake, Lake Baikal, is in Russia.

In Asia there are high MOUNTAIN ranges, DESERTS, thick forests, great RIVERS, and inland seas. Some of them form barriers which people cannot cross easily. Because of these barriers, the various groups of people in Asia have not mixed and so have developed different ways of life.

U.S.S.R.

The letters U.S.S.R. stand for Union of Soviet Socialist Republics. The U.S.S.R. is also called the Soviet Union, or simply Russia. It is the largest country in the world, covering one-sixth of all the world's land.

A vast plain stretches from west to east across Russia. Most of it is forest, but much of the land is farmed. The Ural Mountains run north-south across the plain. Most people think of the U.S.S.R. west of the Urals as part of EUROPE and not of ASIA. Great ranges of MOUNTAINS lie along the southern border of the U.S.S.R. The north coast is on the ARCTIC OCEAN. The north-east region, called Siberia, is very cold in winter.

Because it is so large, the U.S.S.R. has vast resources. It is one of the world's leading industrial countries. Although much of the land is used for farming, droughts often occur and result in food shortages. Before WORLD WAR I, the U.S.S.R. was a mainly agricultural country, although industry was developing rapidly. Following the REVOLUTION of 1917, a COMMUNIST government was set up. The U.S.S.R. soon became a powerful industrial nation. The government rules 15 regions called republics. The PRESIDENT is the head of state, but real power lies with the First Secretary of the Communist Party.

The chief language of the U.S.S.R. is Russian, a slavonic language written in the Cyrillic alphabet.

Turkey

Most of Turkey occupies a peninsula of land between the Black Sea and the MEDITERRANEAN SEA. This region is known as ASIA Minor. But a small part of Turkey lies on the west side of the Bosporus – the stretch of water that connects the two seas. This part is in EUROPE. Turkey is more like its European than its Asian neighbours. Reforms (changes) made in the 1920s and 1930s ended many Asian features of Turkish life.

Until 1918 Turkey had a powerful empire and controlled large parts of Europe and north AFRICA. The centre of the empire was Constantinople, now renamed ISTANBUL. Great mosques and palaces can still be seen there. Turkey is now governed by a PARLIAMENT. However, the ARMY has taken control of the country on several occasions. The capital of Turkey is Ankara.

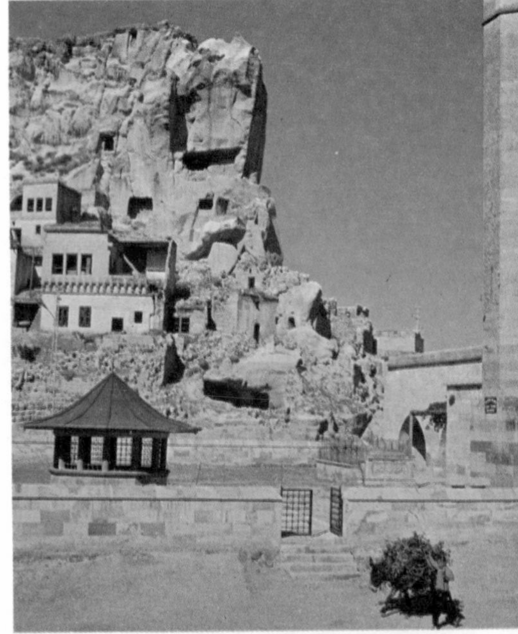

Above: Ancient dwellings in Turkey.
Below: A street in Cyprus.

Cyprus

Cyprus is a large ISLAND at the eastern end of the MEDITERRANEAN SEA. It has a central plain with MOUNTAINS to the north and south. Most people are farmers. There are two main groups of people in Cyprus. The Christian Greek Cypriots make up nearly four-fifths of the population, while most of the others are Moslem Turkish Cypriots. Greek and Turkish are the official languages. There has been much fighting between the two groups over the control of the country. Most of them now live in separate areas. Cyprus is a member of the COMMONWEALTH.

	Turkey	Cyprus	Israel	Syria
Population	40,198,000	639,000	3,600,000	8,300,000
Area (sq. km.)	779,452	9,251	20,700	185,680
Capital	Ankara	Nicosia	JERUSALEM	Damascus

Israel

Israel is a country which contains places that are holy to Jews, Christians, and Moslems. It was created in 1948 as a home for people of the Jewish religion (JUDAISM). The Jews once lived in Palestine, the old name for the area, but they scattered all over the world in the last 2000 years. Today about one-fifth of all Jews live in Israel. About four-fifths of Israel's people are Jews. The others are mostly ARABS. Hebrew and Arabic are the official languages.

Much of Israel consists of dry plains and DESERTS. However, the Israelis have worked hard to irrigate the land for farming and to build a modern nation. Farming is important, but mining and manufacturing are now much more valuable industries than agriculture. Most of the people live in cities and towns.

Israel is a REPUBLIC, governed by the Knesset (PARLIAMENT). In 1948–9 Israel fought with its Arab neighbours who opposed the creation of the new nation. Other short wars in 1956, 1967, and 1973 left Israel in control of much land which belonged to EGYPT, JORDAN, and SYRIA. In 1977–9 Israel negotiated with Egypt to make peace between them. But other Arab nations opposed these negotiations. They still regarded themselves as being at war with Israel.

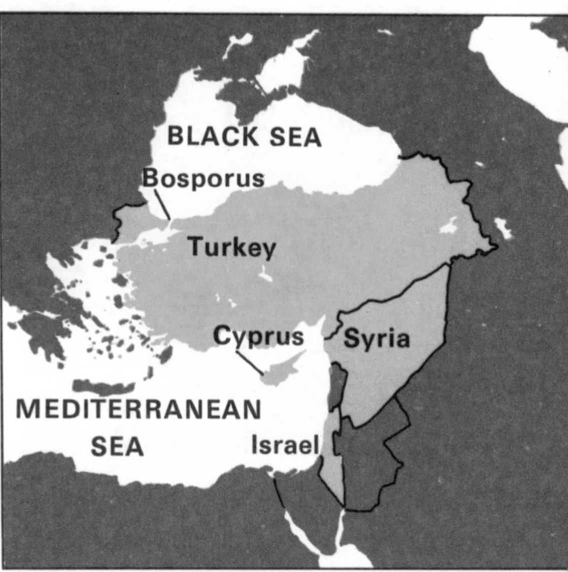

Above: A desert scene in Israel.
Below: Damascus, the capital city of Syria.

Syria

Syria lies to the south of TURKEY. It has a short COAST on the MEDITERRANEAN SEA. There is fertile land in the north, but DESERT covers the south. The River Euphrates flows through the centre of the country. Syria is a mostly agricultural country. Most people are ARABS and speak Arabic.

Syria is governed by its PRESIDENT and an elected People's Council.

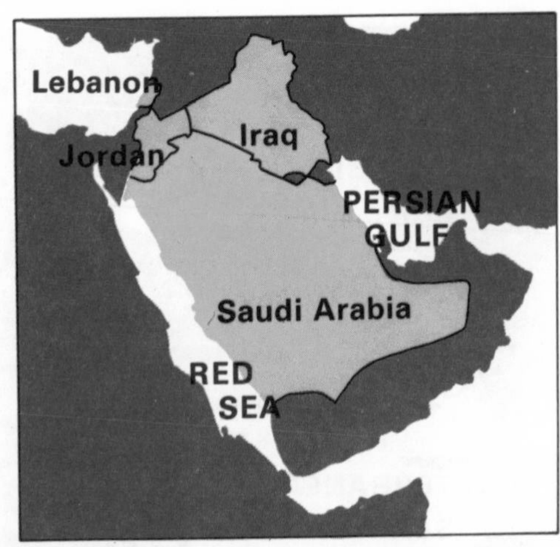

Lebanon

Lebanon borders the MEDITERRANEAN SEA between SYRIA and ISRAEL. It is a mountainous country, but most people are farmers. However, trade and tourism are much more valuable industries. Another important industry is oil-refining. The OIL comes from SAUDI ARABIA and IRAQ through pipelines.

The people are mostly ARABS and Arabic is the official language. However, about two-fifths of the people are Christians, the rest being Moslems. Conflict between Christians and Moslems caused civil wars in the mid-1970s and early 1980s. Lebanon has also suffered by being involved in Arab-Israeli conflicts.

In 1978 and again in 1982 parts of Lebanon were invaded by Israeli troops who wanted to drive out the Palestinians there. The Palestinians are Arab refugees from Israel. Lebanon is a REPUBLIC. In normal times, it is governed by an elected PARLIAMENT which represents all the religious groups.

Above: The famous cedars of Lebanon in the snow.
Below: A view of Amman, Jordan's capital city.

Jordan

Jordan is an ARAB country to the east of ISRAEL. It has no coastline. Before the 1967 Arab-Israeli war, Jordan occupied land on both sides of the River Jordan. The land on the west side is fertile and contains many historical remains. One-third of Jordan's people live there.

Since 1967 this area and its people have been controlled by Israel. Much of eastern Jordan is poor DESERT land. But most people are farmers, and CEREALS, fruits, and vegetables are the chief crops. Jordan's most valuable product is phosphates. These are used to make FERTILIZERS.

Jordan is a MONARCHY and the king is head of state. He rules with an elected PARLIAMENT. Arabic is the official language.

Above: Little market stalls, at Taef, Saudi Arabia.
Below: A market in Baghdad, the capital of Iraq. Behind is the ornate entrance into a mosque, typical of Islamic architecture.

Saudi Arabia

Saudi Arabia is a large country between the Red Sea and the Persian Gulf. Most of the land is hot DESERT. The people protect themselves from the sun by wearing loose, baggy clothes and head-dresses. Outside their homes, most women still wear veils, a custom in most Arab nations.

Bedouin tribesmen roam the deserts. There is some farming in oases and irrigated regions. Saudi Arabia has large deposits of OIL. Money from oil sales abroad has been used to build new SCHOOLS, hospitals, and ROADS.

Near the Red Sea coast is the city of Mecca. This is a holy city in the religion of ISLAM, which most Arabs follow. Mecca was the birthplace of MOHAMMED, who founded Islam. Every year, many thousands of Moslems (followers of Islam) make a pilgrimage to Mecca from all over the world. The king rules Saudi Arabia with a council of ministers. There are no ELECTIONS. Everyone must obey the laws of Islam.

Iraq

Iraq lies between SYRIA and the northern end of the Persian Gulf. Much of the land is DESERT, but a fertile plain lies between the Tigris and Euphrates rivers. The first civilizations began here more than 5000 years ago. Ancient BABYLON was in what is now southern Iraq.

Most of the people live by farming. Iraq has large deposits of OIL. Profits from the sale of oil have improved farming. Iraq is an ARAB nation. It is ruled by a council of army officers. A long war with Iran began in 1980.

	Lebanon	Jordan	Saudi Arabia	Iraq
Population	2,780,000	2,752,000	9,157,000	11,505,000
Area (sq. km.)	10,400	96,000	2,400,000	438,446
Capital	Beirut	Amman	Riyadh	Baghdad

Kuwait

Kuwait lies at the head of the Persian Gulf. This ARAB country consists mostly of hot DESERT. It is one of the world's richest nations because of its large OIL deposits. With money from oil sales, the government provides free health and education services. Even the telephone service is free. The country is a MONARCHY, with a sheikh, (an Arab prince), as head of state. The sheikh rules with an appointed cabinet.

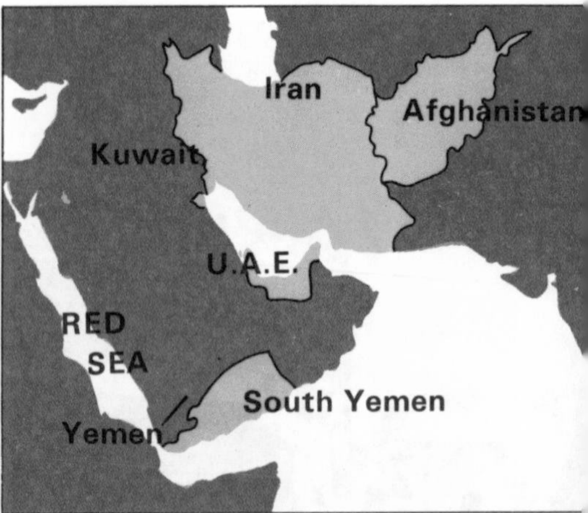

United Arab Emirates

The United Arab Emirates is a country on the south-western coast of the Persian Gulf. It consists of seven emirates, which have joined together. An emirate is the name for a place ruled by a sheikh. The land is mostly DESERT, but there are large OIL deposits. As in other rich ARAB nations, money from oil sales is being used to develop the country and create free services for the people.

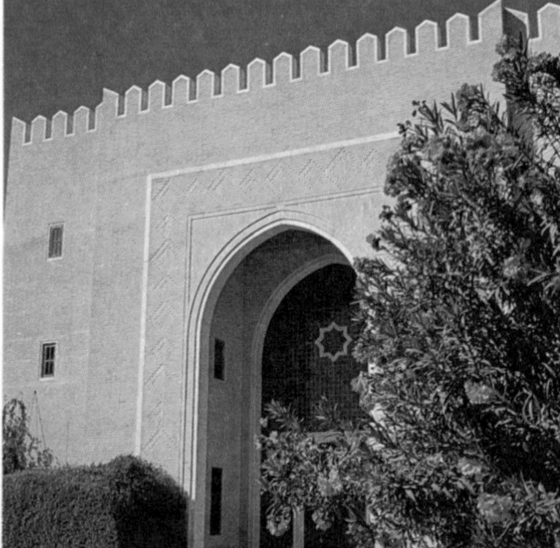

Yemen

The Yemen Arab Republic is on the south-eastern side of the Red Sea, between SAUDI ARABIA and SOUTH YEMEN. It is a poor, mountainous country. Most people farm, and COTTON, COFFEE, and hides are the main products.

Above right: The House of Parliament, Kuwait.
Right: San'a, capital of the Yemen Arab Republic.

South Yemen

South Yemen lies along the Gulf of Aden, to the south of the YEMEN Arab Republic and SAUDI ARABIA. The country is officially called the People's Democratic Republic of Yemen. It is a poor, largely DESERT country. Most people are farmers or fishermen.

	Kuwait	United Arab E
Population	1,066,000	656,000
Area (sq. km.)	24,280	92,100
Capital	Kuwait	Abu Dha

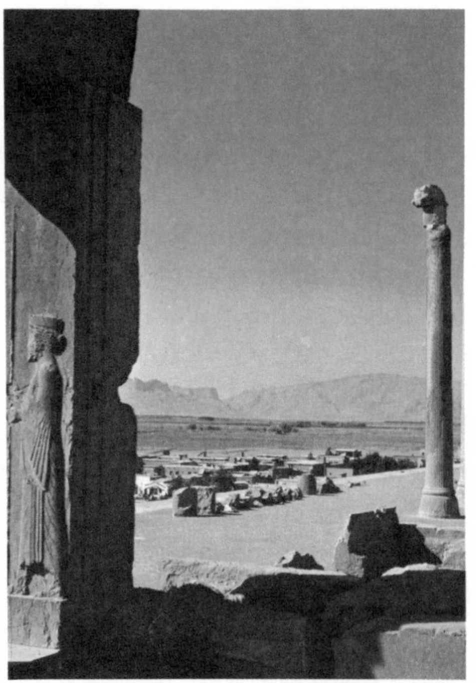

Above: The ruins of Persepolis, the ancient capital of the Persian Empire, in Iran.

Iran

Iran lies between the U.S.S.R. and the Persian Gulf. It used to be called Persia. A high plateau surrounded by MOUNTAINS covers most of Iran. The land is dry, and most of the people make a living by farming. There are vast deposits of OIL, which bring a lot of money to Iran.

The PERSIANS dominated the ancient world in about 500 B.C. Over a thousand years ago Iran was the centre of a great Arab civilisation. The people of modern Iran are not Arabs. But they are Moslems, and write the Persian language in Arabic script. Iran was ruled by an emperor, the Shah, until 1979 when he left the country after many people had rioted against his rule. Iran became an Islamic REPUBLIC. A long war with Iraq began in 1980.

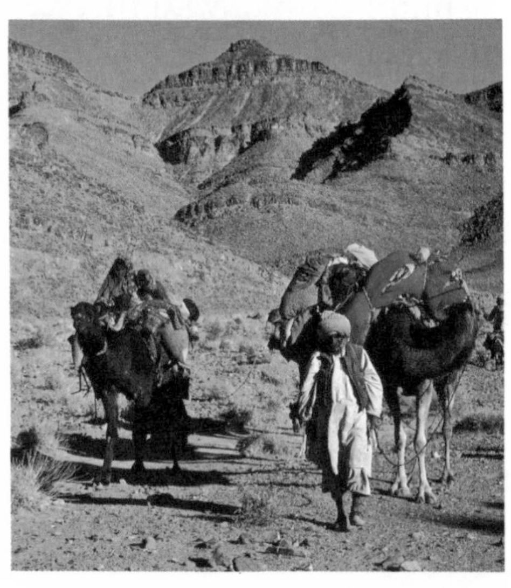

Afghanistan

Afghanistan is bordered by the U.S.S.R. to the north, IRAN to the west, and PAKISTAN to the south and east. The south-west corner is low-lying DESERT. Over the rest of the country rise the great MOUNTAINS of the Hindu Kush. The only farmland is in the mountain VALLEYS. There are few natural resources and little industry. Afghanistan was a MONARCHY until 1973 when it became a REPUBLIC. In 1979 Soviet troops entered Afghanistan. They helped the government to fight Moslem rebels.

Left: Nomads with their camels in Afghanistan.

s	Yemen	South Yemen	Iran	Afghanistan
	5,238,000	1,663,000	34,000,000	19,580,000
	195,000	160,330	1,648,000	657,500
	San'a	Aden	Tehran	Kabul

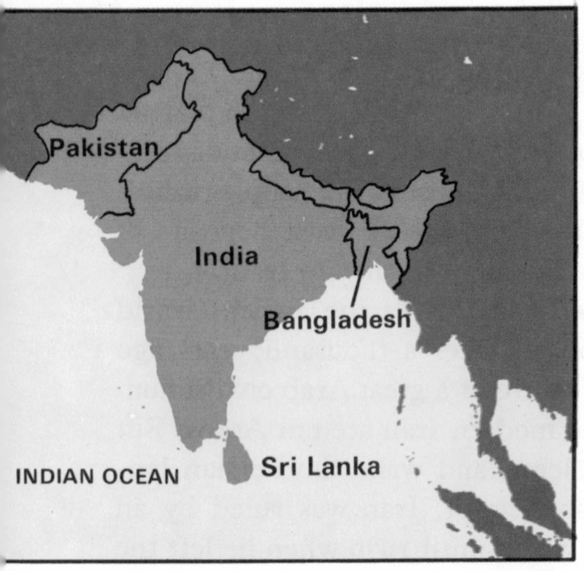

Below: The centre of Calcutta, one of India's largest cities.

India

Before 1947, India, PAKISTAN, and BANGLADESH were all part of the British colony of India. SRI LANKA (Ceylon), the ISLAND to the south of India, was also a British colony. When India became an independent nation in 1947, a separate nation called Pakistan was also formed. In India most people are HINDUS and in Pakistan, Moslems (followers of ISLAM). Ceylon became an independent country in 1948.

Pakistan was in two parts – West Pakistan and East Pakistan – separated by India. In 1971 East Pakistan tried to become an independent nation. Forces from West Pakistan invaded East Pakistan. India came to the help of East Pakistan. After a short war in December 1971, East Pakistan became an independent country and called itself Bangladesh. West Pakistan is now called simply Pakistan. Ceylon changed its name to Sri Lanka in 1972. All these countries are members of the British COMMONWEALTH, except Pakistan, which left in 1972.

India occupies the vast Indian peninsula that juts out into the INDIAN OCEAN. It has more people than any nation except CHINA, and most of them are very poor. Nearly three-quarters of the people work on the land, most on very small farms. Great civilizations flourished in India in the past, and Indian art and music are famous throughout the world.

Many languages are spoken in India, but the main official one is Hindi. Many people also speak English. India is a REPUBLIC, governed by a PARLIAMENT.

	India	Pakistan	Bangladesh	Sri Lanka
Population	605,000,000	74,955,000	76,815,000	14,270,000
Area (sq. km.)	3,166,828	796,095	144,020	65,610
Capital	DELHI	Islamabad	Dakha	Colombo

Pakistan

Pakistan lies to the north-west of INDIA. The River Indus flows through the centre of the country from the HIMALAYA mountains in the north to the coast of the Arabian Sea in the south. Fertile plains surround this river and its tributaries in the north, though further south it flows through DESERT. Farming is very important in Pakistan. Only one-tenth of the people work in industry. The main languages are Urdu and English. The PRESIDENT is head of state.

Left: A mosque in Lahore, Pakistan.

Bangladesh

Bangladesh is almost enclosed by north-eastern India. It was once the eastern province of PAKISTAN. The Ganges, Brahmaputra, and other rivers flow through Bangladesh to the Bay of Bengal. Most people farm the land, and RICE and JUTE are the leading crops. The war with West Pakistan ruined the country. Today the people are very poor. Bengali is the main language, but many people also speak English. Bangladesh is governed by a PARLIAMENT.

Left: Bangladeshi girls dancing in a circle.

Sri Lanka

Sri Lanka used to be called Ceylon. It has a central range of forest-covered MOUNTAINS, surrounded by low plains. Most people work on the land. RICE, TEA, RUBBER, and coconuts are the main crops. The people speak Sinhala or Tamil, but many also speak English. Sri Lanka is a REPUBLIC.

Left: An enclosed pathway leads to a fortress overlooking the forests of Sri Lanka.

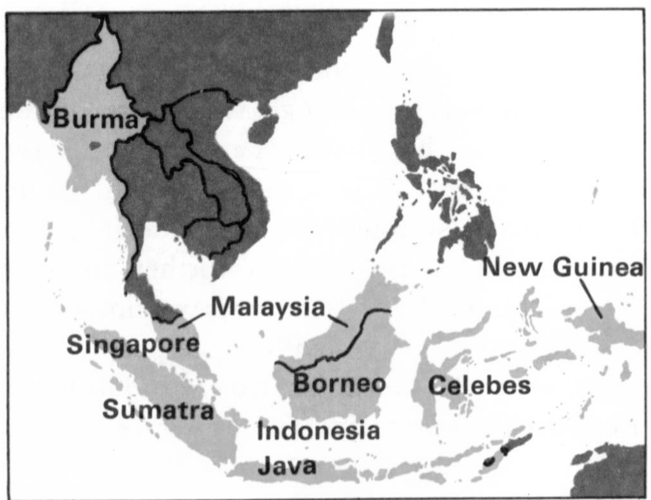

Above: A view of Rangoon, Burma. Below: The old town hall at Malacca in Malaysia was built by Dutch colonists.

Burma

Burma and INDIA are separated by the Bay of Bengal. High forested MOUNTAINS are in northern Burma, but there are fertile plains in the south. RICE is the main food crop in this mainly farming country. Most Burmese are BUDDHISTS and there are many beautiful temples. The main language is Burmese. Burma is a REPUBLIC governed by a People's Assembly.

Malaysia

Malaysia is a country made up of three parts: Malaya, which is at the end of the Malay peninsula, and Sarawak and Sabah on the island of Borneo on the other side of the South China Sea.

Several different peoples live in Malaysia. About half are Malays, but there are also many Chinese and Indians, as well as Dyaks in Sarawak. Malay and English are the official languages, but many people also speak Chinese.

The climate is hot and damp, and dense rainforests cover the land. Malaysia is one of the richest nations in ASIA. It leads the world in producing RUBBER, tin, and palm oil. RICE is the chief food. Malaysia is governed by a PARLIAMENT and is a member of the COMMONWEALTH.

	Burma	Malaysia
Population	28,890,000	12,629,000
Area (sq. km.)	678,000	329,749
Capital	Rangoon	Kuala Lumpur

Singapore

Singapore is a small island REPUBLIC. It occupies an ISLAND at the southern tip of the Malay peninsula in south-east ASIA. It has become rich because of its large, modern port. The exports and imports of many countries pass through its busy harbour. Manufacturing industries are also important in Singapore.

About three-quarters of the people are Chinese. There are also Malays, Indians, and other groups. Singapore was once part of MALAYSIA, but it broke away in 1965. It is a member of the COMMONWEALTH.

Indonesia

Indonesia is made up of a string of islands between MALAYSIA, the Philippines, and AUSTRALIA. The islands include parts of Kalimantan (Borneo) and New Guinea, as well as Sumatra, Java, and Sulawesi (Celebes). The islands are mountainous. They are covered with rain forests that grow thickly in the hot, damp climate.

Indonesia has more volcanoes than any other country. The world's greatest volcanic explosion took place on the island of Krakatoa in 1883.

The people of Indonesia are part Malaysian and part Polynesian in origin. Most are Moslems (followers of ISLAM). Indonesia has more Moslems than any other country. The official language is Indonesian, but there are many different dialects from island to island. Most of the people are farmers, and the two main crops are RICE and RUBBER. There is some mining and oil is the chief export. Indonesia is a REPUBLIC.

Singapore	Indonesia
2,278,000	133,000,000
602	1,903,650
Singapore	Jakarta

Above: The waterfront at Singapore.
Below: The island of Bali in Indonesia is famous for its temples.

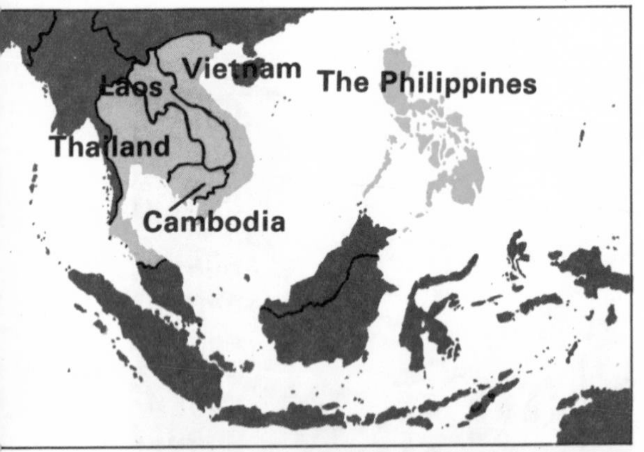

Above: An Indian elephant in Thailand.
Below: The Pagsanjan river on one of the Philippine islands.

Thailand

Thailand is still often called by its old name of Siam. The Thai people are good craftsmen and the country is famous for its beautiful Buddhist TEMPLES and hand-woven silks.

Thailand is bordered by BURMA, Laos, and CAMBODIA. MOUNTAINS lie along the borders. In the centre is the fertile valley of the Menam River. Most Thai people live by farming. RICE, RUBBER, and TIMBER are the main products.

Thailand is a MONARCHY, but an army group took over the government in the 1970s. Fighting between Thais and invaders from the east marred the country's progress in the 1970s. The Thai language is spoken.

Philippines

The Philippines is an island nation to the north of INDONESIA. It consists of more than 7000 islands. The largest are Luzon, where the capital, Manila, is situated, and Mindanao. It is a tropical, mountainous country. Most people are farmers, and RICE and maize are the main crops.

The Philippines is unusual in Asia because more than nine-tenths of the people are Christians. Christianity was introduced in the 1500s. Spain ruled the country until 1898, when the U.S.A. took over. In 1946 the Philippines became an independent REPUBLIC. It is now ruled by the president assisted by a PARLIAMENT. But the president can rule directly. The official language is Pilipino, but many people speak English or Spanish.

	Thailand	Philippines
Population	44,273,000	43,940,000
Area (sq. km.)	514,000	300,000
Capital	Bangkok	Manila

Vietnam

Vietnam borders the South China Sea. It was a French colony until 1954, when it was divided into two countries, North Vietnam and South Vietnam. The North had a COMMUNIST government, but the South was anti-communist. From 1960 North Vietnam and CHINA helped communists in South Vietnam to fight against their government. The communists won control of South Vietnam in 1975 and North and South Vietnam were united in 1976.

This tropical country consists mainly of forest. RICE is the main crop. Industries have been growing quickly.

Above: Ho Chi Minh City, which is in Vietnam. Before 1975 it was called Saigon.

Below: The royal palace, former home of the royal family, at Phnom Penh in Cambodia.

Laos

Laos is a poor country with no coastline. Most of the people are farmers, and RICE, maize, tobacco and cotton are the major crops. The country was formerly a French colony. It became a fully independent MONARCHY in 1954. But in 1975, after a civil war, it became a COMMUNIST REPUBLIC.

Cambodia

Cambodia is now officially called Democratic Kampuchea. Most people are farmers. RICE and RUBBER are the main crops.

A civil war in the early 1970s did much damage. It ended when a COMMUNIST REPUBLIC was set up in 1975. Cambodia became an ally of CHINA. In 1979 Cambodia's government was overthrown. It was replaced by a government friendly to Vietnam and the U.S.S.R.

Vietnam	Laos	Cambodia
47,150,000	2,900,000	8,000,000
329,566	235,700	181,000
Hanoi	Vientiane	Phnom Penh

China

China has more people than any other country. It lies in eastern ASIA and is the third largest country in the world (after the U.S.S.R. and CANADA). High MOUNTAINS and vast DESERTS cover the west and north of China, and winters can be bitterly cold. But the coastal plains and inland river valleys, especially those of the Hwang Ho, Yangtze, and Si Kiang, which lie to the east and south, have a warm, moist climate. These regions are the most thickly populated parts of the country.

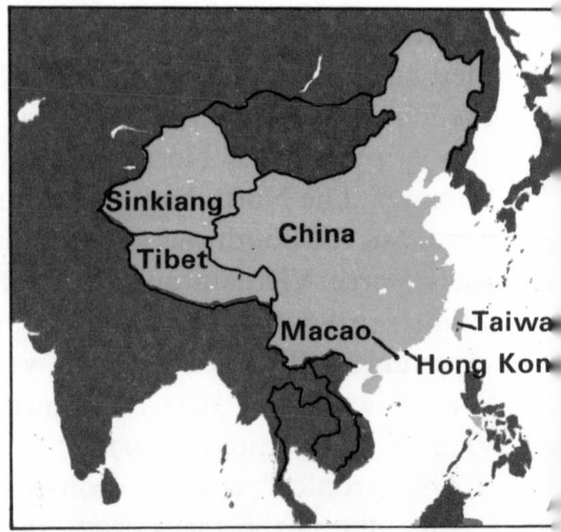

The people work hard to farm the land in order to feed the very large population. RICE and WHEAT are the main crops. Industry is also important in China. IRON and steel are made in the large cities in the north-east, and textiles are made in the east. Many Chinese industries and FACTORIES are very small.

There have been several great civilizations in China. The CHINESE have made many important inventions and Chinese art is world famous. Between about 1800 and 1945, foreign traders and invaders from the West and from JAPAN made a lot of money out of China but left the people poor. After WORLD WAR II there was a civil war. COMMUNIST forces, led by MAO TSE-TUNG, won.

In 1949 they took control of all China except the island of Taiwan. Under communist rule, the government owns all the land, factories, and mines. The communists have concentrated on increasing food production. They have set up many communes, which are groups of villages

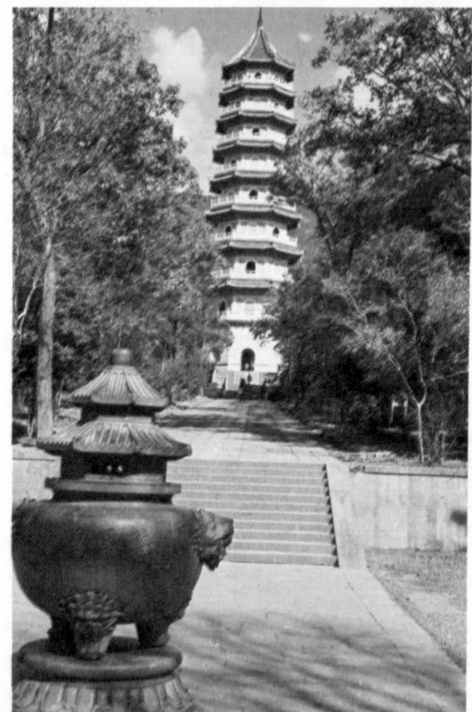

Above: A pagoda, which is an old temple or shrine, near Nanking, in China.

	China	Hong Kong	Macao	Taiwan
Population	1,008,000,000	4,500,000	260,000	16,290,000
Area (sq. km.)	9,597,000	1,046	16	35,981
Capital	PEKING	Victoria	Macao	Taipei

Above: Thousands of people live on boats like these in Hong Kong Harbour.
Below: Taroko Gorge in Taiwan.

where the people work together. They have also developed manufacturing and mining industries. In recent years, China has not been on good terms with the other great communist power, the U.S.S.R.

The Chinese language has many dialects. The one most widely spoken is Mandarin Chinese. Chinese is written with picture symbols instead of letters. Anyone who wishes to read has to learn at least 1000 symbols, or 'characters'. A way of writing Chinese with our Roman alphabet has been invented to help teach Chinese.

Hong Kong

Hong Kong is a prosperous British colony which occupies a peninsula and some offshore islands in southern CHINA. It has many industries and is a major PORT with a deep harbour. Hong Kong's products are sold all over the world. Most of the people are CHINESE, and Hong Kong is one of the world's most thickly populated places. To house many people in this small area many high blocks of flats have been built.

Macao

Macao is a tiny Portuguese territory near HONG KONG on the southern coast of CHINA. It has been ruled by Portugal since 1557. It is a trading and tourist centre. Most people are CHINESE.

Taiwan

Taiwan, once called Formosa, is a large island off China. Nationalist Chinese, who had fought against the COMMUNISTS for control of the mainland, made it their home in 1949. Taiwan is officially called the Republic of CHINA. It represented China in the UNITED NATIONS until 1971, when Communist China took over. The communists claim control over Taiwan.

Mongolia

Mongolia is a large country that lies between CHINA and the U.S.S.R. It has high MOUNTAINS and DESERT to the north and west, and grassy plains to the east. Most Mongolians are herdsmen who roam the plains with their CAMELS, SHEEP, CATTLE, and GOATS. There is some industry, which is mostly based on animal products, such as hides.

Left: Shepherds in the Gobi Desert, Mongolia.
Below left: Bulguk-sa Temple, the oldest in Korea.

In the 1200s Mongolia was the centre of a vast empire that stretched from China across ASIA to EUROPE. GENGHIS KHAN built this empire, but it did not last very long. Today, Mongolia has a COMMUNIST government.

Korea

Korea occupies a peninsula (neck of land) jutting into the sea from north-east CHINA. After WORLD WAR II, U.S. and Russian forces freed the country from the JAPANESE. They divided Korea into two parts: South Korea and North Korea.

	Mongolia	North Korea	South Korea	Japan
Population	1,500,000	16,000,000	34,709,000	113,086,000
Area (sq. km.)	1,565,000	122,370	98,447	372,480
Capital	Ulan Bator	Pyongyang	SEOUL	TOKYO

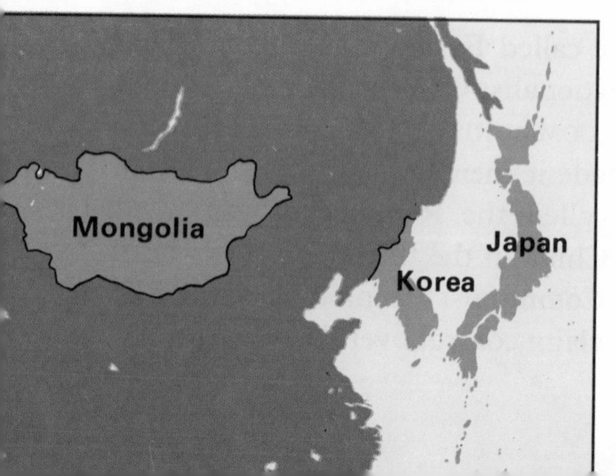

From 1950 to 1953 the two nations fought one another to control the peninsula. A truce was finally agreed, however, and the two remain separate. South Korea is a REPUBLIC governed by a PRESIDENT and a PARLIAMENT. North Korea has a COMMUNIST government.

Most of the people are farmers but industry has progressed greatly in recent years.

Japan

Japan occupies four large ISLANDS and several small ones off the eastern coast of ASIA. The biggest island is Honshu, and all Japan's large cities are on this island. The islands are mountainous. There is little farmland and few minerals.

In spite of this lack of resources, Japan is now one of the world's richest nations. The JAPANESE have made their country into a leading industrial nation during this century alone. Japanese products, such as cameras and TELEVISION sets, are famous throughout the world.

Japanese people are formal and courteous. Their old buildings and ceremonies are very beautiful. But the rapid growth of industry has caused much POLLUTION.

Japan is governed by a PARLIAMENT. The Emperor is head of state. The people speak Japanese, which is written with picture symbols.

Above: A cable car near Lake Kawaguchi in Japan.
Below: The magnificent Tōdaiji Temple at Nara in Japan.

Africa

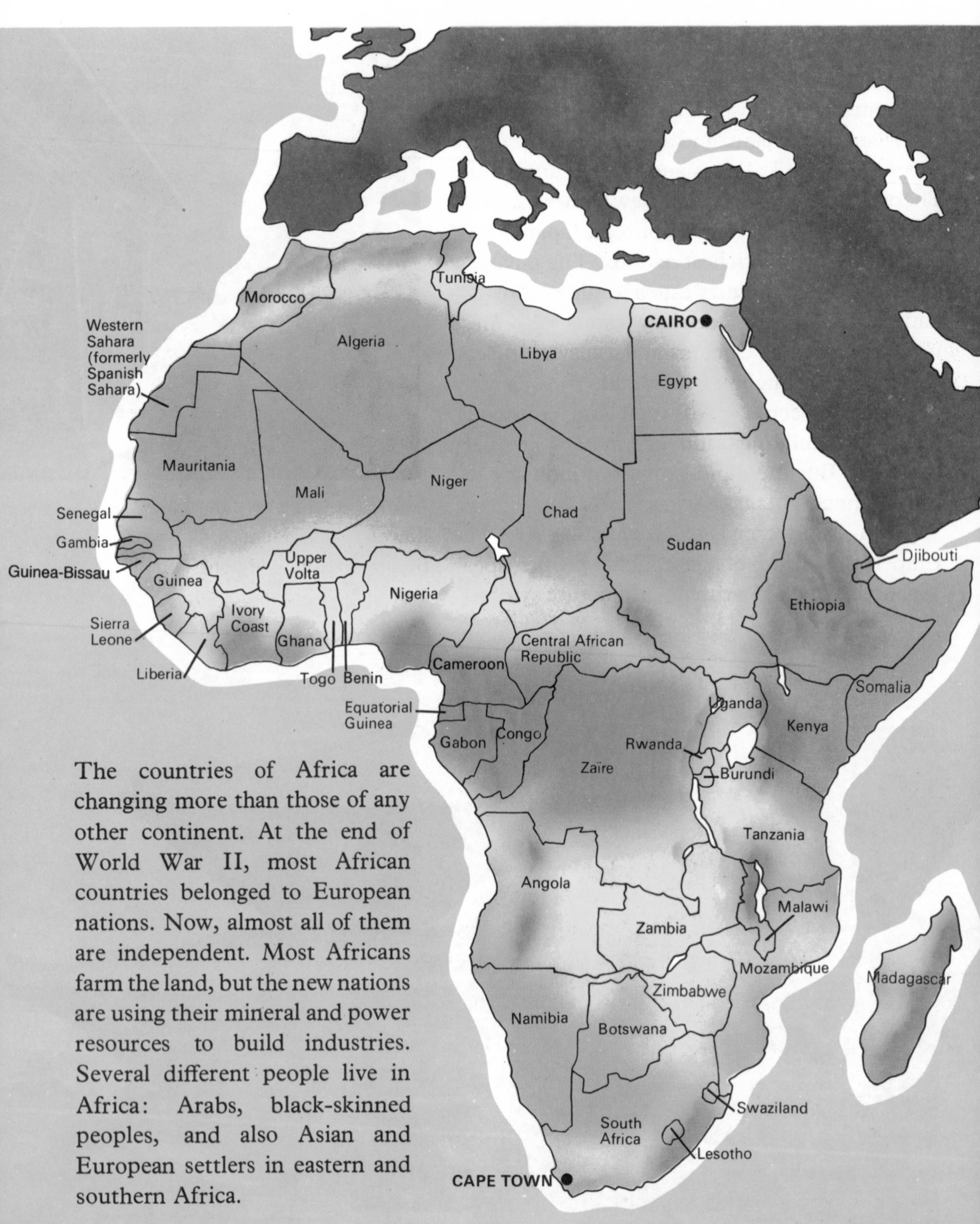

The countries of Africa are changing more than those of any other continent. At the end of World War II, most African countries belonged to European nations. Now, almost all of them are independent. Most Africans farm the land, but the new nations are using their mineral and power resources to build industries. Several different people live in Africa: Arabs, black-skinned peoples, and also Asian and European settlers in eastern and southern Africa.

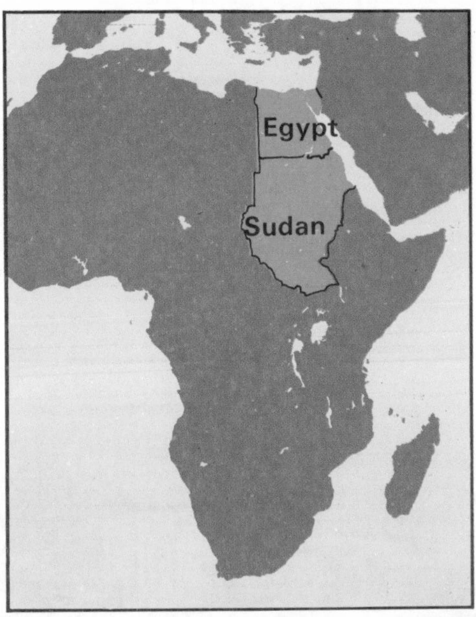

Below: The ancient temples of Abu Simbel lie beside Lake Nasser. Bottom: The palace at Khartoum, capital of the Sudan.

Egypt

Egypt lies in the north-east corner of AFRICA. It is a hot DESERT country. Most people live in the VALLEY of the River Nile, where the land is fertile. They have small farms, and the main crops are COTTON and RICE. Hydro-electric power from the Aswan High Dam across the Nile will help to build industry in Egypt. The ruins of ancient Egypt, such as the PYRAMIDS, the Sphinx, and the tombs of the pharaohs, attract many tourists.

Egypt is an ARAB country and the people speak Arabic. Egypt was for a long time in dispute with ISRAEL. In 1967, Egypt lost the Sinai peninsula to Israel. The SUEZ CANAL runs between the peninsula and the rest of Egypt. Egypt regained some territory in Sinai in the 1973 Arab-Israeli war. In 1977–9 Egypt and Israel negotiated a peace treaty. But other Arab nations did not join in the negotiations. Egypt is governed by a PRESIDENT and PARLIAMENT.

	Egypt	Sudan
Population	39,000,000	17,000,000
Area (sq. km.)	1,000,000	2,500,000
Capital	CAIRO	Khartoum

Sudan

The Sudan lies to the south of EGYPT. It is the largest country in AFRICA. The north is DESERT, but there are GRASSLANDS in the south. The people live by farming, and MILLET and COTTON are the main crops. The Nile and its tributaries flow across the Sudan, producing fertile land in some places and SWAMPS in others.

ARABS live in the north and black peoples in the south. They fought a CIVIL WAR between 1964 and 1972. The country is governed by a PRESIDENT and PARLIAMENT.

Libya

Libya lies along the MEDITERRANEAN SEA between EGYPT and TUNISIA. There is fertile land near the COAST and at oases inland, but most of the country is DESERT. Ancient Roman towns still stand there, preserved in the dry heat. Most Libyans are farmers. They grow MAIZE, olives, and dates. OIL was discovered in the 1960s. Libya now earns a great deal of money by selling oil to other countries.

Libya, an ARAB country, was governed by a king until 1969. Then a group of army officers removed the king from power. Libya is now ruled by the General Secretariat of the General People's Congress. Because of its new wealth, Libya has become a major Arab power.

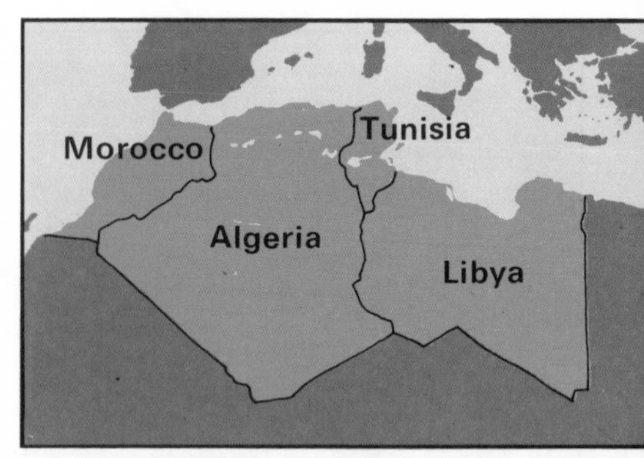

Right: A view of Tripoli, Libya.
Below right: The National Assembly (formerly a royal palace) at Tunis.

Tunisia

Tunisia is situated on the MEDITERRANEAN SEA between LIBYA and ALGERIA. The ATLAS mountains extend into northern Tunisia. RIVERS run from the MOUNTAINS to the sea, and the COAST has a Mediterranean climate with wet winters and dry summers. Most people are farmers or herdsmen. Mining is also important and there is some OIL. The southern part of the country beyond the mountains extends into the Sahara DESERT.

Tunisia is an ARAB country. Until 1956 it was a colony of FRANCE. It is now an independent REPUBLIC governed by a PARLIAMENT.

	Libya	Tunisia	Algeria	Morocco
Population	2,630,000	5,770,000	17,000,000	17,826,000
Area (sq. km.)	1,759,540	164,150	2,381,745	659,670
Capital	Tripoli	Tunis	Algiers	Rabat

Algeria

Algeria lies along the COAST of North AFRICA between TUNISIA and MOROCCO. It is the second largest country in Africa. (The largest is the SUDAN.) Most of Algeria is in the Sahara DESERT.

Groups of nomads (wandering herdsmen) with their CAMELS and other LIVESTOCK roam the desert. Most of Algeria's people live along the coast and farm for a living. They grow MAIZE, and grapes for making wine. Deposits of OIL and NATURAL GAS have been found in the desert.

Most Algerians are ARABS and follow the religion of ISLAM. Algeria was once a colony of FRANCE. The Algerians fought a long war with France to gain independence. When it was granted in 1962, most of the French settlers left. Algeria is now governed by a revolutionary council and a PARLIAMENT.

Above: An oasis in the Sahara desert, Algeria.
Below: Moroccans barter at a market near Marrakesh.

Morocco

Morocco lies in the north-west corner of AFRICA. Its COAST borders the MEDITERRANEAN SEA and the ATLANTIC OCEAN. The ATLAS Mountains cross Morocco from east to west. The land near the sea is fertile, and most Moroccans live there and farm the land. There are rich mineral deposits.

The land on the other side of the Atlas mountains is part of the Sahara DESERT. Three main groups of people live in Morocco. The Berbers are mostly mountain herdsmen. The ARABS and the Moors (descendants of Arabs and Berbers) live on the coastal plains.

Arabic is the official language of Morocco. Many people speak French or Spanish. Morocco is a MONARCHY, governed by PARLIAMENT. The country's area was increased in the late 1970s when Morocco occupied Western (formerly Spanish) Sahara. But some Saharans have fought against the occupation of their country.

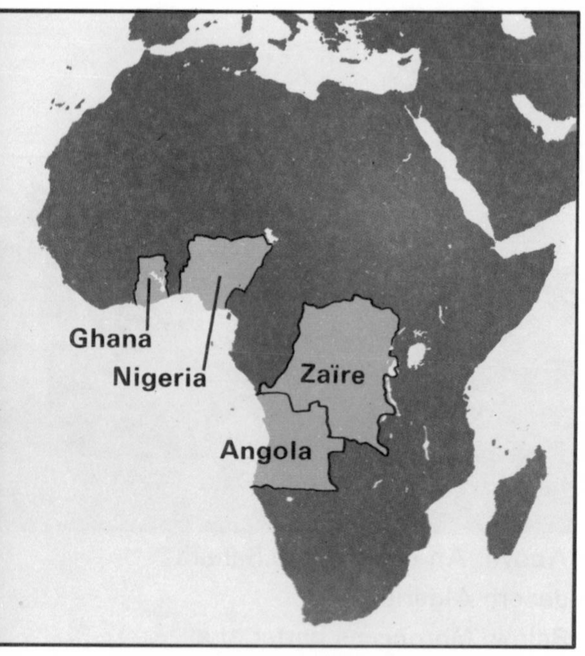

Below: The hospital at Kumasi, which is the second largest city in Ghana.

Ghana

Ghana lies in western AFRICA and borders the Gulf of Guinea. The country is low-lying and covered with forest and GRASSLAND. Most people are farmers, and COCOA and cassava are the main crops. Fishing is important along the coast.

A great DAM has been built across the River Volta in Ghana to create a LAKE 400 kilometres long. The water from the lake is used to irrigate dry land. Hydro-electric power from the dam is helping to build up Ghana's industries especially the manufacture of ALUMINIUM.

Most of the people of Ghana are black. There are several different tribes and languages. Ghana was once a British colony. It was called the Gold Coast, because gold was mined there. In 1957 Ghana became independent. Since then it has had different forms of government. At times, as in 1972, the army has taken control. At present, Ghana is governed by a council of army officers. Ghana is a member of the COMMONWEALTH.

Nigeria

Nigeria is in western AFRICA. It gets its name from the River Niger which flows through the country to the Gulf of Guinea. The country is low-lying in the south, rising to a plateau in the north. There are mangrove SWAMPS along the coast. Inland there are forests and GRASSLANDS. Most of the people are farmers. There is some industry based on timber and animal products. Nigeria is now Africa's leading OIL producer. Profits from oil sales are being used to develop the country, which is changing quickly.

Most Nigerians are black. There are about 250 different groups of people and languages, but English is the official language. Before independence in 1960, Nigeria was a British colony.

In 1967 the people of eastern Nigeria tried to break away from Nigeria and set up an independent nation called Biafra. There was a war, and in 1970 Nigeria regained control. Nigeria had a military government in 1966–79. The army took over again in December 1983.

Left: The market place at Ibadan, Nigeria.

Zaïre

Zaïre (pronounced Za-eer) is the third largest country in AFRICA. It is in the central part of the continent. Zaïre has a tropical climate, and dense rain forest covers most of the land. Palm trees are grown for their oil, and RUBBER, COFFEE, and TIMBER are other agricultural products. Zaïre is also rich in minerals, particularly COPPER, which is mined in Shaba. Most of the people are black, and many speak Swahili.

Zaïre was a colony of BELGIUM until 1960. It was called the Republic of the Congo until 1971. Zaïre is a REPUBLIC governed by a PARLIAMENT. There is only one POLITICAL PARTY.

Above: A fabric shop in Zaïre.

	Ghana	Nigeria	Zaire	Angola
Population	9,600,000	73,000,000	25,600,000	5,673,000
Area (sq. km.)	238,305	923,773	2,345,409	1,246,700
Capital	Accra	Lagos	Kinshasa	Luanda

Angola

Angola lies south of ZAIRE in south-central AFRICA, and has a long coast on the ATLANTIC OCEAN. Almost all of Angola is a high forested plateau. Most of the people are black and work on the land. Angola was a Portuguese territory until 1975. A short civil war followed independence and most Europeans left the country.

Left: A rocky landscape in Angola.

South Africa

South Africa, at the southern tip of AFRICA, is made up of a high plateau edged with higher mountains and a coastal plain. Many rivers, such as the Orange River, have been dammed up to provide water for farming and for electricity.

It is warm on the east coast where sugar and fruit are grown. On the grassland plateau MAIZE and cattle are farmed. Because the west has less rain, some parts are almost desert. The south-west coast is important for fruit and wool.

Gold, diamonds, iron, uranium and platinum are mined. South Africa's income comes from the industries and from her agriculture.

South Africa has four provinces, the Transvaal, the Cape, the Orange Free State, and Natal. The country is governed by a PARLIAMENT with a PRESIDENT as head of state.

The two official languages are English and Afrikaans. The black, or Bantu, people have their own languages. Many black people live in special areas called Homelands. By 1984 four of these Homelands had been recognized as independent by South Africa. But over half of the black people live in European areas.

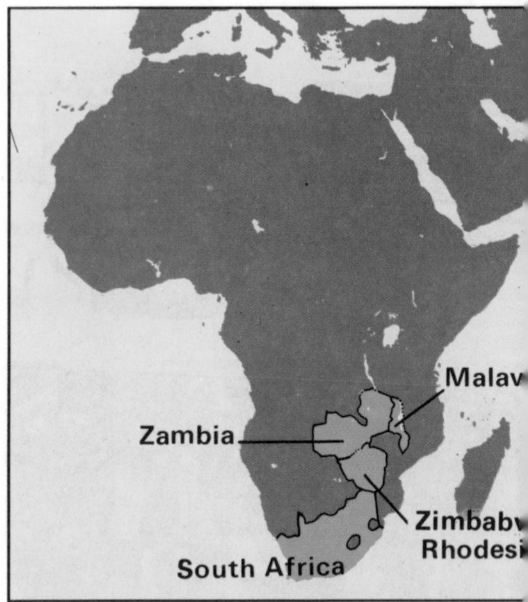

Above: Mountains in South Africa.

	South Africa	Zimbabwe	Zambia	Malawi
Population	21,402,000	6,530,000	5,138,000	5,310,000
Area (sq. km.)	1,221,042	390,622	752,620	118,036
Capital	Pretoria, Cape Town	Harare	Lusaka	Lilongwe

Zimbabwe

Zimbabwe, formerly called Rhodesia, is a grass-covered, plateau country between ZAMBIA and SOUTH AFRICA. The people are mainly black. The country is a REPUBLIC governed by a PARLIAMENT. In 1965 the country, which was

Right: Johannesburg, South Africa.

then ruled by European settlers, declared its independence from Britain. Britain and other nations stopped trading with the country to try to force it to change its policies.

In 1979 a new government headed by a black PRIME MINISTER came to power. This government negotiated a return to British rule in late 1979, leading to independence in 1980.

Zambia

Zambia, in central AFRICA, to the north of Zimbabwe, became independent from Britain in 1964. The name 'Zambia' comes from the Zambezi River which flows along the country's southern border. On the river are the Victoria Falls and the Kariba Dam, which Zambia shares with Zimbabwe. Hydro-electricity from the Dam powers Zambia's industries. Mining is the leading activity and there are large copper deposits. But most people are farmers.

Zambia is independent, and is governed by a PARLIAMENT with only one political party. The PRESIDENT is head of state.

Above left: Victoria Falls on the River Zambezi, which separates Zambia and Zimbabwe.

Malawi

Malawi is a tropical country and lies between ZAMBIA and Lake Malawi, which is one of the Great Rift Valley Lakes. Most of the people are black and farm with crops like MAIZE and sorghum. The important cash crops are tea, COTTON, and tobacco. There is little industry.

The government of Malawi is similar to that of Zambia. Like Zambia, Malawi has a PRESIDENT. It is also a member of the COMMONWEALTH.

Left: Main Street, Blantyre, Malawi.

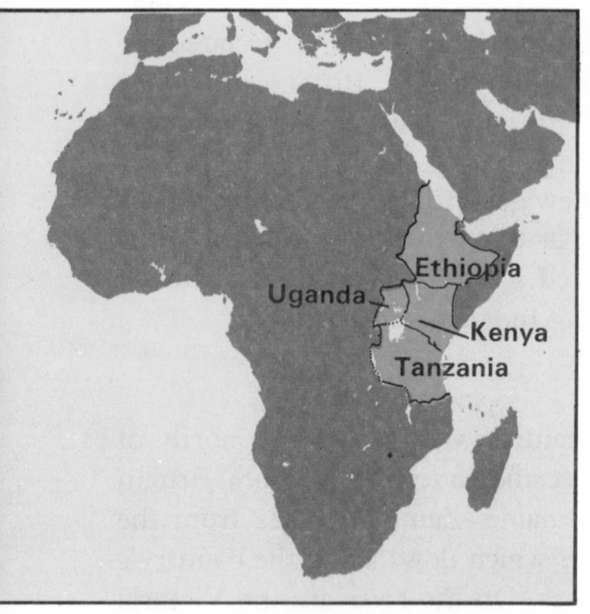

Below: A street in Zanzibar, an island off the mainland of Tanzania.
Bottom: Women watching a tribal hunt in Uganda.

Tanzania

Tanzania lies in eastern AFRICA between Lake Tanganyika and the INDIAN OCEAN. Most of the land is a high, grassy plateau where animals such as ELEPHANTS, GIRAFFES, and lions roam.

Most of the people are black and speak Swahili, but there is also a large Asian population and some ARABS and people of European descent. Most of the people farm the land or keep CATTLE.

Tanzania used to be a British colony called Tanganyika. It gained independence in 1961. In 1964 the offshore ISLAND of Zanzibar joined Tanganyika and the country was renamed Tanzania. The head of state is the PRESIDENT. All the people may vote, but there is only one POLITICAL PARTY. Tanzania is now a member of the COMMONWEALTH.

Uganda

Uganda lies in central AFRICA. Part of the country borders Lake Victoria, Africa's largest LAKE. The land is mainly GRASSLAND, and most people are farmers. COFFEE and COTTON are the most important crops. Mining, particularly of COPPER, is also important. Most of the people are black. Swahili and English are spoken.

Uganda was a British colony until 1962 when it gained independence. The country was then ruled by a military government which expelled most of the Asians who once lived in Uganda. It said that they had too much influence in the country. In 1979 Ugandan rebels backed by TANZANIA invaded and overthrew the PRESIDENT.

	Tanzania	Uganda
Population	15,000,000	11,172,000
Area (sq. km.)	945,578	236,860
Capital	Dodoma	Kampala

Kenya

Kenya lies between UGANDA and the INDIAN OCEAN. Wild animals roam the high grassy plains, and there are many LAKES and MOUNTAINS. Mount Kilimanjaro, Africa's highest mountain, is on the southern border with TANZANIA. There are several national parks, where wildlife is protected. Most of the people are farmers, and COFFEE is a major crop.

Most of the people are black and there are several tribes. They speak Swahili or English. There are also some ARABS as well as people of Asian and European descent. Kenya was a British colony before it became an independent country in 1963. There was fighting before independence, but now the people of Kenya live peacefully together. The PRESIDENT is head of state. Kenya is a member of the COMMONWEALTH.

Above: The market at Nairobi.
Below: Camels carrying loads of salt to market in Ethiopia.

Ethiopia

Ethiopia is a mountainous country bordering the SUDAN, KENYA, and the Red Sea. No other country in AFRICA is so rugged. The scenery and the unusual wildlife attract many visitors. Most Ethiopians are farmers. COFFEE is the most important crop. There is little industry.

Several different peoples live in Ethiopia. Some are black, but others are descended from people of western ASIA. Many are of mixed descent. The official language is Amharic.

Ethiopia was once named Abyssinia. It was ruled by Emperor Haile Selassie until 1974, when the armed forces took power and removed the Emperor.

	Kenya	Ethiopia
Population	13,800,000	29,416,000
Area (sq. km.)	582,600	1,000,000
Capital	Nairobi	Addis Ababa

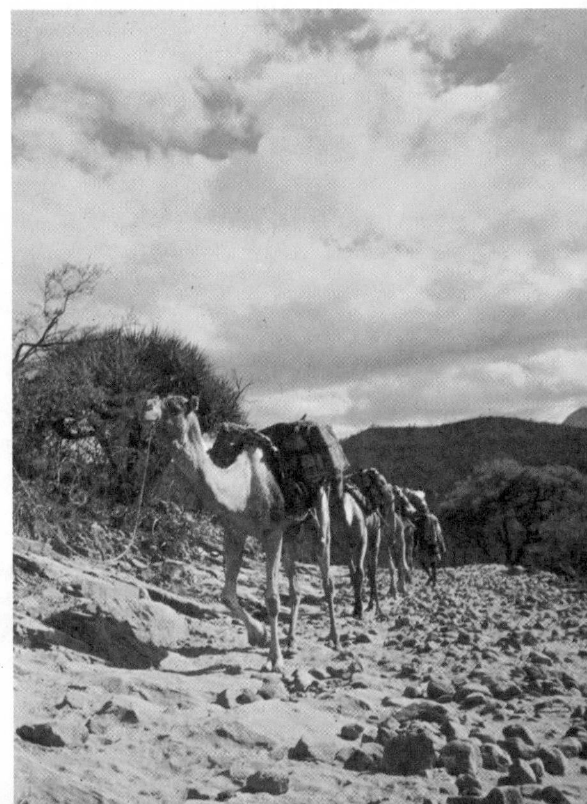

The Americas

The Americas range from the icy wastes of the Arctic to the cool lands of Tierra del Fuego near the ANTARCTIC. The Americas are sometimes called the New World, because they were not known to Europeans until the late fifteenth century.

There are two main parts, NORTH AMERICA and SOUTH AMERICA. Central America is the name sometimes given to the southern part of North America from MEXICO to Panama. Central America is made up of eight nations, including Mexico.

People of European origin have settled in the Americas, and in most cases govern the countries. They outnumber the original people, the AMERICAN INDIANS and ESKIMOS. British and French people occupied North America, and Spanish and Portuguese settlers came to Central and South America.

Because the Spanish and Portuguese are among the MEDITERRANEAN peoples called Latins, the parts of America which they colonized are known as Latin America.

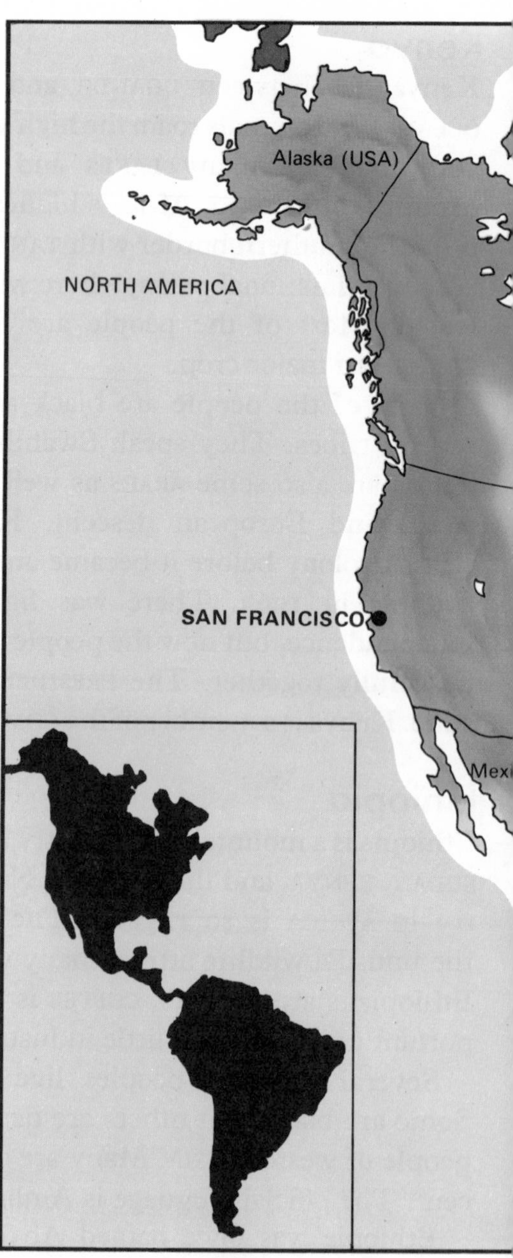

Left: The town of Skagway, Alaska, was built at the time of Klondike Gold Rush of 1897–1898. The buildings are preserved just as they were during this period.
Right: Gardens in Caracas, capital of Venezuela.

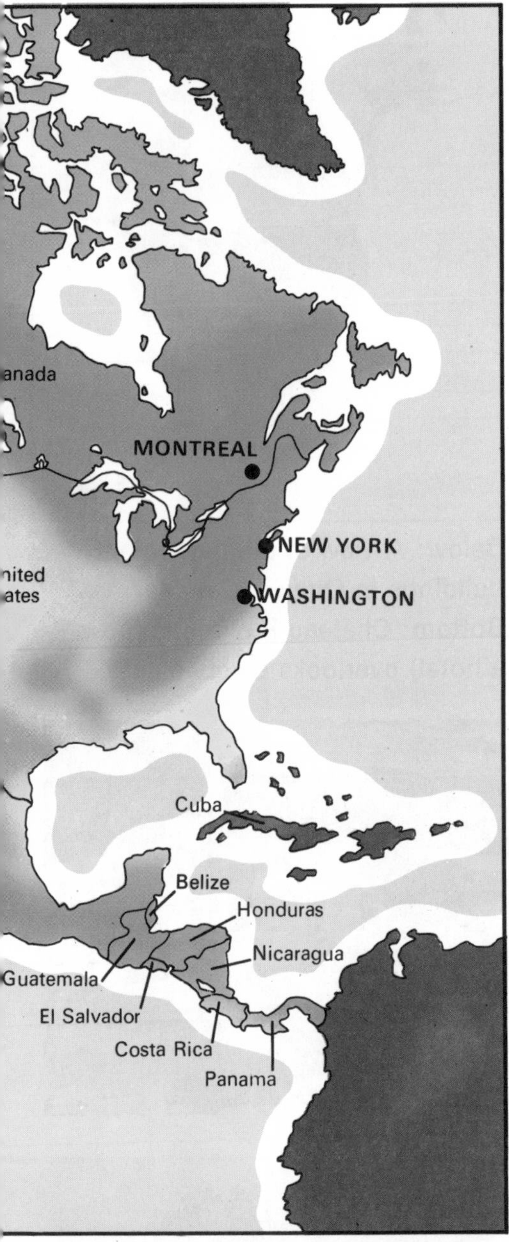

Above: Puerto Montt lies in southern Chile at the end of the great Pan-American Highway.

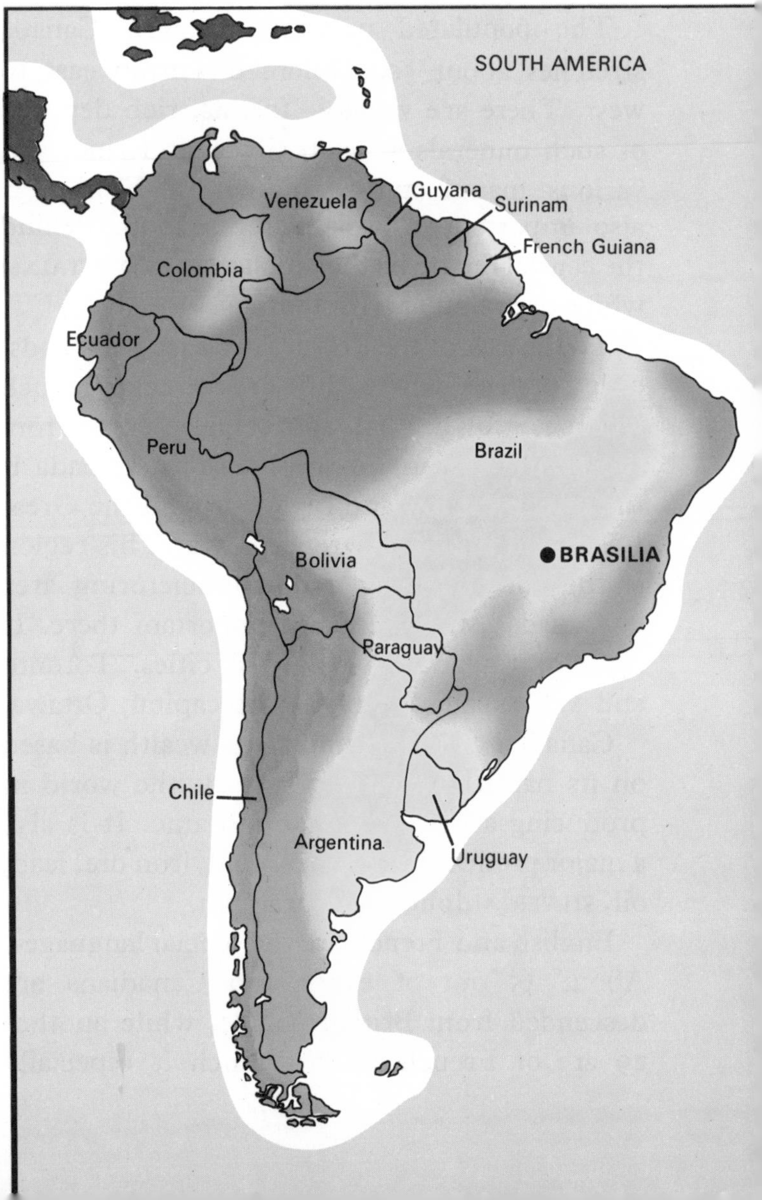

Canada

Canada is the second largest country in the world after the U.S.S.R., but it is thinly populated. Most Canadians live in the south, within about 500 kilometres of the border with the United States.

The far north of Canada lies within the Arctic Circle, where winters are long and bitterly cold. In this region, called the TUNDRA, it is too cold for trees to grow. ESKIMOS live in the Arctic north. South of the tundra is a vast region covered by forests and huge LAKES.

The populated part of southern Canada stretches about 5000 kilometres from east to west. There are valuable forests, rich deposits of such minerals as lead, silver, and zinc, and various manufacturing industries. Fishing is also important, especially for salmon. Behind the coastal region lie the high ROCKY MOUNTAINS, which are popular with tourists.

To the east of the Rockies are vast grasslands, called prairies, where cattle are reared and much wheat is grown. COAL and OIL also come from the prairie region. In south-eastern Canada is the important lowland region around the Great Lakes and the St Lawrence River. This region is the chief farming and manufacturing area in Canada; MINING is also important there. It contains Canada's two largest cities, Toronto and MONTREAL, as well as the capital, Ottawa.

Canada is a rich country. Its wealth is based on its natural resources. It leads the world in producing asbestos, nickel and zinc. It is also a major producer of copper, gold, iron ore, lead, oil, SILVER, sulphur, and uranium.

English and French are the official languages. About 45 out of every 100 Canadians are descended from British people, while another 29 are of French stock. French is especially

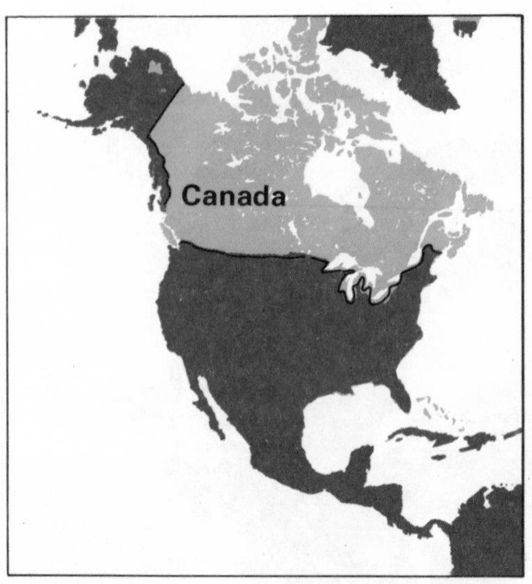

Below: A view of the parliament buildings in Ottawa, Canada. Bottom: Chateau Frontenac (now a hotel) overlooks Quebec.

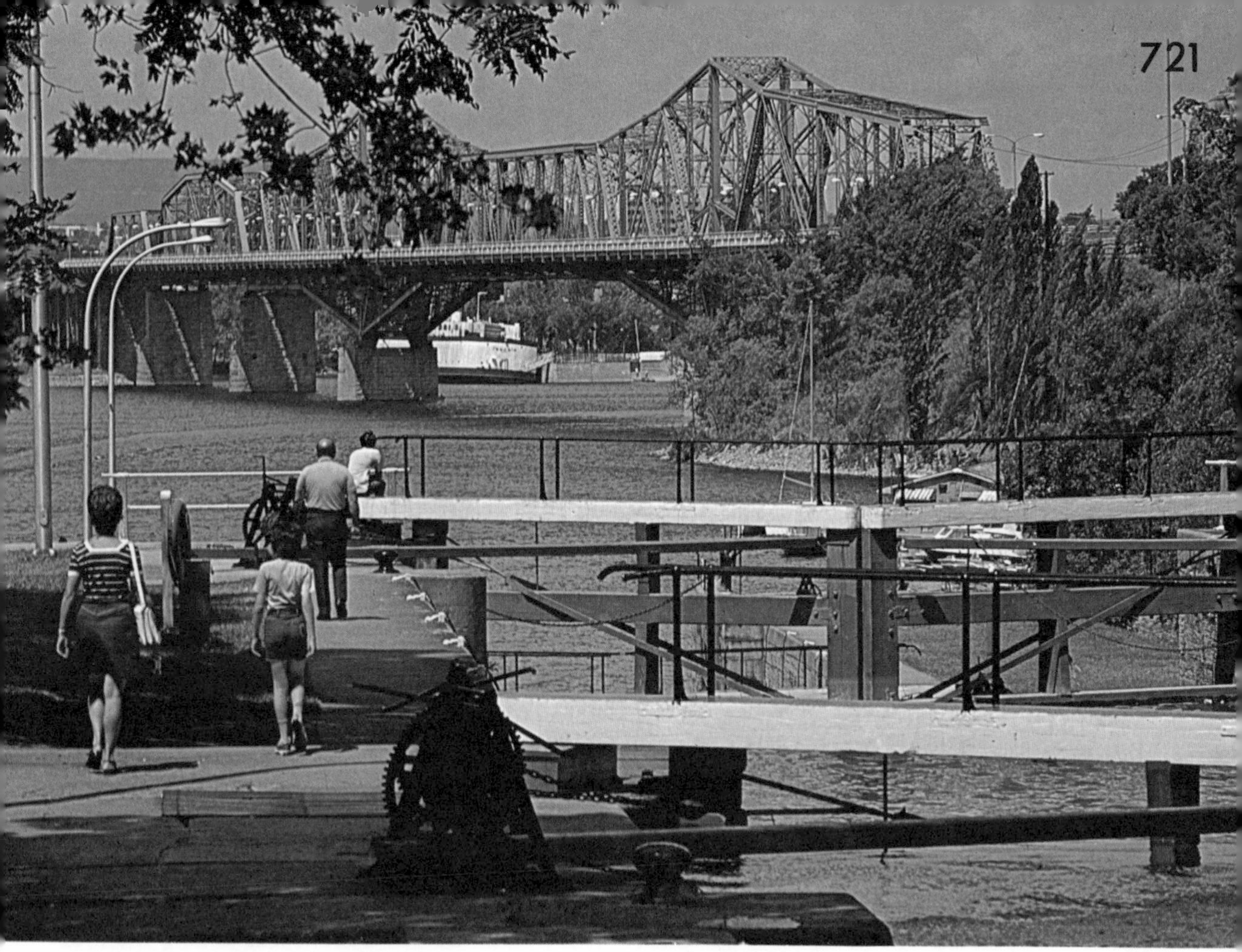

important in Quebec, Canada's largest province, where about 80 out of every 100 people speak French. Some people in Quebec would like to set up their own country.

The country is divided into ten provinces and two thinly populated territories. Each province and territory has its own government. Canada also has a central government, with a PARLIAMENT and a prime minister at its head.

Above: The Alexander Bridge in Ottawa.
Right: A view of Montreal.

	Canada
Population	24,343,000
Area (sq. km.)	9,976,140
Capital	Ottawa

U.S.A.

The United States of America is the richest country in the world. It is also the fourth largest after the U.S.S.R., Canada, and China. The U.S.A. has huge resources of minerals and fuels, which are supplied to the manufacturing industries. The U.S.A. is the world's most industrialized nation, but there are also enormous areas of fertile farmland.

The U.S.A. is a varied country. It includes icy Arctic wastelands in Alaska, barren deserts in the south-west, and sunny beaches in Florida. There are high mountain ranges, deep valleys, such as the scenic Grand Canyon in Arizona, and great inland prairies.

Thousands of years ago there were probably no people in the Americas. Then the ancestors of the American Indians came from northern Asia. They spread slowly southwards throughout the Americas. The Eskimos, who were later arrivals also from Asia, stayed in the north. When European settlers began to colonize North America in the 1600s, most Indians were living as nomadic hunters. The settlers wanted to farm the land on which the Indians hunted.

Above: New Orleans in the deep south of the United States.
Below: Boston was among the first cities founded in the U.S.A.

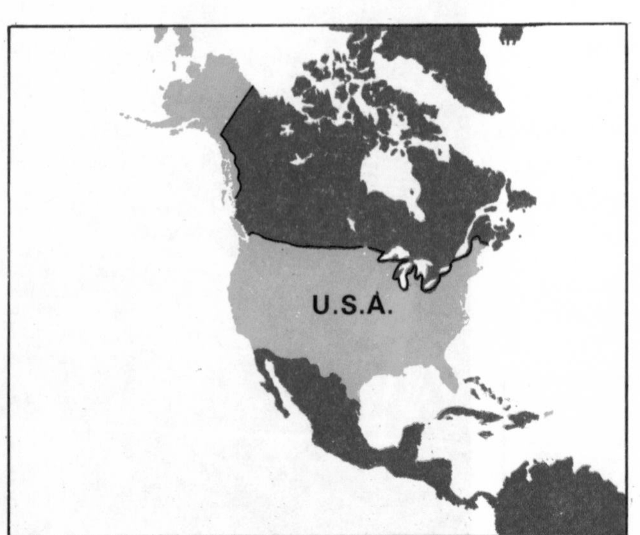

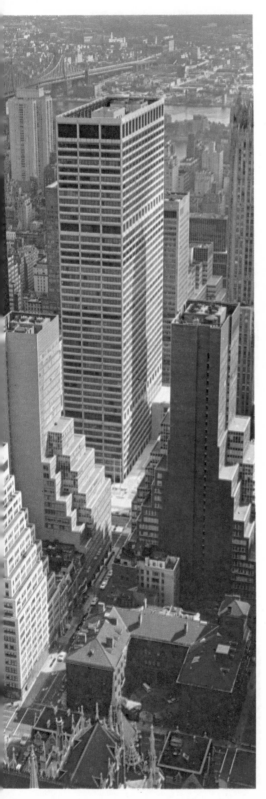

This clash of cultures led to many wars between the Indians and the white settlers. The settlers finally won and the U.S.A. now has about 600,000 Indians.

People of many races live in the U.S.A. About 87 out of every 100 people are of European origin. They are descended from European settlers who went to the U.S.A. often to escape war and famine. About 11 out of every 100 people are blacks.

The U.S.A. is a federal republic. It consists of 50 states and the small District of Columbia, in which the capital, Washington, is situated. Each of the states has its own government. The central government is headed by the president, who is elected to four-year terms. The national legislature is the Congress. It consists of the Senate and the House of Representatives.

	United States
Population	226,546,000
Area (sq. km.)	9,160,412
Capital	Washington D.C.

Left: A view of the skyscrapers in New York.
Below: Rounding up cattle in South Dakota.

Mexico

Mexico lies south of the U.S.A. between the PACIFIC OCEAN and the Gulf of Mexico. Much of the land is mountainous. Long MOUNTAIN ranges, called the east, west and south Sierra Madre, enclose a high plateau, where most Mexicans live. It is cooler there than in the low-lying coastal plains and the tropical lands to the south. About four out of every ten Mexicans are farmers. SILVER and COAL mining are the most valuable industries. There are also important oil deposits and oil is exported. Steel and textiles are the chief manufactured products.

There was a great Indian (AZTEC) civilization in Mexico before the Spaniards conquered the Indians in the early 1500s. Remains of Aztec temples and PYRAMIDS can still be seen. Spanish rule continued until 1822.

More than half of the people are of mixed Indian and European descent, three-tenths are Indians, and most others are of pure European origin. Indian languages are spoken, but Spanish is the official language. Mexico is a REPUBLIC governed by a PARLIAMENT.

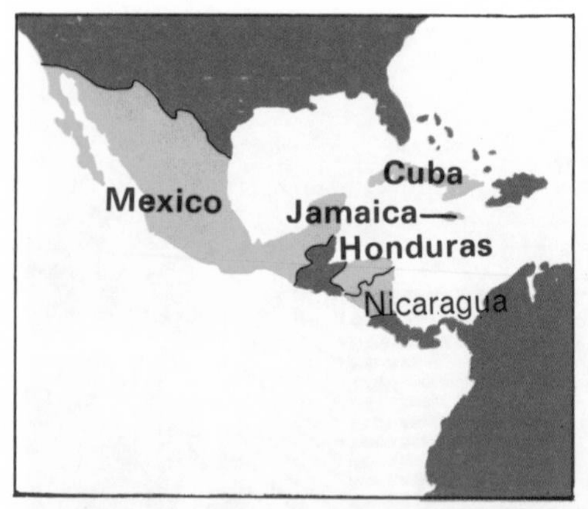

Above: A church in Mexico City, in the Spanish style.
Below: Cattle pulling a cart along the shore of Lake Nicaragua.

Nicaragua

Nicaragua is a Central American country with two coastlines, one facing the Caribbean Sea and the other the PACIFIC OCEAN. The tropical lowlands are separated by central highlands. Volcanic eruptions are common.

Most of the people are farmers living on the western lowlands. These contain two huge lakes, called Nicaragua and Managua. The most valuable products are COTTON, coffee, and sugar. Most of the people, who speak Spanish, are of mixed Indian and European descent, but one-tenth are blacks. Nicaragua is a REPUBLIC governed by a PARLIAMENT.

Jamaica

Jamaica is a beautiful, mountainous West Indian island which attracts many tourists. Most of the people are black, or of mixed black and European origin. Jamaica produces bauxite, which is used to make ALUMINIUM. Sugar-cane, bananas, and coffee are the most valuable crops. Jamaica is a member of the COMMONWEALTH and is ruled by a PARLIAMENT. The official language in the country is English.

Left: A beach on Montego Bay, Jamaica.

Above: Farming in Cuba.
Below: Havana, the modern city capital of Cuba.

Cuba

Cuba is the largest country in the West Indies. Fertile plains cover about half of the country. The rest is mountainous or hilly. Farming is the main activity and sugar-cane is the chief crop. Cuba was ruled by Spain until 1898. It then came under the influence of the U.S.A. In 1959 COMMUNIST forces seized power, and Cuba is now the only communist country in the Americas. It is a REPUBLIC with a PRESIDENT as head of state. Spanish is the official language.

Honduras

Honduras is a wedge-shaped Central American country north of NICARAGUA. It has a long coast bordering the Caribbean Sea, and a narrow outlet to the PACIFIC OCEAN through the Gulf of Fonseca. Most people are of mixed Indian and European origin. They speak Spanish. Bananas are the main export. Since 1972 Honduras has been governed by an army group.

	Mexico	Nicaragua	Jamaica	Cuba	Honduras
Population	62,329,000	2,253,000	2,085,000	9,470,000	3,036,000
Area (sq. km.)	1,972,546	148,000	10,991	114,524	112,088
Capital	Mexico City	Managua	Kingston	Havana	Tegucigalpa

Brazil

Brazil is the largest country in SOUTH AMERICA, and one of the largest in the world. The great Amazon River and its tributaries flow through the northern half of Brazil. In the south, the land rises to form the Brazilian Highlands. Most Brazilians live in this cooler region, particularly on the coast. Farming is important, and the main crops are COFFEE and COTTON. There are large mineral deposits and industry is developing rapidly. In 1960 the capital was moved from Rio de Janeiro to BRASILIA, in order to help develop the interior of the country.

Brazil was first settled by the Portuguese, and Portuguese is the main language. Many people are of European descent. There are also Indians and black people. Brazil is governed by a PARLIAMENT, and the PRESIDENT is head of state.

Colombia

Colombia is in the north-western corner of South America. It contains ranges of the high ANDES MOUNTAINS, surrounded by coastal lowlands to the west and north. The humid forests of the Amazon basin, to the east of the mountains, cover over half of the country. But most people live in the fertile mountain VALLEYS, which are much cooler than the lowlands. Farming is the main activity, and COFFEE, COTTON, and meat are leading exports. Emeralds are also exported, and mining and manufacturing are increasing rapidly.

The people are mostly of mixed Indian and European descent, but nearly 400 small Indian tribes live in the Amazon forests. Spanish is the official language. Colombia is a REPUBLIC.

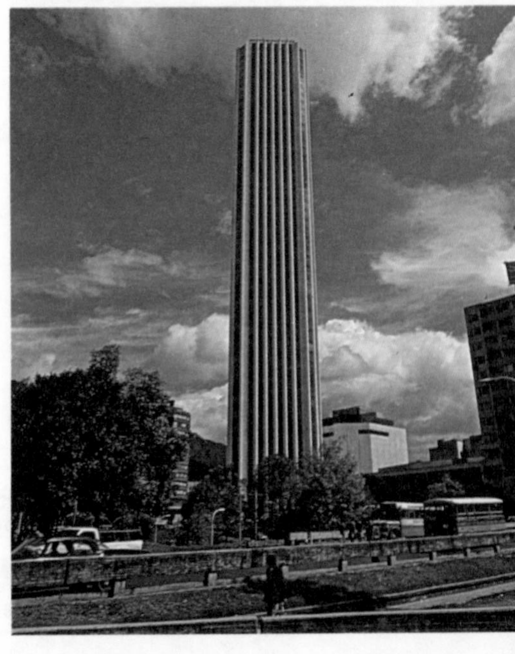

Above right: Rio de Janeiro in Brazil.
Right: Bogota, the capital of Colombia.

Peru

Peru lies along the PACIFIC coast of SOUTH AMERICA, west of BRAZIL and Bolivia. The ANDES MOUNTAINS rise behind a strip of DESERT along the COAST. Beyond the mountains there are vast forested plains. Most Peruvians live among the mountains and farm the land. Others live along the coast, where fishing is important. But mining is the most valuable industry.

Before the Spaniards conquered Peru, there was a great Indian (INCA) civilization there. Remains of the Indian cities can still be seen in the mountains. Today about half of the people are Indians. Most of the others are of mixed Indian and European descent. Spanish is the main language, but Indian languages are also widely spoken.

In 1968 the parliamentary government was overthrown by army officers. This group planned to restore civilian rule in 1980.

Above: The market place in the town of Cuzco, which lies high up among the Andes Mountains that cross Peru from north to south.

Below: A view of Buenos Aires, Argentina's capital and its largest city.

Argentina

Argentina is a large country in the south-eastern part of SOUTH AMERICA. There is forest to the north, and large grassy plains, called the pampas, in the centre. CATTLE and SHEEP graze the pampas in great herds. Most of Argentina's industry is based on animal products.

Argentina has few Indians. Most of the people are descended from the first Spanish settlers and from other European settlers. Spanish is the main language. In 1976 the President was overthrown by army officers. A general became PRESIDENT of the REPUBLIC.

	Brazil	Colombia	Peru	Argentina
Population	110,124,000	25,167,000	15,500,000	25,050,000
Area (sq. km.)	8,511,965	1,138,914	1,285,215	2,771,815
Capital	Brasilia	Bogotá	Lima	Buenos Aires

Australia and Oceania

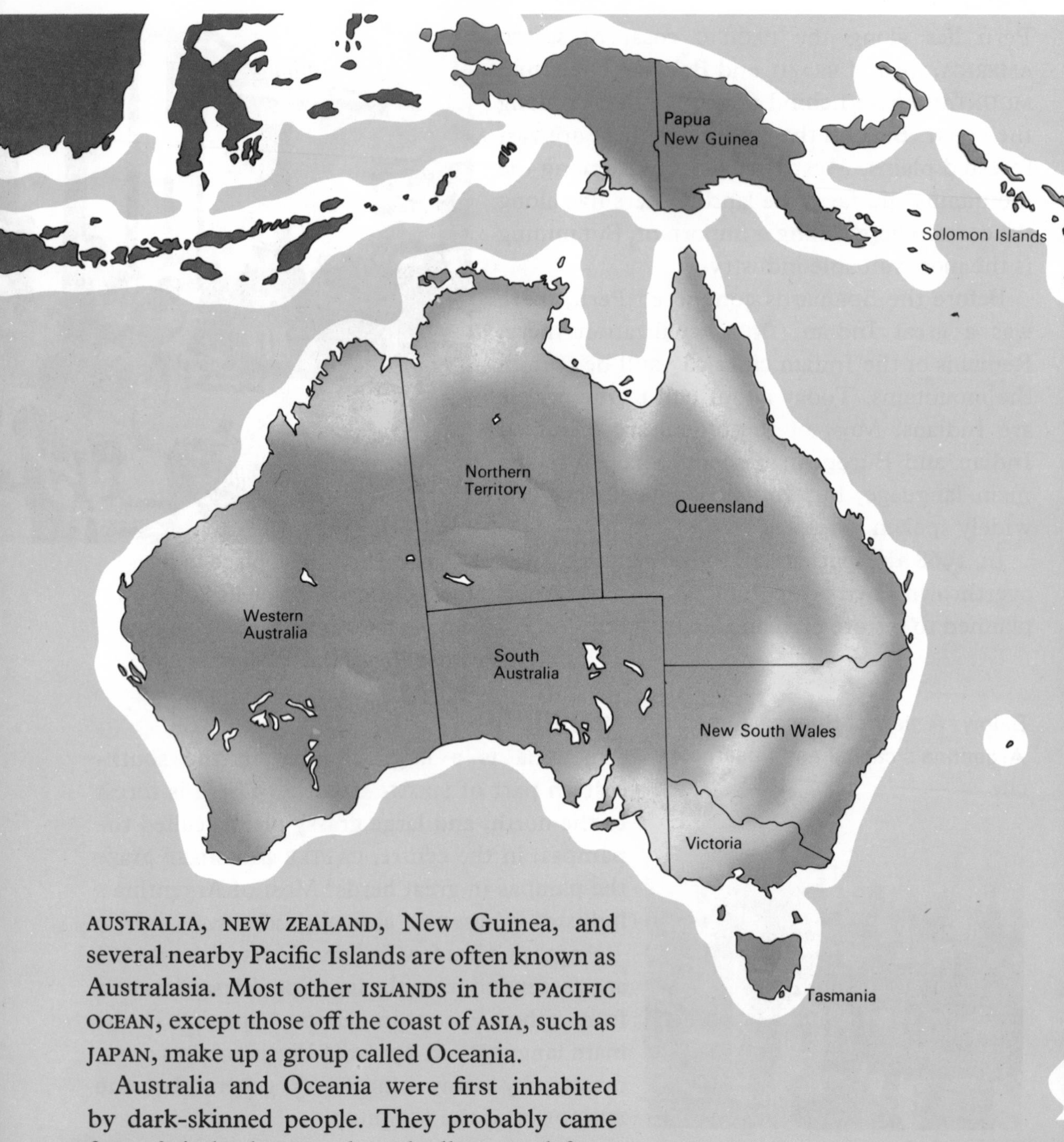

AUSTRALIA, NEW ZEALAND, New Guinea, and several nearby Pacific Islands are often known as Australasia. Most other ISLANDS in the PACIFIC OCEAN, except those off the coast of ASIA, such as JAPAN, make up a group called Oceania.

Australia and Oceania were first inhabited by dark-skinned people. They probably came from Asia by boat, and gradually spread from island to island. It is also possible that some islands in the middle of the Pacific Ocean were settled by people from SOUTH AMERICA. They could have drifted to the islands on rafts.

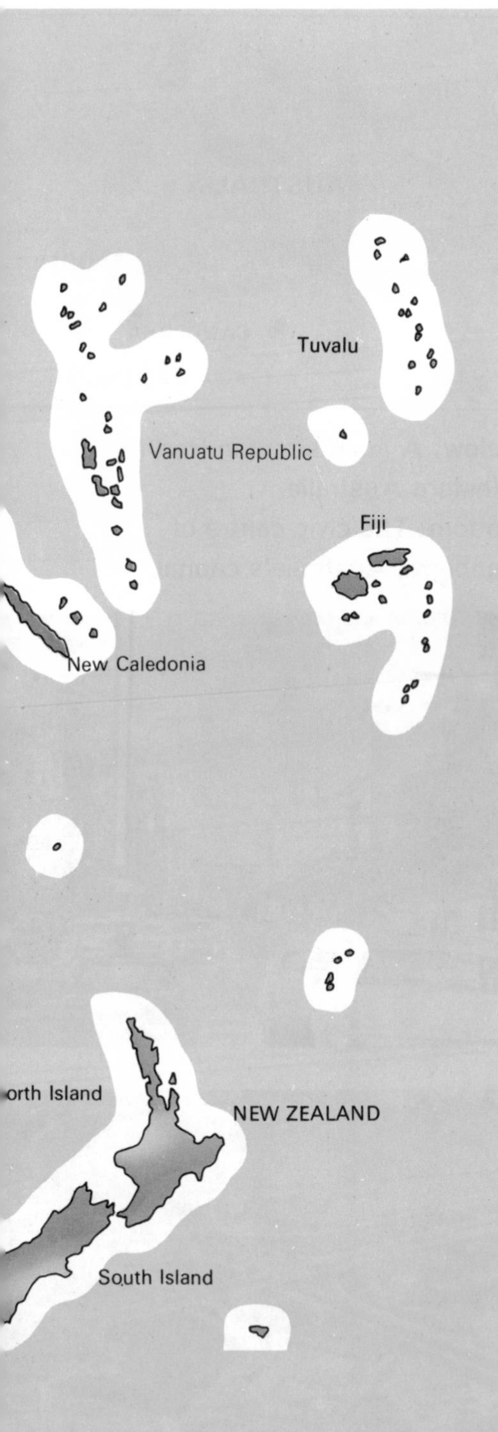

Australia is separated from other continents by water. As a result, many unusual animals live there which are not found anywhere else. They include marsupials (POUCHED MAMMALS) such as the kangaroo. There are also the duck-billed platypus, the kiwi, and the beautiful birds of paradise.

European explorers first came to the Pacific in the early seventeenth century. Australia and New Zealand became known in the eighteenth century and were later colonized by Europeans. The other islands attracted few colonists.

Oceania

There are thousands of small ISLANDS scattered throughout the PACIFIC OCEAN. Some of them are known as south sea islands. The islands are in the tropics and it is always warm. Many have sandy beaches lined with palm trees bearing coconuts. Hills or MOUNTAINS covered with dense forest often rise inland, and fruit trees grow along sheltered streams and VALLEYS. This kind of island is usually of volcanic origin. Volcanic SOIL is very fertile. Many other islands are ATOLLS or coral islands. They are small, flat islands.

Many of the islands of Oceania lie in long rows called archipelagoes. There are three main groups of islands – Melanesia, Micronesia, and Polynesia. Melanesia is in the south-west Pacific, Micronesia in the north-west, and Polynesia in the middle of the Pacific Ocean.

The people of each group of islands are slightly different. In Melanesia, which means black islands, the people are very dark. In Micronesia (meaning small islands) the people have features like those of the Chinese and Japanese. The people of Polynesia (many islands) have light brown skins and look a little like Europeans. The Maoris of NEW ZEALAND are POLYNESIANS.

Australia

Australia is one of the largest countries in the world. Its population, however, is quite small. Most of Australia is dry scrub or DESERT, and few people can live there. Almost all Australians live on, or near, the fertile eastern coast. But there are vast CATTLE stations in parts of Australia's interior where huge herds of cattle are raised for beef. On the eastern highlands, where the climate is wetter, SHEEP and dairy cattle are raised. The country is rich in minerals, and industry is important.

Two groups of BLACK-SKINNED PEOPLE lived in Australia before the European settlers began to arrive. They were the ABORIGINES. There are now fewer aborigines than when the colonists first arrived. One group was exiled to the island of Tasmania off the south coast. These Tasmanian aborigines have now died out.

Many of the first settlers were sent as convicts from Britain in the late eighteenth century. People still go to Australia to make a new start, attracted by the Australian way of life and the warm climate.

Australia is divided into six states and two territories. The states govern themselves in local matters, but the central government governs the territories, and makes the big decisions for all Australia. The government is headed by the PRIME MINISTER. Australia belongs to the COMMONWEALTH. The head of state is the British MONARCH who is represented in Australia by the governor-general. English is spoken in Australia.

	Australia	New Zealand
Population	14,927,000	3,176,000
	Aborigines: 100,000	Maoris: 280,000
Area (sq. km.)	7,682,300	268,704
Capital	Canberra	Wellington

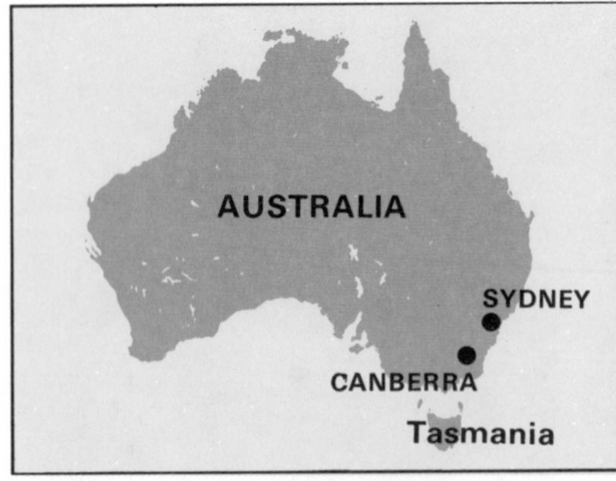

Below: A main street in Perth, Western Australia.
Bottom: The civic centre of Canberra, Australia's capital.

New Zealand

New Zealand mainly consists of two large, mountainous ISLANDS to the east of AUSTRALIA. The islands have beautiful scenery. In North Island there are several VOLCANOES, as well as GEYSERS that spout clouds of hot steam, and hot springs. In South Island there is a range of mountains along the west coast called the Southern Alps. New Zealand is mainly an agricultural country. The farmers raise SHEEP and CATTLE.

The first people to live in New Zealand were the Maoris, who are a light brown POLYNESIAN people. Since the early nineteenth century, the country has been settled by European colonists.

New Zealand is governed by a PARLIAMENT in the same way as Australia. It is a member of the COMMONWEALTH, and the people speak English.

Above left: The harbour at Wellington, New Zealand.
Left: An old port in Tasmania.

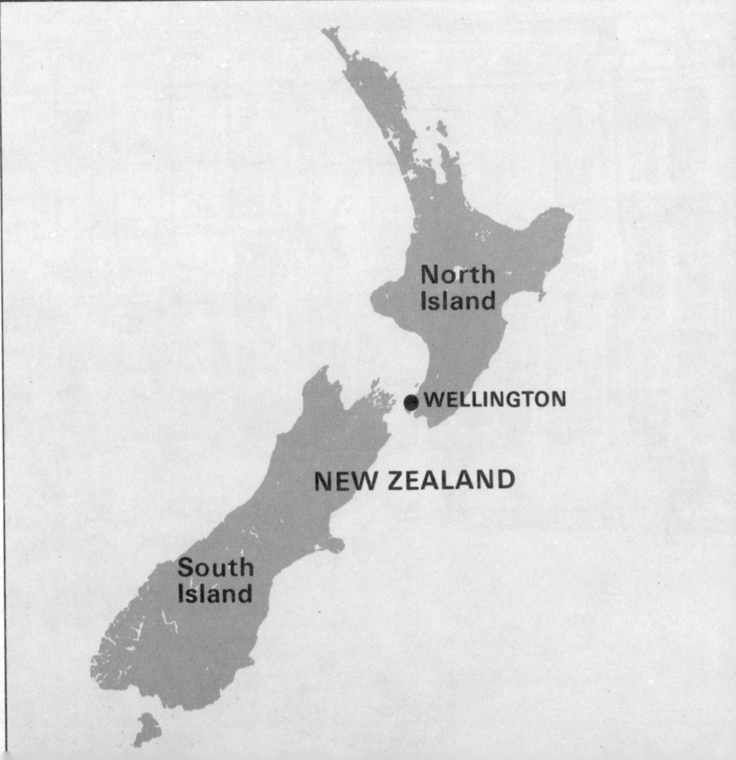

Cities

In the past, cities grew from villages and towns. A village became a town and then a city as more and more people went to live there. Cities grew only where people could trade easily. For this reason, cities began on RIVERS, near the sea, or where several ROADS met. Traders could enter and leave the city by these routes.

Today, cities do not have to grow up slowly. New cities can be built in a few years. They have their own AIRPORTS and roads to carry trade. But they are still often built on rivers, or near the sea. The capital of a country is usually its most important city. The people who govern a country often live and work in the capital. Most of the cities on the following pages are capitals. The population figures include the people in the suburbs (the built-up area around the city).

Great cities all have their famous buildings, such as these two.
Above: The Law Courts, London.
Below: The Town Hall, Brussels.

Above: Tall office blocks rise above London's older buildings.

London

London, the capital of the UNITED KINGDOM, is one of the largest cities in the world. It lies on the River Thames. London is a large port and huge DOCKS line the Thames. Up the river, west of the docks, lies the City of London. This is the oldest part of London. There are many old buildings and narrow streets. The City is one of the world's most important centres of BANKING and INSURANCE.

West of the City is the West End, a busy regions of SHOPS, THEATRES, cinemas, and restaurants. Around the West End are several large parks. Nearby is Buckingham Palace, the main home of the reigning MONARCH of Britain. The outer parts of London contain many districts of houses and industry. The whole city, including both inner and outer parts, is called Greater London.

Above: A boat full of tourists about to go under a bridge on an Amsterdam canal.

Amsterdam

Amsterdam is the capital and the largest city in the NETHERLANDS. It was once an important port, and has many old CANALS that run in a circular pattern through the centre of the city. Because the main ROADS cross one canal after another, Amsterdam has many bridges. Along the canals, the roads are cobbled (made of stones placed together) and there are many tall old buildings.

Once, the canals carried barges, but today they carry boats full of tourists. In the streets that cross the canals there are many SHOPS and restaurants. The Rijksmuseum in Amsterdam is important for its many paintings by REMBRANDT, and the City Museum has many by VAN GOGH.

	Greater London	Amsterdam
Population	6,696,000	976,000

Above: The Gran Via, Madrid.
Below: The Arc de Triomphe in Paris is the largest triumphal arch in the world.

Madrid

Madrid is the capital and largest city of SPAIN. It lies in the centre of Spain on a high plateau. King Philip II chose the site of Madrid as his capital in 1561, and the city has grown slowly since then. It is more important as a centre of government than of industry.

At the centre of Madrid is a large square called the Puerta del Sol. The main streets meet at this square. Stately buildings line the streets. The Prado is one of the most famous ART GALLERIES in the world. It has many important paintings by EL GRECO, Velasquez, GOYA, and Bosch. Another MUSEUM in the National Palace has a famous collection of art treasures.

Paris

Paris is the capital of FRANCE. With its surrounding suburbs, it is one of the world's largest cities. Paris is built on the River Seine. In the river are two islands – the Ile St Louis and the Ile de la Cité. The famous cathedral of Notre Dame is on the Ile de la Cité. Near by is the student quarter and main buildings of the UNIVERSITY of Paris. To the west is the Avenue of the Champs Elysées leading to the Arc de Triomphe, a triumphal arch built by NAPOLEON.

Among the many MUSEUMS and ART GALLERIES is the Louvre, which houses the *Mona Lisa* by LEONARDO DA VINCI as well as other treasures. Paris also has many fine examples of architecture; unlike many other European cities, it has never been bombed.

The most famous landmark of Paris is the EIFFEL TOWER. It has been a symbol of Paris since it was built in 1889.

	Madrid	Paris	Rome	Venice
Population	3,146,000	8,424,000	2,884,000	362,000

Above: The Colosseum, Rome.
Below: A corner of Venice.

Rome

Rome is the capital and largest city of ITALY. It is built on the River Tiber and was once the centre of the Roman Empire. Many ruins date from this time, especially the FORUM and the Colosseum. The Forum was the centre of government of the empire. The Colosseum was an arena seating thousands of spectators who gathered to watch spectacles such as gladiators fighting.

Many buildings in Rome were built after the time of the ANCIENT ROMANS. They include small PALACES and fountains, as well as magnificent churches. The largest church is St Peter's Basilica. It is in the VATICAN CITY, a tiny state within Rome. The Pope governs the ROMAN CATHOLIC Church from the Vatican City. Rome has superb paintings and other works of art, including many by MICHELANGELO.

Venice

Venice, in north Italy, was built many centuries ago on a group of small ISLANDS just off the coast. CANALS cut across the city instead of streets. People travel about the city by boat or by walking along the narrow lanes between the tall old houses. A causeway with a road and railway connects Venice to the mainland. No cars or other vehicles can, however, enter the city.

At the heart of Venice is St Mark's Square. It is lined with fine colonnades, and at one end are the campanile (bell tower), St Mark's Basilica and the Palace of the Doge, who used to rule Venice. The square and its buildings are world famous for their great beauty.

Unfortunately, Venice is slowly sinking into the sea. The Italian government has plans to save it, but the cost will be very great.

Athens

Athens is the largest city and capital of GREECE. Most of Athens is a busy modern city and port. Its port is known as Piraeus. Athens was also the most important city of ancient Greece. On a high hill called the Acropolis stand ruins from that time. They include the PARTHENON, a temple whose design has been copied in many buildings around the world.

Many ANCIENT GREEK statues and carvings can be seen in the National Archaeological MUSEUM in Athens.

Right: The Acropolis dominates Athens.

Above: The Kurfürstendamm in West Berlin.

Berlin

Berlin is inside EAST GERMANY. It is a divided city. West Berlin is part of WEST GERMANY, and East Berlin is part of East Germany.

The two countries have completely different governments, and the border of East Berlin is strongly guarded. Before 1961 people could pass freely from one part of the city to the other. Then a wall was built by the East Germans to prevent people from leaving East Berlin. Today, people need to have passports or permits in order to pass through the gates in the wall.

Berlin was the capital of all Germany before WORLD WAR II. In the war it was heavily bombed, but much of the city has been rebuilt.

The heart of West Berlin is the Kurfürstendamm, a wide tree-lined avenue. The main shops and hotels are on this street.

One of the features of East Berlin is Treptower Park with its massive war memorial. Karl Marx Allee is the principal street in East Berlin.

	Athens	East Berlin	West Berlin	Vienna	Moscow
Population	2,540,000	1,106,000	1,951,000	1,615,000	7,819,000

Vienna

Vienna is the capital of AUSTRIA. In the eighteenth and nineteenth centuries it was a leading centre of art and learning. Elegant buildings and charming parks and squares date from that time. Several of Vienna's famous old buildings were destroyed or damaged during WORLD WAR II, but some have been restored or rebuilt. They include the Opera House and the Cathedral of St Stephen. In the Hofburg palace is the Spanish Riding School, where the famous white horses perform to music.

Vienna is on the River Danube. Today it is also an important industrial centre.

Left: A park in Vienna. In the background is the town hall.

Moscow

Moscow is the capital and largest city of the U.S.S.R. In the centre of Moscow is the KREMLIN. The tsars, the rulers of Russia before the Russian REVOLUTION, lived there. Today, the government has its headquarters in the Kremlin. Inside its walls are bell towers, cathedrals, and palaces. Outside the Kremlin is Red Square, where huge parades take place. There is often a long queue of people waiting on one side of the square to see the tomb of LENIN. On another side is the Cathedral of St Basil. It has nine onion-shaped domes of many colours.

ROADS lead out in all directions from the centre of Moscow. They are crossed by ring roads where Moscow's old walls once stood. The city lies on the Moskva River. Many trade goods between EUROPE and ASIA pass through Moscow.

Right: A long line of people waiting in Red Square, Moscow, to visit Lenin's tomb.

Istanbul

Istanbul is the largest city in TURKEY, although Ankara is the capital. In ancient times Istanbul was called Byzantium. From A.D. 330, the city was called Constantinople. Its Turkish name, Istanbul, became the official name in 1930.

Istanbul lies on the Bosporus, the narrow channel of water that separates EUROPE from ASIA. The city has long been an important trading centre and port. Ferries go back and forth across the Bosporus, and a new bridge also links the two continents.

The minarets and domes of many mosques rise above Istanbul's skyline. The Blue Mosque, with its inside walls of patterned blue tiles, is among the most famous. ST SOPHIA, once a Christian church, dates from the sixth century. It is now a MUSEUM. The Seraglio, part of the old palace, also attracts many tourists.

Left: A view of the Bosporus from Istanbul.

	Istanbul	Jerusalem	Delhi	Bombay
Population	3,864,000	344,000	3,647,000	5,971,000

Jerusalem

Jerusalem was once a divided city as BERLIN is now. One part was in ISRAEL and the other in JORDAN. In the war between the two countries in 1967, Israel took over Jordan's half of Jerusalem. It is now the capital of Israel.

Jerusalem is a holy city to Christians, Jews, and Moslems. There are many important places of worship, including the Dome of the Rock and the Church of the Holy Sepulchre. In the centre of Jerusalem is the Old City, a tangle of old houses and narrow alleys.

Right: Part of the Old City of Jerusalem.

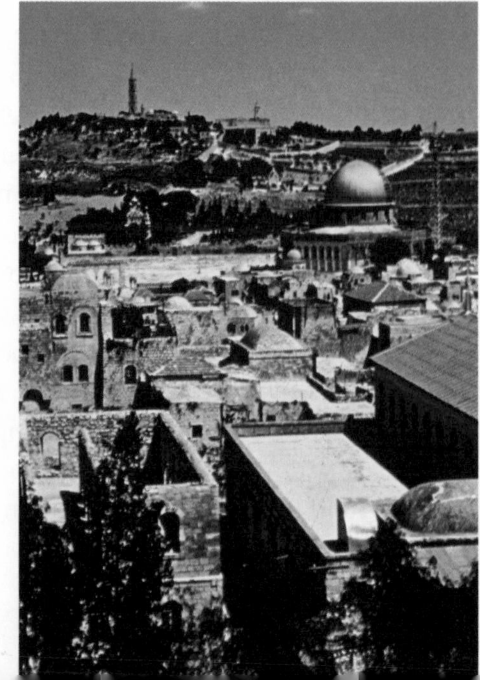

Delhi

Delhi is the capital of INDIA. It has two parts, Old Delhi and New Delhi. They show the influence of India's past rulers – the Mughals and the British. Old Delhi is a walled city with busy streets of small shops and markets. Its great buildings include the magnificent Jama Masjid Mosque, built by the Mughal emperor Shah Jahan in the seventeenth century.

New Delhi was built eight kilometres away from Old Delhi in 1912. It was designed by British architects. There are wide tree-lined streets, shopping centres, and large public buildings. These include the PARLIAMENT building, which is circular and has pillars around the outside. An unusual building is an open-air observatory built in the eighteenth century. The National MUSEUM of India is in New Delhi. It has a superb collection of Indian art.

Above: The huge Red Fort in Delhi was built by Shah Jahan in the seventeenth century.

Bombay

Bombay, India's second largest city after Calcutta, is the country's leading seaport and the main commercial centre. It is sometimes called the Gateway to INDIA. This name is now used for an impressive stone arch which overlooks Bombay's fine, natural harbour.

This crowded, noisy city has many skyscrapers. Textiles are manufactured and there are many light industries. For example, Bombay is a centre of the Indian film industry. Most of the people are HINDUS, but there is also an important Parsee community. In 1534 Bombay became a Portuguese possession. In 1662 Portugal gave it to the wife of the English King, Charles II. In 1668 Charles gave Bombay to the East India Company.

Left: A machine for crushing sugar-cane in a street in Bombay.

Jakarta

Jakarta, also spelled D'jakarta, is the capital of INDONESIA. It lies on the north-western coast of the crowded island of Java. Jakarta is mainly a centre of government and commerce, but there are some industries. The city's port, Tandjung Priok, is linked to Jakarta by a canal.

The city is mostly modern in style. The Old City has a Dutch character, because it was founded by the Dutch in 1610. From 1619 until 1949, when Indonesia became independent, Jakarta was called Batavia. The people are mostly Malays who follow ISLAM. The city has many beautiful mosques, but also BUDDHIST and Confucian temples, and Christian churches.

Above: Life in Hong Kong Harbour.
Below: The Forbidden City, Peking.

Peking

Peking is the capital of CHINA. It is not China's largest city, which is Shanghai. Peking consists of several smaller cities. At the centre is the Forbidden City, once the home of the emperors of China. Inside was the Imperial Palace, now a MUSEUM. Only people who lived or worked there could enter the Forbidden City.

Beyond its walls is the Imperial City, where China's government buildings are. T'ien An Men Square, a huge square used for holding rallies, is in the Imperial City.

Around the Imperial City is the Tartar City. It was the rich part of old Peking, and contains many old temples and elegant houses. Next to the Tartar City is the CHINESE City. At one time poor people and merchants lived there. Today, there are many narrow streets crowded with SHOPS and MARKETS. Beyond the old cities are suburbs of houses, FACTORIES, and offices.

	Jakarta	Peking	Seoul	Tokyo
Population	4,600,000	8,000,000	6,889,000	8,643,000

Seoul

Seoul is the capital and largest city of South KOREA. It was founded in 1392 by the Yi kings, who ruled Korea for more than 500 years. Several of the gates and parts of the wall of the old city can still be seen. Seoul contains many new buildings and modern ROADS.

Many of the old buildings have been torn down, but four of the Yi PALACES remain. In the Palace of Virtuous Longevity are MUSEUMS devoted to the art and history of Korea. Throughout Seoul are many tea rooms, where Koreans meet and relax.

Left: Seoul has many fine modern buildings.

Below: The bright lights of the Ginza district in Tokyo.

Tokyo

Tokyo is the capital of JAPAN. It has more people than any other city in the world except Shanghai. Because it is so crowded, travelling within Tokyo is difficult. The ROADS are packed with traffic and the BUSES and trains are jammed with people. Also, some streets in Tokyo do not have names and so it is not easy to find one's way.

Tokyo is best seen from Tokyo Tower. This tower looks like the EIFFEL TOWER in PARIS, but it is a little higher. At its foot is Shiba Park, with its Buddhist TEMPLE and gate.

To the north is the PARLIAMENT building; beyond that is the Imperial PALACE in its large grounds. The Emperor of Japan lives in the palace. To the east is the harbour and Tokyo Bay. In the north-east are the stores and restaurants of the Ginza district and the entertainment centre of Asakusa district. These districts are lively and colourful, with dazzling lights at night. A few women in Japan wear traditional JAPANESE costume, but most dress in Western-style clothes.

Above: A school in Cairo. It is designed in the traditional Arab style of architecture.

Cairo

Cairo is the capital and largest city of EGYPT. It lies on the River Nile. In the old part of Cairo houses with overhanging balconies cluster along narrow streets. The slender minarets of mosques rise above the houses. People dress in ARAB robes. In the new part of Cairo there are wide avenues lined with hotels and stores.

Many people come to Cairo to see the PYRAMIDS at the edge of the city. The Great Pyramid is the only one of the seven wonders of the ancient world that still stands. Beside it is the Great Sphinx, a huge statue of a lion with the head of a pharaoh, a ruler of ancient Egypt. Treasures of the pharaohs can be seen in Cairo's MUSEUMS.

Above: Looking down over Camps Bay, Cape Town, from the slopes of Table Mountain.

Cape Town

Cape Town lies on Table Bay, near the Cape of Good Hope at the southern tip of AFRICA. The PARLIAMENT of SOUTH AFRICA meets in Cape Town.

The city is well known for Table Mountain. This MOUNTAIN has a flat top like the top of a table. It is often covered with low cloud (the 'Tablecloth'). Table Mountain towers more than a thousand metres above the city. Botanical gardens line its slopes, and cable cars carry people to the top of the mountain.

Cape Town was founded in 1652 and is the oldest city in South Africa. It was built as a port that could be used by ships on their way to INDIA. Today, it is still one of the busiest of South Africa's ports. It became more important when the SUEZ CANAL was closed in 1967. Cape Town is also a centre of light industry.

	Cairo	Cape Town	Montreal	Washington D.C.
Pop.	5,715,000	1,097,000	2,802,000	757,000

Montreal

Montreal and Toronto are Canada's largest cities. They have about the same number of people. Montreal lies on the St Lawrence River, and is one of the biggest inland ports in the world. Montreal is in Quebec province, which is the French-speaking part of Canada. Many of the people speak both English and French.

In the centre of the city rises a high hill called Mount Royal. The city gets its name from this hill, which is called Mont Réal in French.

Beautiful parks cover the hill, and give fine views of the city's modern centre and the great river beyond. Montreal has a new UNDERGROUND RAILWAY. As with the French Métro, the trains run on rubber wheels and are almost silent.

Above: The view over Montreal from Mount Royal, with the St Lawrence River in the background.

Washington, D.C.

Washington is the capital city of the United States and the centre of its government. Its full name is Washington D.C. (District of Columbia), and it is near the east coast of the U.S.A. The *State* of Washington is quite separate. It lies on the west coast.

George WASHINGTON, the first PRESIDENT, chose the site for the city, which is named after him. Wide streets, squares, and parks were built in great patterns, with main avenues leading to the government buildings. These buildings have domes and colonnades like those of the great old buildings of EUROPE. They include the Capitol, where CONGRESS meets, and the White House, which is the president's home. Among other buildings are the Library of Congress, one of the greatest LIBRARIES in the world, and the Supreme Court of the United States.

Washington lies on the Potomac River. Beside the RIVER is the Pentagon, the huge five-sided headquarters of the U.S. armed forces.

Above: The White House, in Washington D.C., is the home of the president of the United States.

San Francisco

Many people consider San Francisco, in California, to be the most beautiful city in the United States. It lies on a tongue of land surrounded by the PACIFIC OCEAN, San Francisco Bay, and the Golden Gate – a channel from the sea to the bay. The city is built on steep hills and its elegant homes and offices look down to the water on almost all sides. Trams hauled by cables run up and down the steep streets. Long suspension bridges span the Golden Gate and San Francisco Bay.

Above: Telegraph Hill, one of San Francisco's steep hills.
Below: Central Park in New York is overlooked by skyscrapers.

New York

New York is the largest city in the United States. It is divided into five boroughs, or sections. The centre of New York is the borough of Manhattan. It is a long, narrow island between the Hudson River and the East River. Many of the streets in Manhattan have numbers instead of names, making it easy to find places.

Off the southern tip of Manhattan is the STATUE OF LIBERTY. The city's BANKING and financial area is at the south end of Manhattan. It is the oldest part of New York. Two of the tallest buildings in the world, the World Trade Centre and the EMPIRE STATE BUILDING, are also there. Not far from the financial district is Greenwich Village, where many artists and writers have lived. Chinatown is also nearby.

Some of New York's most famous SKYSCRAPERS, such as the Empire State Building, are in the centre of Manhattan. Further north is Central Park, a large open area of trees and grass. Harlem, the largest black community in America, is north of Central Park.

	New York	Brasilia	Sydney
Population	7,896,000	537,000	3,281,000

Brasilia

Brasilia has been the capital of BRAZIL since 1960. Before that, Rio de Janeiro on the south-east coast was Brazil's capital. The new capital was built 1000 kilometres inland in order to develop Brazil's vast interior. Now Brasilia has grown into a great city, full of very modern buildings. The PRESIDENT has a home there, and it is Brazil's centre of government. Brasilia also acts as a trading centre for goods from Brazil's interior.

Above: A view over Brasilia.
Right: National Congress Building, Brasilia.
Below: Modern office buildings in the centre of Sydney.

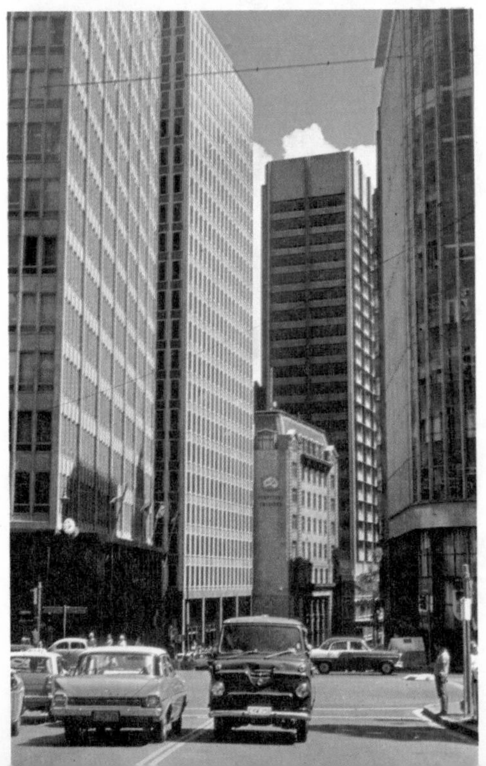

Sydney

Sydney is the largest city of AUSTRALIA, although Canberra is the capital. It is also Australia's oldest city. In 1770 Captain COOK landed at Botany Bay. Eight years later, the first Europeans settled on an inlet where Sydney Harbour is now. Modern Sydney lies around the harbour and Botany Bay.

The great arch of the Sydney Harbour BRIDGE spans the harbour. At the southern end of the bridge is the centre of Sydney. The new opera house with its unusual sail-like domes stands on a small headland. Beyond is the business district and Kings Cross, a district of restaurants and entertainment. Sydney is Australia's leading port, and it is also an important industrial centre.

Famous Monuments

When we think of a city, we usually remember certain great buildings or monuments in or near it, rather than the city as a whole. To many people, ATHENS is known for the PARTHENON, and NEW YORK for the EMPIRE STATE BUILDING and other skyscrapers.

A monument is a construction which reminds us of some person or event. Every civilization builds monuments. In ancient times, the most famous were the Seven Wonders of the World. Of these, only the great PYRAMID in EGYPT remains today.

Certain memorable buildings and monuments were built for religious purposes. The ANGKOR WAT was built as a HINDU temple and SAINT SOPHIA as a Christian church. Palaces may remind us of great rulers, past and present. Other monuments, such as the GREAT WALL OF CHINA, were built as defences against enemies.

A few structures, like the EIFFEL TOWER in PARIS, have become symbols of their cities.

Below: Building Stonehenge.

Above: The Great Pyramid built for King Cheops is on the left.

Below: Stonehenge as it can be seen today.

Pyramids

A PYRAMID has a square base and triangular sides that slope to meet at a point at the top of the pyramid. Pyramids were built by the ANCIENT EGYPTIANS and also by the AZTECS and other Indian tribes in Central America. The Egyptian pyramids were built as long as 4500 years ago. The American pyramids are younger and most were built from 800 to 1400 years ago. Pyramids were used as tombs and as TEMPLES. The best-known pyramid is the Great Pyramid near CAIRO, the tomb of King Cheops.

Stonehenge

Stonehenge is an ancient group of stones standing on Salisbury Plain in southern England. It was completed in about 1300 B.C. Many of the stones are still standing. Originally, there were two main circles of stones, one inside the other. At the centre were two horseshoe-shaped rows of stones around a central block. No one knows quite why Stonehenge was built. If it was used as a temple, the block would probably have been the altar.

Eiffel Tower

The Eiffel Tower is a huge iron tower in PARIS, in FRANCE. It was designed by Alexandre Eiffel for an exhibition there in 1889. It was originally 300.51 metres high. Now, with a TELEVISION mast on top, it rises to 320.75 metres. The Eiffel Tower was the tallest tower in the world before high television masts were built in the 1950s.

The Eiffel Tower rises from a square base to a point. It is made of a network of iron girders. There are two lower platforms and an observation station at the top. These are reached by a lift or by spiral staircases. There are magnificent views of Paris from the tower.

Left: The Eiffel Tower in Paris is one of the most famous landmarks in the world.

Leaning Tower of Pisa

The marble tower at Pisa in Italy is perhaps the strangest tower in the world. It leans so much to one side that it looks as if it is going to topple over.

The tower was started in 1173. It is, in fact, the campanile (bell-tower) of Pisa cathedral. As soon as three storeys had been built, it began to lean as the ground beneath subsided (sank). The tower, which is 56.2 metres high, was finished in 1350. Since then it has continued to move very slowly in spite of measures to prevent it leaning more. It now leans three metres to one side.

It is still safe to climb the tower. But unless its movement is stopped, the tower will one day fall over.

Left: The bell tower of Pisa Cathedral leans to one side because the ground beneath has sunk. The Cathedral is shown on the left.

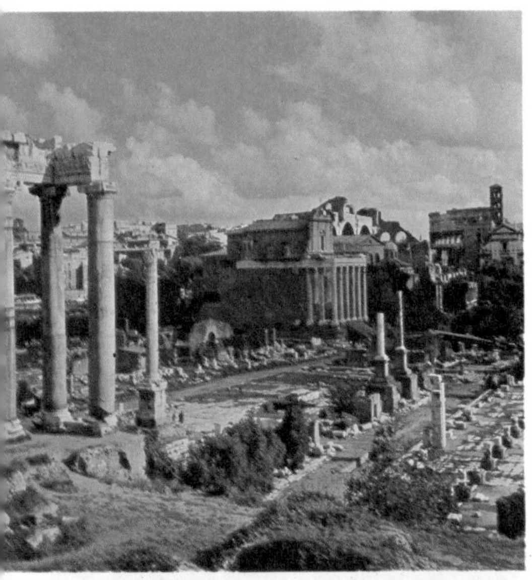

Above: The ruins of the Forum which stood in Ancient Rome.
Below: The Parthenon, built on the Acropolis in Athens.

Forum

The centre of an ANCIENT ROMAN town was known as the forum. It acted as a MARKET place and a centre of government. The Forum at ROME must have been a splendid place. Around the market place were marble halls and temples with pillars, the Curia, or Senate House, great statues, and huge arches.

The Romans, dressed in their flowing togas (robes), gathered in the Forum to discuss business and government. After victories in battle, parades of soldiers with their captives were held in the Forum and captured treasures were displayed.

The buildings of the Forum became ruins after the fall of the Roman Empire. But enough of the ruins remain to give a good impression of the magnificence of ancient Rome.

Parthenon

The Parthenon was the most important temple of ancient ATHENS. It stands on a steep-sided hill, called the Acropolis, which overlooks the city of Athens. It was built for the worship of Athena, the goddess of Athens. Around the marble temple were rows of columns and a frieze of life-like sculptures. Inside the temple were two rooms, in one of which stood a huge statue of Athena.

The Parthenon was built between 447 and 432 B.C. It remained in good condition until 1687. The Turks, who then occupied Athens, were using the temple to store gunpowder when the Venetians invaded. In the fighting the powder exploded and the temple was badly damaged. Some of the sculptures from the frieze were later brought to LONDON and are in the British MUSEUM. The Parthenon has now been partly restored.

Saint Sophia

Saint Sophia is a superb Byzantine church in Istanbul, TURKEY. The Byzantine Empire was the eastern part of the Roman Empire. Saint Sophia was built on the site of an earlier church between A.D. 532 and 537 at the order of Justinian I. It was called Hagia Sophia, or the Church of Holy Wisdom.

Saint Sophia extends 76 metres from east to west and 72 metres from north to south. The great dome, 56 metres high and 31 metres across, was built between 558 and 563. The first dome was damaged during an earthquake. In 1453, the Turks conquered the Byzantine Empire. Saint Sophia then became a mosque (a Moslem place of worship).

Right: Saint Sophia in Istanbul. It used to be a mosque but now it is a museum.

Peterhof Palace

Peterhof is a magnificent palace which stands on the south shore of the Gulf of Finland, 29 kilometres from Leningrad, in RUSSIA. It has superb parks with beautiful fountains, cascades and statues. The palace, now called Petrodvorets, was the home of the Russian Emperor Peter I. It was built between 1714 and 1728 in a very decorative style of architecture known as rococo.

From 1747 to 1752, a great architect, Bartolommeo Rastrelli (1700–71) largely rebuilt and enlarged it. In WORLD WAR II, the Peterhof was badly damaged and many of its treasures were lost. Since 1945, it has been restored by artists and craftsmen.

Right: The Peterhof Palace near Leningrad with the fountains playing in the gardens.

Kremlin

A kremlin is an old fortress or citadel in the centre of a Russian town. In MOSCOW, the Kremlin lies on the banks of the River Moskva. Its three walls are more than two kilometres long, and contain 18 towers and five gates. The tsars (former rulers) of Russia once lived there.

Within the Kremlin is the Grand Palace which overlooks the river, and also several cathedrals. Some of the buildings are now MUSEUMS, displaying the treasures of the tsars.

The Kremlin houses the largest bell in the world, which weighs 196 metric tons. It is cracked and has a piece missing so that it will not ring.

The Kremlin is also the main government centre of the U.S.S.R.

Right: One of the gates of the Kremlin.

Taj Mahal

The Taj Mahal is considered to be one of the world's most beautiful buildings. Its slender minarets and elegant domes of white marble rise above walls of delicate stonework. The Taj Mahal is at Agra in northern INDIA. It lies beside the River Jumna amid gardens with quiet pools. The Taj Mahal was built by the Mughal emperor Shah Jahan, who ruled India in the seventeenth century. It is in memory of his favourite wife, Mumtaz Mahal.

The Taj Mahal took 22 years to build. Shah Jahan planned a similar building, in black, to be sited on the other side of the river. But before it could be built, Shah Jahan was imprisoned by his son Aurangzeb, who had seized the throne. Shah Jahan was buried next to his wife.

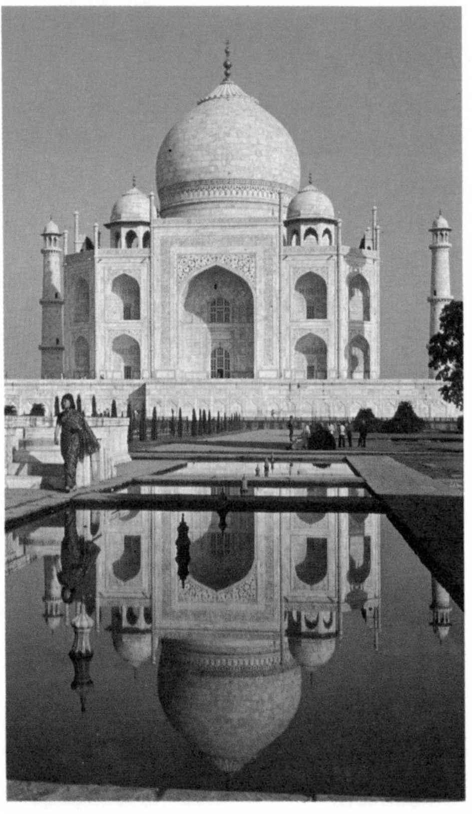

Right: The Taj Mahal at Agra, India.

Great Wall of China

Over 2000 years ago, an army of CHINESE labourers completed the largest structure that man has ever made – the Great Wall of China. It was built across northern CHINA to keep out invaders. It wound over MOUNTAINS and VALLEYS for more than 4000 kilometres – a tenth of the distance around the world.

In some places the wall was as much as 12 metres high and nine metres thick. The wall was made of stone and earth, with brick on the outside. Every 100 metres or so there were guard towers, and there was a roadway along the top. Much of the Great Wall has been preserved or rebuilt, especially at the eastern end, near PEKING.

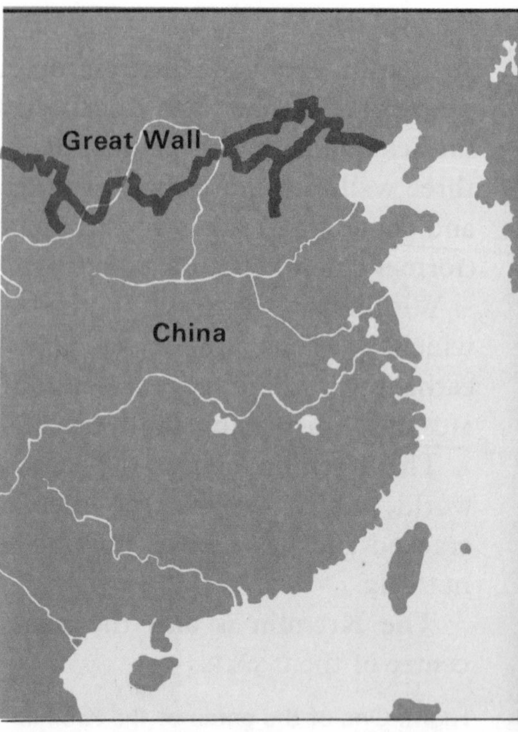

Right: The Great Wall made a vast barrier across northern China.

Angkor Wat

Angkor Wat is the ruin of one of the largest religious buildings in the world. It is in CAMBODIA in south-east ASIA. It was built by King Suryavarman in the twelfth century for the worship of the HINDU god Vishnu.

Angkor Wat consists of three temples, each inside the other and higher than the surrounding temple. The temples, with their beautiful columns and towers, rise like a PYRAMID towards the centre. The outside wall, nearly a kilometre long, is decorated with carvings showing Hindu legends and events of the king's life.

Angkor Wat was abandoned in the fifteenth century when its Hindu rulers were conquered by invaders from Siam (modern THAILAND).

Right: The great temple of Angkor Wat. It was rediscovered in the 1860s in dense jungle by a French explorer.

Statue of Liberty

The Statue of Liberty stands at the entrance to NEW YORK Harbour on a small island called Liberty Island. The statue was given to the United States by FRANCE in 1885. The Statue of Liberty symbolizes the land of freedom that the U.S.A. became to many people fleeing from hardship, war and persecution in other lands. In one hand she holds a tablet bearing the date of the Declaration of Independence. With the other she raises a flaming torch in welcome.

The statue is made of COPPER. With its pedestal, it rises 93 metres above the ground. There is a STAIRCASE inside the statue, and visitors can climb to the statue's crown.

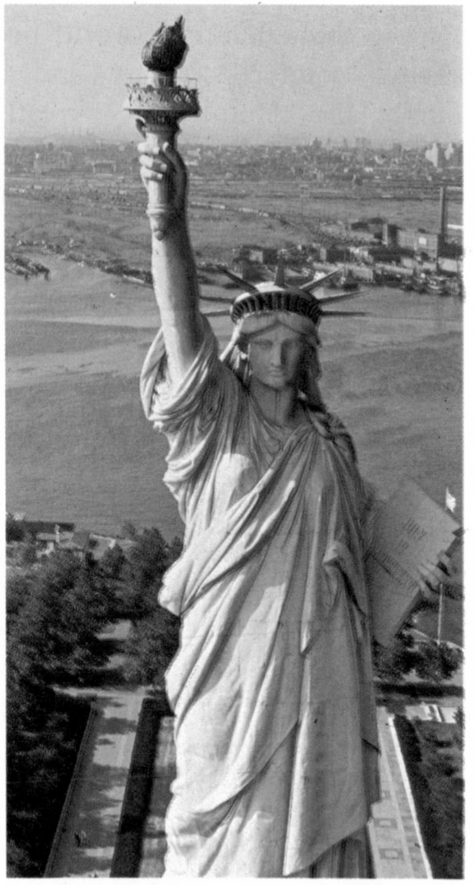

Right: The Statue of Liberty greets people arriving in New York by sea.

Empire State Building

High in Manhattan, in the centre of NEW YORK city, rises the Empire State Building. (The Empire State is another name for the State of New York.) From 1931, the year it was completed, until 1970, it was the tallest inhabited building in the world. The Empire State Building has 102 floors and was originally 381 metres high. A TELEVISION mast erected on the top in 1951 brought the total height to 449 metres.

Like many other New York skyscrapers, the Empire State Building is so tall that its top is often lost in CLOUD. On a clear day, however, one can see for well over 100 kilometres from the observatory on the top floor. Thousands of people visit the building every day, but it is mainly occupied by offices, with SHOPS on the ground floor.

Right: The Empire State Building, New York.

Homes Around the World

People throughout the world need homes for shelter, comfort, security, and as centres for family life. Homes vary greatly from one-roomed huts to flats, semi-detached houses, and large mansions. The ways of life of different people affect the style of their homes. Tents, for example are the most suitable homes for nomadic people because they move around a lot. However, people who live settled lives in villages and towns need secure, solid houses.

Climate is a major factor which determines house styles. Broadly, there are five main climatic regions. These are; the polar regions; the cold forest lands in the northern hemisphere and the mountain lands which have cool or cold climates because of their height above sea-level; temperate mid-latitude zones; tropical rainy regions near the equator; and hot, dry deserts.

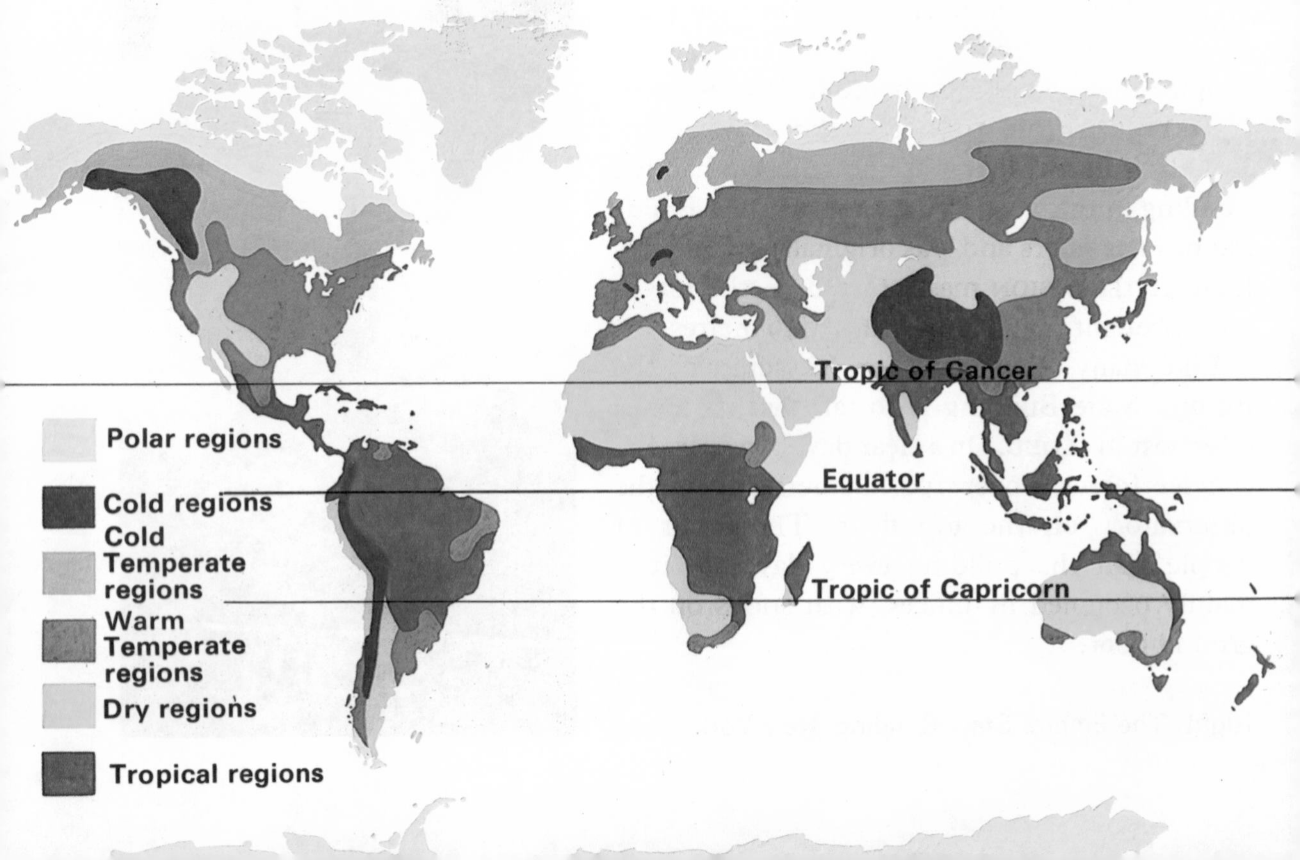

Tropic of Cancer
Equator
Tropic of Capricorn

Polar regions
Cold regions
Cold Temperate regions
Warm Temperate regions
Dry regions
Tropical regions

Polar regions

Polar regions have an average temperature in the warmest month of less than 10°C. The continent of ANTARCTICA, around the South Pole, is much colder than this. It has no permanent population, but scientists work there. Their homes are mostly 10 metres or so below the surface.

The north polar regions include parts of northern Europe, ASIA and North America. ESKIMOS live in Alaska, CANADA, Greenland and Siberia and they call their homes igloos. Igloos can be summer tents, houses made of driftwood, earth and stone, and also snowhouses. Snowhouses are used in winter. They are made from blocks of compacted snow, piled up to produce a domed structure. The entrance is a tunnel which is lower than the floor of the snowhouse. This keeps cold air out of the igloo.

Snowhouses are still used, but many Eskimos now live in modern, prefabricated houses, usually made of wood.

Above: A town in Greenland at night. Below: Most Eskimos now live in prefabricated houses. In winter they are often buried under the snow (right).

Cold regions

South of the icy regions of the ARCTIC lies the TUNDRA. Trees do not grow there because it is too cold. However, in summer, the temperature rises to about 10°C, and for a short period MOSSES, LICHENS and some flowering plants grow in abundance. The summer vegetation provides pasture for REINDEER. Some reindeer are wild, but others are kept in herds by the LAPPS of Scandinavia and various other peoples in the northern U.S.S.R.

Many Lapps now live in villages and they have permanent, modern homes. But some still follow their old nomadic way of life, following the annual migrations (movements north and south) of the reindeer. The traditional summer home of Lapps is a tent made from reindeer skins wrapped around a frame of about 12 poles. Winter tents are made from wool. Furs are used to carpet the tents and fires are lit for heating and cooking. The smoke escapes through a hole in the top of the tent.

Top: A tent in Mongolia.
Above: A timbered house in Canada.
Below: A Lapp tent.

South of the tundra lies a vast region of FORESTS consisting of conifers (evergreens), such as larch, pine, fir, and spruce. These forests can grow because the climate is milder. Conifers provide building material for log cabins and houses made of planks. Such houses were used by trappers in northern CANADA and wood is still an important building material in Siberia. However, many people in these regions now live in modern, centrally-heated houses.

Some people in this region are still nomads and they live in tents. For example, the Khalkha people of MONGOLIA spend winters in circular tents. These tents, called yurts, have a wooden framework, covered by felt and roofed by canvas.

Mountain regions, even in temperate and tropical zones, can be as cold as the Arctic. This is because, on average, temperatures fall by about 7°C for every 1000 metres. Mountains provide rich summer pasture for livestock.

Homes in mountain regions include the wooden chalets of SWITZERLAND. Some chalets have gently sloping wooden roofs. Snow piles up on the roofs and helps to keep the heat inside the chalets.

Most people in Switzerland live in the lower, sheltered parts of the country. But, in summer, many farmers take their animals up the mountains. They spend the summer in simple log cabins, roofed by slate. They gather hay for winter feed for their cattle and, at the end of the summer, return to their homes in the valleys.

A special way of heating homes is used in the bleak mountain lands of Nepal and Tibet. There, many of the stone or brick houses have two storeys. The family lives upstairs and the ground floor is a stable. The heat given off by the animals warms the upper storey of the house.

Above: A Swiss chalet with steeply sloping roofs.

Below: A village in Switzerland.

Temperate regions

The largest temperate regions are in the middle latitudes of the northern hemisphere, between the cold coniferous forests in the north and the hot tropical lands to the south. In these areas the average temperature in the coldest month is never more than 18°C, never less than −3°C.

The original vegetation of these regions was either deciduous forest, with trees that shed their leaves in winter, grasslands, or evergreen woodlands in the drier, warmer parts. Today most of the forest has been cut down. However, wood was once an important building material as we can see from the old timber-frame houses which still stand in some places.

The climate in temperate zones varies from north to south and so do the kinds of homes.

Top right: Japanese houses are made of light materials in case they collapse during earthquakes.
Right: A newly-planned town centre in England.
Below: Terraced houses in Sydney, Australia.

In cool, wet areas, the houses must be kept warm in winter. But in warm and dry areas, flat-roofed, thick-walled houses with high windows are designed to keep homes cool in summer. Many houses are built from local stone. Others are made of BRICKS, and some modern homes are made of concrete, containing STEEL rods.

The temperate regions are thickly populated and contain many of the world's largest cities. The greatest expansion of cities began in the late 1700s, when the INDUSTRIAL REVOLUTION started in Britain. In the 1800s many other countries became industrialized. People flocked to the cities to find jobs in the new FACTORIES. The sudden increase in population caused much over-crowding and squalor. Many houses were built quickly and were of poor quality.

Above: Old houses in Venice, Italy.
Left: A thatched cottage in England.

Modern cities in developed countries contain different kinds of homes. A detached house is one building which houses one family. A semi-detached house contains two self-contained homes. Some homes are built in long, continuous rows, called terraces, while many other people live in flats, or apartments. Some apartment blocks contain hundreds of self-contained homes, sometimes in tall buildings. These buildings cause problems for the people who live in them.

Tropical regions

The tropical rainy regions have average temperatures of over 18°C for every month of the year. In some places, rain falls only in one season. In other areas, close to the equator, rain falls in every month of the year. Great heat combined with regular, heavy rainfall has produced dense rain FORESTS. In these forests, the trees blot out most of the sunlight from the forest floor. Most people live in forest clearings or on rivers.

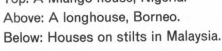

Top: A Miango house, Nigeria.
Above: A longhouse, Borneo.
Below: Houses on stilts in Malaysia.

A typical house in African tropical grasslands, which are called savanna, is the round, mud hut. These houses consist of a wooden frame covered with wet earth. When the earth dries, it forms a strong wall. The roofs of these huts are usually thatched. The thatch consists of such materials as grasses, reeds, or bamboo, which are woven around a wooden frame. The roof slopes so that rainwater will drain off it. The roof also overhangs the walls and protects them from the rain. These huts have no windows and so sunlight can enter them. This helps to keep them cool.

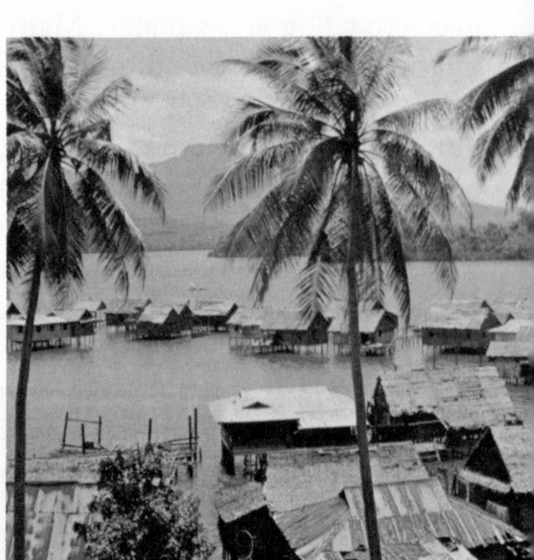

In rain forests, nomads, such as the pygmies of central Africa, make temporary shelters. These crude homes often consist of a wooden frame covered by leaves. Some American Indians, in the Amazon River basin, build simple wooden shelters. They are closed in at the back, but open at the front. They provide shade and let air flow freely through them.

Along rivers in the Amazon basin and also in various parts of tropical south-east Asia, people build houses on stilts. By raising their homes above ground level, they are protected against floods. Air can also flow beneath the floors which has a cooling effect. Raised homes also keep out wild animals and many insects. One well known type of house on stilts is the longhouse, used by the Dyaks of Borneo. These long, wooden buildings are fronted by a roofed verandah. They are divided into rooms and one longhouse may contain between 20 and 50 families.

There are many modern cities in the tropics. Manufacturing industries are developing rapidly in many of these. They offer the chance of jobs and attract many poor families from the countryside into the cities. But many people cannot find work because they lack skills. As a result, these people live in slums. In parts of Africa, Asia and South America, large slums are forming around the fast-growing cities. This development is similar to the growth of slums in cities in temperate nations in the 1800s. The slums lack all hygienic facilities, so illnesses are common. Epidemics which start in the slums sometimes spread through the city.

Above: A shanty-town in Calcutta, India where homes are built out of anything left lying around.

Right: The modern centre of Sao Paulo, Brazil. In this huge, fast-growing city, there are still many people who live in shanty-towns.

Dry regions

DESERTS are places where the total average rainfall is less than 250 millimetres per year. The Sahara is the world's largest desert and the sunniest place on earth. There are some places in hot deserts where there is enough water for people to live. These are called oases. Oases can be small ponds formed where underground, water-bearing rocks meet the surface in a hollow. Other oases can be very large. A large oasis is the Nile valley which gets its water from the River Nile.

Around oases, people have permanent homes. These usually have flat roofs, because tilted roofs are not needed to drain rain-water. Instead the flat roof is often used as an extra room. People can sit out on it or sleep there once the sun has gone down. There are no trees in the desert so houses are often made of stone or

Above: A mud house in North Africa.

Right: Mud huts in North West Syria.
Below: An oasis town in Algeria, North Africa.

sun-dried bricks. These bricks are made from clay mixed with straw, grass, or some similar substance. They would crumble if they were exposed to frequent rain storms or to frost.

Houses in the desert have thick walls and sometimes no windows. This helps to keep hot air out and cool air in. The outside walls are often painted white, because white reflects the heat. Such houses are found in North Africa and the Middle East. Similar houses are also built in the hot deserts of the south-western United States.

Other desert homes are built below the ground. Rooms are cut out of the rock around a pit which is dug about 10 metres below the surface. Homes like these are cool and protected from sandstorms.

Some houses in desert towns are built with wind towers. These are used to cool the house. Any breezes are trapped in the tower and channelled down into the house. Many ARAB houses are built around courtyards and all the rooms face on to them. In the courtyards, there are often beautiful flower gardens and fountains. The water helps to cool the air.

Some desert people are nomads. They make their living from trading or rearing livestock. They take their animals to regions, such as mountain areas, where there is enough rain to support grasses. The Bedouin of the Arabian desert are typical desert nomads. They live in tents which are open on one side during the day to let the air circulate. The tents are often black and made from woven goat hair. Some tents are large and divided into several rooms by curtains. A simple tent has two rooms. The Bedouin nomads do not use furniture. Instead, they sit on rugs which they place on the floor of their tents.

Above: Homes in a desert area of the Sudan, Africa. They have mud walls and thatched roofs.
Below and bottom: Bedouin tents.

Clothes

In ancient times, people wore simple clothes. In hot regions, men and women dressed in loose robes. In cold places, clothes were made of furs or hides. In EUROPE about a thousand years ago, rich people began to wear more attractive clothes. They used cloth of many different colours and patterns. Women wore long dresses and men had fine coats and hose (a kind of stocking). The clothes were often trimmed with fur or lace, and people wore elaborate hats, sometimes decorated with feathers.

Fashions in extravagant styles continued for the rich until WORLD WAR I. Poor people, however, could not afford such clothes. They had to dress in rough clothes of leather, COTTON, and wool. After World War I, most people in Europe and NORTH AMERICA began to dress alike. Clothes became more comfortable to wear. Apart from working clothes and UNIFORMS, men wore suits. The style of men's suits has changed little, but women's clothes have changed a great deal. In the late 1960s, young men began to wear more colourful clothes.

In the older countries of the world, there are national costumes of traditional styles. They are usually elaborate clothes, and their design has not changed for centuries. Few people now wear their national costume, except on special occasions.

1. A primitive hunter of northern Europe.
2. A prince and princess of ancient Egypt.
3. The ancient Aztec Indians of Mexico.
4. English costumes of 1490.
5. Fine clothes of the seventeenth century.
6. An eighteenth-century costume.
7. A French family in about 1900.
8. The fashions of the 1920s.
9. A young man of the early 1970s.

Above: The national dress of the people of the Ukraine, Russia.
Below: Traditional Italian dress.
Bottom: Old Swiss costumes.

Uniforms

Uniforms are special clothes worn by people to show that they have a certain job. Most policemen could not easily do their job unless people could immediately see that they belong to the POLICE force. Their uniform tells everyone that they are people of authority.

Soldiers, sailors, and airmen also wear uniforms. Forces of different countries have different uniforms. Their uniform helps to make them feel that they belong to a certain organization. People of different rank or position in the forces have slightly different uniforms. The differences may also show that they have particular skills, just as SCOUTS and GUIDES wear special badges. Many uniforms are splendid to look at.

In many jobs, people do not wear uniforms. In some, people are expected to wear clothes in a certain style. The businessman who dresses in a dark suit every day could be said to be wearing a uniform.

Beefeater, England

Evzone (guard) Greece

Cook

Bandsman, Jamaica

Swiss Guard, Vatican City

Air Hostess

Jewellery

Throughout history, people have liked to adorn themselves with jewellery. They have worn rings, brooches, necklaces, bracelets, earrings, pendants, and lockets either to improve their appearance or just because they like wearing pretty things. Nowadays, most jewellery is worn by women. Most men wear little jewellery, apart from rings.

Jewellery can be made of any material. Simple things can be used, such as pebbles, shells or pieces of wood. Much jewellery is made from costly materials, however, because of their beauty as well as their value. Pieces of jewellery are usually made of precious metals such as gold or SILVER. Gems such as diamonds, rubies, sapphires, and emeralds are often set in bright mounts of gold or silver. Gems are pieces of PRECIOUS MINERALS that are cut in special ways. They gleam and flash as they catch the light.

Some precious materials used for jewellery are not minerals but come from living things. Pearls are produced by oysters, and ivory comes from ELEPHANT tusks. Nowadays, jewellers can make pieces of jewellery from cheap materials that look like precious materials. To many people, it is the appearance of a piece of jewellery that matters and not its value.

Top: Diamond engagement rings.
Above: A Celtic gold collar.
Below: Ancient arm bands.
Below left: Necklaces from tenth century Sweden.

COUNTRIES AND HOMES FACTS AND FIGURES

EUROPE. The world's smallest country, the Vatican City State, has an area of less than half a square kilometre and a population of about 1,000. On average, men live longest in Norway, women in the Netherlands. About 230,000 people emigrate from the U.K. every year.

ASIA. About a third of the world's land and two-thirds of its people are in Asia. The Trans-Siberian Railway which crosses Asia from east to west, is nearly 10,000 kilometres long. The highest and lowest points on land, Mount Everest and the Dead Sea shore, are both in Asia.

AFRICA. In 1950 there were only four independent African nations; by 1979 there were 50, including many small island nations. Liberia, founded as a home for freed American slaves, became the first independent nation in Africa in 1847. The largest African city is Cairo in Egypt.

AFRICA. In 1950 there were only four independent African nations; by 1983 there were 51, including many small island nations. Ethiopia was never colonized, although it was conquered by Italy in 1935 and occupied until 1941. The largest African city is Cairo in Egypt.

AUSTRALIA AND OCEANIA. There are more than 30,000 islands in Australia and Oceania. The smallest independent country is Nauru with a population of 8,000. The largest atoll, Christmas Island, has an area of nearly 500 square kilometres.

CITIES. The world's oldest city, Jericho on the west bank of the River Jordan, dates back to 7800 B.C. The world's most populous city, Shanghai in China, has a population of 11 million. The world's highest city – Lhasa in Tibet – is 3,684 metres above sea level.

FAMOUS MONUMENTS. The biggest monument ever built – a pyramid at Cholula, Mexico – has a volume of over three million cubic metres. The world's tallest monument is the 192-metre arch at St Louis, Missouri. The tallest statue in the world is that of 'Motherland' in the U.S.S.R.

HOMES AROUND THE WORLD. The tallest block of flats is almost 200 metres high; it is in Chicago. As many as 50 families may live together in a longhouse in Borneo. The fastest lifts in skyscrapers move at a speed of 550 metres per minute (33 kilometres per hour).

CLOTHES. A legend says that silk was invented in 2700 B.C. when a Chinese empress dropped a silk cocoon in a cup of tea. The largest diamond, the Star of Africa, weighs 106 grammes. One shearing of a Merino sheep provides enough wool to make eight suits.

THE ARTS AND ENTERTAINMENT

Painting

When an artist paints a picture, he tries to show other people what he feels is important about living in our world.

We do not know when man first began to paint, but the oldest paintings in the world are over 20,000 years old. They were discovered early this century and are pictures of hunters and animals. We do not know exactly how they were painted, but experts think that the materials used were charcoal and CLAY mixed with animal fat.

Pictures like these are still painted by primitive tribesmen, such as some ABORIGINES in AUSTRALIA. These people believe that the painted pictures will attract the animals so that they can be killed and eaten. It seems likely that the cavemen had the same idea.

Until a few hundred years ago, most paintings were of religious subjects. Then, during the Renaissance, artists began to paint people's

Above: A prehistoric painting of a horse on the wall of a cave at Lascaux, France.
Below: An illustration from an early Irish book of psalms.

Below: A richly coloured religious painting of the angel's appearance to Mary. Many medieval painters used flat gold backgrounds.

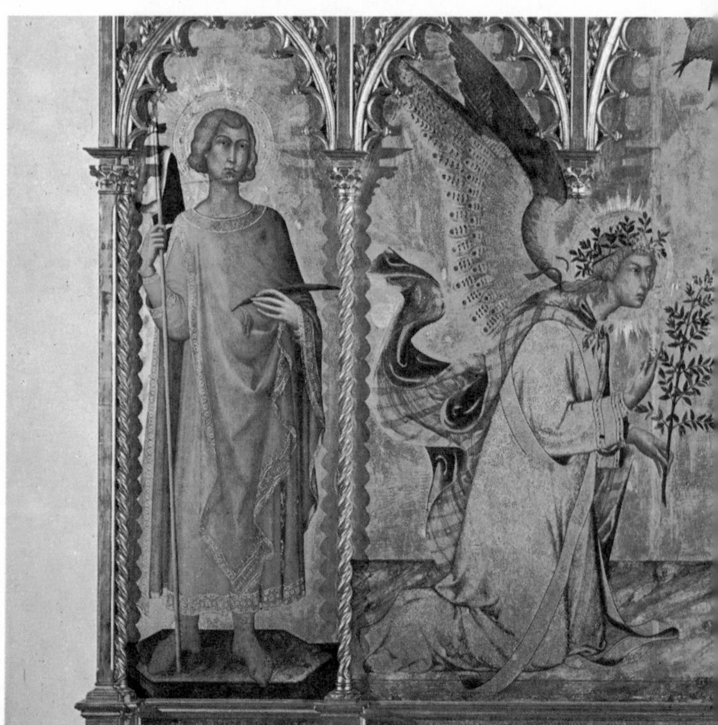

faces (PORTRAITS) and whole figures, too, without adding any religious meaning. (The Renaissance was a great period of rebirth in thinking and the arts that took place during the fourteenth, fifteenth, and sixteenth centuries.) Paintings of the countryside (LANDSCAPES) and of town scenes also became common.

Today, anything can be the subject of a painting. Modern artists, for example, may make paintings which show only lines, curves, or other simple shapes.

Paintings vary greatly in size. Some cover whole walls (murals or wall paintings) and others can be hung from a girl's neck (miniatures). Sometimes paintings are light and airy to look at (many WATERCOLOURS), and sometimes they are rich and dark (some OIL PAINTINGS).

Paints are made from powdered colours, called pigments. These are mixed with a liquid (the binding medium) which allows the artist to work the colours freely for a time before they dry and stick to the surface, to form a hard and lasting layer.

Above: A child's painting.
Below: Some artists like the freshness of children's work so much that they use a child's style in their own paintings.

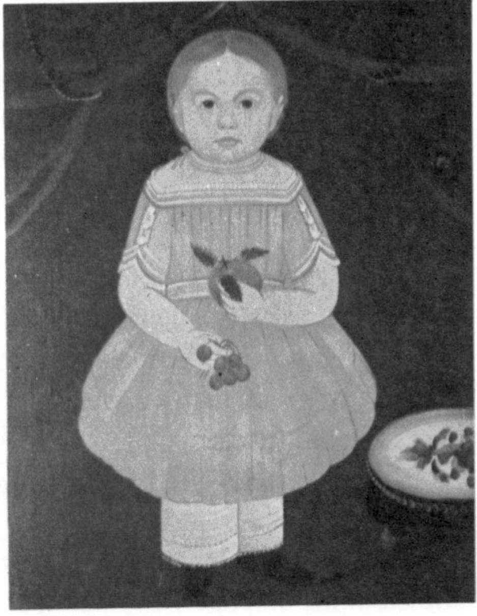

Oriental painting

The word 'oriental' means 'eastern'. Long before the rise of European painting, great works of art were produced in INDIA, CHINA, and JAPAN. No drawings or paintings survive from the very earliest periods. The earliest works from India are carvings and statues from the ancient city of Mohenjo-daro. This city was inhabited as early as 2500 B.C.

Indian art flourished once again when the BUDDHIST religion began in about 500 B.C. Buddhist art includes statues of the Buddha, paintings of stories from his life, and carved TEMPLES. The HINDU religion has also inspired much Indian art.

The style of CHINESE painting is very different from that of Europe. Chinese painting developed from the art of Chinese handwriting with pen and brush. The Chinese artists used coloured inks rather than paint and often used one colour only. This made their work very fine and delicate. Sometimes they painted on long rolls of paper which told a story as they were unrolled. Other paintings were done on silk. The JAPANESE artists also painted on long rolls of paper in the same way.

When Buddhism came to China from India, Indian art influenced the Chinese craftsmen, particularly in temples, and in statues of the Buddha.

Many FRESCOES were painted in temples and MONASTERIES. Not all artists worked on religious themes, however. Scenes from the life of the court and from history were also popular subjects for paintings.

Chinese art reached a very high standard in

Above: An Indian painting of a lady on a swing, surrounded by her attendants.

Right: This lively Japanese street scene was drawn in ink on paper, and painted.

the Sung period (960–1279). Artists made many pictures of LANDSCAPES (hills, rocks, trees, fields and rivers). It became the fashion to paint lonely mountains and WATERFALLS. This was long before such pictures were made in EUROPE where painters have usually preferred people, rather than nature, as subjects. Animals, birds, and plants were also popular subjects. A fluttering bird or a spray of blossom was enough to make a picture.

The Chinese emperor Hui Tsung was a famous painter. He helped and encouraged other artists in their work. However, the names of many of the earlier oriental artists have been lost. It is only comparatively recently that they began to sign their paintings. A famous late Japanese artist, Hokusai (1760–1849), specialised in wood ENGRAVINGS. One of his most famous pictures is *The great wave of Kanagawa* in which the foam on the top of the wave is made to look like claws about to seize two small boats.

Above: A painted Chinese vase.
Below: A Persian manuscript painting from the Middle Ages.

Schools of painting

A group of painters that have similar ideas is often known as a school of painting. There is an Italian school of painting, a Flemish school, a French school and many others. The ANCIENT EGYPTIANS, GREEKS, and ROMANS all produced fine painters, but unfortunately few of their works have survived.

After the decay of the Roman Empire, although interest in painting never died, artists produced less work than before. Some of the pictures that were painted tended to have the rich, patterned quality of MOSAICS. Many artists were influenced by the beautiful mosaics of the BYZANTINE EMPIRE.

The Italian painter Giotto (1267–1337), however, began to paint in quite a different way. His pictures have depth as well as very real feeling. Much of Giotto's work is in the form of FRESCOES. His work looks a little primitive to us, but it was greeted with wonder by the people of Florence. Soon dozens of Italian artists were imitating and developing his style.

On the other side of EUROPE, another great school of painting grew up. The rich Dutch and Flemish tradesmen wanted their PORTRAITS painted, and the walls of their houses decorated. They supported great artists like the brothers Hubert and Jan van Eyck and BRUEGHEL.

Some artists became so busy that they started 'FACTORIES' where they would paint only faces and hands and leave the rest to assistants.

Meanwhile, in ITALY, the Church and the great Italian nobles were supporting the artists, and the churches and PALACES were filled with masterpieces of painting.

Above: A picture in the Byzantine style by the Italian artist Fra Angelico. It shows Jesus surrounded by many angels.

Right: A famous Flemish painting by Jan van Eyck of a rich man and his wife.

Below: A landscape with figures by the French artist Claude. Its subject is from the Bible – David before the Cave of Adullam.

One of the finest periods in Italian art began with the Renaissance (the rebirth of learning). Painters moved away from purely religious subjects (although these were still popular). They became more interested in man. LEONARDO DA VINCI and MICHELANGELO were great artists of the Florentine school; Giovanni Bellini (1430–1516) and TITIAN belonged to the Venetian school.

It was not long before painting began to develop in different ways in different countries, and there were a number of fashions and movements in art. However, in the eighteenth century there was a new interest in the art of GREECE and ROME. The new classical painting (called neo-classical) was most important in FRANCE. Among the greatest neo-classical painters were David (1748–1825) and Ingres (1780–1867).

Above: A picture by Renoir of people in a shower of rain.
Below: This airy springtime landscape was painted by Pissarro.

The Impressionists

Until the nineteenth century, European artists tried to paint things as accurately as possible. They looked at a LANDSCAPE, a face, or a vase, and they tried to copy it in paint on canvas. However, the invention of PHOTOGRAPHY showed how impossible it was to represent solid objects on a flat surface. Artists began to think again about what they were trying to do.

The Impressionists were a group of French artists who found a new answer to this problem. Among the first members of the group were Edouard Manet, Claude Monet, and Pierre Auguste Renoir. They did not try to copy accurately from nature. Instead, they gave their *impression* of things, and tried to show how a scene appeared at one particular moment.

This idea gave artists a new freedom. Monet, for example, could treat a landscape as a pattern of splashes of light and shade. Renoir could show the human body as a collection of soft, rounded shapes. Honoré Daumier could suggest the shape of a man on a horse with a few bold strokes of a brush.

Among other Impressionist painters were Camille Pissarro, Alfred Sisley, and Edgar Degas. Pissarro and Sisley often painted landscapes, but Degas was fascinated by human figures, particularly dancers, whom he often painted.

The Post- (after) Impressionists were a group of painters who were greatly influenced by the Impressionists. The greatest of these was Paul CÉZANNE. Cézanne was more interested in the use of colour than the difference between light and shade. Henri de Toulouse-Lautrec painted a series of vivid impressions of PARIS in the 1890s. He also produced fine THEATRE posters.

Another group of Impressionist painters painted their pictures by means of many tiny dots of colour, in much the same way as colour pictures are printed. One artist who painted in this way was Georges Seurat (1859–91).

Above: *In the Park* by Monet.
Below: The effect of the bright light and heat of a sunny day was the main concern of Alfred Sisley in this landscape.

Modern painting

Although in some ways Seurat was an IMPRESSIONIST painter, he was also one of the first modern painters. Vincent VAN GOGH was a Dutch painter of the same period. His paintings are full of life, movement, and bright colours.

CÉZANNE had already painted many of his LANDSCAPES as though the scenery was made up of blocks or cubes. Early in the twentieth century, a number of artists took this idea even further. They painted straight lines and regular shapes. This movement was called Cubism. The two greatest cubist painters were Georges Braque (1882–1963) and Pablo PICASSO. However, Picasso changed his style away from cubism as his painting developed.

Another group of modern artists included Henri MATISSE. This group was known as the *Fauves* (French for 'wild beasts') because of their daring use of bright colour, and their direct way of painting.

Above: *The First Marriage* (detail) by David Hockney.

Below: A day beside a river, painted as many dots by Seurat.

Yet another movement in painting was Surrealism. Surrealist artists painted a fantastic dream world in which the imagination could run wild. But although this world was imaginary, the paintings were very realistic. The most famous surrealist painter was Salvador Dali.

Many modern artists paint abstract pictures. In these pictures, the artists do not try to copy objects. Instead, they try to express ideas and feelings. These paintings can be difficult to understand. Kandinsky and Mondrian were famous abstract artists. Kandinsky painted free curving shapes. Mondrian often used straight lines in his pictures.

Some abstract artists have been interested only in the way that paint is put onto a canvas. They have tried to forget that it is anything else but what it really is: coloured paint. Action painters work by flinging paint at the canvas from a distance. Sometimes they have dribbled paint out of a tin onto a big picture laid flat on the floor. Jackson Pollock was one of a group of action painters.

Above: A painting in the Cubist style by Braque. He painted the mandolin as though it were made of broken stone.
Below: An example of Op Art, by Vasarely. The shapes seem to move about and confuse the eye.

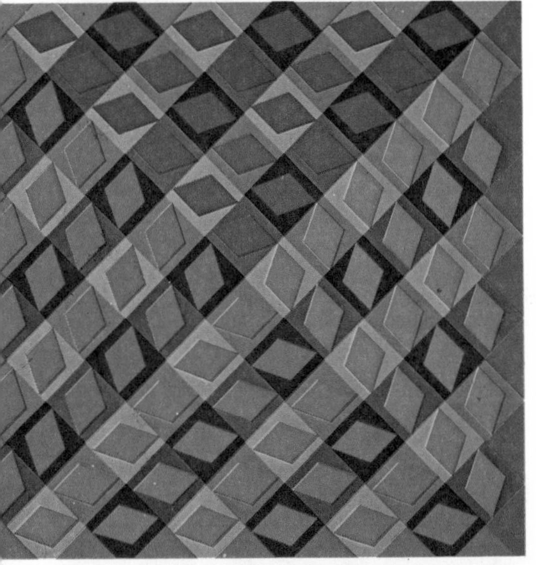

There have been many other movements in modern painting. In England the Kitchen Sink artists were interested in very simple harsh subjects such as cold-looking sculleries and bathrooms. Pop artists produce pictures in the style of advertisements or illustrations in children's comics. They love brightness. Today many artists are turning away from abstract work towards more realistic paintings.

Watercolour painting

For a long time, some paints have been made from pigments (colours) mixed with water and gum. Such paints are often called watercolours. An artist using true watercolours does not paint with white. Instead, he lets the material he is painting on (usually paper) show through the paint to give a light and airy look. This is why, in true watercolour paintings, the colours need to be transparent or partly transparent. True watercolours are well suited to pictures that are painted out-of-doors.

Another kind of watercolour is called poster paint or gouache. These paints are opaque, which means the paper will not show through them. True watercolours have to be put on quickly and surely, without mistakes. Poster paints are easier to use because mistakes can be hidden by over-painting.

A watercolour painting over a sketch made by a pen is known as pen and wash.

FRESCOES, which are painted on the plaster of walls, are also a kind of watercolour painting. The first important western watercolours were painted by British artists in the second half of the eighteenth century.

Most of the British watercolour painters specialized in LANDSCAPES. Some of the best-known of these artists were Francis Towne, Thomas Girtin, J.M.W. TURNER, John Sell Cotman and Peter de Wint.

These artists usually chose to paint scenes from nature. They particularly favoured wild and romantic scenes. The colours they worked with were often quiet.

One artist who used watercolours in a different way was William Blake (1757–1827). Blake was a very religious man who painted his own visions of heaven and hell, as well as scenes

Above: A powerful painting by Blake – *The Good and Evil Angels Struggling for a Child*.
Below: *Chirk Aqueduct* by Cotman.

from the Bible. His style is unlike that of any other painter.

Today, many people paint in watercolours for fun because the equipment needed is cheap and easy to use.

Recently, chemists have invented new materials to help artists with their paintings. One of the most important of these is acrylic paint, which is mixed with water, like watercolours, and which dries very quickly. If you work with acrylics you can paint on many different surfaces – such as glass or cardboard – without preparing them beforehand.

If you would like to use poster paints you will need:

- A set of poster paints.
- Large, medium, and small brushes.
- A piece of paper on a board.
- A palette with wells in it.
- Water in a container.
- Clothes pegs to hold the paper down.

Below: A girl using poster colours in the open air.
Below right: A child's painting of farmers at harvest time.

Oil painting

Oil paints are pure pigments (colours) ground up and mixed with a drying oil. It is possible to use them in many different ways. They can be brushed on to give thin or thick effects. They can be put on with a special tool called a painting knife. The pigments may either be light and delicate or dark. The colours dry so slowly that it is easy to move them about for a day or two in order to blend them or to change the picture.

Oil painting was first done in Germany and the NETHERLANDS during the fourteenth century. Certain artists realised that they could use pigments mixed with oil in new and exciting ways. They could produce results that were impossible for anyone working in WATERCOLOURS.

Right: *Sunflowers* by Vincent van Gogh.

The new method became very popular. The brothers Jan and Hubert van Eyck were the first great painters in oils. Since their time, oils have been used for all kinds of subjects. Most important western painters have worked in oils. MICHELANGELO sometimes painted with oil and tempera paints on the same picture. (In tempera painting, the binding medium is often egg yolk.) REMBRANDT, GOYA, and TURNER all used oil paints.

An oil painting is made on a prepared support. This can be a canvas, a wooden panel, or a piece of board. If canvas is used, it must first be stretched carefully on a frame called a stretcher. The canvas is tightened by means of wedges.

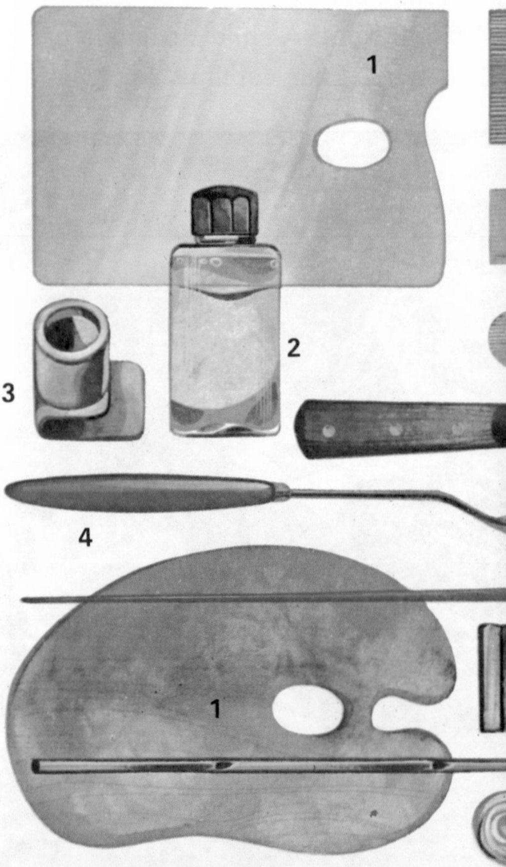

Right: Oil painting materials: (1) Palettes. (2) Linseed oil. (3) Dipper. (4) Painting knife. (5) Flat brushes. (6) Round brush. (7) Palette knife. (8) Filbert brush. (9) Sable brush. (10) Oil paint. (11) Charcoal. (12) Mahl stick. (13) Canvas.

Above: *The Painter's Workshop* by Courbet. A naked model looks over the artist's shoulder.

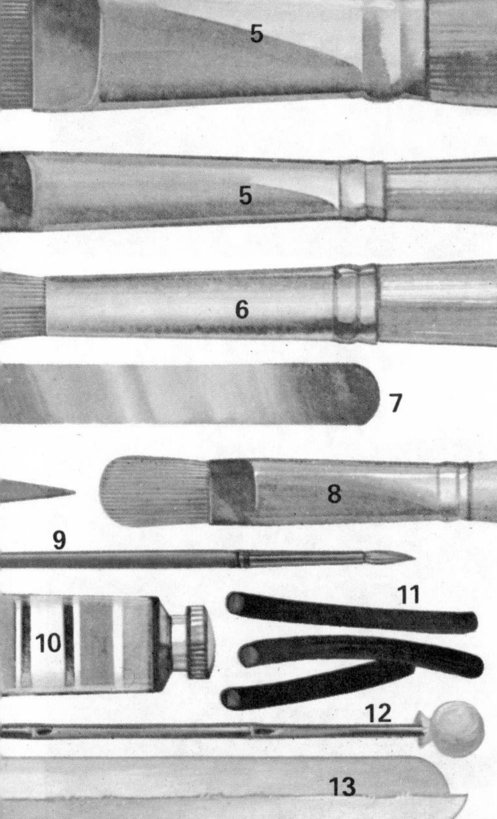

One or two thin layers of glue are often first painted on the support. A white or coloured background is then applied over the glue. This makes the surface slightly absorbent.

The paints are usually prepared with a painting knife on a thin board called a palette. The oil used for mixing with the pigments has to dry within a few days. Linseed oil and poppy oil are the most common drying oils used in oil painting. The paints are usually put on with hog's bristle brushes. Delicate work is sometimes done with a sable brush.

An artist thins his oil paints with turpentine or with one of the other liquid mixtures known as painting mediums. He keeps his painting medium in a small flat tin called a dipper, which clips on to the top of his palette.

Landscapes

To early painters, the countryside was only a background to the people in their paintings.

In the fifteenth century, a number of Italian and Flemish artists realised that nature itself was beautiful. They began to paint the countryside without human figures, or in a way in which human figures played only a small part. These landscape paintings became very popular and more and more artists painted them.

The seventeenth century was a great period for landscape painting, with the Dutch producing many fine landscape painters, such as Ruisdael. Realistic painting of landscapes continued into the eighteenth century. John Constable painted typical English scenes, mainly in oils. The British WATERCOLOUR painters of the eighteenth and nineteenth centuries also liked to paint landscapes.

Nowadays some artists use spades, picks and bulldozers on real stretches of landscape to alter them to their own ways of feeling and thinking. This is called Land Art.

Top right: Constable's *Hay Wain*, and (right) the scene he painted as it is today.
Below: A watercolour of mountains in Australia.

Above: An eighteenth-century portrait by Sir Joshua Reynolds.

Portraits

About six centuries ago, artists were often paid by great Italian nobles and rich Flemish merchants. Such people were called patrons. They sometimes had their portraits painted to show how rich and handsome they were. The artists often painted pictures showing their patrons in the company of saints.

Later, artists began to paint their patrons much more naturally, perhaps playing with a child or a pet DOG. They also sometimes painted ordinary people, like tailors and farmers, just because they had interesting faces. Both these types of portraits give us a good idea of how people dressed and how they lived. Today, wealthy people still get artists to paint their portraits.

Left: A modern portrait — the writer Somerset Maugham by Graham Sutherland.

Frescoes

A fresco is a picture painted on to the plaster of a wall. The colours, or pigments, in fresco painting are usually mixed with limewater.

Some of the finest frescoes still to be seen are those painted in ITALY during the Renaissance, especially by the artists of Florence. Giotto and Masaccio were among the great fresco painters.

In order to paint a fresco, the artist would make a big drawing, called a cartoon, of the same size as the picture he planned to paint. He copied the drawing on to the wall. Then, if he were painting in true fresco, he would lay pure colours, mixed with limewater, straight on to a coat of smooth wet plaster. The colours sank into the plaster and dried hard with it. True fresco lasts as long as the plaster on which it is painted. Many true frescoes are now cracked.

Above: A Byzantine mosaic in Ravenna, Italy. The main colour in the picture is seen again in the

Below: A modern mural from Australia.

decorated ceiling. The artist has cleverly fitted the design into the curve.

An artist working in 'dry fresco' would lay his paint on plaster that was already dry and hard. Although this was a simpler way of painting, it did not make such a lasting piece of work as true fresco, since the paint could flake off.

Modern wall paintings are often known as murals.

Mosaics

Small pieces of coloured material, such as stone or GLASS, can be fitted together to make pictures or patterns known as mosaics. A mosaic is ornamental or decorative. It can be put on a wall, a CEILING, or a floor. Children sometimes cut, decorate, and fire pieces of CLAY at school to make into mosaics on tables or floors.

When a mosaic is being made, the small squares or rectangles of marble or glass are pressed into wet cement or plaster. In some wall mosaics, the pieces (tesserae) are left sticking out very slightly at different angles, so as to catch the light. When you walk round a building with good mosaics on the walls, you will see these little pieces of material glittering like jewels.

Mosaics were known to the ANCIENT GREEKS and ROMANS, and there are parts of mosaic pavements still to be seen in Roman ruins in many countries. Hadrian's villa in Tivoli, ITALY has some fine Roman mosaics.

The Christians of the BYZANTINE EMPIRE probably made the most beautiful mosaics. The church of San Vitale in Ravenna, Italy, is covered inside with sparkling gold, red, green and purple mosaics.

Mosaics are still sometimes used today in or around buildings.

Left: A medieval wall painting of a city under good government by A. Lorenzetti of Siena.

Still-life

A still-life is a painting of a group of household objects, often arranged on a table. The patrons who helped to support early Italian artists liked to be painted surrounded by their possessions. However, it was not until the sixteenth century that a painter called Caravaggio actually painted a study of household objects on their own, without the presence of the patron.

Later artists painted arrangements of things they found of interest or beauty – pots and pans, bowls of fruit, piles of food and FLOWERS. Among the greatest still-life painters were those of the seventeenth-century Dutch school. They painted objects with great realism, sometimes adding guns and dead animals such as RABBITS and GAME BIRDS.

Right: An example of a still-life of flowers and fruit, painted by the Dutch artist Jan van Huysum. Notice the detail in the picture.

Many people consider a Frenchman called Chardin to be the greatest still-life painter ever. He was less concerned with absolute realism than the Dutch painters, and he liked rich and glowing colours.

Two Post-IMPRESSIONIST artists who painted still-life pictures were CÉZANNE and VAN GOGH. Their paintings are not at all realistic. Instead, they show the way in which the artists saw the objects they were painting. The objects are also more homely – APPLES, onions, a pot of flowers, or a pipe.

Right: A painting in quiet colours by the famous French still-life painter Jean Baptiste Chardin. The outlines of the objects are less distinct than those in the painting above.

Above: Two examples of simple collages made by children. The top collage is made with fabric, and the other with tissue paper.

Collage

A collage is a design made by an artist using all kinds of materials that have taken his fancy. It may be a picture of something we can recognise easily, or it may be simply a pattern or abstract. The objects are usually stuck with glue on to a piece of wood, cardboard, or similar supporting material. Sometimes they are painted.

The Cubist painters invented collage. Early collages (known as *papiers collés*) were made from pieces of different kinds of paper cut into shapes and stuck together to make a picture. Wallpapers and NEWSPAPER were used for this. Afterwards, the shapes were worked on with pencil, ink, or paint. Later, different materials were used, such as oilcloth, sand and GLASS. In most good picture collages the objects are not what they portray. For instance, a piece of fabric can become a leaf, and a leaf a ship.

A collage may be in high RELIEF (well raised above the surface it is stuck to) or it may be almost flat. Wire, pieces of wood or metal, newspaper, tissue paper, twigs, matchboxes, brick-ends, and slate have all been stuck to canvas or board to make exciting designs. Today, some artists use many unexpected materials in their work, including cloth, refuse and earth.

To make a collage, you will need:

- A collection of suitable objects.
- A board or similar support.
- Some glue.

It is best to draw a design first in a sand tray or drawing book. Transfer your drawing to the background. Arrange your objects on the background following the drawing only as much as you feel you need to. Then put glue on parts of the background and stick the objects down. Go on doing this till you have a good design.

Drawing

Painters usually make drawings or studies for their pictures before they begin to paint. In some cases they fit into their pictures ideas from drawings made many years earlier. Today, it is often thought that a few lines drawn by a gifted artist may be as interesting as a finished painting.

Some of the world's finest drawings were made by LEONARDO DA VINCI, RAPHAEL, REMBRANDT, and GOYA. A good artist does more than simply draw objects; he can express ideas, moods, and feelings too.

Drawings may be used both to make notes of ideas and to express those ideas clearly. Architects, sculptors, and painters all use drawings in this way. For example, an architect may make rough drawings to work out details of a new building. Later, he will make finished drawings from which the builders can work.

Artists can use different tools and materials for drawing with. These include brushes, metal points, crayons, pens and pencils.

Charcoal is sometimes used for drawing with. Sticks of drawing charcoal are brittle and black; they are usually made from half-burnt WILLOW twigs. Drawings done in charcoal often have a free and lively feeling about them. Big pictures can be worked out in charcoal, which is easily changed with a rubber, or by flicking with a rag. Two coats of fixative (a clear varnish) should be sprayed on to a charcoal drawing to stop it from smudging.

Black and red chalks were often used by artists in the past, for making both rough early drawings and final ones.

Right: A drawing by Tiepolo of a man wearing a hat. It is done with ink washes of different strengths combined with lines.

Crayons are formed from powdered colours called pigments, held together by a binder like oil or wax. They do not smudge easily. They are good for making coloured drawings out-of-doors.

Pencil drawing was not popular until the nineteenth century. Pencils are usually formed from powdered graphite and CLAY baked together. They vary in hardness from 6H (very hard) to 6B (very soft). Like charcoal, the softer kinds need two coats of fixative to prevent smudging.

Left: A strong and imaginative landscape drawing by Samuel Palmer. This is done in sepia (brown) washes and pen and ink.

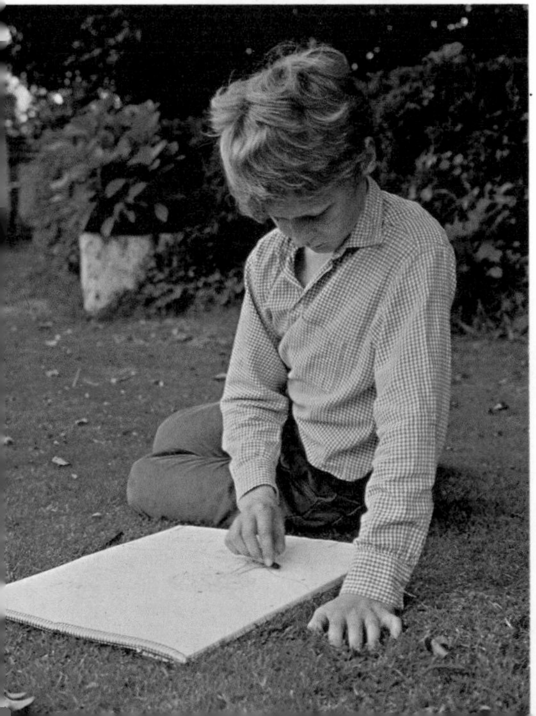

Once it is dry, ink does not smudge, and it lasts for a long time. Inks are mixed with water to make washes of different strengths. Black can be used to make lines, the spaces between often being filled with washes of different colours.

Sometimes a design is drawn in a form that allows it to be printed. It can then be repeated again and again. There are many different ways of printing. Some of them need great skill. They include ENGRAVING, ETCHING, WOODCUTS, and SURFACE PRINTING. In most cases, the design needs to be drawn in reverse. When it is printed, we get a MIRROR image of the original.

If you are interested in art, you should have a drawing book of your own, and practise drawing a great deal. Try crayons, charcoal and pencil first. Anything that appeals to you is worth drawing. Sometimes you may decide to work in a careful and painstaking way. At other times you may draw rapidly and freely, as Tiepolo has done opposite.

Left: A child making a drawing out-of-doors.

Engraving

An artist makes an engraving by cutting or scratching a design on a smooth piece of wood or metal with a sharp tool.

Today, engraving is mostly used for PRINTING designs. There are two main ways of doing this: relief and intaglio.

In relief engraving, the artist first cuts his design into the smooth surface of a wood block or metal plate. Ink is rolled on to this surface and then paper is carefully laid over it and pressed down. When the artist pulls the paper off he finds his design printed in reverse (back-to-front) on the paper. Only those parts of the surface that were not cut away will have printed. WOODCUTS and wood engravings are engraved in relief.

Intaglio engraving is the opposite of relief engraving. The ink is held in the lines and wiped off the plate's smooth surface. Then, soft damp paper is put on the plate and a press squeezes it down into the inky lines. The raised parts do not print but the paper picks up the ink from the lines. Line (or metal) engraving and ETCHING are examples of intaglio engraving.

Above: Durer's *Rhinoceros* is an

Above: A seventeenth-century engraved glass from England.

Below: Engraving with hardboard.
(1) Scratch your design in deep lines on the smooth side of à piece of hardboard. (2) Roll paint or ink over the hardboard with a roller.

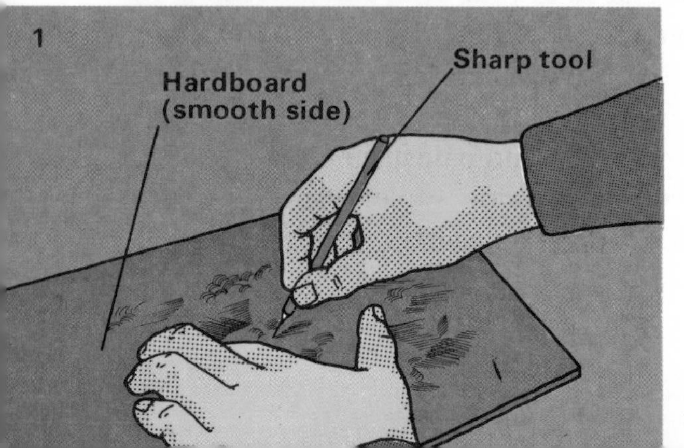

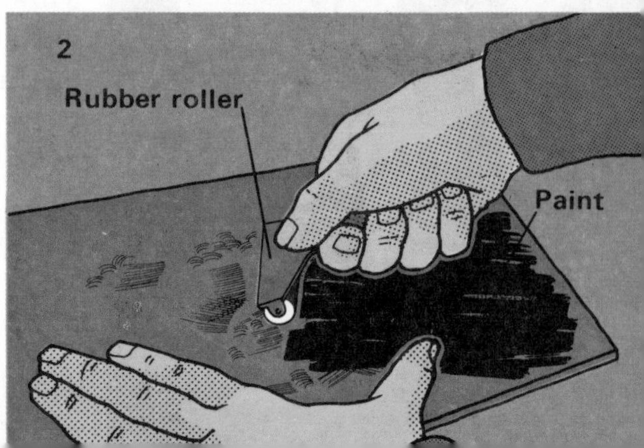

xample of intaglio engraving.

Above: An etching of a wharf by J. M. Whistler.

Etching

An etching is a special kind of ENGRAVING. It is made by using acid to eat away lines cut in a COPPER or zinc plate.

First, the plate is coated with a waxy material. This coat is smoked black, so that when the artist 'draws' his design through the smoked surface, his lines will show up clearly.

Next, he lowers the plate into a bath (dish) of acid. This eats into the metal where the covering has been scratched away. The back of the plate is protected from the acid by a coat of varnish.

The artist lifts out the plate, and puts varnish on the parts of his design that he wants to keep fine and delicate. Then he repeats the process until the acid has bitten deeply into his strongest lines.

Afterwards, he dabs ink on to the plate and wipes the surface clean. Then he puts a piece of paper on the plate, lays a blanket over the paper, and runs it between the rollers of a strong press. The paper is pushed on to the ink held in the lines to give a print. Sometimes a little ink is left between the lines, as in relief engraving.

Below: (3) The ink is wiped from the surface with a cloth and paper is pressed on to it.
(4) When the paper is pulled off the surface you will have an intaglio engraving.

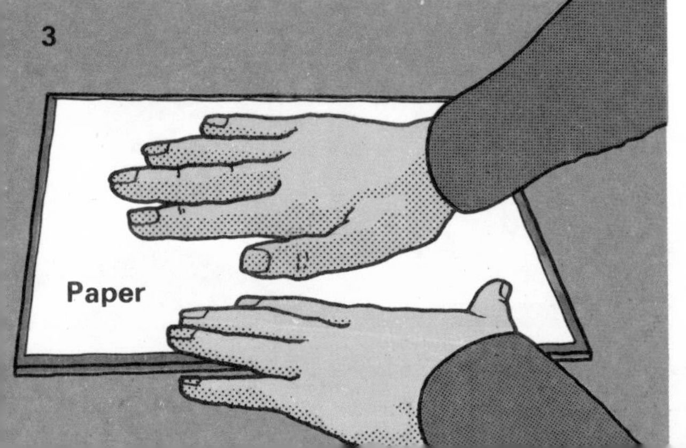

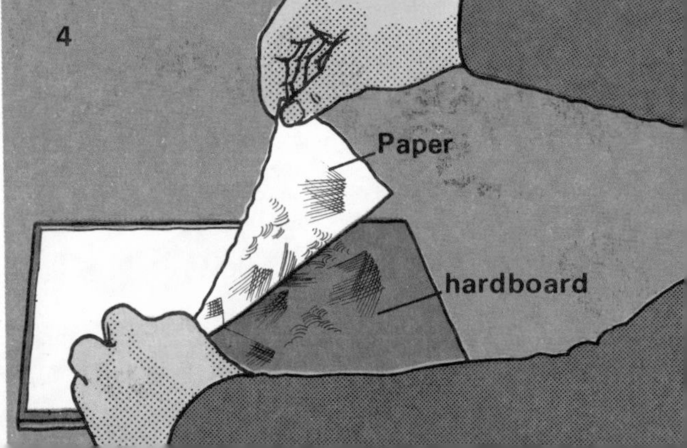

Woodcuts

Making a woodcut is an old way of printing on paper. The CHINESE were using woodcuts in the ninth century A.D. A print taken from a woodcut is usually bold and simple and it can be in colour.

To make a woodcut, an artist cuts V-shaped lines with a sharp knife in a soft wood. Nowadays, he may use such materials as sandpaper to give special effects. He cuts away with a gouge whatever parts he does not want to print. (A gouge is a U- or V-shaped chisel.)

Afterwards, he presses a piece of printing paper on to the inked surface with a burnisher or spoon handle.

A wood ENGRAVING can have almost as much detail in it as a metal engraving. The artist cuts his drawing across the end grain of a block of box wood with a sharp tool which is called a burin or scraper.

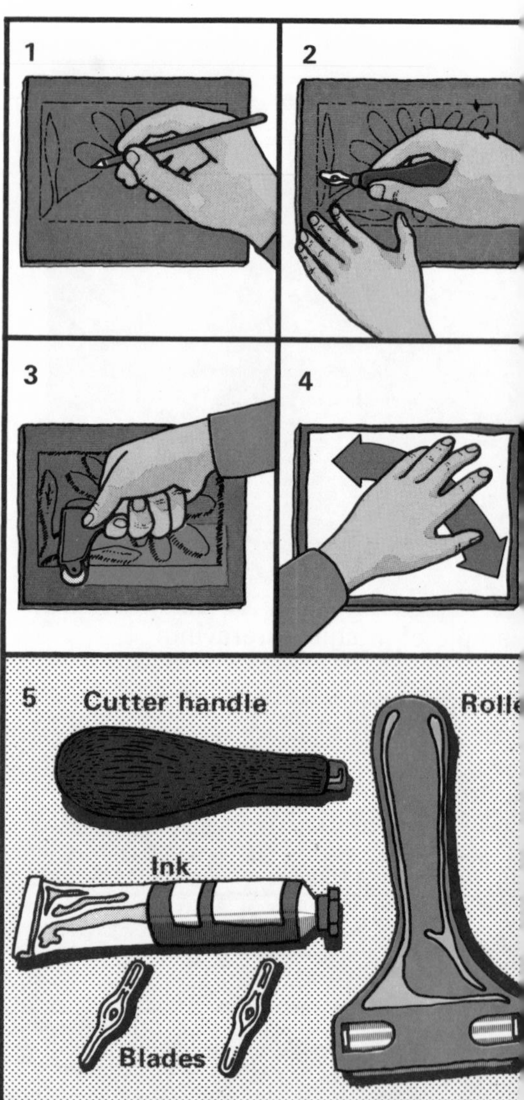

Right (top to bottom): Making a lino-cut. Lino-cuts are made in much the same way as woodcuts. (1) Draw the design on to a block of lino. (2) Cut out the parts you do *not* want to print. (3) Roll ink on to the surface. (4) Press the paper on to the lino block. (5) Some lino-cutting equipment. (6) The finished print.
Below: A wood engraving by Thomas Bewick.

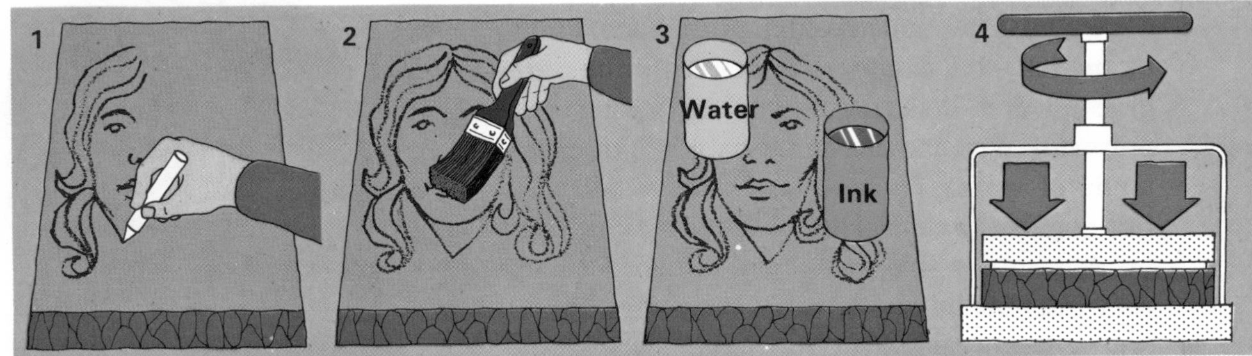

Surface printing

An artist who prints his designs from a smooth surface, without cutting any of it away, is making a surface print. Lithography is the main kind of surface printing.

A German called Senefelder invented lithography in about 1798. It is made possible by the fact that grease repels (throws off) water. In lithography, an artist may use a greasy crayon to draw his image, or he may have a special ink and various types of brushes. He can also use tools for scratching the surface.

The artist first draws his design on the smooth surface of a metal plate or on to a piece of special limestone. He usually does this with a greasy crayon or ink. Then he fixes the marks he has made, which means he keeps his drawing on the stone by coating it with gum and acid. He damps the stone with water and rolls a layer of printing ink over it. The greasy ink is thrown off by the clean damp stone, but it sticks to the marks of the drawing.

The artist takes a print by laying a piece of printing paper on the inked stone and putting it through a press.

Nowadays, metal plates are used in lithography for PRINTING photographs and other things besides artists' designs. Posters and maps are examples of this.

Above: Making a lithograph.
(1) The artist draws a portrait with greasy chalk on the stone. (2) A coating of gum and acid is laid over the whole surface of the stone with a brush. (3) The stone is damped with water, and then a layer of ink is rolled over it. (4) A piece of paper is placed on the stone and pressed down.
Below: *May Belfort* – a lithograph by Toulouse-Lautrec.

Sculpture

Sculpture is the name given to a number of kinds of models and carvings. Some sculptures are graceful and delicate; others are strong and powerful. Wax and CLAY are very good for many kinds of work. They are easily modelled and built up from a central lump. Wood carvings can be delicate, or like many sculptures in stone, they can be solid and firm in feeling. Both wood and stone are carved from a solid block.

Some sculptures have lasted for thousands of years. Little figures of stone or ivory, often representing their gods, were made by early man.

Right: An example of free-standing sculpture. A head, cast in bronze, from Benin in Nigeria, West Africa.

Much later, the EGYPTIANS, GREEKS, and ROMANS made sculptures from many different substances, including marble and METAL. During the Renaissance, sculptors like Donatello and MICHELANGELO made powerful and beautiful sculptures in stone.

Until recently, most sculpture represented gods, animals, or men. It was usually made to decorate important buildings. Much sculpture also used to be painted.

Modern sculptors, however, often take shapes or patterns as their subjects, and they rarely paint on stone. They put into sculptured form ideas and feelings about the nature of modern life. Some of them have been very much affected by science, showing great interest in lines, circles, and machine-like forms.

The best sculptors are careful to choose the right material for the kinds of feelings or ideas they are working with. Modern sculptors have tried out new materials, such as expanded polystyrene, PLASTICS and fibre glass.

Relief sculpture

When a piece of sculpture is flattish or shallow-looking, it is known as a relief. This means that those of its proportions that give it depth have been shortened, while its other proportions have not been changed.

In some senses, a relief sculpture is half way between a picture and a solid piece of FREE-STANDING SCULPTURE (sculpture that we can walk around). Relief sculptures were often used to decorate the walls of buildings or other flat surfaces.

Left: A medium relief modelled in clay. A terracotta (red clay) bust of Dionysus, the Ancient Greek god of wine.

Reliefs may be high, medium, or low. In high relief, the proportion of the depth of the piece is not greatly reduced.

The forms may be undercut to allow them to stand out sharply from their background. Shadows play an important part in high reliefs. A low relief has no undercutting and the forms seem flat.

In ancient times, the Sumerians used to make high reliefs by hammering COPPER sheets over wooden moulds. Among the finest relief sculptures of animals ever carved were those of the Assyrians. The GREEKS carved bands of reliefs (friezes) in marble on important buildings. An Italian named Lorenzo Ghiberti modelled and cast two sets of bronze doors in relief for a building in Florence.

Left: A very high relief in metal. A panel from the bronze door of the Baptistery, Florence, Italy. The sculptor, Ghiberti, has used low relief for objects in the background.

Above: A head modelled by Manzu in terracotta (red clay).
Below: An early king of Syria.

Free-standing sculpture

Pictures and low RELIEFS can be looked at only from the front. Free-standing sculpture can be walked around and viewed from all sides. This makes special problems for the sculptor. (A painter does not have to consider his pictures from every angle.) However, all the objects around us have three dimensions – height, breadth, and depth – and so it is perhaps more natural to work in-the-round, as it is called, rather than in-the-flat, as a painter does.

A sculptor working on a piece of free-standing sculpture has to use his materials in such a way that they will support their own weight. If he is modelling materials like CLAY or plaster he will probably use some kind of supporting skeleton (armature). This is often made of wire or lead tubing. It will hold up tall or overhanging forms.

If he is carving out of stone or wood, he must leave enough material in the lower parts to hold up the whole piece. To support figures, for example, sculptors have used carved tree-trunks, rocks, and the limbs of other figures. In general, however, a good design does not rely greatly on supports.

The EGYPTIANS and ANCIENT GREEKS carved figures out of stone in such a way that it did not lose its solid and powerful nature. Later Greeks were so skilful that their marble figures of perfectly formed people often look as if they would have been better suited to METAL SCULPTURE.

Epstein and Henry MOORE are modern sculptors who have suited their designs to their materials. Their ideas have come partly from the sculpture of primitive peoples.

For several centuries, most sculpture has been left unpainted. Recently, however, some sculptors have again begun painting such materials as wood.

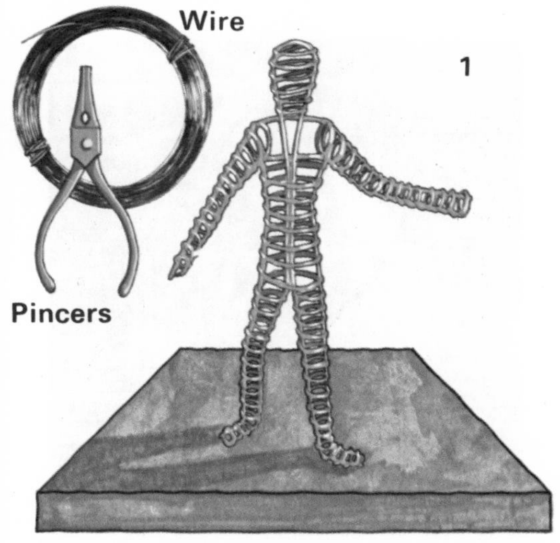

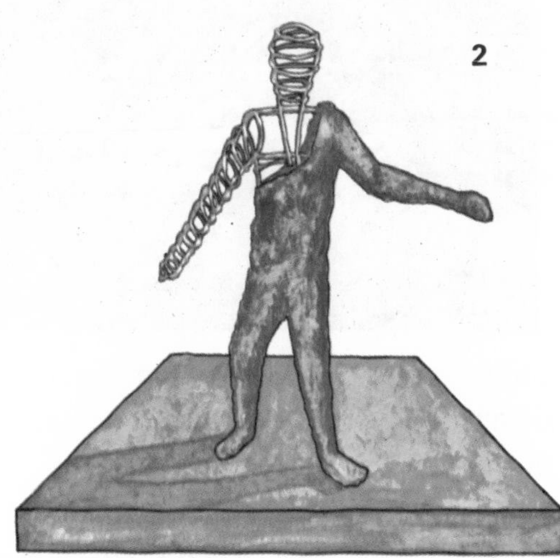

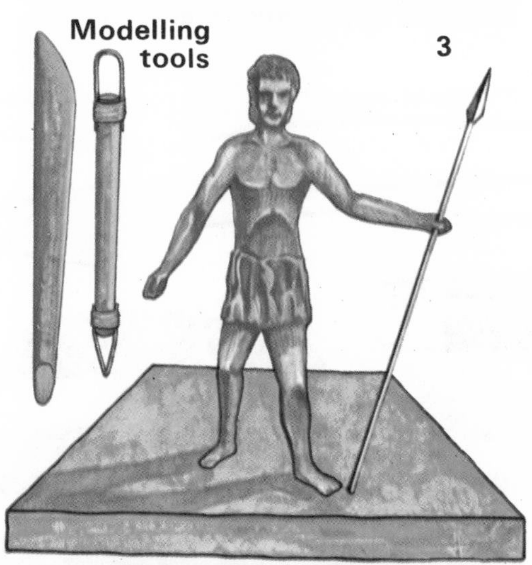

Modelling

To make a model, a sculptor uses a soft material such as CLAY, wax, or plaster. The model may be left as it is or used to make a mould for casting.

Clay. To prevent clay from falling over and losing shape while it is being modelled, it is often built up on a support. A sculptor who is making a portrait in clay sometimes wraps a rope around a tapered post and builds up the clay on the rope. When the clay is firm, he first takes out the post and then the rope. After it has dried, his model is fired in a kiln. Clay can be given many different kinds of surface, from very rough to perfectly smooth.

Metal. A metal sculpture that has been cast from a clay model is not brittle (easily broken) as fired clay is. When the sculpture is cast, the metal holds every mark the sculptor has made on the clay.

Wax. Big or small wax models have often been used by sculptors to guide them in their carving of wood or stone.

Plaster. Plaster is generally used for making models to cast in another material. It can be built up like clay on a support of wood or lead tubing wrapped with straw or rags.

Left: How to make a model. You will need:
- Clay, papier mâché, or a similar material.
- Wire and a base board.
- Pincers and modelling tools.

METHOD

An armature (supporting skeleton) is made from wire and fastened to a base board (1). The sculpture is built up in stages on top of the armature. The clay must be kept damp (2). Modelling tools are used for finishing (3).

Wood-carving

If you have ever whittled away at a stick with a penknife, you will know that wood can be a most enjoyable material to work with. It can be carved to make both RELIEF and FREE-STANDING shapes. Wood is also carved to make parts of buildings or pieces of FURNITURE.

Soft woods are more difficult to carve than harder ones. The best wood-carvers have a strong feeling for the way the wood grew while it was alive (shown by its grain) and for the movement this suggests to them. Wood is a light and slender material compared with stone. Forms that stand out sharply from their background are more natural to wood than they are to stone. But wood does not last as long as stone or METAL. It may rot or woodworm may attack it.

African sculptors have used hard wood to carve fantastic religious MASKS and statues of gods. The great seventeenth-century English sculptor, Grinling Gibbons, made many carvings of fruit, GAME BIRDS, and FLOWERS.

The sap must dry out from a piece of wood before it is cut. That is, the wood must be well seasoned. The main tools used in carving wood are V- or U-shaped gouges, which are hit with a mallet or pushed carefully with both hands.

Top: A cravat, carved in wood by Grinling Gibbons. Gibbons produced many fine pieces of carving for Sir Christopher Wren.
Above: A carving in wood on a religious theme, from France.

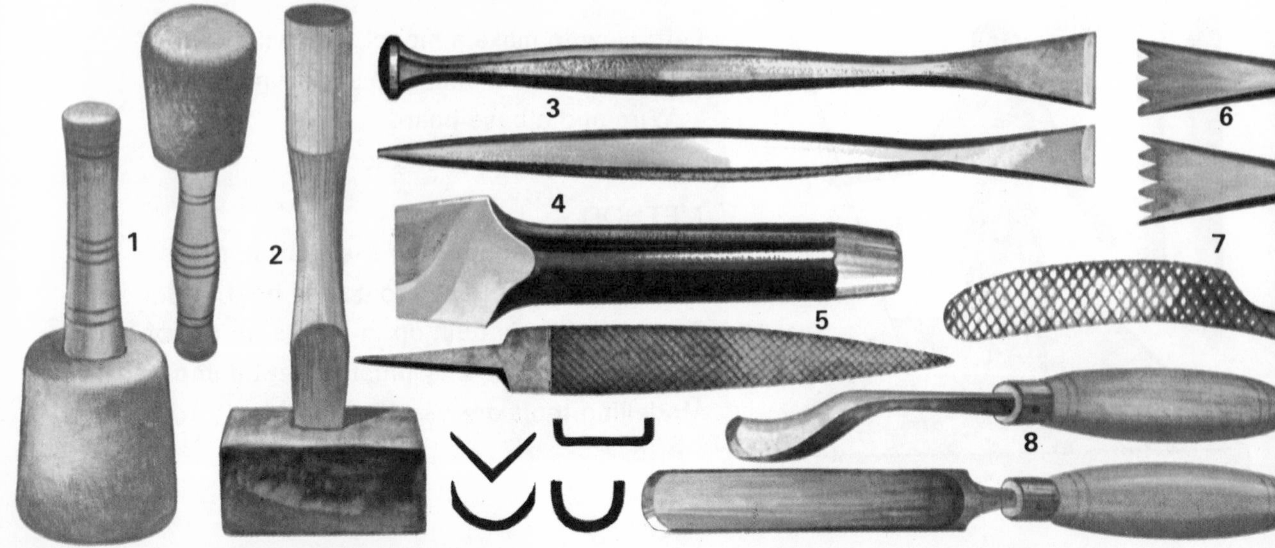

Stone-carving

Very many different kinds of stone have been used in the past for sculpture. Like wood, stone can be soft or hard. But, unlike wood, the softer stones are easier to shape than the hard ones.

During the Middle Ages, English craftsmen were famous for carvings done in alabaster, which is a soft pink or whitish stone. Soap-stone, sometimes used for carving by ESKIMOS, cuts easily too.

Limestone was carved by the EGYPTIANS, who were among the finest sculptors in stone that the world has ever seen. They also made sculptures out of very hard stones, such as granite. MICHELANGELO, like the GREEKS and ROMANS, used marble, which is very hard. Eric Gill and Henry MOORE are two English sculptors who have worked successfully with stone.

Most modern sculptors carve stone directly. This means that they do not rely on measuring devices to find the correct proportions. Often they will try to 'release' the form (which they hold in their minds) from the rough stone block. It is as if their idea was imprisoned in the stone.

Among the tools used for carving stone are the point and the claw. The point is a short pointed steel bar. The claw is a chisel with teeth. Both tools are hit with a hammer.

Limestone and alabaster are both suitable for beginners to work on. The blocks may be placed in a wooden box filled with sand. They can then be moved about to face in different directions, as required.

Left: Tools for carving stone and wood:
(1) Mallets. (2) Hammer. (3) Chisels. (4) Pitcher.
(5) Rasp. (6) Claw chisels. (7) Riffler. (8) Gouges.
The hammer, chisels, pitcher, and claws are for stone; the gouges are for wood.

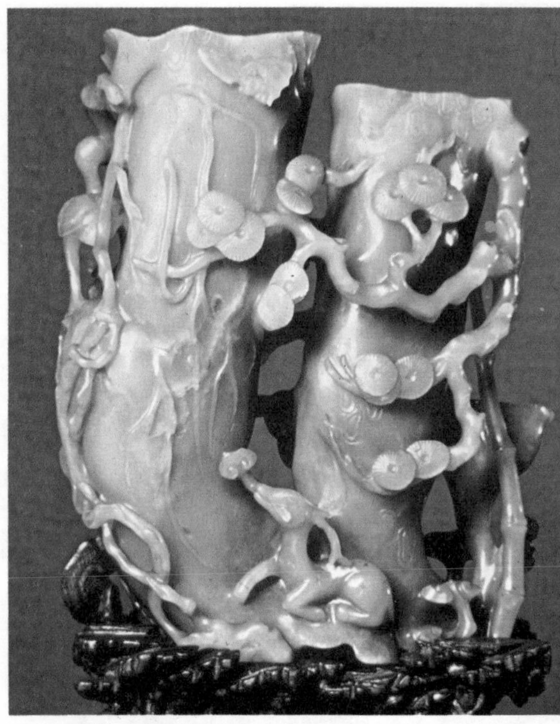

Above: A Chinese jade vase of the eighteenth century. Jade is a very hard stone and needs careful workmanship.
Below: *The Crucifixion* by Eric Gill.

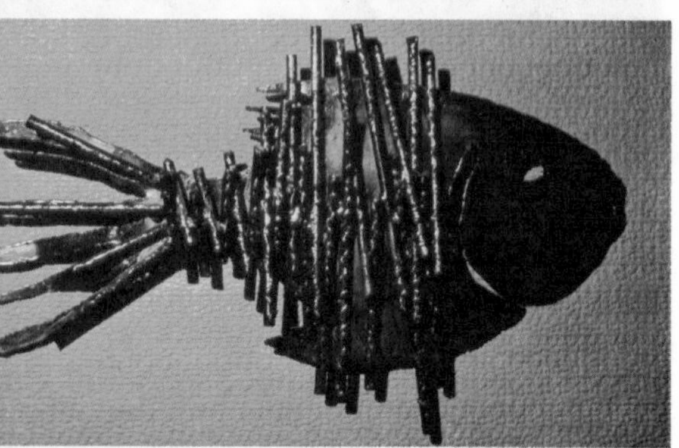

Metal sculpture

Like stone, METAL can be made to express bulkiness and weight. But it is also possible to form all kinds of shapes in metal that would not stand upright in stone. Tall graceful shapes, long wiry shapes and shapes that are thin or overhanging are suited to metal sculpture.

CLAY or wax models may sometimes be cast in metal to produce a less fragile, and therefore longer-lasting, sculpture. Bronze is the most common metal used in CASTING sculptures. It is made from COPPER, to which is added a little tin, or some other metal, such as zinc or lead, which will harden the copper.

The unfinished surface left after casting is often cleaned off by the sculptor himself. As time passes, bronze takes on a most beautiful green or brown surface called a patina. Today, this green surface can be produced artificially after the sculpture has been cast.

During the twentieth century, sculptors have used other metals besides bronze for their work. The invention of electric WELDING made it possible to join pieces of metal together without using bolts or rivets. Sculptures have been made from rods, beams and sheets of steel, ALUMINIUM, and other metals. Metal is also sometimes used together with other materials, such as wood or PLASTICS.

In much modern metal sculpture it is possible to see the influence of work done by the engineers and architects who design objects used in everyday life.

Top left: *Structure* by Stephen Gilbert.
Middle left: *The Fish*, a wall sculpture made of steel.
Below left: Making a cast of a metal sculpture in a foundry.

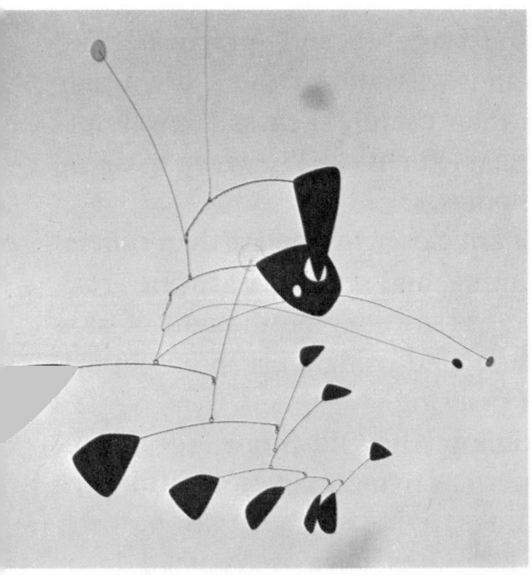

Paper sculpture and mobiles

Today, many artists and sculptors are interested in the shapes and patterns that lie within natural objects. They may also be interested in the forms suggested by a material itself.

Paper is a good material to use for sculpture that is not meant to last a long time. Paper can be cut, torn, curled and folded to form figures, animals and plants. The Japanese have a kind of paper sculpture called origami. In origami, the paper is always folded into shape and never cut or torn.

Mobiles are pieces of abstract sculpture that are usually moved by the currents of air in a room or by the wind outside. Other pieces are moved by motors and look like complicated machines. Simple mobiles can be made with shapes cut from thick paper or card.

Top left: A mobile made by Alexander Calder. It is made of painted metal.
Left: A sheep made from coloured paper.
Below: Making a mobile. If you wish to make a mobile (4) you will need: (1) Pieces of wire or wood for the arms. (2) Thread. (3) Colourful objects cut from card, tinfoil, or thin metal. Try to invent your own shapes.

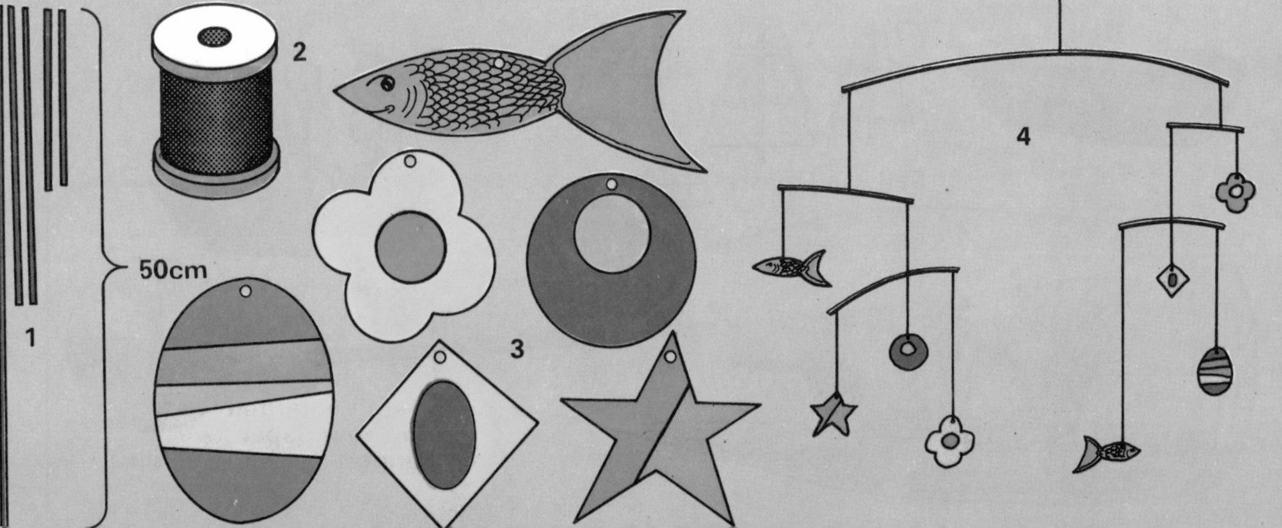

Crafts

Some crafts are useful and practical, like BASKETWORK and WEAVING. Others are ornamental rather than useful, such as FLOWER ARRANGING and BRASS RUBBING. They help to decorate people's homes.

Some crafts are closer to fine art than others. (Drawing, painting, and sculpture are fine arts.) For example, POTTERY may be thought of as a kind of sculpture, and using a brush on pottery as a branch of painting.

Since the time of the Old Stone Age, crafts have been important to men's lives. Skilful ways of making things by hand, such as baskets, water pots, or harnesses, have been passed down from fathers to sons for generations. This has led to the growth of specialist craft traditions or styles in different areas.

When machines began to make things quickly, many of the old crafts died out. Today, when people have noticed this happening, a new interest in hand crafts has often started to grow up again.

Top left: Two ornamental candles.
Left: A corn dolly and other straw shapes.
Below: Putting a boat into a bottle. A blob of glue on the hinge will hold the mast firm.

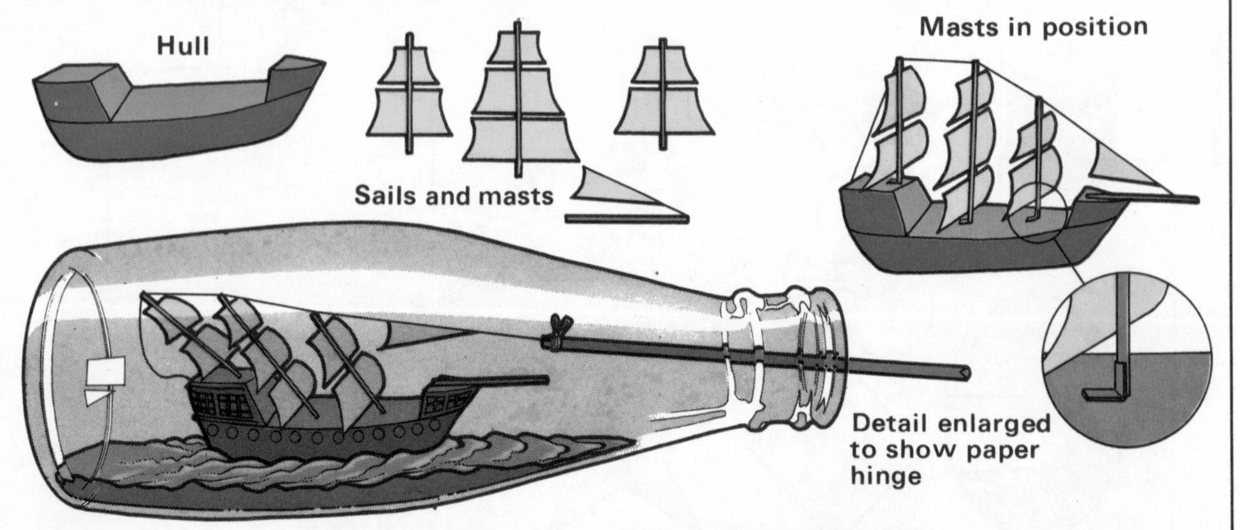

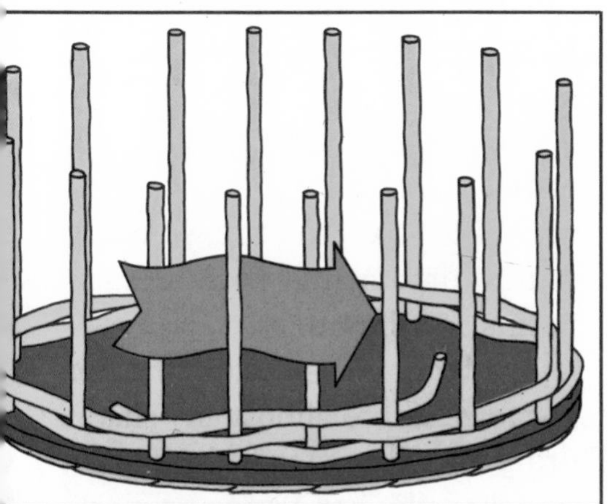

Basketwork

Basketwork is the weaving together of roots, twigs or other springy parts of some kinds of plants. It is still used for the weaving of shopping baskets, lobster pots, chairs, tables, hats, and even small boats called coracles. Different kinds of shopping and gardening baskets are often made from WILLOW twigs. The young thin stems are woven and plaited. Raffia (the leaf of a palm tree) is also used to make baskets. Rushes can be woven to make linen baskets and mats.

Until the nineteenth century, the basket-maker used the plants that grew nearest to his workshop. Then rattan cane began to prove suitable for so much basketwork that it often took the place of the local products. Rattan is a creeping palm with long thorny feelers, which grows in INDONESIA.

Baskets were probably made even earlier than CLAY pots. The EGYPTIANS and ancient Britons built huts of simple basketwork smeared with clay. Some of the most beautiful baskets have been made by AMERICAN INDIANS.

The basket-maker needs only a few simple tools. Among them are bodkins, round-nosed pliers, shears, and knives.

A simple basket may be woven on a specially prepared wooden base. The base may also be woven as a part of the basket. The upright canes rising from the base are called stakes. When a basket-maker weaves a single cane in and out of the stakes he is 'randing'. When he does this with two canes alternately he is 'pairing'.

Above left: Different kinds of basketwork. (1) Lobster pot. (2) Stone jar holder. (3) Wine basket. (4) Table mat. (5) Coracle.

Left: Weaving a basket with a wooden base. 'Randing' a cane between the stakes.

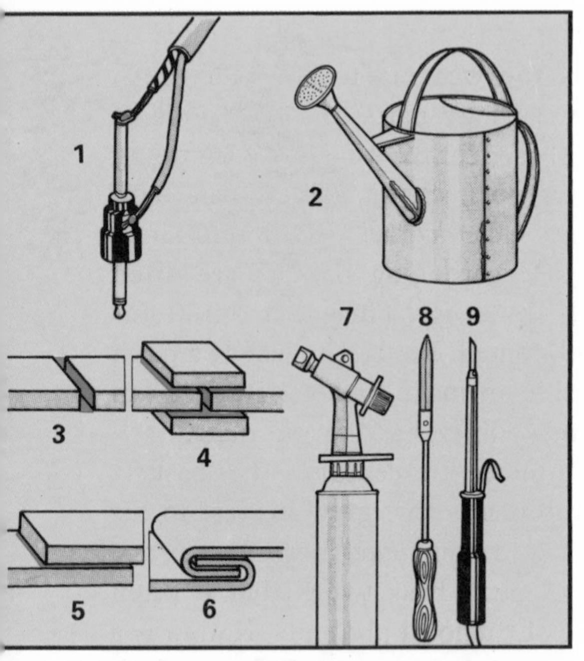

Above: Joints and tools in metalwork: **Joints:** (1) Electrical. (2) A break repaired. (3) A butt join. (4) A double-strap joint. (5) A lap joint. (6) A fold joint. **Tools:** (7) A gas blow-lamp. (8) A soldering iron. (9) An electrical soldering iron. Below: A girl punching a pattern on a silver bowl in Thailand.

Metalwork

METAL is usually strong and hard but it can be shaped by cutting and hammering. This is why useful articles and ornaments have been made in metal for a very long time. Metal has been shaped into such things as cups, plates, bowls, knives, candlesticks, urns, gates, and hinges. Often these are beautiful and intricate in design.

SILVER and gold, two precious metals, are not very hard. In order to give them strength they are often mixed with another metal to form an ALLOY. COPPER and tin make an alloy called bronze. Tin and lead make pewter. Metal that has been shaped into a flat sheet is called sheet metal. It can be hammered by hand into such things as bowls and plates.

There are many ways of working metal. Among them are FORGING, beating, planishing, and soldering.

Forging is shaping metal by hammering it or squeezing it when hot.

Planishing is smoothing metal by light hammering.

Solder can be made from an alloy of tin and lead. This is melted to join two pieces of some metals together.

Besides other methods, metal can be decorated by ENGRAVING, chasing (cutting a design with a tool), polishing, and by the use of enamel (a shiny glass-like substance).

Pottery-making

Anything made in baked CLAY is POTTERY. Tiles, cups, saucers, plates, ornamental pots, storage jars, and wash basins are all pottery.

As long as clay is damp it is possible for the potter to model or form it into almost any shape he chooses. During this first stage, the potter works his clay into shape by hand or on a wheel.

If he is making a pot by hand, he waits until it is dry enough to stand stiffly before beating or scraping it into its final form.

When the clay has dried, it will still hold the shape the potter has given it. It may then be fired (baked) in a kiln. It must be completely dry before firing. After this first firing, it is known as 'biscuit' pottery. The potter covers the biscuit with a layer of wet glaze, which goes shiny and hard at the second firing.

The potter can decorate his pots by painting, incising (a kind of ENGRAVING), scratching, or by pressing different tools into them.

Right: Making a coil pot. (1) Cutting out the base. A flat 'skin' of clay is rolled out and cut into a circle. (2) Thin coils are laid on top of each other. (3) The coils are 'luted' (joined) for strength. (4) Luting can be done by hand or with a tool. Below: *The Trumpeter* by John Perceval is pottery that has been given a coat of glaze.

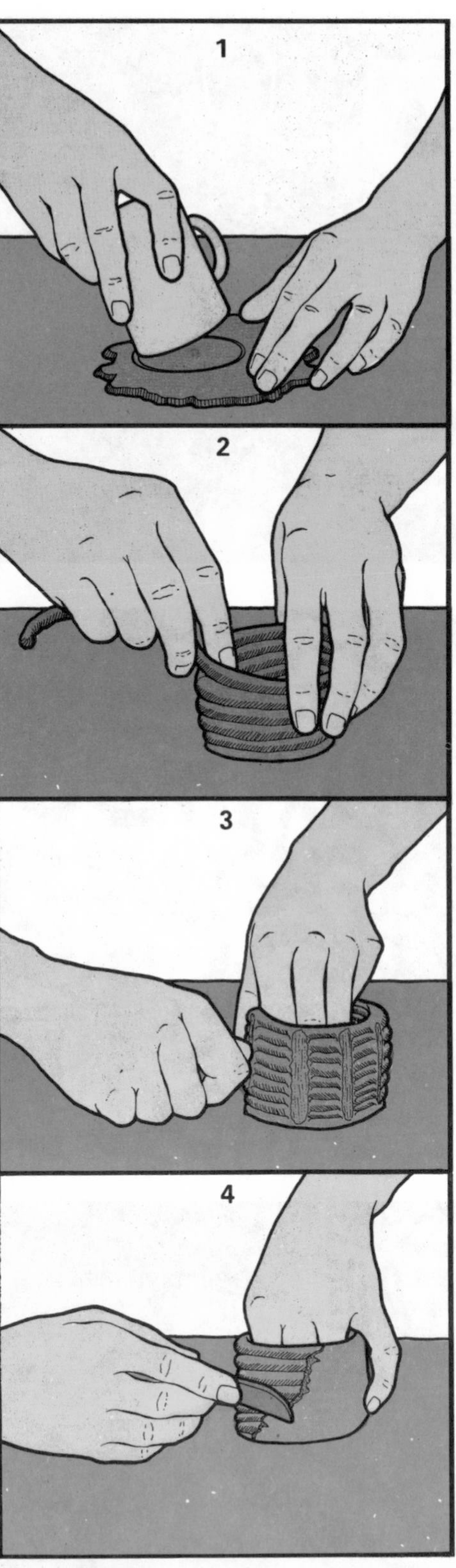

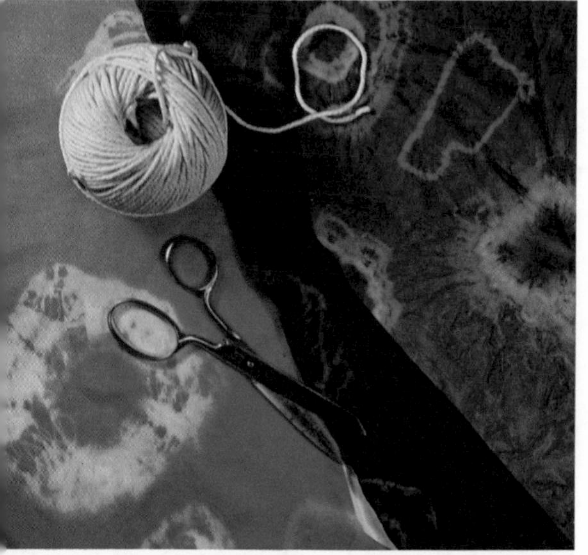

Fabric printing

Designs are often printed on fabrics. One way of doing this is called block PRINTING. In block printing, a pattern is cut into a wood block. The block is coloured with a dye or other colouring substance, and pressed hard on to the fabric.

In screen printing, you usually make a design by fixing a stencil (pattern) to a silk screen. You then place both stencil and screen on the fabric and force paint through them on to it. The pattern of the stencil is reproduced on the fabric. You can also use a varnish on the screen in place of a stencil.

Many fabrics are given a pattern by dyeing. Two common ways of dyeing are tie-dye and batik.

In tie-dye, the fabric is first knotted, sewn, or bound up with string. It is then dipped in a bath of dye. After a short time, the fabric is lifted out of the dye and left to drain. When dry, it is opened out. The dye will not have reached the parts of the fabric that have been tightly tied or sewn up. These parts will still be the original colour. The rest of the fabric will be coloured by the dye.

In batik, a pattern is 'painted' on to a piece of fabric with hot wax. Then the fabric is dyed. The dye will be thrown off the wax, but it will colour the rest of the fabric.

Top left: Some examples of tie-dye. Circular patterns are often made by this way of dyeing. Many edges are blurred.
Centre left: Block printing. To make this design, ink was rolled on to the engraved block, which was pressed on to the fabric.
Left: Batik. Wax 'resists' the dye. Often a batik is crossed by very thin lines.
Right: English embroidery—the Syon Cope.

Embroidery

Embroidery is the decorating of a surface with various kinds of stitches and threads. The surface (or backing) is usually a piece of fabric, but in modern embroidery, leather, PLASTIC, or even METAL gauze are used.

Stitches can be worked in embroidery silks, wool, metallic threads, or even string and wire. Embroidery is often found on useful objects such as clothing, tablecloths, and aprons. It can also be used to make purely decorative things, such as pictures or wall hangings.

There are four main kinds of embroidery stitches: (1) Flat stitches, such as stem and satin stitch. (2) Chain stitches. (3) Blanket stitches, which include feather stitches and buttonhole loops. (4) Knotted stitches, for example French knots.

Modern embroidery uses a wide variety of materials. Strands of string, rope, and wool are often worked together with materials like hessian or sacking. More delicate effects come with the use of gold and silver threads. Net can give a feeling of depth to an embroidered design.

Right: Some of the stitches used in embroidery. Below right: Some embroidery equipment.

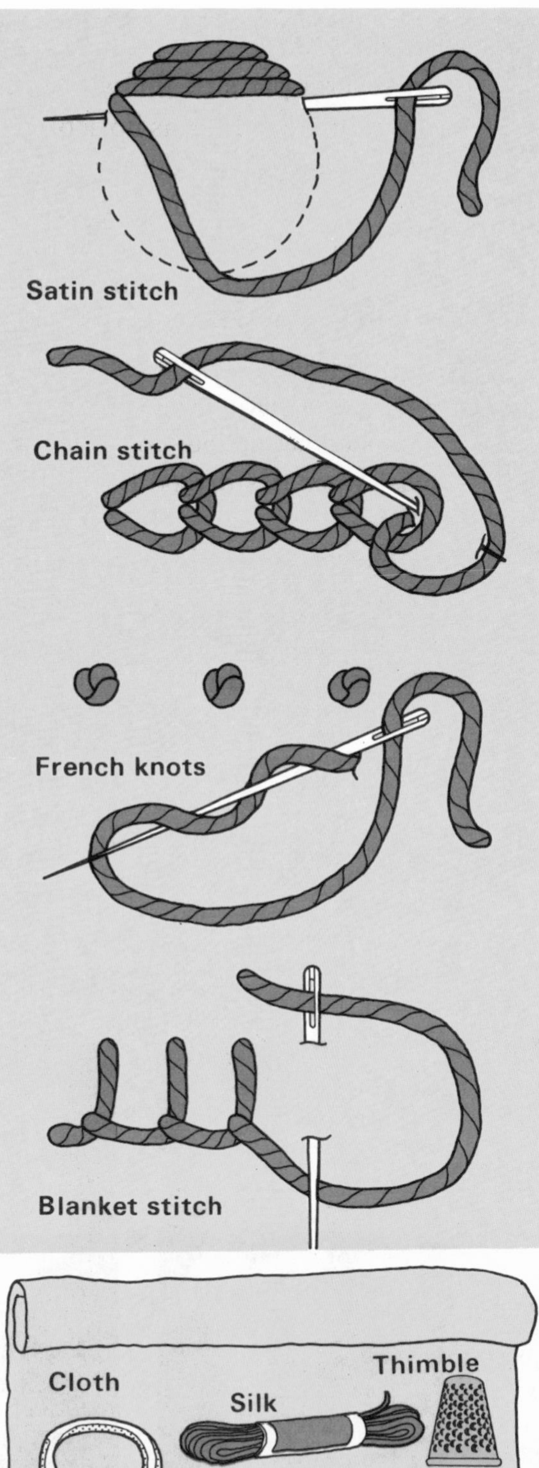

Masks

In several parts of the world, masks are sometimes made to look as horrible as possible. They are worn by witch doctors to frighten away evil spirits. Some primitive peoples believed that if you put on a mask to look like an animal, you would turn into that animal yourself.

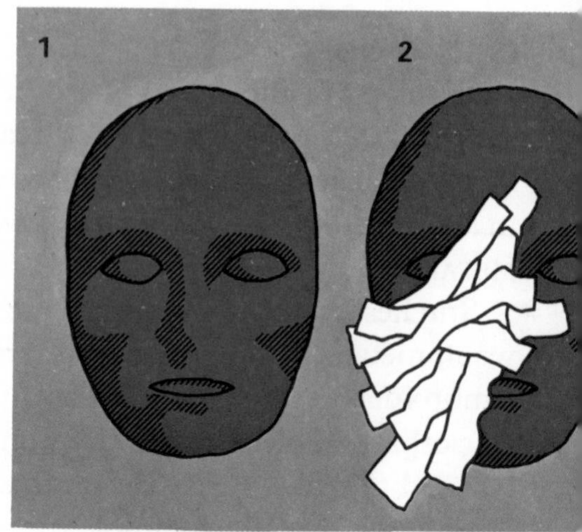

Right: Making a papier mâché mask. (1) Mould a face in papier mâché on a board. (2) Lay strips of pasted newspaper on the face. (3) Remove the mask when it is dry. (4) Paint it.

There are people in New Guinea who talk to masks because they think they are spirits that can help them. In many countries today, masks are mainly used for amusement or disguise.

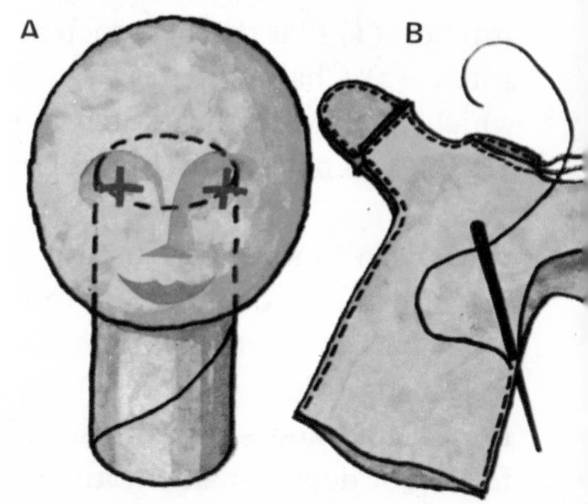

Right: Making a glove puppet. (A) Build a papier mâché ball on a tube of card. (B) Sew a felt dress with a draw-string at the neck. (C) Add wool for hair. (D) Put your hand in the puppet to work it.
Below left: A frightening mask from Switzerland.
Below centre: An Aztec mask made from mosaic.
Below right: *Mr Punch*, a glove puppet.

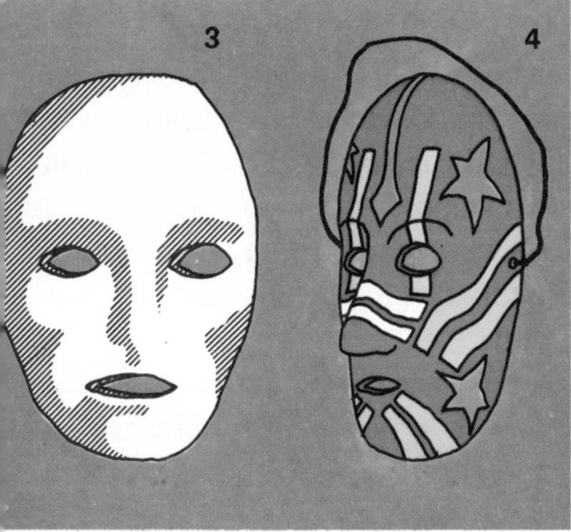

Puppets

A puppet play is a play in miniature (on a small scale) with moving dolls for ACTORS. There are many different kinds of puppets. One kind is made of wood, with joints, and is controlled by wires or strings. Glove puppets and shadow puppets are other kinds. The figures of shadow puppets are made from flat card or wood, and they are moved about behind a screen. A bright light behind the puppets throws their shadows on to the screen.

In the past, puppets were used by the ANCIENT GREEKS and ROMANS. In more modern times, one of the most popular forms of puppet THEATRE has been the Punch and Judy show.

Today, most puppet theatres use glove puppets. A glove puppet usually has a papier mâché head built up on a cardboard tube. The puppet-master puts his forefinger in the tube, and his thumb and middle finger in the arms.

Below left: Stick puppets. Their feet are kept level with the puppet theatre stage.
Below right: String puppets (sometimes called marionettes).

Dolls

Some of the earliest dolls in EUROPE came from the Black Forest in Germany. This area was famous for its wood carving, and the early dolls were made out of wood.

Later on, dolls were made from rags or leather stuffed with sawdust. These dolls are soft and are called rag dolls.

Today, many dolls are made of PLASTIC. Some have arms and legs that move and eyes that open and close. Some walk automatically and others 'talk'.

Most countries have a national costume, and when you visit them you can usually buy a doll in national dress.

Left: Making a dish-mop doll. Shape the 'face' with an elastic band, and paint it. Use felt for the arms and legs.
Below left: A dressed doll of about 1900.
Below right: A doll made from a clog.

Flower arranging

Many flowers can be arranged to make pleasing designs. Most often the flowers are freshly picked. But dried FLOWERS and LEAVES can also be used for decoration.

Flowers have been used as decoration for centuries. JAPANESE flower arrangement may have begun in the sixth century A.D. The Flemish and Dutch flower painters of the seventeenth and eighteenth centuries were a major influence on European flower arranging.

Picked flowers must be made to last as long as possible. The moisture they lose must be replaced by standing them in water.

In order to allow the flowers to draw up as much moisture as they can, their STEMS should be cut at an angle (slopingly). About five centimetres of BARK should be scraped off woody stems, and the ends bruised by gentle hammering, or by slitting. The lower leaves should be taken off.

Above: A flower arrangement using dahlias. Flowers are held up with vases, wire, plastic foam and pin-holders (nails in a base).

Brass rubbing

A memorial brass is a brass plate that has an ENGRAVING – usually the figure of a person. There are many such plates on the floors and walls of old churches.

To make a rubbing, dust the whole plate carefully. Spread strong, thin paper over the plate and stick it with tape at the corners. Then, feel for the edges of the plate with your fingertips and rub black cobblers' wax all the way round. This will give you a dark boundary line. Go on rubbing all over the brass until a clear picture appears. The lines on the brass will show white in your rubbing.

Left: Making a brass rubbing in Ely Cathedral, England.

Dancing

Dancing is one of the oldest human activities. The very earliest EGYPTIAN pictures show complicated dances.

The earliest dances have been long forgotten. They developed over the centuries into a number of special dances – war dances, fire dances, rain dances, courting dances, and so on.

These dances vary widely in different parts of the world. AMERICAN INDIAN dances, for instance, are fast and vigorous, while most Asian dances are slow and stately.

In EUROPE, dancing has often been banned because people enjoyed it so much that rulers and religious leaders thought it made them forget work and prayer.

People in many parts of the world believe in dancing as a kind of religious ceremony. They believe that a certain kind of dance will influence their gods.

Right: The Little Angels, a world-famous dance group from Korea, performing a fan dance.

They hope that the gods will protect them from disease, bring RAIN, ensure a good harvest, or give them many children.

These ritual dances go back long before any written or spoken records. Although nobody knows why certain steps have to be danced in a particular order, it is known that this is the only way the dance must be done.

The Navaho Indians in the United States have a famous rain dance. Many African tribes also have magnificent dances. MASKS often play an important part in ritual dances.

Below: Ritual dancers from several different parts of the world:
1. A Hawaiian dancer with a grass skirt.
2. A dancer from Thailand.
3. A dancer from Sri Lanka (Ceylon).
4. A kathakali dancer of India.
5. The buffalo dance of the Sioux Indians.
6. A Japanese kabuki dancer.
7. A Zulu dancer from southern Africa.

Folk dance

Nobody really knows how European folk dances began but some experts believe they were religious in origin. Certainly many of them take place at the time of ancient pagan festivals. Some of them are also connected with natural events, such as the longest day of the year, seed-time, or harvest.

What we do know is that by medieval times all European countries had their own traditional folk dances with their own traditional dress. These dances varied from place to place, and even neighbouring villages would have different dances. In England the maypole dance was common and in Scotland sword dancing was popular.

In many countries, especially in rural areas, folk dancing is still part of everyday life. People gather on holidays to dance their own special dances.

In other countries, however, such as Britain, the tradition of folk dancing has been largely lost. The old folk dances, such as Morris dancing, are performed only by enthusiasts.

Above: A group of Swiss dancers perform a folk dance in their national costume.

Below: Morris dancers at a folk dance festival in England.

Ballroom dancing

Ballroom dancing developed at the beginning of this century in the United States. It had its own rules, which were followed in many other countries. The chief dance was the waltz.

Other ballroom dances were the foxtrot, the quickstep, and the tango. Later, more dances were introduced, many from Latin America, such as the rumba and the cha cha cha from Cuba, and the samba from BRAZIL.

Because many people liked ballroom dancing, a number of cafés were turned into dance halls. Tea-time dances were held in hotels and other places. Special clubs were opened where people could go and dance together.

Ballroom dancing continues to be popular among older people. Teams of dancers often take part in competitions. They dance in couples, and also in large groups in formation dances.

Modern dancing

Modern dancing is usually more energetic than ballroom dancing. Though each dance has its own movements, dancers are freer to make up their own variations.

The first modern dance was the jitterbug which started in the United States. It developed into the jive, and then into rock and roll, which was danced to the rock music of the 1950s.

During the 1960s, dance halls began to be replaced by discotheques, places where people could go to dance to the latest popular music. Today there are a variety of modern dance styles, which can be danced with or without a partner. Modern dancing is particularly popular among young people who enjoy its powerful rhythms.

Above right: The 'Hesitation Waltz' in 1919.
Right: Young dancers in a discotheque.

Ballet

Ballet (pronounced *ba-lay*) is a kind of theatre. It is a mixture of dancing, music and painting. The dancers do not speak or sing but through their movements they tell a story or create a mood, of, for example, love, friendship or hate.

Ballet is a very formal style of dancing, because every step and movement is carefully worked out. If it is well performed, however, it looks effortless and graceful to the audience.

Many people like to watch ballet because of the daring leaps and clever steps of the dancers. But there is much more to ballet than this. There is great beauty in the moving shapes and patterns of the dancers' limbs and bodies. The dancing should go so perfectly with the music that you get more pleasure and feeling from watching a ballet than from listening to its music alone.

You can enjoy ballet from your very first visit, yet the more you learn about it the more you will enjoy it. Once you know what the various gestures mean, you can follow the story more easily. You will also enjoy ballet more by learning the names of the many different poses and movements the dancers make, and which are the most brilliant and difficult.

Above: Margot Fonteyn, Britain's most famous ballerina.

Ballet dancers

Ballet dancers lead a very tough life. They must always be fit. The dancers' MUSCLES must be trained to give any possible movement at any time. This requires hours of practice every day.

In order to give a good performance, dancers must learn and rehearse their parts (roles). This takes a long time for there are many thousands of separate movements in one ballet. Many rehearsals are necessary to perfect the dancing.

To become a ballet dancer, it is necessary to train for many years before trying to join a ballet company. A company may have its own theatre and will also tour other theatres.

We know little about the way famous dancers of a century or more ago danced as there were no films to record their dancing. The most famous ballet dancers of our century belonged to the *Ballet Russe* which toured Europe in the early 1900s. They included Nijinsky and the ballerinas Pavlova and Karsavina. Other famous dancers of the past and present in our century include Alicia Markova, Rudolf Nureyev, Natalia Makarova and Mikhail Baryshnikov. Leading companies presenting modern dance include the Martha Graham Dance Company and the Ballet Rambert.

Left: The five basic positions of ballet, which were laid down in the seventeenth century. Although a ballet has many thousands of separate movements, they are all based on these positions.

Above right: A performance of the ballet *Electra* by an Australian company.

Right: A class of dancers rehearsing together at a ballet school. The bar that runs along the wall is always found in ballet schools. The dancers grip it when doing some of their exercises.

Above: Rudolf Nureyev at a rehearsal.
Below: *La Fille Mal Gardée*, a romantic ballet.

Choreographer

The choreographer (pronounced *ko-ri-og-ra-fa*) is the person who decides how the dancers in a ballet will move. He may take a piece of music that he knows and loves and then work out the best way in which it can become a ballet. A choreographer may also work with a composer to create a ballet to a new piece of music.

The choreographer has to arrange all the movements of the dancers, down to the least movement of the head, hands, and feet, as well as the overall pattern of the ballet.

The choreographer also works with the designer, who decides on the costumes and STAGE setting. Then he starts working with the dancers and teaches them his ballet. The ballet may be performed for many years and other companies may dance it. Ballets, like music, can be written down so that other ballet dancers can perform them. A system of symbols known as 'dance notation' is used for this.

Romantic and classical ballet

Ballet began as dances at the royal courts of ITALY and FRANCE in the 1600s. As dancers invented more steps and movements, so ballet became a special entertainment and moved from the courts to THEATRES. Though all ballets created before our century are really 'classical' ballets, some are also called 'romantic'. In romantic ballets, atmosphere and the feelings of the characters are even more important than usual. The most famous of such ballets is *Giselle*, which dates from 1841.

Later in the 1800s, ballet started to decline. All that seemed to matter was the ballerina. Even in Russia, where standards of dancing stayed high, there were few good ballets. The few included *Swan Lake* and *The Sleeping Beauty* with music by TCHAIKOVSKY. Classical ballet seemed to have come to a dead end.

Modern ballet

In the early 1900s, a Russian company called the *Ballet Russe* became famous. It was directed by Serge Diaghilev. The company created many important ballets for which the music was written by famous composers. The best-known of these ballets include *The Firebird* and *Petrouchka* with choreography by Mikhail Fokine and thrilling music by STRAVINSKY.

In recent times, some dancers have rejected the steps and movements of classical ballet. Instead they prefer to dance naturally to music. As they do not always use ballet steps, their dancing is often called modern dance. Abstract ballet has also become popular. In this kind of ballet, there is no story.

The American CHOREOGRAPHER, George Balanchine, has developed abstract ballet, especially to Stravinsky's later music. Nowadays, ballets are danced to all kinds of music, including jazz, pop, and electronic music. Some modern ballets have no music and are danced in silence.

Above: A scene from *The Sleeping Beauty*, one of the best-loved of classical ballets.

Below: *The Rite of Spring* caused a sensation when it was first performed in 1913 because of Stravinsky's revolutionary music.

Opera

An opera is a play with music. The ACTORS sing some of the words instead of speaking them. In GRAND OPERA, they sing all the words. The music and singing portray the moods of the story and the feelings of the characters in it.

To appreciate an opera, you should go and see one. Listening to opera on the RADIO or on records does not give much idea of what it is really like. Going to an opera can be very exciting. There is usually a large ORCHESTRA, and a chorus of singers as well as the leading singers. The scenery is colourful and the STAGE lighting often very dramatic. Although parts of an opera are treated in such detail that the action is rather slow, the beauty of the songs compensates for the breaks in the action.

However, it is not always easy to appreciate opera. Sometimes the words are in a foreign language, often Italian. Even if the opera is sung in English, it is sometimes difficult to make out the words. It helps if you get to know the story first. The programme always contains an outline of the story, so make sure you buy one at the opera house or THEATRE and read it before the curtain goes up.

Above: Shirley Verrett in *Don Carlos* by Verdi, an opera based on the life of a Spanish prince.

Below: The opera house at Sydney, Australia.

Above: Boris Christoff in *Boris Godunov* by Mussorgsky, an opera about a Russian emperor.

Opera singers

Singing opera is a difficult task. Opera singers must have powerful voices that can be heard above the ORCHESTRA. It helps if they can read music easily, and they must be fit, for some operas are very long. Singers must be prepared to sing in several languages, especially Italian and German. There are many famous Italian and German operas, and operas are not always sung in the singer's own language. Singers also have to act, which some do better than others.

Learning and rehearsing an opera takes a long time. First, the singer must learn the part with the aid of a coach, who accompanies the singer at the PIANO. Then the singers rehearse the music with the CONDUCTOR of the opera. Next, they learn and rehearse their STAGE movements with the producer of the opera. The final rehearsals are carried out with the orchestra, and in full costume, on the stage.

The best singers get the principal solo roles in an opera. But a company also needs many good singers to make up the chorus of an opera.

The part that a singer is given in an opera depends on the range of his or her voice. A female with a high voice is a *soprano*, and with a low one, a *contralto*. In between is a *mezzo soprano*. A *tenor* is a male singer with a high voice. Next comes a *baritone*, and the lowest voice is a *bass* one. Famous opera singers of the century have included the tenor Caruso, the Russian bass, Chaliapin, and Maria Callas. Today's stars include Placido Domingo, Janet Baker, Grace Bumbry, Luciano Pavarotti and Kiri Te Kanawa from New Zealand. All are thrilling performers.

Left: The Australian Joan Sutherland (centre) in Donizetti's *The Daughter of the Regiment*, which is about a girl brought up by soldiers.

Making an opera

Apart from the performers – the singers, ORCHESTRA and CONDUCTOR – several people work together to create an opera. The composer writes the music. The librettist writes the libretto, or words. The designer creates the costumes and the STAGE setting. The director works out the stage actions and helps the singers with their acting.

None of these jobs is easy, but the composer probably has the hardest task. Composing an opera may take years. An opera composer must consider many things. He must express the atmosphere of the story and the feelings of the characters in his music. He must keep the story moving, and bring it to a climax where necessary. He must also try to give the whole opera a complete musical design.

The composer works closely with the librettist. The librettist may write a new story for the opera, or he may take a previous story of his own or one already written.

Above: An opera singer rehearses with the conductor.

Below: A scene from *La Bohème* by Puccini.

Above: Recording an opera. The conductor is in the centre.

Grand opera

Grand opera is the kind of opera in which every word is sung. The main songs are called *arias*. These are the best-known parts of operas. But ordinary speech is sung as well. It may seem odd to hear everyday talk in song, but the composer can heighten the drama and create a complete musical design if every word is set to music. GRAND OPERA can be based on both serious and amusing subjects.

In early operas, in the seventeenth century, speech was often set to simple music consisting of a repeated note and a few accompanying chords. This style of music is called recitative (pronounced *re-si-ta-teev*).

In later operas, the music that goes with speech is more interesting. If you have a friend who likes opera, ask him or her for advice on which ones to see first. Once you can accept that ordinary speech may be sung and not seem odd, you will probably enjoy opera yourself.

Light opera

Light opera has almost as long a history as opera itself. In it, the ordinary speech is spoken instead of being sung, and it becomes more like a play than grand opera. Many different words are used to describe it, including operetta (little opera) and comic opera. Among the best comic operas were written by Gilbert and Sullivan in the 1800s. Many of them are still popular today. Many 'musicals' can be described as operettas, such as *West Side Story*, *My Fair Lady* and *Oliver*. Some light operas need operatic voices, others do not. All, if well performed, can be powerful entertainment.

Left: *La Périchole* (The Street Singer), a light opera by Offenbach, which was first produced in 1868.

Famous operas

The first great opera was *Orpheus* by Monteverdi, who worked in the early 1600s. He combined recitative and arias to make a dramatic whole. His example was followed for a short while, but opera gradually lost this unity. The Austrian composer Gluck restored the balance of song and action in the late 1700s with his *Orpheus* and *Alcestis*. MOZART followed him, writing many famous operas, including *The Marriage of Figaro*, *Don Giovanni*, and *The Magic Flute*.

The Italian operas of the 1800s are still among the most popular for their tuneful arias. They include *The Barber of Seville* by Rossini and *Norma* by Bellini. The greatest Italian opera composer of this time was Verdi, whose operas *Rigoletto*, *La Traviata*, and *Aida* are still world famous.

In Germany, WAGNER, like Gluck before him, wrote operas that contained much drama. These included *The Flying Dutchman*, *Lohengrin*, *Tristan and Isolde*, and *The Ring of the Nibelungs*. All were masterpieces of GRAND OPERA.

Tuneful LIGHT OPERAS developed in France in the 1800s. The best known are probably *Carmen* by Bizet, and the lively *Orpheus in the Underworld* by Offenbach.

In the 1900s, the old Italian tradition continued in the operas of Puccini, such as *Tosca* and *Madame Butterfly*. In Germany, Richard Strauss composed highly dramatic operas such as *Elektra*. Other important composers of this century include Berg of Austria with *Wozzeck* and *Lulu*, and the British composer Benjamin BRITTEN whose works include *Billy Budd* and *Death in Venice*.

Right: A scene from *Ariadne auf Naxos*, an opera written by Richard Strauss in 1912.

Music is an art that almost everyone enjoys. Everyone can make sound in some way – by singing, banging a stick, plucking a tight string, or blowing through a pipe. All over the world, many kinds of music have developed as people found out how to make sound in different ways. There are so many kinds of music to hear that you can soon find a kind that you like. As you get older you can explore music, finding more and more music that interests you.

People can get all kinds of feelings from hearing music. Music can make you want to march or dance, it can make you feel happy or sad. More than other arts, music can affect our moods and feelings. This is why music is so popular. But if you get to know music well, you may also be able to hear the ways in which the music is put together. The best and most lasting music can do both these things to its listeners. It should have an effect on their feelings and it should have interesting patterns of sound.

Every country has its own kind of music. In FRANCE, many people like dance music played on

Above: African music is well known for its powerful rhythm.

Below: Playing a grand piano, with lid raised.

the ACCORDION. The Irish and the people of eastern EUROPE are fond of energetic music played on the violin and many Americans enjoy banjo music. SPAIN is famous for its GUITAR music, and INDIA for the twanging sound of the sitar. The Scots enjoy the skirl of the bagpipes, and the Greeks dance and sing to the lively strains of bouzouki music.

Many people like music in their own national style. But there are also people who enjoy CLASSICAL MUSIC and pop music, which has spread throughout the world with the aid of the record-player and RADIO.

However, there are still great differences between the music of the west and that of the east. Many of the instruments are very different. The guitar and the sitar are both instruments in which strings are plucked by the fingers, but they do not sound alike. The musical differences between east and west are not only in the instruments, but also in the ways the notes are put together.

Below: The vina (right) is a popular instrument in India.

Below: A Scottish military band with massed drums and bagpipes.

Making music

Learning to play any instrument may take years of practice. You have to train certain MUSCLES to act in complicated ways. Some instruments, such as the PIANO and GUITAR, are easier at first than others. But no instrument is easy to play well. You must also learn to read music, and this too takes practice.

To make your own music, you must know how music is put together. You can compose music simply by playing some on the piano and recording your work on a tape recorder. But if you want to compose well, you must know about the theory of music.

There are four main elements of music: melody, harmony, counterpoint, and rhythm. A melody is simply a tune. Some tunes, like those of folk songs and pop songs, are easy to follow and sing. The melodies of music such as symphonies may be more difficult to recognise.

Harmony is the sound of two or more notes played at once. The music that accompanies a tune has a harmony. Composers try to make the harmony interesting.

Counterpoint happens when two or more different tunes are played or sung together, or when the same tunes are played or sung some time apart. The tunes must fit well together and produce good harmony. A composer must be good at counterpoint so that every singer or musician in a choir or ORCHESTRA always has a good melody, even if it is not the main melody.

Rhythm is the way the notes are connected in time. It is not the same as the speed of a piece which is called its tempo.

The illustration on the far right shows these four elements in the same piece of music. Ask someone to play you the music on the piano, if you cannot play yourself.

Above: The koto of Japan has 13 silk strings.

Right: Elements of music. The first six bars of music of *God Save the Queen*–the British national anthem.

Above: This school orchestra has percussion instruments and recorders.

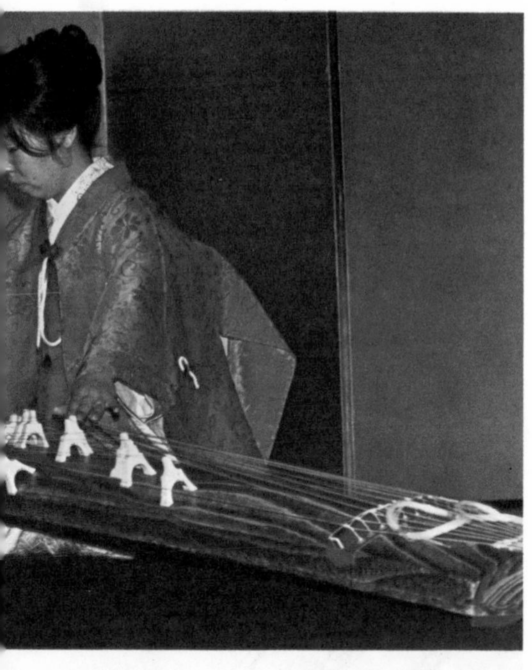

The first section of music (1) shows the melody, or tune. With every note of the melody, other notes can be played to give a harmony. The second section (2) shows the harmony to the first note of the melody.

The third section of music (3) shows counterpoint. Here, three more melodies are shown underneath the tune. Each of these melodies can be played on its own. But you can also play them with the tune, and they fit together and give a good harmony. Notice that the first note of each of the melodies is the same as that in the second section of music.

The fourth section (4) shows the rhythm of the tune. It is written on only one line of music instead of a staff (group of five lines).

1

2

3

4

Musical instruments

There are many different kinds of musical instruments. They all make sound by vibration in three basic ways. The vibrations can be caused by a tight string or skin, a column of air, or a solid piece of metal or wood. The vibration makes a sound wave in the air that reaches our ears. Most instruments fit into four main classes: STRINGS, WOODWIND, BRASS, and PERCUSSION. These are the sections of a symphony ORCHESTRA.

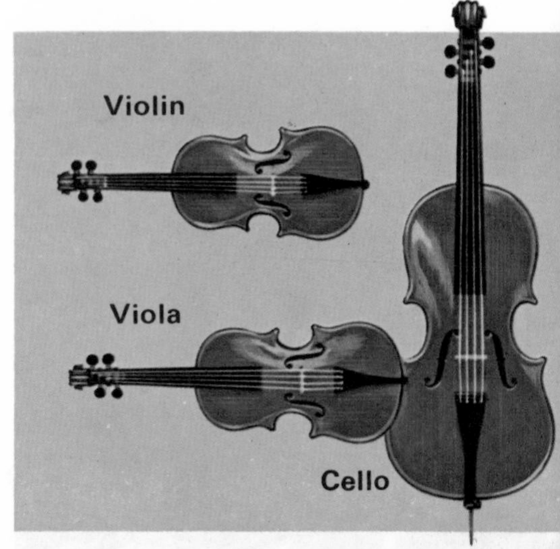

Strings

'Strings' is the name of the family of instruments which includes the violin, viola, cello, and double bass. The violin is the smallest and plays the highest notes. The double bass is the largest and plays the lowest notes. They each have four tight strings that run from the centre of the instrument over a 'bridge' to the long neck. At the end of the neck the strings are wound around pegs. They are tuned (given the right note) by turning the pegs.

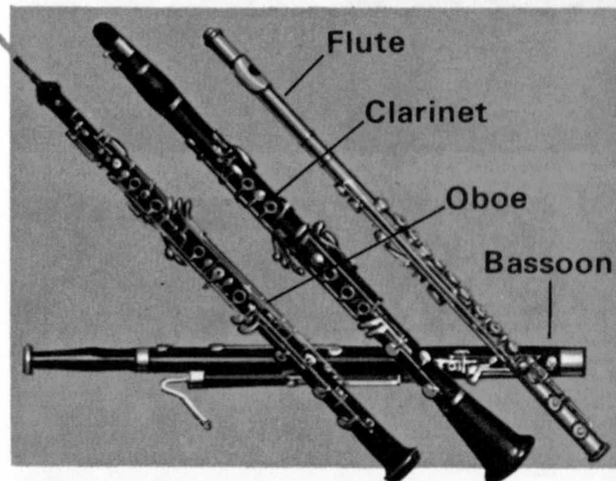

A stringed instrument is played by holding its neck in the left hand and a bow in the right. The bow is moved lightly across one or more of the strings to vibrate them and make a sound. Sometimes a string is plucked with a finger instead. The fingers of the other hand push the strings down on the finger board on the neck of a stringed instrument, making the sound higher or lower. The violin and viola are held under the chin, but the cello and double bass rest on the floor.

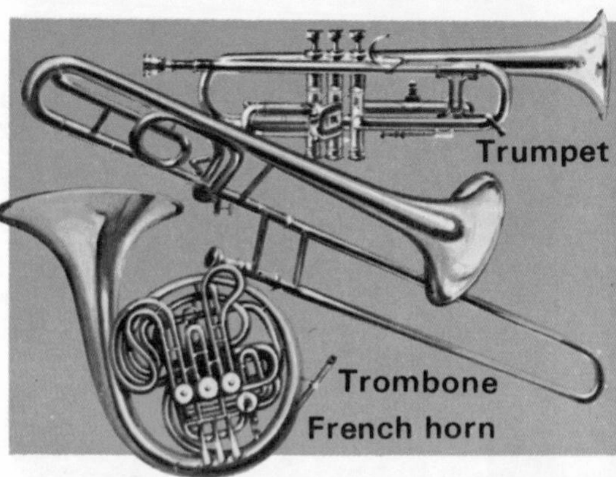

Every symphony ORCHESTRA has a large string section, and there is a lot of solo music for the violin and the cello. Stringed instruments are often played in chamber music, which is music for small groups of musicians.

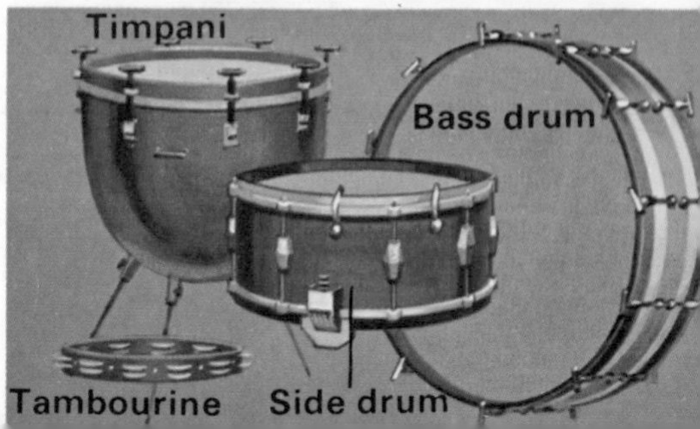

Woodwind

The piccolo, flute, clarinet, oboe, cor anglais, bassoon, saxophone, and recorder are all woodwind instruments. They are all hollow inside, and the sound is produced by vibrating the air inside them. The player blows across or into a hole at one end of the instrument, or into a mouthpiece containing a reed that vibrates. Along the pipe of the instrument are holes that can be covered by the fingers, or by keys that operate pads. This alters the length of the air column inside the instrument and makes the notes higher or lower.

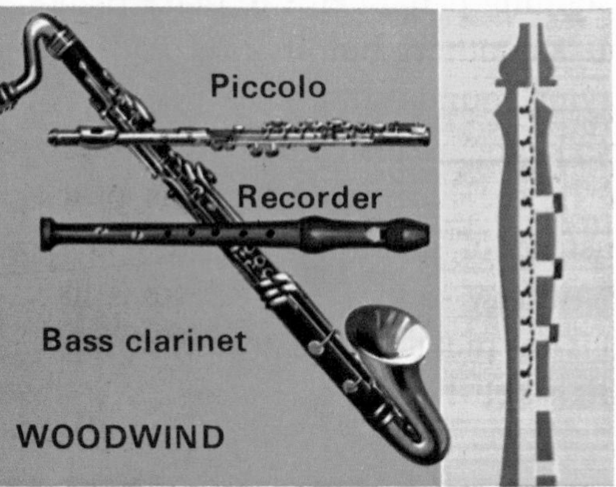

Brass

Brass instruments include the trumpet, trombone, horn and tuba. Like the WOODWIND instruments, these contain a column of air. To set it vibrating and make a sound, the player blows into a cup-shaped or cone-shaped mouthpiece at one end. His tongue is pressed against his gums or teeth. His lips vibrate and set the air column vibrating. The player can get several different notes just by changing the pressure of his lips against the mouthpiece. He gets other notes by altering the length of the air column. In most brass instruments he presses valves to do this, but a trombonist uses a slide.

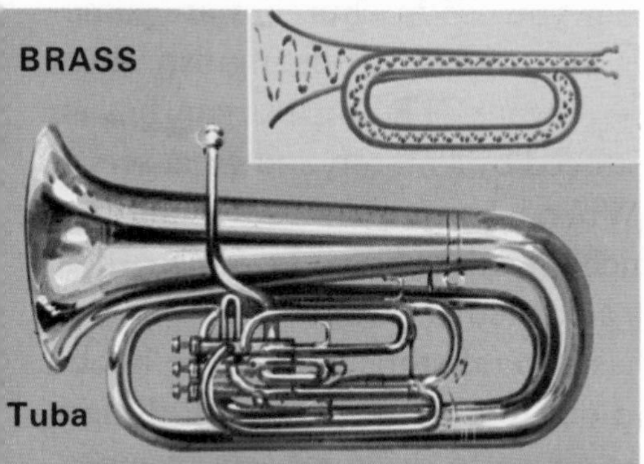

Percussion

Percussion instruments are sounded by striking them with a stick or mallet. Indefinite pitch instruments, such as drums, gongs, cymbals, the tambourine, and triangle, give out a sound without any particular note. Definite pitch instruments, or tuned percussion, give out actual notes. These instruments include the timpani or kettle-drums, the xylophone, and the vibraphone and glockenspiel which give bell-like sounds.

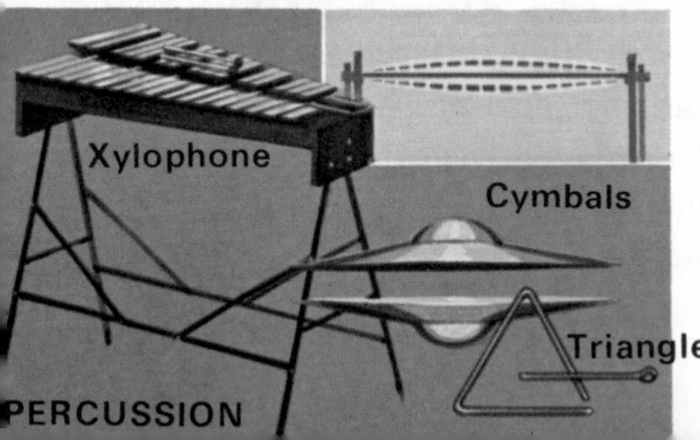

Above: A grand piano with its lid open.
Below: This picture of an organ shows the pipes clearly.

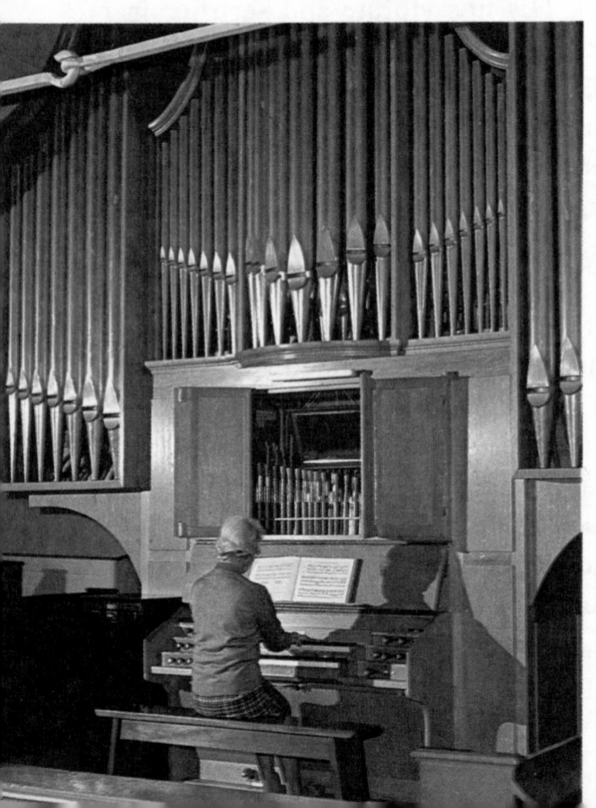

Piano

The piano has a keyboard on which the player's fingers can press the keys and produce sounds. Each key operates levers that make a felt-tipped hammer strike a tight string. (The strings are in fact made of wire, and most strings consist of two or three separate wires tuned to the same note.)

A piano has two pedals. The left-hand pedal makes the sound softer. The right-hand pedal is often called the loud pedal, but this is misleading. This pedal does not make the notes louder but sustains them (makes them last longer). Using the sustaining pedal helps to make piano playing sound smoother, but if used badly it makes the playing sound 'muddy'.

Several other keyboard instruments are similar to the piano. In the harpsichord, quills pluck the strings instead of hammers striking them, giving a short twangy sound. The celeste is like the piano, but it has metal bars instead of strings. It produces high bell-like notes.

Organ

The organs that you see in churches are sometimes called pipe organs to distinguish them from electronic organs. The pipe organ has an air supply produced by a motor, and great sets of organ pipes. When a key is pressed, the air goes to a pipe, which is rather like a huge recorder. Each pipe has a particular note.

An organ has several stops, which are knobs that are pulled out to alter the sound. Pulling a stop makes the air go to different sets of pipes.

An organ may have several keyboards, so that the organist can play different sets of sounds with each hand. It also has a set of keys called pedals that are played with the feet at the same time that the hands are playing. The pedals produce very deep notes.

The electronic organ produces similar sounds by electronics and has no pipes. The sound comes from a LOUDSPEAKER like that in a record player.

Guitar

The guitar is one of the most popular musical instruments. It is not difficult to play simple tunes and accompaniments on the guitar. A guitar usually has six strings that are plucked with the fingers of one hand. The other fingers press the strings against frets (ridges) on the fingerboard to vary the notes. The banjo and lute work in much the same way. In the electric guitar, the vibration of the strings is turned into an electric signal that operates a LOUDSPEAKER.

Above: A harp.
Below: A synthesizer.

Harp

The harp is one of the oldest instruments. It has a set of strings like those on the PIANO. The strings are sounded by plucking them with the fingers of both hands. The harp has fewer strings than the piano, and so cannot make all the notes that a piano can. While the harp is being played, the harpist can press foot pedals to alter the lengths of the strings. By running the fingers over the strings, cascades of notes can be produced.

Electronic instruments

Electronic instruments are new kinds of instruments that work by electricity. They produce electric signals that go to a LOUDSPEAKER to make sounds. Most of these instruments, like the electronic ORGAN and the synthesizer, have keyboards. The keys work like switches to turn the sounds on and off. Other controls alter the kinds of sounds made. Synthesizers can make entirely new sounds.

Orchestra

An orchestra is a large group of musicians playing together. It usually contains many different instruments so that the orchestra can produce a variety of sounds. The largest, a symphony orchestra, may have more than a hundred players. Symphony orchestras play all kinds of concert music as well as symphonies, and they also provide music for ballets and operas.

More than half the instruments are STRINGS, which are in the front of the orchestra. They include two groups of violins – first violins and second violins. In the centre comes the WOODWIND section. Finally, towards the back are the BRASS and PERCUSSION. With this placing, the quieter instruments are at the front and can be heard better. Solo performers, such as singers, violinists and pianists, are placed nearest to the CONDUCTOR at the front.

A small symphony orchestra of about 30 players is called a chamber orchestra. The string section of a symphony orchestra may play alone as a string orchestra. But groups of similar instruments are usually called bands. A brass band may consist only of brass instruments, although clarinets and drums are often added. They play special music and also arrangements of orchestral music. A big band is used for some jazz and dance music. It has sections of brass and saxophones, as well as a rhythm section of PIANO, double bass, and drums to provide a beat. A variety orchestra or light orchestra is a big band with a string section.

Large orchestras are not common outside western countries. But in INDONESIA there are *gamelan* orchestras made up of percussion instruments, especially xylophones and gongs. They play beautiful music of chiming bell sounds with very complex rhythms.

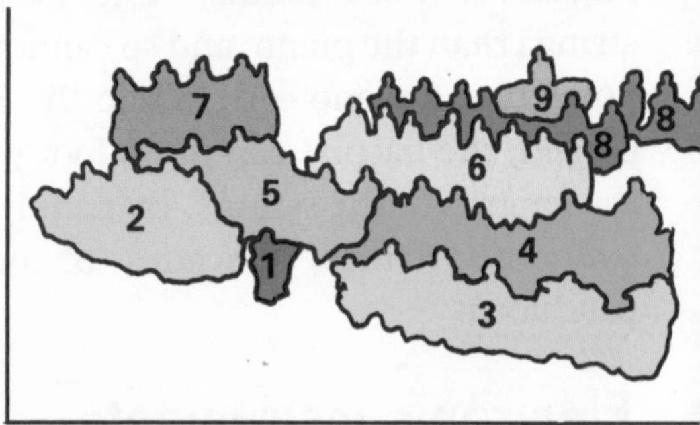

Top: Otto Klemperer conducting the New Philharmonia Orchestra. The diagram (above) shows the layout of this orchestra. (1) Conductor. (2) First violins. (3) Second violins. (4) Violas. (5) Cellos. (6) Woodwind. (7) Double basses. (8) Brass. (9) Percussion.

Conductor

A large ORCHESTRA needs someone to direct the music. This person is the conductor. Usually he does not play and stands in front of the orchestra. But sometimes he plays the solo part of a concerto as well as conducting. The conductor has the score of the music before him or he may even learn the score by heart. The score has the music that everyone is playing, and the conductor must be able to take in all the different parts at the same time.

The conductor directs the performance by using gestures of his hands and face. He sets the speed of the music by beating time with one hand. He also cues the players (indicates when they should start to play), and makes some parts of the music loud or soft. The players glance at the conductor as they play. Most conductors hold a baton in one hand to make their gestures clear. Without the conductor, the orchestra could still play the music but the performance would probably seem lifeless.

The leader of an orchestra is the principal player. In a symphony orchestra, he is the first violin. He assists the conductor when necessary.

Below: Colin Davis gives a firm direction during rehearsal.
Below right: André Previn uses a more delicate gesture.

Above: A picture from an old manuscript showing nuns singing.

Classical music

The best meaning of the term 'classical music' is music so finely composed that it goes on being enjoyed by people down the years and centuries. There is also a second meaning which is explained below.

Classical music can be composed for many different combinations of players and singers, from solo performers and quartets up to large choirs and symphony ORCHESTRAS.

From pictures and writings we know that music is a very old art. Yet we can only guess how early musicians sounded because their music was not written down. The earliest written music is church music. In the Middle Ages, monks sang chants consisting of simple melodies. Gradually more complicated melodies were added.

Not all musicians were monks and priests. There were wandering singers all over Europe. Soon there were fine composers in places like Italy, England and France.

Early music had mainly been sung, but music for instruments became popular as well. In the late 1600s and early 1700s composers appeared whose music for orchestras, singers and choirs is still loved by millions. The greatest, perhaps, was J.S. BACH. Other composers include another German, HANDEL, the Italians, Scarlatti, father and son, and Vivaldi.

Now for the second meaning of 'classical'. The music of the eighteenth century is often described as classical. This is because it is so beautifully shaped. Although it is lovely to

Above left: Part of a painting by Veronese showing instruments of the sixteenth century.
Bottom left: A seventeenth-century painting of an early keyboard instrument called a virginal.

listen to, the feelings of eighteenth-century composers are not expressed as freely as in the music of many later 'romantic' composers.

The greatest classical composers of all time were probably HAYDN, MOZART and BEETHOVEN. Beethoven, who died in 1827, is the composer who links the classical age with the romantic age. The Romantics were not shy of showing their feelings. Some painted pictures in music. Beethoven, for example, expressed his feelings about the countryside in his 'Pastoral' Symphony.

Above right: Many pieces of music are composed for dances, such as this eighteenth-century minuet.
Right: Tchaikovsky's *1812* overture commemorates Napoleon's retreat from Moscow.
Below right: Fingal's Cave in Scotland inspired Mendelssohn to write an overture.

Other composers of the 1800s used their own nation's musical rhythms and sometimes folk tunes in their music. Franz Liszt, the Hungarian composer and pianist, wrote piano pieces in Hungarian gypsy style. CHOPIN often used Polish dance rhythms.

The great line of German composers was continued by SCHUBERT, Mendelssohn, Schumann and BRAHMS. His four symphonies were more classical than romantic. Romantic music came to a climax with the great operas of the German genius WAGNER, the music of the Russians TCHAIKOVSKY and Gustav Mahler, and the music and operas of Richard Strauss.

Strauss, who lived until 1948, and Mahler, often used enormous orchestras.

Bottom right: A sixteenth-century Italian painting showing a lute being played.

Modern music

Classical music is now more popular than ever before. In contrast, much modern music is quite unpopular, because ordinary listeners find it unharmonious and difficult to understand.

In order to try to find out why this is, we must go back some years. In the late nineteenth and early twentieth centuries, Debussy began writing music that did not use any of the musical forms that existed at the time. Other composers also experimented with new forms. But until about 50 years ago, most modern music could be understood and enjoyed by the average music lover. Modern composers whose music was popular included Sibelius (Finnish), Vaughan Williams and BRITTEN (British), Ravel (French), Copland (American), Stravinsky, Prokofiev and Shostakovich (Russian).

Right: The American Leonard Bernstein, composer of *West Side Story*, conducts one of his works.

All these composers wrote melodies, though some of their tunes seemed strange at first. But other composers were following a different road. The Austrian Schoenberg (1874–1951) was the first of them. He wanted to compose music that broke away from traditional rules even more sharply. He developed what became known as 'serial' music. He was followed by two more Austrians, Berg and Webern. Both are regarded as great musicians but ordinary listeners often find their music hard to follow. Later composers went even further. Some, like Stockhausen, use electronic as well as ordinary instruments to experiment with new sounds.

Music seems to some people to have reached a dead end. Some composers are now looking back to the more melodious music of the past.

Jazz

The word jazz was first used about 75 years ago to describe a popular form of American music. This music had begun in the city of New Orleans, where it was played by black people in the streets, at weddings and funerals, and finally in dance halls and restaurants too.

Jazz took many forms, but most jazz fans only use the word about music which includes 'improvisation'. This means that the musicians play their version of a tune in their own way. This style is called traditional jazz, and one of its greatest composers is Duke Ellington (1899–1970). In the 1950s a new style called modern jazz also became popular. Jazz has strong rhythms, and some jazz songs which are slow and sad are called 'Blues'.

Left: The jazz musician Dizzie Gillespie is well known for his unique upturned trumpet.

Popular music

The beginnings of popular music are lost in history. Such music has always been 'people's music', easy to listen to and enjoy. Most of it is soon forgotten and only the best examples become 'standards'.

People still enjoy old folk songs, and some of the lively MUSIC HALL songs of Victorian times. They also enjoy the best songs from old MUSICALS like *Oklahoma* and *West Side Story*. The songs of the Beatles – unlike most pop – seem certain to survive as 'standards' and so do some of those sung by such popular entertainers as Bing Crosby and Frank Sinatra.

Popular music never stands still and it is interesting to try to guess which tunes will last.

Left: A group of singers at a pop concert.

Theatre

For more than 2000 years people have been going to the theatre to enjoy plays. Long before that, our prehistoric ancestors had added words to the dances that they performed before hunting or fighting or in honour of their gods. These words, sung or spoken, were early forms of play, though they were not written down.

The very first real plays were acted in ANCIENT EGYPT and ANCIENT GREECE. Egyptian temples were sometimes used for plays about gods and goddesses.

European theatre began about 2500 years ago in Greece. It sprang from religious festivals. Gradually, singing to the gods gave way to written plays. These were acted in the open air in front of an audience looking down from a hillside. Over the years a proper stage and seating for the audience was added.

Above: The theatre at Epidaurus is the best preserved of ancient Greek theatres.

Below: A play of the Japanese Noh theatre, which developed from religious dances.

Plays can be divided into types. The best known are probably tragedies and comedies. Tragedy is often about the downfall of great men. The finest tragedies are by SHAKESPEARE, whose plays are acted in nearly every country on earth. Comedies can be about any subject as long as they are funny. Today, all kinds of plays are performed. There are thrillers and detective plays. Some of the most popular of these are by Agatha Christie.

Farce is a special kind of comedy which some people have called tragedy turned upside down! In a farce, amazing things happen to ordinary people but the effect is funny rather than sad.

Drama reaches a bigger audience than ever before, now that plays are transmitted on RADIO and TELEVISION and in the CINEMA.

Left: A scene from *The Taming of the Shrew* — one of Shakespeare's most popular comedies.
Below: Every action and line in a play has to be practised over and over again. Here the actors take a break in rehearsal.

Greek drama

The Greeks acted their plays in huge stone theatres out of doors. The actors wore magnificent costumes and tall headdresses to make them seem larger than life. Tragic actors also wore masks to show clearly what sort of a person the character was. Greek plays were about the gods, and the heroes of Greek legend and history. There was always a chorus of actors, as well as the main characters, who explained and commented on what was going on.

The great writers of Greek drama were Aeschylus, Sophocles, Euripides and Aristophanes.

Right: A modern performance of a Greek tragedy.
Below: A performance of a play as it might have looked in Ancient Greece.

Miracle plays

Around A.D. 1000, churches began putting on plays telling Bible stories, for few people at that time could read. These plays gradually spread outside the churches and were performed by tradesmen in the streets and market places of Europe. Each group of tradesmen acted suitable stories, for instance, fishmongers might act Jonah and the Whale, the shipbuilders would present Noah's Ark. Soon the ACTORS added their own details and comments, making some of these plays an interesting mixture of Bible stories and everyday life.

Elizabethan theatre

During Queen Elizabeth I's reign, the first public playhouse opened in London in 1576.

The great genius of this age was, of course, SHAKESPEARE. Huge audiences flocked to watch his plays. The performances took place in the daytime, and the theatres were usually roofless. Smaller indoor theatres were also built. The female parts were always taken by boys, because the theatre-hating religious sect (known as Puritans) did not allow women to appear on the stage.

In the 1640s, the Puritans closed down all the theatres. It was not until Charles II restored the throne in 1660 that the theatre flourished again in England.

Harlequin

In Italy a form of theatre sprang up in the sixteenth century called the *commedia dell'arte*. Troupes of actors went from place to place playing unwritten comedies. The characters and costumes were always the same and the plots were agreed on beforehand. The best known character is probably Harlequin.

Above: A sixteenth-century theatre.
Below: The characters of the *commedia dell'arte*—(1) Harlequin. (2) Columbine. (3) Pantaloon.

Left: Miracle plays were performed on simple platforms with no background scenery. There was a space under the platform so that evil characters could fall through a trapdoor into 'hell'.

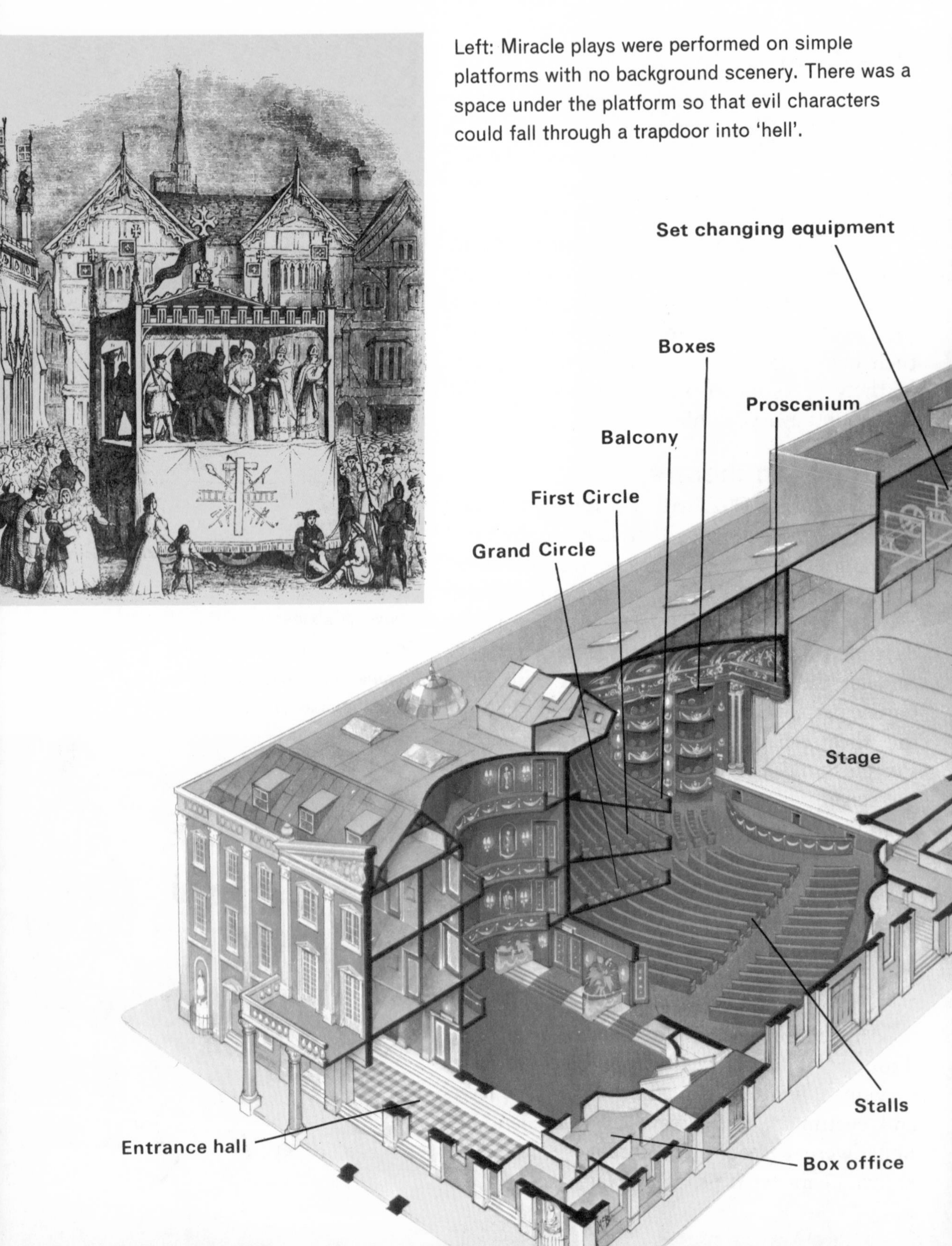

Below: The kind of theatre that is most common today. The stage has a proscenium arch. Behind the stage there must be accommodation for changing rooms and for storing 'props'. There is usually space below the stage to store away scenery when it is not in use.

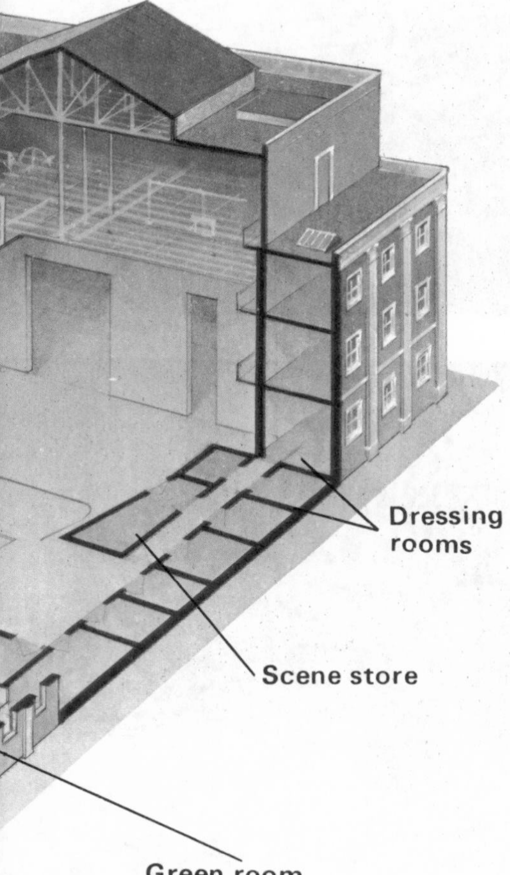

Right: A play being performed 'in the round'. The disadvantage is that the actors have their backs to some of the audience.

Stages

Down the ages many different kinds of stage have been used by actors. The very first stages were simple platforms. By Shakespeare's time, the stage jutted out into the audience and important people were even allowed to sit on the stage to watch the action.

Most of today's stages, in theatres built more than 20 years ago, are based on ones used in Italy nearly 400 years ago. Audiences sit looking at a 'picture frame' stage, with actors performing behind an arch called a proscenium. These theatres have a curtain which cuts off the audience from the stage until the play begins.

Lately, some theatre people have begun to rebel against the picture frame stage. They want to bring the action forward among the audience as it was in Shakespeare's day.

There are even 'theatres in the round' today where the action takes place right in the middle of the audience. Some larger theatres are built with more than one type of stage to suit different kinds of play.

Actors

The life of an actor or actress may seem exciting, but it is also very hard work. Most, though not all, actors begin by training at a drama school. There they learn to use their voices properly, to move well and to act a wide range of parts. Yet they cannot really be taught to act. If a person has not got the ability in the first place, no amount of training will help.

In the old days the single aim of an actor was to act in the theatre, but now he or she also hopes to act on TELEVISION and in the CINEMA.

Some actors are remembered years after their deaths. Shakespeare's friend, Richard Burbage, the very first Hamlet, is still remembered. So is Sir Henry Irving, the first actor to be knighted.

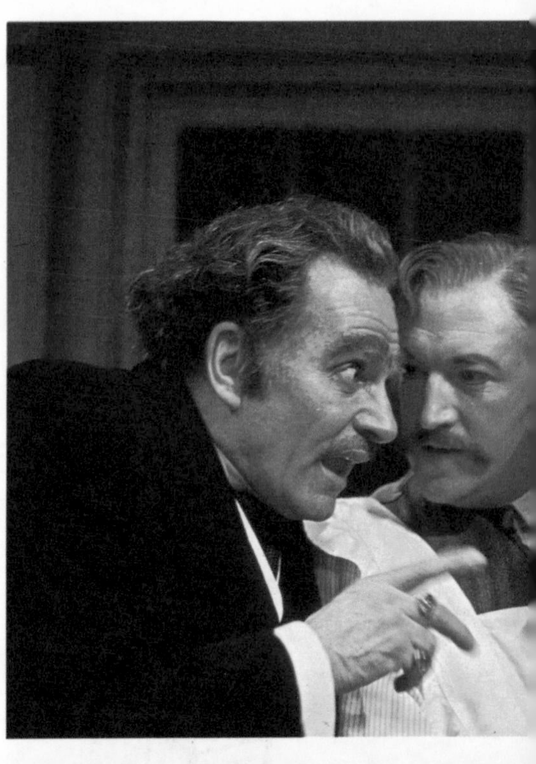

Two famous British actors.
Above right: Laurence Olivier (left of picture).
Below: David Garrick lived in the seventeenth century. This painting by Hogarth shows him in the title part of Shakespeare's Richard III.

Costumes

The right costumes can make all the difference to the success or failure of a play. If a play is set in an earlier time, the costume designer might look back at old books and paintings to get the details right. What you see on the stage does not have to be absolutely accurate, but it must look as if it is.

Sometimes 'period' costume is only hinted at. In Shakespeare's time, actors wore 'modern' clothes but if the play was set in Ancient Rome, for example, Roman-style helmets would be worn.

Actors and actresses may have to wear several different outfits during one performance. As well as looking good, costumes have to be quick and easy to change. They must also stand up to hard wear, because a successful play may run for years!

Scenery

Throughout the early history of the THEATRE, scenery was not used at all. But in the fifteenth century, Italian architects began to design painted backcloths for plays. These could easily be changed to represent a change of place. This custom eventually spread throughout EUROPE. By the eighteenth century, designing and installing scenery had become a full-time job. The invention of the proscenium arch made possible the placing of machinery behind it to make it easy to change sets quickly.

In the nineteenth century, designers often went in for very realistic settings. Today, however, some designers prefer to suggest the mood of the play by using simple costumes and little or no scenery.

Left: An attractive set designed for a musical.

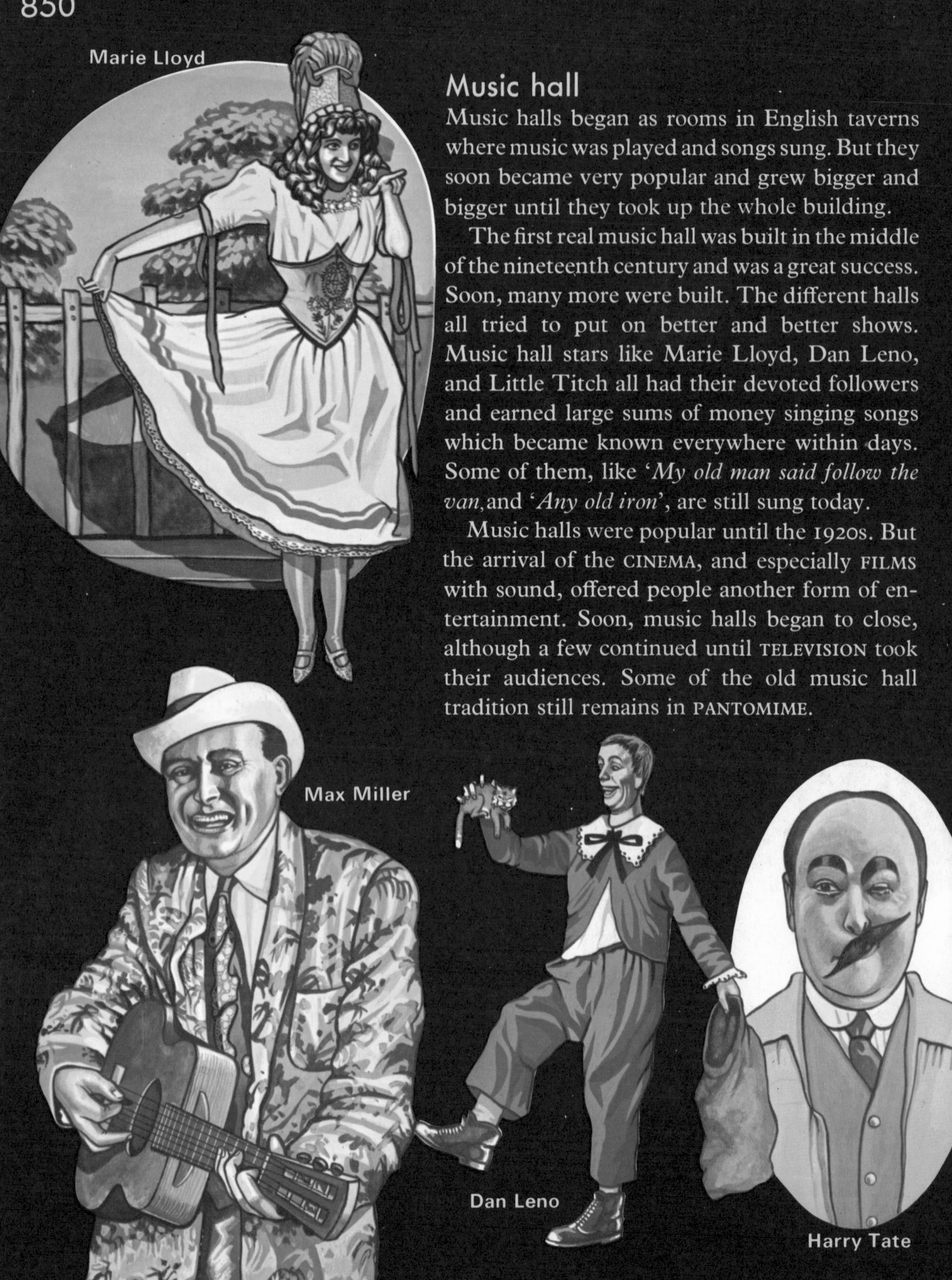

Music hall

Music halls began as rooms in English taverns where music was played and songs sung. But they soon became very popular and grew bigger and bigger until they took up the whole building.

The first real music hall was built in the middle of the nineteenth century and was a great success. Soon, many more were built. The different halls all tried to put on better and better shows. Music hall stars like Marie Lloyd, Dan Leno, and Little Titch all had their devoted followers and earned large sums of money singing songs which became known everywhere within days. Some of them, like '*My old man said follow the van,*and '*Any old iron*', are still sung today.

Music halls were popular until the 1920s. But the arrival of the CINEMA, and especially FILMS with sound, offered people another form of entertainment. Soon, music halls began to close, although a few continued until TELEVISION took their audiences. Some of the old music hall tradition still remains in PANTOMIME.

Pantomime

Pantomime today is a purely British entertainment although at one time it was popular in many parts of EUROPE. It takes place only at, and just after, Christmas and is mainly for children. Pantomimes are based on well-known fairy tales or legends – such as *The Babes in the Wood, Cinderella, Aladdin, Dick Whittington,* and *Robin Hood*.

By tradition the 'principal boy' is always played by an actress, while the 'dame', the principal boy's mother, is always a man. There is also always a villain, whom the audience is encouraged to boo.

The SCENERY is always very colourful and the costumes equally so. Pantomimes have lots of songs and the audience is invited to join in some of them. Acting in pantomimes is hard work because children like a lot of action, but pantomime is popular with ACTORS because children respond so well. A new form of pantomime is pantomime on ice.

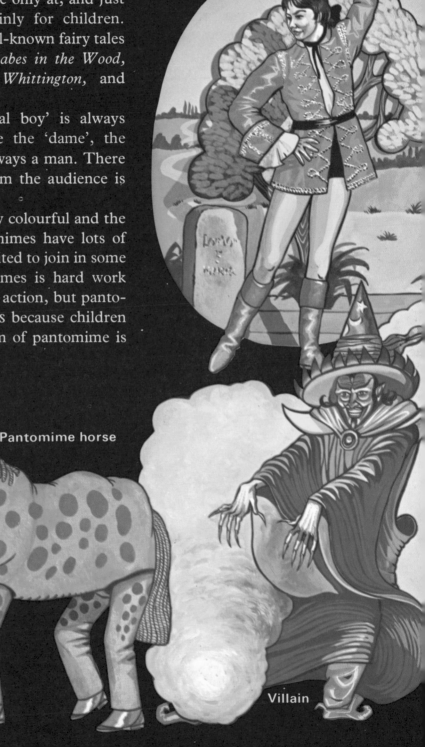

Dame

Pantomime horse

Circuses and Fairs

The first circuses were built by the ROMANS and used for chariot races and fights between gladiators. The rise of CHRISTIANITY put a stop to these, however. During the Middle Ages there were wandering bands of ACROBATS and JUGGLERS, but proper circuses were not built again until the nineteenth century.

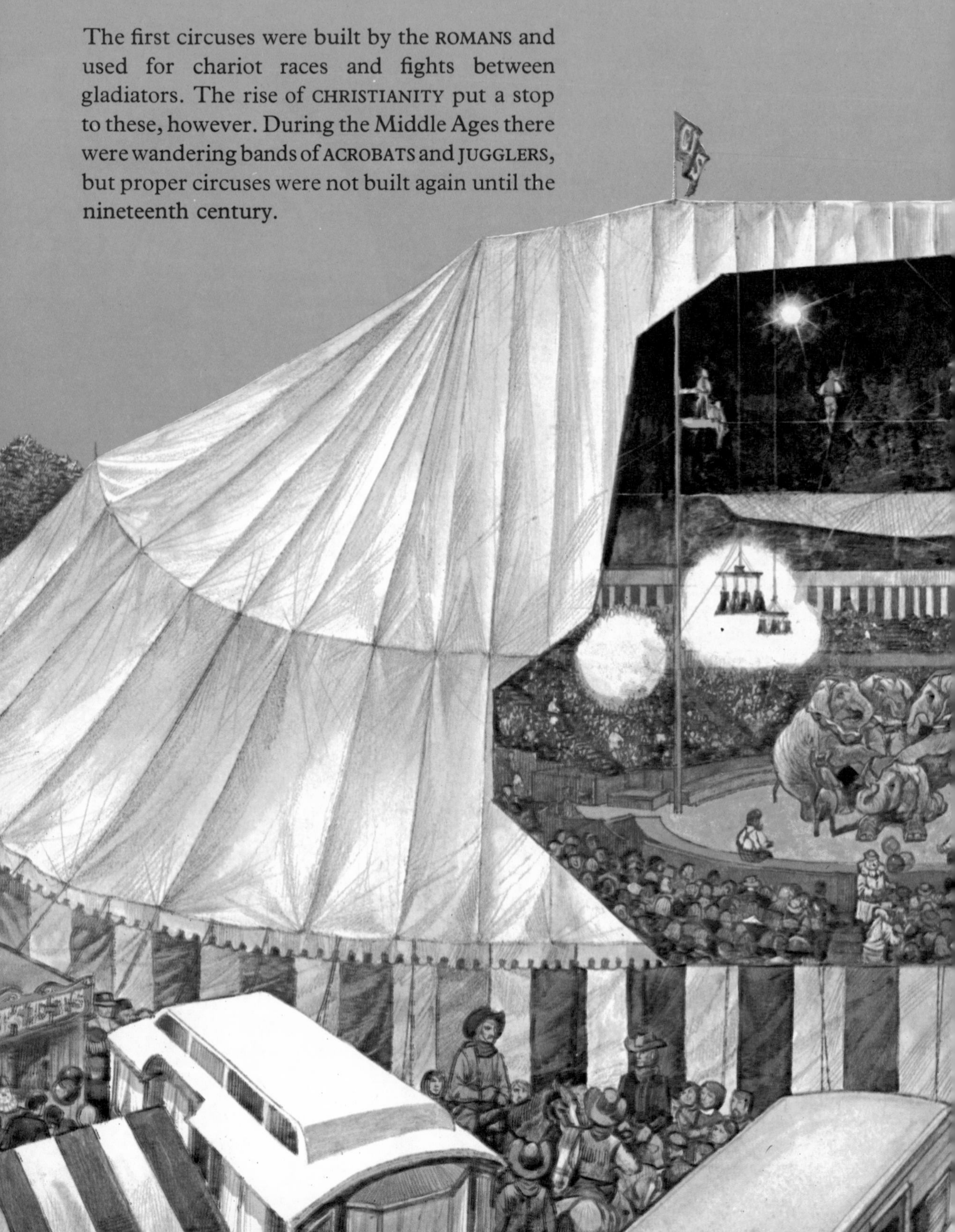

The first of these modern circuses were built of wood or brick, but they were soon replaced by a tent or 'big top'. This meant that the circus could travel from town to town. Some famous circuses travel all over the world. European circuses usually have a single ring, but Americans prefer a three-ring circus.

Circus animals

The first modern circuses were really exhibitions of trained HORSES and this tradition is still very strong. But since the middle of the nineteenth century other animals have become popular – SEALS, ELEPHANTS, LIONS, TIGERS, and BEARS.

Training circus animals needs great patience. Every action has to be rehearsed hundreds of times before the animal performs it automatically. Clever trainers have trained animals to do some very unusual things. Elephants have been trained to ride BICYCLES, lions to walk tight-ropes, and seals to play tunes on motor horns.

Circus animals today are protected by animal welfare societies, although most circuses take good care of the animals since they are their most valuable possessions.

Circus animals can be trained to perform amazing feats. These include balancing acts, and even making some kind of music.

Acrobats

No circus is complete without its acrobats, whether they be tight-rope walkers, bareback HORSE riders, or somersaulters. To succeed as an acrobat requires not only great skill and strength, but also great patience. The only way to success is by constant practice from early childhood. Many acrobatic acts look very dangerous but such is the skill of the acrobats that they are not usually in danger.

One of the most famous acrobats in history was a Frenchman called Blondin, who lived in the middle of the nineteenth century. He performed many famous and spectacular feats. The most famous was when he walked across Niagara Falls on a rope nearly 50 metres above the river, stopping only to stand on his head in the middle.

Acrobats thrill audiences with their extraordinary feats of balance. It takes years of practice to develop such skill.

Jugglers

Jugglers are shown in ANCIENT EGYPTIAN wall-paintings and they have been popular throughout history. Both ROMAN emperors and medieval kings kept troupes of jugglers to entertain them. Like ACROBATS, jugglers often train from childhood and practise continually.

Most jugglers specialise in one particular form of juggling, either with plates, bells, glasses or skittles. Probably the greatest juggler of all time was an Italian, Enrico Rastelli, who died in 1931. He was able to keep ten balls or eight plates in the air at once.

Left: Daviso Martini is one of the world's finest jugglers. Here he performs five separate actions at once. He balances on one leg while using the other leg, both hands and even his mouth to do difficult balancing and juggling acts.

Clowns

The circus would not be complete without its clowns. Their funny clothes and painted faces are an essential part of the show. Yet they only appeared comparatively recently, long after ACROBATS and JUGGLERS. The first real clown, Joe Grimaldi, died in 1837.

Clowns are often skilful acrobats and musicians, and there is a great deal more to their acts than just falling about and pouring water over one another. Some clowns have become world-famous – Grock, Popov, Kelly, and Coco. There is a belief that beneath their funny costumes clowns are sad men, but this is no more true of clowns than of anyone else.

Right: Grimaldi was the first real clown. Here he looks as if he is about to drench someone with a tub full of water.

Fairs

The first fairs were gatherings of merchants who traded their goods. Then, a little later in history, entertainers began to set up sideshows to amuse the merchants in their leisure hours. Today, the merchants have disappeared and only the entertainment remains.

Some of the older fairs are always held in the same place. Others, like circuses, travel from town to town and usually arrive at the same time each year so that they are expected. Fairs include many amusements – shooting galleries, coconut shies, helter-skelters, and dodgem cars.

Working on fairgrounds is often traditional in a family, and it is quite likely that the lady who collects your money at the swings is the seventh or eighth generation to work in fairs. The biggest fair ever held was in NEW YORK in 1939. It covered more than a thousand acres.

Above: A roundabout at a fair.
Below left: A busy fairground.
Below: A troupe of clowns in action in the ring.

Cinema, Television and Radio

Radio, television and the cinema have revolutionized the world's entertainment industry. They have brought marvellous music, art and theatre into the homes of more people than ever before.

The invention of photography in the last century paved the way for moving pictures. In 1895, the first public performance on a screen was given in Paris by the Lumière brothers. Early films were silent. A pianist or orchestra provided a musical accompaniment. Snatches of written speech and story were flashed onto the screen to make the story easier to follow.

In 1927, *The Jazz Singer* was screened. It was the first film with sound. The 'talkies' were born. The cinema grew into an enormous in-

Right: An early film advertising poster.

Below: A scene from an old film called *The Sheik.*

Below: The pioneer of radio was the Italian, Marconi. He sent a radio message between England and France in 1898.

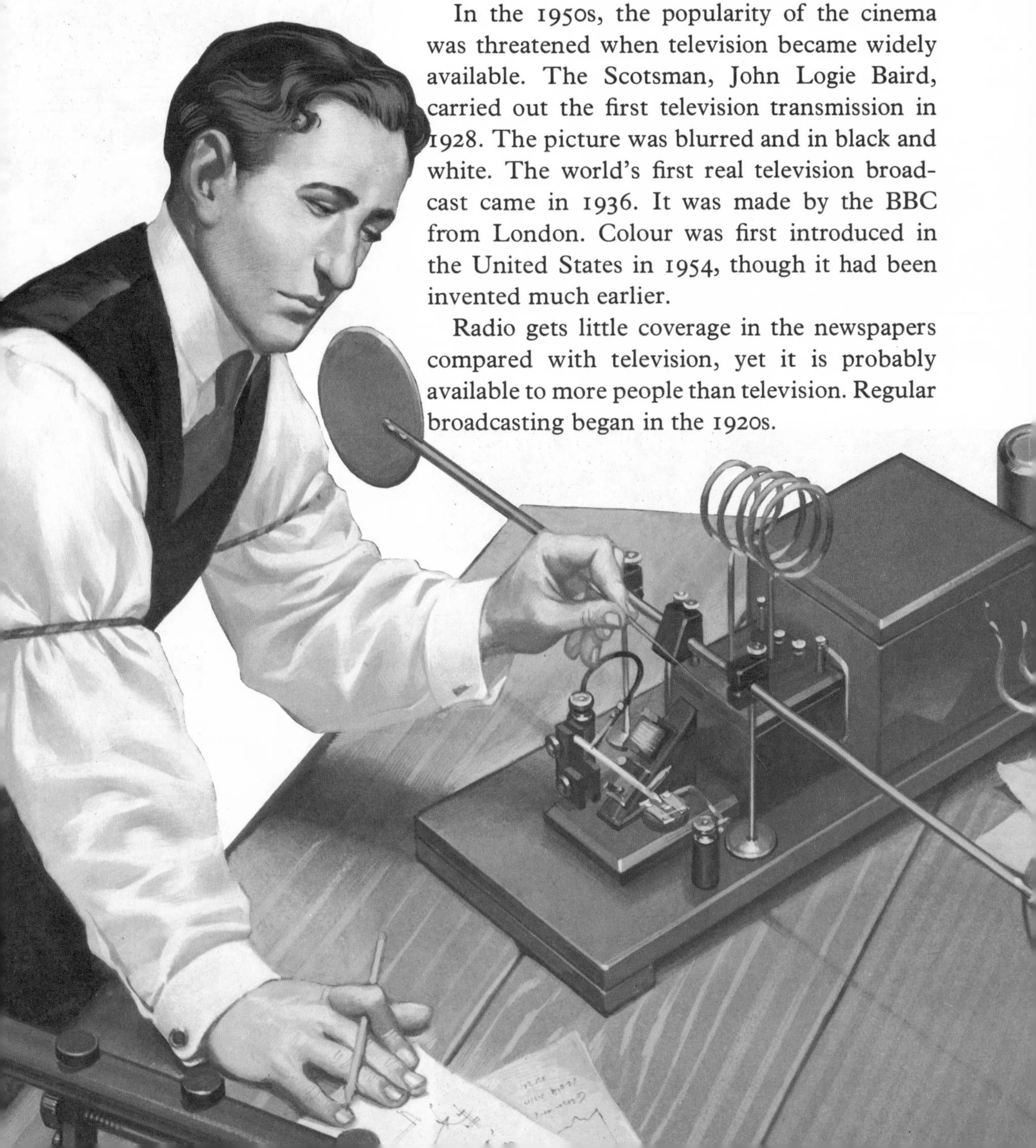

dustry. Hollywood, a tiny village near Los Angeles in the United States, grew into the film capital of the world. Today, tens of thousands of cinemas have been built to bring films to people all round the world.

In the 1950s, the popularity of the cinema was threatened when television became widely available. The Scotsman, John Logie Baird, carried out the first television transmission in 1928. The picture was blurred and in black and white. The world's first real television broadcast came in 1936. It was made by the BBC from London. Colour was first introduced in the United States in 1954, though it had been invented much earlier.

Radio gets little coverage in the newspapers compared with television, yet it is probably available to more people than television. Regular broadcasting began in the 1920s.

Film-making

To make a FILM you need more than just ACTORS and a camera. Making films is usually extremely expensive, and so the first person needed is a producer who will find the money as well as look after the business side of the film. Secondly, a film needs a director. The director decides how the film should be made, and how the actors should act. The director has a number of assistants.

The lighting man is important because the clever use of light can build up mood and hint at ideas behind the story. The sound man controls the strength and quality of the sound. The camera crew is headed by the chief camera-man.

Above: A camera-man at work in Kenya.

Below: All kinds of effects can be created in a film studio.

He controls exactly what is being filmed. He also decides where to move the camera and when to change the camera LENSES.

The continuity girl has to ensure that when one scene follows another, everything in the second scene follows on smoothly. The wardrobe mistress and the MAKE-UP man see that the actors look right for their parts.

If a film has to be shot outside the studio, the team has to go out 'on location' and this may take them thousands of miles. Finally, the film has to be processed, cut and edited, and music and sound effects added.

The box-office success of a film often depends on how well it is publicized. Much money has to be spent even when the film is complete. The heyday of films was in the 1930s and 40s. Today, far fewer people go to the cinema regularly.

Below: Preparing to film a scene on location in the desert.

Broadcasting

By the mid 1950s, television had replaced films as the favourite form of entertainment in the United States. Since then, it has become equally popular in many European countries.

The range of programmes now broadcast on television is enormous. It covers films, plays, music, sports, schools programmes, news and current affairs, as well as comedy shows, games, quizzes and many more.

Getting a programme on the air needs a large number of people and a vast amount of complex equipment. The roles of the producer and director are rather different in the film and television worlds. In television, the producer is responsible for the content of the programme. Once the planning stages are complete, the programme is usually recorded in a studio. A

Left: Actress Glenda Jackson before and after being made up as Elizabeth I for a television series.
Below: Final preparations in a television studio.

bove: An actor holds a microphone
ıring a rehearsal.
elow: Inside a studio in a popular
ıusic radio station.

number of cameras are used, each filming a different view of the action. It is the job of the director to select the camera shots.

In addition to the producer and director, there are camera-men, sound and lighting men and various engineers, as well as the performers in front of the cameras. Then, once the programme has been recorded, it has to be edited, when any unwanted material is cut out. Additional sound is often added at this stage as well.

Of course different kinds of programmes need different people and conditions to make them. Actors and actresses are needed to make films and plays. Reporters and journalists work on news programmes. Like films, many television programmes are filmed on location as well as in the studio. Very often, sports and other programmes are transmitted to our homes 'live' in outside broadcasts.

The first real radio programme was broadcast in Massachusetts in the United States in 1906. Radio stations began to appear in the 1920s.

THE ARTS AND ENTERTAINMENT FACTS AND FIGURES

PAINTING. Many prehistoric paintings were made in caves that were without any natural light at all. The largest painting ever made, a panorama of the Mississippi, was about 1·5 kilometres long and 3·6 metres wide. In his lifetime, Turner made over 20,000 watercolours and drawings.

DRAWING. X-rays of Old Masters often reveal the painter's original drawing, or cartoon, underneath the oil painting. The most valuable drawing is Leonardo da Vinci's cartoon of *The Virgin and Child.* It is now in the National Gallery in London.

SCULPTURE. The world's largest sculptures are the mounted figures of Jefferson Davis, Robert E. Lee, and Stonewall Jackson, carved on the face of Stone Mountain in Georgia, U.S.A. The most valuable sculpture is a polished bronze by Constantin Brancusi.

CRAFTS. The Bayeux tapestry, 70 metres long, is the world's longest piece of embroidery. The most valuable piece of pottery, the Portland Vase, is a Roman vase about 2000 years old. Some people can knit by hand at an average speed of more than a hundred stitches per minute.

DANCING. Morris dances originated in the military dances of the Moors in Spain. The Dervishes, a Moslem sect, dance in whirls until they go into a trance. The first ballet of importance was produced in 1581 by the valet of Catherine de' Medici, the Queen of France.

OPERA. The longest opera now performed, *The Mastersingers* by Wagner, lasts five and a quarter hours. A prima donna is the principal woman singer in an opera. *Amahl and the Night Visitors,* composed by Menotti in 1951, was the first opera to be written for television.

MUSIC. The oldest written music dates back to about 1800 B.C. The gamelan instruments of Indonesia are tuned to the highest note that their maker can sing. The pipe organ produces the highest and lowest notes of any non-electric musical instrument.

THEATRE. The largest building to be used as a theatre is in Peking, China; it seats 10,000 people. Professional actresses first appeared in England in 1660. The Great Spanish dramatist, Lope de Vega (1562-1635), is credited with writing over 2,000 plays.

CIRCUSES AND FAIRS. As many as 87,000 people at one time could watch a circus in the Colosseum in Ancient Rome. In 1969 Henri Rochetain made a record tightrope walk of 3,465 metres. The highest human pyramid ever achieved contained five rows of acrobats.

CINEMA, TELEVISION AND RADIO. In 1895 the Lumière brothers opened the first cinema in a Paris hotel. Financially, the most successful film ever made is *Star Wars.* The first television news item was transmitted in New York in 1928.

SPORTS AND PASTIMES

Team Sports

A sports team is a number of people playing together. In team sports, two teams are matched against each other. The aim is for one team to score more goals, more points, or more runs than the other team.

Whether the sport is football, HOCKEY, or BASKETBALL, every player tries to work with his team-mates. The number of players in a team varies, depending on the sport. In hockey and SOCCER there are 11 players on the field. In AUSTRALIAN FOOTBALL, there are 18.

Teams often have a manager or coach. They train the players in teamwork and help them to improve their skills. They also see that they are physically fit. During matches a referee or umpire is there to see that the game is played according to the rules.

Team sports are popular around the world. People in many different countries follow the success of their teams. They attend the games, listen to them on RADIO, or watch on TELEVISION. Team sports are played both nationally and internationally.

Below: The goalkeeper dives to save a goal. He is the only player in a football team who is allowed to handle the ball.

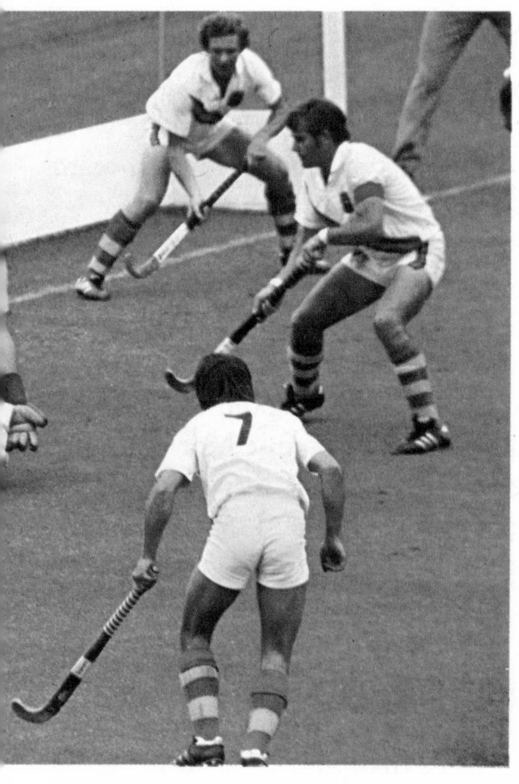

Hockey

Hockey is often called field hockey to distinguish it from ICE HOCKEY. It is played by men, women, and by mixed teams. There are 11 players in each team.

The players use specially-shaped sticks to hit the hard leather ball. They can only hit the ball with the flat front side of the stick. They must not raise the stick above shoulder level.

The goalkeeper wears heavy leg padding. He can use his feet as well as his stick to defend the goal.

A game of hockey is played in two halves of 35 minutes each. It is played all the year round. In ASIA, hockey is often played on hard pitches. This makes the game very fast.

Left: A hockey goalmouth scene. The goalkeeper has rushed out in defence.

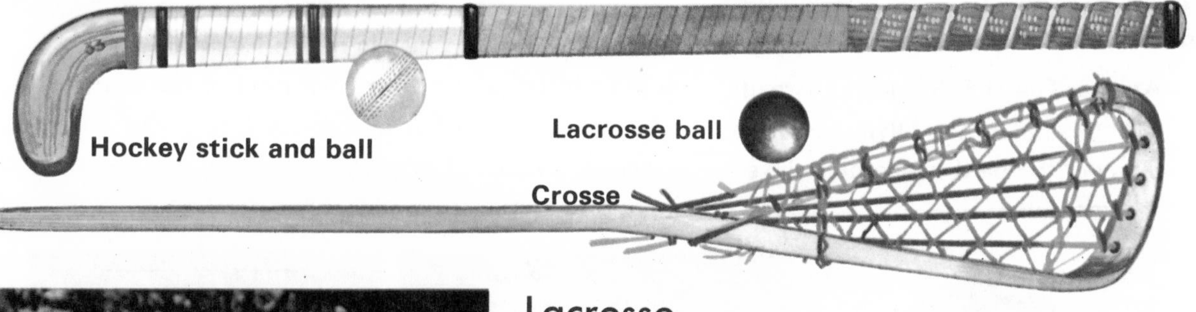

Above: In lacrosse, the goalkeeper wears protective clothing.

Lacrosse

Lacrosse probably developed from a game once played by AMERICAN INDIANS. It is mainly played in the U.S.A., CANADA, England, and AUSTRALIA. The rules are slightly different in each of these countries.

Men's teams have 10 players and women's have 12. Players pick up, carry, and throw a solid rubber ball with a three-cornered net at the end of the lacrosse stick, or crosse. They score goals by using the crosse to throw the ball between the goalposts.

Above: The U.S.A. playing Brazil at basketball in the Olympic Games. Many of the best basketball players are very tall.

Basketball and netball

Basketball was invented in 1891 by a U.S. professor, Dr James Naismith. Peach baskets were placed at opposite ends of a hall and each team tried to throw a soccer ball into the basket.

Today, the basket is a metal ring with an open net attached beneath. A player throwing the ball into the basket in the normal course of play scores two points for a field goal. A goal scored from a free throw is worth one point.

The ball can be thrown, tapped, or dribbled (bounced with one hand) in any direction. There are five players in each team and up to five substitutes may also be chosen. The game is very fast. It is the most popular sport after SOCCER. The Harlem Globetrotters is a famous U.S. team that plays all over the world.

Netball is an amateur game played by women. It is similar to basketball and used to have the same name. There are seven players on each side and the game can be played indoors or out. Each player must stay in her own part of the court. If she moves out of it a free pass is given to the opposing team. The player with the ball can only take one step before passing.

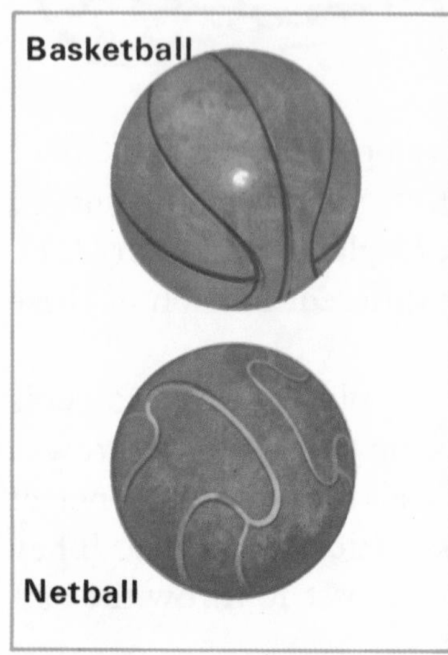

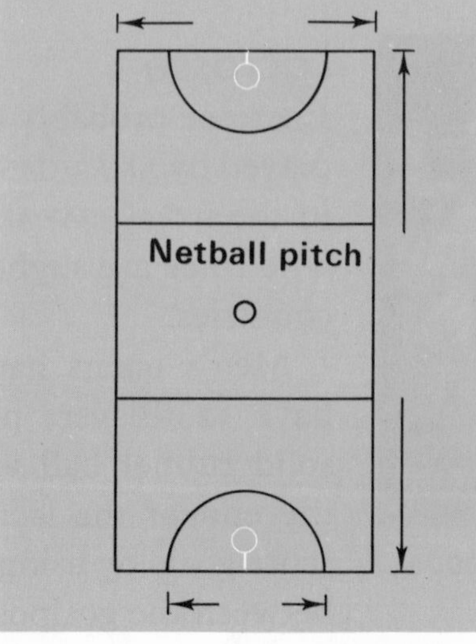

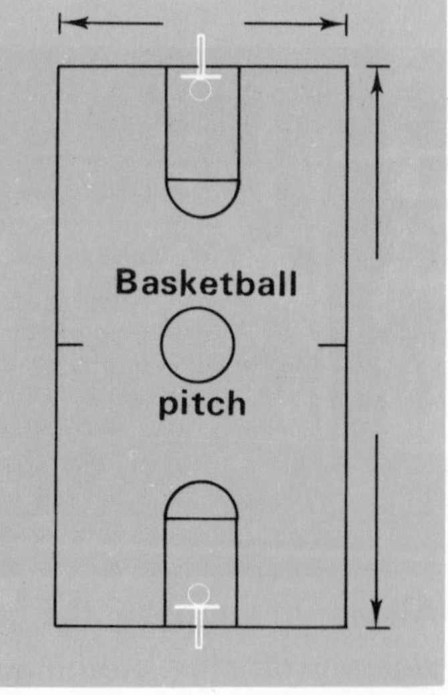

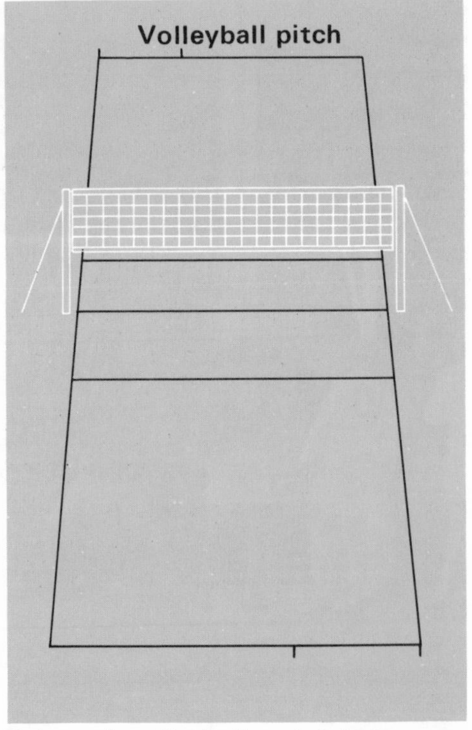

Below: A volleyball match between Japan and the U.S.S.R.

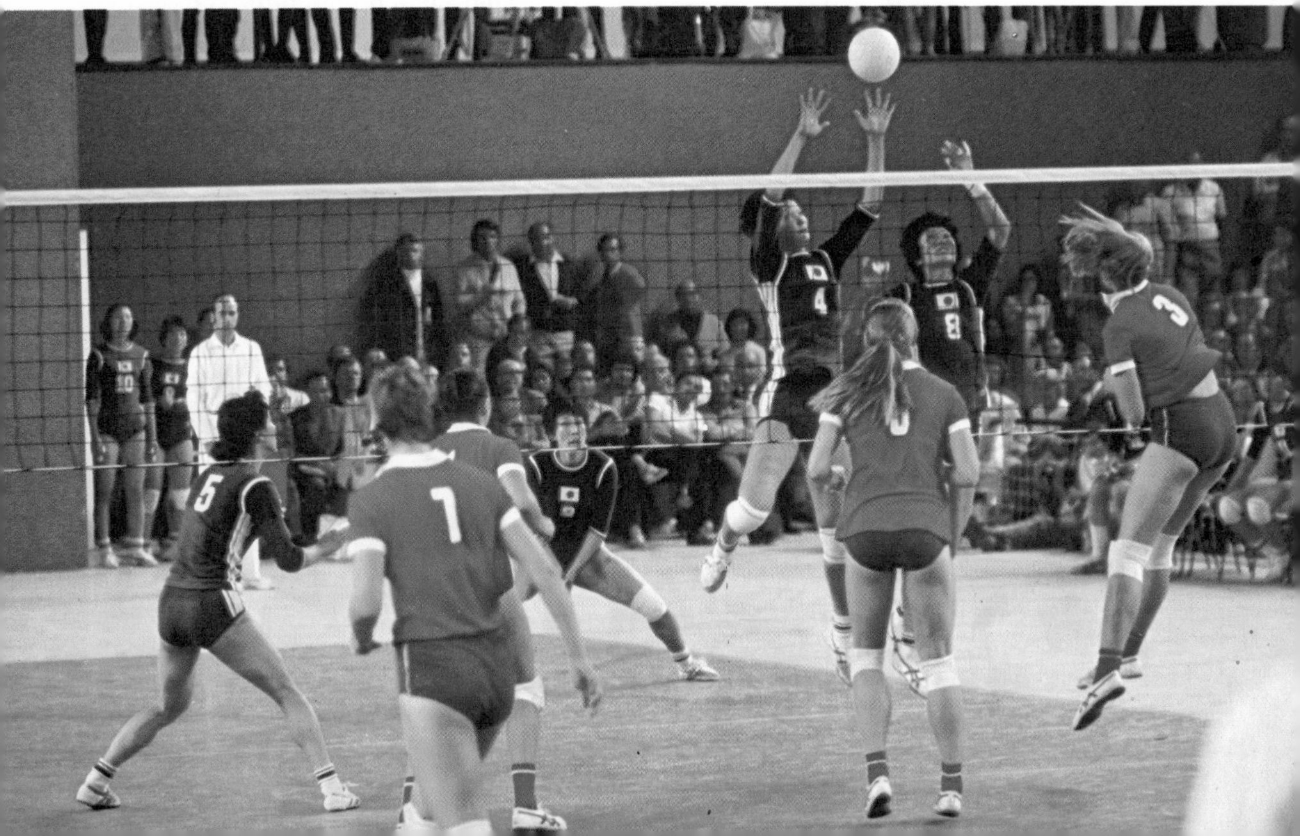

Volleyball

Volleyball, like netball, is based on the game of BASKETBALL. It was invented by an American in 1895, and is a very fast and skilful game.

Two teams face each other across a high net. A player serves the ball over the net with his hand or arm. The receiving team must keep the ball off the ground. They can touch the ball three times before returning it over the net. No player can touch the ball twice in a row.

Only the team that serves the ball can score points. It gets one point if the ball hits the ground in the opposing team's court. It can also score a point if the other team hits the ball into the net or out of bounds. When the receiving team wins a rally, it serves next and then tries to score one or more points.

Volleyball is a very popular international sport for men and women. It was introduced into the OLYMPIC GAMES in 1964.

Soccer

Soccer (short for Association Football) is the world's most popular team sport. Men have enjoyed kicking a ball around in rough games of different kinds for hundreds of years. Organized soccer began in 1863 when the Football Association was formed in LONDON. Soccer is now played in more than 130 countries.

A football team has 11 players whose aim is to score goals. They are allowed to kick, or hit the ball with their head, but only the goalkeeper can handle it. Soccer clubs play one another in various competitions. These are held in most countries and large crowds support their teams.

The first international match was between England and Scotland in 1872. Other international matches began in the early part of this century. The most important international competition is the World Cup. BRAZIL won the competition for the third time in 1970.

There is a great contrast in clothing and style of play between soccer (above) and American football (below).

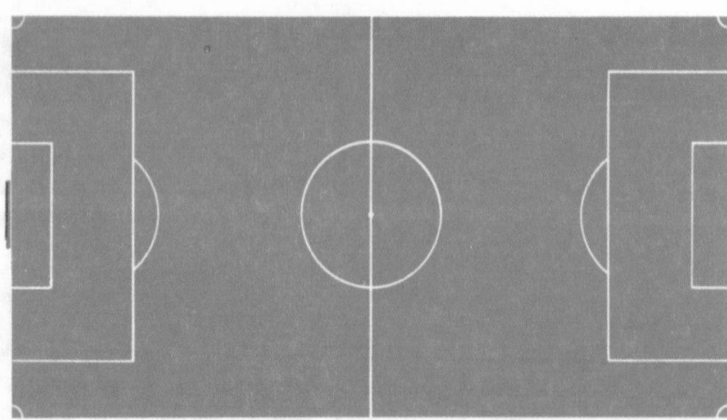

Above: A soccer pitch.
Below: A ball and boots used in soccer.

American football

American football developed from RUGBY FOOTBALL. As in rugby, the ball is oval and the object is to carry the ball over the opposing team's goal-line. This is called a touchdown and scores six points. After a touchdown, a conversion kick – over the crossbar and between the uprights of the goal – scores one point. A similar kick in the course of play is called a field goal and earns three points.

As in the English game, players can tackle only the man with the ball. They can, however, block opponents who do not have the ball. There are 11 players on each side and several substitutes are allowed. Players always wear padded equipment and helmets. Play is divided into four 15-minute periods, with a 15-minute interval after the second period.

American football is not played widely outside the U.S.A.

Right: An American football pitch. This is called a gridiron because of the markings on it which occur at regular intervals.

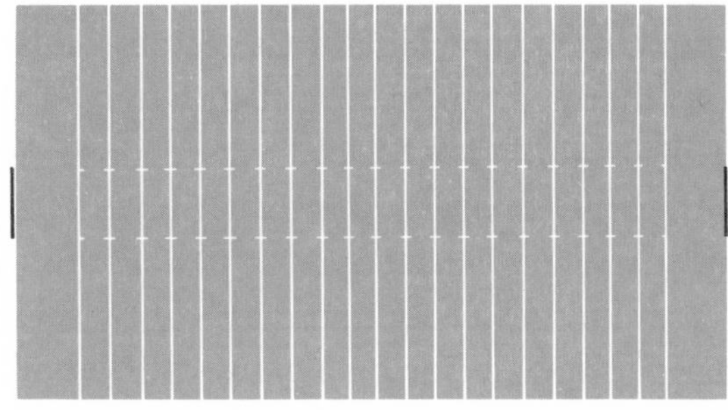

Below: Some items of American football equipment.

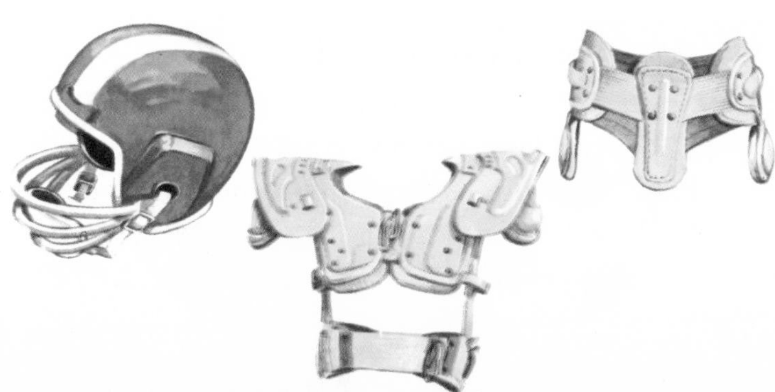

Rugby football

Rugby Union football is played by amateurs and has 15 players a side. Rugby League is amateur and professional and has 13 players a side. Rugby League dates from 1895 when some clubs in the North of England broke away from the Rugby Union, the governing body of the amateur game.

The object in Rugby football is to carry an oval-shaped ball over the opposing goal-line and touch it down on the ground for a try. This scores four points in Rugby Union and three in Rugby League. A conversion kick at the goal follows a try. It is worth two points. Penalty kicks are worth three points in Union and two in League. For conversion kicks and penalty kicks to score points, the ball must pass over the crossbar and between the uprights. In both kinds of Rugby, passing the ball forward is illegal. Only the man with the ball may be tackled.

The main difference between the two games is the play-the-ball rule in Rugby League. Another difference is when the ball goes out of play over the touchline at the side of the pitch. In Rugby Union, there is a lineout, but in Rugby League there is a scrum-down.

Both games are played internationally, mainly in the COMMONWEALTH and EUROPE. Rugby football is said to have originated at Rugby school in England in 1823. During a game of football, one of the boys, William Webb Ellis, picked up the ball and began running towards the opposing goal.

Rugby League. Playing-the-ball (above) and (below) an example of field placing at a kick-off.

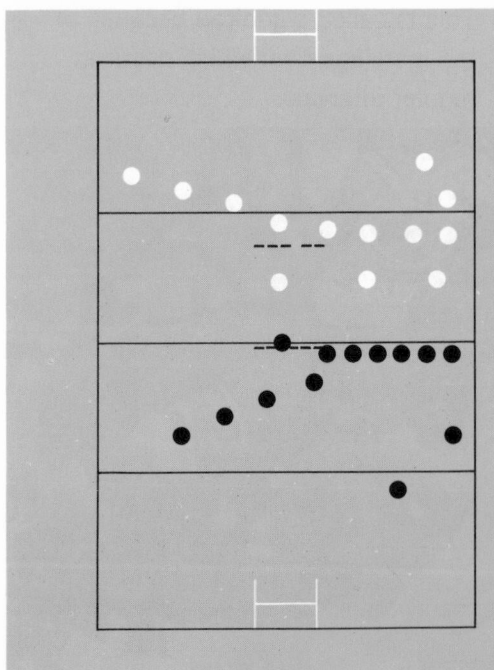

Australian football

Australian football, once called Australian Rules, developed from SOCCER, RUGBY, and Gaelic football. It was first played in the nineteenth century by English and Irish immigrants to AUSTRALIA. The field is oval and much larger than for other

Above: The scrum-half passes the ball to his fly-half after a Rugby Union scrum.
Right: High leaps for the ball and the unusual goal are features of Australian football.

football games. There are 18 players to each team.

The oval ball can be passed in any direction. Players are allowed to kick or punch the ball, or to tap it in the air to a team–mate. This is known as palming. High leaps to catch the ball are a spectacular part of the game. A player running with the ball must bounce it or touch it down every 10 metres. An opposing player tackles by holding him round the waist or by grabbing his vest, which is called a guernsey.

The two goals have four posts each, but no cross-bar. If the ball is kicked between the two inner goalposts without touching them, a goal is scored for six points. A ball passing between the inner and outer posts is called a behind and earns only one point.

Above: W.G. Grace, the most famous cricketer of the nineteenth century. Below: A baseball batter. The catcher is behind him.

Cricket

Cricket is a bat and ball game first played in England at least 300 years ago. The Marylebone Cricket Club, which is responsible for the laws of cricket, has been based at Lord's Cricket Ground in LONDON since 1815.

There are 11 players in each team and the winning team is the one scoring the most runs. When the batsman hits the ball and has time to run from one wicket to the other, he scores a run. If he hits the ball to the boundary he scores four runs. If the ball goes over the boundary, without first hitting the ground, he scores six runs.

The bowler bowls the ball from the far end of the pitch in an attempt to dismiss the batsman. He does this by hitting the wickets which the batsman is defending or trapping him leg-before-wicket. The batsman is also out if his hit is caught on the full by a fielder, if he is stumped by the wicket-keeper, or is run out. When 10 of the 11 batsmen are out, the fielding team takes its turn to bat.

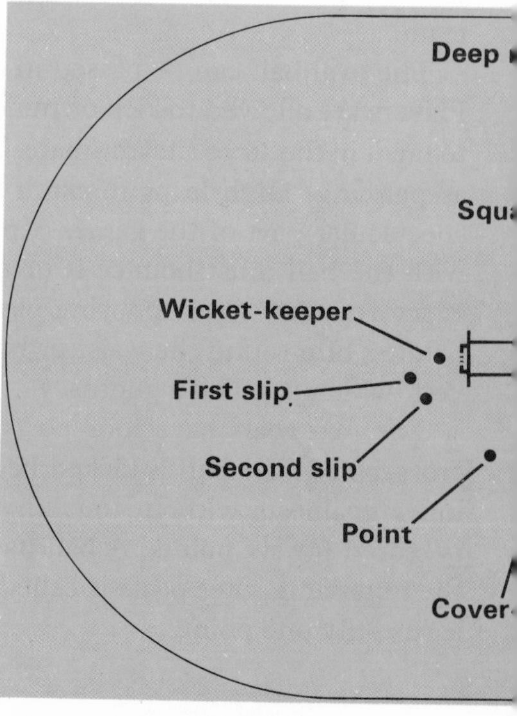

Above: Australia and the West Indies playing in a Test match at Sydney. The placing of this field shows the wicket-keeper, left, and three slips and two gulleys on his right. Two umpires are used in cricket.

Below: An alternative placing of the field for a slow or medium pace bowler.

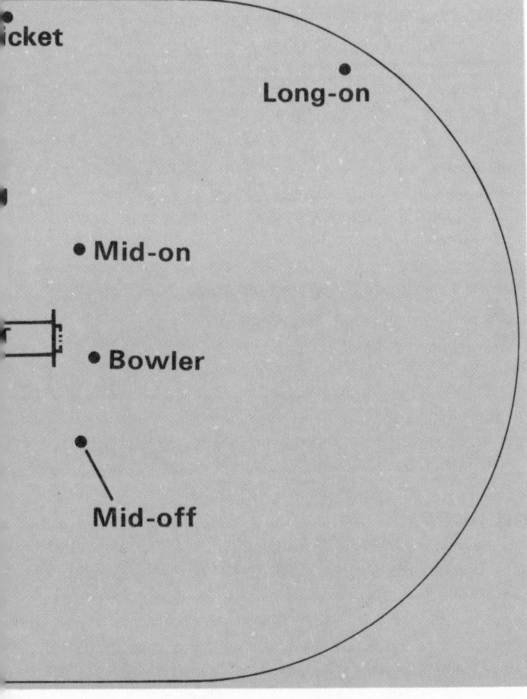

Baseball

Baseball is an American game, first played in about 1839. It developed from the English game of rounders. A similar game, called softball, is played in AUSTRALIA and NEW ZEALAND.

There are nine players in each team, and substitutes are allowed. One team is at bat while the other team is in the field. The pitcher of the fielding team throws the ball to the batter, who stands at home plate. If the batter tries to hit and misses, or if the ball goes over the plate, a strike is called. After three strikes the batter is out. If the pitcher throws four balls outside the strike area, the batter is allowed to walk to first base.

If the batter hits the ball into fair territory, he must drop his bat and run to first base. There are four bases, arranged in the shape of a diamond. If he gets to first base before the ball is thrown there, he is safe. Whenever the pitcher throws the ball or it is hit, he tries to run to another base. If the batter gets around all four bases, he completes a run, which is worth one point. A run off one hit is called a home run. A batter is out if his hit is caught or the ball is returned to the base before he gets there.

Individual Sports

In individual sports the athlete competes on his or her own. These include the oldest sports, such as running, WRESTLING, and BOXING.

Although athletes in these sports compete alone, they often train together. Some have coaches, who play an important part in improving skill and fitness.

Some individual sports, such as TENNIS, can be played either as singles, or as doubles, with two players on each side.

In many of these sports, records are kept. Breaking a record is the aim of many individual sportsmen.

Below: All these athletics field events are in the women's programme except for the hammer and the pole vault.

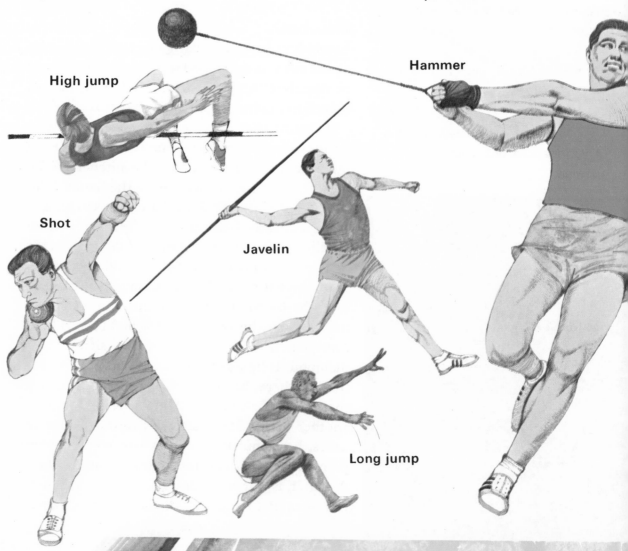

Hammer

High jump

Shot

Javelin

Long jump

Above: Women take part in most athletics events. In this 100 metres hurdles race, the hurdles are 840 millimetres high.

Track and field athletics

Athletics is the main sport in the OLYMPIC GAMES. The International Amateur Athletic Federation has members in over 140 countries. Athletics is not just one sport but several. The track events include the sprints (short races up to 400 metres), longer races up to 10,000 metres, hurdle races, relay races, and the steeplechase. The field events are the jumps, the pole vault, and the throwing events. Then there is the marathon, a road race of just over 42 kilometres, and also race walking.

In athletics, fitness and skill are equally important. Technique does not win points, as it does in diving and gymnastics, but it is often essential to have good technique if you are to win. Thus coaching plays a very important part, especially in events like pole vaulting and hurdling. Some experts believe that the throwing events – the shot, discus, hammer, and javelin – are technically the most difficult.

There have been very big improvements in athletics performances since records were first officially kept in 1913. Olympic standards are now much better than the timings or distances which used to be good enough for gold medals.

Performance in athletic events is measured, and records are broken regularly. The fastest sprinters can run at a speed of over 35 kilometres an hour, and the best long distance runners can cover over 20 kilometres in an hour.

In the men's decathlon, 10 events are spread over two days. In the women's pentathlon, five events are contested in two days. In both the decathlon and pentathlon, competitors receive points for their performances. The winner is the athlete who builds up the biggest total over the two days.

Modern pentathlon

The modern pentathlon consists of five sports held on five consecutive days. The events are riding, FENCING, SHOOTING, SWIMMING, and running. It used to be called the military pentathlon because it demanded all the physical qualities of the ideal soldier.

The competitor must be a first-class athlete. He needs speed for fencing, steadiness for shooting, and toughness for swimming and running. He must also know how to handle a horse.

The riding course is 800 metres with 15 jumps. An épée is used in the fencing. The shooting is with a pistol at a target 25 metres away. The swimming is a freestyle race of 300 metres, and the footrace is 4000 metres across country.

Points are awarded for a competitor's performances in each of the sports and the man with the highest total is the winner. The modern pentathlon is in the OLYMPIC GAMES and there is also a World Championship.

Below: The five sports in the pentathlon.

Fencing

Fencing has been a sport as well as a military skill for many hundreds of years. Men used swords in the BRONZE AGE. Modern fencing is performed with three kinds of weapons – the foil, épée, and sabre.

In foil and épée, the fencer wears a jacket of metal covered with canvas. The jacket is connected to an electrical device that signals when he is hit by his opponent. In sabre, the edge of the weapon is used as well as the point.

Fencing is an Olympic sport.

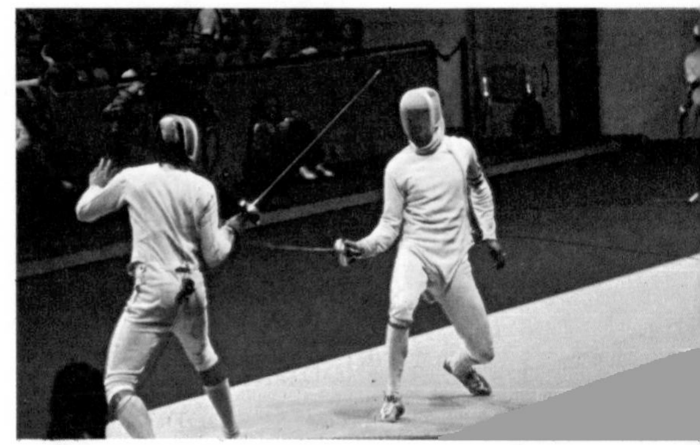

Above: The wire from the fencer's back connects the judging apparatus with his weapon.

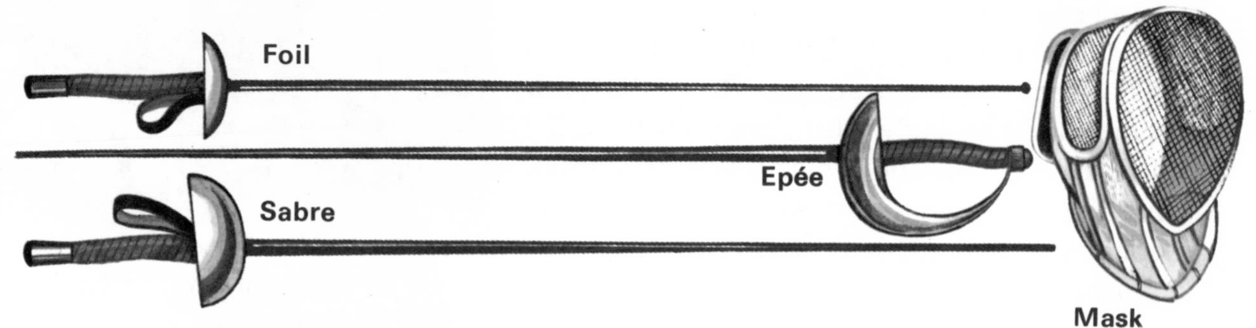

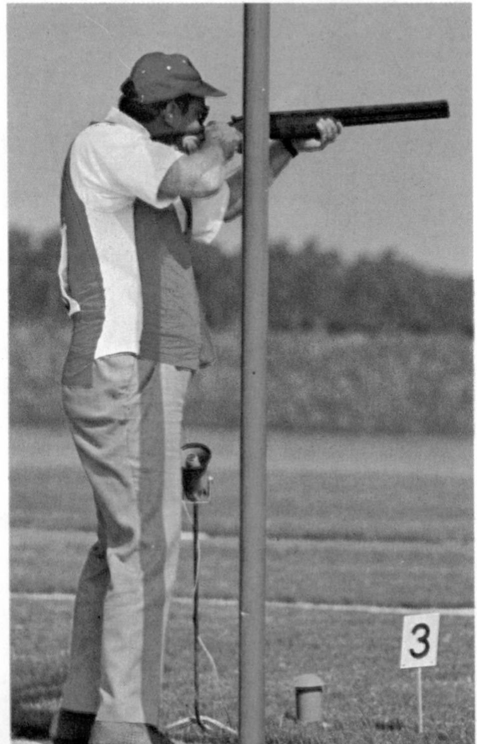

Shooting

Shooting, as a competitive sport, has two main branches. One is target shooting, a sport which is about 500 years old. In target shooting, various kinds of guns are used, from pistols to rifles.

The other is clay-pigeon shooting, sometimes called trap shooting. Moving targets – saucer-shaped clay pigeons – are catapulted into the air, and the marksman aims to hit as many in succession as he can. In championships each competitor shoots at 200 targets.

Skeet shooting is similar, with two targets moving in opposite directions.

Left: The trap shooter does not know the angle from which the target will appear.

Wrestling

Wrestling is one of the oldest sports. It was part of the ANCIENT GREEK Olympic Games in 704 B.C. The ROMANS took it up, and Greco-Roman wrestling is one of the styles contested in the modern Olympics. The other is freestyle. Each has 10 body weight classes.

In Greco-Roman, the wrestler is not allowed to use his legs on his opponent and cannot hold him below the waist. In both styles, the aim is to pin your opponent with his shoulders flat on the ground for the count of 'one'.

There are different kinds of wrestling in various parts of the world. In JAPAN there is sumo wrestling. The aim is to force the other man out of the ring or to make him touch the ground with some part of his body other than his feet. In the U.S.S.R. there is sambo, which is similar to JUDO. In Turkish yagli wrestling the competitors smear their bodies with grease so that it is difficult to take hold of them.

Above: One of the many different holds in freestyle wrestling.

Judo

Judo is a form of unarmed combat invented in JAPAN. The aim of each fighter is to throw his opponent or to force him to submit. Judo is practised by men and women, boys and girls. A judo contest may last up to twenty minutes. It is controlled by a referee.

The wrestlers wear loose-fitting clothes tied at the waist with a belt. The colour of the belt shows the grade of the judoka.

Pupils are known as *kyu* and experienced judoka are graded in twelve levels of *dan*, which means degree. There are six weight classes in judo.

Right: Judoka may catch hold of each other by the costume, or judogi.

Weight lifting

Weight lifting is a competitive sport for men consisting of raising barbells. These are iron bars evenly loaded with metal discs. Weight lifting competitions have taken place in the OLYMPIC GAMES since 1920. Lifters are classed in ten different weight categories, from flyweight to super-heavyweight.

There are now two main kinds of lift: the snatch, and the jerk. In the snatch, the lifter lifts the barbell above his head in one movement before standing up. In the jerk, he uses two movements.

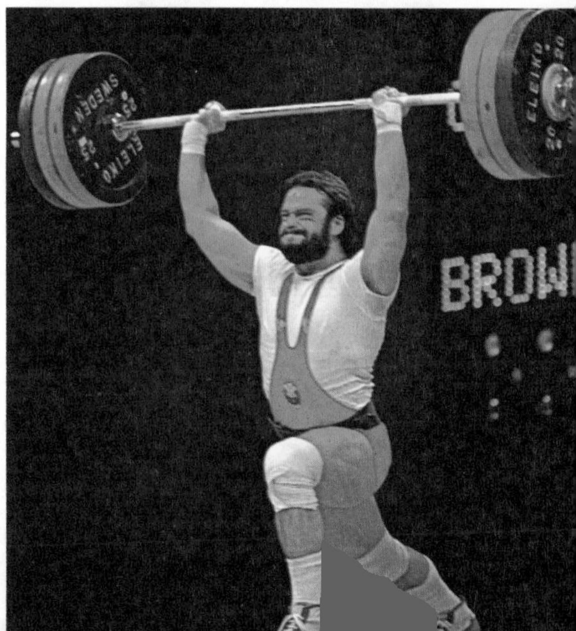

Above right: Vasili Alexeev (U.S.S.R.) was Olympic super-heavyweight champion in 1972 and 1976.
Right: A competitor in the 1978 Commonwealth Games.

Boxing

In ancient times, the Greeks held boxing matches. The ROMANS fought with metal guards on their hands, sometimes to the death. Bare-knuckle fighting, usually between servants, was a popular sport in England until the Marquess of Queensberry drew up the rules of boxing.

A modern boxer wears gloves weighing about 200 grammes. He is not allowed to punch his rival below the belt or on the back of the head or body.

A bout can be won by a knockout, when one boxer is knocked down by his opponent. He loses the fight if he cannot rise to his feet before the referee counts to ten. A referee can also stop the fight if he feels that one boxer is badly hurt, or can no longer defend himself.

A fight can also be won on points. This means that one boxer has attacked more often and made more clean punches. Amateur boxing bouts are of three rounds. Professional championships

Left: James ('Gentleman Jim') Corbett became world heavyweight champion in 1892.
Below: Ex-world heavyweight champion Muhammad Ali in the ring with Floyd Patterson.

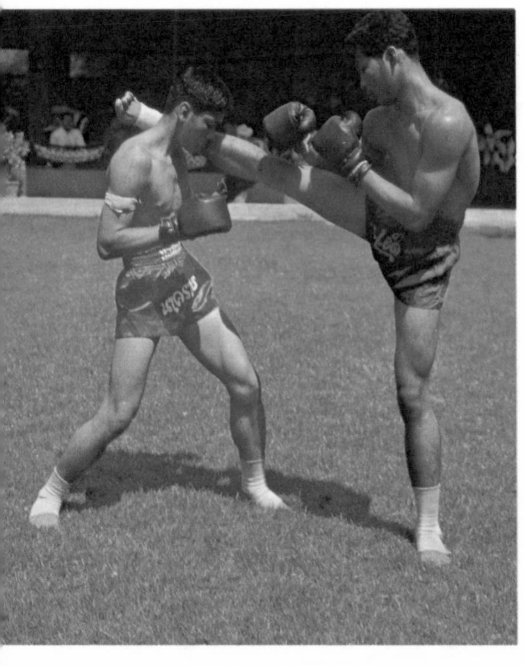

are fought for ten, twelve, or fifteen rounds.

There are 11 weight divisions recognized by world amateur boxing authorities. These are: light-fly, fly, bantam, feather, light, light-welter, welter, light middle, middle, light-heavy, and heavy.

Professional boxing has become one of the highest-paid sports. A heavyweight champion can expect to earn several million dollars from one fight in defence of his title. Film, radio, and television fees help to increase the sums which can be paid both to the winner and loser.

Left: In Thai boxing, fighters may use their feet, legs, and elbows as well as fists.

Gymnastics

Gymnastics, according to the ANCIENT GREEK philosopher Aristotle, is both an art and a science. Modern gymnastics came into existence less than a hundred years ago. It has been an event in the OLYMPIC GAMES since 1896.

The usual competition events for men are combined exercises, horizontal bar, parallel bars, pommel horse, rings, vault, and floor exercises. The women do the first and the last two exercises and also the beam and asymmetrical bars.

There are four judges who award up to a maximum of 10 points for each event. The highest and lowest of the four scores are dropped. The average of the remaining scores is the one that counts.

Trampolining is a form of gymnastics performed on a spring bed. The gymnast does a sequence of movements interrupted by rebounds from the bed. He may land on his feet, his seat, his back, or his front before rebounding into the next somersault or twist.

Above: Balance, control, agility, and poise are some of the skills required of the gymnast on the parallel bars.

Tennis

Tennis was first played in FRANCE about 600 years ago. It was usually played indoors. This old kind of tennis is now called *real* (meaning *royal*) tennis. The first lawn tennis club was formed in England in 1872 and the first Wimbledon championship was played five years later.

The aim of the game is to hit the ball over the net and into your opponent's court. If he misses, or returns into the net or outside your court, you win the rally. A rally is a series of strokes leading to one point being scored.

A game begins with one player serving. If his opponent fails to return the ball over the net after one bounce or misses it altogether, the server wins the point. The score is 15-love. If he continues to win points, the score progresses to 30-love, 40-love, and then game. If the opposing player wins the same number of rallies the score will go to 15-all, 30-all, and 40-all (usually called deuce). At deuce, one player must win two rallies in succession to win the game. The first player to win six games wins the set, providing he is two games ahead at the end.

At the end of each set the player who has been serving becomes the receiver. The first player to win two sets in a three-set match, or three sets if it is a five-set match, is the match winner.

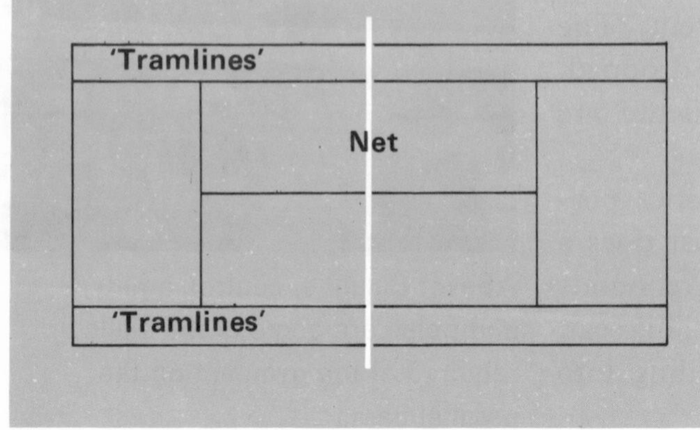

Above: A doubles tennis match. In singles the outer 'tramlines' are not part of the court. Tournaments are more often played on grass courts than on hard ones.

Above: Mrs Evonne Cawley, the Australian player, has been among the world's leading tennis stars in recent years.

Left: A tennis court.

Right: A stroke in table tennis.

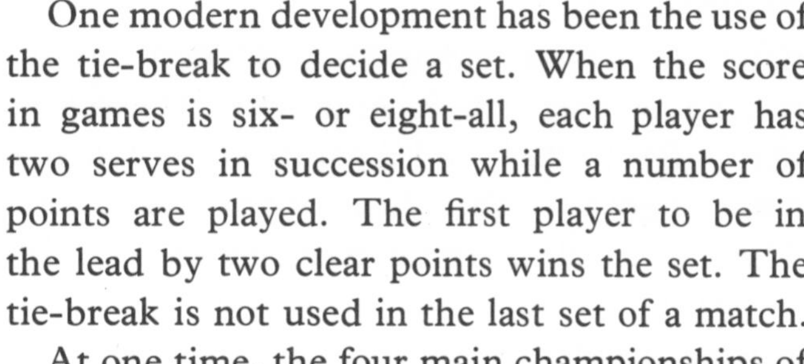

One modern development has been the use of the tie-break to decide a set. When the score in games is six- or eight-all, each player has two serves in succession while a number of points are played. The first player to be in the lead by two clear points wins the set. The tie-break is not used in the last set of a match.

At one time, the four main championships of international tennis were the Australian, French, British (Wimbledon) and American. In 1969, Rod Laver of AUSTRALIA became the first player to win all four in a year (the Grand Slam) for the second time. Today there are many important events with rich prize-money for the winners.

Table tennis

Table tennis is an indoor game played with bats and a plastic ball. For each rally (exchange of strokes) that a player wins, he scores one point. The first player to reach 21 points is the winner. If the score reaches 20-all, play goes on until one player is two points ahead.

The ball is served by hitting it so that it bounces on the server's side of the net and then again on the receiver's side. The receiver must return it after one bounce on his side, as in TENNIS. If he misses the ball, or hits it into the net, or off the table, the server wins the point.

A player must master forehand and backhand strokes. In addition there are various types of spin – topspin, backspin, and sidespin – which can cause the ball to behave in different ways and defeat an opponent. Western players usually hold the bat as they would a handle. Asian players grip the bat as they would a pen.

Table tennis, which used to be called ping-pong, was first played in England in the 1880s and the English Table Tennis Association was formed in 1927.

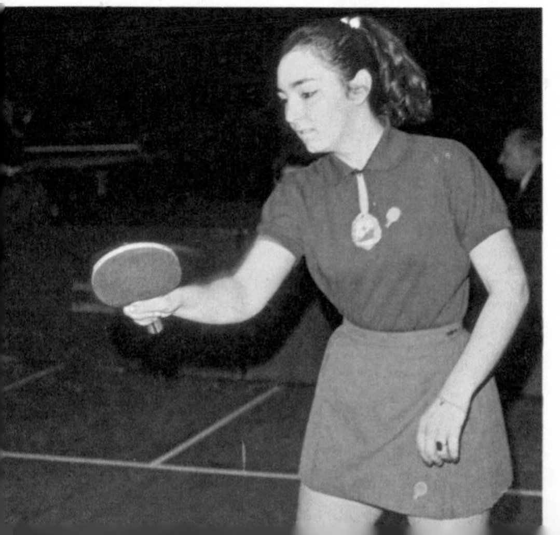

Badminton

Badminton is an indoor or outdoor game for men and women, singles or doubles. It is played with a light racket and a shuttlecock, which is made of goose feathers in a cork or plastic base. The shuttlecock is served from below the level of the waist. The other side must return it before it touches the ground.

If the server wins the rally, he gets one point. If he loses, the service goes to the other player who then tries to win a point. In doubles, both players serve before the service is passed to the other side. A game is usually to 15 points. A match is the best of three games.

Badminton is an extremely fast game but slow drop shots are often used. This results in changes of pace which are one of the features of the game. Quick reactions and a strong wrist are essential.

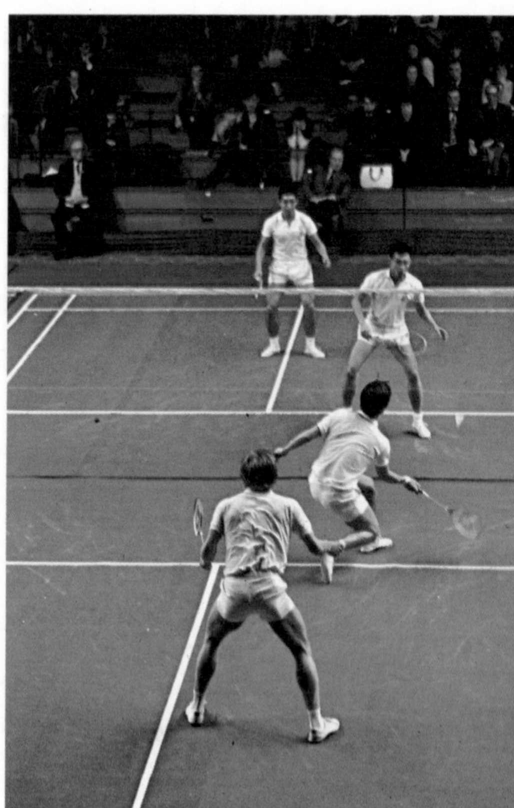

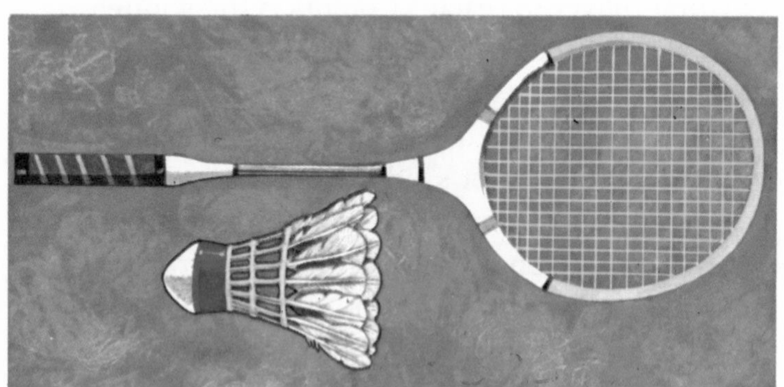

Above: Badminton doubles.
Left: A badminton racket and shuttlecock.

Squash

Squash is an indoor game played in an enclosed court. Only the server can score points. He must serve the hollow rubber ball against the front wall above the cut line. This is the second of the three lines across the front wall. The top line marks the court boundary; the bottom one is the tell-tale line. The other player must return the ball after no more than one bounce.

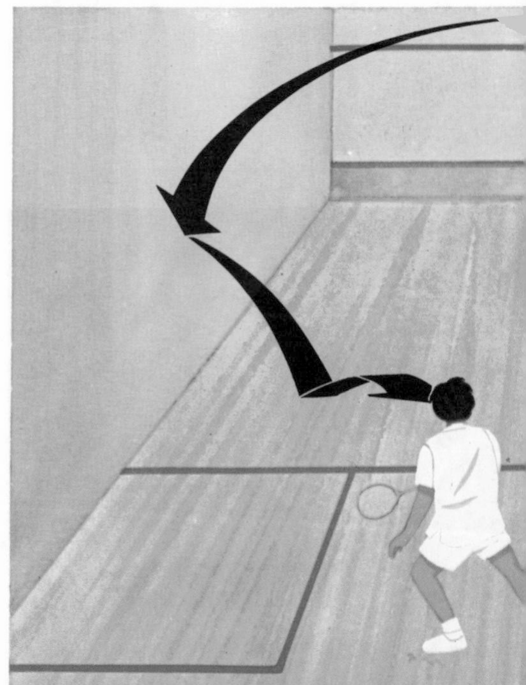

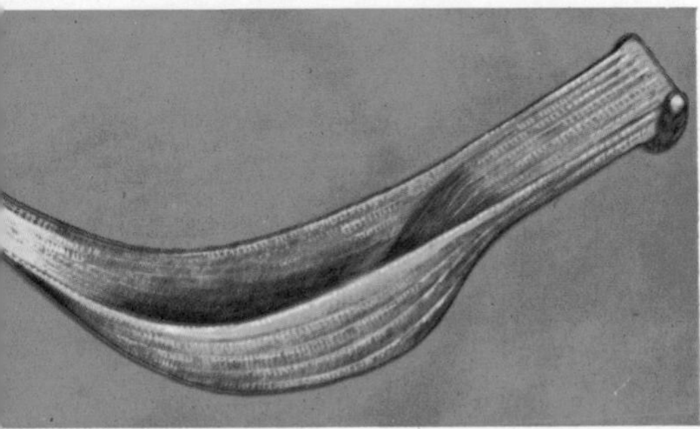

Top: Pelota on an open court.
Above: The *cesta* used in pelota.
Below: A squash rally in progress.

The return shot can bounce off any part of the other three walls, but it must hit the front wall below the boundary line and above the tell-tale line. A sheet of tin below the tell-tale line tells when the ball is out. The first player to score nine points wins.

Pelota

Pelota is the name given to ball and court games played in Northern SPAIN. The French call them *Pelotê Basque*. In the U.S.A., pelota is called *jai alai* after the court in which one of the fastest pelota games is played. This game is *cesta punta*. It is played with the *cesta*, a long wicker-work basket in which the ball is caught and thrown.

Cesta punta is among the most popular pelota games because it is so exciting. The ball travels at speeds of over 250 kilometres an hour and players throw themselves about spectacularly. The *jai alai* court has three walls: front, side, and back. The players catch the ball in the basket after it hits the front or back wall, and return it so that it hits the front wall. They must not return it after more than one bounce.

Other pelota games are played on open courts and players use rackets, bats, or *cestas*.

Handball

Handball is a very old game in which players hit the ball against a wall with their hands. There are three main kinds. Irish handball, the most popular, was exported to the United States. It is played with a hard ball and the court has four walls. In this game players can also kick the ball. There are also two soft ball games, one played with four walls and the other with only one. In all three versions only the server can score points and the first player to reach 21 points is the winner.

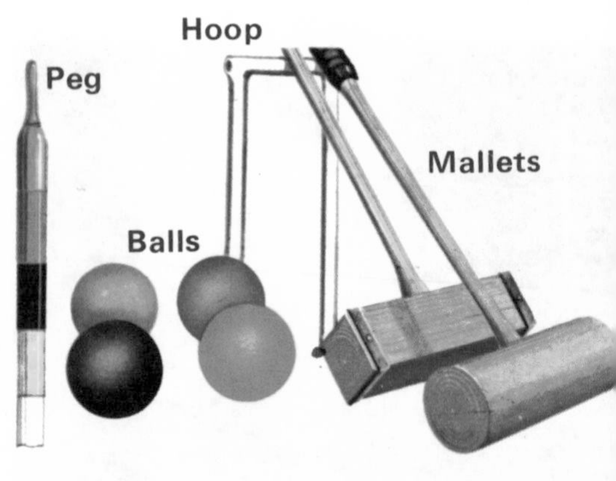

Above: Items of croquet equipment.

Archery

Archery was a warlike art for thousands of years. The longbow, made of wood, was an important weapon during the Middle Ages and is used today for target shooting. However, the bow used most often is the composite bow, which is made from wood, plastic and FIBRE GLASS. It is a development of the bow used by warriors in ASIA. Another bow is the crossbow. Today, this is more often used for hunting.

In target shooting, competitors shoot from various distances from the target, up to 90 metres away. There are a number of competitions, or rounds. A round consists of a set number of arrows shot from different distances. In men's tournaments, the distances are 90, 70, 50, and 30 metres. The women's distances are 70, 60, 50, and 30 metres.

Normally, six arrows are shot at a time. There are five colours on a target. The gold circle in the centre scores 9 points. The red scores seven; the blue, five; the black, three; and the white scores one point. On international targets, each colour is divided into two, and scoring goes from one point to 10 points.

Another form of archery is flight shooting. A special short bow is used, and the object is to fire an arrow as far as possible. Some archers have shot arrows over 1000 metres away.

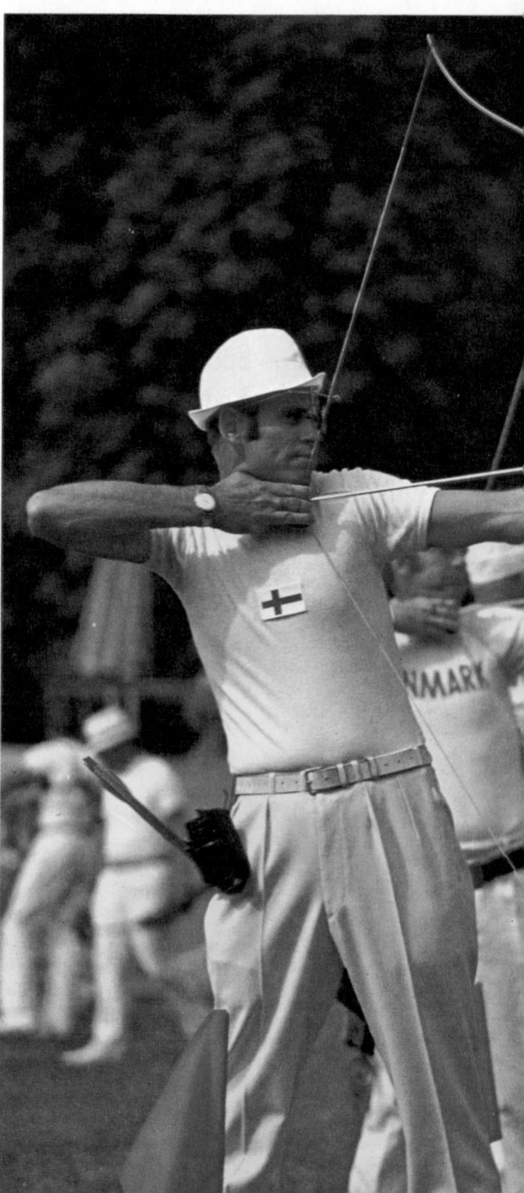

Quoits

Quoits is an old English game. The quoit is an iron ring. The player throwing the quoit tries to make it land exactly over a post (the pin), or to get it nearer to the pin than the opponent's quoit. The pin is usually 25 centimetres high, and 12 metres away from where the player stands.

Deck quoits is a similar game played on board ship, using rope rings.

Croquet

Croquet is a game that came from France more than a hundred years ago. In singles croquet, each player hits two balls through a number of hoops, using a mallet. The object of the game is to hit the balls through all the hoops in order, and then to hit a peg.

In doubles, the two teams take alternate shots. Players try to hinder their opponents by making them take shots from difficult positions, as in BILLIARDS.

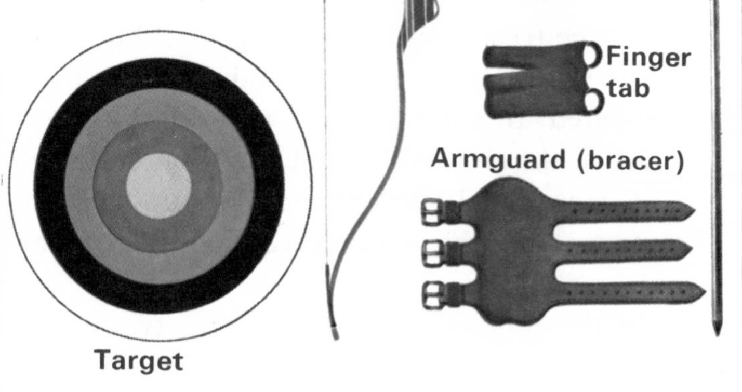

Above: Archery equipment. The finger tab helps the archer to release the arrow smoothly. The armguard protects the forearm from the bowstring.
Left: The string is held with three fingers, and drawn back to the lips.

Bowls

In the game of bowls, each player has four bowls (or woods). The aim is to roll your bowl as close as possible to the jack, which is a small white ball. The jack is bowled from the mat by the first player. If your bowl stops closer to the jack than your opponent's, it is called a shot and scores one point. Bowls can also be played with two, three, or four players to a side.

Bowls were first played in England in about 1300.

Cycling

A BICYCLE is normally a means of transport. Many people ride only for convenience or pleasure, and cycling is good exercise. But it is natural that men and women should want to see who can cycle fastest. Cycle racing, which began more than 150 years ago, takes several different forms, both on track and road.

In the OLYMPIC GAMES, there are track sprints, pursuit races, and a time trial. There is a time trial on the road as well as a longer road race.

A time trial is really a race against the clock. Competitors start separately and their times are compared. In a pursuit race, two riders start at the same time but at different points on the track. The winner is the one who catches up with his opponent, or who rides a given number of laps quickest.

In the professional six-day race, two riders cycle as a team. They keep going round an indoor track for six consecutive nights. One of them must always be in the saddle.

The most important professional road race is the Tour de France.

Above: In road racing, riders compete in daily stages for more than three weeks. They may ride total distances of more than 4000 kilometres.

Road racing bicycle

Golf

Golf is an open-air game. Each player uses a number of clubs to hit a ball into a series of holes (usually 18). There are two main kinds of golf match: stroke, or medal, play and match play. In stroke play, the player who takes the fewest strokes to get to the end of the course wins. In match play, the winner is the player who wins most holes.

The length of each hole (the distance between the tee and the green) varies. It can be less than 200 metres or more than 500 metres. A player may use up to 14 clubs. Woods are for driving from the tee and fairways; irons are for medium-range shots. The putter is used on the green to hit the ball into the hole. Each course has a 'par' in the number of strokes a first-class player will take to play it. On most courses this is about 70.

Golf was first played in Scotland. The Royal and Ancient Golf Club was founded in 1754. It controls the rules of the game and conducts its famous tournament, the British Open. The three other major tournaments take place in the U.S.A. They are the U.S. Open, Masters', and P.G.A.

Below: A player uses an iron to take a shot at the green (not shown). The man carrying his clubs is called a caddy.
Below right: Different golf clubs.

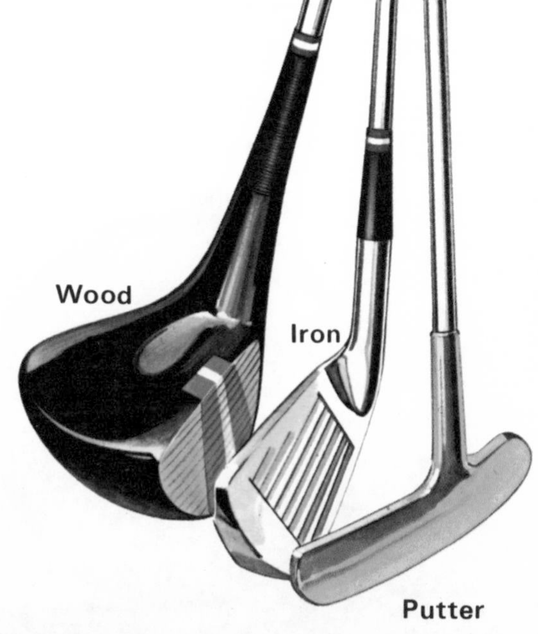

Winter Sports

Winter sports all take place on either SNOW or ice. They include some of the fastest and more dangerous sports.

SKIING and BOBSLEDDING are the main snow sports. Not every country, however, has resorts where the weather and snowfall are suitable. So people often travel to other countries. There they can enjoy winter sports and a winter holiday at the same time.

In the past, people had to wait for cold weather before they could skate on frozen ponds or rivers. Electrically frozen ice rinks can now be found in many cities and large towns. So you can go SKATING at any time of the year.

Many countries also have artificial ski slopes, where people can learn or practise skiing even when there is no snow.

Some people find that winter sports help to keep them fit for other activities in the summer. Others simply prefer winter sports to other kinds. Winter sports are among the most exciting of all outdoor activities.

Right: A competitor makes a turn in an Olympic giant slalom event.
Below: The spectacular sport of ski jumping.

Skiing

Many hundreds of years ago, men travelled over the SNOW on long boards. However, skiing did not start to become popular as a sport until a hundred years ago. The International Ski Federation was formed in 1924 – this was also the year of the first winter OLYMPIC GAMES.

The art of skiing was first developed in Scandinavia, and in the ALPS. Today, people ski wherever conditions are right. Many people who do not live near skiing areas go on winter holidays.

The skier's basic equipment consists of the skis themselves, usually made of metal, or PLASTIC with metal edges. Strong boots are used which can be attached to the skis with special bindings. The skier carries two poles, which help him to make turns and to keep his balance.

Competitive skiing has four main forms. They are ski jumping, Alpine racing, Nordic skiing, and biathlon. All four are in the winter Olympics.

Ski jumping is a most spectacular sport. The jumper skis down a long ramp, and is launched into the air. Points are given for style, as well as for distance. Today, some ski jumpers are able to travel through the air for over 150 metres before landing.

Alpine racing includes the downhill race which is a time trial. The winner is the person who skis from top to bottom of the course in the shortest time. Slalom is the second kind of Alpine race. In slalom, the skier has to turn and twist between more than 50 gates – posts set in the ground at intervals down the slope.

Nordic racing is a cross-country race of up to 50 kilometres. In the biathlon, competitors have to cover a cross-country course carrying a rifle with them. They stop at four points on the way to shoot at a target. In Nordic racing the skis are longer than in Alpine racing.

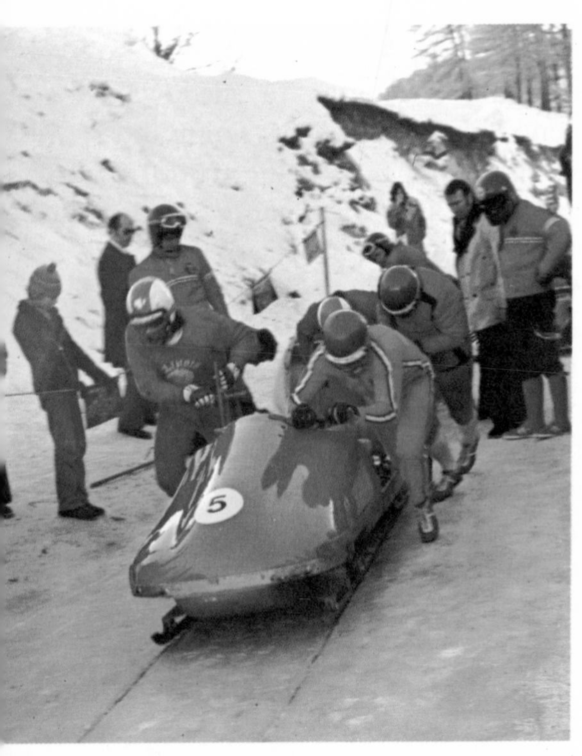

Above: The crew of a four-man bob give their sled a push before jumping into their seats. The sled is made of aluminium and steel.

Bobsledding

Speeds over 140 kilometres an hour make bobsledding a very fast and sometimes dangerous sport. Bobsledding is a team sport. In the winter OLYMPIC GAMES there are two-man and four-man bobs. The man in front steers with a wheel or ropes. The man at the back works the brakes. In the four-man bob, the two men in the middle can help to correct skids by moving their weight from side to side. Championship courses are about 1500 metres long with at least 15 steeply banked turns. Bobsledding is also sometimes called bobsleigh.

Luge tobogganing is another sport that was once a means of transport. There are men's and women's luge events in the winter Olympics. Unlike bobsledding, there are no mechanical means of steering or braking. The riders lean backwards and wear steel-tipped boots which they use to guide or brake the toboggan. The course is usually about 1000 metres long, with twelve turns.

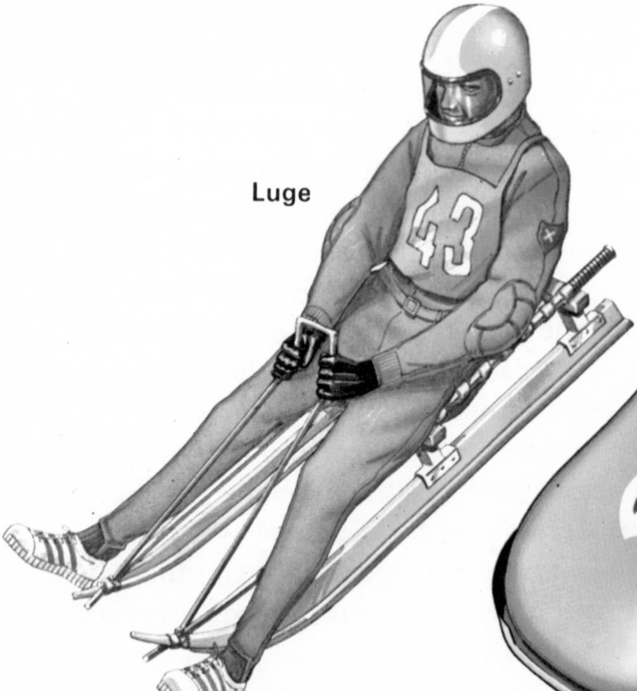

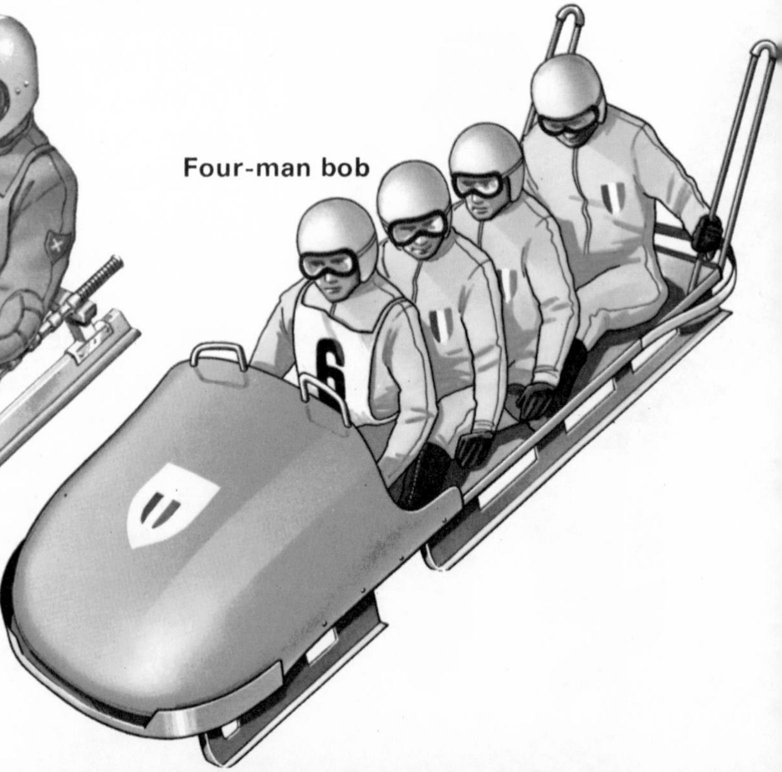

Luge

Four-man bob

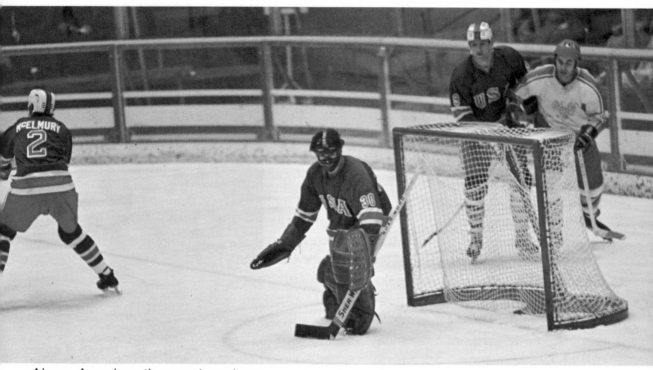

Above: A goalmouth scene in an ice hockey match between the U.S.A. and Poland. The goal-minder wears additional protective clothing.

Ice hockey

Ice HOCKEY is the world's fastest game. Players can skate at nearly 50 kilometres an hour. The object of the game is to score by hitting the puck – a flat rubber disc – into the opposite goal. Players hit the puck with a specially shaped stick, but they are not allowed to kick it with their skates. If the puck leaves the ice, players may strike it down with their hands.

The puck can travel as fast as 190 kilometres an hour. At these speeds it is often impossible for spectators to see the puck. Therefore, a red light is used to tell when a goal is scored.

Players wear padded clothing and helmets. There are six players in each team and up to 12 reserves who may be brought on at any time. A player may pass only to a team–mate in the same zone or, in defence, in his own half.

The most important professional hockey league is in NORTH AMERICA.

Ice skating

Ice skating takes three forms in the Winter Olympics: speed skating, figure skating, and ice dancing. The men's speed skating events are 500, 1000, 1500, 5000 and 10,000 metres: women's events are 500, 1000, 1500 and 3000 metres. The skaters race in pairs, in different lanes so as not to collide. The faster skater wins. In the short races, skaters can travel at an average speed of about 50 kilometres an hour.

Figure skating is divided into compulsory skating and free skating. A skater gets points for his performance, and each section counts for half the points. In compulsory skating, competitors have to skate set movements, such as the figure of eight. In free skating, competitors invent their own series of movements and do them for up to five minutes with music.

Figure skating is also performed in pairs. In all figure skating, the complicated jumps, spins, and other acrobatics call for excellent balance. Hard practice and skilful coaching are essential.

Ice dancing, like figure skating, has compulsory and freestyle sections. Pairs may skate the waltz, tango, rumba, and other dances on ice. They must dance close together for good control of their movements.

People have skated on ice for hundreds of years. Skating has been a sport since the fourteenth century. The first club was founded at Edinburgh in Scotland in 1742. In those days skaters were dependent on natural ice, and so skating was mainly a winter sport. With the invention of electrical refrigeration, skating became a sport for all seasons. The first mechanically frozen rink opened in LONDON in 1876.

Above: An East German pair combine gracefully in figure skating.

Right: The long bladed skate is for speed skating, the short for figure skating.

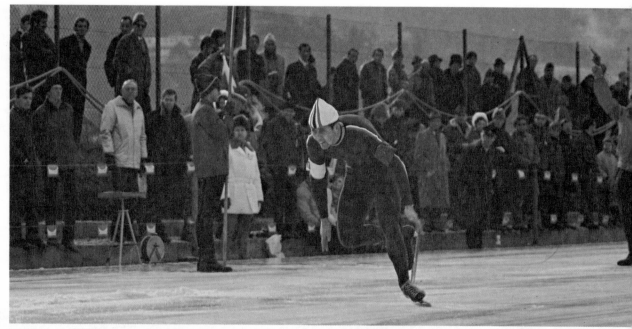

Above: The starter fires his gun and a speed skater gets away to a fast start.

Curling

Curling is an ice sport similar to BOWLS. There are two teams of four players. Each player has two heavy stones. They aim to slide the stone as near as possible to the tee (target) which is just over 38 metres away. A stone that stops nearer the tee than an opponent's scores one point.

A player can make his stone spin by turning the handle as he releases it. This makes the stone curve as it slides along the rink. This is where the name curling comes from.

Teammates are allowed to sweep the ice ahead of a moving stone to help it along. This is called sooping and can add as much as three metres to the distance travelled by the stone.

Curling was played in Scotland at least 400 years ago. It is still popular there and also in CANADA. World Championships have been held since 1959 and Canada were winners eight times in the first ten years.

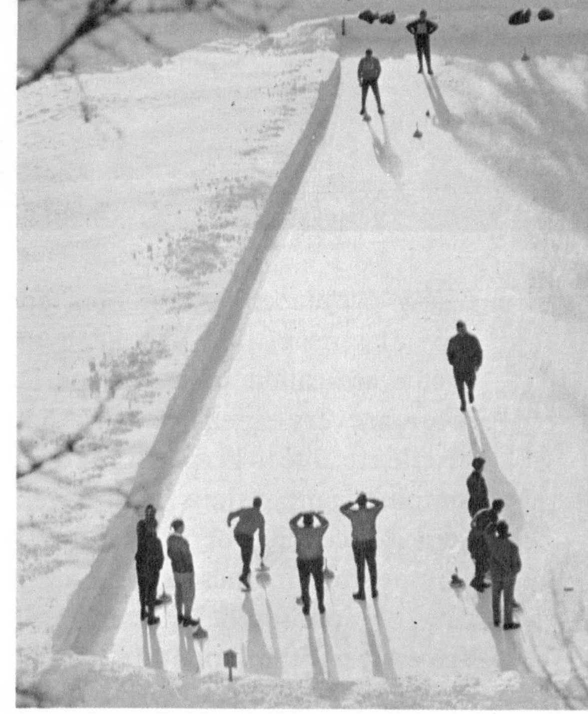

Above: A curling rink at St Moritz, in Switzerland. This is an outdoor rink, but curling is sometimes played indoors.

Spectator Sports

Many people enjoy watching sporting events they may never take part in themselves. These events are called spectator sports. Often these sports are very expensive. For example, not many people are able to keep a HORSE and enter in show jumping competitions. Still fewer can afford to own a racehorse or a Grand Prix racing car. Competitors in these sports are usually either rich or sponsored by someone else. Racing drivers are often sponsored by large car companies. Because these sports have the backing of big money, they are lavishly presented to the public. This helps them to attract large crowds.

Right: The Olympic Games closing ceremony.

Above: Teams marching into the arena for the Opening Ceremony at Munich in 1972.
Below: The Olympic flame.

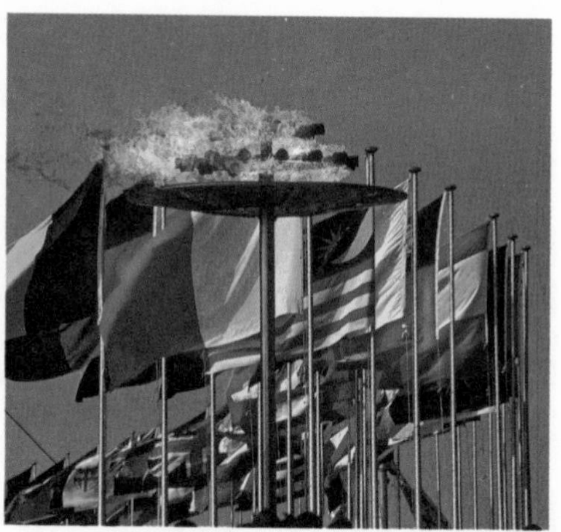

Olympic Games

The Olympic Games is the event with the biggest audience of all. Amateur sportsmen and women from over a hundred nations take part, and hundreds of millions of spectators all over the world watch on TELEVISION.

The modern Olympic Games date from 1896. The French Baron Pierre de Coubertin copied the idea from the ANCIENT GREEK Olympic Games. These were stopped in A.D. 393 by the Roman emperor.

Athletes who compete in the Games have to promise to follow the rules, and to compete in a spirit of true sportsmanship. One competitor takes the oath on behalf of all the others. Today, the competition is so fierce that it is more difficult for the competitors to live up to these ideals.

In Ancient Greece, the winners were given crowns of olive leaves. Today, they get gold medals. Competitors who come second and third get silver and bronze medals. To win a medal in the Olympics is considered the highest honour in amateur sport.

The Olympic Games take place every four years. Each year a different country has the honour of staging the Games. Holding the Games today costs the host country a lot of money. The programme for the summer Games includes about 20 sports. The most important of these is TRACK AND FIELD ATHLETICS.

The host country may introduce a new sport. JUDO was included for the first time when the Olympic Games were staged at Tokyo in JAPAN.

The first Winter Olympic Games were held in 1924. They are held in the same year as the summer Games, but usually in a different country. The main events in the Winter Olympics are Alpine and Nordic SKIING, BOBSLEDDING, SKATING, and ICE HOCKEY.

Horse-riding events

Horse-riding (equestrian) events test the skills of a rider and a horse. The three main sports are dressage, show jumping, and the three-day event. All are in the OLYMPIC GAMES.

Dressage is a series of set exercises that the horse is trained to carry out perfectly. One of them, for example, is called the piaffe, a kind of high-stepping trot. The winner is judged on a points basis.

Show jumping is a course of various kinds of jumps. Competitors must try to finish without a fault. Hitting a fence counts as four faults; a refusal is three faults. The winner is the rider with the fewest faults in the round. A clear round is one where no faults are collected. If more than one competitor has the same number of faults, the rider with the fastest time wins. A typical course is about 800 metres long with a dozen jumps. Show jumping is also one of the events in the MODERN PENTATHLON.

There are three types of show jumping competitions. Some are timed contests. Others are mainly tests of jumping ability with timing only used to decide the result if there is a tie. A third kind is a trial of jumping ability alone.

One of the most difficult things in show jumping is that a rider does not know his course until he walks it immediately before the competition.

The three-day event consists of dressage (first stage), cross-country speed and endurance (second stage), and show jumping (third stage). These contests used to be part of the military training of army cavalry officers.

Above: A horse and rider descend a bank in a show jumping derby competition at Hickstead, England.

Right: A competitor from Argentina clearing a wall in a show jumping event.

Polo

Polo was developed during the British rule in INDIA in about 1868. A similar game had been played in Persia (modern IRAN) long before that. Polo is a goal-scoring game, and skill in hitting the ball is just as important as riding ability. The ball is made of bamboo and the stick has a mallet-shaped head.

Because it is such a hard game for the ponies, play is divided into periods of seven and a half minutes. In a tournament match, there are six of these periods, or chukkas. The ponies are rested or changed between chukkas. There are four players on each side, and teams change ends after each goal. The penalty for offences, such as bumping, is a free hit at the goal from 60, 40, or 30 metres.

Few people can afford to play polo. Buying and keeping a polo pony is expensive. The game is popular in England, the U.S.A., and ARGENTINA.

Below: A player taking a shot in a game of polo. Behind the goal are the scoreboard and clock for timing chukkas.

Horse racing

There are two main kinds of racing: flat racing, which takes place in the spring and summer months, and jump racing, or steeplechasing. Many races are handicaps. In these the best HORSES carry more weight. The idea is that all the horses should have a more equal chance of winning. This makes the sport more interesting and the results more open to chance. Horses usually start racing as two-year-olds. They are entered in the important races, known as classics, as three-year-olds.

The big race in the United States is the Kentucky Derby. The most important international flat race is the Prix de l'Arc de Triomphe in FRANCE. The jump season is notable for the British Grand National which was first run in 1837. It has 30 fences in a course of over seven kilometres.

Horse racing is as much an industry as a sport. Millions of spectators follow it on television as well as at the track. Many people like to bet money on the results. In some countries, such as the United States and France, betting is government-controlled. The profits are used for the benefit of the sport.

In many countries, horse racing is among the leading spectator sports. The prizes at the most important races are very valuable. Really good horses change hands for enormous sums of money. Wealthy owners send their most successful horses to stud, so that they will produce more good horses.

Horse racing has been called 'the sport of kings'. This is because, in 1377, the Prince of Wales (later King Richard II of England) rode a race against the Earl of Arundel. The first horse races took place even earlier, but it was the kings and queens of England who made the sport fashionable.

Above: Flat racing

Below: Jockeys wear the racing colours of the horse's owner. They also wear crash helmets.

Above: Jump racing, or steeple-chasing, is a winter sport in Britain. It is more dangerous for the jockey than flat racing.

Greyhound racing

Greyhound racing is a popular betting sport in Britain and the United States. The distances are between 200 metres and 1000 metres, usually on an oval track. An electric hare runs on rails. As it passes the traps it operates a switch that opens the grille and releases the dogs. The fastest dogs can travel over 60 kilometres an hour. Some are good at both flat and hurdle races.

Hundreds of years ago, greyhounds were used for hunting. Their name comes from an Icelandic word meaning dog hunter. These hounds follow by sight and not by scent. This is why a dummy hare is essential to make them run.

The mechanical hare was invented in 1919 by an American named Owen Patrick Smith. The first greyhound races took place in England seven years later.

Right: The start of a greyhound race.

Motor racing

Motor racing takes many different forms. The best known kind is the World Drivers' Championship. The winner is the best driver of Formula One cars – the fastest cars in motor racing.

The winner is decided on a points basis from the results of about 13 races known as Grand Prix. These may vary from year to year but generally include the British, French, United States, South African and Italian Grands Prix. Only a selection of a driver's best races count towards the final result. Juan Fangio of ARGENTINA won the Championship five times between 1951 and 1957.

The most important long distance race for sports cars is the Le Mans 24-hour race in FRANCE. In this race, two drivers share the work of driving each car, stopping only for fuel and service. Average speeds of over 220 kilometres an hour are maintained for over 5000 kilometres. As many as half a million spectators watch this race, which is the climax of the World Sports Car Manufacturer's Championship.

Above: Formula One motor racing – a Tyrrell Ford taking part in the 1972 British Grand Prix.

Below: A Lotus 80 driven by the 1978 World Motor Racing Champion, Mario Andretti.

Apart from Formula One, there are other classes of motor racing for single-seat cars. Formulas Two, Three, and 5000 are some of these. Formula One drivers often start their careers in one or other of these. In the U.S.A., drivers often race on banked, oval speedways.

Rally driving is quite a different sport. The cars are specially tuned models of cars that you can see on ordinary ROADS. A rally is not so much a race as a test of efficiency in getting from one place to another by a given route and in a given time. Drivers are paired, one driving and the other navigating with a map. The Monte Carlo, the East African Safari, and the RAC in Britain are among the best-known rallies.

There are several other kinds of motor racing. Drag racing is a test of acceleration. Cars are timed over a measured distance, usually a quarter-mile (about 400 metres). Hot rod racing is for privately designed cars, built for maximum performance. Vintage car rallies are a newer feature of the motoring scene. Cars built before 1930 may compete in such events.

Below: Rally driving tests cars to the limit on the worst roads in all weathers.

Below: The start of the Monaco Grand Prix, a race for Formula One cars.

Karting

Karting is a form of motor racing which was first introduced in California in 1956. The machines used are the smallest possible four-wheelers. A two-stroke engine and a basic frame made of steel tubing is all that is required. Karts are thus cheap to buy and run, and also easy to maintain. They can be transported by an ordinary car. Despite their tiny size, karts can reach speeds of 200 kilometres per hour. Drivers from the age of 12 upwards compete together. There are international events, including world championships.

Above: The kart driver sits very close to the ground and has a great sense of speed.

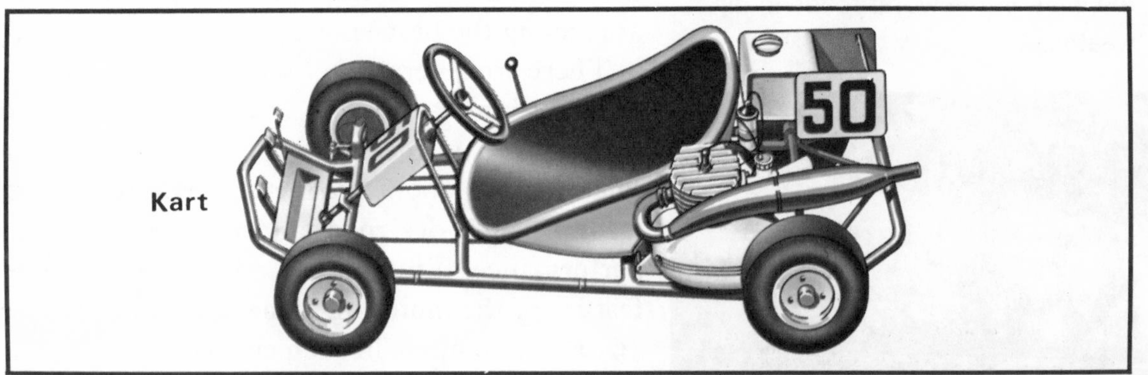

Motorcycle racing

There are several different kinds of motorcycle racing. These include ROAD racing, trials-riding, grass-track racing, sprints, scrambles and side-car racing. The Isle of Man TT (Tourist Trophy) is the most famous road race. It was first held in 1907. The British Government had refused to close a section of road for racing, but the Government of the Isle of Man agreed to do so.

The World Road Racing Championship consists of races for eight categories of machines – 50, 125, 250, 350 and 500 cc, Formula 750, Formula One (over 750 cc), and sidecars. In the U.S.A., dirt track racing with powerful bikes is popular.

Since WORLD WAR II, road racing has largely consisted of a contest between the manufacturers to produce faster and better machines. Italian and Japanese companies have been the most successful. Lap speeds of over 200 kilometres an hour have been recorded.

Trials-riding takes place over difficult country. The riders are given penalty points for putting a foot on the ground, or for stopping. Grass-track racing is similar to SPEEDWAY. Scrambling takes place on tracks of mud or ice.

In sidecar racing, the passenger leans out to help balance the machine as it corners.

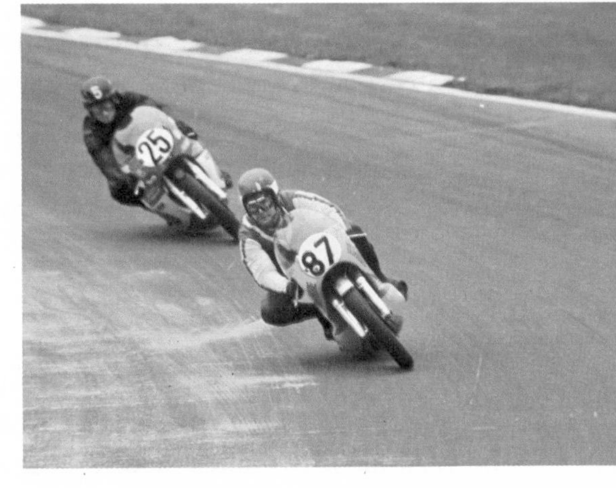

Above: Two racing motorcyclists cornering at speed.

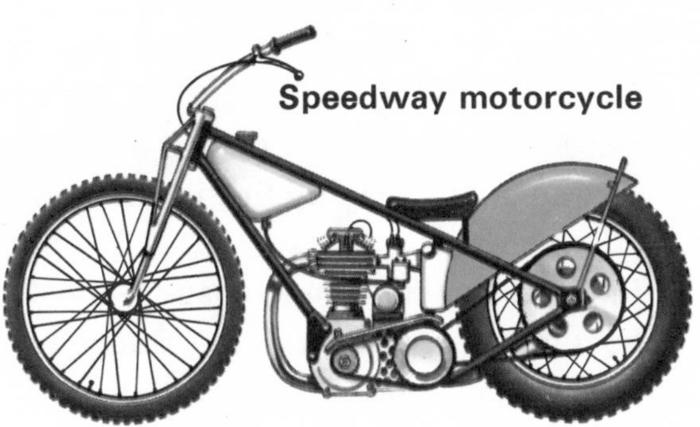

Speedway

Speedway began in AUSTRALIA in 1923. Races are held on short circuits of less than 400 metres. Four riders usually race for four laps on 500 cc machines. Surfaces may be of grass, dirt, cinder, or even ice. Riders wear a metal-tipped boot on their left foot. They use their foot to keep the bicycle from overbalancing on the corners.

The World Championship is decided over 20 races. Each competitor has five rides and meets each opponent once. There is also a World Team Cup.

Left: The starting gate at a speedway track. This track has a dirt surface.

Water Sports

Water sports, like most of the winter sports, are often enjoyed by people on holiday. Some water sports can be very competitive and involve hard work. But people can also enjoy them at an easier level. For example, SWIMMING, which demands enormous effort from an Olympic competitor, can also be pleasant exercise for people of almost any age.

Water sports fall into three groups. There are those in the water, like swimming. Boating in its various forms takes place on the surface of the water. Skin diving, on the other hand, is an underwater sport.

To be good at these sports it is not enough just to keep fit. Competitors must also get to know the water and how it behaves. Large numbers of people find water sports are not only enjoyable but an aid to keeping fit for other sports.

Right: Competitors in a cross-Channel power boat race shoot under Tower Bridge on the River Thames in London.

Above: A sailing regatta in Chesapeake Bay, U.S.A. The brightly coloured sails are called spinnakers.

Right: A water-skier on mono-ski. He has one ski instead of two.

Water skiing

People can ski on water by balancing on two special skis (or sometimes one) as they are pulled along by a boat. It looks easy, but for the beginner it is best to practise with an instructor on land first. Water ski championships are of three types: slalom, jumping, and figures. In the slalom, skiers have to weave their way between a series of six BUOYS. In jumping, they are towed at speed up a waxed ramp. This launches them into the air. Distances of 50 metres have been cleared by men, and over 30 metres by women. Figures include turns and other tricks designed to show each skier's skills. The competitor has two runs of 20 seconds each, and scores points for his performance. Ski racing is another form of competition. Speeds of over 160 kilometres an hour have been reached.

Water skiing is a fairly new sport. The first public demonstration was given in Florida in 1928. The United States has frequently won the World Championships.

Power boat racing

Power boat racing can be a very expensive sport. There are two main types of power boat racing: circuit racing on LAKES and offshore racing at sea. Circuit racing has a bigger following because the spectators can see more of the race. Boats used in hydroplaning – one kind of power boat racing – have specially designed hulls. These allow the boats to skim the water to increase their speed.

Ocean races are longer and more dangerous. The Round Britain race takes the boats over a course of 2240 kilometres in 10 stages. Speeds of over 110 kilometres an hour have been reached on calm water in offshore trials. The world championship is organized by the Union Internationale Motonautique in BELGIUM.

Rowing

Rowing is a sport with a very long history. There are records of rowing races in ancient Greece thousands of years ago. A regatta is a series of rowing races. Regattas have been held in England since 1775.

International rowing events, including the OLYMPIC GAMES, are between eights, fours, or pairs. Rowing, strictly speaking, means pulling the boat with one oar to each man. In sculling, each man has two oars (sculls), and races are between singles, doubles, and fours. In some events a coxswain, or cox, is a member of the crew. He steers the boat. The oarsman nearest the stern is called the stroke. He sets the rate of striking (pulling the oars).

The Henley Royal Regatta in England is one of the major annual rowing occasions. The Thames Cup and the Diamond Sculls are two of the main events at Henley. Apart from regattas, there are head of the river races. In these the boats set off at intervals and the winner is the crew with the best time.

The first Oxford and Cambridge Boat Race took place in 1829. It is rowed every year on a course almost seven kilometres long on the Thames in LONDON.

Right: Cambridge University leading Oxford in the annual Boat Race. Spectators follow the two crews in motor launches.

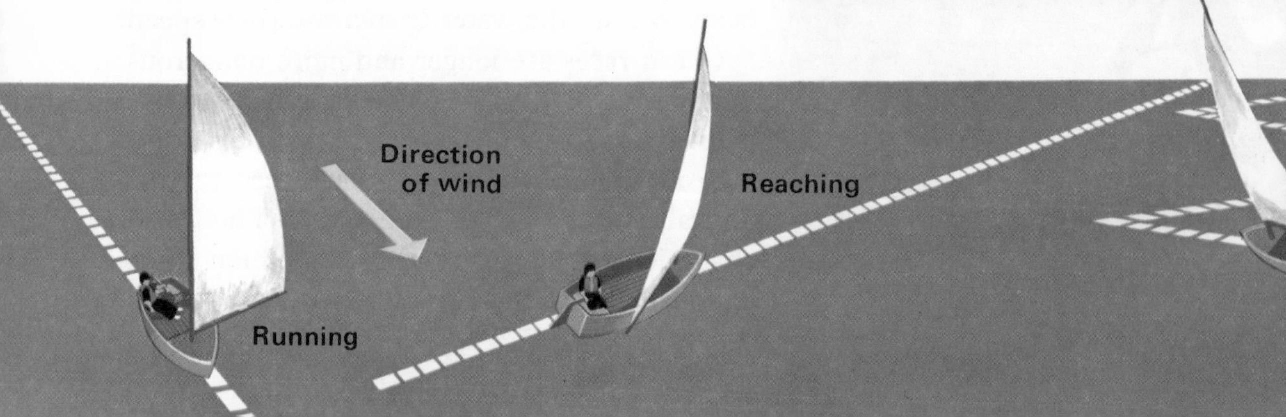

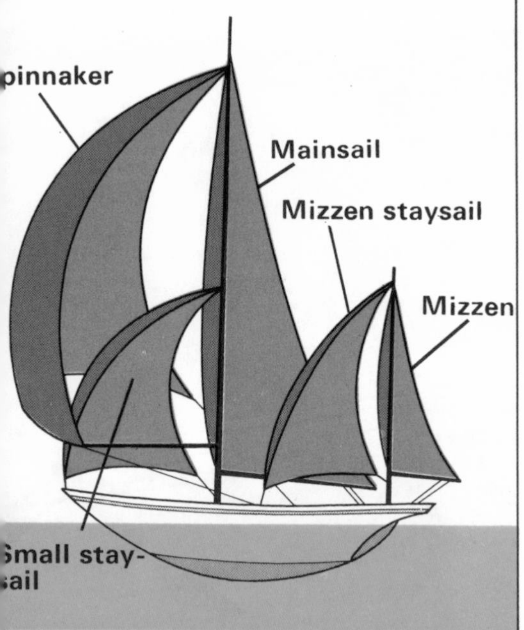

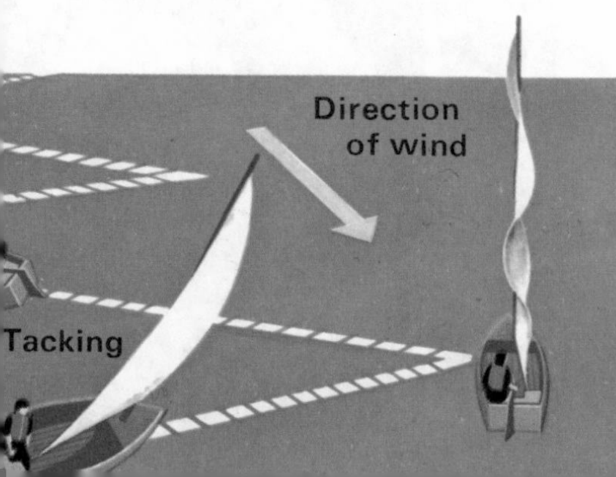

Yachting

Yachting is the art and skill of handling a boat. There are many types of sailing boat. These range from a small dinghy of no more than three metres in length to an ocean racer. Most racing is between boats of the same class (or type), but when boats of different classes compete in the same race, a system of handicap is used.

There are three main classes in international yachting, the Star, the Soling, and the Tempest. Each requires an experienced crew. The biggest ocean race is the America's Cup. This is named after a schooner called *America* that beat all the best British yachts in 1851. The race is for 12-metre yachts and takes place off Rhode Island on the east coast of the United States. The event is not held every year but whenever the last winner is challenged.

Sailing boats are designed so that they can travel in any direction except directly into the WIND. If you want to sail in the direction from which the wind is coming, you have to take a zigzag course. This is called tacking. When a boat sails with the wind behind it, it is running. If the wind is across the boat, it is reaching. Sailing almost into the wind is known as beating.

Small boat sailing is becoming more and more popular as a sport, and most countries have sailing clubs. Sailing a small dinghy need not be very expensive, but it can be dangerous for people with no experience. It is necessary to know about TIDES and currents and to follow the safety rules.

Top: The names of different kinds of sails.
Above: A sailing boat with spinnaker set.
Left: The diagram shows the three points of sailing. (Far left) With the wind astern; (centre) with the wind abeam, and (right) into the wind.

Canoeing

The two main modern canoe sports are kayak and Canadian canoeing. The kayak was developed by Eskimos, who used a paddle with a blade at both ends. The AMERICAN INDIANS invented what is now known as Canadian canoeing. In this the paddle has only one blade.

The Olympic canoe events include these races for men and women: kayak singles (K1), kayak doubles (K2), kayak fours (K4), Canadian singles (C1), and Canadian pairs (C2). In the 1972 Olympics, canoe slalom took place for the first time. This is similar to slalom in SKIING. Canoes are paddled down a rough course as quickly as possible and have to be guided between 30 pairs of poles, called gates.

World championships have been staged since 1949 both for kayak and Canadian canoeing and for canoe sailing.

Right: Rounding a gate in a canoe slalom competition.

Skin-diving

Skin-diving is an underwater sport. Originally people could only go under the water by holding their breath. Now, BREATHING apparatus is used. The simplest kind is the snorkel. This is a short tube to breathe through while the nose and mouth are just below the surface.

SCUBA (Self-Contained Underwater Breathing Apparatus) divers can go under the water and stay down for a long time, breathing from cylinders of compressed air. They can enjoy exploring, PHOTOGRAPHY, FISHING, and other activities. The sport became popular after WORLD WAR II when naval FROGMEN did much work.

Right: Scuba divers in Australia.

Surfing

Surfing was enjoyed by Pacific Islanders centuries ago. However, it has only become a major sport since the 1950s, when the first lightweight boards were invented. Today, there are more than half a million surfers in the United States alone.

Surfing is most popular in places such as California and AUSTRALIA, where there are big WAVES. Body surfers ride the waves without a board, and this is more difficult. Australian surfers sometimes also use surf skis and surfboats.

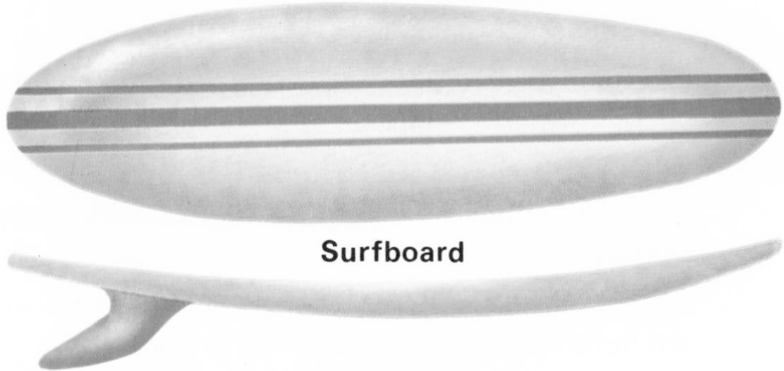
Surfboard

Below: Surfing in a wetsuit.

Swimming and diving

Swimming is the most popular water sport of all. In the OLYMPIC GAMES, swimming is second in importance only to TRACK AND FIELD ATHLETICS. There are freestyle, breaststroke, backstroke, and butterfly events for men and women, as well as several relays.

The breaststroke – using both arms and legs together – and the front crawl were the earliest strokes. PACIFIC islanders have probably used the crawl action for hundreds of years. The butterfly did not become an official stroke until after 1952.

Swimming records are constantly broken. Women are now able to swim faster than men of less than 50 years ago. World records can only be set in 50-metre pools.

Long distance swimming attempts are often made in various parts of the world, in the sea or along RIVERS. The most famous of these is the English Channel swim. Better ways of swimming are developing all the time and it is advisable to learn with a good coach.

Experts can make diving look effortless. But it is actually one of the most demanding of sports. In its simplest form, diving is the quickest method of getting into action in a swimming race. Competitive diving means moving your body in the air and making a perfect entry into the water.

There are 73 different types of dive in international competitions. They are grouped according to how difficult they are. There are seven judges in Olympic events and they give competitors up to 10 points for each dive. The highest and lowest scores are cancelled and the diver's performance is represented by the average of the remaining scores.

Olympic divers compete in springboard and highboard events. They must attempt a certain number of set dives and then some voluntary

dives to test their individual ability. A backward $2\frac{1}{2}$ somersault or a plunge from the highboard into the water at 50 kilometres an hour are difficult and sometimes dangerous feats. They can only be mastered with good coaching, but even boys and girls in their teens can excel.

Top: Australian children swimming on holiday.
Centre left: A perfect diving action.
Centre right: America's Mark Spitz, winner of nine Olympic gold medals for swimming.

Water polo

Water polo is a goal-scoring ball game played in a swimming pool. The game demands fitness and stamina. Being a good swimmer is most important.

There are seven players to a team and four substitutes are allowed. Play is divided into four periods of five minutes. The rules of water polo are complicated, but the aim is to pass or dribble the ball and then throw it into the opposing goal.

The ball can be pushed or thrown but not punched. Except for the goalkeeper, no player can use two hands on the ball. Players are not allowed to put their feet on the floor of the pool while taking an active part in the game. Interception is vital, but the player handling the ball cannot be tackled.

The penalty for ordinary fouls is a free throw. For major fouls, such as rough play, a swimmer can be ordered out of the pool for one minute or until the next goal.

A kind of water polo was played in England about a hundred years ago. East European teams have won most of the Olympic medals.

Left: The goalkeeper, in red cap, can stand but may not throw the ball past the halfway line.

Outdoor Activities

Unlike competitive sports, outdoor activities are not usually based on winning or breaking a record. They include two of the most popular pastimes, GARDENING and ANGLING. Almost everyone can enjoy these open-air activities.

Other outdoor activities demand skill and training. MOUNTAINEERING AND ROCK-CLIMBING are physically trying and often dangerous. It would be unwise to attempt these activities without the advice and help of experienced people. There are clubs and societies that provide this help.

HIKING is a pleasant way of taking exercise. This activity helps people to keep physically fit, and it lets them enjoy the pleasures of the open air. Some outdoor activities are for groups of people. Others are individual pastimes.

Below: A guided horseback tour in the Yosemite National Park in California, U.S.A.

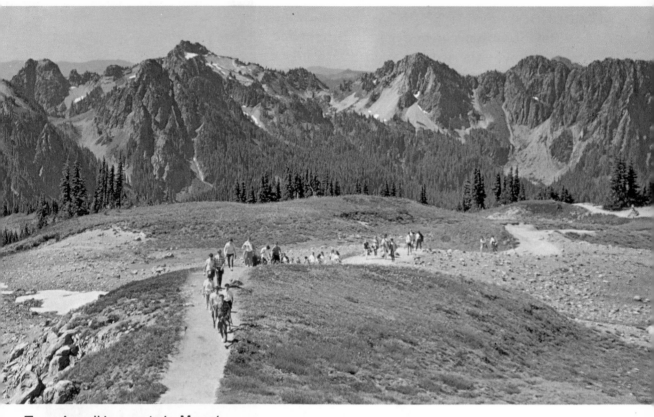

Top: A walking party in Mount Rainier National Park, U.S.A.
Below: Climbing in Switzerland.

Hiking

A hiker does not have to spend much money on equipment. Good comfortable shoes and weatherproof clothes are important, however, and a map and COMPASS can be helpful.

A hike can last just a few hours or a number of days or weeks. Hikers' associations have information on where to go and how long it will take. In many countries there are YOUTH HOSTELS that offer cheap accommodation to hikers.

When hiking, it is best to plan ahead. Hikes should be arranged so that you can reach some place of special interest after a few hours. There are many historic landmarks that attract the hiker. There you can see for yourself the settings of some of the great events of world history. There are also places of great natural beauty – VALLEYS, WATERFALLS, LAKES and hills.

Scouting

The Boy Scout movement began in Britain and spread all over the world. Soon afterwards a similar organization for girls – the Girl Guides – was started. The U.S. equivalent is the Girl Scouts.

Scouts learn many useful outdoor skills, such as CAMPING, map reading, and swimming. They are trained to be responsible members of the community. They are expected to follow the Scout Law, which is a code of correct conduct.

There are various awards open to scouts. The highest is the Advanced Scout Standard in which he has to pass tests in camping skills, physical fitness, and self-reliance. Every four years a World Jamboree is held and scouts from more than a hundred nations get together. Scouting is for boys of 11 years or older. Younger boys can become Cub Scouts.

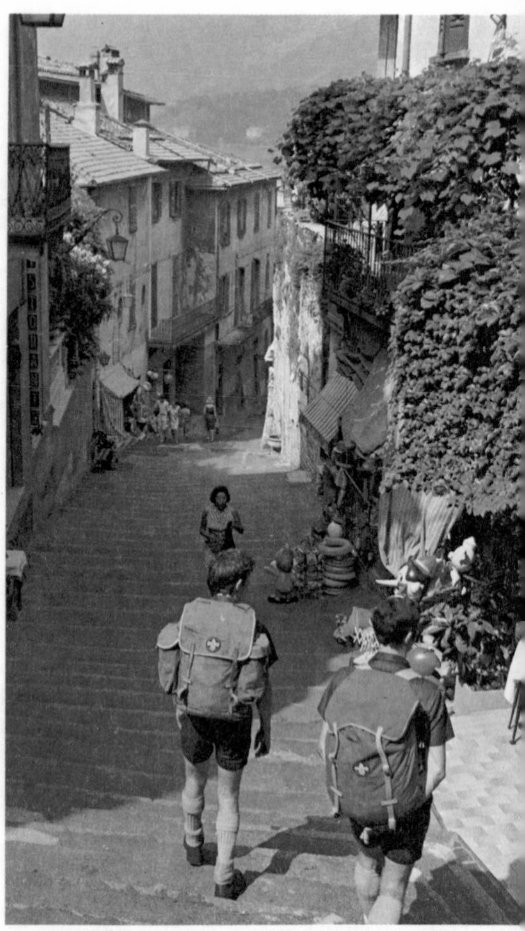

Right: Boy Scouts returning after a long day out. Far right: Venture Scouts carry out services such as visiting old people (above); Girls can become Brownies when they are seven and a half (centre).

Girl Guides and Girl Scouts have a similar code of living. They take part in homemaking as well as outdoor activities. They are also over 11 years old.

The Boy Scout movement was started by Lord Baden-Powell. He was a professional soldier and a hero of the Boer War in SOUTH AFRICA at the turn of the century.

The world headquarters of the Scout movement is in LONDON.

Right: Girl Guides making camp. A sleeping bag is a useful piece of equipment when living outdoors.

Above: A youth hostel in Surrey, England.

Youth hostels and clubs

Youth hostels provide simple and cheap overnight accommodation for young people on hiking or cycling holidays. Members of one youth hostel association can use hostels in other countries when travelling abroad. There are associations in over 30 countries. Members must usually be over nine years old, but family groups are also welcomed.

Many young people also belong to youth clubs which provide a regular meeting-place for their members and help them to organise their own entertainment. Many youth clubs also do social work, often together with a local church.

Camping

Camping is a pleasant way of spending a weekend or a holiday away from home. It is a popular family activity. Many people like camping because it gives them the freedom to go where they please. There are other advantages as well. Campers can stop more or less when they want to and pitch their tent or park their camping vehicles. They can move or drive on if the weather is bad. They can also cook their own meals.

Camping sites can be found from guide books and reports in camping magazines. Many countries have public camping grounds. Most people get to their site by car. However, by using a small tent, and carrying only light equipment, it is possible to travel to the site by MOTORCYCLE, BICYCLE, or even on foot.

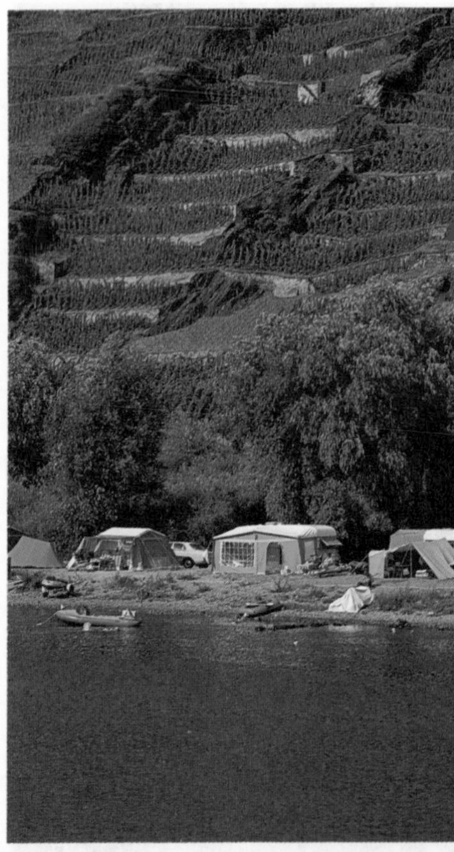

Right: Campers on a river bank in Germany.
Below: Camping near Mont Blanc, in France.

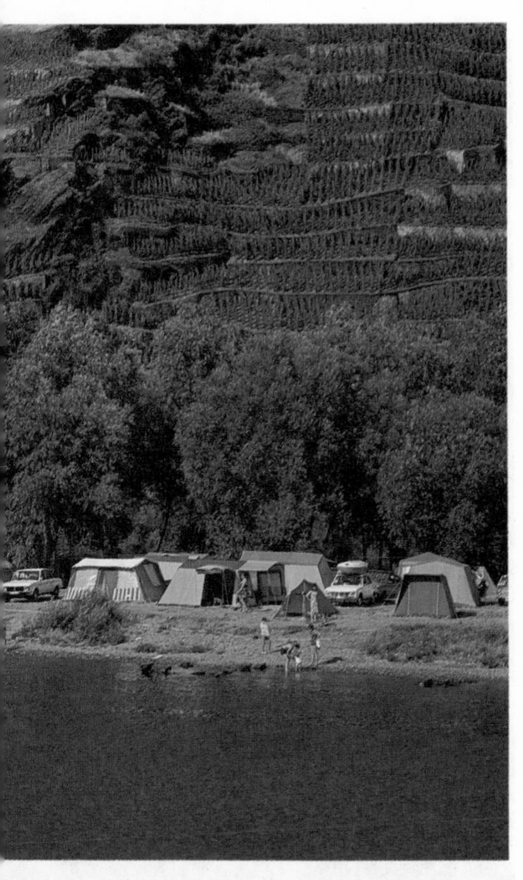

Campers should choose their equipment carefully. Equipment should be easy to carry or pack, and be suitable for its purpose. For example, there are many kinds of tents. Hikers or climbers obviously prefer lightweight tents. A family might need a larger one, with two or even three bedrooms and a living room.

Other people prefer caravan holidays. Today, caravans are towed by cars. They are usually more comfortable than tents, but there are fewer places to stop. Tents can be pitched in places that cannot be reached by caravan.

However, a caravan has more space for storing food, spare clothing, and other equipment. Most modern caravans are fitted with cookers, and some even have such things as refrigerators and showers. There are also motor caravans which have their own engines.

Below: An old-style caravan (left) more ornate but less comfortable than the modern one (right).

Mountaineering and rock climbing

Mountaineering became a sport in the nineteenth century. Climbers from AUSTRIA, Britain, FRANCE, GERMANY, and ITALY made regular attempts on the Alpine peaks in SWITZERLAND. In 1897 the highest ANDES summit, Aconcagua, was conquered. The world's highest point, Everest in the HIMALAYAS, defied all climbers until 1953. The first successful ascent of Everest was made by Edmund Hilary (later Sir Edmund) of NEW ZEALAND, and Sherpa Tenzing Norgai.

The science of climbing depends a great deal on careful planning. On the highest mountains, bases are established at increasing heights. The best climbers are given the least work so that they will be fresh for the final attack on the summit. Climbers must wear oxygen equipment for BREATHING at very high altitudes.

Many mountaineers begin with rock climbing. There are three main kinds: outcrop climbing, crag climbing, and big wall climbing.

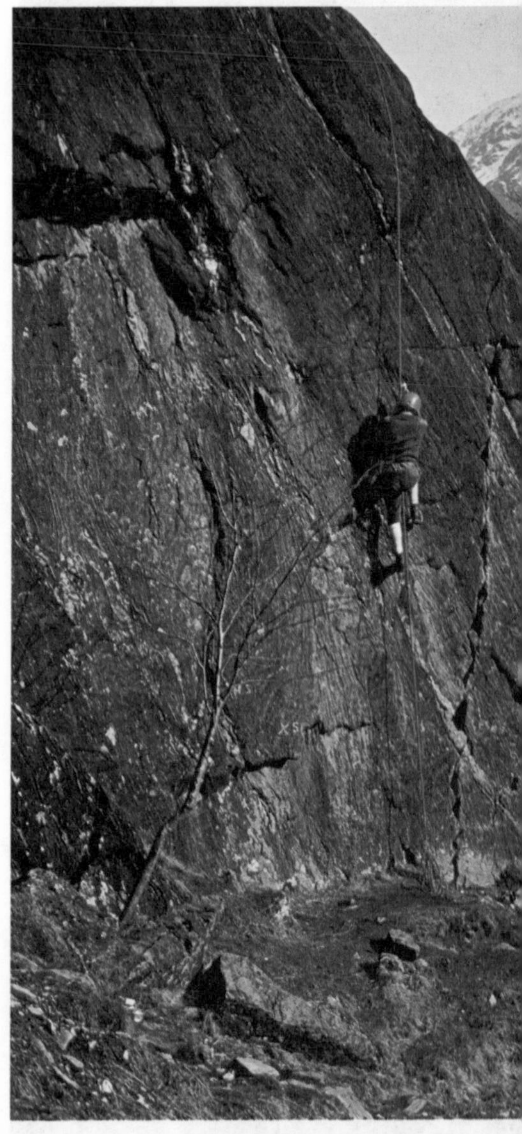

Right: Rock climbing in Glen Nevis, Scotland.
Below: A mountaineer needs a lot of equipment. Some of the most important items are: (1) Climbing boots. (2) Safety helmet. (3) Crampons. (4) Snap links (karabiners). (5) Pitons. (6) Anorak. (7) Piton hammer. (8) Nylon rope. (9) Ice screw. (10) Ice axe.

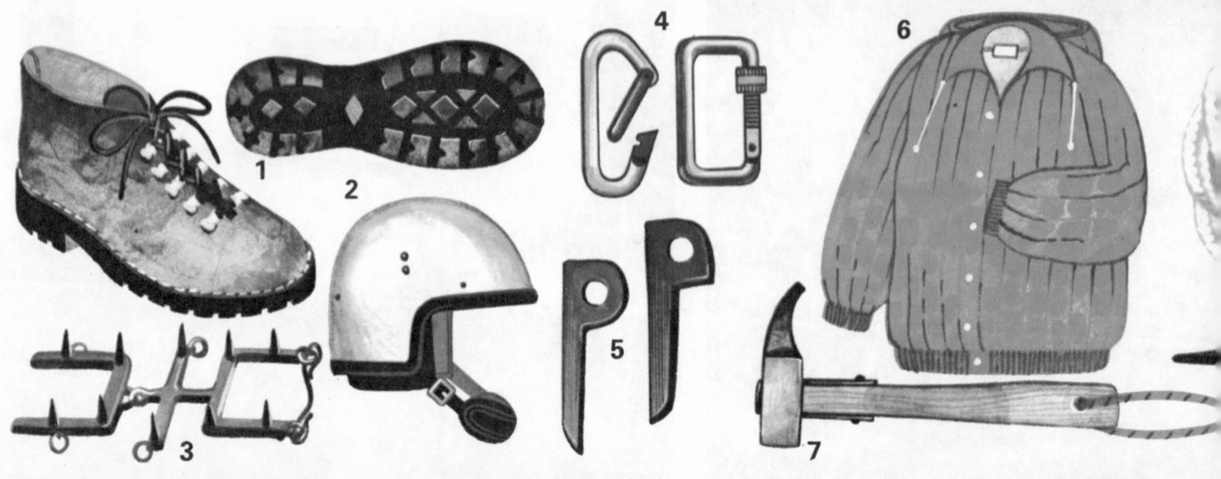

Potholing and caving

CAVES are formed by the continual action of water on limestone for thousands of years. Scientists can learn many things from discoveries made underground.

Curiosity about the unknown inspires men to explore the dark places under the earth. But caving is not a sport for children. Clubs exist where you can learn about CAVE exploration. Special equipment and miners' lamps are necessary. Sometimes diving equipment and wet suits are used to swim along underground streams. Cavers, like mountaineers, usually work in teams to reduce the danger of getting lost. In SWITZERLAND and the United States, explorers have gone as far as 100 kilometres through underground caves. There are a good number of active cavers also in Australia, New Zealand, and South Africa. Many other countries have cave systems which are unexplored.

Cave exploration became popular in EUROPE early in this century. Some of the largest cave systems were found under the Pyrenees between FRANCE and SPAIN. In that area, men have descended over a kilometre into the earth.

Below: A miner's helmet with a light is essential when moving about underground in the dark.

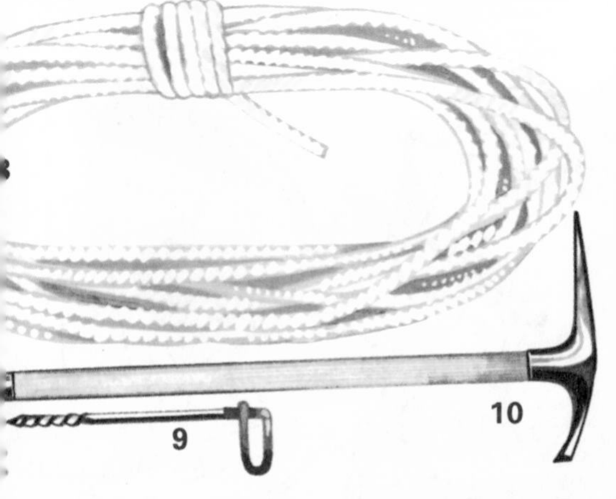

Gardening

Gardening is one of the oldest pastimes in the world. We know that there were ROSES on the earth before there were human beings. Now over 300 kinds of roses have been listed. Gardening is such a big subject that you can spend your whole life learning about it.

There are several different kinds of gardening. You may enjoy having your own flower garden and cutting flowers for your home. Or you may prefer to grow fruit and vegetables for food.

There is something different to be done in a garden every month. There is, according to the seasons in the country where you live, a time to sow, to prune the shrubs, or to stake perennial plants and many other jobs.

You must also know something about the SOIL in your garden, and about FERTILISERS and weed killers, in order to get the best results.

Right: How to make a garden in an old sink.
1. Cover the bottom with pieces of broken pottery. Fill the sink up with potting compost to within a few centimetres of the top.
2. Add one or two small rocks. Put in the plants and label them carefully with marking pegs.
Below: How to make a small vegetable garden. Dig a shallow trench; sprinkle in your seeds; cover over and label with a marking peg.

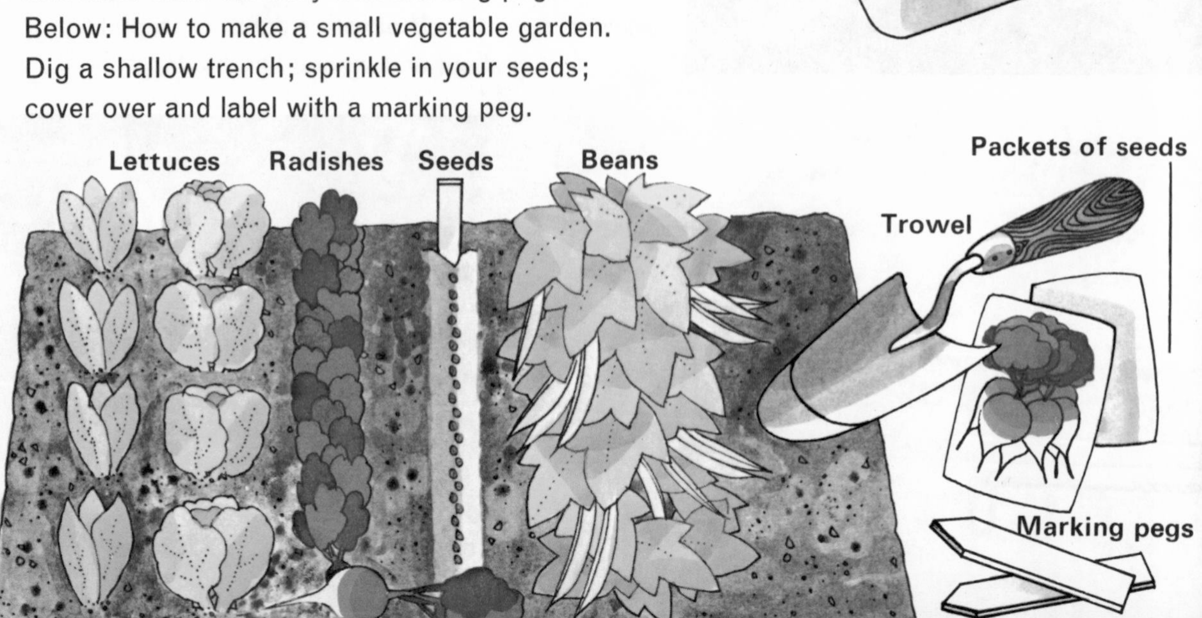

Many people enjoy keeping plants in their homes. The work is light, and a room with flowers and other plants can make a house more beautiful.

Today, there are hundreds of plants that can be grown indoors. Plants such as philodendron, sansevieria, and African violets are kept in many homes. Various kinds of ivy and cactus are also popular.

The indoor gardener has to follow certain rules to keep the plants healthy. Plants kept in heated rooms need plenty of moisture. They have to be carefully watered, and the LEAVES should be sprayed. It is a good idea to keep potted plants on a window-sill. The SUN and daylight help to keep the leaves green. In good weather, indoor plants will also benefit from a little fresh air.

Many different and exotic kinds of indoor plants can be seen at botanical gardens which are open to the public. There are many famous ones in the world, including Kew Gardens in LONDON, the NEW YORK Botanical Gardens, and the Jardin des Plantes in PARIS.

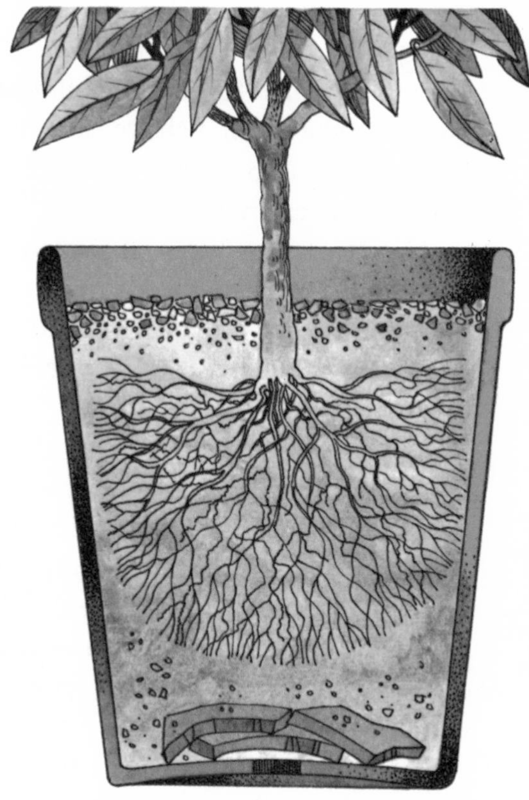

Above: The way to pot a plant.
Below: A greenhouse enables a gardener to have flowers blooming all the year round.

Angling

Men have fished for food for thousands of years. Today, most of the fish we eat is caught by professional fishermen, but the sport of fishing, or angling, is very popular.

The two main ways of fishing for sport are casting and trolling. In casting, the angler throws a lure into the water with a rod and reel. The bait on the line can be live, such as worms or bread, or it can be man-made.

Fly fishermen use either a dry fly or a wet fly. The dry fly looks like an insect and is tied to a float. It is used on slow-moving water. The wet fly is mostly used in fast-moving waters. It sinks and is carried down to where the fish are. Some of the fish we eat, such as SALMON and trout, are caught by casting. These are known as game fish and are much sought after.

Trolling is fishing from a moving boat. The fisherman usually has a rod and reel and tows the bait behind the boat. Trolling is used in the most spectacular kind of deep-sea fishing. A fisherman may land a blue marlin weighing as much as 300 kilogrammes. For safety, he has to be strapped into a chair on the boat and has to wear a harness.

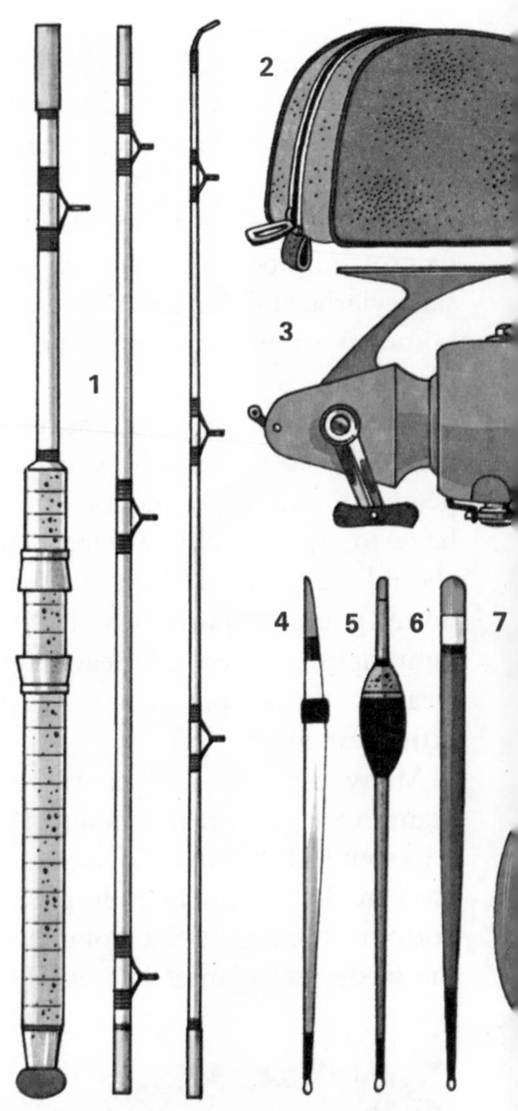

Above: Anglers' equipment. (1) Three-piece rod. (2) Case for reel. (3) Fixed-spool reel. (4) to (8) Different kinds of floats. (9) Swivel link. (10) to (13) Different kinds of hooks. (14) Split shot weights. (15) Pear weight. (16) Barrel weight. (17) to (19) Different kinds of lures. (20) Disgorger. (21) Sea fishing weights. Far left: Salmon fishing in Scotland. Left: The sea angler often wears oilskins and uses a heavier rod.

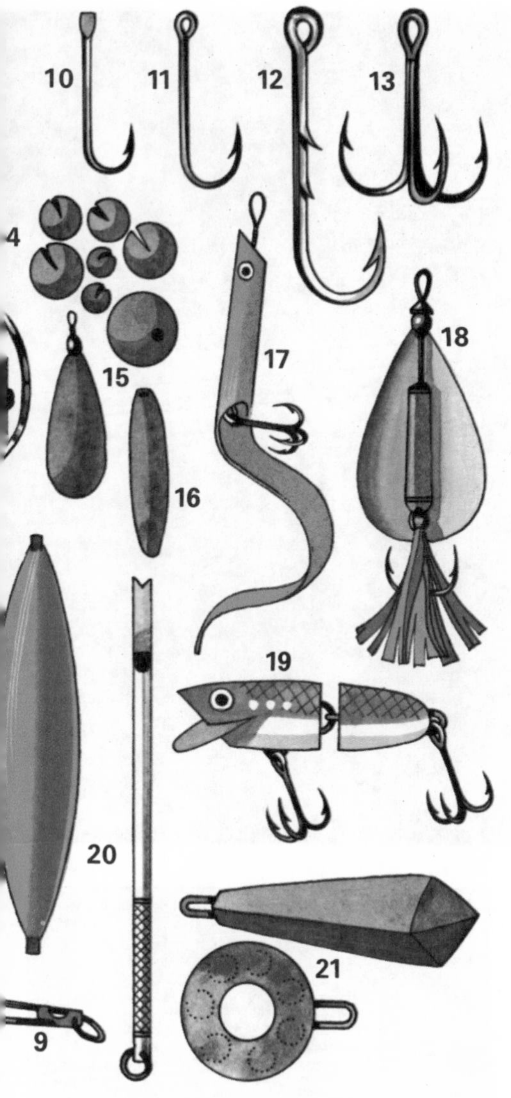

Bird watching

Birds have always fascinated man. Drawings of birds have been found in old CAVES, and the ANCIENT EGYPTIANS put birds in their paintings and carvings. Bird watching as a hobby began in the late nineteenth century. Until then many birds had been killed for sport. Some became extinct. People began to realize that it was better to enjoy the sight and sounds of birds. They kept lists of the birds they saw. In particular, they looked for rare or unusual birds.

Almost anyone can bird-watch. Birds are attracted by scraps of food left for them. They are fond of natural food, such as rotten APPLES or grain.

When bird watching, it is a good idea to have a pair of binoculars, and to take notes. Bird books will help you to identify birds you do not know. You can also obtain recordings of bird song and birdcalls. Some bird watchers take photographs; others use tape recorders to pick up birdsongs.

There are sanctuaries and refuges where bird life is protected by law. You can learn about these places from any national bird organization.

Below: Some aids to bird watching.

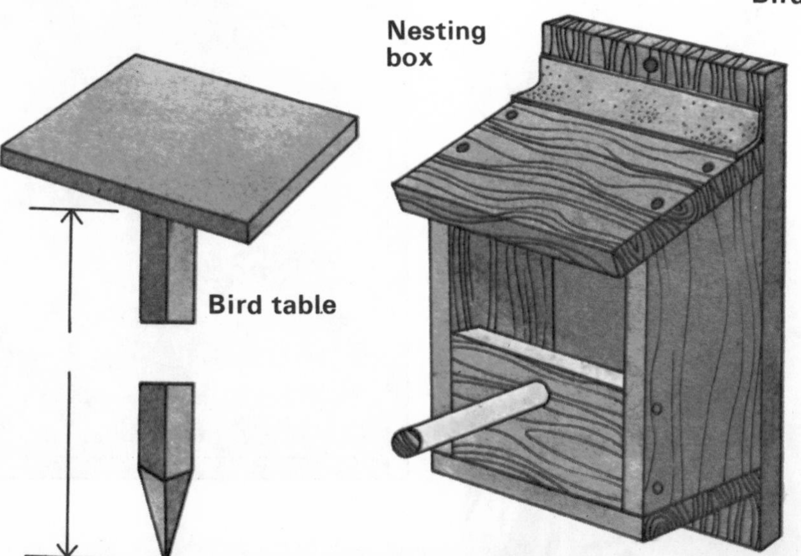

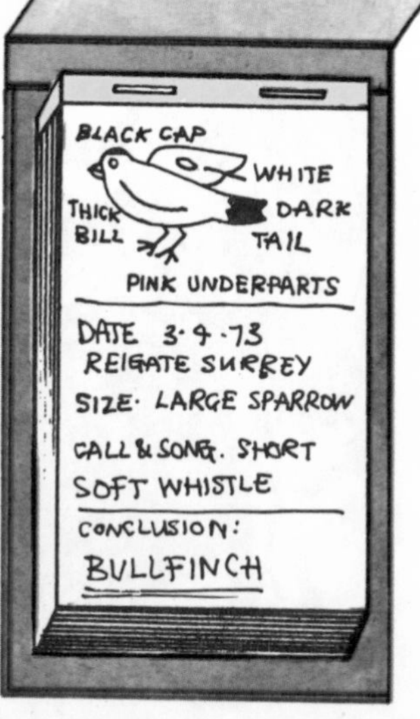

Indoor Games

Many indoor games are played for relaxation. Skittles and darts, for example, have been popular games in Britain for a long time. Bowling is another social game. BILLIARDS and SNOOKER are indoor games that demand great accuracy and control. Such pastimes are easy to understand and most people can play them reasonably well. It is, however, impossible to reach championship class without a lot of practice.

CHESS and CARD GAMES are quite different. Physical skill is not involved. But it takes skill of a special kind to excel at them. They are games that require thought.

Right: A snooker champion in action.
Below: A game of billiards in 1690.
Below right: The arrangement of the balls for a game of snooker.

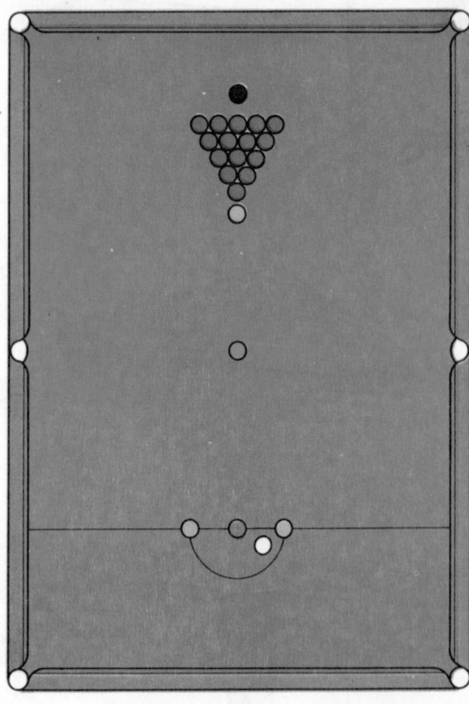

Billiards and snooker

Billiards and snooker are the two most popular cue-and-ball games. Billiards has the longer history. Mary, Queen of Scots, played billiards in the sixteenth century. Billiards is normally played by two people.

Each player has a white ball (the cue ball). The third ball on the table is red. The object of the game is to score points by hitting the balls into any of the six pockets around the side of the table. The highest score wins.

When a player pots (knocks into a pocket) his opponent's cue ball, he scores two. When he pots the red ball, he scores three and when he pots his own cue ball after hitting the red, he also scores three. A cannon is when a player's cue ball strikes both the other balls. This scores two points.

Left: In billiards a ball cannot be potted unless it has first been hit by another ball. Each shot must be played with a view to scoring, and also leaving the balls in a position to score again.
Below left: Balls arranged for a game of pool (American billiards).

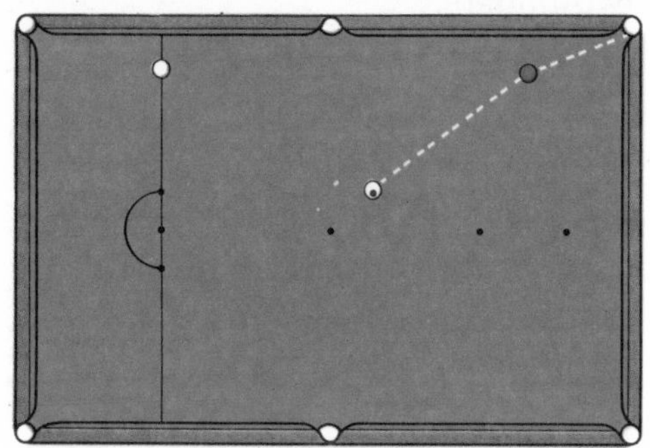

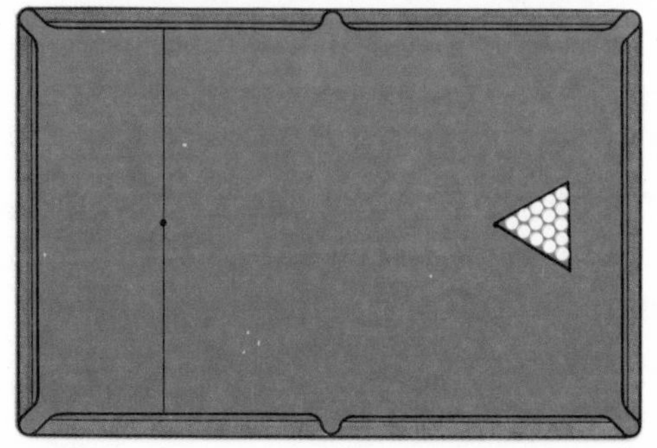

In snooker, a group of 15 red balls are arranged in a triangle. There are six other object balls with different score values. These are: black (7), pink (6), blue (5), brown (4), green (3), and yellow (2). There is also a white cue ball.

The player strikes off with the cue ball. He must first knock a red into a pocket for one point before he can choose another colour and score with that. The reds stay in the pockets but the colours are returned to the table. A red must be potted before each colour. When all the reds are potted, the other colours are potted in turn, starting with yellow.

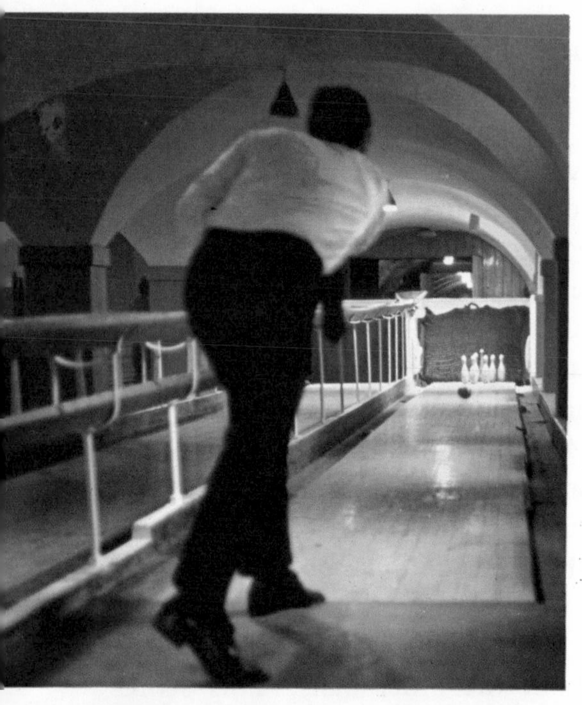

Skittles

Skittles is an ancient game which was probably first played in FRANCE. Today it is played, in different forms, in a number of European countries. In the most common kind there are nine wooden skittles, or pins, arranged in a diamond shape. The game is played on an alley about seven metres long. The balls may be round, or slightly flattened.

The object is to throw the ball so as to knock over as many pins as possible. A game usually consists of three sets of throws for each player. One point is scored for each pin knocked down by each shot. After each shot the pins are replaced in position. The highest possible score in a set of three shots is 27. To obtain this score, a player must knock all the pins over three times.

Above left: Long alley skittles. The balls can be returned to the player along the ramp at the left. Below left: In tenpin bowling, the ball has holes for a thumb and two fingers.

Tenpin bowling

Tenpin bowling grew out of Dutch skittles which was brought to the United States in the eighteenth century. At first, nine pins were used, but when the game was made illegal, an extra pin was added to get around the law.

The ball is made of solid rubber with three finger holes. The player with the highest score after 10 frames is the winner. A frame is two shots, or one if all ten skittles go down with the first shot. This is called a strike and earns ten points, plus a bonus equal to the points score in the next two frames. If the player takes two shots to flatten all the pins, he scores 10 plus a bonus equal to his score for the next frame only.

Otherwise the player scores one for each pin he knocks down. If he misses altogether, this is called an error or spare. A perfect score is 300, which is given for 12 strikes in a row. Tenpin bowling is played in about 50 countries.

Darts

Darts is mostly played in Britain. Each player has three darts, and throws them at a circular board. Each sector on the board scores a different number. A dart landing in the outer ring scores double the number. The inner ring trebles the number. The outer bull's-eye scores 25, and the inner bull's-eye scores 50. Players must start and finish with a 'double' in the outer ring.

Above right: A darts player about to throw.
Right: A dart board. There are 20 sectors, each with a number. One dart has landed in the 18. The second dart has landed in the 1, but in the inner ring. The score of this dart is trebled, making 3. The dart in the 20 sector is in the double ring, and scores 40. The total score is therefore 61.

There are many different kinds of darts games. The most popular one can be played by two or four people. Each player or pair starts with a number of points. The players subtract their score for each turn. The winner is the player who first reduces his points to nothing.

Slot-car racing

Slot-cars are model cars that are raced on a special track. The 'drivers' control their speed by altering the electric current. The game needs great skill because if the cars go too fast they will leave the track.

Right: Two boys racing model cars.

Chess

Chess is a game of skill played on a board marked with 64 squares. Each player has 16 chessmen. The black chessmen are on one side of the board, and the whites on the other. The main object of the game is to capture the opposing king. The game can also be won in other ways or may end in a draw.

Chessmen move in different ways. A bishop, for example, can only move diagonally along squares of the colour on which it started. A rook, or castle, moves in a straight line either forward or sideways. The queen is the most powerful piece on the board. It combines the moves of both rooks and bishops. When a king is in a position to be captured on the next move, the attacking player calls 'check'. If the king is so blocked that it cannot escape, the king is checkmated and the game is over.

Above: Students playing chess.

Below: The start of a game of chess.

Below: (1) A king may be moved one square in any direction.
Right: (2) A queen can move any number of squares; either forwards or sideways like a rook, or diagonally, like a bishop. (3) A knight moves two squares forward and one square sideways.

1

Draughts

Draughts is played on the same board as chess. However, all the pieces look the same. You can only move your pieces on the black squares, and you cannot move backwards. If an opposing piece is in a neighbouring square, and there is a free square on the other side of it, you can take it. You jump your piece over into the free square and the taken piece is removed from the board.

When a piece has reached the opposing base line, it is crowned king. A king usually consists of two pieces – one on top of the other. It can move in any direction, including backwards.

It may be possible to get your opponent into a position where you can take several of his pieces in one move. The winner is the player who succeeds in removing all the opposing pieces from the board. Unlike CHESS, a player must take an opposing piece if he has the chance.

Below: The start of a game of draughts.

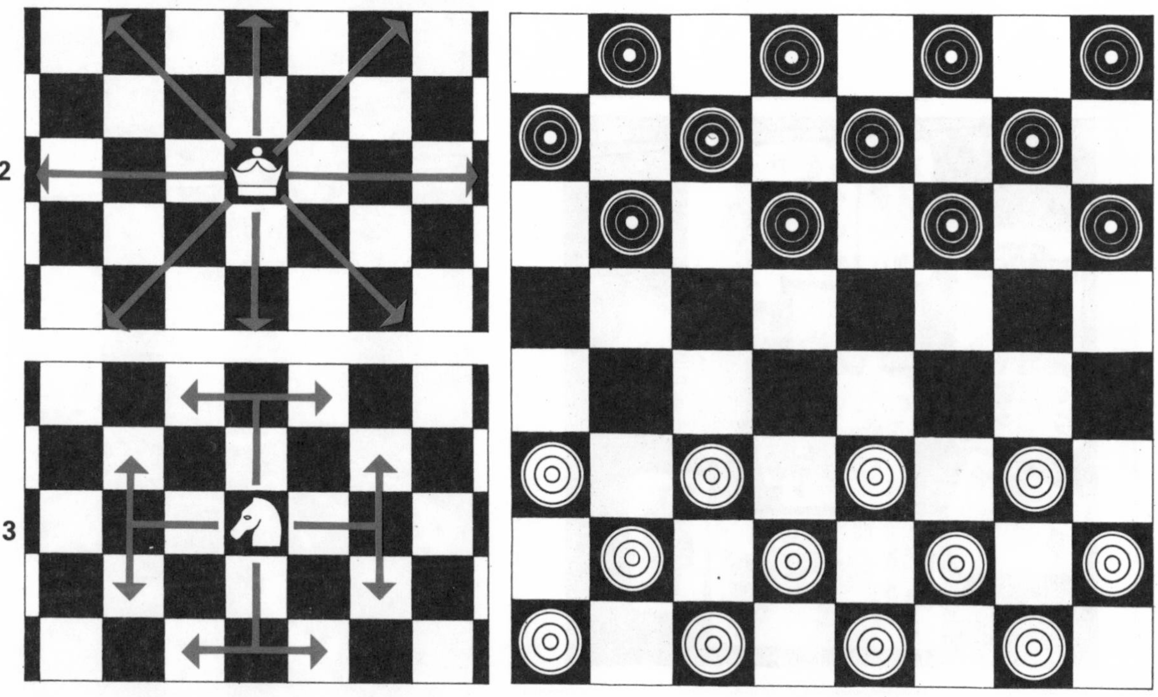

Card games

Most card games are played with ordinary playing cards. There are usually 52 cards in a pack. A few games, such as Happy Families and Canasta, need special packs of cards.

The simplest card games are games of pure chance. Games of chance include Snap, Cheat, Fish, and Slap Jack.

Whist and Bridge are two card games where skill is more important than luck. The four players are each dealt 13 cards. They divide their cards up into suits (Spades, Hearts, Diamonds, and Clubs). One suit is made trumps, which gives it a higher value than the other pair. Many people learn whist before moving on to the more difficult game of bridge.

There are several games in the Rummy family.

Above right: A hand at whist or bridge, sorted into suits.
Below: There are 52 cards in a pack.
Below right: A game of Patience (Solitaire).

These can be played by between two and seven players. Canasta is a development of Rummy. The Canasta pack has 108 cards.

Some card games are almost always played for money. Poker is the most popular of these games. The players are dealt five or seven cards, and there are several scoring combinations. *Vingt-et-un*, or pontoon, is another game that is played for money. The players try to get a hand where the total value is 21. The numbers on the cards are added up. Kings, queens, and jacks score ten. An ace can score either one or 11.

Games of Solitaire, or Patience, can be played by just one person on their own. These games take many forms. The object in most of them is to arrange the cards in a particular order, and in doing so to use up the whole pack.

Above left: Tarot cards are used for fortune-telling.
Below left: A house built from playing cards.
Below: Playing cards in the sixteenth century.

Party games

There are some games that everyone can play. They are especially fun at parties or on holidays.

In one game, the players sit in a large circle on the floor. One of them spins a plate in the middle of the room and calls out a name. The person called must run and take hold of the plate before it falls flat. Then he spins the plate and calls another player. If the player is too slow to catch the plate before it falls, he or she is out of the game. As the number of players gets smaller, they make it more difficult for each other by spinning the plate more slowly and moving farther away. The last person in the game is the winner.

Donkey's tail is played with an outline of a donkey without a tail, drawn on a board. A tail is made with a pin in the end. Each player, in turn, is blindfolded. He is turned around several times so that he loses his sense of direction. He then tries to find the donkey and to pin the tail in the right place. The player who is nearest wins.

There are several target games. One of these involves cutting a number of holes in a large piece of cardboard. The value of each hole is marked on the board. Players take turns throwing balls of various sizes through the holes. The player with the highest score after five or ten turns is the winner.

Shove-halfpenny is an old English game that can be adapted for parties. A chalk line is marked at one end of a polished table. Each player tries to slide a coin as close as possible to the line. The person who gets his coin closest wins the round. The winner is the player who wins the most of a fixed number of rounds.

In the summer, there are many games that can be played outdoors. Hide and seek is a good outdoor game.

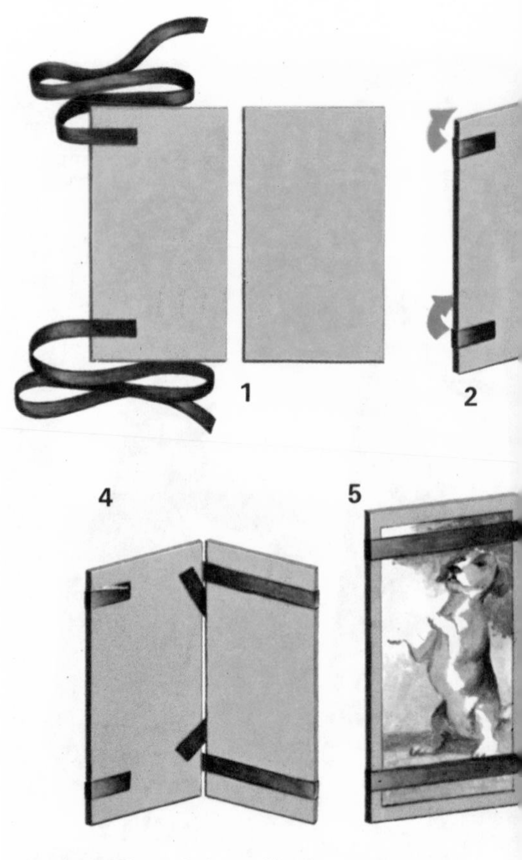

Above: The picture that moves. Take two pieces of thick card and bind them together with ribbon as shown. Slot in your picture. When you open and shut the cards, the

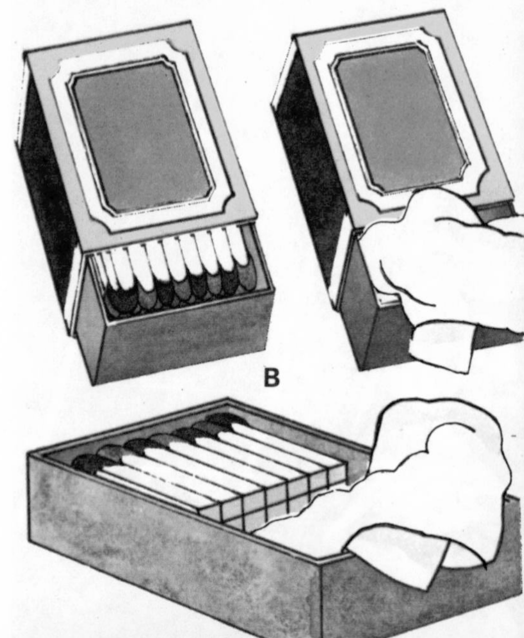

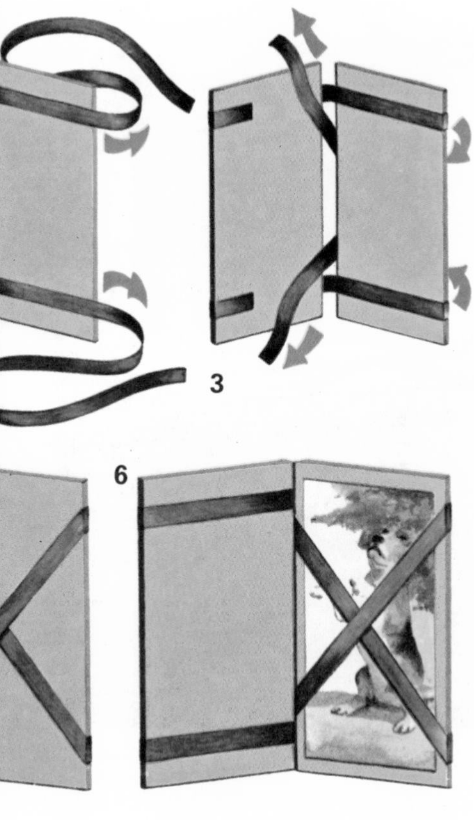

picture seems to move from one card to the other.
Below: Two ways of fixing a 'full' matchbox so that you can produce a handkerchief from it.

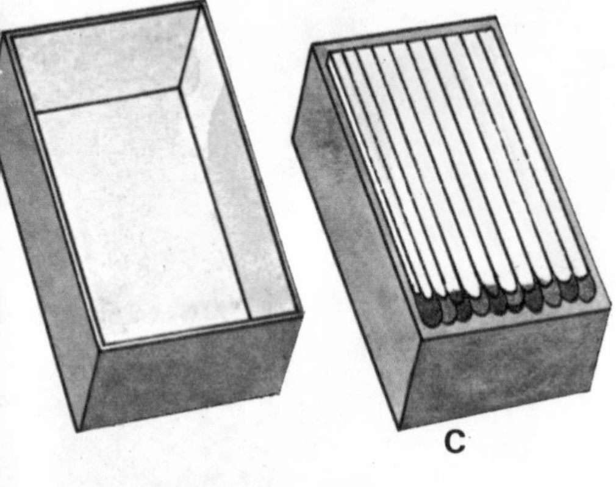

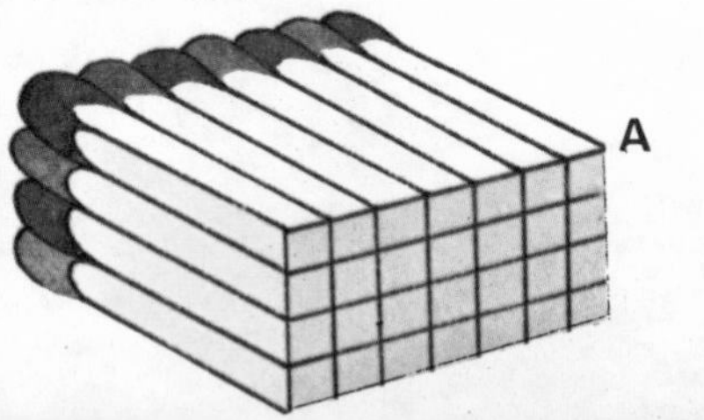

Conjuring

Magic tricks are fascinating to watch and fun to perform. Professional magicians (sometimes called conjurors) often need lots of equipment for their performances. All you will need, however, are a few simple items. A matchstick, some string, a pack of cards, or a few coins will be enough. With practice you will be able to do tricks while disguising the method you have used.

Some tricks are sold in shops. You can buy packs of cards that let you cut the cards automatically into red and black suits. Disappearing tricks can be performed with just a handkerchief and a pencil. More difficult tricks need a conjuror's table – the most useful part of a magician's equipment. Boxes with false bottoms and secret linings can also create the impression that things have disappeared.

Charades

A charade is a word game. The idea is to make your audience guess the word you have in mind by giving them a series of clues. The word must be of two or more syllables. You give one clue for each syllable, and a further clue to the whole word. Suppose the word you choose is *donkey*. You might say to your audience: 'My first is a Spanish nobleman, my second opens doors, and my whole is a four-legged animal.' The audience would then have to guess *don* from the first clue, and *key* from the second. The last should tell them that the word is donkey.

A charade can also be an acting game. Suppose you choose the word *Sunday*. Your first act would be about the word *sun* and your second about the word *day*. Finally, you would do an act about the whole word, *Sunday*, perhaps by kneeling down as though in a church. In this kind of charade you are not allowed to speak.

Hobbies

Hobbies are special interests for your spare time. They are not sports or games. They are things people do because they want to, not because they have to. To a hotel chef, COOKING is not a hobby, but a job of work. But to another person, cooking might well be a hobby if they do not really need to do it.

As your knowledge of a hobby grows, you may find that it will help you to decide what you want to do when you grow up. A boy who is clever at making MODEL AIRCRAFT may well decide that he has a future in AIRCRAFT engineering or design. Many well-known photographers first learned their art as a hobby.

Many young people get satisfaction from collecting things. AUTOGRAPHS, stamps, and coins are some of the most sought-after collector's items. With patience you can build up an interesting and valuable collection.

There are clubs and societies connected with most of these hobbies. There you can meet people who share your interest and exchange ideas with them.

Above: Flying a bird-shaped kite.
Below left: A girl making ornaments out of soft drink cans.
Below: A scale model of a traction engine.

Above: An unusual kite, made up of triangular shapes. When flying a kite, avoid electricity cables. You might get an electric shock if the kite's cord is damp.

Kite flying

Kites are usually made of paper, plastic, or cloth, and can be of various shapes. The simplest are diamond-shaped. Kites can also be shaped like boxes, birds, fish, or butterflies. The principle of kite flying is that the wind is used to gain lift. As the kite climbs, the line on which it is held unwinds from its reel. The best results are obtained in winds of up to about 30 kilometres an hour.

Below: Making a simple kite. You will first need a ball of string (1) and two light wooden struts (2). Cut notches in the ends of the struts (3) and bind them together (4). (5) Cut out a shape slightly larger than the finished kite from light cloth. Cut the edges as shown. Tie string around the outside, fixing it to the notches in the struts. Then glue the flaps over the string. (6) Tie a small ring to a short piece of string, and fix it to the other side of the kite (7). Tie one end of the ball of string to the ring, and wrap the rest round a reel (8). Add the tail (9). The kite (10) is now ready for flying.

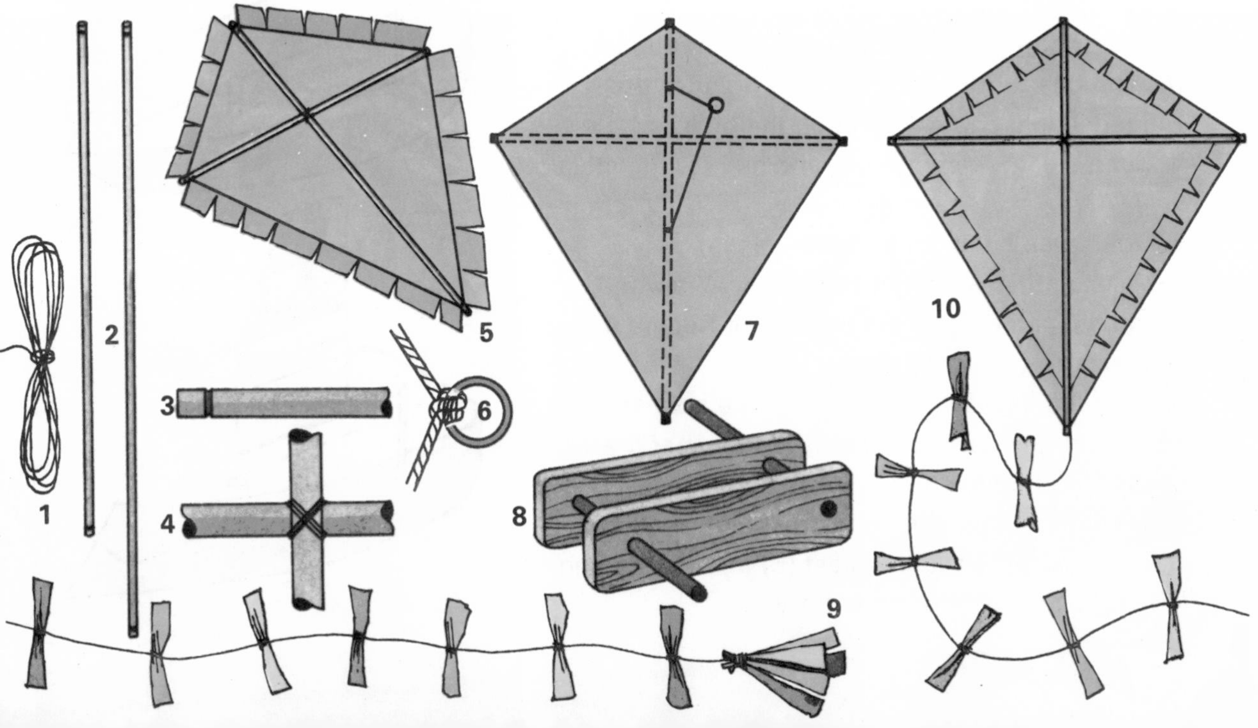

Model ships

The EGYPTIANS made model ships in about 2000 B.C. Some of them have been found in the tombs of the Pharaohs. MUSEUMS in many countries display models of SAILING SHIPS. You can see scale models of ships from the great days of sail, of lake and river craft, of ocean LINERS, warships, TANKERS, and even of nuclear-powered vessels. Most people do not have the knowledge and skill required to construct these kinds of models.

Some modellers make miniature ships as ornaments. Others prefer to make boats that will actually float. Some of these are sail models; others work by electrically operated motors or small combustion engines. There is almost no limit to the amount of detail you can reproduce in a model.

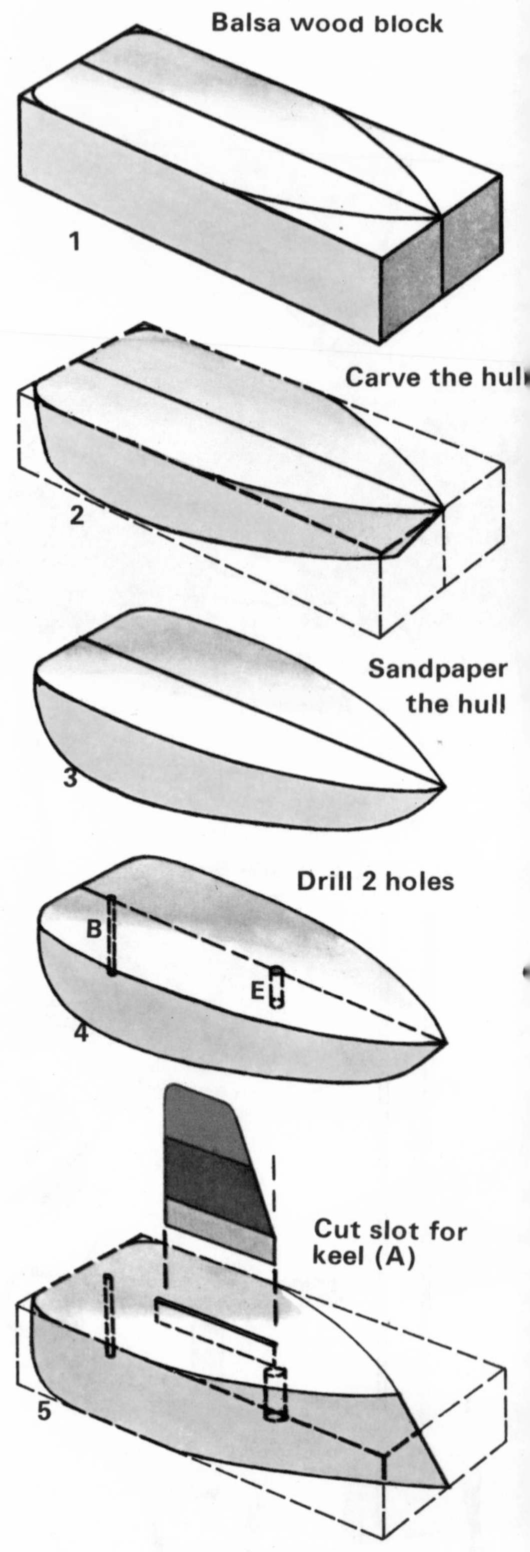

HOW TO MAKE A MODEL SHIP

1. Take a block of balsa wood. This can be any size, but it might be about 30 cm. long. Draw the outline of your boat's hull on it.
2. Carve out the shape of the hull.
3. Sandpaper the hull smooth.
4. Drill two holes in the hull, one for the rudder (B) and one for the mast (E). The hole for the rudder should go right through the hull.
5. Cut a slot in the bottom of the hull for the metal keel (A).
6. Drill seven holes for the tiller bar (b).
7. Make up the sail out of thin cloth. Wrap it round the gaff (F) and the boom (G). Secure it with small tacks or pins.
8. Push the thick wire (b) through the hole at the stern, and glue on the rudder (B). Hammer a wire staple (C) into the stern. Tie the boom to the staple with string, using an adjustable cleat (D).
9. Paint the hull. Add the mast (E) and the rigging (H). Your boat is now ready for use.

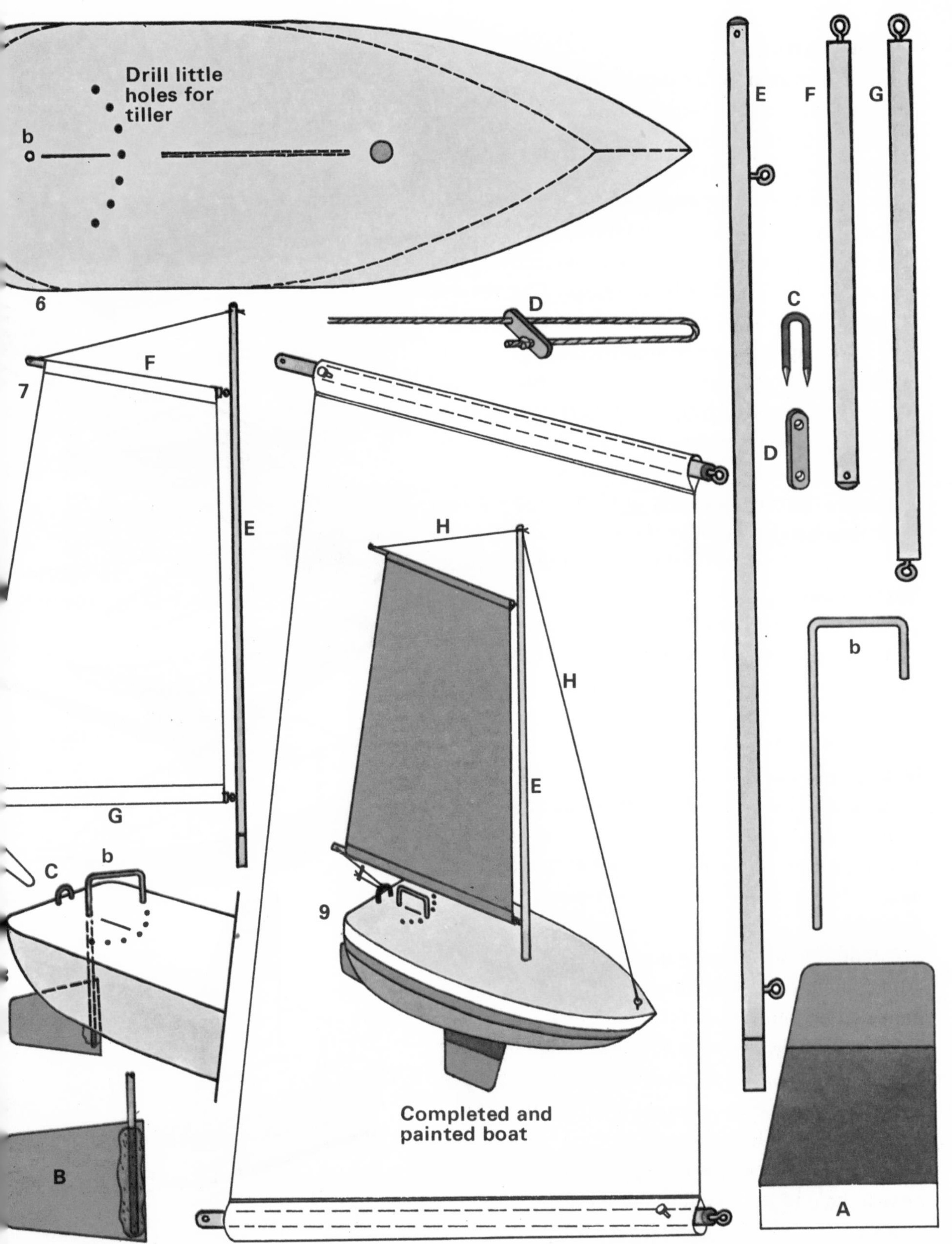
Drill little holes for tiller
b
6
7
F
E
G
C
b
B
D
D
C
D
E
F
G
H
H
E
9
b
A
Completed and painted boat

Model aircraft

Model aircraft are of two main kinds. There are scale models you can build and collect that do not fly. Then there are flying models. You can buy assembly kits for many different aircraft models. Instructions are supplied with the kit.

Flying models may be gliders, or they may be powered. The simplest kind of powered model is driven by a twisted rubber band. The rubber band unwinds and turns the propeller. Quite powerful engines – even small jets – are used in some models. All these models fly through the air without outside help. They are called free-flight models. There are also free-flight models operated by radio control.

Line-controlled models are attached by two lines to a handle held by the operator. They fly in circles, and therefore do not need much space. The operator must keep the lines taut. The lines control how the plane flies.

There are world championships for several branches of model aircraft flying.

HOW TO MAKE A MODEL AIRCRAFT

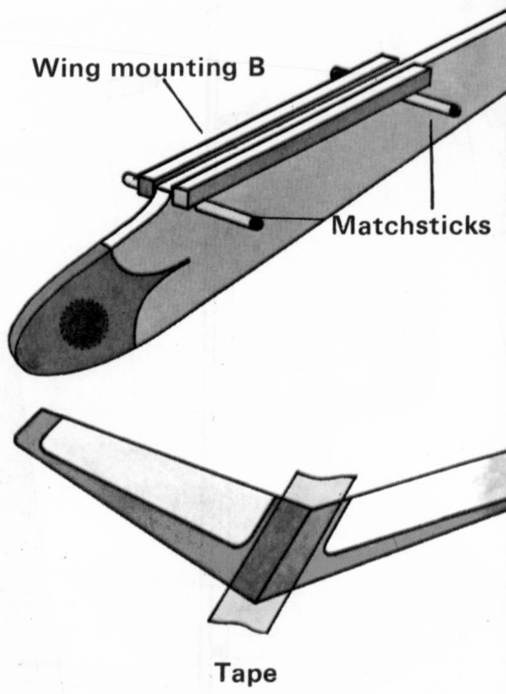

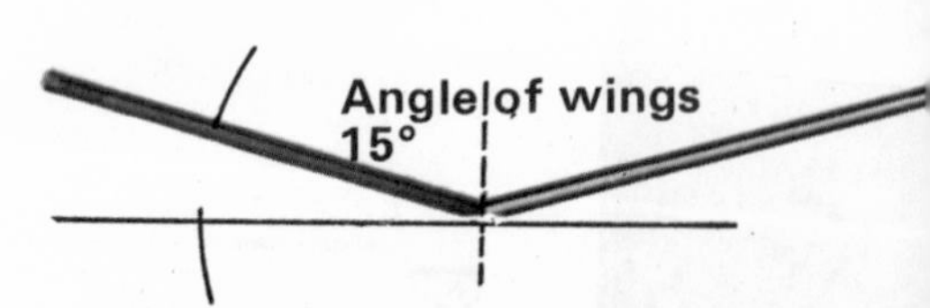

To make a model plane, cut the shape of the fuselage (A) out of a sheet of balsa wood. The wings and tailplane can be made of balsa or stiff card.

2. Make the wing mounting (B) out of thin strips of balsa, resting on matchsticks, and glued to the fuselage.
3. Cut out the wings and tape them together. Attach them to the wing mounting with elastic bands, at an angle of about 15 degrees.
4. Very carefully, cut slots in the fuselage for the fin and tailplane. Cut out the tailplane in one piece. It should stay in place without glue, but the fin may have to be glued in position.
5. Finally, fix a small lead weight to the plane's nose to help to balance it in flight.

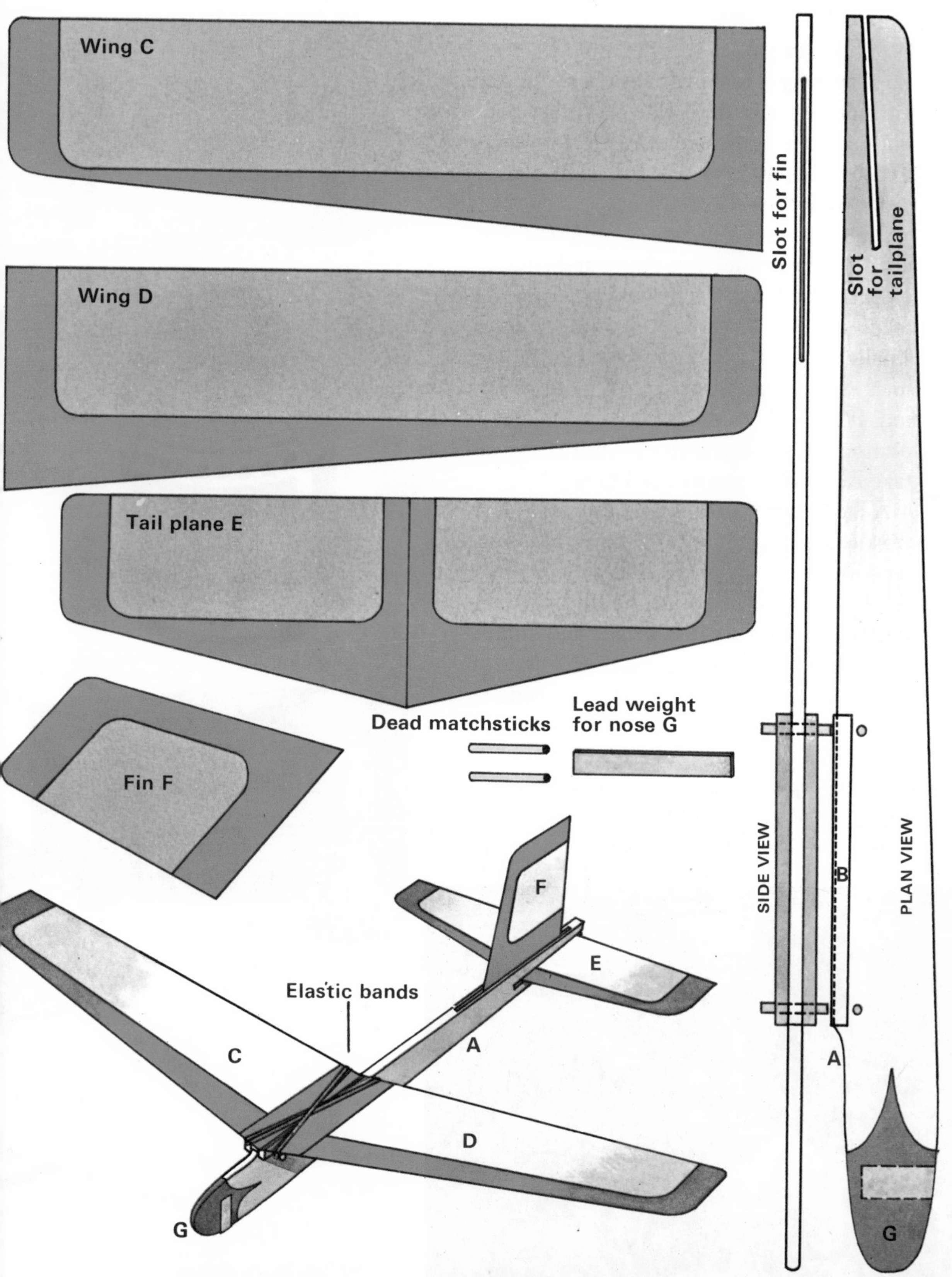
Wing C
Wing D
Tail plane E
Fin F
Slot for fin
Slot for tailplane
Dead matchsticks
Lead weight for nose G
SIDE VIEW
PLAN VIEW
B
A
G
F
E
Elastic bands
C
A
D
G

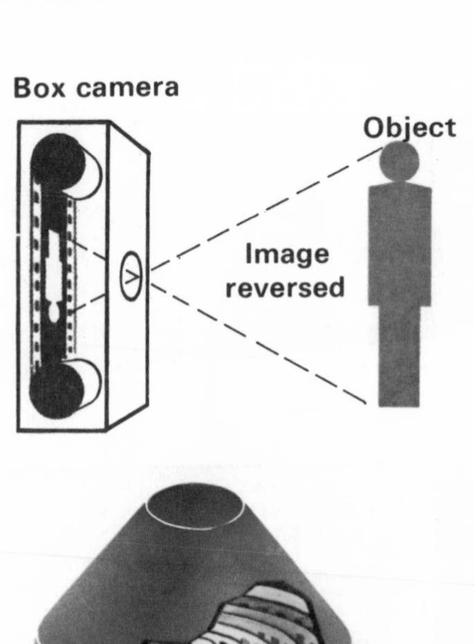

Photography

Photography is making pictures by the action of light on sensitive film. The first black and white photographs were taken about 150 years ago. Colour photography was introduced about 100 years later.

There are a number of different kinds of cameras. One difference between them is the size of the photograph they take. A plate camera takes a large picture. Roll film cameras take smaller ones. An even smaller size is 35 millimetre – this is the size of most colour slides taken today. Polaroid cameras take, develop, and print photographs in less than a minute. Ciné cameras take continuous moving pictures.

A camera is basically a light-proof box. The LENS focuses light on to the film. A shutter controls the amount of light that gets in (the exposure). If there is not much light, you will need a longer exposure. If it is bright and sunny, you will need a shorter exposure. For indoor photos or at night you can create light by using a flash bulb attachment.

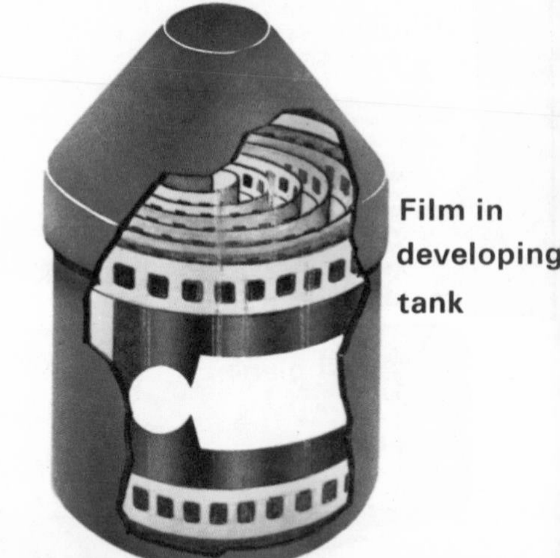

Right: A simple camera complete with the film cartridge which fits inside it.
Below: Some modern photographic equipment.

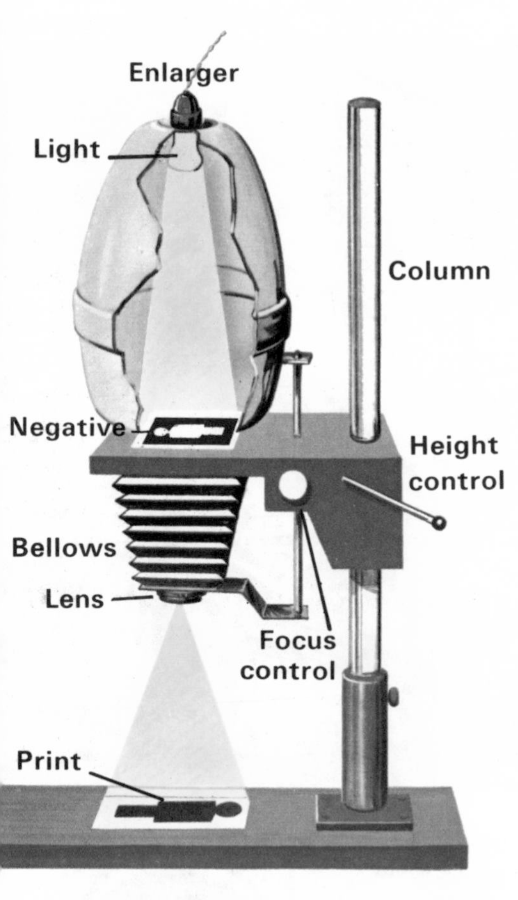

Cooking

It is not necessary to have a lot of equipment or expensive food to cook well. With practice, you can learn to make such things as cakes, sweets, and puddings, as well as main course dishes.

Eggs are one of the most important kinds of food used in cooking. They can be boiled, fried, scrambled, poached, and used to make omelettes. They also have many other uses.

When you have learned to make one dish, try making another. You will soon find that you are able to cook several different complete meals. Children's cook books will give you recipes and ideas.

It is important to be very careful when using a cooker. Make sure you do not get too near to the flame or hotplate. Do not have anything that will burn too near to the cooker. Above all, leave the kitchen tidy and clean when you have finished.

Left: Stages in making a black and white photograph.
Below: A girl learning to cook vegetables in a school cookery lesson.

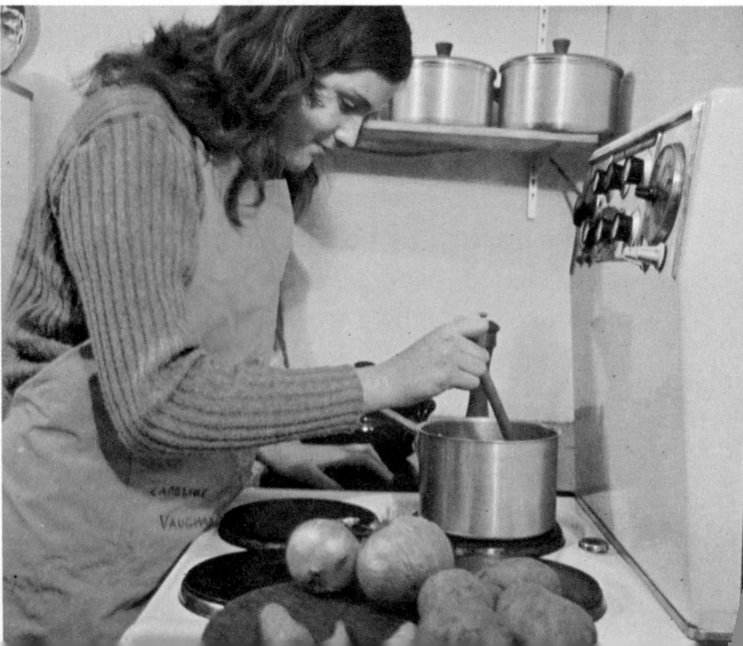

Stamp collecting

Stamp collecting can be started in a small way, but it can be a very big subject. At first you will want to keep all the stamps you receive. In time, you may prefer to collect a particular kind of postage stamp, perhaps from one country, or a group of countries. Or you may wish to collect stamps on a particular subject, such as sport. If you have a stamp with a slight flaw in the design, this makes it rare and more valuable.

Above: Stamp collectors' equipment. The little book (1) is for keeping stamps before they are stuck in the album. The tweezers (2) are for handling the stamps, which may be examined in detail through the lens (3). The paper hinges (4) are for sticking the stamps on to a page (5) in the album (in this case special Olympic stamps).

A stamp catalogue is very useful. It can tell you nearly everything you want to know about your stamps, including their present value. Your catalogue will also give you an accurate description of stamps. There are also weekly and monthly magazines in which collectors and stamp dealers advertise.

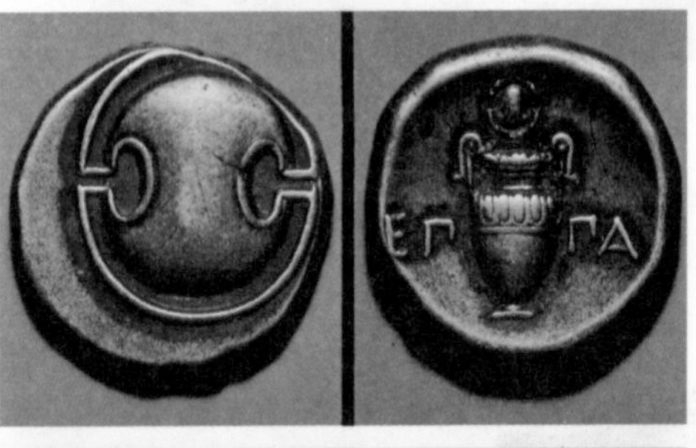

Autographs

Autographs are specimens of handwriting. A single word or a letter in the person's writing is an autograph. The French Emperor, NAPOLEON, often signed papers with the letter N. This signature would be a treasured item in an autograph hunter's collection.

Many young people ask for signatures only. These can be valuable, but a document or letter written and signed by a famous person is worth much more.

You can collect autographs generally, or you can specialise in a particular subject such as sport or politics. Your relatives and friends may help you and you can always trade your duplicates for ones that you do not have.

When writing to famous people for their autographs, remember that they get hundreds of requests. It will help if you send a stamped, addressed envelope for their reply. Show business personalities usually have agents who deal with fan mail. You can often find their addresses in public LIBRARIES.

Coins and medals

Coin collecting is an ancient hobby. The ROMANS used to collect GREEK coins over 2000 years ago. The value of a coin depends partly on its condition. If it is in perfect condition it may be worth ten times as much as a worn or bent coin. The number of coins minted in the year of issue also affects the value. The fewer coins there are of a particular value, the greater their rarity value to the collector. You can collect coins in series – say, one of each English king or queen. Or you can collect all the dates of a particular series. This is a popular form of collecting in the United States.

Some coins are not really intended to buy things. In 1965 a CHURCHILL memorial crown was issued. Millions of people like to keep such coins as souvenirs.

Souvenir medals are also in great demand. They are issued from time to time to commemorate some important historic event or anniversary. A Hawaiian Statehood medal was issued in 1959 when Hawaii became the fiftieth state of the United States.

Coin catalogues will help you to find the value of any coin you may collect or buy.

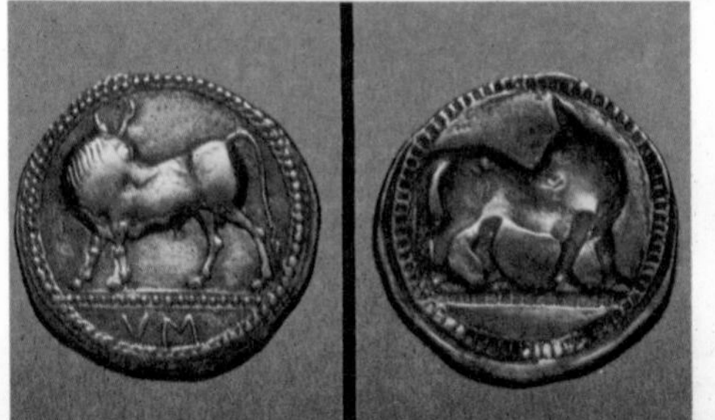

Left: A selection of coins from Ancient Greece.

Pets

People have pets for many reasons. A DOG can be a faithful friend and good company for the whole family. On the other hand, a fish in the pond is little more than an attractive ornament. But in either case you should always remember that a pet is not only your property; it is also your responsibility. It depends on you for food and for the care of its health.

In most cities and towns there are pet shops where you can obtain advice on feeding your animals. Animals cannot tell you when they are not well, so you should see the vet if you are in doubt about your pet's health. When you go away from home, do not forget to have your pet cared for by someone else.

Keeping a pet can be expensive. Make sure that you can afford to look after your pet before you decide to keep one.

Gerbil (desert rat)

Right: Two popular kinds of pets.
Below: A vivarium. This one is lined with moss and bark. It contains frogs and toads.

Dogs and cats

DOGS are the most affectionate of household pets. They are usually loyal, and often courageous. If you want to buy a puppy, you should wait until it is about six weeks old, when it is big enough to leave its mother. Cocker spaniels, sealyhams, dachshunds, poodles, and various types of terrier are among the most popular kinds of dog.

Left: Basset hounds have long ears, a long body, and short legs.

Tortoise

Puppies have to be house-trained. They should also be given a name as soon as possible. Once they learn their names, they will then learn to obey simple commands such as 'sit' or 'wait'. It never helps to get angry when training a puppy.

After they are three months old, puppies need regular exercise. You will need a lead to take a dog through traffic or into parks where they are not allowed to run free. Your name and address should be on the dog's collar.

Unlike dogs, cats lead their own lives. They are usually more attached to their home than to their owner. Most cats will not come when called. They can be good companions, however, especially if they are obtained when young. For this reason, it is a good idea to get a kitten only a few weeks old. It will settle down more easily than a grown cat. Ordinary cats can be just as good pets as pedigree animals such as Persians and Siamese.

Cats do not need a lot of exercise. In fact, some city cats never go outdoors. All cats do need to be kept well fed, however.

Left: Although this cat is mostly white, it is called a tortoiseshell because of its black and brown markings.

Ponies

Ponies can be hired for riding, even in a city. But some people, especially those living in the country, prefer to keep their own. A pony needs plenty of space. In the summer, grass alone is sufficient food.

Some of the stronger breeds of pony can live outside all the year round. Their thick winter coats give them protection. But even they should have a shed for shelter in the worst weather.

Most ponies need a stable during the winter. Hay is then the major part of their fodder, and it should be kept in a rack, not on the ground. A water trough and a salt lick are also necessary to keep them in good health.

In addition to hay, ponies need an occasional meal of oats mixed with bran, particularly if they are getting a lot of exercise. They also need regular grooming. After exercise, they should be rubbed down and covered with a blanket. Every six weeks, their hoofs should be examined in case they need to be trimmed or the shoes changed.

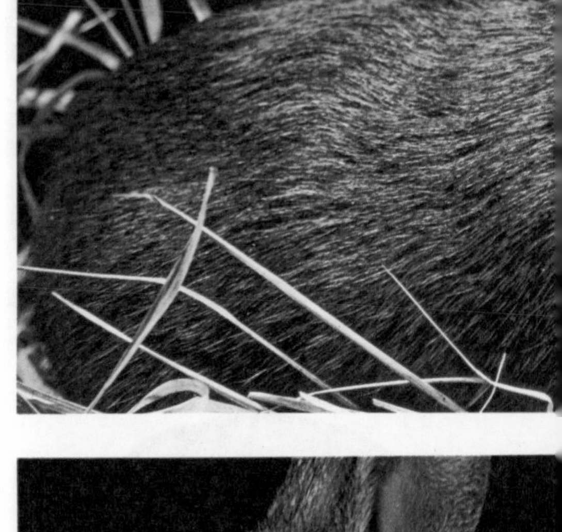

Below: A pony wearing a saddle and bridle. These are made of leather and should be cleaned with a special polish.

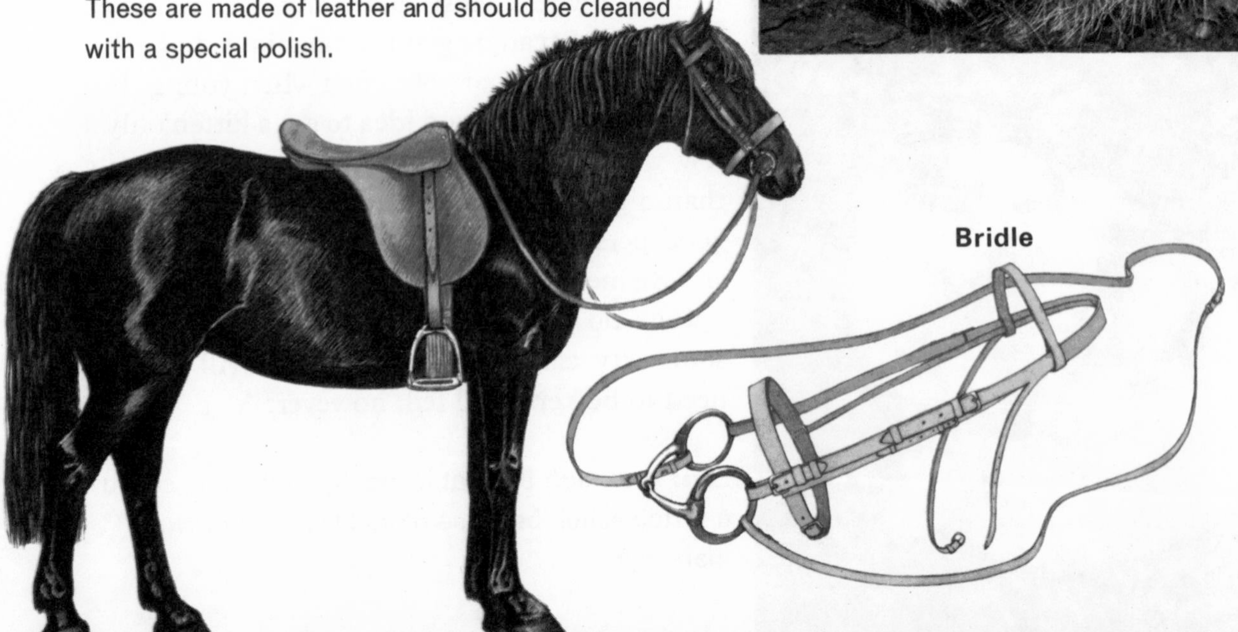

Top: A guinea pig, or cavy.
Left: A baby rabbit.
Below: A white-tailed rat.

Rodent pets

Mice make good pets for some people. They need only a small cage with a sawdust tray in the bottom as a home. A ladder should lead to an upper level with a nesting box and some straw. Mice eat dandelions and other fresh green things as well as SEEDS and brown bread. They produce their young within about three weeks after mating.

Golden hamsters like a warm room. They came originally from a warm climate. They should have a hutch of hard wood or they will bite their way out. They eat WEEDS and also harder food like chestnuts and acorns. Hamsters have a little pouch inside their mouth in which they hoard food.

Gerbils, sometimes called desert rats, can be kept as pets. They should be fed on grain and fresh vegetables. Gerbils are very clean and do not smell. They are most active at dawn and dusk.

Guinea pigs, now more often called cavies, are rodents of South American origin. Green and root vegetables, and other scraps of food keep them well satisfied.

Below: A wood mouse.

Caged birds

Canaries became popular as pets in the nineteenth century. In the wild, most canaries are dark green, but in captivity they are often a bright yellow. They are quite happy in a cage and do not seem to mind living alone. They are noted for their beautiful singing. Ordinary bird seed is their favourite food, but they also need green vegetables in their diet. They enjoy bathing and drinking water every day.

Budgerigars, a kind of PARROT, are even more popular today than canaries. Though their feathers are brighter and more decorative, they cannot sing. They need the same kind of care as canaries. Budgies are good performers and like to have a swing in their cage. They turn somersaults and enjoy playing with tiny objects. Unlike canaries, they are at home outside their cages. Some budgies can learn to say a few words.

The larger parrots are also playful creatures. They usually become attached to one person and will learn to say some simple words. Parakeets, cockatoos, and lovebirds are other birds of tropical origin that make good pets.

Top: The greater crested cockatoo.
Below: A caged canary.
Below left: A greater hill mynah.
Mynah birds can imitate human voices and other noises very well.

Tropical fish

Tropical fish must have heated water to live in. Their tank must have a fitted heater. It should also have a thermostat. This is an automatic device to keep the temperature at a constant level. The tank should have a little sand in it, and WEEDS that can live in warm water.

The number of fish in any one tank depends on the size of the tank. Pet shop owners will tell you how many fish should go in the tank.

Guppies, or rainbow fish, are among the easiest tropical fish to keep. They are not fussy about their food and can stand changes in temperature more than most other kinds. Mollies, platies, barbs, zebra fish, beacon fish, and labyrinth fish are a few of the many varieties.

Dry fish foods are available, as are live foods such as water fleas and worms. Keep a jar of water near a sunny window and it will turn green because tiny floating plants will grow in it. Pour a little of this water into the tank from time to time.

Above: A tropical fish tank, with glass tetra fish, and the brightly coloured cardinal tetras.
Below: Goldfish in a pond.

Pond fish

Pond fish are very little trouble to keep. They breed easily and need hardly any feeding.

The pond should have both deep and shallow water. Fish like to have places where they can be in the light. On the other hand, the deeper water does not freeze so easily in the winter.

Water plants and sand will make the pond a better home for fish. If the pond is new, do not put in any fish for a few weeks. A few water fleas and snails are useful as live food. Clear away leaves and other rubbish that may foul the water.

The most popular freshwater fish is the goldfish. It was first bred in captivity in CHINA. Other attractive pond fish are the Japanese golden carp and the golden or silver orfe.

Places to Visit

Modern means of travel have opened up the marvels of the world to many people. Travellers can see famous landmarks and places of great natural beauty. They can go to Agra, INDIA, to see the TAJ MAHAL. They can visit the great cities of EUROPE, or the plains of AFRICA. In the United States, they can see the STATUE OF LIBERTY as they arrive in NEW YORK by sea. Many visit Niagara Falls on the border between the United States and CANADA. Even the jungles of SOUTH AMERICA and the islands of the PACIFIC can be visited by the adventurous traveller.

Not everyone has the time or money to visit far-away places. However, every country has many places of interest to visit. The homes of famous people who lived long ago are often open to the public. The magnificent palace of Versailles near PARIS was once the residence of King LOUIS XIV of FRANCE. It is now a great tourist attraction.

Most cities have parks, and some also have botanical gardens. These are gardens where interesting and unusual plants are grown. They are important for experts who wish to study the plants. They are also usually of interest to other visitors. The Botanical Gardens at Cambridge, Massachusetts, in the United States, and Kew Gardens in LONDON, England are among the best known.

In addition, most cities – and many smaller towns – have MUSEUMS, ART GALLERIES, and exhibitions. And you do not have to go to Africa to see wildlife. A visit to a ZOO or a GAME RESERVE is a way to enjoy and study wild animals and their habits.

Right: Many tourists in Northern Ireland pay a visit to the Giant's Causeway. It is formed from regular-shaped blocks of volcanic rock.

Above: The Botanical Gardens at Taranto, Italy.
Below: A statue in the grounds of the Palace of Versailles near Paris, in France.

Museums

Museums are buildings where objects of particular interest are stored and arranged for public display. A museum may be concerned with almost any subject in history, science, or the arts. To learn more about the sky, for example, you can visit a planetarium where the night sky is pictured on a dome.

Some museums deal with the life of a famous person. These are often located in the building that used to be the person's home. The rooms may be arranged just as they were in his or her lifetime. Other museums have models of streets and houses from different periods in history.

Sometimes articles of special value or interest are loaned by one museum to another for a special exhibition. CHINESE objects may come to LONDON, or great French paintings be loaned to the United States. Thus, people can see the masterpieces of different countries without having to travel great distances.

Many museums and art galleries are in old buildings and palaces. The Louvre in Paris was once a royal palace. Other museums, such as the Smithsonian Institution in WASHINGTON, were built specially.

Above: An art expert repairing an oriental painting in a museum.
Below: This museum in Mexico contains a model of an Aztec market.
Below right: A reconstruction of an eighteenth-century American tavern in the American Museum in England.

Art galleries

Art galleries are really MUSEUMS of paintings and sculpture. Like museums, the biggest art galleries have a wide variety of exhibits. The smaller ones often contain works by groups of painters of a particular style, or period in history. The National Portrait Gallery in LONDON has paintings of kings and queens, and other important figures from British history. The Museum of Modern Art in NEW YORK is another specialist gallery. On the other hand, the Prado in MADRID has a magnificent collection of paintings of many kinds.

The largest art gallery in the world is in the Winter Palace near Leningrad, in the U.S.S.R. It would require a 24-kilometre walk to see all the exhibits housed there.

Larger galleries have a staff of experts who supervise the cleaning and restoring of works of art. Many are government-supported, partly because of the high cost of buying new exhibits. They may also charge an entrance fee, but some are either free or are free on certain days. Good galleries supply booklets about the works they display. It is a good idea to read one when visiting a gallery.

Top: Napoleon turned the Louvre into a museum for the works of art his army brought back from Italy.
Below left: The Museum of Fine Arts in Boston, U.S.A., houses many famous paintings.
Below: The Cairo Museum, Egypt.

Zoos

The word zoo is short for zoological garden. Zoology is the study of animals. At one time, zoos and menageries were used to entertain royalty. The emperor of CHINA imported a giraffe from AFRICA in the fifteenth century. Today, there are probably over 500 public zoos around the world. The one with the greatest variety of animals is in West BERLIN.

Years ago, zoos always kept animals in barred cages. Today, many zoos try to keep their animals in more natural surroundings. The study of animals in captivity can tell scientists a great deal about the way they live in the wild. It also helps them to find cures for animal diseases. One of the best zoos in the United States is at San Diego in California. There, the climate makes it possible for the animals to live outdoors for most of the year.

As civilization spreads, and natural wildernesses are reduced, zoos are becoming more important. They provide places where rare animals can be preserved from extinction.

Above: Deer in a zoo in Maine, U.S.A.
Below: Tame dolphins leaping over a line in a Honolulu lagoon.

Game reserves

Game reserves have existed in parts of EUROPE for hundreds of years for hunting purposes. Today, reserves are usually sanctuaries where wildlife is safe from hunters and can live and breed undisturbed by man. Over 20 species of animals have become extinct this century, so conservation of certain species is essential.

In AUSTRALIA there are many reserves for the protection of bird life and the smaller kinds of POUCHED MAMMALS. The United States has over 250 game reserves. The most important is Yellowstone National Park, which overlaps the states of Wyoming, Montana, and Idaho. Mount McKinley National Park in Alaska is the home of the caribou. A herd of the almost extinct BUFFALO can be seen at Wind Cave National Park in South Dakota. One of the largest reserves in the world is the Kruger National Park in SOUTH AFRICA, where ELEPHANTS, RHINOCEROSES, GIRAFFES, ZEBRA, and LIONS are among the attractions.

Left: Lions are undisturbed by a passing jeep at a wild life park in California, U.S.A.
Below: Zebras at a water hole at Hkuzi Game Reserve.

SPORTS AND PASTIMES FACTS AND FIGURES

TEAM SPORTS. The greatest goalscorer in soccer is Brazil's Pelé. In about 21 years of first-class football, he scored over 1200 goals, 139 of them in a single year. Wilt Chamberlain was one of the most outstanding of all basketball players. In one season he averaged 50 points a game.

INDIVIDUAL SPORTS. The marathon is the longest race in the Olympic programme. Over the 42 or so kilometres, the runner's feet may hit the ground about 30,000 times. In tennis, the ball may travel at over 240 kilometres an hour as it leaves the server's racquet.

WINTER SPORTS. Winter sports are among the fastest of all sports. Krynica in Poland has the fastest luge run in the world; speeds of over 140 kilometres an hour have been recorded there. When ski-jumping, the skier may land at a speed of over 100 kilometres an hour.

SPECTATOR SPORTS. In drag racing, the fastest time achieved has been under seven seconds, and the highest speed attained, over 430 kilometres an hour – both over a 400-metre track. Polo has the largest pitch of any ball game. It is about 183 metres long and 274 metres wide.

WATER SPORTS. The first man to swim the English Channel both ways between Dover and Calais was Antonio Abertondo of Argentina in 1961. The Dogget's Coat and Badge race between London Bridge and Chelsea was first rowed in 1716. It is the earliest established boat race.

OUTDOOR ACTIVITIES. In A.D. 130 a Greek naturalist described the first artificial fishing bait on record. It was made up of feathers to look like a bee. The first youth hostel was opened at Burg Altena in Germany in 1907. Today there are Girl Guide associations in over 60 different countries.

INDOOR GAMES. The largest bowling centre in the world is in Tokyo. It has over 250 lanes. Chess is derived from a game called Chaturanga which was played in India over 1300 years ago. Whist, first recorded in 1529, was the most popular card game until 1930 when Bridge took over.

HOBBIES. The world's first postage stamps were the Penny Black and Twopence Blue issued by Great Britain on 1st May 1840. Kite fighting is a sport in parts of South America and Asia. The kite's second cord, coated with powdered glass, is used to cut the cords of other kites.

PETS. Tortoises are probably the longest-lived of all animals. One, kept in France, lived for 152 years. The East Indian X-ray fish is so transparent that most of its skeleton is visible through its skin. An alsatian's sense of smell is one million times better than that of a man.

PLACES TO VISIT. Old Faithful, a geyser in Yellowstone National Park, sends a fountain of steam and hot water 50 metres in the air every hour. The city of Pompeii in Italy can be seen today much as it was in A.D. 79, when it was buried in lava and ashes by an eruption of Mount Vesuvius.

INDEX

HOW TO USE THE INDEX

The index is arranged in alphabetical order, so that you can quickly find the subject you are interested in, and the pages on which it is mentioned.

For example, suppose you want to find out about the planet Jupiter. Under J you will find this:

Jupiter (planet), 300, 308, 309

This tells you that Jupiter is mentioned in the text, or shown in a picture, on pages 300, 308 and 309. The word 'planet' in brackets tells you that you are reading about Jupiter the planet, not Jupiter the Roman god (who is indexed separately in the next line).

At the beginning of the index you will find a table showing the pages that appear in each volume of OUR WORLD. The pages from 290 to 383 are in Volume 4, so you should look in that volume for the pages on which Jupiter is mentioned.

IMPORTANT PAGES

You may find that a subject in the index has a page number in **bold type**. This means that on that page there is a complete article, with a heading in **bold type**, on the subject you have looked up. This is usually the place where you will find the most information about the subject. For example, if you look up the composer Johann Sebastian Bach, you will find two page numbers: **397** and 838. On page 397 there is an article about Bach, while on page 838 he is only mentioned very briefly.

SUB-ENTRIES

Sometimes you will find that a subject listed in the index (it is called an 'entry'), has another line just below it, starting a little way across to the right. This is called a 'sub-entry'. For example, if you look under B you will find an entry for BEARS and a sub-entry for POLAR BEARS as well:

bears, **162**
  polar, 162, 365

This tells you that there is an article about bears in general on page 162, while polar bears are mentioned on this page and also on page 365. Sub-entries refer you to a smaller part of the subject that you have looked up.

SMALL SUBJECTS AND LARGE SUBJECTS

As you can see from the previous section about sub-entries, a small subject is often part of a larger subject. If you remember this, it will help you to find things in the index. For example, under ANIMALS you will find sub-entries for animals as pets, domestic animals, prehistoric animals, and several more. But you will not find a sub-entry for every kind of animal mentioned in OUR WORLD. They are indexed separately, under their own names – bears, lions, and so on.

'SEE ALSO' AND 'SEE'

Sometimes, to help you find an entry that is connected with the subject you have looked up, you will find what is called a 'cross-reference', beginning 'see also'. This means you will find more information by looking up the subject of the cross-reference.

For example, under AMERICA there is a cross-reference which reads: '*see also* North America; South America'. This tells you that you will find more about North America under NORTH and more about South America under SOUTH. Similarly, under ANIMALS there is a long cross-reference which reads: '*see also* birds; fish; insects; mammals; reptiles; and individual species'. In other words, birds, fish and the others are different kinds of animal and are indexed separately under these words.

There is also another kind of cross-reference, that begins with just the one word 'see'. This tells you that you will find the subject somewhere else in the index. For example:

Ceylon, *see* Sri Lanka

This cross-reference has been included because people may look for the country under its old name, which was used for a long while and is well known.

A '*see*' cross-reference is also used to tell you which word has been used in the index when there was a choice. For example:

energy, *see* power

Pages referring to energy, power and fuel have been grouped in one entry, and this cross-reference tells you which entry it is.

There was no room to include every cross-reference that might have been useful, so if you cannot find what you are looking for, try to think of another word that might have been used instead. If you still cannot find the subject you want, ask yourself whether it is part of a larger subject that might be in the index or – more likely – whether it may have been divided into smaller subjects.

A

To find the volume of OUR WORLD that contains the page you want, look at the list of volumes and page numbers at the front of this book.

B

To find the volume of OUR WORLD that contains the page you want, look at the list of volumes and page numbers at the front of this book.

To find the volume of OUR WORLD that contains the page you want, look at the list of volumes and page numbers at the front of this book.

To find the volume of OUR WORLD that contains the page you want, look at the list of volumes and page numbers at the front of this book.

D

To find the volume of OUR WORLD that contains the page you want, look at the list of volumes and page numbers at the front of this book.

F

To find the volume of OUR WORLD that contains the page you want, look at the list of volumes and page numbers at the front of this book.

H

I

To find the volume of OUR WORLD that contains the page you want, look at the list of volumes and page numbers at the front of this book.

J

K

L

To find the volume of OUR WORLD that contains the page you want, look at the list of volumes and page numbers at the front of this book.

M

To find the volume of OUR WORLD that contains the page you want, look at the list of volumes and page numbers at the front of this book.

N

To find the volume of OUR WORLD that contains the page you want, look at the list of volumes and page numbers at the front of this book.

O

P

To find the volume of OUR WORLD that contains the page you want, look at the list of volumes and page numbers at the front of this book.

To find the volume of OUR WORLD that contains the page you want, look at the list of volumes and page numbers at the front of this book.

S

To find the volume of OUR WORLD that contains the page you want, look at the list of volumes and page numbers at the front of this book.

To find the volume of OUR WORLD that contains the page you want, look at the list of volumes and page numbers at the front of this book.

T

U

To find the volume of OUR WORLD that contains the page you want, look at the list of volumes and page numbers at the front of this book.

V

W

PAGE NUMBERS AND VOLUME TITLES

From this list of volume titles and page numbers, you can find the volume of OUR WORLD that contains the page or pages you want.

PHOTO CREDITS

A-Z Botanical Collection Ltd, Ace Caravan Company, Air France, Air Portraits, Brian and Cherry Alexander, Allied Breweries Ltd, Allsport, American Museum in Britain, Amey Roadstone Corporation Ltd, Amoco International, Heather Angel M.Sc., F.R.P.S., Anti-Locust Research Centre, Apple and Pear Development Council, Architects Slide Library, Archiv Richard Wagner Gedenstraffe Bayreuth, Ardea Photographics, Ashmolean Museum and P F Purvey, Australian Information Service, Australian News and Information Bureau, Australian Tourist Office, Chris Barker, Barnaby's Picture Library, Beecham Research Laboratories Ltd, Ron Boardman, Bodleian Library, Boosey and Hawkes, Boston Medical Library, Bowater Organisation, Pat Brindley, British Aircraft Corporation, British Antarctic Survey, British Broadcasting Corporation, British European Airways, British Film Institute, British Insulated Callender's Cables Ltd, British Museum, B.P.C. Publishing Ltd, British Railways, British Red Cross, British Steel Corporation, British Sugar Bureau, British Tourist Authority, British Transport, J.E. Bulloz, Robert Burton, Camera Press Ltd, Canadian High Commission, Canadian National Railways, Canadian Pacific, J. Allan Cash, CBS Records, Central Office of Information, Centrehurst, Michael Chinery, Christian Science Publishing Society, Citibank, City Museum Bristol, Civil Service Commission, Bruce Coleman Ltd, Denis Collings, Colorsport, Conseil National du Tourisme au Liban, Conservative Central Office, Christopher Cormack, Coty, Courtaulds, Gerry Cranham F.I.I.P., Dakota Department of Highways, Danish Tourist Office, De Beer's Consolidated Mines Ltd, Decca Radar Ltd, Decca Record Company Ltd, Delaware State Bureau of Travel Development, The Dickens House, Douglas Dickens F.R.P.S., Walt Disney Productions Ltd, Samuel Dobie and Son Ltd, Daniel Doncaster and Sons Ltd, Tony Duffy, Dutch Dairy Bureau, Education Service, EEC, Anne-Marie Ehrlich, Electricity Council, EMI Elstree Studios Ltd, English China Clay, ESSO, Ethiopian Tourist Organisation, Mary Evans Picture Library, Keith Faulkner, Featurepix, Fibreglass Ltd, Fiore, Fisons, Forestry Commission, French Government Tourist Office, French Railways, Sigmund Freud, Fox Photos, Free China Centre, Keith Geary, Geographical Colour Slides, Gesellschaft der Musikfreunde in Wien, Stanley Gibbons, Gibraltar Tourist Office, Girl Guides Association, Charles Grant, Ronald Grant, Greek Tourist Office, Susan Griggs, Guide Dogs for the Blind, Gulf Oil, Hale Observatories, Sonia Halliday Photos, Hamlyn Picture Gallery, Hanil Colour Studios, Harland and Wolf Ltd, Harvard University, Havenbedrijt der Germeente Roterdam, Historiska Museet Stockholm, House of Representatives, Huntington Library, Anwar Hussain, Alan Hutchison, I.B.M., Icelandic Embassy, Imperial War Museum, Industrial Photolabs, International Foundation Mozarteum Salzburg, International Youth Hostel Federation, Mat Irvine, Israel Government Tourist Office, Italian State Tourist Office, Jabatan Penerangan Malaysia, Japanese Embassy, Japan Information Centre, Thomas Jefferson Memorial Foundation, Jodrell Bank, John Lewis Partnership, Victor Kennet, Kenya Coffee Board, Keystone Press Agency, Kitt Peak National Observatory, Koninklijk Instituut Voor de Tropen, Kunsthistoriches Museum Vienna, Kodak, A. Lambert, Lexington International, Lighthouse Service, Lincoln National Life Foundation, London Arts Ltd, London Brick Company, London Hospital, London Transport, Luxembourg Tourist Office, William MacQuitty F.R.G.S., F.R.P.S., Maine Department of Economic Development, Malayan Rubber Fund, Mansell Collection, Marconi Company Ltd, Marylebone Cricket Club, May and Baker, Colin Mayer, Meteorological Office, Metropolitan Museum of Art, Mexico Government Tourist Office, Mexico National Tourist Council, Middle East Airlines, Ministry of Defence, Montana Chamber of Commerce, Moroccan Tourist Office, Museum of African Art Ray Nash, National Aeronautics and Space Administration, National Coal Board, National Film Archive, National Gallery London, National Geographic Society, National Institute of Agricultural Botany, National Maritime Museum, National Park Service, Department of the Interior, National Park Service South West Region, National Portrait Gallery, Natural History Museum, Natural History Photographic Agency, Natural Science Photos, National Scout Caving Activity Centre, Nebraska Game and Parks Commission, Nestlé Company Ltd, Netherlands Tourist Office, New Scotland Yard, New Zealand High Commission, N.A.T.O., Northern Ireland Tourist Board, Nova Scotia Communications and Information Centre, Novosti Press Agency, Gilbert Odd, Olympic Airways, Ontario Ministry of Housing, Osterreichische Nationalbibliothek, Outlook Films Ltd, Pan Korea Book Corporation, The Peninsular and Oriental Steam Navigation Company, Jacques Penry, Philips, Phipps Photographic, Pictorial Colour Slides, Picturepoint, K. Pilsbury, Popperfoto, The Post Office, Potato Marketing Board, Philip Prain, Radiation Ltd, Radio Times Hulton Picture Library, Rank Film Laboratories, David Redfern, Régie Autonome des Transports Parisiens, Religious Society of Friends, Rex Features, Reyolle and Company, G.R. Roberts, Ronan Picture Library, Royal Academy of Arts, Royal Astronomical Society, Royal College of Surgeons, Royal Institute of British Architects, Royal National Lifeboat Institute, Royal Netherlands Embassy, Royal Norwegian Embassy, St Batholomew's Hospital, St John's College Cambridge, St Lawrence Seaway Authority, Satour, La Scala, Science Museum, Scott Polar Research Institute, Scottish National Portrait Gallery, Scouts Association, Scottish Tourist Board, Seaphot, Securicor, Sheffield Art Gallery, Smithsonian Institution, Snark International, Société de l'Aerotrain, Sotherby's, South African Co-operative Citrus Exchange Ltd, South African Tourist Corporation, South Dakota Department of Highways, Space Frontiers, Spalding Bulb Co Ltd, Spectrum Colour Library, Stadelsches Kunstinstitut Frankfurt, Standard Telephones and Cables, State of Minnesota Department of Economic Development, Duncan Stewart, Swiss National Tourist Office, Syndication International, Tate Gallery London, Tate and Lyle Ltd, Tea Council Ltd, Telecommunications Headquarters, Tesco, Tropical Products Institute, Mark Twain Home Board, Twentieth Century Fox, United Arab Airlines, United Glass, United Kingdom Atomic Energy Authority, United Nations, United States Embassy, United States Naval Observatory, United States Travel Service, University College Hospital Dental School, Utah Travel Service, Robert Updegraff, Unilever Ltd, Venezuelan Embassy, Vickers, Victoria and Albert Museum, Walker Art Gallery, Warner Columbia, Watch Tower Bible Tract Society, Wattle Export Development, John Watney, Wedgwood Group, Westminister Hospital, Reg Wilson, Woodmansterne, Yarrow, Zefa Picture Library, Zoological Society of London. the photograph of Caerphilly Castle on page 81 is reproduced by permission of the controller of Her Britannic Majesty's Stationery Office. The painting 'Three Dancers' by P. Picasso on page 394 is copyright S.A.D.E.M. Paris 1973. The chart on page 515 is reproduced from BA chart no. 3204 with the sanction of the Controller, H.M. Stationery Office and of the Hydrographer of the Navy.